EVERYMAN, I will go with thee,
and be thy guide,
In thy most need to go by thy side

THOMAS CARLYLE

Born in 1795 at Ecclefechan, the son of a stone-
mason. Educated at Edinburgh University.
Schoolmaster for a short time, but decided on a
literary career, visiting Paris and London.
Retired in 1828 to Craigenputtock to write.
In 1834 moved to Cheyne Row, Chelsea, and
died there in 1881.

THOMAS CARLYLE

The French Revolution

INTRODUCTION BY
HILAIRE BELLOC

Dent London Melbourne Toronto
EVERYMAN'S LIBRARY
Dutton New York

All rights reserved
Printed in Great Britain by
Biddles Ltd, Guildford, Surrey for
J. M. DENT & SONS LTD
Aldine House, 33 Welbeck St, London
First included in Everyman's Library 1906
Last reprinted 1980

Published in the USA by arrangement with
J. M. Dent & Sons Ltd

No 31 Hardback ISBN 0 460 10031 9

INTRODUCTION

THE position of Carlyle in English Literature will necessarily be twofold, for he chose to add to his general survey of thought the particular task of the historian.

The number of men who have chosen the field of letters in general, and who have added to it in any important degree the department of History, is very small. Dickens cannot be said to have done it seriously in his little history, nor Thackeray in his Essay on the Georges, and if we consider the literature of other nations the same holds good.

Conversely, though the historian properly so called who has dipped into general letters is common enough, yet there have been very few historians, whether in England, France, or Germany, who did not profess to stand upon their history rather than upon their other work.

Two men, however, have particularly chosen to combine the functions of philosopher and of historian, and to express their philosophy in many works as serious and as profound as their historical writings ; these two men are Taine and Carlyle.

It must be clearly recognised in any approach to an appreciation of their position, that a man who so attempts the double function stands under a sharper light than can any other sort of writer. And that for this reason : that the work of the historian is justly recognised by men to be one of supreme importance, and to be one that, while it requires literary power for its fulfilment, requires also twenty other qualities as rarely possessed or as difficult of attainment. It is of supreme importance, because upon a just presentation of the past depends all our concrete judgment of the present. History is the object-lesson of politics, and unless history is presented to us truly, it had better not be presented to us at all ; upon History is based our judgment of men so far as long experience can inform it, and if the picture is false, rather than receive it we had better be left to our instinct and to the little circle of exact knowledge conveyed to us by our own experience.

It is, therefore, principally as an historian that Carlyle in England (as Taine in France) will be judged. His position as a writer is secure; his wisdom in entering the field of history is one upon which debate can still be fruitful, and criticism of value.

What motive was it which moved such men, and Carlyle especially, to enter that field? It was the great expansion of historical knowledge which coincided with the moment when his own powers were at the fullest, coupled with the fact that all the reaction which Carlyle himself represented could find its best arguments in the domain of human actions.

If a thesis has to be maintained which purports to be "practical," and to chastise the tendency to abstraction, that thesis is best maintained by a continual appeal to fact. The vague and generous ideals of the young are combated in this way by the old, and it is generally true that anyone who quarrels with a deductive and ideal system bases his quarrel upon direct, concrete, and personal experience. History is but such experience enlarged.

It is remarkable that with so incisive and so rebellious a mind Carlyle should have fallen so easily, where history was concerned, into the general current of his generation. Indeed, the further we are separated in time from the men of that generation, the more shall we wonder that such doubtful and ill-supported theories should have obtained not only an universal recognition, but a sort of 'passive obedience' from the men who filled what is called the 'Victorian Era' in literature. For example—the whole of that group was filled with "Teutonians." To study the 'Teutonic Race,' as it was called—that is, to study North Germany, and to confirm the cousinship between the English and the North German peoples— was nearly all the task of history. There went with this a strong appetite for the romantic in history as in every other department of letters. Violent action, characters in high light and in deep shadow were compelled to appear in chronicles as much as in novels; in rhetoric as in poetry, and indeed throughout the whole literary effort of the time. To both these tendencies Carlyle easily succumbed.

It might be advanced that he was not a disciple but an originator, and that but for him neither would the English of the middle nineteenth century have developed that passion of theirs for things German, nor would the picturesque, vivid and romantic history which Green, Freeman, and even Kinglake wrote, have come into existence. It is certain that but for Carlyle the double current would not have become so strong as it did become. It is equally certain that but for him the two influences of admiration for the German and the romantic would hardly have coalesced. Yet it is true that he did not originate either the one tendency or the other; the one proceeded from the natural religious sympathy between all Protestant peoples; the other, upon the contrary, from the maturing of French influence upon England, and that enormously increasing power which the Revolution bequeathed to the Latins, and which is only now beginning to bear fruit.

The romantic movement began not with Byron or with Wordsworth, but with Rousseau; the natural alliance of the Protestant peoples began not with Waterloo, but with that treaty between Austria and France in the middle of the eighteenth century, which is perhaps the greatest turning-point in the story of European relations.

It must also be remembered that in England there were separate causes all making both for the Teutonic sentiment and for the romantic. England had never possessed a continuous classical tradition. What Milton had begun and Dryden continued withered long before the first of them had been dead a hundred years. In England, again, the romantic spirit had received no chastisement from the facts of war. England alone of European nations had not suffered invasion, dynastic change or serious internal disorder, and it is in peace and in leisure that the romantic illusion flourishes best. England was passing also through a period of abnormal expansion; all her energies were strained to the utmost; there was a vast growth everywhere. As for the German influence, a German dynasty, German allies, the momentary eclipse of the Italian spirit throughout Europe, and the crude beginnings of philology, all helped to foster it and to maintain it.

All this is passing to-day; much of it has already passed. The theories of race based on Max Müller's researches are doubted; they have certainly failed at the test. The rudimentary anthropology of our grandfathers has been corrected by innumerable experiments and by a vastly extended research. Catholicism has organised a full defensive system, and has proceeded from that to carry the war into Africa, and though we have not had in England itself an experience of disaster, yet the pleasing and somewhat virile illusions of romanticism have been so bled out of Europe in general that we ourselves can hardly maintain them.

In a word, we are in a position to look steadily back at the whole historical work of Carlyle and to judge it, as yet, without undue lack of sympathy, but already with sufficient detachment. We are able to present to ourselves and to answer without passion (and with a considerable certainty) the great question which must be asked of all historians, Did he make dead men live again? There are many who call up phantoms, and many who can present the corpse of the past; there are few who can cause it to rise and act before you with its own body and its own soul. To what extent was he of these few?

In order to answer that question the very first thing to be done is to consider the defects which have been noted in his writings.

It has been said (we will see in a moment with how much or how little justice) that Carlyle could not sympathise with things separate from the conditions of his own birth. He was a peasant and a Calvinist, and it is maintained that to things of which the peasant or the Calvinist are incapable he had no avenue of approach, and therefore that he had no understanding of them.

If that be so, his book upon the French Revolution must be the very best test which we could apply to his powers, for the French Revolution was essentially the work of leisured men, of highly trained intelligences, and of men whom the process of academic education had removed as far as possible from the peasant-life of Europe. Again, it was distinctly the product of a Catholic nation—of a nation, that is, with a contempt for fatalism, an adherence to abstract dogmas, and a military hatred of mere force and of the religions of fear.

It is secondly objected to Carlyle that he could not justly deal with history on account of a constant preoccupation of his: the desire to excite the emotions of his readers.

It has been thirdly objected to him that in the particular case of the French Revolution he could not properly delineate the French character, because he had a most imperfect acquaintance with the language of France, and no acquaintance whatever with its people.

Added to these criticisms, another of some weight has often been heard. It is the criticism which all can make against the few historians of modern times: the accusation of inaccuracy.

Now if Carlyle's work be examined upon such lines, it is not difficult to conclude that the main part of the charge against him is false.

Every man is something; if he is not a Calvinist he is a Catholic, an Agnostic or a Mohammedan; if he is not a peasant, he is a shop-keeper or a noble or a soldier. Every man that writes History must therefore have an initial difficulty in comprehending some, and probably most of the characters he sets out to portray. The measure of his power is not to be found in the extent of this difficulty, but in his success in overcoming it. For instance, the best monograph on Robert Burns has been written by a quiet, wealthy man, a foreigner, and a Picard at that, writing in Paris and in the French tongue; and success of that sort, precisely because it has overcome so much initial difficulty, is the prime success of the historian. So with Carlyle. It is not astonishing that he should have written the " Frederick," it is astonishing that he should have written the " Revolution"; and our admiration for the effort and for its result increases with every new thing we learn about Carlyle, and with every new difficulty which we discover to have lain in his way.

A particular instance of this will emphasise my contention. It has been truly remarked of Carlyle as of Dickens, that there was never a single gentleman in his books. The French Revolution was crammed with gentlemen ; very few indeed of the actors in it were of another social rank than that which is called in England by the name of ' the gentry.' Consider, then, Carlyle's portrait of Mirabeau; he certainly makes him something too much of an actor, and something too little of an artist. The inherited dignity of bearing, the firmness of gesture, and the regard for proportion which mark his rank are not present in these pages.[1] But read this passage, and ask yourself whether it has ever been excelled by any writer but Michelet.

"Towards such work, in such manner, marches he, this singular Riquetti Mirabeau. In fiery rough figure, with black Samson-locks under the slouch-hat, he steps along there. A fiery fuliginous mass, which could not be choked and smothered, but would fill all France with smoke. And now it has got *air;* it will burn its whole substance, its whole smoke-atmosphere too, and fill all France with flame. Strange lot ! Forty years of that smouldering, with foul fire-damp and vapour enough ;—and like a burning mountain he blazes heaven-high ; and for twenty-three resplendent months, pours out, in flame and molten fire-torrents, all that is in him, the Pharos and Wonder-sign of an amazed Europe ;—and then lies hollow, cold forever ! Pass on, thou questionable Gabriel Honoré, the greatest of them all : in the whole National Deputies, in the whole Nation, there is none like and none second to thee."

The words are theatrical. 'Whole national deputies' is simply bad English. The 'thou' and the 'thee' are grotesque—but the touch is true.

[1] In the fourth chapter of the fourth book of Part I.

What I mean is this, that if you had known Mirabeau yourself and had read this passage long after his death, you would have said, 'Good lord! how vivid!' long before you had begun to criticise this or that slip in the appreciation. You would in that portrait of Mirabeau have had called up before you Mirabeau as you had known him. So powerful is the modelling that its failure to give the *refinement* of the original would have lain lightly upon your mind, as you were filled with a recollection of his *force*. Carlyle would seem to you to have put a living spirit again into the body of the man, and that living spirit would have been the spirit that you had known.

So is it almost universally where he has to draw the portrait of a man.

Whether the second of the Lameths knew English (I believe he did), or whether in his old age he ever read this book (he had ample time to do it, for he survived its publication by seventeen years), whether he was even acquainted with the name of Carlyle—I do not know; but I am certain that he, who had known Mirabeau, did, if ever he read this passage, stand startled at a resurrection from the dead.

There are exceptions. It is no just appreciation of Carlyle's work to ignore them; on the contrary, these exceptions help us even better than his successes to appreciate the quality of his genius. These exceptions are even numerous. They are to be discovered wherever a character of some complexity and, if I may so express myself, of 'varying grain,' is presented to Carlyle's deep and rapid carving, where the man he is dealing with is not of one stuff throughout.

Two very excellent examples of such failures are his pictures of the King and of Robespierre. In both, the delineation is a task of very considerable difficulty; both had characters highly complex and to some extent self-contradictory; both escape from the power of a pen which was creative, but incapable of analysis.

Louis XVI. was not a weak lump of a man. He never upon any single occasion—and he lived through greater dangers than any modern ruler has lived—showed a sign of fear. He fought for his principles to the very end; he conscientiously deliberated every act of importance which he undertook, and that is a rare and convincing sort of strength. Louis XVI. came of a stock nervous to the point of disease. He would have grown up (under most circumstances) shy, thin, perhaps consumptive, and even more terrified than was his grandfather of intercourse with statesmen

and soldiers. He would probably have died young. The extreme
care spent upon him by doctors, a careful and continually ordered
diet, perpetual exercise in the open air, all these artifices bestowed
upon him before he was twenty a sort of factitious health. He
grew up robust, somnolent, of a large appetite, and with all his
nervous weakness run to lethargy. Here was a man who could
not be jotted down in a few deep strokes of the graver, nor to be
seen clearly in high lights and shadows. Here was a man who
could not by any manipulation be made into a dramatic figure;
therefore, to put it bluntly, Carlyle dismisses him.

Robespierre was descended from a long line of squires, probably
Irish. He was eloquent, pedantic, enthusiastic, cold, of excellent
breeding, of a convinced faith, readily angered against persons,
passionately loved, of a valueless judgment in dealing with masses
of men, and often at fault with individuals. Here, again, is a
character which cannot by any possibility serve the purposes of
melodrama; he was not a monster or a coward, nor even a great
ideal figure, as Hamel would regard him. You cannot deal with
Robespierre unless you deal with the complexity of his position
and of his mind. You must analyse the phenomenon closely, and
you must put him in a separate place right aside from the furious and
simple passions by which he was surrounded but from which he
lived apart. Carlyle was either unable to do this or did not know
that he had to do it; the result is that his Robespierre has no
resemblance either to the original or to any possible man. He is
of wax.[1]

But these, I repeat, are exceptions, and the very causes which
make Louis and Robespierre escape him are proofs of the driving
energy which lay behind his mind. The very fact that he cannot
work in some material enhances the extraordinary power with
which he moulded all other material that fell to his hand.

When it is objected that Carlyle could not deal justly with
history on account of his preoccupation of exciting the emotions,
we are on firmer ground. We are dealing here with his art rather
than with his history, and we are dealing with the great vice to
which art such as his is tempted.

In very early youth a man capable by his style of violently
arousing the emotions of his readers, of striking time and again
the spring which moves us like a phrase of music, may forget him-

---

1 For instance, the famous epithet "Sea-green," is based on *one* phrase of Mme. de
Staël's misread. What Madame de Staël said was that the prominent veins in Robespierre's forehead showed greenish-blue against his fair and somewhat pale skin. But
his complexion was healthy, and his expression, if anything, winning.

self, and may merely over-indulge his power. He will fall into such an excess as it were unconsciously. But as his life proceeds, as his style is criticised and acquires public recognition, he cannot but become conscious of his art; he will tend to repeat certain tricks of it, and he cannot but depend too much upon those tricks to secure him a perpetuity of success and save him the fatigue of creation. He suffers the temptation which falls in another sphere to the orator (for both are rhetoricians), and he tends to yield to that temptation; to force the note. From this fault Carlyle's style after his thirtieth year undoubtedly suffers. As he grew older his straining for the vivid got worse and worse, like Swinburne's alliterations, Browning's obscurity, Wordsworth's "common phrases," or Gladstone's trick of a verbose confusion. Such temptations come only to the great, and it behoves us to be very careful how we charge them with their faults, for we must remember how hardly any great man has escaped them, and how, to lesser men, the temptation itself is impossible. Nevertheless, it is true that the temptation, as it was presented to Carlyle, was only too successful. His art is spoilt by a perpetual tautening of the bow.

I will here quote two passages which should support my contention: the first, as I think, spontaneous; the second false.

The first is near the opening of the seventh chapter of Book IV. in Part III., and begins the trial of the Queen: it is as follows:—

"There are few Printed things one meets with, of such tragic, almost ghastly, significance as those bald pages of the *Bulletin du Tribunal Révolutionnaire*, which bear Title *Trial of the Widow Capet*. Dim, dim, as if in disastrous eclipse; like the pale kingdoms of Dis! Plutonic Judges, Plutonic Tinville; encircled, nine times, with Styx and Lethe, with Fire-Phlegethon and Cocytus named of Lamentation! The very witnesses summoned are like Ghosts . . . they themselves are all hovering over death and doom. . . ."

Consider the qualities of these lines. They open with a simple phrase. The phrase, the consideration of his subject, excite him at once to dithyramb. The rhythm is natural and open. The very vowels of the syllables are consonant to horror, the cadence rises to the wail of the word 'Lamentation.' Its consonants possess the regular though not excessive alliteration of poetical English. It falls and ends like a gong sounding the word "Doom."

Turn now to the second, and see whether these same qualities are not here purposely and forcibly struck upon the metal of his writing rather than appearing as something inherent to the quality of that writing itself.

"One other thing, or rather other things, we will mention; and no more: The Blond Perukes; the Tannery at Meudon. Great talk is of these *Perruques Blondes:* O Reader, they are made from the heads of guillotined Women! The locks of a Duchess, etc., etc." . . ., and so forth to the end of the chapter, twenty lines more: "Alas! then, is man's civilisation only a wrapping through which the savage of him . . ." and so on.

This is bad. It is all forced. The perpetual 'we' of his emphatic manner is introduced to no great purpose. He is writing rapidly. He intended to 'mention' one thing—he thinks of a second (both are false) and is too hasty to remould the sentence. He adds 'no more,' to hide his error and make it pompous. Each phrase is affected. Why 'Great talk is'? Why 'O reader'? Why the excessive commonplace and well-worn tags of the last sentence picked out in an unusual order? It was because he felt his own interest flagging and his pen at fault that he had deliberate recourse to tinsel of this kind.

So much then for the chief fault which can justly be discovered in this great and enduring work. It is easier to take up again the task of defence. I will allude in particular to the charge of inaccuracy, and say at once that Carlyle is without question one of the most accurate historians that ever put pen to paper.

He writes in that method which of all others most compels a man to errors in matters of detail. Fugue: a very vivid presentment: the making of one's subject move before one; the giving of its characters a life of their own such as we give to the characters of fiction—all these high efforts in an historian are direct causes of minute inaccuracy. The extent to which Carlyle escaped that inaccuracy is positively astounding. Many years ago I was requested to comment upon one of the latest editions of his work which was produced with voluminous footnotes at Oxford. Here there was no excuse at all for inaccuracy. The book was dull, pedantic, and badly put together. It was a purely mechanical piece of work, and all the Editor had to do was to verify every reference he made and to see that the spelling and the dates were correct.

Yet I found in this edition at least five errors to one of Carlyle's.

Here is a curious and instructive instance. In speaking of Napoleon's rank before Toulon, Carlyle calls him a major at a

moment when he *may* have held that rank or *may* have been
colonel: it is a point not yet decided, and perhaps never to
be decided. The records are imperfect: the time was a hurried
and muddled one. Napoleon was certainly in a higher than a
battery command, but not yet a general officer. The Oxford
edition elaborately corrects Carlyle and makes Napoleon a captain!

It cannot be too often repeated by those who have the honour
of English historical science at heart that we have in Carlyle not
only in his "Frederick"—where every one concedes it—but
here in the Revolution an admirable instance of care and of
correction. Michelet is perhaps a greater man, and certainly
a greater historian, but in accuracy Carlyle is his superior.
Mignet's little book alone perhaps of the early authorities falls
into less errors, while in the midst of modern research Aulard is
perhaps the only worker who would have a right to contrast his
painstaking with that of the English writer. Taine is nowhere;
but then Taine was not even trying to tell the truth, and that
makes a vast difference where accuracy is concerned.

It is again true of Carlyle that he had but an imperfect acquaintance with the French language, and hardly any acquaintance with the French character. It remains true that by some
sort of miracle he accomplished successfully the task he had set
himself. It is somewhat as though Victor Hugo had managed
to write not a great play (which he did write), but a thorough
history of Oliver Cromwell.

Thus Carlyle comprehended one chief factor of the Revolution:
the mob. Alone of all European peoples, the French are able to
organise themselves from below in large masses, and Paris,
which wrought the Revolution, can do it better than the rest of
France. A French mob can march in column without a leader,
and a Parisian mob can not only march in column, but in a rough
fashion deploy when the column debouches upon some open
space. It is almost incredible, but it is true.

Now of all the writers of his time Carlyle was, one would have
thought, the least able to understand this. He could see nothing
in acephalous mankind. It was the whole of his philosophy that
men cannot so organize themselves, that they need leaders and
strong men, and all the rest of it. Yet so thoroughly has he got
inside his subject, so vitally has he raised it up and made it move
of its own life that in his book you see the French mob doing
precisely what he would have told you, had you asked him, no

mob could do. When he describes them you see them doing
what as a fact they did, and moving in a fashion which, as a fact,
was their own. When he stops to comment upon them, as he
does from time to time, he is often wrong, but when the description begins he becomes right again by a pure instinct for visual-
ising, and for making men act in harmony and in consort in his
book.

His inacquaintance with the French character does certainly
make him misunderstand the battles. Where he is at his best in
his other works, there he is at his worst in the Revolution. His
fighting is all wrong. Everybody knows for instance that Bonaparte lost one of his guns in Vendémiaire, there was no "whiff of
grape shot," and what is worse he does not present the great
battles of '93 and '94 in their true perspective. He does not show
the victories "Pursuing the Terror like furies," and throughout
the work the armies which are the meaning and the guidance
of the Revolution come in as it were by accident and give no
clue.

But there is another point where his ignorance of the French
people and his peculiar ignorance of their religion might have led
him far more astray, and where he is triumphantly successful;
and that is in his portraiture of French violence, and of French
ferocity. He had not in his life seen anything violent or
ferocious. It was sheer creative power which enabled him to
project upon his screen the actualities of which he had read, and
there is perhaps no other English writer who has done it; so alien
is violence to our national character and so utterly removed is it
from our national experience.

The energy of the Revolution, one might conclude, found in the
depths of this man who had never been near the sound of arms or
the vision of an insurgent populace, something congenial: some
ancient strength in the Scotch inherited from mediæval freedom
arose in him and answered the French appeal. It did for him
what the story of Napoleon did for Victor Hugo: it 'blew the
creative gale'—'le souffle createur.'

Here is the peculiar merit of this book, and here is what may
preserve it even when taste has so changed that its rhetoric shall
have become tedious and that a classical reaction shall have
rendered repulsive the anarchic outbursts of its prose. He was
inspired. The enormity of the action moved him as the
Marseillaise can still move the young conscripts upon the march
when they hear it from a distant place and go forward to the call

of it. The Revolution filled him as he proceeded, and was, in a sense, co-author with him of the shock, the flames and the roar, the innumerable feet, and the songs which together build up what we read achieved in these volumes.

H. BELLOC.

SELECT BIBLIOGRAPHY

WORKS: *Elements of Geometry and Trigonometry* (from the French of A. M. Legendre), 1824; *Wilhelm Meister's Apprenticeship*, 3 vols., 1824; *The Life of Schiller* (*London Magazine*, 1823–4), 1825; *German Romance*, 4 vols., 1827; *Sartor Resartus* (*Fraser's Magazine*, 1833–4), Boston, 1836 (also in Everyman's Library); *The French Revolution*, 3 vols., 1837 (also in Everyman's Library, 2 vols.); *Lectures on the History of Literature*, 1838; *Critical and Miscellaneous Essays*, 4 vols., Boston, 1838 (also in Everyman's Library, 2 vols.); *Chartism*, 1840; *On Heroes, Hero-Worship, and the Heroic in History*, 1841; *Past and Present*, 1843 (also in Everyman's Library); *Oliver Cromwell's Letters and Speeches: With Elucidation*, 2 vols., 1845 (also in Everyman's Library, 3 vols.); *Latter-Day Pamphlets*, 1850; *Life of John Stirling*, 1851; *The History of Friedrich II of Prussia*, 6 vols., 1858–65; *Inaugural Address at Edinburgh, April 2nd, 1866*; *On the Choice of Books*, 1866; *The Early Kings of Norway: Also an Essay on the Portraits of John Knox* (*Fraser's Magazine* 1875), 1875; *Reminiscences*, ed. J. A. Froude, 2 vols., 1881 (also in Everyman's Library); *Reminiscences of my Irish Journey in 1849*, 1882; *Last Words of Thomas Carlyle on Trades Unions*, etc., ed. J. C. Aitken, 1882; *Historical Sketches of Notable Persons in the Reigns of James I and Charles I*, ed. A. Carlyle, 1898; *Two Notebooks of Thomas Carlyle*, ed. C. E. Norton, New York, 1898.

COLLECTED WORKS: First collected edition, 16 vols., 1857–8; Ashburton edition, 17 vols. (with three supplementary volumes), 1885–8; Centenary edition (most complete), ed. H. D. Traill, 30 vols., 1896–9; Standard edition, 18 vols., New York, 1905.

LETTERS: *Correspondence of Carlyle and Emerson*, ed. C. E. Norton, 2 vols., 1883; *Correspondence between Goethe and Carlyle*, ed. C. E. Norton, 1887; *Letters of Thomas Carlyle*, ed. C. E. Norton, 2 vols., 1888; *New Letters of Thomas Carlyle*, ed. A. Carlyle, 2 vols., 1904; *Letters of Thomas Carlyle to John Stuart Mill, John Stirling, and Robert Browning*, ed. A. Carlyle, 1923.

BIOGRAPHY AND CRITICISM: B. W. Matz: *Thomas Carlyle, a Brief Account of his Life and Writings*, 1902; D. A. Wilson and D. W. MacArthur: *Life of Thomas Carlyle*, 6 vols., 1923–34; S. Sagar: *Round by Repentance Tower. A Study of Carlyle*, 1930; J. Symons: *Thomas Carlyle: The Life and Ideas of a Prophet*, 1952; Jules Paul Seigel: *Thomas Carlyle* (Critical Heritage Series), 1971.

Carlyle also contributed to the following: Brewster's *Edinburgh Encyclopaedia*, vols. xiv–xvi; *Edinburgh Review*, xlvi, xlviii, xlix, liii–lv; *New Edinburgh Review*, i, ii; *Foreign Review*, i–v; *Fraser's Magazine*, i–viii, xi, xv, xx, xxx, xl; *Westminster Review*, xv, xxvi–xxviii, xxxii, 2nd series vii; *Foreign Quarterly Review*, viii, x, xi, xxxi; *New Monthly Magazine*, xxxiv; *Macmillan's Magazine*, vi, viii, xvi; *Examiner*, 7th April 1839, 4th March, 29th April, 13th May, 2nd December 1848; *Spectator*, 13th May 1848; *Nation* (Dublin), 1st December 1849; *Leigh Hunt's Journal*, 7th, 21st, December 1850, 11th January 1851; *Keepsake*, 1852; *The Times*, 19th June 1844, 28th November 1876, 5th May 1877.

CONTENTS
(Former Volume 1)

Introduction by Hilaire Belloc · · · · · · PAGE v

PART I
THE BASTILLE

BOOK I
DEATH OF LOUIS XV.

CHAPTER
I. Louis the Well-beloved · · · · · · 1
II. Realised Ideals · · · · · · 4
III. Viaticum · · · · · · 12
IV. Louis the Unforgotten · · · · · · 15

BOOK II
THE PAPER AGE

I. Astræa Redux · · · · · · 22
II. Petition in Hieroglyphs · · · · · · 27
III. Questionable · · · · · · 29
IV. Maurepas · · · · · · 32
V. Astræa Redux without Cash · · · · · · 35
VI. Windbags · · · · · · 39
VII. Contrat Social · · · · · · 42
VIII. Printed Paper · · · · · · 45

BOOK III
THE PARLEMENT OF PARIS

I. Dishonoured Bills · · · · · · 50
II. Controller Calonne · · · · · · 54
III. The Notables · · · · · · 57
IV. Loménie's Edicts · · · · · · 64
V. Loménie's Thunderbolts · · · · · · 68
VI. Loménie's Plots · · · · · · 72
VII. Internecine · · · · · · 76
VIII. Loménie's Death-throes · · · · · · 81
IX. Burial with Bonfire · · · · · · 89

BOOK IV

STATES-GENERAL

CHAPTER		PAGE
I.	The Notables again	93
II.	The Election	97
III.	Grown electric	103
IV.	The Procession	106

BOOK V

THE THIRD ESTATE

I.	Inertia	122
II.	Mercury de Brézé	129
III.	Broglie the War-god	135
IV.	To Arms!	140
V.	Give us Arms	145
VI.	Storm and Victory	150
VII.	Not a Revolt	158
VIII.	Conquering your King	161
IX.	The Lanterne	165

BOOK VI

CONSOLIDATION

I.	Make the Constitution	170
II.	The Constituent Assembly	175
III.	The General Overturn	179
IV.	In Queue	187
V.	The Fourth Estate	189

BOOK VII

THE INSURRECTION OF WOMEN

I.	Patrollotism	192
II.	O Richard, O my King	195
III.	Black Cockades	199
IV.	The Menads	201
V.	Usher Maillard	204
VI.	To Versailles	209
VII.	At Versailles	212
VIII.	The Equal Diet	215
IX.	Lafayette	219
X.	The Grand Entries	223
XI.	From Versailles	227

Contents

PART II

THE CONSTITUTION

BOOK I

THE FEAST OF PIKES

CHAPTER		PAGE
I.	In the Tuileries	233
II.	In the Salle de Manége	236
III.	The Muster	246
IV.	Journalism	252
V.	Clubbism	256
VI.	Je le jure	259
VII.	Prodigies	262
VIII.	Solemn League and Covenant . . .	265
IX.	Symbolic	270
X.	Mankind	271
XI.	As in the Age of Gold	276
XII.	Sound and Smoke	281

BOOK II

NANCI

I.	Bouillé	288
II.	Arrears and Aristocrats	290
III.	Bouillé at Metz	295
IV.	Arrears at Nanci	298
V.	Inspector Malseigne	302
VI.	Bouillé at Nanci	306

BOOK III

THE TUILERIES

I.	Epimenides	314
II.	The Wakeful	318
III.	Sword in Hand	323
IV.	To fly or not to fly	328
V.	The Day of Poniards	335
VI.	Mirabeau	341
VII.	Death of Mirabeau	344

Contents

(Former Volume 2)

PART II—THE CONSTITUTION (*continued*)

BOOK IV
VARENNES

CHAPTER		PAGE
I.	Easter at Saint-Cloud	1
II.	Easter at Paris	5
III.	Count Fersen	7
IV.	Attitude	13
V.	The New Berline	16
VI.	Old-Dragoon Drouet	20
VII.	The Night of Spurs	23
VIII.	The Return	30
IX.	Sharp Shot	33

BOOK V
PARLIAMENT FIRST

I.	Grande Acceptation	38
II.	The Book of the Law	44
III.	Avignon	51
IV.	No Sugar	58
V.	Kings and Emigrants	61
VI.	Brigands and Jalès	69
VII.	Constitution will not march	72
VIII.	The Jacobins	76
IX.	Minister Roland	80
X.	Pétion-National-Pique	83
XI.	The Hereditary Representative	85
XII.	Procession of the Black Breeches	88

BOOK VI
THE MARSEILLESE

I.	Executive that does not act	94
II.	Let us march	100
III.	Some Consolation to Mankind	102
IV.	Subterranean	106
V.	At Dinner	108
VI.	The Steeples at Midnight	112
VII.	The Swiss	119
VIII.	Constitution burst in Pieces	125

Contents

PART III

THE GUILLOTINE

BOOK I

SEPTEMBER

CHAPTER   PAGE

    I. The Improvised Commune 130
   II. Danton 140
  III. Dumouriez 144
  IV. September in Paris 147
   V. A Trilogy 154
  VI. The Circular 160
 VII. September in Argonne 168
VIII. Exeunt 176

BOOK II

REGICIDE

    I. The Deliberative 183
   II. The Executive 191
  III. Discrowned 194
  IV. The Loser pays 197
   V. Stretching of Formulas 199
  VI. At the Bar 204
 VII. The Three Votings 211
VIII. Place de la Révolution 216

BOOK III

THE GIRONDINS

    I. Cause and Effect 222
   II. Culottic and Sansculottic 227
  III. Growing shrill 232
  IV. Fatherland in Danger 235
   V. Sansculottism accoutred 243
  VI. The Traitor 246
 VII. In Fight 249
VIII. In Death-Grips 252
  IX. Extinct 257

Contents

BOOK IV
TERROR

CHAPTER									PAGE
I.	Charlotte Corday	.	.	.	.	.	.	.	262
II.	In Civil War	.	.	.	.	.	.	.	269
III.	Retreat of the Eleven	.	.	.	.	.	.	.	272
IV.	O Nature	.	.	.	.	.	.	.	275
V.	Sword of Sharpness	.	.	.	.	.	.	.	279
VI.	Risen against Tyrants	.	.	.	.	.	.	.	282
VII.	Marie-Antoinette	.	.	.	.	.	.	.	286
VIII.	The Twenty-Two	.	.	.	.	.	.	.	288

BOOK V
TERROR THE ORDER OF THE DAY

I.	Rushing down	.	.	.	.	.	.	.	292
II.	Death	.	.	.	.	.	.	.	296
III.	Destruction	.	.	.	.	.	.	.	301
IV.	Carmagnole complete	.	.	.	.	.	.	.	309
V.	Like a Thunder-Cloud	.	.	.	.	.	.	.	315
VI.	Do thy Duty	.	.	.	.	.	.	.	318
VII.	Flame-Picture	.	.	.	.	.	.	.	324

BOOK VI
THERMIDOR

I.	The Gods are athirst	.	.	.	.	.	.	.	329
II.	Danton, no Weakness	.	.	.	.	.	.	.	334
III.	The Tumbrils	.	.	.	.	.	.	.	339
IV.	Mumbo-Jumbo	.	.	.	.	.	.	.	343
V.	The Prisons	.	.	.	.	.	.	.	346
VI.	To finish the Terror	.	.	.	.	.	.	.	349
VII.	Go down to	.	.	.	.	.	.	.	354

BOOK VII
VENDÉMIAIRE

I.	Decadent	.	.	.	.	.	.	.	361
II.	La Cabarus	.	.	.	.	.	.	.	364
III.	Quiberon	.	.	.	.	.	.	.	368
IV.	Lion not dead	.	.	.	.	.	.	.	371
V.	Lion sprawling its last	.	.	.	.	.	.	.	374
VI.	Grilled Herrings	.	.	.	.	.	.	.	380
VII.	The Whiff of Grapeshot	.	.	.	.	.	.	.	383
VIII.	Finis	.	.	.	.	.	.	.	388

GENERAL INDEX	.	.	.	.	.	.	.	.	391

CHRONOLOGICAL TABLE

1774.	May 10.	Death of Louis XV. Accession of Louis XVI.
		Maurepas Prime Minister.
		Dismissal of 'Parlement Maupeou,' and recall of the old Parlement.
	Aug. 24.	Turgot Controller-General of Finance.
1776.	May.	Dismissal of Turgot. Ministry of Necker.
	July 15.	American declaration of Independence.
1778.		War between France and England.
1781.	May.	Dismissal of Necker.
	Nov.	Death of Maurepas.
1783.	Jan. 20.	Peace of Versailles. Recognition of American Independence.
	Nov. 3.	Ministry of Calonne.
1787.	Feb. 22.	Convocation of Notables.
	April 8.	Dismissal of Calonne, ministry of Loménie de Brienne.
	May 25.	Dismissal of Notables.
		Contest of the Paris Parlement with the King as to the registration of Loménie's edicts.
	Aug. 6.	King holds a 'bed of justice' to force the Parlement to register the edicts.
	Aug. 15.	Exile of the Parlement to Troyes.
	Sept. 20.	Return of the Parlement.
	Nov. 19.	'Royal Séance' to invite the Parlement to register edicts.
1788.		Continued struggle between the King and the Parlement; scheme of the 'Bailliages' and 'Plenary Court.'
	May 5.	Arrest of d'Espréménil and Goeslard de Monsabert.
	Aug. 8.	Royal Edict that States-General shall assemble in the following May.
	Aug. 16.	The Treasury insolvent.
	Aug. 25.	Dismissal of Loménie, recall of Necker.
	Nov. 6–Dec. 12.	Second Convocation of Notables.
1789.	April 27–8.	Riot at Réveillon's warehouse.
	May 4.	Procession of the States-General.
	May 4–June 20.	Contest as to whether the Orders shall vote separately, or as one Assembly.
	June 17.	The Third Estate adopt the title of 'National Assembly.'

1789.	June 20.	Oath of the Tennis Court.
	June 23.	Séance royale.
		Triumph of the Third Estate, and union of the Orders.
	July 12.	Dismissal of Necker. Insurrection of Paris.
	July 14.	Fall of the Bastille.
	July 15.	Recall of Necker to the Ministry of Finance.
	July–August.	Peasants' Revolt.
	Aug. 4.	Abolition of feudal dues, &c.
	Oct. 1.	Banquet at Versailles.
	Oct. 5.	Insurrection of women.
	Oct. 6.	King removes to Paris.
1790.	Feb. 4.	Visit of the King to the Assembly, and National Oath.
		During these months all France is 'federating.'
	June.	Anacharsis Clootz and his deputation of Mankind in the Assembly.
		Titles of nobility abolished.
	July 1–12.	All Paris turns out to prepare the Champ-de-Mars for the Federation fête.
	July 14.	The Federation fête, or 'Feast of Pikes.'
	Aug. 24–31.	The mutiny at Nanci, suppressed by Bouillé.
	Sept. 3.	Necker resigns office and leaves France.
	Sept. 20.	Funeral service for the slain at Nanci.
1791.	Feb. 28.	Attack upon Vincennes. The 'day of poniards.'
	April 2.	Death of Mirabeau.
	April 4.	Funeral of Mirabeau.
	April 18.	King's proposed visit to Saint-Cloud stopped by the mob.
	May 4.	Saint-Huruge burns the Pope in effigy.
	June 20.	The flight to Varennes.
	July 17.	'Massacre' of the Champ-de-Mars.
	Aug. 27.	Declaration of Pilnitz.
	Sept. 30.	End of the Constituent Assembly.
	Oct. 1.	Meeting of the Legislative Assembly.
	Oct. 16.	Murder of L'Escuyer at Avignon, followed by Jourdan's massacres there.
1792.	March.	Girondin ministry appointed.
	April 20.	Declaration of War.
	April 29.	Panic at Lille and murder of Dillon by his soldiers.
	June 9.	Skirmish of Maubeuge.
	June 12.	Dismissal of the Girondin ministry.
	June 19.	King vetoes the two decrees concerning (a) the non-juring priests, (b) the camp of Fédérés.
	June 20.	The 'Procession of Black Breeches' invades the Tuileries.
	June 28.	Lafayette at the bar of the Assembly.
	July 6.	Pétion, mayor of Paris, 'suspended.'

1792.   July   7.   The scene of the 'Baiser de Lamourette.'

July   11.   Decree that the 'country is in danger.'

July   14.   Federation fête.

July   25.   Brunswick's manifesto published.

July   30.   Skirmish between the Marseillese and the Grenadiers of Filles-Saint-Thomas.

Aug.   8.   Acquittal of Layafette.

Aug.   9–10.   The 'Central Committee of the Sections' usurps the place of the Paris municipality.

             Arrest and Murder of Mandat.

Aug.   10.   The Insurrection. Sack of the Tuileries and 'suspension' of the King. Fall of the monarchy.

Aug.   10, 12.   New 'Patriot' Ministry, including Danton as Minister of Justice.

Aug.   13.   The royal family imprisoned at the Temple.

Aug.   23.   Capitulation of Longwy.

Sept.   2–6.   September massacres.

Sept.   2.   Brunswick occupies Verdun. Dumouriez occupies the passes of the Argonne.

Sept.   20.   Cannonade of Valmy.

Sept.   21.   Meeting of the Convention.

Sept.   22.   Proclamation of the Republic.

Nov.   6.   Defeat of the Austrians by Dumouriez at Jemappes.

Nov.   19.   Decree of the Convention offering assistance to all nations to throw off despotism.

Dec.   11.   Opening of the king's trial.

1793.   Jan.   21.   Execution of the king.

Feb.   1.   Declaration of war between France and England.

Mar.   7.   Declaration of war between France and Spain.

Mar.   10.   Insurrection of La Vendée.

Mar.   18.   Defeat of the French by the Austrians at Neerwinden.

Mar.   25.   Constitution of the Committee of Public Safety.

April   4.   Dumouriez deserts to the Austrians.

May   31.   The Commune 'in insurrection.' Abolition of the Girondin 'Commission of Twelve.'

June   2.   Insurrection; expulsion of the Girondin deputies.

July   12.   Capitulation of Condé.

July   13.   Assassination of Marat.

July   25.   Capitulation of Maintz.

July   28.   Capitulation of Valenciennes.

Aug.   23.   Levy *en masse*.

Aug.   29.   Capitulation of Toulon to the English.

Sept.   17.   Law against suspected persons.

Oct.   7.   Capitulation of Lyons to the Convention.

Oct.   16.   Execution of the queen.

1793.   Oct. 31.   Execution of the Girondins.

        Nov. 10.   Feast of Reason.

        Dec. 19.   Recapture of Toulon from the English.

1794.   Mar. 15.   Arrest of the Hébertists.

        Mar. 24.   Execution of the Hébertists.

        April 5.   Execution of Dantonists.

        June 1.   Defeat of the French by the English off Brest. Sinking of the *Vengeur*.

        June 8.   Feast of the Être Suprême.

        July 27 (Thermidor 9).   Fall of Robespierre.

        July 28.   Execution of Robespierre.

        Nov. 12.   Closing of the Jacobin Club.

        Dec. 8.   Readmission to the Convention of the seventy-three Girondin deputies.

1795.   January.   Conquest of Holland by the French under Pichegru.

        April 1 (Germinal 12).   Abortive insurrection against the Convention.

        April 5.   Treaty of Bâle. Peace between France and Prussia.

        May 20 (Prairial 1).   Second abortive insurrection against the Convention.

        July 10.   Peace between France and Spain.

        July 21.   Repulse of the Emigrants, assisted by the English, at Quiberon.

        Sept. 23.   Proclamation of the constitution of the Directorate.

        Oct. 5 (Vendémiaire 13).   Last insurrection against the Convention; the 'whiff of grape-shot.'

September 22nd of 1792 is Vendémiaire 1st of Year One, and the new months are all of 30 days each; therefore:

Chronological Table

To the number of the day in				ADD	We have the number of the day in					DAYS
	Vendémiaire	.	.	. 21		September	.	.	.	30
	Brumaire	.	.	. 21		October .	.	.	.	31
	Frimaire .	.	.	. 20		November	.	.	.	30
	Nivose .	.	.	. 20		December	.	.	.	31
	Pluviose .	.	.	. 19		January .	.	.	.	31
	Ventose .	.	.	. 18		February	.	.	.	28
	Germinal	.	.	. 20		March	.	.	.	31
	Floréal .	.	.	. 19		April	.	.	.	30
	Prairial .	.	.	. 19		May	.	.	.	31
	Messidor .	.	.	. 18		June	.	.	.	30
	Thermidor	.	.	. 18		July	.	.	.	31
	Fructidor	.	.	. 17		August	.	.	.	31

There are 5 Sansculottides, and in leap-year a sixth, to be added at the end of Fructidor.

The New Calendar ceased on the 1st of January 1806. See *Choix des Rapports*, xiii. 83–99; xix. 199.

PART I—THE BASTILLE

BOOK I

DEATH OF LOUIS XV

CHAPTER I

LOUIS THE WELL-BELOVED

PRESIDENT HÉNAULT, remarking on royal Surnames of Honour how difficult it often is to ascertain not only why, but even when, they were conferred, takes occasion in his sleek official way to make a philosophical reflection. 'The Surname of *Bien-aimé* (Well-beloved),' says he, 'which Louis XV. bears, will not leave posterity in the same doubt. This Prince, in the year 1744, while hastening from one end of his kingdom to the other, and suspending his conquests in Flanders that he might fly to the assistance of Alsace, was arrested at Metz by a malady which threatened to cut short his days. At the news of this, Paris, all in terror, seemed a city taken by storm: the churches resounded with supplications and groans; the prayers of priests and people were every moment interrupted by their sobs; and it was from an interest so dear and tender that this Surname of *Bien-aimé* fashioned itself,—a title higher still than all the rest which this great Prince has earned.'

So stands it written; in lasting memorial of that year 1744. Thirty other years have come and gone; and 'this great Prince' again lies sick; but in how altered circumstances now! Churches resound not with incessant groanings; Paris is stoically calm: sobs interrupt no prayers, for indeed none are offered; except Priests' Litanies, read or chanted at fixed money-rate per hour, which are not liable to interruption. The shepherd of the people has been carried home from Little Trianon, heavy of heart, and been put to bed in his own Château of Versailles; the flock knows it, and heeds it not. At most, in the immeasurable tide of French Speech (which ceases not day after day, and only ebbs towards the short hours of night), may this of the royal sickness emerge from time to time as an article of news. Bets are doubtless depending; nay, some people 'express themselves loudly in the streets.' But for the rest, on green field and steepled city, the May sun shines out, the May evening fades; and men ply their useful or useless business as if no Louis lay in danger.

Dame Dubarry, indeed, might pray, if she had a talent for it; Duke d'Aiguillon too, Maupeou and the Parlement Maupeou: these, as they sit in their high places, with France harnessed under their feet, know well on what basis they continue there. Look to it, d'Aiguillon; sharply as thou didst, from the Mill of St. Cast, on Quiberon and the invading English; thou 'covered if not with glory yet with meal!' Fortune was ever accounted inconstant: and each dog has but his day.

Forlorn enough languished Duke d'Aiguillon, some years ago; covered, as we said, with meal; nay with worse. For La Chalotais, the Breton Parlementeer, accused him not only of poltroonery and tyranny, but even of *concussion* (official plunder of money); which accusations it was easier to get 'quashed' by backstairs Influences than to get answered: neither could the thoughts, or even the tongues, of men be tied. Thus, under disastrous eclipse, had this grand-nephew of the great Richelieu to glide about; unworshipped by the world; resolute Choiseul, the abrupt proud man, disdaining him, or even forgetting him. Little prospect but to glide into Gascony, to rebuild Châteaus there, and die inglorious killing game! However, in the year 1770, a certain young soldier, Dumouriez by name, returning from Corsica, could see 'with sorrow, at Compiègne, the old King of France, on foot, with doffed hat, in sight of his army, at the side of a magnificent phaeton, doing homage to the—Dubarry.'

Much lay therein! Thereby, for one thing, could d'Aiguillon postpone the rebuilding of his Château, and rebuild his fortunes first. For stout Choiseul would discern in the Dubarry nothing but a wonderfully dizened Scarlet-woman; and go on his way as if she were not. Intolerable: the source of sighs, tears, of pettings and poutings; which would not end till 'France' (La France, as she named her royal valet) finally mustered heart to see Choiseul; and with that 'quivering in the chin' (*tremblement du menton*) natural in such case, faltered out a dismissal: dismissal of his last substantial man, but pacification of his scarlet-woman. Thus d'Aiguillon rose again, and culminated. And with him there rose Maupeou, the banisher of Parlements; who plants you a refractory President 'at Croc in Combrailles on the top of steep rocks, inaccessible except by litters,' there to consider himself. Likewise there rose Abbé Terray, dissolute Financier, paying eightpence in the shilling,—so that wits exclaim in some press at the playhouse, "Where is Abbé Terray, that he might reduce us to two-thirds!" And so have these individuals (verily by black-art) built them a Domdaniel, or enchanted Dubarrydom; call it an Armida-Palace, where they dwell pleasantly; Chancellor Maupeou 'playing blind-man's-buff' with the scarlet Enchantress; or gallantly presenting her with dwarf Negroes; —and a Most Christian King has unspeakable peace within doors, whatever he may have without. "My Chancellor is a scoundrel; but I cannot do without him."

Beautiful Armida-Palace, where the inmates live enchanted lives; lapped in soft music of adulation; waited on by the splendours of the world;—which nevertheless hangs wondrously as by a single hair. Should the Most Christian King die; or even get seriously afraid of dying! For, alas, had not the fair haughty Chateauroux to fly, with wet cheeks and flaming heart, from that Fever-scene at Metz, long since; driven forth by sour shavelings? She hardly returned, when fever and shavelings were both swept into the background. Pompadour too, when Damiens wounded Royalty 'slightly, under the fifth rib,' and our drive to Trianon went off futile, in shrieks and madly shaken torches,—had to pack, and be in readiness: yet did not go, the wound not proving poisoned. For his Majesty has religious faith; believes, at least in a Devil. And now a third peril; and who knows what may be in it! For the Doctors look grave; ask privily, If his Majesty had not the smallpox long ago?—and doubt it may have been a false kind. Yes, Maupeou, pucker those sinister brows of thine, and peer out on it with thy malign rat-eyes: it is a questionable case. Sure only that man is mortal; that with the life of one mortal snaps irrevocably the wonderfulest talisman, and all Dubarrydom rushes off, with tumult, into infinite Space; and ye, as subterranean Apparitions are wont, vanish utterly,—leaving only a smell of sulphur!

These, and what holds of these may pray,—to Beelzebub, or whoever will hear them. But from the rest of France there comes, as was said, no prayer; or one of an *opposite* character, 'expressed openly in the streets.' Château or Hôtel, where an enlightened Philosophism scrutinises many things, is not given to prayer: neither are Rossbach victories, Terray Finances, nor, say only 'sixty thousand *Lettres-de-Cachet*' (which is Maupeou's share), persuasives towards that. O Hénault! Prayers? From a France smitten (by black-art) with plague after plague; and lying now, in shame and pain, with a Harlot's foot on its neck, what prayer can come? Those lank scarecrows, that prowl hunger-stricken through all highways and byways of French Existence, will they pray? The dull millions that, in the workshop or furrowfield, grind foredone at the wheel of Labour, like haltered gin-horses, if blind so much the quieter? Or they that in the Bicêtre Hospital, 'eight to a bed,' lie waiting their manumission? Dim are those heads of theirs, dull stagnant those hearts: to them the great Sovereign is known mainly as the great Regrater of Bread. If they hear of his sickness, they will answer with a dull *Tant pis pour lui;* or with the question, Will he die?

Yes, will he die? that is now, for all France, the grand question, and hope; whereby alone the King's sickness has still some interest.

CHAPTER II

REALISED IDEALS

SUCH a changed France have we; and a changed Louis. Changed, truly; and further than thou yet seest!—To the eye of History many things, in that sick-room of Louis, are now visible, which to the Courtiers there present were invisible. For indeed it is well said, 'in every object there is inexhaustible meaning; the eye sees in it what the eye brings means of seeing.' To Newton and to Newton's Dog Diamond, what a different pair of Universes; while the painting on the optical retina of both was, most likely, the same! Let the Reader here, in this sick-room of Louis, endeavour to look with the mind too.

Time was when men could (so to speak) of a given man, by nourishing and decorating him with fit appliances, to the due pitch, *make* themselves a King, almost as the Bees do; and what was still more to the purpose, loyally obey him when made. The man so nourished and decorated, thenceforth named royal, does verily bear rule; and is said, and even thought, to be, for example, 'prosecuting conquests in Flanders,' when he lets himself like luggage be carried thither: and no light luggage; covering miles of road. For he has his unblushing Chateauroux, with her bandboxes and rouge-pots, at his side; so that, at every new station, a wooden gallery must be run up between their lodgings. He has not only his *Maison-Bouche*, and *Valetaille* without end, but his very Troop of Players, with their pasteboard coulisses, thunder-barrels, their kettles, fiddles, stage-wardrobes, portable larders, (and chaffering and quarrelling enough); all mounted in wagons, tumbrils, second-hand chaises,—sufficient not to conquer Flanders, but the patience of the world. With such a flood of loud jingling appurtenances does he lumber along, prosecuting his conquests in Flanders: wonderful to behold. So nevertheless it was and had been: to some solitary thinker it might seem strange; but even to him, inevitable, not unnatural.

For ours is a most fictile world; and man is the most fingent plastic of creatures. A world not fixable; not fathomable! An unfathomable Somewhat, which is *Not we;* which we can work with, and live amidst,—and model, miraculously in our miraculous Being, and name World.—But if the very Rocks and Rivers (as Metaphysic teaches) are, in strict language, *made* by those outward Senses of ours, how much more, by the Inward Sense, are all Phenomena of the spiritual kind: Dignities, Authorities, Holies, Unholies! Which inward sense, moreover, is not permanent like the outward ones, but forever growing and changing. Does not the Black African take of Sticks and Old Clothes (say, exported Monmouth-Street cast-clothes) what will suffice; and of these, cunningly combining them, fabricate for himself an Eidolon (Idol, or *Thing Seen*), and name it *Mumbo-Jumbo;* which he can thenceforth pray to, with upturned awe-struck eye, not without hope? The white European mocks; but ought rather to consider; and see whether he, at home, could not do the like a little more wisely.

So it *was*, we say, in those conquests of Flanders, thirty years ago: but so it no longer is. Alas, much more lies sick than poor Louis: not the French King only, but the French Kingship; this too, after long rough tear and wear, is breaking down. The world is all so changed; so much that seemed

vigorous has sunk decrepit, so much that was not is beginning
to be !—Borne over the Atlantic, to the closing ear of Louis,
King by the Grace of God, what sounds are these; muffled
ominous, new in our centuries? Boston Harbour is black
with unexpected Tea: behold a Pennsylvanian Congress
gather; and ere long, on Bunker Hill, DEMOCRACY announcing,
in rifle-volleys death-winged, under her Star Banner, to the
tune of Yankee-doodle-doo, that she is born, and, whirlwind-
like, will envelope the whole world !

Sovereigns die and Sovereignties: how all dies, and is for
a Time only; is a 'Time-phantasm, yet reckons itself real !'
The Merovingian Kings, slowly wending on their bullock-carts
through the streets of Paris, with their long hair flowing, have
all wended slowly on,—into Eternity. Charlemagne sleeps at
Salzburg, with truncheon grounded; only Fable expecting that
he will awaken. Charles the Hammer, Pepin Bow-legged, where
now is their eye of menace, their voice of command? Rollo and
his shaggy Northmen cover not the Seine with ships; but have
sailed off on a longer voyage. The hair of Towhead (*Tête
d'étoupes*) now needs no combing; Iron-cutter (*Taillefer*)
cannot cut a cobweb; shrill Fredegonda, shrill Brunhilda have
had out their hot life-scold, and lie silent, their hot life-frenzy
cooled. Neither from that black Tower de Nesle descends
now darkling the doomed gallant, in his sack, to the Seine
waters; plunging into Night: for Dame de Nesle now cares
not for this world's gallantry, heeds not this world's scandal;
Dame de Nesle is herself gone into Night. They are all
gone; sunk,—down, down, with the tumult they made; and
the rolling and the trampling of ever new generations passes
over them; and they hear it not any more forever.

And yet withal has there not been realised somewhat ?
Consider (to go no further) these strong Stone-edifices, and
what they hold ! Mud-Town of the Borderers (*Lutetia Paris-
iorum* or *Barisiorum*) has paved itself, has spread over all
the Seine Islands, and far and wide on each bank, and become
City of Paris, sometimes boasting to be 'Athens of Europe,'
and even 'Capital of the Universe.' Stone towers frown aloft;
long-lasting, grim with a thousand years. Cathedrals are there,
and a Creed (or memory of a Creed) in them; Palaces, and
a State and Law. Thou seest the Smoke-vapour; unextinguished Breath as of a thing living. Labour's thousand
hammers ring on her anvils: also a more miraculous Labour

works, noiselessly, not with the Hand but with the Thought. How have cunning workmen in all crafts, with their cunning head and right-hand, tamed the Four Elements to be their ministers; yoking the Winds to their Sea-chariot, making the very Stars their Nautical Timepiece;—and written and collected a *Bibliothèque du Roi;* among whose Books is the Hebrew Book! A wondrous race of creatures: *these* have been realised, and what of Skill is in these: call not the Past Time, with all its confused wretchednesses, a lost one.

Observe, however, that of man's whole terrestrial possessions and attainments, unspeakably the noblest are his Symbols, divine or divine-seeming; under which he marches and fights, with victorious assurance, in this life-battle: what we can call his Realised Ideals. Of which realised Ideals, omitting the rest, consider only these two: his Church, or spiritual Guidance; his Kingship, or temporal one. The Church: what a word was there; richer than Golconda and the treasures of the world! In the heart of the remotest mountains rises the little Kirk; the Dead all slumbering round it, under their white memorial-stones, 'in hope of a happy resurrection:'—dull wert thou, O Reader, if never in any hour (say of moaning midnight, when such Kirk hung spectral in the sky, and Being was as if swallowed up of Darkness) it spoke to thee—things unspeakable, that went to thy soul's soul. Strong was he that had a Church, what we can call a Church: he stood thereby, though 'in the centre of Immensities, in the conflux of Eternities,' yet manlike towards God and man; the vague shoreless Universe had become for him a firm city, and dwelling which he knew. Such virtue was in Belief; in these words, well spoken: *I believe.* Well might men prize their *Credo*, and raise stateliest Temples for it, and reverend Hierarchies, and give it the tithe of their substance; it was worth living for and dying for.

Neither was that an inconsiderable moment when wild armed men first raised their Strongest aloft on the buckler-throne, and, with clanging armour and hearts, said solemnly: Be thou our Acknowledged Strongest! In such Acknowledged Strongest (well-named King, *Kön-ning*, Can-ning, or Man that was Able) what a Symbol shone now for them,— significant with the destinies of the world! A Symbol of true Guidance in return for loving Obedience; properly, if he knew it, the prime want of man. A Symbol which might be called sacred; for is there not, in reverence for what is better than we, an indestructible sacredness? On which ground, too, it was well said there lay in the Acknowledged Strongest a divine right; as surely there might in the Strongest, whether Acknowledged or not,—considering *who* it was that made him strong. And so, in the midst of confusions and unutterable incongruities (as all growth is confused), did this of Royalty, with Loyalty environing it, spring up; and grow mysteriously, subduing and assimilating (for a principle of Life was in it); till it also had grown world-great, and was among the main Facts of our modern existence. Such a Fact, that Louis XIV., for example, could answer the expostulatory Magistrate with his " *L'État c'est moi* (The State? I am the State);" and be replied to by silence and abashed looks. So far had accident and forethought; had your Louis Elevenths, with the leaden Virgin in their hat-band, and torture-wheels and conical *oubliettes* (man-eating!) under their feet; your Henri Fourths, with their prophesied social millennium, 'when every peasant should have his fowl in the pot;' and on the whole, the fertility of this most fertile Existence (named of Good and Evil)—brought it, in the matter of the Kingship. Wondrous! Concerning which may we not again say, that in the huge mass of Evil, as it rolls and swells. there is ever some Good working imprisoned, working towards deliverance and triumph?

How such Ideals do realise themselves; and grow, wondrously, from amid the incongruous ever-fluctuating chaos of the Actual: this is what World-History, if it teach anything, has to teach us. How they grow; and, after long stormy growth, bloom out mature, supreme; then quickly (for the blossom is brief) fall into decay; sorrowfully dwindle; and crumble down, or rush down, noisily or noiselessly disappearing. The blossom is so brief; as of some centennial Cactus-flower, which after a century of waiting shines out for hours! Thus from the day when rough Clovis, in the Champ de Mars, in sight of his whole army, had to cleave retributively the head of that rough Frank, with sudden battle-axe, and the fierce words, "It was thus thou clavest the vase" (St. Remi's and mine) "at Soissons," forward to Louis the Grand and his *L'État c'est moi*, we count some twelve hundred years: and now this the very next Louis is dying, and so much dying with him!— Nay, thus too, if Catholicism, with and against Feudalism (but *not* against Nature and her bounty), gave us English a Shakespeare and Era of Shakespeare, and so produced a blossom of Catholicism—it was not till Catholicism itself, so far as Law could abolish it, had been abolished here.

But of those decadent ages in which no Ideal either grows or blossoms? When Belief and Loyalty have passed away, and only the cant and false echo of them remains; and all Solemnity has become Pageantry; and the Creed of persons in authority has become one of two things: an Imbecility or a Machiavelism? Alas, of these ages World-History can take no notice; they have to become compressed more and more, and finally suppressed in the Annals of Mankind: blotted out as spurious,—which indeed they are. Hapless ages: wherein, if ever in any, it is an unhappiness to be born. To be born, and to learn only, by every tradition and example, that God's Universe is Belial's and a Lie; and 'the Supreme Quack' the hierarch of men! In which mournfulest faith, nevertheless, do we not see whole generations (two, and sometimes even three successively) live, what they call living; and vanish,—without chance of reappearance?

In such a decadent age, or one fast verging that way, had our poor Louis been born. Grant also that if the French Kingship had not, by course of Nature, long to live, he of all men was the man to accelerate Nature. The Blossom of French Royalty, cactus-like, has accordingly made an astonishing progress. In those Metz days, it was still standing with all its petals, though bedimmed by Orleans Regents and *Roué* Ministers and Cardinals; but now, in 1774, we behold it bald, and the virtue nigh gone out of it.

Disastrous indeed does it look with those same 'realised ideals,' one and all! The Church, which in its palmy season, seven hundred years ago, could make an Emperor wait barefoot, in penance-shirt, three days, in the snow, has for centuries seen itself decaying; reduced even to forget old purposes and enmities, and join interest with the Kingship: on this younger strength it would fain stay its decrepitude; and these two will henceforth stand and fall together. Alas, the Sorbonne still sits there, in its old mansion; but mumbles only jargon of dotage, and no longer leads the consciences of men: not the Sorbonne; it is *Encyclopédies*, *Philosophie*, and who knows what nameless innumerable multitude of ready Writers, profane Singers, Romancers, Players, Disputators, and Pamphleteers, that now form the Spiritual Guidance of the world. The world's Practical Guidance too is lost, or has glided into the same miscellaneous hands. Who is it that the King

(*Ableman*, named also *Roi*, *Rex*, or Director) now guides?
His own huntsman and prickers: when there is to be no hunt,
it is well said, '*Le Roi ne fera rien* (To-day his Majesty will
do *nothing*).' He lives and lingers there, because he is living
there, and none has yet laid hands on him.

The nobles, in like manner, have nearly ceased either to
guide or misguide; and are now, as their master is, little more
than ornamental figures. It is long since they have done
with butchering one another or their king: the Workers, pro-
tected, encouraged by Majesty, have ages ago built walled
towns, and there ply their crafts; will permit no Robber Baron
to 'live by the saddle,' but maintain a gallows to prevent it.
Ever since that period of the *Fronde*, the Noble has changed
his fighting sword into a court rapier; and now loyally attends
his king as ministering satellite; divides the spoil, not now
by violence and murder, but by soliciting and finesse. These
men call themselves supports of the throne: singular gilt-paste-
board *caryatides* in that singular edifice! For the rest, their
privileges every way are now much curtailed. That Law
authorising a Seigneur, as he returned from hunting, to kill
not more than two Serfs, and refresh his feet in their warm
blood and bowels, has fallen into perfect desuetude,—and
even into incredibility; for if Deputy Lapoule can believe in
it, and call for the abrogation of it, so cannot we. No
Charolois, for these last fifty years, though never so fond
of shooting, has been in use to bring down slaters and
plumbers, and see them roll from their roofs; but contents
himself with partridges and grouse. Close-viewed, their industry
and function is that of dressing gracefully and eating sump-
tuously. As for their debauchery and depravity, it is perhaps
unexampled since the era of Tiberius and Commodus. Nevertheless, one has still partly a feeling with the lady Maréchale:
"Depend upon it, Sir, God thinks twice before damning a man
of that quality." These people of old, surely had virtues,
uses; or they could not have been there. Nay, one virtue
they are still required to have (for mortal man cannot live
without a conscience): the virtue of perfect readiness to fight
duels.

Such are the shepherds of the people: and now how fares it
with the flock? With the flock, as is inevitable, it fares ill, and
ever worse. They are not tended, they are only regularly
shorn. They are sent for, to do statute-labour, to pay statute-
taxes; to fatten battlefields (named 'bed of honour') with

their bodies, in quarrels which are not theirs; their hand and toil is in every possession of man; but for themselves they have little or no possession. Untaught, uncomforted, unfed; to pine stagnantly in thick obscuration, in squalid destitution and obstruction: this is the lot of the millions; *peuple taillable et corvéable à merci et miséricorde.* In Brittany they once rose in revolt at the first introduction of Pendulum Clocks; thinking it had something to do with the *Gabelle.* Paris requires to be cleared out periodically by the Police; and the horde of hunger-stricken vagabonds to be sent wandering again over space—for a time. 'During one such periodical clearance,' says Lacretelle, 'in May, 1750, the Police had presumed withal to carry off some reputable people's children, in the hope of extorting ransoms for them. The mothers fill the public places with cries of despair; crowds gather, get excited; so many women in distraction run about exaggerating the alarm: an absurd and horrid fable rises among the people; it is said that the doctors have ordered a Great Person to take baths of young human blood for the restoration of his own, all spoiled by debaucheries. Some of the rioters,' adds Lacretelle, quite coolly, 'were hanged on the following days:' the Police went on. O ye poor naked wretches! and this then is your inarticulate cry to Heaven, as of a dumb tortured animal, crying from uttermost depths of pain and debasement? Do these azure skies, like a dead crystalline vault, only reverberate the echo of it on you? Respond to it only by 'hanging on the following days?'—Not so: not for ever! Ye are heard in Heaven. And the answer too will come,—in a horror of great darkness, and shakings of the world, and a cup of trembling which all the nations shall drink.

Remark, meanwhile, how from amid the wrecks and dust of this universal Decay new Powers are fashioning themselves, adapted to the new time, and its destinies. Besides the old Noblesse, originally of Fighters, there is a new recognised Noblesse of Lawyers; whose gala-day and proud battle-day even now is. An unrecognised Noblesse of Commerce; powerful enough, with money in its pocket. Lastly, powerfulest of all, least recognised of all, a Noblesse of Literature; without steel on their thigh, without gold in their purse, but with the 'grand thaumaturgic faculty of Thought' in their head. French Philosophism has arisen; in which little word how much do we include! Here, indeed, lies properly the cardinal symptom of the whole widespread malady. Faith is gone out; Scepticism is come in. Evil abounds and accumulates; no man has Faith to withstand it, to amend it, to begin by amending himself; it must even go on accumulating. While hollow languor and vacuity is the lot of the Upper, and want and stagnation of the Lower, and universal misery is very certain, what other thing is certain? That a Lie cannot be believed! Philosophism knows only this: her other belief is mainly, that in spiritual supersensual matters no Belief is possible. Unhappy! Nay, as yet the Contradiction of a Lie is some kind of Belief; but the Lie with its Contradiction once swept away, what will remain? The five unsatiated Senses will remain, the sixth insatiable Sense (of vanity); the whole *dæmonic* nature of man will remain,—hurled forth to rage blindly without rule or rein; savage itself, yet with all the tools and weapons of civilisation: a spectacle new in History.

In such a France, as in a Powder-tower, where fire unquenched and now unquenchable is smoking and smouldering all round, has Louis XV. lain down to die. With Pompadourism and Dubarryism, his Fleur-de-lis has been shamefully struck down in all lands and on all seas; Poverty invades even the Royal Exchequer, and Tax-farming can squeeze out no more; there is a quarrel of twenty-five years' standing with the Parlement; everywhere Want, Dishonesty, Unbelief, and hot-brained Sciolists for state-physicians: it is a portentous hour.

Such things can the eye of History see in this sick-room of King Louis, which were invisible to the Courtiers there. It is twenty years, gone Christmas-day, since Lord Chesterfield, summing up what he had noted of this same France, wrote, and sent off by post, the following words, that have become memorable: 'In short, all the symptoms which I have ever met with in History, previous to great Changes and Revolutions in government, now exist and daily increase in France.'

CHAPTER III

VIATICUM

FOR the present, however, the grand question with the Governors of France is: Shall extreme unction, or other ghostly viaticum (to Louis, not to France), be administered?

It is a deep question. For, if administered, if so much as spoken of, must not, on the very threshold of the business, Witch Dubarry vanish; hardly to return should Louis even recover? With her vanishes Duke d'Aiguillon and Company, and all their Armida-Palace, as was said; Chaos swallows the whole again, and there is left nothing but a smell of brimstone. But then, on the other hand, what will the Dauphinists and Choiseulists say? Nay, what may the royal martyr himself say, should he happen to get deadly-worse, without getting delirious? For the present, he still kisses the Dubarry hand; so we, from the anteroom, can note: but afterwards? Doctors' bulletins may run as they are ordered, but it is 'confluent small-pox,'—of which, as is whispered too, the Gatekeeper's once so buxom Daughter lies ill: and Louis XV. is not a man to be trifled with in his viaticum. Was he not wont to cate-chise his very girls in the *Parc-aux-cerfs*, and pray with and for them, that they might preserve their—orthodoxy? A strange fact, not an unexampled one; for there is no animal so strange as man.

For the moment, indeed, it were all well, could Archbishop Beaumont but be prevailed upon—to wink with one eye! Alas, Beaumont would himself so fain do it: for singular to tell, the Church too, and whole posthumous hope of Jesuitism, now hangs by the apron of this same unmentionable woman. But then 'the force of public opinion!' Rigorous Christophe de Beaumont, who has spent his life in persecuting hysterical Jansenists and incredulous Non-confessors; or even their dead bodies, if no better might be,—how shall he now open Heaven's gate, and give absolution with the *corpus delicti* still under his nose? Our Grand-Almoner Roche-Aymon, for his part, will not higgle with a royal sinner about turning of the key: but there are other Churchmen; there is a King's Confessor, foolish Abbé Moudon; and Fanaticism and Decency are not yet extinct. On the whole, what is to be done? The doors can be well watched; the Medical Bulletin adjusted; and much, as usual, be hoped for from time and chance.

The doors are well watched, no improper figure can enter. Indeed, few wish to enter; for the putrid infection reaches even to the *Œil de Bœuf;* so that 'more than fifty fall sick, and ten die.' Mesdames the Princesses alone wait at the loathsome sick bed; impelled by filial piety. The three Princesses, *Graille*, *Chiffe*, *Coche* (Rag, Snip, Pig, as he was wont to name them), are assiduous there; when all have fled. The fourth Princess, *Loque* (Dud), as we guess, is already in the Nunnery, and can only give her orisons. Poor *Graille* and Sisterhood, they have never known a Father; such is the hard bargain Grandeur must make. Scarcely at the *Débotter* (when Royalty took off its boots) could they snatch up their 'enormous hoops, gird the long train round their waists, huddle on their black cloaks of taffeta up to the very chin'; and so, in fit appearance of full dress, 'every evening at six,' walk majestically in; receive their royal kiss on the brow; and then walk majestically out again, to embroidery, small-scandal, prayers, and vacancy. If Majesty came some morning, with coffee of its own making, and swallowed it with them hastily while the dogs were uncoupling for the hunt, it was received as a grace of Heaven. Poor withered ancient women! in the wild tossings that yet await your fragile existence, before it be crushed and broken; as ye fly through hostile countries, over tempestuous seas, are almost taken by the Turks; and wholly, in the Sansculottic Earthquake, know not your right hand from your left, be this always an assured place in your remembrance: for the act was good and loving! To us also it is a little sunny spot in that dismal, howling waste, where we hardly find another.

Meanwhile, what shall an impartial, prudent Courtier do? In these delicate circumstances, while not only death or life, but even sacrament or no sacrament, is a question, the skilfulest may falter. Few are so happy as the Duke d'Orléans and the Prince de Condé; who can themselves, with volatile salts, attend the King's antechamber; and, at the same time, send their brave sons (Duke de Chartres, *Égalité*, that is to be: Duke de Bourbon, one day Condé too, and famous among Dotards) to wait upon the Dauphin. With another few, it is a resolution taken; *jacta est alea.* Old Richelieu, when Archbishop of Beaumont, driven by public opinion, is at last for entering the sick room,—will twitch him by the rochet, into a recess; and there, with his old dissipated mastiff-face, and the oiliest vehemence, be seen pleading (and even, as we judge by Beaumont's change of colour, prevailing) 'that the King be not killed by a proposition in Divinity.' Duke Fronsac, son of Richelieu, can follow his father: when the Curé of Versailles whimpers something about sacraments, he will threaten to 'throw him out of the window if he mention such a thing.'

Happy these, we may say; but to the rest that hover between two opinions, is it not trying? He who would understand to what a pass Catholicism, and much else, had now got, and how the symbols of the Holiest have become gambling-dice of the basest—must read the narrative of those things by Besenval and Soulavie, and the other Court Newsmen of the time. He will see the Versailles galaxy all scattered asunder, grouped into new ever-shifting constellations. There are nods and sagacious glances; go-betweens, silk dowagers mysteriously gliding, with smiles for this constellation, sighs for that: there is tremor, of hope or desperation, in several hearts. There is the pale grinning Shadow of Death, ceremoniously ushered along by another grinning Shadow, of Etiquette: at intervals the growl of Chapel Organs, like prayer by machinery proclaiming, as in a kind of horrid, diabolic horse-laughter, *Vanity of Vanities, all is Vanity!*

CHAPTER IV

LOUIS THE UNFORGOTTEN

POOR Louis! With these it is a hollow phantasmagory, where like mimes they mope and mowl, and utter false sounds for hire; but with thee it is frightful earnest.

Frightful to all men is Death; from of old named King of Terrors. Our little compact home of an Existence, where we dwelt complaining, yet as in a home, is passing, in dark agonies, into an Unknown of Separation, Foreignness, unconditioned Possibility. The Heathen Emperor asks of his soul: Into what places art thou now departing? The Catholic King must answer: To the Judgment-bar of the Most High God! Yes, it is a summing up of Life; a final settling, and giving in the 'account of the deeds done in the body': they are done now; and lie there unalterable, and do bear their fruits, long as Eternity shall last.

Louis XV. had always the kingliest abhorrence of Death. Unlike that praying Duke of Orleans, *Égalité's* grandfather,—for indeed several of them had a touch of madness,—who honestly believed that there was no Death! He, if the Court Newsmen can be believed, started up once on a time, glowing with sulphurous contempt and indignation on his poor Secretary, who had stumbled on the words, *feu roi d'Espagne* (the late King of Spain): "*Feu roi, Monsieur?*"—"Monseigneur," hastily answered the trembling but adroit man of business, "*c'est une titre qu'ils prennent* ('tis a title they take)." Louis, we say, was not so happy; but he did what he could. He would not suffer Death to be spoken of; avoided the sight of churchyards, funereal monuments, and whatsoever could bring it to mind. It is the resource of the Ostrich; who, hard hunted, sticks his foolish head in the ground, and would fain forget that his foolish unseeing body is not unseen too. Or sometimes, with a spasmodic antagonism, significant of the same thing, and of more, he *would* go; or stopping his court carriages, would send into churchyards, and ask, "how many new graves there were to-day," though it gave his poor Pompadour the disagreeablest qualms. We can figure the thought of Louis that day, when, all royally caparisoned for hunting, he met, at some sudden turning in the Wood of Senart, a ragged Peasant with a coffin: "For whom?"—It was for a poor brother slave, whom Majesty had sometimes noticed slaving in those quarters: "What did he die of?"—"Of hunger:"—the King gave his steed the spur.

But figure his thought, when Death is now clutching at his own heart-strings; unlooked for, inexorable! Yes, poor Louis, Death has found thee. No palace walls or life-guards, gorgeous tapestries or gilt buckram of stiffest ceremonial could keep him out; but he is here, here at thy very life-breath, and will extinguish it. Thou, whose whole existence hitherto was a chimera and scenic show, at length becomest a reality: sumptuous Versailles bursts asunder, like a dream, into void Immensity; Time is done, and all the scaffolding of Time falls wrecked with hideous clangour round thy soul: the pale Kingdoms yawn open; there must thou enter, naked, all unking'd, and await what is appointed thee! Unhappy man, there as thou turnest, in dull agony, on thy bed of weariness, what a thought is thine! Purgatory and Hell-fire, now all too possible, in the prospect: in the retrospect,—alas, what thing didst thou do that were not better undone; what mortal didst thou generously help; what sorrow hadst thou mercy on? Do the 'five hundred thousand' ghosts, who sank shamefully on so many battle-fields from Rossbach to Quebec, that thy Harlot might take revenge for an epigram,—crowd round thee in this hour? Thy foul Harem; the curses of mothers, the tears and infamy of daughters? Miserable man! thou 'hast done evil as thou couldst:' thy whole existence seems one hideous abortion and mistake of Nature; the use and meaning of thee not yet known. Wert thou a fabulous Griffin, *devouring* the works of men; daily dragging virgins to thy cave;—clad also in scales that no spear would pierce: no spear but Death's? A Griffin not fabulous but real! Frightful, O Louis, seem these moments for thee.—We will pry no further into the horrors of a sinner's death-bed.

And yet let no meanest man lay flattering unction to his soul. Louis was a Ruler; but art not thou also one? His wide France, look at it from the Fixed Stars (themselves not yet Infinitude), is no wider than thy narrow brickfield, where thou too didst faithfully, or didst unfaithfully. Man, 'Symbol of Eternity imprisoned into Time!' it is not thy works, which are all mortal, infinitely little, and the greatest no greater than the least, but only the Spirit thou workest in, that can have worth or continuance.

But reflect, in any case, what a life-problem this of poor Louis, when he rose as *Bien-Aimé* from that Metz sick-bed, really was. What son of Adam could have swayed such incoherences into coherence? Could he? Blindest Fortune alone has cast *him* on the top of it: he swims there; can as little sway it as the drift-log sways the wind-tossed moon-stirred Atlantic. "What have I done to be so loved?" he said then. He may say now: What have I done to be so hated? Thou hast done nothing, poor Louis! Thy fault is properly even this, that thou didst *nothing*. What could poor Louis do? Abdicate, and wash his hands of it,—in favour of the first that would accept! Other clear wisdom there was none for him. As it was, he stood gazing dubiously, the absurdest mortal extant (a very Solecism Incarnate) into the absurdest confused world;—wherein at last nothing seemed so certain as this, That he, the incarnate Solecism, had five senses; that there were Flying (*Tables Volantes*, which vanish through the floor, to come back reloaded), and a *Parc-aux-cerfs*.

Whereby at least we have again this historical curiosity: a human being in an original position; swimming passively, as on some boundless 'Mother of Dead Dogs,' towards issues which he partly saw. For Louis had withal a kind of insight in him. So when a new Minister of Marine, or what else it might be, came announcing his new era, the Scarlet-woman would hear from the lips of Majesty at supper: "Yes, he spread out his ware like another; promised the beautifulest things in the world; not a thing of which will come: he does not know this region; he will see." Or again: "'Tis the twentieth time I have heard all that; France will never get a Navy, I believe." How touching also was this: "If *I* were Lieutenant of Police, I would prohibit those Paris cabriolets."

Doomed mortal;—for is it not a doom to be Solecism incarnate! A new *Roi Fainéant*, King Donothing; but with the strangest new *Mayor of the Palace*: no bow-legged Pepin

now for *Mayor*, but that same cloud-capt, fire-breathing
Spectre of DEMOCRACY; incalculable, which is enveloping the
world!——Was Louis, then, no wickeder than this or the
other private Donothing and Eatall; such as we often enough see,
under the name of Man of Pleasure, cumbering God's diligent
Creation, for a time? Say, wretcheder! His Life-solecism
was seen and felt of a whole scandalised world; him endless
Oblivion cannot engulf, and swallow to endless depths,—not
yet for a generation or two.

However, be this as it will, we remark, not without interest,
that 'on the evening of the 4th,' Dame Dubarry issues from
the sick-room, with perceptible 'trouble in her visage.' It is
the fourth evening of May, year of Grace, 1774. Such a
whispering in the Œil-de-Bœuf! Is he dying then? What
can be said, is that Dubarry seems making up her packages;
she sails weeping through her gilt boudoirs, as if taking leave.
D'Aiguillon and Company are near their last card; nevertheless they will not yet throw up the game. But as for the
sacramental controversy, it is as good as settled without being
mentioned; Louis sends for his Abbé Moudon in the course
of next night; is confessed by him, some say for the space of
'seventeen minutes,' and demands the sacraments of his own
accord.

Nay already, in the afternoon, behold is not this your
Sorceress Dubarry with the handkerchief at her eyes, mounting D'Aiguillon's chariot; rolling off in his Duchess's consolatory arms? She is gone: and her place knows her no
more. Vanish, false Sorceress; into Space! Needless to
hover at neighbouring Ruel; for thy day is done. Shut are
the royal palace-gates for evermore; hardly in coming years
shalt thou, under cloud of night, descend once, in black
domino, like a black night-bird, and disturb the fair
Antoinette's music-party in the Park; all Birds of Paradise
flying from thee, and musical windpipes growing mute. Thou
unclean, yet unmalignant, not unpitiable thing! What a
course was thine: from that first trucklebed (in Joan of Arc's
country) where thy mother bore thee, with tears, to an unnamed father: forward, through lowest subterranean depths,
and over highest sunlit heights, of Harlotdom and Rascaldom
—to the guillotine-axe, which sheers away thy vainly whimpering head? Rest there uncursed; only buried and abolished;
what else befitted thee?

Louis, meanwhile, is in considerable impatience for his sacraments; sends more than once to the window, to see whether they are not coming. Be of comfort, Louis, what comfort thou canst: they are under way, these sacraments. Towards six in the morning, they arrive. Cardinal Grand-Almoner Roche-Aymon is here in pontificals, with his pyxes and his tools: he approaches the royal pillow; elevates his wafer; mutters or seems to mutter somewhat;—and so (as the Abbé Georgel, in words that stick to one, expresses it) has Louis 'made the *amende honorable* to God:' so does your Jesuit construe it.—" *Wa, Wa,*" as the wild Clotaire groaned out, when life was departing, "what great God is this that pulls down the strength of the strongest kings."

The *amende honorable*, what 'legal apology' you will, to God:—but not, if D'Aiguillon can help it, to man. Dubarry still hovers in his mansion at Ruel; and while there is life, there is hope. Grand-Almoner Roche-Aymon, accordingly (for he seems to be in the secret), has no sooner seen his pyxes and gear repacked, than he is stepping majestically forth again, as if the work were done! But King's Confessor Abbé Moudon starts forward; with anxious acidulent face, twitches him by the sleeve; whispers in his ear. Whereupon the poor Cardinal has to turn round; and declare audibly, "that his Majesty repents of any subjects of scandal he may have given (*a pu donner*); and purposes, by the strength of Heaven assisting him, to avoid the like—for the future!" Words listened to by Richelieu with mastiff-face, growing blacker; and answered to, aloud, 'with an epithet,'—which Besenval will not repeat. Old Richelieu, conqueror of Minorca, companion of Flying-Table orgies, perforator of bedroom walls, is thy day also done?

Alas, the Chapel organs may keep going; the Shrine of Sainte Geneviève be let down, and pulled up again,—without effect. In the evening the whole Court, with Dauphin and Dauphiness, assist at the Chapel: priests are hoarse with chanting their 'Prayers of Forty Hours;' and the heaving bellows blow. Almost frightful! For the very heaven blackens; battering rain-torrents dash, with thunder; almost drowning the organ's voice: and electric fire-flashes make the very flambeaux on the altar pale. So that the most, as we are told, retired, when it was over, with hurried steps, 'in a state of meditation (*recueillement*),' and said little or nothing.

So it has lasted for the better half of a fortnight; the

Dubarry gone almost a week. Besenval says, all the world was getting impatient *que cela finît;* that poor Louis would have done with it. It is now the 10th of May, 1774. He will soon have done now.

This tenth May day falls into the loathsome sick-bed; but dull, unnoticed there: for they that look out of the windows are quite darkened; the cistern-wheel moves discordant on its axis; Life, like a spent steed, is panting towards the goal. In their remote apartments, Dauphin and Dauphiness stand road-ready; all grooms and equerries booted and spurred: waiting for some signal to escape the house of pestilence. And, hark! across the Œil-de-Bœuf, what sound is that; sound terrible and absolutely like thunder?' It is the rush of the whole Court, rushing as in wager, to salute the new Sovereigns: Hail to your Majesties! The Dauphin and Dauphiness are King and Queen! Overpowered with many emotions, they two fall on their knees together, and, with streaming tears, exclaim: "O God, guide us, protect us; we are too young to reign!"—Too young indeed.

But thus, in any case, 'with a sound absolutely like thunder,' has the Horologe of Time struck, and an old Era passed away. The Louis that was, lies forsaken, a mass of abhorred clay; abandoned 'to some poor persons, and priests of the *Chapelle Ardente,*'—who make haste to put him 'in two lead coffins, pouring in abundant spirits of wine.' The new Louis with his Court is rolling towards Choisy, through the summer afternoon: the royal tears still flow; but a word mispronounced by Monseigneur d'Artois sets them all laughing, and they weep no more. Light mortals, how ye walk your light life-minuet, over bottomless abysses, divided from you by a film!

For the rest, the proper authorities felt that no funeral could be too unceremonious. Besenval himself thinks it was un-ceremonious enough. Two carriages containing two noble-men of the usher species, and a Versailles clerical person; some score of mounted pages, some fifty palfreniers: these, with torches, but not so much as in black, start from Versailles on the second evening, with their leaden bier. At a high trot, they start; and keep up that pace. For the jibes (*brocards*) of those Parisians, who stand planted in two rows, all the way to St. Denis, and 'give vent to their pleasantry, the character-istic of the nation,' do not tempt one to slacken. Towards midnight the vaults of St. Denis receive their own: unwept by any eye of all these; if not by poor *Loque* his neglected Daughter's, whose Nunnery is hard by.

Him they crush down, and huddle underground, in this impatient way; him and his era of sin and tyranny and shame: for behold a New Era is come; the future all the brighter that the past was base.

BOOK II

THE PAPER AGE

CHAPTER I

ASTRÆA REDUX

A PARADOXICAL philosopher, carrying to the uttermost length that aphorism of Montesquieu's 'Happy the people whose annals are tiresome,' has said, ' Happy the people whose annals are vacant.' In which saying, mad as it looks, may there not still be found some grain of reason ? For truly, as it has been written, 'Silence is divine,' and of Heaven ; so in all earthly things too there is a silence which is better than any speech. Consider it well, the Event, the thing which can be spoken of and recorded, is it not, in all cases, some disruption, some solution of continuity ? Were it even a glad Event, it involves change, involves loss (of active Force) ; and so far, either in the past or in the present, is an irregularity, a disease. Stillest perseverance were our blessedness ; not dislocation and alteration,—could they be avoided.

The oak grows silently, in the forest, a thousand years ; only in the thousandth year, when the woodman arrives with his axe, is there heard an echoing through the solitudes ; and the oak announces itself when, with far-sounding crash, it *falls*. How silent too was the planting of the acorn ; scattered from the lap of some wandering wind ! Nay, when our oak flowered, or put on its leaves (its glad Events), what shout of proclamation could there be ? Hardly from the most observant a word of recognition. These things *befell* not, they were slowly *done* ; not in an hour, but through the flight of days : what was to be said of it ? This hour seemed altogether as the last was, as the next would be.

It is thus everywhere that foolish Rumour babbles not of what is done, but of what was misdone or undone ; and foolish History (ever, more or less, the written epitomised synopsis of Rumour) knows so little that were not as well unknown. Attila Invasions, Walter-the-Penniless Crusades, Sicilian Vespers, Thirty-Years' Wars : mere sin and misery : not work, but hindrance of work! For the Earth, all this while, was yearly green and yellow with her kind harvests; the hand of the craftsman, the mind of the thinker rested not: and so, after all and in spite of all, we have this so glorious high-domed blossoming World; concerning which, poor History may well ask, with wonder, Whence *it* came? She knows so little of it, knows so much of what obstructed it, what would have rendered it impossible. Such, nevertheless, by necessity or foolish choice, is her rule and practice: whereby that paradox, 'Happy the people whose annals are vacant,' is not without its true side.

And yet, what seems more pertinent to note here, there is a stillness, not of unobstructed growth, but of passive inertness, the symptom of imminent downfall. As victory is silent, so is defeat. Of the opposing forces the weaker has resigned itself; the stronger marches on, noiseless now, but rapid, inevitable: the fall and overturn will not be noiseless. How all grows, and has its period, even as the herbs of the fields, be it annual, centennial, millennial! All grows and dies, each by its own wondrous laws in wondrous fashion of its own; spiritual things most wondrously of all. Inscrutable, to the wisest, are these latter; not to be prophesied of, or understood. If when the oak stands proudliest flourishing to the eye, you know that its heart is sound, it is not so with the man; how much less with the Society, with the Nation of men! Of such it may be affirmed even that the superficial aspect, that the inward feeling of full health, is generally ominous. For indeed it is of apoplexy, so to speak, and a plethoric lazy habit of body, that Churches, Kingships, Social Institutions, oftenest die. Sad, when such Institution plethorically says to itself, Take thy ease, thou hast goods laid up;—like the fool of the Gospel, to whom it was answered, Fool, *this night* thy life shall be required of thee!

Is it the healthy peace, or the ominous unhealthy, that rests on France, for these next Ten Years? Over which the Historian can pass lightly, without call to linger: for as yet events are not, much less performances. Time of sunniest stillness;—shall we call it, what all men thought it, the new Age of Gold? Call it at least, of Paper; which in many ways is the succedaneum of Gold. Bank-paper, wherewith you can still buy when there is no gold left; Book-paper, splendent with Theories, Philosophies, Sensibilities,—beautiful art, not only of revealing Thought, but also of so beautifully hiding from us the want of Thought! Paper is made from the *rags* of things that did once exist; there are endless excellences in Paper.—What wisest Philosophe, in this halcyon uneventful period, could prophesy that there was approaching, big with darkness and confusion, the event of events? Hope ushers in a Revolution,—as earthquakes are preceded by bright weather. On the Fifth of May, fifteen years hence, old Louis will not be sending for the Sacraments; but a new Louis, his grandson, with the whole pomp of astonished intoxicated France, will be opening the States General.

Dubarrydom and its D'Aiguillons are gone forever. There is a young, still docile, well-intentioned King; a young, beautiful and bountiful, well-intentioned Queen; and with them all France, as it were, become young. Maupeou and his Parlement have to vanish into thick night; respectable Magistrates, not indifferent to the Nation, were it only for having been opponents of the Court, descend now unchained from their 'steep rocks at Croc in Combrailles' and elsewhere, and return singing praises: the old Parlement of Paris resumes its functions. Instead of a profligate bankrupt Abbé Terray, we have now, for Controller-General. a virtuous philosophic Turgot, with a whole Reformed France in his head. By whom whatsoever is wrong. in Finance or otherwise, will be righted,—as far as possible. It is not as if Wisdom herself were henceforth to have seat and voice in the Council of Kings? Turgot has taken office with the noblest plainness of speech to that effect; been listened to with the noblest royal trustfulness. It is true, as King Louis objects, "They say he never goes to mass;" but liberal France likes him little worse for that; liberal France answers, "The Abbé Terray always went." Philosophism sees, for the first time, a Philosophe (or even a Philosopher) in office: she in all things will applausively second him; neither will light old Maurepas obstruct, if he can easily help it.

Then how 'sweet' are the manners; vice 'losing all its deformity;' becoming *decent* (as established things, making regulations for themselves, do); becoming almost a kind of 'sweet' virtue! Intelligence so abounds; irradiated by wit and the art of conversation. Philosophism sits joyful in her glittering saloons, the dinner-guest of Opulence grown ingenuous, the very nobles proud to sit by her; and preaches, lifted up over all Bastilles, a coming millennium. From far Fernay, Patriarch Voltaire given sign: veterans Diderot, D'Alembert have lived to see this day; these with their younger Marmontels, Morellets, Chamforts, Raynals, make glad the spicy board of rich ministering Dowager, of philosophic Farmer-General. O nights and suppers of the gods! Of a truth, the long-demonstrated will now be done: 'the Age of Revolutions approaches' (as Jean Jacques wrote), but then of happy blessed ones Man awakens from his long somnambulism; chases the Phantasms that beleaguered and bewitched him. Behold the new morning glittering down the eastern steeps; fly, false Phantasms, from its shafts of light; let the Absurd fly utterly, forsaking this lower earth forever. It is Truth and *Astræa Redux* that (in the shape of Philosophism) henceforth reign. For what imaginable purpose was man made, if not to be 'happy?' By victorious Analysis, and Progress of the Species happiness enough now awaits him. Kings can become philosophers; or else philosophers Kings. Let but Society be once rightly constituted,—by victorious Analysis. The stomach that is empty shall be filled; the throat that is dry shall be wetted with wine. Labour itself shall be all one as rest; not grievous, but joyous. Wheatfields, one would think, cannot come to grow untilled; no man made clayey, or made weary thereby;—unless indeed machinery will do it? Gratuitous Tailors and Restaurateurs may start up, at fit intervals, one as yet sees not how. But if each will, according to rule of Benevolence, have a care for all, then surely—no one will be uncared for. Nay, who knows but, by sufficiently victorious Analysis, 'human life may be indefinitely lengthened,' and men get rid of Death, as they have already done of the Devil? We shall then be happy in spite of Death and the Devil.—So preaches magniloquent Philosophism her *Redeunt Saturnia regna*.

The prophetic song of Paris and its Philosophes is audible enough in the Versailles Œil-de-Bœuf; and the Œil-de-Bœuf, intent chiefly on nearer blessedness, can answer, at worst, with a polite "Why not?" Good old cheery Maurepas is too joyful a Prime Minister to dash the world's joy. Sufficient for the day be its own evil. Cheery old man, he cuts his jokes, and hovers careless along; his cloak well adjusted to the wind, if so be he may please all persons. The simple young King, whom a Maurepas cannot think of troubling with business, has retired into the interior apartments; taciturn, irresolute; though with a sharpness of temper at times: he, at length, determines on a little smith-work; and so, in apprenticeship with a Sieur Gamain (whom one day he shall have little cause to bless), is learning to make locks. It appears further, he understood Geography; and could read English. Unhappy young King, his childlike trust in that foolish old Maurepas deserved another return. But friend and foe, destiny and himself have combined to do him hurt.

Meanwhile the fair young Queen, in her halls of state, walks like a goddess of Beauty, the cynosure of all eyes; as yet mingles not with affairs; heeds not the future; least of all, dreads it. Weber and Campan have pictured her, there within the royal tapestries, in bright boudoirs, baths, peignoirs, and the Grand and Little Toilette; with a whole brilliant world waiting obsequious on her glance: fair young daughter of Time, what things has Time in store for thee! Like Earth's brightest Appearance, she moves gracefully, environed with the grandeur of Earth: a reality, and yet a magic vision; for, behold, shall not utter Darkness swallow it! The soft young heart adopts orphans, portions meritorious maids, delights to succour the poor,—such poor as come picturesquely in her way; and sets the fashion of doing it; for, as was said, Benevolence has now begun reigning. In her Duchess de Polignac, in her Princess de Lamballe, she enjoys something almost like friendship: now too, after seven long years, she has a child, and soon even a Dauphin, of her own; can reckon herself, as Queens go, happy in a husband.

Events? The grand events are but charitable Feasts of Morals (*Fêtes des mœurs*), with their Prizes and Speeches; Poissarde Processions to the Dauphin's cradle; above all, Flirtations, their rise, progress, decline and fall. There are Snow-statues raised by the poor in hard winter, to a Queen who has given them fuel. There are masquerades, theatricals; beautifyings of little Trianon, purchase and repair of St. Cloud; journeyings from the summer Court-Elysium to the winter one. There are poutings and grudgings from the Sardinian Sisters-in-law (for the Princes too are wedded); little jealousies, which Court-Etiquette can moderate. Wholly the lightest-hearted frivolous foam of Existence; yet an artfully refined foam; pleasant were it not so costly, like that which mantles on the wine of Champagne!

Monsieur, the King's elder Brother, has set up for a kind of wit; and leans towards the Philosophe side. Monseigneur d'Artois pulls the mask from a fair impertinent; fights a duel in consequence,—almost drawing blood. He has breeches of a kind new in this world;—a fabulous kind; 'four tall lackeys,' says Mercier, as if he had seen it, 'hold him up in the air, that he may fall into the garment without vestige of wrinkle; from which rigorous encasement the same four, in the same way, and with more effort, have to deliver him at night.' This last is he who now, as a gray timeworn man, sits desolate at Grätz; having winded up his destiny with the Three days. In such sort are poor mortals swept and shovelled to and fro.

CHAPTER II

PETITION IN HIEROGLYPHS

WITH the working people, again, it is not so well. Unlucky! For there are from twenty to twenty-five millions of them. Whom, however, we lump together into a kind of dim compendious unity, monstrous but dim, far off, as the *canaille;* or, more humanely, as 'the masses.' Masses indeed: and yet, singular to say, if, with an effort of imagination, thou follow them, over broad France, into their clay hovels, into their garrets and hutches, the masses consist all of units. Every unit of whom has his own heart and sorrows; stands covered there with his own skin, and if you prick him, he will bleed. O purple Sovereignty, Holiness, Reverence; thou, for example, Cardinal Grand-Almoner, with thy plush covering of honour, who hast thy hands strengthened with dignities and monies, and art set on thy world-watchtower solemnly, in sight of God, for such ends,—what a thought: that every unit of these masses is a miraculous Man, even as thyself art; struggling, with vision or with blindness, for *his* infinite Kingdom (this life which he has got, once only, in the middle of Eternities); with a spark of the Divinity, what thou callest an immortal soul, in him!

Dreary, languid do these struggle in their obscure remoteness; their hearth cheerless, their diet thin. For them, in this world, rises no Era of Hope; hardly now in the other,—if it be not hope in the gloomy rest of Death, for their faith too is failing. Untaught, uncomforted, unfed! A dumb generation; their voice only an inarticulate cry: spokesman, in the King's Council, in the world's forum, they have none that finds credence. At rare intervals (as now, in 1775), they will fling down their hoes and hammers; and, to the astonishment of thinking mankind, flock hither and thither, dangerous, aimless; get the length even of Versailles. Turgot is altering the Corn-trade,

abrogating the absurdest Corn-laws; there is dearth, real, or
were it even 'factitious;' an indubitable scarcity of bread. And
so, on the 2nd day of May, 1775, these waste multitudes do
here, at Versailles Château, in widespread wretchedness, in
sallow faces, squalor, winged raggedness, present, as in legible
hieroglyphic writing, their Petition of Grievances. The Château-
gates must be shut; but the King will appear on the balcony,
and speak to them. They have seen the King's face; their
Petition of Grievances has been, if not read, looked at. For
answer, two of them are hanged, on a 'new gallows forty feet
high;' and the rest driven back to their dens,—for a time.

Clearly a difficult 'point' for Government, that of dealing
with these masses;—if indeed it be not rather the sole point
and problem of Government, and all other points mere accidental crotchets, superficialities, and beatings of the wind!
For let Charter-Chests, Use and Wont, Law common and
special say what they will, the masses count to so many millions
of units; made, to all appearance, by God,—whose earth this
is declared to be. Besides, the people are not without ferocity;
they have sinews and indignation. Do but look what holiday
old Marquis Mirabeau, the crabbed old Friend of Men, looked
on, in these same years, from his lodging, at the Baths of
Mont d'Or: 'The savages descending in torrents from the
mountains; our people ordered not to go out. The Curate in
surplice and stole; Justice in its peruke; Marechausées sabre
in hand, guarding the place, till the bagpipes can begin. The
dance interrupted, in a quarter of an hour, by battle; the cries,
the squealings of children, of infirm persons, and other assistants,
tarring them on, as the rabble does when dogs fight; frightful
men, or rather frightful wild-animals, clad in jupes of coarse
woollen, with large girdles of leather studded with copper nails;
of gigantic stature, heightened by high wooden-clogs (sabots);
rising on tiptoe to see the fight; tramping time to it; rubbing
their sides with their elbows: their faces haggard (figures hâves),
and covered with their long greasy hair; the upper part of the
visage waxing pale, the lower distorting itself into the attempt
at a cruel laugh and a sort of ferocious impatience. And these
people pay the taille! And you want further to take their salt
from them! And you know not what it is you are stripping
barer, or as you call it, governing; what, by the spurt of your
pen, in its cold dastard indifference, you will fancy you can
starve always with impunity; always till the catastrophe come!
—Ah Madame, such Government by Blindman's-buff, stum-

bling along too far, will end in the General Overturn (*culbute générale*).'

Undoubtedly a dark feature this in an Age of Gold,—Age, at least, of Paper and Hope! Meanwhile, trouble us not with thy prophecies, O croaking Friend of Men: 'tis long that we have heard such; and still the old world keeps wagging, in its old way.

CHAPTER III

QUESTIONABLE

Or is this same Age of Hope itself but a simulacrum; as Hope too often is? Cloud-vapour with rainbows painted on it, beautiful to see, to sail towards,—which hovers over Niagara Falls? In that case, victorious Analysis will have enough to do.

Alas, yes! a whole world to remake, if she could see it: work for another than she! For all is wrong, and gone out of joint; the inward spiritual, and the outward economical; head or heart, there is no soundness in it. As indeed, evils of all sorts are more or less of kin, and do usually go together: especially it is an old truth, that wherever huge physical evil is, there, as the parent and origin of it, has moral evil to a proportionate extent been. Before those five-and-twenty labouring Millions, for instance, could get that haggardness of face, which old Mirabeau now looks on, in a Nation calling itself Christian, and calling man the brother of man,—what unspeakable, nigh infinite Dishonesty (of *seeming* and not *being*) in all manner of Rulers, and appointed Watchers, spiritual and temporal, must there not, through long ages, have gone on accumulating! It will accumulate: moreover, it will reach a head; for the first of all Gospels is this, that a Lie cannot endure forever.

In fact, if we pierce through that rosepink vapour of Sentimentalism, Philanthropy, and Feasts of Morals, there lies behind it one of the sorriest spectacles. You might ask, What bonds that ever held a human society happily together, or held it together at all, are in force here? It is an unbelieving people; which has suppositions, hypotheses, and froth-systems of victorious Analysis; and for *belief* this mainly, that Pleasure is pleasant. Hunger they have for all sweet things; and the law of Hunger: but what other law? Within them, or over them, properly none!

Their King has become a King Popinjay: with his Maurepas Government, gyrating as the weather-cock does, blown about by every wind. Above them they see no God; or they even do not look above, except with astronomical glasses. The Church indeed still is; but in the most submissive state; quite tamed by Philosophism; in a singularly short time; for the hour was come. Some twenty years ago, your Archbishop Beaumont would not even let the poor Jansenists get buried: your Loménie Brienne (a rising man, whom we shall meet with yet) could, in the name of the Clergy, insist on having the Antiprotestant Laws, which condemn to death for preaching, 'put in execution.' And alas, now not so much as Baron Holbach's Atheism can be burnt,—except as pipe-matches by the private speculative individual. Our Church stands haltered, dumb, like a dumb ox; lowing only for provender (of tithes); content if it can have that; or, with dumb stupor, expecting its further doom. And the Twenty Millions of 'haggard faces;' and, as finger-post and guidance to them in their dark struggle, 'a gallows forty feet high!' Certainly a singular Golden Age; with its Feasts of Morals, its 'sweet manners,' its sweet institutions (*institutions douces*); betokening nothing but peace among men!—Peace? O Philosophe-Sentimentalism, what hast thou to do with peace, when thy mother's name is Jezebel? Foul Product of still fouler Corruption, thou with the corruption art doomed!

Meanwhile it is singular how long the rotten will hold together, provided you do not handle it roughly. For whole generations it continues standing, 'with a ghastly affectation of life,' after all life and truth has fled out of it: so loth are men to quit their old ways; and, conquering indolence and inertia, venture on new. Great truly is the Actual; is the Thing that has rescued itself from bottomless deeps of theory and possibility, and stands there as a definite indisputable Fact, whereby men do work and live, or once did so. Wisely shall men cleave to that, while it will endure; and quit it with regret, when it gives way under them. Rash enthusiast of Change, beware! Hast thou well considered all that Habit does in this life of ours; how all Knowledge and all Practice hang wondrous over infinite abysses of the Unknown, Impracticable; and our whole being is an infinite abyss, *overarched* by Habit, as by a thin Earth-rind, laboriously built together?

But if 'every man,' as it has been written, 'holds confined within him a *mad*-man,' what must every Society do;—Society, which in its commonest state is called 'the standing miracle of this world!' 'Without such Earth-rind of Habit,' continues our author, 'call it System of Habits, in a word, *fixed ways* of acting and of believing,—Society would not exist at all. With such it exists, better or worse. Herein too, in this its System of Habits, acquired, retained how you will, lies the true Law-Code and Constitution of a Society; the only Code, though an unwritten one, which it can in no wise *dis*obey. The thing we call written Code, Constitution, Form of Government, and the like, what is it but some miniature image, and solemnly expressed summary of this unwritten Code? *Is*,—or rather, alas, is *not*; but only should be, and always tends to be! In which latter discrepancy lies struggle without end.' And now, we add in the same dialect, let but, by ill chance, in such ever-enduring struggle,—your 'thin Earth-rind' be once *broken!* The fountains of the great deep boil forth; fire-fountains, enveloping, engulfing. Your 'Earth-rind' is shattered, swallowed up; instead of a green flowery world there is a waste wild-weltering chaos;—which has again, with tumult and struggle, to *make* itself into a world.

On the other hand, be this conceded: Where thou findest a lie that is oppressing thee, extinguish it. Lies exist there only to be extinguished; they wait and cry earnestly for extinction. Think well, meanwhile, in what spirit thou wilt do it: not with hatred, with headlong selfish violence; but in clearness of heart, with holy zeal, gently, almost with pity. Thou wouldst not *replace* such extinct Lie by a new Lie, which a new Injustice of thy own were; the parent of still other Lies? Whereby the latter end of that business were worse than the beginning.

So, however, in this world of ours, which has both an indestructible hope in the Future, and an indestructible tendency to persevere as in the Past, must Innovation and Conservation wage their perpetual conflict, as they may and can. Wherein the 'dæmonic element,' that lurks in all human things, *may* doubtless, some once in the thousand years,—get vent! But indeed may we not regret that such conflict,—which, after all, is but like that classical one of 'hate filled Amazons with heroic Youths,' and will end in *embraces*,—should usually be so spasmodic? For Conservation, strengthened by that mightiest quality in us, our indolence, sits for long ages, not victorious only, which she should be; but tyrannical, incommunicative. She holds her adversary as if annihilated; such adversary lying, all the while, like some buried Enceladus; who, to gain the smallest freedom, has to stir a whole Trinacria with its Ætnas.

Wherefore, on the whole, we will honour a Paper Age too; an Era of hope! For in this same frightful process of Enceladus Revolt; when the task, on which no mortal would willingly enter, has become imperative, inevitable,—is it not even a kindness of Nature that she lures us forward by cheerful promises, fallacious or not; and a whole generation plunges into the Erebus Blackness, lighted on by an Era of Hope? It has been well said: 'Man is based on Hope; he has properly no other possession but Hope; this habitation of his is named the Place of Hope.'

CHAPTER IV

MAUREPAS

BUT now, among French hopes, is not that of old M. de Maurepas one of the best-grounded; who hopes that he, by dexterity, shall contrive to continue Minister? Nimble old man, who for all emergencies has his light jest; and ever in the worst confusion will emerge, cork-like, unsunk! Small care to him is Perfectibility, Progress of the Species, and *Astræa Redux:* good only, that a man of light wit, verging towards fourscore, can in the seat of authority feel himself important among men. Shall we call him, as haughty Châteauroux was wont, of old, '*M. Faquinet* (Diminutive of Scoundrel)?' In courtier dialect, he is now named 'the Nestor of France;' such governing Nestor as France has.

At bottom, nevertheless, it might puzzle one to say where the Government of France, in these days, specially is. In that Château of Versailles, we have Nestor, King, Queen, ministers and clerks, with paper-bundles tied in tape: but the Government? For Government is a thing that *governs*, that guides; and if need be, compels. Visible in France there is not such a thing. Invisible, inorganic, on the other hand, there is: in Philosophe saloons, in Œil-de-Bœuf galleries : in the tongue of the babbler, in the pen of the pamphleteer. Her Majesty appearing at the Opera is applauded; she returns all radiant with joy. Anon the applauses wax fainter, or threaten to cease; she is heavy of heart, the light of her face has fled. Is Sovereignty some poor Montgolfier; which, blown into by the popular wind, grows great and mounts; or sinks flaccid, if the wind be withdrawn? France was long a 'Despotism tempered by Epigrams;' and now, it would seem, the Epigrams have got the upper hand.

Happy were a young 'Louis the Desired' to make France happy; if it did not prove too troublesome, and he only knew the way. But there is endless discrepancy round him; so many claims and clamours; a mere confusion of tongues. Not reconcilable by man; not manageable, suppressible, save by some strongest and wisest man;—which only a lightly-jesting lightly gyrating M. de Maurepas can so much as subsist amidst. Philosophism claims her new Era, meaning thereby innumerable things. And claims it in no faint voice; for France at large, hitherto mute, is now beginning to speak also; and speaks in that same sense. A huge, many-toned sound; distant, yet not unimpressive. On the other hand, the Œil-de-Bœuf, which, as nearest, one can hear best, claims with shrill vehemence that the Monarchy be as heretofore a Horn of Plenty; wherefrom loyal courtiers may draw,—to the just support of the throne. Let Liberalism and a New Era, if such is the wish, be introduced; only no curtailment of the royal moneys! Which latter condition, alas, is precisely the impossible one.

Philosophism, as we saw, has got her Turgot made Controller-General; and there shall be endless reformation. Unhappily this Turgot could continue only twenty months. With a miraculous *Fortunatus' Purse* in his Treasury, it might have lasted longer; with such Purse indeed, every French Controller-General, that would prosper in these days, ought first to provide himself. But here again may we not remark the bounty of Nature in regard to Hope? Man after man advances confident to the Augean Stable, as if *he* could clean it; expends his little fraction of an ability on it, with such cheerfulness; does, in so far as he was honest, accomplish something. Turgot has faculties; honesty, insight, heroic volition; but the Fortunatus' Purse he has not. Sanguine Controller-General! a whole pacific French Revolution may stand schemed in the head of the thinker; but who shall pay the unspeakable 'indemnities' that will be needed? Alas, far from that: on the very threshold of the business, he proposes that the Clergy, the Noblesse, the very Parlements be subjected to taxes like the People! One shriek of indignation and astonishment reverberates through all the Château galleries; M. de Maurepas has to gyrate: the poor King, who had written few weeks ago, '*Il n'y a que vous et moi qui aimions le peuple* (There is none but you and I that has the people's interest at heart),' must write now a dismissal; and let the French Revolution accomplish itself, pacifically or not, as it can.

Hope then is deferred? Deferred; not destroyed, or abated. Is not this, for example, our Patriarch Voltaire, after long years of absence, revisiting Paris? With face shrivelled to nothing; with 'huge peruke *à la Louis Quatorze*, which leaves only two eyes visible, glittering like carbuncles,' the old man is here. What an outburst! Sneering Paris has suddenly grown reverent; devotional with Hero-worship. Nobles have disguised themselves as tavern-waiters to obtain sight of him: the loveliest of France would lay their hair beneath his feet. 'His chariot is the nucleus of a Comet; whose train fills whole streets:' they crown him in the theatre, with immortal vivats; finally 'stifle him under roses,'—for old Richelieu recommended opium in such state of the nerves, and the excessive Patriarch took too much. Her Majesty herself had some thought of sending for him, but was dissuaded. Let Majesty consider it nevertheless. The purport of this man's existence has been to wither up and annihilate all whereon Majesty and Worship for the present rests: and is it *so* that the world recognises him? With Apotheosis, as its Prophet and Speaker, who has spoken wisely the thing it longed to say? Add only that the body of this same rose-stifled, beatified Patriarch cannot get buried except by stealth. It is wholly a notable business; and France, without doubt, is *big* (what the Germans call 'Of good Hope'): we shall wish her a happy birth-hour, and blessed fruit.

Beaumarchais, too, has now winded up his Law Pleadings (*Mémoires*); not without result to himself and to the world. Caron Beaumarchais (or de Beaumarchais, for he got ennobled) had been born poor, but aspiring, esurient; with talents, audacity, adroitness; above all, with the talent for intrigue; a lean, but also a tough, indomitable man. Fortune and dexterity brought him to the harpsichord of Mesdames, our good Princesses, *Loque, Graille* and Sisterhood. Still better, Pâris Duvernier, the Court-Banker, honoured him with some confidence;

to the length even of transactions in cash. Which confidence, however, Duvernier's Heir, a person of quality, would not continue. Quite otherwise; there springs a Lawsuit from it: wherein tough Beaumarchais, losing both money and repute, is, in the opinion of Judge-Reporter Goezman of the Parlement Maupeou, and of a whole indifferent acquiescing world, miserably beaten. In all men's opinions, only not in his own! Inspired by the indignation which makes, if not verses, satirical law-papers, the withered Music-master, with a desperate heroism, takes up his lost cause in spite of the world; fights for it, against Reporters, Parlements, and Principalities, with light banter, with clear logic; adroitly, with an inexhaustible toughness and resource, like the skilfulest fencer; on whom, so skilful is he, the whole world now looks. Three long years it lasts; with wavering fortune. In fine, after labours comparable to the Twelve of Hercules, our unconquerable Caron triumphs; regains his Lawsuit and Lawsuits; strips Reporter Goezman of the judicial ermine; covering him with a perpetual garment of obloquy instead;—and in regard to the Parlement Maupeou (which he has helped to extinguish), to Parlements of all kinds, and to French Justice generally, gives rise to endless reflections in the minds of men. Thus has Beaumarchais, like a lean French Hercules, ventured down, driven by destiny, into the Nether Kingdoms; and victoriously tamed hell-dogs there. He also is henceforth among the notabilities of his generation.

CHAPTER V

ASTRÆA REDUX WITHOUT CASH

OBSERVE, however, beyond the Atlantic, has not the new day verily dawned! Democracy, as we said, is born; storm-girt, is struggling for life and victory. A sympathetic France rejoices over the Rights of Man; in all saloons, it is said, What a spectacle! Now, too, behold our Deane, our Franklin, American Plenipotentiaries, here in person soliciting: the sons of the Saxon Puritans, with their Old-Saxon temper, Old-Hebrew culture, sleek Silas, sleek Benjamin, here on such errand, among the light children of Heathenism, Monarchy, Sentimentalism, and the Scarlet-woman. A spectacle indeed; over which saloons may cackle joyous,—though Kaiser Joseph, questioned on it, gave this answer, most unexpected from a

Philosophe: "Madame, the trade I live by is that of royalist (*Mon métier à moi c'est d'être royaliste*)."

So thinks light Maurepas too; but the wind of Philosophism and force of public opinion will blow him round. Best wishes, meanwhile, are sent; clandestine privateers armed. Paul Jones shall equip his *Bon Homme Richard*: weapons, military stores can be smuggled over (if the English do not seize them); wherein once more Beaumarchais, dimly as the Giant Smuggler, becomes visible,—filling his own lank pocket withal. But surely, in any case, France should have a Navy. For which great object were not now the time; now when that proud Termagant of the Seas has her hands full? It is true, an impoverished Treasury cannot build ships; but the hint once given (which Beaumarchais says *he* gave), this and the other loyal Seaport, Chamber of Commerce, will build and offer them. Goodly vessels bound into the waters, a *Ville de Paris*, Leviathan of ships.

And now when gratuitous three-deckers dance there at anchor, with streamers flying; and eleutheromaniac Philosophedom grows ever more clamorous, what can a Maurepas do—but gyrate? Squadrons cross the ocean; Gateses, Lees, rough Yankee Generals, 'with woollen night-caps under their hats,' present arms to the far-glancing Chivalry of France; and new-born Democracy sees, not without amazement, 'Despotism tempered by Epigrams' fight at her side. So, however, it is. King's forces and heroic volunteers; Rochambeaus, Bouillés, Lameths, Lafayettes, have drawn their swords in this sacred quarrel of mankind;—shall draw them again elsewhere, in the strangest way.

Off Ushant some naval thunder is heard. In the course of which did our young Prince, Duke de Chartres, 'hide in the hold;' or did he materially, by *active* heroism, contribute to the victory? Alas, by a second edition, we learn that there was no victory; or that English Keppel had it. Our poor young Prince gets his Opera plaudits changed into mocking tehees; and cannot become Grand-Admiral,—the source to him of woes which one may call endless.

Wo also for *Ville de Paris*, the Leviathan of ships! English Rodney has clutched it, and led it home, with the rest; so successful was his 'new manœuvre of breaking the enemy's line.' It seems as if, according to Louis XV., 'France were never to have a Navy.' Brave Suffren must return from

Hyder Ally and the Indian Waters; with small result; yet with great glory for 'six' *non-defeats;*—which indeed, with such seconding as he had, one may reckon heroic. Let the old sea-hero rest now, honoured of France, in his native Cevennes mountains; send smoke, not of gunpowder, but mere culinary smoke, through the old chimneys of the Castle of Jalès,—which one day, in other hands, shall have other fame. Brave Lapérouse shall by and by lift anchor, on philanthropic Voyage of Discovery; for the King knows Geography. But alas this also will not prosper: the brave Navigator goes, and returns not; the Seekers search far seas for him in vain. He has vanished trackless into blue Immensity; and only some mournful mysterious shadow of him hovers long in all heads and hearts.

Neither, while the War yet lasts, will Gibraltar surrender. Not though Crillon, Nassau-Siegen, with the ablest projectors extant, are there; and Prince Condé and Prince d'Artois have hastened to help. Wondrous leather-roofed Floating-batteries, set afloat by French-Spanish *Pacte de Famille,* give gallant summons: to which, nevertheless, Gibraltar answers Plutonically, with mere torrents of red-hot iron,—as if stone Calpe had become a throat of the Pit; and utters such a Doom's-blast of a *No,* as all men must credit.

And so, with this loud explosion, the noise of War has ceased; an Age of Benevolence may hope, for ever. Our noble volunteers of Freedom have returned, to be her missionaries. Lafayette, as the matchless of his time, glitters in the Versailles Œil-de-Bœuf; has his Bust set up in the Paris Hôtel-de-Ville. Democracy stands inexpugnable, immeasurable, in her New World; has even a foot lifted towards the Old;—and our French Finances, little strengthened by such work, are in no healthy way.

What to do with the Finances? This indeed is the great question: a small but most black weather-symptom, which no radiance of universal hope can cover. We saw Turgot cast forth from the Controllership, with shrieks,—for want of a Fortunatus' Purse. As little could M. de Clugny manage the duty; or indeed do any thing, but consume his wages; attain 'a place in History,' where as an ineffectual shadow thou beholdest him still lingering;—and let the duty manage itself. Did Genevese Necker *possess* such a Purse then? He possessed banker's skill, banker's honesty; *credit* of all kinds, for

he had written Academic Prize Essays, struggled for India
Companies, given dinners to Philosophes, and 'realised a fortune in twenty years.' He possessed further a taciturnity and
solemnity; of depth, or else of dullness. How singular for
Celadon Gibbon, false swain as he had proved; whose father,
keeping most probably his own gig, 'would not hear of such
a union,'—to find now his forsaken Demoiselle Curchod sitting in the high places of the world, as Minister's Madame,
and 'Necker not jealous!'

A new young Demoiselle, one day to be famed as a Madame
and De Stael, – was romping about the knees of the Decline
and Fall: the lady Necker founds Hospitals; gives solemn
Philosophe dinner-parties, to cheer her exhausted Controller-
General.   Strange things have happened: by clamour of
Philosophism, management of Marquis de Pezay, and Poverty
constraining even Kings. And so Necker, Atlas-like, sustains
the burden of the Finances, for five years long. Without
wages, for he refused such; cheered only by Public Opinion,
and the ministering of his noble Wife. With many thoughts
in him, it is hoped;—which however he is shy of uttering. His
Compte Rendu, published by the royal permission, fresh sign
of a New Era. shows wonders ;—which what but the genius of
some Atlas-Necker can prevent from becoming portents? In
Necker's head too there is a whole pacific French Revolution,
of its kind; and in that taciturn dull depth, or deep dullness,
ambition enough.

Meanwhile, alas, his Fortunatus' Purse turns out to be little
other than the old "*vectigal* of Parsimony." Nay, he too has
to produce his scheme of taxing: Clergy, Noblesse to be taxed;
Provincial Assemblies, and the rest,—like a mere Turgot! The
expiring M. de Maurepas must gyrate one other time. Let
Necker also depart; not unlamented.

Great in a private station, Necker looks on from the distance;
abiding his time. 'Eighty thousand copies' of his new book,
which he calls *Administration des Finances*, will be sold in few
days. He is gone; but shall return, and that more than once,
borne by a whole shouting Nation. Singular Controller-
General of the Finances; once Clerk in Thelusson's Bank.

CHAPTER VI

WINDBAGS

So marches the world, in this its Paper Age, or Era of Hope.
Not without obstructions, war explosions; which however,
heard from such distance, are little other than a cheerful
marching-music. If indeed that dark living chaos of Ignorance
and Hunger, five and twenty million strong, under your feet,—
were to begin playing!

For the present, however, consider Longchamp; now when
Lent is ending, and the glory of Paris and France has gone
forth, as in annual wont. Not to assist at *Tenebris* Masses,
but to sun itself and show itself, and salute the Young
Spring. Manifold, bright-tinted, glittering with gold; all
through the Bois de Boulogne, in long-drawn variegated rows;
—like long-drawn living flower-borders, tulips, dahlias. lilies of
the valley; all in their moving flower pots (of newgilt carriages):
pleasure of the eye, and pride of life! So rolls and dances
the Procession: steady, of firm assurance, as if it rolled on
adamant and the foundations of the world; not on mere
heraldic parchment,—under which smoulders a lake of fire.
Dance on. ye foolish ones; ye sought not wisdom, neither
have ye found it. Ye and your fathers have sown the wind, ye
shall reap the whirlwind. Was it not, from of old, written:
The wages of sin is death?

But at Longchamp. as elsewhere, we remark for one thing,
that dame and cavalier are waited on each by a kind of human
familiar, named *jokei*. Little elf, or imp; though young, already
withered; with its withered air of premature vice, of knowing-
ness, of completed elf-hood: useful in various emergencies.
The name *jokei* (jockey) comes from the English; as the thing
also fancies that it does. Our Anglomania, in fact, is grown
considerable; prophetic of much. If France is to be free, why
shall she not, now when mad war is hushed, love neighbouring
Freedom? Cultivated men, your Dukes de Liancourt, de la
Rochefoucault admire the English Constitution, the English
National Character; would import what of it they can.

Of what is lighter, especially if it be light as wind, how much
easier the freightage! Non-Admiral Duke de Chartres (not
yet d'Orléans or Egalité) flies to and fro across the Strait; im-
porting English Fashions: this he, as hand-and-glove with an

English Prince of Wales, is surely qualified to do. Carriages
and saddles; top-boots and *redingotes*, as we call riding-coats.
Nay the very mode of riding: for now no man on a level with
his age but will trot *à l'Anglais*, rising in the stirrups; scornful
of the old sitfast method, in which, according to Shakespeare,
'butter and eggs' go to market. Also, he can urge the fervid
wheels, this brave Chartres of ours; no whip in Paris is rasher
and surer than the unprofessional one of Monseigneur.

Elf *jokeis*, we have seen; but see now real Yorkshire jockeys,
and what they ride on, and train; English racers for French
Races. These likewise we owe first (under the Providence of
the Devil) to Monseigneur. Prince d'Artois also has his stud
of racers. Prince d'Artois has withal the strangest horseleech:
a moon-struck, much enduring individual, of Neuchâtel in
Switzerland,—named *Jean Paul Marat*. A problematic
Chevalier d'Éon, now in petticoats, now in breeches, is no less
problematic in London than in Paris; and causes bets and law-
suits. Beautiful days of international communion! Swindlery
and Blackguardism have stretched hands across the Channel,
and saluted mutually: on the race-course of Vincennes or
Sablons, behold, in English curricle-and-four, wafted glorious
among the principalities and rascalities, an English Dr. Dodd,
—for whom also the too early gallows gapes.

Duke de Chartres was a young Prince of great promise, as
young princes often are; which promise unfortunately has
belied itself. With the huge Orleans Property, with the Duke
de Penthièvre for Father-in-law (and now the young Brother-
in-law Lamballe killed by excesses),—he will one day be the
richest man in France. Meanwhile, 'his hair is all falling out,
his blood is quite spoiled,'—by early transcendentalism of debauchery. Carbuncles stud his face; dark studs on a ground
of burnished copper. A most signal failure, this young Prince!
The stuff prematurely burnt out of him: little left but foul
smoke and ashes of expiring sensualities: what might have
been Thought, Insight. and even Conduct, gone now or fast
going,—to confused darkness, broken by bewildering dazzle-
ments; to obstreperous crotchets; to activities which you may
call semi-delirious, or even semi-galvanic! Paris affects to laugh
at his charioteering: but he heeds not such laughter.

On the other hand, what a day, not of laughter, was that,
when he threatened, for lucre's sake, to lay sacrilegious hand
on the Palais-Royal Garden! The flower-parterres shall be
riven up; the Chestnut Avenues shall fall: time-honoured bos-

cages, under which the Opera Hamadryads were wont to wander, not inexorable to men. Paris moans aloud. Philidor, from his Café de la Régence, shall no longer look on greenness; the loungers and losels of the world, where now shall they haunt? In vain is moaning. The axe glitters; the sacred groves fall crashing,—for indeed Monseigneur was short of money; the Opera Hamadryads fly with shrieks. Shriek not, ye Opera Hamadryads; or not as those that have no comfort. He will surround your Garden with new edifices and piazzas: though narrowed, it shall be replanted; dizened with hydraulic jets, cannon which the sun fires at noon; things bodily, things spiritual, such as man has not imagined;—and in the Palais-Royal shall again, and more than ever, be the *Sorcerer's Sabbath* and *Satan-at-Home* of our Planet.

What will not mortals attempt? From remote Annonay in the Vivarais, the Brothers Montgolfier send up their paper-dome, filled with the smoke of burnt wool. The Vivarais Provincial Assembly is to be prorogued this same day: Vivarais Assembly-members applaud, and the shouts of congregated men. Will victorious Analysis scale the very Heavens then?

Paris hears with eager wonder; Paris shall ere long see. From Réveillon's Paper-warehouse there, in the Rue St. Antoine (a noted Warehouse),—the new Montgolfier air-ship launches itself. Ducks and poultry have been borne skyward: but now shall men be borne. Nay, Chemist Charles thinks of hydrogen and glazed silk. Chemist Charles will himself ascend, from the Tuileries Garden; Montgolfier solemnly cutting the cord. By Heaven, this Charles does also mount, he and another! Ten times ten thousand hearts go palpitating; all tongues are mute with wonder and fear;—till a shout, like the voice of seas, rolls after him, on his wild way. He soars, he dwindles upwards; has become a mere gleaming circlet,—like some Turgotine snuffbox, what we call "*Turgotine-Platitude;*" like some new daylight Moon! Finally he descends; welcomed by the universe. Duchess Polignac, with a party, is in the Bois de Boulogne, waiting; though it is drizzly winter, the 1st of December 1783. The whole chivalry of France, Duke de Chartres foremost, gallops to receive him.

Beautiful invention; mounting heavenward, so beautifully,—so unguidably! Emblem of much, and of our Age of Hope itself; which shall mount, specifically-light, majestically in this same manner; and hover,—tumbling whither Fate will. Well if it do not, Pilâtre-like, explode; and *de*mount all the more tragically!—So, riding on windbags, will men scale the Empyrean.

Or observe Herr Doctor Mesmer, in his spacious Magnetic Halls. Long-stoled he walks: reverend, glancing upwards, as in rapt commerce; an Antique Egyptian Hierophant in this new age. Soft music flits; breaking fitfully the sacred stillness. Round their Magnetic Mystery, which to the eye is mere tubs with water,—sit breathless, rod in hand, the circles of Beauty and Fashion, each circle a living circular *Passion Flower*: expecting the magnetic afflatus, and new-manufactured Heaven-on-Earth. O women, O men, great is your infidel-faith! A Parlementary Duport, a Bergasse, D'Espréménil we notice there; Chemist Berthollet too,—on the part of Monseigneur de Chartres.

Had not the Academy of Sciences, with its Baillys, Franklins, Lavoisiers, interfered! But it did interfere. Mesmer may pocket his hard money, and withdraw. Let him walk silent by the shore of the Bodensee, by the ancient town of Constance; meditating on much. For so, under the strangest new vesture, the old great truth (since no vesture can hide it) begins again to be revealed. That man is what we call a miraculous creature, with miraculous power over men; and, on the whole, with such a Life in him, and such a World round him, as victorious Analysis, with her Physiologies, Nervous-systems, Physic and Metaphysic, will never completely *name*, to say nothing of explaining. Wherein also the Quack shall, in all ages, come in for his share.

CHAPTER VII

CONTRAT SOCIAL

IN such succession of singular prismatic tints, flush after flush suffusing our horizon, does the Era of Hope dawn on towards fulfilment. Questionable! As indeed, with an Era of Hope that rests on mere universal Benevolence, victorious Analysis, Vice cured of its deformity; and, in the long run, on Twenty-five dark savage Millions, looking up, in hunger and weariness, to that *Ecce-signum* of theirs 'forty feet high,'—how could it be but questionable?

Through all time, if we read aright, sin was, is, will be, the parent of misery. This land calls itself most Christian, and has crosses and cathedrals; but its High-priest is some Roche-Aymon, some Necklace-Cardinal Louis de Rohan. The voice of the poor, through long years, ascends inarticulate, in *Jacqueries*, meal-mobs; low-whimpering of infinite moan: unheeded of the Earth; not unheeded of Heaven. Always moreover where the Millions are wretched, there are the Thousands straitened, unhappy; only the Units can flourish; or say rather, be ruined the last. Industry, all noosed and haltered, as if it too were some beast of chase for the mighty hunters of this world to bait, and cut slices from,—cries passionately to these its well-paid guides and watchers, not, *Guide me;* but, *Laissez faire,* Leave me alone of *your* guidance! What market has Industry in this France? For two things there may be market and demand: for the coarser kind of field-fruits, since the Millions will live: for the finer kinds of luxury and spicery,—of multiform taste, from opera-melodies down to racers and courtesans; since the Units will be amused. It is at bottom but a mad state of things.

To mend and remake all which, we have, indeed, victorious Analysis. Honour to victorious Analysis; nevertheless, out of the Workshop and Laboratory, what thing was victorious Analysis yet known to make? Detection of incoherences, mainly; destruction of the incoherent. From of old, Doubt was but half a magician: she evokes the spectres which she cannot quell. We shall have 'endless vortices of froth-logic;' whereon first words, and then things, are whirled and swallowed. Remark, accordingly, as acknowledged grounds of Hope, at bottom mere precursors of Despair, this perpetual theorising about Man, the Mind of Man, Philosophy of Government, Progress of the Species, and such like; the main thinking furniture of every head. Time, and so many Montesquieus, Mablys, spokesmen of Time, have discovered innumerable things: and now has not Jean Jacques promulgated his new Evangel of a *Contrat Social;* explaining the whole mystery of Government, and how it is *contracted* and bargained for,—to universal satisfaction? Theories of Government! Such have been, and will be; in ages of decadence. Acknowledge them in their degree; as processes of Nature, who does nothing in vain; as steps in her great process. Meanwhile, what theory is so certain as this, That all theories, were they never so earnest, painfully elaborated, are, and by the very conditions of them, must be incomplete, questionable, and even false? Thou shalt know that this Universe is, what it professes to be, an *infinite* one. Attempt not to swallow *it*, for thy logical digestion; be thankful, if skilfully planting down this and the other fixed pillar in the chaos, thou prevent its swallowing *thee*. That a new young generation has exchanged the Sceptic Creed, *What shall I believe?* for passionate Faith in this Gospel according to Jean Jacques, is a further step in the business; and betokens much

Blessed also is Hope; and always from the beginning there was some Millennium prophesied; Millennium of Holiness; but (what is notable) never till this new Era, any Millennium of mere Ease and plentiful Supply. In such prophesied Lubberland, of Happiness, Benevolence, and Vice cured of its deformity, trust not my friends! Man is not what one calls a happy animal; his appetite for sweet victual is so enormous. How, in this wild Universe, which storms-in on him, infinite, vague-menacing, shall poor man find, say not happiness, but existence, and footing to stand on, if it be not by girding himself together for continual endeavour and endurance? Wo, if in his heart there dwelt no devout Faith; if the word Duty had lost its meaning for him! For as to this of Sentimentalism, so useful for weeping with over romances and on pathetic occasions, it otherwise verily will avail nothing; nay less. The healthy heart that said to itself, "How healthy am I!" was already fallen into the fatallest sort of disease. Is not Sentimentalism twin-sister to Cant, if not one and the same with it? Is not Cant the *materia prima* of the Devil; from which all falsehoods, imbecilities, abominations body themselves; from which no true thing *can* come? For Cant is itself properly a double-distilled Lie; the second-power of a Lie.

And now if a whole Nation fall into that? In such case, I answer, infallibly they will return out of it! For life is no cunningly-devised deception or self deception: it is a great truth that thou art alive, that thou hast desires, necessities; neither can these subsist and satisfy themselves on delusions, but on fact. To fact, depend on it, we shall come back; to such fact, blessed or cursed, as we have wisdom for. The lowest, least blessed fact one knows of, on which necessitous mortals have ever based themselves, seems to be the primitive one of Cannibalism: That *I* can devour *Thee*. What if such Primitive Fact were precisely the one we had (with our improved methods) to revert to, and begin anew from!

CHAPTER VIII

PRINTED PAPER

IN such a practical France, let the theory of Perfectibility say what it will, discontents cannot be wanting: your promised Reformation is so indispensable; yet it comes not; who will begin it—with himself? Discontent with what is around us, still more with what is above us, goes on increasing; seeking ever new vents.

Of Street Ballads, of Epigrams that from of old tempered Despotism, we need not speak. Nor of Manuscript News-papers (*Nouvelles à la main*) do we speak. Bachaumont and his journeymen and followers may close those 'thirty volumes of scurrilous eaves-dropping,' and quit that trade; for at length if not liberty of the Press, there is license. Pamphlets can be surreptitiously vended and read in Paris, did they even bear to be 'Printed at Pekin' We have a *Courrier de l' Europe* in those years, regularly published at London; by a De Morande, whom the guillotine has not yet devoured. There too an unruly Linguet, still unguillotined, when his own country has become too hot for him, and his brother Advocates have cast him out, can emit his hoarse wailings, and *Bastille Dévoilée* (Bastille Unveiled). Loquacious Abbé Raynal, at length, has his wish; sees the *Histoire Philosophique*, with its 'lubricity,' unveracity, loose loud eleutheromaniac rant (contributed, they say, by Philosophedom at large, though in the Abbé's name, and to his glory), burnt by the common hangman;—and sets out on his travels as a martyr. It was the Edition of 1781; perhaps the last notable Book that had such fire-beatitude,—the hangman discovering now that it did not serve.

Again, in Courts of Law, with their money-quarrels, divorce-cases, wheresoever a glimpse into the household existence can be had, what indications! The Parlements of Besançon and Aix ring, audible to all France, with the amours and destinies of a young Mirabeau. He, under the nurture of a 'Friend of Men,' has, in State Prisons, in marching Regiments, Dutch Author's-garrets, and quite other scenes, 'been for twenty years learning to resist despotism:' despotism of men and alas also of gods. How, beneath this rose-coloured veil of Universal Benevolence and *Astræa Redux*, is the sanctuary of Home so often a dreary void, or a dark contentious Hell-on-Earth! The old Friend of Men has his own divorce-case too; and at times, 'his whole family but one' under lock and key: he writes much about reforming and enfranchising the world; and for his own private behoof, he has needed sixty *Lettres-de-Cachet.* A man of insight too; with resolution, even with manful principle: but in such an element, inward and outward: which he could not rule, but only madden. Edacity, rapacity;—quite contrary to the finer sensibilities of the heart! Fools, that expect your verdant Millennium, and nothing but Love and Abundance, brooks running wine, winds whispering Music,—with the whole ground and basis of your existence champed into a mud of Sensuality; which, daily growing deeper, will soon have no bottom but the Abyss!

Or consider that unutterable business of the Diamond Necklace. Red-hatted Cardinal Louis de Rohan; Sicilian jailbird Balsamo Cagliostro; milliner Dame de Lamotte, 'with a face of some piquancy:' the highest Church Dignitaries waltzing, in Walpurgis Dance, with quack-prophets, pickpurses and public women;—a whole Satan's Invisible World displayed; working there continually under the daylight visible one; the smoke of its torment going up for ever! The Throne has been brought into scandalous collision with the Treadmill. Astonished Europe rings with the mystery for nine months; sees only lie unfold itself from lie; corruption among the lofty and the low, gulosity, credulity, imbecility, strength nowhere but in the hunger. Weep, fair Queen, thy first tears of unmixed wretchedness! Thy fair name has been tarnished by foul breath; irremediably while life lasts. No more shalt thou be loved and pitied by living hearts, till a new generation has been bòrn, and thy own heart lies cold, cured of all its sorrows.—The Epigrams henceforth become, not sharp and bitter; but cruel, atrocious, unmentionable. On that 31st of May 1786, a miserable Cardinal Grand-Almoner Rohan, on issuing from his Bastille, is escorted by hurrahing crowds: unloved he, and worthy of no love; but important since the Court and Queen are his enemies.

How is our bright Era of Hope dimmed; and the whole sky growing bleak with signs of hurricane and earthquake! It is a doomed world: gone all 'obedience that made men free;' fast going the obedience that made men slaves,—at least to one another. Slaves only of their own lusts they are now, and will be. Slaves of sin; inevitably also of sorrow. Behold the mouldering mass of Sensuality and Falsehood; round which plays foolishly, itself a corrupt phosphorescence, some glimmer of Sentimentalism;—and over all, rising, as Ark of *their* Covenant, the grim Patibulary Fork 'forty feet high;' which also is now nigh rotted. Add only that the French Nation distinguishes itself among Nations by the characteristic of Excitability; with the good, but also with the perilous evil, which belongs to that. Rebellion, explosion, of unknown extent is to be calculated on. There are, as Chesterfield wrote, 'all the symptoms I have ever met with in History!'

Shall we say then: Wo to Philosophism. that it destroyed Religion, what it called 'extinguishing the abomination (*écraser l'infâme*)?' Wo rather to those that made the Holy an abomination, and extinguishable; wo to all men that live in such a time of world-abomination and world-destruction! Nay, answer the Courtiers, it was Turgot, it was Necker, with their mad innovating; it was the Queen's want of etiquette; it was he, it was she, it was that. Friends! it was every scoundrel that had lived, and quack-like pretended to be doing, and been only eating and *mis*doing, in all provinces of life, as Shoeblack or as Sovereign Lord, each in his degree, from the time of Charlemagne and earlier. All this (for be sure no falsehood perishes, but is as seed sown out to grow) has been storing itself for thousands of years; and now the account-day has come. And rude will the settlement be: of wrath laid up against the day of wrath. O my Brother, be not thou a Quack! Die rather, if thou wilt take counsel; 'tis but dying once, and thou art quit of it forever. Cursed is that trade; and bears curses, thou knowest not how, long ages after thou art departed, and the wages thou hadst are all consumed; nay, as the ancient wise have written,—through Eternity itself, and is verily marked in the Doom-Book of a God!

Hope deferred maketh the heart sick. And yet, as we said, Hope is but deferred; not abolished, not abolishable. It is very notable, and touching, how this same Hope does still light onwards the French Nation through all its wild destinies. For we shall still find Hope shining, be it for fond invitation, be it for anger and menace; as a mild heavenly light it shone; as a red conflagration it shines: burning sulphurous blue, through darkest regions of Terror, it still shines; and goes not out at all, since Desperation itself is a kind of Hope. Thus is our Era still to be named of Hope, though in the saddest sense,—when there is nothing left but Hope.

But if any one would know summarily what a Pandora's Box lies there for the opening, he may see it in what by its nature is the symptom of all symptoms, the surviving Literature of the Period. Abbé Raynal, with his lubricity and loud loose rant, has spoken *his* word; and already the fast-hastening generation responds to another. Glance at Beaumarchais' *Mariage de Figaro;* which now (in 1784), after difficulty enough, has issued on the stage; and 'runs its hundred nights,' to the admiration of all men. By what virtue or internal vigour it so ran, the reader of our day will rather wonder: —and indeed will know so much the better that it flattered some pruriency of the time; that it spoke what all were feeling, and longing to speak. Small substance in that *Figaro:* thin wiredrawn intrigues, thin wiredrawn sentiments and sarcasms; a thing lean, barren; yet which winds and whisks itself, as through a wholly mad universe, adroitly, with a high-sniffing air: wherein each, as was hinted, which is the grand secret, may see some image of himself, and of his own state and ways. So it runs its hundred nights, and all France runs with it; laughing applause. If the soliloquising Barber ask: "What has your Lordship done to earn all this?" and can only answer: "You took the trouble to be born (*Vous vous êtes donné la peine de naître*),"—all men must laugh: and a gay horse-racing Anglomaniac Noblesse loudest of all. For how can small books have a great danger in them? asks the Sieur Caron; and fancies his thin epigram may be a kind of reason. Conqueror of a golden fleece, by giant smuggling; tamer of hell-dogs, in the Parlement Maupeou; and finally crowned Orpheus in the *Théâtre Français*, Beaumarchais has now culminated, and unites the attributes of several demigods. We shall meet him once again, in the course of his decline.

Still more significant are two Books produced on the eve of the ever-memorable Explosion itself, and read eagerly by all the world: Saint-Pierre's *Paul et Virginie*, and Louvet's *Chevalier de Faublas*. Noteworthy Books; which may be considered as the last-speech of old Feudal France. In the first there rises melodiously, as it were, the wail of a moribund world: everywhere wholesome Nature in unequal conflict with diseased perfidious Art; cannot escape from it in the lowest hut, in the remotest island of the sea. Ruin and death must strike down the loved one; and, what is most significant of all, death even here not by necessity but by etiquette. What a world of prurient corruption lies visible in that super-

sublime of modesty! Yet, on the whole, our good Saint-
Pierre is musical, poetical though most morbid: we will call
his Book the swan-song of old dying France.

Louvet's, again, let no man account musical. Truly, if this
wretched *Faublas* is a death-speech, it is one under the
gallows, and by a felon that does not repent. Wretched *cloaca*
of a Book; without depth even as a *cloaca*! What 'picture of
French society' is here? Picture properly of nothing, if not
of the mind that gave it out as some sort of picture. Yet
symptom of much; above all of the world that could nourish
itself thereon.

BOOK III

THE PARLEMENT OF PARIS

CHAPTER I

DISHONOURED BILLS

WHILE the unspeakable confusion is everywhere weltering within, and through so many cracks in the surface sulphur-smoke is issuing, the question arises: Through what crevice will the main Explosion carry itself? Through which of the old craters or chimneys; or must it, at once, form a new crater for itself? In every Society are such chimneys, are Institutions serving as such: even Constantinople is not without its safety-valves; there, too, Discontent can vent itself,—in material fire; by the number of nocturnal conflagrations, or of hanged bakers, the Reigning Power can read the signs of the times, and change course according to these.

We may say that this French Explosion will doubtless first try all the old Institutions of escape; for by each of these there is, or at least there used to be, some communication with the interior deep; they are national Institutions in virtue of that. Had they even become personal Institutions, and what we can call choked up from their original uses, there nevertheless must the impediment be weaker than elsewhere. Through which of them, then? An observer might have guessed: Through the Law Parlements; above all, through the Parlement of Paris.

Men, though never so thickly clad in dignities, sit not inaccessible to the influences of their time; especially men whose life is business; who at all turns, were it even from behind judgment-seats, have come in contact with the actual workings of the world. The Counsellor of Parlement, the President himself, who has bought his place with hard money that he might be looked up to by his fellow-creatures, how shall he, in all Philosophe-soirées, and saloons of elegant culture, become notable as a Friend of Darkness? Among the Paris Longrobes there may be more than one patriotic Malesherbes, whose rule is conscience and the public good;

there are clearly more than one hot-headed D'Esprém#nil, to
whose confused thought any loud reputation of the Brutus sort
may seem glorious. The Lepelletiers, Lamoignons have titles
and wealth; yet at Court are only styled 'Noblesse of the
Robe.' There are Duports of deep scheme: Fréteaus, Saba-
tiers, of incontinent tongue: all nursed more or less on the
milk of the *Contrat Social*. Nay, for the whole Body, is not
this patriotic opposition also a fighting for oneself? Awake,
Parlement of Paris, renew thy long warfare! Was not the
Parlement Maupeou abolished with ignominy? Not now hast
thou to dread a Louis XIV., with the crack of his whip, and
his Olympian looks; not now a Richelieu and Bastilles: no,
the whole Nation is behind thee. Thou too (O heavens!)
mayest become a Political Power; and with the shakings of
thy horse-hair wig, shake principalities and dynasties, like a very
Jove with his ambrosial curls!

Light old M. de Maurepas, since the end of 1781, has been
fixed in the frost of death: "Never more," said the good
Louis, "shall I hear his step in the room there overhead";
his light jestings and gyratings are at an end. No more can
the importunate reality be hidden by pleasant wit, and to-day's
evil be deftly rolled over upon to-morrow. The morrow itself
has arrived; and now nothing but a solid phlegmatic M. de
Vergennes sits there, in dull matter of fact, like some dull
punctual Clerk (which he originally was); admits what cannot
be denied, let the remedy come whence it will. In him is no
remedy; only clerk-like 'despatch of business' according
to routine. The poor King, grown older yet hardly more
experienced, must himself, with such no-faculty as he has,
begin governing; wherein also his Queen will give help. Bright
Queen, with her quick clear glances and impulses; clear, and
even noble; but all-too superficial, vehement-shallow, for that
work! To govern France were such a problem; and now it
has grown well-nigh too hard to govern even the Œil-de-Bœuf.
For if a distressed People has its cry, so likewise, and more
audibly, has a bereaved Court. To the Œil-de-Bœuf it remains
inconceivable how, in a France of such resources, the Horn of
Plenty should run dry: did it not *use* to flow? Nevertheless
Necker, with his revenue of parsimony, has 'suppressed above
six hundred places,' before the Courtiers could oust him; par-
simonious finance-pedant as he was. Again, a military pedant,
Saint-Germain, with his Prussian manœuvres; with his Prussian

notions, as if merit and not coat-of-arms should be the rule of promotion, has disaffected military men; the Mousquetaires, with much else are suppressed: for he too was one of your suppressors; and unsettling and oversetting, did mere mischief —to the Œil-de-Bœuf. Complaints abound; scarcity, anxiety: it is a changed Œil-de-Bœuf. Besenval says, already in these years (1781) there was such a melancholy (such a *tristesse*) about Court, compared with former days, as made it quite dispiriting to look upon.

No wonder that the Œil-de-Bœuf feels melancholy, when you are suppressing its places? Not a place can be suppressed, but some purse is the lighter for it; and more than one heart the heavier; for did it not employ the working classes too,— manufacturers, male and female, of laces, essences; of Pleasure generally, whosoever could manufacture Pleasure? Miserable economies; never felt over Twenty-five Millions! So, however, it goes on: and is not yet ended. Few years more and the Wolf-hounds shall fall suppressed, the Bear-hounds, the Falconry; places shall fall, thick as autumnal leaves. Duke de Polignac demonstrates, to the complete silencing of ministerial logic, that his place cannot be abolished; then gallantly, turning to the Queen, surrenders it, since her Majesty so wishes. Less chivalrous was Duke de Coigny, and yet not luckier: "We got into a real quarrel, Coigny and I," said King Louis; "but if he had even struck me, I could not have blamed him." In regard to such matters there can be but one opinion. Baron Besenval, with that frankness of speech which stamps the independent man, plainly assures her Majesty that it is frightful (*affreux*); "you go to bed, and are not sure but you shall rise impoverished on the morrow: one might as well be in Turkey." It is indeed a dog's life.

How singular this perpetual distress of the royal treasury! And yet it is a thing not more incredible than undeniable. A thing mournfully true: the stumbling-block on which all Ministers successively stumble, and fall. Be it 'want of fiscal genius,' or some far other want, there is the palpablest discrepancy between Revenue and Expenditure; a *Deficit* of the Revenue: you must 'choke (*combler*) the Deficit,' or else it will swallow you! This is the stern problem; hopeless seemingly as squaring of the circle. Controller Joly de Fleury, who succeeded Necker, could do nothing with it; nothing but propose loans, which were tardily filled up; impose new taxes, unproductive of money, productive of clamour and discontent. As little could Controller d'Ormesson do, or even less; for if Joly maintained himself beyond year and day, D'Ormesson reckons only by months: till 'the King purchased Rambouillet without consulting him,' which he took as a hint to withdraw. And so, towards the end of 1783, matters threaten to come to a still-stand. Vain seems human ingenuity. In vain has our newly-devised 'Council of Finances' struggled, our Intendants of Finance, Controller-General of Finances: there are unhappily no finances to control. Fatal paralysis invades the social movement; clouds, of blindness or of blackness, envelop us: are we breaking down, then, into the black horrors of NATIONAL BANKRUPTCY?

Great is Bankruptcy: the great bottomless gulf into which all Falsehoods, public and private, do sink, disappearing; whither, from the first origin of them, they were all doomed. For Nature is true and not a lie. No lie you can speak or act but it will come, after longer or shorter circulation, like a Bill drawn on Nature's Reality, and be presented there for payment,—with the answer, *No effects*. Pity only that it often had so long a circulation: that the original forger were so seldom he who bore the final smart of it! Lies, and the burden of evil they bring, are passed on; shifted from back to back, and from rank to rank, and so land ultimately on the dumb lowest rank, who with spade and mattock, with sore heart and empty wallet, daily come in *contact* with reality, and can pass the cheat no further.

Observe nevertheless how, by a just compensating law, if the lie with its burden (in this confused whirlpool of Society) sinks and is shifted ever downwards, then in return the distress of it rises ever upwards and upwards. Whereby, after the long pining and demi-starvation of those Twenty Millions, a Duke de Coigny and his Majesty come also to have their 'real quarrel.' Such is the law of just Nature; bringing, though at long intervals, and were it only by Bankruptcy, matters round again to the mark.

But with a Fortunatus' Purse in its pocket, through what length of time might not almost any Falsehood last! Your Society, your Household, practical or spiritual Arrangement, is untrue, unjust, offensive to the eye of God and man. Nevertheless its hearth is warm, its larder well replenished: the innumerable Swiss of Heaven, with a kind of natural loyalty, gather round it; will prove, by pamphleteering, musketeering, that it is a truth; or if not an unmixed (unearthly, impossible)

Truth, then better, a wholesomely attempered one (as wind is to the shorn lamb), and works well. Changed outlook, however, when purse and larder grow empty! Was your Arrangement so true, so accordant to Nature's ways, then how, in the name of wonder, has Nature, with her infinite bounty, come to leave it famishing there? To all men, to all women and all children, it is now indubitable that your Arrangement was *false.* Honour to Bankruptcy; ever righteous on the great scale, though in detail it is so cruel. Under all falsehoods it works, unweariedly mining. No Falsehood, did it rise heaven-high and cover the world, but Bankruptcy, one day, will sweep it down, and make us free of it.

CHAPTER II

CONTROLLER CALONNE

UNDER such circumstances of *tristesse,* obstruction and sick languor, when to an exasperated Court it seems as if fiscal genius had departed from among men, what apparition could be welcomer than that of M. de Calonne? Calonne, a man of indisputable genius; even fiscal genius, more or less; of experience both in managing Finance and Parlements, for he has been Intendant at Metz, at Lille; King's Procureur at Douai. A man of weight, connected with the moneyed classes; of unstained name,—if it were not some peccadillo (of showing a Client's Letter) in that old D'Aiguillon-Lachalotais business, as good as forgotten now. He has kinsmen of heavy purse, felt on the Stock Exchange. Our Foulons, Berthiers intrigue for him :—old Foulon, who has now nothing to do but intrigue; who is known and even seen to be what they call a scoundrel; but of unmeasured wealth; who, from Commissariat-clerk which he once was, may hope, some think, if the game go right, to be Minister himself some day.

Such propping and backing has M. de Calonne; and then intrinsically such qualities! Hope radiates from his face; persuasion hangs on his tongue. For all straits he has present remedy, and will make the world roll on wheels before him. On the 3rd of November 1783, the Œil-de-Bœuf rejoices in its new Controller-General. Calonne also shall have trial; Calonne also, in his way, as Turgot and Necker had done in theirs, shall forward the consummation; suffuse, with one other flush of brilliancy, our now too leaden-coloured Era of Hope, and wind it up—into fulfilment.

Great, in any case, is the felicity of the Œil-de-Bœuf. Stinginess has fled from these royal abodes : suppression ceases ; your Besenval may go peaceably to sleep, sure that he shall awake unplundered. Smiling Plenty, as if conjured by some enchanter, has returned ; scatters contentment from her new-flowing horn. And mark what suavity of manners ! A bland smile distinguishes our Controller : to all men he listens with an air of interest, nay of anticipation ; makes their own wish clear to themselves, and grants it ; or at least, grants conditional promise of it. "I fear this is a matter of difficulty," said her Majesty.—" Madame," answered the Controller, "if it is but difficult, it is done ; if it is impossible, it shall be done (*se fera*)." A man of such 'facility' withal. To observe him in the pleasure-vortex of society, which none partakes of with more gusto, you might ask, When does he work ? And yet his work, as we see, is never behindhand ; above all, the fruit of his work : ready-money. Truly a man of incredible facility : facile action, facile elocution, facile thought : how, in mild suasion, philosophic depth sparkles up from him, as mere wit and lambent sprightliness ; and in her Majesty's Soirées, with the weight of a world lying on him, he is the delight of men and women ! By what magic does he accomplish miracles? By the only true magic, that of genius. Men name him '*the* Minister ;' as indeed, when was there another such ? Crooked things are become straight by him, rough places plain ; and over the Œil-de-Bœuf there rests an unspeakable sunshine.

Nay, in seriousness, let no man say that Calonne had not genius ; genius for Persuading ; before all things, for Borrowing. With the skilfulest judicious appliances of underhand money, he keeps the Stock Exchanges flourishing ; so that Loan after Loan is filled up as soon as opened. 'Calculators likely to know' have calculated that he spent, in extraordinaries, 'at the rate of one million daily ;' which indeed is some fifty thousand pounds sterling : but did he not produce something with it ; namely peace and prosperity, for the time being? Philosophedom grumbles and croaks ; buys, as we said, 80,000 copies of Necker's new Book, but Nonpareil Calonne, in her Majesty's Apartment, with the glittering retinue of Dukes, Duchesses, and mere happy admiring faces, can let Necker and Philosophedom croak.

The misery is, such a time cannot last! Squandering, and Payment by Loan is no way to choke a Deficit. Neither is oil the substance for quenching conflagrations;—alas no, only for assuaging them, *not* permanently! To the Nonpareil himself, who wanted not insight, it is clear at intervals, and dimly certain at all times, that his trade is by nature temporary, growing daily more difficult; that changes incalculable lie at no great distance. Apart from financial Deficit, the world is wholly in such a new-fangled humour; all things working loose from their old fastenings, towards new issues and combinations. There is not a dwarf *jokei*, a cropt Brutus'-head, or Anglo-maniac horseman rising on his stirrups, that does not betoken change. But what then? The day, in any case, passes pleasantly; for the morrow, if the morrow come, there shall be counsel too. Once mounted (by munificence, suasion, magic of genius) high enough in favour with the Œil-de-Bœuf, with the King, Queen, Stock Exchange, and so far as possible with all men, a Nonpareil Controller may hope to go careering through the Inevitable, in some unimagined way, as handsomely as another.

At all events, for these three miraculous years, it has been expedient heaped on expedient: till now, with such cumulation and height, the pile topples perilous. And here has this world's-wonder of a Diamond Necklace brought it at last to the clear verge of tumbling. Genius in that direction can no more: mounted high enough, or not mounted, we must fare forth. Hardly is poor Rohan, the Necklace-Cardinal, safely bestowed in the Auvergne Mountains, Dame de la Motte (unsafely) in the Salpêtrière, and that mournful business hushed up, when our sanguine Controller once more astonishes the world. An expedient, unheard of for these hundred and sixty years, has been propounded; and, by dint of suasion (for his light audacity, his hope and eloquence are matchless) has been got adopted,—*Convocation of the Notables*.

Let notable persons, the actual or virtual rulers of their districts, be summoned from all sides of France: let a true tale, of his Majesty's patriotic purposes and wretched pecuniary impossibilities, be suasively told them; and then the question put: What are we to do? Surely to adopt healing measures; such as the magic of genius will unfold; such as, once sanctioned by Notables, all Parlements and all men must, with more or less reluctance, submit to.

CHAPTER III

THE NOTABLES

HERE then is verily a sign and wonder; visible to the whole world; bodeful of much. The Œil-de-Bœuf dolorously grumbles; were we not well as we stood,—quenching conflagrations by oil? Constitutional Philosophedom starts with joyful surprise; stares eagerly what the result will be. The public creditor, the public debtor, the whole thinking and thoughtless public have their several surprises, joyful or sorrowful. Count Mirabeau, who has got his matrimonial and other Lawsuits huddled up, better or worse; and works now in the dimmest element at Berlin; compiling *Prussian Monarchies,* Pamphlets *On Cagliostro;* writing, with pay, but not with honourable recognition, innumerable Despatches for his Government,—scents or descries richer quarry from afar. He, like an eagle or vulture, or mixture of both, preens his wings for flight homewards.

M. de Calonne has stretched out an Aaron's Rod over France; miraculous; and is summoning quite unexpected things. Audacity and hope alternate in him with misgivings; though the sanguine-valiant side carries it. Anon he writes to an intimate friend, "*Je me fais pitié à moi-même* (I am an object of pity to myself);" anon, invites some dedicating Poet or Poetaster to sing 'this Assembly of the Notables, and the Revolution that is preparing.' Preparing indeed; and a matter to be sung,—only not till we have *seen* it, and what the issue of it is. In deep obscure unrest, all things have so long gone rocking and swaying: will M. de Calonne, with this his alchemy of the Notables, fasten all together again and get new revenues? Or wrench all asunder; so that it go no longer rocking and swaying, but clashing and colliding?

Be this as it may, in the bleak short days, we behold men of weight and influence threading the great vortex of French Locomotion, each on his several line, from all sides of France, towards the Château de Versailles: summoned *de par le roi.* There, on the 22nd day of February 1787, they have met, and got installed: Notables to the number of a Hundred and Thirty-seven, as we count them name by name; add Seven Princes of the Blood, it makes the round Gross of Notables. Men of the sword, men of the robe; Peers, dignified Clergy, Parlementary Presidents; divided into Seven Boards

(*Bureaux*); under our Seven Princes of the Blood, Monsieur, D'Artois, Penthièvre, and the rest; among whom let not our new Duke d'Orléans (for, since 1785, he is Chartres no longer) be forgotten. Never yet made Admiral, and now turning the corner of his fortieth year, with spoiled blood and prospects; half weary of a world which is more than half-weary of him, Monseigneur's future is most questionable. Not an illumination and insight, not even in conflagration; but, as was said, 'in dull smoke and ashes of outburnt sensualities,' does he live and digest. Sumptuosity and sordidness; revenge, life-weariness, ambition, darkness, putrescence; and, say, in sterling money, three hundred thousand a year,—were this poor Prince once to burst loose from his Court-moorings, to what regions, with what phenomena, might he not sail and drift! Happily as yet he 'affects to hunt daily;' sits there, since he must sit, presiding that Bureau of his, with dull moon-visage, dull glassy eyes, as if it were a mere tedium to him.

We observe finally, that Count Mirabeau has actually arrived. He descends from Berlin, on the scene of action; glares into it with flashing sun-glance; discerns that it will do nothing for him. He had hoped these Notables might need a Secretary. They do need one; but have fixed on Dupont de Nemours; a man of smaller fame, but then of better;—who indeed, as his friends often hear, labours under this complaint, surely not a universal one, of having 'five kings to correspond with.' The pen of a Mirabeau cannot become an official one; nevertheless it remains a pen. In defect of Secretaryship, he sets to denouncing Stock-brokerage (*Dénonciation de l'Agiotage*); testifying, as his wont is, by loud bruit, that he is present and busy;—till, warned by friend Talleyrand, and even by Calonne himself underhand, that 'a seventeenth *Lettre-de-Cachet* may be launched against him,' he timefully flits over the marches.

And now, in stately royal apartments, as Pictures of that time still represent them, our hundred and forty-four Notables sit organised; ready to hear and consider. Controller Calonne is dreadfully behindhand with his speeches, his preparatives; however the man's 'facility of work' is known to us. For freshness of style, lucidity, ingenuity, largeness of view, that opening Harangue of his was unsurpassable:—had not the subject-matter been so appalling. A Deficit, concerning which accounts vary, and the Controller's own account is not unquestioned; but which all accounts agree in representing as 'enormous.' This is the epitome of our Controller's difficulties: and then his means? Mere Turgotism; for thither, it seems, we must come at last: Provincial Assemblies; new Taxation; nay, strangest of all, new Landtax, what he calls *Subvention Territoriale*, from which neither Privileged nor Unprivileged, Noblemen, Clergy, nor Parlementeers, shall be exempt!

Foolish enough! These Privileged Classes have been used to tax; levying toll, tribute and custom, at all hands, while a penny was left: but to be themselves taxed! Of such Privileged persons, meanwhile, do these Notables, all but the merest fraction, consist. Headlong Calonne had given no heed to the 'composition,' or judicious packing of them; but chosen such Notables as were really notable; trusting for the issue to off-hand ingenuity, good fortune, and eloquence that never yet failed. Headlong Controller-General! Eloquence can do much, but not all. Orpheus, with eloquence grown rhythmic, musical (what we call Poetry), drew iron tears from the cheek of Pluto; but by what witchery of rhyme or prose wilt thou from the pocket of Plutus draw gold?

Accordingly, the storm that now rose and began to whistle round Calonne, first in these Seven Bureaus, and then on the outside of them, awakened by them, spreading wider and wider over all France, threatens to become unappeasable. A Deficit so enormous! Mismanagement, profusion is too clear. Peculation itself is hinted at; nay, Lafayette and others go so far as to speak it out, with attempts at proof. The blame of his Deficit our brave Calonne, as was natural, had endeavoured to shift from himself on his predecessors; not excepting even Necker. But now Necker vehemently denies; whereupon an 'angry Correspondence,' which also finds its way into print.

In the Œil-de-Bœuf, and her Majesty's private Apartments, an eloquent Controller, with his "Madame, if it is but difficult," had been persuasive: but, alas, the cause is now carried elsewhither. Behold him, one of these sad days, in Monsieur's Bureau; to which all the other Bureaus have sent deputies. He is standing at bay: alone; exposed to an incessant fire of questions, interpellations, objurgations, from those 'hundred and thirty-seven' pieces of logic-ordnance,—what we may well call *bouches à feu*, fire-mouths literally! Never, according to Besenval, or hardly ever, had such a display of intellect, dexterity, coolness, suasive eloquence, been made by man. To the raging play of so many fire-mouths he opposes nothing angrier than light-beams, self-possession and fatherly smiles. With the imperturbablest bland clearness, he, for five hours long, keeps answering the incessant volley of fiery captious questions, reproachful interpellations; in words prompt as lightning, quiet as light. Nay, the cross-fire too: such side-questions and incidental interpellations as, in the heat of the main-battle, he (having only one tongue) could not get answered; these also he takes up, at the first slake; answers even those. Could blandest suasive eloquence have saved France, she were saved.

Heavy-laden Controller! In the Seven Bureaus seems nothing but hindrance: in Monsieur's Bureau, a Loménie de Brienne, Archbishop of Toulouse, with an eye himself to the Controllership, stirs up the Clergy; there are meetings, underground intrigues. Neither from without anywhere comes sign of help or hope. For the Nation (where Mirabeau is now, with stentor-lungs, 'denouncing Agio') the Controller has hitherto done nothing, or less. For Philosophedom he has done as good as nothing.—sent out some scientific Lapérouse, or the like: and is he not in 'angry correspondence' with its Necker? The very Œil-de-Bœuf looks questionable; a fallen Controller has no friends. Solid M. de Vergennes, who with his phlegmatic judicious punctuality might have kept down many things, died the very week belore these sorrowful Notables met. And now a Seal-keeper, *Garde-des-Sceaux* Miroménil is thought to be playing the traitor: spinning plots for Loménie-Brienne! Queen's-Reader Abbé de Vermond, unloved individual, was Brienne's creature, the work of his hands from the first: it may be feared the backstairs passage is open, the ground getting mined under our feet. Treacherous Garde-des-Sceaux Miroménil, at least, should be dismissed: Lamoignon, the eloquent Notable, a stanch man, with con- nections. and even ideas. Parlement-President yet intent on reforming Parlements, were not he the right Keeper? So, for one, thinks busy Besenval; and, at dinner-table, rounds the same into the Controller's ear,—who always, in the intervals of landlord-duties, listens to him as with charmed look, but answers nothing positive.

Alas, what to answer? The force of private intrigue, and then also the force of public opinion, grows so dangerous, confused! Philosophedom sneers aloud, as if its Necker already triumphed. The gaping populace gapes over Wood- cuts or Copper-cuts; where, for example, a Rustic is repre-

sented convoking the Poultry of his barnyard, with this opening
address: "Dear animals, I have assembled you to advise me
what sauce I shall dress you with;" to which a Cock respond-
ing: "We don't want to be eaten," is checked by "You wander
from the point (*Vous vous écartez de la question*)." Laughter
and logic; ballad-singer, pamphleteer; epigram and caricature:
what wind of public opinion is this,—as if the Cave of the
Winds were bursting loose! At nightfall. President Lamoignon
steals over to the Controller's; finds him 'walking with large
strides in his chamber, like one out of himself.' With rapid
confused speech the Controller begs M. de Lamoignon to give
him 'an advice.' Lamoignon candidly answers that, except in
regard to his own anticipated Keepership, unless that would
prove remedial, he really cannot take upon him to advise.

'On the Monday after Easter,' the 9th of April 1787, a date
one rejoices to verify, for nothing can excel the indolent falsehood of these *Histoires* and *Mémoires*,—'On the Monday after
Easter, as I, Besenval, was riding towards Romainville to the
Maréchal de Ségur's, I met a friend on the Boulevards, who
told me that M. de Calonne was out. A little further on came
M. the Duke d'Orléans, dashing towards me, head to the
wind' (trotting *à l' Anglaise*) 'and confirmed the news.' It is
true news. Treacherous Garde-des-Sceaux Miroménil is gone,
and Lamoignon is appointed in his room: but appointed for
his own profit only, not for the Controller's: 'next day' the
Controller also has had to move. A little longer he may linger
near; be seen among the money-changers, and even 'working
in the Controller's office,' where much lies unfinished: but
neither will that hold. Too strong blows and beats this tempest
of public opinion, of private intrigue, as from the Cave of all
the winds; and blows him (higher Authority giving sign) out
of Paris and France,—over the horizon, into Invisibility, or
outer Darkness.

Such destiny the magic of genius could not forever avert.
Ungrateful Œil-de-Bœuf! did he not miraculously rain gold
manna on you; so that, as a Courtier said, "All the world held
out its hand, and I held out my hat,"—for a time? Himself
is poor, penniless, had not a 'Financier's widow in Lorraine'
offered him, though he was turned of fifty, her hand and the
rich purse it held. Dim henceforth shall be his activity, though
unwearied: Letters to the King, Appeals, Prognostications;
Pamphlets (from London), written with the old suasive facility;
which however do not persuade. Luckily his widow's purse

fails not. Once, in a year or two, some shadow of him shall be seen hovering on the Northern Border, seeking election as National Deputy; but be sternly beckoned away. Dimmer then, far-borne over utmost European lands, in uncertain twilight of diplomacy, he shall hover, intriguing for 'Exiled Princes,' and have adventures; be overset into the Rhine-stream and half-drowned, nevertheless save his papers dry. Unwearied, but in vain! In France he works miracles no more; shall hardly return thither to find a grave. Farewell, thou facile sanguine Controller-General, with thy light rash hand, thy suasive mouth of gold: worse men there have been, and better; but to thee also was allotted a task,—of raising the wind, and the winds; and thou hast done it.

But now, while Ex-Controller Calonne flies storm-driven over the horizon, in this singular way, what has become of the Controllership? It hangs vacant, one may say; extinct, like the Moon in her vacant interlunar cave. Two preliminary shadows, poor M. Fourqueux, poor M. Villedeuil, do hold, in quick succession, some simulacrum of it,—as the new Moon will sometimes shine out with a dim preliminary old one in her arms. Be patient, ye Notables! An actual new Controller is certain, and even ready; were the indispensable manœuvres but gone through. Long-headed Lamoignon, with Home-Secretary Breteuil, and Foreign Secretary Montmorin have exchanged looks; let these three once meet and speak. Who is it that is strong in the Queen's favour, and the Abbé de Vermond's? That is a man of great capacity? Or at least that has struggled, these fifty years, to have it thought great; now, in the Clergy's name, demanding to have Protestant death-penalties 'put in execution;' now flaunting it in the Œil-de-Bœuf, as the man-pleaser and woman-pleaser; gleaning even a good word from Philosophedom and your Voltaires and D'Alembert's? That has a party ready-made for him in the Notables?—Loménie de Brienne, Archbishop of Toulouse! answer all the three, with the clearest instantaneous concord; and rush off to propose him to the King; 'in such haste,' says Besenval, 'that M. de Lamoignon had to borrow a *simarre*,' seemingly some kind of cloth apparatus necessary for that.

Loménie-Brienne, who had all his life 'felt a kind of pre-destination for the highest offices,' has now therefore obtained them. He presides over the Finances; he shall have the title

of Prime Minister itself, and the effort of his long life be
realised. Unhappy only that it took such talent and industry
to *gain* the place; that to *qualify* for it hardly any talent or
industry was left disposable! Looking now into his inner
man, what qualifications he may have, Loménie beholds, not
without astonishment, next to nothing but vacuity and possibility. Principles or methods, acquirement outward or inward
(for his very body is wasted, by hard tear and wear) he finds
none; not so much as a plan, even an unwise one. Lucky, in
these circumstances, that Calonne has had a plan! Calonne's
plan was gathered from Turgot's and Necker's by compilation;
shall become Loménie's by adoption. Not in vain has Loménie
studied the working of the British Constitution; for he professes to have some Anglomania, of a sort. Why, in that free
country, does one Minister, driven out by Parliament, vanish
from his King's presence, and another enter, borne in by Parliament? Surely not for mere change (which is ever wasteful);
but that all men may have share of what is going; and so the
strife of Freedom indefinitely prolong itself, and no harm be
done.

The Notables, mollified by Easter festivities, by the sacrifice
of Calonne, are not in the worst humour. Already his Majesty,
while the 'interlunar shadows' were in office, had held session
of Notables; and from his throne delivered promissory conciliatory eloquence: 'the Queen stood waiting at a window,
till his carriage came back; and Monsieur from afar clapped
hands to her,' in sign that all was well. It has had the best
effect; if such do but last. Leading Notables meanwhile can
be 'caressed;' Brienne's new gloss, Lamoignon's long head
will profit somewhat; conciliatory eloquence shall not be
wanting. On the whole, however, is it not undeniable that this
of ousting Calonne and adopting the plans of Calonne, is a
measure, which to produce its best effect, should be looked at
from a certain distance, cursorily; not dwelt on with minute
near scrutiny? In a word, that no service the Notables could
now do were so obliging as, in some handsome manner, to—
take themselves away? Their 'Six Propositions' about Provisional Assemblies, suppression of *Corvées* and such like, can
be accepted without criticism. The *Subvention* or Land-tax,
and much else, one must glide hastily over; safe nowhere but
in flourishes of conciliatory eloquence. Till at length, on this
25th of May, year 1787, in solemn final session, there bursts
forth what we can call an explosion of eloquence; King,

Loménie, Lamoignon and retinue taking up the successive strain ; in harangues to the number of ten, besides his Majesty's, which last the livelong day ;—whereby, as in a kind of choral anthem. or bravura peal, of thanks, praises, promises, the Notables are, so to speak, organed out, and dismissed to their respective places of abode. They had sat, and talked, some nine weeks : they were the first Notables since Richelieu's, in the year 1626.

By some Historians, sitting much at their ease, in the safe distance, Loménie has been blamed for this dismissal of Notables : nevertheless it was clearly time. There are things, as we said, which should not be dwelt on with minute close scrutiny : over hot coals you cannot glide too fast. In these Seven Bureaus. where no work could be done, unless talk were work. the questionablest matters were coming up. Lafayette, for example, in Monseigneur d'Artois' Bureau, took upon him to set forth more than one deprecatory oration about *Lettres-de-Cachet*, Liberty of the Subject, *Agio*, and such like ; which Monseigneur endeavouring to repress, was answered that a Notable being summoned to speak his opinion must speak it.

Thus too his Grace the Archbishop of Aix perorating once, with a plaintive pulpit-tone, in these words : "Tithe, that free-will offering of the piety of Christians"—"Tithe," interrupted Duke la Rochefoucault, with the cold business-manner he has learned from the English, "that free-will offering of the piety of Christians ; on which there are now forty-thousand law-suits in this realm." Nay Lafayette, bound to speak his opinion, went the length, one day, of proposing to convoke a 'National Assembly.' "You demand States-General?"asked Monseigneur with an air of minatory surprise.—"Yes, Monseigneur ; and even better than that."—"Write it," said Monseigneur to the Clerks.—Written accordingly it is ; and what is more, will be acted by and by.

CHAPTER IV

LOMÉNIE'S EDICTS

THUS then have the Notables returned home ; carrying, to all quarters of France, such notions of deficit, decrepitude, distraction ; and that States-General will cure it, or will not cure it but kill it. Each Notable, we may fancy, is as a funereal torch ; disclosing hideous abysses, better left hid ! The unquietest humour possesses all men; ferments, seeks issue, in pamphleteering, caricaturing, projecting, declaiming; vain jangling of thought, word and deed.

It is Spiritual Bankruptcy, long tolerated; verging now towards Economical Bankruptcy, and become intolerable. For from the lowest dumb rank, the inevitable misery as was predicted, has spread upwards. In every man is some obscure feeling that his position, oppressive or else oppressed, is a false one: all men, in one or the other acrid dialect, as assaulters or as defenders, must give vent to the unrest that is in them. Of such stuff national well-being, and the glory of rulers, is not made. O Loménie, what a wild-heaving, waste-looking, hungry and angry world hast thou, after lifelong effort, got promoted to take charge of!

Loménie's first Edicts are mere soothing ones: creation of Provincial Assemblies, 'for apportioning the imposts,' when we get any; suppression of *Corvées* or statute-labour; alleviation of *Gabelle.* Soothing measures, recommended by the Notables, long clamoured for by all liberal men. Oil cast on the waters has been known to produce a good effect. Before venturing with great essential measures, Loménie will see this singular 'swell of the public mind' abate somewhat.

Most proper, surely. But what if it were not a swell of the abating kind? There are swells that come of upper tempest and wind-gust. But again there are swells that come of subterranean pent wind, some say; and even of inward decomposition, of decay that has become self-combustion:—as when, according to Neptuno-Plutonic Geology, the World is all decayed down into due attritus of this sort; and shall now be *exploded*, and new-made! These latter abate not by oil.—The fool says in his heart, How shall not to-morrow be as yesterday; as all days,—which were once to-morrows? The wise man, looking on this France, moral intellectual, economical, sees, 'in short, all the symptoms he has ever met with in history,'— *un*abateable by soothing Edicts.

Meanwhile, abate or not, cash must be had; and for that, quite another sort of Edicts, namely 'bursal' or fiscal ones. How easy were fiscal Edicts, did you know for certain that the Parlement of Paris would what they call 'register' them! Such right of registering, properly of mere *writing down*, the Parlement has got by old wont; and, though but a Law-Court, can remonstrate, and higgle considerably about the same. Hence many quarrels; desperate Maupeou devices, and victory and defeat;—a quarrel now near forty years long. Hence fiscal Edicts, which otherwise were easy enough, become such problems. For example, is there not Calonne's *Subvention Territoriale*, universal, unexempting Landtax; the sheet-anchor of Finance? Or, to show, so far as possible, that one is not without original finance talent, Loménie himself can devise an *Édit du Timbre* or Stamptax,—borrowed also, it is true; but then from America: may it prove luckier in France than there!

France has her resources: nevertheless, it cannot be denied, the aspect of that Parlement is questionable. Already among the Notables, in that final symphony of dismissal, the Paris President had an ominous tone. Adrien Duport, quitting magnetic sleep, in this agitation of the world, threatens to rouse himself into preternatural wakefulness. Shallower but also louder, there is magnetic D'Espréménil, with his tropical heat (he was born at Madras); with his dusky confused violence; holding of Illumination, Animal Magnetism, Public Opinion, Adam Weisshaupt, Harmodius and Aristogiton, and all manner of confused violent things: of whom can come no good. The very Peerage is infected with the leaven. Our Peers have, in too many cases, laid aside their frogs, laces, bagwigs; and go about in English costume, or ride rising in their stirrups,—in the most headlong manner; nothing but insubordination, eleutheromania, confused unlimited opposition in their heads. Questionable: not to be ventured upon, if we had a Fortunatus' Purse! But Loménie has waited all June, casting on the waters what oil he had; and now, betide as it may, the two Finance Edicts must out. On the 6th of July, he forwards his proposed Stamptax and Landtax to the Parlement of Paris; and, as if putting his own leg foremost, not his borrowed Calonne's-leg,—places the Stamptax first in order.

Alas, the Parlement will *not* register: the Parlement demands instead a 'state of the expenditure,' a 'state of the contemplated reductions'; 'states' enough; which his Majesty must decline to furnish! Discussions arise; patriotic eloquence: the Peers are summoned. Does the Nemean Lion begin to bristle? Here surely is a duel, which France and the Universe may look upon: with prayers; at lowest, with curiosity and bets. Paris stirs with new animation. The outer courts of the Palais de Justice roll with unusual crowds,

coming and going; their huge outer hum mingles with the
clang of patriotic eloquence within, and gives vigour to it.
Poor Loménie gazes from the distance, little comforted; has his
invisible emissaries flying to and fro, assiduous, without result.
So pass the sultry dog-days, in the most electric manner;
and the whole month of July. And still, in the Sanctuary of
Justice, sounds nothing but Harmodius-Aristogiton eloquence,
environed with the hum of crowding Paris; and no registering
accomplished, and no 'states' furnished. "States?" said
a lively Parlementeer: "Messieurs, the states that should be
furnished us, in my opinion, are the STATES-GENERAL." On
which timely joke there follow cachinnatory buzzes of approval.
What a word to be spoken in the Palais de Justice! Old
D'Ormesson (the Ex-Controller's uncle) shakes his judicious
head; far enough from laughing. But the outer courts, and
Paris and France, catch the glad sound, and repeat it; shall
repeat it, and re-echo and reverberate it, till it grow a deafening
peal. Clearly enough here is no registering to be thought of.

The pious Proverb says, 'There are remedies for all things
but death.' When a Parlement refuses registering, the remedy,
by long practice, has become familiar to the simplest: a Bed
of Justice. One complete month this Parlement has spent in
mere idle jargoning, and sound and fury; the *Timbre* Edict
not registered or like to be; the *Subvention* not yet so much
as spoken of. On the 6th of August let the whole refractory
Body roll out, in wheeled vehicles, as far as the King's Château
of Versailles; there shall the King, holding his Bed of Justice,
order them, by his own royal lips, to register. They may
remonstrate, in an under tone; but they must obey, lest a
worse unknown thing befall them.

It is done: the Parlement has rolled out, on royal summons;
has heard the express royal order to register. Whereupon it
has rolled back again, amid the hushed expectancy of men.
And now, behold, on the morrow, this Parlement, seated once
more in its own Palais, with 'crowds inundating the outer
courts,' not only does not register, but (O portent!) declares
all that was done on the prior day to be *null*, and the Bed of
Justice as good as a futility! In the history of France here
verily is a new feature. Nay, better still, our heroic Parlement, getting suddenly enlightened on several things, declares
that, for its part, it is incompetent to register Tax-edicts at all,
—having done it by mistake, during these late centuries; that

for such act one authority is only competent: the assembled
Three Estates of the Realm!

To such length can the universal spirit of a Nation penetrate
the most isolated Body-corporate: say rather, with such
weapons, homicidal and suicidal, in exasperated political
duel, will Bodies-corporate fight! But, in any case, is not
this the real death-grapple of war and internecine duel,
Greek meeting Greek; whereon men, had they even no interest in it, might look with interest unspeakable? Crowds, as
was said, inundate the outer courts: inundation of young
eleutheromaniac Noblemen in English costume, uttering audacious speeches; of Procureurs, Basoche-Clerks, who are idle
in these days; of Loungers, Newsmongers, and other nondescript classes,—rolls tumultuous there. 'From three to four
thousand persons,' waiting eagerly to hear the *Arrêtés* (Resolutions) you arrive at within; applauding with bravos, with the
clapping of from six to eight thousand hands! Sweet also is
the meed of patriotic eloquence, when your D'Espréménil,
your Fréteau, or Sabatier, issuing from his Demosthenic
Olympus, the thunder being hushed for the day, is welcomed,
in the outer courts, with a shout from four thousand throats;
is borne home shoulder-high 'with benedictions,' and strikes
the stars with his sublime head.

CHAPTER V

LOMÉNIE'S THUNDERBOLTS

ARISE, Loménie-Brienne: here is no case for 'Letters of
Jussion'; for faltering or compromise. Thou seest the whole
loose *fluent* population of Paris (whatsoever is not solid, and
fixed to work) inundating these outer courts, like a loud
destructive deluge; the very Basoche of Lawyers' Clerks talks
sedition. The lower classes, in this duel of Authority with
Authority, Greek throttling Greek, have ceased to respect the
City Watch: Police-satellites are marked on the back with
chalk (the M signifies *mouchard*, spy); they are hustled, hunted
like *feræ naturæ*. Subordinate rural Tribunals send messengers
of congratulation, of adherence. Their Fountain of Justice is
becoming a Fountain of Revolt. The Provincial Parlements
look on, with intent eye, with breathless wishes, while their
elder sister of Paris does battle: the whole Twelve are of one
blood and temper; the victory of one is that of all.

Ever worse it grows: on the 10th of August, there is '*Plainte*' emitted touching the 'prodigalities of Calonne,' and permission to 'proceed' against him. No registering, but instead of it, denouncing: of dilapidation, peculation; and ever the burden of the song, States-General! Have the royal armories no thunderbolt, that thou couldst, O Loménie, with red right-hand, launch it among these Demosthenic theatrical thunder-barrels, mere resin and noise for most part;—and shatter, and smite them silent? On the night of the 14th of August Loménie launches his thunderbolt, or handful of them. Letters named of the Seal (*de Cachet*), as many as needful, some six score and odd, are delivered overnight. And so, next day be-times, the whole Parlement, once more set on wheels, is rolling incessantly towards Troyes in Champagne; 'escorted,' says History, 'with the blessings of all people;' the very inn-keepers and postilions looking gratuitously reverent. This is the 15th of August 1787.

What will not people bless; in their extreme need! Seldom had the Parlement of Paris deserved much blessing, or re-ceived much. An isolated Body-corporate, which, out of old confusions (while the Sceptre of the Sword was confusedly struggling to become a Sceptre of the Pen), had got itself together, better and worse, as Bodies-corporate do; to satisfy some dim desire of the world, and many clear desires of individuals: and so had grown, in the course of centuries, on concession, on acquirement and usurpation, to be what we see it: a prosperous Social Anomaly, deciding Law-suits, sanction-ing or rejecting Laws; and withal disposing of its places and offices by sale for ready money,—which method sleek President Hénault, after meditation, will demonstrate to be the in-different-best.

In such a Body, existing by purchase for ready money, there could not be excess of public spirit; there might well be excess of eagerness to divide the public spoil. Men in helmets have divided that, with swords; Men in wigs, with quill and inkhorn, do divide it: and even more hatefully these latter, if more peaceably; for the wig-method is at once irresistibler and baser. By long experience, says Besenval, it has been found useless to sue a Parlement at law; no Officer of Justice will serve a writ on one: his wig and gown are his Vulcan's-panoply, his enchanted cloak of darkness.

The Parlement of Paris may account itself an unloved body,

mean, not magnanimous, on the political side. Were the King weak, always (as now) has his Parlement barked, cur-like, at his heels ; with what popular cry there might be. Were he strong, it barked before his face ; hunting for him as his alert beagle. An unjust Body ; where foul influences have more than once worked shameful perversion of judgment. Does not, in these very days, the blood of murdered Lally cry aloud for vengeance ? Baited, circumvented, driven mad like the snared lion, Valour had to sink extinguished under vindictive Chicane. Behold him, that hapless Lally, his wild dark soul looking through his wild dark face ; trailed on the ignominious death-hurdle ; the voice of his despair choked by a wooden gag ! The wild fire-soul that has known only peril and toil ; and, for threescore years, has buffeted against Fate's obstruction and men's perfidy, like genius and courage amid poltroonery, dishonesty and commonplace ; faithfully enduring and endeavouring,—O Parlement of Paris, dost thou reward it with a gibbet and a gag ? The dying Lally bequeathed his memory to his boy ; a young Lally has arisen, demanding redress in the name of God and man. The Parlement of Paris does its utmost to defend the indefensible, abominable ; nay, what is singular, dusky-glowing Aristogiton d'Espréménil is the man chosen to be its spokesman in that.

Such Social Anomaly is it that France now blesses. An unclean Social Anomaly ; but in duel against another worse ! The exiled Parlement is felt to have 'covered itself with glory.' There are quarrels in which even Satan, bringing help, were not unwelcome ; even Satan, fighting stiffly, might cover himself with glory,—of a temporary sort.

But what a stir in the outer courts of the Palais, when Paris finds its Parlement trundled off to Troyes in Champagne ; and nothing left but a few mute Keepers of Records ; the Demosthenic thunder become extinct, the martyrs of liberty clean gone ! Confused wail and menace rise from the four thousand throats of Procureurs, Basoche-Clerks, Nondescripts, and Anglomaniac Noblesse ; ever new idlers crowd to see and hear : Rascality, with increasing numbers and vigour, hunts *mouchards.* Loud whirlpool rolls through these spaces ; the rest of the City, fixed to its work, cannot yet go rolling. Audacious placards are legible ; in and about the Palais, the speeches are as good as seditious. Surely the temper of Paris is much changed. On the third day of this business (18th of

August), Monsieur and Monseigneur D'Artois, coming in state-carriages, according to use and wont, to have these late obnoxious *Arrêts* and Protests " expunged " from the Records, are received in the most marked manner. Monsieur, who is thought to be in opposition, is met with vivats and strewed flowers : Monseigneur, on the other hand, with silence ; with murmurs, which rise to hisses and groans ; nay an irreverent Rascality presses towards him in floods, with such hissing vehemence, that the Captain of the Guards has to give order, " *Haut les armes* (Handle arms) ! "—at which thunder-word, indeed, and the flash of the clear iron, the Rascal flood recoils, through all avenues, fast enough. New features these. Indeed, as good M. de Malesherbes pertinently remarks, " it is a quite new kind of contest this with the Parlement : " no transitory sputter, as from collision of hard bodies ; but more like " the first sparks of what, if not quenched, may become a great conflagration."

This good Malesherbes sees himself now again in the King's Council, after an absence of ten years : Loménie would profit if not by the faculties of the man, yet by the name he has. As for the man's opinion, it is not listened to ;—wherefore he will soon withdraw, a second time ; back to his books and his trees. In such King's Council what can a good man profit ? Turgot tries it not a second time : Turgot has quitted France and this Earth, some years ago ; and now cares for none of these things. Singular enough : Turgot, this same Loménie, and the Abbé Morellet were once a trio of young friends ; fellow-scholars in the Sorbonne. Forty new years have carried them severally thus far.

Meanwhile the Parlement sits daily at Troyes, calling cases, and daily adjourns, no Procureur making his appearance to plead. Troyes is as hospitable as could be looked for : nevertheless one has comparatively a dull life. No crowds now to carry you, shoulder-high, to the immortal gods ; scarcely a Patriot or two will drive out so far, and bid you be of firm courage. You are in furnished lodgings, far from home and domestic comfort : little to do, but wander over the unlovely Champagne fields ; seeing the grapes ripen ; taking counsel about the thousand-times consulted : a prey to tedium ; in danger even that Paris may forget you. Messengers come and go : pacific Loménie is not slack in negotiating, promising, D'Ormesson and the prudent elder Members see no good in strife.

After a dull month, the Parlement, yielding and retaining, makes truce, as all Parlements must. The Stamptax is withdrawn: the *Subvention* Landtax is also withdrawn; but, in its stead, there is granted, what they call a 'Prorogation of the Second Twentieth,'—itself a kind of Landtax, but not so oppressive to the Influential classes; which lies mainly on the Dumb class. Moreover, secret promises exist (on the part of the Elders), that finances may be raised by Loan. Of the ugly word States-General there shall be no mention.

And so, on the 20th of September, our exiled Parlement returns: D'Espréménil said, 'it went out covered with glory, but had come back covered with mud (*de boue*).' Not so, Aristogiton; or if so, thou surely art the man to clean it.

CHAPTER VI

LOMÉNIE'S PLOTS

Was ever unfortunate Chief Minister so bested as Loménie-Brienne? The reins of the State fairly in his hand these six months; and not the smallest motive-power (of Finance) to stir from the spot with, this way or that! He flourishes his whip, but advances not. Instead of ready money, there is nothing but rebellious debating and recalcitrating.

Far is the public mind from having calmed; it goes chafing and fuming ever worse: and in the royal coffers, with such yearly Deficit running on, there is hardly the colour of coin. Ominous prognostics! Malesherbes, seeing an exhausted, exasperated France grow hotter and hotter, talks of "conflagration:" Mirabeau, without talk, has, as we perceive, descended on Paris again, close on the rear of the Parlement,—not to quit his native soil any more.

Over the Frontiers, behold Holland invaded by Prussia; the French party oppressed, England and the Stadtholder triumphing: to the sorrow of War-secretary Montmorin and all men. But without money, sinews of war, as of work, and of existence itself, what can a Chief Minister do? Taxes profit little: this of the Second Twentieth falls not due till next year; and will then, with its "strict valuation," produce more controversy than cash. Taxes on the Privileged Classes cannot be got registered: are intolerable to our supporters themselves: taxes on the Unprivileged yield nothing,—as from a thing drained dry more cannot be drawn. Hope is nowhere, if not in the old refuge of Loans.

To Loménie, aided by the long head of Lamoignon, deeply pondering this sea of troubles, the thought suggested itself: Why not have a Successive Loan (*Emprunt Successif*), or Loan that went on lending, year after year, as much as needful; say, till 1792? The trouble of registering such Loan were the same: we had then breathing time; money to work with, at least to subsist on. Edict of a Successive Loan must be proposed. To conciliate the Philosophes, let a liberal Edict walk in front of it, for emancipation of Protestants; let a liberal Promise guard the rear of it, then when our Loan ends, in that final 1792, the States-General shall be convoked.

Such liberal Edict of Protestant Emancipation, the time having come for it shall cost a Loménie as little as the 'Death-penalties to be put in execution' did. As for the liberal Promise, of States-General, it can be fulfilled or not: the fulfilment is five good years off; in five years much intervenes. But the registering? Ah, truly, there is the difficulty?—However, we have that promise of the Elders, given secretly at Troyes. Judicious gratuities, cajoleries, underground intrigues; with old Foulon, named "*Ame damnée* Familiar-demon, of the Parlement," may perhaps do the rest. At worst and lowest, the Royal Authority has resources,—which ought it not to put forth? If it cannot realise money, the Royal Authority is as good as dead; dead of that surest and miserablest death, inanition. Risk and win; without risk all is already lost? For the rest, as in enterprises of pith, a touch of stratagem often proves furthersome, his Majesty announces *a Royal Hunt*, for the 19th of November next; and all whom it concerns are joyfully getting their gear ready.

Royal hunt indeed; but of two-legged unfeathered game! At eleven in the morning of that Royal-Hunt day, 19th of November 1787, unexpected blare of trumpeting, tumult of charioteering and cavalcading disturbs the Seat of Justice: his Majesty is come with Garde-des-Sceaux Lamoignon, and Peers and retinue, to hold Royal Session and have Edicts registered. What a change, since Louis XIV. entered here, in boots; and, whip in hand, ordered his registering to be done,—with an Olympian look, which none durst gainsay; and did, without stratagem, in such unceremonious fashion, hunt as well as register! For Louis XVI., on this day, the

Registering will be enough; if indeed he and the day suffice for it.

Meanwhile, with fit ceremonial words, the purpose of the royal breast is signified:—Two Edicts, for Protestant Emancipation, for Successive Loan: of both which Edicts our trusty Garde-des-Sceaux Lamoignon will explain the purport; on both which a trusty Parlement is requested to deliver its opinion, each member having free privilege of speech. And so, Lamoignon too having perorated not amiss, and wound up with that Promise of States-General,—the Sphere-music of Parlementary eloquence begins. Explosive, responsive. sphere answering sphere, it waxes louder and louder. The Peers sit attentive; of diverse sentiment: unfriendly to States-General; unfriendly to Despotism, which cannot reward merit, and is suppressing places. But what agitates his Highness d'Orléans? The rubicund moonhead goes wagging; darker beams the copper visage, like unscoured copper; in the glazed eye is disquietude; he rolls uneasy in his seat, as if he meant something. Amid unutterable satiety, has sudden new appetite, for new forbidden fruit, been vouchsafed him? Disgust and edacity; laziness that cannot rest; futile ambition, revenge, non-admiralship:—O, within that carbuncled skin what a confusion of confusions sits bottled!

'Eight Couriers,' in the course of the day, gallop from Versailles, where Loménie waits palpitating; and gallop back again, not with the best news. In the outer Courts of the Palais, huge buzz of expectation reigns; it is whispered the Chief Minister has lost six votes overnight. And from within, resounds nothing but forensic eloquence, pathetic and even indignant; heartrending appeals to the royal clemency, that his Majesty would please to summon States-General forthwith, and be the Saviour of France:—wherein dusky-glowing D'Esprémenil, but still more Sabatier de Cabre, and Fréteau, since named *Commère* Fréteau (Goody Fréteau), are among the loudest. For six mortal hours it lasts, in this manner; the infinite hubbub unslackened.

And so now, when brown dusk is falling through the windows, and no end visible, his Majesty, on hint of Garde-des-Sceaux Lamoignon, opens his royal lips once more to say, in brief, That he must have his Loan-Edict registered.—Momentary deep pause!—See! Monseigneur d'Orléans rises; with moon-visage turned towards the royal platform, he asks, with a delicate graciosity of manner covering unutterable things: " Whether it is a Bed of Justice, then, or a Royal Session?" Fire flashes on him from the throne and neighbourhood : surly answer that "it is a Session." In that case, Monseigneur will crave leave to remark that Edicts cannot be registered by *order* in a Session ; and indeed to enter, against such registry, his individual humble Protest. "*Vous êtes bien le maître* (You will do your pleasure)," answers the King; and thereupon, in high state, marches out, escorted by his Court-retinue : D'Orléans himself, as in duty bound, escorting him, but only to the gate. Which duty done, D'Orléans returns in from the gate; redacts his Protest, in the face of an applauding Parlement, an applauding France; and so—has *cut* his Court-moorings, shall we say? And will now sail and drift, fast enough, towards Chaos?

Thou foolish D'Orléans; Equality that art to be! Is Royalty grown a mere wooden Scarecrow; whereon thou, pert scald headed crow, mayest alight at pleasure, and peck? Not yet wholly.

Next day, a Lettre-de-Cachet sends D'Orléans to bethink himself in his Château of Villers-Cotterets, where, alas, is no Paris with its joyous necessaries of life ; no fascinating, indispensable Madame de Buffon,—light wife of a great Naturalist much too old for her. Monseigneur, it is said, does nothing but walk distractedly, at Villers-Cotterets; cursing his stars. Versailles itself shall hear penitent wail from him, so hard is his doom. By a second simultaneous Lettre-de-Cachet, Goody Fréteau is hurled into the Stronghold of Ham, amid the Norman marshes ; by a third, Sabatier de Cabre into Mont St. Michel, amid the Norman quicksands. As for the Parlement, it must, on summons, travel out to Versailles, with its Register-book under its arm, to have the Protest *biffé* (expunged); not without admonition, and even rebuke. A stroke of authority, which, one might have hoped, would quiet matters.

Unhappily, no: it is a mere taste of the whip to rearing coursers, which makes them rear worse! When a team of Twenty-five Millions begins rearing, what is Loménie's whip? The Parlement will nowise acquiesce meekly ; and set to register the Protestant Edict, and do its other work, in salutary fear of these three Lettres-de-Cachet. Far from that, it begins questioning Lettres-de-Cachet generally, their legality, endurability ; emits dolorous objurgation, petition on petition to have its three Martyrs delivered ; cannot, till that be complied with, so much as think of examining the Protestant Edict, but puts it off always 'till this day week.'

In which objurgatory strain Paris and France joins it, or rather has preceded it; making fearful chorus. And now also the other Parlements, at length opening their mouths, begin to join; some of them, as at Grenoble and at Rennes, with portentous emphasis,—threatening, by way of reprisal, to interdict the very Taxgatherer. "In all former contests," as Malesherbes remarks, "it was the Parlement that excited the Public; but here it is the Public that excites the Parlement."

CHAPTER VII

INTERNECINE

WHAT a France, through these winter months of the year 1787! The very Œil-de-Bœuf is doleful, uncertain; with a general feeling, among the Suppressed, that it were better to be in Turkey. The Wolf-hounds are suppressed, the Bear-hounds; Duke de Coigny, Duke de Polignac: in the Trianon little-heaven, her Majesty, one evening, takes Besenval's arm; asks his candid opinion. The intrepid Besenval, having, as he hopes, nothing of the sycophant in *him*,—plainly signifies that, with a Parlement in rebellion, and an Œil-de-Bœuf in suppression, the King's Crown is in danger;—whereupon, singular to say, her Majesty, as if hurt, changed the subject, *et ne me parla plus de rien!*

To whom, indeed, can this poor Queen speak! In need of wise counsel, if ever mortal was; yet beset here only by the hubbub of chaos! Her dwelling-place is so bright to the eye, and confusion and black care darkens it all. Sorrows of the Sovereign, sorrows of the woman, thick-coming sorrows environ her more and more. Lamotte, the Necklace-Countess, has in these late months escaped, perhaps been suffered to escape from the Salpêtrière. Vain was the hope that Paris might thereby forget her; and this ever-widening lie, and heap of lies, subside. The Lamotte, with a V (for *Voleuse*, Thief) branded on both shoulders, has got to England; and will therefrom emit lie on lie; defiling the highest queenly name mere distracted lies; which, in its present humour, France will greedily believe.

For the rest, it is too clear our Successive Loan is not filling. As indeed, in such circumstances, a Loan registered by ex punging of Protests was not the likeliest to fill. Denunciation of *Lettres-de-Cachet*, of Despotism generally, abates not : the Twelve Parlements are busy; the Twelve hundred Placarders, Balladsingers, Pamphleteers. Paris is what, in figurative speech, they call "flooded with pamphlets (*regorgé de brochures*)"; flooded and eddying again. Hot deluge,—from so many Patriot ready-writers, all at the *fervid* or boiling point; each ready-writer, now in the hour of eruption, going like an Iceland Geyser! Against which what can a judicious Friend Morellet do; a Rivarol, an unruly Linguet (well paid for it),—spouting *cold !*

Now also, at length, does come discussion of the Protestant Edict : but only for new embroilment; in pamphlet and counter-pamphlet, increasing the madness of men. Not even Orthodoxy, bedrid as she seemed, but will have a hand in this confusion. She once again in the shape of Abbé Lenfant, 'whom Prelates drive to visit and congratulate,'—raises audible sound from her pulpit-drum. Or mark how D'Espréménil, who has his own confused way in all things, produces at the right moment in Parlementary harangue, a pocket Crucifix, with the apostrophe : 'Will ye crucify him afresh?' *Him*, O D'Espréménil, without scruple;—considering what poor stuff, of ivory and filigree, *he* is made of !

To all which add only, that poor Brienne has fallen sick; so hard was the tear and wear of his sinful youth, so violent, incessant is this agitation of his foolish old age. Baited, bayed at through so many throats, his Grace, growing consumptive, inflammatory (with *humeur de dartre*), lies reduced to milk diet; in exasperation, almost in desperation; with 'repose,' precisely the impossible recipe, prescribed as the indispensable.

On the whole, what can a poor Government do, but once more recoil ineffectual ? The King's Treasury is running towards the less; and Paris 'eddies with a flood of pamphlets.' At all rates, let the *latter* subside a little ! D'Orléans gets back to Raincy, which is nearer Paris and the fair frail Buffon; finally to Paris itself: neither are Fréteau and Sabatier banished forever. The Protestant Edict is registered; to the joy of Boissy d'Anglas and good Malesherbes : Successive Loan, all protests expunged or else withdrawn, remains open, —the rather as few or none come to fill it. States-General, for which the Parlement has clamoured, and now the whole Nation clamours, will follow 'in five years,'—if indeed not

sooner. O Parlement of Paris, what a clamour was that!
" Messieurs," said old D'Ormesson, "you will get States-
General, and you will repent it."   Like the Horse in the
Fable, who, to be avenged of his enemy, applied to the Man.
The Man mounted ; did swift execution on the enemy ; but,
unhappily, would not dismount !   Instead of five years, let
three years pass, and this clamorous Parlement shall have
both seen its enemy hurled prostrate, and been itself ridden
to foundering (say rather jugulated for hide and shoes), and
lie dead in the ditch.

Under such omens, however, we have reached the spring of
1788.   By no path can the King's Government find passage
for itself, out is everywhere shamefully flung back.   Beleaguered by Twelve rebellious Parlements, which are grown
to be the organs of an angry Nation, it can advance no-
whither ; can accomplish nothing, obtain nothing, not so
much as money to subsist on ; but must sit there, seemingly,
to be eaten up of Deficit.

The measure of the Iniquity, then, of the Falsehood which
has been gathering through long centuries, is nearly full?   At
least, that of the Misery is !   From the hovels of the Twenty-
five Millions, the misery, permeating upwards and forwards, as
its laws is, has got so far,—to the very Œil-de-Bœuf of
Versailles.   Man's hand, in this blind pain, is set against
man : not only the low against the higher, but the higher
against each other ; Provincial Noblesse is bitter against
Court Noblesse ; Robe against Sword ; Rochet against Pen.
But against the King's Government who is *not* bitter?   Not
even Besenval, in these days.   To it all men and bodies
of men are become as enemies ; it is the centre whereon
infinite contentions unite and clash.   What new universal
vertiginous movement is this ; of Institutions, social Arrangements, individual Minds, which once worked co-operative ;
now rolling and grinding in distracted collision ?   Inevitable :
it is the breaking up of a World-Solecism, worn out at last,
down even to bankruptcy of money !   And so this poor
Versailles Court, as the chief or central Solecism, finds all the
other Solecisms arrayed against it.   Most natural !   For your
human Solecism, be it Person or Combination of Persons,
is ever, by law of Nature, uneasy ; if verging towards bankruptcy, it is even miserable :—and when would the meanest
Solecism consent to blame or amend *itself*, while there remained another to amend ?

These threatening signs do not terrify Loménie, much less teach him. Loménie, though of light nature, is not without courage, of a sort. Nay, have we not read of lightest creatures, trained Canary-birds, that could fly cheerfully with lighted matches, and fire cannon; fire whole powder-magazines? To sit and die of Deficit is no part of Loménie's plan. The evil is considerable; but can he not remove it, can he not attack it? At lowest, he can attack the *symptom* of it: these rebellious Parlements he can attack, and perhaps remove. Much is dim to Loménie, but two things are clear: that such Parlementary duel with Royalty is growing perilous, nay internecine; above all, that money must be had. Take thought, brave Loménie; thou Garde-des-Sceaux Lamoignon, who hast ideas! So often defeated, balked cruelly when the golden fruit seemed within clutch, rally for one other struggle. To tame the Parlement, to fill the King's coffers; these are now life-and-death questions.

Parlements have been tamed, more than once. Set to perch ' on the peaks of rocks inaccessible except by litters,' a Parlement grows reasonable. O Maupeou, thou bold bad man, had we left thy work where it was!—But apart from exile, or other violent methods, is there not one method whereby all things are tamed, even lions? The method of hunger? What if the Parlement's supplies were cut off; namely its Law-suits!

Minor Courts, for the trying of innumerable minor causes, might be instituted: these we could call *Grand Bailliages*. Whereon the Parlement, shortened of its prey, would look with yellow despair; but the Public, fond of cheap justice, with favour and hope. Then for Finance, for registering of Edicts, why not, from our own Œil-de-Bœuf Dignitaries, our Princes, Dukes, Marshals, make a thing we could call *Plenary Court*; and there, so to speak, do our registering ourselves? Saint Louis had his Plenary Court, of Great Barons; most useful to him: our Great Barons are still here (at least the Name of them is still here); our necessity is greater than his.

Such is the Loménie-Lamoignon device; welcome to the King's Council, as a light-beam in great darkness. The device seems feasible, it is eminently needful: be it once well executed, great deliverance is wrought. Silent, then, and steady; now or never!—the World shall see one other Historical Scene; and so singular a man as Loménie de Brienne still the Stage-manager there.

Behold, accordingly, a Home-Secretary Breteuil 'beautifying

Paris,' in the peaceablest manner. in this hopeful spring weather of 1788; the old hovels and hutches disappearing from our Bridges: as if for the State too there were halcyon weather, and nothing to do but beautify.   Parlement seems to sit acknowledged victor.   Brienne says nothing of Finance; or even says, and prints, that it is all well.   How is this; such halcyon quiet; though the Successive Loan did not fill?   In a victorious Parlement, Counsellor Goeslard de Monsabert even denounces that 'levying of the Second Twentieth on strict valuation,' and gets decree that the valuation shall not be strict,—not on the Privileged classes.   Nevertheless Brienne endures it, launches no Lettre-de-Cachet against it.   How is this?

Smiling is such vernal weather; but treacherous, sudden! For one thing, we hear it whispered, 'the Intendants of Provinces have all got order to be at their posts on a certain day.'   Still more singular, what incessant Printing is this that goes on at the King's Château, under lock and key?   Sentries occupy all gates and windows; the Printers come not out; they sleep in their work-rooms; their very food is handed in to them!   A victorious Parlement smells new danger.   D'Espréménil has ordered horses to Versailles; prowls round that guarded Printing-Office; prying, snuffing, if so be the sagacity and ingenuity of man may penetrate it.

To a shower of gold most things are penetrable.   D'Espréménil descends on the lap of a Printer's Danaë, in the shape of 'five hundred louis d'or': the Danaë's Husband smuggles a ball of clay to her; which she delivers to the golden Counsellor of Parlement.   Kneaded within it, there stick printed proof-sheets:—by Heaven! the royal Edict of that same self-registering *Plenary Court*; of those *Grand Bailliages* that shall cut short our Law-suits!   It is to be promulgated over all France in one and the same day.

This, then, is what the Intendants were bid wait for at their posts: this is what the Court sat hatching, as its accursed cockatrice-egg; and would not stir, though provoked, till the brood were out!   Hie with it, D'Espréménil, home to Paris; convoke instantaneous Sessions; let the Parlement, and the Earth, and the Heavens know it.

CHAPTER VIII

LOMÉNIE'S DEATH-THROES

On the morrow, which is the 3d of May 1788, an astonished Parlement sits convoked; listens speechless to the speech of D'Espréménil, unfolding the infinite misdeed. Deed of treachery; of unhallowed darkness, such as Despotism loves! Denounce it, O Parlement of Paris; awaken France and the Universe; roll what thunder-barrels of forensic eloquence thou hast: with thee too it is verily Now or never!

The Parlement is not wanting at such juncture. In the hour of his extreme jeopardy, the lion first incites himself by roaring, by lashing his sides. So here the Parlement of Paris. On the motion of D'Espréménil, a most patriotic Oath, of the One-and-all sort, is sworn, with united throat; an excellent new idea, which, in these coming years, shall not remain unimitated. Next comes indomitable Declaration, almost of the rights of man, at least of the rights of Parlement; Invocation to the friends of French Freedom, in this and in subsequent time. All which, or the essence of all which, is brought to paper; in a tone wherein some thing of plaintiveness blends with, and tempers, heroic valour. And thus, having sounded the storm-bell,—which Paris hears, which all France will hear; and hurled such defiance in the teeth of Loménie and Despotism, the Parlement retires as from a tolerable first day's work.

But how Loménie felt to see his cockatrice-egg (so essential to the salvation of France) broken in this premature manner, let readers fancy! Indignant he clutches at his thunderbolts (*de Cachet*, of the Seal); and launches two of them: a bolt for D'Espréménil; a bolt for that busy Goeslard, whose service in the Second Twentieth and 'strict valuation' is not forgotten. Such bolts clutched promptly overnight, and launched with the early new morning, shall strike agitated Paris if not into re-quiescence, yet into wholesome astonishment.

Ministerial thunderbolts may be launched; but if they do not *hit*? D'Espréménil and Goeslard, warned, both of them, as is thought, by the singing of some friendly bird, elude the Loménie Tipstaves; escape disguised through skywindows, over roofs, to their own Palais de Justice: the thunderbolts have *missed*. Paris (for the buzz flies abroad) is struck into astonishment *not* wholesome. The two Martyrs of Liberty doff their

disguises; don their long gowns: behold! in the space of an
hour, by aid of ushers and swift runners, the Parlement, with
its Counsellors, Presidents, even Peers, sits anew assembled.
The assembled Parlement declares that these its two Martyrs
cannot be given up, to any sublunary authority; moreover that
the 'session is permanent,' admitting of no adjournment, till
pursuit of them has been relinquished.

And so, with forensic eloquence, denunciation and protest,
with couriers going and returning, the Parlement, in this state
of continual explosion that shall cease neither night nor day,
waits the issue.   Awakened Paris once more inundates those
outer courts; boils, in floods wilder than ever, through all
avenues.   Dissonant hubbub there is; jargon as of Babel, in
the hour when they were first smitten (as here) with mutual
unintelligibility, and the people had not yet dispersed!

Paris City goes through its diurnal epochs, of working and
slumbering; and now, for the second time, most European
and African mortals are asleep.   But here, in this Whirlpool of
Words, sleep falls not; the Night spreads her coverlid of
Darkness over it in vain.   Within is the sound of mere
martyr invincibility; tempered with the due tone of plaintiveness.   Without is the infinite expectant hum,—growing
drowsier a little.   So has it lasted for six-and-thirty hours.

But hark! through the dead of midnight what tramp is this?
Tramp as of armed men, foot and horse; Gardes Françaises,
Gardes Suisses: marching hither; in silent regularity; in the
flare of torchlight!   There are Sappers too, with axes and crowbars: apparently, if the doors open not, they will be forced!—
It is Captain D'Agoust, missioned from Versailles.   D'Agoust, a
man of known firmness;—who once forced Prince Condé
himself, by mere incessant looking at him, to give satisfaction
and fight: he now, with axes and torches, is advancing on the
very sanctuary of Justice.   Sacrilegious; yet what help?   The
man is a soldier; looks merely at his orders; impassive, moves
forward like an inanimate engine.

The doors open on summons, there need no axes; door
after door.   And now the innermost door opens; discloses the
long-gowned Senators of France: a hundred and sixty-seven by
tale, seventeen of them Peers; sitting there, majestic, 'in permanent session.'   Were not the man military, and of cast-iron,
this sight, this silence re-echoing the clank of his own boots,
might stagger him!   For the hundred and sixty-seven receive
him in perfect silence; which some liken to that of the

Roman Senate overfallen by Brennus; some to that of a nest of coiners surprised by officers of the Police. *Messieurs*, said D'Agoust, *De par le Roi!* Express order has charged D'Agoust with the sad duty of arresting two individuals: M. Duval d'Esprémenil and M. Goeslard de Monsabert. Which respectable individuals, as he has not the honour of knowing them, are hereby invited, in the King's name, to surrender themselves.—Profound silence! Buzz, which grows a murmur: "We are all D'Esprémenils!" ventures a voice; which other voices repeat. The President inquires, Whether he will employ violence? Captain D'Agoust, honoured with his Majesty's commission, has to execute his Majesty's order; would so gladly do it without violence, will in any case do it; grants an august Senate space to deliberate which method *they* prefer. And thereupon D'Agoust, with grave military courtesy, has withdrawn for the moment.

What boots it, august Senators? All avenues are closed with fixed bayonets. Your Courier gallops to Versailles, through the dewy Night; but also gallops back again, with tidings that the order is authentic, that it is irrevocable. The outer courts simmer with idle population; but D'Agoust's grenadier-ranks stand there as immovable floodgates: there will be no revolting to deliver you. "Messieurs!" thus spoke D'Esprémenil, "when the victorious Gauls entered Rome, which they had carried by assault, the Roman Senators, clothed in their purple, sat there, in their curule chairs, with a proud and tranquil countenance, awaiting slavery or death. Such too is the lofty spectacle, which you, in this hour, offer to the universe (*à l'univers*), after having generously"—with much more of the like, as can still be read.

In vain, O D'Esprémenil! Here is this cast-iron Captain D'Agoust, with his cast-iron military air, come back. Despotism, constraint, destruction sit waving in his plumes. D'Esprémenil must fall silent; heroically give himself up, lest worse befall. Him Goeslard heroically imitates. With spoken and speechless emotion, they fling themselves into the arms of their Parliamentary brethren, for a last embrace: and so amid plaudits and plaints, from a hundred and sixty-five throats; amid wavings, sobbings, a whole forest-sigh of Parlementary pathos,—they are led through winding passages, to the reargate; where, in the gray of the morning, two Coaches with *Exempts* stand waiting. There must the victims mount; bayonets menacing behind. D'Esprémenil's stern question to

the populace, 'Whether they have courage?' is answered by
silence. They mount, and roll; and neither the rising of the
May sun (it is the 6th morning), nor its setting shall lighten
their heart: but they fare forward continually; D'Espréménil
towards the utmost Isles of St. Marguerite, or Hières (supposed
by some, if that is any comfort, to be Calypso's Island); Goeslard towards the land-fortress of Pierre-en-Cize, extant then,
near the City of Lyons.

Captain D'Agoust may now therefore look forward to Major-
ship, to Commandantship of the Tuileries;—and withal vanish
from History; where nevertheless he has been fated to do a
notable thing. For not only are D'Espréménil and Goeslard
safe whirling southward, but the Parlement itself has straightway to march out: to that also his inexorable order reaches.
Gathering up their long skirts, they file out, the whole Hundred and Sixty-five of them, through two rows of unsympathetic grenadiers: a spectacle to gods and men. The people
revolt not; they only wonder and grumble: also, we remark,
these unsympathetic grenadiers are *Gardes Françaises*,—who,
one day, will sympathise! In a word, the Palais de Justice is
swept clear, the doors of it are locked; and D'Agoust returns
to Versailles with the key in his pocket,—having, as was said,
merited preferment.

As for this Parlement of Paris, now turned out to the street,
we will without reluctance leave it there. The Beds of Justice
it had to undergo, in the coming fortnight, at Versailles, in
registering, or rather refusing to register, those new-hatched
Edicts; and how it assembled in taverns and taprooms there,
for the purpose of Protesting; or hovered disconsolate, with
outspread skirts, not knowing where to assemble; and was
reduced to lodge Protest ' with a Notary;' and in the end, to
sit still (in a state of forced 'vacation'), and do nothing: all
this, natural now, as the burying of the dead after battle,
shall not concern us. The Parlement of Paris has as good as
performed its part; doing and misdoing, so far, but hardly
further, it could stir the world.

Loménie has removed the evil then? Not at all; not so
much as the symptom of the evil; scarcely the *twelfth* part of
the symptom, and exasperated the other eleven! The intendants of Provinces, the military Commandants are at their
posts, on the appointed 8th of May; but in no Parlement, if
not in the single one of Douai, can these new Edicts get

registered. Not peaceable signing with ink; but browbeating, bloodshedding, appeal to primary club-law! Against these Bailliages, against this Plenary Court, exasperated Themis everywhere shows face of battle: the Provincial Noblesse are of her party, and whoever hates Loménie and the evil time; with her Attorneys and Tipstaves, she enlists and operates down even to the populace. At Rennes, in Brittany, where the historical Bertrand de Moleville is Intendant, it has passed from fatal continual duelling, between the military and gentry, to street-fighting; to stone-volleys and musket-shot: and still the Edicts remain unregistered. The afflicted Bretons send remonstrance to Loménie, by a Deputation of Twelve; whom, however, Loménie, having heard them, shuts up in the Bastille. A second larger Deputation he meets, by his scouts, on the road, and persuades or frightens back. But now a third largest Deputation is indignantly sent by *many* roads: refused audience on arriving, it meets to take counsel; invites Lafayette and all Patriot Bretons in Paris to assist; agitates itself; becomes the *Breton Club*, first germ of—the *Jacobins' Society*.

So many as eight Parlements get exiled: others might need that remedy, but it is one not always easy of appliance. At Grenoble, for instance, where a Mounier, a Barnave have not been idle, the Parlement had due order (by *Lettres-de-Cachet*) to depart, and exile itself: but on the morrow, instead of coaches getting yoked, the alarm-bell bursts forth, ominous; and peals and booms all day; crowds of mountaineers rush down, with axes, even with firelocks,—whom (most ominous of all!) the soldiery shows no eagerness to deal with. 'Axe over head,' the poor General has to sign capitulation; to engage that the *Lettres-de-Cachet* shall remain unexecuted, and a beloved Parlement stay where it is. Besançon, Dijon, Rouen, Bourdeaux, are not what they should be! At Pau in Béarn, where the old Commandant had failed, the new one (a Grammont, native to them) is met by a Procession of townsmen with the Cradle of Henri Quatre, the Palladium of their Town; is conjured as he venerates this old Tortoise-shell, in which the great Henri was rocked, not to trample on Bearnese liberty; is informed, withal, that his Majesty's cannon are all safe—in the keeping of his Majesty's faithful Burghers of Pau, and do now lie pointed on the walls thereof; ready for action!

At this rate, your Grand Bailliages are like to have a stormy infancy. As for the Plenary Court, it has literally expired in the birth. The very Courtiers looked shy at it; old Marshal Broglie declined the honour of sitting therein. Assaulted by a universal storm of mingled ridicule and execration, this poor Plenary Court met once, and never any second time. Distracted country! Contention hisses up, with forked hydra-tongues, wheresoever poor Loménie sets his foot. 'Let a Commandant, a Commissioner of the King,' says Weber, 'enter one of these Parlements to have an Edict registered, the whole Tribunal will disappear, and leave the Commandant alone with the Clerk and First President. The Edict registered and the Commandant gone, the whole Tribunal hastens back, to declare such registration null. The highways are covered with *Grand Deputations* of Parlements, proceeding to Versailles, to have their registers expunged by the King's hand; on returning home, to cover a new page with a new resolution still more audacious.'

Such is the France of this year 1788. Not now a Golden or Paper Age of Hope; with its horse-racings, balloon-flyings, and finer sensibilities of the heart: ah, gone is that; its golden effulgence paled, bedarkened in *this* singular manner,—brewing towards preternatural weather! For, as in that wreck-storm of *Paul et Virginie* and Saint-Pierre,—'One huge motionless cloud' (say, of Sorrow and Indignation) 'girdles our whole horizon; streams up, hairy, copper-edged, over a sky of the colour of lead' Motionless itself; but 'small clouds' (as exiled Parlements and such like), 'parting from it, fly over the zenith, with the velocity of birds:'—till at last, with one loud howl, the whole Four Winds be dashed together, and all the world exclaim There is the tornado! *Tout le monde s'écria, Voilà l'ouragan!*

For the rest, in such circumstances, the Successive Loan, very naturally, remains unfilled; neither, indeed, can that impost of the Second Twentieth, at least not on 'strict valuation,' be levied to good purpose: 'Lenders,' says Weber, in his hysterical vehement manner, 'are afraid of ruin; tax-gatherers of hanging.' The very Clergy turn away their face: convoked in Extraordinary Assembly, they afford no gratuitous gift (*don gratuit*),—if it be not that of advice; here too instead of cash is clamour for States-General.

O Loménie-Brienne, with thy poor flimsy mind all bewildered, and now 'three actual cauteries' on thy worn-out body; who art like to die of inflammation, provocation, milk-diet,

dartres vives and *maladie*—(best untranslated); and presidest
over a France with innumerable *actual cauteries*, which also is
dying of inflammation and the rest! Was it wise to quit the
bosky verdures of Brienne, and thy new ashlar Château there,
and what it held, for *this?* Soft were those shades and lawns;
sweet the hymns of Poetasters, the blandishments of high-
rouged Graces: and always this and the other Philosophe
Morellet (nothing deeming himself or thee a questionable
Sham-Priest) could be so happy in making happy :—and also
(hadst thou known it), in the Military School hard by, there
sat, studying mathematics, a dusky-complexioned taciturn Boy,
under the name of: NAPOLEON BONAPARTE!—With fifty years
of effort, and one final dead-lift struggle, thou hast made an
exchange! Thou hast got thy robe of office,—as Hercules
had his Nessus'-shirt.

On the 13th of July, of this 1788, there fell, on the very
edge of harvest, the most frightful hail-storm; scattering into
wild waste the Fruits of the Year; which had otherwise
suffered grievously by drought. For sixty leagues round
Paris especially, the ruin was almost total. To so many
other evils, then, there is to be added, that of dearth, perhaps
of famine.

Some days before this hailstorm, on the 5th of July; and
still more decisively some days after it, on the 8th of August,
—Loménie announces that the States-General are actually to
meet in the following month of May. Till after which period,
this of the Plenary Court, and the rest, shall remain *postponed*.
Futher, as in Loménie there is no plan of forming or holding
these most desirable States-General, 'thinkers are invited' to
furnish him with one,—through the medium of discussion by
the public press!

What could a poor Minister do? There are still ten months
of respite reserved : a sinking pilot will fling out all things, his
very biscuit-bags, lead, log, compass and quadrant, before flinging out *himself*. It is on this principle, of sinking, and the
incipient delirium of despair, that we explain likewise the
almost miraculous 'invitation to thinkers.' Invitation to Chaos
to be so kind as build, out of its tumultuous drift-wood, an
Ark of Escape for him! In these cases, not invitation but
command has usually proved serviceable.—The Queen stood,
that evening, pensive, in a window, with her face turned
towards the Garden. The *Chef de Goblet* had followed her
with an obsequious cup of coffee; and then retired till it were

sipped. Her Majesty beckoned Dame Campan to approach. "*Grand Dieu!*" murmured she, with the cup in her hand, "what a piece of news will be made public to-day! The King grants States-General." Then raising her eyes to Heaven (if Campan were not mistaken), she added: "'Tis a first beat of the drum, of ill omen for France. This Noblesse will ruin us."

During all that hatching of the Plenary Court, while Lamoignon looked so mysterious, Besenval had kept asking him one question: Whether they had cash? To which as Lamoignon always answered (on the faith of Loménie) that the cash was safe, judicious Besenval rejoined that then all was safe. Nevertheless the melancholy fact is, that the royal coffers are almost getting literally void of coin. Indeed, apart from all other things, this 'invitation to thinkers,' and the great change now at hand are enough to 'arrest the circulation of capital,' and forward only that of pamphlets. A few thousand gold louis are now all of money or money's worth that remains in the King's Treasury. With another movement as of desperation, Loménie invites Necker to come and be Controller of Finances! Necker has other work in view than controlling Finances for Loménie: with a dry refusal he stands taciturn; awaiting his time.

What shall a desperate Prime Minister do? He has grasped at the strongbox of the King's Theatre: some Lottery had been set on foot for the sufferers by the hailstorm; in his extreme necessity, Loménie lays hands even on this. To make provision for the passing day, on any terms, will soon be impossible.—On the 16th of August, poor Weber heard, at Paris and Versailles, hawkers 'with a hoarse stifled tone of voice (*voix étouffée, sourde*),' trawling and snuffling, through the streets, an *Edict concerning Payments* (such was the soft title Rivarol had contrived for it): all Payments at the Royal Treasury shall be henceforth, three-fifths in Cash, and the remaining two-fifths—in Paper bearing interest! Poor Weber almost swooned at the sound of these cracked voices, with their bodeful raven-note; and will never forget the effect it had on him.

But the effect on Paris, on the world generally? From the dens of Stock-brokerage, from the heights of Political Economy, of Neckerism and Philosophism; from all articulate and inarticulate throats, rise hootings and howlings, such as ear had not yet heard. Sedition itself may be imminent! Monseigneur d'Artois, moved by Duchess Polignac, feels called to wait upon her Majesty; and explain frankly what crisis matters stand in. 'The Queen wept;' Brienne himself wept;—for it is now visible and palpable that he must go.

Remains only that the Court, to whom his manners and garrulities were always agreeable, shall make his fall soft. The grasping old man has already got his Archbishopship of Toulouse exchanged for the richer one of Sens: and now, in this hour of pity, he shall have the Coadjutorship for his nephew (hardly yet of due age); a Dameship of the Palace for his niece; a Regiment for her husband; for himself a red Cardinal's-hat, a *Coup de Bois* (cutting from the royal forests), and on the whole 'from five to six hundred thousand livres of revenue:' finally his Brother, the Comte de Brienne, shall still continue War-minister. Buckled round with such bolsters and huge feather-beds of Promotion, let him now fall as soft as he can!

And so Loménie departs: rich if Court-titles and Money-bonds can enrich him; but if these cannot, perhaps the poorest of all extant men. 'Hissed at by the people of Versailles,' he drives forth to Jardi; southward to Brienne,—for recovery of health. Then to Nice, to Italy; but shall return; shall glide to and fro, tremulous, faint-twinkling, fallen on awful times: till the Guillotine—snuff out his weak existence? Alas, worse: for it is *blown* out, or choked out, foully, pitiably, on the way to the Guillotine! In his Palace of Sens, rude Jacobin Bailiffs made him drink with them from his own wine-cellars, feast with them from his own larder; and on the morrow morning, the miserable old man lies dead. This is the end of Prime Minister, Cardinal Archbishop Loménie de Brienne. Flimsier mortal was seldom fated to do as weighty a mischief; to have a life as despicable-envied, an exit as frightful. *Fired*, as the phrase is, with ambition: blown, like a kindled rag, the sport of winds, not this way, not that way, but of all ways, straight towards *such* a powder-mine,—which he kindled! Let us pity the hapless Loménie; and forgive him; and, as soon as possible, forget him.

CHAPTER IX

BURIAL WITH BONFIRE

BESENVAL, during these extraordinary operations, of Payment two-fifths in Paper, and change of Prime Minister, had been out on a tour through his District of Command; and indeed,

for the last months, peacefully drinking the waters of Contrexé-
ville.   Returning now, in the end of August towards Moulins,
and 'knowing nothing,' he arrives one evening at Langres;
finds the whole Town in a state of uproar (*grande rumeur*).
Doubtless some sedition; a thing too common in these days!
He alights nevertheless; inquires of a 'man tolerably dressed,'
what the matter is?—"How?" answers the man, "you have
not heard the news?   The Archbishop is thrown out, and M.
Necker is recalled; and all is going to go well!"

Such *rumeur* and vociferous acclaim has risen round M.
Necker, ever from 'that day when he issued from the Queen's
Apartments,' a nominated Minister.   It was on the 24th of
August: 'the galleries of the Château, the courts, the streets
of Versailles; in few hours, the Capital; and, as the news
flew, all France resounded with the cry of *Vive le Roi, Vive
M. Necker!*'   In Paris indeed it unfortunately got the length
of 'turbulence.'   Petards, rockets go off, in the Place Dauphine, more than enough.   A 'wicker Figure (*Mannequin
d'osier*),' in Archbishop's stole, made emblematically, three-
fifths of it satin, two-fifths of it paper, is promenaded, not in
silence, to the popular judgment-bar; is doomed; shriven by
a mock Abbé de Vermond; then solemnly consumed by fire,
at the foot of Henri's Statue on the Pont Neuf;—with such
petarding and huzzaing that Chevalier Dubois and his City-
watch see good finally to make a charge (more or less ineffectual); and there wanted not burning of sentry-boxes,
forcing of guard-houses, and also 'dead bodies thrown into the
Seine over-night,' to avoid new effervescence.

Parlements therefore shall return from exile: Plenary Court,
Payments two-fifths in Paper have vanished; gone off in smoke
at the foot of Henri's Statue.   States-General (with a Political
Millennium) are now certain; nay, it shall be announced, in our
fond haste, for January next: and all, as the Langres man said,
is 'going to go.'

To the prophetic glance of Besenval, one other thing is too
apparent: that Friend Lamoignon cannot keep his Keepership.
Neither he nor War-minister Comte de Brienne!   Already old
Foulon, with an eye to be war-minister himself, is making
underground movements.   This is that same Foulon named
âme damnée du Parlement; a man grown gray in treachery, in
griping, projecting, intriguing and iniquity; who once when
it was objected, to some finance-scheme of his, "What will the
people do?"—made answer, in the fire of discussion, "The

people may eat grass:" hasty words, which fly abroad irrevocable,—and will send back tidings!

Foulon, to the relief of the world, fails on this occasion; and will always fail. Nevertheless it steads not M. de Lamoignon. It steads not the doomed man that he have interviews with the King; and be 'seen to return *radieux*,' emitting *rays*. Lamoignon is the hatred of Parlements: Comte de Brienne is Brother to the Cardinal Archbishop. The 24th of August has been; and the 14th September is not yet, when they two, as their great Principal had done, descend, —made to fall *soft*, like him.

And now, as if the last burden had been rolled from its heart, and assurance were at length perfect, Paris bursts forth anew into extreme jubilee. The Basoche rejoices aloud, that the foe of Parlements is fallen; Nobility, Gentry, Commonalty have rejoiced; and rejoice. Nay now, with new emphasis, Rascality itself, starting suddenly from its dim depths, will arise and do it,—for down even thither the new Political Evangel, in some rude version or other, has penetrated. It is Monday, the 14th of September, 1788: Rascality assembles anew, in great force, in the Place Dauphine; lets off petards, fires blunderbusses, to an incredible extent, without interval, for eighteen hours. There is again a wicker Figure, '*Mannequin* of osier;' the centre of endless howlings. Also Necker's Portrait snatched. or purchased, from some Print-shop, is borne processionally, aloft on a perch, with huzzas;—an example to be remembered.

But chiefly on the Pont Neuf, where the Great Henri, in bronze, rides sublime; there do the crowds gather. All passengers must stop. till they have bowed to the People's King, and said audibly: *Vive Henri Quatre: au diable Lamoignon!* No carriage but must stop; not even that of his Highness d'Orléans. Your coach-doors are opened: Monsieur will please to put forth his head and bow; or even, if refractory, to alight altogether, and kneel: from Madame a wave of her plumes, a smile of her fair face, there where she sits, shall suffice:—and surely a coin or two (to buy *fusées*) were not unreasonable, from the Upper Classes, friends of Liberty? In this manner it proceeds for days; in such rude horse-play,—not without kicks. The City-watch can do nothing; hardly save its own skin: for the last twelvemonth, as we have sometimes seen, it has been a kind of pastime to

hunt the Watch. Besenval indeed is at hand with soldiers;
but they have orders to avoid firing, and are not prompt
to stir.

On Monday morning the explosion of petards began: and
now it is near midnight of Wednesday; and the 'wicker
Mannequin' is to be buried,—apparently in the Antique
fashion. Long rows of torches, following it, move towards
the Hôtel Lamoignon; but a 'servant of mine' (Besenval's)
has run to give warning, and there are soldiers come. Gloomy
Lamoignon is not to die by conflagration, or this night;—not
yet for a year, and then by gunshot (suicidal or accidental is
unknown). Foiled Rascality burns its 'Mannikin of osier,'
under his windows; 'tears up the sentry-box,' and rolls off: to
try Brienne; to try Dubois Captain of the Watch. Now,
however, all is bestirring itself; Gardes Françaises, Invalides,
Horse-patrol: the Torch Procession is met with sharp shot,
with the thrusting of bayonets, the slashing of sabres. Even
Dubois makes a charge, with that Cavalry of his, and the
cruellest charge of all: 'there are a great many killed and
wounded.' Not without clangour, complaint; subsequent
criminal trials, and official persons dying of heart-break! So,
however, with steel-besom Rascality is brushed back into its
dim depths, and the streets are swept clear.

Not for a century and a half had Rascality ventured to step
forth in this fashion; not for so long, showed its huge rude
lineaments in the light of day. A Wonder and new Thing:
as yet gamboling merely, in awkward Brobdignag sport, not
without quaintness; hardly in anger: yet in its huge half-
vacant laugh lurks a shade of grimness,—which could unfold
itself!

However, the thinkers invited by Loménie are now far on
with their pamphlets: States-General, on one plan or another,
will infallibly meet: if not in January, as was once hoped, yet
at latest in May. Old Duke de Richelieu, moribund in these
autumn days, opens his eyes once more, murmuring, "What
would Louis Fourteenth" (whom he remembers) "have said!"
—then closes them again, forever, before the evil time.

BOOK IV

STATES-GENERAL

CHAPTER I

THE NOTABLES AGAIN

THE universal prayer, therefore, is to be fulfilled! Always in days of national perplexity, when wrong abounded and help was not, this remedy of States-General was called for: by a Malesherbes, nay by a Fénelon; even Parlements calling for it were 'escorted with blessings.' And now behold it is vouchsafed us; States-General shall verily be!

To say, let States-General be, was easy; to say in what manner they shall be, is not so easy. Since the year 1614, there have no States-General met in France, all trace of them has vanished from the living habits of men. Their structure, powers, methods of procedure, which were never in any measure fixed, have now become wholly a vague possibility. Clay which the potter may shape, this way or that:—say rather, the twenty-five millions of potters; for so many have now, more or less, a vote in it! How to shape the States-General? There is a problem. Each Body-corporate, each privileged, each organised Class has secret hopes of its own in that matter; and also secret misgivings of its own,—for, behold, this monstrous twenty-million Class, hitherto the dumb sheep which these others had to agree about the manner of shearing, is now also arising with hopes! It has ceased or is ceasing to be dumb; it speaks through Pamphlets, or at least brays and growls behind them, in unison,—increasing wonderfully their volume of sound.

As for the Parlement of Paris, it has at once declared for the 'old form of 1614.' Which form had this advantage, that the *Tiers État*, Third Estate, or Commons, figured there as a show mainly: whereby the Noblesse and Clergy had but to avoid quarrel between themselves, and decide unobstructed what *they* thought best. Such was the clearly declared opinion of the Paris Parlement. But, being met by a storm of mere hooting and howling from all men, such opinion was blown straightway to the winds; and the popularity of the Parlement along with it,—never to return. The Parlement's part, we said above, was as good as played. Concerning which, however, there is this further to be noted: the proximity of dates. It was on the 22nd of September that the Parlement returned from 'vacation' or 'exile in its estates;' to be reinstalled amid boundless jubilee from all Paris. Precisely next day it was, that this same Parlement came to its 'clearly declared opinion;' and then on the morrow after that, you behold it, 'covered with outrages;' its outer court, one vast sibilation, and the glory departed from it for evermore. A popularity of twenty-four hours was, in those times, no uncommon allowance.

On the other hand, how superfluous was that invitation of Loménie: the invitation to thinkers! Thinkers and unthinkers, by the million. are spontaneously at their post, doing what is in them. Clubs labour: *Société Publicole;* Breton Club; Enraged Club, *Club des Enragés.* Likewise Dinnerparties in the Palais Royal; your Mirabeaus, Talleyrands dining there, in company with Chamforts, Morellets, with Duponts and hot Parlementeers, not without object! For a certain *Necker*ean Lion's-provider, whom one could name, assembles them there;—or even their own private determination to have dinner does it. And then as to Pamphlets—in figurative language, 'it is a sheer snowing of pamphlets; like to snow up the Government thoroughfares!' Now is the time for Friends of Freedom; sane, and even insane.

Count, or self-styled Count, d'Antraigues, 'the young Languedocian gentleman,' with perhaps Chamfort the Cynic to help him, rises into furor almost Pythic; highest, where many are high. Foolish young Languedocian gentleman; who himself so soon, 'emigrating among the foremost,' has to fly indignant over the marches, with the *Contrat Social* in his pocket,—towards outer darkness, thankless intriguings, *ignis-fatuus* hoverings, and death by the stiletto! Abbé Sieyès has left Chartres Cathedral, and canonry and book-shelves there: has let his tonsure grow, and come to Paris with a secular head, of the most irrefragable sort, to ask three questions, and answer them: *What is the third Estate? All. —What has it hitherto been in our form of government? Nothing.— What does it want? To become Something.*

D'Orléans, for be sure he, on his way to Chaos, is in the thick of this,—promulgates his *Deliberations;* fathered by him, written by Laclos of the *Liaisons Dangereuses.* The result of which comes out simply : 'The Third Estate is the Nation.' On the other hand, Monseigneur d'Artois, with other Princes of the Blood, publishes in solemn *Memorial* to the King, that if such things be listened to, Privilege, Nobility, Monarchy, Church, State and Strongbox are in danger. In danger truly : and yet if you do not listen, are they out of danger ? It is the voice of all France, this sound that rises. Immeasurable, manifold ; as the sound of outbreaking waters : wise were he who knew what to do in it,—if not to fly to the mountains, and hide himself ?

How an ideal, all-seeing Versailles Government, sitting there on such principles, in such an environment, would have determined to demean itself at this new juncture, may even yet be a question. Such a Government would have felt too well that its long task was now drawing to a close ; that, under the guise of these States-General, at length inevitable, a new omnipotent Unknown of Democracy was coming into being ; in presence of which no Versailles Government either could or should, except in a provisory character, continue extant. To enact which provisory character, so unspeakably important, might its whole faculties but have sufficed ; and so a peaceable, gradual, well-conducted Abdication and *Domine-dimittas* have been the issue !

This for our ideal, all-seeing Versailles Government. But for the actual irrational Versailles Government ? Alas ! that is a Government existing there only for its own behoof : without right, except possession ; and now also without might. It foresees nothing, sees nothing ; has not so much as a purpose, but has only purposes,—and the instinct whereby all that exists will struggle to keep existing. Wholly a vortex ; in which vain counsels, hallucinations, falsehoods, intrigues, and imbecilities whirl ; like withered rubbish in the meeting of winds ! The Œil-de-Bœuf has its irrational hopes, if also its fears. Since hitherto all States-General have done as good as nothing, why should these do more ? The Commons, indeed, look dangerous ; but on the whole is not revolt, unknown now for five generations, an impossibility ? The Three Estates can, by management, be set against each other ; the Third will, as heretofore, join with the King ; will, out of mere spite and self-interest, be eager to tax and vex the other two. The other two are thus delivered bound into our hands, that we may fleece them likewise. Whereupon, money being got, and the Three Estates all in quarrel, dismiss them, and let the future go as it can! As good Archbishop Loménie was wont to say: "There are so many accidents; and it needs but one to save us."—Yes; and how many to destroy us?

Poor Necker in the midst of such an anarchy does what is possible for him. He looks into it with obstinately hopeful face; lauds the known rectitude of the kingly mind; listens indulgent-like to the known perverseness of the queenly and courtly;—emits if any proclamation or regulation, one favouring the *Tiers État;* but settling nothing; hovering afar off rather, and advising all things to settle themselves. The grand questions, for the present, have got reduced to two: the Double Representation, and the Vote by Head. Shall the Commons have a 'double representation,' that is to say, have as many members as the Noblesse and Clergy united? Shall the States-General, when once assembled, vote and deliberate, in one body, or in three separate bodies; 'vote by head, or vote by class,'—*ordre* as they call it? These are the moot-points now filling all France with jargon, logic and eleuthero-mania. To terminate which, Necker bethinks him, Might not a second Convocation of the Notables be fittest? Such second Convocation is resolved on.

On the 6th of November of this year 1788, these Notables accordingly have reassembled; after an interval of some eighteen months. They are Calonne's old Notables, the same Hundred and Forty-four,—to show one's impartiality; likewise to save time. They sit there once again, in their Seven Bureaus, in the hard winter weather: it is the hardest winter seen since 1709; thermometer below zero of Fahrenheit, Seine River frozen over. Cold, scarcity and eleuthero-maniac clamour: a changed world since these Notables were 'organned out,' in May gone a year! They shall see now whether, under their Seven Princes of the Blood, in their Seven Bureaus, they can settle the moot-points.

To the surprise of Patriotism, these Notables, once so patriotic, seem to incline the wrong way; towards the anti-patriotic side. They stagger at the Double Representation, at the Vote by Head: there is not affirmative decision; there is mere debating, and that not with the best aspects. For, indeed, were not these Notables themselves mostly of the

Privileged Classes? They clamoured once; now they have their misgivings; make their dolorous representations. Let them vanish, ineffectual; and return no more! They vanish, after a month's session, on this 12th day of December, year 1788: the *last* terrestrial Notables; not to reappear any other time, in the History of the World.

And so, the clamour still continuing, and the Pamphlets; and nothing but patriotic Addresses, louder and louder, pouring in on us from all corners of France,—Necker himself some fortnight after, before the year is yet done, has to present his *Report;* recommending at his own risk that same Double Representation; nay almost enjoining it, so loud is the jargon and eleutheromania. What dubitating, what circumambulating! These whole six noisy months (for it began with Brienne in July), has not *Report* followed *Report,* and one Proclamation flown in the teeth of the other?

However, that first moot-point, as we see, is now settled. As for the second, that of voting by Head or by Order, it unfortunately is still left hanging. It hangs there, we may say, between the Privileged Orders and the Unprivileged; as a ready-made battle-prize, and necessity of war, from the very first: which battle-prize whosoever seizes it—may thenceforth bear as battle-flag, with the best omens!

But so, at least, by Royal Edict of the 24th of January, does it finally, to impatient expectant France, become not only indubitable that National Deputies *are* to meet, but possible (so far and hardly further has the royal Regulation gone) to begin electing them.

CHAPTER II

THE ELECTION

Up, then, and be doing! The royal signal-word flies through France, as through vast forests the rushing of a mighty wind. At Parish Churches, in Townhalls, and every House of Convocation; by Bailliages, by Seneschalsies, in whatsoever form men convene; there, with confusion enough, are Primary Assemblies forming. To elect your Electors; such is the form prescribed: then to draw up your "Writ of Plaints and Grievances (*Cahier de plaintes et doléances*)," of which latter there is no lack.

With such virtue works this Royal January Edict; as it
rolls rapidly, in its leathern mails, along these frostbound
highways, towards all the four winds. Like some *fiat*, or
magic spell-word,—which such things do resemble! For
always, as it sounds out 'at the market-cross,' accompanied
with trumpet-blast; presided by Bailli, Seneschal, or other
minor Functionary, with beef-eaters; or, in country churches,
is droned forth after sermon, '*au prône des messes parois-
sales;*' and is registered, posted and let fly over all the world,
—you behold how this multitudinous French People, so long
simmering and buzzing in eager expectancy, begins heaping and shaping itself into organic groups. Which organic
groups, again, hold smaller organic grouplets: the inarticulate buzzing becomes articulate speaking and acting. By
Primary Assembly, and then by Secondary; by 'successive
elections,' and infinite elaboration and scrutiny, according
to prescribed process,—shall the genuine 'Plaints and Grievances' be at length got to paper; shall the fit National
Representative be at length laid hold of.

How the whole People shakes itself, as if it had one life;
and, in thousand-voiced rumour, announces that it is awake,
suddenly out of long death-sleep, and will thenceforth sleep no
more! The long looked-for has come at last; wondrous
news, of Victory, Deliverance, Enfranchisement, sounds
magical through every heart. To the proud strong man it
has come; whose strong hands shall no more be gyved; to
whom boundless unconquered continents lie disclosed. The
weary day-drudge has heard of it; the beggar with his crust
moistened in tears. What! To us also has hope reached;
down even to us? Hunger and hardship are not to be
eternal? The bread we extorted from the rugged glebe, and,
with the toil of our sinews, reaped and ground, and kneaded
into loaves, was not wholly for another, then; but we also
shall eat of it, and be filled? Glorious news (answer the
prudent elders), but all-too unlikely!—Thus, at any rate, may
the lower people, who pay no money taxes and have no right
to vote, assiduously crowd round those that do; and most
Halls of Assembly, within doors and without, seem animated
enough.

Paris, alone of Towns, is to have Representatives; the
number of them twenty. Paris is divided into Sixty Districts;
each of which (assembled in some church, or the like) is
choosing two Electors. Official deputations pass from District

to District, for all is inexperience as yet, and there is endless consulting. The streets swarm strangely with busy crowds, pacific yet restless and loquacious; at intervals, is seen the gleam of military muskets; especially about the Palais, where the Parlement, once more on duty, sits querulous, almost tremulous.

Busy is the French world! In those great days, what poorest speculative craftsman but will leave his workshop; if not to vote, yet to assist in voting? On all highways is a rustling and bustling. Over the wide surface of France, ever and anon, through the spring months, as the Sower casts his corn abroad upon the furrows, sounds of congregating and dispersing; of crowds in deliberation, acclamation, voting by ballot and by voice,—rise discrepant towards the ear of Heaven. To which political phenomena add this economical one, that Trade is stagnant, and also Bread getting dear; for before the rigorous winter there was, as we said, a rigorous summer, with drought, and on the 13th of July with destructive hail. What a fearful day! all cried while that tempest fell. Alas, the next anniversary of it will be a worse. Under such aspects is France electing National Representatives.

The incidents and specialties of these Elections belong not to Universal, but to Local or Parish History: for which reason let not the new troubles of Grenoble or Besançon; the bloodshed on the streets of Rennes, and consequent march thither of the Breton 'Young Men' with Manifesto by their 'Mothers, Sisters and Sweethearts'; not such like, detain us here. It is the same sad history everywhere; with superficial variations. A reinstated Parlement (as at Besançon), which stands astonished at this Behemoth of a States-General it had itself evoked, starts forward, with more or less audacity, to fix a thorn in its nose; and, alas, is instantaneously struck down, and hurled quite out,—for the new popular force can use not only arguments but brickbats! Or else, and perhaps combined with this, it is an order of Noblesse (as in Brittany), which will beforehand tie up the Third Estate, that it harm not the old privileges. In which act of tying up, never so skilfully set about, there is likewise no possibility of prospering; but the Behemoth-Briareus snaps your cords like green rushes. Tie up? Alas, Messieurs! And then, as for your chivalry rapiers, valour and wager-of-battle, think one moment, how can that answer? The plebeian heart, too, has red life in

it, which changes not to paleness at glance even of you ; and
'the six hundred Breton gentlemen assembled in arms, for
seventy-two hours, in the Cordeliers' Cloister, at Rennes,'—
have to come out again, *wiser* than they entered. For the
Nantes Youth, the Angers Youth, all Brittany was astir ;
'mothers, sisters and sweethearts' shrieking after them,
March ! The Breton Noblesse must even let the mad world
have its way.

In other Provinces, the Noblesse, with equal goodwill, finds
it better to stick to Protests, to well-redacted '*Cahiers* of
grievances,' and satirical writings and speeches. Such is
partially their course in Provence ; whither indeed Gabriel
Honoré Riquetti Comte de Mirabeau has rushed down from
Paris, to speak a word in season. In Provence, the Privileged,
backed by their Aix Parlement, discover that such novelties,
enjoined though they be by Royal Edict, tend to National
detriment ; and what is still more indisputable, 'to impair the
dignity of the Noblesse.' Whereupon Mirabeau protesting
aloud, this same Noblesse, amid huge tumult within doors and
without, flatly determines to expel him from their Assembly.
No other method, not even that of successive duels, would
answer with him, the obstreperous fierce-glaring man. Expelled he accordingly is.

'In all countries, in all times,' exclaims he departing, 'the
Aristocrats have implacably pursued every friend of the
People ; and with tenfold implacability, if such a one were
himself born of the Aristocracy. It was thus that the last of
the Gracchi perished, by the hands of the Patricians. But
he, being struck with the mortal stab, flung dust towards
heaven, and called on the Avenging Deities ; and from this
dust there was born Marius,—Marius not so illustrious for
exterminating the Cimbri, as for overturning in Rome the
tyranny of the Nobles.' Casting up *which* new curious handful of dust (through the Printing-press), to breed what it can
and may, Mirabeau stalks forth into the Third Estate.

That he now, to ingratiate himself with this Third Estate,
'opened a cloth-shop in Marseilles,' and for moments became
a furnishing tailor, or even the fable that he did so, is to us
always among the pleasant memorabilities of this era.
Stranger Clothier never wielded the ell-wand ; and rent webs
for men, or fractional parts of men. The *Fils Adoptif* is
indignant at such disparaging fable,—which nevertheless was
widely believed in those days. But indeed, if Achilles, in the

heroic ages, killed mutton, why should not Mirabeau, in the unheroic ones, measure broadcloth?

More authentic are his triumph-progresses through that disturbed district, with mob jubilee, flaming torches, 'windows hired for two louis,' and voluntary guard of a hundred men. He is Deputy Elect, both of Aix and of Marseilles; but will prefer Aix. He has opened his far-sounding voice, the depths of his far-sounding soul; he can quell (such virtue is in a spoken word) the pride-tumults of the rich, the hunger-tumults of the poor; and wild multitudes move under him, as under the moon do billows of the sea: he has become a world-compeller, and ruler over men.

One other incident and specialty we note; with how different an interest! It is of the Parlement of Paris; which starts forward, like the others (only with less audacity, seeing better how it lay), to nose-ring that Behemoth of a States-General. Worthy Doctor Guillotin, respectable practitioner in Paris, has drawn up his little 'Plan of a *Cahier* of *doléances;*' —as had he not, having the wish and gift, the clearest liberty to do? He is getting the people to sign it; whereupon the surly Parlement summons him to give account of himself. He goes; but with all Paris at his heels; which floods the outer courts, and copiously signs the *Cahier* even there, while the Doctor is giving account of himself within! The Parlement cannot too soon dismiss Guillotin, with compliments; to be borne home shoulder-high. This respectable Guillotin we hope to behold once more, and perhaps only once; the Parlement not even once, but let it be engulfed unseen by us.

Meanwhile such things, cheering as they are, tend little to cheer the national creditor, or indeed the creditor of any kind. In the midst of universal portentous doubt, what certainty can seem so certain as money in the purse, and the wisdom of keeping it there? Trading Speculation, Commerce of all kinds, has as far as possible come to a dead pause; and the hand of the industrious lies idle in his bosom. Frightful enough, when now the rigour of seasons has also done its part, and to scarcity of work is added scarcity of food! In the opening spring, there come rumours of forestalment, there come King's Edicts, Petitions of bakers against millers; and at length, in the month of April,—troops of ragged Lackalls, and fierce cries of starvation! These are the thrice-famed *Brigands:* an actual existing quotity of persons; who long reflected and reverberated through so many millions of heads, as in concave multiplying mirrors, become a whole Brigand World; and, like a kind of Supernatural Machinery, wondrously move the Epos of the Revolution. The Brigands are here; the Brigands are there: the Brigands are coming! Not otherwise sounded the clang of Phœbus Apollo's silver bow, scattering pestilence and pale terror: for this clang too was of the imagination; preternatural; and it too walked in formless immeasurability, *having made itself like to the Night* (νυκτì ἐοικώς)!

But remark at least, for the first time, the singular empire of Suspicion, in those lands, in those days. If poor famishing men shall, prior to death, gather in groups and crowds, as the poor fieldfares and plovers do in bitter weather, were it but that they may chirp mournfully together, and misery look in the eyes of misery; if famishing men (what famishing fieldfares cannot do) should discover, once congregated, that they need not die while food is in the land, since they are many, and with empty wallets have right hands: in all this, what need were there of Preternatural Machinery? To most people none; but not to French people, in a time of Revolution. These Brigands (as Turgot's also were, fourteen years ago) have all been set on; enlisted, though without tap of drum,—by Aristocrats, by Democrats, by D'Orléans, D'Artois, and enemies of the public weal. Nay Historians, to this day, will prove it by one argument: these Brigands, pretending to have no victual, nevertheless contrive to drink, nay have been seen drunk. An unexampled fact! But on the whole, may we not predict that a people, with such a width of Credulity and of Incredulity (the proper union of which makes Suspicion, and indeed unreason generally), will see Shapes enough of Immortals fighting in its battle-ranks, and never want for Epical Machinery?

Be this as it may, the Brigands are clearly got to Paris, in considerable multitudes; with sallow faces, lank hair (the true enthusiast complexion), with sooty rags; and also with large clubs, which they smite angrily against the pavement! These mingle in the Election tumult; would fain sign Guillotin's *Cahier*, or any *Cahier* or Petition whatsoever, could they but write. Their enthusiast complexion, the smiting of their sticks bodes little good to any one; least of all to rich master-manufacturers of the Suburb Saint-Antoine, with whose workmen they consort.

CHAPTER III

GROWN ELECTRIC

BUT now also National Deputies from all ends of France are in Paris, with their commissions, what they call *pouvoirs*, or powers, in their pockets; inquiring, consulting; looking out for lodgings at Versailles. The States-General shall open there, if not on the First, then surely on the Fourth of May; in grand procession and gala. The *Salle des Menus* is all new-carpentered, bedizened for them; their very costume has been fixed: a grand controversy which there was, as to 'slouch-hats or slouched-hats,' for the Commons Deputies, has got as good as adjusted. Ever new strangers arrive: loungers, miscellaneous persons, officers on furlough, as the worthy Captain Dampmartin, whom we hope to be acquainted with: these also, from all regions, have repaired hither, to see what is toward. Our Paris Committees, of the Sixty Districts, are busier than ever; it is now too clear, the Paris Elections will be late.

On Monday, the 27th day of April, Astronomer Bailly notices that the Sieur Réveillon is not at his post. The Sieur Réveillon, 'extensive Paper Manufacturer of the Rue Saint-Antoine:' he, commonly so punctual, is absent from Electoral Committee:—and even will never reappear there. In those 'immense Magazines of velvet paper,' has aught befallen? Alas, yes! Alas, it is no Montgolfier rising there to-day; but Drudgery, Rascality and the Suburb that is rising! Was the Sieur Réveillon, himself once a journeyman, heard to say that 'a journeyman might live handsomely on fifteen *sous* a day?' Some sevenpence halfpenny: 'tis a slender sum! Or was he only thought, and believed, to be heard saying it? By this long chafing and friction, it would appear, the National temper has got *electric*.

Down in those dark dens, in those dark heads and hungry hearts, who knows in what strange figure the new Political Evangel may have shaped itself; what miraculous 'Communion of Drudges' may be getting formed! Enough: grim individuals, soon waxing to grim multitudes, and other multitudes crowding to see, beset that Paper-Warehouse; demonstrate, in loud ungrammatical language (addressed to the passions too), the insufficiency of sevenpence halfpenny a-day. The City-watch cannot dissipate them; broils arise and bellowings: Réveillon, at his wits' end entreats the Populace, entreats the Authorities. Besenval, now in active command, Commandant of Paris, does, towards evening, to Réveillon's earnest prayer, send some thirty Gardes Françaises. These clear the street, happily without firing: and take post there for the night, in hope that it may be all over.

Not so: on the morrow it is far worse. Saint-Antoine has arisen anew, grimmer than ever;—reinforced by the unknown Tatterdemalion Figures, with their enthusiast complexion, and large sticks. The City, through all streets, is flowing thitherward to see: 'two cartloads of paving-stones, that happened to pass that way,' have been seized as a visible godsend. Another detachment of Gardes Françaises must be sent; Besenval and the Colonel taking earnest counsel. Then still another; they hardly, with bayonets and menace of bullets, penetrate to the spot. What a sight! A street choked up, with lumber, tumult and the endless press of men. A Paper-Warehouse eviscerated by axe and fire: mad din of Revolt; musket-volleys responded to by yells, by miscellaneous missiles, by tiles raining from roof and window,—tiles, execrations and slain men!

The Gardes Françaises like it not, but have to persevere. All day it continues, slackening and rallying; the sun is sinking, and Saint-Antoine has not yielded. The City flies hither and thither: alas, the sound of that musket-volleying booms into the far dining-rooms of the Chaussée d'Antin; alters the tone of the dinner-gossip there. Captain Dampmartin leaves his wine; goes out with a friend or two, to see the fighting. Unwashed men growl on him, with murmurs of "*À bas les Aristocrates* (Down with the Aristocrats);" and insult the cross of St. Louis! They elbow him, and hustle him; but do not pick his pocket;—as indeed at Réveillon's too there was not the slightest stealing.

At fall of night, as the thing will not end, Besenval takes his resolution: orders out the *Gardes Suisses* with two pieces of artillery. The Swiss Guards shall proceed thither; summon that rabble to depart, in the King's name. If disobeyed, they shall load their artillery with grape-shot, visibly to the general eye; shall again summon; if again disobeyed, fire,—and keep firing 'till the last man' be in this manner blasted off, and the street clear. With which spirited resolution, as might have been hoped, the business is got ended. At sight of the lit matches, of the foreign red-coated Switzers, Saint-Antoine dissipates; hastily, in the shades of dusk. There is an encumbered street; there are 'from four to five hundred' dead men. Unfortunate Réveillon has found shelter in the Bastille; does therefrom, safe behind stone bulwarks, issue plaint, protestation, explanation, for the next month. Bold Besenval has thanks from all the respectable Parisian classes; but finds no special notice taken of him at Versailles,—a thing the man of true worth is used to.

But how it originated, this fierce electric sputter and explosion? From D'Orléans; cries the Court-party: he, with his gold, enlisted these Brigands,—surely in some surprising manner, without sound of drum: he raked them in hither, from all corners; to ferment and take fire; evil is his good. From the Court! cries enlightened Patriotism: it is the cursed gold and wiles of Aristocrats that enlisted them; set them upon ruining an innocent Sieur Réveillon; to frighten the faint, and disgust men with the career of Freedom.

Besenval, with reluctance, concludes that it came from 'the English, our natural enemies.' Or, alas, might one not rather attribute it to Diana in the shape of Hunger? To some twin *Dioscuri*, OPPRESSION and REVENGE; so often seen in the battles of men? Poor Lackalls, all betoiled, besoiled, encrusted into dim defacement;—into whom nevertheless the breath of the Almighty has breathed a living soul! To them it is clear only that eleutheromaniac Philosophism has yet baked no bread; that Patriot Committee-men will level down to their own level, and no lower. Brigands or whatever they might be, it was bitter earnest with them. They bury their dead with the title of *Défenseurs de la Patrie*, Martyrs of the good Cause.

Or shall we say: Insurrection has now *served* its Apprenticeship; and this was its proof-stroke, and no inconclusive one? Its next will be a master-stroke; announcing indisputable Mastership to a whole astonished world. Let that rock-fortress, Tryanny's stronghold, which they name *Bastille* or *Building*, as if there were no other building,—look to its guns!

But, in such wise, with primary and secondary Assemblies, and *Cahiers* of Grievances; with motions, congregations of all kinds; with much thunder of froth-eloquence, and at last with thunder of platoon-musquetry,—does agitated France accomplish its Elections. With confused winnowing and sifting, in this rather tumultuous manner, it has now (all except some remnants of Paris) sifted out the true wheat-grains of National Deputies, Twelve Hundred and Fourteen in number; and will forthwith open its States-General.

CHAPTER IV

THE PROCESSION

ON the first Saturday of May, it is gala at Versailles; and Monday, fourth of the month, is to be a still greater day. The Deputies have mostly got thither, and sought out lodgings; and are now successively, in long well-ushered files, kissing the hand of Majesty in the Château. Supreme Usher de Brézé does not give the highest satisfaction: we cannot but observe that in ushering Noblesse or Clergy into the anointed Presence, he liberally opens *both* his folding-doors; and on the other hand, for members of the Third Estate, opens only one! However, there is room to enter; Majesty has smiles for all.

The good Louis welcomes his Honourable Members, with smiles of hope. He has prepared for them the Hall of *Menus*, the largest near him; and often surveyed the workmen as they went on. A spacious Hall: with raised platform for Throne, Court and Blood-royal; space for six hundred Commons Deputies in front; for half as many Clergy on this hand, and half as many Noblesse on that. It has lofty galleries; where-from dames of honour, splendent in *gaze d'or;* foreign Diplomacies, and other gilt-edged white-frilled individuals, to the number of two thousand,—may sit and look. Broad passages flow through it; and, outside the inner wall, all round it. There are committee-rooms, guard-rooms, robing-rooms: really a noble Hall; where upholstery, aided by the subject fine-arts, has done its best; and crimson tasselled cloths, and emblematic *fleurs-de-lys* are not wanting.

The Hall is ready: the very costume, as we said, has been settled; and the Commons are *not* to wear that hated slouch-hat (*chapeau clabaud*), but one not quite so slouched (*chapeau rabattu*). As for their manner of *working*, when all dressed; for their "voting by head or by order" and the rest,—this, which it were perhaps still time to settle, and in few hours will be no longer time, remains unsettled; hangs dubious in the breast of Twelve Hundred men.

But now finally the Sun, on Monday the 4th of May, has risen;—unconcerned, as if it were no special day. And yet, as his first rays could strike music from the Memnon's Statue on the Nile, what tones were these, so thrilling, tremulous, of preparation and foreboding, which he awoke in every bosom at Versailles! Huge Paris, in all conceivable and inconceivable vehicles, is pouring itself forth; from each Town and Village come subsidiary rills: Versailles is a very sea of men. But above all, from the Church of St. Louis to the Church of Notre-Dame: one vast suspended-billow of Life,—with *spray* scattered even to the chimney-tops! For on chimney-tops too, as over the roofs, and up thitherwards on every lamp-iron, signpost, breakneck coign of vantage, sits patriotic Courage; and every window bursts with patriotic Beauty: for the Deputies are gathering at St. Louis Church; to march in procession to Notre-Dame, and hear sermon.

Yes, friends, ye may sit and look: bodily or in thought, all France, and all Europe, may sit and look; for it is a day like few others. Oh, one might weep like Xerxes:—So many serried rows sit perched there; like winged creatures, alighted out of Heaven: all these and so many more that follow them, shall have wholly fled aloft again, vanishing into the blue Deep; and the memory of this day still be fresh. It is the baptism day of Democracy; sick Time has given it birth, the numbered months being run. The extreme-unction day of Feudalism! A superannuated System of Society, decrepit with toils (for has it not done much; produced *you*, and what ye have and know!)—and with thefts and brawls, named glorious victories; and with profligacies, sensualities, and on the whole with dotage and senility,—is now to die: and so, with death-throes, and birth-throes a new one is to be born. What a work, O Earth and Heaven, what a work! Battles and bloodshed, September Massacres, Bridges of Lodi, retreats of Moscow, Waterloos, Peterloos, Tenpound Franchises, Tar-barrels and Guillotines;——and from this present date, if one might prophesy, some two centuries of it still to fight! Two centuries; hardly less; before Democracy go through its due, most baleful, stages of *Quack*ocracy; and a pestilential World be burnt up, and have begun to grow green and young again.

Rejoice nevertheless, ye Versailles multitudes; to you from whom all this is hid, the glorious end of it is visible. This day, sentence of death is pronounced on Shams; judgment of resuscitation, were it but afar off, is pronounced on Realities. This day, it is declared aloud, as with a Doom-trumpet, that *a Lie is unbelievable.* Believe that, stand by that, if more there be not; and let what thing or things soever will follow it follow. "Ye can no other; God be your help!" So spake a greater than any of you; opening *his* Chapter of World-History.

Behold, however! The doors of St. Louis Church flung wide; and the Procession of Processions advancing towards Notre-Dame! Shouts rend the air; one shout, at which Grecian birds might drop dead. It is indeed a stately, solemn sight. The Elected of France, and then the Court of France; they are marshalled and march there, all in prescribed place and costume. Our Commons 'in plain black mantle and white cravat;' Noblesse, in gold-worked, bright-dyed cloaks of velvet. resplendent, rustling with laces, waving with plumes; the Clergy in rochet, alb, or other best *pontificalibus:* lastly comes the King himself, and King's Household, also in their brightest blaze of pomp,—their brightest and final one. Some Fourteen Hundred Men blown together from all winds, on the deepest errand.

Yes, in that silent marching mass there lies Futurity enough. No symbolic Ark, like the old Hebrews, do these men bear: yet with them too is a Covenant; they too preside at a new Era in the History of Men. The whole Future is there, and Destiny dim-brooding over it; in the hearts and unshaped thoughts of these men, it lies illegible, inevitable. Singular to think: *they* have it in them; yet not they, not mortal, only the Eye above can read it,—as it shall unfold itself, in fire and thunder, of siege, and field artillery; in the rustling of battle-banners, the tramp of hosts, in the glow of burning cities, the shriek of strangled nations! Such things lie hidden, safe-wrapt in this Fourth day of May;—say rather, had lain in some other unknown day, of which this latter is the public fruit and outcome. As indeed what wonders lie in every Day,—had we the sight, as happily we have not, to decipher it: for is not every meanest Day 'the conflux of two Eternities!'

Meanwhile, suppose we too, good reader, should, as now without miracle Muse Clio enables us,—take *our* station also on some coign of vantage; and glance momentarily over this Procession, and this Life-sea; with far other eyes than the rest do,—namely with prophetic? We can mount, and stand there, without fear of falling.

As for the Life-sea, or onlooking unnumbered Multitude, it is unfortunately all-too dim. Yet as we gaze fixedly, do not nameless Figures not a few, which shall not always be nameless, disclose themselves; visible or presumable there? Young Baroness de Staël—she evidently looks from a window; among older honourable women. Her father is Minister, and one of the gala personages; to his own eyes the chief one. Young spiritual Amazon, thy rest is not there; nor thy loved Father's: 'as Malebranche saw all things in God, so M. Necker sees all things in Necker'—a theorem that will not hold.

But where is the brown-locked, light-behaved, fire-hearted Demoiselle Théroigne? Brown eloquent Beauty; who, with thy winged words and glances, shalt thrill rough bosoms, whole steel battalions, and persuade an Austrian Kaiser,— pike and helm lie provided for thee in due season; and, alas, also strait-waistcoat and long lodging in the Salpêtrière! Better hadst thou staid in native Luxemburg, and been the mother of some brave man's children: but it was not thy task, it was not thy lot.

Of the rougher sex how, without tongue, or hundred tongues, of iron, enumerate the notabilities! Has not Marquis Valadi hastily quitted his Quaker broadbrim; his Pythagorean Greek in Wapping, and the city of Glasgow? De Morande from his *Courier de l'Europe*; Linguet from his *Annales*, they looked eager through the London fog, and became, Ex-Editors,—that they might feed the guillotine, and have their due. Does Louvet (of *Faublas*) stand a-tiptoe? And Brissot, hight De Warville, friend of the Blacks? He, with Marquis Condorcet, and Clavière the Genevese 'have created the *Moniteur* Newspaper,' or are about creating it. Able Editors must give account of such a day.

Or seest thou with any distinctness, low down probably, not in places of honour, a Stanislas Maillard, riding-tipstaff (*huissier à cheval*) of the Châtelet; one of the shiftiest of men? A Captain Hulin of Geneva, Captain Élie of the Queen's Regiment; both with an air of half-pay? Jourdan, with tile-coloured whiskers, not yet with tile-beard; an unjust dealer in mules? He shall be, in few months, Jourdan the Headsman, and have other work.

Surely also, in some place not of honour, stands or sprawls up querulous, that he too, though short, may see,—one

squalidest bleared mortal, redolent of soot and horse-drugs:
Jean Paul Marat of Neuchâtel! O Marat, Renovator of
Human Science, Lecturer on Optics; O thou remarkablest
Horseleech, once in D'Artois' Stables,—as thy bleared soul
looks forth, through thy bleared, dull-acrid, wo-stricken face,
what sees it in all this? Any faintest light of hope; like day-
spring after Nova-Zembla night? Or is it but *blue* sulphur-
light, and spectres; wo, suspicion, revenge without end?

Of Draper Lecointre, how he shut his cloth-shop hard by,
and stepped forth, one need hardly speak. Nor of Santerre,
the sonorous Brewer from the Faubourg St Antoine. Two
other Figures, and only two, we signalise there. The huge,
brawny Figure; through whose black brows, and rude flattened
face (*figure écrasée*), there looks a waste energy as of Hercules
not yet furibund,—he is an esurient, unprovided advocate;
Danton by name: him mark. Then that other, his slight-built
comrade, and craft-brother; he with the long curling locks;
with the face of dingy blackguardism, wondrously irradiated
with genius, as if a naphtha-lamp burnt within it: that Figure
is Camille Desmoulins. A fellow of infinite shrewdness, wit,
nay humour; one of the sprightliest, clearest souls in all these
millions. Thou poor Camille, say of thee what they may, it
were but falsehood to pretend one did not almost love thee,
thou headlong lightly sparkling man! But the brawny, not
yet furibund Figure, we say, is Jacques Danton; a name that
shall be 'tolerably known in the Revolution.' He is President
of the electoral Cordeliers District at Paris, or about to be it;
and shall open his lungs of brass.

We dwell no longer on the mixed shouting Multitude: for
now, behold, the Commons Deputies are at hand!

Which of these Six Hundred individuals, in plain white
cravat, that have come up to regenerate France, might one
guess would become their *king?* For a king or leader they, as
all bodies of men, must have: be their work what it may,
there is one man there who, by character, faculty, position,
is fittest of all to do it; that man, as future not yet elected
king, walks there among the rest. He with the thick black
locks, will it be? With the *hure*, as himself calls it, or black
boar's-head, fit to be 'shaken' as a senatorial portent? Through
whose shaggy beetle-brows, and rough-hewn, seamed, carbuncled face, there look natural ugliness, smallpox, inconti-
nence, bankruptcy,—and burning fire of genius; like comet-fire

glaring fuliginous through murkiest confusions? It is *Gabriel Honoré Riquetti de Mirabeau*, the world-compeller; man-ruling Deputy of Aix! According to the Baroness de Staël, he steps proudly along, though looked at askance here; and shakes his black *chevelure*, or lion's-mane,; as if prophetic of great deeds.

Yes, Reader, that is the Type-Frenchman of this epoch; as Voltaire was of the last. He is French in his aspirations, acquisitions, in his virtues, in his vices; perhaps more French than any other man;—and intrinsically such a mass of manhood too. Mark him well. The National Assembly were all different without that one; nay, he might say with the old Despot: "The National Assembly? I am that."

Of a southern climate, of wild southern blood: for the Riquettis, or Arrighettis, had to fly from Florence and the Guelfs, long centuries ago, and settled in Provence; where from generation tò generation they have ever approved themselves a peculiar kindred: irascible, indomitable, sharp-cutting, true, like the steel they wore; of an intensity and activity that sometimes verged towards madness, yet did not reach it. One ancient Riquetti, in mad fulfilment of a mad vow, chains two Mountains together; and the chain, with its 'iron star of five rays,' is still to be seen. May not a modern Riquetti *un*chain so much, and set it drifting,—which also shall be seen?

Destiny has work for that swart burly-headed Mirabeau: Destiny has watched over him, prepared him from afar. Did not his Grandfather, stout *Col-d'Argent* (Silver-Stock, so they named him), shattered and slashed by seven-and-twenty wounds in one fell day, lie sunk together on the Bridge at Casano; while Prince Eugene's cavalry galloped and regalloped over him,—only the flying sergeant had thrown a camp-kettle over that loved head; and Vendôme, dropping his spy-glass, moaned out, "Mirabeau is *dead*, then!" Nevertheless he was not dead, he awoke to breath, and miraculous surgery;—for Gabriel was yet to be. With his *silver stock* he kept his scarred head erect, through long years; and wedded; and produced tough Marquis Victor, the *Friend of Men*. Whereby at last in the appointed year 1749, this long-expected rough-hewn Gabriel Honoré did likewise see the light: roughest lion's whelp ever littered of that rough breed. How the old lion (for our old Marquis too was lion-like, most unconquerable, kingly-genial, most perverse) gazed wondering on his offspring; and determined to train him as no lion had yet been! It is in vain, O Marquis! This cub, though thou slay him and flay him, will not learn to draw in dogcart of Political Economy, and be a *Friend of Men*; he will not be Thou, but must and will be Himself, another than Thou. Divorce lawsuits, 'whole family save one in prison and three-score *Lettres-de-Cachet*' for thy own sole use, do but astonish the world.

Our luckless Gabriel, sinned against and sinning, has been in the Isle of Rhé and heard the Atlantic from his tower; in the Castle of If, and heard the Mediterranean at Marseilles. He has been in the Fortress of Joux; and forty-two months, with hardly clothing to his back, in the Dungeon of Vincennes; —all by *Lettre-de-Cachet*, from his lion father. He has been in Pontarlier Jails (self-constituted prisoner); was noticed fording estuaries of the sea (at low water), in flight from the face of men. He has pleaded before Aix Parlements (to get back his wife); the public gathering on roofs, to see since they could not hear: "the clatter-teeth (*claque-dents*)!" snarls singular old Mirabeau; discerning in such admired forensic eloquence nothing but two clattering jaw-bones, and a head vacant, sonorous, of the drum species.

But as for Gabriel Honoré, in these strange wayfarings, what has he not seen and tried? From drill-sergeants, to prime ministers, to foreign and domestic booksellers, all manner of men he has seen. All manner of men he has gained; for at bottom it is a social, loving heart, that wild unconquerable one:—more especially all manner of women. From the Archer's Daughter at Saintes to that fair young Sophie Madame Monnier, whom he could not but "steal," and be beheaded for—in effigy! For indeed, hardly since the Arabian Prophet lay dead to Ali's admiration, was there seen such a Love-hero, with the strength of thirty men. In War, again, he has helped to conquer Corsica; fought duels, irregular brawls; horse-whipped calumnious barons. In Literature, he has written on *Despotism*, on *Lettres-de-Cachet*; Erotics Sapphic-Werterean, Obscenities, Profanities; Books on the *Prussian Monarchy*, on *Cagliostro*, on *Calonne*, on *the Water Companies of Paris*:— each Book comparable, we will say, to a bituminous alarum-fire; huge, smoky, sudden! The firepan, the kindling, the bitumen were his own; but the lumber, of rags, old wood and nameless combustible rubbish (for all is fuel to him), was gathered from hucksters, and ass paniers, of every description under heaven. Whereby, indeed, hucksters enough have been heard to exclaim: Out upon it, the fire is *mine!*

Nay, consider it more generally, seldom had man such a

talent for borrowing. The idea, the faculty of another man he can make his; the man himself he can make his. "All reflex and echo (*tout de reflet et de réverbère*)!" snarls old Mirabeau, who can see, but will not. Crabbed old Friend of Men! it is his sociality, his aggregative nature; and will now be the quality of qualities for him. In that forty years' 'struggle against despotism,' he has gained the glorious faculty of *self-help*, and yet not lost the glorious natural gift of *fellowship*, of being helped. Rare union: this man can live self-sufficing—yet lives also in the life of other men; can make men love him, work with him; a born king of men!

But consider further how, as the old Marquis still snarls, he has "made away with (*humé*, swallowed) all *Formulas*";—a fact which, if we meditate it, will in these days mean much. This is no man of system, then; he is only a man of instincts and insights. A man nevertheless who will glare fiercely on any object; and see through it, and conquer it: for he has intellect, he has will, force beyond other men. A man not with *logic-spectacles;* but with an *eye!* Unhappily without Decalogue, moral Code or Theorem of any fixed sort; yet not without a strong living Soul in him, and Sincerity there: a Reality, not an Artificiality, not a Sham! And so he, having struggled 'forty years against despotism,' and 'made away with all formulas,' shall now become the spokesman of a Nation bent to do the same. For is it not precisely the struggle of France also to cast off despotism; to make away with *her* old formulas,—having found them naught, worn out, far from the reality? She will make away with *such* formulas; and even go *bare*, if need be, till she have found new ones.

Towards such work, in such manner, marches he, this singular Riquetti Mirabeau. In fiery rough figure, with black Samson-locks under the slouch-hat, he steps along there. A fiery fuliginous mass, which could not be choked and smothered, but would fill all France with smoke. And now it has got *air*; it will burn its whole substance, its whole smoke-atmosphere too, and fill all France with flame. Strange lot! Forty years of that smouldering, with foul fire-damp and vapour enough; then victory over that;—and like a burning mountain he blazes heaven-high; and for twenty-three resplendent months, pours out, in flame and molten fire-torrents, all that is in him, the Pharos and Wonder sign of an amazed Europe;—and then lies hollow, cold forever! Pass on, thou questionable Gabriel Honoré, the greatest of them all: in the whole National

Deputies, in the whole Nation, there is none like and none second to thee.

But now if Mirabeau is the greatest, who of these Six Hundred may be the meanest? Shall we say, that anxious, slight, ineffectual-looking man, under thirty, in spectacles; his eyes (were the glasses off) troubled, careful; with upturned face, snuffing dimly the uncertain future times; complexion of a multiplex atrabiliar colour, the final shade of which may be the pale sea-green. That greenish-coloured (*verdâtre*) individual is an Advocate of Arras; his name is *Maximilien Robespierre*. The son of an Advocate; his father founded mason-lodges under Charles Edward, the English Prince or Pretender. Maximilien the first-born was thriftily educated; he had brisk Camille Desmoulins for schoolmate in the College of Louis le Grand, at Paris. But he begged our famed Necklace-Cardinal, Rohan, the patron, to let him depart thence, and resign in favour of a younger brother. The strict-minded Max departed; home to paternal Arras; and even had a Law-case there and pleaded, not unsuccessfully, 'in favour of the first Franklin thunder-rod.' With a strict painful mind, an understanding small but clear and ready, he grew in favour with official persons, who could foresee in him an excellent man of business, happily quite free from genius. The Bishop, therefore, taking counsel, appoints him Judge of his diocese; and he faithfully does justice to the people: till behold, one day, a culprit comes whose crime merits hanging; and the strict-minded Max must abdicate, for his conscience will not permit the dooming of any son of Adam to die. A strict-minded, strait-laced man! A man unfit for Revolutions? Whose small soul, transparent wholesome-looking as small-ale, could by no chance ferment into virulent *alegar*,—the mother of ever new alegar, till all France were grown acetous virulent? We shall see.

Between which two extremes of grandest and meanest, so many grand and mean roll on, towards their several destinies, in that Procession! There is *Cazalès*, the learned young soldier; who shall become the eloquent orator of Royalism, and earn the shadow of a name. Experienced *Mounier*, experienced *Malouet*; whose Presidential Parlementary experience the stream of things shall soon leave stranded. A *Pétion* has left his gown and briefs at Chartres for a stormier sort of pleading; has not forgotten his violin, being fond of music. His hair is grizzled, though he is still young: convictions,

beliefs placid-unalterable are in that man; not hindmost of
them, belief in himself. A Protestant-clerical *Rabaut-St-
Étienne*, a slender young eloquent and vehement *Barnave*,
will help to regenerate France. There are so many of them
young. Till thirty the Spartans did not suffer a man to
marry: but how many men here under thirty; coming to produce not one sufficient citizen, but a nation and a world of
such! The old to heal up rents; the young to remove
rubbish:—which latter, is it not, indeed, the task here?

Dim, formless from this distance, yet authentically there,
thou noticest the Deputies from Nantes? To us mere clothes-
screens, with slouch-hat and cloak, but bearing in their pocket
a *Cahier* of *doléances* with this singular clause, and more such,
in it: 'That the master wigmakers of Nantes be not troubled
with new guild-brethren, the actually existing number of ninety-
two being more than sufficient!' The Rennes people have
elected Farmer *Gérard;* 'a man of natural sense and rectitude, without any learning.' He walks there, with solid step;
unique, 'in his rustic farmer-clothes;' which he will wear
always, careless of short-cloaks and costumes. The name
Gérard, or '*Père Gérard*, Father Gérard,' as they please to
call him, will fly far: borne about in endless banter; in
Royalist satires, in Republican didactic Almanacks. As for
the man Gérard, being asked once, what he did, after trial
of it, candidly think of this Parlementary work,—"I think,"
answered he, "that there are a good many scoundrels among
us." So walks Father Gérard; solid in his thick shoes,
whithersoever bound.

And worthy *Doctor Guillotin*, whom we hoped to behold
one other time? If not here, the Doctor should be here, and
we see him with the eye of prophecy: for indeed the Parisian
Deputies are all a little late. Singular Guillotin, respectable
practitioner; doomed by a satiric destiny to the strangest
immortal glory that ever kept obscure mortal from his resting-place, the bosom of oblivion! Guillotin can improve the
ventilation of the Hall; in all cases of medical police and
hygiène be a present aid: but, greater far, he can produce his
'Report on the Penal Code;' and reveal therein a cunningly
devised Beheading Machine, which shall become famous and
world-famous. This is the product of Guillotin's endeavours,
gained not without meditation and reading; which product
popular gratitude or levity christens by a feminine derivative
name, as if it were his daughter: *La Guillotine!* "With my

machine, Messieurs, I whisk off your head (*vous fais sauter la tête*) in a twinkling, and you have no pain ;"—whereat they all laugh. Unfortunate Doctor ! For two-and-twenty years he, unguillotined, shall hear nothing but guillotine, see nothing but guillotine; then dying, shall through long centuries wander, as it were, a disconsolate ghost, on the wrong side of Styx and Lethe ; his name like to outlive Cæsar's.

See *Bailly*, likewise of Paris, time-honoured Historian of Astronomy Ancient and Modern. Poor Bailly, how thy serenely beautiful Philosophising, with its soft moonshiny clearness and thinness, ends in foul thick confusion — of Presidency, Mayorship, diplomatic Officiality, rabid Triviality, and the throat of everlasting Darkness ! Far was it to descend from the heavenly galaxy to the *Drapeau Rouge :* beside that fatal dung-heap, on that last hell-day, thou must 'tremble,' though only with cold, '*de froid.*' Speculation is not practice : to be weak is not so miserable ; but to be weaker than our task. Wo the day when they mounted thee, a peaceable pedestrian, on that wild Hippogryff of a Democracy ; which, spurning the firm earth, nay lashing at the very *stars,* no yet known Astolpho could have ridden !

In the Commons Deputies there are Merchants, Artists, Men of Letters ; three hundred and seventy-four Lawyers ; and at least one Clergyman : the *Abbé Sieyès.* Him also Paris sends, among its twenty. Behold him, the light thin man ; cold, but elastic, wiry; instinct with the pride of Logic ; passionless, or with but one passion, that of self-conceit. If indeed that can be called a passion, which, in its independent concentrated greatness, seems to have soared into transcendentalism ; and to sit there with a kind of god-like indifference, and look down on passion ! He is the man, and wisdom shall die with him. This is the Sieyès who shall be System-builder, Constitution-builder General ; and build Constitutions (as many as wanted) skyhigh,—which shall all unfortunately fall before he get the scaffolding away. "*La Politique,*" said he to Dumont, "Polity is a science I think I have completed (*achevée*)." What things, O Sieyès, with thy clear assiduous eyes, art thou to see ! But were it not curious to know how Sieyès, now in these days (for he is said to be still alive) looks out on all that Constitution masonry, through the rheumy soberness of extreme age ? Might we hope, still with the old irrefragable transcendentalism ? The victorious cause pleased the gods, the vanquished one pleased Sieyès (*victa Catoni*).

Thus, however, amid skyrending *vivats*, and blessings from every heart, has the Procession of the Commons Deputies rolled by.

Next follow the Noblesse, and next the Clergy; concerning both of whom it might be asked, What they specially have come for? Specially, little as they dream of it, to answer this question, put in a voice of thunder: What are you doing in God's fair Earth and Task-garden; where whosoever is not working is begging or stealing? Wo, wo to themselves and to all, if they can only answer: Collecting tithes, Preserving game!—Remark meanwhile how *D'Orléans* affects to step before his own Order, and mingle with the Commons. For him are *vivats*: few for the rest, though all wave in plumed 'hats of a feudal cut,' and have sword on thigh; though among them is *D'Antraigues*, the young Languedocian gentleman,—and indeed many a Peer more or less noteworthy.

There are *Liancourt*, and *La Rochefoucault*; the liberal Anglo-maniac Dukes. There is a filially pious *Lally*; a couple of liberal *Lameths*. Above all, there is a *Lafayette*; whose name shall be Cromwell-Grandison, and fill the world Many a 'formula' has this Lafayette too made away with; yet not *all* formulas. He sticks by the Washington-formula; and by that he will stick;—and hang by it, as by sure bower-anchor hangs and swings the tight warship, which, after all changes of wildest weather and water, is found still hanging. Happy for him; be it glorious or not! Alone of all Frenchmen he has a theory of the world, and right mind to conform thereto; he can become a hero and perfect character, were it but the hero of one idea. Note further our old Parlementary friend, *Crispin-Catiline d'Esprémenil*. He is returned from the Mediterranean Islands, a redhot royalist, repentant to the finger ends;—unsettled-looking; whose light, dusky-glowing at best, now flickers foul in the socket: whom the National Assembly will by and by, to save time, 'regard as in a state of distraction.' Note lastly that globular *Younger* Mirabeau: indignant that his elder Brother is among the Commons: it is *Viscomte* Mirabeau: named oftener Mirabeau *Tonneau* (Barrel Mirabeau), on account of his rotundity, and the quantities of strong liquor he contains.

There then walks our French Noblesse. All in the old pomp of chivalry: and yet, alas, how changed from the old position; drifted far down from their native latitude, like Arctic icebergs got into the Equatorial sea, and fast thawing there! Once these Chivalry *Duces* (Dukes, as they are still named) did actually *lead* the world,—were it only towards battle-spoil, where lay the world's best wages then: moreover, being the ablest Leaders going, they had their lion's share, those *Duces*; which none could grudge them. But now, when so many Looms, improved Ploughshares, Steam-Engines, and Bills of Exchange have been invented; and, for battle-brawling itself, men hire Drill-Sergeants at eighteen-pence a-day,—what mean these goldmantled Chivalry Figures, walking there 'in black velvet cloaks,' in high-plumed 'hats of a feudal cut?' Reeds shaken in the wind!

The Clergy have got up; with *Cahiers* for abolishing pluralities, enforcing residence of bishops, better payment of tithes. The Dignitaries, we can observe, walk stately, apart from the numerous Undignified,—who indeed are properly little other than Commons disguised in Curate-frocks. Here, however, though by strange ways, shall the Precept be fulfilled, and they that are greatest (much to their astonishment) become least. For one example, out of many, màrk that plausible *Grégoire*; one day Curé Grégoire shall be a Bishop, when the now stately are wandering distracted, as Bishops *in partibus*. With other thought, mark also the *Abbé Maury*; his broad bold face; mouth accurately primmed; full eyes, that ray out intelligence, falsehood,—the sort of sophistry which is astonished you should find it sophistical. Skilfullest vamper up of old rotten leather, to make it look like new; always a rising man; he used to tell Mercier, "You will see; I shall be in the Academy before you." Likely indeed, thou skilfullest Maury; nay thou shalt have a Cardinal's Hat, and plush and glory; but alas, also, in the longrun—mere oblivion, like the rest of us; and six feet of earth! What boots it, vamping rotten leather on these terms? Glorious in comparison is the livelihood thy good old Father earns, by making shoes,—one may hope, in a sufficient manner. Maury does not want for audacity. He shall wear pistols, by and by; and, at death-cries of "*La Lanterne*, The Lamp-iron!"—answer coolly, "Friends, will you see better there?"

But yonder, halting lamely along, thou noticest next *Bishop Talleyrand-Périgord*, his Reverence of Autun. A sardonic grimness lies in that irreverend Reverence of Autun. He will do and suffer strange things; and will *become* surely one of the strangest things ever seen, or like to be seen. A man living in falsehood, and on falsehood; yet not what you can call a false

man: there is the specialty! It will be an enigma for future
ages, one may hope: hitherto such a product of Nature and
Art was possible only for this age of ours,—Age of Paper, and
of the Burning of Paper. Consider Bishop Talleyrand and
Marquis Lafayette as the topmost of their two kinds; and say
once more, looking at what they did and what they were, *O
Tempus ferax rerum!*

On the whole, however, has not this unfortunate Clergy also
drifted in the Time-stream, far from its native latitude? An
anomalous mass of men; of whom the whole world has already
a dim understanding that it can understand nothing. They
were once a Priesthood, interpreters of Wisdom, revealers of
the Holy that is in Man; a true *Clerus* (or Inheritance of God
on Earth): but now?—They pass silently, with such *Cahiers*
as they have been able to redact; and none cries, God bless
them.

King Louis with his Court brings up the rear: he cheerful,
in this day of hope, is saluted with plaudits; still more Necker
his Minister. Not so the Queen; on whom hope shines not
steadily any more. Ill-fated Queen! Her hair is already gray
with many cares and crosses; her first-born son is dying in
these weeks: black falsehood has ineffaceably soiled her name;
ineffaceably while this generation lasts. Instead of *Vive la
Reine*, voices insult her with *Vive d'Orléans*. Of her queenly
beauty little remains except its stateliness; not now gracious,
but haughty, rigid, silently enduring. With a most mixed
feeling, wherein joy has no part, she resigns herself to a day
she hoped never to have seen. Poor Marie Antoinette; with
thy quick noble instincts; vehement glancings, vision all-
too fitful narrow for the work thou hast to do! O there are
tears in store for thee; bitterest wailings, soft womanly meltings,
though thou hast the heart of an imperial Theresa's Daughter.
Thou doomed one, shut thy eyes on the future!—

And so, in stately Procession, have passed the Elected of
France. Some towards honour and quick fire-consummation;
most towards dishonour; not a few towards massacre, confusion,
emigration, desperation: all towards Eternity!—So many heterogeneities cast together into the fermenting-vat; there, with
incalculable action, counteraction, elective affinities, explosive
developments, to work out healing for a sick moribund System
of Society! Probably the strangest Body of Men, if we consider well, that ever met together on our Planet on such an

errand. So thousandfold complex a Society, ready to burst up from its infinite depths; and these men, its rulers and healers, without life-rule for themselves—other life-rule than a Gospel according to Jean Jacques! To the wisest of them, what we must call the wisest, man is properly an Accident under the sky. Man is without Duty round him; except it be 'to make the Constitution.' He is without Heaven above him, or Hell beneath him; he has no God in the world.

What further or better belief can be said to exist in these Twelve Hundred? Belief in high-plumed hats of a feudal cut; in heraldic scutcheons; in the divine right of Kings, in the divine right of Game-destroyers. Belief, or what is still worse, canting half-belief; or worst of all, mere Machiavelic pretence-of-belief,—in consecrated dough-wafers, and the godhood of a poor old Italian Man! Nevertheless in that immeasurable Confusion and Corruption, which struggles there so blindly to become less confused and corrupt, there is, as we say, this one salient-point of a New Life discernible; the deep fixed Determination to have done with Shams. A determination, which, consciously or unconsciously, is *fixed;* which waxes ever more fixed, into every madness and fixed-idea; which in such embodiment as lies provided there, shall now unfold itself rapidly: monstrous, stupendous, unspeakable; new for long thousands of years!—How has the Heaven's *light,* oftentimes in this Earth, to clothe itself in thunder and electric murkiness; and descend as molten *lightning,* blasting, if purifying! Nay is it not rather the very murkiness, and atmospheric suffocation, that *brings* the lightning and the light? The new Evangel, as the old had been, was it to be born in the Destruction of a World?

But how the Deputies assisted at High Mass, and heard sermon, and applauded the preacher, church as it was, when he preached politics; how, next day, with sustained pomp, they are, for the first time, installed in their *Salle des Menus* (Hall no longer of *Amusements*), and become a States-General, —readers can fancy for themselves. The King from his *estrade,* gorgeous as Solomon in all his glory, runs his eye over that majestic Hall; many-plumed, many-glancing; bright-tinted as rainbow, in the galleries and near side-spaces, where Beauty sits raining bright influence. Satisfaction, as one that after long voyaging had got to port, plays over his broad simple face: the innocent King! He rises and speaks, with sonorous tone, a conceivable speech. With which, still more with the succeeding one-hour and two-hour speeches of Garde-des-Sceaux and M. Necker, full of nothing but patriotism, hope, faith, and deficiency of the revenue,—no reader of these pages shall be tried.

We remark only that, as his Majesty, on finishing the speech, put on his plumed hat, and the Noblesse according to custom imitated him, our Tiers-Etat Deputies did mostly, not without a shade of fierceness, in like manner clap on, and even crush on their slouched hats: and stand there awaiting the issue. Thick buzz among them, between majority and minority of *Couvrez-vous*, *Découvrez-vous* (Hats off, Hats on)! To which his Majesty puts end, by taking *off* his own royal hat again.

The session terminates without further accident or omen than this; with which, significantly enough, France has opened her States-General.

BOOK V

THE THIRD ESTATE

CHAPTER I

INERTIA

THAT exasperated France, in this same National Assembly of hers, has got something, nay something great, momentous, indispensable, cannot be doubted; yet still the question were: Specially *what?* A question hard to solve, even for calm onlookers at this distance; wholly insoluble to actors in the middle of it. The States-General, created and conflated by the passionate effort of the whole Nation, is there as a thing high and lifted up. Hope, jubilating, cries aloud that it will prove a miraculous Brazen Serpent in the Wilderness; whereon whosoever looks, with faith and obedience, shall be healed of all woes and serpent-bites.

We may answer, it will at least prove a symbolic Banner; round which the exasperated complaining Twenty-five Millions, otherwise isolated and without power, may rally, and work— what it is in them to work. If battle must be the work, as one cannot help expecting, then shall it be a battle-banner (say, an Italian Gonfalon, in its old Republican *Carroccio*); and shall tower up, car-borne, shining in the wind; and with iron tongue peal forth many a signal. A thing of prime necessity; which whether in the van or in the centre, whether leading or led and driven, must do the fighting multitude incalculable services. For a season, while it floats in the very front, nay as it were stands solitary there, waiting whether force will gather round it, this same National *Carroccio*, and the signal peals it rings, are a main object with us.

The omen of the 'slouch-hats clapt on' shows the Commons Deputies to have made up their minds on one thing: that neither Noblesse nor Clergy shall have precedence of them; hardly even Majesty itself. To such length has the *Contrat Social*, and force of public opinion, carried us. For what is

Majesty but the Delegate of the Nation; delegated, and bargained with (even rather tightly),—in some very singular posture of affairs, which Jean Jacques has not fixed the date of?

Coming therefore into the Hall, on the morrow, an inorganic mass of Six Hundred individuals, these Commons Deputies perceive, without terror, that they have it all to themselves. Their Hall is also the Grand or General Hall for all the Three Orders. But the Noblesse and Clergy, it would seem, have retired to their two separate Apartments, or Halls; and are there 'verifying their powers,' not in a conjoint but in a separate capacity. They are to constitute two separate, perhaps separately-voting Orders, then? It is as if both Noblesse and Clergy had silently taken for granted that they already are such! Two Orders against one; and so the Third Order to be left in a perpetual minority?

Much may remain unfixed; but the negative of that is a thing fixed: in the Slouch-hatted heads, in the French Nation's head. Double representation, and all else hitherto gained, were otherwise futile, null. Doubtless, the 'powers must be verified;'—doubtless the Commission, the electoral Documents of your Deputy must be inspected by his brother Deputies, and found valid: it is the preliminary of all. Neither is this question, of doing it separately or doing it conjointly, a vital one: but if it lead to such? It must be resisted? wise was that maxim, Resist the beginnings! Nay were resistance unadvisable, even dangerous, yet surely pause is very natural: pause, with Twenty-five Millions behind you, may become resistance enough.—The inorganic mass of Commons Deputies will restrict itself to a 'system of inertia,' and for the present remain inorganic.

Such methods, recommendable alike to sagacity, and to timidity, do the Commons Deputies adopt; and, not without adroitness, and with ever more tenacity, they persist in it, day after day, week after week. For six weeks their history is of the kind named barren; which indeed, as Philosophy knows, is often the fruitfullest of all. These were their still creation-days; wherein they sat incubating! In fact, what they did was to do nothing, in a judicious manner. Daily the inorganic body reassembles; regrets that they cannot get organisation, 'verification of powers in common,' and begin regenerating France. Headlong motions may be made, but let such be repressed; inertia alone is at once unpunishable and unconquerable.

Cunning must be met by cunning; proud pretension by inertia, by a low tone of patriotic sorrow; low, but incurable, unalterable. Wise as serpents; harmless as doves: what a spectacle for France. Six hundred inorganic individuals, essential for its regeneration and salvation, sit there, on their elliptic benches, longing passionately towards life; in painful durance; like souls waiting to be born. Speeches are spoken; eloquent; audible within doors and without. Mind agitates itself against mind; the Nation looks on with ever deeper interest. Thus do the Commons Deputies sit incubating.

There are private conclaves, supper-parties, consultations; Breton Club, Club of Viroflay; germs of many Clubs. Wholly an element of confused noise, dimness, angry heat;—wherein, however, the Eros-egg, kept at the fit temperature, may hover safe, unbroken till it be hatched. In your Mouniers, Malouets, Lechapeliers is science sufficient for that; fervour in your Barnaves, Rabauts. At times shall come an inspiration from royal Mirabeau: he is nowise yet recognised as royal; nay he was 'groaned at,' when his name was first mentioned: but he is struggling towards recognition.

In the course of the week, the Commons having called their Eldest to the chair, and furnished him with young stronger-lunged assistants,—can speak articulately; and, in audible lamentable words, declare, as we said, that they are an inorganic body, longing to become organic. Letters arrive; but an inorganic body cannot open letters; they lie on the table unopened. The Eldest may at most procure for himself some kind of List or Muster-roll, to take the votes by; and wait what will betide. Noblesse and Clergy are all elsewhere: however, an eager public crowds all galleries and vacancies; which is some comfort. With effort, it is determined, not that a Deputation shall be sent, for how can an inorganic body send deputations?—but that certain individual Commons Members shall, in an accidental way, stroll into the Clergy Chamber, and then into the Noblesse one; and mention there, as a thing they have happened to observe, that the Commons seem to be sitting waiting for them, in order to verify their powers. That is the wiser method!

The Clergy, among whom are such a multitude of Undignified, of mere Commons in Curates' frocks, depute instant respectful answer that they are, and will now more than ever

be, in deepest study as to that very matter. Contrariwise the
Noblesse, in cavalier attitude. reply, after four days, that they,
for their part, are all verified and constituted; which, they had
trusted, the Commons also were; such *separate* verification
being clearly the proper constitutional wisdom-of-ancestors
method;—as they the Noblesse will have much pleasure in
demonstrating by a Commission of their number, if the
Commons will meet them, Commission against Commission !
Directly in the rear of which comes a deputation of Clergy,
reiterating, in their insidious conciliatory way, the same proposal. Here then is a complexity: what will wise Commons
say to this ?

Warily, inertly, the wise Commons, considering that they
are, if not a French Third Estate, at least an Aggregate of
individuals pretending to some title of that kind, determine,
after talking on it five days, to name such a Commission,—
though, as it were, with proviso not to be convinced: a sixth
day is taken up in naming it ; a seventh and an eighth day in
getting the forms of meeting, place, hour and the like, settled :
so that it is not till the evening of the 23d of May that
Noblesse Commission first meets Commons Commission,
Clergy acting as Conciliators ; and begins the impossible task
of convincing it. One other meeting, on the 25th, will suffice:
the Commons are inconvincible, the Noblesse and Clergy
irrefragably convincing ; the Commissions retire ; each Order
persisting in its first pretensions.

Thus have three weeks passed. For three weeks, the Third
Estate Carroccio, with far-seen Gonfalon, has stood stockstill,
flouting the wind ; waiting what force would gather round it.

Fancy can conceive the feeling of the Court ; and how
counsel met counsel and loud-sounding inanity whirled in that
distracted vortex, where wisdom could not dwell. Your cunningly devised Taxing-Machine has been got together ; set up
with incredible labour ; and stands there, its three pieces in
contact ; its two fly-wheels of Noblesse and Clergy, its huge
working-wheel of Tiers État. The two fly-wheels whirl in the
softest manner ; but, prodigious to look upon, the huge working-wheel hangs motionless, refuses to stir ! The cunningest
engineers are at fault. How *will* it work, when it does begin ?
Fearfully, my Friends ; and to many purposes ; but to gather
taxes, or grind court-meal, one may apprehend, never. Could
we but have continued gathering taxes *by hand !* Messeigneurs
d'Artois, Conti, Condé (named Court Triumvirate), they of

the anti-democratic *Mémoire au Roi*, has not their foreboding proved true? They may wave reproachfully their high heads; they may beat their poor brains; but the cunningest engineers can do nothing. Necker himself, were he even listened to, begins to look blue. The only thing one sees advisable is to bring up soldiers. New regiments, two, and a battalion of a third, have already reached Paris; others shall get in march. Good were it in all circumstances, to have troops within reach; good that the command were in sure hands. Let Broglie be appointed: old Marshal Duke de Broglie: veteran disciplinarian, of a firm drill-sergeant morality, such as may be depended on.

For, alas, neither are the Clergy, or the very Noblesse what they should be; and might be, when so menaced from without: entire, undivided within. The Noblesse, indeed, have their Catiline or Crispin D'Espréménil, dusky-glowing, all in renegade heat: their boisterous Barrel-Mirabeau; but also they have their Lafayettes, Liancourts, Lameths, above all, their D'Orléans, now cut forever from his Court-moorings, and musing drowsily of high and highest sea-prizes (for is not he too a son of Henri Quatre, and partial potential Heir-Apparent?)—on his voyage towards Chaos. From the Clergy again, so numerous are the Curés, actual deserters have run over: two small parties; in the second party Curé Grégoire. Nay there is talk of a whole Hundred and Forty-nine of them about to desert in mass, and only restrained by an Archbishop of Paris. It seems a losing game.

But judge if France, if Paris sat idle, all this while! Addresses from far and near flow in: for our Commons have now grown organic enough to open letters. Or indeed to cavil at them! Thus poor Marquis de Brézé, Supreme Usher, Master of Ceremonies, or whatever his title was, writing about this time on some ceremonial matter, sees no harm in winding up with a 'Monsieur, yours with sincere attachment.'—"To whom does it address itself, this sincere attachment?" inquires Mirabeau, "To the Dean of the Tiers-État."—"There is no man in France entitled to write that," rejoins he; whereat the Galleries and the world will not be kept from applauding. Poor De Brézé! These Commons have a still older grudge at him; nor has he yet done with them.

In another way, Mirabeau has had to protest against the quick suppression of his newspaper, *Journal of the States-General;*—and to continue it under a new name. In which

act of valour, the Paris Electors, still busy redacting their
Cahier, could not but support him, by Address to his Majesty:
they claim utmost 'provisory freedom of the press;' they
have spoken even about demolishing the Bastille, and erecting
a Bronze Patriot King on the site!—These are the rich
Burghers: but now consider how it went, for example, with
such loose miscellany, now all grown eleutheromanaic, of
Loungers, Prowlers, social Nondescripts (and the distilled
Rascality of our Planet), as whirls forever in the Palais Royal;
—or what low infinite groan, fast changing into a growl, comes
from Saint Antoine, and the Twenty-five Millions in danger of
starvation!

There is the indisputablest scarcity of corn;—be it Aristo-
crat-plot, D'Orléans-plot, of this year; or drought and hail of
last year: in city and province, the poor man looks
desolately towards a nameless lot. And this States-General,
that could make us an age of gold, is forced to stand motionless; cannot get its powers verified! All industry necessarily
languishes, if it be not that of making motions.

In the Palais Royal there has been erected, apparently by
subscription, a kind of Wooden Tent (*en planches de bois*);
—most convenient; where select Patriotism can now redact
resolutions, deliver harangues, with comfort, let the weather
be as it will. Lively is that Satan-at-Home! On his table,
on his chair, in every *café*, stands a patriotic orator; a crowd
round him within; a crowd listening from without, open-
mouthed, through the door and window; with 'thunders of
applause for every sentiment of more than common hardiness.'
In Monsieur Dessein's Pamphlet-shop, close by, you cannot
without strong elbowing get to the counter: every hour produces its pamphlet, or litter of pamphlets; 'there were thirteen
today, sixteen yesterday, ninety-two last week.' Think of
Tyranny and Scarcity; Fervid-eloquence, Rumour, Pamphleteering; *Société Publicole*, Breton Club, Enraged Club;—and
whether every tap-room, coffee-room, social reunion, accidental
street group, over wide France, was not an Enraged Club!

To all which the Commons Deputies can only listen with
a sublime inertia of sorrow; reduced to busy themselves 'with
their internal police.' Surer position no Deputies ever occupied; if they keep it with skill. Let not the temperature rise
too high; break not the Eros-egg till it be hatched, till it
break itself! An eager public crowds all Galleries and vacancies; 'cannot be restrained from applauding.' The two

Privileged Orders, the Noblesse all verified and constituted, may look on with what face they will; not without a secret tremor of heart. The Clergy, always acting the part of conciliators, make a clutch at the Galleries, and the popularity there; and miss it. Deputation of them arrives, with dolorous message about the 'dearth of grains,' and the necessity there is of casting aside vain formalities, and deliberating on this. An insidious proposal; which, however, the Commons (moved thereto by sea-green Robespierre) dexterously accepts as a sort of hint, or even pledge, that the clergy will forthwith come over to them, constitute the States-General, and *so* cheapen grains!—Finally, on the 27th day of May, Mirabeau, judging the time now nearly come, proposes that 'the inertia cease;' that, leaving the Noblesse to their own stiff ways, the Clergy be summoned, 'in the name of the God of Peace,' to join the Commons, and begin. To which summons if they turn a deaf ear,—we shall see! Are not one Hundred and Forty-nine of them ready to desert?

O Triumvirate of Princes, new Garde-des-Sceaux Barentin, thou Home-Secretary Breteuil, Duchess Polignac, and Queen eager to listen,—what is now to be done? This Third Estate will get in motion, with the force of all France in it; Clergy-machinery with Noblesse-machinery, which were to serve as beautiful counterbalances and drags, will be shamefully dragged after it,—and take fire along with it. What is to be done? The Œil-de-Bœuf waxes more confused than ever. Whisper and counter-whisper; a very tempest of whispers! Leading men from all the Three Orders are nightly spirited thither; conjurors many of them; but can they conjure this? Necker himself were now welcome, could he interfere to purpose.

Let Necker interfere, then; and in the King's name! Happily that incendiary 'God-of-Peace' message is not yet *answered*. The Three Orders shall again have conferences; under this Patriot Minister of theirs, somewhat may be healed, clouted up;—we meanwhile getting forward Swiss Regiments, and a 'hundred pieces of field-artillery.' This is what the Œil-de-Bœuf, for its part, resolves on.

But as for Necker—Alas, poor Necker, thy obstinate Third Estate has one first-last word, *verification in common*, as the pledge of voting and deliberating in common! Half-way proposals, from such a tried friend, they answer with a stare. The tardy conferences speedily break up: the Third Estate, now ready and resolute, the whole world backing it, returns to its Hall of the Three Orders; and Necker to the Œil-de-Bœuf with the character of a disconjured conjuror there,—fit only for dismissal.

And so the Commons Deputies are at last on their own strength getting under way? Instead of Chairman, or Dean, they have now got a President: Astronomer Bailly. Under way, with a vengeance! With endless vociferous and temperate eloquence, borne on Newspaper wings to all lands, they have now, on this 17th day of June, determined that their name is not *Third Estate*, but—*National Assembly!* They then are the Nation? Triumvirate of Princes, Queen, refractory Noblesse and Clergy, what then are *you?* A most deep question;—scarcely answerable in living political dialects.

All regardless of which, our new National Assembly proceeds to appoint a 'committee of subsistences:' dear to France, though it can find little or no grain. Next, as if our National Assembly stood quite firm on its legs,—to appoint 'four other standing committees:' then to settle the security of the National Debt: then that of the Annual Taxation: all within eight-and-forty hours. At such rate of velocity it is going: the conjurors of the Œil-de-Bœuf may well ask themselves, Whither?

CHAPTER II

MERCURY DE BRÉZÉ

Now surely were the time for a 'god from the machine;' there is a *nodus* worthy of one. The only question is, Which god? Shall it be Mars de Broglie, with his hundred pieces of cannon?—Not yet, answers prudence; so soft irresolute is King Louis. Let it be Messenger *Mercury*, our Supreme Usher de Brézé!

On the morrow, which is the 20th of June, these Hundred and Forty-nine false Curates, no longer restrainable by his Grace of Paris, will desert in a body: let De Brézé intervene, and produce—closed doors! Not only shall there be Royal Session, in that Salle des Menus; but no meeting, nor working (except by carpenters), till then. Your Third Estate, self-styled 'National Assembly,' shall suddenly see itself extruded from its Hall, by carpenters, in this dexterous way; and reduced to do nothing, not even to meet, or articulately lament,—till Majesty, with *Séance Royale* and new miracles, be ready! In this manner shall De Brézé, as Mercury *ex machinâ*, intervene; and, if the Œil-de-Bœuf mistake not, work deliverance from the *nodus*.

Of poor De Brézé we can remark that he has yet prospered in none of his dealings with these Commons. Five weeks ago, when they kissed the hand of Majesty, the mode he took got nothing but censure; and then his 'sincere attachment,' how was it scornfully whiffed aside! Before supper, this night, he writes to President Bailly, a new Letter, to be delivered shortly after dawn tomorrow, in the King's name. Which Letter however, Bailly, in the pride of office, will merely crush together into his pocket, like a bill he does not mean to pay.

Accordingly on Saturday morning the 20th of June, shrill-sounding heralds proclaim, through the streets of Versailles, that there is to be *Séance Royale* next Monday; and no meeting of the States-General till then. And yet, we observe, President Bailly, in sound of this, and with De Brézé's Letter in his pocket, is proceeding, with National Assembly at his heels, to the accustomed Salle des Menus; as if De Brézé and heralds were mere wind. It is shut, this Salle; occupied by Gardes Françaises. "Where is your Captain?" The Captain shows his royal order: workmen, he is grieved to say, are all busy setting up the platform for his Majesty's *Séance;* most unfortunately, no admission; admission, at furthest, for President and Secretaries to bring away papers, which the joiners might destroy! President Bailly enters with Secretaries; and returns bearing papers: alas, within doors, instead of patriotic eloquence, there is now no noise but hammering, sawing, and operative screeching and rumbling! A profanation without parallel.

The Deputies stand grouped on the Paris Road, on this umbrageous *Avenue de Versailles;* complaining aloud of the indignity done them. Courtiers, it is supposed, look from their windows, and giggle. The morning is none of the comfortablest: raw; it is even drizzling a little. But all travellers pause; patriot gallery men, miscellaneous spectators increase the groups. Wild counsels alternate. Some desperate Deputies propose to go and hold session on the great outer Staircase at Marly, under the King's windows; for his Majesty, it seems, has driven over thither. Others talk of making the Château Forecourt, what they call *Place d'Armes*, a Runnymede and new *Champ de Mai* of free Frenchmen: nay of awakening, to sounds of indignant Patriotism, the echoes of the Œil-de-Bœuf itself.—Notice is given that President Bailly, aided by judicious Guillotin and others, has found place in the Tennis-Court of the Rue St. François. Thither, in long-drawn files, hoarse-jingling, like cranes on wing, the Commons Deputies angrily wend.

Strange sight was this in the Rue St. François, Vieux Versailles! A naked Tennis-Court, as the Pictures of that time still give it: four walls; naked, except aloft some poor wooden pent-house, or roofed spectators'-gallery, hanging round them: —on the floor not now an idle teeheeing, a snapping of balls and rackets; but the bellowing din of an indignant National Representation, scandalously exiled hither! However, a cloud of witnesses looks down on them, from wooden pent-house, from wall-top, from adjoining roof and chimney; rolls towards them from all quarters, with passionate spoken blessings. Some table can be procured to write on; some chair, if not to sit on, then to stand on. The Secretaries undo their tapes; Bailly has constituted the Assembly.

Experienced Mounier, not wholly new to such things, in Parlementary revolts, which he has seen or heard of, thinks that it were well, in these lamentable threatening circumstances, to unite themselves by an oath.—Universal acclamation, as from smouldering bosoms getting vent! The Oath is redacted; pronounced aloud by President Bailly,—and indeed in such a sonorous tone, that the cloud of witnesses, even out doors, hear it, and bellow response to it. Six hundred right-hands rise with President Bailly's, to take God above to witness that they will not separate for man below, but will meet in all places, under all circumstances, wheresoever two or three can get together, till they have made the Constitution. Made the Constitution, Friends! That is a long task. Six hundred hands, meanwhile, will sign as they have sworn; six hundred save *one;* one Loyalist Abdiel, still visible by this sole light-point, and namable, poor 'M. Martin d'Auch, from Castelnaudary, in Languedoc.' Him they permit to sign or signify refusal; they even save him from the cloud of witnesses, by declaring 'his head deranged.' At four o'clock, the signatures are all appended; new meeting is fixed for Monday morning, earlier than the hour of the Royal Session; that our Hundred and Forty-nine Clerical deserters be not balked: we will meet 'at the Recollets Church or else-

where,' in hope that our Hundred and Forty-nine will join us;
—and now it is time to go to dinner.

This then is the Session of the Tennis-court, famed *Séance
du Jeu de Paume;* the fame of which has gone forth to all
lands. This is Mercurius de Brézé's appearance as *Deus ex
machinâ;* this is the fruit it brings! The giggle of Courtiers
in the Versailles Avenue has already died into gaunt silence.
Did the distracted Court, with Garde-des-Sceaux Barentin,
Triumvirate and Company, imagine that they could scatter six
hundred National Deputies, big with a National Constitution,
like as much barndoor poultry, big with next to nothing,—by
the white or black rod of a Supreme Usher? Barndoor poultry
fly cackling: but National Deputies turn round, lion-faced;
and, with uplifted right-hand, swear an Oath that makes the
four corners of France tremble.

President Bailly has covered himself with honour; which
shall become rewards. The National Assembly is now doubly
and trebly the Nation's Assembly; not militant, martyred
only, but triumphant; insulted, and which could not *be* insulted. Paris disembogues itself once more, to witness, 'with
grim looks,' the *Séance Royale:* which, by a new felicity, is
postponed till Tuesday. The Hundred and Forty-nine, and
even with Bishops among them, all in processional mass, have
had free leisure to march off, and solemnly join the Commons
sitting waiting in their Church. The Commons welcomed
them with shouts, with embracings, nay with tears; for it is
growing a life-and-death matter now.

As for the *Séance* itself, the Carpenters seem to have accomplished their platform; but all else remains unaccomplished.
Futile, we may say fatal, was the whole matter. King Louis
enters, through seas of people, all grim-silent, angry, with many
things,—for it is a bitter rain too. Enters, to a Third Estate,
likewise grim-silent; which has been wetted waiting under
mean porches, at back-doors, while Court and Privileged were
entering by the front. King and Garde-des-Sceaux (there is
no Necker visible) made known, not without long-windedness,
the determinations of the royal breast. The Three Orders
shall vote separately. On the other hand, France may look
for considerable constitutional blessings; as specified in these
Five-and-thirty Articles, which Garde-des-Sceaux is waxing
hoarse with reading. Which Five-and-thirty Articles, adds his
Majesty again rising, if the Three Orders most unfortunately
cannot agree together to effect them, I myself will effect: "*seul*

je ferai le bien de mes peuples,"—which being interpreted may
signify, You, contentious Deputies of the States-General, have
probably not long to be here! But, in fine, all shall now withdraw for this day; and meet again, each Order in its separate
place, tomorrow morning for despatch of business. *This* is
the determination of the royal breast: pithy and clear. And
herewith King, retinue, Noblesse, majority of Clergy file out,
as if the whole matter were satisfactorily completed.

These file out; through grim-silent seas of people. Only
the Commons Deputies file not out; but stand there in gloomy
silence, uncertain what they shall do. One man of them is
certain; one man of them discerns and dares! It is now that
King Mirabeau starts to the Tribune, and lifts up his lion-
voice. Verily a word in season; for, in such scenes, the
moment is the mother of ages! Had not Gabriel Honoré
been there,—one can well fancy, how the Commons Deputies,
affrighted at the perils which now yawned dim all round them,
and waxing ever paler in each other's paleness, might very
naturally, one after one, have *glided off;* and the whole course
of European History have been different!

But he is there. List to the *brool* of that royal forest-voice;
sorrowful, low; fast swelling to a roar! Eyes kindle at the
glance of his eye:—National Deputies were missioned by a
Nation; they have sworn an Oath; they—But lo! while the
lion's voice roars loudest, what Apparition is this? Apparition
of Mercurius de Brézé, muttering somewhat!—"Speak out,"
cry several.—"Messieurs," shrills De Brézé, repeating himself,
"You have heard the King's orders!"—Mirabeau glares on
him with fire-flashing face; shakes the black lion's mane:
"Yes, Monsieur, we have heard what the King was advised to
say: and you, who cannot be the interpreter of his orders to
the States-General; you, who have neither place nor right of
speech here; *you* are not the man to remind us of it. Go,
Monsieur, tell those who sent you that we are here by the will
of the People, and that nothing but the force of bayonets shall
send us hence!" And poor De Brézé shivers forth from the
National Assembly;—and also (if it be not in one faintest
glimmer, months later) finally from the page of History!—

Hapless De Brézé; doomed to survive long ages, in men's
memory, in this faint way, with tremulent white rod! He was
true to Etiquette, which was his Faith here below; a martyr
to respect of persons. Short woollen cloaks could not kiss
Majesty's hand as long velvet ones did. Nay lately, when the

poor little Dauphin lay dead, and some ceremonial Visitation came, was he not punctual to announce it even to the Dauphin's *dead body*: "Monseigneur, a Deputation of the States-General!" *Sunt lachrymæ rerum.*

But what does the Œil-de-Bœuf, now when De Brézé shivers back thither? *Despatch* that same force of bayonets? Not so: the seas of people still hang multitudinous, intent on what is passing; nay rush and roll, loud-billowing, into the Courts of the Château itself; for a report has arisen that Necker is to be dismissed. Worst of all, the Gardes Françaises seem indisposed to act: 'two Companies of them *do not fire* when ordered!' Necker, for not being at the ·*Séance*, shall be shouted for, carried home in triumph; and must not be dismissed. His Grace of Paris, on the other hand, has to fly with broken coach-panels, and owe his life to furious driving. The *Gardes-du-Corps* (Body-Guards), which you were drawing out, had better be drawn in again. There is no sending of bayonets to be thought of.

Instead of soldiers, the Œil-de-Bœuf sends—carpenters, to take down the platform. Ineffectual shift! In few instants, the very carpenters cease wrenching and knocking at their platform; standing on it, hammer in hand, and listen open-mouthed. The Third Estate is decreeing that it is, was, and will be, nothing but a National Assembly; and now, moreover, an inviolable one, all members of it inviolable; 'infamous, traitorous, towards the Nation, and guilty of capital crime, is any person, body-corporate, tribunal, court or commission that now or henceforth, during the present session or after it, shall dare to pursue, interrogate, arrest, or cause to be arrested, detain or cause to be detained, any,' &c., &c., 'on *whose part soever* the same be commanded.' Which done, one can wind up with this comfortable reflection from Abbé Sieyès: "Messieurs, you are today what you were yesterday."

Courtiers may shriek; but it is, and remains, even so. Their well-charged explosion has exploded *through the touchhole;* covering themselves with scorches, confusion, and unseemly soot! Poor Triumvirate, poor Queen; and above all, poor Queen's Husband, who means well, had he any fixed meaning! Folly is that wisdom which is wise only behindhand. Few months ago these Thirty-five Concessions had filled France with a rejoicing, which might have lasted for several years. Now it is unavailing, the very mention of it slighted; Majesty's express orders set at naught.

All France is in a roar; a sea of persons, estimated at 'ten thousand,' whirls 'all this day in the Palais Royal.' The remaining Clergy, and likewise some Forty-eight Noblesse, D'Orléans among them, have now forthwith gone over to the victorious Commons;—by whom, as is natural, they are received 'with acclamation.'

The Third Estate triumphs; Versailles Town shouting round it; ten thousand whirling all day in the Palais Royal; and all France standing a-tiptoe, not unlike whirling! Let the Œil-de-Bœuf look to it. As for King Louis, he will swallow his injuries; will temporise, keep silence; will at all costs have present peace. It was Tuesday, the 23d of June, when he spoke that peremptory royal mandate; and the week is not done till he has written to the remaining obstinate Noblesse, that they also must oblige him, and give in. D'Espréménil rages his last; Barrel Mirabeau 'breaks his sword,' making a vow,—which he might as well have kept. The 'Triple Family' is now therefore complete; the third erring brother, the Noblesse, having joined it;—erring but pardonable; soothed, as far as possible, by sweet eloquence from President Bailly.

So triumphs the Third Estate; and States-General are become National Assembly; and all France may sing *Te Deum*. By wise inertia, and wise cessation of inertia, great victory has been gained. It is the last night of June: all night you meet nothing on the streets of Versailles but 'men running with torches,' with shouts and jubilation. From the 2nd of May when they kissed the hand of Majesty, to this 30th of June, when men run with torches, we count eight weeks and three days. For eight weeks the National Carroccio has stood far-seen, ringing many a signal; and, so much having now gathered round it, may hope to stand.

CHAPTER III

BROGLIE THE WAR-GOD

The Court feels indignant that it is conquered; but what then? Another time it will do better. Mercury descended in vain; now has the time come for Mars.—The gods of the Œil-de-Bœuf have withdrawn into the darkness of their cloudy Ida; and sit there, shaping and forging what may be needful, be it 'billets of a new National Bank,' munitions of war, or things for ever inscrutable to men.

Accordingly, what means this 'apparatus of troops?' The National Assembly can get no furtherance for its Committee of Subsistences; can hear only that, at Paris, the Bakers' shops are besieged; that, in the Provinces, people are 'living on meal-husks and boiled grass.' But on all highways there hover dust-clouds, with the march of regiments, with the trailing of cannon: foreign Pandours, of fierce aspect; Salis-Samade, Esterhazy, Royal-Allemand; so many of them foreign; to the number of thirty thousand,—which fear can magnify to fifty: all wending towards Paris and Versailles! Already, on the heights of Montmartre, is a digging and delving; too like a scarping and trenching. The effluence of Paris is arrested Versailles-ward by a barrier of cannon at Sèvres Bridge. From the Queen's Mews, cannon stand pointed on the National Assembly Hall itself. The National Assembly has its very slumbers broken by the tramp of soldiery, swarming and de-filing, endless, or seemingly endless, all round those spaces, at dead of night, 'without drum-music, without audible word of command.' What means it?

Shall eight, or even shall twelve Deputies, our Mirabeaus, Barnaves at the head of them, be whirled suddenly to the Castle of Ham; the rest ignominiously dispersed to the winds? No National Assembly can make the Constitution with cannon levelled on it from the Queen's Mews! What means this reticence of the Œil-de-Bœuf, broken only by nods and shrugs? In the mystery of that cloudy Ida, what is it that they forge and shape?—Such questions must distracted Patriotism keep asking, and receive no answer but an echo.

Questions and echo bad enough in themselves:—and now, above all, while the hungry food-year, which runs from August to August, is getting older; becoming more and more a famine-year! With 'meal-husks and boiled grass,' Brigands may actually collect; and, in crowds, at farm and mansion, howl angrily, *Food! Food!* It is in vain to send soldiers against them: at sight of soldiers they disperse, they vanish as under ground; then directly reassemble elsewhere for new tumult and plunder. Frightful enough to look upon; but what to *hear* of, reverberated through Twenty-five Millions of suspicious minds! Brigands and Broglie, open Conflagration, preternatural Rumour are driving mad most hearts in France. What will the issue of these things be?

At Marseilles, many weeks ago, the Townsmen have taken arms : for 'suppressing of Brigands,' and other purposes : the military Commandant may make of it what he will. Elsewhere, everywhere, could not the like be done? Dubious, on the distracted Patriot Imagination, wavers, as a last deliverance, some foreshadow of a *National Guard*. But conceive, above all, the Wooden Tent in the Palais Royal! A universal hubbub there, as of dissolving worlds : there loudest bellows the mad, mad-making voice of Rumour ; there sharpest gazes Suspicion into the pale dim World-Whirlpool ; discerning shapes and phantasms : imminent bloodthirsty Regiments camped on the Champ-de-Mars ; dispersed National Assembly ; redhot cannon-balls (to burn Paris) :—the mad War-god and Bellona's sounding thongs. To the calmest man it is becoming too plain that battle is inevitable.

Inevitable, silently nod Messeigneurs and Broglie : Inevitable and brief! Your National Assembly, stopped short in its Constitutional labours, may fatigue the royal ear with addresses and remonstrances : those cannon of ours stand duly levelled ; those troops are here. The King's Declaration, with its Thirty-five too generous Articles, was spoken, was not listened to ; but remains yet unrevoked : he himself shall effect it, *seul il fera !*

As for Broglie, he has his head-quarters at Versailles, all as in a seat of war : clerks writing ; significant staff-officers inclined to taciturnity : plumed aide-de-camps, scouts, orderlies flying or hovering. He himself looks forth, important, impenetrable ; listens to Besenval Commandant of Paris, and his warning and earnest counsels (for he has come out repeatedly on purpose), with a silent smile. The Parisians resist? scornfully cry Messeigneurs. As a meal-mob may! They have sat quiet, these five generations, submitting to all. Their Mercier declared, in these very years, that a Parisian revolt was henceforth 'impossible.' Stand by the royal Declaration, of the Twenty-third of June. The Nobles of France, valorous, chivalrous as of old, will rally round us with one heart ;—and as for this which you call Third Estate, and which we call *canaille* of unwashed Sansculottes, of Patelins, Scribblers, factious Spouters,—brave Broglie, 'with a whiff of grape-shot (*salve de canons*),' if need be, will give quick account of it. Thus reason they : on their cloudy Ida ; hidden from men,—men also hidden from them.

Good is grapeshot, Messeigneurs, on one condition : that

the shooter also were made of metal! But unfortunately h
is made of flesh; under his buffs and bandoleers, your hire
shooter has instincts, feelings, even a kind of thought. It i
his kindred, bone of his bone, this same *canaille* that shall b
whiffed; he has brothers in it, a father and mother,—living o
meal-husks and boiled grass. His very doxy, not yet 'dead i
the spital,' drives him into military heterodoxy; declares tha
if he shed Patriot blood, he shall be accursed among men
The soldier, who has seen his pay stolen by rapacious Foulons
his blood wasted by Soubises, Pompadours, and the gates o
promotion shut inexorably on him if he were not born noble
—is himself not without griefs against you. Your cause i
not the soldier's cause; but, as would seem, your own only
and no other god's nor man's.

For example, the world may have heard how, at Béthun
lately, when there rose some 'riot about grains,' of which sor
there are so many, and the soldiers stood drawn out, an
the word 'Fire!' was given,—not a trigger stirred; only th
butts of all muskets rattled angrily against the ground; and
the soldiers stood glooming, with a mixed expression o
countenance;—till clutched 'each under the arm of a patrio
householder,' they were all hurried off, in this manner, t
be treated and caressed, and have their pay increased by sub
scription!

Neither have the Gardes Françaises, the best regiment of th
line, shown any promptitude for street-firing lately. The
returned grumbling from Réveillon's; and have not burn
a single cartridge since; nay, as we saw, not even when bid
A dangerous humour dwells in these Gardes. Notable me
too, in their way! Valadi the Pythagorean was, at one time
an officer of theirs. Nay, in the ranks, under the three
cornered felt and cockade, what hard heads may there not be
and reflections going on,—unknown to the public! One hea
of the hardest we do now discern there: on the shoulder
of a certain Sergeant Hoche. Lazare Hoche, that is the nam
of him; he used to be about the Versailles Royal Stables
nephew of a poor herb-woman; a handy lad; exceedingl
addicted to reading. He is now Sergeant Hoche, and can ris
no further: he lays out his pay in rushlights, and chea
editions of books.

On the whole, the best seems to be: Consign these Garde
Françaises to their Barracks. So Besenval thinks, and orders
Consigned to their barracks, the Gardes Françaises do bu

form a 'Secret Association,' an Engagement not to act against
the National Assembly. Debauched by Valadi the Pythagorean; debauched by money and women! cry Besenval and
innumerable others. Debauched by what you will, or in need
of no debauching, behold them, long files of them, their consignment broken, arrive, headed by their Sergeants, on the
26th day of June, at the Palais Royal! Welcome with vivats,
with presents, and a pledge of patriot liquor; embracing and
embraced; declaring in words that the cause of France is their
cause! Next day and the following days the like. What
is singular too, except this patriot humour and breaking of
their consignment, they behave otherwise with 'the most
rigorous accuracy.'

They are growing questionable, these Gardes! Eleven
ring-leaders of them are put in the Abbaye Prison. It boots
not in the least. The imprisoned Eleven have only, 'by the
hand of an individual,' to drop, towards nightfall, a line in the
Café de Foy; where Patriotism harangues loudest on its
table. 'Two hundred young persons, soon waxing to four
thousand,' with fit crowbars roll towards the Abbaye; smite
asunder the needful doors; and bear out their Eleven, with
other military victims:—to supper in the Palais Royal Garden:
to board, and lodging 'in camp-beds, in the *Théâtre des
Variétés;*' other national *Prytaneum* as yet not being in readiness. Most deliberate! Nay so punctual were these young
persons, that finding one military victim to have been imprisoned for real civil crime, they returned him to his cell, with
protest.

Why new military force was not called out? New military
force was called out. New military force did arrive, full
gallop, with drawn sabre; but the people gently 'laid hold of
their bridles;' the dragoons sheathed their swords; lifted their
caps by way of salute, and sat like mere statues of dragoons,
—except indeed that a drop of liquor being brought them, they
'drank to the King and Nation with the greatest cordiality!'

And now, ask in return, why Messeigneurs and Broglie the
great god of war, on seeing these things did not pause; and
take some other course, any other course? Unhappily, as we
said, they could see nothing. Pride, which goes before a fall;
wrath, if not reasonable, yet pardonable, most natural, had
hardened their hearts and heated their heads: so with imbecility and violence (ill-matched pair) they rush to seek their
hour. All Regiments are not Gardes Françaises, or de-

bauched by Valadi the Pythagorean : let fresh undebauched
Regiments come up ; let Royal-Allemand, Salis-Samade, Swiss
Château-Vieux come up,—which can fight, but can hardly
speak except in German gutturals ; let soldiers march, and
highways thunder with artillery-waggons : Majesty has a *new*
Royal Session to hold,—and miracles to work there ! The
whiff of grape-shot can, if needful, become a blast and
tempest.

In which circumstances, before the redhot balls begin raining, may not the Hundred-and-twenty Paris Electors, though
their *Cahier* is long since finished, see good to meet again
daily, as an ' Electoral Club ?' They meet first 'in a Tavern ;
where ' a large wedding-party ' cheerfully gives place to them.
But latterly they meet in the *Hôtel-de-Ville*, in the Townhall
itself. Flesselles, Provost of Merchants, with his Four
Echevins (*Scabins*, Assessors) could not prevent it ; such was
the force of public opinion. He, with his Echevins, and
the Six-and-Twenty Town-Councillors, all appointed from
Above, may well sit silent there, in their long gowns ; and
consider, with awed eye, what prelude this is of convulsion
coming from Below, and how they themselves shall fare in
that !

CHAPTER IV

TO ARMS !

So hangs it, dubious, fateful, in the sultry days of July. It is
the passionate printed *advice* of M. Marat, to abstain, of all
things, from violence. Nevertheless the hungry poor are
already burning Town Barriers, where Tribute on eatables
is levied ; getting clamorous for food.

The twelfth July morning is Sunday: the streets are all placarded with an enormous-sized *De par le Roi*, 'inviting peaceable citizens to remain within doors,' to feel no alarm, to gather
in no crowd. Why so? What mean these 'placards of enormous
size?' Above all, what means this clatter of military; dragoons,
hussars, rattling in from all points of the compass towards the
Place Louis Quinze : with a staid gravity of face, though
saluted with mere nicknames, hootings and even missiles?
Besenval is with them. Swiss Guards of his are already in the
Champs Elysées, with four pieces of artillery.

Have the destroyers descended on us, then? From the Bridge of Sèvres to utmost Vincennes. from Saint-Denis to the Champ-des-Mars, we are begirt! Alarm, of the vague unknown, is in every heart. The Palais Royal has become a place of awestruck interjections, silent shakings of the head: one can fancy with what dolorous sound the noontide cannon (which the Sun fires at crossing of his meridian) went off there; bodeful, like an inarticulate voice of doom. Are these troops verily come out 'against Brigands?' Where are the Brigands? What mystery is in the wind?—Hark! a human voice reporting articulately the Job's-news: *Necker, People's Minister, Saviour of France, is dismissed.* Impossible, incredible! Treasonous to the public peace! Such a voice ought to be choked in the water-works;—had not the news-bringer quickly fled. Nevertheless, friends, make of it what ye will, the news is true. Necker is gone. Necker hies north-ward incessantly, in obedient secrecy, since yesternight. We have a new Ministry: Broglie the War-god; Aristocrat Breteuil; Foulon who said the people might eat grass!

Rumour, therefore, shall arise; in the Palais Royal, and in broad France. Paleness sits on every face: confused tremor and fremescence; waxing into thunder-peals, of Fury stirred on by Fear.

But see Camille Desmoulins, from the Café de Foy, rushing out, sibylline in face; his hair streaming, in each hand a pistol! He springs to a table: the Police satellites are eyeing him; alive they shall not take him, not they alive him alive. This time he speaks without stammering:—Friends! shall we die like hunted hares? Like sheep hounded into their pin-fold; bleating for mercy, where is no mercy, but only a whetted knife? The hour is come; the supreme hour of Frenchman and Man; when Oppressors are to try conclusions with Oppressed; and the word is, swift Death, or Deliverance forever. Let such hour be *well*-come! Us, meseems, one cry only befits: To Arms! Let universal Paris, universal France, as with the throat of a whirlwind, sound only: To arms!—"To arms!" yell responsive the innumerable voices; like one great voice, as of a Demon yelling from the air: for all faces wax fire-eyed. all hearts burn up into madness. In such, or fitter words, does Camille evoke the Elemental Powers, in this great moment.—Friends, continues Camille, some rallying sign! Cockades; green ones;—the colour of

Hope!—As with the flight of locusts, these green tree-leaves
green ribands from the neighbouring shops; all green thing
are snatched, and made cockades of. Camille descends from
his table; 'stifled with embraces, wetted with tears;' has a
bit of green ribbon handed him; sticks it in his hat. And
now to Curtius' Image-shop there; to the Boulevards; to the
four winds, and rest not till France be on fire!

France, so long shaken and wind-parched, is probably at the
right inflammable point.—As for poor Curtius, who, one
grieves to think, might be but imperfectly paid,—he cannot
make two words about his Images. The Wax-bust of Necker
the Wax-bust of D'Orléans, helpers of France: these, covered
with crape, as in funeral procession, or after the manner of
suppliants appealing to Heaven, to Earth, and Tartarus itself
a mixed multitude bears off. For a sign! As indeed man
with his singular imaginative faculties, can do little or nothing
without signs; thus Turks look to their Prophet's Banner
also Osier *Mannikins* have been burnt, and Necker's Portrait
has erewhile figured, aloft on its perch (p. 91).

In this manner march they, a mixed, continually increasing
multitude; armed with axes, staves and miscellanea; grim
many-sounding, through the streets. Be all Theatre shut; le
all dancing on planked floor, or on the natural greensward
cease! Instead of a Christian Sabbath, and feast of *guinguette*
tabernacles, it shall be a Sorcerer's Sabbath; and Paris, gone
rabid, dance,—with the Fiend for piper!

However, Besenval, with horse and foot, is in the Place
Louis Quinze. Mortals promenading homewards, in the fall
of the day, saunter by, from Chaillot or Passy, from flirtation
and a little thin wine; with sadder step than usual. Will the
Bust-Procession pass that way? Behold it; behold also
Prince Lambesc dash forth on it, with his Royal-Allemands
Shots fall, and sabre-strokes; Busts are hewed asunder; and
alas, also heads of men. A sacred Procession has nothing
for it but to *explode*, along what streets, alleys, Tuilerie
Avenues it finds; and disappear. One unarmed man lie
hewed down; a Garde Française by his uniform: bear him
(or bear even the report of him) dead and gory to his
Barracks;—where he has comrades still alive!

But why not now, victorious Lambesc, charge through that
Tuileries Garden itself, where the fugitives are vanishing
Not show the Sunday promenaders too how steel glitters

besprent with blood; that it be told of, and men's ears tingle?—Tingle alas, they did; but the wrong way. Victorious Lambesc, in this his second or Tuileries charge, succeeds but in overturning (call it not slashing, for he struck with the flat of his sword) one man, a poor old schoolmaster, most pacifically tottering there; and is driven out, by barricade of chairs, by flights of 'bottles and glasses,' by execrations in bass-voice and treble. Most delicate is the mob-queller's vocation; wherein Too-much may be as bad as Not-enough. For each of these bass-voices, and more each treble voice, borne to all parts of the City, rings now nothing but distracted indignation; will ring all night. The cry, *To arms*, roars tenfold; steeples with their metal storm-voice boom out, as the sun sinks; armorers' shops are broken open, plundered; the streets are a living foam sea, chafed by all the winds.

Such issue came of Lambesc's charge on the Tuileries Garden; no striking of salutary terror into Chaillot promenaders; a striking into broad wakefulness of Frenzy and the three Furies,—which otherwise were not asleep! For they lie always, those subterranean Eumenides (fabulous and yet so true), in the dullest existence of man;—and can dance, brandishing their dusky torches, shaking their serpent-hair. Lambesc with Royal-Allemand may ride to his barracks, with curses for his marching-music; then ride back again, like one troubled in mind: vengeful Gardes Françaises, *sacre*ing, with knit brows, start out on him, from their barracks in the Chaussé d'Antin; pour a volley into him (killing and wounding); which he must not answer, but ride on.

Counsel dwells not under the plumed hat. If the Eumenides awaken, and Broglie has given no orders, what can a Besenval do? When the Gardes Françaises, with Palais-Royal volunteers, roll down, greedy of more vengeance, to the Place Louis Quinze itself, they find neither Besenval, Lambesc, Royal-Allemand, nor any soldier now there. Gone is military order. On the far Eastern Boulevard, of Saint-Antoine, the Chasseurs Normandie arrive, dusty, thirsty, after a hard day's ride; but can find no billet-master, see no course in this City of confusions; cannot get to Besenval, cannot so much as discover where he is: Normandie must even bivouack there, in its dust and thirst,—unless some patriot will treat it to a cup of liquor, with advices.

Raging multitudes surround the Hôtel-de-Ville, crying: Arms! Orders! The Six-and-twenty Town-Councillors, with

their long gowns, have ducked under (into the raging chaos);
—shall never emerge more. Besenval is painfully wriggling
himself out, to the Champ-de-Mars; he must sit there 'in the
cruellest uncertainty!' courier after courier may dash off for
Versailles; but will bring back no answer, can hardly bring
himself back. For the roads are all blocked with batteries
and pickets, with floods of carriages arrested for examination:
such was Broglie's one sole order; the Œil-de-Bœuf, hearing
in the distance such mad din, which sounded almost like
invasion, will before all things keep its own head whole. A
new Ministry, with, as it were, but one foot in the stirrup,
cannot take leaps. Mad Paris is abandoned altogether to
itself.

What a Paris, when the darkness fell! A European metro-
politan City hurled suddenly forth from its old combinations
and arrangements; to crash tumultuously together, seeking
new. Use and wont will now no longer direct any man;
each man with what of originality he has, must begin thinking; or following those that think. Seven hundred thousand
individuals, on the sudden, find all their old paths, old ways of
acting, and deciding, vanish from under their feet. And so
there go they, with clangour and terror, they know not as yet
whether running, swimming, or flying,—headlong into the
New Era. With clangour and terror: from above, Broglie,
the war-god, impends, preternatural, with his redhot cannon-
balls; and from below a preternatural Brigand-world menaces
with dirk and firebrand: madness rules the hour.

Happily, in place of the submerged Twenty-six, the Electoral
Club is gathering; has declared itself a 'Provisional Municipality.' On the morrow, it will get Provost Flesselles, with an
Échevin or two, to give help in many things. For the present
it decrees one most essential thing: that forthwith a 'Parisian
Militia' shall be enrolled. Depart, ye heads of Districts, to
labour in this great work; while we here, in Permanent Committee, sit alert. Let fencible men, each party in its own
range of streets, keep watch and ward, all night. Let Paris
court a little fever-sleep; confused by such fever-dreams, of
'violent motions at the Palais Royal;'—or from time to time
start awake, and look out, palpitating, in its nightcap, at the
clash of discordant mutually-unintelligible Patrols; on the
gleam of distant Barriers, going up all-too ruddy towards the
vault of Night.

CHAPTER V

GIVE US ARMS

On Monday, the huge City has awoke, not to its week-day industry: to what a different one! The working man has become a fighting man; has one want only: that of arms. The industry of all crafts has paused;—except it be the smith's, fiercely hammering pikes; and, in a faint degree, the kitchener's, cooking offhand victuals, for *bouche va toujours*. Women too are sewing cockades;— not now of *green*, which being D'Artois colour, the Hôtel-de-Ville has had to interfere in it; but of *red* and *blue*, our old Paris colours: these, once based on a ground of constitutional *white*, are the famed TRICOLOR,—which (if Prophecy err not) 'will go round the world.'

All shops, unless it be the Bakers' and Vintners', are shut: Paris is in the streets;—rushing, foaming like some Venice wine-glass into which you had dropped poison. The tocsin, by order, is pealing madly from all steeples. Arms, ye Elector Municipals; thou Flesselles with thy Échevins give us arms! Flesselles gives what he can: fallacious, perhaps insidious promises of arms from Charleville; order to seek arms here, order to seek them there. The new Municipals give what they can; some three hundred and sixty indifferent firelocks, the equipment of the City-watch: 'a man in wooden shoes, and without coat, directly clutches one of them, and mounts guard.' Also as hinted, an order to all Smiths to make pikes with their whole soul.

Heads of Districts are in fervent consultation; subordinate Patriotism roams distracted, ravenous for arms. Hitherto at the Hôtel-de-Ville was only such modicum of indifferent fire-locks as we have seen. At the so-called Arsenal, there lies nothing but rust, rubbish and saltpetre,—overlooked too by the guns of the Bastille. His Majesty's Repository, what they call *Garde-Meuble*, is forced and ransacked: tapestries enough, and gauderies; but of serviceable fighting-gear small stock! Two silver-mounted cannons there are; an ancient gift from his Majesty of Siam to Louis Fourteenth; gilt sword of the Good Henri; antique Chivalry arms and armour. These, and such as these, a necessitous Patriotism snatches greedily, for want of better. The Siamese cannons go trundling, on an errand they were not meant for. Among the indifferent fire-locks are seen tournay-lances; the princely helm and hauberk glittering amid ill-hatted heads,—as in a time when all times and their possessions are suddenly sent jumbling!

At the *Maison de Saint-Lazare*, Lazar-House once, now a Correction-House with Priests, there was no trace of arms; but, on the other hand, corn, plainly to a culpable extent. Out with it, to market; in this scarcity of grains! Heavens, will 'fifty-two carts,' in long row, hardly carry it to the *Halle aux Bleds*? Well truly, ye reverend Fathers, was your pantry filled; fat are your larders; over-generous your wine-bins, ye plotting exasperators of the Poor; traitorous forestallers of bread!

Vain is protesting, entreaty on bare knees: the House of Saint-Lazarus has that in it which comes not out by protesting. Behold, how, from every window, it *vomits:* mere torrents of furniture, of bellowing and hurlyburly;—the cellars also leaking wine. Till, as was natural, smoke rose,—kindled, some say, by the desperate Saint-Lazaristes themselves, desperate of other riddance! and the Establishment vanished from this world in flame. Remark nevertheless that 'a thief' (set on or not by Aristocrats), being detected there, is 'instantly hanged.'

Look also at the Châtelet Prison. The Debtors' Prison of La Force is broken from without; and they that sat in bondage to Aristocrats go free: hearing of which the Felons at the Châtelet do likewise 'dig up their pavements,' and stand on the offensive; with the best prospects,—had not Patriotism, passing that way, 'fired a volley' into the Felon-world; and crushed it down again under hatches. Patriotism consorts not with thieving and felony: surely also Punishment, this day, hitches (if she still hitch) after Crime, with frightful shoes-of-swiftness! 'Some score or two' of wretched persons, found prostrate with drink in the cellars of that Saint-Lazare, are indignantly haled to prison: the Jailor has no room; whereupon, other place of security not suggesting itself, it is written, '*on les pendit*, they hanged them.' Brief is the word; not without significance, be it true or untrue!

In such circumstances, the Aristocrat, the unpatriotic rich man is packing up for departure. But he shall not get departed. A wooden-shod force has seized all Barriers, burnt or not: all that enters, all that seeks to issue, is stopped there, and dragged to the Hôtel-de-Ville: coaches, tumbrils, plate, furniture, 'many meal-sacks,' in time even 'flocks and herds' encumber the Place de Grève.

And so it roars, and rages, and brays: drums beating, steeples pealing; criers rushing with hand-bells: "Oyez, oyez, All men to their Districts to be enrolled!" The Districts have met in gardens, open squares; are getting marshalled into volunteer troops. No redhot ball has yet fallen from Besenval's Camp; on the contrary, Deserters with their arms are continually dropping in: nay now, joy of joys, at two in the afternoon, the Gardes Françaises, being ordered to Saint-Denis, and flatly declining, have come over in a body! It is a fact worth many. Three thousand six hundred of the best fighting men, with complete accoutrement; with cannoneers even, and cannon! Their officers are left standing alone; could not so much as succeed in 'spiking the guns.' The very Swiss, it now may be hoped, Château-Vieux and the others, will have doubts about fighting.

Our Parisian Militia, which some think it were better to name National Guard,—is prospering as heart could wish. It promised to be forty-eight thousand; but will in few hours double and quadruple that number: invincible, if we had only arms!

But see, the promised **Charleville Boxes**, marked *Artillerie!* Here then are arms enough?—Conceive the blank face of Patriotism, when it found them filled with rags, foul linen, candle-ends, and bits of wood! Provost of the Merchants, how is this? Neither at the Chartreux Convent, whither we were sent with signed order, is there or ever was there any weapon of war. Nay here, in this Seine Boat, safe under tarpaulings (had not the nose of Patriotism been of the finest), are 'five thousand-weight of gunpowder;' not coming *in*, but surreptitiously going out! What meanest thou, Flesselles? 'Tis a ticklish game, that of 'amusing' us. Cat plays with captive mouse: but mouse with enraged cat, with enraged National Tiger?

Meanwhile, the faster, O ye black-aproned Smiths, smite; with strong arm and willing heart. This man and that, all stroke from head to heel, shall thunder alternating, and ply the great forge-hammer, till stithy reel and ring again; while ever and anon, overhead, booms the alarm-cannon,—for the City has now got gunpowder. Pikes are fabricated; fifty thousand of them, in six-and-thirty hours: judge whether the Black-aproned have been idle. Dig trenches, unpave the streets, ye others, assiduous, man and maid; cram the earth in barrel-barricades, at each of them a volunteer sentry; pile the whinstones in window-sills and upper rooms. Have scalding pitch, at least boiling water ready, ye weak old women, to pour it and dash it on Royal-Allemand, with your old skinny arms: your shrill curses along with it will not be wanting!—Patrols of the new-born National Guard, bearing torches, scour the streets, all that night; which otherwise are vacant, yet illuminated in every window by order. Strange-looking; like some naphtha-lighted City of the Dead, with here and there a flight of perturbed Ghosts.

O poor mortals, how ye make this Earth bitter for each other; this fearful and wonderful Life fearful and horrible; and Satan has his place in all hearts! Such agonies and ragings and wailings ye have, and have had, in all times:—to be buried all, in so deep silence; and the salt sea is not swoln with your tears.

Great meanwhile is the moment, when tidings of Freedom reach us; when the long-enthralled soul, from amid its chains and squalid stagnancy, arises, were it still only in blindness and bewilderment, and swears by Him that made it, that it will be *free!* Free? Understand that well, it is the deep commandment, dimmer or clearer, of our whole being, to be *free*. Freedom is the one purport, wisely aimed at, or unwisely, of all man's struggles, toilings and sufferings, in this Earth. Yes, supreme is such a moment (if thou have known it): first vision as of a flame-girt Sinai, in this our waste Pilgrimage,—which thenceforth wants not its pillar of cloud by day, and pillar of fire by night! Something it is even,—nay, something considerable, when the chains have grown *corrosive*, poisonous,—to be free 'from oppression by our fellow-man.' Forward, ye maddened sons of France; be it towards this destiny or towards that! Around you is but starvation, falsehood, corruption and the clam of death. Where ye are is no abiding.

Imagination may, imperfectly, figure how Commandant Besenval, in the Champ-de-Mars, has worn out these sorrowful hours. Insurrection raging all round; his men melting away! From Versailles, to the most pressing messages, comes no answer; or once only some vague word of answer which is worse than none. A Council of Officers can decide merely that there is no decision: Colonels inform him, 'weeping,' that they do not think their men will fight. Cruel uncertainty is here: war-god Broglie sits yonder, inaccessible in his Olympus; does not descend terror-clad, does not produce his whiff of grape-shot; sends no orders.

Truly, in the Château of Versailles all seems mystery: in the Town of Versailles, were we there, all is rumour, alarm and indignation. An august National Assembly sits, to appearance, menaced with death; endeavouring to defy death. It has resolved 'that Necker carries with him the regrets of the Nation.' It has sent solemn Deputation over to the Château, with entreaty to have these troops withdrawn. In vain: his Majesty, with a singular composure, invites us to be busy rather with our own duty, making the constitution! Foreign Pandours, and such like, go pricking and prancing, with a swashbuckler air; with an eye too probably to the *Salle des Menus*,—were it not for the 'grim-looking countenances' that crowd all avenues there. Be firm, ye National Senators; the cynosure of a firm, grim-looking people!

The august National Senators determine that there shall, at least, be Permanent Session till this thing end. Wherein however, consider that worthy Lafranc de Pompignan, our new President, whom we have named Bailly's successor, is an old man, wearied with many things. He is the Brother of that Pompignan who meditated lamentably on the Book of *Lamentations*:

> *Savez-vous pourquoi Jérémie*
> *Se lamentait toute sa vie?*
> *C'est qu'il prévoyait*
> *Que Pompignan le traduirait!*

Poor Bishop Pompignan withdraws; having got Lafayette for helper or substitute: this latter, as nocturnal Vice-President, with a thin house in disconsolate humour, sits sleepless, with lights unsnuffed;—waiting what the hours will bring.

So at Versailles. But at Paris, agitated Besenval, before retiring for the night, has stept over to old M. de Sombreuil, of the *Hôtel des Invalides* hard by. M. de Sombreuil has, what is a great secret, some eight-and-twenty-thousand stand of muskets deposited in his cellars there; but no trust in the temper of his Invalides. This day, for example, he sent twenty of the fellows down to unscrew those muskets; lest Sedition might snatch at them: but scarcely, in six hours, had the twenty unscrewed twenty gun-locks, or dogsheads (*chiens*) of locks,—each Invalide his dogshead! If ordered to fire, they would, he imagines, turn their cannon against himself.

Unfortunate old military gentlemen, it is your hour, not of

glory! Old Marquis de Launay too, of the Bastille, has pulled up his drawbridges long since, 'and retired into his interior;' with sentries walking on his battlements, under the midnight sky, aloft over the glare of illuminated Paris;—whom a National Patrol passing that way, takes the liberty of firing at: 'seven shots towards twelve at night,' which do not take effect. This was the 13th day of July 1789; a worse day, many said, than the last 13th was, when only hail fell out of Heaven, not madness rose out of Tophet, ruining worse than crops!

In these same days, as Chronology will teach us, hot old Marquis Mirabeau lies stricken down, at Argenteuil,—*not* within sound of these alarm-guns; for *he* properly is not there, and only the body of him now lies, deaf and cold forever. It was on Saturday night that he, drawing his last life-breaths, gave up the ghost there;—leaving a world, which would never go to his mind, now broken out, seemingly, into deliration, and the *culbute général*. What is it to him, departing else-whither, on his long journey? The old Château Mirabeau stands silent, far off, on its scarped rock, in that 'gorge of two windy valleys;' the pale-fading spectre now of a Château: this huge World-riot, and France, and the World itself, fades also, like a shadow on the great still mirror-sea; and all shall be as God wills.

Young Mirabeau, sad of heart, for he loved this crabbed brave old Father, sad of heart, and occupied with sad cares,— is withdrawn from Public History. The great crisis transacts itself without him.

CHAPTER VI

STORM AND VICTORY

BUT, to the living and the struggling, a new, Fourteenth morning dawns. Under all roofs of this distracted City is the nodus of a drama, not untragical, crowding towards solution. The bustlings and preparings, the tremors and menaces; the tears that fell from old eyes! This day, my sons, ye shall quit you like men. By the memory of your fathers' wrongs, by the hope of your children's rights! Tyranny impends in red wrath: help for you is none, if not in your own right hands. This day ye must do or die.

From earliest light, a sleepless Permanent Committee has

heard the old cry, now waxing almost frantic, mutinous: Arms!
Arms! Provost Flesselles, or what traitors there are among
you, may think of those Charleville Boxes. A hundred-and-
fifty-thousand of us; and but the third man furnished with so
much as a pike! Arms are the one thing needful: with arms
we are an unconquerable man-defying National Guard; without
arms, a rabble to be whiffed with grapeshot.

Happily the word has arisen, for no secret can be kept,—
that there lie muskets at the *Hôtel des Invalides*. Thither will
we: King's Procureur M. Ethys de Corny, and whatsoever of
authority a Permanent Committee can lend, shall go with us.
Besenval's Camp is there; perhaps he will not fire on us; if
he kills us, we shall but die.

Alas, poor Besenval, with his troops melting away in that
manner, has not the smallest humour to fire! At five o'clock
this morning, as he lay dreaming, oblivious in the *École
Militaire*, a 'figure' stood suddenly at his bedside; 'with
face rather handsome; eyes inflamed, speech rapid and curt,
air audacious;' such a figure drew Priam's curtains! The
message and monition of the figure was, that resistance would
be hopeless; that if blood flowed, woe to him who shed it.
Thus spoke the figure: and vanished. 'Withal there was a
kind of eloquence that struck one.' Besenval admits that he
should have arrested him, but did not. Who this figure with
inflamed eyes, with speech rapid and curt, might be? Besenval
knows, but mentions not. Camille Desmoulins? Pythagorean
Marquis Valadi, inflamed with 'violent motions all night at
the Palais Royal?' Fame names him, 'Young M. Meillar';
then shuts her lips about him forever.

In any case, behold about nine in the morning, our National
Volunteers rolling in long wide flood, south-westward to the
Hôtel des Invalides; in search of the one thing needful. King's
Procureur M. Ethys de Corny and officials are there; the Curé
of Saint-Étienne du Mont marches unpacific, at the head of
his militant Parish; the Clerks of the Basoche in red coats
we see marching, now Volunteers of the Basoche; the Volunteers of the Palais Royal:—National Volunteers, numerable
by tens of thousands; of one heart and mind. The King's
muskets are the Nation's; think, old M. de Sombreuil, how,
in this extremity, thou wilt refuse them! Old M. de Sombreuil
would fain hold parley, send couriers; but it skills not: the
walls are scaled, no Invalide firing a shot; the gates must be
flung open. Patriotism rushes in, tumultuous, from grunsel

up to ridge-tile, through all rooms and passages; rummaging
distractedly for arms. What cellar, or what cranny can escape
it? The arms are found; all safe there; lying packed in
straw,—apparently with a view to being burnt! More ravenous
than famishing lions over dead prey, the multitude, with clangour and vociferation, pounces on them; struggling, dashing,
clutching:—to the jamming-up, to the pressure, fracture and
probable extinction of the weaker Patriot. And so, with such
protracted crash of deafening, most discordant Orchestra-music,
the Scene is changed; and eight-and-twenty thousand sufficient
firelocks are on the shoulders of as many National Guards,
lifted thereby out of darkness into fiery light.

Let Besenval look at the glitter of these muskets, as they
flash by: Gardes Françaises, it is said, have cannon levelled on
him; ready to open, if need were, from the other side of the
River. Motionless sits he; 'astonished,' one may flatter oneself, 'at the proud bearing (*fière contenance*) of the Parisians.'
—And now to the Bastille, ye intrepid Parisians! There
grapeshot still threatens: thither all men's thoughts and steps
are now tending.

Old De Launay, as we hinted, withdrew 'into his interior'
soon after midnight of Sunday. He remains there ever since,
hampered, as all military gentlemen now are, in the saddest
conflict of uncertainties. The Hôtel-de-Ville 'invites' him to
admit National Soldiers, which is a soft name for surrendering.
On the other hand, His Majesty's orders were precise. His
garrison is but eighty-two old Invalides, reinforced by thirty-
two young Swiss; his walls indeed are nine feet thick, he has
cannon and powder; but, alas, only one day's provision of
victuals. The city, too, is French, the poor garrison mostly
French. Rigorous old De Launay, think what thou wilt do!

All morning, since nine, there has been a cry every where:
To the Bastille! Repeated 'deputations of citizens' have been
here, passionate for arms; whom De Launay has got dismissed
by soft speeches through portholes. Towards noon, Elector
Thuriot de la Rosière gains admittance; finds De Launay indisposed for surrender; nay, disposed for blowing up the place
rather. Thuriot mounts with him to the battlements: heaps of
paving-stones, old iron and missiles lie piled; cannon all duly
levelled; in every embrasure a cannon,—only drawn back a
little! But outwards, behold, O Thuriot, how the multitude
flows on, welling through every street: tocsin furiously pealing,

all drums beating the *générale*: the Suburb Saint-Antoine
rolling hitherward wholly, as one man! Such vision (spectral
yet real) thou, O Thuriot, as from thy Mount of Vision,
beholdest in this moment: prophetic of what other Phantasmagories, and loud-gibbering Spectral Realities, which thou yet
beholdest not, but shalt! " *Que voulez-vous ?* " said De Launay,
turning pale at the sight, with an air of reproach, almost of
menace. "Monsieur," said Thuriot, rising into the moral
sublime, "what mean *you*? Consider if I could not precipi-
tate *both* of us from this height,"—say only a hundred feet, exclusive of the walled ditch! Whereupon De Launay fell
silent. Thuriot shows himself from some pinnacle, to comfort
the multitude becoming suspicious, fremescent: then descends;
departs with protest; with warning addressed also to the
Invalides,—on whom, however, it produces but a mixed indis-
tinct impression. The old heads are none of the clearest;
besides, it is said, De Launay has been profuse of beverages
(*prodigua des buissons*). They think they will not fire,—if not
fired on, if they can help it; but must, on the whole, be ruled
considerably by circumstances.

Wo to thee, De Launay, in such an hour, if thou canst not,
taking some one firm decision, *rule* circumstances! Soft
speeches will not serve; hard grapeshot is questionable; but
hovering between the two is *un*questionable. Ever wilder
swells the tide of men; their infinite hum waxing ever louder,
into imprecations, perhaps into crackle of stray musketry,—
which latter, on walls nine feet thick, cannot do execution.
The Outer Drawbridge has been lowered for Thuriot; new
deputation of citizens (it is the third, and noisiest of all) penetrates that way into the Outer Court: soft speeches producing
no clearance of these, De Launay gives fire; pulls up his
Drawbridge. A slight sputter;—which has *kindled* the too
combustible chaos; made it a roaring fire-chaos! Bursts forth
Insurrection, at sight of its own blood (for there were deaths
by that sputter of fire), into endless rolling explosion of
musketry, distraction, execration;—and over head, from the
Fortress, let one great gun, with its grapeshot, go booming, to
show what we *could* do. The Bastille is besieged!

On, then, all Frenchmen, that have hearts in your bodies!
Roar with all your throats, of cartilage and metal, ye Sons of
Liberty; stir spasmodically whatsoever of utmost faculty is in
you, soul, body, or spirit; for it is the hour! Smite, thou
Louis Tournay, cartwright of the Marais, old-soldier of the

Regiment Dauphiné; smite at that Outer Drawbridge chain, though the fiery hail whistles round thee! Never, over nave or felloe, did thy axe strike such a stroke. Down with it, man; down with it to Orcus: let the whole accursed Edifice sink thither, and Tyranny be swallowed up forever! Mounted, some say, on the roof of the guard-room, some 'on bayonets stuck into joints of the wall,' Louis Tournay smites, brave Aubin Bonnemère (also an old soldier) seconding him: the chain yields, breaks; the huge Drawbridge slams down, thundering (*avec fracas*). Glorious: and yet, alas, it is still but the outworks. The Eight grim Towers, with their Invalide musketry, their paving stones and cannon-mouths, still soar aloft intact;—Ditch yawning impassable, stone-faced; the inner Drawbridge with its *back* towards us: the Bastille is still to take!

To describe this Siege of the Bastille (thought to be one of the most important in History) perhaps transcends the talent of mortals. Could one but, after infinite reading, get to understand so much as the plan of the building! But there is open Esplanade, at the end of the Rue Saint-Antoine; there are such Forecourts, *Cour Avancée, Cour de l'Orme*, arched Gateway (where Louis Tournay now fights); then new draw-bridges, dormant-bridges, rampart-bastions, and the grim Eight Towers; a labyrinthic Mass, high-frowning there, of all ages from twenty years to four hundred and twenty;—beleaguered, in this its last hour, as we said, by mere Chaos come again! Ordnance of all calibres; throats of all capacities; men of all plans, every man his own engineer: seldom since the war of Pygmies and Cranes was there seen so anomalous a thing. Half-pay Elie is home for a suit of regimentals; no one would heed him in coloured clothes: half-pay Hulin is haranguing Gardes Françaises in the Place de Grève. Frantic Patriots pick up the grapeshots; bear them, still hot (or seemingly so), to the Hôtel-de-Ville;—Paris, you perceive, is to be burnt! Flesselles is 'pale to the very lips,' for the roar of the multitude grows deep. Paris wholly has got to the acme of its frenzy; whirled, all ways, by panic madness. At every street-barricade, there whirls simmering a minor whirlpool,—strengthening the barricade, since God knows what is coming; and all minor whirlpools play distractedly into that grand Fire-Mahlstrom which is lashing round the Bastille.

And so it lashes and it roars. Cholat the wine-merchant

has become an impromptu cannoneer. See Georget, of the Marine Service, fresh from Brest, ply the King of Siam's cannon. Singular (if we were not used to the like): Georget lay, last night, taking his ease at his inn; the King of Siam's cannon also lay, knowing nothing of *him*, for a hundred years. Yet now, at the right instant, they have got together, and discourse eloquent music. For, hearing what was toward, Georget sprang from the Brest Diligence, and ran. Gardes Françaises also will be here, with real artillery: were not the walls so thick!—Upwards from the Esplanade, horizontally from all neighbouring roofs and windows, flashes one irregular deluge of musketry, without effect. The Invalides lie flat, firing comparatively at their ease from behind stone; hardly through portholes, show the tip of a nose. We fall, shot; and make no impression!

Let conflagration rage; of whatsoever is combustible! Guard-rooms are burnt, Invalides mess-rooms. A distracted 'Peruke-maker with two fiery torches' is for burning 'the saltpetres of the Arsenal;'—had not a woman run screaming; had not a Patriot, with some tincture of Natural Philosophy, instantly struck the wind out of him (butt of musket on pit of stomach), overturned barrels, and stayed the devouring element. A young beautiful lady, seized escaping in these Outer Courts, and thought falsely to be De Launay's daughter, shall be burnt in De Launay's sight; she lies swooned on a paillasse: but again a Patriot, it is brave Aubin Bonnemère the old soldier, dashes in, and rescues her. Straw is burnt; three cartloads of it, hauled thither, go up in white smoke: almost to the choking of Patriotism itself; so that Elie had, with singed brows, to drag back one cart; and Réole the 'gigantic haberdasher' another. Smoke as of Tophet; confusion as of Babel; noise as of the Crack of Doom!

Blood flows; the aliment of new madness. The wounded are carried into houses of the Rue Cerisaie; the dying leave their last mandate not to yield till the accursed Stronghold fall. And yet, alas, how fall? The walls are so thick! Deputations, three in number, arrive from the Hôtel-de-Ville; Abbé Fauchet (who was of one) can say, with what almost superhuman courage of benevolence. These wave their Town-flag in the arched Gateway; and stand, rolling their drum; but to no purpose. In such Crack of Doom, De Launay cannot hear them, dare not believe them: they return, with justified rage, the whew of lead still singing in their ears.

What to do? The Firemen are here, squirting with their fire pumps on the Invalides cannon. to wet the touchholes; they unfortunately cannot squirt so high; but produce only clouds of spray. Individuals of classical knowledge propose *catapults*. Santerre, the sonorous Brewer of the Suburb Saint-Antoine, advises rather that the place be fired, by a 'mixture of phosphorus and oil-of-turpentine spouted up through forcing pumps:' O Spinola-Santerre, hast thou the mixture *ready*? Every man his own engineer! And still the fire-deluge abates not: even women are firing, and Turks; at least one woman (with her sweetheart), and one Turk. Gardes Françaises have come: real cannon, real cannoneers. Usher Maillard is busy; half-pay Elie, half-pay Hulin rage in the midst of thousands.

How the great Bastille Clock ticks (inaudible) in its Inner Court there, at its ease, hour after hour; as if nothing special, for it or the world, were passing! It tolled One when the firing began; and is now pointing towards Five, and still the firing slakes not.—Far down, in their vaults, the seven Prisoners hear muffled din as of earthquakes; their Turnkeys answer vaguely.

Wo to thee, De Launay, with thy poor hundred Invalides! Broglie is distant, and his ears heavy: Besenval hears, but can send no help. One poor troop of Hussars has crept, reconnoitering, cautiously along the Quais, as far as the Pont Neuf. "We are come to join you," said the Captain; for the crowd seems shoreless. A large-headed dwarfish individual of smoke-bleared aspect, shambles forward, opening his blue lips, for there is sense in him; and croaks: "Alight then, and give up your arms!" The Hussar-Captain is too happy to be escorted to the Barriers, and dismissed on parole. Who the squat individual was? Men answer, It is M. Marat, author of the excellent pacific *Avis au Peuple*! Great truly, O thou remarkable Dogleech, is this thy day of emergence and new-birth: and yet this same day come four years——!—But let the curtains of the Future hang.

What shall De Launay do? One thing only De Launay could have done: what he said he would do. Fancy him sitting, from the first, with lighted taper, within arm's length of the Powder-Magazine; motionless, like old Roman Senator, or Bronze Lamp-holder; coldly apprising Thuriot, and all men, by a slight motion of his eye, what his resolution was:—Harmless, he sat there, while unharmed; but the King's Fortress, meanwhile, could, might, would, or should, in nowise be surrendered, save to the King's Messenger: one old man's life is worthless, so it be lost with honour; but think, ye brawling *canaille*, how will it be when a whole Bastille springs skyward!—In such statuesque, taper-holding attitude, one fancies De Launay might have left Thuriot, the red Clerks of the Basoche, Curé of Saint-Stephen and all the tag-rag-and-bobtail of the world, to work their will.

And yet, withal, he could not do it. Hast thou considered how each man's heart is so tremulously responsive to the hearts of all men; hast thou noted how omnipotent is the very sound of many men? How their shriek of indignation palsies the strong soul; their howl of contumely withers with unfelt pangs? The Ritter Gluck confessed that the ground-tone of the noblest passage, in one of his noblest Operas, was the voice of the Populace he had heard at Vienna, crying to their Kaiser: Bread! Bread! Great is the combined voice of men; the utterance of their *instincts*, which are truer than their *thoughts:* it is the greatest a man encounters, among the sounds and shadows which make up this World of Time. He who can resist that, has his footing somewhere *beyond* Time. De Launay could not do it. Distracted, he hovers between two; hopes in the middle of despair; surrenders not his Fortress; declares that he will blow it up, seizes torches to blow it up, and does not blow it. Unhappy old De Launay, it is the death-agony of thy Bastille and thee! Jail, Jailor-ing, and Jailor, all three, such as they may have been, must finish.

For four hours now has the World-Bedlam roared: call it the World-Chimæra, blowing fire! The poor Invalides have sunk under their battlements, or rise only with reversed mus-kets: they have made a white flag of napkins; go beating the *chamade*, or seeming to beat, for one can hear nothing. The very Swiss at the Portcullis look weary of firing; disheartened in the fire-deluge: a porthole at the drawbridge is opened, as by one that would speak. See Huissier Maillard, the shifty man! On his plank, swinging over the abyss of that stone Ditch; plank resting on parapet, balanced by weight of Patriots, —he hovers perilous: such a Dove towards such an Ark! Deftly, thou shifty Usher: one man already fell; and lies smashed, far down there, against the masonry; Usher Maillard falls not: deftly, unerring he walks, with outspread palm. The Swiss holds a paper through his porthole; the shifty Usher snatches it, and returns. Terms of surrender: Pardon, immunity to all! Are they accepted?—"*Foi d'officier*, On the word of an officer," answers half-pay Hulin,—or half-pay Élie, for men do not agree on it, "they are!" Sinks the drawbridge,—Usher Maillard bolting it when down; rushes-in the living deluge: the Bastille is fallen! *Victoire! La Bastille est prise!*

CHAPTER VII

NOT A REVOLT

WHY dwell on what follows? Hulin's *foi d'officier* should have been kept, but could not. The Swiss stand drawn up, disguised in white canvass smocks; the Invalides without disguise; their arms all piled against the wall. The first rush of victors, in ecstasy that the death-peril is passed, 'leaps joyfully on their necks;' but new victors rush, and ever new, also in ecstasy not wholly of joy. As we said, it was a living deluge, plunging headlong: had not the Gardes Françaises, in their cool military way, 'wheeled round with arms levelled,' it would have plunged suicidally, by the hundred or the thousand, into the Bastille-ditch.

And so it goes plunging through court and corridor; billowing uncontrollable, firing from windows—on itself; in hot frenzy of triumph, of grief and vengeance for its slain. The poor Invalides will fare ill; one Swiss, running off in his white smock, is driven back, with a death-thrust. Let all Prisoners be marched to the Townhall, to be judged!—Alas, already one poor Invalide has his right hand slashed off him; his maimed body dragged to the Place de Grève, and hanged there. This same right hand, it is said, turned back De Launay from the Powder-Magazine, and saved Paris.

De Launay, 'discovered in gray frock with poppy-coloured ribbon,' is for killing himself with the sword of his cane. He shall to the Hôtel-de-Ville; Hulin, Maillard and others escorting him; Élie marching foremost 'with the capitulation paper on his sword's point.' Through roarings and cursings; through hustlings, clutchings, and at last through strokes! Your escort is hustled aside, felled down; Hulin sinks exhausted on a heap of stones. Miserable De Launay! He shall never enter the Hôtel-de-Ville: only his 'bloody hairqueue, held up in a bloody-hand;' that shall enter, for a sign. The bleeding trunk lies on the steps there; the head is off through the streets; ghastly, aloft on a pike.

Rigorous De Launay has died; crying out, "O friends, kill me fast!" Merciful De Losme must die; though Gratitude embraces him, in this fearful hour, and will die for him; it avails not. Brothers, your wrath is cruel! Your Place de Grève is become a Throat of the Tiger; full of mere fierce bellowings, and thirst of blood. One other officer is massacred; one other Invalide is hanged on the Lamp-iron; with difficulty, with generous perseverance, the Gardes Françaises will save the rest. Provost Flesselles, stricken long since with the paleness of death, must descend from his seat, 'to be judged at the Palais Royal:' alas, to be shot dead, by an unknown hand, at the turning of the first street!—

O evening sun of July, how, at this hour, thy beams fall slant on reapers amid peaceful woody-fields; on old women spinning in cottages; on ships far out in the silent main; on Balls at the Orangerie of Versailles, where high-rouged Dames of the Palace are even now dancing with double-jacketed Hussar-Officers;—and also on this roaring Hell-porch of a Hôtel-de-Ville! Babel Tower, with the confusion of tongues, were not Bedlam added with the conflagration of thoughts, was no type of it. One forest of distracted steel bristles, endless, in front of an Electoral Committee; points itself in horrid radii, against this and the other accused breast. It was the Titans warring with Olympus; and they, scarcely crediting it, have *conquered:* prodigy of prodigies; delirious,—as it could not but be. Denunciation, vengeance: blaze of triumph on a dark ground of terror; all outward, all inward things fallen into one general wreck of madness!

Electoral Committee? Had it a thousand throats of brass, it would not suffice. Abbé Lefèvre, in the Vaults down below, is black as Vulcan, distributing that 'five-thousand weight of Powder;' with what perils, these eight-and-forty hours! Last night, a Patriot, in liquor, insisted on sitting to smoke on the edge of one of the Powder-barrels: there smoked he, independent of the world,—till the Abbé 'purchased his pipe for three francs,' and pitched it far.

Élie, in the grand Hall, Electoral Committee looking on, sits 'with drawn sword bent in three places;' with battered helm, for he was of the Queen's Regiment, Cavalry; with torn regimentals, face singed and soiled; comparable, some think, to 'an antique warrior;'—judging the people; forming a list of Bastille Heroes. O Friends, stain not with blood the greenest laurels ever gained in this world: such is the burden of Élie's song: could it but be listened to. Courage, Élie! Courage, ye Municipal Electors! A declining sun; the need of victuals, and of telling news, will bring assuagement, dispersion: all earthly things must end.

Along the streets of Paris circulate Seven Bastille Prisoners, borne shoulder-high; seven heads on pikes; the Keys of the Bastille; and much else. See also the Gardes Françaises, in their stedfast military way, marching home to their barracks, with the Invalides and Swiss kindly enclosed in hollow square. It is one year and two months since these same men stood unparticipating, with Brennus d'Agoust at the Palais de Justice, when Fate overtook D'Espréménil; and now they have participated; and will participate. Not Gardes Françaises henceforth, but *Centre Grenadiers of the National Guard:* men of iron discipline and humour—not without a kind of thought in them!

Likewise ashlar stones of the Bastille continue thundering through the dusk; its paper archives shall fly white. Old secrets come to view; and long-buried Despair finds voice. Read this portion of an old Letter: 'If for my consolation Monseigneur would grant me, for the sake of God and the Most Blessed Trinity, that I could have news of my dear wife; were it only her name on a card, to show that she is alive! It were the greatest consolation I could receive; and I should forever bless the greatness of Monseigneur.' Poor Prisoner, who namest thyself *Quéret-Démery,* and hast no other history, —she is *dead,* that dear wife of thine, and thou art dead! 'Tis fifty years since thy breaking heart put this question; to be heard now first, and long heard, in the hearts of men.

But so does the July twilight thicken; so must Paris, as sick children, and all distracted creatures do, brawl itself finally into a kind of sleep. Municipal Electors, astonished to find their heads still uppermost, are home: only Moreau de Saint-Méry of tropical birth and heart, of coolest judgment; he, with two others, shall sit permanent at the Townhall. Paris sleeps; gleams upward the illuminated City: patrols go clashing, without common watchword; there go rumours; alarms of war, to the extent of 'fifteen thousand men marching through the Suburb Saint-Antoine,'—who never got it marched through. Of the day's distraction judge by this of the night: Moreau de Saint-Méry, 'before rising from his seat, gave upwards of three thousand orders.' What a head: comparable to Friar Bacon's

Brass Head! Within it lies all Paris. Prompt must the answer be, right or wrong; in Paris is no other Authority extant. Seriously, a most cool clear head;—for which also thou, O brave Saint-Méry, in many capacities, from august Senator to Merchant's-Clerk, Book-dealer, Vice-King; in many places, from Virginia to Sardinia, shalt, ever as a brave man, find employment.

Besenval has decamped, under cloud of dusk, 'amid a great affluence of people,' who did not harm him; he marches, with faint-growing tread, down the left bank of the Seine, all night, —towards infinite space. Re-summoned shall Besenval himself be; for trial, for difficult acquittal. His King's-troops, his Royal-Allemand, are gone hence forever.

The Versailles Ball and lemonade is done; the Orangerie is silent except for nightbirds. Over in the Salle des Menus, Vice-president Lafayette, with unsnuffed lights, 'with some Hundred or so of Members, stretched on tables round him,' sits erect; out-watching the Bear. This day, a second solemn Deputation went to his Majesty; a second and then a third: with no effect. What will the end of these things be?

In the Court, all is mystery, not without whisperings of terror; though ye dream of lemonade and epaulettes, ye foolish women! His Majesty, kept in happy ignorance, perhaps dreams of double-barrels and the Woods of Meudon. Late at night, the Duke de Liancourt, having official right of entrance, gains access to the Royal Apartments; unfolds, with earnest clearness, in his constitutional way, the Job's-news. " *Mais*," said poor Louis, "*c'est une révolte,* Why, that is a revolt!"— "Sire," answered Liancourt, "it is not a revolt,—it is a revolution."

CHAPTER VIII

CONQUERING YOUR KING

ON the morrow a fourth Deputation to the Château is on foot: of a more solemn, not to say awful character; for, besides 'orgies in the Orangery,' it seems 'the grain-convoys are all stopped;' nor has Mirabeau's thunder been silent. Such Deputation is on the point of setting out,—when lo, his Majesty himself, attended only by his two Brothers, steps in; quite in the paternal manner; announces that the troops, and all causes of offence, are gone, and henceforth there shall be nothing but trust, reconcilement, goodwill; whereof he 'permits, and even requests,' a National Assembly to assure Paris in his name! Acclamation, as of men suddenly delivered from death, gives answer. The whole Assembly spontaneously rises to escort his Majesty back; 'interlacing their arms to keep off the excessive pressure from him;' for all Versailles is crowding and shouting. The Château Musicians, with a felicitous promptitude, strike up the *Sein de sa Famille* (Bosom of one's Family); the Queen appears at the Balcony with her little boy and girl, 'kissing them several times;' infinite *Vivats* spread far and wide;—and suddenly there has come, as it were, a new Heaven-on-Earth.

Eighty-eight august Senators, Bailly, Lafayette and our repentant Archbishop among them, take coach for Paris, with the great intelligence; benedictions without end on their heads. From the Place Louis Quinze, where they alight, all the way to the Hôtel-de-Ville, it is one sea of Tricolor cockades, of clear National muskets; one tempest of huzzaings, hand-clappings, aided by 'occasional rollings' of drum-music. Harangues of due fervour are delivered, especially by Lally Tollendal, pious son of the ill-fated murdered Lally; on whose head, in consequence, a civic crown (of oak or parsley) is forced,—which he forcibly transfers to Bailly's.

But, surely, for one thing, the National Guard should have a General! Moreau de Saint-Méry, he of the 'three thousand orders,' casts one of his significant glances on the Bust of Lafayette, which has stood there ever since the American War of Liberty. Whereupon, by acclamation, Lafayette is nominated. Again, in room of the slain traitor or quasi-traitor Flesselles, President Bailly shall be—Provost of the Merchants? No: Mayor of Paris! So be it. *Maire de Paris!* Mayor Bailly, General Lafayette; *vive Bailly, vive Lafayette!* the universal out-of-doors multitude rends the welkin in confirmation.—And now, finally, let us to Notre-Dame for a *Te Deum.*

Towards Notre-Dame Cathedral, in glad procession, these Regenerators of the Country walk, through a jubilant people; in fraternal manner; Abbé Lefèvre, still black with his gunpowder services, walking arm in arm with the white-stoled Archbishop. Poor Bailly comes upon the Foundling Children, sent to kneel to him; and 'weeps.' *Te Deum,* our Archbishop officiating, is not only sung, but *shot*—with blank cartridges.

Our joy is boundless, as our woe threatened to be. Paris, by her own pike and musket, and the valour of her own heart, has conquered the very war-gods,—to the satisfaction now of Majesty itself. A courier is, this night, getting under way for Necker: the People's Minister, invited back by King, by National Assembly, and Nation, shall traverse France amid shoutings, and the sound of trumpet and timbrel.

Seeing which course of things, Messeigneurs of the Court Triumvirate, Messieurs of the dead-born Broglie Ministry, and others such, consider that their part also is clear; to mount and ride. Off, ye too-royal Broglies, Polignacs and Princes of the Blood; off while it is yet time! Did not the Palais-Royal, in its late nocturnal 'violent motions,' set a specific price (place of payment not mentioned) on each of your heads?— With precautions, with the aid of pieces of cannon and regiments that can be depended on, Messeigneurs, between the 16th night and the 17th morning, get to their several roads. Not without risk! Prince Condé has (or seems to have) 'men galloping at full speed;' with a view, it is thought, to fling him into the river Oise, at Pont-Sainte-Mayence. The Polignacs travel disguised; friends, not servants, on their coach-box. Broglie has his own difficulties at Versailles, runs his own risks at Metz and Verdun; does nevertheless get safe to Luxemburg, and there rests.

This is what they call the First Emigration; determined on, as appears, in full Court-conclave; his Majesty assisting; prompt he, for his share of it, to follow any counsel whatsoever. 'Three Sons of France, and four Princes of the blood of Saint Louis,' says Weber, 'could not more effectually humble the Burghers of Paris than by appearing to withdraw in fear of their life.' Alas, the Burghers of Paris bear it with unexpected stoicism! The Man D'Artois indeed is gone; but has he carried, for example, the Land D'Artois with him? Not even Bagatelle the Country-house (which shall be useful as a Tavern); hardly the four-valet Breeches, leaving the Breeches-maker!—As for old Foulon, one learns that he is dead; at least 'a sumptuous funeral' is going on; the undertakers honouring him, if no other will. Intendant Berthier, his son-in-law, is still living; lurking; he joined Besenval, on that Eumenides Sunday; appearing to treat it with levity; and is now fled no man knows whither.

The Emigration is not gone many miles, Prince Condé hardly across the Oise, when his Majesty, according to arrangement, for the Emigration also thought it might do good,—undertakes a rather daring enterprise: that of visiting Paris in person. With a Hundred Members of Assembly; with small or no military escort, which indeed he dismissed at the Bridge of Sèvres, poor Louis sets out; leaving a desolate Palace; a Queen weeping, the Present, the Past and the Future all so unfriendly for her.

At the Barrier of Passy, Mayor Bailly, in grand gala, presents him with the keys; harangues him, in Academic style; mentions that it is a great day; that in Henri Quatre's case, the King had to make conquest of his People; but in this happier case, the People makes conquest of its King (*a conquis son Roi*). The King, so happily conquered, drives forward, slowly, through a steel people, all silent, or shouting only *Vive la Nation;* is harangued at the Townhall, by Moreau of the three thousand orders, by King's Procureur M. Ethys de Corny, by Lally Tollendal, and others; knows not what to think of it or say of it; learns that he is 'Restorer of French Liberty,'—as a Statue of him, to be raised on the site of the Bastille, shall testify to all men. Finally, he is shown at the Balcony, with a Tricolor cockade in his hat; is greeted now, with vehement acclamation, from Square and Street, from all windows and roofs:—and so drives home again amid glad mingled and, as it were, intermarried shouts, of *Vive le Roi* and *Vive la Nation;* wearied but safe.

It was Sunday when the red-hot balls hung over us, in mid air: it is now but Friday, and 'the Revolution is sanctioned.' An august National Assembly shall make the Constitution; and neither foreign Pandour, domestic Triumvirate, with levelled Cannon, Guy-Faux powder-plots (for that too was spoken of); nor any tyrannic Power on the Earth or under the Earth, shall say to it, What dost thou?—So jubilates the People; sure now of a Constitution. Cracked Marquis Saint-Huruge is heard under the windows of the Château; murmuring sheer speculative-treason.

CHAPTER IX

THE LANTERNE

THE Fall of the Bastille may be said to have shaken all France to the deepest foundations of its existence. The rumour of these wonders flies every where: with the natural speed of Rumour; with an effect thought to be preternatural, produced by plots. Did D'Orléans or Laclos, nay did Mirabeau (not overburdened with money at this time) send riding Couriers out from Paris; to gallop 'or all radii,' or highways, towards all points of France! It is a miracle, which no penetrating man will call in question.

Already in most towns, Electoral Committees were met; to regret Necker, in harangue and resolution. In many a Town, as Rennes, Caen, Lyons, an ebullient people was already regretting him in brickbats and musketry. But now, at every Town's-end in France, there do arrive, in these days of terror, —'men,' as men will arrive; nay 'men on horseback,' since Rumour oftenest travels riding. These men declare, with alarmed countenance, *The* BRIGANDS to be coming, to be just at hand; and do then—ride on, about their further business, be what it might! Whereupon the whole population of such Town defensively flies to arms. Petition is soon thereafter forwarded to National Assembly; in such peril and terror of peril, leave to organise yourself cannot be withheld: the armed population becomes every where an enrolled National Guard. Thus rides Rumour, careering along all radii, from Paris outwards, to such purpose: in few days, some say in not many hours, all France to the utmost borders bristles with bayonets. Singular, but undeniable,—miraculous or not!— But thus may any chemical liquid, though cooled to the freezing-point, or far lower, still continue liquid; and then, on the slightest stroke or shake, it at once rushes wholly into ice. Thus has France, for long months and even years, been chemically dealt with; brought below zero; and now, shaken by the Fall of a Bastille, it instantaneously congeals: into one crystallised mass, of sharp-cutting steel! *Guai a chi la tocca,* 'Ware who touches it!

In Paris, an Electoral Committee, with a new Mayor and General, is urgent with belligerent workmen to resume their handicrafts. Strong Dames of the Market (*Dames de la Halle*) deliver congratulatory harangues; present 'bouquets to the Shrine of Sainte Genéviève.' Unenrolled men deposit their arms.—not so readily as could be wished: and receive 'nine francs.' With *Te Deums*, Royal Visits, and sanctioned Revolution, there is halcyon weather; weather even of preternatural brightness; the hurricane being overblown.

Nevertheless, as is natural, the waves still run high, hollow rocks retaining their murmur. We are but at the 22d of the month, hardly above a week since the Bastille fell, when it suddenly appears that old Foulon is alive; nay, that he is here, in early morning, in the streets of Paris: the extortioner, the plotter, who would make the people eat grass, and was a liar from the beginning!— It is even so. The deceptive 'sumptuous funeral' (of some domestic that died); the hiding-place at Vitry towards Fontainebleau, have not availed that wretched old man. Some living domestic or dependant, for none loves Foulon, has betrayed him to the Village. Merciless boors of Vitry unearth him; pounce on him, like hell-hounds: Westward, old Infamy; to Paris, to be judged at the Hôtel-de-Ville! His old head, which seventy-four years have bleached, is bare; they have tied an emblematic bundle of grass on his back; a garland of nettles and thistles is round his neck: in this manner; led with ropes; goaded on with curses and menaces, must he, with his old limbs, sprawl forward; the pitiablest, most unpitied of all old men.

Sooty Saint-Antoine, and every street, musters its crowds as he passes;—the Hall of the Hôtel-de-Ville, the Place de Grève itself, will scarcely hold his escort and him. Foulon must not only be judged righteously, but judged there where he stands, without any delay. Appoint seven judges, ye Municipals, or seventy-and-seven; name them yourselves, or we will name them: but judge him! Electoral rhetoric, eloquence of Mayor Bailly, is wasted, for hours, explaining the beauty of the Law's delay. Delay, and still delay! Behold, O Mayor of the People, the morning has worn itself into noon: and he is still unjudged!—Lafayette, pressingly sent for, arrives; gives voice: This Foulon, a known man, is guilty almost beyond doubt; but may he not have accomplices? Ought not the truth to be cunningly pumped out of him,—in the Abbaye Prison? It is a new light! Sansculottism claps hands;—at which handclapping, Foulon (in his fainness, as his Destiny would have it) also claps. "See!

they understand one another!" cries dark Sansculottism,
blazing into fury of suspicion,—"Friends," said 'a person in
good clothes,' stepping forward, "what is the use of judging
this man? Has he not been judged these thirty years?"
With wild yells, Sansculottism clutches him, in its hundred
hands: he is whirled across the Place de Grève, to the
'*Lanterne*,' Lamp-iron which there is at the corner of the *Rue
de la Vannerie*; pleading bitterly for life,—to the deaf winds.
Only with the third rope (for two ropes broke, and the quaver-
ing voice still pleaded), can he be so much as got hanged! His
Body is dragged through the streets; his Head goes aloft on
a pike, the mouth filled with grass: amid sounds as of Tophet,
from a grass-eating people.

Surely if Revenge is a 'kind of Justice,' it is a 'wild'
kind! O mad Sansculottism, hast thou risen, in thy mad
darkness, in thy soot and rags; unexpectedly, like an Enceladus, living-buried, from under his Trinacria? They that
would make grass be eaten do now eat grass, in *this* manner?
After long dumb-groaning generations, has the turn suddenly
become thine?—To such abysmal overturns, and frightful
instantaneous inversions of the centre of gravity, are human
Solecisms all liable, if they but knew it; the more liable, the
falser (and top-heavier) they are!—

To add to the horror of Mayor Bailly and his Municipals,
word comes that Berthier has also been arrested; that he is
on his way hither from Compiègne. Berthier, Intendant (say
Tax-levier) of Paris; sycophant and tyrant; forestaller of
Corn; contriver of Camps against the people;—accused of
many things: is he not Foulon's son-in-law; and, in that one
point, guilty of all? In these hours, too, when Sansculottism
has its blood up! The shuddering Municipals send one of
their number to escort him, with mounted National Guards.

At the fall of day, the wretched Berthier, still wearing a
face of courage, arrives at the Barrier; in an open carriage;
with the Municipal beside him; five hundred horsemen with
drawn sabres; unarmed footmen enough: not without noise!
Placards go brandished round him; bearing legibly his indictment, as Sansculottism, with unlegal brevity, 'in huge letters',
draws it up. Paris is come forth to meet him: with hand-
clappings, with windows flung up; with dances, triumph-songs,
as of the Furies. Lastly, the Head of Foulon; this also
meets him on a pike. Well might his 'look become glazed,'

and sense fail him, at such sight!—Nevertheless, be the man's conscience what it may, his nerves are of iron. At the Hôtel-de-Ville, he will answer nothing. He says he obeyed superior orders; they have his papers; they may judge and determine: as for himself, not having closed an eye these two nights, he demands, before all things, to have sleep. Leaden sleep, thou miserable Berthier! Guards rise with him, in motion towards the Abbaye. At the very door of the Hôtel-de-Ville, they are clutched; flung asunder, as by a vortex of mad arms; Berthier whirls towards the Lanterne. He snatches a musket; fells and strikes, defending himself like a mad lion: he is borne down, trampled, hanged, mangled: his Head, too, and even his Heart, flies over the City on a pike.

Horrible, in Lands that had known equal justice! Not so unnatural in Lands that had never known it. "*Le sang qui coule, est il donc si pur?*" asks Barnave; intimating that the Gallows, though by irregular methods, has its own.—Thou thyself, O Reader, when thou turnest that corner of the Rue de la Vannerie, and discernest still that same grim Bracket of old Iron, wilt not want for reflections. 'Over a grocer's shop,' or otherwise; with 'a bust of Louis XIV. in the niche under it,' now no longer in the niche,—*it* still sticks there; still holding out an ineffectual light, of fish-oil; and has seen worlds wrecked, and says nothing.

But to the eye of enlightened Patriotism, what a thunder-cloud was this; suddenly shaping itself in the radiance of the halcyon weather! Cloud of Erebus blackness; betokening latent electricity without limit. Mayor Bailly, General Lafayette throw up their commissions, in an indignant manner;—need to be flattered back again. The cloud disappears, as thunder-clouds do. The halcyon weather returns, though of a grayer complexion; of a character more and more evidently *not* supernatural.

Thus, in any case, with what rubs soever, shall the Bastille be abolished from our Earth; and with it, Feudalism, Despotism, and, one hopes, Scoundrelism generally, and all hard usage of man by his brother man. Alas, the Scoundrelism and hard usage are not so easy of abolition! But as for the Bastille, it sinks day after day, and month after month; its ashlars and boulders tumbling down continually, by express order of our Municipals. Crowds of the curious roam through its caverns; gaze on the skeletons found walled-up, on the *oubliettes*, iron cages, monstrous stone-blocks with padlock chains. One day we discern Mirabeau there; along with the Genevese Dumont. Workers and onlookers make reverent way for him; fling verses, flowers on his path, Bastille-papers and curiosities into his carriage with *vivats*.

Able Editors compile Books from the *Bastille Archives;* from what of them remain unburnt. The Key of that Robber-Den shall cross the Atlantic; shall lie on Washington's hall-table. The great Clock ticks now in a private patriotic Clockmaker's apartment; no longer measuring hours of mere heaviness. Vanished is the Bastille, what we call vanished: the *body*, or sand-stones, of it hanging, in benign metamorphosis, for centuries to come, over the Seine waters, as *Pont Louis Seize;* the soul of it living, perhaps still longer, in the memories of men.

So far, ye august Senators, with your Tennis-Court Oaths, your inertia and impetus, your sagacity and pertinacity, have ye brought us. "And yet think, Messieurs," as the Petitioners justly urged, "you who were our saviours did yourselves need saviours,"—the brave Bastillers, namely; workmen of Paris; many of them in straitened pecuniary circumstances! Subscriptions are opened; Lists are formed, more accurate than Élie's; harangues are delivered. A Body of *Bastille Heroes*, tolerably complete, did get together;—comparable to the Argonauts; hoping to endure like them. But in little more than a year, the whirlpool of things threw them asunder again, and they sank. So many highest superlatives achieved by man are followed by new higher; and dwindle into comparatives and positives! The Siege of the Bastille, weighed with which, in the Historical balance, most other sieges, including that of Troy Town, are gossamer, cost, as we find, in killed and mortally wounded, on the part of the Besiegers, some Eighty-three persons: on the part of the Besieged, after all that straw-burning, fire-pumping, and deluge of musketry, One poor solitary Invalid, shot stone-dead (*roide-mort*) on the battlements! The Bastille Fortress, like the City of Jericho, was overturned by miraculous *sound*.

BOOK VI

CONSOLIDATION

CHAPTER I

MAKE THE CONSTITUTION

HERE perhaps is the place to fix, a little more precisely, what these two words, *French Revolution*, shall mean; for, strictly considered, they may have as many meanings as there are speakers of them. All things are in revolution; in change from moment to moment, which becomes sensible from epoch to epoch: in this Time-World of ours there is properly nothing else but revolution and mutation, and even nothing else conceivable. Revolution, you answer, means *speedier* change. Whereupon one has still to ask: How speedy? At what degree of speed; in what particular points of this variable course, which varies in velocity, but can never stop till Time itself stops, does revolution begin and end; cease to be ordinary mutation, and again become such? It is a thing that will depend on definition more or less arbitrary.

For ourselves, we answer that French Revolution means here the open violent Rebellion, and Victory, of disimprisoned Anarchy against corrupt worn-out Authority: how Anarchy breaks prison; bursts up from the infinite Deep, and rages uncontrollable, immeasurable, enveloping a world; in phasis after phasis of fever-frenzy;—till the frenzy burning itself out, and what elements of new Order it held (since all Force holds such) developing themselves, the Uncontrollable be got, if not reimprisoned, yet harnessed, and its mad forces made to work towards their object as sane regulated ones. For as Hierarchies and Dynasties of all kinds, Theocracies, Aristocracies, Autocracies, Strumpetocracies, have ruled over the world; so it was appointed, in the decrees of Providence, that this same Victorious Anarchy, Jacobinism, Sansculottism, French Revolution, Horrors of French Revolution, or what else mortal name it, should have its turn. The 'destructive wrath' of Sansculottism: this is what we speak, having unhappily no voice for singing.

Surely a great Phenomenon: nay it is a *transcendental* one, overstepping all rules and experience; the crowning Phenomenon of our Modern Time. For here again, most unexpectedly, comes antique Fanaticism in new and newest vesture; miraculous, as all Fanaticism is. Call it the Fanaticism of 'making away with formulas, *de humer les formules.*' The world of formulas, the *formed* regulated world, which all habitable world is,—must needs hate such Fanaticism like death; and be at deadly variance with it. The world of formulas must conquer it; or failing that, must die execrating it, anathematising it;—can nevertheless in nowise prevent its being and its having been. The Anathemas are there, and the miraculous Thing is there.

Whence it cometh? Whither it goeth? These are questions! When the age of Miracles lay faded into the distance as an incredible tradition, and even the age of Conventionalities was now old; and Man's Existence had for long generations rested on mere formulas which were grown hollow by course of time; and it seemed as if no Reality any longer existed, but only Phantasms of realities, and God's Universe were the work of the Tailor and Upholsterer mainly, and men were buckram masks that went about becking and grimacing there,—on a sudden, the Earth yawns asunder, and amid Tartarean smoke, and glare of fierce brightness, rises SANSCULOTTISM, many-headed, fire-breathing, and asks: What think ye of *me?* Well may the buckram masks start together, terror-struck; 'into expressive well-concerted groups!' It is indeed, Friends, a most singular, most fatal thing. Let whosoever is but buckram and a phantasm look to it: ill verily may it fare with him; here methinks he cannot much longer be. Wo also to many a one who is not wholly buckram, but partly real and human! The age of Miracles has come back! 'Behold the World-Phœnix, in fire-consummation and fire-creation: wide are her fanning wings; loud is her death-melody, of battle-thunders and falling-towns; skyward lashes the funeral flame, enveloping all things: it is the Death-Birth of a World!'

Whereby, however, as we often say, shall one unspeakable blessing seem attainable. This, namely: that Man and his Life rest no more on hollowness and a Lie, but on solidity and some kind of Truth. Welcome the beggarliest truth, so it *be* one, in exchange for the royallest sham! Truth of any kind breeds ever new and better truth; thus hard granite rock will crumble down into soil, under the blessed skyey influences; and cover itself with verdure, with fruitage and umbrage. But as for Falsehood, which, in like contrary manner, grows ever falser,—what can it, or what should it do but decease, being ripe; decompose itself, gently or even violently, and return to the Father of it,—too probably in flames of fire?

Sansculottism will burn much; but what is incombustible it will not burn. Fear not Sansculottism; recognise it for what it is, the portentous inevitable end of much, the miraculous beginning of much. One other thing thou mayest understand of it: that it too came from God; for has it not *been*? From of old, as it is written, are His goings forth; in the great Deep of things; fearful and wonderful now as in the beginning: in the whirlwind also He speaks; and the wrath of men is made to praise him.—But to gauge and measure this immeasurable Thing, and what is called *account for it*, and reduce it to a dead logic-formula, attempt not! Much less shalt thou shriek thyself hoarse, cursing it; for that, to all needful lengths, has been already done. As an actually existing Son of Time, *look*, with unspeakable manifold interest, oftenest in silence, at what the Time did bring: therewith edify, instruct, nourish thyself, or were it but amuse and gratify thyself, as it is given thee.

Another question which at every new turn will rise on us, requiring ever new reply, is this: Where the French Revolution specially *is*? In the King's Palace, in his Majesty's or her Majesty's managements, and maltreatments, cabals, imbecilities and woes, answer some few:—whom we do not answer. In the National Assembly, answer a large mixed multitude: who accordingly seat themselves in the Reporter's Chair; and therefrom noting what Proclamations, Acts, Reports, passages of logic-fence, bursts of parliamentary eloquence seem notable within doors, and what tumults and rumours of tumult become audible from without, produce volume on volume; and, naming it History of the French Revolution, contentedly publish the same. To do the like, to almost any extent, with so many Filed Newspapers, *Choix des Rapports, Histoires Parlementaires* as there are, amounting to many horseloads, were easy for us. Easy but unprofitable. The National Assembly, named now Constituent Assembly, goes its course; making the Constitution; but the French Revolution also goes *its* course.

In general, may we not say that the French Revolution lies

in the heart and head of every violent-speaking, of every violent-thinking French Man? How the Twenty-five Millions of such, in their perplexed combination, acting and counteracting may give birth to events; which event successively is the cardinal one; and from what point of vision it may best be surveyed: this is a problem. Which problem the best insight, making light from all possible sources, shifting its point of vision whithersoever vision or glimpse of vision can be had, may employ itself in solving; and be well content to solve in some tolerably approximate way.

As to the National Assembly, in so far as it still towers eminent over France, after the manner of a car-borne *Carroccio*, though now no longer in the van; and rings signals for retreat or for advance,—it is and continues a reality among other realities. But in so far as it sits making the Constitution, on the other hand, it is a fatuity and chimera mainly. Alas, in the never so heroic building of Montesquieu-Mably card-castles, though shouted over by the world, what interest is there? Occupied in that way, an august National Assembly becomes for us little other than a Sanhedrim of Pedants, not of the gerund-grinding, yet of no fruitfuller sort; and its loud debatings and recriminations about Rights of Man, Right of Peace and War, *Veto suspensif*, *Veto absolu*, what are they but so many Pedant's-curses, "May God confound you for your *Theory of Irregular Verbs!*"

A Constitution can be built, Constitutions enough *à la Sieyès*: but the frightful difficulty is, that of getting men to come and live in them! Could Sieyès have drawn thunder and lightning out of Heaven to sanction his Constitution, it had been well: but without any thunder? Nay, strictly considered, is it not still true that without some such celestial sanction, given visibly in thunder or invisibly otherwise, no Constitution can in the longrun be worth much more than the waste-paper it is written on? The Constitution, the set of Laws, or prescribed Habits of Acting, that men will live under, is the one which images their Convictions,—their Faith as to this wondrous Universe, and what rights, duties, capabilities they have there: which stands sanctioned, therefore, by Necessity itself; if not by a seen Deity, then by an unseen one. Other Laws, whereof there are always enough *ready*-made, are usurpations; which men do not obey, but rebel against, and abolish, at their earliest convenience.

The question of questions accordingly was, Who is it that especially for rebellers and abolishers, can make a Constitution? He that can image forth the general Belief when there is one; that can impart one when, as here, there is none. A most rare man; ever, as of old, a god-missioned man! Here however, in defect of such transcendent supreme man, Time with its infinite succession of merely superior men, each yielding his little contribution does much. Force likewise (for, as Antiquarian Philosophers teach, the royal Sceptre was from the first something of a Hammer, to *crack* such heads as could not be convinced) will all along find somewhat to do. And thus in perpetual abolition and reparation, rending and mending, with struggle and strife, with present evil, and the hope and effort towards future good, must the Constitution, as all human things do, build itself forward; or unbuild itself, and sink, as it can and may. O Sieyès, and ye other Committeemen, and Twelve Hundred miscellaneous individuals from all parts of France! what is the Belief of France, and yours, if ye knew it? Properly that there shall be no belief; that all formulas be swallowed. The Constitution which will suit that? Alas, too clearly, a No-Constitution, an Anarchy;—which also in due season, shall be vouchsafed you.

But, after all, what can an unfortunate National Assembly do? Consider only this, that there are Twelve Hundred miscellaneous individuals; not a unit of whom but has his own thinking-apparatus, his own speaking-apparatus! In every unit of them is some belief and wish, different for each, both that France should be regenerated, and also that he individually should do it. Twelve Hundred separate Forces, yoked miscellaneously to any object, miscellaneously to all sides of it and bidden pull for life!

Or is it the nature of National Assemblies generally to do, with endless labour and clangour, Nothing? Are representative Governments mostly at bottom Tyrannies too? Shall we say, the *Tyrants*, the ambitious contentious Persons, from all corners of the country do, in this manner, get gathered into one place; and there, with motion and counter-motion, with jargon and hubbub, *cancel* one another, like the fabulous Kilkenny Cats; and produce, for net-result, *zero;*—the country meanwhile *governing* or guiding *itself*, by such wisdom, recognised, or for most part unrecognised, as may exist in individual heads here and there?—Nay, even that were a great improvement: for of old, with their Guelf Factions and Ghibelline actions, with their Red Roses and White Roses, they were wont to cancel the whole country as well. Besides they do it now in a much narrower cockpit; within the four walls of their Assembly House, and here and there an out-post of Hustings and Barrel-heads; do it with tongues too, not with swords:— All which improvements, in the art of producing zero, are they not great? Nay, best of all, some happy Continents (as the Western one, with its Savannahs, where whosoever has four willing limbs, finds food under his feet, and an infinite sky over his head) can do without governing.—What Sphinx-questions; which the distracted world, in these very generations, must answer or die!

CHAPTER II

THE CONSTITUENT ASSEMBLY

ONE thing an elected Assembly of Twelve Hundred is fit for: Destroying. Which indeed is but a more decided exercise of its natural talent for Doing Nothing. Do nothing, only keep agitating, debating; and things will destroy themselves.

So and not otherwise proved it with an august National Assembly. It took the name Constituent, as if its mission and function had been to construct or build; which also, with its whole soul, it endeavoured to do: yet, in the fates, in the nature of things, there lay for it precisely of all functions the most opposite to that. Singular, what Gospels men will believe; even Gospels according to Jean Jacques! It was the fixed Faith of these National Deputies, as of all thinking Frenchmen, that the Constitution could be *made;* that they, there and then, were called to make it. How, with the tough-ness of old Hebrews or Ishmaelite Moslem, did the otherwise light unbelieving People persist in this their *Credo quia impossibile;* and front the armed world with it; and grow fanatic, and even heroic, and do exploits by it! The Constituent Assembly's Constitution, and several others, will, being printed and not manuscript, survive to future generations, as an in-structive well-nigh incredible document of the Time: the most significant Picture of the then existing France: or at lowest, Picture of these men's Picture of it.

But in truth and seriousness, what could the National Assembly have done? The thing to *be* done was, actually as they said, to regenerate France; to abolish the old France, and make a new one, quietly or forcibly, by concession or by violence: this by the Law of Nature has become inevitable. With what degree of violence, depends on the wisdom of those that preside over it. With perfect wisdom on the part of the National Assembly, it had all been otherwise; but whether, in any wise, it could have been pacific, nay other than bloody and convulsive, may still be a question.

Grant, meanwhile, that this Constituent Assembly does to the last continue to be something. With a sigh, it sees itself incessantly forced away from its infinite divine task of perfecting 'the Theory of Irregular Verbs,'—to finite terrestrial tasks which latter have still a significance for us. It is the cynosure of revolutionary France, this National Assembly. All work of Government has fallen into its hands, or under its control; all men look to it for guidance. In the middle of that huge Revolt of Twenty-five Millions, it hovers always aloft as *Carroccio* or Battle-Standard, impelling and impelled, in the most confused way: if it cannot give much guidance, it will still seem to give some. It emits pacificatory Proclamations, not a few; with more or with less result. It authorises the enrolment of National Guards,—lest Brigands come to devour us, and reap the unripe crops. It sends missions to quell 'effervescences;' to deliver men from the Lanterne. It can listen to congratulatory Addresses, which arrive daily by the sackful; mostly in King Cambyses' vein: also to Petitions and complaints from all mortals; so that every mortal's complaint, if it cannot get redressed, may at least hear itself complain. For the rest, an august National Assembly can produce Parliamentary Eloquence; and appoint Committees. Committees of the Constitution, of Reports, of Researches; and of much else: which again yield mountains of Printed Paper; the theme of new Parliamentary Eloquence, in bursts, or in plenteous smooth-flowing floods. And so, from the waste vortex whereon all things go whirling and grinding, Organic Laws, or the similitude of such, slowly emerge.

With endless debating, we get the *Rights of Man* written down and promulgated: true paper basis of all paper Constitutions. Neglecting, cry the opponents, to declare the Duties of Man! Forgetting, answer we, to ascertain the *Mights* of Man;—one of the fatallest omissions!—Nay, sometimes, as on the Fourth of August, our National Assembly, fired suddenly by an almost preternatural enthusiasm, will get through whole masses of work in one night. A memorable night, this Fourth of August: Dignitaries temporal and spiritual; Peers, Arch-bishops, Parlement-Presidents, each outdoing the other in patriotic devotedness, come successively to throw their now untenable possessions on the 'altar of the fatherland.' With louder and louder vivats,—for indeed it is 'after dinner' too, —they abolish Tithes, Seignorial Dues, Gabelle, excessive Preservation of Game; nay Privilege, Immunity, Feudalism root and branch; then appoint a *Te Deum* for it; and so, finally, disperse about three in the morning, striking the stars with their sublime heads. Such night, unforeseen but for ever memorable, was this of the Fourth of August 1789. Miraculous, or semi-miraculous, some seem to think it. A new Night of Pentecost, shall we say, shaped according to the new Time, and new Church of Jean Jacques Rousseau? It had its causes; also its effects.

In such manner labour the National Deputies; perfecting their Theory of Irregular Verbs; governing France, and being governed by it; with toil and noise; cutting asunder ancient intolerable bonds; and, for new ones, assiduously spinning ropes of sand. Were their labours a nothing or a something, yet the eyes of all France being reverently fixed on them, History can never very long leave them altogether out of sight.

For the present, if we glance into that Assembly Hall of theirs, it will be found, as is natural, 'most irregular.' As many as a 'hundred members are on their feet at once;' no rule in making motions, or only commencements of a rule; Spectators' Gallery allowed to applaud, and even to hiss; President, appointed once a fortnight, raising many times no serene head above the waves. Nevertheless, as in all human Assemblages, like does begin arranging itself to like; the perennial rule, *Ubi homines sunt modi sunt*, proves valid. Rudiments of Methods disclose themselves; rudiments of Parties. There is a Right Side (*Côté Droit*), a Left Side (*Côté Gauche*); sitting on M. le President's right hand, or on his left; the *Côté Droit* conservative; the *Côté Gauche* destructive. Intermediate is Anglomaniac Constitutionalism, or Two-Chamber Royalism; with its Mouniers, its Lallys,— fast verging towards nonentity. Pre-eminent, on the Right Side, pleads and perorates Cazalès the Dragoon-captain, eloquent, mildly fervent; earning for himself the shadow of a name. There also blusters Barrel-Mirabeau, the Younger

Mirabeau, not without wit; dusky D'Espréménil does nothing but sniff and ejaculate; *might*, it is fondly thought, lay prostrate the Elder Mirabeau himself, would he but try,—which he does not. Last and greatest, see, for one moment, the Abbé Maury; with his jesuitic eyes, his impassive brass face, 'image of all the cardinal sins.' Indomitable, unquenchable, he fights jesuitico-rhetorically; with toughest lungs and heart; for Throne, especially for Altar and Tithes. So that a shrill voice exclaims once, from the Gallery : "Messieurs of the Clergy, you *have* to be shaved; if you wriggle too much, you will get cut."

The Left Side is also called the D'Orléans side; and sometimes, derisively, the Palais Royal. And yet, so confused, real-imaginary seems everything, 'it is doubtful,' as Mirabeau said, 'whether D'Orléans himself belong to that same D'Orléans party.' What can be known and seen is, that his moon-visage does beam forth from that point of space. There likewise sits seagreen Robespierre; throwing in his light weight, with decision, not yet with effect. A thin lean Puritan and Precisian, he would make away with formulas; yet lives, moves and has his being wholly in formulas, of another sort. ' *Peuple*,' such, according to Robespierre, ought to be the Royal method of promulgating Laws, '*Peuple*, this is the Law I have framed for thee; dost thou accept it ?'—answered, from Right Side, from Centre and Left, by inextinguishable laughter. Yet men of insight discern that the Seagreen may by chance go far: "This man," observes Mirabeau, "will do somewhat; he believes every word he says."

Abbé Sieyès is busy with mere Constitutional work; wherein, unluckily, fellow-workmen are less pliable than, with one who has completed the Science of Polity, they ought to be. Courage, Sieyès, nevertheless! Some twenty months of heroic travail, of contradiction from the stupid, and the Constitution shall be built; the top-stone of it brought out with shouting,—say rather, the top-paper, for it is all Paper; and *thou* hast done in it what the Earth or the Heaven could require, thy utmost. Note likewise this Trio; memorable for several things; memorable were it only that their history is written in an epigram : 'whatsoever these Three have in hand,' it is said, 'Duport thinks it, Barnave speaks it, Lameth does it.'

But royal Mirabeau? Conspicuous among all parties, raised above and beyond them all, this man rises more and more. As we often say, he has an *eye*, he is a reality; while others are formulas and eye-*glasses*. In the Transient he will detect the Perennial; find some firm footing even among Paper-vortexes. His fame is gone forth to all lands; it gladdened the heart of the crabbed old Friend of Men himself before he died. The very Postilions of inns have heard of Mirabeau: when an impatient Traveller complains that the team is in-sufficient, his Postilion answers, "Yes, Monsieur, the wheelers are weak; but my *mirabeau* (main horse), you see, is a right one, *mais mon mirabeau est excellent.*"

And now, Reader, thou shalt quit this noisy Discrepancy of a National Assembly; not (if thou be of humane mind) without pity. Twelve Hundred brother men are there, in the centre of Twenty-five Millions; fighting so fiercely with Fate and with one another; struggling their lives out, as most sons of Adam do, for that which profiteth not. Nay, on the whole, it is admitted further to be very *dull*. "Dull as this day's Assembly," said some one. "Why date, *Pourquoi dater?*" answered Mirabeau.

Consider that they are Twelve Hundred: that they not only speak, but *read* their speeches; and even borrow and steal speeches to read! With Twelve Hundred fluent speakers, and their Noah's Deluge of vociferous commonplace, silence unattainable may well seem the one blessing of Life. But figure Twelve Hundred pamphleteers; droning forth perpetual pamphlets: and no man to gag them! Neither, as in the American congress, do the arrangements seem perfect. A Senator has not his own Desk and Newspaper here; of Tobacco (much less of Pipes) there is not the slightest provision. Con-versation itself must be transacted in a low tone, with continual interruption: only 'pencil Notes' circulate freely; 'in incredi ble numbers, to the foot of the very tribune.' Such work is it, regenerating a Nation; perfecting one's Theory of Irregular Verbs !

CHAPTER III

THE GENERAL OVERTURN

OF the King's Court, for the present, there is almost nothing whatever to be said. Silent, deserted are these halls; Royalty languishes forsaken of its war-god and all its hopes, till once the Œil-de-Bœuf rally again. The sceptre is departed from King Louis; is gone over to the *Salle des Menus*, to the Paris

Townhall, or one knows not whither. In the July days, while all ears were yet deafened by the crash of the Bastille, and Ministers and Princes were scattered to the four winds, it seemed as if the very Valets had grown heavy of hearing. Besenval, also in flight towards Infinite Space, but hovering a little at Versailles, was addressing his Majesty personally for an Order about post-horses; when, lo, 'the Valet in waiting places himself familiarly between his Majesty and me,' stretching out his rascal neck to learn what it was! His Majesty, in sudden choler, whirled round; made a clutch at the tongs: 'I gently prevented him; he grasped my hand in thankfulness; and I noticed tears in his eyes.'

Poor King; for French Kings also are men! Louis Fourteenth himself once clutched the tongs, and even smote with them; but then it was at Louvois, and Dame Maintenon ran up.—The Queen sits weeping in her inner apartments, surrounded by weak women: she is 'at the height of unpopularity'; universally regarded as the evil genius of France. Her friends and familiar counsellors have all fled; and fled, surely, on the foolishest errand. The Château Polignac still frowns aloft, on its 'bold and enormous cubical rock,' amid the blooming champaigns, amid the blue girdling mountains of Auvergne: but no Duke and Duchess Polignac look forth from it; they have fled, they have 'met Necker at Bâle;' they shall not return. That France should see her Nobles resist the Irresistible, Inevitable, with the face of angry men, was unhappy, not unexpected; but with the face and sense of pettish children? This was her peculiarity. They understood nothing; would understand nothing. Does not, at this hour, a new Polignac, firstborn of these Two, sit reflective in the Castle of Ham; in an astonishment he will never recover from; the most confused of existing mortals?

King Louis has his new Ministry: mere Popularities; Old-President Pompignan; Necker, coming back in triumph; and other such. But what will it avail him? As was said, the sceptre, all but the wooden gilt sceptre, has departed elsewhither. Volition, determination is not in this man: only innocence, indolence; dependence on all persons but himself, on all circumstances but the circumstances he were lord of. So troublous internally is our Versailles and its work. Beautiful, if seen from afar, resplendent like a Sun; seen near at hand, a mere Sun's-Atmosphere, hiding darkness, confused ferment of ruin!

But over France, there goes on the indisputablest 'destruction of formulas;' transaction of realities that follow therefrom. So many millions of persons, all gyved, and nigh strangled, with formulas; whose Life nevertheless, at least the digestion and hunger of it, was real enough! Heaven has at length sent an abundant harvest: but what profits it the poor man, when Earth with her formulas interposes? Industry, in these times of insurrection, must needs lie dormant; capital, as usual, not circulating, but stagnating timorously in nooks. The poor man is short of work, is therefore short of money; nay even had he money, bread is not to be bought for it. Were it plotting of Aristocrats, plotting of D'Orléans; were it Brigands, preternatural terror, and the clang of Phœbus Apollo's silver bow,—enough, the markets are scarce of grain, plentiful only in tumult. Farmers seem lazy to thresh;—being either 'bribed;' or needing no bribe, with prices ever rising, with perhaps rent itself no longer so pressing. Neither, what is singular, do municipal enactments. 'That along with so many measures of wheat you shall sell so many of rye,' and other the like, much mend the matter. Dragoons with drawn swords stand ranked among the corn-sacks, often more dragoons than sacks. Meal-mobs abound; growing into mobs of a still darker quality.

Starvation has been known among the French Commonalty before this: known and familiar. Did we not see them, in the year 1775, presenting, in sallow faces, in wretchedness and raggedness, their Petition of Grievances; and, for answer, getting a brand-new Gallows forty feet high? (p. 28). Hunger and Darkness, through long years! For look back on that earlier Paris Riot, when a Great Personage, worn out by debauchery, was believed to be in want of Blood-baths; and Mothers, in worn raiment, yet with living hearts under it, 'filled the public places' with their wild Rachel-cries, stilled also by the Gallows. Twenty years ago, the Friend of Men (preaching to the deaf) described the Limousin Peasants as wearing a pain-stricken (souffre-douleur) look, a look past complaint, 'as if the oppression of the great were like the hail and the thunder, a thing irremediable, the ordinance of Nature.' And now if in some great hour, the shock of a falling Bastille should awaken you; and it were found to be the ordinance of Art merely; and remediable, reversible!

Or has the Reader forgotten that 'flood of savages,' which, in sight of the same Friend of Men, descended from the mountains at Mont d'Or? Lank-haired haggard faces; shapes rawboned, in high sabots; in woollen jupes, with leather girdles studded with copper-nails! They rocked from foot to foot, and beat time with their elbows too, as the quarrel and battle, which was not long in beginning, went on; shouting fiercely; the lank faces distorted into the similitude of a cruel laugh. For they were darkened and hardened: long had they been the prey of excise-men and tax-men; of 'clerks with the cold spurt of their pen.' It was the fixed prophecy of our old Marquis, which no man would listen to, that 'such Government by Blind-man's-buff, stumbling along too far, would end by the General Overturn, the *Culbute Générale !*'

No man would listen, each went his thoughtless way;— and Time and Destiny also travelled on. The Government by Blind-man's-buff, stumbling along, has reached the precipice inevitable for it. Dull Drudgery, driven on, by clerks with the cold dastard spurt of their pen, has been driven—into a Communion of Drudges! For now, moreover, there have come the strangest confused tidings; by Paris Journals with their paper wings; or still more portentous, where no Journals are, by rumour and conjecture: Oppression *not* inevitable; a Bastille prostrate, and the Constitution fast getting ready! Which Constitution, if it be something and not nothing, what can it be but bread to eat?

The Traveller, 'walking up hill bridle in hand,' overtakes 'a poor woman;' the image, as such commonly are, of drudgery and scarcity; 'looking sixty years of age, though she is not yet twenty-eight.' They have seven children, her poor drudge and she: a farm, with one cow, which helps to make the children soup; also one little horse, or garron. They have rents and quit-rents, Hens to pay to this Seigneur, Oat-sacks to that; King's taxes, Statute labour, Church-taxes, taxes enough;—and think the times inexpressible. She has heard that some*where*, in some manner, some*thing* is to be done for the poor: "God send it soon; for the dues and taxes crush us down (*nous écrasent*)!"

Fair prophecies are spoken, but they are not fulfilled. There have been Notables, Assemblages, turnings out and comings in. Intriguing and manœuvring; Parlementary eloquence and arguing, Greek meeting Greek in high places, has long gone on; yet still bread comes not. The harvest is reaped and garnered: yet still we have no bread. Urged by despair and by hope, what can Drudgery do, but rise, as predicted, and produce the General Overturn?

Fancy, then, some Five full-grown Millions of such gaunt figures, with their haggard faces (*figures hâves*); in woollen jupes, with copper-studded leather girths, and high sabots,—starting up to ask, as in forest-roarings, their washed Upper-Classes, after long unreviewed centuries, virtually this question: How have ye treated us; how have ye taught us, fed us, and led us, while we toiled for you? The answer can be read in flames, over the nightly summer-sky. *This* is the feeding and leading we have had of you: EMPTINESS,—of pocket, of stomach, of head and of heart. Behold there is *nothing in us;* nothing but what Nature gives her wild children of the desert: Ferocity and Appetite: Strength grounded on Hunger. Did ye mark among your Rights of Man, that man was not to die of starvation, while there was bread reaped by him? It is among the Mights of Man.

Seventy-two Châteaus have flamed aloft in the Mâconnais and Beaujolais alone: this seems the centre of the conflagration; but it has spread over Dauphiné, Alsace, the Lyonnais; the whole South-East is in a blaze. All over the North, from Rouen to Metz, disorder is abroad: smugglers of salt go openly in armed bands; the barriers of towns are burnt; toll-gatherers, tax-gatherers, official persons put to flight. 'It was thought,' says Young, 'the people, from hunger, would revolt:' and we see they have done it. Desperate Lackalls, long prowling aimless, now finding hope in desperation itself, everywhere form a nucleus. They ring the Church-bell by way of tocsin: and the Parish turns out to the work. Ferocity, atrocity; hunger and revenge: such work as we can imagine!

Ill stands it now with the Seigneur, who, for example, 'has walled up the only Fountain of the Township;' who has ridden high on his *chartier* and parchments; who has preserved Game not wisely but too well. Churches also, and Canonries, are sacked, without mercy; which have shorn the flock too close, forgetting to feed it. Woe to the land over which Sansculottism, in its day of vengeance, tramps rough-shod,—shod in sabots! Highbred Seigneurs, with their delicate women and little ones, had to 'fly half-naked,' under cloud of night: glad to escape the flames, and even worse. You meet them at the *tables-d'hôte* of inns; making wise reflexions or foolish, that 'rank is destroyed;' uncertain whither they shall now wend. The *métayer* will find it convenient to be slack in paying rent. As for the Tax-gatherer, he, long hunting as a biped of prey, may now find himself hunted as one; his Majesty's Exchequer will not 'fill up the Deficit,' this season: it is the notion of many that a Patriot Majesty, being the Restorer of French Liberty, has abolished most taxes, though, for their private ends, some men make a secret of it.

Where this will end? In the Abyss, one may prophesy; whither all Delusions are, at all moments, travelling; where this Delusion has now arrived. For if there be a Faith, from of old, it is this, as we often repeat, that no Lie can live forever. The very Truth has to change its vesture, from time to time; and be born again. But all Lies have sentence of death written down against them, in Heaven's Chancery itself; and, slowly or fast, advance incessantly towards their hour. 'The sign of a Grand Seigneur being landlord,' says the vehement plain-spoken Arthur Young, 'are wastes, *landes*, deserts, ling: go to his residence, you will find it in the middle of a forest, peopled with deer, wild boars and wolves. The fields are scenes of pitiable management, as the houses are of misery. To see so many millions of hands, that would be industrious, all idle and starving: Oh, if I were legislator of France for one day, I would make these great lords skip again!' O Arthur, thou now beholdest them *skip*;—wilt thou grow to grumble at that too?

For long years and generations it lasted; but the time came. Featherbrain, whom no reasoning and no pleading could touch, the glare of the firebrand had to illuminate: there remained but that method. Consider it, look at it! The widow is gathering nettles for her children's dinner; a perfumed Seigneur, delicately lounging in the Œil-de-Bœuf, has an alchemy whereby he will extract from her the third nettle, and name it Rent and Law: such an arrangement must end. Ought it not? But, O most fearful is *such* an ending! Let those, to whom God, in his great mercy, has granted time and space, prepare another and milder one.

To some it is a matter of wonder that the Seigneurs did not do something to help themselves; say, combine and arm: for there were a 'hundred and fifty thousand of them,' all valiant enough. Unhappily, a hundred and fifty thousand scattered over wide Provinces, divided by mutual ill-will, cannot combine. The highest Seigneurs, as we have seen, had already emigrated,—with a view of putting France to the blush. Neither are arms now the peculiar property of Seigneurs; but of every mortal who has ten shillings, wherewith to buy a secondhand firelock.

Besides, those starving Peasants, after all, have not four feet and claws, that you could keep them down permanently in that manner. They are not even of black colour: they are mere Unwashed Seigneurs; and a Seigneur too has human bowels!—the Seigneurs did what they could; enrolled in National Guards; fled, with shrieks, complaining to Heaven and Earth. One Seigneur, famed Memmay of Quincey, near Vesoul, invited all the rustics of his neighbourhood to a banquet; blew up his Château and them with gunpowder; and instantaneously vanished, no man yet knows whither. Some half-dozen years after, he came back; and demonstrated that it was by accident.

Nor are the Authorities idle; though unluckily, all Authorities, Municipalities and such like, are in the uncertain transitionary state; getting regenerated from old Monarchic to new Democratic; no Official yet knows clearly what he is. Nevertheless, Mayors old or new do gather *Marechaussées*, National Guards, Troops of the line; justice, of the most summary sort, is not wanting. The Electoral Committee of Mâcon, though but a Committee, goes the length of hanging, for its own behoof, as many as twenty. The Prévôt of Dauphiné traverses the country 'with a movable column,' with tipstaves, gallowsropes; for gallows any tree will serve, and suspend its culprit, or 'thirteen' culprits.

Unhappy country! How is the fair gold-and-green of the ripe bright Year defaced with horrid blackness; black ashes of Châteaus, black bodies of gibbeted Men! Industry has ceased in it; not sounds of the hammer and saw, but of the tocsin and alarm-drum. The sceptre has departed, *whither* one knows not;—breaking itself in pieces: here impotent, there tyrannous. National Guards are unskilful, and of doubtful purpose; Soldiers are inclined to mutiny: there is danger that they two may quarrel, danger that they may *agree*. Strasburg has seen riots: a Townhall torn to shreds, its archives scattered white on the winds; drunk soldiers embracing drunk citizens for three days, and Mayor Dietrich and Marshal Rochambeau reduced nigh to desperation.

Through the middle of all which phenomena is seen, on his triumphant transit, 'escorted,' through Béfort for instance, 'by fifty National Horsemen and all the military music of the place,'—M. Necker, returning from Bâle! Glorious as the meridian; though poor Necker himself partly guesses whither it is leading. One highest culminating day, at the Paris Townhall; with immortal vivats, with wife and daughter kneeling publicly to kiss his hand; with Besenval's pardon granted,—but indeed revoked before sunset: one highest day, but then lower days, and ever lower, down even to lowest! Such magic is in a name; and in the want of a name. Like some enchanted Mambrino's Helmet, essential to victory, comes this 'Saviour of France;' beshouted, becymballed by the world: alas, so soon to be *dis*enchanted, to be pitched shamefully over the lists as a Barber's Bason! Gibbon 'could wish to show him' (in this ejected, Barber's-Bason state) to any man of solidity, who were minded to have the soul burnt out of him, and become a *caput mortuum*, by Ambition, unsuccessful or successful.

Another small phasis we add, and no more: how, in the Autumn months, our sharp-tempered Arthur has been 'pestered for some days past,' by shot, lead-drops and slugs, 'rattling five or six times into my chaise and about my ears;' all the mob of the country gone out to kill Game! It is even so. On the Cliffs of Dover, over all the Marches of France, there appear, this autumn, two signs on the Earth; emigrant flights of French Seigneurs; emigrant winged flights of French Game! Finished, one may say, or as good as finished, is the Preservation of Game on this Earth; completed for endless Time. What part *it* had to play in the History of Civilisation is played: *plaudite; exeat!*

In this manner does Sansculottism blaze up, illustrating many things; producing, among the rest, as we saw, on the Fourth of August, that semi-miraculous Night of Pentecost in the National Assembly; semi-miraculous, which had its causes, and its effects. Feudalism is struck dead; not on parchment only, and by ink; but in very fact, by fire; say, by self-combustion. This conflagration of the South-East will abate; will be got scattered, to the West, or elsewhither: extinguish it will not, till the *fuel* be all done.

CHAPTER IV

IN QUEUE

IF we look now at Paris, one thing is too evident: that the Bakers' shops have got their *Queues*, or Tails; their long strings of purchasers, arranged *in tail*, so that the first come be the first served,—were the shop once open! This waiting in tail, not seen since the early days of July, again makes its appearance in August. In time, we shall see it perfected by practice to the rank almost of an art; and the art, or quasi-art, of standing in tail become one of the characteristics of the Parisian People, distinguishing them from all other Peoples whatsoever.

But consider, while work itself is so scarce, how a man must not only realise money, but stand waiting (if his wife is too weak to wait and struggle) for half-days in the Tail, till he get it changed for dear bad bread! Controversies, to the length sometimes of blood and battery, must arise in these exasperated Queues. Or if no controversy, then it is but one accordant *Pange Lingua* of complaint against the Powers that be. France has begun her long Curriculum of Hungering, instructive and productive beyond Academic Curriculums; which extends over some seven most strenuous years. As Jean Paul says of his own Life, 'to a great height shall the business of Hungering go.'

Or consider, in strange contrast, the jubilee Ceremonies; for, in general, the aspect of Paris presents these two features: jubilee ceremonials and scarcity of victual. Processions enough walk in jubilee; of Young Women, decked and dizened, their ribands all tricolor; moving with song and tabor, to the Shrine of Sainte Geneviève, to thank her that the Bastille is down. The Strong Men of the Market, and the Strong Women, fail not with their bouquets and speeches. Abbé Fauchet, famed in such work (for Abbé Lefèvre could only distribute powder) blesses tricolor cloth for the National Guard; and makes it a National Tricolor Flag; victorious, or to be victorious, in the cause of civil and religious liberty all over the world. Fauchet, we say, is the man for *Te-Deums*, and public Consecrations;—to which, as in this instance of the Flag, our National Guard will 'reply with volleys of musketry,' Church and Cathedral though it be; filling Notre Dame with such noisest fuliginous *Amen*, significant of several things.

On the whole, we will say our new Mayor Bailly, our new
Commander Lafayette named also 'Scipio-Americanus,' have
bought their preferment dear. Bailly rides in gilt state-coach,
with beef-eaters and sumptuosity; Camille Desmoulins, and
others, sniffing at him for it: Scipio bestrides the 'white
charger,' and waves with civic plumes in sight of all France.
Neither of them, however, does it for nothing; but, in truth, at
an exorbitant rate. At this rate, namely: of feeding Paris, and
keeping it from fighting. Out of the City-funds, some seventeen thousand of the utterly destitute are employed digging on
Montmartre, at ten pence a day, which buys them, at market
price, almost two pounds of bad bread:—they look very
yellow, when Lafayette goes to harangue them. The Townhall
is in travail, night and day; it must bring forth Bread, a Municipal Constitution, regulations of all kinds, curbs on the
Sansculottic Press; above all, Bread, Bread.

Purveyors prowl the country far and wide, with the appetite
of lions; detect hidden grain, purchase open grain; by gentle
means or forcible, must and will find grain. A most thankless
task; and so difficult, so dangerous,—even if a man did gain
some trifle by it! On the 19th of August, there is food for
one day. Complaints there are that the food is spoiled, and
produces an effect on the intestines: not corn but plaster-of
Paris! Which effect on the intestines, as well as that 'smart-
ing in the throat and palate,' a Townhall Proclamation warns
you to disregard, or even to consider as drastic-beneficial. The
Mayor of Saint-Denis, so black was his bread, has, by a
dyspeptic populace, been hanged on the Lanterne there.
National Guards protect the Paris Corn-Market: first ten
suffice; then six hundred. Busy are ye, Bailly, Brissot de
Warville, Condorcet, and ye others!

For, as just hinted, there is a Municipal Constitution to be
made too. The old Bastille Electors, after some ten days of
psalmodying over their glorious victory, began to hear it asked,
in a splenetic tone, Who put *you* there? They accordingly had
to give place, not without moanings, and audible growlings on
both sides, to a new larger Body, specially elected for that
post. Which new Body, augmented, altered, then fixed finally
at the number of Three Hundred, with the title of Town
Representatives (*Représentans de la Commune*), now sits there;
rightly portioned into Committees; assiduous making a Constitution; at all moments when not seeking flour.

And such a Constitution; little short of miraculous: one

that shall 'consolidate the Revolution !' The Revolution is finished, then? Mayor Bailly and all respectable friends of Freedom would fain think so. Your Revolution, like jelly sufficiently *boiled*, needs only to be poured into *shapes*, of Constitution, and 'consolidated' therein? Could it, indeed, contrive to *cool;* which last, however, is precisely the doubtful thing, or even the not doubtful !

Unhappy Friends of Freedom ; consolidating a Revolution ! They must sit at work there, their pavilion spread on very Chaos ; between two hostile worlds, the Upper Court-world, the nether Sansculottic one ; and, beaten on by both, toil painfully, perilously,—doing, in sad literal earnest, 'tne impossible.'

CHAPTER V

THE FOURTH ESTATE

PAMPHLETEERING opens its abysmal throat wider and wider ; never to close more. Our Philosophes, indeed, rather withdraw ; after the manner of Marmontel, 'retiring in disgust the first day.' Abbé Raynal, grown gray and quiet in his Marseilles domicile, is little content with this work : the last literary act of the man will again be an act of rebellion ; an indignant *Letter to the Constituent Assembly ;* answered by 'the order of the day.' Thus also Philosophe Morellet puckers discontented brows ; being indeed threatened in his benefices by that Fourth of August : it is clearly going too far. How astonishing that those 'haggard figures in woollen jupes' would not rest as satisfied with Speculation, and victorious Analysis, as we !

Alas, yes: Speculation, Philosophism, once the ornament and wealth of the saloon, will now coin itself into mere Practical Propositions, and circulate on street and highway, universally ; with results ! A fourth Estate, of Able Editors, springs up ; increases and multiplies ; irrepressible, incalculable. New Printers, new Journals, and ever new (so prurient is the world), let our Three Hundred curb and consolidate as they can ! Loustalot, under the wing of Prudhomme dull-blustering Printer, edits weekly his *Révolutions de Paris ;* in an acrid, emphatic manner. Acrid, corrosive, as the spirit of sloes and copperas, is Marat, *Friend of the People ;* struck already with the fact that the National Assembly, so full of

Aristocrats, 'can do nothing,' except dissolve itself, and make way for a better; that the Townhall Representatives are little other than babblers and imbeciles, if not even knaves. Poor is this man; squalid, and dwells in garrets; a man unlovely to the sense, outward and inward; a man forbid;—and is becoming fanatical, possessed with fixed-idea. Cruel *lusus* of Nature! Did Nature, O poor Marat, as in cruel sport, knead thee out of her *leavings*, and miscellaneous waste clay; and fling thee forth, stepdame-like, a Distraction into this distracted Eighteenth Century? Work is appointed thee there; which thou shalt do. The Three Hundred have summoned and will again summon Marat: but always he croaks forth answer sufficient; always he will defy them, or elude them; and endure no gag.

Carra, 'Ex-secretary of a decapitated Hospodar,' and then of a Necklace-Cardinal; likewise Pamphleteer, Adventurer, in many scenes and lands,—draws nigh to Mercier, of the *Tableau de Paris;* and, with foam on his lips, proposes an *Annales Patriotiques.* The *Moniteur* goes its prosperous way; Barrère 'weeps,' on Paper as yet loyal; Rivarol, Royou are not idle. Deep calls to deep: your *Domine Salvum Fac Regem* shall awaken *Pange Lingua;* with an *Ami-du-Peuple* there is a King's-Friend Newspaper, *Ami-du-Roi.* Camille Desmoulins has appointed himself *Procureur-Général de la Lanterne,* Attorney-General of the Lamp-iron; and pleads, *not* with atrocity, under an atrocious title; editing weekly his brilliant *Revolutions of Paris and Brabant.* Brilliant, we say; for if, in that thick murk of Journalism, with its dull blustering, with its fixed or loose fury, any ray of genius greet thee, be sure it is Camille's. The thing that Camille touches, he with his light finger adorns: brightness plays, gentle, unexpected, amid horrible confusions; often is the word of Camille worth reading, when no other's is. Questionable Camille, how thou glitterest with a fallen, rebellious, yet still semi-celestial light; as is the starlight on the brow of Lucifer! Son of the Morning, into what times and what lands art thou fallen!

But in all things there is good;—though it be not good for 'consolidating Revolutions.' Thousand wagon-loads of this Pamphleteering and Newspaper matter lie rotting slowly in the Public Libraries of our Europe. Snatched from the great gulf, like oysters by bibliomaniac pearl-divers, there must they first *rot,* then what was pearl, in Camille or others, may be seen as such, and continue as such.

Nor has public speaking declined, though Lafayette and his Patrols look sour on it. Loud always is the Palais Royal, loudest the Café de Foy; such a miscellany of Citizens and Citizenesses circulating there. 'Now and then,' according to Camille, 'some Citizens employ the liberty of the *press* for a private purpose; so that this or the other Patriot finds himself short of his watch or pocket-handkerchief!' But for the rest, in Camille's opinion, nothing can be a livelier image of the Roman Forum. 'A Patriot proposes his motion; if it finds any supporters, they make him mount on a chair, and speak. If he is applauded, he prospers and redacts; if he is hissed, he goes his ways.' Thus they, circulating and perorating. Tall shaggy Marquis Saint-Huruge, a man that has had losses, and has deserved them, is seen eminent, and also heard. 'Bellowing' is the character of his voice, like that of a Bull of Bashan; voice which drowns all voices, which causes frequently the hearts of men to leap. Cracked or half-cracked is this tall Marquis's head; uncracked are his lungs; the cracked and the uncracked shall alike avail him.

Consider further that each of the Forty-eight Districts has its own Committee; speaking and motioning continually; aiding in the search for grain, in the search for a Constitution; checking and spurring the poor Three Hundred of the Townhall. That Danton, with a 'voice reverberating from the domes,' is President of the Cordeliers District; which has already become a Goshen of Patriotism. That apart from the 'seventeen thousand utterly necessitous, digging on Montmartre,' most of whom, indeed, have got passes, and been dismissed into Space 'with four shillings,—there is a *strike*, or union, of Domestics out of place; who assemble for public speaking: next, a strike of Tailors, for even they will strike and speak; further, a strike of Journeymen Cordwainers; a strike of Apothecaries: so dear is bread.' All these, having struck, must speak; generally under the open canopy; and pass resolutions;—Lafayette and his Patrols watching them suspiciously from the distance.

Unhappy mortals: such tugging and lugging, and throttling of one another, to divide, in some not intolerable way, the joint Felicity of man in this Earth; when the whole lot to be divided is such a 'feast of *shells!*'—Diligent are the Three Hundred; none equals Scipio-Americanus in dealing with mobs. But surely all these things bode ill for the consolidating of a Revolution.

BOOK VII

THE INSURRECTION OF WOMEN

CHAPTER I

PATROLLOTISM

No, Friends, this Revolution is not of the consolidating kind. Do not fires, fevers, sown seeds, chemical mixtures, men, events; all embodiments of Force that work in this miraculous Complex of Forces, named Universe—go on *growing*, through their natural phases and developments, each according to its kind; reach their height, reach their visible decline; finally sink under, vanishing, and what we call *die*? They all grow; there is nothing but what grows, and shoots forth into its special expansion,—once give it leave to spring. Observe too that each grows with a rapidity proportioned, in general, to the madness and unhealthiness there is in it: slow regular growth, though this also ends in death, is what we name health and sanity.

A Sansculottism, which has prostrated Bastilles, which has got pike and musket, and now goes burning Châteaus, passing resolutions and haranguing under roof and sky, may be said to have sprung; and, by law of Nature, must grow. To judge by the madness and diseasedness both of itself, and of the soil and element it is in, one might expect the rapidity and monstrosity would be extreme.

Many things too, especially all diseased things, grow by shoots and fits. The first grand fit and shooting forth of Sansculottism was that of Paris conquering its King; for Bailly's figure of rhetoric was all-too sad a reality. The King is conquered; going at large on his parole; on condition, say, of absolutely good behaviour,—which, in these circumstances, will unhappily mean no behaviour whatever. A quite untenable position, that of Majesty put on its good behaviour! Alas, is it not natural that whatever lives try to keep itself living? Whereupon his Majesty's behaviour will soon become exceptionable; and so the Second grand Fit of Sansculottism, that of putting him in durance, cannot be distant.

Necker, in the National Assembly, is making moan, as usual, about his Deficit: Barriers and Customhouses burnt; the Tax-gatherer hunted, not hunting; his Majesty's Exchequer all but empty. The remedy is a Loan of thirty millions; then, on still more enticing terms, a Loan of eighty millions: neither of which Loans, unhappily, will the Stockjobbers venture to lend. The Stockjobber has no country, except his own black pool of *Agio*.

And yet, in those days, for men that have a country, what a glow of patriotism burns in many a heart; penetrating inwards to the very purse! So early as the 7th of August, a *Don Patriotique*, 'Patriotic Gift of jewels to a considerable extent,' has been solemnly made by certain Parisian women; and solemnly accepted with honourable mention. Whom forthwith all the world takes to imitating and emulating. Patriotic Gifts, always with some heroic eloquence, which the President must answer and the Assembly listen to, flow in from far and near: in such number that the honourable mention can only be performed in 'lists published at stated epochs.' Each gives what he can: the very cordwainers have behaved munificently; one landed proprietor gives a forest; fashionable society gives its shoebuckles, takes cheerfully to shoe-ties. Unfortunate-females give what they have 'amassed in loving.' The smell of all cash, as Vespasian thought, is good.

Beautiful, and yet inadequate! The Clergy must be 'invited' to melt their superfluous Church-plate,—in the Royal Mint. Nay finally, a Patriotic Contribution, of the forcible sort, has to be determined on, though unwillingly: let the fourth part of your declared yearly revenue, for this once only, be paid down; so shall a National Assembly make the Constitution, undistracted at least by insolvency. Their own wages, as settled on the 17th of August, are but Eighteen Francs a day, each man; but the Public Service must have sinews, must have money. To *appease* the Deficit; not to '*combler*, or choke, the Deficit,' if you or mortal could! For withal, as Mirabeau was heard saying, "it is the Deficit that saves us."

Towards the end of August, our National Assembly in its constitutional labours has got so far as the question of *Veto*: shall Majesty have a Veto on the National Enactments; or not have a Veto? What speeches were spoken, within doors and without; clear, and also passionate logic; imprecations,

comminations; gone happily, for most part, to Limbo!
Through the cracked brain and uncracked lungs of Saint-
Huruge, the Palais Royal rebellows with Veto. Journalism is
busy, France rings with Veto. 'I shall never forget,' says
Dumont, 'my going to Paris, one of those days, with Mirabeau; and the crowd of people we found waiting for his
carriage, about Le Jay the Bookseller's shop. They flung
themselves before him; conjuring him with tears in their eyes
not to suffer the *Veto Absolu*. They were in a frenzy:
"Monsieur le Comte, you are the People's father, you must
save us; you must defend us against those villains who are
bringing back Despotism. If the King get this Veto, what is
the use of National Assembly? We are slaves; all is done."'
Friends, *if* the sky fall, there will be catching of larks!
Mirabeau, adds Dumont, was eminent on such occasions: he
answered vaguely, with a Patrician imperturbability, and
bound himself to nothing.

Deputations go to the Hôtel-de-Ville; anonymous Letters
to Aristocrats in the National Assembly, threatening that
fifteen thousand, or sometimes that sixty thousand, 'will
march to illuminate you.' The Paris Districts are astir;
Petitions signing: Saint-Huruge sets forth from the Palais
Royal with an escort of fifteen hundred individuals, to petition
in person. Resolute, or seemingly so, is the tall shaggy
Marquis, is the Café de Foy: but resolute also is Com-
mandant-General Lafayette. The streets are all beset by
Patrols: Saint-Huruge is stopped at the *Barrière des Bons
Hommes*; he may bellow like the bulls of Bashan, but abso-
lutely must return. The brethren of the Palais Royal 'circu-
late all night,' and make motions, under the open canopy; all
Coffeehouses being shut. Nevertheless Lafayette and the
Townhall do prevail; Saint-Huruge is thrown into prison;
Veto Absolu adjusts itself into *Suspensive Veto*, prohibition not
forever, but for a term of time; and this doom's-clamour will
grow silent, as the others have done.

So far has Consolidation prospered, though with difficulty;
repressing the Nether Sansculottic world; and the Constitution
shall be made. With difficulty: amid jubilee and scarcity;
Patriotic Gifts, Bakers'-queues; Abbé-Fauchet Harangues,
with their *Amen* of platoon-musketry! Scipio-Americanus has
deserved thanks from the National Assembly and France.
They offer him stipends and emoluments to a handsome
extent; all which stipends and emoluments he, covetous of fame

other blessedness than mere money, does, in his chivalrous
way, without scruple, refuse.

To the Parisian common man, meanwhile, one thing remains inconceivable : that now when the Bastille is down, and
French Liberty restored, grain should continue so dear. Our
Rights of Man are voted, Feudalism and all Tyranny
abolished; yet behold we stand *in queue!* Is it Aristocrat
forestallers; a Court still bent on intrigues? Something is
rotten, somewhere.

And yet, alas, what to do? Lafayette, with his Patrols,
prohibits every thing, even complaint. Saint-Huruge and
other heroes of the *Veto* lie in durance. People's-Friend
Marat was seized; Printers of Patriotic Journals are fettered
and forbidden; the very Hawkers cannot cry, till they get
license, and leaden badges. Blue National Guards ruthlessly
dissipate all groups; scour, with levelled bayonets, the Palais
Royal itself. Pass, on your affairs, along the Rue Taranne,
the Patrol, presenting his bayonet, cries, *To the left!* Turn
into the Rue Saint-Bénoit, he cries, *To the right!* A judicious
Patriot (like Camille Desmoulins, in this instance) is driven,
for quietness' sake, to take the gutter.

O much-suffering People, our glorious Revolution is evapora-
ing in tricolor ceremonies, and complimentary harangues!
Of which latter, as Loustalot acridly calculates, 'upwards
of two thousand have been delivered within the last month, at
the Townhall alone.' And our mouths unfilled with bread,
are to be shut, under penalties? The Caricaturist promulgates
his emblematic Tablature: *Le Patrouillotisme chassant le
Patriotisme*, Patriotism driven out by Patrollotism. Ruthless
Patrols; long superfine harangues; and scanty ill-baked loaves,
more like baked Bath bricks,—which produce an effect on the
intestines! Where will this end? In consolation?

CHAPTER II

O RICHARD, O MY KING

FOR, alas, neither is the Townhall itself without misgivings.
The Nether Sansculottic world has been suppressed hitherto:
but then the Upper Court-world! Symptoms there are that
the Œil-de-Bœuf is rallying.

More than once in the Townhall Sanhedrim, often enough

from those outspoken Bakers'-queues, has the wish uttered itself: O that our Restorer of French Liberty were here; that he could see with his own eyes, not with the false eyes of Queens and Cabals, and his really good heart be enlightened! For falsehood still environs him; intriguing Dukes de Guiche, with Bodyguards; scouts of Bouillé; a new flight of intriguers, now that the old is flown. What else means this advent of the *Régiment de Flandre;* entering Versailles, as we hear, on the 23d of September, with two pieces of cannon? Did not the Versailles National Guard do duty at the Château? Had they not Swiss; Hundred Swiss; *Gardes-du-Corps,* Bodyguards so-called? Nay, it would seem, the number of Bodyguards on duty has, by a manœuvre, been doubled: the new relieving Battalion of them arrived at its time; but the old relieved one does not *depart!*

Actually, there runs a whisper through the best-informed Upper-Circles, or a nod still more portentous than whispering, of his Majesty's flying to Metz; of a Bond (to stand by him therein), which has been signed by Noblesse and Clergy, to the incredible amount of thirty, or even of sixty thousand. Lafayette coldly whispers it, and coldly asseverates it, to Count d'Estaing at the Dinner-table; and D'Estaing, one of the bravest men, quakes to the core lest some lackey overhear it; and tumbles thoughtful, without sleep, all night. Régiment de Flandre, as we said, is clearly arrived. His Majesty, they say, hesitates about sanctioning the Fourth of August; makes observations, of chilling tenor, on the very Rights of Man! Likewise, may not all persons, the Bakers'-queues themselves discern, on the streets of Paris, the most astonishing number of Officers on furlough, Crosses of St. Louis, and such like? Some reckon 'from a thousand to twelve hundred.' Officers of all uniforms; nay one uniform never before seen by eye: green faced with red! The tricolor cockade is not always visible: but what, in the name of Heaven, may these *black* cockades, which some wear, foreshadow?

Hunger whets everything, especially Suspicion and Indignation. Realities, themselves, in this Paris, have grown unreal; preternatural. Phantasms once more stalk through the brain of hungry France. O ye laggards and dastards, cry shrill voices from the Queues, if ye had the hearts of men, ye would take your pikes and secondhand firelocks, and look into it; not leave your wives and daughters to be starved, murdered and worse!—Peace, women! The heart of man is bitter and heavy; Patriotism, driven out by Patrollotism, knows not what to resolve on.

The truth is, the Œil-de-Bœuf has rallied; to a certain unknown extent. A changed Œil-de-Bœuf; with Versailles National Guards, in their tricolor cockades, doing duty there; a Court all flaring with tricolor! Yet even to a tricolor Court men will rally. Ye loyal hearts, burnt-out Seigneurs, rally round your Queen! With wishes; which will produce hopes, which will produce attempts!

For indeed self-preservation being such a law of Nature, what can a rallied Court do, but attempt and endeavour, or call it *plot*,—with such wisdom and unwisdom as it has? They will fly, escorted, to Metz, where brave Bouillé commands; they will raise the Royal Standard: the Bond-signatures shall become armed men. Were not the King so languid! Their Bond, if at all signed, must be signed without his privity.—Unhappy King, *he* has but one resolution: not to have a civil war. For the rest, he still hunts, having ceased lockmaking; he still dozes, and digests; is clay in the hands of the potter. Ill will it fare with him, in a world where all is helping itself; where, as has been written, 'whosoever is not hammer must be stithy;' and 'the very hyssop on the wall grows there, in that chink, because the whole Universe could not prevent its growing!'

But as for the coming up of this Régiment de Flandre, may it not be urged that there were Saint-Huruge Petitions, and continual meal-mobs? Undebauched Soldiers, be there plot, or only dim elements of a plot, are always good. Did not the Versailles Municipality (an old Monarchic one, not yet refounded into a Democratic) instantly second the proposal? Nay the very Versailles National Guard, wearied with continual duty at the Château, did not object; only Draper Lecointre, who is now Major Lecointre, shook his head.—Yes, Friends, surely it was natural this Régiment de Flandre should be sent for, since it could be got. It was natural that, at sight of military bandoleers, the heart of the rallied Œil-de-Bœuf should revive; and Maids of Honour, and gentlemen of honour, speak comfortable words to epauletted defenders, and to one another. Natural also, and mere common civility that the Bodyguards, a Regiment of Gentlemen, should invite their Flandre brethren to a Dinner of welcome!—Such invitation, in the last days of September, is given and accepted.

Dinners are defined as ' the *ultimate* act of communion:' men that can have communion in nothing else, can sympathetically eat together, can still rise into some glow of brotherhood over food and wine. The Dinner is fixed on, for Thursday the First of October; and ought to have a fine effect. Further, as such Dinner may be rather extensive, and even the Non-commissioned and the Common man be introduced, to see and to hear, could not his Majesty's Opera Apartment, which has lain quite silent ever since Kaiser Joseph was here, be obtained for the purpose?—The Hall of the Opera is granted; the Salon d'Hercule shall be drawing-room. Not only the Officers of Flandre but of the Swiss, of the Hundred Swiss; nay of the Versailles National Guard, such of them as have any loyalty, shall feast: it will be a Repast like few.

And now suppose this Repast, the solid part of it, trans-acted; and the first bottle over. Suppose the customary loyal toasts drunk; the King's health, the Queen's with deafening vivats ;—that of the Nation ' omitted,' or even ' rejected.' Suppose champagne flowing; with pot-valorous speech, with instrumental music, empty featherheads growing ever the noisier, in their own emptiness, in each other's noise. Her Majesty, who looks unusually sad to-night (his Majesty sitting dulled with the day's hunting), is told that the sight of it would cheer her. Behold! She enters there, issuing from her State-rooms, like the Moon from clouds, this fairest un-happy Queen of Hearts; royal Husband by her side, young Dauphin in her arms! She descends from the Boxes, amid splendour and acclaim; walks queenlike round the Tables; gracefully escorted, gracefully nodding; her looks full of sorrow, yet of gratitude and daring, with the hope of France on her mother-bosom! And now, the band striking up, *O Richard, O mon Roi, l'univers t'abandonne* (O Richard, O my King, the world is all forsaking thee) — could man do other than rise to height of pity, of loyal valour? Could featherheaded young ensigns do other than, by white Bourbon Cockades, handed them from fair fingers; by waving of swords, drawn to pledge the Queen's health; by trampling of National Cockades; by scaling the Boxes, whence in-trusive murmurs may come; by vociferation, tripudiation, sound, fury and distraction, within doors and without,—testify what tempest-tost state of vacuity they are in? Till cham-pagne and tripudiation do their work; and all lie silent, hori-zontal; passively slumbering with meed-of-battle dreams!—

A natural Repast; in ordinary times, a harmless one: now fatal, as that of Thyestes; as that of Job's Sons, when a strong wind smote the four corners of their banquet-house! Poor ill-advised Marie Antoinette, with a woman's vehemence, not with a sovereign's foresight! It was so natural, yet so unwise. Next day, in public speech of ceremony, her Majesty declares herself 'delighted with the Thursday.'

The heart of the Œil-de-Bœuf glows into hope; into daring, which is premature. Rallied Maids of Honour, waited on by Abbés, sew 'white cockades;' distribute them, with words, with glances, to epauletted youths; who, in return, may kiss, not without fervour, the fair sewing fingers. Captains of horse and foot go swashing with 'enormous white cockades;' nay one Versailles National Captain has mounted the like, so witching were the words and glances, and laid aside his tricolor! Well may Major Lecointre shake his head with a look of severity; and speak audible resentful words. But now a swashbuckler, with enormous white cockade, over-hearing the Major, invites him insolently, once and then again elsewhere, to recant; and failing that, to duel. Which latter feat Major Lecointre declares that he will not perform, not at least by any known laws of fence; that he nevertheless will, according to mere law of Nature, by dirk and blade, 'ex-erminate' any 'vile gladiator' who may insult him or the Nation;—whereupon (for the Major is actually drawing his implement) 'they are parted,' and no weasands slit.

CHAPTER III

BLACK COCKADES

BUT fancy what effect this Thyestes Repast, and trampling on the National Cockade, must have had in the *Salle des Menus;* in the famishing Bakers'-queues at Paris! Nay, such Thyestes Repasts, it would seem, continue. Flandre has given its Counter-Dinner to the Swiss and Hundred Swiss; then on Saturday there has been another.

Yes, here with us is famine; but yonder at Versailles is food, enough and to spare! Patriotism stands in queue, shivering hungerstruck, insulted by Patrollotism; while bloody-minded Aristocrats, heated with excess of high living, trample on the National Cockade. Can the atrocity be true? Nay, look: green uniforms faced with red; black cockades,—the colour of Night! Are we to have military onfall; and death also by starvation? For behold the Corbeil Cornboat, which used to come twice a-day, with its Plaster-of-Paris meal, now comes only once. And the Townhall is deaf; and the men are laggard and dastard!—At the Café de Foy, this Saturday evening, a new thing is seen, not the last of its kind: a woman engaged in public speaking. Her poor man, she says, was put to silence by his District; their Presidents and Officials would not let him speak. Wherefore she here with her shrill tongue will speak; denouncing, while her breath endures, the Corbeil Boat, the Plaster-of-Paris bread, sacrilegious Opera-dinners, green uniforms, Pirate Aristocrats, and those black cockades of theirs!—

Truly, it is time for the black cockades at least to vanish. Them Patrollotism itself will not protect. Nay, sharp-tempered 'M. Tassin,' at the Tuileries parade on Sunday morning, forgets all National military rule; starts from the ranks, wrenches down one black cockade which is swashing ominous there and tramples it fiercely into the soil of France. Patrollotism itself is not without suppressed fury. Also the Districts begin to stir; the voice of President Danton reverberates in the Cordeliers: People's-Friend Marat has flown to Versailles and back again;—swart bird, not of the halcyon kind.

And so Patriot meets promenading Patriot, this Sunday; and sees his own grim care reflected on the face of another. Groups, in spite of Patrollotism, which is not so alert as usual, fluctuate deliberative; groups on the Bridges, on the Quais, at the patriotic Cafés. And ever as any black cockade may emerge, rises the many voiced growl and bark: *À bas*, Down! All black cockades are ruthlessly plucked off: one individual picks his up again; kisses it, attempts to refix it; but a 'hundred canes start into the air,' and he desists. Still worse went it with another individual; doomed, by extempore *Plebiscitum*, to the Lanterne; saved, with difficulty, by some active *Corps-de-Garde.*—Lafayette sees signs of an effervescence; which he doubles his Patrols, doubles his diligence, to prevent. So passes Sunday, the 4th of October 1789.

Sullen is the male heart, repressed by Patrollotism; vehement is the female, irrepressible. The public-speaking woman at the Palais Royal was not the only speaking one:—Men know not what the pantry is, when it grows empty; only house-mothers know. O women, wives of men that will only calculate and not act! Patrollotism is strong; but Death, by

starvation and military onfall, is stronger. Patrollotism represses male Patriotism : but female Patriotism? Will Guards
named National thrust their bayonets into the bosoms of
women? Such thought, or rather such dim unshaped raw
material of a thought, ferments universally under the female
night-cap; and, by earliest day-break, on slight hint, will
explode.

CHAPTER IV

THE MENADS

IF Voltaire once, in splenetic humour, asked his countrymen :
' But you, *Gualches*, what have you invented ?" they can now
answer : The Art of Insurrection. It was an art needed in
these last singular times : an art for which the French nature,
so full of vehemence, so free from depth, was perhaps of all
others the fittest.

Accordingly, to what a height, one may well say of perfection, has this branch of human industry been carried by
France, within the last half-century ! Insurrection, which
Lafayette thought might be ' the most sacred of duties,' ranks
now, for the French people, among the duties which they
can perform. Other mobs are dull masses; which roll onwards
with a dull fierce tenacity, a dull fierce heat, but emit no light-
flashes of genius as they go. The French mob, again, is
among the liveliest phenomena of our world. So rapid,
audacious ; so clear-sighted, inventive, prompt to seize the
moment; instinct with life to its finger-ends ! That talent,
were there no other, of spontaneously standing in queue,
distinguishes, as we said, the French People from all Peoples,
ancient and modern.

Let the Reader confess too that, taking one thing with
another, perhaps few terrestrial Appearances are better worth
considering than mobs. Your mob is a genuine outburst of
nature; issuing from, or communicating with, the deepest deep
of Nature. When so much goes grinning and grimacing as
a lifeless Formality, and under the stiff buckram no heart can
be felt beating, here once more, if nowhere else, is a Sincerity
and Reality. Shudder at it; or even shriek over it, if thou
must; nevertheless consider it. Such a Complex of human
Forces and Individualities hurled forth, in their transcendental
mood, to act and react, on circumstances and on one another;

to work out what it is in them to work. The thing they will
do is known to no man; least of all to themselves. It is the
inflammablest immeasurable Fire-work, generating, consuming
itself. With what phases, to what extent, with what results
it will burn off, Philosophy and Perspicacity conjecture in
vain.

'Man,' as has been written, 'is for ever interesting to man;
nay properly there is nothing else interesting.' In which light
also, may we not discern why most Battles have become so
wearisome? Battles, in these ages, are transacted by mechanism; with the slightest possible development of human in-
dividuality or spontaneity: men now even die, and kill one
another, in an artificial manner. Battles ever since Homer's
time, when they were Fighting Mobs, have mostly ceased to
be worth looking at, worth reading of or remembering. How
many wearisome bloody Battles does History strive to represent; or even, in a husky way, to sing :—and she would omit
or carelessly slur-over this one Insurrection of Women?

A thought, or dim raw-material of a thought, was fermenting
all night, universally in the female head, and might explode.
In squalid garret, on Monday morning Maternity awakes, to
hear children weeping for bread. Maternity must forth to the
streets, to the herb-markets and Bakers'-queues; meets there
with hunger-stricken Maternity, sympathetic, exasperative.
O we unhappy women! But, instead of Bakers'-queues, why
not to Aristocrats' palaces, the root of the matter? *Allons!*
Let us assemble. To the Hôtel-de-Ville; to Versailles; to
the Lanterne!

In one of the Guardhouses of the Quartier Saint-Eustache,
'a young woman' seizes a drum,—for how shall National
Guards give fire on women, on a young woman? The young
woman seizes the drum; sets forth beating it, 'uttering cries
relative to the dearth of grains.' Descend, O mothers; descend,
ye Judiths, to food and revenge!—All women gather and go;
crowds storm all stairs, force out all women: the female Insurrectionary Force, according to Camille, resembles the English
Naval one; there is a universal 'Press of women.' Robust
Dames of the Halle, slim Mantua-makers, assiduous, risen
with the dawn; ancient Virginity tripping to matins; the
Housemaid, with early broom; all must go. Rouse ye, O
women; the laggard men will not act; they say, we ourselves
may act!

And so, like snowbreak from the mountains, for every staircase is a melted brook, it storms; tumultuous, wild-shrilling,
towards the Hôtel-de-Ville. Tumultuous, with or without drum-
music; for the Faubourg Saint-Antoine also has tucked up its
gown; and with besom-staves, fire-irons, and even rusty pistols
(void of ammunition), is flowing on. Sound of it flies, with
a velocity of sound, to the utmost Barriers. By seven o'clock,
on this raw October morning, fifth of the month, the Townhall will see wonders. Nay, as chance would have it, a male
party are already there; clustering tumultuously round some
National Patrol, and a Baker who has been seized with short
weights. They are there; and have even lowered the rope of
the Lanterne. So that the official persons have to smuggle
forth the short-weighing Baker by back doors, and even send
'to all the Districts' for more force.

Grand it was, says Camille, to see so many Judiths, from
eight to ten thousand of them in all, rushing out to search into
the root of the matter! How unfrightful it must have been;
ludicro-terrific, and most unmanageable. At such hour the
overwatched Three Hundred are not yet stirring: none but
some Clerks, a company of National Guards; and M. de
Gouvion, the Major-general. Gouvion has fought in America
for the cause of civil Liberty; a man of no inconsiderable
heart, but deficient in head. He is, for the moment, in his
back apartment, assuaging Usher Maillard, the Bastille-ser-
geant, who has come, as too many do, with 'representations.'
The assuagement is still incomplete when our Judiths arrive.

The National Guards form on the outer stairs, with levelled
bayonets; the ten thousand Judiths press up, resistless; with
obtestations, with outspread hands,—merely to speak to the
Mayor. The rear forces them; nay, from male hands in
the rear, stones already fly: the National Guard must do one
of two things; sweep the Place de Grève with cannon, or else
open to right and left. They open; the living deluge rushes
in. Through all rooms and cabinets, upwards to the topmost
belfry: ravenous, seeking arms, seeking Mayors, seeking
justice;—while, again, the better-dressed speak kindly to the
Clerks; point out the misery of these poor women; also their
ailments, some even of an interesting sort.

Poor M. de Gouvion is shiftless in this extremity; a man
shiftless, perturbed: who will one day commit suicide. How
happy for him that Usher Maillard the shifty was there, at the
moment, though making representations! Fly back, thou

shifty Maillard : seek the Bastille Company ; and O return fa
with it ; above all, with thy own shifty head ! For, behold, th
Judiths can find no Mayor or Municipal ; scarcely, in the top
most belfry, can they find poor Abbé Lefèvre the Powde
distributor. Him, for want of a better, they suspend there : i
the pale morning light ; over the top of all Paris, which swim
in one's failing eyes :—a horrible end ? Nay, the rope brok
as French ropes often did ; or else an Amazon cut it. Abb
Lefèvre falls; some twenty feet, rattling among the leads ; an
lives long years after, though always with 'a *tremblement* in th
limbs.'

And now doors fly under hatchets ; the Judiths have broke
the Armory ; have seized guns and cannons, three money-bag
paper-heaps ; torches flare : in few minutes, our brave Hôte
de-Ville, which dates from the Fourth Henry, will, with all tha
it holds, be in flames !

CHAPTER V

USHER MAILLARD

In flames, truly,—were it not that Usher Maillard, swift of foo
shifty of head, has returned !

Maillard, of his own motion,—for Gouvion or the rest wou'
not even sanction him,—snatches a drum ; descends th
Porch-stairs, ran-tan, beating sharp, with loud rolls, his Rogues
march : To Versailles ! *Allons ; à Versailles !* As men beat o
kettle or warmingpan, when angry she-bees, or say, flyin
desperate wasps, are to be hived ; and the desperate insec
hear it, and cluster round it,—simply as round *a* guidanc
where there was none: so now these Menads round shift
Maillard, Riding-Usher of the Châtelet. The axe pauses up
lifted ; Abbé Lefèvre is left half-hanged ; from the belfr
downwards all vomits itself. What rub-a-dub is that ? Stanisla
Maillard, Bastille-hero, will lead us to Versailles ? Joy to the
Maillard ; blessed art thou above Riding-Ushers. Away, the
away !

The seized cannon are yoked with seized cart-horses : brow
locked Demoiselle Théroigne, with pike and helmet, sits ther
as gunneress, ' with haughty eye and serene fair countenance;
comparable, some think, to the *Maid* of Orleans, or even r
calling 'the idea of Pallas Athene.' Maillard (for his dru
still rolls) is, by heaven-rending acclamation, admitted Genera

Maillard hastens the languid march. Maillard, beating rhythmic, with sharp rantan, all along the Quais, leads forward, with difficulty, his Menadic host. Such a host—marched not in silence! The bargeman pauses on the River; all wagoners and coach-drivers fly; men peer from windows,—not women, lest they be pressed. Sight of sights: Bacchantes, in these ultimate Formalised Ages! Bronze Henri looks on. from his Pont-Neuf; the Monarchic Louvre, Medicean Tuileries see a day like none heretofore seen.

And now Maillard has his Menads in the *Champs Élysées* Fields *Tartarean* rather); and the Hôtel-de-Ville has suffered comparatively nothing, Broken doors; an Abbé Lefèvre, who shall never more distribute powder; three sacks of money, most part of which (for Sansculottism, though famishing, is not without honour) shall be returned: this is all the damage. Great Maillard! A small nucleus of Order is round his drum; but his outskirts fluctuate, like the mad Ocean: for Rascality male and female is flowing in on him, from the four winds: guidance there is none but in his single head and two drumsticks.

O Maillard, when, since War first was, had General of Force such a task before him, as thou this day? Walter the Penniless still touches the feeling heart: but then Walter had sanction; had space to turn in; and also his Crusaders were of the male sex. Thou, this day, disowned of Heaven and Earth, art General of Menads. Their inarticulate frenzy thou must, on the spur of the instant, render into articulate words, into actions that are not frantic. Fail in it, this way or that? Pragmatical Officiality, with its penalties and law-books, waits before thee; Menads storm behind. If such hewed off the melodious head of Orpheus and hurled it into the Peneus waters, what may they not make of thee,—thee rhythmic merely, with no music but a sheepskin drum?—Maillard did not fail. Remarkable Maillard, if fame were not an accident, and History a distillation of Rumour, how remarkable wert thou!

On the Elysian Fields there is pause and fluctuation; but, for Maillard, no return. He persuades his Menads, clamorous for arms and the Arsenal, that no arms are in the Arsenal; that an unarmed attitude, and petition to a National Assembly, will be the best: he hastily nominates or sanctions generalesses, captains of tens and fifties;—and so, in loosest-flowing order, to the rhythm of some 'eight drums' (having laid aside his own), with the Bastille Volunteers bringing up his rear, once more takes the road.

Chaillot, which will promptly yield baked loaves, is not plundered; nor are the Sèvres Potteries broken. The old arches of Sèvres Bridge echo under Menadic feet; Seine River gushes on with his perpetual murmur; and Paris flings after us the boom of tocsin and alarm-drum,—inaudible, for the present, amid shrill-sounding hosts, and the splash of rainy weather. To Meudon, to Saint-Cloud, on both hands, the report of them has gone abroad; and hearths, this evening, will have a topic. The press of women still continues, for it is the cause of all Eve's Daughters, mothers that are, or that ought to be. No carriage-lady, were it with never such hysterics, but must dismount, in the mud roads, in her silk shoes, and walk. In this manner, amid wild October weather, they, a wild unwinged stork-flight, through the astonished country wend their way. Travellers of all sorts they stop; especially travellers or couriers from Paris. Deputy Lecha-pelier, in his elegant vesture, from his elegant vehicle, looks forth amazed through his spectacles; apprehensive for life;— states eagerly that he is Patriot-Deputy Lechapelier, and even Old-President Lechapelier, who presided on the Night of Pentecost, and is original member of the Breton Club. Thereupon 'rises huge shout of *Vive Lechapelier*, and several armed persons sprang up behind and before to escort him.'

Nevertheless, news, despatches from Lafayette, or vague noise of rumour, have pierced through, by side roads. In the National Assembly, while all is busy discussing the order of the day; regretting that there should be Anti-National Repasts in Opera-Halls; that his Majesty should still hesitate about accepting the Rights of Man, and hang conditions and per-adventures on them:—Mirabeau steps up to the President, experienced Mounier as it chanced to be; and articulates, in bass under-tone: "*Mounier, Paris marche sur nous* (Paris is marching on us)." "May be (*Je n'en sais rien*)!"—"Believe it or disbelieve it, that is not my concern; but Paris, I say, is marching on us. Fall suddenly unwell; go over to the Château; tell them this. There is not a moment to lose "— "Paris marching on us?" responds Mounier, with an atrabiliar accent: "Well, so much the better! We shall the sooner be a Republic." Mirabeau quits him, as one quits an experienced

President getting blindfold into deep waters; and the order of the day continues as before.

Yes, Paris is marching on us; and more than the women of Paris! Scarcely was Maillard gone, when M. de Gouvion's message to all the Districts, and such tocsin and drumming of the *générale*, began to take effect. Armed National Guards from every District; especially the Grenadiers of the Centre, who are our old Gardes Françaises, arrive, in quick sequence, on the Place de Grève. An 'immense people' is there; Saint-Antoine, with pike and rusty firelock, is all crowding thither, be it welcome or unwelcome. The Centre Grenadiers are received with cheering: "it is not cheers that we want," answer they gloomily; "the Nation has been insulted; to arms, and come with us for orders!" Ha, sits the wind *so?* Patriotism and Patrollotism are now one!

The Three Hundred have assembled; 'all the Committees are in activity;' Lafayette is dictating despatches for Versailles, when a Deputation of the Centre Grenadiers introduces itself to him. The Deputation makes military obeisance; and thus speaks, not without a kind of thought in it: "*Mon Général,* we are deputed by the Six Companies of Grenadiers. We do not think you a traitor, but we think the Government betrays you; it is time that this end. We cannot turn our bayonets against women crying to us for bread. The people are miserable, the source of the mischief is at Versailles: we must go seek the King, and bring him to Paris. We must exterminate (*exterminer*) the *Régiment de Flandre* and the *Gardes-du-Corps,* who have dared to trample on the National Cockade. If the King be too weak to wear his crown, let him lay it down. You will crown his Son, you will name a Council of Regency: and all will go better." Reproachful astonishment paints itself on the face of Lafayette; speaks itself from his eloquent chivalrous lips: in vain. "My General, we would shed the last drop of our blood for you; but the root of the mischief is at Versailles; we must go and bring the King to Paris; all the people wish it, *tout le peuple le veut.*"

My General descends to the outer staircase; and harangues once more in vain. "To Versailles! To Versailles!" Mayor Bailly, sent for through floods of Sansculottism, attempts academic oratory from his gilt state-coach; realises nothing but infinite hoarse cries of: "Bread! To Versailles!"—and gladly shrinks within doors. Lafayette mounts the white charger; and again harangues, and reharangues: with elo-

quence, with firmness, indignant demonstration; with all thing
but persuasion. "To Versailles! To Versailles!" So last
it, hour after hour;—for the space of half a day.

The great Scipio-Americanus can do nothing; not so much
as escape. "*Morbleu, mon Général,*" cry the Grenadiers serry
ing their ranks as the white charger makes a motion that way
"you will not leave us, you will abide with us!" A perilou
juncture: Mayor Bailly and the Municipals sit quaking withir
doors; my General is prisoner without: the Place de Grève
with its thirty thousand Regulars, its whole irregular Saint
Antoine and Saint-Marceau, is one minatory mass of clear or
rusty steel; all hearts set, with a moody fixedness, on one
object. Moody, fixed are all hearts: tranquil is no heart,—i
it be not that of the white charger who paws there, with
arched neck, composedly champing his bit; as if no World,
with its Dynasties and Eras, were now rushing down. The
drizzly day bends westward; the cry is still: "To Versailles!'

Nay now, borne from afar, come quite sinister cries
hoarse, reverberating in longdrawn hollow murmurs, with
syllables too like those of "*Lanterne!*" Or else, irregular
Sansculottism may be marching off, of itself; with pikes, nay
with cannon. The inflexible Scipio does at length, by aide-de
camp, ask of the Municipals: Whether or not he may go? A
Letter is handed out to him, over armed heads; sixty thousand
faces flash fixedly on his, there is stillness and no bosom
breathes, till he have read. By Heaven, he grows suddenly
pale! Do the Municipals permit? 'Permit and even order,'
—since he can no other. Clangour of approval rends the
welkin. To your ranks, then; let us march!

It is, as we compute, towards three in the afternoon.
Indignant National Guards may dine for once from their
haversack: dined or undined, they march with one heart.
Paris flings up her windows, claps hands, as the Avengers, with
their shrilling drums and shalms tramp by: she will then sit
pensive, apprehensive, and pass rather a sleepless night. On
the white charger, Lafayette, in the slowest possible manner,
going and coming, and eloquently haranguing among the
ranks, rolls onward with his thirty thousand. Saint-Antoine,
with pike and cannon, has preceded him; a mixed multitude,
of all and of no arms, hovers on his flanks and skirts; the
country once more pauses agape: *Paris marche sur nous.*

CHAPTER VI

TO VERSAILLES

For, indeed, about this same moment, Maillard has halted his
draggled Menads on the last hill-top; and now Versailles, and
the Château of Versailles, and far and wide the inheritance of
Royalty opens to the wondering eye. From far on the right,
over Marly and Saint-Germains-en-Laye; round towards Rambouillet, on the left: beautiful all; softly embosomed; as if in
sadness, in the dim moist weather! And near before us is
Versailles, New and Old; with that broad frondent *Avenue de
Versailles* between,—stately-frondent, broad, three hundred
feet as men reckon, with its four Rows of Elms; and then the
Château de Versailles, ending in royal Parks and Pleasances,
gleaming lakelets, arbours, Labyrinths, the *Ménagerie*, and
Great and Little Trianon. High-towered dwellings, leafy
pleasant places; where the gods of this lower world abide:
whence, nevertheless, black Care cannot be excluded; whither
Menadic Hunger is even now advancing, armed with pike-
thyrsi!

Yes, yonder, Mesdames, where our straight frondent Avenue,
joined, as you note, by Two frondent brother Avenues from
this hand and from that, spreads out into Place Royal and
Palace Forecourt; yonder is the *Salle des Menus*. Yonder an
august Assembly sits regenerating France. Forecourt, Grand
Court, Court of Marble, Court narrowing into Court you may
discern next, or fancy: on the extreme verge of which that
glass-dome, visibly glittering like a star of hope, is the—Œil-
de-Bœuf! Yonder, or nowhere in the world, is bread baked
for us. But, O Mesdames, were not one thing good? That
our cannons, with Demoiselle Théroigne and all show of war,
be put to the rear? Submission beseems petitioners of a
National Assembly; we are strangers in Versailles,—whence,
too audibly, there comes even now a sound as of tocsin and
générale! Also to put on, if possible, a cheerful countenance,
hiding our sorrows; and even to sing? Sorrow, pitied of the
Heavens, is hateful, suspicious to the Earth.—So counsels
shifty Maillard; haranguing his Menads, on the heights near
Versailles.

Cunning Maillard's dispositions are obeyed. The draggled
Insurrectionists advance up the Avenue, 'in three columns,'
among the four Elm-rows; 'singing *Henri Quatre*,' with what

melody they can; and shouting *Vive le Roi*. Versailles, though the Elm-rows are dripping wet, crowds from both sides, with: "*Vivent nos Parisiennes*, Our Paris ones forever!"

Prickers, scouts have been out towards Paris, as the rumour deepened: whereby his Majesty, gone to shoot in the Woods of Meudon, has been happily discovered, and got home; and the *générale* and tocsin set a-sounding. The Bodyguards are already drawn up in front of the Palace Grates; and look down the Avenue de Versailles; sulky, in wet buckskins. Flandre too is there, repentant of the Opera-Repast. Also Dragoons dismounted are there. Finally Major Lecointre, and what he can gather of the Versailles National Guard;—though it is to be observed, our Colonel, that same sleepless Count d'Estaing, giving neither order nor ammunition, has vanished most improperly; one supposes, into the Œil-de-Bœuf. Red coated Swiss stand within the Grates, under arms. There likewise, in their inner room, 'all the Ministers,' Saint-Priest, Lamentation Pompignan and the rest, are assembled with M. Necker: they sit with him there; blank, expecting what the hour will bring.

President Mounier, though he answered Mirabeau with a *tant mieux*, and affected to slight the matter, had his own forebodings. Surely, for these four weary hours he has reclined not on roses! The order of the day is getting forward: a Deputation to his Majesty seems proper, that it might please him to grant 'Acceptance pure and simple' to those Constitution-Articles of ours; the 'mixed qualified Acceptance,' with its peradventures, is satisfactory to neither gods nor men.

So much is clear. And yet there is more, which no man speaks, which all men now vaguely understand. Disquietude, absence of mind is on every face; Members whisper, uneasily come and go: the order of the day is evidently not the day's want. Till at length, from the outer gates, is heard a rustling and justling, shrill uproar and squabbling, muffled by walls; which testifies that the hour is come! Rushing and crushing one hears now; then enter Usher Maillard, with a Deputation of Fifteen muddy dripping Women,—having, by incredible industry, and aid of all the macers, persuaded the rest to wait out of doors. National Assembly shall now, therefore, look its august task directly in the face: regenerative Constitutionalism has an unregenerate Sansculottism bodily in front of it; crying, "Bread! Bread!"

Shifty Maillard, translating frenzy into articulation; repressive with the one hand, expostulative with the other, does his best; and really, though not bred to public speaking, manages rather well:—In the present dreadful rarity of grains, a Deputation of Female Citizens has, as the august Assembly can discern, come out from Paris to petition. Plots of Aristocrats are too evident in the matter; for example, one miller has been bribed 'by a banknote of 200 livres' not to grind,—name unknown to the Usher, but fact provable, at least indubitable. Further, it seems, the National Cockade has been trampled on; also there are Black Cockades, or were. All which things will not an august National Assembly, the hope of France, take into its wise immediate consideration?

And Menadic Hunger, irrepressible, crying "Black Cockades," crying " Bread, Bread," adds, after such fashion : Will it not?—Yes, Messieurs, if a Deputation to his Majesty, for the 'Acceptance pure and simple,' seemed proper,—how much more now, for 'the afflicting situation of Paris;' for the calming of this effervescence! President Mounier, with a speedy Deputation, among whom we notice the respectable figure of Doctor Guillotin, gets himself forthwith on march. Vice-President shall continue the order of the day; Usher Maillard shall stay by him to repress the women. It is four o'clock, of the miserablest afternoon, when Mounier steps out.

O experienced Mounier, what an afternoon; the last of thy political existence! Better had it been to 'fall suddenly unwell,' while it was yet time. For, behold, the Esplanade, over all its spacious expanse, is covered with groups of squalid dripping Women; of lankhaired male Rascality, armed with axes, rusty pikes, old muskets, ironshod clubs (*batons ferrés*, which end in knives or sword-blades, a kind of extempore billhook);—looking nothing but hungry revolt. The rain pours : Gardes-du-Corps go caracoling through the groups 'amid hisses;' irritating and agitating what is but dispersed here to reunite there.

Innumerable squalid women beleaguer the President and Deputation; insist on going with him : has not his Majesty himself, looking from the window, sent out to ask, What we wanted? "Bread, and speech with the King (*Du pain, et parler au Roi*)," that was the answer. Twelve women are clamorously added to the Deputation; and march with it, across the Esplanade; through dissipated groups, caracoling Bodyguards and the pouring rain.

President Mounier, unexpectedly augmented by Twelve women, copiously escorted by Hunger and Rascality, is himself mistaken for a group; himself and his Women are dispersed by caracolers; rally again with difficulty, among the mud. Finally the Grates are opened; the Deputation gets access, with the Twelve women too in it; of which latter, Five shall even see the face of his Majesty. Let wet Menadism, in the best spirits it can, expect their return.

CHAPTER VII

AT VERSAILLES

But already Pallas Athene (in the shape of Demoiselle Théroigne) is busy with Flandre and the dismounted Dragoons. She, and such women as are fittest, go through the ranks; speak with an earnest jocosity; clasp rough troopers to their patriot bosom, crush down spontoons and musketoons with soft arms: can a man, that were worthy of the name of man, attack famishing patriot women?

One reads that Théroigne had bags of money, which she distributed over Flandre:—furnished by whom? Alas, with money-bags one seldom sits on insurrectionary cannon. Calumnious Royalism! Théroigne had only the limited earnings of her profession of unfortunate-female; money she had not, but brown locks, the figure of a Heathen Goddess and an eloquent tongue and heart.

Meanwhile, Saint-Antoine, in groups and troops, is continually arriving; wetted, sulky; with pikes and impromptu billhooks: driven thus far by popular fixed-idea. So many hirsute figures driven hither, in that manner: figures that have come to do they know not what; figures that have come to see it done! Distinguished among all figures, who is this, of gaunt stature, with leaden breastplate, though a small one; bushy in red grizzled locks; nay, with long tile-beard? It is Jourdan, unjust dealer in mules; a dealer no longer, but a Painter's Model, playing truant this day. From the necessities of Art comes his long tile-beard; whence his leaden breastplate (unless indeed he were some Hawker licensed by leaden badge) may have come,—will perhaps remain forever a Historical Problem. Another Saul among the people we discern: '*Pére Adam*, Father Adam,' as the groups name him; to us better known as bull-voiced Marquis Saint-Huruge; hero of the *Veto;* a man that has had losses, and deserved them. The tall Marquis, emitted some days ago from limbo, looks peripatetically on this scene from under his umbrella, not without interest. All which persons and things, hurled together as we see; Pallas Athene, busy with Flandre; patriotic Versailles National Guards, short of ammunition, and deserted by D'Estaing their Colonel, and commanded by Lecointre their Major; then caracoling Bodyguards, sour, dispirited, with their buckskins wet; and finally this flowing sea of indignant Squalor,—may they not give rise to occurrences?

Behold, however, the Twelve She-deputies return from the Château. Without President Mounier, indeed; but radiant with joy, shouting *"Life to the King and his House."* Apparently the news are good, Mesdames? News of the best! Five of us were admitted to the internal splendours, to the Royal Presence. This slim damsel, 'Louison Chabray, worker in sculpture, aged only seventeen,' as being of the best looks and address, her we appointed speaker. On whom, and indeed on all of us, his Majesty looked nothing but graciousness. Nay, when Louison, addressing him, was like to faint, he took her in his royal arms; and said gallantly, "It was well worth while (*Elle en valût bien la peine*)." Consider, O Women, what a King! His words were of comfort, and that only: there shall be provision sent to Paris, if provision is in the world; grains shall circulate free as air; millers shall grind, or do worse, while their millstones endure; and nothing be left wrong which a Restorer of French Liberty can right.

Good news these; but, to wet Menads, all-too incredible! There seems no proof, then? *Words* of comfort,—they are words only; which will feed nothing. O miserable People, betrayed by Aristocrats, who corrupt thy very messengers! In his royal arms, Mademoiselle Louison? In his arms? Thou shameless minx, worthy of a name—that shall be nameless! Yes, thy skin is soft: ours is rough with hardship; and well wetted, waiting here in the rain. No children hast thou hungry at home; only alabaster dolls, that weep not! The traitress! To the Lanterne!—And so poor Louison Chabray, no asseveration or shrieks availing her, fair slim damsel, late in the arms of Royalty, has a garter round her neck, and furibund Amazons at each end; is about to perish so,—when two Bodyguards gallop up, indignantly dissipating; and rescue her. The miscredited Twelve hasten back to the Château, for an 'answer in writing.'

Nay, behold, a new flight of Menads, with 'M. Brunout Bastille Volunteer,' as impressed-commandant, at the head of it. These also will advance to the Grate of the Grand Court, and see what is toward. Human patience, in wet buckskins, has its limits. Bodyguard Lieutenant M. de Savonnières for one moment lets his temper, long provoked, long pent, give way. He not only dissipates these latter Menads; but caracoles and cuts, or indignantly flourishes, at M. Brunout, the impressed-commandant; and, finding great relief in it, even chases him; Brunout flying nimbly, though in a pirouette manner, and now with sword also drawn. At which sight of wrath and victory, two other Bodyguards (for wrath is contagious, and to pent Bodyguards is so solacing) do likewise give way; give chase, with brandished sabre, and in the air make horrid circles. So that poor Brunout has nothing for it but to retreat with accelerated nimbleness, through rank after rank; Parthian-like, fencing as he flies; above all, shouting lustily, "*On nous laisse assassiner*, They are getting us assassinated!"

Shameful! Three against one! Growls come from the Lecointrian ranks; bellowings, — lastly shots. Savonnières' arm is raised to strike: the bullet of a Lecointrian musket shatters it; the brandished sabre jingles down harmless. Brunout has escaped, this duel well ended: but the wild howl of war is everywhere beginning to pipe!

The Amazons recoil; Saint-Antoine has its cannon pointed (full of grapeshot); thrice applies the lit flambeau; which thrice refuses to catch,—the touchholes are so wetted; and voices cry: "*Arrêtez, il n'est pas temps encore*, Stop, it is not yet time!" Messieurs of the Garde-du-Corps, ye had orders not to fire; nevertheless two of you limp dismounted, and one war-horse lies slain. Were it not well to draw back out of shot-range; finally to file off,—into the interior? If in so filing off, there did a musketoon or two discharge itself, at these armed shopkeepers, hooting and crowing, could man wonder? Draggled are your white cockades of an enormous size; would to Heaven they were got exchanged for tricolor ones! Your buckskins are wet, your hearts heavy. Go, and return not!

The Bodyguards file off, as we hint; giving and receiving shots; drawing no life-blood; leaving boundless indignation.

Some three times in the thickening dusk, a glimpse of them is seen, at this or the other Portal: saluted always with execrations, with the whew of lead. Let but a Bodyguard show face, he is hunted by Rascality;—for instance, poor 'M. de Moucheton of the Scotch Company,' owner of the slain war-horse; and has to be smuggled off by Versailles Captains. Or rusty firelocks belch after him, shivering asunder his—hat. In the end, by superior Order, the Bodyguards, all but the few on immediate duty, disappear; or as it were abscond; and march, under cloud of night, to Rambouillet.

We remark also that the Versaillese have now got ammunition: all afternoon, the official Person could find none; till, in these so critical moments, a patriotic Sub-lieutenant set a pistol to his ear, and would thank him to find some,—which he thereupon succeeded in doing. Likewise that Flandre, disarmed by Pallas Athene, says openly, it will not fight with citizens; and for token of peace has exchanged cartridges with the Versaillese.

Sansculottism is now among mere friends; and can 'circulate freely;' indignant at Bodyguards;—complaining also considerably of hunger.

CHAPTER VIII

THE EQUAL DIET

BUT why lingers Mounier; returns not with his Deputation? It is six, it is seven o'clock; and still no Mounier, no Acceptance pure and simple.

And, behold, the dripping Menads, not now in deputation but in mass, have penetrated into the Assembly: to the shamefullest interruption of public speaking and order of the day. Neither Maillard nor Vice-President can restrain them, except within wide limits; not even, except for minutes, can the lion-voice of Mirabeau, though they applaud it; but ever and anon they break in upon the regeneration of France with cries of : "Bread, not so much discoursing! *Du pain; pas tant de longs dicours !*"—So insensible were these poor creatures to bursts of parliamentary eloquence !

One learns also that the royal Carriages are getting yoked, as if for Metz. Carriages, royal or not, have verily showed themselves at the back Gates. They even produced, or

quoted, a written order from our Versailles Municipality,—
which is a Monarchic not a Democratic one. However, Versailles Patrols drove them in again; as the vigilant Lecointre
had strictly charged them to do.

A busy man, truly, is Major Lecointre, in these hours. For
Colonel D'Estaing loiters invisible in the Œil-de-Bœuf; invisible, or still more questionably *visible* for instants: then
also a too loyal Municipality requires supervision: no order,
civil or military, taken about any of these thousand things!
Lecointre is at the Versailles Townhall: he is at the Grate of
the Grand Court; communing with Swiss and Bodyguards.
He is in the ranks of Flandre; he is here, he is there:
studious to prevent bloodshed; to prevent the Royal Family
from flying to Metz; the Menads from plundering Versailles.

At the fall of night, we behold him advance to those armed
groups of Saint-Antoine, hovering all-too grim near the Salle
des Menus. They receive him in a half-circle; twelve speakers
behind cannons with lighted torches in hand, the cannon-
mouths *towards* Lecointre: a picture for Salvator! He asks,
in temperate but courageous language: What they, by this
their journey to Versailles, do specially want? The twelve
speakers reply, in few words inclusive of much: "Bread, and
the end of these brabbles, *Du pain, et la fin des affaires.*"
When the *affairs* will end, no Major Lecointre, nor no mortal,
can say: but as to bread, he inquires, How many are you?—
learns that they are six hundred, that a loaf each will suffice;
and rides off to the Municipality to get six hundred loaves.

Which loaves, however, a Municipality of Monarchic
temper will not give. It will give two tons of rice rather,—
could you but know whether it should be boiled or raw. Nay
when this too is accepted, the Municipals have disappeared;
—ducked under, as the Six-and-twenty Long-gowned of Paris
did; and, leaving not the smallest vestige of rice, in the
boiled or raw state, they there vanish from History!

Rice comes not; one's hope of food is balked; even one's
hope of vengeance: is not M. de Moucheton of the Scotch
Company, as we said, deceitfully smuggled off? Failing all
which, behold only M. de Moucheton's slain warhorse, lying
on the Esplanade there! Saint-Antoine, balked, esurient,
pounces on the slain warhorse; flays it; roasts it, with such
fuel, of paling, gates, portable timber as can be come at,—
not without shouting; *and*, after the manner of ancient Greek
Heroes, *they lifted their hands to the daintily readied repast;*

such as it might be. Other Rascality prowls discursive; seeking what it may devour. Flandre will retire to its barracks; Lecointre also with his Versailles,—all but the vigilant Patrols, charged to be doubly vigilant.

So sink the shadows of night, blustering, rainy and all paths grow dark. Strangest Night ever seen in these regions, —perhaps since the Bartholomew Night, when Versailles, as Bassompierre writes of it, was a *chétif château*. O for the Lyre of some Orpheus, to constrain, with touch of melodious strings, these mad masses into Order! For here all seems fallen asunder, in wide yawning dislocation. The highest, as in down-rushing of a World, is come in contact with the lowest: the Rascality of France beleaguering the Royalty of France; 'iron-shod batons' lifted round the diadem, not to guard it! With denunciations of bloodthirsty Anti-national Bodyguards, are heard dark growlings against a Queenly Name.

The Court sits tremulous, powerless; varies with the varying temper of the Esplanade, with the varying colour of the rumours from Paris. Thick-coming rumours; now of peace, now of war. Necker and all the Ministers consult; with a blank issue. The Œil-de-Bœuf is one tempest of whispers:— We will fly to Metz; we will not fly. The royal Carriages again attempt egress,—though for trial merely; they are again driven in by Lecointre's Patrols. In six hours, nothing has been resolved on; not even the Acceptance pure and simple.

In six hours? Alas, he who, in such circumstances, cannot resolve in six minutes, may give up the enterprise: him Fate has already resolved for. And Menadism, meanwhile, and Sansculottism takes counsel with the National Assembly; grows more and more tumultuous there. Mounier returns not; Authority nowhere shows itself: the Authority of France lies, for the present, with Lecointre and Usher Maillard.— This then is the abomination of desolation; come suddenly, though long foreshadowed as inevitable! For, to the blind, all things are sudden. Misery which, through long ages, had no spokesman, no helper, will now be its own helper and speak for itself. The dialect, one of the rudest, is, what it could be, *this*.

At eight o'clock there returns to our Assembly not the Deputation; but Doctor Guillotin announcing that it will return; also that there is hope of the Acceptance pure and simple. He himself has brought a Royal Letter, authorising and commanding the freest 'circulation of grains.' Which

Royal Letter Menadism with its whole heart applauds. Conformably to which the Assembly forthwith passes a Decree; also received with rapturous Menadic plaudits:—Only could not an august Assembly contrive further to "*fix* the price of bread at eight sous the half-quartern; butchers'-meat at six sous the pound;" which seem fair rates? Such motion do 'a multitude of men and women,' irrepressible by Usher Maillard, now make; does an august Assembly hear made. Usher Maillard himself is not always perfectly measured in speech; but if rebuked, he can justly excuse himself by the peculiarity of the circumstances.

But finally, this Decree well passed, and the disorder continuing; and Members melting away, and no President Mounier returning,—what can the Vice-President do but also melt away? The Assembly melts, under such pressure, into deliquium; or, as it is officially called, adjourns. Maillard is despatched to Paris, with the 'Decree concerning Grains' in his pocket; he and some women, in carriages belonging to the King. Thitherward slim Louison Chabray has already set forth, with that 'written answer' which the Twelve She-deputies returned in to seek. Slim sylph, she has set forth, through the black muddy country : she has much to tell, her poor nerves so flurried; and travels, as indeed today on this road all persons do, with extreme slowness. President Mounier has not come, nor the Acceptance pure and simple; though six hours with their events have come; though courier on courier reports that Lafayette is coming. Coming, with war or with peace? It is time that the Château also should determine on one thing or another; that the Château also should show itself alive, if it would continue living !

Victorious, joyful after such delay, Mounier does arrive at last, and the hard-earned Acceptance with him; which now, alas, is of small value. Fancy Mounier's surprise to find his Senate, whom he hoped to charm by the Acceptance pure and simple,—all gone; and in its stead a Senate of Menads ! For as Erasmus's Ape mimicked, say with wooden splint, Erasmus shaving. so do these Amazons hold, in mock majesty, some confused parody of National Assembly. They make motions; deliver speeches; pass enactments; productive at least of loud laughter. All galleries and benches are filled; a Strong Dame of the Market is in Mounier's Chair. Not without difficulty, Mounier, by aid of macers and persuasive speaking, makes his way to the Female-President; the Strong

Dame, before abdicating, signifies that, for one thing, she and indeed her whole senate male and female (for what was one roasted warhorse among so many?) are suffering very considerably from hunger.

Experienced Mounier, in these circumstances, takes a twofold resolution: To reconvoke his Assembly Members by sound of drum; also to procure a supply of food. Swift messengers fly, to all bakers, cooks, pastrycooks, vintners, restorers; drums beat, accompanied with a shrill vocal proclamation, through all streets. They come: the Assembly Members come; what is still better, the provisions come. On tray and barrow come these latter; loaves, wine, great store of sausages. The nourishing baskets circulate harmoniously along the benches; *nor*, according to the Father of Epics, *did any soul lack a fair share of victual* (δαῖτος ἐΐσης, *an equal diet*); highly desirable at the moment.

Gradually some hundred or so of Assembly Members get edged in, Menadism making way a little, round Mounier's chair; listen to the Acceptance pure and simple; and begin, what is the order of the night, 'discussion of the Penal Code.' All benches are crowded; in the dusky galleries, duskier with unwashed heads, is a strange 'coruscation,'—of impromptu bill-hooks. It is exactly five months this day since these same galleries were filled with high-plumed jewelled Beauty, raining bright influences; and now? To such length have we got in regenerating France. Methinks the travail-throes are of the sharpest!—Menadism will not be restrained from occasional remarks; asks, "What is the use of Penal Code! The thing we want is bread." Mirabeau turns round with lion-voiced rebuke; Menadism applauds him; but recommences.

Thus they, chewing tough sausages, discussing the Penal Code, make night hideous. What the issue will be? Lafayette with his thirty thousand must arrive first; him, who cannot now be distant, all men expect, as the messenger of Destiny.

CHAPTER IX

LAFAYETTE

Towards midnight lights flare on the hill; Lafayette's lights! The roll of his drums comes up the Avenue de Versailles. With peace, or with war! Patience, friends! With neither. Lafayette is come, but not yet the catastrophe.

He has halted and harangued so often, on the march; spent nine hours on four leagues of road. At Montreuil, close on Versailles, the whole host had to pause; and, with uplifted right hand, in the murk of Night, to these pouring skies, swear solemnly to respect the King's dwelling; to be faithful to King and National Assembly. Rage is driven out of sight, by the laggard march; the thirst of vengeance slaked in weariness and soaking clothes. Flandre is again drawn out under arms: but Flandre, grown so patriotic, now needs no 'exterminating.' The wayworn Battalions halt in the Avenue: they have, for the present, no wish so pressing as that of shelter and rest.

Anxious sits President Mounier; anxious the Château. There is a message coming from the Château, that M. Mounier would please to return thither with a fresh Deputation, swiftly; and so at least *unite* our two anxieties. Anxious Mounier does of himself send, meanwhile, to apprise the General that his Majesty has been so gracious as to grant us the Acceptance pure and simple. The General, with a small advance column, makes answer in passing; speaks vaguely some smooth words to the National President,—glances, only with the eye, at that so mixtiform National Assembly; then fares forward towards the Château. There are with him two Paris Municipals; they were chosen from the Three Hundred for that errand. He gets admittance through the locked and padlocked Grates, through sentries and ushers, to the Royal Halls.

The Court, male and female, crowds on his passage, to read their doom on his face; which exhibits, say Historians, a mixture 'of sorrow, of fervour and valour,' singular to behold. The King, with Monsieur, with Ministers and Marshals, is waiting to receive him: He 'is come,' in his highflown chivalrous way, 'to offer his head for the safety of his Majesty's.' The two Municipals state the wish of Paris: four things, of quite pacific tenor. First, that the honour of guarding his sacred person be conferred on patriot National Guards;—say, the Centre Grenadiers, who as Gardes Françaises were wont to have that privilege. Second, that provisions be got, if possible. Third, that the Prisons, all crowded with political delinquents, may have judges sent them. Fourth, *that it would please his Majesty to come and live in Paris.* To all which four wishes, except the fourth, his Majesty answers readily, Yes; or indeed may almost say that he has already answered it. To the fourth he can answer only, Yes or No; would so gladly answer, Yes and No!—But, in any case, are not their dispositions, thank Heaven, so entirely pacific? There is time for deliberation. The brunt of the danger seems past!

Lafayette and D'Estaing settle the watches; Centre Grenadiers are to take the Guard-room they of old occupied as Gardes Françaises;—for indeed the Gardes-du-Corps, its late ill-advised occupants, are gone mostly to Rambouillet. That is the order of *this* night; sufficient for the night is the evil thereof. Whereupon Lafayette and the two Municipals, with highflown chivalry, take their leave.

So brief has the interview been, Mounier and his Deputation were not yet got up. So brief and satisfactory. A stone is rolled from every heart. The fair Palace Dames publicly declare that this Lafayette, detestable though he be, is their saviour for once. Even the ancient vinaigrous *Tantes* admit it; the King's Aunts, ancient *Graille* and Sisterhood, known to us of old. Queen Marie-Antoinette has been heard often say the like. She alone, among all women and all men, wore a face of courage, of lofty calmness and resolve this day. She alone saw clearly what she *meant* to do; and Theresa's Daughter *dares* do what she means, were all France threatening her; abide where her children are, where her husband is.

Towards three in the morning all things are settled: the watches set, the Centre Grenadiers put into their old Guard-room, and harangued; the Swiss, and few remaining Body-guards harangued. The wayworn Paris Battalions, consigned to 'the hospitality of Versailles,' lie dormant in spare-beds, spare-barracks, coffeehouses, empty churches. A troop of them, on their way to the Church of Saint-Louis, awoke poor Weber, dreaming troublous, in the Rue Sartory. Weber has had his waistcoat-pocket full of balls all day; 'two hundred balls, and two *pears* of powder!' For waistcoats were waistcoats then, and had flaps down to mid-thigh. So many balls he has had all day; but no opportunity of using them: he turns over now, execrating disloyal bandits; swears a prayer or two, and straight to sleep again.

Finally the National Assembly is harangued; which thereupon, on motion of Mirabeau, discontinues the Penal Code, and dismisses for this night. Menadism, Sansculottism has cowered into guard-houses, barracks of Flandre, to the light of cheerful fire; failing that, to churches, officehouses, sentry-boxes, wheresoever wretchedness can find a lair.   The troublous Day has brawled itself to rest: no lives yet lost but that of one warhorse.   Insurrectionary Chaos lies slumbering round the Palace, like Ocean round a Diving-bell,—no crevice yet disclosing itself.

Deep sleep has fallen promiscuously on the high and on the low; suspending most things, even wrath and famine.   Darkness covers the Earth.   But, far on the North-east, Paris flings up her great yellow gleam; far into the wet black Night.   For all is illuminated there, as in the old July Nights; the streets deserted for alarm of war; the Municipals all wakeful; Patrols hailing, with their hoarse *Who-goes*.   There, as we discover, our poor slim Louison Chabray, her poor nerves all fluttered, is arriving about this very hour.   There Usher Maillard will arrive, about an hour hence, 'towards four in the morning.' They report, successively, to a wakeful Hôtel-de-Ville what comfort they can; which again, with early dawn, large comfortable Placards shall impart to all men.

Lafayette, in the Hôtel de Noailles, not far from the Château, having now finished haranguing, sits with his Officers consulting: at five o'clock the unanimous best counsel is, that a man so tost and toiled for twenty-four hours and more, fling himself on a bed, and seek some rest.

Thus, then, has ended the First Act of the Insurrection of Women.   How it will turn on the morrow?   The morrow, as always, is with the Fates!   But his Majesty, one may hope, will consent to come honourably to Paris; at all events, he can visit Paris.   Anti-national Bodyguards, here and elsewhere, must take the National Oath; make reparation to the Tricolor; Flandre will swear.   There may be much swearing; much public speaking there will infallibly be: and so, with harangues and vows, may the matter in some handsome way wind itself up.

Or, alas, may it not be all otherwise, *un*handsome; the consent not honourable, but extorted, ignominious?   Boundless Chaos of Insurrection presses slumbering round the Palace, like Ocean round a Diving-bell; and may penetrate at any crevice.   Let but that accumulated insurrectionary mass find entrance!   Like the infinite inburst of water; or say rather, of inflammable, self-igniting fluid; for example, 'turpentine-and-phosphorus oil,'—fluid known to Spinola Santerre!

CHAPTER X

THE GRAND ENTRIES

THE dull dawn of a new morning, drizzly and chill, had but broken over Versailles, when it pleased Destiny that a Bodyguard should look out of window, on the right wing of the Château, to see what prospect there was in Heaven and in Earth. Rascality male and female is prowling in view of him. His fasting stomach is, with good cause, sour; he perhaps cannot forbear a passing malison on them; least of all can he forbear answering such.

Ill words breed worse: till the worst word come; and then the ill deed. Did the maledicent Bodyguard, getting (as was too inevitable) better malediction than he gave, load his musketoon, and threaten to fire; nay actually fire? Were wise who wist! It stands asserted; to us not credibly. But be this as it may, menaced Rascality, in whinnying scorn, is shaking at all Grates: the fastening of one (some write, it was a chain merely) gives way; Rascality is in the Grand Court, whinnying louder still.

The maledicent Bodyguard, more Bodyguards than he do now give fire; a man's arm is shattered. Lecointre will depose that 'the Sieur Cardine, a National Guard without arms, was stabbed.' But see, sure enough, poor Jérôme l'Héritier, an unarmed National Guard he too, 'cabinetmaker, a saddler's son, of Paris,' with the down of youthhood still on his chin,—he reels death-stricken; rushes to the pavement, scattering it with his blood and brains!—Alleleu! Wilder than Irish wakes rises the howl; of pity, of infinite revenge. In few moments, the Grate of the inner and inmost Court, which they name Court of Marble, this too is forced, or surprised, and bursts open: the Court of Marble too is overflowed: up the Grand Staircase, up all stairs and entrances rushes the living Deluge! Deshuttes and Varigny, the two sentry Bodyguards, are trodden down, are massacred with a hundred pikes. Women snatch their cutlasses, or any weapon, and storm-in Menadic:—other women lift the corpse of shot Jérôme; lay it down on the Marble steps; there shall the livid face and smashed head, dumb forever, *speak*.

Wo now to all Bodyguards, mercy is none for them! Miomandre de Sainte-Marie pleads with soft words, on the Grand Staircase, 'descending four steps:'—to the roaring tornado. His comrades snatch him up, by the skirts and belts; literally, from the jaws of Destruction; and slam-to their Door. This also will stand few instants: the panels shivering in, like potsherds. Barricading serves not: fly fast, ye Bodyguards: rabid Insurrection, like the Hellhound Chase, uproaring at your heels!

The terrorstruck Bodyguards fly bolting and barricading; it follows. Whitherward? Through hall on hall: wo, now! towards the Queen's Suite of Rooms, in the furthest room of which the Queen is now asleep. Five sentinels rush through that long Suite; they are in the Anteroom knocking loud: "Save the Queen!" Trembling women fall at their feet with tears: are answered: "Yes, we will die; save ye the Queen!"

Tremble not, women, but haste: for, lo, another voice shouts far through the outermost door, "Save the Queen!" and the door is shut. It is brave Miomandre's voice that shouts this second warning. He has stormed across imminent death to do it; fronts imminent death, having done it. Brave Tardivet du Repaire, bent on the same desperate service, was borne down with pikes; his comrades hardly snatched him in again alive. Miomandre and Tardivet: let the names of these two Bodyguards, as the names of brave men should, live long.

Trembling Maids of Honour, one of whom from afar caught glimpse of Miomandre as well as heard him, hastily wrap the Queen; not in robes of state. She flies for her life, across the Œil-de-Bœuf; against the main door of which too Insurrection batters. She is in the King's Apartment, in the King's arms; she clasps her children amid a faithful few. The Imperial-hearted bursts into mother's tears: "O my friends, save me and my children, *O mes amis, sauvez moi et mes enfans!*" The battering of Insurrectionary axes clangs audible across the Œil-de-Bœuf. What an hour!

Yes, Friends; a hideous fearful hour; shameful alike to Governed and Governor; wherein Governed and Governor ignominiously testify that their relation is at an end. Rage, which had brewed itself in twenty thousand hearts for the last four-and-twenty hours, has taken *fire:* Jérôme's brained corpse lies there as live-coal. It is, as we said, the infinite Element bursting in; wild-surging through all corridors and conduits

Meanwhile the poor Bodyguards have got hunted mostly into the Œil-de-Bœuf. They may die there, at the King's threshold; they can do little to defend it. They are heaping *tabourets* (stools of honour), benches and all movables, against the door; at which the axe of Insurrection thunders.—But did brave Miomandre perish, then, at the Queen's outer-door? No, he was fractured, slashed, lacerated, left for dead; he has nevertheless crawled hither; and shall live, honoured of loyal France. Remark also, in flat contradiction to much which has been said and sung, that Insurrection did *not* burst that door he had defended; but hurried else-whither, seeking new Bodyguards.

Poor Bodyguards, with their Thyestes Opera-Repast! Well for them that Insurrection has only pikes and axes; no right sieging-tools! It shakes and thunders. Must they all perish miserably, and Royalty with them? Deshuttes and Varigny, massacred at the first inbreak, have been beheaded in the Marble Court · a sacrifice to Jérôme's *manes:* Jourdan with the tile-beard did that duty willingly; and asked, If there were no more? Another captive they are leading round the corpse, with howl-chantings: may not Jourdan again tuck up his sleeves?

And louder and louder rages Insurrection within, plundering if it cannot kill; louder and louder it thunders at the Œil-de-Bœuf: what can now hinder its bursting in?—On a sudden it ceases; the battering has ceased! Wild rushing; the cries grow fainter; there is silence, or the tramp of regular steps; then a friendly knocking: "We are the Centre Grenadiers, old Gardes Françaises: Open to us, Messieurs of the Garde-du-Corps; we have not forgotten how you saved us at Fontenoy!" The door is opened; enter Captain Gondran and the Centre Grenadiers: there are military embracings; there is sudden deliverance from death into life.

Strange Sons of Adam! It was to 'exterminate' these Gardes-du-Corps that the Centre Grenadiers left home: and now they have rushed to save them from extermination. The memory of common peril, of old help, melts the rough heart; bosom is clasped to bosom, not in war. The King shows himself, one moment, through the door of his Apartment, with: "Do not hurt my Guards!"—"*Soyons frères,* Let us be brothers!" cries Captain Gondran; and again dashes off, with levelled bayonets, to sweep the Palace clear.

Now too Lafayette, suddenly roused, not from sleep (for his eyes had not yet closed), arrives; with passionate popular eloquence, with prompt military word of command. National

Guards, suddenly roused, by sound of trumpet and alarm-drum, are all arriving. The death-melly ceases: the first sky-lambent blaze of Insurrection is got damped down; it burns now, if unextinguished, yet flameless, as charred coals do, and not inextinguishable. The King's Apartments are safe. Ministers, Officials, and even some loyal National Deputies are assembling round their Majesties. The consternation will, with sobs and confusion, settle down gradually, into plan and counsel, better or worse.

But glance now, for a moment, from the royal windows! A roaring sea of human heads, inundating both Courts; billowing against all passages: Menadic women: infuriated men, mad with revenge, with love of mischief, love of plunder! Rascality has slipped its muzzle; and now bays, three-throated, like the Dog of Erebus. Fourteen Bodyguards are wounded; two massacred, and as we saw, beheaded; Jourdan asking, "Was it worth while to come so far for two?" Hapless Deshuttes and Varigny! Their fate surely was sad. Whirled down so suddenly to the abyss; as men are, suddenly, by the wide thunder of the Mountain Avalanche, awakened not by *them*, awakened far off by others! When the Château Clock last struck, they two were pacing languid, with poised musketoon; anxious mainly that the next hour would strike. It had struck; to them inaudible. Their trunks lie mangled: their heads parade, 'on pikes twelve feet long,' through the streets of Versailles; and shall, about noon, reach the Barriers of Paris,—a too ghastly contradiction to the large comfortable Placards that have been posted there!

The other captive Bodyguard is still circling the corpse of Jérôme, amid Indian war-whooping; bloody Tilebeard, with tucked sleeves, brandishing his bloody axe; when Gondran and the Grenadiers come in sight. "Comrades, will you see a man massacred in cold blood?"—"Off, butchers!" answer they; and the poor Bodyguard is free. Busy runs Gondran, busy run Guards and Captains; scouring all corridors; dispersing Rascality and Robbery; sweeping the Palace clear. The mangled carnage is removed; Jérôme's body to the Townhall, for inquest: the fire of Insurrection gets damped, more and more, into measurable, manageable heat.

Transcendent things of all sorts, as in the general outburst of multitudinous Passion, are huddled together; the ludicrous, nay the ridiculous, with the horrible. Far over the billowy sea of heads, may be seen Rascality, caprioling on horses from the Royal Stud. The Spoilers these; for Patriotism is always infected so, with a proportion of mere thieves and scoundrels. Gondran snatched their prey from them in the Château; whereupon they hurried to the Stables, and took horse there. But the generous Diomedes' steeds, according to Weber, disdained such scoundrel-burden; and, flinging up their royal heels, did soon project most of it, in parabolic curves, to a distance, amid peals of laughter; and were caught. Mounted National Guards secured the rest.

Now too is witnessed the touching last-flicker of Etiquette; which sinks not here, in the Cimmerian World-wreckage, without a sign; as the house-cricket might still chirp in the pealing of a Trump of Doom. "Monsieur," said some Master of Ceremonies (one hopes it might be De Brézé), as Lafayette, in these fearful moments, was rushing towards the inner Royal Apartments, " *Monsieur, le Roi vous accorde les grandes entrées*, Monsieur, the King grants you the Grand Entries,"—not finding it convenient to refuse them!

CHAPTER XI

FROM VERSAILLES

HOWEVER, the Paris National Guard, wholly under arms, has cleared the Palace, and even occupies the nearer external spaces: extruding miscellaneous Patriotism, for most part, into the Grand Court, or even into the Forecourt.

The Bodyguards, you can observe, have now of a verity hoisted the National Cockade:' for they step forward to the windows or balconies, hat aloft in hand, on each hat a new tricolor; and fling over their bandoleers in sign of surrender; and shout *Vive la Nation*. To which how can the generous heart respond but with, *Vive le Roi; vivent les Gardes-du-Corps?* His Majesty himself has appeared with Lafayette on the balcony, and again appears: *Vive le Roi* greets him from all throats; but also from some one throat is heard, "*Le Roi à Paris*, The King to Paris!"

Her Majesty, too, on demand, shows herself, though there is peril in it: she steps out on the balcony, with her little boy and girl. "No children, *Point d'enfans!*" cry the voices. She gently pushes back her children; and stands alone, her hands serenely crossed on her breast: "should I die," she had

said, "I will do it." Such serenity of heroism has its effect.
Lafayette, with ready wit, in his highflown chivalrous way,
takes that fair queenly hand, and, reverently kneeling, kisses
it: thereupon the people do shout *Vive la Reine*. Nevertheless, poor Weber 'saw' (or even thought he saw; for hardly
the third part of poor Weber's experiences, in such hysterical
days, will stand scrutiny) 'one of these brigands level his
musket at her Majesty,'—with or without intention to shoot;
for another of the brigands 'angrily struck it down.'

So that all, and the Queen herself, nay the very Captain of
the Bodyguards, have grown National! The very Captain
of the Bodyguards steps out now with Lafayette. On the hat
of the repentant man is an enormous tricolor; large as a
soup-platter, or sun-flower; visible to the utmost Forecourt.
He takes the National Oath with a loud voice, elevating
his hat; at which sight all the army raise their bonnets on
their bayonets, with shouts. Sweet is reconcilement to the
heart of man. Lafayette has sworn Flandre; he swears the
remaining Bodyguards, down in the Marble Court; the people
clasp them in their arms:—O my brothers, why would ye force
us to slay you? Behold there is joy over you, as over
returning prodigal sons!—The poor Bodyguards, now National
and tricolor, exchange bonnets, exchange arms; there shall be
peace and fraternity. And still "*Vive le Roi;*" and also "*Le
Roi à Paris*," not now from one throat, but from all throats as
one, for it is the heart's wish of all mortals.

Yes, *The King to Paris*: what else? Ministers may consult,
and National Deputies wag their heads: but there is now no other
possibility. You have forced him to go willingly. "At one
o'clock!" Lafayette gives audible assurance to that purpose
and universal Insurrection, with immeasurable shout, and
a discharge of all the fire-arms, clear and rusty, great and
small, that it has, returns him acceptance. What a sound
heard for leagues: a doom-peal!—That sound too rolls away
into the Silence of Ages. And the Château of Versailles
stands ever since vacant, hushed-still; its spacious Courts
grass-grown, responsive to the hoe of the weeder. Times and
generations roll on, in their confused Gulf current; and
buildings, like builders, have their destiny.

Till one o'clock, then, there will be three parties, National
Assembly, National Rascality, National Royalty, all busy
enough. Rascality rejoices; women trim themselves with

tricolor. Nay motherly Paris has sent her Avengers sufficient
'cartloads of loaves;' which are shouted over, which are
gratefully consumed. The Avengers, in return, are searching
for grain-stores; loading them in fifty wagons; that so a
National King, probably harbinger of all blessings, may be
the evident bringer of plenty, for one.

And thus has Sansculottism made prisoner its King;
revoking his parole. The Monarchy has fallen; and not
so much as honourably: no, ignominiously; with struggle,
indeed, oft-repeated; but then with unwise struggle; wasting
its strength in fits and paroxysms; at every new paroxysm
foiled more pitifully than before. Thus Broglie's whiff of
grapeshot, which might have been something, has dwindled to
the pot-valour of an Opera Repast, and *O Richard, O mon
Roi.* Which again we shall see dwindle to a Favras' Conspiracy, a thing to be settled by the hanging of one Chevalier.

Poor Monarchy! But what save foulest defeat can await
that man, who wills, and yet wills not? Apparently the King
either has a right, assertible as such to the death, before God
and man; or else he has no right. Apparently, the one
or the other; could he but know which! May Heaven pity
him! Were Louis wise, he would this day abdicate.—Is
it not strange so few Kings abdicate; and none yet heard of
has been known to commit suicide? Fritz the First, of
Prussia, alone tried it; and they cut the rope.

As for the National Assembly, which decrees this morning
that it 'is inseparable from his Majesty,' and will follow him to
Paris, there may one thing be noted: its extreme want of
bodily health. After the Fourteenth of July there was a
certain sickliness observable among honourable Members; so
many demanding passports, on account of infirm health. But
now, for these following days, there is a perfect murrain:
President Mounier, Lally Tollendal, Clermont Tonnère, and
all Constitutional Two-Chamber Royalists needing change of
air; as most No-Chamber Royalists had formerly done.

For, in truth, it is the *second Emigration* this that has now
come; most extensive among Commons Deputies, Noblesse,
Clergy: so that 'to Switzerland alone there go sixty thousand.'
They will return in the day of accounts! Yes, and have hot
welcome.—But Emigration on Emigration is the peculiarity
of France. One Emigration follows another; grounded on
reasonable fear, unreasonable hope, largely also on childish
pet. The highflyers have gone first, now the lower flyers;

and ever the lower will go, down to the crawlers. Whereby, however, cannot our National Assembly so much the more commodiously make the Constitution; your Two-Chamber Anglomaniacs being all safe, distant on foreign shores? Abbé Maury is seized and sent back again: he, tough as tanned leather, with eloquent Captain Cazalès and some others, will stand it out for another year.

But here, meanwhile, the question arises: Was Philippe d'Orléans seen, this day, 'in the Bois de Boulogne, in gray surtout;' waiting under the wet sere foliage, what the day might bring forth? Alas, yes, the Eidolon of him was,—in Weber's and other such brains. The Châtelet shall make large inquisition into the matter, examining a hundred and seventy witnesses, and Deputy Chabroud publish his Report; but disclose nothing *further*. What then has caused these two unparalleled October Days? For surely such dramatic exhibition never yet enacted itself without Dramatist and Machinist. Wooden Punch emerges not, with his domestic sorrows, into the light of day, unless the wire be pulled: how can human mobs? Was it not D'Orléans then, and Laclos, Marquis Sillery, Mirabeau and the sons of confusion; hoping to drive the King to Metz, and gather the spoil? Nay was it not, quite contrariwise, the Œil-de-Bœuf, Bodyguard Colonel de Guiche, Minister Saint-Priest and highflying Loyalists; hoping also to drive him to Metz, and try it by the sword of civil war? Good Marquis Toulongeon, the Historian and Deputy, feels constrained to admit that it was *both*.

Alas, my Friends, credulous incredulity is a strange matter. But when a whole Nation is smitten with Suspicion, and sees a dramatic miracle in the very operation of the gastric juices, what help is there? Such Nation is already a mere hypochondriac bundle of diseases; as good as changed into glass; atrabiliar, decadent; and will suffer crises. Is not Suspicion itself the one thing to be suspected, as Montaigne feared only fear?

Now, however, the short hour has struck. His Majesty is in his carriage, with his Queen, sister Elizabeth, and two royal children. Not for another hour can the infinite Procession get marshalled and under way. The weather is dim drizzling; the mind confused; the noise great.

Processional marches not a few our world has seen; Roman triumphs and ovations, Cabiric cymbal-beatings, Royal progresses, Irish funerals; but this of the French Monarchy marching to its bed remained to be seen. Miles long, and of breadth losing itself in vagueness, for all the neighbouring country crowds to see. Slow; stagnating along like shoreless Lake, yet with a noise like Niagara, like Babel and Bedlam. A splashing and a tramping; a hurrahing, uproaring, musket-volleying;—the truest segment of Chaos seen in these latter Ages! Till slowly it disembogue itself, in the thickening dusk, into expectant Paris, through a double row of faces all the way from Passy to the Hôtel-de-Ville.

Consider this: Vanguard of National troops; with trains of artillery; of pikemen and pikewomen, mounted on cannons, on carts, hackney-coaches, or on foot;—tripudiating, in tricolor ribbons from head to heel; loaves stuck on the points of bayonets, green boughs stuck in gun-barrels. Next, as main-march, 'fifty cart-loads of corn,' which have been lent, for peace, from the stores of Versailles. Behind which follow stragglers of the Garde-du-Corps; all humiliated, in Grenadier bonnets. Close on these comes the Royal Carriage; come Royal Carriages; for there are a Hundred National Deputies too, among whom sits Mirabeau,—his remarks not given. Then finally, pellmell, as rearguard, Flandre, Swiss, Hundred Swiss, other Bodyguards, Brigands, whosoever cannot get before. Between and among all which masses, flows without limit Saint-Antoine, and the Menadic Cohort. Menadic especially about the Royal Carriage; tripudiating there, covered with tricolor; singing 'allusive songs:' pointing with one hand to the Royal Carriage, which the allusions hit, and pointing to the Provision wagons with the other hand, and these words: "Courage, Friends! We shall not want bread now; we are bringing you the Baker, the Bakeress and the Baker's Boy (*le Boulanger, la Boulangère et le petit Mitron*)."

The wet day draggles the tricolor, but the joy is unextinguish-able. Is not all well now? "*Ah, Madame, notre bonne Reine,*" said some of these Strong-women some days hence, "Ah, Madame, our good Queen, don't be a traitor any more (*ne soyez plus traître*), and we will all love you!" Poor Weber went splashing along, close by the Royal carriage, with the tear in his eye: 'their Majesties did me the honour,' or I thought they did it, 'to testify, from time to time, by shrugging of the shoulders, by looks directed to Heaven, the emotions they felt.' Thus, like frail cockle, floats the royal Life-boat, helm-less, on black deluges of Rascality.

Mercier, in his loose way, estimates the Procession and assistants at two hundred thousand. He says it was one boundless inarticulate Haha;—*transcendent* World-Laughter; comparable to the Saturnalia of the Ancients. Why not? Here too, as we said, is Human Nature once more human; shudder at it whoso is of shuddering humour: yet behold it is human. It has 'swallowed all formulas;' it tripudiates even so. For which reason they that collect Vases and Antiques, with figures of Dancing Bacchantes 'in wild and all-but impossible positions' may look with some interest on it.

Thus, however, has the slow-moving Chaos, or modern Saturnalia of the Ancients, reached the Barrier; and must halt, to be harangued by Mayor Bailly. Thereafter it has to lumber along, between the double row of faces, in the transcendent heaven-lashing Haha; two hours longer, towards the Hôtel-de-Ville. Then again to be harangued there, by several persons; by Moreau de Saint-Méry among others; Moreau of the Three-thousand orders, now National Deputy for St. Domingo. To all which poor Louis, 'who seemed to experience a slight emotion' on entering this Townhall, can answer only that he "comes with pleasure, with confidence among his people." Mayor Bailly, in reporting it, forgets 'confidence:' and the poor Queen says eagerly: "Add, with confidence."—"Messieurs," rejoins Mayor Bailly, "you are happier than if I had not forgotten."

Finally, the King is shown on an upper balcony, by torch-light, with a huge tricolor in his hat: 'and all the people,' says Weber, 'grasped one another's hand;'—thinking *now* surely the New Era was born. Hardly till eleven at night can Royalty get to its vacant, long-deserted Palace of the Tuileries; to lodge there, somewhat in stroller-player fashion. It is Tuesday the sixth of October, 1789.

Poor Louis has Two other Paris Processions to make: one ludicrous-ignominious like this: the other not ludicrous nor ignominious, but serious, nay sublime.

PART II—THE CONSTITUTION

BOOK I

THE FEAST OF PIKES

CHAPTER I

IN THE TUILERIES

THE victim having once got his stroke-of-grace, the catastrophe can be considered as almost come. There is small interest now in watching his long low moans: notable only are his sharper agonies, what convulsive struggles he may make to cast the torture off from him; and then finally the last departure of life itself, and how he lies extinct and ended, either wrapt like Cæsar in decorous mantle-folds, or unseemly sunk together, like one that had not the force even to die.

Was French Royalty, when wrenched forth from its tapestries in that fashion, on that Sixth of October 1789, such a victim? Universal France, and Royal Proclamation to all the Provinces, answers anxiously, *No*. Nevertheless one may fear the worst. Royalty was beforehand so decrepit, moribund, there is little life in it to heal an injury. How much of its strength, which was of the imagination merely, has fled; Rascality having looked plainly in the King's face, and not died! When the assembled crows can pluck up their scarecrow, and say to it, Here shalt thou stand and not there; and can treat with it, and make it, from an infinite, a quite finite Constitutional scarecrow,—what is to be looked for? Not in the finite Constitutional scarecrow, but in what still unmeasured infinite-seeming force may rally round it, is there thenceforth any hope. For it is most true that all available Authority is *mystic* in its conditions, and comes 'by the grace of God.'

Cheerfuller than watching the death-struggles of Royalism will it be to watch the growth and gambollings of Sansculottism; for, in human things, especially in human society, all death is but a death-birth: thus if the sceptre is departing from Louis, it is only that, in other forms, other sceptres, were it even pike-sceptres, may bear sway. In a prurient element, rich with nutritive influences, we shall find that Sansculottism grows lustily, and even frisks in not ungraceful sport: as indeed most young creatures are sportful; nay, may it not be noted further, that as the grown cat, and cat-species generally, is the cruellest thing known, so the merriest is precisely the kitten, or growing cat?

But fancy the Royal Family risen from its truckle-beds on the morrow of that mad day: fancy the Municipal inquiry, "How would your Majesty please to lodge?"—and then that the King's rough answer, "Each may lodge as he can, I am well enough," is congeed and bowed away in expressive grins, by the Townhall Functionaries, with obsequious upholsterers at their back; and how the Château of the Tuileries is repainted, regarnished into a golden Royal Residence; and Lafayette with his blue National Guards lies encompassing it, as blue Neptune (in the language of poets) does an island, wooingly. Thither may the wrecks of re-habilitated Loyalty gather, if it will become Constitutional; for Constitutionalism thinks no evil; Sansculottism itself rejoices in the King's countenance. The rubbish of a Menadic Insurrection, as in this ever-kindly world all rubbish can and must be, is swept aside; and so again, on clear arena, under new conditions, with something even of a new stateliness, we begin a new course of action.

Arthur Young has witnessed the strangest scene: Majesty walking unattended in the Tuileries Gardens; and miscellaneous tricolor crowds, who cheer it, and reverently make way for it: the very Queen commands at lowest respectful silence, regretful avoidance. Simple ducks, in those royal waters, quackle for crumbs from young royal fingers: the little Dauphin has a little railed garden, where he is seen delving, with ruddy cheeks and flaxen curled hair; also a little hutch to put his tools in, and screen himself against showers. What peaceable simplicity! Is it peace of a Father restored to his children? Or of a Taskmaster who has lost his whip? Lafayette, and the Municipality and universal Constitutionalism assert the former, and do what is in them to realise it. Such Patriotism as snarls dangerously and shows teeth, Patrollotism shall suppress; or far better, Royalty shall soothe down the angry hair of it, by gentle pattings; and, most effectual of all, by fuller diet. Yes, not only shall Paris be fed, but the King's hand be seen in that work. The household goods of the Poor shall, up to a certain amount, by royal bounty, be disengaged from pawn, and that insatiable *Mont de Piété* shall disgorge; rides in the city with their *Vive le-Roi* need not fail: and so by substance and show, shall Royalty, if man's art can popularise it, be popularised.

Or, alas, is it neither restored Father nor diswhipped Task-master that walks there, but an anomalous complex of both these, and of innumerable other heterogeneities: reducible to no rubric, if not to this newly devised one: *King Louis Re-storer of French Liberty?* Man indeed, and King Louis like other men, lives in this world to make rule out of the ruleless; by his living energy, he shall force the absurd itself to become less absurd. But then if there *be* no living energy; living passivity only? King Serpent, hurled into its unexpected watery dominion, did at least bite, and assert credibly that he was there: but as for the poor King Log, tumbled hither and thither as thousandfold chance and other will than his might direct, how happy for him that he was indeed wooden; and, doing nothing, could also see and suffer nothing! It is a dis-tracted business.

For his French Majesty, meanwhile, one of the worst things is, that he can get no hunting. Alas, no hunting henceforth; only a fatal being-hunted! Scarcely, in the next June weeks, shall he taste again the joys of the game-destroyer; in next June, and never more. He sends for his smith-tools; gives, in the course of the day, official or ceremonial business being ended, 'a few strokes of the file, *quelques coups de lime.*' Inno-cent brother mortal, why wert thou not an obscure substantial maker of locks; but doomed in that other far-seen craft, to be a maker only of world-follies, unrealities; things self-destruc-tive, which no mortal hammering could rivet into coherence!

Poor Louis is not without insight, nor even without the elements of will; some sharpness of temper, spurting at times from a stagnating character. If harmless inertness could save him, it were well; but he will slumber and painfully dream, and to *do* aught is not given him. Royalist Anti-quarians still show the rooms where Majesty and suite, in these extraordinary circumstances, had their lodging. Here sat the Queen; reading,—for she had her library brought hither, though the King refused his; taking vehement counsel of the vehement uncounselled; sorrowing over altered times; yet with sure hope of better: in her young rosy Boy has she not the living emblem of hope! It is a murky, working sky; yet with golden gleams—of dawn, or of deeper meteoric night? Here again this chamber, on the other side of the main entrance, was the King's: here his Majesty breakfasted and did official work; here daily after breakfast he received the Queen; sometimes in pathetic friendliness; sometimes in human sulkiness, for flesh is weak; and when questioned about business, would answer: "Madame, your business is with the children." Nay, Sire, were it not better you, your Majesty's self, took the children? So asks impartial History scornful that the *thicker* vessel was not also the stronger; pity struck for the porcelain clay of humanity rather than for the tile-clay,—though indeed *both* were broken!

So, however, in this Medicean Tuileries, shall the French King and Queen now sit for one-and-forty months; and see a wild-fermenting France work out its own destiny, and theirs. Months bleak, ungenial, of rapid vicissitude; yet with a mild pale splendour, here and there: as of an April that were leading to leafiest Summer; as of an October that led only to everlasting Frost. Medicean Tuileries, how changed since it was a peaceful Tile-field! Or is the ground itself fate-stricken, accursed; an Atreus' Palace; for that Louvre window is still nigh, out of which a Capet, whipt of the Furies, fired his signal of the Saint Bartholomew! Dark is the way of the Eternal as mirrored in this world of Time: God's way is in the sea, and His path in the great deep.

CHAPTER II

IN THE SALLE DE MANÉGE

To believing Patriots, however, it is now clear, that the Constitution will march, *marcher*,—had it once legs to stand on. Quick, then, ye Patriots, bestir yourselves, and make it; shape legs for it! In the *Archevêché*, or Archbishop's Palace, his Grace himself having fled; and afterwards in the Riding-hall, named Manége, close on the Tuileries: there does a National Assembly apply itself to the miraculous work. Successfully, had there been any heaven-scaling Prometheus among them; not successfully, since there was none! There, in noisy debate, for the sessions are occasionally 'scandalous,' and as many as three speakers have been seen in the Tribune at once,—let us continue to fancy it wearing the slow months.

Tough, dogmatic, long of wind is Abbé Maury; Ciceronian pathetic is Cazalès. Keen-trenchant, on the other side, glitters

young Barnave; abhorrent of sophistry; shearing, like
keen Damascus sabre, all sophistry asunder,—reckless what
else he shear with it. Simple seemest thou, O solid
Dutch-built Pétion; if solid, surely dull. Nor life-giving is
that tone of thine, livelier polemical Rabaut. With ineffable
serenity sniffs great Sieyès, aloft, alone; his Constitution ye
may babble over, ye may mar, but can by no possibility mend:
is not Polity a science he has exhausted? Cool, slow, two
military Lameths are visible, with their quality sneer, or demi-
sneer; they shall gallantly refund their Mother's Pension,
when the Red Book is produced; gallantly be wounded in
duels. A Marquis Toulongeon, whose Pen we yet thank, sits
here; in stoical meditative humour, oftenest silent, accepts
what Destiny will send. Thouret and Parlementary Duport
produce mountains of Reformed Law; liberal, Anglomaniac;
available and unavailable. Mortals rise and fall. Shall goose
Gobel, for example,—or Göbel, for he is of Strasburg German
breed,—be a Constitutional Archbishop?

Alone of all men there, Mirabeau may begin to discern
clearly whither all this is tending. Patriotism, accordingly,
regrets that his zeal seems to be getting cool. In that famed
Pentecost-Night of the Fourth of August, when new Faith
rose suddenly into miraculous fire, and old Feudality was
burnt up, men remarked that Mirabeau took no hand in it;
that, in fact, he luckily happened to be absent. But did he
not defend the *Veto*, nay *Veto Absolu;* and tell vehement
Barnave that six hundred irresponsible senators would make
of all tyrannies the insupportablest? Again, how anxious was
he that the King's Ministers should have seat and voice in the
National Assembly;—doubtless with an eye to being Minister
himself! Whereupon the National Assembly decides, what is
very momentous, that no Deputy shall be Minister; he, in
his haughty stormful manner, advising us to make it, "no
Deputy called Mirabeau." A man of perhaps inveterate
feudalisms; of stratagems; too often visible leanings towards
the Royalist side: a man suspect; whom Patriotism will
unmask! Thus, in these June days, when the question, *Who
shall have right to declare war?* comes on, you hear hoarse
Hawkers sound dolefully through the streets, "Grand Treason
of Count Mirabeau, price only one sou;"—because he pleads
that it shall be not the Assembly, but the King! Pleads;
nay prevails: for, in spite of the hoarse Hawkers, and an
endless Populace raised by them to the pitch even of

'*Lanterne*,' he mounts the Tribune next day; grim-resolute, murmuring aside to his friends that speak of danger: " I know it : I must come hence either in triumph, or else torn in fragments:" and it was in triumph that he came.

A man stout of heart; whose popularity is not of the populace, '*pas populacière*;' whom no clamour of unwashed mobs without doors, or of washed mobs within, can scare from his way! Dumont remembers hearing him deliver a Report on Marseilles; 'every word was interrupted on the part of the *Côté Droit* by abusive epithets ; calumniator, liar, assassin, scoundrel (*scélérat*) : ' Mirabeau pauses a moment, and in a honeyed tone, addressing the most furious, says : " I wait, Messieurs, till these amenities be exhausted."' A man enigmatic, difficult to unmask ! For example, whence comes his money? Can the profit of a newspaper, sorely eaten into by Dame Le Jay ; can this, and the eighteen francs a-day your National Deputy has, be supposed equal to this expenditure ? House in the Chaussée d'Antin ; Country-house at Argenteuil ; splendours, sumptuosities, orgies ;—living as if he had a mint ! All saloons, barred against Adventurer Mirabeau, are flung wide-open to King Mirabeau, the cynosure of Europe, whom female France flutters to behold,—though the man Mirabeau is one and the same. As for money, one may conjecture that Royalism furnishes it ; which, if Royalism do, will not the same be welcome, as money always is to him ?

'Sold,' whatever Patriotism thinks, he cannot readily be : the spiritual fire which is in that man ; which shining through such confusions is nevertheless Conviction, and makes him strong, and without which he had no strength,—is not buyable nor saleable; in such transference of barter, it would vanish and not *be*. Perhaps 'paid and not sold, *payé pas vendu :*' as poor Rivarol, in the unhappier converse way, calls himself 'sold and not paid !' A man travelling, comet-like, in splendour and nebulosity, his wild way ; whom telescopic Patriotism may long watch, but, without higher mathematics, will not make out. A questionable, most blameable man; yet to us the far notablest of all. With rich munificence, as we often say, in a most blinkard, bespectacled, logic-chopping generation, Nature has gifted this man with an eye. Welcome is his word, there where he speaks and works ; and growing ever welcomer ; for it alone goes to the heart of the business : logical cobwebbery shrinks itself together ; and thou seest a *thing*, how it is, how it may be worked with.

Unhappily our National Assembly has much to do: a
France to regenerate; and France is short of so many requi-
sites, short even of cash. These same Finances give trouble
enough; no choking of the Deficit; which gapes ever, *Give,
give!* To appease the Deficit we venture on a hazardous step,
sale of the Clergy's Lands and superfluous Edifices; most
hazardous. Nay, given the sale, who is to buy them, ready-
money having fled? Wherefore, on the 19th day of December,
a paper-money of '*Assignats*,' of Bonds secured, or *assigned*,
on that Clerico-National Property, and unquestionable at least
in payment of that,—is decreed: the first of a long series of
like financial performances, which shall astonish mankind So
that now, while old rags last, there shall be no lack of circulating medium: whether of commodities to circulate thereon,
is another question. But, after all, does not this Assignat
business speak volumes for modern science? Bankruptcy, we
may say, was come, as the *end* of all Delusions needs must
come: yet how gently, in softening diffusion, in mild succession, was it hereby made to fall;—like no all destroying
avalanche; like gentle showers of a powdery impalpable snow,
shower after shower, till all was indeed buried, and yet little
was destroyed that could not be replaced, be dispensed with!
To such length has modern machinery reached. Bankruptcy,
we said, was great; but indeed Money itself is a standing
miracle.

On the whole, it is a matter of endless difficulty, that of the
Clergy. Clerical property may be made the Nation's, and the
Clergy hired servants of the State; but if so, is it not an
altered Church? Adjustment enough, of the most confused
sort, has become unavoidable. Old landmarks, in any sense,
avail not in a new France. Nay, literally, the very Ground is
new divided; your old parti-coloured *Provinces* become new
uniform *Departments* Eighty-three in number;—whereby, as in
some sudden shifting of the Earth's axis, no mortal knows his
new latitude at once. The Twelve old Parlements too, what
is to be done with them? The old Parlements are declared to
be all 'in permanent vacation,'—till once the new equal-justice,
of Departmental Courts, National Appeal-Court, of elective
Justices, Justices of Peace, and other Thouret-and-Duport
apparatus be got ready. They have to sit there, these old
Parlements, uneasily waiting; as it were, with the rope round
their neck; crying as they can, *Is there none to deliver us?*
But happily the answer being *None, none,* they are a manage-

able class, these Parlements. They can be bullied, even, into silence; the Paris Parlement, wiser than most, has never whimpered. They will and must sit there; in such vacation as is fit: their Chamber of Vacation distributes in the interim what little justice is going. With the rope round their neck, their destiny may be succinct! On the 13th of November 1790, Mayor Bailly shall walk to the Palais de Justice, few even heeding him; and with municipal seal-stamp and a little hot wax, seal up the Parlementary Paper-rooms,—and the dread Parlement of Paris pass away, into Chaos, gently as does a Dream! So shall the Parlements perish, succinctly; and innumerable eyes be dry.

Not so the Clergy. For granting even that Religion were dead; that it had died, half-centuries ago, with unutterable Dubois; or emigrated lately to Alsace, with Necklace-Cardinal Rohan; or that it now walked as goblin *revenant*, with Bishop Talleyrand of Autun; yet does not the Shadow of Religion, the Cant of Religion, still linger? The Clergy have means and material: means, of number, organisation, social weight; a material, at lowest, of public ignorance, known to be the mother of devotion. Nay, withal, is it incredible that there might, in simple hearts, latent here and there like gold-grains in the mud-beach, still dwell some real Faith in God, of so singular and tenacious a sort that even a Maury or a Talleyrand could still be the symbol for it?—Enough, the Clergy has strength, the Clergy has craft and indignation. It is a most fatal business this of the Clergy. A weltering hydra-coil, which the National Assembly has stirred up about its ears; hissing, stinging; which cannot be appeased, alive; which cannot be trampled dead! Fatal, from first to last! Scarcely after fifteen months' debating, can a *Civil Constitution of the Clergy* be so much as got to paper; and then for getting it into reality? Alas, such Civil Constitution is but an agreement to disagree. It divides France from end to end, with a new split, infinitely complicating all the other splits:—Catholicism, what of it there is left, with the Cant of Catholicism, raging on the one side, and sceptic Heathenism on the other; both, by contradiction, waxing fanatic. What endless jarring, of Refractory hated Priests, and Constitutional despised ones; of tender consciences, like the King's, and consciences hot-seared, like certain of his People's: the whole to end in Feasts of Reason and a War of La Vendée! So deep-seated is Religion in the heart of man, and holds of all infinite passions. If the dead

echo of it still did so much, what could not the living voice of
it once do?

Finance and Constitution, Law and Gospel: this surely
were work enough; yet this is not all. In fact, the Ministry,
and Necker himself, whom a brass inscription, 'fastened by the
people over his door-lintel,' testifies to be the '*Ministre adoré*,'
are dwindling into clearer and clearer nullity. Execution or
legislation, arrangement or detail, from their nerveless fingers
all drops undone; all lights at last on the toiled shoulders
of an august Representative Body. Heavy-laden National
Assembly! It has to hear of innumerable fresh revolts,
Brigand expeditions; of Châteaus in the West, especially of
Charter-chests, *Chartiers*, set on fire; for there too the over-
loaded Ass frightfully recalcitrates. Of Cities in the South
full of heats and jealousies; which will end in crossed sabres,
Marseilles against Toulon, and Carpentras beleagured by
Avignon;—of so much Royalist collision in a career of
Freedom; nay of patriot collision, which a mere difference of
velocity will bring about! Of a Jourdan Coupe-tête, who has
skulked thitherward, to those southern regions, from the claws
of the Châtelet; and will raise whole scoundrel-regiments.

Also it has to hear of Royalist *Camp of Jalès:* Jalès moun-
tain-girdled Plain, amid the rocks of the Cevennes; whence
Royalism, as is feared and hoped, may dash down like a
mountain deluge, and submerge France! A singular thing
this Camp of Jalès; existing mostly on paper. For the
Soldiers at Jalès, being peasants or National Guards, were in
heart sworn Sansculottes; and all that the Royalist Captains
could do was, with false words, to keep them, or rather keep
the report of them, drawn up there, visible to all imaginations,
for a terror and a sign,—if peradventure France might be reconquered by theatrical machinery, by the *picture* of a Royalist
Army done to the life! Not till the third summer was this
portent, burning out by fits and then fading, got finally extinguished; was the old Castle of Jalès, no Camp being
visible to the bodily eye, got blown asunder by some National
Guards.

Also it has to hear not only of Brissot and his *Friends of the
Blacks*, but by and by of a whole St. Domingo blazing skyward; blazing in literal fire, and in far worse metaphorical;
beaconing the nightly main. Also of the shipping interest,
and the landed interest, and all manner of interests, reduced
to distress. Of Industry everywhere manacled, bewildered;

and only Rebellion thriving. Of sub-officers, soldiers and sailors in mutiny by land and water. Of soldiers, at Nanci, as we shall see, needing to be cannonaded by a brave Bouillé. Of sailors, nay the very galley-slaves, at Brest, needing also to be cannonaded, but with no Bouillé to do it. For indeed, to say it in a word, in those days there was *no King* in Israel, and every man did that which was right in his own eyes.

Such things has an august National Assembly to hear of, as it goes on regenerating France. Sad and stern: but what remedy? Get the Constitution ready; and all men will swear to it: for do not 'Addresses of adhesion' arrive by the cart-load? In this manner, by Heaven's blessing, and a Constitution got ready, shall the bottomless fire-gulf be vaulted in, with rag-paper; and Order will wed Freedom, and live with her there,—till it grow too hot for them. O *Côté Gauche*, worthy are ye, as the adhesive Addresses generally say, to 'fix the regards of the Universe;' the regards of this one poor Planet, at lowest!—

Nay, it must be owned, the *Côté Droit* makes a still madder figure. An irrational generation; irrational, imbecile, and with the vehement obstinacy characteristic of that; a generation which will not learn. Falling Bastilles, Insurrections of Women, thousands of smoking Manorhouses, a country bristling with no crop but that of Sansculottic steel: these were tolerably didactic lessons; but them they have not taught. There are still men, of whom it was of old written, Bray them in a mortar! Or, in milder language, They have *wedded* their delusions: fire nor steel, nor any sharpness of Experience, shall sever the bond; till *death* do us part! On such may the Heavens have mercy; for the Earth, with her rigorous Necessity, will have none.

Admit, at the same time, that it was most natural. Man lives by Hope: Pandora, when her box of gods'-gifts flew all out, and became gods'-curses, still retained Hope. How shall an irrational mortal, when his highplace is never so evidently pulled down, and he, being irrational, is left resourceless,—part with the belief that it will be rebuilt? It would make all so straight again; it seems so unspeakably desirable; so reasonable,—would you but look at it aright! For, must not the thing which was continue to be; or else the solid World dissolve? Yes, persist, O infatuated Sansculottes of France! Revolt against constituted Authorities; hunt out your rightful Seigneurs, who at bottom so loved you, and readily shed their

blood for you,—in country's battles as at Rossbach and elsewhere; and, even in preserving game, were preserving *you*,
could ye but have understood it: hunt them out, as if they
were wild wolves; set fire to their Châteaus and Chartiers as
to wolf-dens; and what then? Why, then turn every man his
hand against his fellow! In confusion, famine, desolation,
regret the days that are gone; rueful recall them, recall us
with them. To repentant prayers we will not be deaf.

So, with dimmer or clearer consciousness, must the Right
Side reason and act. An inevitable position perhaps; but a
most false one for them. Evil, be thou our good: this henceforth must virtually be their prayer. The fiercer the effervescence grows, the sooner will it pass; for, after all, it is but
some mad effervescence; the World is solid, and cannot dissolve.

For the rest, if they have any positive industry, it is that
of plots, and backstairs conclaves. Plots which cannot be
executed; which are mostly theoretic on their part;—for which
nevertheless this and the other practical Sieur Augeard, Sieur
Maillebois, Sieur Bonne Savardin, gets into trouble, gets imprisoned and escapes with difficulty. Nay there is a poor
practical Chevalier Favras, who, not without some passing
reflex on Monsieur himself, gets hanged for them, amid loud
uproar of the world. Poor Favras, he keeps dictating his last
will 'at the Hôtel-de-Ville, through the whole remainder of
the day,' a weary February day; offers to reveal secrets if they
will save him; handsomely declines since they will not; then
dies, in the flare of torchlight, with politest composure; remarking, rather than exclaiming, with outspread hands:
"People, I die innocent; pray for me." Poor Favras;—
type of so much that has prowled indefatigable over France,
in days now ending; and, in freer field, might have *earned*
instead of prowling,—to thee it is no theory!

In the Senate-house again, the attitude of the Right Side
is that of calm unbelief. Let an august National Assembly
make a Fourth-of-August Abolition of Feudality; declare the
Clergy State-servants who shall have wages; vote Suspensive
Vetos, new Law-Courts: vote or decree what contested thing
it will; have it responded to from the four corners of France,
nay, get King's Sanction, and what other Acceptance were
conceivable,—the Right Side, as we find, persists, with imperturbablest tenacity, in considering, and ever and anon
shows that it still considers, all these so-called Decrees as

mere temporary whims, which indeed stand on paper, but in practice and fact are not, and cannot be. Figure the brass head of an Abbé Maury flooding forth jesuitic eloquence in this strain; dusky D'Espréménil, Barrel Mirabeau (probably in liquor), and enough of others, cheering him from the Right: and, for example, with what visage a seagreen Robespierre eyes him from the Left. And how Sieyès ineffably sniffs on him, or does not deign to sniff; and how the Galleries groan in spirit, or bark rabid on him: so that to escape the Lanterne, on stepping forth, he needs presence of mind, and a pair of pistols in his girdle! For he is one of the toughest of men.

Here indeed becomes notable one great difference between our two kinds of civil war; between the modern *lingual* or Parliamentary-logical kind, and the ancient or *manual* kind in the steel battlefield;—much to the disadvantage of the former. In the manual kind, where you front your foe with drawn weapon, one right stroke is final; for, physically speaking. when the brains are out the man does honestly die, and trouble you no more. But how different when it is with argument you fight! Here no victory yet definable can be considered as final. Beat him down with Parliamentary invective, till sense be fled; cut him in two, hanging one half on this dilemma-horn, the other on that; blow the brains or thinking faculty quite out of him for the time: it kills not; he rallies and revives on the morrow; to-morrow he repairs his golden fires! The thing that *will* logically extinguish him is perhaps still a desideratum in Constitutional civilisation. For how, till a man know, in some measure, at what point he becomes logically defunct, can Parliamentary Business be carried on, and Talk cease or slake?

Doubtless it was some feeling of this difficulty; and the clear insight how little such knowledge yet existed in the French nation, new in the Constitutional career, and how defunct Aristocrats would continue to walk for unlimited periods, as Partridge the Almanac-maker did,—that had sunk into the deep mind of People's-friend Marat, an eminently practical mind; and had grown there, in that richest putrescent soil, into the most original plan of action ever submitted to a People. Nor yet has it grown; but it has germinated, it is growing; rooting itself into Tartarus, branching towards Heaven; the second season hence, we shall see it risen out of the bottomless Darkness, full-grown, into disastrous Twilight,—a Hemlock-tree, great as the world; on or under whose boughs all the People's-friends of the world may lodge. 'Two hundred and Sixty thousand Aristocrat heads:' that is the precisest calculation, though one would not stand on a few hundreds; yet we never rise as high as the round three hundred thousand. Shudder at it, O People; but it is as true, as that ye yourselves, and your People's-friend, are alive. These prating Senators of yours hover ineffectual on the barren letter, and will never save the Revolution. A Cassandra-Marat cannot do it, with his single shrunk arm; but with a few determined men it were possible. "Give me," said the People's-friend, in his cold way, when young Barbaroux, once his pupil in a course of what was called Optics, went to see him, "Give me two hundred Naples Bravoes, armed each with a good dirk, and a muff on his left arm by way of shield: with them I will traverse France, and accomplish the Revolution." Nay, be grave, young Barbaroux; for thou seest, there is no jesting in those rheumy eyes, in that soot-bleared figure, most earnest of created things; neither indeed is there madness, of the strait-waistcoat sort.

Such produce shall the Time ripen in cavernous Marat, the man forbid; living in Paris cellars, lone as fanatic Anchorite in his Thebaid; say, as far-seen Simon on his Pillar,—taking peculiar views therefrom. Patriots may smile; and, using him as a bandog now to be muzzled, now to be let bark, name him, as Desmoulins does, 'Maximum of Patriotism' and 'Cassandra-Marat': but were it not singular if this dirk-and-muff plan of his (with superficial modifications) proved to be precisely the plan adopted?

After this manner, in these circumstances, do august Senators regenerate France. Nay, they are, in very deed, *believed* to be regenerating it; on account of which great fact, main fact of their history, the wearied eye can never be permitted wholly to ignore them.

But, looking away now from these precincts of the Tuileries, where Constitutional Royalty, let Lafayette water it as he will, languishes too like a cut branch; and august Senators are perhaps at bottom only perfecting their 'theory of defective verbs,'—how does the young Reality, young Sansculottism thrive? The attentive observer can answer: It thrives bravely; putting forth new buds; expanding the old buds into leaves, into boughs. Is not French Existence, as before, most prurient, all *loosened*, most nutrient for it? Sansculottism has the property of growing by what other things die of: by agitation, contention, disarrangement; nay in a word, by what is the symbol and fruit of all these: Hunger.

In such a France as this, Hunger, as we have remarked, can hardly fail. The Provinces, the Southern Cities feel it in their turn; and what it brings: Exasperation, preternatural Suspicion In Paris some halcyon days of abundance followed the Menadic Insurrection, with its Versailles grain-carts, and recovered Restorer of Liberty; but they could not continue. The month is still October, when famishing Saint-Antoine, in a moment of passion, seizes a poor Baker, innocent 'François the Baker;' and hangs him, in Constantinople wise;—but even this, singular as it may seem, does not cheapen bread! Too clear it is, no Royal bounty, no Municipal dexterity can adequately feed a Bastille-destroying Paris. Wherefore, on view of the hanged Baker, Constitutionalism in sorrow and anger demands '*Loi Martiale*,' a kind of Riot Act;—and indeed gets it most readily, almost before the sun goes down.

This is that famed *Martial Law*, with its Red Flag, its '*Drapeau Rouge*,' in virtue ot which Mayor Bailly, or any Mayor, has but henceforth to hang out that new *Oriflamme* of his; then to read or mumble something about the King's peace; and, after certain pauses, serve any undispersing Assemblage with musket-shot, or whatever shot will disperse it. A decisive Law; and most just on one proviso: that all Patrollotism be of God, and all mob-assembling be of the Devil;—otherwise not so just. Mayor Bailly, be unwilling to use it! Hang not out that new Oriflamme, *flame* not *of gold* but of the want of gold! The thrice-blessed Revolution is *done*, thou thinkest? If so, it will be well with thee.

But now let no mortal say henceforth that an august National Assembly wants riot: all it ever wanted was riot enough to balance Court-plotting; all it now wants. of Heaven or of Earth, is to get its theory of defective verbs perfected.

CHAPTER III

THE MUSTER

WITH Famine and a Constitutional theory of defective verbs going on, all other excitement is conceivable. A universal shaking and sifting of French Existence this is: in the course of which, for one thing, what a multitude of low-lying figures are sifted to the top, and set busily to work there!

Dogleech Marat, now far-seen as Simon Stylites, we already know; him and others, raised aloft. The mere sample these, of what is coming, of what continues coming, upwards from the realm of night!—Chaumette, by and by Anaxagoras Chaumette, one already descries: mellifluous in street groups; not now a seaboy on the high and giddy mast: a mellifluous tribune of the common people, with long curling locks, on *bourne*stone of the thoroughfares; able sub-editor too; who shall rise,—to the very gallows. Clerk Tallien, he also is become sub-editor; shall become able-editor; and more. Bibliopolic Momoro, Typographic Prudhomme see new trades opening. Collot d'Herbois, tearing a passion to rags, pauses on the Thespian boards; listens, with that black bushy head, to the sound of the world's drama: shall the Mimetic become Real? Did ye hiss him, O men of Lyons? Better had ye clapped!

Happy now, indeed, for all manner of *mimetic*, half-original men! Tumid blustering, with more or less of sincerity, which need not be entirely sincere, yet the sincerer the better, is like to go far. Shall we say, the Revolution-element works itself rarer and rarer; so that only lighter and lighter bodies will float in it; till at last the mere blown-bladder is your only swimmer? Limitation of mind, then vehemence, promptitude, audacity, shall all be available; to which add only these two: cunning and good lungs. Good fortune must be presupposed. Accordingly, of all classes the rising one, we observe, is now the Attorney class: witness Bazires, Carriers, Fouquier-Tinvilles, Basoche-Captain Bourdons: more than enough. Such figures shall Night, from her wonder-bearing bosom, emit; swarm after swarm. Of another deeper and deepest swarm, not yet dawned on the astonished eye; of pilfering Candle-snuffers, Thief-valets, disfrocked Capuchins, and so many Héberts, Henriots, Ronsins, Rossignols, let us, as long as possible, forbear speaking.

Thus, over France, all stirs that has what the Physiologists call *irritability* in it: how much more all wherein irritability has perfected itself into vitality, into actual vision, and force that can will! All stirs, and if not in Paris, flocks thither. Great and greater waxes President Danton in his Cordeliers Section; his rhetorical tropes are all 'gigantic:' energy flashes from his black brows, menaces in his athletic figure, rolls in the sound of his voice 'reverberating from the domes:' this man also, like Mirabeau, has a natural *eye*, and begins to see whither Constitutionalism is tending, though with a wish in it different from Mirabeau's.

Remark, on the other hand, how General Dumouriez has quitted Normandy and the Cherbourg Breakwater, to come—whither we may guess. It is his second or even third trial at Paris, since this New Era began; but now it is in right earnest, for he has quitted all else. Wiry, elastic unwearied man; whose life was but a battle and a march! No, *not* a creature of Choiseul's; "the creature of God and of my sword,"—he fiercely answered in old days. Overfalling Corsican batteries, in the deadly fire-hail; wriggling invincible from under his horse, at Closterkamp of the Netherlands, though tethered with 'crushed stirrup-iron and nineteen wounds;' tough, minatory, standing at bay, as forlorn hope, on the skirts of Poland; intriguing, battling in cabinet and field; roaming far out, obscure, as King's spial, or sitting sealed up, enchanted in Bastille; fencing, pamphleteering, scheming and struggling from the very birth of him,—the man has come thus far. How represssed, how irrepressible! Like some incarnate spirit in prison, which indeed he *was*; hewing on granite walls for deliverance: striking fire-flashes from them. And now has the general earthquake rent his cavern too? Twenty years younger, what might he not have done! But his hair has a shade of gray; his way of thought is all fixed, military. He can *grow* no further, and the new world is in such growth. We will name him, on the whole, one of Heaven's Swiss; without faith; wanting above all things work, work on *any* side. Work also is appointed him; and he will do it.

Not from over France only are the unrestful flocking towards Paris; but from all sides of Europe. Where the carcass is, thither will the eagles gather. Think how many a Spanish Guzman, Martinico Fournier named 'Fournier *l'Américain*,' Engineer Miranda from the very Andes, were flocking or had flocked. Walloon Pereyra might boast of the strangest parentage: him, they say, Prince Kaunitz the Diplomatist heedlessly dropped; like ostrich-egg, to be hatched of Chance,—into an ostrich-*eater!* Jewish or German Freys do business in the great Cesspool of *Agio;* which Cesspool this *Assignat*-fiat has quickened, into a Mother of dead dogs. Swiss Clavière could found no Socinian Genevese Colony in

Ireland; but he paused, years ago, prophetic, before the Minister's Hôtel at Paris; and said, it was borne on his mind that *he* one day was to be Minister, and laughed. Swiss Pache, on the other hand, sits sleekheaded, frugal; the wonder of his own alley, and even of neighbouring ones, for humility of mind, and a thought deeper than most men's: sit there, Tartuffe, till wanted! Ye Italian Dufournys, Flemish Prolys, flit hither all ye bipeds of prey! Come whosesoever head is hot; thou of mind *ungoverned*, be it chaos as of undevelopment or chaos as of ruin; the man who cannot get known, the man who is too well known; if thou have any vendible faculty, nay if thou have but edacity and loquacity, come! They come; with hot unutterabilities in their heart; as Pilgrims towards a miraculous shrine. Nay how many come as vacant Strollers, aimless, of whom Europe is full, merely towards *something!* For benighted fowls, when you beat their bushes, rush towards any light. Thus Frederick Baron Trenck too is here; mazed, purblind, from the cells of Magdeburg; Minotauric cells, and his Ariadne lost! Singular to say, Trenck, in these years, sells wine; not indeed in bottle, but in wood.

Nor is our England without her missionaries. She has her life-saving Needham; to whom was solemnly presented a 'civic sword,' — long since rusted into nothingness. Her Paine: rebellious Staymaker; unkempt; who feels that he, a single Needleman, did, by his *Common Sense* Pamphlet, free America; that he can and will free all this World; perhaps even the other. Price-Stanhope Constitutional Association sends over to congratulate; welcomed by National Assembly, though they are but a London Club; whom Burke and Toryism eye askance.

On thee too, for country's sake, O Chevalier John Paul, be a word spent, or misspent! In faded naval uniform, Paul Jones lingers visible here; like a wineskin from which the wine is all drawn. Like the ghost of himself! Low is his once loud bruit; scarcely audible, save, with extreme tedium, in ministerial ante-chambers, in this or the other charitable dining-room, mindful of the past. What changes; culminatings and declinings! Not now, poor Paul, thou lookest wistful over the Solway brine, by the foot of native Criffel, into blue mountainous Cumberland, into blue Infinitude; environed with thrift, with humble friendliness; thyself, young fool, longing to be aloft from it, or even to be away from it Yes, beyond that sapphire Promontory, which men name St. Bees, which is not sapphire either, but dull sandstone, when one gets *close* to it, there is a world. Which world thou too shalt taste of!—From yonder White Haven rise his smoke-clouds; ominous though ineffectual. Proud Forth quakes at his bellying sails; had not the wind suddenly shifted. Flamborough reapers, homegoing, pause on the hill-side: for what sulphur-cloud is that that defaces the sleek sea; sulphur-cloud spitting streaks of fire? A sea cockfight it is, and of the hottest; where British *Serapis* and the French-American *Bonne Homme Richard* do lash and throttle each other, in their fashion; and lo the desperate valour has suffocated the deliberate, and Paul Jones too is of the Kings of the Sea!

The Euxine, the Meotian waters felt thee next, and long-skirted Turks, O Paul; and thy fiery soul has wasted itself in thousand contradictions;—to no purpose. For, in far lands, with scarlet Nassau-Siegens, with sinful Imperial Catherines, is not the heart broken, even as at home with the mean? Poor Paul! hunger and dispiritment track thy sinking footsteps: once or at most twice, in this Revolution-tumult the figure of thee emerges; mute, ghost-like, as 'with stars dim-twinkling through.' And then, when the light is gone quite out, a National Legislature grants 'ceremonial funeral!' As good had been the natural Presbyterian Kirk-bell, and six feet of Scottish earth, among the dust of thy loved ones.—*Such* world lay beyond the Promontory of St. Bees. Such is the life of sinful mankind here below.

But of all strangers, far the notablest for us is Baron Jean Baptiste de Clootz;—or, dropping baptisms and feudalisms, World-Citizen Anacharsis Clootz, from Cleves. Him mark, judicious Reader. Thou hast known his Uncle, sharp-sighted thorough-going Cornelius de Pauw, who mercilessly cuts down cherished illusions; and of the finest antique Spartans will make mere modern cut-throat Mainots. The like stuff is in Anacharsis: hot metal; full of scoriæ, which should and could have been smelted out, but which will not. He has wandered over this terraqueous Planet; seeking, one may say, the Paradise we lost long ago. He has seen English Burke; has been seen of the Portugal Inquisition; has roamed, and fought, and written; is writing, among other things, 'Evidences of the *Mahometan* Religion.' But now, like his Scythian adoptive godfather, he finds himself in the Paris Athens;

surely, at last, the haven of his soul. A dashing man, beloved at Patriotic dinner-tables; with gaiety, nay with humour; headlong, trenchant, of free purse; in suitable costume; though what mortal ever more despised costumes? Under all costumes Anacharsis seeks the man; not Stylites Marat will more freely trample costumes, if they hold no man. This is the faith of Anacharsis: That there is a Paradise discoverable; that all costumes ought to hold men. O Anacharsis, it is a headlong, swift-going faith. Mounted thereon, meseems, thou art bound hastily for the City of *Nowhere;* and wilt *arrive!* At best, we may say, arrive *in good riding attitude;* which indeed is something.

So many new persons and new things have come to occupy this France. Her old Speech and Thought, and Activity which springs from these, are all changing; fermenting towards unknown issues. To the dullest peasant, as he sits sluggish, overtoiled, by his evening hearth, one idea has come: that of Châteaus burnt; of Châteaus combustible. How altered all Coffeehouses, in Province or Capital! The *Antre de Procope* has now other questions than the Three Stagyrite Unities to settle; not theatre-controversies, but a world-controversy: there, in the ancient pigtail mode, or with modern Brutus' heads, do well-frizzed logicians hold hubbub, and Chaos umpire sits. The ever-enduring melody of Paris Saloons has got a new ground-tone: ever-enduring; which has been heard, and by the listening Heaven too, since Julian the Apostate's time and earlier; mad now as formerly.

Ex-Censor Suard, *Ex*-Censor, for we have freedom of the Press; he may be seen there; impartial, even neutral. Tyrant Grimm rolls large eyes, over a questionable coming Time. Atheist Naigeon, beloved-disciple of Diderot, crows, in his small difficult way, heralding glad dawn. But on the other hand, how many Morellets, Marmontels, who had sat all their life hatching Philosophe eggs, cackle now, in a state bordering on distraction, at the brood they have brought out! It was so delightful to have one's Philosophe Theorem demonstrated, crowned in the saloons: and now an infatuated people will not continue speculative, but have Practice?

There also observe Preceptress Genlis, or Sillery, or Sillery-Genlis,—for our husband is both Count and Marquis, and we have more than one title. Pretentious, frothy; a puritan yet creedless; darkening counsel by words without wisdom! For, it is in that thin element of the Sentimentalist and Distinguished-Female that Sillery-Genlis works; she would gladly be sincere, yet can grow no sincerer than sincere-cant: sincere-cant of many forms, ending in the devotional form. For the present, on a neck still of moderate whiteness, she wears as jewel a miniature Bastille, cut on mere sandstone, but then actual Bastille sandstone. M. le Marquis is one of D'Orléans's errandmen; in National Assembly, and elsewhere. Madame, for her part, trains up a youthful D'Orléans generation in what superfinest morality one can; gives meanwhile rather enigmatic account of fair Mademoiselle Pamela, the daughter whom she has *adopted*. Thus she, in Palais Royal saloon;— whither, we remark, D'Orléans himself, spite of Lafayette, has returned from that English 'mission' of his: surely no pleasant mission: for the English would not speak to him; and Saint Hannah More of England, so unlike Saint Sillery-Genlis of France, saw him shunned, in Vauxhall Gardens, like one pest-struck, and his red-blue impassive visage waxing hardly a shade bluer.

CHAPTER IV

JOURNALISM

As for Constitutionalism, with its National Guards, it is doing what it can; and has enough to do; it must, as ever, with one hand wave persuasively, repressing Patriotism; and keep the other clenched to menace Royalist plotters. A most delicate task; requiring tact.

Thus, if People's-friend Marat has to-day his writ of '*prise de corps*, or seizure of body,' served on him, and dives out of sight, to-morrow he is left at large; or is even encouraged, as a sort of bandog whose baying may be useful. President Danton, in open Hall, with reverberating voice, declares that, in a case like Marat's, 'force may be resisted by force.' Whereupon the Châtelet serves Danton also with a writ;— which, however, as the whole Cordeliers District responds to it, what Constable will be prompt to execute? Twice more, on new occasions, does the Châtelet launch its writ; and twice more in vain: the body of Danton cannot be seized by Châtelet; he unseized, should he even fly for a season, shall behold the Châtelet itself flung into limbo.

Municipality and Brissot, meanwhile, are far on with their Municipal Constitution. The Sixty *Districts* shall become Forty-eight *Sections*; much shall be adjusted, and Paris have its Constitution. A Constitution wholly Elective; as indeed all French Government shall and must be. And yet, one fatal element has been introduced: that of *citoyen actif*. No man who does not pay the *marc d'argent*, or yearly tax equal to three days' labour, shall be other than a *passive* citizen: not the slightest vote for him; were he *acting*, all the year round, with sledge-hammer, with forest-levelling axe! Unheard of! cry Patriot Journals. Yes truly, my Patriot Friends, if Liberty, the passion and prayer of all men's souls, means Liberty to send your fifty-thousandth part of a new Tongue-fencer into National Debating-club, then, be the gods witness, ye are hardly entreated. Oh, if in National *Palaver* (as the Africans name it) such blessedness is verily found, what tyrant would deny it to Son of Adam! Nay, might there not be a Female Parliament too, with 'screams from the Opposition benches,' and 'the honourable Member borne out in hysterics?' To a Children's Parliament would I gladly consent; or even lower if ye wished it. Beloved Brothers! Liberty, one may fear, is actually, as the ancient wise men said, of Heaven. On this Earth, where, thinks the enlightened public, did a brave little Dame de Staal (not Necker's Daughter, but a far shrewder than she) find the nearest approach to Liberty? After mature computation, cool as Dilworth's, her answer is, *In the Bastille.* "Of Heaven?" answer many, asking. Wo that they should *ask*; for that is the very misery! "Of Heaven" means much; share in the National Palaver it may, or may as probably *not* mean.

One Sansculottic bough that cannot fail to flourish is Journalism. The voice of the People *being* the voice of God, shall not such divine voice make itself heard? To the ends of France; and in as many dialects as when the *first* great Babel was to be built! Some loud as the lion; some small as the sucking dove. Mirabeau himself has his instructive Journal or Journals, with Geneva hodmen working in them; and withal has quarrels enough with Dame Le Jay, his Female Bookseller, so ultra-compliant otherwise.

King's-friend Royou still prints himself. Barrère sheds tears of loyal sensibility in *Break of Day* Journal, though with declining sale. But why is Fréron so hot, democratic; Fréron, the King's-friend's Nephew? He has it by kind, that heat of his: *wasp* Fréron begot him; Voltaire's *Frélon*; who fought stinging, while sting and poison-bag were left, were it only as Reviewer, and over printed Waste-paper. Constant, illuminative, as the nightly lamplighter, issues the useful *Moniteur*, for it is now become diurnal: with facts and few commentaries; official, safe in the middle;—its able Editors sunk long since, recoverably or irrecoverably, in deep darkness. Acid Loustalot, with his 'vigour,' as of young sloes, shall never ripen, but die untimely: his Prudhomme, however, will not let that *Révolutions de Paris* die; but edit it himself, with much else,—dull-blustering Printer though he be.

Of Cassandra-Marat we have spoken often; yet the most surprising truth remains to be spoken; that he actually does not want sense; but, with croaking gelid throat, croaks out masses of the truth, on several things. Nay sometimes, one might almost fancy he had a perception of humour, and were laughing a little, far down in his inner man. Camille is wittier than ever, and more outspoken, cynical; yet sunny as ever. A light melodious creature; 'born,' as he shall yet say with bitter tears, 'to write verses;' light Apollo, so clear, soft-lucent, in this war of the Titans, wherein he shall not conquer!

Folded and hawked Newspapers exist in all countries; but, in such a Journalistic element as this of France, other and stranger sorts are to be anticipated. What says the English reader to a *Journal Affiche*, Placard Journal; legible to him that has no half-penny; in bright prismatic colours, calling the eye from afar? Such, in the coming months, as Patriot Associations, public and private, advance, and can subscribe funds, shall plenteously hang themselves out: *leaves*, limed leaves, to catch what they can! The very Government shall have its Pasted Journal; Louvet, busy yet with a new 'charming romance,' shall write *Sentinelles*, and post them with effect; nay Bertrand de Moleville, in his extremity, shall still more cunningly try it. Great is Journalism. Is not every able Editor a Ruler of the World, being a persuader of it; though self-elected, yet sanctioned, by the sale of his Numbers? Whom indeed the world has the readiest method of deposing, should need be: that of merely doing *nothing* to him; which ends in starvation.

Nor esteem it small what those Bill-stickers had to do in Paris: above Three-score of them: all with their crosspoles, haversacks, pastepots; nay with leaden badges, for the Municipality licenses them. A Sacred College, properly of World-rulers' Heralds, though not respected as such, in an Era still incipient and raw. They made the walls of Paris didactic, suasive, with an ever fresh Periodical Literature, wherein he that ran might read: Placard Journals, Placard Lampoons, Municipal Ordinances, Royal Proclamations; the whole other or vulgar Placard-department superadded,—or omitted from contempt! What unutterable things the stone-walls spoke, during these five years! But it is all gone: Today swallowing Yesterday, and then being in its turn swallowed of Tomorrow, even as Speech ever is. Nay what, O thou immortal Man of Letters, is Writing itself but speech conserved for a time? The Placard Journal conserved it for one day; some Books conserve it for the matter of ten years; nay some for three thousand; but what then? Why, *then*, the years being all run, it also dies, and the world is rid of it. Oh, were there not a spirit in the word of man, as in man himself, that survived the audible bodied word, and tended either godward or else devilward forevermore, why should he trouble himself much with the truth of it, or the falsehood of it, except for commercial purposes? His immortality indeed, and whether it shall last half a lifetime or a lifetime and half; is not that a very considerable thing? Immortality, mortality:—there were certain runaways whom Fritz the Great bullied back into the battle with a: "*R—, wollt ihr ewig leben,* Unprintable Offscouring of Scoundrels, would ye live forever!"

This is the Communication of Thought; how happy when there is any Thought to communicate! Neither let the simpler old methods be neglected, in their sphere. The Palais-Royal Tent, a tyrannous Patrollotism has removed; but can it remove the lungs of man? Anaxagoras Chaumette we saw mounted on bournestones, while Tallien worked sedentary at the sub-editorial desk. In any corner of the civilised world, a tub can be inverted, and an articulate-speaking biped mount thereon. Nay, with contrivance, a portable trestle, or folding-stool, can be procured, for love or money; this the peripatetic Orator can take in his hand, and, driven out here, set it up again there: saying mildly, with a Sage Bias, *Omnia mea mecum porto.*

Such is Journalism, hawked, pasted, spoken. How changed since one old Métra walked this same Tuileries Garden, in gilt cocked hat, with Journal at his nose, or held loose-folded behind his back; and was a notability of Paris, 'Metra the

Newsman;' and Louis himself was wont to say: *Qu'en dit Métra?* Since the first Venetian News-sheet was sold for a *gazza*, or farthing, and named *Gazette*. We live in a fertile world.

CHAPTER V

CLUBBISM

WHERE the heart is full, it seeks, for a thousand reasons, in a thousand ways, to impart itself. How sweet, indispensable, in such cases, is fellowship; soul mystically strengthening soul! The meditative Germans, some think, have been of opinion that Enthusiasm in general means simply excessive Congregating—*Schwärmerey*, or *Swarming*. At any rate, do we not see glimmering half-red embers, if laid *together*, get into the brightest white glow?

In such a France, gregarious Reunions will needs multiply, intensify; French Life will step out of doors, and, from domestic, become a public Club Life. Old Clubs, which already germinated, grow and flourish; new everywhere bud forth. It is the sure symptom of Social Unrest; in such way, most infallibly of all, does Social Unrest exhibit itself; find solacement, and also nutriment. In every French head there hangs now, whether for terror or for hope, some prophetic picture of a New France: prophecy which brings, nay which almost *is*, its own fulfilment; and in all ways, consciously, and unconsciously, works towards that.

Observe, moreover, how the Aggregative Principle, let it be but deep enough, goes on aggregating, and this even in a geometrical progression; how when the whole world, in such a plastic time, is forming itself into Clubs, some One Club, the strongest or luckiest, shall by friendly attracting, by victorious compelling, grow ever stronger, till it becomes immeasurably strong; and all the others, with their strength, be either lovingly absorbed into it, or hostilely abolished by it. This if the Club-spirit is universal; if the time *is* plastic. Plastic enough is the time, universal the Club-spirit: such an all-absorbing, paramount One Club cannot be wanting.

What a progress, since the first salient-point of the Breton Committee! (p. 85). It worked long in secret, not languidly; it has come with the National Assembly to Paris; calls itself *Club*: calls itself, in imitation, as is thought, of those generous

Price-Stanhope English who sent over to congratulate, *French Revolution Club;* but soon, with more originality, *Club of Friends of the Constitution.* Moreover, it has leased for itself, at a fair rent, the Hall of the Jacobins Convent, one of our 'superfluous edifices:' and does therefrom now, in these spring months, begin shining out on an admiring Paris. And so, by degrees, under the shorter popular title of *Jacobins Club,* it shall become memorable to all times and lands. Glance into the interior: strongly yet modestly benched and seated; as many as Thirteen Hundred chosen Patriots; Assembly Members not a few. Barnave, the two Lameths are seen there; occasionally Mirabeau, perpetually Robespierre; also the ferret-visage of Fouquier-Tinville with other attorneys; Anacharsis of Prussian Scythia, and miscellaneous Patriots,—though all is yet in the most perfectly cleanwashed state; decent, nay dignified. President on platform, President's bell are not wanting; oratorical Tribune high-raised; nor strangers' galleries, wherein also sit women. Has any French Antiquarian Society preserved that written Lease of the Jacobins Convent Hall? Or was it, unluckier even than Magna Charta, *clipt* by sacrilegious Tailors? Universal History is not indifferent to it.

These Friends of the Constitution have met mainly, as their name may foreshadow, to look after Elections when an Election comes, and procure fit men: but likewise to consult generally that the Commonweal take no damage; one as yet sees not how. For indeed let two or three gather together anywhere, if it be not in Church, where all are bound to the *passive* state; no mortal can say accurately, themselves as little as any, for *what* they are gathered. How often has the broached barrel proved not to be for joy and heart-effusion, but for duel and head-breakage; and the promised feast become a Feast of the Lapithæ! This Jacobins Club, which at first shone resplendent, and was thought to be a new celestial Sun for enlightening the Nations, had, as things have, to work through its appointed phases: it burned unfortunately more and more lurid, more sulphurous, distracted;—and swam at last, through the astonished Heaven, like a Tartarean Portent, and lurid-burning Prison of Spirits in Pain.

Its style of eloquence? Rejoice, Reader, that thou knowest it not, that thou canst never perfectly know. The Jacobins published a Journal of Debates, where they that have the heart may examine: impassioned, dull-droning, Patriotic-eloquence; implacable, unfertile—save for Destruction, which was indeed its work: most wearisome, though most deadly. Be thankful that Oblivion covers so much; that all carrion is by and by buried in the green Earth's bosom, and even makes her grow the greener. The Jacobins are buried; but their work is not; it continues 'making the tour of the world,' as it can. It might be seen lately, for instance, with bared bosom and death-defiant eye, as far on as Greek Missolonghi; strange enough, old slumbering Hellas was resuscitated, into *somnambulism* which will become clear wakefulness, by a voice from the Rue St. Honoré! All dies, as we often say; except the spirit of man, of what man *does*. Thus has not the very House of the Jacobins vanished: scarcely lingering in a few old men's memories? The St. Honoré Market has brushed it away, and now where dull-droning eloquence, like a Trump of Doom, once shook the world, there is a pacific chaffering for poultry and greens. The Sacred National Assembly Hall itself has become common ground; President's platform permeable to wain and dust-cart; for the Rue de Rivoli runs there. Verily, at Cockcrow (of this Cock or the other), *all* Apparitions do melt and dissolve in space.

The Paris *Jacobins* became 'the Mother-Society, *Société Mère;*' and had as many as 'three hundred' shrill-tongued daughters in 'direct correspondence' with her. Of indirectly corresponding, what we may call grand-daughters and minute progeny, she counted 'forty-four thousand!'—But for the present we note only two things: the first of them a mere anecdote. One night, a couple of brother Jacobins are doorkeepers; for the members take this post of duty and honour in rotation, and admit none that have not tickets: one doorkeeper was the worthy Sieur Laïs, a patriotic Opera-singer, stricken in years, whose windpipe is long since closed without result; the other, young, and named Louis Philippe, D'Orléan's firstborn, has in this latter time, after unheard-of destinies, become Citizen-King, and struggles to rule for a season. All flesh is grass; higher reedgrass or creeping herb.

The second thing we have to note is historical: that the Mother-Society, even in this its effulgent period, cannot content all Patriots. Already it must throw off, so to speak, two dissatisfied swarms; a swarm to the right, a swarm to the left. One party, which thinks the Jacobins lukewarm, constitutes itself into *Club of the Cordeliers;* a hotter Club: it is Danton's element; with whom goes Desmoulins. The other party, again, which thinks the Jacobins scalding-hot, flies off to the right, and becomes 'Club of 1789, Friends of the *Monarchic* Constitution.' They are afterwards named '*Feuillans Club;*' their place of meeting being the Feuillans Convent. Lafayette is, or becomes, their chief man; supported by the respectable Patriot everywhere, by the mass of Property and Intelligence, —with the most flourishing prospects. They, in these June days of 1790, do, in the Palais Royal, dine solemnly with open windows; to the cheers of the people; with toasts, with inspiriting songs,—with one song at least, among the feeblest ever sung. They shall, in due time, be hooted forth, over the borders, into Cimmerian night.

Another expressly Monarchic or Royalist Club, '*Club des Monarchiens,*' though a Club of ample funds, and all sitting on damask sofas, cannot realise the smallest momentary cheer: realises only scoffs and groans :—till, ere long, certain Patriots in disorderly sufficient number, proceed thither, for a night or for nights, and groan it out of pain. Vivacious alone shall the Mother-Society and her family be. The very Cordeliers may, as it were, return into her bosom, which will have grown warm enough.

Fatal-looking! Are not such Societies an incipient New Order of Society itself? The Aggregative Principle anew at work in a Society grown obsolete cracked asunder, dissolving into rubbish and primary atoms?

CHAPTER VI

JE LE JURE

WITH these signs of the times, is it not surprising that the dominant feeling all over France was still continually Hope? O blessed Hope, sole boon of man: whereby, on his strait prison-walls, are painted beautiful far-stretching landscapes; and into the night of very Death is shed holiest dawn! Thou art to all an indefeasible possession in this God's-world; to the wise a sacred Constantine's-banner, written on the eternal skies; under which they *shall* conquer, for the battle itself is victory: to the foolish some secular *mirage*, or shadow of still waters, painted on the parched earth; whereby at least their dusty pilgrimage, if devious, becomes cheerfuller, becomes possible.

In the death-tumults of a sinking Society, French Hope sees

only the birth-struggles of a new unspeakably better Society
and sings, with full assurance of faith, her brisk Melody
which some inspired fiddler has in these very days composed
for her,—the world-famous *Ça-ira*. Yes; 'that will go;' and
then there will *come*—? All men hope; even Marat hopes—
that Patriotism will take muff and dirk. King Louis is not
without hope : in the chapter of chances; in a flight to some
Bouillé; in getting popularised at Paris. But what a hoping
People he had, judge by the fact, and series of facts, now to be
noted.

Poor Louis, meaning the best, with little insight and even
less determination of his own, has to follow, in that dim wayfaring of his, such signal as may be given him; by backstair
Royalism, by official or backstairs Constitutionalism, whichever
for the month may have convinced the royal mind. If flight
to Bouillé, and (horrible to think!) a *drawing* of the civil
sword do hang as theory, portentous in the background, much
nearer is this fact of these Twelve Hundred Kings, who sit in
the *Salle de Manége*. Kings uncontrollable by him, not yet
irreverent to him. Could kind management of these but
prosper, how much better were it than armed Emigrants,
Turin intrigues, and the help of Austria ! Nay, are the two
hopes inconsistent? Rides in the suburbs, we have found
cost little ; yet they always brought *vivats*. Still cheaper is
a soft word; such as has many times turned away wrath. In
these rapid days, while France is all getting divided into
Departments, Clergy about to be remodelled, Popular Societies
rising, and Feudalism and so much else is ready to be hurled
into the melting-pot,—might one not try?

On the 4th of February, accordingly, M. le Président read
to his National Assembly a short autograph, announcing that
his Majesty will step over, quite in an unceremonious way,
probably about noon. Think, therefore, Messieurs, what it
may mean; especially, how ye will get the Hall decorated
a little. The Secretaries' Bureau can be shifted down from
the platform ; on the President's chair be slipped this cover of
velvet, 'of a violet colour sprigged with gold fleur-de-lys ;'—
for indeed M. le Président has had previous notice underhand
and taken counsel with Doctor Guillotin. Then some fraction
of 'velvet carpet,' of like texture and colour, cannot that be
spread in front of the chair, where the Secretaries usually sit?
So has judicious Guillotin advised : and the effect is found
satisfactory. Moreover, as it is probable that his Majesty, in

spite of the fleur-de-lys velvet, will stand and not sit at all, the President himself, in the interim, presides standing. And so, while some honourable Member is discussing, say, the division of a Department, Ushers announce: " His Majesty! " In person, with small suite, enter Majesty: the honourable Member stops short; the Assembly starts to its feet: the Twelve Hundred Kings 'almost all,' and the Galleries no less, do welcome the Restorer of French Liberty with loyal shouts. His Majesty's Speech, in diluted conventional phraseology, expresses this mainly: That he, most of all Frenchmen, rejoices to see France getting regenerated; is sure, at the same time, that they will deal gently with her in the process. and not regenerate her *roughly*. Such was his Majesty's Speech: the feat he performed was coming to speak it, and going back again.

Surely, except to a very hoping People, there was not much here to build upon. Yet what did they not build! The fact that the King has spoken, that he has voluntarily come to speak, how inexpressibly encouraging! Did not the glance of his royal countenance, like concentrated sunbeams, kindle all hearts in an august Assembly; nay thereby in an inflammable enthusiastic France? To move 'Deputation of thanks' can be the happy lot of but one man; to go in such Deputation the lot of not many. The Deputed have gone, and returned with what highest-flown compliment they could; whom also the Queen met, Dauphin in hand. And still do not our hearts burn with insatiable gratitude; and to one other man a still higher blessedness suggests itself: To move that we all renew the National Oath.

Happiest honourable Member, with his word so in season as word seldom was; magic Fugleman of a whole National Assembly, which sat there bursting to do somewhat; Fugleman of a whole on-looking France! The President swears; declares that every one shall swear, in distinct *je le jure*. Nay the very gallery sends him down a written slip signed, with their Oath on it; and as the Assembly now casts an eye that way, the Gallery all stands up and swears again. And then out of doors, consider at the Hôtel-de-Ville how Bailly, the great Tennis-Court swearer, again swears, towards nightfall, with all the Municipals, and Heads of Districts assembled there. And 'M. Danton suggests that the public would like to partake:' whereupon Bailly, with escort of Twelve, steps forth to the great outer staircase; sways the ebullient multitude with stretched hand; takes their oath, with a thunder of 'rolling drums,' with shouts that rend the welkin. And on all streets the glad people, with moisture and fire in their eyes, 'spontaneously formed groups, and swore one another,'—and the whole City was illuminated. This was the Fourth of February 1790: a day to be marked white in Constitutional annals.

Nor is the illumination for a night only, but partially or totally it lasts a series of nights. For each District, the Electors of each District will swear specially; and always as the District swears, it illuminates itself. Behold them, District after District, in some open square, where the Non-Electing People can all see and join: with their uplifted right-hands, and *je le jure;* with rolling drums, with embracings, and that infinite hurrah of the enfranchised,—which any tyrant that there may be can consider! Faithful to the King, to the Law, to the Constitution which the National Assembly *shall* make.

Fancy, for example, the Professors of Universities parading the streets with their young France, and swearing, in an enthusiastic manner, not without tumult. By a larger exercise of fancy expand duly this little word: The like was repeated in every Town and District in France! Nay one Patriot Mother, in Lagnon of Brittany, assembles her ten children; and, with her own aged hand, swears them all herself, the high-souled venerable woman. Of all which, moreover, a National Assembly must be eloquently apprised. Such three weeks of swearing? Saw the Sun ever such a swearing people? Have they been bit by a swearing tarantula? No: but they are men and Frenchmen; they have Hope; and, singular to say, they have Faith, were it only in the Gospel according to Jean Jacques O my Brothers, would to Heaven it were even as ye think and have sworn! But there are Lover's Oaths, which, had they been true as love itself, *cannot* be kept; not to speak of Dicer's Oaths, also a known sort.

CHAPTER VII

PRODIGIES

To such length had the *Contrat Social* brought it, in believing hearts. Man, as is well said, lives by faith; each generation has its own faith, more or less; and laughs at the faith of its predecessor,—most unwisely. Grant indeed that this faith in the Social Contract belongs to the stranger sorts; that an unborn generation may very wisely, if not laugh, yet stare at it, and piously consider. For, alas, what is *Contrat*? If all men were such that a mere spoken or sworn Contract would bind them, all men were then true men, and Government a superfluity. Not what thou and I have promised to each other, but what the balance of our forces can make us perform to each other: that, in so sinful a world as ours, is the thing to be counted on. But above all, a People and a Sovereign promising to one another; as if a whole People, changing from generation to generation, nay from hour to hour, could ever by any method be made to *speak* or promise; and to speak mere solecisms: "We, be the Heavens witness, which Heavens however do no miracles now; we, ever-changing Millions, will *allow* thee, changeful Unit, to *force* us or govern us!" The world has perhaps seen few faiths comparable to that.

So nevertheless had the world then construed the matter. Had they *not* so construed it, how different had their hopes been, their attempts, their results! But so and not otherwise did the Upper Powers will it to be. Freedom by social Contract; such was verily the Gospel of that Era. And all men had believed in it, as in a Heaven's Glad-tidings men should; and with overflowing heart and uplifted voice clave to it, and stood fronting Time and Eternity on it. Nay smile not; or only with a smile sadder than tears! This too was a better faith than the one it had replaced; than faith merely in the Everlasting Nothing and man's Digestive Power; lower than *which* no faith can go.

Not that such universally prevalent, universally jurant, feeling of Hope, could be a unanimous one. Far from that. The time was ominous: social dissolution near and certain; social renovation still a problem, difficult and distant, even though sure. But if ominous to some clearest onlooker, whose faith stood not with the one side or with the other, nor in the evervexed jarring of Greek with Greek at all,—how unspeakably ominous to dim Royalist participators; for whom Royalism was Mankind's palladium; for whom, with the abolition of Most-Christian Kingship and most Talleyrand Bishopship, all loyal obedience, all religious faith was to expire, and final Night envelope the Destinies of Man! On serious hearts, of that persuasion, the matter sinks down deep; prompting, as we have seen, to backstairs plots, to Emigration

with pledge of war, to Monarchic clubs; nay to still madde
things.

The Spirit of Prophecy, for instance, had been considere
extinct for some centuries: nevertheless these last-times, a
indeed is the tendency of last-times, do revive it; that so, c
French mad things, we might have sample also of the maddes
In remote rural districts, whither Philosophism has not ye
radiated, where a heterodox Constitution of the Clergy i
bringing strife round the altar itself, and the very Churcl
bells are getting melted into small money-coin, it appear
probable that the End of the World cannot be far off. Deep
musing atrabiliar old men, especially old women, hint in a
obscure way that they know what they know. The Hol
Virgin, silent so long, has not gone dumb;—and truly now
if ever more in this world, were the time for her to speal
One Prophetess, though careless historians have omitted he
name, condition and whereabout, becomes audible to th
general ear; credible to not a few; credible to Friar Gerle
poor Patriot Chartreux, in the National Assembly itself! She
in Pythoness recitative, with wildstaring eye, sings that ther
shall be a Sign; that the heavenly Sun himself will han,
out a Sign, or Mock-Sun,—which, many say, shall be stampe
with the Head of hanged Favras. List, Dom Gerle, with tha
poor addled poll of thine; list, O list;—and hear nothing.

Notable, however. was that 'magnetic vellum, *vélin mag
nétique*,' of the Sieurs d'Hozier and Petit-Jean, Parlementeer
of Rouen. Sweet young D'Hozier, 'bred in the faith of hi
Missal, and of parchment genealogies,' and of parchmen
generally; adust, melancholic, middle-aged Petit-Jean: wh
came these two to Saint-Cloud, where his Majesty was hunt
ing, on the festival of St. Peter and St. Paul; and waite
there, in antechambers, a wonder to whispering Swiss, th
livelong day; and even waited without the Grates, whe
turned out; and had dismissed their valets to Paris, as wit
purpose of endless waiting? They have a *magnetic vellum*
these two; whereon the Virgin, wonderfully clothing hersel
in Mesmerean Cagliostric Occult-Philosophy, has inspire
them to jot down instructions and predictions for a much
straitened King. To whom, by Higher Order, they will thi
day present it; and save the Monarchy and World. Un
accountable pair of visual-objects! Ye should be men, an
of the Eighteenth Century; but your magnetic vellum forbid
us so to interpret. Say, are ye aught? Thus ask the Guard

house Captains, the Mayor of Saint-Cloud; nay, at great
length, thus asks the Committee of Researches, and not the
Municipal, but the National Assembly one. No distinct
answer, for weeks. At last it becomes plain that the right
answer is *negative.* Go, ye Chimeras, with your magnetic
vellum; sweet young Chimera, adust middle-aged one! The
Prison-doors are open. Hardly again shall ye preside the
Rouen Chamber of Accounts; but vanish obscurely into
Limbo.

CHAPTER VIII

SOLEMN LEAGUE AND COVENANT

SUCH dim masses, and specks of even deepest black, work in
that white-heat glow of the French mind, now wholly in fusion
and *con*fusion. Old women here swearing their ten children
on the new Evangel of Jean Jacques; old women there looking up for Favras' Heads in the celestial Luminary: these *are*
preternatural signs, prefiguring somewhat.

In fact, to the Patriot children of Hope themselves it is
undeniable that difficulties exist: emigrating Seigneurs; Parlements in sneaking but most malicious mutiny (though the rope
is round their neck); above all, the most decided ' deficiency
of grains.' Sorrowful; but, to a Nation that hopes, not irremediable. To a Nation which is in fusion and ardent communion of thought; which, for example, on signal of one
Fugleman, will lift its right-hand like a drilled regiment, and
swear and illuminate, till every village from Ardennes to the
Pyrenees has rolled its village-drum, and sent up its little oath,
and glimmer of tallow-illumination some fathoms into the
reign of Night!

If grains are defective, the fault is not of Nature or National
Assembly, but of Art and Anti-national Intriguers. Such
malign individuals, of the scoundrel species, have power to
vex us, while the Constitution is a-making. Endure it, ye
heroic Patriots: nay rather, why not cure it? Grains do
grow, they lie extant there in sheaf or sack; only that regraters
and Royalist plotters, to provoke the People into illegality,
obstruct the transport of grains. Quick, ye organised Patriot
Authorities, armed National Guards, meet together; unite your
goodwill; in union is tenfold strength: let the concentred flash
of your Patriotism strike stealthy Scoundrelism blind, paralytic,
as with a *coup de soleil.*

Under which hat or nightcap of the Twenty-five millions thi
pregnant idea first arose, for in some one head it did rise, no
man can now say. A most small idea, near at hand for the
whole world: but a living one, fit; and which waxed, whether
into greatness or not, into immeasurable size. When a Nation
is in this state that the Fugleman can operate on it, what will
the word in season, the act in season, not do! It will grow
verily, like the Boy's Bean, in the Fairy-Tale, heaven-high
with habitations and adventures on it, in one night. It is
nevertheless unfortunately still a Bean (for your long-lived Oak
grows *not* so); and the next night, it may lie felled, horizontal,
trodden into common mud.—But remark, at least, how natural
to any agitated Nation, which has Faith, this business of Cov
enanting is. The Scotch, believing in a righteous Heaven
above them, and also in a Gospel, far other than the Jean-
Jacques one, swore, in their extreme need, a Solemn League
and Covenant,—as Brothers on the forlorn-hope, and imminence of battle, who embrace, looking godward: and got the
whole Isle to swear it; and even, in their tough Old-Saxon
Hebrew-Presbyterian way, to keep it more or less;—for the
thing, as such things are, was heard in Heaven and partially
ratified there: neither is it yet dead, if thou wilt look, nor like
to die. The French too, with their Gallic-Ethnic excitability
and effervescence, have, as we have seen, real Faith, of a sort;
they are hard bested, though in the middle of Hope: a
National Solemn League and Covenant there may be in
France too; under how different conditions; with how different development and issue!

Note, accordingly, the small commencement; first spark of
a mighty firework: for if the particular *hat* cannot be fixed
upon, the particular District can. On the 29th day of last
November, were National Guards by the thousand seen filing,
from far and near, with military music, with Municipal officers
in tricolor sashes, towards and along the Rhone-stream, to
the little town of Étoile. There with ceremonial evolution
and manœuvre, with fanfaronading, musketry salvoes, and what
else the Patriot genius could devise, they made oath and
obtestation to stand faithfully by one another, under Law and
King; in particular, to have all manner of grains, while grains
there were, freely circulated, in spite both of robber and
regrater. This was the meeting of Étoile, in the mild end of
November 1789.

But now, if a mere empty Review, followed by Review-dinner, ball, and such gesticulation and flirtation as there may be, interests the happy County-town, and makes it the envy of surrounding County-towns, how much more might this! In a fortnight, larger Montélimart, half ashamed of itself, will do as good, and better. On the Plain of Montélimart, or what is equally sonorous, 'under the Walls of Montélimart,' the 13th of December sees new gathering and obtestation; six thousand strong; and now indeed, with these three remarkable improvements, as unanimously resolved on there. First, that the men of Montélimart do federate with the already federated men of Étoile. Second, that, implying not expressing the circulation of grain, they 'swear in the face of God and their Country' with much more emphasis and comprehensiveness, 'to obey all decrees of the National Assembly, and see them obeyed, till death, *jusqu'à la mort.*' Third, and most important, that official record of all this be solemnly delivered in, to the National Assembly, to M. de Lafayette, and 'to the Restorer of French Liberty;' who shall all take from it what comfort they can. Thus does large Montélimart vindicate its Patriot importance, and maintain its rank in the municipal scale.

And so, with the New-year, the signal is hoisted: for is not a National Assembly, and solemn deliverance there, at lowest a National Telegraph? Not only grain shall circulate, while there is grain, on highways or the Rhone-waters, over all that South-Eastern region,—where also if Monseigneur d'Artois saw good to break in from Turin, hot welcome might await him; but whatsoever Province of France is straitened for grain, or vexed with a mutinous Parlement, unconstitutional plotters, Monarchic Clubs, or any other Patriot ailment,—can go and do likewise, or even do better. And now, especially, when the February swearing has set them all agog! From Brittany to Burgundy, on most Plains of France, under most City-walls, it is a blaring of trumpets, waving of banners, a Constitutional manœuvring: under the vernal skies, while Nature too is putting forth her green Hopes, under bright sunshine defaced by the stormful East; like Patriotism victorious, though with difficulty, over Aristocracy and defect of grain! There march and constitutionally wheel, to the *ça-ira*-ing mood of fife and drum, under their tricolor Municipals, our clear-gleaming Phalanxes; or halt, with uplifted right-hand, and artillery salvoes that imitate Jove's thunder; and all the Country, and metaphorically all 'the Universe,' is looking on. Wholly, in their best apparel, brave men and beautifully dizened women, most o. whom have lovers there; swearing, by the eternal Heavens and this green-growing all-nutritive Earth, that France is free!

Sweetest days, when (astonishing to say) mortals have actually met together in communion and fellowship; and man, were it only once through long despicable centuries, is for moments verily the brother of man!—And then the Deputations to the National Assembly, with high-flown descriptive harangue; to M. de Lafayette, and the Restorer; very frequently moreover to the Mother of Patriotism, sitting on her stout benches in that Hall of the Jacobins! The general ear is filled with Federation. New names of Patriots emerge, which shall one day become familiar: Boyer-Fonfrède, eloquent denunciator of a rebellious Bordeaux Parlement; Max Isnard, eloquent reporter of the Federation of Draguignan; eloquent pair, separated by the whole breadth of France, who are nevertheless to meet. Ever wider burns the flame of Federation; ever wider and also brighter. Thus the Brittany and Anjou brethren mention a Fraternity of *all* true Frenchmen; and go the length of invoking 'perdition and death' on any renegade: moreover, if in their National-Assembly harangue, they glance plaintively at the *marc d'argent* which makes so many citizens *passive*, they, over in the Mother-Society, ask, being henceforth themselves 'neither Bretons nor Angevins but French,' Why all France has not one Federation, and universal Oath of Brotherhood, once for all? A most pertinent suggestion; dating from the end of March. Which pertinent suggestion the whole Patriot world cannot but catch, and reverberate and agitate till it become *loud*;—which in that case, the Townhall Municipals had better take up, and meditate.

Some universal Federation seems inevitable: the Where is given; clearly Paris: only the When, the How? These also productive Time will give; is already giving. For always as the Federative work goes on, it perfects itself, and Patriot genius adds contribution after contribution. Thus, at Lyons, in the end of the May month, we behold as many as fifty, or some say sixty thousand, met to federate: and a multitude looking on, which it would be difficult to number. From dawn to dusk! For our Lyons Guardsmen took rank, at five in the bright dewy morning; came pouring in, bright-gleaming, to the Quai de Rhone, to march thence to the Federation-field; amid wavings of hats and lady-handkerchiefs; glad shoutings of some two hundred thousand Patriot voices and hearts; the beautiful and brave! Among whom, courting no notice, and yet the notablest of all, what queenlike Figure is this; with her escort of house-friends and Champagneux the Patriot Editor; come abroad with the earliest? Radiant with enthusiasm are those dark eyes, is that strong Minerva-face, looking dignity and earnest joy; joyfullest she where all are joyful. It is Roland de la Platrière's Wife! Strict elderly Roland, King's Inspector of Manufactures here; and now likewise, by popular choice, the strictest of our new Lyons Municipals: a man who has gained much, if worth and faculty be gain: but, above all things, has gained to wife Phlipon the Paris Engraver's daughter. Reader, mark that queenlike burgher-woman: beautiful, Amazonian-graceful to the eye; more so to the mind. Unconscious of her worth (as all worth is), of her greatness, of her Crystal clearness; genuine, the creature of Sincerity and Nature, in an age of Artificiality, Pollution and Cant; there, in her still completeness, in her still invincibility, *she*, if thou knew it, is the noblest of all living French-women,—and will be seen, one day. O blessed rather while *un*seen, even of herself! For the present she gazes, nothing doubting, into this grand theatricality; and thinks her young dreams are to be fulfilled.

From dawn to dusk, as we said, it lasts; and truly a sight like few. Flourishes of drums and trumpets are something: but think of an 'artificial Rock fifty feet high,' all cut into crag-steps, not without the similitude of 'shrubs!' The interior cavity, for in sooth it is made of deal,—stands solemn, a 'Temple of Concord:' on the outer summit rises 'a Statue of Liberty,' colossal, seen for miles, with her Pike and Phrygian Cap, and civic column: at her feet a Country's Altar, *'Autel de la Patrie:'*—on all which neither deal-timber nor lath and plaster, with paint of various colours, have been spared. But fancy then the banners all placed on the steps of the Rock; high-mass chanted: and the civic oath of fifty thousand: with what volcanic outburst of sound from iron and other throats, enough to frighten back the very Soane and Rhone; and how the brightest fireworks, and balls, and even repasts closed in that night of the gods! And so the Lyons Federation vanishes too, swallowed of darkness;—and yet not wholly, for our brave fair Roland was there; also she, though in the deepest privacy, writes her Narrative of it in Champagneux's *Courrier de Lyons;* a piece which 'circulates to the extent of sixty thousand;' which one would like now to read.

But on the whole, Paris, we may see, will have little t
devise; will only have to borrow and apply. And then as t
the day, what day of all the calendar is fit, if the Bastille Ann
versary be not? The particular spot too, it is easy to see
must be the Champ-de-Mars; where many a Julian the Apo
tate has been lifted on bucklers, to France's or the world'
sovereignty; and iron Franks, loud-clanging, have responde
to the voice of a Charlemagne; and from of old mere sub
limities have been familiar.

CHAPTER IX

SYMBOLIC

How natural, in all decisive circumstances, is Symbolic Repre
sentation to all kinds of men! Nay, what is man's whol
terrestrial Life but a Symbolic Representation, and makin;
visible, of the Celestial invisible Force that is in him? By ac
and word he strives to do it; with sincerity, if possible; failin
that, with theatricality, which latter also may have its meaning
An Almacks Masquerade is not nothing; in more genial ages
your Christmas Guisings, Feasts of the Ass, Abbots of Un
reason, were a considerable something: sincere sport the;
were; as Almacks may still be sincere wish for sport. Bu
what, on the other hand, must not sincere earnest have been
say, a Hebrew Feast of Tabernacles have been! A whol
nation gathered, in the name of the Highest, under the eye o
the Highest; imagination herself flagging under the reality
and all noblest Ceremony as yet not grown ceremonial, bu
solemn, significant to the outmost fringe! Neither, in moder
private life, are theatrical scenes, of tearful women wetting
whole ells of cambric in concert, of impassioned bushy
whiskered youth threatening suicide, and such like, to be s
entirely detested: drop thou a tear over them thyself rather.

At any rate, one can remark that no Nation will throw-by its
work, and deliberately go out to make a scene, without mean
ing something thereby. For indeed no scenic individual, with
knavish hypocritical views, will take the trouble to *soliloquise* a
scene; and now consider, is not a scenic Nation placed pre
cisely in that predicament of soliloquising; for its own behoo
alone; to solace its own sensibilities, maudlin or other?—Yet
in this respect, of readiness for scenes, the difference o
Nations, as of men, is very great. If our Saxon Puritanic

friends, for example, swore and signed their National Covenant, without discharge of gunpowder, or the beating of any drum, in a dingy Covenant-Close of the Edinburgh High-street, in a mean room, where men now drink mean liquor, it was consistent with their ways so to swear it. Our Gallic-Encyclopedic friends, again, must have a Champ-de-Mars, seen of all the world, or universe; and such a Scenic Exhibition, to which the Coliseum Amphitheatre was but a stroller's barn, as this old Globe of ours had never or hardly ever beheld. Which method also we reckon natural, then and there. Nor perhaps was the respective *keeping* of these two Oaths far out of due proportion to such respective display in taking them: inverse proportion, namely. For the theatricality of a people goes in a compound ratio; ratio indeed of their trustfulness, sociability, fervency; but then also of their excitability, of their porosity, not *continent;* or say, of their explosiveness, hot-flashing, but which does not last.

How true also, once more, is it that no man or Nation of men, *conscious* of doing a great thing, was ever, in that thing, doing other than a small one! O Champ-de-Mars Federation, with three hundred drummers, twelve hundred wind musicians, and artillery planted on height after height to boom the tidings of it all over France, in few minutes! Could no Atheist-Naigeon contrive to discern, eighteen centuries off, those Thirteen most poor mean-dressed men. at frugal Supper, in a mean Jewish dwelling, with no symbol but hearts god-initiated into the 'Divine depth of Sorrow,' and a *Do this in remembrance of me;*—and so cease that small difficult crowing of his, if he were not doomed to it?

CHAPTER X

MANKIND

PARDONABLE are human theatricalities; nay, perhaps touching, like the passionate utterance of a tongue which with sincerity *stammers;* of a head which with insincerity *babbles,*—having gone distracted. Yet, in comparison with unpremeditated outbursts of Nature, such as Insurrection of Women, how foisonless, unedifying, undelightful: like small ale palled, like an effervescence that has effervesced! Such scenes, coming of forethought, were they world-great, and never so cunningly devised, are at bottom mainly pasteboard and paint.

But the others are original; emitted from the great everliving heart of Nature herself: what figure *they* will assume is unspeakably significant. To us, therefore, let the French National Solemn League and Federation be the highest recorded triumph of the Thespian Art: triumphant surely, since the whole Pit, which was of Twenty-five Millions, not only claps hands, but does itself spring on the boards and passionately set to playing there. And being such, be it treated as such: with sincere cursory admiration; with wonder from afar. A whole Nation gone mumming deserves so much; but deserves not that loving minuteness a Menadic Insurrection did. Much more let prior, and as it were, rehearsal scenes of Federation come and go, henceforward, as they list; and, on Plains and under City-walls, innumerable regimental bands blare off into the Inane, without note from us.

One scene, however, the hastiest reader will momentarily pause on: that of Anacharsis Clootz and the Collective sinful Posterity of Adam.—For a Patriot Municipality has now, on the 4th of June, got its plan concocted, and got it sanctioned by National Assembly; a Patriot King assenting; to whom, were he even free to dissent, Federative harangues, overflowing with loyalty, have doubtless a transient sweetness. There shall come Deputed National Guards, so many in the hundred, from each of the Eighty-three Departments of France. Likewise from all Naval and Military King's forces, shall Deputed quotas come; such Federation of National with Royal Soldier has, taking place spontaneously, been already seen and sanctioned. For the rest, it is hoped, as many as forty thousand may arrive: expenses to be borne by the Deputing District; of all which let District and Department take thought, and elect fit men,—whom the Paris brethren will fly to meet and welcome.

Now, therefore, judge if our Patriot artists are busy; taking deep counsel how to make the Scene worthy of a look from the Universe! As many as fifteen thousand men, spademen, barrowmen, stonebuilders, rammers, with their engineers, are at work on the Champ-de-Mars; hollowing it out into a National Amphitheatre, fit for such solemnity. For one may hope it will be annual and perennial; a 'Feast of Pikes, *Fête des Piques*,' notablest among the high tides of the year; in any case, ought not a scenic Free Nation to have some permanent National Amphitheatre? The Champ-de-Mars is getting hollowed out; and the daily talk and the nightly dream in most Parisian heads is of Federation, and that only. Federate

Deputies are already under way. National Assembly, what with its natural work, what with hearing and answering harangues of these Federates, of this Federation, will have enough to do! Harangue of 'American Committee,' among whom is that faint figure of Paul Jones as 'with the stars dimwinkling through it,'—come to congratulate us on the prospect of such auspicious day. Harangue of Bastille Conquerors, come to 'renounce' any special recompense, any peculiar place at the solemnity;—since the Centre Grenadiers rather rumble. Harangue of 'Tennis-Court Club,' who enter with far-gleaming Brass-plate, aloft on a pole, and the Tennis-Court Oath engraved thereon; which far-gleaming Brass-plate they purpose to affix solemnly in the Versailles original locality, on the 20th of this month, which is the anniversary, as a deathless memorial, for some years: they will then dine, as they come back, in the Bois de Boulogne;—cannot, however, do it without apprising the world. To such things does the August National Assembly ever and anon cheerfully listen, suspending its regenerative labours; and with some touch of impromptu eloquence make friendly reply;—as indeed the wont has long been; for it is a gesticulating, sympathetic People, and has a heart, and wears it on its sleeve.

In which circumstances, it occurred to the mind of Anacharsis Clootz, that while so much was embodying itself into Club or Committee, and perorating applauded, there yet remained a greater and greatest; of which, if *it* also took body and perorated, what might not the effect be: Humankind namely, *le Genre Humain* itself! In what rapt creative moment the Thought rose in Anacharsis's soul; all his throes, while he went about giving shape and birth to it; how he was sneered at by cold worldlings; but did sneer again, being a man of polished sarcasm; and moved to and fro persuasive in coffeehouse and soirée, and dived down assiduous-obscure in the great deep of Paris, making his Thought a Fact: of all this the spiritual biographies of that period say nothing. Enough that on the 19th evening of June 1790, the sun's slant rays lighted a spectacle such as our foolish little Planet has not often had to show: Anacharsis Clootz entering the august Salle de Manége, with the Human Species at his heels. Swedes, Spaniards, Polacks; Turks, Chaldeans, Greeks, dwellers in Mesopotamia; behold them all; they have come to claim place in the grand Federation, having an undoubted interest in it.

"Our Ambassador titles," said the fervid Clootz, "are not written on parchment, but on the living hearts of all men." These whiskered Polacks, long-flowing turbaned Ishmaelites, astrological Chaldeans, who stand so mute here, let them plead with you, august Senators, more eloquently than eloquence could. They are the mute representatives of their tongue-tied, befettered, heavyladen Nations; who from out of that dark bewilderment gaze wistful, amazed, with half-incredulous hope, towards you, and this your bright light of a French Federation: bright particular daystar, the herald of universal day. We claim to stand there, as mute monuments, pathetically adumbrative of much.—From bench and gallery comes 'repeated applause;' for what august Senator but is flattered even by the very shadow of human Species depending on him? From President Sieyès, who presides this remarkable fortnight, in spite of his small voice, there comes eloquent though shrill reply. Anacharsis, and the 'Foreigners Committee' shall have place at the Federation; on condition of telling their respective Peoples what they see there. In the mean time, we invite them to the 'honours of the sitting, *honneur de la séance*.' A long-flowing Turk, for rejoinder, bows with Eastern solemnity, and utters articulate sounds: but owing to his imperfect knowledge of the French dialect, his words are like spilt water; the thought he had in him remains conjectural to this day.

Anacharsis and Mankind accept the honours of the sitting; and have forthwith, as the old Newspapers still testify, the satisfaction to see several things. First and chief, on the motion of Lameth, Lafayette, Saint-Fargeau and other Patriot Nobles, let the others repugn as they will: all Titles of Nobility, from Duke to Esquire, or lower, are henceforth *abolished*. Then, in like manner, Livery Servants, or rather the Livery of Servants. Neither, for the Future, shall any man or woman, self-styled noble, be 'incensed,'—foolishly fumigated with incense, in Church; as the wont has been. In a word, Feudalism being dead these ten months, why should her empty trappings and scutcheons survive? The very Coats-of-arms will require to be obliterated;—and yet Cassandra-Marat on this and the other coach-panel notices that they 'are but painted over,' and threaten to peer through again.

So that henceforth De Lafayette is but the Sieur Motier, and Saint-Fargeau is plain Michel Lepelletier; and Mirabeau soon after has to say huffingly, "With your *Riquetti* you have set Europe at cross-purposes for three days." For his Counthood

is not indifferent to this man; which indeed the admiring
People treat him with to the last. But let extreme Patriotism
rejoice, and chiefly Anacharsis and Mankind; for now it seems
to be taken for granted that one Adam is Father of us all!—

Such was, in historical accuracy, the famed feat of Anacharsis.
Thus did the most extensive of Public Bodies find a sort of
spokesman. Whereby at least we may judge of one thing:
what a humour the once sniffing mocking City of Paris and
Baron Clootz had got into; when such exhibition could
appear a propriety, next door to a sublimity. It is true, Envy
did, in after times, pervert this success of Anacharsis; making
him, from incidental 'Speaker of the Foreign Nations Committee,' claim to be official permanent 'Speaker, *Orateur*, of
the Human Species,' which he only deserved to be; and
alleging, calumniously, that his astrological Chaldeans, and the
rest, were a mere French tag-rag-and-bobtail disguised for the
nonce; and, in short, sneering and fleering at him in *her* cold
barren way: all which, however, he, the man he was, could
receive on thick enough panoply, or even rebound therefrom,
and also go *his* way.

Most extensive of Public Bodies, we may call it; and also
the most unexpected: for who could have thought to see All
Nations in the Tuileries Riding-Hall? But so it is; and truly
as strange things may happen when a whole People goes
mumming and miming. Hast not thou thyself perchance seen
diademed Cleopatra, daughter of the Ptolemies, pleading,
almost with bended knee, in unheroic tea-parlour, or dimlit
retail-shop, to inflexible gross Burghal Dignitary, for leave to
reign and die; being dressed for it, and moneyless, with small
children;—while suddenly Constables have shut the Thespian
barn, and her Antony pleaded in vain? Such visual spectra
flit across this Earth, if the Thespian Stage be rudely interfered
with: but much more, when, as was said, Pit jumps on Stage,
then is it verily, as in Herr Tieck's Drama, a *Verkehrte Welt*,
or World Topsyturvied!

Having seen the Human Species itself, to have seen the
'*Dean*' of the Human Species' ceased now to be a miracle.
Such '*Doyen du Genre Humain*, Eldest of Men,' had shown
himself there, in these weeks: Jean Claude Jacob, a born Serf,
deputed from his native Jura Mountains to thank the National
Assembly for enfranchising them. On his bleached worn face
are ploughed the furrowings of one hundred and twenty years.

He has heard dim *patois*-talk, of immortal Grand-Monarch victories; of a burned Palatinate, as *he* toiled and moiled to make a little speck of this Earth greener; of Cevennes Dragoonings; of Marlborough going to the war. Four generations have bloomed out, and loved and hated, and rustled off: he was forty-six when Louis Fourteenth died. The Assembly, as one man, spontaneously rose, and did reverence to the Eldest of the World; old Jean is to take *séance* among them, honourably, with covered head. He gazes feebly there, with his old eyes, on that new wonder-scene; dreamlike to him, and uncertain, wavering amid fragments of old memories and dreams. For Time is all growing unsubstantial, dreamlike; Jean's eyes and mind are weary, and about to close,—and open on a far other wonder-scene, which shall be real. Patriot Subscription, Royal Pension was got for him, and he returned home glad; but in two months more he left it all, and went on his unknown way.

CHAPTER XI

AS IN THE AGE OF GOLD

MEANWHILE to Paris, ever going and returning, day after day, and all day long, towards that Field of Mars, it becomes painfully apparent that the spadework there cannot be got done in time. There is such an area of it; three hundred thousand square feet: for from the École Militaire (which will need to be done up in wood with balconies and galleries) westward to the Gate by the River (where also shall be wood, in triumphal arches), we count some thousand yards of length: and for breadth, from this umbrageous Avenue of eight rows, on the South side, to that corresponding one on the North, some thousand feet more or less. All this to be scooped out, and wheeled up in slope along the sides; high enough; for it must be rammed down there, and shaped stair-wise into as many as 'thirty ranges of convenient seats,' firm-trimmed with turf, covered with enduring timber;—and then our huge pyramidal Fatherland's-Altar, *Autel de la Patrie*, in the centre, also to be raised and stair-stepped. Force-work with a vengeance; it is a World's Amphitheatre! There are but fifteen days good: and at this languid rate, it might take half as many weeks. What is singular too, the spademen seem to work lazily; they will not work double-tides, even for offer of more wages, though their tide is but seven hours; they declare angrily that the human tabernacle requires occasional rest!

Is it Aristocrats secretly bribing? Aristocrats were capable of that. Only six months since, did not evidence get afloat that subterranean Paris,—for we stand over quarries and catacombs, dangerously, as it were midway between Heaven and the Abyss, and are hollow underground,—was charged with gunpowder, which should make us 'leap?' Till a Cordeliers Deputation actually went to examine, and found it—carried off again! An accursed, incurable brood; all asking for 'passports' in these sacred days. Trouble, of rioting, Château-burning, is in the Limousin and elsewhere; for they are busy! Between the best of Peoples and the best of Restorer Kings they would sow grudges; with what a fiend's grin would they see this Federation, looked for by the Universe, fail!

Fail for want of spadework, however, it shall not. He that has four limbs and a French heart can do spadework; and will! On the first July Monday, scarcely has the signal-cannon boomed; scarcely have the languescent mercenary Fifteen Thousand laid down their tools, and the eyes of onlookers turned sorrowfully to the still high Sun; when this and the other Patriot, fire in his eye, snatches barrow and mattock, and himself begins indignantly wheeling. Whom scores and then hundreds follow; and soon a volunteer Fifteen Thousand are shovelling and trundling; with the heart of giants: and all in right order, with that extemporaneous adroitness of theirs: whereby *such* a lift has been given, worth three mercenary ones;—which may end when the late twilight thickens, in triumph-shouts, heard or heard of beyond Montmartre!

A sympathetic population will *wait*, next day, with eagerness, till the tools are free. Or why wait? Spades elsewhere exist! And so now bursts forth that effulgence of Parisian enthusiasm, good-heartedness and brotherly love; such, if Chroniclers are trustworthy, as was not witnessed since the Age of Gold. Paris, male and female, precipitates itself towards its Southwest extremity, spade on shoulder. Streams of men, without order; or in order, as ranked fellow-craftsmen, as natural or accidental reunions, march towards the Field of Mars. Three-deep these march; to the sound of stringed music; preceded by young girls with green boughs and tricolor streamers: they have shouldered, soldier-wise, their shovels and picks; and with one throat are singing ça-ira. Yes, *pardieu ça-ira*, cry the passengers on the streets. All corporate Guilds, and public and private Bodies of Citizens, from the highest to the lowest, march; the very Hawkers, one finds, have ceased bawling for one day. The neighbouring Villages turn out: their able men come marching, to village fiddle or tambourine and triangle, under their Mayor, or Mayor and Curate, who also walk bespaded, and in tricolor sash. As many as one hundred and fifty thousand workers; nay at certain seasons, as some count, two hundred and fifty thousand; for, in the afternoon especially, what mortal but, finishing his hasty day's work, would run! A stirring City: from the time you reach the Place Louis-Quinze, southward over the River, by all Avenues, it is one living throng. So many workers; and no mercenary mock-workers, but real ones that lie freely to it: each Patriot *stretches* himself against the stubborn glebe; hews and wheels with the whole weight that is in him.

Amiable infants, *aimables enfans!* They do the '*police de l'atelier*' too, the guidance and governance, themselves; with that ready will of theirs, with that extemporaneous adroitness. It is a true brethren's work; all distinctions confounded, abolished; as it was in the beginning, when Adam himself delved. Long-frocked tonsured Monks, with short-skirted Water-carriers, with swallow-tailed well-frizzled *Incroyables* of a Patriot turn; dark Charcoalmen, meal-white Peruke-makers; or Peruke-wearers, for Advocate and Judge are there, and all Heads of Districts: sober Nuns sisterlike with flaunting Nymphs of the Opera, and females in common circumstances named unfortunate: the patriot Rag-picker, and perfumed dweller in palaces; for Patriotism like New-birth, and also like Death, levels all. The Printers have come marching, Prud-homme's all in Paper-caps with *Révolutions de Paris* printed on them;—as Camille notes; wishing that in these great days there should be a *Pacte des Écrivains* too, or Federation of Able Editors. Beautiful to see! The snowy linen and deli-cate pantaloon alternates with the soiled check-shirt and bushel-breeches; for both have cast their coats, and under both are four limbs and a set of Patriot muscles. There do they pick and shovel; or bend forward, yoked in long strings to box-barrow or over-loaded tumbril; joyous with one mind. Abbé Sieyès is seen pulling, wiry, vehement, if too light for draught; by the side of Beauharnais, who shall get Kings though he be none. Abbé Maury did not pull; but the

Charcoalmen brought a mummer guised like him, and he had to pull in effigy. Let no august Senator disdain the work: Mayor Bailly, Generalissimo Lafayette are there; and, alas, shall be there *again* another day! The King himself comes to see: sky-rending *Vive-le-roi!* 'and suddenly with shouldered spades they form a guard of honour round him.' Whosoever can come comes; to work, or to look, and bless the work.

Whole families have come. One whole family we see clearly of three generations: the father picking, the mother shovelling, the young ones wheeling assiduous; old grandfather, hoary with ninety-three years, holds in his arms the youngest of all: frisky, not helpful this one; who nevertheless may tell it to *his* grandchildren; and how the Future and the Past alike looked on, and with failing or with half-formed voice, faltered their *ça-ira.* A vintner has wheeled in, on Patriot truck, beverage of wine: "Drink not, my brothers, if ye are not thirsty; that your cask may last the longer:" neither did any drink but men 'evidently exhausted.' A dapper Abbé looks on, sneering: "To the barrow!" cry several; whom he, lest a worse thing befall him, obeys: nevertheless one wiser Patriot barrowman, arriving now, interposes his *"arrêtez;"* setting down his own barrow, he snatches the Abbé's; trundles it fast, like an infected thing, forth of the Champ-de-Mars circuit, and discharges it *there.* Thus too a certain person (of some quality, or private capital, to appearance), entering hastily, flings down his coat, waistcoat and two watches, and is rushing to the thick of the work: "But your watches?" cries the general voice.—"Does one distrust his brothers?" answers he; nor were the watches stolen. How beautiful is noble-sentiment: like gossamer gauze, beautiful and cheap; which will stand no tear and wear! Beautiful cheap gossamer gauze, thou film-shadow of a raw-material of Virtue, which art *not* woven, nor likely to be, into Duty; thou art better than nothing, and also worse!

Young Boarding-school Boys, College Students, shout *Vive la Nation*, and regret that they have yet 'only their sweat to give.' What say we of Boys? Beautifullest Hebes; the loveliest of Paris, in their light air-robes, with riband girdle of tricolor, are there; shovelling and wheeling with the rest; their Hebe eyes brighter with enthusiasm and long hair in beautiful dishevelment; hard-pressed are their small fingers; but they make the patriot barrow go, and even force it to the summit of the slope (with a little tracing, which what man's arm were not too happy to lend?)—then bound down with it again, and go for more; with their long locks and tricolors blown back; graceful as the rosy Hours. O, as that evening Sun fell over the Champ-de-Mars, and tinted with fire the thick umbrageous boscage that shelters it on this hand and on that, and struck direct on those domes and two-and-forty Windows of the École Militaire, and made them all of burnished gold,—saw he on his wide zodiac road other such sight? A living garden spotted and dotted with such flowerage; all colours of the prism; the beautifullest blent friendly with the usefullest? all growing and working brotherlike there, under one warm feeling, were it but for days; once and no second time! But night is sinking; these Nights too, into Eternity. The hastiest traveller Versailles-ward has drawn bridle on the heights of Chaillot: and looked for moments over the River; reporting at Versailles what he saw, not without tears.

Meanwhile, from all points of the compass, Federates are arriving; fervid children of the South, 'who glory in their Mirabeau;' considerate North-blooded Mountaineers of Jura; sharp Bretons, with their Gaelic suddenness; Normans, not to be overreached in bargain; all now animated with one noblest fire of Patriotism. Whom the Paris brethren march forth to receive; with military solemnities, with fraternal embracing, and a hospitality worthy of the heroic ages. They assist at the Assembly's Debates, these Federates; the Galleries are reserved for them. They assist in the toils of the Champ-de-Mars; each new troop will put its hand to the spade; lift a hod of earth on the Altar of the Fatherland. But the flourishes of rhetoric, for it is a gesticulating People; the Moral Sublime of those Addresses to an august Assembly, to a Patriot Restorer! Our Breton Captain of Federates kneels even in a fit of enthusiasm, and gives up his sword; he wet-eyed to a King wet-eyed. Poor Louis! These, as he said afterwards, were among the bright days of his life.

Reviews also there must be; Royal Federate-reviews, with King, Queen and tricolor Court looking on: at lowest, if, as is too common, it rains, our Federate Volunteers will file through the inner gateways, Royalty standing dry. Nay there, should some stop occur, the beautifullest fingers in France may take you softly by the lapelle, and, in mild flute-voice ask : "Monsieur, of what Province are you ?" Happy he who can reply, chivalrously lowering his sword's point, "Madame, from the Province your ancestors reigned over." He, that happy 'Provincial Advocate,' now Provincial Federate, shall be rewarded by a sun-smile, and such melodious glad words addressed to a King : "Sire, these are your faithful Lorrainers." Cheerier verily, in these holidays, is this 'skyblue faced with red' of a National Guardsman, than the dull black and gray of a Provincial Advocate, which in workdays one was used to. For the same thrice-blessed Lorrainer shall, this evening, stand sentry at a Queen's door ; and feel that he could die a thousand deaths for her : then again, at the outer gate, and even a third time, she shall see him ; nay, he will make her do it, presenting arms with emphasis, 'making his musket jingle again :' and in her salute there shall again be a sunsmile, and that little blonde-locked too hasty Dauphin shall be admonished, "Salute then, Monsieur, don't be unpolite ;' and therewith she, like a bright Sky-wanderer or Planet with her little Moon, issues forth peculiar.

But at night, when Patriot spadework is over, figure the sacred rights of hospitality ! Lepelletier Saint-Fargeau, a mere private senator, but with great possessions, has daily his ' hundred dinner-guests ;' the table of Generalissimo Lafayette may double that number. In lowly parlour, as in lofty saloon, the wine-cup passes round ; crowned by the smiles of Beauty ; be it of lightly-tripping Grisette or of high-sailing Dame, for both equally have beauty, and smiles precious to the brave.

CHAPTER XII

SOUND AND SMOKE

AND so now, in spite of plotting Aristocrats, lazy hired spademen, and almost of Destiny itself (for there has been much rain too), the Champ-de-Mars, on the 13th of the month, is fairly ready : trimmed, rammed, buttressed with firm masonry ; and Patriotism can stroll over it admiring ; and as it were rehearsing, for in every head is some unutterable image of the morrow. Pray Heaven there be not clouds. Nay what far worse cloud is this. of a misguided Municipality that talks of admitting Patriotism to the solemnity by tickets ! Was it by tickets we were admitted to the work ; and to what brought the work ? Did we take the Bastille by tickets ? A misguided

Municipality sees the error; at late midnight, rolling drums announce to Patriotism starting half out of its bedclothes, that it is to be ticketless. Pull down thy night-cap therefore; and, with demi-articulate grumble, significant of several things, go pacified to sleep again. Tomorrow is Wednesday morning; unforgettable among the *fasti* of the world.

The morning comes, cold for a July one; but such a festivity would make Greenland smile. Through every inlet of that National Amphitheatre (for it is a league in circuit, cut with openings at due intervals), floods-in the living-throng; covers, without tumult, space after space. The École Militaire has galleries and overvaulting canopies, wherein Carpentry and Painting have vied, for the Upper Authorities; triumphal arches, at the Gate by the River, bear inscriptions, if weak, yet well-meant, and orthodox. Far aloft, over the Altar of the Fatherland, on their tall crane standards of iron, swing pensile our antique *Cassolettes* or Pans of Incense; dispensing sweet incense-fumes,—unless for the Heathen Mythology, one sees not for whom. Two hundred thousand Patriotic Men; and, twice as good, one hundred thousand Patriotic Women, all decked and glorified as one can fancy, sit waiting in this Champ-de-Mars.

What a picture: that circle of bright-dyed Life, spread up there, on its thirty-seated Slope; leaning, one would say, on the thick umbrage of those Avenue-Trees, for the stems of them are hidden by the height; and all beyond it mere greenness of Summer Earth, with the gleams of waters, or white sparklings of stone edifices: little circular enamel-picture in the centre of such a vase—of emerald! A vase not empty: the Invalides Cupolas want not their population, nor the distant Windmills of Montmartre: on remotest steeple and invisible village belfry, stand men with spy-glasses. On the heights of Chaillot are many-coloured undulating groups; round and far on, over all the circling heights that embosom Paris, it is as one more or less peopled Amphitheatre, which the eye grows dim with measuring. Nay heights, as was before hinted, have cannon: and a floating-battery of cannon is on the Seine. When eye fails, ear shall serve; and all France properly is but one Amphitheatre; for in paved town and unpaved hamlet, men walk listening; till the muffled thunder sound audible on their horizon, that they too may begin swearing and firing! But now, to streams of music, come Federates enough,—for they have assembled on the Boulevard Saint-Antoine or thereby, and come marching through the City, with their Eighty-three Department Banners, and blessings not loud but deep; comes National Assembly, and takes seat under its Canopy; comes Royalty, and takes seat on a throne beside it. And Lafayette, on white charger, is here, and all the civic Functionaries; and the Federates form dances, till their strictly military evolutions and manœuvres can begin.

Evolutions and manœuvres? Task not the pen of mortal to describe them: truant imagination droops;—declares that it is not worth while. There is wheeling and sweeping, to slow, to quick and double-quick time: Sieur Motier, or Generalissimo Lafayette, for they are one and the same, and he is General of France, in the King's stead, for four-and-twenty hours; Sieur Motier must step forth, with that sublime chivalrous gait of his; solemnly ascend the steps of the Fatherland's Altar, in sight of Heaven and of the scarcely breathing Earth; and, under the creak of those swinging *Cassolettes*, 'pressing his sword's point firmly there,' pronounce the Oath, *To King, to Law, and Nation* (not to mention 'grains' with their circulating), in his own name and that of armed France. Whereat there is waving of banners, and acclaim sufficient. The National Assembly must swear, standing in its place; the King himself audibly. The King swears; and now *be* the welkin split with vivats: let citizens enfranchised embrace, each smiting heartily his palm into his fellow's; and armed Federates clang their arms; above all, that floating battery speak! It has spoken,—to the four corners of France. From eminence to eminence bursts the thunder; faint-heard, loud-repeated. What a stone, cast into what a lake; in circles that do *not* grow fainter. From Arras to Avignon; from Metz to Bayonne! Over Orleans and Blois it rolls, in cannon-recitative; Puy bellows of it amid his granite mountains; Pau where is the shell-cradle of Great Henri. At far Marseilles, one can think, the ruddy evening witnesses it; over the deep blue Mediterranean waters, the Castle of If ruddy-tinted darts forth, from every cannon's mouth, its tongue of fire; and all the people shout: Yes, France is Free. O glorious France, that has burst out so; into universal sound and smoke; and attained—the Phrygian *Cap* of Liberty! In all Towns, Trees of Liberty also may be planted; with or without advantage. Said we not, it was the highest stretch attained by the Thespian Art on this Planet, or perhaps attainable?

The Thespian Art, unfortunately, one must still call it; for behold there, on this Field of Mars, the National Banners, before there could be any swearing, were to be all blessed. A most proper operation; since surely without Heaven's blessing bestowed, say even, audibly or inaudibly *sought*, no Earthly banner or contrivance can prove victorious; but now the means of doing it? By what thrice-divine Franklin thunder-rod shall miraculous fire be drawn out of Heaven; and descend gently, life-giving, with health to the souls of men? Alas, by the simplest: by Two Hundred shaven-crowned Individuals, 'in snow-white albs, with tricolor girdles,' arranged on the steps of Fatherland's Altar; and, at their head for spokesman, Soul's Overseer Talleyrand-Périgord! These shall act as miraculous thunder-rod,—to such length as they can. O ye deep azure Heavens and thou green allnursing Earth; ye Streams everflowing; deciduous Forests that die and are born again, continually, like the sons of men; stone Mountains that die daily with every rain-shower, yet are not dead and levelled for ages of ages, nor born again (it seems) but with new world-explosions, and such tumultuous seething and tumbling, steam half-way to the Moon; O thou unfathomable mystic All, garment and dwellingplace of the UNNAMED; and thou, articulate-speaking Spirit of Man, who mouldest and modellest that Unfathomable Unnameable even as we see,—is not *there* a miracle: That some French mortal should, we say not have believed, but pretended to imagine he believed that Talleyrand and Two Hundred pieces of white Calico could do it!

Here, however, we are to remark with the sorrowing Historians of that day, that suddenly, while Episcopus Talleyrand, long-stoled, with mitre and tricolor belt, was yet but hitching up the Altar-steps to do his miracle, the material Heaven grew black; a north-wind, moaning cold moisture, began to sing; and there descended a very deluge of rain. Sad to see! The thirty-staired Seats, all round our Amphitheatre, get instantaneously slated with mere umbrellas, fallacious when so thick-set: our Antique *Cassolettes* become water-pots; their incense-smoke gone hissing, in a whiff of muddy vapour. Alas, instead of vivats, there is nothing now but the furious peppering and rattling. From three to four hundred thousand human individuals feel that they have a skin; happily *impervious*. The General's sash runs water: how all military banners droop; and will not wave, but lazily flap, as if metamorphosed into painted tin-banners! Worse, far worse, these

hundred thousand, such is the Historian's testimony, of the
fairest of France! Their snowy muslins all splashed and
draggled; the ostrich-feather shrunk shamefully to the back-
bone of a feather: all caps are ruined; innermost pasteboard
molten into its original pap: Beauty no longer swims decorated in her garniture, like Love-goddess hidden-revealed
in her Paphian clouds, but struggles in disastrous imprisonment in it, for 'the shape was noticeable;' and now only
sympathetic interjections, titterings, teeheeings, and resolute
good-humour will avail. A deluge; an incessant sheet or
fluid-column of rain; such that our Overseer's very mitre must
be filled; not a mitre, but a filled and leaky fire-bucket on his
reverend head!—Regardless of which, Overseer Talleyrand
performs his miracle: the Blessing of Talleyrand, another than
that of Jacob, is on all the Eighty-three departmental flags of
France; which wave or flap, with such thankfulness as needs.
Towards three o'clock, the sun beams out again: the remaining evolutions can be transacted under bright heavens, though
with decorations much damaged.

On Wednesday our Federation is consummated: but the
festivities last out the week, and over into the next. Festivities
such as no Bagdad Caliph, or Aladdin with the Lamp, could
have equalled. There is a Jousting on the River; with its
water-somersets, splashing and haha-ing: Abbé Fauchet, *Te
Deum* Fauchet, preaches, for his part, in the 'rotunda of the
Corn-market,' a funeral harangue on Franklin; for whom
the National Assembly has lately gone three days in black.
The Motier and Lepelletier tables still groan with viands;
roofs ringing with patriotic toasts. On the fifth evening, which
is the Christian Sabbath, there is a Universal Ball. Paris, out
of doors and in, man, woman and child, is jigging it, to the
sound of harp and four-stringed fiddle. The hoariest-headed
man will tread one or other measure, under this nether Moon;
speechless nurselings, *infants* as we call them, νήπια τέκνα,
crow in arms; and sprawl out numb-plump little limbs,—impatient for muscularity, they know not why. The stiffest balk
bends more or less; all joists creek.

Or out, on the Earth's breast itself, behold the Ruins of
the Bastille. All lamplit, allegorically decorated; a Tree of
Liberty sixty feet high; and Phrygian Cap on it, of size
enormous, under which King Arthur and his round-table
might have dined! In the depths of the background is a
single lugubrious lamp, rendering dim-visible one of your iron

cages, half-buried, and some Prison stones,—Tyranny vanish
ing downwards, all gone but the skirt: the rest wholly lamp-
festoons, trees real or of pasteboard; in the similitude of a
fairy grove; with this inscription, readable to runner: '*Ici l'on
danse*, Dancing Here.' As indeed had been obscurely foreshadowed by Cagliostro prophetic Quack of Quacks, when he,
four years ago, quitted the grim durance;—to fall into a
grimmer, of the Roman Inquisition, and not quit it.

But after all, what is this Bastille business to that of the
Champs Élysées? Thither, to these Fields well named Elysian,
all feet tend. It is radiant as day with festooned lamps; little
oil-cups, like variegated fire-flies, daintily illume the highest
leaves: trees there are all sheeted with variegated fire, shedding
far a glimmer into the dubious wood. There, under the free
sky, do tight-limbed Federates, with fairest newfound sweethearts, elastic as Diana, and not of that coyness and tart
humour of Diana, thread their jocund mazes, all through the
ambrosial night; and hearts were touched and fired; and
seldom surely had our old Planet, in that huge conic Shadow
of hers 'which goes beyond the Moon, and is named *Night*,'
curtained such a Ball-room. O if, according to Seneca, the
very gods look down on a good man struggling with adversity,
and smile; what must they think of Five-and-twenty million
indifferent ones victorious over it,—for eight days and more?

In this way, and in such ways, however, has the Feast of
Pikes danced itself off: gallant Federates wending homewards,
towards every point of the compass, with feverish nerves, heart
and head much heated; some of them, indeed, as Dampmartin's elderly respectable friend from Strasburg, quite 'burnt
out with liquors,' and flickering towards extinction. The
Feast of Pikes has danced itself off, and become defunct,
and the ghost of a Feast;—nothing of it now remaining but
this vision in men's memory; and the place that knew it (for
the slope of that Champ-de-Mars is crumbled to half the
original height) now knowing it no more. Undoubtedly one
of the memorablest National Hightides. Never or hardly
ever, as we said, was Oath sworn with such heart-effusion,
emphasis and expenditure of joyance; and then it was broken
irremediably within year and day. Ah, why? When the
swearing of it was so heavenly-joyful, bosom clasped to bosom,
and Five-and-twenty million hearts all burning together; O
ye inexorable Destinies, why?—Partly *because* it was sworn

with such overjoyance; but chiefly, indeed, for an older reason: that Sin had come into the world, and Misery by Sin! These Five-and-twenty millions, if we will consider it, have now henceforth, with that Phrygian Cap of theirs, no force *over* them, to bind and guide; neither *in* them, more than heretofore, is guiding force, or rule of just living: how then, while they all go rushing at such a *pace*, on unknown ways, with no bridle, towards no aim, can hurlyburly unutterable fail? For verily not Federation-rosepink is the colour of this Earth and her work: not by outbursts of noble-sentiment, but with far other ammunition, shall a man front the world.

But how wise, in all cases, to 'husband your fire;' to keep it deep down, rather, as genial radical-heat! Explosions, the forciblest, and never so well directed, are questionable; far oftenest futile, always frightfully wasteful: but think of a man, of a Nation of men, spending its whole stock of fire in one artificial Firework! So have we seen fond weddings (for individuals, like Nations, have their Hightides) celebrated with an outburst of triumph and deray, at which the elderly shook their heads. Better had a serious cheerfulness been; for the enterprise was great. Fond pair! the more triumphant ye feel, and victorious over terrestrial evil, which seems all abolished, the wider-eyed will your disappointment be to find terrestrial evil still extant. "And why extant?" will each of you cry: "Because my false mate has played the traitor: evil was abolished; I, for one, meant faithfully, and did, or would have done!" Whereby the over-sweet moon of honey changes itself into long years of vinegar: perhaps divulsive vinegar, like Hannibal's.

Shall we say then, the French Nation has led Royalty, or wooed and teased poor Royalty to lead *her*, to the hymeneal Fatherland's Altar, in such over-sweet manner; and has, most thoughtlessly, to celebrate the nuptials with due shine and demonstration,—burnt her bed?

BOOK II

NANCI

CHAPTER I

BOUILLÉ

DIMLY visible, at Metz on the North-Eastern frontier, a certain brave Bouillé, last refuge of Royalty in all straits and meditations of flight, has for many months hovered occasionally in our eye; some name or shadow of a brave Bouillé: let us now, for a little, look fixedly at him, till he become a substance and person for us. The man himself is worth a glance; his position and procedure there, in these days, will throw light on many things.

For it is with Bouillé as with all French Commanding Officers; only in a more emphatic degree. The grand National Federation, we already guess, was but empty sound, or worse: a last loudest universal *Hep-hep-hurrah*, with full bumpers, in the National Lapithæ-feast of Constitution-making; as in loud denial of the palpably existing; as if, with hurrahings, you would shut out notice of the inevitable, already knocking at the gates! Which new National bumper, one may say, can but deepen the drunkenness; and so, the *louder* it swears Brotherhood, will the sooner and the more surely lead to Cannibalism. Ah, under that fraternal shine and clangour, what a deep world of irreconcilable discords lie momentarily assuaged, damped down for one moment! Respectable military Federates have barely got home to their quarters; and the inflammablest, 'dying, burnt up with liquors, and kindness' has not yet got extinct; the shine is hardly out of men's eyes, and still blazes filling all men's memories,—when your discords burst forth again very considerably darker than ever. Let us look at Bouillé, and see how.

Bouillé for the present commands in the Garrison of Metz, and far and wide over the East and North; being indeed, by a late act of Government with sanction of National Assembly, appointed one of our Four supreme Generals. Rochambeau and Mailly, men and Marshals of note in these days, though

288

to us of small moment, are two of his colleagues; tough old babbling Lückner, also of small moment for us, will probably be the third. Marquis de Bouillé is a determined Loyalist; not indeed disinclined to moderate reform, but resolute against immoderate. A man long suspect to Patriotism; who has more than once given the august Assembly trouble; who would not, for example, take the National Oath, as he was bound to do, but always put it off on this or the other pretext, till an autograph of Majesty requested him to do it as a favour. There, in this post, if not of honour yet of eminence and danger, he waits, in a silent concentred manner; very dubious of the future. 'Alone,' as he says, or almost alone, of all the old military Notabilities, he has not emigrated; but thinks always, in atrabiliar moments, that there will be nothing for him too but to cross the marches. He might cross, say, to Trèves or Coblentz where Exiled Princes will be one day ranking; or say, over into Luxemburg, where old Broglie loiters and languishes. Or is there not the great dim Deep of European Diplomacy; where your Calonnes, your Breteuils are beginning to hover, dimly discernible?

With immeasurable confused outlooks and purposes, with no clear purpose but this of still trying to do his Majesty a service, Bouillé waits; struggling what he can to keep his district loyal, his troops faithful, his garrisons furnished. He maintains, as yet, with his Cousin Lafayette some thin diplomatic correspondence, by letter and messenger; chivalrous constitutional professions on the one side, military gravity and brevity on the other; which thin correspondence one can see growing ever the thinner and hollower, towards the verge of entire vacuity. A quick, choleric, sharply discerning, stubbornly endeavouring man; with suppressed-explosive resolution, with valour, nay headlong audacity: a man who was more in his place, lionlike defending those Windward Isles, or, as with military tiger-spring, clutching Nevis and Montserrat from the English,—than here in this suppressed condition, muzzled and fettered by diplomatic packthreads; looking out for a civil war, which may never arrive. Few years ago Bouillé was to have led a French East-Indian Expedition, and reconquered or conquered Pondicherri and the Kingdoms of the Sun: but the whole world is suddenly changed, and he with it; Destiny willed it not in that way, but in this.

CHAPTER II

ARREARS AND ARISTOCRATS

INDEED, as to the general outlook of things, Bouillé himself augurs not well of it. The French Army, ever since those old Bastille days, and earlier, has been universally in the questionablest state, and growing daily worse. Disipline, which is at all times a kind of miracle, and works by faith, broke down then; one sees not with what near prospect of recovering itself. The Gardes Françaises played a deadly game; but how they won it, and wear the prizes of it, all men know. In that general overturn, we saw the Hired Fighters refuse to fight. The very Swiss of Château-Vieux, which indeed is a kind of French Swiss, from Geneva and the Pays de Vaud, are understood to have declined. Deserters glided over; Royal-Allemand itself looked disconsolate, though stanch of purpose. In a word, we there saw *Military Rule*, in the shape of poor Besenval with that convulsive unmanageable Camp of his, pass twó martyr days on the Champ-de-Mars; and then, veiling itself, so to speak, 'under cloud of night,' depart 'down the left bank of the Seine,' to seek refuge elsewhere; *this* ground having clearly become too hot for it (p. 161).

But what new ground to seek, what remedy to try? Quarters that were 'uninfected:' this doubtless, with judicious strictness of drilling, were the plan. Alas, in all quarters and places, from Paris onward to the remotest hamlet, is infection, is seditious contagion: inhaled, propagated by contact and converse, till the dullest soldier catch it! There is speech of men in uniform with men not in uniform; men in uniform read journals, and even write in them. There are public petitions or remonstrances, private emissaries and associations; there is discontent, jealousy, uncertainty, sullen suspicious humour. The whole French Army, fermenting in dark heat, glooms ominous, boding good to no one.

So that, in the general social dissolution and revolt, we are to have this deepest and dismallest kind of it, a revolting soldiery? Barren, desolate to look upon is this same business of revolt under all its aspects; but how infinitely more so, when it takes the aspect of military mutiny! The very implement of rule and restraint, whereby all the rest was managed and held in order, has become precisely the frightfullest immeasurable implement of misrule; like the element of Fire, our indispensable all-ministering servant, when it gets the *mastery*, and becomes conflagration. Discipline we called a kind of miracle : in fact, is it not miraculous how one man moves hundreds of thousands : each unit of whom, it may be, loves him not, and singly fears him not, yet has to obey him, to go hither or go thither, to march and halt, to give death, and even to receive it, as if a Fate had spoken : and the word-of-command becomes, almost in the literal sense, a magic-word?

Which magic-word, again, if it be once *forgotten ;* the spell of it once broken ! The legions of assiduous ministering spirits rise on you now as menacing fiends ; your free orderly arena becomes a tumult-place of the Nether Pit, and the hapless magician is rent limb from limb. Military mobs are mobs with muskets in their hands ; and also with death hanging over their heads, for death is the penalty of disobedience, and they have disobeyed. And now if all mobs are properly frenzies, and work frenetically with mad fits of hot and of cold, fierce rage alternating so incoherently with panic terror, consider what your military mob will be, with such a conflict of duties and penalties, whirled between remorse and fury, and, for the hot fit, loaded firearms in its hand ! To the soldier himself, revolt is frightful, and oftenest perhaps pitiable ; and yet so dangerous, it can only be hated, cannot be pitied. An anomalous class of mortals these poor Hired Killers ! With a frankness, which to the Moralist in these times seems surprising, they have sworn to become machines ; and nevertheless they are still partly men. Let no prudent person in authority remind them of this latter fact ; but always let force, let injustice above all, stop short clearly on *this* side of the rebounding point ! Soldiers, as we often say, do revolt : were it not so, several things which are transient in this world might be perennial.

Over and above the general quarrel which all sons of Adam maintain with their lot here below, the grievances of the French soldiery reduce themselves to two. First, that their Officers are Aristocrats ; secondly, that they cheat them of their Pay. Two grievances ; or rather we might say one, capable of becoming a hundred ; for in that single first proposition, that the Officers are Aristocrats, what a multitude of corollaries lie ready ! It is a bottomless ever-flowing fountain of grievances this ; what you may call a general raw-material of grievance, wherefrom individual grievance after grievance will daily body itself forth. Nay there will even be a kind of comfort in getting it, from time to time, so embodied. Peculation of one's Pay! It is embodied; made tangible, made denounceable; exhalable, if only in angry words.

For unluckily that grand fountain of grievances does exist: Aristocrats almost all our Officers necessarily are; they have it in the blood and bone. By the law of the case, no man can pretend to be the pitifullest lieutenant of Militia till he have first verified, to the satisfaction of the Lion-King, a Nobility of four generations. Not nobility only, but four generations of it: this latter is the improvement hit upon, in comparatively late years, by a certain War-minister much pressed for commissions. An improvement which did relieve the over-pressed War-minister, but which split France still further into yawning contrasts of Commonalty and Nobility, nay of new Nobility and old; as if already with your new and old, and then with your old, older and oldest, there were not contrasts and discrepancies enough;—the general clash whereof men now see and hear, and in the singular whirlpool, all contrasts gone together to the bottom! Gone to the bottom or going; with uproar, without return; going everywhere save in the Military section of things; and there, it may be asked, can they hope to continue always at the top? Apparently, not.

It is true, in a time of external Peace, when there is no fighting, but only drilling, this question, How you rise from the ranks, may seem theoretical rather. But in reference to the Rights of Man it is continually practical. The soldier has sworn to be faithful not to the King only, but to the Law and the Nation. Do our Commanders love the Revolution? ask all soldiers. Unhappily no, they hate it, and love the Counter-Revolution. Young epauletted men, with quality-blood in them, poisoned with quality-pride, do sniff openly, with indignation struggling to become contempt, at our Rights of Man, as at some new-fangled cobweb, which shall be brushed down again. Old Officers, more cautious, keep silent, with closed uncurled lips; but one guesses what is passing within. Nay who knows, how, under the plausiblest word of command, might lie Counter-Revolution itself, sale to Exiled Princes and the Austrian Kaiser: treacherous Aristocrats hoodwinking the small insight of us common men?—In such manner works that general raw-material of grievance; disastrous; instead of trust and reverence, breeding hate, endless suspicion, the impossibility of commanding and obeying. And now when this second more tangible grievance has articulated itself universally in the mind of the common man: Peculation of his Pay! Peculation of the despicablest sort does exist, and has long existed; but, unless the new-declared Rights of Man, and all rights whatsoever, *be* a cobweb, it shall no longer exist.

The French Military System seems dying a sorrowful suicidal death. Nay more, citizen, as is natural, ranks himself against citizen in this cause. The soldier finds audience, of numbers and sympathy unlimited, among the Patriot lower-classes. Nor are the higher wanting to the officer. The officer still dresses and perfumes himself for such sad unemigrated *soirée* as there may still be; and speaks his woes,— which woes, are they not Majesty's and Nature's? Speaks, at the same time, his gay defiance, his firm-set resolution. Citizens, still more Citizenesses, see the right and the wrong; not the Military System alone will die by suicide, but much along with it. As was said, there is yet possible a deeper overturn than any yet witnessed; that deepest *up*turn of the black-burning sulphurous stratum whereon all rests and grows!

But how these things may act on the rude soldier-mind, with its military pedantries, its inexperience of all that lies off the parade-ground; inexperience as of a child, yet fierceness of a man, and vehemence of a Frenchman! It is long that secret communings in mess-room and guard-room, sour looks, thousandfold petty vexations between commander and commanded, measure everywhere the weary military day. Ask Captain Dampmartin; an authentic, ingenious literary officer of horse; who loves the Reign of Liberty, after a sort: yet has had his heart grieved to the quick many times, in the hot South-Western region and elsewhere; and has seen riot, civil battle by daylight and by torchlight, and anarchy hatefuller than death. How insubordinate Troopers, with drink in their heads, meet Captain Dampmartin and another on the ramparts, where there is no escape or side-path; and make military salute punctually, for we look calm on them: yet make it in a snappish, almost insulting manner: how one morning they 'leave all their chamois shirts' and superfluous buffs, which they are tired of, laid in piles at the Captains' doors; whereat 'we laugh,' as the ass does eating thistles: nay how they 'knot two forage-cords together,' with universal noisy cursing, with evident intent to hang the Quartermaster:—all this the worthy

Captain, looking on it through the ruddy-and-sable of fon
regretful memory, has flowingly written down. Men growl i
vague discontent; officers fling up their commissions, an
emigrate in disgust.

Or let us ask another literary Officer; not yet Captain; Sub
lieutenant only, in the Artillery Regiment La Fère: a youn,
man of twenty-one, not unentitled to speak; the name of hin
is *Napoleon Buonaparte.* To such height of Sub-lieutenanc
has he now got promoted, from Brienne School, five year
ago; 'being found qualified in mathematics by La Place.' H
is lying at Auxonne, in the West, in these months; not sump
tuously lodged—'in the house of a Barber, to whose wife h
did not pay the customary degree of respect;' or even over a
the Pavillon, in a chamber with bare walls; the only furnitur
an indifferent 'bed without curtains, two chairs, and in th
recess of a window a table covered with books and papers: hi
Brother Louis sleeps on a coarse mattress in an adjoinin,
room.' However, he is doing something great: writing hi
first Book or Pamphlet,—eloquent vehement *Letter to M
Matteo Buttafuoco,* our Corsican Deputy, who is not a Patrio
but an Aristocrat, unworthy of Deputyship. Joly of Dôle i
Publisher. The literary Sublieutenant corrects the proofs
'sets out on foot from Auxonne, every morning at four o'cloc
for Dôle: after looking over the proofs, he partakes of a
extremely frugal breakfast with Joly, and immediately prepare
for returning to his Garrison; where he arrives before noon
having thus walked above twenty miles in the course of th
morning.'

This Sublieutenant can remark that, in drawing-rooms, o
streets, on highways, at inns, everywhere men's minds ar
ready to kindle into a flame. That a Patriot, if he appear i
the drawing-room, or amid a group of officers, is liable enoug
to be discouraged, so great is the majority against him: but n
sooner does he get into the street, or among the soldiers, tha
he feels again as if the whole Nation were with him. Tha
after the famous Oath, *To the King, to the Nation, and Law*
there was a great change; that before this, if ordered to fire o
the people, he for one would have done it in the King's name
but that after this, in the Nation's name, he would not have don
it. Likewise that the Patriot officers, more numerous too i
the Artillery and Engineers than elsewhere, were few i
number; yet that having the soldiers on their side, they rule
the regiment; and did often deliver the Aristocrat brothe

ficer out of peril and strait. One day, for example, 'a member of our own mess roused the mob, by singing, from the windows of our dining-room, *O Richard, O my King;* and I had to snatch him from their fury.'

All which let the reader multiply by ten thousand; and read it, with slight variations, over all the camps and garrisons of France. The French Army seems on the verge of universal mutiny.

Universal mutiny! There is in that what may well make Patriot Constitutionalism and an august Assembly shudder. Something behoves to be done; yet what to do no man can tell. Mirabeau proposes even that the Soldiery, having come to such a pass, be forthwith disbanded, the whole Two Hundred and Eighty Thousand of them; and organised anew. Impossible this, in so sudden a manner! cry all men. And yet literally, answer we, it is inevitable, in one manner or another. Such an army, with its four-generation Nobles, its peculated Pay, and men knotting forage-cords to hang their quartermaster, cannot subsist beside such a Revolution. Your alternative is a slow-pining chronic dissolution and new organisation; or a swift decisive one; the agonies spread over years, or concentred into an hour. With a Mirabeau for Minister or Governor, the latter had been the choice; with no Mirabeau for Governor, it will naturally be the former.

CHAPTER III

BOUILLÉ AT METZ

To Bouillé, in his North-Eastern circle, none of these things are altogether hid. Many times flight over the marches gleams on him as a last guidance in such bewilderment: nevertheless he continues here; struggling always to hope the best, not from new organisation, but from happy Counter-Revolution and return to the old. For the rest, it is clear to him that this same National Federation, and universal swearing and fraternising of People and Soldiers, has done 'incalculable mischief.' So much that fermented secretly has hereby got vent, and become open: National Guards and Soldiers of the line, solemnly embracing one another on all parade-fields, drinking, swearing patriotic oaths, fall into disorderly street-processions, constitutional unmilitary exclamations and hurrahings. On which account the Regiment Picardie, for one,

has to be drawn out in the square of the barracks, here a
Metz, and sharply harangued by the General himself; bu
expresses penitence.

Far and near, as accounts testify, insubordination has begun
grumbling louder and louder. Officers have been seen shut u
in their mess-rooms; assaulted with clamorous demands, no
without menaces. The insubordinate ringleader is dismisse
with 'yellow furlough,' yellow infamous thing they call *cu*
touche jaune: but ten new ringleaders rise in his stead, an
the yellow *cartouche* ceases to be thought disgraceful. 'Withi
a fortnight,' or at furthest a month, of that sublime Feast o
Pikes, the whole French Army, demanding Arrears, formin
Reading Clubs, frequenting Popular Societies, is in a stat
which Bouillé can call by no name but that of mutiny. Bouill
knows it as few do; and speaks by dire experience. Take on
instance instead of many.

It is still an early day of August, the precise date now
undiscoverable, when Bouillé, about to set out for the water
of Aix-la-Chapelle, is once more suddenly summoned to th
barracks of Metz. The soldiers stand ranged in fighting order
muskets loaded, the officers all there on compulsion; an
require with many-voiced emphasis to have their arrears paid
Picardie was penitent; but we see it has relapsed: the wid
space bristles and lours with mere mutinous armed men
Brave Bouillé advances to the nearest Regiment, opens hi
commanding lips to harangue; obtains nothing but querulous
indignant discordance, and the sound of so many thousan
livres legally due. The moment is trying; there are some ten
thousand soldiers now in Metz, and one spirit seems to hav
spread among them.

Bouillé is firm as the adamant; but what shall he do? *A*
German Regiment, named of Salm, is thought to be of bette
temper: nevertheless, Salm too may have heard of the precept
Thou shalt not steal; Salm too may know that money is money
Bouillé walks trustfully towards the Régiment de Salm, speak
trustful words; but here again is answered by the cry of forty-fou
thousand livres odd sous. A cry waxing more and more voci
ferous, as Salm's humour mounts; which cry, as it will produc
no cash or promise of cash, ends in the wild simultaneou
whirr of shouldered muskets, and a determined quick-tim
march on the part of Salm—towards its Colonel's house, in
the next street, there to seize the colours and military chest
Thus does Salm, for its part; strong in the faith that *meum*

not *tuum*, that fair speeches are not forty-four thousand livres odd sous.

Unrestrainable! Salm tramps to military time, quick consuming the way. Bouillé and the officers, drawing swords, have to dash, into double-quick *pas-de-charge*, or unmilitary running; to get the start; to station themselves on the outer staircase, and stand there with what of death-defiance and sharp steel they have; Salm truculently coiling itself up, rank after rank, opposite them, in such humour as we can fancy, which happily has not yet mounted to the murder-pitch. There will Bouillé stand, certain at least of *one* man's purpose: in grim calmness, awaiting the issue. What the intrepidest of men and generals can do is done. Bouillé, though there is a barricading picket at each end of the street, and death under his eyes, contrives to send for a Dragoon Regiment with orders to charge: the dragoon officers mount; the dragoon men will not: hope is none there for him. The street, as we say, barricaded; the Earth all shut out, only the indifferent heavenly Vault overhead: perhaps here or there a timorous householder peering out of window, with prayer for Bouillé; copious Rascality, on the pavement, with prayer for Salm: there do the two parties stand;—like chariots locked in a narrow thoroughfare; like locked wrestlers at a dead-grip! For two hours they stand: Bouillé's sword glittering in his hand, adamantine resolution clouding his brows: for two hours by the clocks of Metz. Moody-silent stands Salm, with occasional clangour; but does not fire. Rascality, from time to time, urges some grenadier to level his musket at the General; who looks on as a bronze General would: and always some corporal or other strikes it up.

In such remarkable attitude, standing on that staircase for two hours, does brave Bouillé, long a shadow, dawn on us visibly out of the dimness, and become a person. For the rest, since Salm has not shot him at the first instant, and since in himself there is no variableness, the danger will diminish. The Mayor, 'a man infinitely respectable,' with his Municipals and tricolor sashes, finally gains entrance; remonstrates, perorates, promises; gets Salm persuaded home to its barracks. Next day, our respectable Mayor lending the money, the officers pay down *half* of the demand in ready cash. With which liquidation Salm pacifies itself; and for the present all is hushed up, as much as may be.

Such scenes as this of Metz, or preparations and demon-

strations towards such, are universal over France; Dampmartin, with his knotted forage-cords and piled chamois-jackets,
is at Strasburg in the South-east; in these same days or rather
nights, Royal Champagne is 'shouting *Vive la Nation, au
diable les Aristocrates* with some thirty lit candles,' at Hesdin,
on the far North-West. "The garrison of Bitche," Deputy
Rewbell is sorry to state, "went out of town with drums beating; deposed its officers; and then returned into the town,
sabre in hand." Ought not a National Assembly to occupy
itself with these objects? Military France is everywhere full of
sour inflammatory humour, which exhales itself fuliginously,
this way or that: a whole continent of smoking flax; which,
blown on here or there by any angry wind, might so easily
start into a blaze, into a continent of fire.

Constitutional Patriotism is in deep natural alarm at these
things. The august Assembly sits diligently deliberating;
dare nowise resolve, with Mirabeau, on an instantaneous dis-
bandment and extinction; finds that a course of palliatives is
easier. But at least and lowest, this grievance of the Arrears
shall be rectified. A plan, much noised of in those days,
under the name 'Decree of the Sixth of August,' has been
devised for that. Inspectors shall visit all armies; and, with
certain elected corporals and 'soldiers able to write,' verify
what arrears and peculations do lie due, and make them good.
Well, if in this way the smoky heat be cooled down; if it be
not, as we say, ventilated overmuch, or by sparks and collision
somewhere, sent *up* !

CHAPTER IV

ARREARS AT NANCI

WE are to remark, however, that of all districts, this of Bouillé's
seems the inflammablest. It was always to Bouillé and Metz
that Royalty would fly: Austria lies near; here more than
elsewhere must the disunited People look over the borders, into
a dim sea of Foreign Politics and Diplomacies, with hope or
apprehension, with mutual exasperation.

It was but in these days that certain Austrian troops, marching peaceably across an angle of this region, seemed an Invasion realised; and there rushed towards Stenai, with musket
on shoulder, from all the winds, some thirty thousand National
Guards, to inquire what the matter was. A matter of mere

diplomacy it proved; the Austrian Kaiser, in haste to get to Belgium, had bargained for this short cut. The infinite dim movement of European Politics waved a skirt over these paces, passing on its way; like the passing shadow of a condor; and such a winged flight of thirty thousand, with mixed cackling and crowing, rose in consequence! For, in addition to all, this people, as we said, is much divided: Aristocrats abound; Patriotism has both Aristocrats and Austrians to watch. It is Lorraine, this region; not so illuminated as old France: it remembers ancient Feudalisms; nay, within man's memory it had a Court and King of its own, or indeed the splendour of a Court and King, without the burden. Then, contrariwise, the Mother Society, which sits in the Jacobins Church at Paris, has Daughters in the Towns here; shrill-tongued, driven acrid: consider how the memory of good King Stanislaus, and ages of Imperial Feudalism, may comport with this New acrid Evangel, and what a virulence of discord here may be! In all which, the Soldiery, officers on one side, private men on the other, takes part, and now indeed principal part; a Soldiery, moreover, all the hotter here as it lies the denser, the frontier Province requiring more of it.

So stands Lorraine: but the capital City more especially so. The pleasant City of Nanci, which faded Feudalism loves, where King Stanislaus personally dwelt and shone, has an Aristocrat Municipality, and then also a Daughter Society: it has some forty thousand divided souls of population; and three large Regiments, one of which is Swiss Château-Vieux, dear to Patriotism ever since it refused fighting, or was thought to refuse, in the Bastille days. Here unhappily all evil influences seem to meet concentred; here, of all places, may jealousy and heat evolve itself. These many months, accordingly, man has been set against man, Washed against Unwashed; Patriot Soldier against Aristocrat Captain, ever the more bitterly: and a long score of grudges has been running up.

Nameable grudges, and likewise unnameable: for there is a punctual nature in Wrath; and daily, were there but glances of the eye, tones of the voice, and minutest commissions or omissions, it will jot down somewhat, to account, under the head of sundries, which always swells the sum-total. For example, in April last, in those times of preliminary Federation, when National Guards and Soldiers were everywhere swearing brotherhood, and all France was locally federating,

preparing for the grand National Feast of Pikes, it w
observed that these Nanci Officers threw cold water on tl
whole brotherly business; that they first hung back fro
appearing at the Nanci Federation; then did appear, but
mere *redingote* and undress, with scarcely a clean shirt o
nay that one of them, as the National Colours flaunted by
that solemn moment, did, without visible necessity, take occ
sion to *spit*.

Small 'sundries as per journal,' but then incessant one
The Aristocrat Municipality, pretending to be Constitution
keeps mostly quiet; not so the Daughter Society, the fi
thousand adult male Patriots of the place, still less the fi
thousand female: not so the young, whiskered or whiskerles
four-generation Noblesse in epaulettes; the grim Patriot Swi
of Château-Vieux, effervescent infantry of Régiment du Rc
hot troopers of Mestre-de-Camp! Walled Nanci, which stan
so bright and trim, with its straight streets, spacious square
and Stanislaus' Architecture, on the fruitful alluvium of tl
Meurthe; so bright, amid the yellow cornfields in the
Reaper-Months,—is inwardly but a den of discord, anxiet
inflammability, not far from exploding. Let Bouillé look to i
If that universal military heat, which we liken to a vast co
tinent of smoking flax, do anywhere take fire, his beard, he
in Lorraine and Nanci, may the most readily of all get singe
by it.

Bouillé, for his part, is busy enough, but only with tl
general superintendence; getting his pacified Salm, and a
other still tolerable Regiments, marched out of Metz, t
southward towns and villages; to rural Cantonments as at Vi
Marsal and thereabout, by the still waters; where is plenty
horse-forage, sequestered parade-ground, and the soldier
speculative faculty can be stilled by drilling. Salm, as w
said, received only half payment of arrears; naturally n
without grumbling. Nevertheless that scene of the draw
sword may, after all, have raised Bouillé in the mind of Salm
for men and soldiers love intrepidity and swift inflexible dec
sion, even when they suffer by it. As indeed is not this fund
mentally the quality of qualities for a man? A quality whic
by itself is next to nothing; since inferior animals, asses, dog
even mules have it; yet, in due combination, it is the indi
pensable basis of all.

Of Nanci and its heats, Bouillé, commander of the whol

nows nothing special: understands generally that the troops
that City are perhaps the *worst*. The Officers there have it
l, as they have long had it, to themselves; and unhappily
em to manage it ill. 'Fifty yellow furloughs,' given out in
ne batch, do surely betoken difficulties. But what was
atriotism to think of certain light-fencing Fusileers 'set on,'
r supposed to be set on, 'to insult the Grenadier-club,'—con-
derate speculative Grenadiers and that reading-room of theirs?
'ith shoutings, with hootings; till the speculative Grenadier
rew his side-arms too; and there ensued battery and duels!
'ay more, are not swash-bucklers of the same stamp 'sent out'
isibly, or sent out presumably, now in the dress of Soldiers, to
ick quarrels with the Citizens; now, disguised as Citizens, to
ick quarrels with the Soldiers? For a certain Roussière, expert
n fence, was taken in the very fact; four Officers (presumably
f tender years) hounding him on, who thereupon fled precipi-
itely! Fence-master Roussière, haled to the guard-house, had
entence of three months' imprisonment: but his comrades
emanded 'yellow furlough' for *him* of all persons; nay,
hereafter they produced him on parade; capped him in
aper-helmet, inscribed *Iscariot;* marched him to the gate of
he City; and there sternly commanded him to vanish for-
vermore.

On all which suspicions, accusations and noisy procedure,
nd on enough of the like continually accumulating, the
)fficer could not but look with disdainful indignation; per-
aps disdainfully express the same in words, and 'soon after
y over to the Austrians.'

So that when it here, as elsewhere, comes to the question of
.rrears, the humour and procedure is of the bitterest: Regi-
nent Mestre-de-Camp getting, amid loud clamour, some three
old louis a man,—which have, as usual, to be borrowed from
he municipality; Swiss Château-Vieux applying for the like,
ut getting instead instantaneous *courrois*, or cat-o'-nine-tails,
ith subsequent unsufferable hisses from the women and
hildren: Régiment du Roi, sick of hope deferred, at length
eizing its military chest, marching it to quarters, but next day
narching it back again, through streets all struck silent:—un-
rdered paradings and clamours, not without strong liquor;
bjurgation, insubordination; your military ranked Arrange-
nent going all (as the Typographers say of set types, in a
imilar case) rapidly *to pie*! Such is Nanci in these early days
f August; the sublime Feast of Pikes not yet a month old.

Constitutional Patriotism, at Paris and elsewhere, may well quake at the news. War-Minister Latour du Pin runs breathless to the National Assembly, with a written message that 'all is burning, *tout brûle, tout presse*.' The National Assembly, on the spur of the instant, renders such *Décret*, and 'order to submit and repent,' as he requires; if it will avail anything. On the other hand, Journalism, through all its throats, gives hoarse outcry, condemnatory, elegiac-applausive. The Fortyeight Sections lift up voices; sonorous Brewer, or call him now *Colonel* Santerre, is not silent, in the Faubourg Saint-Antoine. For, meanwhile, the Nanci Soldiers have sent a Deputation of Ten, furnished with documents and proofs; who will tell another story than the 'all-is-burning' one. Which deputed Ten, before ever they reach the Assembly Hall, assiduous Latour du Pin picks up, and on warrant of Mayor Bailly, claps in prison! Most unconstitutionally; for they had Officers' furloughs. Whereupon Saint-Antoine, in indignant uncertainty of the future, closes its shops. Is Bouillé a traitor then, sold to Austria? In that case, these poor private sentinels have revolted mainly out of Patriotism?

New Deputation, Deputation of National Guardsmen now, sets forth from Nanci to enlighten the Assembly. It meets the old deputed Ten returning, quite unexpectedly *un*hanged; and proceeds thereupon with better prospects; but effects nothing. Deputations, Government Messengers, Orderlies at hand-gallop, Alarms, thousand-voiced Rumours, go vibrating continually; backwards and forwards,—scattering distraction. Not till the last week of August does M. de Malseigne, selected as Inspector, get down to the scene of mutiny; with Authority, with cash, and 'Decree of the Sixth of August.' He now shall see these Arrears liquidated, justice done, or at least tumult quashed.

CHAPTER V

INSPECTOR MALSEIGNE

OF Inspector Malseigne we discern, by direct light, that he is 'of Herculean stature;' and infer with probability, that he is of truculent moustachioed aspect,—for *Royalist* Officers now leave the upper lip unshaven; that he is of indomitable bull-heart; and also, unfortunately, of thick bull-head.

On Tuesday the 24th of August 1790, he opens session as

Inspecting Commissioner; meets those 'elected corporals, and soldiers that can write.' He finds the accounts of Château-Vieux to be complex; to require delay and reference: he takes to haranguing, to reprimanding; ends amid audible grumbling. Next morning, he resumes session, not at the Townhall as prudent Municipals counselled, but once more at the barracks. Unfortunately Château-Vieux, grumbling all night, will now hear of no delay or reference; from reprimanding on his part, it goes to bullying,—answered with continual cries of "*Jugez toute de suite*, Judge it at once;" whereupon M. de Malseigne will off in a huff. But lo, Château-Vieux, swarming all about the barrack-court, has sentries at every gate; M. de Malseigne, demanding egress, cannot get it, not though Commandant Denoue backs him; can get only "*Jugez tout de suite.*" Here is a nodus!

Bull-hearted M. de Malseigne draws his sword; and will force egress. Confused splutter. M. de Malseigne's sword breaks: he snatches Commandant Denoue's: the sentry is wounded. M. de Malseigne, whom one is loath to kill, does force egress,—followed by Château-Vieux all in disarray; a spectacle to Nanci. M. de Malseigne walks at a sharp pace, yet never runs, wheeling from time to time with menaces and movements of fence; and so reaches Denoue's house, unhurt; which house Château-Vieux, in an agitated manner, invests,—hindered as yet from entering, by a crowd of officers formed on the staircase. M. de Malseigne retreats by back ways to the Townhall, flustered though undaunted; amid an escort of National Guards. From the Townhall he, on the morrow, emits fresh orders, fresh plans of settlement with Château-Vieux: to none of which will Château-Vieux listen: whereupon he finally, amid noise enough, emits order that Château-Vieux shall march on the morrow morning, and quarter at Sarre Louis. Château-Vieux flatly refuses marching; M. de Malseigne 'takes *act*,' due notarial protest, of such refusal,—if happily that may avail him.

This is the end of Thursday; and indeed, of M. de Malseigne's Inspectorship, which has lasted some fifty hours. To such length, in fifty hours, has he unfortunately brought it. Mestre-de-Camp and Régiment du Roi hang, as it were, fluttering; Château-Vieux is clean gone, in what way we see. Overnight, an Aide-de-Camp of Lafayette's, stationed here for such emergency, sends swift emissaries far and wide to summon National Guards. The slumber of the country is broken by clattering hoofs, by loud fraternal knockings; everywhere the Constitutional Patriot must clutch his fighting-gear, and take the road for Nanci.

And thus the Herculean Inspector has sat all Thursday, among terror-struck Municipals, a centre of confused noise all Thursday, Friday, and till Saturday towards noon. Château-Vieux, in spite of the notarial protest, will not march a step. As many as four thousand National Guards are dropping or pouring in; uncertain what is expected of them; still more uncertain what will be obtained of them. For all is uncertainty, commotion and suspicion: there goes a word that Bouillé, beginning to bestir himself in the rural Cantonments eastward, is but a Royalist traitor; that Château-Vieux and Patriotism are sold to Austria, of which latter M. de Malseigne is probably some agent. Mestre-de-Camp and Roi flutter still more questionably: Château-Vieux, far from marching, 'waves red flags out of two carriages,' in a passionate manner, along the streets; and next morning answers its Officers: "Pay us, then; and we will march with you to the world's end!"

Under which circumstances, towards noon on Saturday, M. de Malseigne thinks it were good perhaps to inspect the ramparts,—on horseback. He mounts, accordingly, with escort of three troopers. At the gate of the City, he bids two of them wait for his return; and with the third, a trooper to be depended upon, he—gallops off for Lunéville; where lies a certain Carbineer Regiment not yet in a mutinous state! The two left troopers soon get uneasy; discover how it is, and give the alarm. Mestre-de-Camp, to the number of a hundred, saddles in frantic haste, as if sold to Austria; gallops out pell-mell in chase of its Inspector. And so they spur, and the Inspector spurs; careering, with noise and jingle, up the valley of the River Meurthe, towards Lunéville and the midday sun: through an astonished country; indeed almost to their own astonishment.

What a hunt; Actæon like; which Actæon de Malseigne happily *gains*. To arm, ye Carbineers of Lunéville: to chastise mutinous men, insulting your General Officer, insulting your own quarters;—above all things, fire *soon*, lest there be parleying and ye refuse to fire! The Carbineers fire soon, exploding upon the first stragglers of Mestre-de-Camp; who shriek at the very flash and fall back hastily on Nanci, in a state not far from distraction. Panic and fury: sold to Austria without an *if;* so much per regiment, the very sums can be specified; and raitorous Malseigne is fled! Help, O Heaven; help, thou Earth,—ye unwashed Patriots; ye too are sold like us!

Effervescent Régiment du Rio primes its firelocks, Mestre-de-Camp saddles wholly: Commandant Denoue is seized, s flung in prison with a 'canvass shirt (*sarreau de toile*)' about im; Château-Vieux bursts up the magazines; distributes three thousand fusils' to a Patriot people: Austria shall have hot bargain. Alas, the unhappy hunting-dogs, as we said, ave *hunted away* their huntsman; and do now run howling nd baying, on what trail they know not; nigh rabid!

And so there is tumultuous march of men, through the ight; with halt on the heights of Flinval, whence Lunéville an be seen all illuminated. Then there is parley, at four n the morning; and reparley; finally there is agreement: the Carbineers give in; Malseigne is surrendered, with apologies n all sides. After weary confused hours, he is even got nder way; the Lunévillers all turning out, in the idle Sunday, o see such departure: home-going of mutinous Mestre-de-Camp with its Inspector captive. Mestre-de Camp accordingly narches; the Lunévillers look. See! at the corner of the irst street, our Inspector bounds off again, bull-hearted as he s; amid the slash of sabres, the crackle of musketry; and scapes, full gallop, with only a ball lodged in his buff-*jerkin*. The Herculean man! And yet it is an escape to no purpose. or the Carbineers, to whom after the hardest Sunday's ride n record, he has come circling back, 'stand deliberating by heir nocturnal watch-fires;' deliberating of Austria, of traitors, nd the rage of Mestre-de-Camp. So that, on the whole, the next sight we have is that of M. de Malseigne, on the Monday fternoon, faring bull-hearted through the streets of Nanci; in pen carriage, a soldier standing over him with drawn sword; mid the 'furies of the women,' hedges of National Guards, nd confusion of Babel: to the Prison beside Commandant Denoue! That finally is the lodging of Inspector Malseigne.

Surely it is time Bouillé were drawing near. The Country ll round, alarmed with watchfires, illuminated towns, and narching and rout, has been sleepless these several nights. Nanci, with its uncertain National Guards, with its distributed usils, mutinous soldiers, black panic and redhot ire, is not a City but a Bedlam.

CHAPTER VI

BOUILLÉ AT NANCI

HASTE with help, thou brave Bouillé: if swift help come no
all is now verily 'burning;' and may burn,—to what length
and breadths! Much, in these hours, depends on Bouillé
as it shall now fare with him, the whole Future may be th
way or be that. If, for example, he were to loiter dubitatin,
and not come; if he were to come, and fail: the who
Soldiery of France to blaze into mutiny, National Guar
going some this way, some that; and Royalism to draw i
rapier, and Sansculottism to snatch its pike; and the Spirit o
Jacobinism, as yet young, girt with sun-rays, to grow insta
taneously mature, girt with hell-fire,—as mortals, in one nigl
of deadly crisis, have had their heads turned gray!

Brave Bouillé is advancing fast, with the old inflexibility
gathering himself, unhappily 'in small affluences,' from Eas
from West and North; and now on Tuesday morning, the la
day of the month, he stands all concentred, unhappily still i
small force, at the village of Frouarde, within some few mile
Son of Adam with a more dubious task before him is nc
in the world this Tuesday morning. A weltering inflammabl
sea of doubt and peril, and Bouillé sure of simply one thing
his own determination. Which one thing, indeed, may b
worth many. He puts a most firm face on the matter: 'Sub
mission, or unsparing battle and destruction; twenty-fou
hours to make your choice:' this was the tenor of his Pro
clamation; thirty copies of which he sent yesterday to Nanci
—all of which, we find, were intercepted and not posted.
Nevertheless, at half-past eleven this morning, seemingly b
way of answer, there does wait on him at Frouarde som
Deputation from the mutinous Regiments, from the Nanc
Municipals, to see what can be done. Bouillé receives thi
Deputation 'in a large open court adjoining his lodging:
pacified Salm, and the rest, attend also, being invited to do it
—all happily still in the right humour. The Mutineers pro
nounce themselves with a decisiveness, which to Bouillé seem
insolence; and happily to Salm also. Salm, forgetful of th
Metz staircase and sabre, demands that the scoundrels 'b
hanged' there and then. Bouillé represses the hanging; bu
answers that mutinous Soldiers have one course, and not mor

than one: To liberate, with heartfelt contrition, Messieurs Denoue and De Malseigne; to get ready forthwith for marching off, whither he shall order; and 'submit and repent,' as the National Assembly has decreed, as he yesterday did in thirty printed Placards proclaim. These are his terms, unalterable as the decrees of Destiny. Which terms as they, the Mutineer deputies, seemingly do not accept, it were good for them to vanish from this spot, and even to do it promptly; with him too, in few instants, the word will be, Forward! The Mutineer deputies vanish, not unpromptly; the Municipal ones, anxious beyond right for their own individualities, prefer abiding with Bouillé.

Brave Bouillé, though he puts a most firm face on the matter, knows his position full well: how at Nanci, what with rebellious soldiers, with uncertain National Guards, and so many distributed fusils, there rage and roar some ten thousand fighting men; while with himself is scarcely the third part of that number, in National Guards also uncertain, in mere pacified Regiments,—for the present full of rage, and clamour to march; but whose rage and clamour may next moment take such a fatal *new* figure. On the top of one uncertain billow, therewith to calm billows! Bouillé must 'abandon himself to Fortune;' who is said sometimes to favour the brave. At half-past twelve, the Mutineer deputies having vanished, our drums beat; we march: for Nanci! Let Nanci bethink itself, then; for Bouillé has thought and determined.

And yet how shall Nanci think: not a City but a Bedlam! Grim Château-Vieux is for defence to death; forces the municipality to order, by tap of drum, all citizens acquainted with artillery to turn out, and assist in managing the cannon. On the other hand, effervescent Régiment du Roi is drawn up in its barracks; quite disconsolate, hearing the humour Salm is in; and ejaculates dolefully from its thousand throats: "*La loi, la loi*, Law, law!" Mestre-de-Camp blusters, with profane swearing, in mixed terror and furor; National Guards look this way and that, not knowing what to do. What a Bedlam-City: as many plans as heads; all ordering, none obeying: quiet none,—except the Dead, who sleep underground, having *done* their fighting.

And, behold, Bouillé proves as good as his word: 'at half-past two' scouts report that he is within half a league of the gates; rattling along, with cannon, and array; breathing nothing but destruction. A new Deputation, Municipals,

Mutineers, Officers, goes out to meet him; with passionate entreaty for yet one other hour. Bouillé grants an hour. Then, at the end thereof, no Denoue or Malseigne appearing as promised, he rolls his drums, and again takes the road. Towards four o'clock, the terrorstruck Townsmen may see him face to face. His cannons rattle there, in their carriages; his vanguard is within thirty paces of the Gate Stanislaus. Onward like a Planet, by appointed times, by law of Nature! What next? Lo, flag of truce and chamade; conjuration to halt: Malseigne and Denoue are on the street, coming hither; the soldiers all repentant, ready to submit and march! Adamantine Bouillé's look alters not; yet the word *Halt* is given: gladder moment he never saw. Joy of joys! Malseigne and Denoue do verily issue; escorted by National Guards; from streets all frantic, with sale to Austria and so forth: they salute Bouillé, unscathed. Bouillé steps aside to speak with them, and with other heads of the Town there; having already ordered by what Gates and Routes the mutineer Regiments shall file out.

Such colloquy with these two General Officers and other principal Townsmen, was natural enough; nevertheless one wishes Bouillé had postponed it, and *not* stepped aside. Such tumultuous inflammable masses, tumbling along, making way for each other; this of keen nitrous oxide, that of sulphurous firedamp,—were it not well to stand *between* them, keeping them well separate, till the space be cleared? Numerous stragglers of Château-Vieux and the rest have not marched with their main columns, which are filing out by the appointed Gates, taking station in the open meadows. National Guards are in a state of nearly distracted uncertainty; the populace, armed and unarmed, roll openly delirious,—betrayed, sold to the Austrians, sold to the Aristocrats. There are loaded cannon with lit matches among them, and Bouillé's vanguard is halted within thirty paces of the Gate. Command dwells not in that mad inflammable mass; which smoulders and tumbles there, in blind smoky rage; which will not open the Gate when summoned; says it will open the cannon's throat sooner!—Cannonade not, O Friends, or be it through my body! cries heroic young Desilles, young Captain of *Roi*, clasping the murderous engine in his arms, and holding it. Château-Vieux Swiss, by main force, with oaths and menaces, wrench off the heroic youth; who undaunted, amid still louder oaths, seats himself on the touch-hole. Amid still louder oaths, with even louder clangour,—and, alas, with the loud

crackle of first one, and then of three other muskets;
which explode into his body; which roll *it* in the dust,—and
do also, in the loud madness of such moment, bring lit cannon-
match to ready priming; and so, with one thunderous belch of
grapeshot, blast some fifty of Bouillé's vanguard into air!

Fatal! That sputter of the first musket-shot has kindled
such a cannon-shot, such a death-blaze; and all is now redhot
madness, conflagration as of Tophet. With demoniac rage,
the Bouillé vanguard storms through that Gate Stanislaus;
with fiery sweep, sweeps Mutiny clear away, to death, or into
shelters and cellars; from which latter, again, Mutiny continues
firing. The ranked Regiments hear it in their meadow; they
rush back again through the nearest Gate; Bouillé gallops in,
distracted, inaudible;—and now has begun, in Nanci, as
in that doomed Hall of the Nibelungen, 'a murder grim and
great.'

Miserable: such scene of dismal aimless madness as the
anger of Heaven but rarely permits among men! From cellar
or from garret, from open street in front, from successive
corners of cross-streets on each hand, Château-Vieux and
Patriotism keep up the murderous rolling-fire, on murderous
not Unpatriotic fires. Your blue National Captain, riddled with
balls, one hardly knows on whose side fighting, requests to be
laid on the colours to die: the patriotic Woman (name not
given, deed surviving) screams to Château-Vieux that it must
not fire the other cannon: and even flings a pail of water on it,
since screaming avails not. Thou shalt fight; thou shalt not
fight; and with whom shalt thou fight! Could tumult awaken
the old Dead, Burgundian Charles the Bold might stir from
under that Rotunda of his: never since he, raging, sank in the
ditches, and lost Life and Diamond, was such a noise heard
here.

Three thousand, as some count, lie mangled, gory: the half
of Château-Vieux has been shot, without need of Court-
Martial. Cavalry, of Mestre-de-Camp or their foes, can do
little. Régiment du Roi, was persuaded to its barracks;
stands there palpitating. Bouillé, armed with the terrors of the
Law, and favoured of Fortune, finally triumphs. In two
murderous hours, he has penetrated to the grand Squares,
dauntless, though with loss of forty officers and five hundred
men: the shattered remnants of Château-Vieux are seeking
covert. Régiment du Roi, not effervescent now, alas no, but
having effervesced, will offer to ground its arms; will 'march

in a quarter of an hour.' Nay these poor effervesced require 'escort' to march with, and get it; though they are thousands strong, and have thirty ball-cartridges a man! The sun is not yet down, when Peace, which might have come bloodless, has come bloody: the mutinous Regiments are on march, doleful, on their three Routes: and from Nanci rises wail of women and men, the voice of weeping and desolation; the City weeping for its slain who awaken not. These streets are empty but for victorious patrols.

Thus has Fortune, favouring the brave, dragged Bouillé, as himself says, out of such a frightful peril 'by the hair of the head.' An intrepid adamantine man, this Bouillé; had *he* stood in old Broglie's place in those Bastille days, it might have been all different! He has extinguished mutiny, and immeasurable civil war. Not for nothing, as we see; yet at a rate which he and Constitutional Patriotism consider cheap. Nay, as for Bouillé, he, urged by subsequent contradiction which arose, declares coldly, it was rather against his own private mind, and more by public military rule of duty, that he did extinguish it,—immeasurable civil war being now the only chance. Urged, we say, by subsequent contradiction! Civil war, indeed, is Chaos; and in all vital Chaos there is new Order shaping itself free: but what a faith this, that of all new Orders out of Chaos and Possibility of Man and his Universe, Louis Sixteenth and Two-Chamber Monarchy were precisely the one that would shape itself! It is like undertaking to throw deuce-ace, say only five hundred successive times, and *any* other throw to be fatal—for Bouillé. Rather thank Fortune, and Heaven, always, thou intrepid Bouillé; and let contradiction go its way! Civil war, conflagrating universally over France at this moment, might have led to one thing or to another thing: meanwhile, to *quench* conflagration, wheresoever one finds it, wheresoever one can; this, in all times, is the rule for man and General Officer.

But at Paris, so agitated and divided, fancy how it went, when the continually vibrating Orderlies vibrated *thither* at hand-gallop, with such questionable news! High is the gratulation; and also deep the indignation. An august Assembly, by overwhelming majorities, passionately thanks Bouillé; a King's autograph, the voices of all Loyal, all Constitutional men run to the same tenor. A solemn National funeral-service, for the Law-defenders slain at Nanci, is said and sung in the Champ-de-Mars; Bailly, Lafayette and National Guards, all except the few that protested, assist. With pomp and circumstance, with Episcopal Calicoes in tricolor girdles, Altar of Fatherland smoking with cassolettes, or incense-kettles; the vast Champ-de-Mars wholly hung round with black mortcloth, —which mortcloth and expenditure Marat thinks had better have been laid out in bread, in these dear days, and given to the hungry living Patriot. On the other hand, living Patriotism, and Saint-Antoine, which we have seen noisily closing its shops and such like, assembles now 'to the number of forty thousand;' and, with loud cries, under the very windows of the thanking National Assembly, demands revenge for murdered Brothers, judgment on Bouillé and instant dismissal of War-Minister Latour du Pin.

At sound and sight of which things, if not War-Minister Latour, yet 'Adored Minister' Necker, sees good on the 3rd of September 1790, to withdraw softly, almost privily,—with an eye to the 'recovery of his health.' Home to native Switzerland; not as he last came; lucky to reach it alive! Fifteen months ago, we saw him coming, with escort of horse, with sound of clarion and trumpet (p. 186); And now, at Arcis-sur-Aube, while he departs, unescorted, soundless, the Populace and Municipals stop him as a fugitive, are not unlike massacring him as a traitor; the National Assembly, consulted on the matter, gives him free egress as a nullity. Such an unstable 'drift-mould of Accident' is the substance of this lower world, for them that dwell in houses of clay; so, especially in hot regions and times, do the proudest palaces we build of it take wings, and become Sahara sand-palaces, spinning many-pillared in the whirlwind, and bury us under their sand!—

In spite of the forty thousand, the National Assembly persists in its thanks; and Royalist Latour du Pin continues Minister. The forty thousand assemble next day, as loud as ever; roll towards Latour's Hôtel; find cannon on the porch, steps with flambeau lit; and have to retire elsewhither, and digest their spleen, or reabsorb it into the blood.

Over in Lorraine meanwhile, they of the distributed fusil, ringleaders of Mestre-de-Camp, of Roi, have got marked out for judgment;—yet shall never get judged. Briefer is the doom of Château-Vieux. Château-Vieux is, by Swiss law, given up for instant trial in Court-Martial of its own officers. Which Court-Martial, with all brevity (in not many hours), has hanged some Twenty-three, on conspicuous gibbets; marched some Three-score in chains to the Galleys; and so, to appearance, finished the matter off. Hanged men do cease for ever from this Earth; but out of chains and the Galleys there may be resuscitation in triumph. Resuscitation for the chained Hero; and even for the chained Scoundrel, or Semi-scoundrel! Scottish John Knox, such World-Hero as we know, sat once nevertheless pulling grim-taciturn at the oar of French Galley, 'in the *Water of Lore*;' and even flung their Virgin-Mary over, instead of kissing her,—as a '*pented bredd*,' or timber Virgin, who could naturally swim. So, ye of Château-Vieux, tug patiently, not without hope!

But indeed at Nanci generally, Aristocracy rides triumphant, rough. Bouillé is gone again, the second day; an Aristocrat Municipality, with free course, is as cruel as it had before been cowardly. The Daughter Society, as the mother of the whole mischief, lies ignominiously suppressed; the Prisons can hold no more; bereaved down-beaten Patriotism murmurs, not loud but deep. Here and in the neighbouring Towns, 'flattened balls' picked from the streets of Nanci are worn at button-holes: balls flattened in carrying death to Patriotism; men wear them there, in perpetual memento of revenge. Mutineer deserters roam the woods; have to demand charity at the musket's end. All is dissolution, mutual rancour, gloom and despair: till National Assembly Commissioners arrive, with a steady gentle flame of Constitutionalism in their hearts; who gently lift up the down-trodden, gently pull down the too-uplifted; reinstate the Daughter Society, recall the mutineer deserter; gradually levelling, strive in all wise ways to smooth and soothe. With such gradual mild levelling on the one side; as with solemn funeral-service, cassolettes, Courts-Martial, National thanks, on the other,—all that Officiality can do is done. The buttonhole will drop its flat ball; the black ashes, so far as may be, get green again.

This is the 'Affair of Nanci;' by some called the 'Massacre of Nanci;'—properly speaking, the unsightly *wrong-side* of that thrice-glorious Feast of Pikes, the right-side of which formed a spectacle for the very gods. Right-side and wrong lie always so near: the one was in July, in August the other! Theatres, the theatres over in London, are bright with their pasteboard simulacrum of that 'Federation of the French people,' brought out as Drama: this of Nanci, we may say, though not played in any pasteboard Theatre, did for many months enact itself, and even walk spectrally,—in all French heads. For the news of it fly pealing through all France: awakening, in town and village, in clubroom, messroom, to the utmost borders, some mimic reflex or imaginative repetition of the business; always with the angry questionable assertion: It was right; It was wrong. Whereby come controversies, duels; embitterment, vain jargon; the hastening forward, the augmenting and intensifying of whatever new explosions lie in store for us.

Meanwhile, at this cost or at that, the mutiny, as we say, is stilled. The French Army has neither burst up in universal simultaneous delirium; nor been at once disbanded, put an end to, and made new again. It must die in the chronic manner, through years, by inches; with partial revolts, as of Brest Sailors or the like, which dare not spread; with men unhappy, insubordinate; officers unhappier, in Royalist moustachioes, taking horse, singly or in bodies, across the Rhine: sick dissatisfaction, sick disgust on both sides; the Army moribund, fit for no duty:—till it do, in that unexpected manner, Phœnix-like, with long throes, get both dead and newborn: then start forth strong, nay stronger and even strongest.

Thus much was the brave Bouillé hitherto fated to do. Wherewith let him again fade into dimness; and, at Metz or the rural Cantonments, assiduously drilling, mysteriously diplomatising, in scheme within scheme, hover as formerly a faint shadow, the hope of Royalty.

BOOK III

THE TUILERIES

CHAPTER I

EPIMENIDES

How true, that there is nothing dead in this Universe; that what we call dead is only changed, its forces working in inverse order! 'The leaf that lies rotting in moist winds,' says one, 'has still force; else how could it *rot?*' Our whole Universe is but an infinite Complex of Forces; thousandfold, from Gravitation up to Thought and Will; man's Freedom environed with Necessity of Nature: in all which nothing at any moment slumbers, but all is forever awake and busy. The thing that lies isolated inactive thou shalt nowhere discover; seek everywhere, from the granite mountain, slow-mouldering since Creation, to the passing cloud-vapour, to the living man; to the action, to the spoken word of man. The word that is spoken, as we know, flies irrevocable: not less, but more, the action that is done. 'The gods themselves,' sings Pindar, 'cannot annihilate the action that is done.' No: this, once done, is done always: cast forth into endless Time; and, long conspicuous or soon hidden, must verily work and grow forever there, an indestructible new element in the Infinite of Things. Or, indeed, what *is* this Infinite of Things itself, which men name Universe, but an Action, a total-sum of Actions and Activities? The living ready-made sum-total of these three,—which Calculation cannot add, cannot bring on its tablets; yet the sum, we say, is written visible: All that has been done, All that is doing, All that will be done! Understand it well, the Thing thou beholdest, that Thing is an Action, the product and expression of exerted Force: the All of Things is an infinite conjugation of the verb *To do*. Shoreless Fountain-Ocean of Force, of power *to do*; wherein Force rolls and circles, billowing, many-streamed, harmonious; wide as Immensity, deep as Eternity; beautiful and terrible, not to be comprehended: this is what man names Existence and Universe; this thousand-tinted

Flame-image, at once veil and revelation, reflex such as he, in his poor brain and heart, can paint, of One Unnameable dwelling in inaccessible light! From beyond the Star-galaxies, from before the Beginning of Days, it billows and rolls,—round *thee*, nay thyself art of it, in this point of Space where thou now standest, in this moment which thy clock measures.

Or apart from all Transcendentalism, is it not a plain truth of sense, which the duller mind can even consider as a truism, that human things wholly are in continual movement, and action and reaction; working continually forward; phasis after phasis, by unalterable laws, towards prescribed issues? How often must we say, and yet not rightly lay to heart: The seed that is sown, it will spring! Given the summer's blossoming, then there is also given the autumnal withering: so is it ordered not with seedfields only, but with transactions, arrangements, philosophies, societies, French Revolutions, whatsoever man works with in this lower world. The Beginning holds in it the End, and all that leads thereto; as the acorn does the oak and its fortunes. Solemn enough, did we think of it,—which unhappily, and also happily, we do not very much! Thou there canst begin; the Beginning is for thee, and there: but where, and of what sort, and for whom will the End be? All grows, and seeks and endures its destinies: consider likewise how much grows, as the trees do, whether *we* think of it or not. So that when your Epimenides, your somnolent Peter Klaus, since named Rip van Winkle, awakens again, he finds it a changed world. In that seven-years sleep of his, so much has changed! All that is without us will change while we think not of it; much even that is within us. The truth that was yesterday a restless Problem, has to-day grown a Belief burning to be uttered: on the morrow, contradiction has exasperated it into mad Fanaticism; obstruction has dulled it into sick Inertness; it is sinking towards silence, of satisfaction or of resignation. Today is not Yesterday, for man or for thing. Yesterday there was the oath of Love; today has come the curse of Hate. Not willingly: ah, no; but it could not help coming. The golden radiance of youth, would it willingly have tarnished itself into the dimness of old age?—Fearful: how we stand enveloped, deep-sunk, in that Mystery of TIME; and are Sons of Time; fashioned and woven out of Time; and on us, and on all that we have, or see, or do, is written: Rest not, Continue not, Forward to thy doom!

But in seasons of Revolution, which indeed distinguish themselves from common seasons by their *velocity* mainly, your miraculous Seven-sleeper might, with miracle enough, awake *sooner:* not by the century, or seven years, need he sleep; often not by the seven months. Fancy, for example, some new Peter Klaus sated with the jubilee of that Federation day, had lain down, say directly after the Blessing of Talleyrand; and, reckoning it all safe *now*, had fallen composedly asleep under the timber-work of the Fatherland's Altar; to sleep there, not twenty-one years, but as it were year and day. The cannonading of Nanci, so far off, does not disturb him; nor does the black mortcloth, close at hand, nor the requiems chanted, and minute-guns, incense-pans and concourse right over his head: none of these; but Peter sleeps through them all. Through one circling year, as we say; from July the 14th of 1790, till July the 17th of 1791: but on that latter day, no Klaus, nor most leaden Epimenides, only the Dead could continue sleeping: and so our miraculous Peter Klaus awakens. With what eyes, O Peter! Earth and sky have still their joyous July look, and the Champ-de-Mars is multitudinous with men: but the jubliee-huzzahing has become Bedlam-shrieking, of terror and revenge; not blessing of Talleyrand, or any blessing, but cursing, imprecation and shrill wail; our cannon-salvoes are turned to sharp shot; for swinging of incense-pans and Eighty-three Departmental Banners, we have waving of the one sanguineous *Drapeau-Rouge.*—Thou foolish Klaus! The one lay in the other, the one *was* the other *minus* Time; even as Hannibal's rock-rending vinegar lay in the sweet new wine. That sweet Federation was of last year; this sour Divulsion is the selfsame substance, only older by the appointed days.

No miraculous Klaus or Epimenides sleeps in these times; and yet, may not many a man, if of due opacity and levity, act the same miracle in a natural way; we mean, with his eyes open? Eyes has he, but he sees not, except what is under his nose. With a sparkling briskness of glance, as if he not only saw but saw through, such a one goes whisking, assiduous, in his circle of officialities; not dreaming but that *it* is the whole world: as indeed, where your vision terminates, does not inanity begin *there*, and the world's end clearly disclose itself— to you? Whereby our brisk-sparkling assiduous official person (call him, for instance, Lafayette), suddenly startled, after year and day, by huge grapeshot tumult, stares not less astonished at it than Peter Klaus would have done. Such natural-miracle can Lafayette perform; and indeed not he only but most other officials, non-officials, and generally the whole French people can perform it; and do bounce up, ever and anon, like amazed Seven-sleepers awakening; awakening amazed at the noise they themselves *make*. So strangely is Freedom, as we say, environed in Necessity; such a singular Somnambulism, of Conscious and Unconscious, of Voluntary and Involuntary, is this life of man. If anywhere in the world there was astonishment that the Federation Oath went into grapeshot, surely of all persons the French, first swearers and then shooters, felt astonished the most.

Alas, offences must come. The sublime Feast of Pikes, with its effulgence of brotherly love, unknown since the Age of Gold, has changed nothing. That prurient heat in Twenty-five millions of hearts is not cooled thereby; but is still hot, nay hotter. Lift off the pressure of command from so many millions; all pressure or binding rule, except such melo-dramatic Federation Oath as they have bound *themselves* with! For *Thou shalt* was from of old the condition of man's being, and his weal and blessedness was in obeying that. Wo for him when, were it on the hest of the clearest necessity, rebel-lion, disloyal isolation, and mere *I will*, becomes his rule! But the Gospel of Jean-Jacques has come, and the first Sacrament of it has been celebrated: all things, as we say, are got into hot and hotter prurience; and must go on pruriently fermenting, in continual change noted or unnoted.

'Worn out with disgusts,' Captain after Captain, in Royalist moustachioes, mounts his war-horse, or his Rozinante war-garron, and rides minatory across the Rhine; till all have ridden. Neither does civic Emigration cease; Seigneur after Seigneur must, in like manner, ride or roll; impelled to it, and even compelled. For the very Peasants despise him, in that he dare not join his order and fight. Can he bear to have a Distaff, a *Quenouille* sent to him: say in copper-plate shadow, by post; or fixed up in wooden reality over his gate-lintel: as if he were no Hercules, but an Omphale? Such scutcheon they forward to him diligently from beyond the Rhine; till he too bestir himself and march, and in sour humour another Lord of Land is gone, *not* taking the Land with him. Nay, what of Captains and emigrating Seigneurs? There is not an angry word on any of those Twenty-five million French tongues, and indeed not an angry thought in their hearts, but is some fraction of the great Battle. Add many successions of angry words together, you have the manual brawl; add brawls together, with the festering sorrows they leave, and they rise to riots and revolts. One reverend thing after another ceases to meet reverence: in visible material combustion, château after château mounts up; in spiritual invisible combustion, one authority after another. With noise and glare, or noiselessly and unnoted, a whole Old System of things is vanishing piecemeal: the morrow thou shalt look, and it is not.

CHAPTER II

THE WAKEFUL

SLEEP who will, cradled in hope and short vision, like Lafayette, who 'always in the danger done sees the last danger that will threaten him,'—Time is not sleeping, nor Time's seedfield.

That sacred Herald's-College of a *new* Dynasty; we mean the Sixty and odd Billstickers with their leaden badges, are not sleeping. Daily they, with pastepot and cross-staff, new-clothe the walls of Paris in colours of the rainbow: authoritative-heraldic, as we say, or indeed almost magical-thaumaturgic; for no Placard-Journal that they paste but will convince some soul or souls of men. The Hawkers bawl; and the Balladsingers: great Journalism blows and blusters, through all its throats, forth from Paris towards all corners of France, like an Æolus' Cave; keeping alive all manner of fires.

Throats or Journals there are, as men count, to the number of some Hundred and thirty-three. Of Various calibre; from your Chéniers, Gorsases, Camilles, down to your Marat, down now to your incipient Hébert of the *Père Duchesne;* these blow, with fierce weight of argument or quick light banter, for the Rights of Man: Durosoys, Royous, Peltiers, Sulleaus, equally with mixed tactics (inclusive, singular to say, of much profane Parody), are blowing for Altar and Throne. As for Marat the People's-Friend, his voice is as that of the bullfrog, or bittern by the solitary pools; he, unseen of men, croaks harsh thunder, and that alone continually,—of indignation, suspicion, incurable sorrow. The People are sinking toward ruin, near starvation itself: 'My dear friends,' cries he, 'your indigence is not the fruit of vices nor of idleness; you have a right to life, as good as Louis XVI., or the happiest of the century. What man can say he has a right to dine, when you have no bread?' The People sinking on the one hand: on the other hand, nothing but wretched Sieur Motiers, treasonous Riquetti Mirabeaus; traitors, or else shadows and simulacra of Quacks to be seen in high places, look where you will! Men that go mincing, grimacing, with plausible speech and brushed raiment; hollow within: Quacks political; Quacks scientific, academical: all with a fellow-feeling for each other, and kind of Quack public-spirit! Not great Lavoisier himself, or any of the Forty can escape this rough tongue; which wants not frantic sincerity, nor, strangest of all, a certain rough caustic sense. And then the 'three thousand gaming-houses' that are in Paris; cesspools for the scoundrelism of the world; sinks of iniquity and debauchery,—whereas without good morals Liberty is impossible! There, in these Dens of Satan, which one knows, and perseveringly denounces, do Sieur Motier's *mouchards* consort and colleague; battening vampyre-like on a People next-door to starvation. '*O Peuple!*' cries he ofttimes, with heart-rending accent. Treason, delusion, vampyrism, scoundrelism, from Dan to Beersheba! The soul of Marat is sick with the sight: but what remedy? To erect 'Eight Hundred gibbets,' in convenient rows, and proceed to hoisting; 'Riquetti on the first of them!' Such is the brief recipe of Marat, Friend of the People.

So blow and bluster the Hundred and thirty-three: nor, as would seem, are these sufficient: for there are benighted nooks in France, to which Newspapers do not reach; and everywhere is 'such an appetite for news as was never seen in any country.' Let an expeditious Dampmartin, on furlough, set out to return home from Paris, he cannot get along for 'peasants stopping him on the highway;' overwhelming him with questions:' the *Maître de Poste* will not send out the horses till you have well nigh quarrelled with him, but asks always, What news? At Autun, in spite of the dark night and 'rigorous frost,' for it is now January 1791, nothing will serve but you must gather your wayworn limbs and thoughts, and 'speak to the multitudes from a window opening into the market-place.' It is the shortest method: *This*, good Christian people, is verily what an august Assembly seemed to me to be doing; this and no other is the news:

> Now my weary lips I close;
> Leave me, leave me to repose!

The good Dampmartin!—But, on the whole, are not Nations

astonishingly true to their National character; which indeed runs in the blood? Nineteen hundred years ago, Julius Cæsar, with his quick sure eye, took note how the Gauls waylaid men. 'It is a habit of theirs,' says he, 'to stop travellers, were it even by constraint, and inquire whatsoever each of them may have heard or known about any sort of matter: in their towns, the common people beset the passing trader; demanding to hear from what regions he came, what things he got acquainted with there. Excited by which rumours and hearsays they will decide about the weightiest matters; and necessarily repent next moment that they did it, on such guidance of uncertain reports, and many a traveller answering with mere fictions to please them, and get off.' Nineteen hundred years; and good Dampmartin, wayworn, in winter frost, probably with scant light of stars and fish-oil, still perorates from the Inn-window! This people is no longer called Gaulish; and it has *wholly* become *braccatus*, has got breeches, and suffered change enough: certain fierce German *Franken* came storming over; and, so to speak, vaulted on the back of it; and always after, in their grim tenacious way, have ridden it bridled; for German is, by his very name, *Guerre*-man, or man that *wars* and *gars*. And so the People, as we say, is now called French or Frankish: nevertheless, does not the old Gaulish and Gaelic Celthood, with its vehemence, effervescent promptitude, and what good and ill it had, still vindicate itself little adulterated?—

For the rest, that in such prurient confusion, Clubbism thrives and spreads, need not be said. Already the Mother of Patriotism, sitting in the Jacobins, shines supreme over all; and has paled the poor lunar light of that Monarchic Club near to final extinction. She, we say, shines supreme, girt with sun-light, not yet with infernal lightning; reverenced, not without fear, by Municipal Authorities; counting her Barnaves, Lameths, Pétions, of a National Assembly; most gladly of all, her Robespierre. Cordeliers, again, your Hébert, Vincent, Bibliopolist Momoro, groan audibly that a tyrannous Mayor and Sieur Motier harrow them with the sharp *tribula* of Law, intent apparently to suppress them by tribulation. How the Jacobin Mother-Society, as hinted formerly, sheds forth Cordeliers on this hand, and then Feuillans on that; the Cordeliers 'an elixir or double distillation of Jacobin Patriotism;' the other a widespread weak dilution thereof: how she will reabsorb the former into her Mother-bosom, and stormfully

dissipate the latter into Nonentity: how she breeds and brings
forth Three Hundred Daughter-Societies; her rearing of them,
her correspondence, her endeavourings and continual travail:
how, under an old figure, Jacobinism shoots forth organic fila-
ments to the utmost corners of confused dissolved France;
organising it anew:—this properly is the grand fact of the
Time.

To passionate Constitutionalism, still more to Royalism,
which see all their own Clubs fail and die, Clubbism will
naturally grow to seem the root of all evil. Nevertheless
Clubbism is not death, but rather new organisation, and life
out of death: destructive, indeed, of the remnants of the Old;
but to the New important, indispensable. That man can cooperate and hold communion with man, herein lies his miraculous strength. In hut or hamlet, Patriotism mourns not now
like voice in the desert: it can walk to the nearest Town; and
there, in the Daughter-Society, make its ejaculation into an
articulate oration, into an action, guided forward by the
Mother of Patriotism herself. All Clubs of Constitutionalists,
and such like, fail, one after another, as shallow fountains:
Jacobinism alone has gone down to the deep subterranean
lake of waters; and may, unless *filled in*, flow there, copious,
continual, like an Artesian well. Till the Great Deep have
drained itself up; and all be flooded and submerged, and
Noah's Deluge out-deluged!

On the other hand, Claude Fauchet, preparing mankind for
a Golden Age now apparently just at hand, has opened his
Cercle Social, with clerks, corresponding boards, and so forth;
in the precincts of the Palais Royal. It is *Te-Deum* Fauchet;
the same who preached on Franklin's Death, in that huge
Medicean rotunda of the *Halle-aux-bleds*. He here, this
winter, by Printing-press and melodious Colloquy, spreads
bruit of himself to the utmost City-barriers. 'Ten thousand
persons of respectability' attend there; and listen to this
'*Procureur-Général de la Vérité*, Attorney-General of Truth,'
so has he dubbed himself; to his sage Condorcet, or other
eloquent coadjutor. Eloquent Attorney-General! He blows
out from him, better or worse, what crude or ripe thing he
holds: not without result to himself; for it leads to a
Bishopric, though only a Constitutional one. Fauchet ap-
proves himself a glib-tongued, strong-lunged, whole-hearted
human individual: much flowing matter there is, and really of
the better sort, about Right, Nature, Benevolence, Progress;

which flowing matter, whether 'it is pantheistic,' or is pot-theistic, only the greener mind, in these days, need examine. Busy Brissot was long ago of purpose to establish precisely same such regenerative *Social Circle*: nay he had tried it in 'Newman-street Oxford-street,' of the Fog Babylon; and failed,—as some say, surreptitiously pocketing the cash. Fauchet, not Brissot, was fated to be the happy man; whereat, however, generous Brissot will with sincere heart sing a timber-toned *Nunc Domine*. But 'ten thousand persons of respectability': what a bulk have many things in proportion to their magnitude! This *Cercle Social*, for which Brissot chants in sincere timber-tones such *Nunc Domine*, what is it? Unfortunately wind and shadow. The main reality one finds in it now, is perhaps this: that an 'Attorney-General of Truth' did once take shape of a body, as Son of Adam, on our Earth, though but for months or moments; and ten thousand persons of respectability attended, ere yet Chaos and Nox had reabsorbed him.

Hundred and thirty-three Paris Journals; regenerative Social Circle; oratory, in Mother and Daughter Societies, from the balconies of Inns, by chimney-nook, at dinner-table, —polemical, ending many times in duel! Add ever, like a constant growling accompaniment of bass Discord: scarcity of work, scarcity of food. The winter is hard and cold; ragged Bakers'-queues, like a black tattered flag-of-distress, wave out ever and anon. It is the third of our Hunger-years, this new year of a glorious Revolution. The rich man when invited to dinner, in such distress-seasons, feels bound in politeness to carry his own bread in his pocket: how the poor dine? And your glorious Revolution has done it, cries one. And our glorious Revolution is subtilely, by black traitors worthy of the Lamp-iron, *perverted* to do it, cries another. Who will paint the huge whirlpool wherein France, all shivered into wild incoherence, whirls? The jarring that went on under every French roof, in every French heart; the diseased things that were spoken, done, the sum-total whereof is the French Revolution, tongue of man cannot tell. Nor the laws of action that work unseen in the depths of that huge blind Incoherence! With amazement, not with measurement, men look on the Immeasurable; not knowing its laws; *seeing*, with all different degrees of knowledge, what new phases, and results of event, its laws bring forth. France is as a monstrous Galvanic Mass, wherein all sorts of far stranger than chemical galvanic or electric forces and substances are at work; electrifying one another, positive and negative; filling with electricity your Leyden-jars,—Twenty-five millions in number! As the jars get full, there will, from time to time, be, on slight hint, an explosion.

CHAPTER III

SWORD IN HAND

On such wonderful basis, however, has Law, Royalty, Authority, and whatever yet exists of visible Order, to maintain itself, while it can. Here, as in that commixture of the Four Elements did the Anarch Old, has an august Assembly spread its pavilion; curtained by the dark infinite of discords; founded on the wavering bottomless of the Abyss; and keeps continual hubbub. Time is around it, and Eternity, and the Inane; and it does what it can, what is given it to do.

Glancing reluctantly in, once more, we discern little that is edifying: a Constitutional Theory of Defective Verbs struggling forward, with perseverance, amid endless interruptions: Mirabeau, from his tribune, with the weight of his name and genius, awing down much Jacobin violence; which in return vents itself the louder over in its Jacobins' Hall, and even reads him sharp lectures there. This man's path is mysterious, questionable; difficult, and he walks without companion in it. Pure Patriotism does not now count him among her chosen; pure Royalism abhors him, yet his weight with the world is overwhelming. Let him travel on, companionless, unwavering, whither he is bound,—while it is yet day with him, and the night has not come.

But the chosen band of pure Patriot brothers is small; counting only some Thirty, seated now on the extreme tip of the Left, separate from the world. A virtuous Pétion; an incorruptible Robespierre, most consistent, incorruptible of thin acrid men; Triumvirs Barnave, Duport, Lameth, great in speech, thought, action, each according to his kind; a lean old Goupil de Prefeln: on these and what will follow them has pure Patriotism to depend.

There too, conspicuous among the Thirty, if seldom audible, Philippe d'Orléans may be seen sitting: in dim fuliginous bewilderment; having, one might say, *arrived* at Chaos! Gleams there are, at once of a Lieutenancy and Regency;

debates in the Assembly itself, of succession to the Throne
'in case the present Branch should fail;' and Philippe, they
say, walked anxiously in silence, through the corridors, till
such high argument were done: but it came all to nothing;
Mirabeau, glaring into the man, and through him, had to
ejaculate in strong untranslatable language: "*Ce j— f— ne
vaut pas la peine qu'on se donne pour lui.*" It came all to nothing; and in the meanwhile Philippe's money, they say, is
gone! Could he refuse a little cash to the gifted Patriot, in
want only of that; he himself in want of all *but* that? Not
a pamphlet can be printed without cash; or indeed written,
without food purchasable by cash. Without cash your hope-
fullest Projector cannot stir from the spot; individual patriotic
or other Projects require cash: how much more do widespread
Intrigues, which live and exist by cash; lying wide-spread,
with dragon-appetite for cash; fit to swallow Princedoms!
And so Prince Philippe, amid his Sillerys, Lacloses and confused Sons of Night, has rolled along: the centre of the
strangest cloudy coil; out of which has visibly come, as we
often say, an Epic Preternatural Machinery of SUSPICION;
and *within* which there has dwelt and worked,—what specialities of treason, stratagem, aimed or aimless endeavour towards
mischief, no party living (if it be not the presiding Genius of
it, Prince of the Power of the Air) has now any chance to
know. Camille's conjecture is the likeliest: that poor Philippe
did mount up, a little way, in treasonable speculation, as he
mounted formerly in one of the earliest Balloons; but,
frightened at the new position he was getting into, had soon
turned the cock again, and come down. More fool than he
rose! To create Preternatural Suspicion, this was his function
in the Revolutionary Epos. But now if he have lost his
cornucopia of ready-money, what else had he to lose? In
thick darkness, inward and outward, he must welter and
flounder on, in that piteous death-element, the hapless man.
Once, or even twice, we shall still behold him emerged; struggling out of thick death-element: in vain. For one moment,
it is the last moment, he starts aloft, or is flung aloft, even into
clearness and a kind of memorability,—to sink then forevermore!

The *Côté Droit* persists no less; nay with more animation
than ever, though hope has now well nigh fled. Tough Abbé
Maury, when the obscure country Royalist grasps his hand
with transport of thanks, answers, rolling his indomitable

brazen head : " *Hélas, Monsieur,* all that I do here is as good as simply *nothing.*" Gallant Faussigny, visible this one time in History, advances frantic, into the middle of the Hall, exclaiming : "There is but one way of dealing with it, and that is to fall sword in hand on those gentry there, *sabre à la main sur ces gaillards là,*" frantically indicating our chosen Thirty on the extreme tip of the Left ! Whereupon is clangour and clamour, debate, repentance,—evaporation. Things ripen towards downright incompatibility, and what is called 'scission:' that fierce theoretic onslaught of Faussigny's was in August 1790 ; next August will not have come, till a famed Two Hundred and Ninety-two, the chosen of Royalism, make solemn final 'scission' from an Assembly given up to faction ; and depart, shaking the dust off their feet.

Connected with this matter of sword in hand, there is yet another thing to be noted. Of duels we have sometimes spoken : how, in all parts of France, innumerable duels were fought ; and argumentative men and messmates, flinging down the wine-cup and weapons of reason and repartee, met in the measured field ; to part bleeding ; or perhaps *not* to part, but to fall mutually skewered through with iron, their wrath and life alike ending,—and die as fools die. Long has this lasted, and still lasts. But now it would seem as if in an august Assembly itself, traitorous Royalism, in its despair, had taken to a new course : that of cutting off Patriotism by systematic duel ! Bully-swordsmen, '*Spadassins*' of that party, go swaggering ; or indeed they can be had for a trifle of money. '*Twelve Spadassins*' were *seen,* by the yellow eye of Journalism, 'arriving recently out of Switzerland ;' also 'a considerable number of Assassins, *nombre considérable d'assassins,* exercising at fencing-schools and at pistol-targets.' Any Patriot-Deputy of mark can be called out ; let him escape one time, or ten times, a time there necessarily is when he must fall, and France mourn. How many cartels has Mirabeau had ; especially while he was the People's champion ! Cartels by the hundred : which he, since the Constitution must be made first, and his time is precious, answers now always with a kind of stereotype formula : ' Monsieur, you are put upon my List ; but I warn you that it is long, and I grant no preferences.'

Then, in Autumn, had we not the Duel of Cazalès and Barnave ; the two chief masters of tongue-shot meeting now to exchange pistol-shot? For Cazalès, chief of the Royalists, whom we call 'Blacks or *Noirs*,' said in a moment of passion, "the Patriots were sheer Brigands," nay in so speaking, he darted, or seemed to dart, a fire-glance specially at Barnave; who thereupon could not but reply by fire-glances,—by adjournment to the Bois-de-Boulogne. Barnave's second shot took effect: on Cazalès' *hat*. The 'front nook' of a triangular Felt, such as mortals then wore, deadened the ball; and saved that fine brow from more than temporary injury. But how easily might the lot have fallen the other way, and Barnave's hat not been so good! Patriotism raises its loud denunciations of Duelling in general: petitions an august Assembly to stop such Feudal barbarism by law. Barbarism and solecism: for will it convince or convict any man to blow half an ounce of lead through the head of him? Surely not.—Barnave was received at the Jacobins with embraces, yet with rebukes.

Mindful of which, and also that his reputation in America was that of headlong foolhardiness rather, and want of brain not of heart, Charles Lameth does, on the eleventh day of November, with little emotion, decline attending some hot young Gentleman from Artois, come expressly to challenge him: nay indeed he first coldly engages to attend; then coldly permits two Friends to attend instead of him, and shame the young Gentleman out of it, which they successfully do. A cold procedure; satisfactory to the two Friends, to Lameth and the hot young Gentleman; whereby, one might have fancied, the whole matter was cooled down.

Not so, however: Lameth, proceeding to his senatorial duties, in the decline of the day, is met in those Assembly corridors by nothing but Royalist *brocards:* sniffs, huffs and open insults. Human patience has its limits: "Monsieur," said Lameth, breaking silence to one Lautrec, a man with hunchback, or natural deformity, but sharp of tongue, and a *Black* of the deepest tint, "Monsieur, if you were a man to be fought with!"—"I am one," cries the young Duke de Castries. Fast as fireflash Lameth replies, "*Tout à l'heure*, On the instant, then!" And so, as the shades of dusk thicken in that Bois-de-Boulogne, we behold two men with lion-look, with alert attitude, side foremost, right foot advanced; flourishing and thrusting, stoccado and passado, in tierce and quart; intent to skewer one another. See, with most skewering purpose, headlong Lameth, with his whole weight, makes a furious lunge; but deft Castries whisks aside: Lameth skewers only the air,—and slits deep and far, on Castries' sword's-point, his own extended left arm! Whereupon, with bleeding, pallor, surgeon's-lint and formalities, the Duel is considered satisfactorily done.

But will there be no end, then? Beloved Lameth lies deep-slit, not out of danger. Black traitorous Aristocrats kill the People's defenders, cut up not with arguments, but with rapier-slits. And the Twelve *Spadassins* out of Switzerland, and the considerable number of Assassins exercising at the pistol-target? So meditates and ejaculates hurt Patriotism, with ever-deepening, ever-widening fervour, for the space of six and thirty hours.

The thirty-six hours past, on Saturday the 13th, one beholds a new spectacle: The Rue de Varennes, and neighbouring Boulevard des Invalides, covered with a mixed flowing multitude: the Castries Hôtel gone distracted, devil-ridden, belching from every window, 'beds with clothes and curtains,' plate of silver and gold with filigree, mirrors, pictures, images, commodes, chiffoniers, and endless crockery and jingle: amid steady popular cheers, absolutely without theft: for there goes a cry, "He shall be hanged that steals a nail." It is a *Plebiscitum*, or informal iconoclastic Decree of the Common People, in the course of being executed!—The Municipality sits tremulous; deliberating whether they will hang out the *Drapeau Rouge* and Martial Law: National Assembly, part in loud wail, part in hardly suppressed applause; Abbé Maury unable to decide whether the iconoclastic Plebs amount to forty thousand or to two hundred thousand.

Deputations, swift messengers, for it is at a distance over the River, come and go. Lafayette and National Guards, though without *Drapeau Rouge*, get under way; apparently in no hot haste. Nay, arrived on the scene, Lafayette salutes with doffed hat, before ordering to fix bayonets. What avails it? The Plebeian 'Court of *Cassation*,' as Camille might punningly name it, has done its work; steps forth, with unbuttoned vest, with pockets turned inside out: sack, and just ravage, not plunder! With inexhaustible patience, the Hero of two Worlds remonstrates; persuasively, with a kind of sweet constraint, though also with fixed bayonets, dissipates, hushes down: on the morrow it is once more all as usual.

Considering which things, however, Duke Castries may justly 'write to the President,' justly transport himself across

the Marches; to raise a corps, or do what else is in hir
Royalism totally abandons that Bobadilian method of contes
and the twelve *Spadassins* return to Switzerland,—or even
Dreamland through the Horn-gate, whichsoever their tru
home is. Nay Editor Prudhomme is authorised to publis
a curious thing: 'We are authorised to publish,' says he, dul
blustering Publisher, 'that M. Boyer champion of goo
Patriots, is at the head of Fifty *Spadassinicides* or Bully-*killer*
His Address is: Passage du Bois de Boulogne, Faubourg S
Denis.' One of the strangest Institutes, this of Champio
Boyer and the Bully-killers! Whose services, however, a
not wanted; Royalism having abandoned the rapier metho
as plainly impracticable.

CHAPTER IV

TO FLY OR NOT TO FLY

THE truth is, Royalism sees itself verging towards sad e
tremities; nearer and nearer daily. From over the Rhine
comes asserted that the King in his Tuileries is not free: th
the poor King may contradict, with the official mouth, but i
his heart feels often to be undeniable. Civil Constitution
the Clergy; Decree of ejectment against Dissidents from it
not even to this latter, though almost his conscience rebel
can he say Nay; but, after two months' hesitating, signs th
also. It was 'on January 21st,' of this 1791, that he signe
it; to the sorrow of his poor heart yet, on *another* Twenty
first of January! Whereby come Dissident ejected Priests
unconquerable Martyrs according to some, incurable chicanin
Traitors according to others. And so there has arrived wh
we once foreshadowed: with Religion, or with the Cant an
Echo of Religion, all France is rent asunder in a new ruptu
of continuity; complicating, embittering all the older;—to b
cured only by stern surgery, in La Vendée!

Unhappy Royalty, unhappy Majesty, Hereditary Represe
tative, *Représentant Héréditaire*, or howsoever they may nam
him; of whom much is expected, to whom little is given
Blue National Guards encircle that Tuileries; a Lafayett
thin constitutional Pedant; clear, thin, inflexible, as wat
turned to thin ice; whom no Queen's heart can love. Nation
Assembly, its pavilion spread where we know, sits near b
keeping continual hubbub. From without, nothing but Nan

Revolts, sack of Castries Hôtels, riots and seditions; riots North and South, at Aix, at Douai, at Béfort, Usez, Perpignan, at Nismes, and that incurable Avignon of the Pope's: a continual crackling and sputtering of riots from the whole face of France;—testifying how electric it grows. Add only the hard winter, the famished *strikes* of operatives; that continual running-bass of Scarcity, ground-tone and basis of all other Discords!

The plan of Royalty, so far as it can be said to have any fixed plan, is still, as ever, that of flying towards the frontiers. In very truth, the only plan of the smallest promise for it! Fly to Bouillé; bristle yourself round with cannon, served by your 'forty-thousand undebauched Germans:' summon the National Assembly to follow you, summon what of it is Royalist, Constitutional, gainable by money; dissolve the rest, by grapeshot if need be. Let Jacobinism and Revolt, with one wild wail, fly into Infinite Space; driven by grapeshot. Thunder over France with the cannon's mouth; commanding, not entreating, that this riot cease. And then to rule afterwards with utmost possible Constitutionality; doing justice, loving mercy; *being* Shepherd of this indigent People, not Shearer merely, and Shepherd's similitude! All this, if ye dare. If ye dare not, then, in Heaven's name, go to sleep: other handsome alternative seems none.

Nay, it were perhaps possible; with a man to do it. For if such inexpressible whirlpool of Babylonish confusions (which our Era is) cannot be stilled by man, but only by Time and men, a man may moderate its paroxysms, may balance and sway, and keep himself unswallowed on the top of it,—as several men and Kings in these days do. Much is possible for a man; men will obey a man that *kens* and *cans*, and name him reverently their *Ken-ning* or King. Did not Charlemagne rule? Consider too whether he had smooth times of it; hanging 'four-thousand Saxons over the Weser-Bridge,' at one dread swoop! So likewise, who knows but, in this same distracted fanatic France, the right man may verily exist? An olive-complexioned taciturn man; for the present, Lieutenant in the Artillery-service, who once sat studying Mathematics at Brienne? The same who walked in the morning to correct proof-sheets at Dôle, and enjoyed a frugal breakfast with M. Joly? (p. 294). Such a one is gone, whither also famed General Paoli his friend is gone, in these very days, to see old scenes

in native Corsica, and what Democratic good can be do⌐
there.

Royalty never executes the evasion-plan, yet never abando⌐
it; living in variable hope; undecisive, till fortune shall decid⌐
In utmost secrecy, a brisk Correspondence goes on wi⌐
Bouillé; there is also a plot, which emerges more than onc⌐
for carrying the King to Rouen: plot after plot, emerging ar⌐
submerging, like *ignes fatui* in foul weather, which lea⌐
nowhither. 'About ten o'clock at night,' the Heredita⌐
Representative, in *partie quarrée*, with the Queen, with Broth⌐
Monsieur, and Madame, sits playing '*wisk*,' or whist. Ush⌐
Campan enters mysteriously, with a message he only ha⌐
comprehends: How a certain Comte D'Inisdal waits anxiou⌐
in the outer antechamber; National Colonel, Captain of t⌐
watch for this night, is gained over; post-horses ready all t⌐
way; party of Noblesse sitting armed, determined; will h⌐
Majesty, before midnight, consent to go? Profound silence⌐
Campan waiting with upturned ear. "Did your Majesty he⌐
what Campan said?" asks the Queen. "Yes, I heard⌐
answers Majesty, and plays on. "'Twas a pretty couplet, th⌐
of Campan's," hints Monsieur, who at times showed a pleasa⌐
wit: Majesty, still unresponsive, plays wisk. "After all, or⌐
must say something to Campan," remarks the Queen. "Te⌐
M. D'Inisdal," said the King, and the Queen puts an emphas⌐
on it, "That the King cannot *consent* to be forced away."-⌐
"I see!" said D'Inisdal, whisking round, peaking himself int⌐
flame of irritancy: "we have the risk; we are to have all t⌐
blame if it fail,"—and vanishes, he and his plot, as will-o'-wisp⌐
do. The Queen sat till far in the night, packing jewels: b⌐
it came to nothing; in that peaked flame of irritancy t⌐
will-o'-wisp had gone *out*.

Little hope there is in all this. Alas, with whom to fly⌐
Our loyal *Gardes-du-Corps*, ever since the Insurrection ⌐
Women, are disbanded; gone to their homes, gone, mar⌐
of them, across the Rhine towards Coblentz and Exile⌐
Princes: brave Miomandre and brave Tardivet, these faithf⌐
Two, have received, in nocturnal interview with both Majestie⌐
their *viaticum* of gold louis, of heartfelt thanks from a Queen⌐
lips, though unluckily 'his Majesty stood, back to fire, n⌐
speaking;' and do now dine through the Provinces; recountir⌐
hairbreadth escapes, insurrectionary horrors. Great horror⌐
to be swallowed yet of greater. But, on the whole, wh⌐

a falling off from the old splendour of Versailles! Here
in this poor Tuileries a National Brewer-Colonel, sonorous
Santerre, parades officially behind her Majesty's chair. Our
high dignitaries all fled over the Rhine: nothing now to be
gained at Court; but hopes, for which life itself must be
risked! Obscure busy men frequent the back stairs; with
hearsays, wind-projects, unfruitful fanfaronades. Young Royalists, at the *Théâtre de Vaudeville*, 'sing couplets;' if that
could do anything. Royalists enough, Captains on furlough,
burnt-out Seigneurs, may likewise be met with, 'in the Café
de Valois, and at Méot the Restaurateur's.' There they fan
one another into high loyal glow; drink, in such wine as can
be procured, confusion to Sansculottism; show purchased
dirks, of an improved structure, made to order; and, greatly
daring, dine. It is in these places, in these months, that the
epithet *Sansculotte* first gets applied to indigent Patriotism;
in the last age we had Gilbert *Sansculotte*, the indigent Poet.
Destitute-of-Breeches: a mournful Destitution; which however,
if Twenty millions share it, may become more effective than
most Possessions!

Meanwhile, amid this vague dim whirl of fanfaronades,
wind-projects, poniards made to order, there does disclose
itself one *punctum-saliens* of life and feasibility: the finger of
Mirabeau! Mirabeau and the Queen of France have met;
have parted with mutual trust! It is strange; secret as the
Mysteries; but it is indubitable. Mirabeau took horse, one
evening; and rode westward, unattended,—to see Friend
Clavière in that country house of his? Before getting to
Clavière's, the much-musing horseman struck aside to a back
gate of the Garden of Saint-Cloud: some Duke D'Aremberg,
or the like, was there to introduce him; the Queen was not
far; on a 'round knoll, *rond point*, the highest of the Garden
of Saint-Cloud,' he beheld the Queen's face; spake with her,
alone, under the void canopy of Night. What an interview;
fateful secret for us, after all searching; like the colloquies of
the gods! She called him 'a Mirabeau:' elsewhere we read
that she 'was charmed with him,' the wild submitted Titan; as
indeed it is among the honourable tokens of this high ill-fated
heart that no mind of any endowment, no Mirabeau, nay no
Barnave, no Dumouriez, ever came face to face with her but,
in spite of all prepossessions, she was forced to recognise it, to
draw nigh to it, with trust. High imperial heart; with the
instinctive attraction towards all that had any height! "You

know not the Queen," said Mirabeau once in confidence
"her force of mind is prodigious; she is a man for courage
—And so, under the void Night, on the crown of that knol
she has spoken with a Mirabeau; he has kissed loyally th
queenly hand, and said with enthusiasm: "Madame, th
Monarchy is saved!"—Possible? The Foreign Power
mysteriously sounded, gave favourable guarded response
Bouillé is at Metz, and could find forty-thousand sure German
With a Mirabeau for head, and a Bouillé for hand, somethir
verily is possible,—if Fate intervene not.

But figure under what thousandfold wrappages, and cloak
of darkness, Royalty, meditating these things, must involv
itself. There are men with 'Tickets of Entrance;' there ar
chivalrous consultings, mysterious plottings. Consider als
whether, involve as it like, plotting Royalty can escape th
glance of Patriotism; lynx-eyes, by the ten thousand, fixed o
it, which see in the dark! Patriotism knows much: know
the dirks made to order, and can specify the shops; know
Sieur Motier's legions of *mouchards;* the Tickets of *Entré*
and men in black; and how plan of evasion succeeds plan,—
or may be supposed to succeed it. Then conceive the couplet
chanted at the *Théâtre de Vaudeville;* or worse, the whisper
significant nods of traitors in moustachios. Conceive, on th
other hand, the loud cry of alarm that came through th
Hundred-and-Thirty Journals; the Dionysius'-Ear of each c
the Forty-Eight Sections, wakeful night and day.

Patriotism is patient of much; not patient of all. Th
Café de Procope has sent, visibly along the streets, a Deputa
tion of Patriots, 'to expostulate with bad Editors,' by trustfu
word of mouth: singular to see and hear. The bad Editor
promise to amend, but do not. Deputations for change c
Ministry were many; Mayor Bailly joining even with Cordelie
Danton in such; and they have prevailed. With what profit
Of Quacks, willing or constrained to be Quacks, the race i
everlasting: Ministers Duportail and Dutertre will have t
manage much as Ministers Latour-du-Pin and Cice did. S
welters the confused world.

But now, beaten on forever by such inextricable contradic
tory influences and evidences, what *is* the indigent Frenc
Patriot, in these unhappy days, to believe, and walk by? Un
certainty all; except that he is wretched, indigent; tha
a glorious Revolution, the wonder of the Universe, ha
hitherto brought neither Bread nor Peace; being marred b

aitors, difficult to discover. Traitors that dwell in the dark,
visible there;—or seen for moments, in pallid dubious twi-
ght, stealthily vanishing thither! Preternatural Suspicion
nce more rules the minds of men.

'Nobody here,' writes Carra, of the *Annales Patriotiques*, so
arly as the first of February, 'can entertain a doubt of the
onstant obstinate project these people have on foot to get the
.ing away; or of the perpetual succession of manœuvres they
mploy for that.' Nobody: the watchful Mother of Patriotism
eputed two Members to her daughter at Versailles, to examine
ow the matter looked there. Well, and there? Patriotic
arra continues: 'The Report of these two deputies we all
eard with our own ears last Saturday. They went with others
f Versailles, to inspect the King's Stables, also the stables of
e whilom *Gardes-du-Corps;* they found there from seven to
ight hundred horses standing always saddled and bridled,
eady for the road at a moment's notice. The same deputies,
oreover, saw with their own two eyes several Royal Carriages,
hich men were even then busy loading with large well-stuffed
ggage-bags,' leather *cows*, as we call them, '*vaches de cuir;*
he Royal Arms on the panels almost entirely effaced.'
Momentous enough! Also 'on the same day the whole
Maréchaussée, or Cavalry Police, did assemble with arms,
orses and baggage,'—and disperse again. They want the
King over the marches, that so Emperor Leopold and the
German Princes, whose troops are ready, may have a pretext
or beginning: 'this,' adds Carra, 'is the word of the riddle:
his is the reason why our fugitive Aristocrats are now making
evies of men on the frontiers; expecting that, one of these
nornings, the Executive Chief Magistrate will be brought over
o them, and the civil war commence.'

If indeed the Executive Chief Magistrate, bagged, say in
ne of these leather *cows*, were once brought safe over to
hem! But the strangest thing of all is, that Patriotism,
hether barking at a venture, or guided by some instinct
f preternatural sagacity, is actually barking *aright* this time;
t something, not at nothing. Bouillé's Secret Correspondence,
ince made public, testifies as much.

Nay, it is undeniable, visible to all, that *Mesdames* the
King's Aunts are taking steps for departure: asking passports
f the Ministry, safe-conducts of the Municipality; which
Marat warns all men to beware of. They will carry gold with
hem, 'these old *Béguines;*' nay they will carry the little

Dauphin, 'having nursed a changeling, for some time, to leave in his stead!' Besides, they are as some light substance flung up, to show how the wind sits; a kind of proof-kite you fly of to ascertain whether the grand paper-kite, Evasion of the King may mount!

In these alarming circumstances, Patriotism is not wanting to itself. Municipality deputes to the King; Sections depute to the Municipality; a National Assembly will soon stir. Meanwhile, behold, on the 19th of February 1791, Mesdames quitting Bellevue and Versailles with all privacy, are off Towards Rome, seemingly; or one knows not whither. They are not without King's passports, countersigned; and what i more to the purpose, a serviceable Escort. The Patriotic Mayor or Mayorlet of the Village of Moret tried to detain them: but brisk Louis de Narbonne, of the Escort, dashed off at handgallop; returned soon with thirty dragoons, and victoriously cut them out. And so the poor ancient women go their way; to the terror of France and Paris, whose nervou excitability is become extreme. Who else would hinder poo *Loque* and *Graille*, now grown so old, and fallen into such unexpected circumstances, when gossip itself turning only on terrors and horrors is no longer pleasant to the mind, and you cannot get so much as an orthodox confessor in peace,—from going what way soever the hope of any solacement might lead them?

They go, poor ancient dames,—whom the heart were hard that did not pity: they go; with palpitations, with unmelodiou suppressed screechings; all France screeching and cackling, in loud *un*suppressed terror, behind, and on both hands of them such mutual suspicion is among men. At Arnay le Duc above half-way to the frontiers, a Patriotic Municipality and populace again takes courage to stop them: Louis Narbonne must now back to Paris, must consult the National Assembly. National Assembly answers, not without an effort, that Mes dames may go. Whereupon Paris rises worse than ever screeching half-distracted. Tuileries and precincts are filled with women and men, while the National Assembly debate this question of questions; Lafayette is needed at night for dispersing them, and the streets are to be illuminated. Com mandant Berthier, a Berthier before whom are great thing unknown, lies for the present under blockade at Bellevue i Versailles. By no tactics could he get Mesdames' Luggag stirred from the Courts there; frantic Versaillese women cam creaming about him : his very troops cut the wagon-traces ; e 'retired to the interior,' waiting better times.

Nay in these same hours, while Mesdames, hardly cut out om Moret by the sabre's edge, are driving rapidly, to foreign arts, and not yet stopped at Arnay, their august Nephew poor Monsieur, at Paris, has dived deep into his cellars of the Luxembourg for shelter ; and, according to Montgaillard, can ardly be persuaded up again. Screeching multitudes environ hat Luxembourg of his ; drawn thither by report of his eparture : but at sight and sound of Monsieur, they become rowing multitudes ; and escort Madame and him to the Tuileries with vivats. It is a state of nervous excitability such s few nations know.

CHAPTER V

THE DAY OF PONIARDS

Or, again, what means this visible reparation of the Castle of Vincennes? Other Jails being all crowded with prisoners, ew space is wanted here : that is the Municipal account. For in such changing of Judicatures, Parlements being abolished, and New Courts but just set up, prisoners have accumulated. Not to say that in these times of discord and club-law, offences and committals are, at any rate, more numerous. Which Municipal account, does it not sufficiently explain the phenomenon? Surely, to repair the Castle of Vincennes was of all enterprises that an enlightened Municipality could undertake, the most innocent.

Not so, however, does neighbouring Saint-Antoine look on it : Saint-Antoine to whom these peaked turrets and grim donjons, all-too near her own dark dwelling, are of themselves an offence. Was not Vincennes a kind of minor Bastille? Great Diderot and Philosophes have lain in durance here ; great Mirabeau, in disastrous eclipse, for forty-two months. And now when the old Bastille has become a dancing-ground (had any one the mirth to dance), and its stones are getting built into the Pont Louis-Seize, does this minor, comparative insignificance of a Bastille flank itself with fresh-hewn mullions, spread out tyrannous wings ; menacing Patriotism? New space for prisoners : and what prisoners? A D'Orléans, with the chief Patriots on the tip of the Left? It is said, there runs 'a subterranean passage' all the way from the Tuileries

hither. Who knows? Paris, mined with quarries and cata
combs, does hang wondrous over the abyss; Paris was once
to be blown up,—though the powder, when we went to look
had got withdrawn. A Tuileries, sold to Austria, and
Coblentz, should have no subterranean passage. Out o
which might not Coblentz or Austria issue, some morning
and, with cannon of long range, '*foudroyer*,' bethunder a
patriotic Saint-Antoine into smoulder and ruin!

So meditates the benighted soul of Saint-Antoine, as it see
the aproned workmen, in early spring, busy on these towers
An official-speaking Municipality, a Sieur Motier with his
legions of *mouchards*, deserve no trust at all. Were Patrio
Santerre, indeed, Commander! But the sonorous Brewe
commands only our own Battalion: of such secrets he ca
explain nothing, knows nothing, perhaps suspects much. And
so the work goes on; and afflicted benighted Saint-Antoine
hears rattle of hammers, sees stones suspended in air.

Saint-Antoine prostrated the first great Bastille: will i
falter over this comparative insignificance of a Bastille.
Friends, what if we took pikes, fire-locks, sledgehammers
and helped ourselves!—Speedier is no remedy; nor so certain
On the 28th day of February, Saint-Antoine turns out, as
it has now often done; and, apparently with little superfluou
tumult, moves eastward to that eye-sorrow of Vincennes
With grave voice of authority, no need of bullying and
shouting, Saint-Antoine signifies to parties concerned there
that its purpose is, To have this suspicious Stronghold razed
level with the general soil of the country. Remonstrance
may be proffered, with zeal; but it avails not. The outer
gate goes up, drawbridges tumble; iron window-stanchions
smitten out with sledgehammers, become iron-crowbars: it
rains a rain of furniture, stone-masses, slates: with chaotic
clatter and rattle, Demolition clatters down. And now hasty
expresses rush through the agitated streets, to warn Lafayette
and the Municipal and Departmental Authorities; Rumou
warns a National Assembly; a Royal Tuileries, and all men
who care to hear it: That Saint-Antoine is up; that Vincennes,
and probably the last remaining Institution of the Country,
is coming down.

Quick, then! Let Lafayette roll his drums and fly eastward; for to all Constitutional Patriots this is again bad news.
And you, ye Friends of Royalty, snatch your poniards of
improved structure, made to order; your sword-canes, secret

rms, and tickets of entry; quick, by backstairs passages, rally
ound the Son of Sixty Kings. An effervescence probably got
p by D'Orléans and Company, for the overthrow of Throne
nd Altar: it is said her Majesty shall be put in prison, put
ut of the way; what then will *his* Majesty be? Clay for the
ansculottic Potter! Or were it impossible to fly this day; a
rave Noblesse suddenly all rallying? Peril threatens, hope
nvites; Dukes de Villequier, de Duras, Gentlemen of the
Chamber give Tickets and admittance; a brave Noblesse is
uddenly all rallying. Now were the time to 'fall sword in
and on those gentry there,' could it be done with effect.

The Hero of two Worlds is on his white charger: blue
Nationals, horse and foot, hurrying eastward; Santerre, with
he Saint-Antoine Battalion, is already there,—apparently
ndisposed to act. Heavy-laden Hero of two Worlds, what
asks are these! The jeerings, provocative gambollings of that
Patriot Suburb, which is all out on the streets now, are hard
o endure; unwashed Patriots jeering in sulky sport; one
nwashed Patriot 'seizing the General by the boot,' to unhorse
im. Santerre, ordered to fire, makes answer obliquely,
"These are the men that took the Bastille;" and not a trigger
tirs. Neither dare the Vincennes Magistracy give warrant of
rrestment, or the smallest countenance: wherefore the Gen-
ral 'will take it on himself' to arrest. By promptitude, by
heerful adroitness, patience and brisk valour without limits,
he riot may be again bloodlessly appeased.

Meanwhile, the rest of Paris, with more or less unconcern,
nay mind the rest of its business: for what is this but an
ffervescence, of which there are now so many? The National
Assembly, in one of its stormiest moods, is debating a Law
gainst Emigration; Mirabeau declaring aloud, "I swear
eforehand that I will not obey it." Mirabeau is often at the
Tribune this day; with endless impediments from without;
vith the old unabated energy from within. What can mur-
nurs and clamours, from Left or from Right, do to this man;
ike Teneriffe or Atlas unremoved? With clear thought; with
trong bass-voice, though at first low, uncertain, he claims audi-
nce, sways the storm of men: anon the sound of him waxes,
oftens; he rises into far-sounding melody of strength, triumphant, which subdues all hearts; his rude seamed face, deso-
ate, fire-scathed, becomes fire-lit, and radiates: once again
nen feel, in these beggarly ages, what is the potency and
mnipotency of man's word on the souls of men. "I will

triumph or be torn in fragments," he was once heard to say. "Silence," he cries now, in strong word of command, in imperial consciousness of strength. "Silence, the thirty voices, *Silence aux trente voix!*"—and Robespierre and the Thirty Voices die into mutterings; and the Law is once more as Mirabeau would have it.

How different, at the same instant, is General Lafayette's street-eloquence; wrangling with sonorous Brewers, with an ungrammatical Saint-Antoine! Most different, again, from both is the Café-de-Valois eloquence, and suppressed fanfaronade, of this multitude of men with Tickets of Entry; who are now inundating the Corridors of the Tuileries. Such things can go on simultaneously in one City. How much more in one Country; in one Planet with its discrepancies, every Day a mere crackling infinitude of discrepancies,—which nevertheless do yield some coherent net-product, though an infinitesimally small one!

But be this as it may, Lafayette has saved Vincennes; and is marching homewards with some dozen of arrested demolitionists. Royalty is not yet saved;—nor indeed specially endangered. But to the King's Constitutional Guard, to these Old Gardes Françaises, or Centre Grenadiers, as it chanced to be, this affluence of men with Tickets of Entry is becoming more and more unintelligible. Is his Majesty verily for Metz, then; to be carried off by these men, on the spur of the instant? That revolt of Saint-Antoine, got up by traitor Royalists for a stalking-horse? Keep a sharp outlook, ye Centre Grenadiers on duty here: good never came from the 'men in black.' Nay they have cloaks, *redingotes;* some of them leather-breeches, boots,—as if for instant riding! Or what is this that sticks visible from the lapelle of the Chevalier de Court? Too like the handle of some cutting or stabbing instrument! He glides and goes; and still the dudgeon sticks from his left lapelle. "Hold, Monsieur!"—a Centre Grenadier clutches him; clutches the protrusive dudgeon, whisks it out in the face of the world: by Heaven, a very dagger; hunting-knife or whatsoever you will call it; fit to drink the life of Patriotism!

So fared it with Chevalier de Court, early in the day; not without noise; not without commentaries. And now this continually increasing multitude at nightfall? Have they daggers too? Alas, with them too, after angry parleyings, there has begun a groping and a rummaging; all men in black, spite of their Tickets of Entry, are clutched by the collar, and groped. Scandalous to think of: for always, as the dirk, sword-cane, pistol, or were it but tailor's bodkin, is found on him, and with loud scorn drawn forth from him, he, the hapless man in black, is flung all-too rapidly down stairs. Flung; and ignominiously descends, head foremost; accelerated by ignominious shovings from sentry after sentry; nay, as is written, by smitings, twitchings,—spurnings *à posteriori*, not to be named. In this accelerated way, emerges, uncertain which end uppermost, man after man in black, through all issues, into the Tuileries Garden. Emerges, alas, into the arms of an indignant multitude, now gathered and gathering there, in the hour of dusk, to see what is toward, and whether the Hereditary Representative is carried off or not. Hapless men in black; at last *convicted* of poniards made to order; convicted 'Chevaliers of the Poniard!' Within is as the burning ship; without is as the deep sea. Within is no help; his Majesty, looking forth, one moment, from his interior sanctuaries, coldly bids all visitors 'give up their weapons;' and shuts the door again. The weapons given up form a heap: the convicted Chevaliers of the Poniard keep descending pellmell, with impetuous velocity; and at the bottom of all staircases, the mixed multitude receives them, hustles, buffets, chases, and disperses them.

Such sight meets Lafayette, in the dusk of the evening, as he returns, successful with difficulty at Vincennes: Sansculotte Scylla hardly weathered, here is Aristocrat Charybdis gurgling under his lee! The patient Hero of two Worlds almost loses temper. He accelerates, does not retard, the flying Chevaliers; delivers, indeed, this or the other hunted Loyalist of quality, but rates him in bitter words, such as the hour suggested; such as no saloon could pardon. Hero ill-bested; hanging, so to speak, in mid air; hateful to Rich divinities above; hateful to Indigent mortals below! Duke de Villequier, Gentleman of the Chamber, gets such contumelious rating, in presence of all people there, that he may see good first to exculpate himself in the Newspapers; then, that not prospering, to retire over the Frontiers, and begin plotting at Brussels. His Apartment will stand vacant; usefuller, as we may find, than when it stood occupied. .

So fly the Chevaliers of the Poniard; hunted of Patriotic men, shamefully in the thickening dusk. A dim miserable business; born of darkness; dying away there in the thickening dusk and dimness. In the midst of which, however, let the reader discern clearly one figure running for its life: Crispin-Catiline d'Espréménil,—for the last time, or the last but one. It is not yet three years since these same Centre Grenadiers, Gardes Françaises then, marched him towards the Calypso Isles, in the gray of the May morning (p. 84); and he and they have got thus far. Buffeted, beaten down, delivered by popular Pétion, he might well answer bitterly: "And I too, Monsieur, have been carried on the People's shoulders." A fact which popular Pétion, if he like, can meditate.

But happily, one way and another, the speedy night covers up this ignominious Day of Poniards; and the Chevaliers escape, though maltreated, with torn coat-skirts and heavy hearts, to their respective dwelling-houses. Riot twofold is quelled; and little blood shed, if it be not insignificant blood from the nose: Vincennes stands undemolished, reparable; and the Hereditary Representative has not been stolen, nor the Queen smuggled into Prison. A day long remembered: commented on with loud hahas and deep grumblings; with bitter scornfulness of triumph, bitter rancour of defeat. Royalism, as usual, imputes it to D'Orléans and the Anarchists intent on insulting Majesty: Patriotism, as usual, to Royalists, and even Constitutionalists, intent on stealing Majesty to Metz: we, also as usual, to Preternatural Suspicion, and Phœbus Apollo having made himself like the Night.

Thus, however, has the reader seen, in an unexpected arena, on this last day of February 1791, the Three long-contending elements of French Society dashed forth into singular comico-tragico collision; acting and reacting openly to the eye. Constitutionalism, at once quelling Sansculottic riot at Vincennes, and Royalist treachery in the Tuileries, is great, this day, and prevails. As for poor Royalism, tossed to and fro in that manner, its daggers all left in a heap, what can one think of it? Every dog, the adage says, has its day: *has* it; has had it; or will have it. For the present, the day is Lafayette's and the Constitution's. Nevertheless Hunger and Jacobinism, fast growing fanatical, still work; their day, were they once fanatical, will come. Hitherto, in all tempests, Lafayette, like some divine Sea-ruler, raises his serene head: the upper Æolus' blasts fly back to their caves, like foolish unbidden winds: the under sea-billows they had vexed into froth allay themselves. But if, as we often write, the *sub*marine Titanic Fire-powers came into play, the Ocean-bed from beneath being *burst?* If they hurled Poseidon Lafayette and his Constitution out of Space; and in the Titanic melly, sea were mixed with the sky?

CHAPTER VI

MIRABEAU

THE spirit of France waxes ever more acrid, fever-sick: towards the final outburst of dissolution and delirium. Suspicion rules all minds: contending parties cannot now commingle; stand separated sheer asunder, eyeing one another, in most aguish mood, of cold terror or hot rage. Counter-Revolution, Days of Poniards, Castries Duels; Flight of Mesdames, of Monsieur and Royalty! Journalism shrills ever louder its cry of alarm. The sleepless Dionysius's Ear of the Forty-eight Sections, how feverishly quick has it grown; convulsing with strange pangs the whole sick Body, as in such sleeplessness and sickness the ear will do!

Since Royalists get Poniards made to order, and a Sieur Motier is no better than he should be, shall not Patriotism too, even of the indigent sort, have Pikes, secondhand Firelocks, in readiness for the worst? The anvils ring, during this March month, with hammering of Pikes. A Constitutional Municipality promulgated its Placard, that no citizen except the 'active' or cash-citizen was entitled to have arms; but there rose, instantly responsive, such a tempest of astonishment from Club and Section, that the Constitutional Placard, almost next morning, had to cover itself up, and die away into inanity, in a second improved edition. So the hammering continues; as all that it betokens does.

Mark, again, how the extreme tip of the Left is mounting in favour, if not in its own National Hall, yet with the Nation, especially with Paris. For in such universal panic of doubt, the opinion that is sure of itself, as the meagrest opinion may the soonest be, is the one to which all men will rally. Great is Belief, were it never so meagre; and leads captive the doubting heart. Incorruptible Robespierre has been elected Public Accuser in our new Courts of Judicature; virtuous Pétion, it is thought, may rise to be Mayor, Cordelier Danton,

called also by triumphant majorities, sits at the Departmental
Council-table; colleague there of Mirabeau. Of incorruptible
Robespierre it was long ago predicted that he might go far,
mean meagre mortal though he was; for Doubt dwelt not in
him.

Under which circumstances ought not Royalty likewise to
cease doubting, and begin deciding and acting? Royalty has
always that sure trump-card in its hand: Flight out of Paris.
Which sure trump-card Royalty, as we see, keeps ever and
anon clutching at, grasping; and swashes it forth tentatively;
yet never tables it, still puts it back again. Play it, O Royalty!
If there be a chance left, this seems it, and verily the last
chance; and now every hour is rendering this a doubtfuller.
Alas, one would so fain both fly and not fly; play one's card
and have it to play. Royalty, in all human likelihood, will not
play its trump-card till the honours, one after one, be mainly
lost; and such trumping of it prove to be the sudden finish of
the game!

Here accordingly a question always arises; of the prophetic
sort; which cannot now be answered. Suppose Mirabeau,
with whom Royalty takes deep counsel, as with a Prime
Minister that cannot yet legally avow himself as such, had got
his arrangements *completed*? Arrangements he has; far-stretching plans that dawn fitfully on us, by fragments, in the confused
darkness. Thirty Departments ready to sign loyal Addresses,
of prescribed tenor: King carried out of Paris, but only to
Compiègne and Rouen, hardly to Metz, since, once for all, no
Emigrant rabble shall take the lead in it: National Assembly
consenting, by dint of loyal Addresses, by management, by
force of Bouillé, to hear reason, and follow thither! Was it so,
on *these* terms, that Jacobinism and Mirabeau were then to
grapple, in their Hercules-and-Typhon duel; Death inevitable
for the one or the other? The duel itself is determined on,
and sure: but on what terms; much more, with what issue,
we in vain guess. It is vague darkness all: unknown what is
to be; unknown even what has already been. The giant
Mirabeau walks in darkness, as we said; companionless on
wild ways: what his thoughts during these months were, no
record of Biographer, nor vague *Fils Adoptif*, will now ever
disclose.

To us, endeavouring to cast his horoscope, it of course
remains doubly vague. There is one Herculean Man; in
internecine duel with him, there is Monster after Monster.

Emigrant Noblesse return, sword on thigh, vaunting of their Loyalty never sullied; descending from the air, like Harpy-swarms, with ferocity, with obscene greed. Earthward there is the Typhon of Anarchy, Political, Religious; sprawling hundred-headed, say with Twenty-five million heads; wide as the area of France; fierce as Frenzy; strong in very Hunger. With these shall the Serpent-queller do battle continually, and expect no rest.

As for the King, he as usual will go wavering chameleon-like, changing colour and purpose with the colour of his environment;—good for no Kingly use. On one royal person, on the Queen only, can Mirabeau perhaps place dependence. It is possible, the greatness of this man, not unskilled too in blandishments, courtiership, and graceful adroitness, might, with most legitimate sorcery fascinate the volatile Queen, and fix her to him. She has courage for all noble daring; an eye and a heart: the soul of Theresa's Daughter. 'Faut-il donc, Is it fated then,' she passionately writes to her Brother, 'that I, with the blood I am come of, with the sentiments I have, must live and die among such mortals?' Alas, poor Princess, Yes. 'She is the only *man*,' as Mirabeau observes, 'whom his Majesty has about him.' Of one other man Mirabeau is still surer: of himself. There lie his resources; sufficient or insufficient.

Dim and great to the eye of Prophecy looks that future. A perpetual life-and-death battle; confusion from above and from below;—mere confused darkness for us; with here and there some streak of faint lurid light. We see a King perhaps laid aside; not tonsured, tonsuring is out of fashion now; but say, sent away anywhither, with handsome annual allowance, and stock of smith-tools. We see a Queen and Dauphin, Regent and Minor; a Queen 'mounted on horseback,' in the din of battles, with *Moriamur pro rege nostro!* 'Such a day,' Mirabeau writes, 'may come.'

Din of battles, wars more than civil, confusion from above and from below: in such environment the eye of Prophecy sees Comte de Mirabeau, like some Cardinal de Retz, storm-fully maintain himself; with head all-devising, heart all-daring, if not victorious, yet unvanquished, while life is left him. The specialities and issues of it, no eye of Prophecy can guess at: it is clouds, we repeat, and tempestuous night; and in the middle of it, now visible, far-darting, now labouring in eclipse, is Mirabeau indomitably struggling to be Cloud-Compeller!—

One can say that, had Mirabeau lived, the History of France and of the World had been different. Further, that the man would have needed, as few men ever did, the whole compass of that same ' Art of Daring, *Art d'Oser*,' which he so prized; and likewise that he, above all men then living, would have practised and manifested it. Finally, that some substantiality, and no empty simulacrum of a formula, would have been the result realised by him : a result you could have loved, a result you could have hated; by no likelihood, a result you could only have rejected with closed lips, and swept into quick forgetfulness forever. Had Mirabeau lived one other year !

CHAPTER VII

DEATH OF MIRABEAU

But Mirabeau could not live another year, any more than he could live another thousand years. Men's years are numbered, and the tale of Mirabeau's was now complete. Important or unimportant ; to be mentioned in World-History for some centuries, or not to be mentioned there beyond a day or two, —it matters not to peremptory Fate. From amid the press of ruddy busy Life, the Pale Messenger beckons silently : widespreading interests, projects, salvation of French Monarchies, what thing soever man has on hand, he must suddenly quit it all, and go. Wert thou saving French Monarchies ; wert thou blacking shoes on the Pont Neuf ! The most important of men cannot stay ; did the World's History depend on an hour, that hour is not to be given. Whereby indeed, it comes that these same *would-have-beens* are mostly a vanity ; and the World's History could never in the least be what it would, or might, or should, by any manner of potentiality, but simply and altogether what it *is*.

The fierce wear and tear of such an existence has wasted out the giant oaken strength of Mirabeau. A fret and fever that keeps heart and brain on fire : excess of effort, of excitement ; excess of all kinds : labour incessant, almost beyond credibility ! ' If I had not lived with him,' says Dumont, ' I never should have known what a man can make of one day ; what things may be placed within the interval of twelve hours. A day for this man was more than a week or a month is for others : the mass of things he guided on together was prodigious ; from the scheming to the executing not a moment lost.'—" Monsieur le Comte," said his Secretary to him once, "what you require is impossible."—"Impossible!"—answered he, starting from his chair, "*Ne me dites jamais ce bête de mot*, Never name to me that blockhead of a word." And then the social repasts; the dinner which he gives as Commandant of National Guards, which 'cost five hundred pounds:' alas, and 'the Syrens of the Opera;' and all the ginger that is hot in the mouth:—down what a course is this man hurled! Cannot Mirabeau stop; cannot he fly, and save himself alive? No! There is a Nessus' Shirt on this Hercules; he must storm and burn there, without rest, till he be consumed. Human strength, never so Herculean, has its measure. Herald shadows flit pale across the fire-brain of Mirabeau; heralds of the pale repose. While he tosses and storms, straining every nerve, in that sea of ambition and confusion, there comes, sombre and still, a monition that for him the issue of it will be swift death.

In January last, you might see him as President of the Assembly; 'his neck wrapt in linen cloths, at the evening session:' there was sick heat of the blood, alternate darkening and flashing in the eyesight; he had to apply leeches, after the morning labour, and preside bandaged. 'At parting he embraced me,' says Dumont, 'with an emotion I had never seen in him: "I am dying, my friend; dying as by slow fire; we shall perhaps not meet again. When I am gone, they will know what the value of me was. The miseries I have held back will burst from all sides on France."' Sickness gives louder warning; but cannot be listened to. On the 27th day of March, proceeding towards the Assembly, he had to seek rest and help in Friend de Lamarck's, by the road; and lay there, for an hour, half-fainted, stretched on a sofa. To the Assembly nevertheless he went, as if in spite of Destiny itself; spoke, loud and eager, five several times; then quitted the Tribune—forever. He steps out, utterly exhausted, into the Tuileries Gardens; many people press round him, as usual, with applications, memorials; he says to the Friend who was with him: "Take me out of this!"

And so, on the last day of March 1791, endless anxious multitudes beset the Rue de la Chaussée d'Antin; incessantly inquiring; within doors there, in that House numbered, in our time, 42, the overwearied giant has fallen down, to die. Crowds of all parties and kinds; of all ranks from the King to the meanest man! The King sends publicly twice a-day to inquire; privately besides: from the world at large there is no end of inquiring. 'A written bulletin is handed out every three hours,' is copied and circulated; in the end, it is printed. The People spontaneously keep silence; no carriage shall enter with its noise: there is crowding pressure; but the Sister of Mirabeau is reverently recognised, and has free way made for her. The People stand mute, heart-stricken; to all it seems as if a great calamity were nigh: as if the last man of France, who could have swayed these coming troubles, lay there at hand-grips with the unearthly Power.

The silence of a whole People, the wakeful toil of Cabanis, Friend and Physician, skills not: on Saturday, the second day of April, Mirabeau feels that the last of the Days has risen for him; that on this day he has to depart and be no more. His death is Titanic, as his life has been! Lit up, for the last time, in the glare of coming dissolution, the mind of the man is all glowing and burning; utters itself in sayings, such as men long remember. He longs to live, yet acquiesces in death, argues not with the inexorable. His speech is wild and wondrous: unearthly Phantasms dancing now their torch-dance round his soul; the soul itself looking out, fire-radiant, motionless, girt together for that great hour! At times comes a beam of light from him on the world he is quitting. " I carry in my heart the death-dirge of the French Monarchy; the dead remains of it will now be the spoil of the factious." Or again, when he heard the cannon fire, what is characteristic too: "Have we the Achilles' Funeral already?" So likewise, while some friend is supporting him: "Yes, support that head; would I could bequeath it thee!" For the man dies as he has lived; self-conscious, conscious of a world looking on. He gazes forth on the young Spring, which for him will never be Summer. The Sun has risen; he says, "*Si ce n'est pas là Dieu, c'est du moins son cousin germain.*"—Death has mastered the out-works; power of speech is gone; the citadel of the heart still holding out: the moribund giant, passionately, by sign, demands paper and pen; writes his passionate demand for opium, to end these agonies. The sorrowful Doctor shakes his head: *Dormir*, 'To sleep,' writes the other, passionately pointing at it! So dies a gigantic Heathen and Titan; stumbling blindly, undismayed, down to his rest. At half-past eight in the morning, Doctor Petit, standing at the foot of the bed, says, "*Il ne souffre plus.*" His suffering and his working are now ended.

Even so, ye silent Patriot multitudes, all ye men of France; this man is rapt away from you. He has fallen suddenly, without bending till he broke; as a tower falls, smitten by sudden lightning. His word ye shall hear no more, his guidance follow no more.—The multitudes depart, heartstruck; spread the sad tidings. How touching is the loyalty of men to their Sovereign Man! All theatres, public amusements close; no joyful meeting can be held in these nights, joy is not for them: the People break in upon private dancing-parties, and sullenly command that they cease. Of such dancing-parties apparently but two came to light; and these also have gone out. The gloom is universal; never in this City was such sorrow for one death; never since that old night when Louis XII. departed, 'and the *Crieurs des Corps* went sounding their bells, and crying along the streets: *Le bon roi Louis, père du peuple, est mort,* The Good King Louis, Father of the People, is dead!' King Mirabeau is now the lost King; and one may say with little exaggeration, all the People mourns for him.

For three days there is low wide moan; weeping in the National Assembly itself. The streets are all mournful; orators mounted on the *bornes*, with large silent audience, preaching the funeral sermon of the dead. Let no coachman whip fast, distractively with his rolling wheels, or almost at all, through these groups! His traces may be cut; himself and his fare, as incurable Aristocrats, hurled sulkily into the kennels. The bournestone orators speak as it is given them; the Sansculottic People, with its rude soul, listens eager,—as men will to any Sermon, or *Sermo*, when it *is* a spoken Word meaning a Thing, and not a Babblement meaning No-thing. In the Restaurateur's of the Palais-Royal, the waiter remarks, "Fine weather, Monsieur:"—"Yes, my friend," answers the ancient Man of Letters, "very fine; but Mirabeau is dead." Hoarse rhythmic threnodies come also from the throats of ballad-singers; are sold on gray-white paper at a *sou* each. But of Portraits, engraved, painted, hewn and written; of Eulogies, Reminiscences, Biographies, nay *Vaudevilles*, Dramas and Melodramas, in all Provinces of France, there will, through these coming months, be the due immeasurable crop; thick as the leaves of Spring. Nor, that a tincture of burlesque might be in it, is Gobel's Episcopal *Mandement* wanting; goose Gobel, who has just been made Constitutional Bishop of Paris. A Mandement wherein *Ça ira* alternates very

strangely with *Nomine Domini;* and you are, with a grave
countenance, invited to 'rejoice at possessing in the midst
of you a body of Prelates created by Mirabeau, zealous
followers of his doctrine, faithful imitators of his virtues.'
So speaks, and cackles manifold, the Sorrow of France;
wailing articulately, inarticulately, as it can, that a Sovereign Man is snatched away. In the National Assembly,
when difficult questions are astir, all eyes will 'turn mechanic-
ally to the place where Mirabeau sat,'—and Mirabeau is
absent now.

On the third evening of the lamentation, the fourth of April,
there is solemn Public Funeral; such as deceased mortal
seldom had. Procession of a league in length; of mourners
reckoned loosely at a hundred thousand. All roofs are
thronged with onlookers, all windows, lamp-irons, branches of
trees. 'Sadness is painted on every countenance; many
persons weep.' There is double hedge of National Guards;
there is National Assembly in a body; Jacobin Society, and
Societies; King's Ministers, Municipals, and all Notabilities,
Patriot or Aristocrat. Bouillé is noticeable there, 'with his
hat on;' say, hat drawn over his brow, hiding many thoughts!
Slow-wending, in religious silence, the Procession of a league
in length, under the level sun-rays, for it is five o'clock, moves
and marches: with its sable plumes; itself in a religious
silence; but, by fits with the muffled roll of drums, by fits with
some long-drawn wail of music, and strange clangour of trom-
bones, and metallic dirge-voice; amid the infinite hum of men.
In the Church of Saint-Eustache, there is funeral oration by
Cerutti; and discharge of fire-arms, which 'brings down
pieces of the plaster.' Thence, forward again to the Church
of Sainte-Geneviève; which has been consecrated, by supreme
decree, on the spur of this time, into a Pantheon for the Great
Men of the Fatherland, *Aux Grands Hommes la Patrie recon-
naissante.* Hardly at midnight is the business done; and
Mirabeau left in his dark dwelling: first tenant of that Fatherland's Pantheon.

Tenant, alas, who inhabits but at will, and shall be cast out.
For, in these days of convulsion and disjection, not even the
dust of the dead is permitted to rest. Voltaire's bones are,
by and by, to be carried from their stolen grave in the Abbey
of Scellières, to an eager *stealing* grave, in Paris his birth-
city: all mortals processioning and perorating there; cars
drawn by eight white horses, goadsters in classical costumes,

Death of Mirabeau 349

with fillets and wheat-ears enough,—though the weather is of the wettest. Evangelist Jean Jacques too, as is most proper, must be dug up from Ermenonville, and processioned, with pomp, with sensibility, to the Pantheon of the Fatherland. He and others: while again Mirabeau, we say, is cast forth from it, happily incapable of being *re*placed; and rests now, irrecognisable, reburied hastily at dead of night 'in the central part of the Churchyard Sainte-Catherine, in the Suburb Saint-Marceau,' to be disturbed no further.

So blazes out, farseen, a Man's Life, and becomes ashes and a *caput mortuum*, in this World-Pyre, which we name French Revolution: not the first that consumed itself there; nor, by thousands and many millions, the last! A man who 'had swallowed all formulas;' who, in these strange times and circumstances, felt called to live Titanically, and also to die so. As he, for his part, had swallowed all formulas, what Formula is there, never so comprehensive, that will express truly the *plus* and the *minus* of him, give us the accurate net-result of him? There is hitherto none such. Moralities not a few must shriek condemnatory over this Mirabeau; the Morality by which he could be judged has not yet got uttered in the speech of men. We will say this of him again: That he is a Reality and no Simulacrum; a living Son of Nature our general Mother; not a hollow artifice, and mechanism of Conventionalities, son of nothing, *brother* to nothing. In which little word, let the earnest man, walking sorrowful in a world mostly of 'Stuffed Clothes-suits,' that chatter and grin meaningless on him, quite *ghastly* to the earnest soul,—think what significance there is!

Of men who, in such sense, are alive, and see with eyes, the number is now not great: it may be well, if in this huge French Revolution itself, with its all-developing fury, we find some Three. Mortals driven rabid we find; sputtering the acridest logic; baring their breast to the battle-hail, their neck to the guillotine:—of whom it is so painful to say that they too are still, in good part, manufactured Formalities, not Facts but Hearsays!

Honour to the strong man, in these ages, who has shaken himself loose of shams, and *is* something. For in the way of being *worthy*, the first condition surely is that one *be*. Let Cant cease, at all risks and at all cost: till Cant cease, nothing else can begin. Of human Criminals, in these centuries, writes the Moralist, I find but one unforgivable: the Quack.

' Hateful to God,' as divine Dante sings, 'and to the Enemies of God,

' A Dio spiacente ed a' nemici sui!'

But whoever will, with sympathy, which is the first essential towards insight, look at this questionable Mirabeau, may find that there lay verily in him, as the basis of all, a Sincerity, a great free Earnestness; nay call it Honesty, for the man did before all things see, with that clear flashing vision, into what *was*, into what existed as fact; and did, with his wild heart, follow that and no other. Whereby on what ways soever he travels and struggles, often enough falling, he is still a brother man. Hate him not; thou canst not hate him! Shining through such soil and tarnish, and now victorious effulgent, and oftenest struggling eclipsed, the light of genius itself is in this man; which was never yet base and hateful; but at worst was lamentable, loveable with pity. They say that he was ambitious, that he wanted to be Minister. It is most true. And was he not simply the one man in France who could have done any good as Minister? Not vanity alone, not pride alone; far from that! Wild burstings of affection were in this great heart; of fierce lightning, and soft dew of pity. So sunk bemired in wretchedst defacements, it may be said of him, like the Magdalen of old, that he loved much: his Father, the harshest of old crabbed men, he loved with warmth, with veneration.

Be it that his falls and follies are manifold,—as himself often lamented even with tears. Alas, is not the Life of every such man already a poetic Tragedy; made up 'of Fate and of one's own Deservings,' of *Schicksal und eigene Schuld;* full of the elements of Pity and Fear? This brother man, if not Epic for us, is Tragic; if not great, is large; large in his qualities, world-large in his destinies. Whom other men, recognising him as such, may, through long times, remember, and draw nigh to examine and consider: these, in their several dialects, will say of him and sing of him,—till the right thing be said; and so the Formula that *can* judge him be no longer an undiscovered one.

Here then the wild Gabriel Honoré drops from the tissue of our History; not without a tragic farewell. He is gone: the flower of the wild Riquetti or Arrighetti kindred; which seems as if in him, with one last effort, it had done its best, and then expired, or sunk down to the undistinguished level. Crabbed old Marquis Mirabeau, the Friend of Men, sleeps sound. The Bailli Mirabeau, worthy Uncle, will soon die forlorn, alone. Barrel-Mirabeau, already gone across the Rhine, his Regiment of Emigrants will drive nigh desperate. 'Barrel-Mirabeau,' says a biographer of his, 'went indignantly across the Rhine, and drilled Emigrant Regiments. But as he sat one morning in his tent, sour of stomach doubtless and of heart, meditating in Tartarean humour on the turn things took, a certain Captain or Subaltern demanded admittance on business. Such Captain is refused; he again demands, with refusal; and then again; till Colonel Viscount Barrel-Mirabeau, blazing up into a mere burning brandy-barrel, clutches his sword, and tumbles out on this *canaille* of an intruder,—alas, on the *canaille* of an intruder's sword-point, who had drawn with swift dexterity; and dies, and the Newspapers name it *apoplexy* and *alarming accident*.' So die the Mirabeaus.

New Mirabeaus one hears not of: the wild kindred, as we said, is gone out with this its greatest. As families and kindreds sometimes do; producing, after long ages of un-noted notability, some living quintessence of all the qualities they had, to flame forth as a man world-noted; after whom they rest as if exhausted; the sceptre passing to others. The chosen Last of the Mirabeaus is gone; the chosen man of France is gone. It was he who shook old France from its basis; and, as if with his single hand, has held it toppling there, still unfallen. What things depended on that one man! He is as a ship suddenly shivered on sunk rocks: much swims on the waste waters, far from help.

Part II, Book IV and following were published in a separate volume in the previous Everyman edition.

PART II—THE CONSTITUTION

(*continued*)

BOOK IV

VARENNES

CHAPTER I

EASTER AT SAINT-CLOUD

THE French Monarchy may now therefore be considered as, in all human probability, lost; as struggling henceforth in blindness as well as weakness, the last light of reasonable guidance having gone out. What remains of resources their poor Majesties will waste still further, in uncertain loitering and wavering. Mirabeau himself had to complain that they only gave him half confidence, and always had some plan within his plan. Had they fled frankly with him to Rouen or anywhither, long ago! They may fly now with chance immeasurably lessened; which will go on lessening towards absolute zero. Decide, O Queen; poor Louis can decide nothing: execute this Flight-project, or at least abandon it. Correspondence with Bouillé there has been enough, what profits consulting, and hypothesis, while all around is in fierce activity of practice? The Rustic sits waiting till the river run dry: alas, with you it is not a common river, but a Nile Inundation; snows melting in the unseen mountains; till all, and you where you sit, be submerged.

Many things invite to flight. The voice of Journals invites; Royalist Journals proudly hinting it as a threat, Patriot Journals rabidly denouncing it as a terror. Mother Society, waxing more and more emphatic, invites;—so emphatic that, as was prophesied, Lafayette and your limited Patriots have ere long to branch off from her, and form themselves into Feuillans; with infinite public controversy; the victory in which, doubtful though it look, will remain with the *un*limited Mother. Moreover, ever since the Day of Poniards, we have seen unlimited Patriotism openly equipping itself with arms. Citizens denied 'activity,' which is facetiously made to signify a certain weight of purse, cannot buy blue uniforms, and be Guardsmen; but man is greater than blue cloth; man can fight, if need be, in multiform cloth, or even almost without cloth,—as Sansculotte. So pikes continue to be hammered, whether those Dirks of improved structure with barbs be 'meant for the West-India market,' or not meant. Men beat, the wrong way, their ploughshares into swords. Is there not what we may call an 'Austrian Committee,' *Comité Autrichien*, sitting daily and nightly in the Tuileries? Patriotism, by vision and suspicion, knows it too well! If the King fly, will there not be Aristocrat-Austrian invasion; butchery; replacement of Feudalism; wars more than civil? The hearts of men are saddened and maddened.

Dissident Priests likewise give trouble enough. Expelled from their Parish Churches, where Constitutional Priests, elected by the Public, have replaced them, these unhappy persons resort to Convents of Nuns, or other such receptacles; and there, on Sabbath, collecting assemblages of Anti-Constitutional individuals, who have grown devout all on a sudden, they worship or pretend to worship in their strait-laced contumacious manner; to the scandal of Patriotism. Dissident Priests, passing along with their sacred wafer for the dying, seem wishful to be massacred in the streets; wherein Patriotism will not gratify them. Slighter palm of martyrdom, however, shall not be denied: martyrdom not of massacre, yet of fustigation. At the refractory places of worship, Patriot men appear; Patriot women with strong hazel wands, which they apply. Shut thy eyes, O Reader; see not this misery, peculiar to these later times,—of martyrdom without sincerity, with only cant and contumacy! A dead Catholic Church is not allowed to lie dead; no, it is *galvanised* into the detestablest death-life; whereat Humanity, we say, shuts its eyes. For the Patriot women take their hazel wands, and fustigate, amid laughter of bystanders, with alacrity: broad bottom of Priests alas, Nuns too, reversed and *cotillons retroussés!* The National Guard does what it can: Municipality 'invokes the Principle of Toleration;' grants Dissident worshippers the Church of the *Théatins;* promising protection. But it is to no purpose at the door of that *Théatins* Church appears a Placard, and suspended atop, like Plebeian Consular *fasces*,—a Bundle of Rods! The Principles of Toleration must do the best they

may: but no Dissident man shall worship contumaciously;
there is a *Plebiscitum* to that effect; which, though unspoken,
is like the laws of the Medes and Persians. Dissident contumacious Priests ought not to be harboured, even in private,
by any man: the Club of the Cordeliers openly denounces
Majesty himself as doing it.

Many things invite to flight: but probably this thing above
all others, that it has become impossible! On the 15th of
April, notice is given that his Majesty, who has suffered much
from catarrh lately, will enjoy the Spring weather for a few
days, at Saint-Cloud. Out at Saint-Cloud? Wishing to
celebrate his Easter, his *Pâques* or Pasch, there; with refractory Anti-Constitutional Dissidents?—Wishing rather to
make off for Compiègne, and thence to the Frontiers? As
were, in good sooth, perhaps feasible, or would once have
been; nothing but some two *chasseurs* attending you;
chasseurs easily corrupted! It is a pleasant possibility, execute it or not. Men say there are thirty thousand Chevaliers
of the Poniard lurking in the woods there: lurking in the
woods, and thirty thousand,—for the human Imagination is
not fettered. But now, how easily might these, dashing out
on Lafayette, snatch off the Hereditary Representative; and
roll away with him, after the manner of a whirlblast, whither
they listed!—Enough, it were well the king did not go. Lafayette is forewarned and forearmed: but, indeed, is the risk his
only; or his and all France's?

Monday the eighteenth of April is come; the Easter journey
to Saint-Cloud shall take effect. National Guard has got its
orders; a First Division, as Advanced Guard, has even
marched, and probably arrived. His Majesty's *Maison-bouche*,
they say, is all busy stewing and frying at Saint-Cloud; the
King's dinner not far from ready there. About one o'clock,
the Royal Carriage, with its eight royal blacks, shoots stately
into the Place du Carrousel; draws up to receive its royal
burden. But hark! from the neighbouring Church of Saint-
Roch, the tocsin begins ding-dong-ing. Is the King stolen
then; is he going; gone? Multitudes of persons crowd the
Carrousel: the Royal Carriage still stands there;—and, by
Heaven's strength, shall stand!

Lafayette comes up, with aides-de-camp and oratory; pervad-
ing the groups: "*Taisez-vous*," answer the groups, "the King
shall not go." Monsieur appears, at an upper window: ten
thousand voices bray and shriek, "*Nous ne voulons pas que le*

Roi parte." Their Majesties have mounted. Crack go the whips; but twenty Patriot arms have seized each of the eight bridles: there is rearing, rocking, vociferation; not the smallest headway. In vain does Lafayette fret, indignant; and perorate and strive: Patriots in the passion of terror bellow round the Royal Carriage; it is one bellowing sea of Patriot terror run frantic. Will Royalty fly off towards Austria; like a lit rocket towards endless Conflagration of Civil War? Stop it, ye Patriots, in the name of Heaven! Rude voices passionately apostrophise Royalty itself. Usher Campan, and other the like official persons, pressing forward with help or advice, are clutched by the sashes, and hurled and whirled, in a confused perilous manner; so that her Majesty has to plead passion ately from the carriage-window.

Order cannot be heard, cannot be followed; National Guards know not how to act. Centre Grenadiers, of the Observatoire Battalion, are there; not on duty; alas, in quasi mutiny; speaking rude disobedient words; threatening the mounted Guards with sharp shot if they hurt the people Lafayette mounts and dismounts; runs haranguing, panting on the verge of despair. For an hour and three-quarters 'seven quarters of an hour,' by the Tuileries Clock! Desperate Lafayette will open a passage, were it by the cannon's mouth if his Majesty will order. Their Majesties, counselled to it by Royalist friends, by Patriot foes, dismount; and retire in, with heavy indignant heart; giving up the enterprise. *Maison bouche* may eat that cooked dinner themselves: his Majesty shall not see Saint-Cloud this day,—nor any day.

The pathetic fable of imprisonment in one's own Palace has become a sad fact, then? Majesty complains to Assembly Municipality deliberates, proposes to petition or address Sections respond with sullen brevity of negation. Lafayette flings down his Commission; appears in civic pepper-and-salt frock; and cannot be flattered back again; not in less than three days; and by unheard-of entreaty; National Guards kneeling to him, and declaring that it is not sycophancy, that they are free men kneeling here to the *Statue of Liberty*. For the rest, those Centre Grenadiers of the Observatoire are disbanded,—yet indeed are re-inlisted, all but fourteen, under a new name, and with new quarters. The King must keep his Easter in Paris; meditating much on this singular posture of things; but as good as determined now to fly from it, desire being whetted by difficulty.

CHAPTER II

EASTER AT PARIS

For above a year, ever since March 1790, it would seem, there has hovered a project of Flight before the royal mind; and ever and anon has been condensing itself into something like a purpose; but this or the other difficulty always vaporised it again. It seems so full of risks, perhaps of civil war itself; above all, it cannot be done without effort. Somnolent laziness will not serve: to fly, if not in a leather *vache*, one must verily stir himself. Better to adopt that Constitution of theirs; execute it so as to show all men that it is *in*executable? Better or not so good: surely it is *easier*. To all difficulties you need only say, There is a lion in the path, behold your Constitution will not act! For a somnolent person it requires no effort to counterfeit death,—as Dame de Staël and Friends of Liberty can see the King's Government long doing, *faisant la mort.*

Nay now, when desire whetted by difficulty has brought the matter to a head, and the royal mind no longer halts between two, what can come of it? Grant that poor Louis were safe with Bouillé, what, on the whole, could he look for there? Exasperated Tickets of Entry answer: Much, all. But cold Reason answers: Little, almost nothing. Is not loyalty a law of Nature? ask the Tickets of Entry. Is not love of your King, and even death for him, the glory of all Frenchmen,— except these few Democrats? Let Democrat Constitution-builders see what they will do without their Keystone; and France rend its hair, having lost the Hereditary Representative!

Thus will King Louis fly; one sees not reasonably towards what. As a maltreated Boy, shall we say, who, having a Step-mother, rushes sulkily into the wide world; and will wring the paternal heart?—Poor Louis escapes from known unsupportable evils, to an unknown mixture of good and evil, coloured by Hope. He goes, as Rabelais did when dying, to seek a great May-be: *je vais chercher un grand Peut-être!* As not only the sulky Boy but the wise grown Man is obliged to do, so often, in emergencies.

For the rest, there is still no lack of stimulants, and step-dame maltreatments, to keep one's resolution at the due pitch. Factious disturbances cease not: as indeed how can they, unless authoritatively *conjured*, in a Revolt which is by Nature bottomless? If the ceasing of faction be the price of the

King's somnolence, he may awake when he will, and take
wing.

Remark, in any case, what somersets and contortions a dead
Catholicism is making,—skilfully galvanised : hideous, and
even piteous, to behold ! Jurant and Dissident, with their
shaved crowns, argue frothing everywhere ; or are ceasing to
argue, and stripping for battle. In Paris was scourging while
need continued : contrariwise in the Morbihan of Brittany
without scourging, armed Peasants are up, roused by pulpit
drum, they know not why. General Dumouriez, who has got
missioned thitherwards, finds all in sour heat of darkness
finds also that explanation and conciliation will still do much.

But again, consider this : that his Holiness, Pius Sixth, has
seen good to excommunicate Bishop Talleyrand ! Surely, we
will say then, considering it, there is no living or dead Church
in the Earth that has not the indubitablest right to excommunicate Talleyrand. Pope Pius has right and might, in his way.
But truly so likewise has Father Adam, *ci-devant* Marquis
Saint-Huruge, in his way. Behold, therefore, on the Fourth
of May, in the Palais-Royal, a mixed loud-sounding multitude,
in the middle of whom, Father Adam, bull-voiced Saint
Huruge, in white hat, towers visible and audible. With him
it is said, walks Journalist Gorsas, walk many others of the
washed sort ; for no authority will interfere. Pius Sixth, with
his plush and tiara, and power of the Keys, they bear aloft
of natural size,—made of lath and combustible gum. Royou,
the King's Friend, is borne too in effigy ; with a pile of Newspaper *King's-Friends*, condemned Numbers of the *Ami-du-Roi*,
fit fuel of the sacrifice. Speeches are spoken ; a judgment is
held, a doom proclaimed, audible in bull-voice, towards the four
winds. And thus, amid great shouting, the holocaust is consummated, under the summer sky ; and our lath-and-gum
Holiness, with the attendant victims, mounts up in flame, and
sinks down in ashes ; a decomposed Pope : and right or might
among all the parties, has better or worse accomplished itself
as it could. But, on the whole, reckoning from Martin Luther
in the Market-place of Wittenberg to Marquis Saint-Huruge
in this Palais-Royal of Paris, what a journey have we gone ; into
what strange territories has it carried us ! No Authority can
now interfere. Nay Religion herself, mourning for such things,
may after all ask, What have *I* to do with them ?

In such extraordinary manner does dead Catholicism somer-
set and caper, skilfully galvanised. For, does the reader

inquire into the subject-matter of controversy in this case; what the difference between Orthodoxy or *My-doxy* and Heterodoxy or *Thy-doxy* might here be? My-doxy is, that an august National Assembly can equalise the extent of Bishop-ricks; that an equalised Bishop, his Creed and Formularies being left quite as they were, can swear Fidelity to King, Law and Nation, and so become a Constitutional Bishop. Thy-doxy, if thou be Dissident, is that he cannot; but that he must become an accursed thing. Human ill-nature needs but some Homoiousian *iota*, or even the pretence of one; and will flow copiously through the eye of a needle: thus always must mortals go jargoning and fuming,

> And, like the ancient Stoics in their porches,
> With fierce dispute maintain their churches.

This *Auto-da-fé* of Saint-Huruge's was on the Fourth of May 1791. Royalty sees it; but says nothing.

CHAPTER III

COUNT FERSEN

ROYALTY, in fact, should, by this time, be far on with its preparations. Unhappily much preparation is needful. Could a Hereditary Representative be carried in leather *vache*, how easy were it! But it is not so.

New Clothes are needed; as usual, in all Epic transactions, were it in the grimmest iron ages; consider 'Queen Chrimhilde, with her sixty sempstresses, in that iron *Nibelungen Song!* No Queen can stir without new clothes. Therefore, now, Dame Campan whisks assiduous to this mantua-maker and to that: and there is clipping of frocks and gowns, upper clothes and under, great and small; such a clipping and sewing, as might have been dispensed with. Moreover, her Majesty cannot go a step anywhither without her *Nécessaire;* dear *Nécessaire*, of inlaid ivory and rosewood, cunningly devised; which holds perfumes, toilette-implements, infinite small queenlike furnitures: necessary to terrestrial life. Not without a cost of some five hundred louis, of much precious time, and difficult hood-winking which does not blind, can this same Necessary of life be forwarded by the Flanders Carriers,—never to get to hand. All which, you would say, augurs ill for the prospering of the enterprise. But the whims of women and queens must be humoured.

Bouillé, on his side, is making a fortified camp at Mont
médi; gathering Royal-Allemand, and all manner of othe
German and true French Troops thither, 'to watch th
Austrians.' His Majesty will not cross the frontiers, unles
on compulsion. Neither shall the Emigrants be much em
ployed, hateful as they are to all people. Nor shall old
war-god Broglie have any hand in the business; but solely
our brave Bouillé; to whom, on the day of meeting, a
Marshal's Baton shall be delivered, by a rescued King, amid
the shouting of all the troops. In the meanwhile, Paris being
so suspicious, were it not good to write your Foreign Am
bassadors an ostensible Constitutional Letter; desiring al
Kings and men to take heed that King Louis loves the Con
stitution, that he has voluntarily sworn, and does again swear
to maintain the same, and will reckon those his enemies who
affect to say otherwise? Such a Constitutional Letter is
despatched by Couriers, is communicated confidentially to the
Assembly, and printed in all Newspapers; with the finest
effect. Simulation and dissimulation mingle extensively in
human affairs.

We observe, however, that Count Fersen is often using his
Ticket of Entry; which surely he has clear right to do.
A gallant soldier and Swede, devoted to this fair Queen;—as
indeed the Highest Swede now is. Has not King Gustav,
famed fiery *Chevalier du Nord*, sworn himself, by the old laws
of chivalry, her Knight? He will descend on fire-wings of
Swedish musketry, and deliver her from these foul dragons,—
if, alas, the assassin's pistol intervene not!

But, in fact, Count Fersen does seem a likely young soldier,
of alert decisive ways: he circulates widely, seen, unseen; and
has business on hand. Also Colonel the Duke de Choiseul,
nephew of Choiseul the great, of Choiseul the now deceased;
he and Engineer Goguelat are passing and repassing between
Metz and the Tuileries: and Letters go in cipher,—one of
them, a most important one, hard to *de*cipher; Fersen having
ciphered it in haste. As for Duke de Villequier, he is gone
ever since the Day of Poniards; but his Apartment is useful
for her Majesty.

On the other side, poor Commandant Gouvion, watching at
the Tuileries, second in National command, sees several things
hard to interpret. It is the same Gouvion who sat, long
months ago, at the Townhall, gazing helpless into that In-

surrection of Women; motionless, as the brave stabled steed
when conflagration rises, till Usher Maillard snatched his
drum. Sincerer Patriot there is not; but many a shiftier.
He, if Dame Campan gossip credibly, is paying some similitude of love-court to a certain false Chambermaid of the
Palace, who betrays much to him: the *Nécessaire*, the clothes,
the packing of jewels,—could he understand it when betrayed.
Helpless Gouvion gazes with sincere glassy eyes into it; stirs
up his sentries to vigilance; walks restless to and fro; and
hopes the best.

But, on the whole, one finds that, in the second week of
June, Colonel de Choiseul is privately in Paris; having come
' to see his children.' Also that Fersen has got a stupendous
new Coach built, of the kind named *Berline*; done by the
first artists; according to a model: they bring it home to him,
in Choiseul's presence; the two friends take a proof-drive in
it, along the streets; in meditative mood; then send it up to
' Madame Sullivan's, in the Rue de Clichy,' far North, to wait
there till wanted. Apparently a certain Russian Baroness de
Korff, with Waiting-woman, Valet, and two Children, will travel
homewards with some state: in whom these young military
gentlemen take interest? A Passport has been procured for
her; and much assistance shown, with Coach-builders and such
like;—so helpful-polite are young military men. Fersen has
likewise purchased a Chaise fit for two, at least for two waiting-
maids; further, certain necessary horses: one would say, he
is himself quitting France, not without outlay? We observe
finally that their Majesties, Heaven willing, will assist at
Corpus-Christi Day, this blessed Summer Solstice, in Assump-
tion Church, here at Paris, to the joy of all the world. For
which same day, moreover, brave Bouillé, at Metz, as we find,
has invited a party of friends to dinner; but indeed is gone
from home, in the interim, over to Montmédi.

These are of the Phenomena, or visual Appearances, of this
wide-working terrestrial world: which truly is all phenomenal,
what they call spectral; and never rests at any moment; one
never at any moment can know why.

On Monday night, the Twentieth of June 1791, about
eleven o'clock, there is many a hackney-coach, and glass-
coach (*carrosse de remise*), still rumbling, or at rest, on the
streets of Paris. But of all glass-coaches, we recommend this
to thee, O Reader, which stands drawn up in the Rue de

l'Echelle, hard by the Carrousel and out-gate of the Tuileries
in the Rue de l'Échelle that then was; 'opposite Ronsin the
saddler's door,' as if waiting for a fare there! Not long does
it wait : a hooded Dame, with two hooded Children has issued
from Villequier's door, where no sentry walks, into the Tuilerie
Court-of-Princes; into the Carrousel; into the Rue de l'Échelle
where the Glass-coachman readily admits them; and again
waits. Not long; another Dame, likewise hooded or shrouded
leaning on a servant, issues in the same manner; bids the
servant good night; and is, in the same manner, by the Glass-
coachman, cheerfully admitted. Whither go so many Dames?
'Tis his Majesty's *Couchée*, Majesty just gone to bed, and all
the Palace-world is retiring home. But the Glass-coachman
still waits; his fare seemingly incomplete.

By and by, we note a thickset Individual, in round hat and
peruke, arm-and-arm with some servant, seemingly of the Runner or Courier sort; he also issues through Villequier's door;
starts a shoebuckle as he passes one of the sentries, stoops
down to clasp it again; is however, by the Glass-coachman
still more cheerfully admitted. And *now*, is his fare complete?
Not yet; the Glass-coachman still waits.—Alas! and the false
Chambermaid has warned Gouvion that she thinks the Royal
Family will fly this very night; and Gouvion distrusting his
own glazed eyes, has sent express for Lafayette; and Lafayette's
Carriage, flaring with lights, rolls this moment through the
inner Arch of the Carrousel,—where a Lady shaded in broad
gypsy-hat, and leaning on the arm of a servant, also of the
Runner or Courier sort, stands aside to let it pass, and has
even the whim to touch a spoke of it with her *badine*,—light
little magic rod which she calls *badine*, such as the Beautiful
then wore. The flare of Lafayette's Carriage rolls past : all
is found quiet in the Court-of-Princes; sentries at their post;
Majesties' Apartments closed in smooth rest. Your false
Chambermaid must have been mistaken? Watch thou,
Gouvion, with Argus' vigilance; for, of a truth, treachery is
within these walls.

But where is the Lady that stood aside in gypsy-hat, and
touched the wheel-spoke with her *badine?* O Reader, that
Lady that touched the wheel-spoke was the Queen of France!
She has issued safe through that inner Arch, into the Carrousel
itself; but not into the Rue de l'Échelle. Flurried by the
rattle and rencounter, she took the right hand not the left;
neither she nor her Courier knows Paris; he indeed is no

Courier, but a loyal stupid *ci-devant* Bodyguard disguised as
one. They are off, quite wrong, over the Pont Royal and
River; roaming disconsolate in the Rue de Bac; far from the
Glass-coachman, who still waits. Waits, with flutter of heart;
with thoughts—which he must button close up, under his
jarvie-surtout!

Midnight clangs from all the City-steeples; one precious
hour has been spent so; most mortals are asleep. The Glass-
coachman waits; and in what mood! A brother jarvie drives
up, enters into conversation; is answered cheerfully in jarvie-
dialect: the brothers of the whip exchange a pinch of snuff;
decline drinking together, and part with good night. Be the
Heavens blest! here at length is the Queen-lady, in gypsy-hat;
safe after perils; who has had to inquire her way. She too is
admitted; her Courier jumps aloft, as the other, who is also
a disguised Bodyguard, has done; and now, O Glass-coachman
of a thousand,—Count Fersen, for the Reader sees it is thou,
—drive!

Dust shall not stick to the hoofs of Fersen: crack! crack!
the Glass-coach rattles, and every soul breathes lighter. But
is Fersen on the right road? Northeastward, to the Barrier
of Saint-Martin and Metz Highway, thither were we bound:
and lo, he drives right Northward! The royal Individual, in
round hat and peruke, sits astonished; but right or wrong,
there is no remedy. Crack, crack, we go incessant, through
the slumbering City. Seldom, since Paris rose out of mud,
or the Longhaired Kings went in Bullock-carts, was there such
a drive. Mortals on each hand of you, close by, stretched out
horizontal, dormant; and we alive and quaking! Crack, crack,
through the Rue de Grammont; across the Boulevard; up the
Rue de la Chaussée d'Antin,—these windows, all silent, of
Number 42, were Mirabeau's. Towards the Barrier not of
Saint-Martin, but of Clichy on the utmost North! Patience,
ye royal Individuals; Fersen understands what he is about.
Passing up the Rue de Clichy, he alights for one moment at
Madame Sullivan's: "Did Count Fersen's Coachman get the
Baroness de Korff's new Berline?"—"Gone with it an hour-
and-half ago," grumbles responsive the drowsy Porter.—"*C'est
bien.*" Yes, it is well;—though had not such hour-and-half
been *lost*, it were still better. Forth therefore, O Fersen, fast,
by the Barrier de Clichy; then Eastward along the Outer
Boulevard, what horses and whipcord can do!

Thus Fersen drives, through the ambrosial night. Sleeping

Paris is now all on the right-hand of him; silent except fo
some snoring hum : and now he is Eastward as far as the
Barrier de Saint-Martin ; looking earnestly for Baroness de
Korff's Berline. This Heaven's Berline he at length does
descry, drawn up with its six horses, his own German Coach
man waiting on the box. Right, thou good German : now
haste, whither thou knowest !—And as for us of the Glass
coach, haste too, O haste ; much time is already lost ! The
august Glass-Coach fare, six Insides, hastily packs itself into
the new Berline ; two Bodyguard Couriers behind. The
Glass-coach itself is turned adrift, its head towards the City
to wander whither it lists,—and be found next morning tumbled
in a ditch. But Fersen is on the new box, with its brave new
hammer-cloths ; flourishing his whip ; he bolts forward towards
Bondy. There a third and final Bodyguard Courier of ours
ought surely to be, with post-horses ready-ordered. There
likewise ought that purchased Chaise, with the two Waiting
maids and their band-boxes, to be ; whom also her Majesty
could not travel without. Swift, thou deft Fersen, and may
the Heavens turn it well !

Once more, by Heaven's blessing, it is all well. Here is
the sleeping Hamlet of Bondy ; Chaise with Waiting-women ;
horses all ready, and postilions with their churn-boots, impatient in the dewy dawn. Brief harnessing done, the postilions
with their churn-boots vault into the saddles ; brandish circularly their little noisy whips. Fersen, under his jarvie-surtout,
bends in lowly silent reverence of adieu ; royal hands wave
speechless inexpressible response ; Baroness de Korff's Berline, with the Royalty of France, bounds off : forever, as it
proved. Deft Fersen dashes obliquely Northward, through
the country, towards Bougret ; gains Bougret, finds his German
Coachman and chariot waiting there ; cracks off, and drives
undiscovered into unknown space. A deft active man, we
say ; what he undertook to do is nimbly and successfully done.

And so the Royalty of France is actually fled ? This
precious night, the shortest of the year, it flies, and drives !
Baroness de Korff is, at bottom, Dame de Tourzel, Governess
of the Royal Children : she who came hooded with the two
hooded little ones ; little Dauphin ; little Madame Royale,
known long afterwards as Duchesse d'Angoulême. Baroness
de Korff's *Waiting-maid* is the Queen in gypsy-hat. The royal
Individual in round hat and peruke, he is *Valet* for the time

being. That other hooded Dame, styled *Travelling-companion*, is kind Sister Elizabeth; she had sworn, long since, when the Insurrection of Women was, that only death should part her and them. And so they rush there, not too impetuously, through the Wood of Bondy:—over a Rubicon in their own and France's History.

Great; though the future is all vague! If we reach Bouillé? If we do not reach him? O Louis! and this all round thee is the great slumbering Earth (and overhead, the great watchful Heaven); the slumbering Wood of Bondy,—where Long-haired Childeric Do-nothing was struck through with iron; not unreasonably, in a world like ours. These peaked stone-towers are Raincy; towers of wicked D'Orléans. All slumbers save the multiplex rustle of our new Berline. Loose-skirted scarecrow of an Herb-merchant, with his ass and early greens, toilsomely plodding, seems the only creature we meet. But right ahead the great Northeast sends up evermore his gray brindled dawn: from dewy branch, birds here and there, with short deep warble, salute the coming Sun. Stars fade out, and Galaxies; Street-lamps of the City of God. The Universe, O my brothers, is flinging wide its portals for the Levee of the GREAT HIGH KING. Thou, poor King Louis, farest never-theless, as mortals do, towards Orient lands of Hope; and the Tuileries with *its* Levees, and France and the Earth itself, is but a larger kind of doghutch,—occasionally going rabid

CHAPTER IV

ATTITUDE

BUT in Paris, at six in the morning; when some Patriot Deputy, warned by a billet, awoke Lafayette, and they went to the Tuileries?—Imagination may paint, but words cannot, the surprise of Lafayette; or with what bewilderment helpless Gouvion rolled glassy Argus' eyes, discerning now that his false Chambermaid had told true!

However, it is to be recorded that Paris, thanks to an august National Assembly, did, on this seeming doomsday, surpass itself. Never, according to Historian eye-witnesses, was there seen such an 'imposing attitude.' Sections all 'in permanence;' our Townhall too, having first, about ten o'clock, fired three solemn alarm-cannons: above all, our National Assembly! National Assembly, likewise permanent, decides

what is needful; with unanimous consent, for the *Côté Droit*
sits dumb, afraid of the Lanterne. Decides with a calm
promptitude, which rises towards the sublime. One must
needs vote, for the thing is self-evident, that his Majesty has
been *abducted*, or spirited away, '*enlevé*,' by some person or
persons unknown: in which case, what will the Constitution
have us do? Let us return to first principles, as we alway
say: "*revenons aux principes.*"

By first or by second principles, much is promptly decided
Ministers are sent for, instructed how to continue their func
tions; Lafayette is examined; and Gouvion, who gives a most
helpless account, the best he can. Letters are found written
one Letter of immense magnitude; all in his Majesty's hand
and evidently of his Majesty's own composition; addressed
to the National Assembly. It details, with earnestness, with
a childlike simplicity, what woes his Majesty has suffered
Woes great and small: A Necker seen applauded, a Majesty
not; then insurrection; want of due furniture in Tuileries
Palace; want of due cash in Civil List; *general* want of cash,
of furniture and order; anarchy everywhere: Deficit never
yet, in the smallest, 'choked or *comblé*:'—wherefore, in brief,
his Majesty has retired towards a place of Liberty: and,
leaving Sanctions, Federation, and what Oaths there may be,
to shift for themselves, does now refer—to what, thinks an
august Assembly? To that 'Declaration of the Twenty-third
of June,' with its "*Seul il fera*, He alone will make his People
happy." As if *that* were not buried, deep enough, under two
irrevocable Twelvemonths, and the wreck and rubbish of a
whole Feudal World! This strange autograph Letter the
National Assembly decides on printing; on transmitting to
the Eighty-three Departments, with exegetic commentary,
short but pithy. Commissioners also shall go forth on all
sides; the People be exhorted; the Armies be increased; care
taken that the Commonweal suffer no damage.—And now,
with a sublime air of calmness, nay of indifference, 'we pass
to the order of the day!'

By such sublime calmness, the terror of the People is
calmed. These gleaming Pike-forests, which bristled fateful
in the early sun, disappear again; the far-sounding Street-
orators cease, or spout milder. We are to have a civil war;
let us have it then. The King is gone; but National
Assembly, but France and we remain. The People also takes
a great attitude; the People also is calm; motionless as a

ouchant lion. With but a few *broolings*, some waggings of
he tail; to show what it *will* do! Cazalès, for instance, was
eset by street-groups, and cries of *Lanterne;* but National
'atrols easily delivered him. Likewise all King's effigies and
tatues, at least stucco ones, get abolished. Even King's
ames; the word *Roi* fades suddenly out of all shop-signs;
he Royal Bengal Tiger itself on the Boulevards, becomes the
Jational Bengal one, *Tigre National.*

How great is a calm couchant People! On the morrow,
nen will say to one another: "We have no King, yet we
lept sound enough." On the morrow, fervent Achille de
Châtelet, and Thomas Paine the rebellious Needleman, shall
ave the walls of Paris profusely plastered with their Placard;
nnouncing that there must be a *Republic.*—Need we add,
hat Lafayette too, though at first menaced by Pikes, has
aken a great attitude, or indeed the greatest of all? Scouts
nd Aides-de-camp fly forth, vague, in quest and pursuit;
roung Romœuf towards Valenciennes, though with small
hope.

Thus Paris; sublimely calmed, in its bereavement. But
from the *Messageries Royales*, in all Mail-bags, radiates forth
far-darting the electric news: Our Hereditary Representative
is flown. Laugh, black Royalists: yet be it in your sleeve
only; lest Patriotism notice, and waxing frantic, lower the
Lanterne! In Paris alone is a sublime National Assembly
with its calmness; truly, other places must take it as they
can: with open mouth and eyes; with panic cackling, with
wrath, with conjecture. How each one of those dull leathern
Diligences, with its leathern bag and 'The King is fled,'
furrows up smooth France as it goes; through town and
hamlet, ruffles the smooth public mind into quivering agitation of death-terror; then lumbers on, as if nothing had
happened! Along all highways; towards the utmost borders;
till all France is ruffled,—roughened up (metaphorically speaking) into one enormous, desperate-minded, red guggling Turkey
Cock!

For example, it is under cloud of night that the leathern
Monster reaches Nantes; deep sunk in sleep. The word
spoken rouses all Patriot men: General Dumouriez, enveloped
in roquelaures, has to descend from his bedroom; finds the
street covered with 'four or five thousand -citizens in their
shirts.' Here and there a faint farthing rushlight, hastily
kindled; and so many swart-featured haggard faces with night-

caps pushed back; and the more or less flowing drapery of nightshirt: open-mouthed till the General say his word! And overhead, as always, the Great Bear is turning so quiet round Boötes; steady, indifferent as the leathern Diligence itself. Take comfort, ye men of Nantes; Boötes and the steady Bear are turning; ancient Atlantic still sends his brine, loud-billowing, up your Loire-stream; brandy shall be hot in the stomach: this is not the Last of the Days, but one before the Last.— The fools! If they knew what was doing, in these very instants, also by candlelight, in the far Northeast!

Perhaps, we may say, the most terrified man in Paris or France is—who, thinks the Reader?—seagreen Robespierre. Double paleness, with the shadow of gibbets and halters, overcasts the seagreen features: it is too clear to him that there is to be 'a Saint-Bartholomew of Patriots,' that in four-and-twenty hours he will not be in life. These horrid anticipations of the soul he is heard uttering at Pétion's: by a notable witness. By Madame Roland, namely; her whom we saw, last year, radiant at the Lyons Federation. These four months, the Rolands have been in Paris; arranging with Assembly Committees the Municipal affairs of Lyons, affairs all sunk in debt;—communing, the while, as was most natural, with the best Patriots to be found here, with our Brissots, Pétions, Buzots, Robespierres: who were wont to come to us, says the fair Hostess, four evenings in the week. They, running about, busier than ever this day, would fain have comforted the seagreen man; spake of Achille de Châtelet's Placard; of a Journal to be called *The Republican;* of preparing men's minds for a Republic. "A Republic?" said the Seagreen, with one of his dry husky *un*sportful laughs, "What is that?" O seagreen Incorruptible, thou shalt see!

CHAPTER V

THE NEW BERLINE

BUT scouts, all this while, and aides-de-camp, have flown forth faster than the leathern Diligences. Young Romœuf, as we said, was off early towards Valenciennes: distracted Villagers seize him, as a traitor with a finger of his own in the plot; drag him back to the Townhall; to the National Assembly, which speedily grants a new passport. Nay now, that same scarecrow of an Herb-merchant with his ass has bethought him of the grand new Berline seen in the Wood of Bondy; and delivered evidence of it; Romœuf, furnished with new passport, is sent forth with double speed on a hopefuller track; by Bondy, Claye and Châlons, towards Metz, to track the new Berline; and gallops *à franc étrier*.

Miserable new Berline! Why could not Royalty go in some old Berline similar to that of other men? Flying for life, one does not stickle about his vehicle. Monsieur, in a commonplace travelling-carriage, is off Northwards; Madame, his Princess, in another, with variation of route: they cross one another while changing horses, without look of recognition; and reach Flanders, no man questioning them. Precisely in the same manner, beautiful Princess de Lamballe set off, about the same hour; and will reach England safe:—would she had continued there! The beautiful, the good, but the unfortunate; reserved for a frightful end!

All runs along, unmolested, speedy, except only the new Berline. Huge leathern vehicle:—huge Argosy, let us say, or Acapulco-ship; with its heavy stern-boat of Chaise-and-pair; with its three yellow Pilot-boats of mounted Bodyguard Couriers, rocking aimless round it and ahead of it, to bewilder, not to guide! It lumbers along, lurchingly with stress, at a snail's pace; noted of all the world. The Bodyguard Couriers, in their yellow liveries, go prancing and clattering; loyal but stupid: unacquainted with all things. Stoppages occur; and breakages, to be repaired at Étoges. King Louis too will dismount, will walk up hills, and enjoy the blessed sunshine:—with eleven horses and double drink-money, and all furtherances of Nature and Art, it will be found that Royalty, flying for life, accomplishes Sixty-nine miles in Twenty-two incessant hours. Slow Royalty! And yet not a minute of these hours but is precious: on minutes hang the destinies of Royalty now.

Readers, therefore, can judge in what humour Duke de Choiseul might stand waiting, in the village of Pont-de-Sommevelle, some leagues beyond Châlons, hour after hour, now when the day bends visibly westward. Choiseul drove out of Paris, in all privity, ten hours before their Majesties' fixed time; his Hussars, led by Engineer Goguelat, are here duly, come 'to escort a treasure that is expected:' but, hour after hour, is no Baroness de Korff's Berline. Indeed, over all that Northeast Region, on the skirts of Champagne and of Lorraine, where the great Road runs, the agitation is considerable.

For all along, from this Pont-de-Sommevelle Northeastward as far as Montmédi, at Post-villages and Towns, escorts of Hussars and Dragoons do lounge waiting; a train or chain of Military Escorts; at the Montmédi end of it our brave Bouillé: an electric thunder-chain; which the invisible Bouillé, like a Father Jove, holds in his hand—for wise purposes! Brave Bouillé has done what man could; has spread out his electric thunder-chain of Military Escorts, onwards to the threshold of Châlons: it waits but for the new Korff Berline; to receive it, escort it, and, if need be, bear it off in whirlwind of military fire. They lie and lounge there, we say, these fierce Troopers; from Montmédi and Stenai, through Clermont, Sainte-Menehould to utmost Pont-de-Sommevelle, in all Post-villages; for the route shall avoid Verdun and great Towns: they loiter impatient, 'till the Treasure arrive.'

Judge what a day this is for brave Bouillé: perhaps the first day of a new glorious life; surely the last day of the old! Also, and indeed still more, what a day beautiful and terrible, for your young full-blooded Captains: your Dandoins, Comte de Damas, Duke de Choiseul, Engineer Goguelat, and the like; entrusted with the secret!—Alas, the day bends ever more westward; and no Korff Berline comes to sight. It is four hours beyond the time, and still no Berline. In all Village-streets, Royalist Captains go lounging, looking often Paris-ward; with face of unconcern, with heart full of black care: rigorous Quartermasters can hardly keep the private dragoons from *cafés* and dramshops. Dawn on our bewilderment, thou new Berline; dawn on us, thou Sun-Chariot of a new Berline, with the destinies of France!

It was of his Majesty's ordering, this military array of Escorts: a thing solacing the Royal imagination with a look of security and rescue; yet, in reality, creating only alarm, and, where there was otherwise no danger, danger without end. For each Patriot, in these Post-villages, asks naturally: This clatter of cavalry, and marching and lounging of troops, what means it? To escort a Treasure? Why escort, when no Patriot will steal from the Nation; or where is your Treasure? —There has been such marching and counter-marching: for it is another fatality, that certain of these Military Escorts came out so early as yesterday; the Nineteenth not the Twentieth of the month being the day *first* appointed; which her Majesty, for some necessity or other, saw good to alter. And now consider the suspicious nature of Patriotism; suspicious, above all, of Bouillé the Aristocrat; and how the sour doubting humour has had leave to accumulate and exacerbate for four-and-twenty hours!

At Pont-de-Sommevelle, these Forty foreign Hussars of Goguelat and Duke Choiseul are becoming an unspeakable mystery to all men. They lounged long enough, already, at Sainte-Menehould; lounged and loitered till our National Volunteers there, all risen into hot wrath of doubt, 'demanded three hundred fusils of their Townhall,' and got them. At which same moment too, as it chanced, our Captain Dandoins was just coming in, from Clermont with *his* troop, at the other end of the Village. A fresh troop; alarming enough; though happily they are only Dragoons and French! So that Goguelat with his Hussars had to ride, and even to do it fast; till here at Pont-de-Sommevelle, where Choiseul lay waiting, he found resting-place. Resting-place as on burning marle. For the rumour of him flies abroad; and men run to and fro in fright and anger: Châlons sends forth exploratory pickets of National Volunteers towards this hand; which meet exploratory pickets, coming from Sainte-Menehould, on that. What is it, ye whiskered Hussars, men of foreign guttural speech; in the name of Heaven, what is it that brings you? A Treasure?— exploratory pickets shake their heads. The hungry Peasants, however, know too well what Treasure it is; Military seizure for rents, feudalities; which no Bailiff could make us pay! This they know;—and set to jingling their parish-bell by way of tocsin; with rapid effect! Choiseul and Goguelat, if the whole country is not to take fire, must needs, be there Berline, be there no Berline, saddle and ride.

They mount; and this parish tocsin happily ceases. They ride slowly Eastward; towards Sainte-Menehould; still hoping the Sun-Chariot of a Berline may overtake them. Ah me, no Berline! And near now is that Sainte-Menehould, which expelled us in the morning, with its 'three hundred National fusils;' which looks, belike, not too lovingly on Captain Dandoins and his fresh Dragoons, though only French;— which, in a word, one dare not enter the *second* time, under pain of explosion! With rather heavy heart, our Hussar Party strikes off to the left; through byways, through pathless hills and woods, they, avoiding Sainte-Menehould and all places which have seen them heretofore, will make direct for the distant Village of Varennes. It is probable they will have a rough evening-ride.

This first military post, therefore, in the long thunder-chain, has gone off with no effect; or with worse, and your chain threatens to entangle itself!—The Great Road, however, is got hushed again into a kind of quietude, though one of the wakefullest. Indolent Dragoons cannot, by any Quartermaster, be kept altogether from the dramshop; where Patriots drink, and will even treat, eager enough for news. Captains, in a state near distraction, beat the dusty highway, with a face of indifference; and no Sun-Chariot appears. Why lingers it? Incredible, that with eleven horses, and such yellow Couriers and furtherances, its rate should be under the weightiest drayrate, some three miles an hour! Alas, one knows not whether it ever even got out of Paris;—and yet also one knows not whether, this very moment, it is not at the Village-end! One's heart flutters on the verge of unutterabilities.

CHAPTER VI

OLD-DRAGOON DROUET

In this manner, however, has the Day bent downwards. Wearied mortals are creeping home from their field-labour; the village-artisan eats with relish his supper of herbs, or has strolled forth to the village-street for a sweet mouthful of air and human news. Still summer-eventide everywhere! The great Sun hangs flaming on the utmost Northwest; for it is his longest day this year. The hill-tops rejoicing will ere long be at their ruddiest, and blush Good-night. The thrush, in green dells, on long-shadowed leafy spray, pours gushing his glad serenade, to the babble of brooks grown audibler; silence is stealing over the Earth. Your dusty Mill of Valmy, as all other mills and drudgeries, may furl its canvass, and cease swashing and circling. The swenkt grinders in this Treadmill of an Earth have ground out another Day; and lounge there, as we say, in village groups; movable, or ranked on social stone-seats; their children, mischievous imps, sporting about their feet. Unnotable hum of sweet human gossip rises from this Village of Sainte-Menehould, as from all other villages. Gossip mostly sweet, unnotable; for the very Dragoons are French and gallant; nor as yet has the Paris-and-Verdun Diligence, with its leathern bag, rumbled in, to terrify the minds of men.

One figure nevertheless we do note at the last door of

the Village: that figure in loose-flowing nightgown, of Jean
Baptiste Drouet, Master of the Post here. An acrid choleric
man, rather dangerous-looking; still in the prime of life,
though he has served, in his time, as a Condé Dragoon.
This day, from an early hour Drouet got his choler stirred,
and has been kept fretting. Hussar Goguelat in the morning
saw good, by way of thrift, to bargain with his own Inn-
keeper, not with Drouet, regular *Maître de Poste*, about
some gig-horse for the sending back of his gig; which thing
Drouet perceiving came over in red ire, menacing the Inn-
keeper, and would not be appeased. Wholly an unsatisfactory
day. For Drouet is an acrid Patriot too, was at the Paris
Feast of Pikes: and what do these Bouillé soldiers mean?
Hussars,—with their gig, and a vengeance to it!—have hardly
been thrust out, when Dandoins and his fresh Dragoons arrive
from Clermont, and stroll. For what purpose? Choleric
Drouet steps out and steps in, with long-flowing nightgown;
looking abroad, with that sharpness of faculty which stirred
choler gives to man.

On the other hand, mark Captain Dandoins on the street of
that same village; sauntering with a face of indifference, a
heart eaten of black care! For no Korff Berline makes its
appearance. The great Sun flames broader towards setting:
one's heart flutters on the verge of dread unutterabilities.

By Heaven! here is the yellow Bodyguard Courier; spurring
fast, in the ruddy evening light! Steady, O Dandoins, stand
with inscrutable indifferent face; though the yellow blockhead spurs past the Post-house; inquires to find it; and stirs
the village, all delighted with his fine livery.—Lumbering
along with its mountains of bandboxes, and Chaise behind,
the Korff Berline rolls in; huge Acapulco-ship with its Cock-
boat, having got thus far. The eyes of the Villagers look
enlightened, as such eyes do when a coach transit, which is an
event, occurs for them. Strolling Dragoons respectfully, so
fine are the yellow liveries, bring hand to helmet; and a Lady
in gypsy-hat responds with a grace peculiar to her. Dandoins
stands with folded arms, and what look of indifference and
disdainful garrison-air a man can, while the heart is like leaping
out of him. Curled disdainful moustachio; careless glance,—
which however surveys the Village-groups, and does not like
them. With his eye he bespeaks the yellow Courier. Be
quick, be quick! Thick-headed Yellow cannot understand the
eye; comes up mumbling, to ask in words: seen of the village!

Nor is Post-master Drouet unobservant, all this while : but steps out and steps in, with his long-flowing nightgown, in the level sunlight ; prying into several things. When a man's faculties, at the right time, are sharpened by choler, it may lead to much. That Lady in slouched gypsy-hat, though sitting back in the Carriage, does she not resemble some one we have seen, some time ;—at the Feast of Pikes, or elsewhere? And this *Grosse-Tête* in round hat and peruke, which, looking rearward, pokes itself out from time to time, methinks there are features in it——? Quick, Sieur Guillaume, Clerk of the *Directoire*, bring me a new Assignat! Drouet scans the new Assignat ; compares the Paper-money picture with the Gross Head in round hat there : by Day and Night! you might say the one was an attempted Engraving of the other. And this march of Troops ; this sauntering and whispering,—I see it!

Drouet Post-master of this Village, hot Patriot, Old-Dragoon of Condé, consider, therefore, what thou wilt do. And fast, for behold the new Berline, expeditiously yoked, cracks whipcord, and rolls away !—Drouet dare not, on the spur of the instant, clutch the bridles in his own two hands ; Dandoins, with broadsword, might hew you off. Our poor Nationals, not one of them here, have three hundred fusils, but then no powder ; besides one is not sure, only morally-certain. Drouet, as an adroit Old-Dragoon of Condé, does what is advisablest ; privily bespeaks Clerk Guillaume, Old-Dragoon of Condé he too ; privily, while Clerk Guillaume is saddling two of the fleetest horses, slips over to the Townhall to whisper a word ; then mounts with Clerk Guillaume ; and the two bound eastward in pursuit, to *see* what can be done.

They bound eastward, in sharp trot : their moral-certainty permeating the Village, from the Townhall outwards, in busy whispers. Alas ! Captain Dandoins orders his Dragoons to mount ; but they, complaining of long fasts, demand bread-and-cheese first ;—before which brief repast can be eaten, the whole Village is permeated ; not whispering now, but blustering and shrieking ! National Volunteers, in hurried muster, shriek for gunpowder ; Dragoons halt between Patriotism and Rule of the Service, between bread-and-cheese and fixed bayonets : Dandoins hands secretly his Pocket-book, with its secret despatches, to the rigorous Quartermaster : the very Ostlers have Stable-forks and flails. The rigorous Quartermaster, half-saddled, cuts out his way with the sword's edge, amid levelled bayonets, amid Patriot vociferations, adjurations,

flail-strokes; and rides frantic;—few or even none following
him; the rest, so sweetly constrained, consenting to stay there.

And thus the new Berline rolls; and Drouet and Guillaume
gallop after it, and Dandoins' Troopers or Trooper gallops
after them; and Sainte-Menehould, with some leagues of the
King's Highway, is in explosion;—and your Military thunder-
chain has gone off in a self-destructive manner; one may fear,
with the frightfullest issues.

CHAPTER VII

THE NIGHT OF SPURS

THIS comes of mysterious Escorts, and a new Berline with
eleven horses: 'he that has a secret should not only hide it,
but hide that he has it to hide.' Your first Military Escort has
exploded self-destructive; and all Military Escorts, and a
suspicious Country will now be up, explosive; comparable *not*
to victorious thunder. Comparable, say rather, to the first
stirring of an Alpine Avalanche; which, once stir it, as here
at Sainte-Menehould, will spread,—all round, and on and
on, as far as Stenai; thundering with wild ruin, till Patriot
Villagers, Peasantry, Military Escorts, new Berline and Royalty
are down,—jumbling in the Abyss!

The thick shades of Night are falling. Postilions crack and
whip: the Royal Berline is through Clermont, where Colonel
Comte de Damas got a word whispered to it; is safe through,
towards Varennes; rushing at the rate of double drink-money:
an Unknown, '*Inconnu* on horseback,' shrieks earnestly some
hoarse whisper, not audible, into the rushing Carriage-window,
and vanishes, left in the night. August Travellers palpitate;
nevertheless overwearied Nature sinks every one of them into
a kind of sleep. Alas, and Drouet and Clerk Guillaume spur;
taking side-roads, for shortness, for safety; scattering abroad
that moral-certainty of theirs; which flies, a bird of the air
carrying it!

And your rigorous Quartermaster spurs; awakening hoarse
trumpet-tone,—as here at Clermont, calling out Dragoons gone
to bed. Brave Colonel de Damas has them mounted, in part,
these Clermont men; young Cornet Remy dashes off with a
few. But the Patriot Magistracy is out here at Clermont too;
National Guards shrieking for ball-cartridges; and the Village
'illuminates itself;'— deft Patriots springing out of bed;

alertly, in shirt or shift, striking a light; sticking up each his farthing candle, or penurious oil-cruse, till all glitters and glimmers; so deft are they! A *camisado*, or shirt-tumult, everywhere: storm-bell set a-ringing; village-drum beating furious *générale*, as here at Clermont, under illumination; distracted Patriots pleading and menacing! Brave young Colonel de Damas, in that uproar of distracted Patriotism, speaks some fire-sentences to what Troopers he has: "Comrades insulted at Sainte-Menehould: King and Country calling on the brave;" then gives the fire-word, *Draw swords*. Whereupon, alas, the Troopers only *smite* their sword-handles, driving them further home! "To me, whoever is for the King!" cries Damas in despair; and gallops, he with some poor loyal Two, of the Subaltern sort, into the bosom of the Night.

Night unexampled in the Clermontais; shortest of the year; remarkablest of the century: Night deserving to be named of Spurs! Cornet Remy, and those Few he dashed off with, has missed his road; is galloping for hours towards Verdun; then, for hours, across hedged country, through roused hamlets, towards Varennes. Unlucky Cornet Remy; unluckier Colonel Damas, with whom there ride desperate only some loyal Two! More ride not of that Clermont Escort: of other Escorts, in other Villages, not even Two may ride; but only all curvet and prance,—impeded by storm-bell and your Village illuminating itself.

And Drouet rides and Clerk Guillaume; and the Country runs.—Goguelat and Duke Choiseul are plunging through morasses, over cliffs, over stock and stone, in the shaggy woods of the Clermontais; by tracks; or trackless, with guides; Hussars tumbling into pitfalls, and lying 'swooned three quarters of an hour,' the rest refusing to march without them. What an evening-ride from Pont-de-Sommevelle; what a thirty hours, since Choiseul quitted Paris, with Queen's-valet Leonard in the chaise by him! Black Care sits behind the rider. Thus go they plunging; rustle the owlet from his branchy nest; champ the sweet-scented forest-herb, queen-of-the-meadows *spilling* her spikenard; and frighten the ear of Night. But hark! towards twelve o'clock, as one guesses, for the very stars are gone out: sound of the tocsin from Varennes? Checking bridle, the Hussar Officer listens: "Some fire undoubtedly!"—yet rides on, with double breath-lessness, to verify.

Yes, gallant friends that do your utmost, it is a certain sort of fire : difficult to quench.—The Korff Berline, fairly ahead of all this riding Avalanche, reached the little paltry Village of Varennes about eleven o'clock ; hopeful, in spite of that hoarse-whispering Unknown. Do not all Towns now lie behind us ; Verdun avoided on our right ? Within wind of Bouillé himself, in a manner ; and the darkest of midsummer nights favouring us ! And so we halt on the hill-top at the South end of the Village ; expecting our relay ; which young Bouillé, Bouillé's own son, with his Escort of Hussars, was to have ready ; for in this Village is no Post. Distracting to think of : neither horse nor Hussar is here ! Ah, and stout horses, a proper relay belonging to Duke Choiseul, do stand at hay, but in the Upper Village over the Bridge ; and we know not of them. Hussars likewise do wait, but drinking in the taverns. For indeed it is six hours beyond the time ; young Bouillé, silly stripling, thinking the matter over for this night, has retired to bed. And so our yellow Couriers, in-experienced, must rove, groping, bungling, though a Village mostly asleep : Postilions will not, for any money, go on with the tired horses ; not at least without refreshment ; not they, let the Valet in round hat argue as he likes.

Miserable ! 'For five-and-thirty minutes' by the King's watch, the Berline is at a dead stand : Round-hat arguing with Churn-boots ; tired horses slobbering their meal-and-water ; yellow Couriers groping, bungling ;—young Bouillé asleep, all the while, in the Upper Village, and Choiseul's fine team standing at hay. No help for it ; not with a King's ransom ; the horses deliberately slobber, Round-hat argues, Bouillé sleeps. And mark now, in the thick night, do not two Horse-men, with jaded trot, come clank-clanking ; and start with half-pause, if one noticed them, at sight of this dim mass of a Berline, and its dull slobbering and arguing ; then prick off faster, into the Village ? It is Drouet, he and Clerk Guillaume ! Still ahead, they two, of the whole, riding hurly-burly ; unshot, though some brag of having chased them. Perilous is Drouet's errand also ; but he is an Old-Dragoon, with his wits shaken thoroughly awake.

The Village of Varennes lies dark and slumberous ; a most unlevel Village, of inverse saddle-shape, as men write. It sleeps ; the rushing of the River Aire singing lullaby to it. Nevertheless from the Golden Arm, *Bras d'Or* Tavern, across that sloping Marketplace, there still comes shine of social light; comes voice of rude drovers, or the like, who have not yet taken the stirrup-cup; Boniface Le Blanc, in white apron, serving them; cheerful to behold. To this *Bras d'Or*, Drouet enters, alacrity looking through his eyes; he nudges Boniface, in all privacy, " *Camarade, es-tu bon Patriote*, Art thou a good Patriot?"—" *Si je suis!*" answers Boniface.—"In that case," eagerly whispers Drouet—what whisper is needful, heard of Boniface alone.

And now see Boniface Le Blanc bustling, as he never did for the jolliest toper. See Drouet and Guillaume, dexterous Old-Dragoons, instantly down blocking the Bridge, with a 'furniture-wagon they find there,' with whatever wagons, tumbrils, barrels, barrows their hands can lay hold of;—till no carriage can pass. Then swiftly, the Bridge once blocked, see them take station hard by, under Varennes Archway: joined by Le Blanc, Le Blanc's Brother, and one or two alert Patriots he has roused. Some half-dozen in all, with National muskets, they stand close, waiting under the Archway, till that same Korff Berline rumble up.

It rumbles up: *Alte là!* lanterns flash out from under coat-skirts, bridles chuck in strong fists, two National muskets level themselves fore and aft through the two Coach-doors. "Mesdames, your Passports?"—Alas, alas! Sieur Sausse, Procureur of the Township, Tallow-chandler also and Grocer, is there, with official grocer-politeness; Drouet with fierce logic and ready wit:—The respected Travelling Party, be it Baroness de Korff's, or persons of still higher consequence, will perhaps please to rest itself in M. Sausse's till the dawn strike up!

O Louis; O hapless Marie-Antoinette, fated to pass thy life with such men! Phlegmatic Louis, art thou but lazy semi-animate phlegm then, to the centre of thee? King, Captain-General, Sovereign Frank! if thy heart ever formed, since it began beating under the name of heart, any resolution at all, be it now then, or never in this world:—"Violent nocturna individuals, and if it were persons of high consequence? And if it were the King himself? Has the King not the power which all beggars have, of travelling unmolested on his own Highway? Yes: it is the King; and tremble ye to know it The King has said, in this one small matter; and in France or under God's Throne, is no power that shall gainsay. No the King shall ye stop here under this your miserable Arch way; but his dead body only, and answer it to Heaven and

Earth. To me, Bodyguards; Postilions, *en avant!*"—One fancies in that case the pale paralysis of these two Le Blanc musketeers; the drooping of Drouet's underjaw; and how Procureur Sausse had melted like tallow in furnace-heat: Louis faring on; in some few steps awakening Young Bouillé, awakening relays and Hussars: triumphant entry, with caval-cading high-brandishing Escort, and Escorts, into Montmédi; and the whole course of French History different!

Alas, it was not *in* the poor phlegmatic man. Had it been in him, French History had never come under this Varennes Archway to decide itself.—He steps out; all step out. Pro-cureur Sausse gives his grocer-arms to the Queen and Sister Elizabeth, Majesty taking the two Children by the hand. And thus they walk, coolly back, over the Marketplace, to Procureur Sausse's; mount into his small upper story; where straightway his Majesty 'demands refreshments.' Demands refreshments, as is written; gets bread-and-cheese with a bottle of Burgundy; and remarks, that it is the best Burgundy he ever drank!

Meanwhile, the Varennes Notables, and all men, official and non-official, are hastily drawing on their breeches; getting their fighting gear. Mortals half-dressed tumble out barrels, lay felled trees; scouts dart off to all the four winds,—the tocsin begins clanging, 'the Village illuminates itself.' Very singular: how these little Villages do manage, so adroit are they, when startled in midnight alarm of war. Like little adroit municipal rattle-snakes, suddenly awakened: for their storm-bell rattles and rings; their eyes glisten luminous (with tallow-light), as in rattle-snake ire; and the Village will *sting*. Old-Dragoon Drouet is our engineer and generalissimo; valiant as a Ruy Diaz:—Now or never, ye Patriots, for the soldiery is coming; massacre by Austrians, by Aristocrats, wars more than civil, it all depends on you and the hour!— National Guards rank themselves, half-buttoned: mortals, we say, still only in breeches, in under-petticoat, tumble out barrels and lumber, lay felled trees for barricades: the Village will *sting*. Rabid Democracy, it would seem, is *not* confined to Paris, then? Ah no, whatsoever Courtiers might talk; too clearly no. This of dying for one's King is grown into a dying for one's self, *against* the King, if need be.

And so our riding and running Avalanche and Hurlyburly has *reached* the Abyss, Korff Berline foremost; and may pour itself thither, and jumble: endless! For the next six hours, need we ask if there was a clattering far and wide? Clattering and tocsining and hot tumult, over all the Clermontais, spreading through the Three-Bishopricks: Dragoon and Hussar Troops galloping on roads and no-roads; National Guards arming and starting in the dead of night; tocsin after tocsin transmitting the alarm. In some forty minutes, Goguelat and Choiseul, with their wearied Hussars, reach Varennes. Ah, it is no fire, then; or a fire difficult to quench! They leap the tree-barricades, in spite of National sergeant; they enter the village, Choiseul instructing his Troopers how the matter really is; who respond interjectionally, in their guttural dialect, "*Der König; die Königinn!*" and seem stanch. These now, in their stanch humour, will, for one thing, beset Procureur Sausse's house. Most beneficial: had not Drouet stormfully ordered otherwise; and even bellowed in his extremity, "Cannoneers, to your guns!"—two old honeycombed Field-pieces, empty of all but cobwebs; the rattle whereof, as the Cannoneers with assured countenance trundled them up, did nevertheless abate the Hussar ardour, and produce a respect-fuller ranking further back. Jugs of wine, handed over the ranks,—for the German throat too has sensibility,—will complete the business. When Engineer Goguelat, some hour or so afterwards, steps forth, the response to him is—a hiccuping *Vive la Nation!*

What boots it? Goguelat, Choiseul, now also Count Damas, and all the Varennes Officiality are with the King; and the King can give no order, form no opinion; but sits there, as he has ever done, like clay on potter's wheel; perhaps the absurdest of all pitiable and pardonable clay-figures that now circle under the Moon. He will go on, next morning, and take the National Guard *with* him; Sausse permitting! Hapless Queen: with her two children laid there on the mean bed, old Mother Sausse kneeling to Heaven, with tears and an audible prayer, to bless them; imperial Marie-Antoinette near kneeling to Son Sausse and Wife Sausse, amid candle-boxes and treacle-barrels,—in vain! There are Three thousand National Guards got in; before long they will count Ten thousand: tocsins spreading like fire on dry heath, or far faster.

Young Bouillé, roused by this Varennes tocsin, has taken horse, and—fled towards his Father. Thitherward also rides, in an almost hysterically desperate manner, a certain Sieur

Aubriot, Choiseul's Orderly; swimming dark rivers, our Bridge being blocked; spurring as if the Hell-hunt were at his heels. Through the village of Dun, he galloping still on, scatters the alarm; at Dun, brave Captain Deslons and *his* Escort of a Hundred saddle and ride. Deslons too got into Varennes; leaving his Hundred outside, at the tree-barricade; offer to cut King Louis out, if he will order it: but unfortunately "the work *will* prove hot;" whereupon King Louis has "no orders to give."

And so the tocsin clangs, and Dragoons gallop, and can do nothing, having galloped; National Guards stream in like the gathering of ravens: your exploding Thunder-chain, falling Avalanche, or what else we liken it to, does play, with a vengeance,—up now as far as Stenai and Bouillé himself. Brave Bouillé, son of the whirlwind, he saddles Royal-Allemand; speaks fire-words, kindling heart and eyes; distributes twenty-five gold-louis a company:—Ride, Royal-Allemand, long-famed: no Tuileries Charge and Necker-Orleans Bust-Procession (i. 142): a very King made captive, and world all to win!—Such is the Night deserving to be named of Spurs.

At six o'clock two things have happened. Lafayette's Aide-de-camp, Romœuf, riding *à franc étrier*, on that old Herb-merchant's route, quickened during the last stages, has got to Varennes; where the Ten thousand now furiously demand, with fury of panic terror, that Royalty shall forthwith return Paris-ward, that there be not infinite bloodshed. Also, on the other side 'English Tom,' Choiseul's *jokei*, flying with that Choiseul relay, has met Bouillé on the heights of Dun; the adamantine brow flushed with dark thunder; thunderous rattle of Royal-Allemand at his heels. English Tom answers as he can the brief question, How it is at Varennes?—then asks in turn, What he, English Tom, with M. de Choiseul's horses, is to do, and whither to ride?—To the Bottomless Pool! answers a thunder-voice; then again speaking and spurring, orders Royal-Allemand to the gallop; and vanishes, swearing (*en jurant*). 'Tis the last of our brave Bouillé. Within sight of Varennes, he having drawn bridle, calls a council of officers; finds that it is in vain. King Louis has departed, consenting: amid the clangour of universal stormbell; amid the tramp of Ten thousand armed men, already arrived; and say, of Sixty thousand flocking thither. Brave Deslons, even without 'orders,' darted at the River Aire with his Hundred; swam one branch of it, could not the other; and stood there, dripping and panting, with inflated nostril; the Ten thousand answering him with a shout of mockery, the new Berline lumbering Paris-ward its weary inevitable way. No help, then, in Earth; nor, in an age not of miracles, in Heaven!

That night, 'Marquis de Bouillé and twenty-one more of us rode over the Frontiers: the Bernardine monks at Orval in Luxemburg gave us supper and lodging.' With little of speech, Bouillé rides; with thoughts that do not brook speech. Northwards, towards uncertainty, and the Cimmerian Night: towards West-Indian Isles, for with thin Emigrant delirium the son of the whirlwind cannot act; towards England, towards premature Stoical death; not towards France any more. Honour to the Brave; who, be it in this quarrel or in that, *is* a substance and articulate-speaking piece of human Valour, not a fanfaronading hollow Spectrum and squeaking and gibbering shadow! One of the few Royalist Chief-actors this Bouillé, of whom so much can be said.

The brave Bouillé too, then, vanishes from the tissue of our Story. Story and tissue, faint ineffectual Emblem of that grand Miraculous Tissue, and Living Tapestry named *French Revolution*, which did weave itself then in very fact, 'on the loud-sounding Loom of Time!' The old Brave drop out from it, with their strivings; and new acrid Drouets, of new strivings and colour, come in:—as is the manner of that weaving.

CHAPTER VIII

THE RETURN

So, then, our grand Royalist Plot, of Flight to Metz, has *executed* itself. Long hovering in the background, as a dread royal *ultimatum*, it has rushed forward in its terrors: verily to some purpose. How many Royalist Plots and Projects, one after another, cunningly-devised, that were to explode like powder-mines and thunder-claps; not one solitary Plot of which has issued otherwise! Powder-mine of a *Séance Royale* on the Twenty-third of June 1789, which exploded as we then said, 'through the touchhole;' which next, your wargod Broglie having *re*loaded it, brought a Bastille about your ears. Then came fervent Opera-Repast, with flourishing of sabres, and

O Richard, O my King; which, aided by Hunger, produces Insurrection of Women, and Pallas Athene in the shape of Demoiselle Théroigne. Valour profits not; neither has fortune smiled on fanfaronade. The Bouillé Armament ends as the Broglie one had done. Man after man spends himself in this cause, only to work it quicker ruin; it seems a cause doomed, forsaken of Earth and Heaven.

On the Sixth of October gone a year, King Louis, escorted by Demoiselle Théroigne and some two hundred thousand, made a Royal Progress and Entrance into Paris, such as man had never witnessed; we prophesied him Two more such; and accordingly another of them, after this Flight to Metz, is now coming to pass. Théroigne will not escort here; neither does Mirabeau now 'sit in one of the accompanying carriages.' Mirabeau lies dead, in the Pantheon of Great Men. Théroigne lies living, in dark Austrian Prison; having gone to Liège, professionally, and been seized there. Bemurmured now by the hoarse-flowing Danube: the light of her Patriot Supper-parties gone quite out; so lies Théroigne: she shall speak with the Kaiser face to face, and return. And France lies—how! Fleeting time shears down the great and the little; and in two years alters many things.

But at all events, here, we say, is a second Ignominious Royal Procession, though much altered; to be witnessed also by its hundreds of thousands. Patience, ye Paris Patriots; the Royal Berline is returning. Not till Saturday: for the Royal Berline travels by slow stages; amid such loud-voiced confluent sea of National Guards, sixty thousand as they count; amid such tumult of all people. Three National-Assembly Commissioners, famed Barnave, famed Pétion, generally-respectable Latour-Maubourg, have gone to meet it; of whom the two former ride in the Berline itself beside Majesty, day after day. Latour, as a mere respectability, and man of whom all men speak well, can ride in the rear, with Dame de Tourzel and the *Soubrettes*.

So on Saturday evening, about seven o'clock, Paris by hundreds of thousands is again drawn up: not now dancing the tricolor joy-dance of hope; nor as yet dancing in fury-dance of hate and revenge: but in silence, with vague look of conjecture, and curiosity mostly scientific. A Saint-Antoine Placard has given notice this morning that 'whosoever insults Louis shall be caned, whosoever applauds him shall be hanged.' Behold then, at last, that wonderful new Berline; encircled by blue National sea with fixed bayonets, which flows slowly, floating it on, through the silent assembled hundreds of thousands. Three yellow Couriers sit atop bound with ropes. Pétion, Barnave, their Majesties, with Sister Elizabeth, and the Children of France, are within.

Smile of embarrassment, or cloud of dull sourness, is on the broad phlegmatic face of his Majesty; who keeps declaring to the successive Official persons, what is evident, "*Eh bien, me voilà*, Well, here you have me;" and what is not evident, "I do assure you I did not mean to pass the frontiers;" and so forth: speeches natural for that poor Royal Man; which Decency would veil. Silent is her Majesty, with a look of grief and scorn; natural for that Royal Woman. Thus lumbers and creeps the ignominious Royal Procession, through many streets, amid a silent-gazing people: comparable, Mercier thinks, to some *Procession du Roi de Basoche ;* or say, Procession of King Crispin, with his Dukes of Sutor-mania and royal blazonry of Cordwainery. Except indeed that this is *not* comic; ah, no, it is comico-tragic; with bound Couriers, and a Doom hanging over it; most fantastic, yet most miserably real. Miserablest *flebile ludibrium* of a Pickle-herring Tragedy ! It sweeps along there, in most *un*gorgeous Pall, through many streets in the dusty summer evening; gets itself at length wriggled out of sight; vanishing in the Tuileries Palace—towards its doom, of slow torture, *peine forte et dure.*

Populace, it is true, seizes the three rope-bound yellow Couriers; will at least massacre *them.* But our august Assembly, which is sitting at this great moment, sends out Deputation of rescue; and the whole is got huddled up. Barnave, 'all dusty,' is already there, in the National Hall; making brief discreet address and report. As indeed, through the whole journey, this Barnave has been most discreet, sympathetic; and has gained the Queen's trust, whose noble instinct teaches her always who is to be trusted. Very different from heavy Pétion; who, if Campan speak truth, ate his luncheon, comfortably filled his wine-glass, in the Royal Berline; flung out his chicken-bones past the nose of Royalty itself; and, on the King's saying, "France cannot be a Republic," answered, "No, it is not ripe yet." Barnave is henceforth a Queen's adviser, if advice could profit: and her Majesty astonishes Dame Campan by signifying almost a regard for Barnave; and that, in a day of retribution and Royal triumph, Barnave shall *not* be executed.

On Monday night Royalty went; on Saturday evening it
returns: so much, within one short week, has Royalty accomplished for itself. The Pickle-herring Tragedy has vanished
in the Tuileries Palace, towards 'pain strong and hard.'
Watched, fettered and humbled as Royalty never was.
Watched even in its sleeping apartments and inmost recesses:
for it has to sleep with door set ajar, blue National Argus
watching, his eye fixed on the Queen's curtains; nay, on one
occasion, as the Queen cannot sleep, he offers to sit by her
pillow, and converse a little!

CHAPTER IX

SHARP SHOT

In regard to all which, this most pressing question arises:
What is to be done with it? Depose it! resolutely answer
Robespierre and the thoroughgoing few. For, truly, with a
King who runs away, and needs to be watched in his very bedroom that he may stay and govern you, what other reasonable
thing can be done? Had Philippe d'Orléans not been a *caput
mortuum!* But of him, known as one defunct, no man now
dreams. Depose it not; say that it is inviolable, that it was
spirited away, was *enlevé;* at any cost of sophistry and solecism,
reestablish it! so answer with loud vehemence all manner of
constitutional Royalists; as all your pure Royalists do naturally
likewise, with low vehemence, and rage compressed by fear, still
more passionately answer. Nay, Barnave and the two Lameths,
and what will follow them, do likewise answer so. Answer,
with their whole might: terrorstruck at the unknown Abysses
on the verge of which, driven thither by themselves mainly, all
now reels, ready to plunge.

By mighty effort and combination, this latter course is the
course fixed on; and it shall by the strong arm, if not by the
clearest logic, be made good. With the sacrifice of all their
hard-earned popularity, this notable Triumvirate, says Toulongeon, 'set the Throne up again, which they had so toiled to
overturn: as one might set up an overturned pyramid, on its
vertex;' to stand so long as it is *held.*

Unhappy France; unhappy in King, Queen and Constitution; one knows not in which unhappiest! Was the meaning
of our so glorious French Revolution this, and no other, That
when Shams and Delusions, long soul-killing, had become

body-killing, and got the length of Bankruptcy and Inanition, a great People rose and, with one voice, said, in the Name of the Highest: *Shams shall be no more?* So many sorrows and bloody horrors, endured, and to be yet endured through dismal coming centuries, were they not the heavy price paid and payable for this same: Total Destruction of Shams from among men? And now, O Barnave Triumvirate! is it in such *double*-distilled Delusion, and Sham even of a Sham, that an effort of this kind will rest acquiescent? Messieurs of the popular Triumvirate, never!—But after all, what can poor popular Triumvirates, and fallible august Senators, do? They can, when the truth is all too horrible, stick their heads ostrich-like into what sheltering Fallacy is nearest; and wait there, *a posteriori*.

Readers who saw the Clermontais and Three-Bishopricks gallop in the Night of Spurs; Diligences ruffling up all France into one terrific terrified Cock of India; and the Town of Nantes in its shirt,—may fancy what an affair to settle this was. Robespierre, on the extreme Left, with perhaps Pétion and lean old Goupil, for the very Triumvirate has defalcated, are shrieking hoarse; drowned in Constitutional clamour. But the debate and arguing of a whole Nation; the bellowings through all Journals, for and against; the reverberant voice of Danton; the Hyperion shafts of Camille, the porcupine-quills of implacable Marat:—conceive all this.

Constitutionalists in a body, as we often predicted, do now recede from the Mother Society, and become *Feuillans*, threatening her with inanition, the rank and respectability being mostly gone. Petition after Petition, forwarded by Post, or borne in Deputation, comes praying for Judgment and *Déchéance*, which is our name for Deposition; praying at lowest for Reference to the Eighty-three Departments of France. Hot Marseillese Deputation comes declaring, among other things: "Our Phocean Ancestors flung a bar of Iron into the Bay at their first landing: this Bar will float again on the Mediterranean brine before we consent to be slaves." All this for four weeks or more, while the matter still hangs doubtful; Emigration streaming with double violence over the frontiers; France seething in fierce agitation of this question and prize question; What is to be done with the fugitive Hereditary Representative?

Finally, on Friday the 15th of July 1791, the National

Assembly decides; in what negatory manner we know. Whereupon the Theatres all close, the *Bourne*-stones and Portable-chairs begin spouting. Municipal Placards flaming on the walls, and Proclamations published by sound of trumpet, 'invite to repose;' with small effect. And so, on Sunday the 17th, there shall be a thing seen, worthy of remembering. Scroll of a Petition, drawn up by Brissots, Dantons, by Cordeliers, Jacobins; for the thing was infinitely shaken and manipulated, and many had a hand in it : such Scroll lies now visible, on the wooden framework of the Fatherland's Altar, for signature. Unworking Paris, male and female, is crowding thither, all day, to sign or to see. Our fair Roland herself the eye of History can discern there ' in the morning;' not without interest. In few weeks the fair Patriot will quit Paris ; yet perhaps only to return.

But, what with sorrow of balked Patriotism, what with closed theatres, and Proclamations still publishing themselves by sound of trumpet, the fervour of men's minds, this day, is great. Nay, over and above, there has fallen out an incident, of the nature of Farce-Tragedy and Riddle ; enough to stimulate all creatures. Early in the Day, a Patriot (or some say, it was a Patriotess, and indeed the truth is undiscoverable), while standing on the firm deal-board of Fatherland's Altar, feels suddenly, with indescribable torpedo-shock of amazement, his bootsole pricked through from below; clutches up suddenly this electrified bootsole and foot; discerns next instant—the point of a gimlet or bradawl playing up, through the firm deal-board, and now hastily drawing itself back ! Mystery, perhaps Treason ? The wooden framework is impetuously broken up; and behold, verily a mystery, never explicable fully to the end of the world ! Two human individuals of mean aspect, one of them with a wooden leg, lie ensconced there, gimlet in hand : they must have come in overnight; they have a supply of provisions,—no ' barrel of gunpowder' that one can *see;* they affect to be asleep ; look blank enough, and give the lamest account of themselves. " Mere curiosity ; they were boring up, to get an eyehole; to see, perhaps 'with lubricity,' whatsoever, from that *new* point of vision, could be seen :"—little that was edifying, one would think ! But indeed what stupidest thing may not human Dulness, Pruriency, Lubricity, Chance and the Devil, choosing Two out of Half-a-million idle human heads, tempt them to ?

Sure enough, the two human individuals with their gimlet

are there. Ill-starred pair of individuals! For the result o
it all is, that Patriotism, fretting itself, in this state of nervou
excitability, with hypotheses, suspicions and reports, keep
questioning these two distracted human individuals, and agair
questioning them; claps them into the nearest Guardhouse
clutches them out again; one hypothetic group snatching then
from another: till finally, in such extreme state of nervou
excitability, Patriotism hangs them as spies of Sieur Motier
and the life and secret is choked out of them forevermore
Forevermore, alas! Or is a day to be looked for when these
two evidently mean individuals, who are human nevertheless
will become Historical Riddles; and, like him of the *Iror
Mask* (also a human individual, and evidently nothing more)
—have their Dissertations? To us this only is certain, tha
they had a gimlet, provisions and a wooden leg; and have diec
there on the Lanterne, as the unluckiest fools might die.

And so the signature goes on, in a still more excited manner
And Chaumette, for Antiquarians possess the very Paper to thi
hour,—has signed himself 'in a flowing saucy hand slightly
leaned;' and Hébert, detestable *Père Duchesne*, as if 'an inkec
spider had dropped on the paper;' Usher Maillard also ha
signed, and many Crosses, which cannot write. And Paris
through its thousand avenues, is welling to the Champ-de-Mar
and from it, in the utmost excitability of humour; centra
Fatherland's Altar quite heaped with signing Patriots ane
Patriotesses; the Thirty benches and whole internal Space
crowded with onlookers, with comers and goers; one regurgi
tating whirlpool of men and women in their Sunday clothe
All which a Constitutional Sieur Motier sees; and Bailly
looking into it with his long visage made still longer. Augur
ing no good; perhaps *Déchéance* and Deposition after all
Stop it, ye Constitutional Patriots; fire itself is quenchable
yet only quenchable at *first*.

Stop it, truly: but how stop it? Have not the first fre
People of the Universe a right to petition?—Happily, if also
unhappily, here is one proof of riot: these two human in
dividuals hanged at the Lanterne. Proof, O treacherous Sieu
Motier? Were they not two human individuals sent thithe
by *thee* to be hanged; to be a pretext for thy bloody *Drapea*
Rouge? This question shall many a Patriot, one day, ask
and answer affirmatively, strong in Preternatural Suspicion.

Enough, towards half-past seven in the evening the mer
natural eye can behold this thing: Sieur Motier, with Muni

cipals in scarf, with blue National Patrollotism, rank after rank, to the clang of drums; wending resolutely to the Champ-de-Mars; Mayor Bailly, with elongated visage, bearing, as in sad duty bound, the *Drapeau Rouge*. Howl of angry derision rises in treble and bass from a hundred thousand throats, at the sight of Martial Law; which, nevertheless, waving its Red sanguinary Flag, advances there, from the Gros-Caillou Entrance; advances, drumming and waving, towards Altar of Fatherland. Amid still wilder howls, with objurgation, obtestation; with flights of pebbles and mud, *saxa et fæces;* with crackle of a pistol-shot;—finally with volley-fire of Patrollotism; levelled muskets; roll of volley on volley! Precisely after one year and three days, our sublime Federation Field is wetted, in this manner, with French blood.

Some 'Twelve unfortunately shot,' reports Bailly, counting by units; but Patriotism counts by tens and even by hundreds. Not to be forgotten, nor forgiven! Patriotism flies, shrieking, execrating. Camille ceases journalising, this day; Great Danton with Camille and Fréron have taken wing, for their life; Marat burrows deep in the Earth, and is silent. Once more Patrollotism has triumphed; one other time; but it is the last.

This was the Royal Flight to Varennes. Thus was the Throne overturned thereby; but thus also was it victoriously set up again—on its vertex; and will stand while it can be held.

BOOK V

PARLIAMENT FIRST

CHAPTER I

GRANDE ACCEPTATION

In the last nights of September, when the autumnal equinox is past, and gray September fades into brown October, why are the Champs Élysées illuminated; why is Paris dancing, and flinging fire-works? They are gala-nights, these last of September; Paris may well dance, and the Universe: the Edifice of the Constitution is completed! Completed; nay *revised*, to see that there was nothing insufficient in it; solemnly proffered to his Majesty; solemnly accepted by him, to the sound of cannon-salvoes, on the fourteenth of the month. And now by such illumination, jubilee, dancing and fire-working, do we joyously handsel the new Social Edifice, and first raise heat and reek there, in the name of Hope.

The Revision, especially with a throne standing on its vertex, has been a work of difficulty, of delicacy. In the way of propping and buttressing, so indispensable now, something could be done, and yet, as is feared, not enough. A repentant Barnave Triumvirate, our Rabauts, Duports, Thourets, and indeed all Constitutional Deputies did strain every nerve: but the Extreme Left was so noisy; the People were so suspicious, clamorous to have the work ended: and then the loyal Right Side sat feeble-petulant all the while, and as it were, pouting and petting; unable to help, had they even been willing. The Two Hundred and Ninety had solemnly made scission, before that; and departed, shaking the dust off their feet. To such transcendency of fret, and desperate hope that worsening of the bad might the sooner end it and bring back the good, had our unfortunate loyal Right Side now come!

However, one finds that this and the other little prop has been added, where possibility allowed. Civil List and Privy Purse were from of old well cared for. King's Constitutional Guard, Eighteen hundred loyal men from the Eighty-three Departments, under a loyal Duke de Brissac; this, with trust-

38

worthy Swiss besides, is of itself something. The old loyal
Bodyguards are indeed dissolved, in name as well as in fact;
and gone mostly towards Coblentz. But now also those Sansculottic violent Gardes Françaises, or Centre Grenadiers, shall
have their mittimus: they do ere long, in the Journals, not
without a hoarse pathos, publish their Farewell; 'wishing all
Aristocrats the graves in Paris which to us are denied.' They
depart, these first Soldiers of the Revolution; they hover very
dimly in the distance for about another year; till they can be
remodelled, new-named, and sent to fight the Austrians; and
then History beholds them no more. A most notable Corps
of men; which has its place in World-History;—though to
us, so is History written, they remain mere rubrics of men;
nameless; a shaggy Grenadier Mass, crossed with buff-belts.
And yet might we not ask: What Argonauts, what Leonidas'
Spartans had done such a work? Think of their destiny:
since that May morning, some three years ago, when they, unparticipating, trundled off D'Espréménil to the Calypso Isles;
since that July evening, some two years ago, when they, participating, and *sacre*-ing with knit brows, poured a volley into
Besenval's Prince de Lambesc! (i. 84; 143). History waves
them her mute adieu.

So that the Sovereign Power, these Sansculottic Watchdogs,
more like wolves, being leashed and led away from his Tuileries,
breathes freer. The Sovereign Power is guarded henceforth
by a loyal Eighteen Hundred,—whom Contrivance, under
various pretexts, may gradually swell to Six Thousand; who
will hinder no journey to Saint-Cloud. The sad Varennes
business has been soldered up; cemented, even in the blood
of the Champ-de-Mars, these two months and more; and indeed ever since, as formerly. Majesty has had its privileges,
its 'choice of residence,' though, for good reasons, the royal
mind 'prefers continuing in Paris.' Poor royal mind, poor
Paris; that have to go mumming; enveloped in speciosities,
in falsehood which knows itself false; and to enact mutually
your sorrowful farce-tragedy, being bound to it; and on the
whole, to hope always, in spite of hope!

Nay, now that his Majesty has accepted the Constitution, to
the sound of cannon-salvoes, who would not hope? Our good
King was misguided, but he meant well. Lafayette has moved
for an Amnesty, for universal forgiving and forgetting of Revolutionary faults; and now surely the glorious Revolution, cleared
of its rubbish, is complete! Strange enough, and touching in

several ways, the old cry of *Vive le Roi* once more rises roun
King Louis the Hereditary Representative. Their Majestie
went to the Opera; gave money to the Poor: the Queen her
self, now when the Constitution is accepted, hears voice c
cheering. Bygone shall be bygone; the New Era *shall* begin
To and fro, amid those lamp-galaxies of the Elysian Fields
the Royal Carriage slowly wends and rolls; everywhere wit
vivats, from a multitude striving to be glad. Louis looks out
mainly on the variegated lamps and gay human groups, wit
satisfaction enough for the hour. In her Majesty's face, 'unde
that kind graceful smile a deep sadness is legible.' Brilliancie
of valour and of wit stroll here observant: a Dame de Staë
leaning most probably on the arm of her Narbonne. Sh
meets Deputies; who have built this Constitution; who saunte
here with vague communings,—not without thoughts whethe
it will stand. But as yet melodious fiddle-strings twang an
warble everywhere, with the rhythm of light fantastic feet
long lamp-galaxies fling their coloured radiance; and brass
lunged Hawkers elbow and bawl, "*Grande Acceptation, Const
tution Monarchique :*" it behoves the Son of Adam to hope
Have not Lafayette, Barnave and all Constitutionalists set thei
shoulders handsomely to the inverted pyramid of a throne
Feuillans, including almost the whole Constitutional Respecta
bility of France, perorate nightly from their tribune; corre
spond through all Post-offices; denouncing unquiet Jacobinism
trusting well that *its* time is nigh done. Much is uncertain
questionable; but if the Hereditary Representative be wise
and lucky, may one not, with a sanguine Gaelic temper, hop
that he will get in motion better or worse; that what is want
ing to him will gradually be gained and added?

For the rest, as we must repeat, in this building of the
Constitutional Fabric, especially in this Revision of it, nothin
that one could think of to give it new strength, especially to
steady it, to give it permanence, and even eternity, has been
forgotten. Biennial Parliament, to be called Legislative
Assemblée Législative; with Seven Hundred and Forty-five
Members, chosen in a judicious manner by the 'active
citizens' alone, and even by electing of electors still more
active: this, with privileges of Parliament, shall meet, self
authorised if need be, and self-dissolved; shall grant money
supplies and talk; watch over the administration and
authorities; discharge forever the functions of a Constitu
tional Great Council, Collective Wisdom and National Palave

—as the Heavens will enable. Our First biennial Parliament, which indeed has been a-choosing since early in August, is now as good as chosen. Nay it has mostly got to Paris : it arrived gradually; not without pathetic greeting to its venerable Parent, the now moribund Constituent ; and sat there in the Galleries, reverently listening, ready to begin, the instant the ground were clear.

Then as to changes in the Constitution itself? This, impossible for any Legislative, or common biennial Parliament, and possible solely for some resuscitated Constituent or National Convention, is evidently one of the most ticklish points. The august moribund Assembly debated it for four entire days. Some thought a change, or at least a reviewal and new approval, might be admissible in thirty years, some even went lower, down to twenty, nay to fifteen. The august Assembly had once decided for thirty years ; but it revoked that, on better thoughts ; and did not fix any date of time, but merely some vague outline of a posture of circumstances, and, on the whole, left the matter hanging. Doubtless a National Convention can be assembled even *within* the thirty years : yet one may hope, not ; but that Legislatives, biennial Parliaments of the common kind, with their limited faculty, and perhaps quiet successive additions thereto, may suffice, for generations, or indeed while computed Time runs.

Furthermore, be it noted that no member of this Constituent has been, or could be, elected to the new Legislative. So noble-minded were these Law-makers ! cry some : and Solon-like would banish themselves. So splenetic ! cry more : each grudging the other, none daring to be outdone in self-denial by the other. So unwise in either case ! answer all practical men. But consider this other self-denying ordinance, That none of us can be King's Minister, or accept the smallest Court Appointment, for the space of four, or at lowest (and on long debate and Revision), for the space of two years ! So moves the incorruptible seagreen Robespierre ; with cheap magnanimity he ; and none dare be outdone by him. It was such a law, not superfluous *then*, that sent Mirabeau to the gardens of Saint-Cloud, under cloak of darkness, to that colloquy of the gods ; and thwarted many things. Happily and unhappily there is no Mirabeau now to thwart.

Welcomer meanwhile, welcome surely to all right hearts, is Lafayette's chivalrous Amnesty. Welcome too is that hard-wrung Union of Avignon ; which has cost us, first and last,

'thirty sessions of debate,' and so much else : may it at lengt
prove lucky! Rousseau's statue is decreed : virtuous Jean
Jacques, Evangelist of the Contrat Social. Not Drouet c
Varennes; nor worthy Lataille, master of the old world-famou
Tennis-Court in Versailles, is forgotten; but each has hi
honourable mention, and due reward in money. Whereupon
things being all so neatly winded up, and the Deputations
and Messages, and royal and other ceremonials having rustle
by; and the King having now affectionately perorated abou
peace and tranquillisation, and members having answere
"*Oui! oui!*" with effusion, even with tears,—Presiden
Thouret, he of the Law Reforms, rises, and, with a stron
voice, utters these memorable last-words : " The Nationa
Constituent Assembly declares that it has finished its mission
and that its sittings are all ended." Incorruptible Robes
pierre, virtuous Pétion are borne home on the shoulders o
the people; with vivats heaven-high. The rest glide quietl
to their respective places of abode. It is the last afternoo
of September 1791 ; on the morrow morning the new Legisla
tive will begin.

So, amid glitter of illuminated streets and Champs Élysées
and crackle of fireworks and glad deray, has the first Nationa
Assembly vanished ; *dissolving*, as they well say, into blan
Time; and is no more. National Assembly is gone, its wor
remaining; as all Bodies of men go, and as man himself goes
it had its beginning, and must likewise have its end.
Phantasm-Reality born of Time, as the rest of us are; flittin
ever backwards now on the tide of Time : to be long re
membered of men. Very strange Assemblages, Sanhedrims
Amphictyonics, Trades-Unions, Ecumenic Councils, Parlia
ments and Congresses, have met together on this Planet, an
dispersed again; but a stranger Assemblage than this augus
Constituent, or with a stranger mission, perhaps never me
there. Seen from the distance, this also will be a miracle
Twelve Hundred human individuals, with the Gospel of Jean
Jacques Rousseau in their pocket, congregating in the nam
of Twenty-five Millions, with full assurance of faith, to 'mak
the Constitution :' such sight, the acme and main produc
of the Eighteenth Century, our World can witness once only
For Time is rich in wonders, in monstrosities most rich ; an
is observed never to repeat himself, or any of his Gospels :—
surely least of all, this Gospel according to Jean-Jacque

Once it was right and indispensable, since such had become the Belief of men; but once also is enough.

They have made the Constitution, these Twelve Hundred Jean-Jacques Evangelists; not without result. Near twenty-nine months they sat, with various fortune; in various capacity;—always, we may say, in that capacity of car-borne Carroccio, and miraculous Standard of the Revolt of Men, as a Thing high and lifted up; whereon whosoever looked might hope healing. They have seen much, cannons levelled on them; then suddenly, by interposition of the Powers, the cannons drawn back; and a wargod Broglie vanishing, in thunder *not* his own, amid the dust and downrushing of a Bastille and Old Feudal France. They have suffered some-what: Royal Session, with rain and Oath of the Tennis-Court; Nights of Pentecost; Insurrections of Women. Also have they not done somewhat? Made the Constitution, and managed all things the while; passed, in these twenty-nine months, 'twenty-five hundred Decrees,' which on the average is some three for each day, including Sundays! Brevity, one finds, is possible, at times: had not Moreau de Saint-Méry, to give three thousand orders before rising from his seat (i. 160)?—There was valour (or value) in these men; and a kind of faith,—were it only faith in this, That cobwebs are not cloth; that a Constitution could be made. Cobwebs and chimeras ought verily to disappear; for *a* Reality there is. Let formulas, soul-killing, and now grown body-killing, in-supportable, begone, in the name of Heaven and Earth!— Time, as we say, brought forth these Twelve Hundred; Eternity was before them, Eternity behind; they worked, as we all do, in the confluence of Two Eternities; what work was given them. Say not that it was nothing they did. Con-sciously they did somewhat; unconsciously how much! They had their giants and their dwarfs, they accomplished their good and their evil; they are gone, and return no more. Shall they not go with our blessing, in these circumstances; with our mild farewell?

By post, by diligence, on saddle or sole; they are gone: towards the four winds. Not a few over the marches, to rank at Coblentz. Thither wended Maury, among others; but in the end towards Rome,—to be clothed there in red Cardinal plush; in falsehood as in a garment; pet-son (her *last* born?) of the Scarlet Woman. Talleyrand-Périgord, excommunicated Constitutional Bishop, will make his way to London: to be

Ambassador, spite of the Self-denying Law; brisk youn
Marquis Chauvelin acting as Ambassador's-Cloak. In Londo
too, one finds Pétion the virtuous; harangued and haranguing
pledging the wine-cup with Constitutional Reform-Clubs, i
solemn tavern-dinner. Incorruptible Robespierre retires fo
a little to native Arras; seven short weeks of quiet; the las
appointed him in this world. Public Accuser in the Pari
Department, acknowledged highpriest of the Jacobins; th
glass of incorruptible thin Patriotism, for his narrow emphasi
is loved of all the narrow,—this man seems to be rising, some
whither? He sells his small heritage at Arras; accompanie
by a Brother and a Sister, he returns, scheming out witl
resolute timidity a small sure destiny for himself and them
to his old lodging, at the Cabinet-maker's, in the Rue St
Honoré:—O resolute-tremulous incorruptible seagreen man
towards *what* a destiny!

Lafayette, for his part, will lay down the command. He
retires Cincinnatus-like to his hearth and farm; but soon
leaves them again. Our National Guard, however, shall hence
forth have no one Commandant; but all Colonels shall com
mand in succession, month about. Other Deputies we hav
met, or Dame de Staël has met, 'sauntering in a thoughtfu
manner;' perhaps uncertain what to do. Some, as Barnave
the Lameths, and their Duport, will continue here in Paris
watching the new biennial Legislative, Parliament the First
teaching it to walk, if so might be; and the Court to lead it.

Thus these: sauntering in a thoughtful manner; travellin
by post or diligence,—whither Fate beckons. Giant Mirabea
slumbers in the Pantheon of Great Men: and France? and
Europe?—The brass-lunged Hawkers sing "Grand Accepta
tion, Monarchic Constitution" through these gay crowds: the
Morrow, grandson of Yesterday, must be what it can, as To
day its Father is. Our new biennial Legislative begins t
constitute itself on the first of October 1791.

CHAPTER II

THE BOOK OF THE LAW

IF the august Constituent Assembly itself, fixing the regard
of the Universe, could, at the present distance of time and
place, gain comparatively small attention from us, how muc
less can this poor Legislative! It has its Right side and it

left; the less Patriotic and the more, for Aristocrats exist not here or now: it spouts and speaks; listens to Reports, reads Bills and Laws; works in its vocation, for a season: but the History of France, one finds, is seldom or never there. Unhappy Legislative, what can History do with it; if not drop a tear over it, almost in silence? First of the two-year Parliaments of France, which, if Paper Constitution and oft-repeated National Oath could avail aught, were to follow in softly-strong indissoluble sequence while Time ran,—it had to vanish dolefully within *one* year; and there came no second like it. Alas! your biennial Parliaments in endless indis-soluble sequence; they, and all that Constitutional Fabric, built with such explosive Federation Oaths, and its top-stone wrought out with dancing and variegated radiance, went to pieces, like frail crockery, in the crash of things; and already, in eleven short months, were in that Limbo near the Moon, with the ghosts of other Chimeras. There, except for rare specific purposes, let them rest, in melancholy peace.

On the whole, how unknown is a man to himself; or a public Body of men to itself! Æsop's fly sat on the chariot-wheel, exclaiming, What a dust I do raise! Great Governors, clad in purple with fasces and insignia, are governed by their valets, by the pouting of their women and children; or, in Constitutional countries, by the paragraphs of their Able Editors. Say not, I am this or that; I am doing this or that! For thou knowest *it* not, thou knowest only the name it as yet goes by. A purple Nebuchadnezzar rejoices to feel himself now verily Emperor of this great Babylon which he has builded; and *is* a nondescript biped-quadruped, on the eve of a seven-years course of grazing! These Seven Hundred and Forty-five elected individuals doubt not but they are the first biennial Parliament, come to govern France by parlia-mentary eloquence: and they *are* what? And they have come to do what? Things foolish and not wise!

It is much lamented by many that this First Biennial had no members of the old Constituent in it, with their experience of parties and parliamentary tactics; that such was their foolish Self-denying Law. Most surely, old members of the Con-stituent had been welcome to us here. But, on the other hand, what old or what new members of any Constituent under the Sun could have effectually profited? There are first biennial Parliaments so postured as to be, in a sense, *beyond* wisdom; where wisdom and folly differ only in degree, and wreckage and dissolution are the appointed issue for both.

Old-Constituents, your Barnaves, Lameths and the like, for whom a special Gallery has been set apart, where they may sit in honour and listen, are in the habit of sneering at these new Legislators; but let not us! The poor Seven Hundred and Forty-five, sent together by the active citizens of France, are what they could be: do what is fated them. That they are of Patriot temper we can well understand. Aristocrat Noblesse had fled over the marches, or sat brooding silent in their un-burnt Châteaus; small prospect had they in Primary Electoral Assemblies. What with Flights to Varennes, what with Days of Poniards, with plot after plot, the People are left to themselves; the People must needs choose Defenders of the People, such as can be had. Choosing, as *they* also will ever do, 'if not the ablest man, yet the man ablest to be chosen!' Fervour of character, decided Patriot-Constitutional feeling; these are qualities: but free utterance, mastership in tongue-fence; this is the quality of qualities. Accordingly one finds, with little astonishment, in this First Biennial, that as many as Four hundred Members are of the Advocate or Attorney species. Men who can speak, if there be aught to speak: nay here are men also who can think, and even act. Candour will say of this ill-fated First French Parliament, that it wanted not its modicum of talent, its modicum of honesty; that it, neither in the one respect nor in the other, sank below the average of Parliaments, but rose above the average. Let average Parlia-ments, whom the world does *not* guillotine, and cast forth to long infamy, be thankful not to themselves but to their stars!

France, as we say, has once more done what it could: fervid men have come together from wide separation; for strange issues. Fiery Max Isnard is come, from the utmost Southeast; fiery Claude Fauchet, Te-Deum Fauchet Bishop of Calvados, from the utmost Northwest. No Mirabeau now sits here, who had swallowed formulas: our only Mirabeau now is Danton, working as yet out of doors; whom some call 'Mirabeau of the Sansculottes.'

Nevertheless we have our gifts,—especially of speech and logic. An eloquent Vergniaud we have; most mellifluous yet most impetuous of public speakers; from the region named Gironde, of the Garonne: a man unfortunately of indolent habits; who will sit playing with your children, when he ought to be scheming and perorating. Sharp-bustling Guadet; considerate grave Gensonné; kind-sparkling mirthful young Ducos; Valazé doomed to a sad end: all these likewise are of that Gironde or Bordeaux region: men of fervid Constitutional principles; of quick talent, irrefragable logic, clear respectability; who will have the Reign of Liberty establish itself, but only by respectable methods. Round whom others of like temper will gather; known by and by as *Girondins*, to the sorrowing wonder of the world. Of which sort note Condorcet, Marquis and Philosopher; who has worked at much, at Paris Municipal Constitution, Differential Calculus, Newspaper *Chronique de Paris*, Biography, Philosophy; and now sits here as two-years Senator: a notable Condorcet, with stoical Roman face, and fiery heart; 'volcano hid under snow;' styled likewise, in irreverent language, '*mouton enragé*,' peaceablest of creatures bitten rabid! Or note, lastly, Jean-Pierre Brissot; whom Destiny, long working noisily with him, has hurled hither, say, to have done with him. A biennial Senator he too; nay, for the present, the king of such. Restless, scheming, scribbling Brissot; who took to himself the style *de Warville*, heralds know not in the least why;—unless it were that the father of him did, in an unexceptionable manner, perform Cookery and Vintnery in the Village of *Ouar*ville? A man of the windmill species, that grinds always, turning towards all winds, not in the steadiest manner.

In all these men there is talent, faculty to work; and they will do it: working and shaping, not *without* effect, though alas not in marble, only in quicksand!—But the highest faculty of them all remains yet to be mentioned; or indeed has yet to unfold itself for mention: Captain Hippolyte Carnot sent hither from the Pas de Calais; with his cold mathematical head, and silent stubbornness of will: iron Carnot, far-planning, imperturbable, unconquerable; who, in the hour of need, shall not be found wanting. His hair is yet black; and it shall grow gray, under many kinds of fortune, bright and troublous: and with iron aspect this man shall face them all.

Nor is *Côté Droit*, and band of King's friends, wanting: Vaublanc, Dumas, Jaucourt the honoured Chevalier; who love Liberty, yet with Monarchy over it; and speak fearlessly according to that faith;—whom the thick-coming hurricanes will sweep away. With them let a new military Theodore Lameth be named;—were it only for his two Brothers' sake, who look down on him, approvingly there, from the Old-Constituents' Gallery. Frothy professing Pastorets, honey-

mouthed conciliatory Lamourettes, and speechless nameles
individuals sit plentiful, as Moderates, in the middle. Stil
less is a *Côté Gauche* wanting : extreme Left ; sitting on the
topmost benches, as if aloft on its speculatory Height o
Mountain, which will become a practical fulminatory Height
and make the name of Mountain famous-infamous to all time
and lands.

Honour waits not on this Mountain ; nor as yet even lou
dishonour. Gifts it boasts not, nor graces, of speaking or o
thinking ; solely this one gift of assured faith, of audacity tha
will defy the Earth and the Heavens. Foremost here are the
Cordelier Trio : hot Merlin from Thionville, hot Bazire
Attorneys both ; Chabot, disfrocked Capuchin, skilful in agio.
Lawyer Lacroix, who wore once as subaltern the single
epaulette, has loud lungs and a hungry heart. There too is
Couthon, little dreaming *what* he is ;—whom a sad chance has
paralysed in the lower extremities. For, it seems, he sat once
a whole night, not warm in his true-love's bower (who indeed
was by law another's), but sunken to the middle in a cold
peat-bog, being hunted out from her ; quaking for his life, in
the cold quaking morass ; and goes now on crutches to the
end. Cambon likewise, in whom slumbers undeveloped such
a finance-talent for printing of Assignats ; Father of Paper-
money ; who, in the hour of menace, shall utter this stern
sentence, "War to the Manorhouse, peace to the Hut, *Guerre
aux Châteaux, paix aux Chaumières !*" Lecointre, the intrepid
Draper of Versailles, is welcome here : known since the Opera-
Repast and Insurrection of Women. Thuriot too ; Elector
Thuriot, who stood in the embrasures of the Bastille, and saw
Saint-Antoine rising in mass ; who has many other things to
see. Last and grimmest of all, note old Ruhl, with his brown
dusky face and long white hair ; of Alsatian Lutheran breed ;
a man whom age and book-learning have not taught ; who,
haranguing the old men of Rheims, shall hold up the Sacred
Ampulla (Heaven-sent, wherefrom Clovis and all Kings have
been anointed) as a mere worthless oil-bottle, and dash it to
sherds on the pavement there ; who, alas, shall dash much to
sherds, and finally his own wild head by pistol-shot, and *so*
end it.

Such lava welters redhot in the bowels of this Mountain ;
unknown to the world and to itself ! A mere commonplace
Mountain hitherto ; distinguished from the Plain chiefly by its
superior *barrenness*, its baldness of look : at the utmost it may,

o the most observant, perceptibly *smoke*. For as yet all lies
so solid, peaceable; and doubts not, as was said, that it will
endure while Time runs. Do not all love Liberty and the
Constitution? All heartily;—and yet with degrees. Some,
as Chevalier Jaucourt and his Right Side, may love Liberty
ess than Royalty, were the trial made; others, as Brissot and
his Left Side, may love it more than Royalty. Now again, of
these latter some may love Liberty more than Law itself;
others not more. Parties *will* unfold themselves; no mortal
as yet knows how. Forces work within these men and without: dissidence grows opposition; ever widening; waxing
into incompatibility and internecine feud; till the strong is
abolished by a stronger; himself in his turn by a strongest!
Who can help it? Jaucourt and his Monarchists, Feuillans,
or Moderates; Brissot and his Brissotins, Jacobins, or Girondins; these, with the Cordelier Trio, and all men, must work
what is appointed them, and in the way appointed them.

And to think what fate these poor Seven Hundred and
Forty-five are assembled, most unwittingly, to meet! Let no
heart be so hard as not to pity them. Their soul's wish was
to live and work as the First of the French Parliaments; and
make the Constitution march. Did they not, at their very
instalment, go through the most affecting Constitutional ceremony, almost with tears? The Twelve eldest are sent
solemnly to fetch the Constitution itself, the printed Book of
the Law. Archivist Camus, an Old-Constituent appointed
Archivist, he and the Ancient Twelve, amid blare of military
pomp and clangour, enter, bearing the divine Book: and
President and all Legislative Senators, laying their hand on
the same, successively take the Oath, with cheers and heart-
effusion, universal three-times-three. In this manner they
begin their session. Unhappy mortals! For, that same day,
his Majesty having received their Deputation of welcome, as
seemed, rather drily, the Deputation cannot but feel slighted,
cannot but lament such slight: and thereupon our cheering
swearing First Parliament sees itself, on the morrow, obliged to
explode into fierce retaliatory sputter of anti-royal Enactment
as to how they, for their part, will receive Majesty; and how
Majesty shall not be called Sire any more, except they please:
and then, on the following day, to recall this Enactment
of theirs, as too hasty, and a mere sputter, though not un-
provoked.

An effervescent well-intentioned set of Senators; too combustible, where continual sparks are flying! Their History is a series of sputters and quarrels; true desire to do their function, fatal impossibility to do it. Denunciations, reprimandings of King's Ministers, of traitors supposed and real; hot rage and fulmination against fulminating Emigrants; terror of Austrian Kaiser, of 'Austrian Committee' in the Tuileries itself; rage and haunting terror, haste and doubt and dim bewilderment!—Haste, we say; and yet the Constitution had provided against haste. No Bill can be passed till it have been printed, till it have been thrice read, with intervals of eight days;—'unless the Assembly shall beforehand decree that there is urgency.' Which, accordingly, the Assembly, scrupulous of the Constitution, never omits to do: Considering this, and also considering that, and then that other, the Assembly decrees always '*qu'il y a urgence*;' and thereupon 'the Assembly, having decreed that there is urgence,' is free to decree—what indispensable distracted thing seems best to it. Two thousand and odd decrees, as men reckon, within Eleven months! The haste of the Constituent seemed great; but this is treble-quick. For the time itself is rushing treble-quick; and they have to keep pace with that. Unhappy Seven Hundred and Forty-five: true-patriotic, but so combustible; being fired, they must needs fling fire: Senate of touchwood and rockets, in a world of smoke-storm, with sparks wind-driven continually flying!

Or think, on the other hand, looking forward some months, of that scene they call *Baiser de Lamourette!* The dangers of the country are now grown imminent, immeasurable; National Assembly, hope of France, is divided against itself. In such extreme circumstances, honey-mouthed Abbé Lamourette, new Bishop of Lyons, rises, whose name *l'amourette*, signifies *the sweetheart*, or Delilah doxy,—he rises, and with pathetic honeyed eloquence, calls on all august Senators to forget mutual griefs and grudges, to swear a new oath, and unite as brothers. Whereupon they all, with vivats, embrace and swear; Left Side confounding itself with Right; barren Mountain rushing down to fruitful Plain, Pastoret into the arms of Condorcet, injured to the breast of injurer, with tears: and all swearing that whosoever wishes either Feuillant Two-Chamber Monarchy or extreme Jacobin-Republic, or anything but the Constitution and that only, shall be anathema maranatha. Touching to behold! For, literally on the morrow morning, they must again quarrel, driven by Fate; and their sublime reconcilement is called derisively the *Baiser de L'amourette*, or Delilah Kiss.

Like fated Eteocles-Polynices Brothers, embracing, though in vain; weeping that they must not love, that they must hate only, and die by each other's hands! Or say, like doomed Familiar Spirits; ordered, by Art Magic under penalties, to do a harder than twist ropes of sand: 'to make the Constitution march.' If the Constitution would but march! Alas, the Constitution will not stir. It falls on its face; they tremblingly lift it on end again: march, thou gold Constitution! The Constitution will not march.—"He shall march, by —— !" said kind Uncle Toby, and even swore. The Corporal answered mournfully: "He will never march in this world."

A Constitution, as we often say, will march when it images, if not the old Habits and Beliefs of the Constituted; then accurately their Rights, or better indeed, their Mights;—for these two, well understood, are they not one and the same? The old Habits of France are gone: her new Rights and Mights are not yet ascertained, except in Paper-theorem; nor can be, in any sort, till she have *tried*. Till she have measured herself, in fell death-grip, and were it in utmost preter-natural spasm of madness, with Principalities and Powers, with the upper and the under, internal and external; with the Earth and Tophet and the very Heaven! Then will she know.—Three things bode ill for the marching of this French Constitution: the French people; the French King; thirdly, the French Noblesse and an assembled European World.

CHAPTER III

AVIGNON

But quitting generalities, what strange Fact is this, in the far Southwest, towards which the eyes of all men do now, in the end of October, bend themselves? A tragical combustion, long smoking and smouldering unluminous, has now burst into flame there.

Hot is that Southern Provençal blood: alas, collisions, as was once said, must occur in a career of Freedom; different directions will produce such; nay different· *velocities* in the same direction will! To much that went on there, History, busied elsewhere, would not specially give heed: to troubles

of Uzés, troubles of Nismes, Protestant and Catholic, Patriot
and Aristocrat; to troubles of Marseilles, Montpellier, Arles;
to Aristocrat Camp of Jalès, that wondrous real-imaginary
Entity, now fading pale-dim, then always again glowing forth
deep-hued (in the imagination mainly);—ominous magical,
'an Aristocrat *picture* of war done naturally!' All this was a
tragical deadly combustion, with plot and riot, tumult by night
and by day; but a *dark* combustion, not luminous, not
noticed; which now, however, one cannot help noticing.

Above all places, the unluminous combustion in Avignon
and the Comtat Venaissin was fierce. Papal Avignon, with
its Castle rising sheer over the Rhone-stream; beautifullest
Town, with its purple vines and gold-orange groves; why must
foolish old rhyming René, the last Sovereign of Provence,
bequeath it to the Pope and Gold Tiara, not rather to Louis
Eleventh with the Leaden Virgin in his hatband? For good
and for evil! Popes, Antipopes, with their pomp, have dwelt
in that Castle of Avignon rising sheer over the Rhone-stream:
there Laura de Sade went to hear mass; her Petrarch twang-
ing and singing by the Fountain of Vaucluse hard by, surely
in a most melancholy manner. This was in the old days.

And now in these new days, such issues do come from a squirt
of the pen by some foolish rhyming René, after centuries,—
this is what we have: Jourdan *Coupe-tête*, leading to siege and
warfare an Army, from three to fifteen thousand strong, called
the Brigands of Avignon; which title they themselves accept,
with the addition of an epithet, 'The *brave* Brigands of
Avignon!' It is even so. Jourdan the Headsman fled hither
from that Châtelet Inquest, from that Insurrection of Women;
and began dealing in madder: but the scene was rife in other
than dye-stuffs; so Jourdan shut his madder-shop, and has
risen, for he was the man to do it. The tile-beard of Jourdan
is shaven off; his fat visage has got coppered and studded with
black carbuncles; the Silenus trunk is swollen with drink and
high living: he wears blue National uniform with epaulettes,
'an enormous sabre, two horse-pistols crossed in his belt, and
other two, smaller, sticking from his pockets;' styles himself
General, and is the tyrant of men. Consider this one fact, O
Reader; and what sort of facts must have preceded it, must
accompany it! Such things come of old René; and of the
question which has risen, Whether Avignon cannot now cease
wholly to be Papal, and become French and free?

For some twenty-five months the confusion has lasted. Say three months of arguing; then seven of raging; then finally some fifteen months now of fighting, and even of hanging. For already in February 1790, the Papal Aristocrats had set up four gibbets, for a sign; but the people rose in June, in retributive frenzy; and forcing the public Hangman to act, hanged four Aristocrats, on each Papal gibbet a Papal Haman. Then were Avignon Emigrations, Papal Aristocrats emigrating over the Rhone River; demission of Papal Consul, flight, victory: re-entrance of Papal Legate, truce, and new onslaught; and the various turns of war. Petitions there were to National Assembly; Congresses of Townships; three-score and odd Townships voting for French Reunion, and the blessings of Liberty; while some twelve of the smaller, manipulated by Aristocrats, gave vote the other way: with shrieks and discord! Township against Township, Town against Town: Carpentras, long jealous of Avignon, is now turned out in open war with it;—and Jourdan *Coupe-tête*, your first General being killed in mutiny, closes his dye-shop; and does there visibly, with siege-artillery, above all with bluster and tumult, with the 'brave Brigands of Avignon,' beleaguer the rival Town, for two months, in the face of the world.

Feats were done, doubt it not, far-famed in Parish History; but to Universal History unknown. Gibbets we see rise, on the one side and on the other; and wretched carcasses swinging there, a dozen in the row; wretched Mayor of Vaison buried before dead. The fruitful seedfields lie unreaped, the vineyards trampled down; there is red cruelty, madness of universal choler and gall. Havoc and anarchy everywhere; a combustion most fierce, but *un*lucent, not to be noticed here!—Finally, as we saw, on the 14th of September last, the National Constituent Assembly,—having sent Commissioners and heard them; having heard Petitions, held Debates, month after month ever since August 1789; and on the whole 'spent thirty sittings' on this matter,—did solemnly decree that Avignon and the Comtat were incorporated with France, and his Holiness the Pope should have what indemnity was reasonable (pp. 41, 42).

And so hereby all is amnestied and finished? Alas, when madness of choler has gone through the blood of men, and gibbets have swung on this side and on that, what will a parchment Decree and Lafayette Amnesty do? Oblivious

Lethe flows not *above* ground! Papal Aristocrats and Patriot Brigands are still an eye-sorrow to each other; suspected, suspicious, in what they do and forbear. The august Constituent Assembly is gone but a fortnight, when, on Sunday the Sixteenth morning of October 1791, the unquenched combustion suddenly becomes luminous. For Anti-constitutional Placards are up, and the Statue of the Virgin is said to have shed tears, and grown red. Wherefore, on that morning, Patriot l'Escuyer, one of our 'six leading Patriots,' having taken counsel with his brethren and General Jourdan, determines on going to Church, in company with a friend or two: not to hear mass, which he values little; but to meet all the Papalists there in a body, nay to meet that same weeping Virgin, for it is the Cordeliers Church; and give them a word of admonition. Adventurous errand; which has the fatallest issue! What L'Escuyer's word of admonition might be, no History records; but the answer to it was a shrieking howl from the Aristocrat Papal worshippers, many of them women. A thousand-voiced shriek and menace; which, as L'Escuyer did not fly, became a thousand-handed hustle and jostle; a thousand-footed kick, with tumblings and tramplings, with the pricking of sempstress stilettoes, scissors and female pointed instruments. Horrible to behold; the ancient Dead, and Petrarchan Laura, sleeping round it there: high Altar and burning tapers looking down on it; the Virgin quite tearless, and of the natural stone-colour!—L'Escuyer's friend or two rush off, like Job's Messengers, for Jourdan and the National Force. But heavy Jourdan will seize the Town-Gates first; does not run treble-fast as he might: on arriving at the Cordeliers Church, the Church is silent, vacant; L'Escuyer, all alone, lies there, swimming in his blood, at the foot of the high Altar; pricked with scissors, trodden, massacred;—gives one dumb sob, and gasps out his miserable life forevermore.

Sight to stir the heart of any man; much more of many men, self-styled Brigands of Avignon! The corpse of L'Escuyer, stretched on a bier, the ghastly head girt with laurel, is borne through the streets; with many-voiced unmelodious *Nenia;* funeral-wail still deeper than it is loud! The copper face of Jourdan, of bereft Patriotism, has grown black. Patriot Municipality despatches official Narrative and tidings to Paris; orders numerous or innumerable arrestments for inquest and perquisition. Aristocrats male and female are haled to the Castle; lie crowded in subterranean dungeons there, bemoaned by the hoarse rushing of the Rhone; cut out from help.

So lie they; waiting inquest and perquisition. Alas! with a Jourdan Headsman for Generalissimo, with his copper-face grown black, and armed Brigand Patriots chanting their *Nenia*, the inquest is likely to be brief. On the next day and the next, let Municipality consent or not, a Brigand Court-Martial establishes itself in the subterranean stories of the Castle of Avignon; Brigand Executioners, with naked sabre, waiting at the door for a Brigand verdict. Short judgment, no appeal! There is Brigand wrath and vengeance; not unrefreshed by brandy. Close by is the dungeon of the *Glacière*, or Ice-Tower: there may be deeds done—? For which language has no name!—Darkness and the shadow of horrid cruelty envelopes these Castle Dungeons, that *Glacière* Tower: clear only that many have entered, that few have returned. Jourdan and the Brigands, supreme now over Municipals, over all authorities Patriot or Papal, reign in Avignon, waited on by Terror and Silence.

The result of all which is, that, on the 15th of November 1791, we behold Friend Dampmartin, and subalterns beneath him, and General Choisi above him, with Infantry and Cavalry, and proper cannon-carriages rattling in front, with spread banners, to the sound of fife and drum, wend, in a deliberate formidable manner, towards that sheer Castle Rock, towards those broad gates of Avignon; three new National-Assembly Commissioners following at safe distance in the rear. Avignon, summoned in the name of Assembly and Law, flings its Gates wide open; Choisi with the rest, Dampmartin and the ' *Bons Enfans*, Good Boys, of *Baufremont*,' so they name these brave Constitutional Dragoons, known to them of old,—do enter, amid shouts and scattered flowers. To the joy of all honest persons; to the terror only of Jourdan Headsman and the Brigands. Nay next we behold carbuncled swollen Jourdan himself show copper-face, with sabre and four pistols; affecting to talk high; engaging, meanwhile, to surrender the Castle that instant. So the Choisi Grenadiers enter with him there. They start and stop, passing that *Glacière*, snuffing its horrible breath; with wild yell, with cries of " Cut the Butcher down ! " —and Jourdan has to whisk himself through secret passages, and instantaneously vanish.

Be the mystery of iniquity laid bare then! A Hundred and Thirty Corpses, of men, nay of women and even children, (for the trembling mother, hastily seized, could not leave her infant), lie heaped in that *Glacière;* putrid under putridities; the horror of the world. For three days there is mournful lifting out, and recognition; amid the cries and movements of a passionate Southern people, now kneeling in prayer, now storming in wild pity and rage: lastly there is solemn sepulture, with muffled drums, religious requiem, and all the people's wail and tears. Their Massacred rest now in holy ground; buried in one grave.

And Jourdan *Coupe-tête?* Him also we behold again, after a day or two: in flight, through the most romantic Petrarchan hill-country; vehemently spurring his nag; young Ligonnet, a brisk youth of Avignon, with Choisi Dragoons, close in his rear! With such swollen mass of a rider no nag can run to advantage. The tired nag, spur-driven, does take the River Sorgue; but sticks in the middle of it; firm on that *chiaro fondo di Sorga;* and will proceed no further for spurring! Young Ligonnet dashes up; the Copper-face menaces and bellows, draws pistol, perhaps even snaps it; is nevertheless seized by the collar; is tied firm, ancles under horse's belly, and ridden back to Avignon, hardly to be saved from massacre on the streets there.

Such is the combustion of Avignon and the Southwest, when it becomes luminous. Long loud debate is in the august Legislative, in the Mother-Society, as to what now shall be done with it. Amnesty, cry eloquent Vergniaud and all Patriots: let there be mutual pardon and repentance, restoration, pacification, and, if so might anyhow be, an end! Which vote ultimately prevails. So the Southwest smoulders and welters again in an 'Amnesty,' or Non-remembrance, which alas cannot *but* remember, no Lethe flowing above ground! Jourdan himself remains unhanged; gets loose again, as one not yet gallows-ripe; nay, as we transiently discern from the distance, is 'carried in triumph through the cities of the South.' What things men carry!

With which transient glimpse, of a Copper-faced Portent faring in this manner through the cities of the South, we must quit these regions;—and let them smoulder. They want not their Aristocrats; proud old Nobles, not yet emigrated. Arles has its '*Chiffonne,*' so, in symbolical cant, they name that Aristocrat Secret-Association; Arles has its pavements piled up, by and by, into Aristocrat barricades. Against

which Rebecqui, the hot-clear Patriot, must lead Marseillese
with cannon. The Bar of Iron has not yet risen to the top
in the Bay of Marseilles; neither have these hot Sons of the
Phoceans submitted to be slaves. By clear management and
hot instance, Rebecqui dissipates that *Chiffonne*, without
bloodshed; restores the pavement of Arles. He sails in Coast-
barks, this Rebecqui, scrutinising suspicious Martello-towers,
with the keen eye of patriotism; marches overland with
despatch, singly, or in force; to City after City; dim scouring
far and wide;—argues, and if it must be, fights. For there
is much to do: Jalès itself is looking suspicious. So that
Legislator Fauchet, after debate on it, has to propose Commissioners and a Camp on the Plain of Beaucaire; with or
without result.

Of all which, and much else, let us note only this small
consequence, that young Barbaroux, Advocate, Town-Clerk of
Marseilles, being charged to have these things remedied,
arrives at Paris in the month of February 1792. The beautiful and brave: young Spartan, ripe in energy, not ripe in
wisdom: over whose black doom there shall flit nevertheless
a certain ruddy fervour, streaks of bright Southern tint, not
wholly swallowed of Death! Note also that the Rolands of
Lyons are again in Paris; for the second and final time. King's
Inspectorship is abrogated at Lyons, as elsewhere: Roland
has his retiring-pension to claim, if attainable; has Patriot
friends to commune with; at lowest, has a Book to publish.
That young Barbaroux and the Rolands came together; that
elderly Spartan Roland liked, or even loved the young Spartan,
and was loved by him, one can fancy: and Madame————?
Breathe not, thou poison-breath, Evil-speech! That soul is
taintless, clear as the mirror-sea. And yet if they two did
look into each other's eyes, and each, in silence, in tragical
renunciance, did find that the other was all-too lovely? *Honi
soit!* She calls him 'beautiful as Antinous:' he 'will speak
elsewhere of that astonishing woman.'—A Madame d'Udon
(or some such name, for Dumont does not recollect quite
clearly) gives copious Breakfast to the Brissotin Deputies and
us Friends of Freedom, at her house in the Place Vendôme;
with temporary celebrity, with graces and wreathed smiles; not
without cost. There, amid wide babble and jingle, our plan
of Legislative Debate is settled for the day, and much coun-
selling held. Strict Roland is seen there, but does not go
often.

CHAPTER IV

NO SUGAR

SUCH are our inward troubles; seen in the Cities of the South; extant, seen or unseen, in all cities and districts, North as well as South. For in all are Aristocrats, more or less malignant; watched by Patriotism; which again, being of various shades, from light Fayettist-Feuillant down to deep-sombre Jacobin, has to watch even *itself*.

Directories of Departments, what we call County Magistracies, being chosen by Citizens of a too 'active' class, are found to pull one way; Municipalities, Town Magistracies, to pull the other way. In all places too are Dissident Priests; whom the Legislative will have to deal with: contumacious individuals, working on that angriest of passions; plotting, enlisting for Coblentz; or suspected of plotting: fuel of a universal unconstitutional heat. What to do with them? They may be conscientious as well as contumacious: gently they should be dealt with, and yet it must be speedily. In unilluminated La Vendée the simple are like to be seduced by them; many a simple peasant, a Cathelineau the wool-dealer wayfaring meditative with his woolpacks, in these hamlets, dubiously shakes his head! Two Assembly Commissioners went thither last Autumn; considerate Gensonné, not yet called to be a senator; Gallois, an editorial man. These Two, consulting with General Dumouriez, spake and worked, softly, with judgment; they have hushed down the irritation, and produced a soft Report,—for the time.

The General himself doubts not in the least but he can keep peace there; being an able man. He passes these frosty months among the pleasant people of Niort, occupies 'tolerably handsome apartments in the Castle of Niort,' and tempers the minds of men. Why is there but one Dumouriez? Elsewhere you find, South or North, nothing but untempered obscure jarring; which breaks forth ever and anon into open clangour of riot. Southern Perpignan has its tocsin, by torchlight; with rushing and onslaught: Northern Caen not less, by daylight; with Aristocrats ranged in arms at Places of Worship; Departmental compromise proving impossible; breaking into musketry and a Plot discovered! Add Hunger too: for bread, always dear, is getting dearer: not so much as

Sugar can be had ; for good reasons. Poor Simonneau, Mayor of Étampes, in this Northern region, hanging out his Red Flag in some riot of grains, is trampled to death by a hungry exasperated People. What a trade this of Mayor, in these times ! Mayor of Saint-Denis hung at the Lanterne, by Suspicion and Dyspepsia, as we saw long since ; Mayor of Vaison, as we saw lately, buried before dead ; and now this poor Simonneau the Tanner, of Étampes,—whom legal Constitutionalism will not forget.

With factions, suspicions, want of bread and sugar, it is verily what they call *déchiré*, torn asunder, this poor country : France and all that is French. For, over seas too come bad news. In black Saint-Domingo, before that variegated Glitter in the Champs Élysées was lit for an Accepted Constitution, there had risen, and was burning contemporary with it, quite another variegated Glitter and nocturnal Fulgor, had we known it : of molasses and ardent-spirits ; of sugar-boileries, plantations, furniture, cattle and men : sky-high ; the Plain of Cap Français one huge whirl of smoke and flame !

What a change here, in these two years ; since that first 'Box of Tricolor Cockades' got through the Custom-house, and atrabiliar Creoles too rejoiced that there was a levelling of Bastilles ! Levelling is comfortable, as we often say : levelling, yet only down to oneself. Your pale-white Creoles have their grievances :—and your yellow Quarteroons ? And your dark-yellow Mulattoes ? And your Slaves soot-black ? Quarteroon Ogé, Friend of our Parisian-Brissotin *Friends of the Blacks*, felt for his share too, that Insurrection was the most sacred of duties. So the tricolor Cockades had fluttered and swashed only some three months on the Creole hat, when Ogé's signal-conflagrations went aloft ; with the voice of rage and terror. Repressed, doomed to die, he took black powder or seedgrains in the hollow of his hand, this Ogé ; sprinkled a film of white ones on the top, and said to his Judges, "Behold they are white ;" then *shook* his hand, and said, "Where are the whites, *Où sont les blancs* ?"

So now, in the Autumn of 1791, looking from the sky-windows of Cap Français, thick clouds of smoke girdle our horizon, smoke in the day, in the night fire ; preceded by fugitive shrieking white women, by Terror and Rumour. Black demonised squadrons are massacring and harrying, with nameless cruelty. They fight and fire 'from behind thickets and coverts,' for the Black man loves the Bush ; they rush to the attack, thousands strong, with brandished cutlasses and fusils, with caperings, shoutings and vociferation,—which, if the White Volunteer Company stands firm, dwindle into staggerings, into quick gabblement, into panic flight at the first volley, perhaps before it.   Poor Ogé could be broken on the wheel; this fire-whirlwind too can be abated, driven up into the mountains: but Saint-Domingo is *shaken*, as Ogé's seed-grains were; shaking, writhing in long horrid death-throes, it is Black without remedy; and remains, as African Haiti, a monition to the world.

O my Parisian Friends, is not *this*, as well as Regraters and Feuillant Plotters, one cause of the astonishing dearth of Sugar!   The Grocer, palpitant, with drooping lip, sees his Sugar *taxé;* weighed out by female Patriotism, in instant retail, at the inadequate rate of twenty-five sous, or thirteen pence a pound.   "Abstain from it?"   Yes, ye Patriot Sections, all ye Jacobins, abstain!   Louvet and Collot-d'Herbois so advise; resolute to make the sacrifice; though "how shall literary men do without coffee?"   Abstain, with an oath; that is the surest:

Also, for like reason, must not Brest and the Shipping Interest languish? Poor Brest languishes, sorrowing, not without spleen; denounces an Aristocrat Bertrand-Moleville, traitorous Aristocrat Marine-Minister.   Do not her Ships and King's Ships lie rotting piecemeal in harbour; Naval Officers mostly fled, and on furlough too, with pay?   Little stirring there; if it be not the Brest Galleys, whip-driven, with their Galley-Slaves,—alas, with some Forty of our hapless Swiss Soldiers of Château-Vieux, among others!   These Forty Swiss, too mindful of Nanci, do now, in their red wool caps, tug sorrowfully at the oar; looking into the Atlantic brine, which reflects only their own sorrowful shaggy faces; and seem forgotten of Hope.

But, on the whole, may we not say, in figurative language, that the French Constitution which shall march is very *rheumatic*, full of shooting internal pains, in joint and muscle; and will not march without difficulty?

CHAPTER V

KINGS AND EMIGRANTS

EXTREMELY rheumatic Constitutions have been known to march, and keep on their feet, though in a staggering sprawling manner, for long periods, in virtue of one thing only : that the *Head* were healthy. But this Head of the French Constitution ! What King Louis is and cannot help being, Readers already know. A King who cannot take the Constitution, nor reject the Constitution : nor do any thing at all, but miserably ask, What shall I do? A King environed with endless confusions; in whose own mind is no germ of order. Haughty implacable remnants of Noblesse struggling with humiliated repentant Barnave-Lameths ; struggling in that obscure element of fetchers and carriers, of Half-pay braggarts from the Café Valois, of Chambermaids, whisperers, and subaltern officious persons ; fierce Patriotism looking on all the while, more and more suspicious, from without : what, in such struggling, can they do ? At best, *cancel* one another, and produce *zero*. Poor King ! Barnave and your Senatorial Jaucourts speak earnestly into this ear ; Bertrand-Moleville, and Messengers from Coblentz, speak earnestly into that : the poor Royal head turns to the one side and to the other side ; can turn itself fixedly to no side. Let Decency drop a veil over it : sorrier misery was seldom enacted in the world. This one small fact, does it not throw the saddest light on much? The Queen is lamenting to Madame Campan : "What am I to do? When they, these Barnaves, get us advised to any step which the Noblesse do not like, then I am pouted at ; nobody comes to my card-table ; the King's Couchée is solitary." In such a case of dubiety, what *is* one to do? Go inevitably to the ground !

The King has accepted this Constitution, knowing beforehand that it will not serve : he studies it, and executes it in the hope mainly that it will be found inexecutable. King's Ships lie rotting in harbour, their officers gone ; the Armies disorganised ; robbers scour the Highways, which wear down unrepaired ; all Public Service lies slack and waste : the Executive makes no effort, or an effort only to throw the blame on the Constitution. Shamming death, '*faisant la mort !*' What Constitution, use it in this manner, can march ? 'Grow to disgust the Nation,' it will truly, unless *you* first grow to disgust the Nation! It is Bertrand de Moleville's plan, and his Majesty's; the best they can form.

Or if, after all, this best-plan proved too slow; proved a failure? Provident of that too, the Queen, shrouded in deepest mystery, ' writes all day, in cipher, day after day, to Coblentz;' Engineer Goguelat, he of the *Night of Spurs*, whom the Lafayette Amnesty has delivered from Prison, rides and runs. Now and then, on fit occasion, a Royal familiar visit can be paid to that Salle de Manége, an affecting encouraging Royal Speech (sincere, doubt it not, for the moment) can be delivered there, and the Senators all cheer and almost weep;—at the same time Mallet du Pan has visibly ceased editing, and invisibly bears abroad a King's Autograph, soliciting help from the Foreign Potentates. Unhappy Louis, *do* this thing or else that other,—if thou couldst!

The thing which the King's Government did do was to stagger distractedly from contradiction to contradiction; and wedding Fire to Water, envelope itself in hissing, and ashy steam; Danton and needy corruptible Patriots are sopped with presents of cash: they accept the sop; they rise refreshed by it, and—travel their own way. Nay, the King's Government did likewise hire Hand-clappers, or *claqueurs*, persons to applaud. Subterranean Rivarol has Fifteen Hundred Men in King's pay, at the rate of some £10,000 sterling, per month; what he calls 'a staff of genius:' Paragraph-writers, Placard Journalists; 'two hundred and eighty Applauders, at three shillings a day:' one of the strangest Staffs ever commanded by man. The muster-rolls and account-books of which still exist. Bertrand-Moleville himself, in a way he thinks very dexterous, contrives to pack the Galleries of the Legislative; gets Sansculottes hired to go thither, and applaud at a signal given, they fancying it was Pétion that bade them: a device which was not detected for almost a week. Dexterous enough; as if a man, finding the Day fast decline, should determine on altering the Clock-hands: *that* is a thing possible for him.

Here too let us note an unexpected apparition of Philippe d'Orléans at Court: his last at the Levee of any King. D'Orléans, sometime in the winter months seemingly, has been appointed to that old first-coveted rank of Admiral,—though only over ships rotting in port. The wished-for comes too late! However, he waits on Bertrand Moleville to give thanks: nay to state that he would willingly thank his Majesty in person; that, in spite of all the horrible things that men have said and

sung, he is far from being his Majesty's enemy; at bottom,
how far! Bertrand delivers the message, brings about the
royal Interview, which does pass to the satisfaction of his
Majesty; D'Orléans seeming clearly repentant, determined to
turn over a new leaf. And yet, next Sunday, what do we see?
'Next Sunday,' says Bertrand, 'he came to the King's Levee;
but the Courtiers ignorant of what had passed, the Crowd of
Royalists who were accustomed to resort thither on that day
specially to pay their court, gave him the most humiliating
reception. They came pressing round him; managing, as if
by mistake, to tread on his toes, to elbow him towards the
door, and not let him enter again. He went down stairs to her
Majesty's Apartments, where cover was laid; so soon as he
showed face, sounds rose on all sides, "*Messieurs, take care of
the dishes,*" as if he had carried poison in his pockets. The
insults which his presence everywhere excited, forced him to
retire without having seen the Royal Family: the crowd
followed him to the Queen's staircase; in descending, he
received a spitting (*crachat*) on the head, and some others on
his clothes. Rage and spite were seen visibly painted on his
face:' as indeed how could they miss to be? He imputes it
all to the King and Queen, who know nothing of it, who are
even much grieved at it; and so descends to his Chaos again.
Bertrand was there at the Château that day himself, and
an eye-witness to these things.

For the rest, Non-jurant Priests, and the repression of them,
will distract the King's conscience; Emigrant Princes and
Noblesse will force him to double-dealing: there must be *veto*
on *veto*; amid the ever-waxing indignation of men. For
Patriotism, as we said, looks on from without, more and more
suspicious. Waxing tempest, blast after blast, of Patriotic
indignation, from without; dim inorganic whirl of Intrigues,
Fatuities, within! Inorganic, fatuous; from which the eye
turns away. De Staël intrigues for her so gallant Narbonne,
to get him made War-Minister; and ceases not, having got
him made. The King shall fly to Rouen; shall there, with
the gallant Narbonne, properly 'modify the Constitution.'
This is the same brisk Narbonne, who, last year, cut out from
their entanglement, by force of dragoons, those poor fugitive
Royal Aunts: men say he is at bottom their Brother, or even
more, so scandalous is scandal. He drives now, with his De
Staël, rapidly to the Armies, to the Frontier Towns; produces
rose-coloured Reports, not too credible; perorates, gesticu-

lates; wavers poising himself on the top, for a moment, seen of men; then tumbles, dismissed, washed away by the Time-flood.

Also the fair Princess de Lamballe intrigues, bosom-friend of her Majesty: to the angering of Patriotism. Beautiful Unfortunate, why did she ever return from England? Her small silver-voice, what can it profit in that piping of the black World-Tornado? Which will whirl *her*, poor fragile Bird of Paradise, against grim rocks. Lamballe and De Staël intrigue visibly, apart or together: but who shall reckon how many others, and in what infinite ways, invisibly! Is there not what one may call an 'Austrian Committee,' sitting invisible in the Tuileries; centre of an invisible Anti-National Spiderweb, which, for we sleep among mysteries, stretches its threads to the ends of the Earth? Journalist Carra has now the clearest certainty of it: to Brissotin Patriotism, and France generally, it is growing more and more probable.

O Reader, hast thou no pity for this Constitution? Rheumatic shooting pains in its members; pressure of hydrocephale and hysteric vapours on its Brain: a Constitution divided against itself; which will never march, hardly even stagger! Why were not Drouet and Procureur Sausse in their beds, that unblessed Varennes Night! Why did they not, in the name of Heaven, let the Korff Berline go whither it listed! Nameless incoherency, incompatibility, perhaps prodigies at which the world still shudders, had been spared.

But now comes the third thing that bodes ill for the marching of this French Constitution: besides the French People, and the French King, there is thirdly—the assembled European World. It has become necessary now to look at that also. Fair France is so luminous: and round and round it, is troublous Cimmerian Night. Calonnes, Breteuils hover dim, far-flown; overnetting Europe with intrigues. From Turin to Vienna; to Berlin, and utmost Petersburg in the frozen North! Great Burke has raised his great voice long ago; eloquently demonstrating that the end of an Epoch is come, to all appearance the end of Civilised Time. Him many answer: Camille Desmoulins, Clootz Speaker of Mankind, Paine the rebellious Needleman, and honourable Gaelic Vindicators in that country and in this: but the great Burke remains unanswerable; 'the Age of Chivalry *is* gone,' and could not but go, having now produced the still more in-

domitable Age of Hunger. Altars enough, of the Dubois-
Rohan sort, changing to the Gobel-and-Talleyrand sort, are
faring by rapid transmutations to—shall we say, the right
Proprietor of them? French Game and French Game-
Preservers did alight on the Cliffs of Dover, with cries of
distress. Who will say that the end of much is not come?
A set of mortals has risen, who believe that Truth is not
a printed Speculation, but a practical Fact; that Freedom
and Brotherhood are possible in this Earth, supposed always
to be Belial's, which 'the Supreme Quack' was to inherit!
Who will say that Church, State, Throne, Altar are not in
danger; that the sacred Strongbox itself, last Palladium of
effete Humanity, may not be blasphemously blown upon, and
its padlocks undone?

The poor Constituent Assembly might act with what
delicacy and diplomacy it would; declare that it abjured
meddling with its neighbours, foreign conquest, and so forth;
but from the first this thing was to be predicted: that old
Europe and new France could not subsist *together*. A
Glorious Revolution, oversetting State-Prisons and Feudalism; publishing, with outburst of Federative Cannon, in
face of all the Earth, that Appearance is not Reality, how
shall it subsist amid Governments which, if Appearance is
not Reality, are—one knows not what? In death-feud, and
internecine wrestle and battle, it shall subsist with them; not
otherwise.

Rights of Man, printed on Cotton Handkerchiefs, in various
dialects of human speech, pass over to the Frankfort Fair.
What say we, Frankfort Fair? They have crossed Euphrates,
and the fabulous Hydaspes; wafted themselves beyond the
Ural, Altai, Himmalayah; struck off from wood stereotypes,
in angular Picture-writing, they are jabbered and jingled of in
China and Japan. Where will it stop? Kien-Lung smells
mischief; not the remotest Dalai-Lama shall now knead his
dough-pills in peace.—Hateful to us, as is the Night! Bestir
yourselves, ye Defenders of Order! They do bestir themselves: all Kings and Kinglets, with their spiritual temporal
array, are astir; their brows clouded with menace. Diplomatic
emissaries fly swift; Conventions, privy Conclaves assemble;
and wise wigs wag, taking what counsel they can.

Also, as we said, the Pamphleteer draws pen, on this side
and that: zealous fists beat the Pulpit-drum. Not without
issue! Did not iron Birmingham, shouting 'Church and

King,' itself knew not why, burst out, last July, into rage, drunkenness and fire; and your Priestleys, and the like, dining there on that Bastille day, get the maddest singeing : scandalous to consider! In which same days, as we can remark, High Potentates, Austrian and Prussian, with Emigrants, were faring towards Pilnitz in Saxony ; there, on the 27th of August, they, keeping to themselves what further 'secret Treaty' there might or might not be, did publish their hopes and their threatenings, their Declaration that it was 'the common cause of Kings.'

Where a will to quarrel is, there is a way. Our readers remember that Pentecost-Night, Fourth of August 1789, when Feudalism fell in a few hours ? The National Assembly, in abolishing Feudalism, promised that 'compensation' should be given ; and did endeavour to give it. Nevertheless the Austrian Kaiser answers that his German Princes, for their part, cannot be unfeudalised ; that they have Possessions in French Alsace, and Feudal Rights secured to them, for which no conceivable compensation will suffice. So this of the Possessioned Princes, *Princes Possessionnés*,' is bandied from Court to Court ; covers acres of diplomatic paper at this day : a weariness to the world. Kaunitz argues from Vienna ; Delessarts responds from Paris, though perhaps not sharply enough. The Kaiser and his possessioned Princes will too evidently come and *take* compensation,—so much as they can get. Nay might one not *partition* France, as we have done Poland, and are doing ; and so pacify it with a vengeance?

From South to North! For actually it is 'the common cause of Kings.' Swedish Gustav, sworn Knight of the Queen of France, will lead Coalised Armies ;—had not Ankarström treasonously shot him ; for, indeed, there were griefs nearer home. Austria and Prussia speak at Pilnitz ; all men intensely listening. Imperial Rescripts have gone out from Turin ; there will be secret Convention at Vienna. Catherine of Russia beckons approvingly; will help, were she ready. Spanish Bourbon stirs amid his pillows ; from him too, even from him, shall there come help. Lean Pitt, 'the Minister of Preparatives,' looks out from his watch-tower in Saint James's, in a suspicious manner. Councillors plotting, Calonnes dimhovering ;—alas, Sergeants rub-a-dubbing openly through all manner of German market-towns, collecting ragged valour! Look where you will, immeasurable Obscurantism is girdling this fair France ; which, again, will not be girdled by it.

Europe is in travail; pang after pang; what a shriek was that of Pilnitz! The birth will be: War.

Nay the worst feature of the business is this last, still to be named; the Emigrants at Coblentz. So many thousands ranking there, in bitter hate and menace: King's Brothers, all Princes of the Blood except wicked D'Orléans; your duelling De Castries, your eloquent Cazalès; bull-headed Malseignes, a war-god Broglie; Distaff Seigneurs, insulted Officers, all that have ridden across the Rhine-stream;— D'Artois welcoming Abbé Maury with a kiss, and clasping him publicly to his own royal heart! Emigration, flowing over the Frontiers, now in drops, now in streams, in various humours of fear, of petulance, rage and hope, ever since those first Bastille days when D'Artois went, 'to shame the citizens of Paris,'—has swollen to the size of a Phenomenon for the world. Coblentz is become a small extra-national Versailles; a Versailles *in partibus*; briguing, intriguing, favouritism, strumpetocracy itself, they say, goes on there; all the old activities, on a small scale, quickened by hungry Revenge.

Enthusiasm, of loyalty, of hatred and hope, has risen to a high pitch; as, in any Coblentz tavern, you may hear, in speech and in singing. Maury assists in the interior Council; much is decided on: for one thing, they keep lists of the dates of your emigrating; a month sooner, or a month later, determines your greater or your less right to the coming Division of the spoil. Cazalès himself, because he had occasionally spoken with a Constitutional tone, was looked on coldly at first: so pure are our principles. And arms are a-hammering at Liége; 'three thousand horses' ambling hitherward from the Fairs of Germany: Cavalry enrolling; likewise Foot-soldiers, 'in blue coat, red waistcoat and nankeen trousers.' They have their secret domestic correspondences, as their open foreign: with disaffected Crypto-Aristocrats, with contumacious Priests, with Austrian Committee in the Tuileries. Deserters are spirited over by assiduous crimps; Royal-Allemand is gone almost wholly. Their route of march, towards France and the Division of the Spoil, is marked out, were the Kaiser once ready. "It is said, they mean to poison the sources; but," adds Patriotism making report of it, "they will not poison the source of Liberty;" whereat '*on applaudit*,' we cannot but applaud. Also they have manufactories of False Assignats; and men that circulate in the interior, distributing

and disbursing the same ; one of these we denounce now to
Legislative Patriotism : ' a man Lebrun by name; about thirty
years of age, with blonde hair and in quantity; has,' only for
the time being surely, ' a black-eye, *œil poché ;* goes in a *wisk*
with a black horse,'—always keeping his Gig !

Unhappy Emigrants, it was their lot, and the lot of France
They are ignorant of much that they should know : of them
selves, of what is around them. A Political Party that knows
not *when it is beaten,* may become one of the fatallest of things
to itself, and to all. Nothing will convince these men that
they cannot scatter the French Revolution at the first blast o
their war-trumpet; that the French Revolution is other than a
blustering Effervescence, of brawlers and spouters, which, a
the flash of chivalrous broadswords, at the rustle of gallows
ropes, will burrow itself, in dens the deeper the welcomer
But, alas, what man does know and measure himself, and the
things that are round him ;—else where were the need o
physical fighting at all? Never, till they are cleft asunder, car
these heads believe that a Sansculottic arm has any vigour i
it : cleft asunder, it will be too late to believe.

One may say, without spleen against his poor erring brother
of any side, that above all other mischiefs, this of the Emigran
Nobles acted fatally on France. Could they have known
could they have understood ! In the beginning of 1789, a
splendour and a terror still surrounded them : the Conflagra
tion of their Châteaus, kindled by months of obstinacy, wen
out after the Fourth of August; and might have continued
out, had they at all known what to defend, what to relinquish
as indefensible. They were still a graduated Hierarchy o
Authorities, or the accredited similitude of such : they sa
there, uniting King with Commonalty ; transmitting and
translating *gradually*, from degree to degree, the command o
the one into the obedience of the other ; rendering command
and obedience still possible. Had they understood their
place, and what to do in it, this French Revolution, which
went forth explosively in years and in months, might have
spread itself over generations ; and not a torture-death but a
quiet euthanasia have been provided for many things.

But they were proud and high, these men ; they were no
wise to consider. They spurned all from them in disdainfu
hate, they drew the sword and flung away the scabbard
France has not only no Hierarchy of Authorities, to translate

command into obedience; its Hierarchy of Authorities has
fled to the enemies of France; calls loudly on the enemies of
France to interfere armed, who want but a pretext to do that.
Jealous Kings and Kaisers might have looked on long, medi-
tating interference, yet afraid and ashamed to interfere: but
now do not the King's Brothers, and all French Nobles,
Dignitaries and authorities that are free to speak, which the
King himself is not,—passionately invite us, in the name of
Right and of Might? Ranked at Coblentz, from Fifteen to
Twenty thousand stand now brandishing their weapons, with
the cry: On, on! Yes, Messieurs, you shall on ;—and divide
the spoil according to your dates of emigrating.

Of all which things a poor Legislative Assembly, and
Patriot France, is informed: by denunciant friend, by
triumphant foe. Sulleau's Pamphlets, of the Rivarol Staff of
Genius, circulate; heralding supreme hope. Durosoy's Placards tapestry the walls; *Chant du Coq* crows day, pecked at
by Tallien's *Ami des Citoyens*. King's-Friend Royou, *Ami du
Roi*, can name, in exact arithmetical ciphers, the contingents
of the various Invading Potentates; in all, Four hundred and
nineteen thousand Foreign fighting men, with Fifteen thousand Emigrants. Not to reckon these your daily and hourly
desertions, which an Editor must daily record, of whole Companies, and even Regiments, crying *Vive le Roi, Vive la Reine*,
and marching over with banners spread :—lies all, and wind ;
yet to Patriotism not wind; nor, alas, one day, to Royou !
Patriotism, therefore, may brawl and babble yet a little while:
but its hours are numbered: Europe is coming with Four
hundred and nineteen thousand and the Chivalry of France;
the gallows, one may hope, will get its own.

CHAPTER VI

BRIGANDS AND JALÈS

WE shall have War, then; and on what terms! With an
Executive 'pretending,' really with less and less deceptiveness
now, 'to be dead;' casting even a wishful eye towards the
enemy: on such terms we shall have War.

Public Functionary in vigorous action there is none; if it be
not Rivarol with his Staff of Genius and Two hundred and
eighty Applauders. The Public Service lies waste; the very

Taxgatherer has forgotten his cunning: in this and the other
Provincial Board of Management (*Directoire de Département*)
it is found advisable to *retain* what Taxes you can gather, to
pay your own inevitable expenditures. Our Revenue is
Assignats; emission on emission of Paper-money. And the
Army; our Three Grand Armies, of Rochambeau, of Lückner,
of Lafayette? Lean, disconsolate hover these Three grand
Armies, watching the frontiers there; three Flights of long-
necked Cranes in moulting time;—wrecked, disobedient, disorganised; who never saw fire; the old Generals and Officers
gone across the Rhine. War-Minister Narbonne, he of the
Rose-coloured Reports, solicits recruitments, equipments,
money, always money; threatens, since he can get none, to
'take his sword,' which belongs to himself, and go serve his
country with that.

The question of questions is: What shall be done? Shall
we, with a desperate defiance which Fortune sometimes
favours, draw the sword at once, in the face of this in-rushing
world of Emigration and Obscurantism; or wait, and temporise and diplomatise, till, if possible, our resources mature
themselves a little? And yet again, are our resources growing
towards maturity; or growing the *other* way? Dubious: the
ablest Patriots are divided; Brissot and his Brissotins, or
Girondins, in the Legislative, cry aloud for the former defiant
plan; Robespierre, in the Jacobins, pleads as loud for the
latter dilatory one: with responses, even with mutual reprimands; distracting the Mother of Patriotism. Consider also
what agitated Breakfasts there may be at Madame d'Udon's in
the Place Vendôme! The alarm of all men is great. Help,
ye Patriots; and O at least agree; for the hour presses. Frost
was not yet gone, when in that 'tolerably handsome apartment of the Castle of Niort,' there arrived a Letter: General
Dumouriez must to Paris. It is War-Minister Narbonne that
writes; the General shall give counsel about many things. In
the month of February 1792, Brissotin friends welcome their
Dumouriez *Polymetis*,—comparable really to an antique
Ulysses in modern costume; quick, elastic, shifty, insuppres-
sible, a 'many-counselled man.'

Let the Reader fancy this fair France with a whole Cimmerian Europe girdling her, rolling in on her, black, to burst
in red thunder of War; fair France herself hand-shackled and
foot-shackled in the weltering complexities of this Social

Clothing, or Constitution, which they have made for her; a France that, in such Constitution, cannot march! And Hunger too; and plotting Aristocrats, and excommunicating Dissident Priests: 'the man Lebrun by name' urging his black *wiski*, visible to the eye; and, still more terrible in his invisibility, Engineer Goguelat, with Queen's cipher, riding and running!

The excommunicatory Priests give new trouble in the Maine and Loire; La Vendée, nor Cathelineau the wool-dealer, has not ceased grumbling and rumbling. Nay, behold Jalès itself once more: how often does that real-imaginary Camp of the Fiend require to be extinguished! For near two years now, it has waned faint and again waxed bright, in the bewildered soul of Patriotism: actually, if Patriotism knew it, one of the most surprising products of Nature working with Art. Royalist Seigneurs, under this or the other pretext, assemble the simple people of the Cevennes Mountains; men not unused to revolt, and with heart for fighting, could their poor heads be got persuaded. The Royalist Seigneur harangues; harping mainly on the religious string: "True Priests maltreated, false Priests intruded, Protestants (once dragooned) now triumphing, things sacred given to the dogs;" and so produces, from the pious Mountaineer throat, rough growlings:—"Shall we not testify, then, ye brave hearts of the Cevennes; march to the rescue? Holy Religion; duty to God and the King?"—"*Si fait, si fait*, Just so, just so," answer the brave hearts always: "*Mais il y a de bien bonnes choses dans la Révolution*, But there are main good things in the Revolution too!"—And so the matter, cajole as we may, will only turn on its axis, not stir from the spot, and remain theatrical merely.

Nevertheless deepen your cajolery, harp quick and quicker, ye Royalist Seigneurs; with a dead-lift effort you may bring it to that. In the month of June next, this *Camp of Jalès* will step forth as a theatricality suddenly become real; Two thousand strong, and with the boast that it is Seventy thousand: most strange to see; with flags flying, bayonets fixed; with Proclamation, and D'Artois Commission of civil war! Let some Rebecqui, or other the like hot-clear Patriot; let some 'Lieutenant-Colonel Aubry,' if Rebecqui is busy elsewhere, raise instantaneous National Guards, and disperse and dissolve it; and blow the Old Castle asunder, that so, if possible, we hear of it no more!

In the months of February and March, it is recorded, the

terror, especially of rural France, had risen even to the transcendental pitch : not far from madness. In Town and Hamlet is rumour, of war, massacre : that Austrians, Aristocrats, above all, that *The Brigands* are close by. Men quit their houses and huts ; rush fugitive, shrieking, with wife and child, they know not whither. Such a terror, the eye-witnesses say, never fell on a Nation ; nor shall again fall, even in Reigns of Terror expressly so-called. The Countries of the Loire, all the Central and Southeast regions, start up distracted, 'simultaneously as by an electric shock ;'—for indeed grain too gets scarcer and scarcer. 'The people barricade the entrances of Towns, pile stones in the upper stories, the women prepare boiling water ; from moment to moment, expecting the attack. In the Country, the alarm-bell rings incessant ; troops of peasants, gathered by it, scour the highways, seeking an imaginary enemy. They are armed mostly with scythes stuck in wood ; and, arriving in wild troops at the barricaded Towns, are themselves sometimes taken for Brigands.'

So rushes old France : old France is rushing *down*. What the end will be is known to no mortal ; that the end is near all mortals may know.

CHAPTER VII

CONSTITUTION WILL NOT MARCH

To all which our poor Legislative, tied up by an unmarching Constitution, can oppose nothing, by way of remedy, but mere bursts of parliamentary eloquence ! They go on, debating, denouncing, objurgating : loud weltering Chaos, which devours *itself*.

But their two thousand and odd Decrees ? Reader, these happily concern not thee, nor me. Mere Occasional-Decrees, foolish and not foolish ; sufficient for *that* day was its own evil ! Of the whole two thousand there are not now half a score, and these mostly blighted in the bud by royal *Veto*, that will profit or disprofit us. On the 17th of January, the Legislative, for one thing, got its High Court, its *Haute Cour,* set up at Orleans. The theory had been given by the Constituent, in May last, but this is the reality : a Court for the trial of Political offences ; a Court which cannot want work. To this it was decreed that there needed no royal Acceptance, therefore that there could be no *Veto*. Also Priests can now

e married; ever since last October: A patriotic adventurous
priest had made bold to marry himself then; and not thinking
his enough, came to the bar with his new spouse; that the
whole world might hold honeymoon with him, and a Law be
obtained.

Less joyful are the Laws against Refractory Priests; and
yet not less needful! Decrees on Priests and Decrees on
Emigrants: these are the two brief Series of Decrees, worked
out with endless debate, and then cancelled by *Veto*, which
mainly concern us here. For an august National Assembly
must needs conquer these Refractories, Clerical or Laic, and
thumbscrew them into obedience: yet, behold, always as you
turn your legislative thumbscrew, and will press and even
crush till Refractories give way,—King's *Veto* steps in with
magical paralysis and your thumbscrew, hardly squeezing,
much less crushing, does not act!

Truly a melancholy Set of Decrees, a pair of Sets; paralysed
by *Veto!* First, under date the 28th of October 1791, we have
Legislative Proclamation, issued by herald and bill-sticker;
inviting Monsieur, the King's Brother, to return within two
months, under penalties. To which invitation Monsieur replies nothing; or indeed replies by Newspaper Parody, inviting
the august Legislative 'to return to common sense within two
months,' under penalties. Whereupon the Legislative must
take stronger measures. So, on the 9th of November, we
declare all Emigrants to be 'suspect of conspiracy;' and, in
brief, to be 'outlawed,' if they have not returned at Newyear's-
day:—Will the King say *Veto?* That 'triple impost' shall
be levied on these men's Properties, or even their Properties
be 'put in sequestration,' one can understand. But further,
on Newyear's-day itself, not an individual having 'returned,'
we declare, and with fresh emphasis some fortnight later again
declare, That Monsieur is *déchu*, forfeited of his eventful
Heirship to the Crown; nay more, that Condé, Calonne, and
a considerable List of others are accused of high treason; and
shall be judged by our High Court of Orleans: *Veto!*—Then
again as to Non-jurant Priests: it was decreed, in November
last, that they should forfeit what Pensions they had; be 'put
under inspection, under *surveillance*,' and, if need were, be
banished: *Veto!* A still sharper turn is coming, but to this
also the answer will be, *Veto*.

Veto after *Veto*; your thumbscrew paralysed! Gods and
men may see that the Legislative is in a false position. As,

alas, who is in a true one? Voices already murmur for a
'National Convention.' This poor Legislative, spurred and
stung into action by a whole France and a whole Europe,
cannot act; can only objurgate and perorate; with stormy
'motions,' and motion in which is no *way*; with effervescence,
with noise and fuliginous fury!

What scenes in that National Hall! President jingling his
inaudible bell; or, as utmost signal of distress, clapping on
his hat; 'the tumult subsiding in twenty minutes,' and this or
the other indiscreet Member sent to the Abbaye Prison for
three days! Suspected Persons must be summoned and
questioned; old M. de Sombreuil of the *Invalides* has to give
account of himself, and why he leaves his gates open. Unusual smoke rose from the Sèvres Pottery, indicating conspiracy;
the Potters explained that it was Necklace-Lamotte's *Mémoires*,
bought up by her Majesty, which they were endeavouring to
suppress by fire,—which nevertheless he that runs may still
read.

Again, it would seem, Duke de Brissac and the King's
Constitutional-Guard are 'making cartridges secretly in the
cellars:' a set of Royalists, pure and impure; black cut-
throats many of them, picked out of gaming-houses and
sinks; in all Six thousand instead of Eighteen hundred; who
evidently gloom on us every time we enter the Château.
Wherefore, with infinite debate, let Brissac and King's Guard
be *disbanded*. Disbanded accordingly they are; after only
two months of existence, for they did not get on foot till
March of this same year. So ends briefly the King's new
Constitutional *Maison Militaire*; he must now be guarded by
mere Swiss and blue Nationals again. It seems the lot of
Constitutional things. New Constitutional *Maison Civile*
he would never even establish, much as Barnave urged it; old
resident Duchesses sniffed at it, and held aloof; on the whole
her Majesty thought it not worth while, the Noblesse would
so soon be back triumphant.

Or, looking still into this National Hall and its scenes,
behold Bishop Torné, a Constitutional Prelate, not of severe
morals, demanding that 'religious costumes and such carica-
tures' be abolished. Bishop Torné warms, catches fire,
finishes by untying, and indignantly flinging on the table, as
if for gage or bet, his own pontifical cross. Which cross, at
any rate, is instantly covered by the cross of *Te-Deum*
Fauchet, then by other crosses, and insignia, till all are

tripped; this clerical Senator clutching off his skull-cap, that
other his frill-collar,—lest Fanaticism return on us.

Quick is the movement here! And then so confused,
insubstantial, you might call it almost *spectral:* pallid, dim,
inane, like the Kingdoms of Dis! Unruly Linguet, shrunk
to a kind of spectre for us, pleads here some cause that he
has; amid rumour and interruption, which excel human
patience: he 'tears his papers, and withdraws,' the irascible
stout little man. Nay, honourable Members will tear their
papers, being effervescent: Merlin of Thionville tears his
papers, crying: "So, the People cannot be saved by *you!*"
Nor are Deputations wanting: Deputations of Sections,
generally with complaint and denouncement, always with
Patriot fervour of sentiment: Deputation of Women, pleading
that they also may be allowed to take Pikes, and exercise in
the Champ-de-Mars. Why not, ye Amazons, if it be in you?
Then occasionally, having done our message and got answer,
we 'defile through the Hall, singing *ça-ira;*' or rather roll and
whirl through it, 'dancing our *ronde patriotique* the while,'—
our new *Carmagnole,* or Pyrrhic war-dance and liberty-dance.
Patriot Huguenin, Ex-Advocate, Ex-Carbineer, Ex-Clerk of
the Barriers, comes deputed, with Saint-Antoine at his heels;
denouncing Antipatriotism, Famine, Forestalment and Man-
eaters; asks an august Legislative: "Is there not a *tocsin in
your hearts* against these *mangeurs d'hommes!*"

But above all things, for this is a continual business, the
Legislative has to reprimand the King's Ministers. Of his
Majesty's Ministers we have said hitherto, and say, next to
nothing. Still more spectral these! Sorrowful; of no per-
manency any of them, none at least since Montmorin
vanished: the 'eldest of the King's Council' is occasionally
not ten days old. Feuillant-Constitutional, as your respectable Cahier de Gerville, as your respectable unfortunate
Delessarts! or Royalist-Constitutional, as Montmorin last
Friend of Necker; or Aristocrat, as Bertrand-Moleville: they
flit there phantom-like, in the huge simmering confusion;
poor shadows, dashed in the racking winds; powerless, without meaning;—whom the human memory need not charge
itself with.

But how often, we say, are these poor Majesty's Ministers
summoned over; to be questioned, tutored; nay threatened,
almost bullied! They answer what, with adroitest simulation
and casuistry, they can: of which a poor Legislative knows

not what to make. One thing only is clear, That Cimmerian Europe is girdling us in; that France (not actually dead, surely?) cannot march. Have a care, ye Ministers! Sharp Guadet transfixes you with cross-questions, with sudden Advocate-conclusions; the sleeping tempest that is in Vergniaud can be awakened. Restless Brissot brings up Reports, Accusations, endless thin Logic; it is the man's highday even now. Condorcet redacts, with his firm pen, our 'Address of the Legislative Assembly to the French Nation.' Fiery Max Isnard, who, for the rest, will "carry not Fire and Sword" on those Cimmerian Enemies, "but Liberty,"—is for declaring "that we hold Ministers responsible; and that by responsibility we mean death, *nous entendons la mort.*"

For verily it grows serious: the time presses, and traitors there are. Bertrand-Moleville has a smooth tongue, the known Aristocrat; gall in his heart. How his answers and explanations flow ready; jesuitic, plausible to the ear! But perhaps the notablest is this, which befell once when Bertrand had done answering and was withdrawn. Scarcely had the august Assembly begun considering what was to be done with him, when the Hall fills with *smoke*. Thick sour smoke: no oratory, only wheezing and barking;—irremediable; so that the august Assembly has to adjourn! A miracle? Typical miracle? One knows not: only this one seems to know, that 'the Keeper of the Stoves *was appointed* by Bertrand' or by some underling of his!—O fuliginous confused Kingdom of Dis, with thy Tantalus-Ixion toils, with thy angry Fire-floods, and Streams named of Lamentation, why hast thou not thy Lethe too, that so one might *finish*!

CHAPTER VIII

THE JACOBINS

NEVERTHELESS let not Patriotism despair. Have we not, in Paris at least, a virtuous Pétion, a wholly Patriotic Municipality? Virtuous Pétion, ever since November, is Mayor of Paris: in our Municipality, the Public, for the Public is now admitted too, may behold an energetic Danton; further, an epigrammatic slow-sure Manuel; a resolute unrepentant Billaud-Varennes, of Jesuit breeding; Tallien able-editor; and nothing but Patriots, better or worse. So ran the November Elec-

.ons: to the joy of most citizens; nay the very Court sup-
orted Pétion rather than Lafayette. And so Bailly and his
'euillants, long waning like the Moon, had to withdraw then,
naking some sorrowful obeisance, into extinction:—or indeed
nto worse, into lurid half-light, grimmed by the shadow of
hat Red Flag of theirs, and bitter memory of the Champ-de-
Mars. How swift is the progress of things and men! Not
now does Lafayette, as on that Federation-day, when *his* noon
vas, 'press his sword firmly on the Fatherland's Altar,' and
wear in sight of France (i. 283): ah no; he, waning and
etting ever since that hour, hangs now, disastrous, on the
dge of the horizon; commanding one of those Three moult-
ng Crane-flights of Armies, in a most suspected, unfruitful,
ncomfortable manner.

But, at worst, cannot Patriotism, so many thousands strong
n this Metropolis of the Universe, help itself? Has it not
ighthands, pikes? Hammering of Pikes, which was not to
be prohibited by Mayor Bailly, has been sanctioned by
Mayor Pétion; sanctioned by Legislative Assembly. How
not, when the King's so-called Constitutional Guard 'was
naking cartridges in secret?' Changes are necessary for the
National Guard itself; this whole Feuillant-Aristocrat Staff
of the Guard must be disbanded. Likewise, citizens without
uniform may surely rank in the Guard, the pike beside the
nusket, in such a time: the 'active' citizen and the passive
who can fight for us, are they not both welcome?—O my
Patriot friends, indubitably Yes! Nay the truth is, Patriotism
throughout, were it never so white-frilled, logical, respectable,
must either lean itself heartily on Sansculottism, the black,
bottomless; or else vanish, in the fruitfullest way, to Limbo!
Thus some, with upturned nose, will altogether sniff and
disdain Sansculottism; others will lean heartily on it; nay
others again will lean what we call *heartlessly* on it: three
sorts; each sort with a destiny corresponding.

In such point of view, however, have we not for the present
a Volunteer Ally, stronger than all the rest; namely, Hunger?
Hunger; and what rushing of Panic Terror this and the sum-
total of our other miseries may bring! For Sansculottism
grows by what all other things die of. Stupid Peter Baille
almost made an epigram, though unconsciously, and with the
Patriot world laughing not at it but at him, when he wrote:
'*Tout va bien ici, le pain manque*, All goes well here, food is
not to be had.'

Neither, if you knew it, is Patriotism without her Constitution that *can* march; her *not* impotent Parliament; or call it
Ecumenic Council, and General-Assembly of the Jean-Jacques
Churches: the MOTHER-SOCIETY, namely! Mother-Society
with her three hundred full-grown Daughters; with what we
can call little Grand-daughters trying to walk, in every village
of France, numerable, as Burke thinks, by the hundred thousand. This is the true Constitution; made not by Twelve
Hundred august Senators, but by Nature herself; and has
grown, unconsciously, out of the wants and the efforts of these
Twenty-five millions of men. They are 'Lords of the Articles,'
our Jacobins; they originate debates for the Legislative;
discuss Peace and War; settle beforehand what the Legislative is to do. Greatly to the scandal of philosophical men,
and of most Historians;—who do in that judge naturally, and
yet not wisely. A Governing Power must exist: your other
powers here are simulacra; this power is *it*.

Great is the Mother-Society: she has had the honour to
be denounced by Austrian Kaunitz; and is all the dearer to
Patriotism. By fortune and valour she has extinguished
Feuillantism itself, at least the Feuillant Club. This latter,
high as it once carried its head, she, on the 18th of February,
has the satisfaction to see shut, extinct; Patriots having gone
thither, with tumult to hiss it out of pain. The Mother-
Society has enlarged her locality, stretches now over the
whole nave of the Church. Let us glance in, with the worthy
Toulongeon, our old Ex-Constituent Friend, who happily has
eyes to see. 'The nave of the Jacobins Church,' says he,
'is changed into a vast Circus, the seats of which mount up
circularly like an amphitheatre to the very groin of the domed
roof. A high Pyramid of black marble, built against one of
the walls, which was formerly a funeral monument, has alone
been left standing: it serves now as back to the Office-bearers'
Bureau. Here on an elevated Platform sit President and Secretaries, behind and above them the white Busts of Mirabeau, of
Franklin, and various others, nay finally of Marat. Facing
this is the Tribune, raised till it is midway between floor and
groin of the dome, so that the speaker's voice may be in the
centre. From that point thunder the voices which shake all
Europe: down below, in silence, are forging the thunderbolts
and the firebrands. Penetrating into this huge circuit, where
all is out of measure, gigantic, the mind cannot repress some
movement of terror and wonder; the imagination recalls

those dread temples which Poetry, of old, had consecrated to
the Avenging Deities.'

Scenes too are in this Jacobin Amphiteatre,—had History
time for them. Flags of the "Three Free Peoples of the
Universe," trinal brotherly flags of England, America, France,
have been waved here in concert; by London Deputation, of
Whigs or *Wighs* and their Club, on this hand, and by young
French Citoyennes on that; beautiful sweet-tongued Female
Citizens, who solemnly send over salutation and brotherhood,
also Tricolor stitched by their own needle, and finally Ears of
Wheat; while the dome rebellows with *Vivent les trois peuples
libres!* from all throats :—a most dramatic scene. Demoiselle
Théroigne recites, from that Tribune in mid air, her persecu-
tions in Austria; comes leaning on the arm of Joseph Chénier,
Poet Chénier, to demand Liberty for the hapless Swiss of
Château-Vieux (i. 311). Be of hope, ye forty Swiss, tugging
there, in the Brest waters; *not* forgotten!

Deputy Brissot perorates from that Tribune; Desmoulins,
our wicked Camille, interjecting audibly from below, "*Coquin!*"
Here, though oftener in the Cordeliers, reverberates the lion-
voice of Danton; grim Billaud-Varennes is here; Collot
d'Herbois, pleading for the Forty Swiss, tearing a passion to
rags. Apophthegmatic Manuel winds up in this pithy way: " A
Minister must perish!"—to which the Amphitheatre responds:
"*Tous, Tous,* All, All!" But the Chief Priest and Speaker
of this place, as we said, is Robespierre, the long-winded incorruptible man. What spirit of Patriotism dwelt in men in
those times, this one fact, it seems to us, will evince: that
fifteen hundred human creatures, not bound to it, sat quiet
under the oratory of Robespierre; nay, listened nightly, hour
after hour, applausive; and gaped as for the word of life.
More insupportable individual, one would say, seldom opened
his mouth in any Tribune. Acrid, implacable-impotent; dull-
drawling, barren as the Harmattan-wind. He pleads in endless earnest-shallow speech, against immediate War, against
Woollen Caps or *Bonnets Rouges*, against many things; and is
the Trismegistus and Dalai-Lama of Patriot men. Whom
nevertheless a shrill-voiced little man, yet with fine eyes, and a
broad beautifully sloping brow, rises respectfully to controvert;
he is, say the Newspaper Reporters, 'M. Louvet, Author of the
charming Romance of *Faublas.*' Steady, ye Patriots! Pull
not *yet* two ways; with a France rushing panic-stricken in the
rural districts, and a Cimmerian Europe storming in on you!

CHAPTER IX

MINISTER ROLAND

ABOUT the vernal equinox, however, one unexpected gleam of hope does burst forth on Patriotism : the appointment of a thoroughly Patriot Ministry. This also his Majesty, among his innumerable experiments of wedding fire to water, will try. *Quod bonum sit.* Madame d'Udon's Breakfasts have jingled with a new significance ; not even Genevese Dumont but had a word in it. Finally, on the 15th and onwards to the 23rd day of March 1792, when all is negotiated,—this is the blessed issue ; this Patriot Ministry that we see.

General Dumouriez, with the Foreign Portfolio, shall ply Kaunitz and the Kaiser, in another style than did poor Delessarts ; whom indeed we have sent to our High Court of Orleans for his sluggishness. War-Minister Narbonne is washed away by the Time-flood ; poor Chevalier de Grave, chosen by the Court, is fast washing away : then shall austere Servan, able Engineer-Officer, mount suddenly to the War Department. Genevese Clavière sees an omen realised : passing the Finance Hôtel, long years ago, as a poor Genevese exile, it was borne wondrously on his mind that *he* was to be Finance-Minister ; and now he is it ;—and his poor Wife, given up by the Doctors, rises and walks, not the victim of nerves but their vanquisher. And above all, our Minister of the Interior ? Roland de la Platrière, he of Lyons ! So have the Brissotins, public or private Opinion, and Breakfasts in the Place Vendôme, decided it. Strict Roland, compared to a *Quaker endimanché*, or Sunday Quaker, goes to kiss hands at the Tuileries, in round hat and sleek hair, his shoes tied with mere riband or ferrat. The Supreme Usher twitches Dumouriez aside : "*Quoi, Monsieur !* No buckles to his shoes ?"—"Ah, Monsieur," answers Dumouriez, glancing towards the ferrat : "All is lost, *Tout est Perdu.*"

And so our fair Roland removes from her upper-floor in the Rue Saint-Jacques, to the sumptuous saloons once occupied by Madame Necker. Nay still earlier, it was Calonne that did all this gilding ; it was he who ground these lustres, Venetian mirrors ; who polished this inlaying, this veneering and or-moulu ; and made it, by rubbing of the proper *lamp*, an Aladdin's Palace :—and now behold, he wanders dim-flitting over Europe ; half-drowned in the Rhine-stream, scarcely saving his Papers! *Vos non vobis.*—The fair Roland, equal to either fortune, has her public Dinner on Fridays, the Ministers all there in a body: she withdraws to her desk (the cloth once removed), and seems busy writing; nevertheless loses no word: if, for example, Deputy Brissot and Minister Clavière get too hot in argument, she, not without timidity, yet with a cunning gracefulness, will interpose. Deputy Brissot's head, they say, is getting giddy, in this sudden height; as feeble heads do.

Envious men insinuate that the Wife Roland is Minister, and not the Husband: it is happily the worst they have to charge her with. For the rest, let whose head soever be getting giddy, it is not this brave woman's. Serene and queenly here, as she was of old in her own hired garret of the Ursulines Convent! She who has quietly shelled French-beans for her dinner; being led to that, as a young maiden, by quiet insight and computation; and knowing what that was, and what she was: such a one will also look quietly on or-moulu and veneering, not ignorant of these either. Calonne did the veneering: he gave dinners here, old Besenval diplomatically whispering to him; and was great: yet Calonne we saw at last 'walk with long strides.' Necker next: and where now is Necker? Us also a swift change has brought hither; a swift change will send us hence. Not a Palace but a Caravansera!

So wags and wavers this unrestful World, day after day, month after month. The streets of Paris, and all Cities, roll daily their oscillatory flood of men; which flood does nightly disappear, and lie hidden horizontal in beds and trucklebeds; and awakes on the morrow to new perpendicularity and movement. Men go their roads, foolish or wise;—Engineer Goguelat to and fro, bearing Queen's cipher. A Madame de Staël is busy; cannot clutch her Narbonne from the Time-flood: a Princess de Lamballe is busy; cannot help her Queen. Barnave, seeing the Feuillants dispersed, and Coblentz so brisk, begs by way of final recompense to kiss her Majesty's hand; "augurs not well of her new course;" and retires home to Grenoble, to wed an heiress there. The Café Valois and Méot the Restaurateur's hear daily gasconade; loud babble of Half-pay Royalists, with or without poniards. Remnants of Aristrocratic saloons call the new Ministry *Ministère-Sansculotte.* A Louvet, of the Romance *Faublas,* is busy in the Jacobins. A Cazotte, of the Romance *Diable Amoureux,* is busy else-where: better wert thou quiet, old Cazotte; it is a world, this, of magic become *real!* All men are busy; doing they only half guess what :—flinging seeds, of tares mostly, into the 'Seedfield of TIME:' this, by and by, will declare wholly what.

But Social Explosions have in them something dread, and as it were mad and magical; which indeed Life always secretly has : thus the dumb Earth (says Fable), if you pull her mandrake roots, will give a demonic mad-making *moan.* These Explosions and Revolts ripen, break forth like dumb dread Forces of Nature; and yet they are Men's forces; and yet *we* are part of them : the Dæmonic that is in man's life has burst out on us, will sweep us too away!—One day here is like another, and yet it is not like but different. How much is growing, silently resistless, at all moments! Thoughts are growing; forms of Speech are growing; and Customs and even Costumes; still more visibly are actions and transactions growing, and that doomed Strife of France with herself and with the whole world.

The word *Liberty* is never named now except in conjunction with another; *Liberty* and *Equality.* In like manner, what, in a reign of Liberty and Equality, can these words, 'Sir,' 'Obedient Servant,' 'Honour to be,' and such like, signify? Tatters and fibres of old Feudality; which, were it only in the Grammatical province, ought to be rooted out! The Mother-Society has long since had proposals to that effect : these she could not entertain; not, at the moment. Note too how the Jacobin Brethren are mounting new Symbolical head-gear : the Woollen Cap or Night-cap, *bonnet de laine,* better known as *bonnet rouge,* the colour being *red.* A thing one wears not only by way of Phrygian Cap-of-Liberty, but also for convenience'-sake, and then also in compliment to the Lower-class Patriots and Bastille-Heroes; for the Red Nightcap combines all the three properties. Nay cockades themselves begin to be made of wool, of tricolor yarn : the riband-cockade, as a symptom of Feuillant Upper-class temper, is becoming suspicious. Signs of the times.

Still more, note the travail-throes of Europe : or rather, note the birth she brings; for the successive throes and shrieks, of Austrian and Prussian Alliance, of Kaunitz Anti-jacobin Despatch, of French Ambassadors cast out, and so forth, were long to note. Dumouriez corresponds with Kaunitz, Metternich, or Cobentzel, in another style than Delessarts did. Strict becomes stricter; categorical answer, as to this Coblentz work and much else, shall be given. Failing which? Failing which, on the 20th day of April 1792, King and Ministers step over to the Salle de Manège, promulgate how the matter stands; and poor Louis, 'with tears in his eyes,' proposes that the Assembly do now decree War. After due eloquence, War is decreed that night.

War, indeed! Paris came all crowding, full of expectancy, to the morning, and still more to the evening, session. D'Orléans with his two sons is there; looks on, wide-eyed, from the opposite gallery. Thou canst look, O Philippe: it is a War big with issues, for thee and for all men. Cimmerian Obscurantism and this thrice-glorious Revolution shall wrestle for it then: some Four-and-Twenty years; in immeasurable Briareus wrestle; trampling and tearing; before they can come to any, not agreement, but compromise, and approximate ascertainment each of what is in the other.

Let our Three Generals on the Frontiers look to it, therefore; and poor Chevalier de Grave, the War-Minister, consider what he will do. What is in the three Generals and Armies we may guess. As for poor Chevalier de Grave, he, in this whirl of things all coming to a press and pinch upon him, loses head, and merely whirls with them, in a totally distracted manner; signing himself at last, 'De Grave, *Mayor of Paris;*' whereupon he demits, returns over the Channel to walk in Kensington Gardens; and austere Servan, the able Engineer-Officer, is elevated in his stead. To the post of Honour? To that of Difficulty, at least.

CHAPTER X

PÉTION-NATIONAL-PIQUE

AND yet, how, on the dark bottomless Cataracts, there plays the foolishest fantastic-coloured spray and shadow; hiding the Abyss under vapoury rainbows! Alongside of this discussion as to Austrian-Prussian War, there goes on not less but more vehemently a discussion, Whether the Forty or Two-and-forty Swiss of Château-Vieux (i. 311) shall be liberated from the Brest Galleys! And then, Whether, being liberated, they shall have a public Festival, or only private ones?

Théroigne, as we saw, spoke, and Collot took up the tale. Has not Bouillé's final display of himself, in that final Night of Spurs, stamped your so-called 'Revolt of Nanci' into a 'Massacre of Nanci,' for all Patriot judgments? Hateful is that massacre; hateful the Lafayette-Feuillant 'public thanks' given for it! For indeed, Jacobin Patriotism and dispersed Feuillantism are now at death-grips; and do fight with all weapons, even with scenic shows. The walls of Paris, accordingly, are covered with Placard and Counter-Placard, on the subject of Forty Swiss blockheads. Journal responds to Journal; Player Collot to Poetaster Roucher; Joseph Chénier the Jacobin, Squire of Théroigne, to his Brother André the Feuillant; Mayor Pétion to Dupont de Nemours: and for the space of two months, there is nowhere peace for the thought of man,—till this thing be settled.

Gloria in excelsis! The Forty Swiss are at last got 'amnestied.' Rejoice ye Forty; doff your greasy wool Bonnets, which shall become Caps of Liberty. The Brest Daughter-Society welcomes you from on board, with kisses on each cheek: your iron Handcuffs are disputed as Relics of Saints; the Brest Society indeed can have one portion, which it will beat into Pikes, a sort of Sacred Pikes; but the other portion must belong to Paris, and be suspended from the dome there, along with the Flags of the Three Free Peoples! Such a goose is man; and cackles over plush-velvet Grand Monarques and woollen Galley-slaves; over everything and over nothing,— and will cackle with his whole soul, merely if others cackle!

On the ninth morning of April, these Forty Swiss blockheads arrived. From Versailles; with *vivats* heaven-high; with the affluence of men and women. To the Townhall we conduct them; nay to the Legislative itself, though not without difficulty. They are harangued, bedinnered, begifted, —the very Court, *not* for conscience-sake, contributing something; and their Public Festival shall be next Sunday. Next Sunday accordingly it is. They are mounted into a 'triumphal Car resembling a ship;' are carted over Paris, with the clang of cymbals and drums, all mortals assisting applausive; carted to the Champ-de-Mars and Fatherland's Altar; and finally carted, for Time always brings deliverance,—into invisibility forevermore.

Whereupon dispersed Feuillantism, or that Party which loves Liberty, yet *not* more than Monarchy, will likewise have its Festival; Festival of Simonneau, unfortunate Mayor of Étampes, who died for the Law; most surely for the Law, though Jacobinism disputes; being trampled down with his Red Flag in the riot about grains. At which Festival the Public again assists, *un*applausive: not we.

On the whole, Festivals are not wanting; beautiful rainbow-spray when all is now rushing treble-quick towards its Niagara Fall. National Repasts there are; countenanced by Mayor Pétion; Saint-Antoine, and the Strong Ones of the Halles defiling through Jacobin Club, "their felicity," according to Santerre, "not perfect otherwise;" singing many-voiced their *ça-ira*, dancing their *ronde patriotique*. Among whom one is glad to discern Saint-Huruge, expressly 'in white hat,' the Saint-Christopher of the Carmagnole. Nay a certain *Tambour*, or National Drummer, having just been presented with a little daughter, determines to have the new Frenchwoman christened, on Fatherland's Altar, then and there. Repast once over, he accordingly has her christened; Fauchet the Te-Deum Bishop acting in chief, Thuriot and honourable persons standing gossips: by the name Pétion-National-Pique! Does this remarkable Citizeness, now past the meridian of life, still walk the Earth? Or did she die perhaps of teething? Universal History is not indifferent.

CHAPTER XI

THE HEREDITARY REPRESENTATIVE

AND yet it is not by carmagnole-dances, and singing of *ça-ira*, that the work can be done. Duke Brunswick is not dancing carmagnoles, but has his drill-sergeants busy.

On the Frontiers, our Armies, be it treason or not, behave in the worst way. Troops badly commanded shall we say? Or troops intrinsically bad? Unappointed, undisciplined, mutinous; that, in a thirty-years peace, have never seen fire? In any case, Lafayette's and Rochambeau's little clutch, which they made at Austrian Flanders, has prospered as badly as clutch need do: soldiers starting at their own shadow; suddenly shrieking "*On nous trahit*," and flying off in wild panic, at or before the first shot;—managing only to hang some two or three prisoners they had picked up, and massacre their own Commander, poor Théobald Dillon, driven into a granary by them in the Town of Lille.

And poor Gouvion: he who sat shiftless in that Insurrection of Women! Gouvion quitted the Legislative Hall and Parliamentary duties, in disgust and despair, when those Galley-slaves of Château-Vieux were admitted there. He said, "Between the Austrians and the Jacobins there is nothing but a soldier's death for it;" and so 'in the dark stormy night,' he has flung himself into the throat of the Austrian cannon, and perished in the skirmish at Maubeuge on the ninth of June. Whom Legislative Patriotism shall mourn, with black mort-cloths and melody in the Champ-de-Mars: many a Patriot shiftier, truer none. Lafayette himself is looking altogether dubious; in place of beating the Austrians, is about writing to denounce the Jacobins. Rochambeau, all disconsolate, quits the service: there remains only Lückner, the babbling old Prussian Grenadier.

Without Armies, without Generals! And the Cimmerian Night *has* gathered itself; Brunswick preparing his proclamation; just about to march! Let a Patriot Ministry and Legislative say, what in these circumstances it will do? Suppress internal enemies, for one thing, answers the Patriot Legislative; and proposes, on the 24th of May, its Decree for the Banishment of Priests. Collect also some nucleus of determined internal friends, adds War-Minister Servan; and proposes, on the 7th of June, his Camp of Twenty-thousand. Twenty-thousand National Volunteers; Five out of each Canton, picked Patriots, for Roland has charge of the Interior: they shall assemble here in Paris; and be for a defence, cunningly devised, against foreign Austrians and domestic *Austrian Committee* alike. So much can a Patriot Ministry and Legislative do.

Reasonable and cunningly devised as such Camp may, to Servan and Patriotism, appear, it appears not so to Feuillantism; to that Feuillant-Aristocrat Staff of the Paris Guard; a Staff, one would say again, which will need to be *dissolved*. These men see, in this proposed Camp of Servan's, an offence; and even, as they pretend to say, an insult. Petitions there come, in consequence, from blue Feuillants in epaulettes; ill received. Nay, in the end, there comes one Petition, called 'of the Eight-thousand National Guards:' so many names are on it, including women and children. Which famed Petition of the Eight-thousand is indeed received: and the Petitioners, all under arms, are admitted to the honours of the sitting,— if honours or even if sitting there be; for the instant their bayonets appear at the one door, the Assembly 'adjourns,' and begins to flow out at the other.

Also, in these same days, it is lamentable to see how National Guards, escorting *Fête-Dieu*, or *Corpus-Christi* ceremonial, do collar and smite down any Patriot that does not uncover as the Hostie passes. They clap their bayonets to the breast of Cattle-butcher Legendre, a known Patriot ever since the Bastille days; and threaten to butcher him; though he sat quite respectfully, he says, in his Gig, at a distance of fifty paces, waiting till the thing were by. Nay, orthodox females were shrieking to have down the *Lanterne* on him.

To such height has Feuillantism gone in this Corps. For indeed, are not their Officers creatures of the chief Feuillant, Lafayette? The Court too has, very naturally, been tampering with them; caressing them, ever since that dissolution of the so-called Constitutional Guard. Some Battalions are altogether '*pétris*, kneaded full' of Feuillantism, mere Aristocrats at bottom: for instance, the Battalion of the *Filles-Saint-Thomas* made up of your Bankers, Stockbrokers, and other Full-purses of the Rue Vivienne. Our worthy old Friend Weber, Queen's Foster-brother Weber, carries a musket in that Battalion,— one may judge with what degree of Patriotic intention.

Heedless of all which, or rather heedful of all which, the Legislative, backed by Patriotic France and the feeling of Necessity, decrees this Camp of Twenty-thousand. Decisive though conditional Banishment of malign Priests it has already decreed.

It will now be seen, therefore, Whether the Hereditary Representative is for us or against us? Whether or not, to all our other woes, this intolerablest one is to be added; which renders us not a menaced Nation in extreme jeopardy and need, but a paralytic Solecism of a Nation; sitting wrapped as in dead cerements, of a Constitutional-Vesture that were no other than a winding-sheet; our right hand glued to our left: to wait there, writhing and wriggling, unable to stir from the spot, till in Prussian rope we mount to the gallows? Let the Hereditary Representative consider it well: The Decree of Priests? The Camp of Twenty-thousand?—By Heaven, he answers, *Veto! Veto!*—Strict Roland hands-in his *Letter to the King;* or rather it was Madame's Letter, who wrote it all at a sitting; one of the plainest spoken Letters ever handed-in to any King. This plain-spoken Letter King Louis has the benefit of reading over-night. He reads, inwardly digests; and next morning, the whole Patriot Ministry finds itself turned out. It is the 13th of June 1792.

Dumouriez, the many-counselled, he, with one Duranthon, called Minister of Justice, does indeed linger for a day or two; in rather suspicious circumstances; speaks with the Queen, almost weeps with her : but in the end, he too sets off for the Army ; leaving what Un-Patriot or Semi-Patriot Ministry and Ministries can now accept the helm, to accept it. Name them not ; new quick-changing Phantasms, which shift like magic-lantern figures ; more spectral than ever !

Unhappy Queen, unhappy Louis! The two *Vetos* were so natural : are not the Priests martyrs ; also friends ? This Camp of Twenty-thousand, could it be other than of storm-fullest Sansculottes ? Natural ; and yet, to France, unendur-able. Priests that cooperate with Coblentz must go elsewhither with their martyrdom : stormful Sansculottes, these and no other kind of creatures will drive back the Austrians. If thou prefer the Austrians, then for the love of Heaven go join them. If not, join frankly with what will oppose them to the death. Middle course is none.

Or, alas, what extreme course was there left now for a man like Louis? Underhand Royalists, Ex-Minister Bertrand-Moleville, Ex-Constituent Malouet, and all manner of un-helpful individuals, advise and advise. With face of hope turned now on the Legislative Assembly, and now on Austria and Coblentz, and round generally on the Chapter of Chances, an ancient Kingship is reeling and spinning, one knows not whitherward, on the flood of things.

CHAPTER XII

PROCESSION OF THE BLACK BREECHES

BUT is there a thinking man in France who, in these circum-stances, can persuade himself that the Constitution will march? Brunswick is stirring ; *he*, in a few days now, will march. Shall France sit still, wrapped in dead cerements and grave-clothes, its right hand glued to its left, till the Brunswick Saint-Bartholomew arrive ; till France be as Poland, and its Rights of Man become a Prussian Gibbet ?

Verily it is a moment frightful for all men. National Death ; or else some preternatural convulsive outburst of National Life ;—that same *dæmonic* outburst ! Patriots whose audacity has limits had, in truth, better retire like Barnave ; court private felicity at Grenoble. Patriots whose audacity has no limits must sink down into the obscure ; and, daring and defying all things, seek salvation in stratagem, in Plot of Insurrection. Roland and young Barbaroux have spread out the Map of

France before them, Barbaroux says 'with tears:' they consider what Rivers, what Mountain-ranges are in it: they will retire behind this Loire-stream, defend these Auvergne stone-labyrinths; save some little sacred Territory of the Free; die at least in their last ditch. Lafayette indites his emphatic Letter to the Legislative against Jacobinism; which emphatic Letter will not heal the unhealable.

Forward, ye Patriots whose audacity has no limits; it is you now that must either do or die! The Sections of Paris sit in deep counsel; send out Deputation after Deputation to the Salle de Manége, to petition and denounce. Great is their ire against tyrannous *Veto*, *Austrian Committee*, and the combined Cimmerian Kings. What boots it? Legislative listens to the 'tocsin in our hearts;' grants us honours of the sitting, sees us defile with jingle and fanfaronade; but the Camp of Twenty-thousand, the Priest-Decree, bevetoed by Majesty, are become impossible for Legislative. Fiery Isnard says, "We will have Equality, should we descend for it to the tomb." Vergniaud utters, hypothetically, his stern Ezekiel-visions of the fate of Anti-national Kings. But the question is: Will hypothetic prophecies, will jingle and fanfaronade demolish the *Veto;* or will the Veto, secure in its Tuileries Château, remain undemolishable by these? Barbaroux, dashing away his tears, writes to the Marseilles Municipality, that they must send him 'Six-hundred men who know how to die, *qui savent mourir.*' No wet-eyed message this, but a fire-eyed one;—which will be obeyed!

Meanwhile the Twentieth of June is nigh, anniversary of that world-famous Oath of the Tennis-Court: on which day, it is said, certain citizens have in view to plant a *Mai* or Tree of Liberty in the Tuileries Terrace of the Feuillants; perhaps also to petition the Legislative and Hereditary Representative about these Vetos;—with such demonstration, jingle and evolution, as may seem profitable and practicable. Sections have gone singly, and jingled and evolved: but if they all went, or great part of them, and there, planting their *Mai* in these alarming circumstances, sounded the tocsin in their hearts?

Among King's Friends there can be but one opinion as to such a step: among Nation's Friends there may be two. On the one hand, might it not by possibility scare away these unblessed Vetos? Private Patriots and even Legislative Deputies may have each his own opinion, or own no-opinion: but the hardest task falls evidently on Mayor Pétion and the Municipals, at once Patriots and Guardians of the public Tranquillity. Hushing the matter down with the one hand; tickling it up with the other! Mayor Pétion and Municipality may lean this way; Department-Directory with Procureur-Syndic Rœderer, having a Feuillant tendency, may lean that. On the whole, each man must act according to his one opinion or to his two opinions; and all manner of influences, official representations cross one another in the foolishest way. Perhaps after all, the Project, desirable and yet not desirable, will dissipate itself, being run athwart by so many complexities; and come to nothing?

Not so; on the Twentieth morning of June, a large Tree of Liberty, Lombardy Poplar by kind, lies visibly tied on its car, in the Suburb Saint-Antoine. Suburb Saint-Marceau too, in the uttermost Southeast, and all that remote Oriental region, Pikemen and Pikewomen, National Guards, and the unarmed curious are gathering,—with the peaceablest intentions in the world. A tricolor Municipal arrives; speaks. Tush, it is all peaceable, we tell thee, in the way of Law: are not Petitions allowable, and the Patriotism of *Mais*? The tricolor Municipal returns without effect: your Sansculottic rills continue flowing, combining into brooks: towards noontide, led by tall Santerre in blue uniform, by tall Saint-Huruge in white hat, it moves westward, a respectable river, or complication of still-swelling rivers.

What Processions have we not seen: *Corpus-Christi* and Legendre waiting in his Gig; Bones of Voltaire with bullock-chariots, and goadsmen in Roman Costume; Feasts of Château-Vieux and Simonneau; Gouvion Funerals, Rousseau Sham-funeral, and the Baptism of Pétion-National-Pike! Nevertheless this Procession has a character of its own. Tricolor ribands streaming aloft from Pike-heads; ironshod batons; and emblems not a few; among which see specially these two, of the tragic and the untragic sort: a Bull's Heart transfixed with iron, bearing this epigraph, ' *Cœur d'Aristocrate*, Aristocrat's heart,' and, more striking still, properly the standard of the host, a pair of old Black Breeches (silk, they say), extended on cross-staff, high overhead, with these memorable words, ' *Tremblez tyrans, voilà les Sanculottes*, Tremble tyrants, here are the Sans-indispensables!' Also, the Procession trails two cannons.

Scarfed tricolor Municipals do now again meet it, in the Quai Saint Bernard; and plead earnestly, having called halt.

Peaceable, ye virtuous tricolor Municipals, peaceable are we as
the sucking dove. Behold our Tennis-Court *Mai*. Petition
is legal; and as for arms, did not an august Legislative receive
the so-called Eight-thousand in arms, Feuillants though they
were? Our Pikes, are they not of National iron? Law is
our father and mother, whom we will not dishonour; but
Patriotism is our own soul. Peaceable, ye virtuous Municipals;
—and on the whole, limited as to time! Stop we cannot;
march ye with us.—The Black Breeches agitate themselves,
impatient; the cannon-wheels grumble: the many-footed Host
tramps on.

How it reached the Salle de Manége, like an ever-waxing
river; got admittance after debate; read its Address; and
defiled, dancing and *ça-ira*-ing, led by tall sonorous Santerre
and tall sonorous Saint-Huruge: how it flowed, not now a
waxing river but a shut Caspian lake, round all Precincts of
the Tuileries; the front Patriot squeezed by the rearward
against barred iron Grates, like to have the life squeezed out
of him, and looking too into the dread throat of cannon, for
National Battalions stand ranked within: how tricolor Municipals ran assiduous, and Royalists with Tickets of Entry; and
both Majesties sat in the interior surrounded by men in black:
all this the human mind shall fancy for itself, or read in old
Newspapers, and Syndic Rœderer's *Chronicle of Fifty Days*.

Our *Mai* is planted; if not in the Feuillants Terrace,
whither is no ingate, then in the Garden of the Capuchins, as
near as we could get. National Assembly has adjourned till
the Evening Session: perhaps this shut lake, finding no
ingate, will retire to its sources again; and disappear in
peace? Alas, not yet: rearward still presses on; rearward
knows little what pressure is in the front. One would wish at
all events, were it possible, to have a word with his Majesty
first!

The shadows fall longer, eastward; it is four o'clock: will
his Majesty not come out? Hardly he! In that case, Commandant Santerre, Cattlebutcher Legendre, Patriot Huguenin
with the tocsin in his heart; they, and others of authority,
will enter *in*. Petition and request to wearied uncertain
National Guard; louder and louder petition; backed by the
rattle of our two cannons! The reluctant Grate opens: endless Sansculottic multitudes flood the stairs; knock at the
wooden guardian of your privacy. Knocks, in such case,
grow strokes, grow smashings: the wooden guardian flies in

shivers. And now ensues a Scene over which the world has
long wailed; and not unjustly; for a sorrier spectacle, of
Incongruity fronting Incongruity, and as it were recognising
themselves incongruous, and staring stupidly in each other's
face, the world seldom saw.

King Louis, his door being beaten on, opens it; stands
with free bosom; asking, "What do you want?" The Sansculottic flood recoils awestruck; returns however, the rear
pressing on the front, with cries of, "Veto! Patriot Ministers!
Remove Veto!"—which things, Louis valiantly answers, this
is not the time to do, nor this the way to ask him to do.
Honour what virtue is in a man. Louis does not want
courage; he has even the higher kind called moral-courage,
though only the passive-half of that. His few National
Grenadiers shuffle back with him, into the embrasure of a
window: there he stands, with unimpeachable passivity, amid
the shouldering and the braying; a spectacle to men. They
hand him a red Cap of Liberty; he sets it quietly on his head,
forgets it there. He complains of thirst; half-drunk Rascality
offers him a bottle, he drinks of it. "Sire, do not fear," says
one of his Grenadiers. "Fear?" answers Louis: "feel then,"
putting the man's hand on his heart. So stands Majesty in
Red woollen Cap; black Sansculottism weltering round him,
far and wide, aimless, with inarticulate dissonance, with cries
of "Veto! Patriot Ministers!"

For the space of three hours or more! The National
Assembly is adjourned; tricolor Municipals avail almost
nothing: Mayor Pétion tarries absent; Authority is none.
The Queen with her Children and Sister Elizabeth, in tears
and terror not for themselves only, are sitting behind barricaded tables and Grenadiers, in an inner room. The Men
in black have all wisely disappeared. Blind lake of Sansculottism welters stagnant through the King's Château, for the
space of three hours.

Nevertheless all things do end. Vergniaud arrives with
Legislative Deputation, the Evening Session having now
opened. Mayor Pétion has arrived; is haranguing, 'lifted on
the shoulders of two Grenadiers.' In this uneasy attitude and
in others, at various places without and within, Mayor Pétion
harangues; many men harangue; finally Commandant Santerre defiles; passes out, with his Sansculottism, by the
opposite side of the Château. Passing through the room
where the Queen, with an air of dignity and sorrowful resig-

nation, sat among the tables and Grenadiers, a woman offers her too a Red Cap; she holds it in her hand, even puts it on the little Prince Royal. "Madame," said Santerre, "this People loves you more than you think."—About eight o'clock the Royal Family fall into each other's arms amid 'torrents of tears.' Unhappy Family! Who would not weep for it, were there not a whole world to be wept for?

Thus has the Age of Chivalry gone, and that of Hunger come. Thus does all-needing Sansculottism look in the face of its *Roi*, Regulator, King or Able-man; and find that *he* has nothing to give it. Thus do the two Parties, brought face to face after long centuries, stare stupidly at one another, *This, it is I; but, good Heaven, is that Thou?*—and depart, not knowing what to make of it. And yet, Incongruities having recognised themselves to be incongruous, something must be made of it. The Fates know what.

This is the world-famous Twentieth of June, more worthy to be called the *Procession of the Black Breeches*. With which, what we had to say of this First French biennial Parliament, and its products and activities, may perhaps fitly enough terminate.

BOOK VI

THE MARSEILLESE

CHAPTER I

EXECUTIVE THAT DOES NOT ACT

How could your paralytic National Executive be put 'in action,' in any measure, by such a Twentieth of June as this? Quite contrariwise: a large sympathy for Majesty so insulted arises everywhere; expresses itself in Addresses, Petitions, 'Petition of the Twenty-thousand inhabitants of Paris,' and such like, among all Constitutional persons; a decided rallying round the throne.

Of which rallying it was thought King Louis might have made something. However, he does make nothing of it, or attempt to make; for indeed his views are lifted beyond domestic sympathy and rallying, over to Coblentz mainly. Neither in itself is this same sympathy worth much. It is sympathy of men who believe still that the Constitution can march. Wherefore the old discord and ferment, of Feuillant sympathy for Royalty and Jacobin sympathy for Fatherland, acting against each other from within; with terror of Coblentz and Brunswick acting from without:—this discord and ferment must hold on its course, till a catastrophe do ripen and come. One would think, especially as Brunswick is near marching, such catastrophe cannot now be distant. Busy, ye Twenty-five French Millions; ye foreign Potentates, minatory Emigrants, German drill-sergeants; each do what his hand findeth! Thou, O Reader, at such safe distance, wilt see what they make of it among them.

Consider, therefore, this pitiable Twentieth of June as a futility; no catastrophe, rather a *catastasis* or heightening. Do not its Black Breeches wave there, in the Historical Imagination, like a melancholy flag of distress; soliciting help, which no mortal can give? Soliciting pity, which thou wert hard-hearted not to give freely, to one and all! Other such flags, or what are called Occurrences, and black or bright symbolic Phenomena will flit through the Historical Imagination; these, one after one, let us note, with extreme brevity.

The first phenomenon is that of Lafayette at the Bar of the Assembly; after a week and day. Promptly, on hearing of this scandalous Twentieth of June, Lafayette has quitted his Command on the North Frontier, in better or worse order; and got hither, on the 28th, to repress the Jacobins : not by letter now ; but by oral Petition, and weight of character, face to face. The august Assembly finds the step questionable; invites him meanwhile to the honours of the sitting. Other honour, or advantage, there unhappily came almost none ; the Galleries all growling; fiery Isnard glooming; sharp Guadet not wanting in sarcasms.

And out of doors, when the sitting is over, Sieur Resson, keeper of the Patriot *Café* in these regions, hears in the street a hurlyburly ; steps forth to look, he and his Patriot customers : it is Lafayette's carriage, with a tumultuous escort of blue Grenadiers, Cannoneers, even Officers of the Line, hurrahing and capering round it. They make a pause opposite Sieur Resson's door ; wag their plumes at him ; nay shake their fists, bellowing *À bas les Jacobins;* but happily pass on without onslaught. They pass on, to plant a *Mai* before the General's door, and bully considerably. All which the Sieur Resson cannot but report with sorrow, that night in the Mother-Society. But what no Sieur Resson nor Mother-Society can do more than guess is this, That a council of rank Feuillants, your unabolished Staff of the Guard and who else has status and weight, is in these very moments privily diliberating at the General's : Can we not put down the Jacobins by force ? Next day, a Review shall be held, in the Tuileries Garden, of such as will turn out, and try. Alas, says Toulongeon, hardly a hundred turned out. Put it off till to-morrow, then, to give better warning. On the morrow, which is Saturday, there turn out 'some thirty;' and depart shrugging their shoulders ! Lafayette promptly takes carriage again ; returns musing on many things.

The dust of Paris is hardly off his wheels, the summer Sunday is still young, when Cordeliers in deputation pluck up that *Mai* of his : before sunset, Patriots have burnt him in effigy. Louder doubt and louder rises, in Section, in National Assembly, as to the legality of such unbidden Anti-jacobin visit on the part of a General : doubt swelling and spreading all over France, for six weeks or so; with endless talk about usurping soldiers, about English Monk, nay about Cromwell: O thou poor *Grandison*-Cromwell!—What boots it? King Louis himself looked coldly on the enterprise: colossal Hero of two Worlds, having weighed himself in the balance, finds that he is become a gossamer Colossus, only some thirty turning out.

In a like sense, and with a like issue, works our Department-Directory here at Paris; who, on the 6th of July, take upon them to suspend Mayor Pétion and Procureur Manuel from all civic functions, for their conduct, replete, as is alleged, with omissions and commissions, on that delicate Twentieth of June. Virtuous Pétion sees himself a kind of martyr, or pseudo-martyr, threatened with several things; drawls out due heroical lamentation; to which Patriot Paris and Patriot Legislative duly respond. King Louis and Mayor Pétion have already had an interview on that business of the Twentieth; an interview and dialogue, distinguished by frankness on both sides; ending on King Louis's side with the words " *Taisez-vous*, Hold your peace."

For the rest, this of suspending our Mayor does seem a mis-timed measure. By ill chance, it came out precisely on the day of that famous *Baiser de l'amourette*, or miraculous reconciliatory Delilah-Kiss, which we spoke of long ago (p. 51). Which Delilah-Kiss was thereby quite hindered of effect. For now his Majesty has to write, almost that same night, asking a reconciled Assembly for advice! The reconciled Assembly will not advise; will not interfere. The King confirms the suspension; then perhaps, but not till then will the Assembly interfere, the noise of Patriot Paris getting loud. Whereby your Delilah-Kiss, such was the destiny of Parliament First, becomes a Philistine Battle!

Nay there goes a word that as many as Thirty of our chief Patriot Senators are to be clapped in prison, by mittimus and indictment of Feuillant Justices, *Juges de Paix;* who here in Paris were well capable of such a thing. It was but in May last that *Juge-de-Paix Larivière*, on complaint of Bertrand-Moleville touching that *Austrian Committee*, made bold to launch his mittimus against three heads of the Mountain, Deputies Bazire, Chabot, Merlin, the Cordelier Trio; summoning them to appear before *him*, and show where that Austrian Committee was, or else suffer the consequences.

Which mittimus the Trio, on their side, made bold to fling in the fire : and valiantly pleaded privilege of Parliament. So that, for his zeal without knowledge, poor Justice Larivière now sits in the prison of Orleans, waiting trial from the *Haute Cour* there. Whose example, may it not deter other rash Justices ; and so this word of the Thirty arrestments continue a word merely?

But on the whole, though Lafayette weighed so light, and has had his *Mai* plucked up, Official Feuillantism falters not a whit ; but carries its head high, strong in the letter of the Law. Feuillants all of these men ; a Feuillant Directory ; founding on high character, and such like ; with Duke de la Rochefoucault for President,—a thing which may prove dangerous for him ! Dim now is the once bright Anglomania of these admired Noblemen. Duke de Liancourt offers, out of Normandy where he is Lord-Lieutenant, not only to receive his Majesty, thinking of flight thither, but to lend him money to enormous amounts. Sire, it is not a Revolt, it is a Revolution ; and truly no rose-water one ! Worthier Noblemen were not in France nor in Europe than those two : but the Time is crooked, quick-shifting, perverse ; what straightest course will lead to any goal, in *it?*

Another phasis which we note, in these early July days, is that of certain thin streaks of Federate National Volunteers wending from various points towards Paris, to hold a new Federation-Festival, or Feast of Pikes, on the Fourteenth there. So has the National Assembly wished it, so has the Nation willed it. In this way, perhaps, may we still have our Patriot Camp in spite of *Veto.* For cannot these Fédérés, having celebrated their Feast of Pikes, march on to Soissons ; and, there being drilled and regimented, rush to the Frontiers, or whither we like? Thus were the one *Veto* cunningly eluded !

As indeed the other *Veto*, about Priests, is also like to be eluded ; and without much cunning. For Provincial Assemblies, in Calvados as one instance, are proceeding, on their own strength, to judge and banish Anti-national Priests. Or still worse, without Provincial Assembly, a desperate People, as at Bourdeaux, can ' hang two of them on the Lanterne,' on the way towards judgment. Pity for the spoken *Veto*, when it cannot become an acted one !

It is true, some ghost of a War-minister, or Home-minister,

for the time being, ghost whom we do not name, does write to Municipalities and King's Commanders, that they shall, by all conceivable methods, obstruct this Federation, and even turn back the Fédérés by force of arms : a message which scatters mere doubt, paralysis and confusion ; irritates the poor Legislature ; reduces the Fédérés, as we see, to thin streaks. But being questioned, this ghost and the other ghosts, What it is then that they propose to do for saving the country ?—they answer, That they cannot tell ; that indeed they, for their part, have, this morning, resigned in a body ; and do now merely respectfully take leave of the helm altogether. With which words they rapidly walk out of the Hall, *sortent brusquement de la salle,* the 'Galleries cheering loudly,' the poor Legislature sitting 'for a good while in silence!' Thus do Cabinet-ministers themselves, in extreme cases, strike work ; one of the strangest omens. Other complete Cabinet-ministry there will not be ; only fragments, and these changeful, which never get completed ; spectral Apparitions that cannot so much as appear ! King Louis writes that he now views this Federation Feast with approval ; and will himself have the pleasure to take part in the same.

And so these thin streaks of Fédérés wend Paris-ward through a paralytic France. Thin grim streaks ; not thick joyful ranks, as of old to the First Feast of Pikes ! No ; these poor Federates march now towards Austria and Austrian Committee, towards jeopardy and forlorn hope ; men of hard fortune and temper, not rich in the world's goods. Municipalities, paralysed by War-minister, are shy of affording cash ; it may be, your poor Federates cannot arm themselves, cannot march, till the Daughter-Society of the place open her pocket, and subscribe. There will not have arrived, at the set day, Three-thousand of them in all. And yet, thin and feeble as these streaks of Federates seem, they are the only thing one discerns moving with any clearness of aim, in this strange scene. Angry buzz and simmer ; uneasy tossing and moaning of a huge France, all enchanted, spell-bound by unmarching Constitution, into frightful conscious and unconscious Magnetic-sleep ; which frightful Magnetic-sleep must now issue soon in one of two things : Death or Madness ! The Fédérés carry mostly in their pocket some earnest cry and Petition, to have the 'National Executive put in action ;' or as a step towards that, to have the King's *Déchéance*, King's Forfeiture, or at least his Suspension, pronounced. They shall be welcome to the Legislative, to the Mother of Patriotism ; and Paris will provide for their lodging.

Déchéance, indeed : and, what next ? A France spell-free, a Revolution saved ; and any thing, and all things next ! so answer grimly Danton and the unlimited Patriots, down deep in their subterranean region of Plot, whither they have now dived. *Déchéance*, answers Brissot with the limited : and if next the little Prince Royal were crowned, and some Regency of Girondins and recalled Patriot Ministry set over him ? Alas, poor Brissot ; looking, as indeed poor man does always, on the nearest morrow as his peaceable promised land ; deciding what must reach to the world's end, yet with an insight that reaches not beyond his own nose. Wiser are the unlimited subterranean Patriots, who with light for the hour itself, leave the rest to the gods.

Or were it not, as we now stand, the probablest issue of all, that Brunswick, in Coblentz, just gathering his huge limbs towards him to rise, might arrive first ; and stop both *Déchéance*, and theorising on it ? Brunswick is on the eve of marching ; with Eighty-thousand, they say ; fell Prussians, Hessians, feller Emigrants : a General of the Great Frederick, with such an Army. And our Armies ? And our Generals ? As for Lafayette, on whose late visit a Committee is sitting and all France is jarring and censuring, he seems readier to fight *us* than fight Brunswick. Lückner and Lafayette pretend to be interchanging corps, and are making movements, which Patriotism cannot understand. This only is very clear, that their corps go marching and shuttling, in the interior of the country ; much nearer Paris than formerly ! Lückner has ordered Dumouriez down to him ; down from Maulde, and the Fortified Camp there. Which order the many-counselled Dumouriez, with the Austrians hanging close on him, he busy meanwhile training a few thousands to stand fire and be soldiers, declares that, come of it what will, he cannot obey. Will a poor Legislative, therefore, sanction Dumouriez ; who applies to it, 'not knowing whether there is any War-ministry?' Or sanction Lückner and these Lafayette movements ?

The poor Legislative knows not what to do. It decrees, however, that the Staff of the Paris Guard, and indeed all such Staffs, for they are Feuillants mostly, shall be broken and replaced. It decrees earnestly in what manner one can declare that the *Country is in Danger*. And, finally, on the 11th of July, the morrow of that day when the Ministry struck work, it decrees that *the Country be*, with all despatch, *declared in Danger*. Whereupon let the King sanction; let the Municipality take measures: if such Declaration will do service, *it* need not fail.

In danger, truly, if ever Country was! Arise, O Country or be trodden down to ignominious ruin! Nay, are not the chances a hundred to one that no rising of the country will save it; Brunswick, the Emigrants, and Feudal Europe drawing nigh?

CHAPTER II

LET US MARCH

But, to our minds, the notablest of all these moving phenomena is that of Barbaroux's 'Six-hundred Marseillese who know how to die.'

Prompt to the request of Barbaroux, the Marseilles Municipality has got these men together: on the fifth morning of July, the Townhall says, "*Marchez, abattez le Tyran*, March strike down the Tyrant;" and they, with grim appropriate "*Marchons*," are marching. Long journey, doubtful errand, *Enfans de la Patrie*, may a good genius guide you! Their own wild heart and what faith it has will guide them: and is not that the monition of some genius, better or worse? Five hundred and Seventeen able men, with Captains of fifties and tens; well armed all, musket on shoulder, sabre on thigh: nay they drive three pieces of cannon; for who knows what obstacles may occur? Municipalities there are, paralysed by War-minister; Commandants with orders to stop even Federation Volunteers: good, when sound arguments will not open a Towngate, if you have a petard to shiver it! They have left their sunny Phocean City and Seahaven, with its bustle and its bloom: the thronging *Course*, with high frondent Avenues, pitchy dockyards, almond and olive groves, orange-trees on house-tops, and white glittering *bastides* that crown the hills, are all behind them. They wend on their wild way, from the extremity of French land, through unknown cities, toward an unknown destiny; with a purpose that they know.

Much wondering at this phenomenon, and how, in a peaceable trading City, so many householders or hearthholders do severally fling down their crafts and industrial tools; gird themselves with weapons of war, and set out on a journey of six-hundred miles, to 'strike down the tyrant,'—you search in all Historical Books, Pamphlets and Newspapers, for some light on it: unhappily without effect. Rumour and Terror precede this march; which still echo on you; the march itself an unknown thing. Weber, in the backstairs of the Tuileries, has understood that they were *Forçats*, Galley-Slaves and mere scoundrels, these Marseillese; that, as they marched through Lyons, the people shut their shops;—also that the number of them was some Four *Thousand*. Equally vague is Blanc Gilli, who likewise murmurs about *Forçats* and danger of plunder. *Forçats* they were not; neither was there plunder or danger of it. Men of regular life, or of the best-filled purse, they could hardly be; the one thing needful in them was that they 'knew how to die.' Friend Dampmartin saw them, with his own eyes, march 'gradually', through his quarters at Villefranche in the Beaujolais: but saw in the vaguest manner; being indeed preoccupied, and himself minded for marching just then—across the Rhine. Deep was his astonishment to think of such a march, without appointment or arrangement, station or ration; for the rest, it was 'the same men he had seen formerly' in the troubles of the South: 'perfectly civil;' though his soldiers could not be kept from talking a little with them.

So vague are all these; *Moniteur, Histoire Parlementaire* are as good as silent: garrulous History, as is too usual, will say nothing where you most wish her to speak! If enlightened Curiosity ever get sight of the Marseilles Council-Books, will it not perhaps explore this strangest of Municipal procedures; and feel called to fish up what of the Biographies, creditable or discreditable, of these Five-hundred and Seventeen, the stream of Time has not yet irrevocably swallowed?

As it is, these Marseillese remain inarticulate, undistinguishable in feature; a blackbrowed Mass, full of grim fire, who wend there, in the hot sultry weather: very singular to contemplate. They wend; amid the infinitude of doubt and dim peril; they not doubtful: Fate and Feudal Europe, having decided, come girdling in from without; they, having also decided, do march within. Dusty of face, with frugal refreshment, they plod onwards; unweariable, not to be turned aside. Such march will become famous. The Thought, which works voiceless in this blackbrowed mass, an inspired Tyrtæan Colonel, Rouget de Lille, whom the Earth still holds, has translated into grim melody and rhythm; into his *Hymn*

or March *of the Marseillese:* luckiest musical-composition
ever promulgated. The sound of which will make the blood
tingle in men's veins; and whole Armies and Assemblage
will sing it, with eyes weeping and burning, with hearts defiant
of Death, Despot and Devil.

One sees well, these Marseillese will be too late for the
Federation Feast. In fact, it is not Champ-de-Mars Oath
that they have in view. They have quite another feat to do;
a paralytic National Executive to set in action. They must
'strike down' whatsoever 'Tyrant,' or Martyr-Fainéant, there
may be who paralyses it; strike and be struck; and on the
whole prosper, and know how to die.

CHAPTER III

SOME CONSOLATION TO MANKIND

OF the Federation Feast itself we shall say almost nothing.
There are tents pitched in the Champ-de-Mars; tent for
National Assembly; tent for Hereditary Representative,—who
indeed is there too early, and has to wait long in it. There
are Eighty-three symbolic Departmental Trees-of-Liberty;
trees and *mais* enough: beautifullest of all, there is one huge
mai, hung round with effete Scutcheons, Emblazonries and
Genealogy-books, nay better still, with Lawyers'-bags, '*sacs de
procédure;*' which shall be burnt. The Thirty seat-rows of
that famed Slope are again full; we have a bright Sun; and
all is marching, streamering and blaring; but what avails it?
Virtuous Mayor Pétion, whom Feuillantism had suspended,
was reinstated only last night, by Decree of the Assembly.
Men's humour is of the sourest. Men's hats have on them,
written in chalk, '*Vive Pétion;*' and even, '*Pétion or Death,
Pétion ou la Mort.*'

Poor Louis, who has waited till five o'clock before the
Assembly would arrive, swears the National Oath this time,
with a quilted cuirass under his waistcoat which will turn
pistol-bullets. Madame de Staël, from that Royal Tent,
stretches out the neck in a kind of agony, lest the waving
multitude which receive him may not render him back alive.
No cry of *Vive le Roi* salutes the ear; cries only of *Vive
Pétion; Pétion ou la Mort.* The National Solemnity is as
it were huddled by; each cowering off almost before the
evolutions are gone through. The very *Mai* with its Scutch-

ons and Lawyers'-bags is forgotten, stands unburnt; till
certain Patriot Deputies,' called by the people, set a torch
to it, by way of voluntary after-piece. Sadder Feast of Pikes
no man ever saw.

Mayor Pétion, named on hats, is at his zenith in this
Federation; Lafayette again is close upon his nadir. Why
does the storm-bell of Saint-Roch speak out, next Saturday;
why do the citizens shut their shops? It is Sections defiling,
is fear of effervescence. Legislative Committee, long deliberating on Lafayette and that Anti-jacobin visit of his,
reports, this day, that there is 'not ground for Accusation!'
Peace, ye Patriots, nevertheless; and let that tocsin cease:
the Debate is not finished, nor the Report accepted; but
Brissot, Isnard and the Mountain will sift it, and resift it,
perhaps for some three weeks longer.

So many bells, storm-bells and noises do ring;—scarcely
audible; one drowning the other. For example: in this same
Lafayette tocsin, of Saturday, was there not withal some faint
bob-minor, and Deputation of Legislative, ringing the Chevalier
Paul Jones to his long rest; tocsin or dirge now all one to
him! Not ten days hence Patriot Brissot, beshouted this day
by the Patriot Galleries, shall find himself begroaned by them,
on account of his limited Patriotism; nay pelted at while
perorating, and 'hit with two prunes.' It is a distracted
empty-sounding world; of bob-minors and bob-majors, of
triumph and terror, of rise and fall!

The more touching is this other Solemnity, which happens
on the morrow of the Lafayette tocsin: Proclamation that the
Country is in Danger. Not till the present Sunday could
such Solemnity be. The Legislative decreed it almost a fortnight ago; but Royalty and the ghost of a Ministry held back
as they could. Now however on this Sunday, 22nd day of
July 1792, it will hold back no longer; and the Solemnity
in very deed is. Touching to behold! Municipality and
Mayor have on their scarfs; cannon-salvo booms alarm from
the Pont-Neuf, and single-gun at intervals all day. Guards
are mounted, scarfed Notabilities, Halberdiers, and a Cavalcade; with streamers, emblematic flags; especially with one
huge Flag, flapping mournfully: *Citoyens, la Patrie est en
Danger.* They roll through the streets, with stern-sounding
music, and slow rattle of hoofs; pausing at set stations, and,
with doleful blast of trumpet, singing out through Herald's

throat, what the Flag says to the eye: "Citizens, our Countr
is in Danger!"

Is there a man's heart that hears it without a thrill? Th
many-voiced responsive hum or bellow of these multitude
is not of triumph; and yet it is a sound deeper than triumph
But when the long Cavalcade and Proclamation ended; an
our huge Flag was fixed on the Pont-Neuf, another like
on the Hôtel-de-Ville, to wave there till better days; and eac
Municipal sat in the centre of his Section, in a Tent raise
in some open square, Tents surmounted with flags of *Patr
en Danger*, and topmost of all a Pike and *Bonnet Rouge;* and
on two drums in front of him, there lay a plank-table, and o
this an open Book, and a Clerk sat, like recording-ange
ready to write the lists, or as we say to enlist! O, then,
seems, the very gods might have looked down on it. Youn
Patriotism, Culottic and Sansculottic, rushes forward emulous
That is my name; name, blood and life is all my country's
why have I nothing more! Youths of short stature weep tha
they are below size. Old men come forward, a son in eac
hand. Mothers themselves will grant the son of their travail
send him, though with tears. And the multitude bellow
Vive la Patrie, far reverberating. And fire flashes in the eye
of men;—and at eventide, your Municipal returns to th
Townhall followed by his long train of Volunteer valour
hands-in his List; says proudly, looking round, This is m
day's harvest. They will march, on the morrow, to Soissons
small bundle holding all their chattels.

So with *Vive la Patrie, Vive la Liberté*, stone Paris rever
berates like Ocean in his caves; day after day, Municipal
enlisting in tricolor Tent; the Flag flapping on Pont-Neu
and Townhall, *Citoyens, la Patrie est en Danger*. Some Ter
thousand fighters, without discipline but full of heart, are o
march in few days. The like is doing in every Town c
France.—Consider, therefore, whether the Country will wan
defenders, had we but a National Executive? Let the Section
and Primary Assemblies, at any rate, become Permanent
They do become Permanent, and sit continually in Paris, an
over France, by Legislative Decree, dated Wednesday th
25th.

Mark contrariwise how, in these very hours, dated th
25th, Brunswick 'shakes himself, *s'ébranle*,' in Coblentz; an
takes the road! Shakes himself indeed; one spoken wor
becomes such a shaking. Successive, simultaneous *dirl* o

thirty-thousand muskets shouldered; prance and jingle of ten-thousand horsemen, fanfaronading Emigrants in the van; drum, kettledrum; noise of weeping, swearing; and the immeasurable lumbering clank of baggage-wagons and camp-kettles that groan into motion: all this is Brunswick shaking himself; not without all this does the one man march, 'covering a space of forty miles.' Still less without his Manifesto, dated, as we say, the 25th; a State-Paper worthy of attention!

By this Document, it would seem great things are in store for France. The universal French People shall now have permission to rally round Brunswick and his Emigrant Seigneurs; tyranny of a Jacobin faction shall oppress them no more; but they shall return, and find favour with their own good King; who, by Royal Declaration (three years ago) of the Twenty-third of June, said that he would himself make them happy. As for National Assembly, and other Bodies of Men invested with some temporary shadow of authority, they are charged to maintain the King's Cities and Strong Places intact, till Brunswick arrive to take delivery of them. Indeed, quick submission may extenuate many things; but to this end it must be quick. Any National Guard or other unmilitary person found resisting in arms shall be 'treated as a traitor;' that is to say, hanged with promptitude. For the rest, if Paris, before Brunswick gets thither, offer any insult to the King: or, for example, suffer a Faction to carry the King away elsewhither; in that case Paris shall be blasted asunder with cannon-shot and 'military execution.' Likewise all other Cities, which may witness, and not resist to the uttermost, such forced-march of his Majesty, shall be blasted asunder; and Paris and every City of them, starting-place, course and goal of said sacrilegious forced-march, shall, as rubbish and smoking ruin, lie there for a sign. Such vengeance were indeed signal, 'an *insigne vengeance;*'—O Brunswick, what words thou writest and blusterest! In this Paris, as in old Nineveh, are so many score thousands that know not the right hand from the left, and also much cattle. Shall the very milk-cows, hard-living cadgers'-asses, and poor little canary-birds die?

Nor is Royal and Imperial Prussian-Austrian Declaration wanting: setting forth, in the amplest manner, their Sanssouci-Schönbrunn version of this whole French Revolution, since the first beginning of it; and with what grief these high heads have seen such things done under the Sun. However, 'as some small consolation to mankind,' they do now dспatch Brunswick; regardless of expense, as one might saऀ or of sacrifices on their own part; for is it not the first duऀ to console men?

Serene Highnesses, who sit there protocolling and manऀ festoing, and consoling mankind! how were it if, for oncऀ in the thousand years, your parchments, formularies anऀ reasons of state were blown to the four winds; and Realitऀ Sans-indispensables stared you, even you, in the face; anऀ Mankind said for itself what the thing was that would consoऀ it?—

CHAPTER IV

SUBTERRANEAN

But judge if there was comfort in this to the Sections aऀ sitting permanent; deliberating how a National Executivऀ could be put in action!

High rises the response, not of cackling terror but oऀ crowing counter-defiance, and *Vive la Nation;* young Valouऀ streaming towards the Frontiers; *Patrie en Danger* muteऀ beckoning on the Pont-Neuf. Sections are busy, in theiऀ permanent Deep; and down, lower still, works unlimiteऀ Patriotism, seeking salvation in plot. Insurrection, you woulऀ say, becomes once more the sacredest of duties? Committeeऀ self-chosen, is sitting at the Sign of the Golden Sun; Jourऀ nalist Carra, Camille Desmoulins, Alsatian Westermann friencऀ of Danton, American Fournier of Martinique;—a Committeऀ not unknown to Mayor Pétion, who, as an official person. must sleep with one eye open. Not unknown to Procureuऀ Manuel; least of all to Procureur-Substitute Danton! He, wrapped in darkness, being also official, bears it on his gianऀ shoulders; cloudy invisible Atlas of the whole.

Much is invisible; the very Jacobins have their reticences. Insurrection is to be: but when? This only we can discern, that such Fédérés as are not yet gone to Soissons, as indeed are not inclined to go yet, "for reasons," says the Jacobin President, "which it may be interesting not to state,"—have got a *Central Committee* sitting close by, under the roof of the Mother-Society herself. Also, what in such ferment and danger of effervescence is surely proper, the Forty-eight Sections have got their Central Committee; intended 'for prompt communication.' To which Central Committee the

Municipality, anxious to have it at hand, could not refuse an
apartment in the Hôtel-de-Ville.

Singular City! For overhead of all this, there is the
customary baking and brewing; Labour hammers and grinds.
Frilled promenaders saunter under the trees; white-muslin
promenaderess, in green parasol, leaning on your arm. Dogs
dance, and shoeblacks polish, on that Pont-Neuf itself, where
Fatherland is in danger. So much goes its course; and yet
the course of all things is nigh altering and ending.

Look at that Tuileries and Tuileries Garden. Silent all as
Sahara; none entering save by ticket! They shut their Gates,
after the Day of the Black Breeches; a thing they had the
liberty to do. However, the National Assembly grumbled
somewhat about Terrace of the Feuillants, how said Terrace
lay contiguous to the back-entrance to their Salle, and was
partly *National* Property; and so now National Justice has
stretched a Tricolor Riband athwart it, by way of boundary-
line; respected with splenetic strictness by all Patriots. It
hangs there that Tricolor boundary-line; carries 'satirical
inscriptions on cards,' generally in verse; and all beyond this
is called *Coblentz*, and remains vacant; silent as a fateful
Golgotha; sunshine and umbrage alternating on it in vain.
Fateful Circuit; what hope can dwell in it? Mysterious
tickets of Entry introduce themselves; speak of Insurrection
very imminent. Rivarol's Staff of Genius had better purchase
blunderbusses; Grenadier bonnets, red Swiss uniforms may be
useful. Insurrection will come; but likewise will it not be
met? Staved off, one may hope, till Brunswick arrive?

But consider withal if the Bourne-stones and Portable-chairs
remain silent; if the Herald's College of Bill-Stickers sleep!
Louvet's *Sentinel* warns gratis on all walls; Sulleau is busy;
People's-Friend Marat and *King's-Friend* Royou croak and
counter-croak. For the man Marat, though long hidden
since that Champ-de-Mars Massacre, is still alive. He has
lain, who knows in what cellars; perhaps in Legendre's; fed
by a steak of Legendre's killing: but, since April, the bullfrog voice of him sounds again; hoarsest of earthly cries.
For the present, black terror haunts him: O brave Barbaroux,
wilt thou not smuggle me to Marseilles, 'disguised as a
jockey?' In Palais-Royal and all public places, as we read,
there is sharp activity; private individuals haranguing that
Valour may enlist; haranguing that the Executive may be put
in action. Royalist Journals ought to be solemnly burnt:

argument thereupon; debates, which generally end in single-stick, *coups de cannes*. Or think of this; the hour midnight place Salle de Manége; august Assembly just adjoining 'Citizens of both sexes enter in a rush, exclaiming, *Vengeance, they are poisoning our Brothers;*'—baking brayed-glass among their bread at Soissons! Vergniaud has to speak soothing words, How Commissioners are already sent to investigate this brayed-glass, and do what is needful therein;—till the rush of Citizens 'makes profound silence;' and goes home to its bed.

Such is Paris; the heart of a France like to it. Preter-natural suspicion, doubt, disquietude, nameless anticipation, from shore to shore:—and those blackbrowed Marseillese marching, dusty, unwearied, through the midst of it; not doubtful they. Marching to the grim music of their hearts, they consume continually the long road, these three weeks and more; heralded by Terror and Rumour. The Brest Fédérés arrive on the 26th; through hurrahing streets. Determined men are these also, bearing or not bearing the Sacred Pikes of Château-Vieux; and on the whole decidedly disinclined for Soissons as yet. Surely the Marseillese Brethren do draw nigher all days.

CHAPTER V

AT DINNER

It was a bright day for Charenton, that 29th of the month, when the Marseillese Brethren actually came in sight. Barbaroux, Santerre and Patriots have gone out to meet the grim way-farers. Patriot clasps dusty Patriot to his bosom; there is footwashing and refection: 'dinner of twelve-hundred covers at the Blue Dial, *Cadran Bleu;*' and deep interior consulta-tion, that one wots not of. Consultation indeed which comes to little; for Santerre, with an open purse, with a loud voice, has almost no head. Here, however, we repose this night: on the morrow is public entry into Paris.

Of which public entry the Day-Historians, *Diurnalists*, or Journalists as they call themselves, have preserved record enough. How Saint-Antoine male and female, and Paris generally, gave brotherly welcome, with bravo and hand-clapping, in crowded streets; and all passed in the peaceablest manner;—except it might be our Marseillese pointed out here

.nd there a riband-cockade, and beckoned that it should be
natched away, and exchanged for a wool one; which was
lone. How the Mother-Society in a body has come as far as
he Bastille ground, to embrace you. How you then wend
»nwards, triumphant, to the Townhall, to be embraced by
Mayor Pétion; to put down your muskets in the Barracks of
Jouvelle France, not far off;—then towards the appointed
Tavern in the Champs Élysées, to enjoy a frugal Patriot
epast.

Of all which the indignant Tuileries may, by its Tickets of
Entry, have warning. Red Swiss look doubly sharp to their
Château-Grates;—though surely there is no danger? Blue
Grenadiers of the Filles-Saint-Thomas Section are on duty
here this day: men of Agio, as we have seen; with stuffed
»urses, riband-çockades; among whom serves Weber. A
»arty of these latter, with Captains, with sundry Feuillant
Notabilities, Moreau de Saint-Méry of the three-thousand
»rders, and others, have been dining, much more respectably,
n a Tavern hard by. They have dined, and are now drinking
Loyal-Patriotic toasts; while the Marseillese, *National*-Patriotic
merely, are about sitting down to their frugal covers of delf.
How it happened remains to this day undemonstrable; but
he external fact is, certain of these Filles-Saint-Thomas
Grenadiers do issue from their Tavern; perhaps touched,
surely not yet muddled with any liquor they have had;—
issue in the professed intention of testifying to the Marseillese,
or to the multitude of Paris Patriots who stroll in these
spaces, That they, the Filles-Saint-Thomas men, if well seen
into, are not a whit less Patriotic than any other class of
men whatever.

It was a rash errand! For how can the strolling multitude
credit such a thing; or do other indeed than hoot at it, pro-
voking and provoked?—till Grenadier sabres stir in the scabbard, and thereupon a sharp shriek rises: "*À nous, Marseillais*,
Help, Marseillese!" Quick as lightning, for the frugal repast
is not yet served, that Marseillese Tavern flings itself open:
by door, by window; running, bounding, vault forth the Five-
hundred and Seventeen undined Patriots; and, sabre flashing
from thigh, are on the scene of controversy. Will ye parley,
ye Grenadier Captains and Official Persons: 'with faces
grown suddenly pale,' the deponents say? Advisabler were
instant moderately swift retreat! The Filles-Saint-Thomas
men retreat, back foremost; then, alas, face foremost, at treble-

quick time; the Marseillese, according to a Deponent, "clear
ing the fences and ditches after them, like lions: Messieurs, i
was an imposing spectacle."

Thus they retreat, the Marseillese following. Swift an
swifter, towards the Tuileries: where the Drawbridge receive
the bulk of the fugitives; and, then suddenly drawn up, save
them; or else the green mud of the Ditch does it. The bull
of them; not all; ah, no! Moreau de Saint-Méry, for ex
ample, being too fat, could not fly fast; he got a stroke, *fla*
stroke only, over the shoulder-blades and fell prone;—an
disappears there from the History of the Revolution. Cut
also there were, pricks in the posterior fleshy parts; much
rending of skirts, and other discrepant waste. But poor Sub
lieutenant Duhamel, innocent Change-broker, what a lot fo
him! He turned on his pursuer, or pursuers, with a pistol
he fired and missed; drew a second pistol, and again fired an
missed; then ran: unhappily in vain. In the Rue Saint
Florentin, they clutched him; thrust him through, in red rage
that was the end of the new Era, and of all Eras, to poor
Duhamel.

Pacific readers can fancy what sort of grace-before-meat this
was to frugal Patriotism. Also how the Battalion of the Filles
Saint-Thomas 'drew out in arms,' luckily without further
result; how there was accusation at the Bar of the Assembly,
and counter-accusation and defence; Marseillese challenging
the sentence of a free jury-court,—which never got empanneled.
We ask rather, What the upshot of all these distracted wildly
accumulating things may, by probability, be? Some upshot;
and the time draws nigh! Busy are Central Committees, of
Fédérés at the Jacobins Church, of Sections at the Townhall;
Reunion of Carra, Camille and Company at the Golden Sun.
Busy; like submarine deities, or call them mud-gods, working
there in deep murk of waters; till the thing be ready.

And how your National Assembly, like a ship water-logged,
helmless, lies tumbling; the Galleries, of shrill Women, of
Fédérés with sabres, bellowing down on it, not unfrightful;—
and waits where the waves of chance may please to strand it;
suspicious, nay on the Left-side, conscious, what submarine
Explosion is meanwhile a-charging! Petition for King's
Forfeiture rises often there: Petition from Paris Section, from
Provincial Patriot Towns; 'from Alençon, Briançon, and the
Traders at the Fair of Beaucaire.' Or what of these? On the
3rd of August, Mayor Pétion and the Municipality come

petitioning for Forfeiture : they openly, in their tricolor Municipal scarfs. Forfeiture is what all Patriots now want and expect. All Brissotins want Forfeiture, with the little Prince Royal for King, and us for Protector over him. Emphatic Fédérés ask the Legislature : "Can you save us, or not?" Forty-seven Sections have agreed to Forfeiture ; only that of the Filles-Saint-Thomas pretending to disagree. Nay Section Mauconseil declares Forfeiture to be, properly speaking, come ; Mauconseil, for one, 'does from this day,' the last of July, 'cease allegiance to Louis,' and take minute of the same before all men. A thing blamed aloud ; but which will be praised aloud ; and the name *Mauconseil*, of Ill-counsel, be thenceforth changed to *Bon-conseil*, of Good-counsel.

President Danton, in the Cordelier's Section, does another thing : invites all Passive Citizens to take place among the Active in Section-business, one peril threatening all. Thus he, though an official person ; cloudy Atlas of the whole. Likewise he manages to have that blackbrowed Battalion of Marseillese shifted to new Barracks, in his own region of the remote Southeast. Sleek Chaumette, cruel Billaud, Deputy Chabot the Disfrocked, Huguenin with the tocsin in his heart, will welcome them there. Wherefore, again and again : "O Legislators, can you save us or not?" Poor Legislators ; with their Legislature water-logged, volcanic Explosion charging under it ! Forfeiture shall be debated on the ninth of August ; that miserable business of Lafayette may be expected to terminate on the eighth.

Or will the humane Reader glance into the Levee-day of Sunday the fifth? The last Levee ! Not for a long time, 'never,' says Bertrand-Moleville, had a Levee been so brilliant, at least so crowded. A sad presaging interest sat on every face ; Bertrand's own eyes were filled with tears. For, indeed, outside of that Tricolor Riband on the Feuillants Terrace, Legislature is debating, Sections are defiling, all Paris is astir this very Sunday, demanding *Déchéance*. Here, however, within the riband, a grand proposal is on foot, for the hundredth time, of carrying his Majesty to Rouen and the Castle of Gaillon. Swiss at Courbevoye are in readiness ; much is ready ; Majesty himself seems almost ready. Nevertheless, for the hundredth time, Majesty, when near the point of action, draws back ; writes, after one has waited, palpitating, an endless summer day, that 'he has reason to believe the Insurrection is not so ripe as you suppose.' Whereat Bertrand-

Moleville breaks forth 'into extremity at once of spleen and despair, *d'humeur et de désespoir*.'

CHAPTER VI

THE STEEPLES AT MIDNIGHT

For, in truth, the Insurrection is just about ripe. Thursday is the ninth of the month August: if Forfeiture be not pronounced by the Legislature that day, we must pronounce it ourselves.

Legislature? A poor water-logged Legislature can pronounce nothing. On Wednesday the eighth, after endless oratory once again, they cannot even pronounce Accusation against Lafayette; but absolve him, hear it, Patriotism!—by a majority of two to one. Patriotism hears it; Patriotism, hounded on by Prussian Terror, by Preternatural Suspicion, roars tumultuous round the Salle de Manége, all day; insults many leading Deputies, of the absolvent Right-side; nay chases them, collars them with loud menace: Deputy Vaublanc, and others of the like, are glad to take refuge in Guardhouses, and escape by the back window. And so, next day, there is infinite complaint; Letter after Letter from insulted Deputy; mere complaint, debate and self-cancelling jargon: the sun of Thursday sets like the others, and no Forfeiture pronounced. Wherefore in fine, To your tents, O Israel!

The Mother-Society ceases speaking; groups cease haranguing: Patriots, with closed lips now, 'take one another's arm;' walk off, in rows, two and two, at a brisk business-pace; and vanish afar in the obscure places of the East. Santerre is ready; or we will make him ready. Forty-seven of the Forty-eight Sections are ready; nay, Filles-Saint-Thomas itself turns up the Jacobin side of it, turns down the Feuillant side of it, and is ready too. Let the unlimited Patriot look to his weapon, be it pike, be it firelock; and the Brest brethren,—above all, the blackbrowed Marseillese prepare themselves for the extreme hour! Syndic Rœderer knows, and laments or not as the issue may turn, that 'five-thousand ball-cartridges, within these few days, have been distributed to Fédérés, at the Hôtel-de-Ville.'

And ye likewise, gallant gentlemen, defenders of Royalty, crowd ye on your side to the Tuileries. Not to a Levee: no, to a Couchée; where much will be put to bed. Your Tickets

f Entry are needful; needfuller your blunderbusses!—They
ome and crowd, like gallant men who also know how to die:
ld Maillé the Camp-Marshal has come, his eyes gleaming
nce again, though dimmed by the rheum of almost fourscore
ears. Courage, Brothers! We have a thousand red Swiss; men
tanch of heart, stedfast as the granite of their Alps. National
irenadiers are at least friends of Order; Commandant Mandat
reathes loyal ardour, will "answer for it on his head." Mandat
vill, and his Staff; for the Staff, though there stands a doom
nd Decree to that effect, is happily never yet dissolved.

Commandant Mandat has corresponded with Mayor Pétion;
arries a written Order from him these three days, to repel
orce by force. A squadron on the Pont-Neuf with cannon
hall turn back these Marseillese coming across the River: a
quadron at the Townhall shall cut Saint-Antoine in two, 'as
t issues from the Arcade Saint-Jean;' drive one half back to
he obscure East, drive the other half forward 'through the
Vickets of the Louvre.' Squadrons not a few, and mounted
quadrons; squadrons in the Palais Royal, in the Place Ven-
lôme: all these shall charge, at the right moment; sweep this
treet, and then sweep that. Some new Twentieth of June we
hall have; only still more ineffectual? Or probably the In-
urrection will not dare to rise at all? Mandat's Squadrons,
Horse-Gendarmerie and blue Guards march, clattering, tramp-
ng; Mandat's Cannoneers rumble. Under cloud of night; to
he sound of his *générale*, which begins drumming when men
hould go to bed. It is the 9th night of August 1792.

On the other hand, the Forty-eight Sections correspond by
wift messengers; are choosing each their 'three Delegates
vith full powers.' Syndic Rœderer, Mayor Pétion are sent
or to the Tuileries: courageous Legislators, when the drum
eats danger, should repair to their Salle. Demoiselle
Théroigne has on her grenadier-bonnet, short-skirted riding-
abit; two pistols garnish her small waist, and sabre hangs
n baldric by her side.

Such a game is playing in this Paris Pandemonium, or City
f all the Devils!—And yet the Night, as Mayor Pétion
valks here in the Tuileries Garden, 'is beautiful and calm;'
Orion and the Pleiades glitter down quite serene. Pétion has
:ome forth, the 'heat' inside was so oppressive. Indeed, his
Majesty's reception of him was of the roughest; as it well
might be. And now there is no outgate; Mandat's blue

Squadrons turn you back at every Grate; nay the Filles-Sain
Thomas Grenadiers give themselves liberties of tongue, Ho
a virtuous Mayor 'shall pay for it, if there be mischief,' an
the like; though others again are full of civility. Surely
any man in France is in straits this night, it is Mayor Pétion
bound, under pain of death, one may say, to smile dexterousl
with the one side of his face, and weep with the other;—death i
he do it not dexterously enough! Not till four in the mornin
does a National Assembly, hearing of his plight, summon hin
over 'to give account of Paris;' of which he knows nothing
whereby, however, he shall get home to bed, and only hi
gilt coach be left. Scarcely less delicate is Syndic Rœderer'
task; who must wait whether he will lament or not, till he se
the issue. Janus Bifrons, or *Mr. Facing-both-ways*, as ver
nacular Bunyan has it! They walk there, in the meanwhile
these two Januses, with others of the like double conforma
tion; and 'talk of indifferent matters.'

Rœderer, from time to time, steps in; to listen, to speak
to send for the Department-Directory itself, he their Procureu
Syndic not seeing how to act. The Apartments are all
crowded; some seven-hundred gentlemen in black elbowing
bustling; red Swiss standing like rocks; ghost, or partial
ghost of a Ministry, with Rœderer and advisers, hovering
round their Majesties; old Marshal Maillé kneeling at the
King's feet to say, He and these gallant gentlemen are come to
die for him. List! through the placid midnight; clang of
the distant stormbell! So, in very sooth: steeple after steeple
takes up the wondrous tale. Black Courtiers listen at the
windows, opened for air; discriminate the steeple-bells: this
is the tocsin of Saint-Roch; that again, is it not Saint-Jacques,
named *de la Boucherie?* Yes, Messieurs! Or even Saint-
Germain l'Auxerrois, hear ye *it* not? The same metal that
rang storm, two hundred and twenty years ago; but by a
Majesty's order then; on Saint Bartholomew's Eve!—So go
the steeple-bells; which Courtiers can discriminate. Nay,
meseems, there is the Townhall itself; we know it by its
sound! Yes, Friends, that is the Townhall; discoursing *so*,
to the Night. Miraculously; by miraculous metal-tongue and
man's arm: Marat himself, if you knew it, is pulling at the
rope there! Marat is pulling; Robespierre lies deep, invisible for the next forty hours; and some men have heart, and
some have as good as none, and not even frenzy will give
them any.

What struggling confusion, as the issue slowly draws on; and the doubtful Hour, with pain and blind struggle, brings forth its Certainty, never to be abolished!—The Full-power Delegates, three from each Section, a Hundred and forty-four in all, got gathered at the Townhall, about midnight. Mandat's Squadron, stationed there, did not hinder their entering: are they not the 'Central Committee of the Sections' who sit here usually; though in greater number to-night? They are there: presided by Confusion, Irresolution, and the Clack of Tongues. Swift scouts fly; Rumour buzzes, of Black Courtiers, red Swiss, of Mandat and his Squadrons that shall charge. Better put off the Insurrection? Yes, put it off. Ha, Hark! Saint-Antoine booming out eloquent tocsin, of its own accord! —Friends, no: ye cannot put off the Insurrection; but must put it on, and live with it, or die with it.

Swift now, therefore: let these actual Old Municipals, on sight of the Full-powers, and mandate of the Sovereign elective People, lay down their functions; and this New Hundred and Forty-four take them up! Will ye nill ye, worthy Old Municipals, go ye must.. Nay is it not a happiness for many a Muncipal that he can wash his hands of such a business; and sit there paralysed, unaccountable, till the Hour do bring forth; or even go home to his night's rest? Two only of the Old, or at most three, we retain: Mayor Pétion, for the present walking in the Tuileries; Procureur Manuel; Procureur-Substitute Danton, invisible Atlas of the whole. And so, with our Hundred and Forty-four, among whom are a Tocsin-Huguenin, a Billaud, a Chaumette; and Editor-Talliens, and Fabre d'Eglantines, Sergents, Panises; and in brief, either emergent or else emerged and full-blown, the entire Flower of unlimited Patriotism: have we not, as by magic, made a New Municipality, ready to act in the unlimited manner; and declare itself roundly, 'in a State of Insurrection!'—First of all, then, be Commandant Mandat sent for, with that Mayor's-Order of his; also let the New Municipals visit those Squadrons that were to charge; and let the storm-bell ring its loudest;—and, on the whole, Forward, ye Hundred and Forty-four; retreat is now none for you!

Reader, fancy not, in thy languid way, that Insurrection is easy. Insurrection is difficult: each individual uncertain even of his next neighbour; totally uncertain of his distant neighbours, what strength is with him, what strength is against him; certain only that, in case of failure, his individual portion is the gallows! Eight hundred thousand heads, and in each of them a separate estimate of these uncertainties, a separate theorem of action conformable to that: out of so many uncertainties, does the certainty, and inevitable net-result never to be abolished, go on, at all moments, bodying itself forth;—leading thee also towards civic-crowns or an ignominious noose.

Could the reader take an Asmodeus' Flight, and waving open all roofs and privacies, look down from the Tower of Notre-Dame, what a Paris were it! Of treble-voice whimperings or vehemence, of bass-voice growlings, dubitations; Courage screwing itself to desperate defiance; Cowardice trembling silent within barred doors; and all round, Dulness calmly snoring; for much Dulness, flung on its mattresses, always sleeps. O, between the clangour of these high-storming tocsins and that snore of Dulness, what a gamut: of trepidation, excitation, desperation; and above it mere Doubt, Danger, Atropos and Nox!

Fighters of this Section draw out; hear that the next Section does not; and thereupon draw in. Saint-Antoine, on this side the River, is uncertain of Saint-Marceau on that. Steady only is the snore of Dulness, are the Six-hundred Marseillese that know how to die. Mandat, twice summoned to the Townhall, has not come. Scouts fly incessant, in distracted haste; and the many-whispering voices of Rumour. Théroigne and unofficial Patriots flit, dim-visible, exploratory, far and wide; like Night-birds on the wing. Of Nationals some Three-thousand have followed Mandat and his *générale*; the rest follow each his own theorem of the uncertainties: theorem, that one should march rather with Saint-Antoine: innumerable theorems that in such a case, the wholesomest were *sleep*. And so the drums beat, in mad fits, and the stormbells peal. Saint-Antoine itself does but draw out and draw in: Commandant Santerre, over there, cannot believe that the Marseillese and Saint-Marceau will march. Thou laggard sonorous Beer-vat, with the loud voice and timber-head, is it time now to palter? Alsatian Westermann clutches him by the throat with drawn sabre: whereupon the Timber-headed believes. In this manner wanes the slow night; amid fret, uncertainty and tocsin; all men's humour rising to the hysterical pitch; and nothing done.

However, Mandat, on the third summons, does come;—come, unguarded; astonished to find the Municipality *new*.

They question him straitly on that Mayor's-Order to resist force
by force ; on that strategic scheme of cutting Saint-Antoine
in two halves : he answers what he can : they think it were
right to send this strategic National Commandant to the
Abbaye Prison, and let a Court of Law decide on him. Alas,
a Court of Law, not Book-Law but primeval Club-Law,
crowds and jostles out of doors ; all fretted to the hysterical
pitch ; cruel as Fear, blind as the Night : such Court of Law,
and no other, clutches poor Mandat from his constables ;
beats him down, massacres him, on the steps of the Townhall.
Look to it, ye new Municipals ; ye People, in a state of Insurrection ! Blood is shed, blood must be answered for ;—
alas, in such hysterical humour, more blood will flow : for it
is as with the Tiger in that : he has only to begin.

Seventeen Individuals have been seized in the Champs
Élysées, by exploratory Patriotism ; they flitting dim-visible, by
it flitting dim-visible. Ye have pistols, rapiers, ye Seventeen ?
One of those accursed 'false Patrols ;' that go marauding, with
Anti-National intent; seeking what they can spy, what they can
spill ! The Seventeen are carried to the nearest Guardhouse ;
eleven of them escape by back passages. "How is this ?"
Demoiselle Théroigne appears at the front entrance, with
sabre, pistols and a train ; denounces treasonous connivance ;
demands, seizes, the remaining six, that the justice of the
People be not trifled with. Of which six two more escape in
the whirl and debate of the Club-Law Court ; the last unhappy
Four are massacred, as Mandat was : Two Ex-Bodyguards ;
one dissipated Abbé ; one Royalist Pamphleteer, Sulleau,
known to us by name, Able Editor, and wit of all work.
Poor Sulleau : his *Acts of the Apostles*, and brisk Placard-
Journals (for he was an able man) come to *Finis*, in this
manner ; and questionable jesting issues suddenly in horrid
earnest ! Such doings usher-in the dawn of the Tenth of
August 1792.

Or think what a night the poor National Assembly has had :
sitting there 'in great paucity,' attempting to debate ;—quivering and shivering ; pointing towards all the thirty-two azimuths
at once, as the magnet-needle does when thunderstorm is in
the air ! If the Insurrection come ? If it come, and fail ?
Alas, in that case, may not black Courtiers with blunderbusses, red Swiss with bayonets rush over, flushed with victory,
and ask us : Thou undefinable, waterlogged, self-distractive,
self-destructive Legislative, what dost thou here *unsunk ?*—Or

figure the poor National Guards, bivouacking in 'temporary tents' there; or standing ranked, shifting from leg to leg, all through the weary night; New tricolor Municipals ordering one thing, old Mandat Captains ordering another. Procureur Manuel has ordered the cannons to be withdrawn from the Pont-Neuf; none ventured to disobey him. It seems certain, then, the old Staff, so long doomed, has finally been dissolved, in these hours; and Mandat is not our Commandant now, but Santerre? Yes, friends: Santerre henceforth,— surely Mandat no more! The Squadrons that were to charge see nothing certain, except that they are cold, hungry, worn down with watching; that it were sad to slay French brothers; sadder to be slain by them. Without the Tuileries Circuit, and within it, sour uncertain humour sways these men: only the red Swiss stand stedfast. Them their officers refresh now with a slight wetting of brandy; wherein the Nationals, too far gone for brandy, refuse to participate.

King Louis meanwhile had lain him down for a little sleep; his wig when he reappeared had lost the powder on one side. Old Marshal Maillé and the gentlemen in black rise always in spirits, as the Insurrection does not rise: there goes a witty saying now, "*Le tocsin ne rend pas*," The tocsin, like a dry milk-cow, does not yield. For the rest, could not one proclaim Martial Law? Not easily; for now, it seems, Mayor Pétion is gone. On the other hand, our Interim Commandant, poor Mandat being off 'to the Hôtel-de-Ville,' complains that so many Courtiers in black encumber the service, are an eye-sorrow to the National Guards. To which her Majesty answers with emphasis, That they will obey all, will suffer all, that they are sure men these.

And so the yellow lamplight dies out in the gray of morning, in the King's Palace, over such a scene. Scene of jostling, elbowing, of confusion, and indeed conclusion, for the thing is about to end. Rœderer and spectral Ministers jostle in the press; consult, in side-cabinets, with one or with both Majesties. Sister Elizabeth takes the Queen to the window: "Sister, see what a beautiful sunrise," right over the Jacobins Church and that quarter! How happy if the tocsin did not yield! But Mandat returns not; Pétion is gone: much hangs wavering in the invisible Balance. About five o'clock, there rises from the Garden a kind of sound; as of a shout which had become a howl, and instead of *Vive le Roi* were ending in

Vive la Nation. "*Mon Dieu!*" ejaculates a spectral Minister, "what is he doing down there?" For it is his Majesty, gone down with old Marshal Maillé to review the troops; and the nearest companies of them answer *so.* Her Majesty bursts into a stream of tears. Yet on stepping from the cabinet, her eyes are dry and calm, her look is even cheerful. 'The Austrian lip, and the aquiline nose, fuller than usual, gave to her countenance,' says Peltier, 'something of majesty, which they that did not see her in these moments cannot well have an idea of.' O thou Theresa's Daughter!

King Louis enters, much blown with the fatigue; but for the rest with his old air of indifference. Of all hopes now, surely the joyfullest were, that the tocsin did not yield.

CHAPTER VII

THE SWISS

UNHAPPY Friends, the tocsin does yield, has yielded! Lo ye, how with the first sunrays its Ocean-tide, of pikes and fusils, flows glittering from the far East;—immeasurable; born of the Night! They march there, the grim host; Saint-Antoine on this side the River; Saint-Marceau on that, the black-browed Marseillese in the van. With hum, and grim murmur, far-heard; like the Ocean-tide, as we say: drawn up, as if by Luna and Influences, from the great Deep of Waters, they roll gleaming on; no King, Canute or Louis, can bid them roll back. Wide-eddying side-currents, of onlookers, roll hither and thither, unarmed, not voiceless; they, the steel host, roll on. New-Commandant Santerre, indeed, has taken seat at the Townhall; rests there, in his halfway-house. Alsatian Westermann, with flashing sabre, does not rest; nor the Sections, nor the Marseillese, nor Demoiselle Théroigne; but roll continually on.

And now, where are Mandat's Squadrons that were to charge? Not a Squadron of them stirs: or they stir in the wrong direction, out of the way; their officers glad that they will even do that. It is to this hour uncertain whether the Squadron on the Pont-Neuf made the shadow of resistance, or did not make the shadow: enough, the blackbrowed Marseillese, and Saint-Marceau following them, do cross without let; do cross, in sure hope now of Saint-Antoine and the rest; do billow on, towards the Tuileries, where their errand is. **The**

Tuileries, at sound of them, rustles responsive: the red Swiss look to their priming; Courtiers in black draw their blunderbusses, rapiers, poniards, some have even fire-shovels; every man his weapon of war.

Judge if, in these circumstances, Syndic Rœderer felt easy! Will the kind Heavens open no middle-course of refuge for a poor Syndic who halts between two? If indeed his Majesty would consent to go over to the Assembly! His Majesty, above all her Majesty, cannot agree to that. Did her Majesty answer the proposal with a "*Fi donc;*" did she say even, she would be nailed to the walls sooner? Apparently not. It is written also that she offered the King a pistol; saying, Now or else never was the time to show himself. Close eye-witnesses did not see it, nor do we. They saw only that she was queenlike, quiet; that she argued not, upbraided not, with the Inexorable; but, like Cæsar in the Capitol, wrapped her mantle, as it beseems Queens and Sons of Adam to do. But thou, O Louis! of what stuff art thou at all? Is there no stroke in thee, then, for Life and Crown? The silliest hunted deer dies not so. Art thou the languidest of all mortals; or the mildest-minded? Thou art the worst-starred.

The tide advances; Syndic Rœderer's and all men's straits grow straiter and straiter. Fremescent clangour comes from the armed Nationals in the Court; far and wide is the infinite hubbub of tongues. What counsel? And the tide is now nigh! Messengers, forerunners speak hastily through the outer Grates; hold parley sitting astride the walls. Syndic Rœderer goes out and comes in. Cannoneers ask him: Are we to fire against the people? King's Ministers ask him: Shall the King's House be forced? Syndic Rœderer has a hard game to play. He speaks to the Cannoneers with eloquence, with fervour; such fervour as a man can, who has to blow hot and cold in one breath. Hot and cold, O Rœderer? We, for our part, cannot live *and* die! The Cannoneers, by way of answer, fling down their linstocks.— Think of this answer, O King Louis, and King's Ministers; and take a poor Syndic's safe middle-course, towards the Salle de Manège. King Louis sits, his hands leant on his knees, body bent forward; gazes for a space fixedly on Syndic Rœderer; then answers, looking over his shoulder to the Queen: *Marchons!* They march; King Louis, Queen, Sister Elizabeth, the two royal children and governess: these, with Syndic Rœderer, and Officials of the Department; amid a

double rank of National Guards. The men with blunderbusses, the steady red Swiss gaze mournfully, reproachfully ;
but hear only these words from Syndic Rœderer : " The King
is going to the Assembly ; make way." It has struck eight,
on all clocks, some minutes ago : the King has left the
Tuileries—forever.

O ye stanch Swiss, ye gallant gentlemen in black, for what
a cause are ye to spend and be spent ! Look out from the
western windows, ye may see King Louis placidly hold on
his way ; the poor little Prince Royal 'sportfully kicking the
fallen leaves.' Fremescent multitude on the Terrace of the
Feuillants whirls parallel to him ; one man in it, very noisy,
with a long pole : will they not obstruct the outer Staircase,
and back-entrance of the Salle, when it comes to that ? King's
Guards can go no further than the bottom step there. Lo,
Deputation of Legislators come out ; he of the long pole is
stilled by oratory ; Assembly's Guards join themselves to
King's Guards, and all may mount in this case of necessity ;
the outer Staircase is free, or passable. See, Royalty ascends ;
a blue Grenadier lifts the poor little Prince Royal from the
press ; Royalty has entered in. Royalty has vanished forever
from your eyes.—And ye ? Left standing there, amid the
yawning abysses, and earthquake of Insurrection ; without
course ; without command : if ye perish, it must be as more
than martyrs, as martyrs who are now without a cause ! The
black Courtiers disappear mostly ; through such issues as they
can. The poor Swiss know not how to act : one duty only is
clear to them, that of standing by their post ; and they will
perform that.

But the glittering steel tide has arrived ; it beats now
against the Château barriers, and eastern Courts ; irresistible,
loud-surging far and wide ;—breaks in, fills the Court of the
Carrousel, blackbrowed Marseillese in the van. King Louis
gone, say you ; over to the Assembly ! Well and good : but
till the Assembly pronounce Forfeiture of him, what boots it ?
Our post is in that Château or stronghold of his ; there till
then must we continue. Think, ye stanch Swiss, whether it
were good that grim murder began, and brothers blasted one
another in pieces for a stone edifice ?—Poor Swiss ! they know
not how to act : from the southern windows, some fling
cartridges, in sign of brotherhood ; on the eastern outer staircase, and within through long stairs and corridors, they stand
firm-ranked, peaceable and yet refusing to stir. Westermann

speaks to them in Alsatian German ; Marseillese plead, in hot Provençal speech and pantomime; stunning hubbub pleads and threatens, infinite, around. The Swiss stand fast, peaceable and yet immovable ; red granite pier in that waste-flashing sea of steel.

Who can help the inevitable issue; Marseillese and all France on this side; granite Swiss on that? The pantomime grows hotter and hotter ; Marseillese sabres flourishing by way of action ; the Swiss brow also clouding itself, the Swiss thumb bringing its firelock to the cock. And hark ! high thundering above all the din, three Marseillese cannon from the Carrousel, pointed by a gunner of bad aim, come rattling over the roofs ! Ye Swiss, therefore, *Fire !* The Swiss fire; by volley, by platoon, in rolling-fire : Marseillese men not a few, and 'a tall man that was louder than any,' lie silent, smashed upon the pavement;—not a few Marseillese after the long dusty march, have made halt *here*. The Carrousel is void; the black tide recoiling; 'fugitives rushing as far as St. Antoine before they stop.' The Cannoneers without linstock have squatted invisible, and left their cannon; which the Swiss seize.

Think what a volley : reverberating doomful to the four corners of Paris, and through all hearts ; like the clang of Bellona's thongs ! The blackbrowed Marseillese, rallying on the instant, have become black Demons that know how to die. Nor is Brest behindhand ; nor Alsatian Westermann; Demoiselle Théroigne is Sibyl Théroigne : Vengeance, *Victoire ou la mort!* From all Patriot artillery, great and small ; from Feuillants Terrace, and all terraces and places of the widespread Insurrectionary sea, there roars responsive a red blazing whirlwind. Blue Nationals, ranked in the Garden, cannot help their muskets going off, *against* Foreign murderers. For there is a sympathy in muskets, in heaped masses of men : nay, are not Mankind, in whole, like tuned strings, and a cunning infinite concordance and unity ; you smite one string, and all strings will begin sounding,—in soft sphere-melody, in deafening screech of madness ! Mounted Gendarmerie gallop distracted; are fired on merely as a thing running; galloping over the Pont Royal, or one knows not whither. The brain of Paris, brain-fevered in the centre of it here, has gone mad ; what you call, taken fire.

Behold, the fire slackens not ; nor does the Swiss rolling-fire slacken from within. Nay they clutched cannon, as we saw ;

and now, from the other side, they clutch three pieces more; alas, cannon without linstock; nor will the steel-and-flint answer, though they try it. Had it chanced to answer! Patriot onlookers have their misgivings; one strangest Patriot onlooker thinks that the Swiss, had they a commander, would beat. He is a man not unqualified to judge; the name of him Napoleon Buonaparte. And onlookers, and women, stand gazing, and the witty Dr. Moore of Glasgow among them, on the other side of the River; cannon rush rumbling past them; pause on the Pont Royal; belch out their iron entrails there, against the Tuileries; and at every new belch, the women and onlookers 'shout and clap hands.' City of all the Devils! In remote streets, men are drinking breakfast-coffee; following their affairs; with a start now and then, as some dull echo reverberates a note louder. And here? Marseillese fall wounded; but Barbaroux has surgeons; Barbaroux is close by, managing, though underhand, and under cover. Marseillese fall death-struck; bequeath their firelock, specify in which pocket are the cartridges; and die murmuring, "Revenge me, Revenge thy country!" Brest Fédéré Officers, galloping in red coats, are shot as Swiss. Lo you, the Carrousel has burst into flame!—Paris Pandemonium! Nay the poor city, as we said, is in fever-fit and convulsion: such crisis has lasted for the space of some half hour.

But what is this that, with Legislative Insignia, ventures through the hubbub and death-hail, from the back-entrance of the Manége? Towards the Tuileries and Swiss: written Order from his Majesty to cease firing! O ye hapless Swiss, why was there no order not to begin it? Gladly would the Swiss cease firing: but who will bid mad Insurrection cease firing? To Insurrection you cannot speak; neither can it, hydraheaded, hear. The dead and dying, by the hundred, lie all around; are borne bleeding through the streets, towards help; the sight of them, like a torch of the Furies, kindling Madness. Patriot Paris roars; as the bear bereaved of her whelps. On, ye Patriots: Vengeance! Victory or death! There are men seen, who rush on, armed only with walking-sticks. Terror and Fury rule the hour.

The Swiss, pressed on from without, paralysed from within, have ceased to shoot; but not to be shot. What shall they do? Desperate is the moment. Shelter or instant death: yet How, Where? One party flies out by the Rue de l'Échelle; is destroyed utterly, 'en entier.' A second, by the other side, throws itself into the Garden; 'hurrying across a keen fusillade;' rushes suppliant into the National Assembly; finds pity and refuge in the back benches there. The third and largest, darts out in column, three hundred strong, towards the Champs Élysées: Ah, could we but reach Courbevoye, where other Swiss are! Wo! see, in such fusillade the column 'soon breaks itself by diversity of opinion,' into distracted segments, this way and that;—to escape in holes, to die fighting from street to street. The firing and murdering will not cease; not yet for long. The red Porters of Hôtels are shot at, be they *Suisse* by nature, or *Suisse* only in name. The very Firemen, who pump and labour on that smoking Carrousel, are shot at: why should the Carrousel *not* burn? Some Swiss take refuge in private houses; find that mercy too does still dwell in the heart of man. The brave Marseillese are merciful, late so wroth; and labour to save. Journalist Gorsas pleads hard with infuriated groups. Clemence, the Wine-merchant, stumbles forward to the Bar of the Assembly, a rescued Swiss in his hand; tells passionately how he rescued him with pain and peril, how he will henceforth support him, being childless himself; and falls a-swoon round the poor Swiss's neck: amid plaudits. But the most are butchered, and even mangled. Fifty (some say Fourscore) were marched as prisoners, by National Guards, to the Hôtel-de-Ville: the ferocious people bursts through on them, in the Place-de-Grève; massacres them to the last man. '*O Peuple*, envy of the universe!' *Peuple*, in mad Gaelic effervescence!

Surely few things in the history of carnage are painfuller. What ineffaceable red streak, flickering so sad in the memory, is that, of this poor column of red Swiss 'breaking itself in the confusion of opinions;' dispersing, into blackness and death! Honour to you, brave men; honourable pity, through long times! Not martyrs were ye; and yet almost more. He was no king of yours, this Louis; and he forsook you like a King of shreds and patches: ye were but sold to him for some poor sixpence a-day; yet would ye work for your wages, keep your plighted word. The work now was to die; and ye did it. Honour to you, O Kinsmen; and may the old Deutsch *Biederkeit* and *Tapferkeit*, and Valour which is *Worth* and *Truth*, be they Swiss, be they Saxon, fail in no age! Not bastards; true-born were these men: sons of the men of Sempach, of Murten, who knelt, but not to thee, O Burgundy! —Let the traveller, as he passes through Lucerne, turn aside to look a little at their monumental Lion; not for Thorwaldsen's sake alone. Hewn out of living rock, the figure rests there, by the still Lake-waters, in lullaby of distant-tinkling *rance-des-vaches*, the granite Mountains dumbly keeping watch all round; and, though inanimate, speaks.

CHAPTER VIII

CONSTITUTION BURST IN PIECES

THUS is the Tenth of August won and lost. Patriotism reckons its slain by the thousand on thousand, so deadly was the Swiss fire from these windows; but will finally reduce them to some Twelve-hundred. No child's-play was it;—nor is it! Till two in the afternoon the massacring, the breaking and the burning has not ended; nor the loose Bedlam shut itself again.

How deluges of frantic Sansculottism roared through all passages of this Tuileries, ruthless in vengeance; how the Valets were butchered, hewn down; and Dame Campan saw the Marseillese sabre flash over her head, but the Blackbrowed said, "*Va-t-en*, Get thee gone," and flung her from him unstruck; how in the cellars wine-bottles were broken, wine-butts were staved-in and drunk; and, upwards to the very garrets, all windows tumbled out their precious royal furnitures: and, with gold mirrors, velvet curtains, down of ript feather-beds, and dead bodies of men, the Tuileries was like no Garden of the Earth :—all this let him who has a taste for it see amply in Mercier, in acrid Montgaillard, or Beaulieu of the *Deux Amis*. A hundred and eighty bodies of Swiss lie piled there; naked, unremoved till the second day. Patriotism has torn their red coats into snips; and marches with them at the Pike's point: the ghastly bare corpses lie there, under the sun and under the stars; the curious of both sexes crowding to look. Which let us not do. Above a hundred carts, heaped with Dead, fare towards the Cemetery of Sainte-Madeleine; bewailed, bewept; for all had kindred, all had mothers, if not here, then there. It is one of those Carnage-fields, such as you read of by the name 'Glorious Victory,' brought home in this case to one's own door.

But the blackbrowed Marseillese have struck down the tyrant of the Château. He is struck down; low, and hardly again to rise. What a moment for an august Legislative was that when the Hereditary Representative entered, under such circumstances; and the Grenadier, carrying the little Prince Royal out of the press, set him down on the Assembly-table! A moment,—which one had to smooth-off with oratory; waiting what the next would bring! Louis said few words: "He was come hither to prevent a great crime; he believed himself safer nowhere than here." President Vergniaud answered briefly, in vague oratory as we say, about "defence of Constituted Authorities," about dying at our post. And so King Louis sat him down; first here, then there; for a difficulty arose, the Constitution not permitting us to debate while the King is present: finally he settles himself with his Family in the '*Loge* of the *Logographe*,' in the Reporter's-Box of a Journalist; which is beyond the enchanted Constitutional Circuit, separated from it by a rail. To such Lodge of the *Logographe*, measuring some ten feet square, with a small closet at the entrance of it behind, is the King of broad France now limited: here can he and his sit pent, under the eyes of the world, or retire into their closet at intervals; for the space of sixteen hours. Such quite peculiar moment has the Legislative lived to see.

But also what a moment was that other, few minutes later, when the three Marseillese cannon went off, and the Swiss rolling fire and universal thunder, like the crack of Doom, began to rattle! Honourable Members start to their feet; stray bullets singing epicedium even here, shivering in with window-glass and jingle. "No, this is our post; let us die here!" They sit therefore, like stone Legislators. But may not the Loge of the *Logographe* be forced from behind? Tear down the railing that divides it from the enchanted Constitutional Circuit! Ushers tear and tug; his Majesty himself aiding from within: the railing gives way; Majesty and Legislative are united in place, unknown Destiny hovering over both.

Rattle, and again rattle, went the thunder; one breathless wide-eyed messenger rushing in after another: King's order to the Swiss went out. It was a fearful thunder; but, as we know, it ended. Breathless messengers, fugitive Swiss, denunciatory Patriots, trepidation; finally tripudiation!—Before four o'clock much has come and gone.

The New Municipals have come and gone; with Three Flags, *Liberté*, *Égalité*, *Patrie*, and the clang of vivats.

Vergniaud, he who as President few hours ago talked of dying for Constituted Authorities, has moved, as Committee-Reporter, that the Hereditary Representative *be suspended;* that a NATIONAL CONVENTION do forthwith assemble to say what further! An able Report; which the President must have had ready in his pocket? A President, in such cases, must have much ready, and yet not ready; and Janus-like look before and after.

King Louis listens to all; retires about midnight 'to three little rooms on the upper floor;' till the Luxembourg be prepared for him, and 'the safeguard of the Nation.' Safer if Brunswick were once here! Or, alas, not so safe? Ye hapless discrowned heads! Crowds come, next morning, to catch a glimpse of them, in their three upper rooms. Montgaillard says the august Captives wore an air of cheerfulness, even of gaiety; that the Queen and Princess Lamballe, who had joined her overnight, looked out of the open window, 'shook powder from their hair on the people below, and laughed.' He is an acrid distorted man.

For the rest, one may guess that the Legislative, above all that the New Municipality continues busy. Messengers, Municipal or Legislative, and swift despatches rush off to all corners of France; full of triumph, blended with indignant wail, for Twelve-hundred have fallen. France sends up its blended shout responsive; the Tenth of August shall be as the Fourteenth of July, only bloodier and greater. The Court has conspired? Poor Court: the Court has been vanquished; and will have both the scath to bear and the scorn. How the statues of Kings do now all fall! Bronze Henri himself, though he wore a cockade once, jingles down from the Pont Neuf, where *Patrie* floats *in Danger.* Much more does Louis Fourteenth, from the Place Vendôme, jingle down; and even breaks in falling. The curious can remark, written on his horse's shoe: '12 *Août* 1692;' a Century and a day.

The tenth of August was Friday. The week is not done, when our old Patriot Ministry is recalled, what of it can be got: strict Roland, Genevese Clavière; add heavy Monge the Mathematician, once a stone-hewer; and, for Minister of Justice,—Danton, 'led hither,' as himself says, in one of his gigantic figures, 'through the breach of Patriot cannon!' These, under Legislative Committees, must rule the wreck as they can: confusedly enough; with an old Legislative water-logged, with a new Municipality so brisk. But National Convention will get itself together; and *then!* Without delay, however, let a new Jury-Court and Criminal Tribunal be set up in Paris, to try the crimes and conspiracies of the Tenth. High Court of Orleans is distant, slow: the blood of the Twelve-hundred Patriots, whatever become of other blood, shall be inquired after. Tremble, ye Criminals and Conspirators; the Minister of Justice is Danton! Robespierre too, after the victory, sits in the New Municipality; insurrectionary 'improvised Municipality,' which calls itself Council General of the Commune.

For three days now, Louis and his Family have heard the Legislative Debates in the Lodge of the *Logographe;* and retired nightly to their small upper rooms. The Luxembourg and safe-guard of the Nation could not be got ready: nay, it seems the Luxembourg has too many cellars and issues; no Municipality can undertake to watch it. The compact Prison of the Temple, not so elegant indeed, were much safer. To the Temple, therefore. On Monday, the 13th day of August 1792, in Mayor Pétion's carriage, Louis and his sad suspended Household fare thither; all Paris out to look at them. As they pass through the Place Vendôme, Louis Fourteenth's Statue lies broken on the ground. Pétion is afraid the Queen's looks may be thought scornful, and produce provocation; she casts down her eyes, and does not look at all. The 'press is prodigious,' but quiet: here and there, it shouts *Vive la Nation;* but for most part gazes in silence. French Royalty vanishes within the gates of the Temple: these old peaked Towers, like peaked Extinguisher or *Bonsoir,* do cover it up; —from which same Towers, poor Jacques Molay and his Templars were burnt out, by French Royalty, five centuries since. Such are the turns of Fate below. Foreign Ambassadors, English Lord Gower, have all demanded passports; are driving indignantly towards their respective homes.

So, then, the Constitution is over? Forever and a day! Gone is that wonder of the Universe; First biennial Parliament, water-logged, waits only till the Convention come; and will then sink to endless depths. One can guess the silent rage of Old-Constituents, Constitution-builders, extinct Feuillants, men who thought the Constitution would march! Lafayette rises to the altitude of the situation; at the head of his Army. Legislative Commissioners are posting towards

him and it, on the Northern Frontier, to congratulate and
perorate : he orders the Municipality of Sedan to arrest these
Commissioners, and keep them strictly in ward as Rebels, till
he say further. The Sedan Municipals obey.

The Sedan Municipals obey : but the Soldiers of the
Lafayette Army ? The Soldiers of the Lafayette Army have,
as all Soldiers have, a kind of dim feeling that they themselves
are Sansculottes in buff belts, that the victory of the Tenth of
August is also a victory for them. They will not rise and
follow Lafayette to Paris ; they will rise and *send* him thither !
On the 18th, which is but next Saturday, Lafayette, with some
two or three indignant Staff-officers, one of whom is Old-
Constituent Alexandre de Lameth, having first put his Lines
in what order he could,—rides swiftly over the Marches
towards Holland. Rides, alas, swiftly into the claws of
Austrians ! He, long wavering, trembling on the verge of the
Horizon, has set, in Olmutz Dungeons ; this History knows
him no more. Adieu, thou Hero of two Worlds ; thinnest,
but compact honour-worthy man ! Through long rough night
of captivity, through other tumults, triumphs and changes,
thou wilt swing well, 'fast-anchored to the Washington Formula ;' and be the Hero and Perfect-character, were it only of
one idea. The Sedan Municipals repent and protest ; the
Soldiers shout *Vive la Nation.* Dumouriez Polymetis, from
his Camp at Maulde, sees himself made Commander-in-Chief.

And, O Brunswick ! what sort of 'military execution' will
Paris merit now ? Forward, ye well-drilled exterminatory
men ; with your artillery-wagons, and camp-kettles jingling.
Forward, tall chivalrous King of Prussia ; fanfaronading
Emigrants and wargod Broglie, 'for some consolation to man-
kind,' which verily is not without need of some.

PART III—THE GUILLOTINE

BOOK I

SEPTEMBER

CHAPTER I

THE IMPROVISED COMMUNE

YE have roused her, then, ye Emigrants and Despots of the world; France is roused! Long have ye been lecturing and tutoring this poor Nation, like cruel uncalled-for pedagogues, shaking over her your ferulas of fire and steel: it is long that ye have pricked and fillipped and affrighted her, there as she sat helpless in her dead cerements of a Constitution, you gathering in on her from all lands, with your armaments and plots, your invadings and truculent bullyings;—and lo now, ye have pricked her to the quick, and she is up, and her blood is up. The dead cerements are rent into cobwebs, and she fronts you in that terrible strength of Nature, which no man has measured, which goes down to Madness and Tophet: see now how ye will deal with her.

This month of September 1792, which has become one of the memorable months of History, presents itself under two most diverse aspects; all of black on the one side, all of bright on the other. Whatsoever is cruel in the panic frenzy of Twenty-five million men, whatsoever is great in the simultaneous death-defiance of Twenty-five million men, stand here in abrupt contrast, near by one another. As indeed is usual when a man, how much more when a Nation of men, is hurled suddenly beyond the limits. For Nature, as green as she looks, rests everywhere on dread foundations, were we further down; and Pan, to whose music the Nymphs dance, has a cry in him that can drive all men distracted.

Very frightful it is when a Nation, rending asunder its Constitutions and Regulations which were grown dead cerements for it, becomes *trans*-cendental; and must now seek its wild way through the New, Chaotic,—where Force is not yet dis-

tinguished into Bidden and Forbidden, but Crime and Virtue
welter unseparated,—in that domain of what is called the
Passions; of what we call the Miracles and the Portents! It
is thus that, for some three years to come, we are to contemplate France, in this final Third Part of our History. Sansculottism reigning in all its grandeur and in all its hideous-
ness: the Gospel (God's-Message) of Man's Rights, Man's
mights or strengths, once more preached irrefragably abroad;
along with this, and still louder for the time, the fearfullest
Devil's-Message of Man's weaknesses and sins;—and all on
such a scale, and under such aspect: cloudy 'death-birth of a
world:' huge smoke-cloud, streaked with rays as of heaven on
one side; girt on the other as with hell-fire! History tells us
many things: but for the last thousand years and more, what
thing has she told us of a sort like this? Which therefore let
us two, O Reader, dwell on willingly, for a little; and from its
endless significance endeavour to extract what may, in present
circumstances, be adapted for us.

It is unfortunate, though very natural, that the history of
this Period has so generally been written in hysterics. Exaggeration abounds, execration, wailing; and, on the whole,
darkness. But thus too, when foul old Rome had to be swept
from the Earth, and those Northmen, and other horrid sons of
Nature, came in, 'swallowing formulas,' as the French now do,
foul old Rome screamed execratively her loudest; so that the
true shape of many things is lost for us. Attila's Huns had
arms of such length that they could lift a stone without stooping. Into the body of the poor Tartars execrative Roman
History intercalated an alphabetic letter; and so they continue
Tartars, of fell Tartarean nature, to this day. Here, in like
manner, search as we will in these multiform innumerable
French Records, darkness too frequently covers, or sheer distraction bewilders. One finds it difficult to imagine that the
Sun shone in this September month, as he does in others.
Nevertheless it is an indisputable fact that the Sun did shine;
and there was weather and work,—nay, as to that, very bad
weather for harvest-work! An unlucky Editor may do his
utmost; and after all, require allowances.

He had been a wise Frenchman, who, looking close at hand
on this waste aspect of France all stirring and whirling, in
ways new, untried, had been able to discern where the cardinal
movement lay; which tendency it was that had the rule and

primary direction of it then ! But at forty-four years' distance, it is different. To all men now, two cardinal movements or grand tendencies, in the September whirl, have become discernible enough: that stormful effluence towards the Frontiers; that frantic crowding towards Townhouses and Council-halls in the interior. Wild France dashes, in desperate death-defiance, towards the Frontiers, to defend itself from foreign Despots; crowds towards Townhalls and Election Committee-rooms, to defend itself from domestic Aristocrats. Let the Reader conceive well these two cardinal movements; and what sidecurrents and endless vortexes might depend on these. He shall judge too, whether, in such sudden wreckage of all old Authorities, such a pair of cardinal movements, half-frantic in themselves, could be of soft nature? As in dry Sahara, when the winds waken, and lift and winnow the immensity of sand ! The air itself (Travellers say) is a dim sand-air; and dim looming through it, the wonderfullest uncertain colonnades of Sand-Pillars rush whirling from this side and from that, like so many mad Spinning Dervishes, of a hundred feet in stature; and dance their huge Desert-waltz there !—

Nevertheless, in all human movements, were they but a day old, there is order, or the beginning of order. Consider two things in this Sahara-waltz of the French Twenty-five millions; or rather one thing, and one hope of a thing; the *Commune* (Municipality) of Paris, which is already here; the National Convention, which shall in few weeks be here. The Insurrectionary Commune, which, improvising itself on the eve of the Tenth of August, worked this ever-memorable Deliverance by explosion, must needs rule over it,—till the Convention meet. This Commune, which they may well call a spontaneous or 'improvised' Commune, is, for the present, sovereign of France. The Legislative, deriving its authority from the Old, how can *it* now have authority when the Old is exploded by insurrection? As a floating piece of wreck, certain things, persons and interests may still cleave to it : volunteer defenders, riflemen or pikemen in green uniform, or red nightcap (of *bonnet rouge*), defile before it daily, just on the wing towards Brunswick; with the brandishing of arms; always with some touch of Leonidas-eloquence, often with a fire of daring that threatens to out-herod Herod,—the Galleries, 'especially the Ladies, never done with applauding.' Addresses of this or the like sort can be received and answered, in the hearing of all France; the Salle de Manége is still useful as a place of proclamation. For which use, indeed, it now chiefly serves. Vergniaud delivers spirit-stirring orations; but always with a prophetic sense only, looking towards the coming Convention. " Let our memory perish," cries Vergniaud, "but let France be free!"—whereupon they all start to their feet, shouting responsive: "Yes, yes, *périsse notre mémoire, pourvu que la France soit libre.*" Disfrocked Chabot adjures Heaven that at least we may "have done with Kings;" and fast as powder under spark, we all blaze up once move, and with waved hats shout and swear: "Yes, *nous le jurons; plus du rois!*" All which, as method of proclamation, is very convenient.

For the rest, that our busy Brissots, rigorous Rolands, men who once had authority, and now have less and less; men who love law, and will have even an Explosion explode itself as far as possible according to rule, do find this state of matters most unofficial-unsatisfactory,—is not to be denied. Complaints are made; attempts are made: but without effect. The attempts even recoil; and must be desisted from, for fear of worse: the sceptre has departed from this Legislative once and always. A poor Legislative, so hard was fate, had let itself be hand-gyved, nailed to the rock like an Andromeda, and could only wail there to the Earth and Heavens; miraculously a winged Perseus (or Improvised Commune) has dawned out of the void Blue, and cut her loose: but whether now is it she with her softness and musical speech, or is it he, with his hardness and sharp falchion and ægis, that shall have casting-vote? Melodious *agreement* of vote; this were the rule! But if otherwise, and votes diverge, then surely Andromeda's part is to weep,—if possible, tears of gratitude alone.

Be content, O France, with this Improvised Commune, such as it is! It has the Implements and has the hands: the time is not long. On Sunday the twenty-sixth of August, our Primary Assemblies shall meet, begin electing of Electors; on Sunday the second of September (may the day prove lucky!) the Electors shall begin electing Deputies; and so an all-healing National Convention will come together. No *marc d'argent*, or distinction of Active and Passive, now insults the French Patriot: but there is Universal suffrage, unlimited liberty to choose. Old-Constituents, Present-Legislators, all France is eligible. Nay, it may be said, the flower of all the Universe (*de l'Univers*) is eligible; for in

these very days we, by act of Assembly, 'naturalise' the chief
Foreign Friends of Humanity: Priestley, burnt out for us in
Birmingham; Klopstock, a genius of all countries; Jeremy
Bentham, useful Jurisconsult; distinguished Paine, the rebellious Needleman;—some of whom may be chosen. As is
most fit; for a Convention of this kind. In a word, Seven-
hundred and Forty-five unshackled sovereigns, admired of
the universe, shall replace this hapless impotency of a Legislative,—out of which, it is likely, the best Members, and the
Mountain in mass, may be re-elected. Roland is getting
ready the *Salle des Cent Suisses*, as preliminary rendezvous for
them; in that void Palace of the Tuileries, now void and
National, and not a Palace, but a Caravansera.

As for the Spontaneous Commune, one may say that there
never was on Earth a stranger Town-Council. Administration,
not of a great City, but of a great Kingdom in a state of revolt
and frenzy, this is the task that has fallen to it. Enrolling,
provisioning, judging; devising, deciding, doing, endeavouring
to do: one wonders the human brain did not give way under
all this, and reel. But happily human brains have such a
talent of taking up simply what they can carry, and ignoring
all the rest; leaving all the rest, as if it were not there!
Whereby somewhat is verily shifted for; and much shifts for
itself. This improvised Commune walks along, nothing doubting; promptly making front, without fear or flurry, at what
moment soever, to the wants of the moment. Were the world
on fire, one improvised tricolor Municipal has but one life to
lose. They are the elixir and chosen-men of Sansculottic
Patriotism; promoted to the forlorn-hope; unspeakable victory
or a high gallows, this is their meed. They sit there, in the
Townhall, these astonishing tricolor Municipals; in Council
General; in Committee of Watchfulness (*de Surveillance*, which
will even become *de Salut Public*, of Public Salvation), or what
other Committees and Sub-committees are needful;—managing infinite Correspondence, passing infinite Decrees: one
hears of a Decree being 'the ninety-eighth of the day.' Ready
is the word. They carry loaded pistols in their pocket; also
some improvised luncheon by way of meal. Or indeed, by
and by, *traiteurs* contract for the supply of repasts, to be eaten
on the spot,—too lavishly, as it was afterwards grumbled.
Thus they: girt in their tricolor sashes; Municipal note-paper
in the one hand, fire-arms in the other. They have their
Agents out all over France; speaking in town-houses, market-

places, highways and byways; agitating, urging to arm; all hearts tingling to hear. Great is the fire of Anti-aristocrat eloquence: nay some, as Bibliopolic Momoro, seem to hint afar off at something which smells of Agrarian Law, and a surgery of the overswoln dropsical strongbox itself;—whereat indeed the bold Bookseller runs risk of being hanged, and Ex-Constituent Buzot has to smuggle him off.

Governing Persons, were they never so insignificant intrinsically, have for most part plenty of Memoir-writers; and the curious, in after-times, can learn minutely their goings out and comings in: which, as men always love to know their fellow-men in singular situations, is a comfort, of its kind. Not so with these Governing Persons, now in the Townhall! And yet what most original fellow-man, of the Governing sort, high-chancellor, king, kaiser, secretary of the home or the foreign department, ever showed such a phasis as Clerk Tallien, Procureur Manuel, future Procureur Chaumette, here in this Sand-waltz of the Twenty-five millions now do? O brother mortals,—thou Advocate Panis, friend of Danton, kinsman of Santerre; Engraver Sergent, since called *Agate* Sergent; thou Huguenin, with the tocsin in thy heart! But, as Horace says, they wanted the sacred memoir-writer (*sacro vate*); and we know them not. Men bragged of August and its doings, publishing them in high places; but of this September none now or afterwards would brag. The September world remains dark, fuliginous, as Lapland witch-midnight; —from which, indeed, very strange shapes will evolve themselves.

Understand this, however: that incorruptible Robespierre is not wanting, now when the brunt of battle is past; in a stealthy way the seagreen man sits there, his feline eyes excellent in the twilight. Also understand this other, a single fact worth many: that Marat is not only there, but has a seat of honour assigned him, a *tribune particulière*. How changed for Marat; lifted from his dark cellar into this luminous 'peculiar tribune!' All dogs have their day; even rabid dogs. Sorrowful, incurable Philoctetes Marat; without whom Troy cannot be taken! Hither, as a main element of the Governing Power, has Marat been raised. Royalist types, for we have 'suppressed' innumerable Durosoys, Royous, and even clapt them in prison,—Royalist types replace the worn types often snatched from a People's-Friend in old ill days. In our 'peculiar tribune' we write and redact: Placards, of due

monitory terror; *Ami du Peuple* (now under the name o
Journal de la République); and sit obeyed of men. ' Marat
says one, ' is the conscience of the Hôtel-de-Ville.' *Keeper*, a
some call it, of the Sovereign's Conscience; which surely, ii
such hands, will not lie hid in a napkin!

Two great movements, as we said, agitate this distracte
National mind : a rushing against domestic Traitors, a rushin
against foreign Despots. Mad movements both, restrainabl
by no known rule; strongest passions of human nature drivin
them on : love, hatred, vengeful sorrow, braggart Nationalit
also vengeful,—and pale Panic over all! Twelve-hundre
slain Patriots. do they not, from their dark catacombs there, i
Death's dumb-show, plead (O ye Legislators) for vengeance
Such was the destructive rage of these Aristocrats on the ever
memorable Tenth. Nay, apart from vengeance, and with ar
eye to Public Salvation only, are there not still, in this Pari
(in round numbers) 'Thirty-thousand Aristocrats,' of the mos
malignant humour; driven now to their last trump-card?—Be
patient, ye Patriots, our New High Court 'Tribunal of the
Seventeenth,' sits; each Section has sent Four Jurymen; and
Danton, extinguishing improper judges, improper practice
wheresoever found, is 'the same man you have known at th
Cordeliers.' With such a Minister of Justice, shall not Justic
be done?—Let it be swift then, answers universal Patriotism
swift and sure!—

One would hope, this Tribunal of the Seventeenth is swifte
than most. Already on the 21st, while our Court is but fou
days old, Collenot d'Angremont, 'the Royalist enlister' (crimp
embaucheur), dies by torchlight. For, lo, the great *Guillotine*
wondrous to behold, now stands there : the Doctor's *Idea* ha
become Oak and Iron; the huge cyclopean axe 'falls in it
grooves like the ram of the Pile-engine,' swiftly snuffing out th
light of men! "*Mais vous, Gualches*, what have you in
vented?" *This?*—Poor old Laporte, Intendant of the Civi
List, follows next : quietly, the mild old man. Then Durosoy
Royalist Placarder, 'cashier of all the Anti-revolutionists o
the interior:' he went rejoicing; said that a Royalist like hin
ought to die, of all days, on this day, the 25th or Saint Louis'
Day. All these have been tried, cast,—the Galleries shouting
approval; and handed over to the Realised Idea, withii
a week. Besides those whom we have acquitted, the Gallerie
murmuring, and have dismissed; or even have personally

guarded back to Prison, as the Galleries took to howling, and
even to menacing and elbowing. Languid this Tribunal
is not.

Nor does the other movement slacken; the rushing against
foreign Despots. Strong forces shall meet in death-grip;
drilled Europe against mad undrilled France; and singular
conclusions will be tried.—Conceive therefore, in some faint
degree, the tumult that whirls in this France, in this Paris!
Placards from Section, from Commune, from Legislative,
from the individual Patriot, flame monitory on all walls.
Flags of Danger to Fatherland wave at the Hôtel-de-Ville; on
the Pont Neuf—over the prostrate Statues of Kings. There
is universal enlisting, urging to enlist; there is tearful-boastful
leave-taking; irregular marching on the Great Northeastern
Road. Marseillese sing their wild *To Arms*, in chorus; which
now all men, all women and children have learnt, and sing
chorally, in Theatres, Boulevards, Streets; and the heart
burns in every bosom: *Aux armes! Marchons!*—Or think
now your Aristocrats are skulking into covert; how Bertrand-
Moleville lies hidden in some garret "in Aubry-le-boucher
Street, with a poor surgeon who had known me!" Dame de
Staël has secreted her Narbonne, not knowing what in the
world to make of him. The Barriers are sometimes open,
oftenest shut; no passports to be had; Townhall Emissaries,
with the eyes and claws of falcons, flitting watchful on all
points of your horizon! In two words: Tribunal of the
Seventeenth, busy under howling Galleries; Prussian Brunswick, 'over a space of forty miles,' with his war-tumbrils, and
sleeping thunders, and Briarean 'sixty-six thousand' right
hands,—coming, coming!

O Heavens, in these latter days of August, he is come!
Durosoy was not yet guillotined when news had come that the
Prussians were harrying and ravaging about Metz; in some
four days more, one hears that Longwi, our first strong-place
on the borders, is fallen 'in fifteen hours.' Quick, therefore,
O ye improvised Municipals; quick, and ever quicker!—The
improvised Municipals make front to this also. Enrolment
urges itself; and clothing, and arming. Our very officers have
now 'wool epaulettes;' for it is the reign of Equality, and
also of Necessity. Neither do men now *monsieur* and *sir* one
another; *citoyen* (citizen) were suitabler; we even say *thou*, as
the free peoples of Antiquity did:' so have Journals and the
improvised Commune suggested; which shall be well.

Infinitely better, meantime, could we suggest where arms
are to be found. For the present, our *Citoyens* chant chorally
To arms; and have no arms! Arms are searched for; passion
ately; there is joy over any musket. Moreover, entrench
ments shall be made round Paris: on the slopes of Mont
martre men dig and shovel; though even the simple suspec
this to be desperate. They dig: Tricolor sashes speak en
couragement and *well-speed-ye.* Nay finally 'twelve Members
of the Legislative go daily,' not to encourage only, but to bear
a hand, and delve: it was decreed with acclamation. Arms
shall either be provided; or else the ingenuity of man crack
itself, and become fatuity. Lean Beaumarchais, thinking to
serve the Fatherland, and do a stroke of trade in the old way,
has commissioned sixty-thousand stand of good arms out of
Holland; would to Heaven, for Fatherland's sake and his,
they were come! Meanwhile railings are torn up; hammered
into pikes; chains themselves shall be welded together into
pikes. The very coffins of the dead are raised; for melting
into balls. All Church-bells must down into the furnace to
make cannon; all Church-plate into the mint to make money.
Also behold the fair swan-bevies of *Citoyennes* that have
alighted in Churches, and sit there with swan-neck,—sewing
tents and regimentals! Nor are Patriotic Gifts wanting, from
those that have aught left; nor stingily given: the fair
Villaumes, mother and daughter, Milliners in the Rue St.
Martin, give a 'silver thimble, and a coin of fifteen *sous*
(sevenpence halfpenny),' with other similar effects; and offer,
at least the mother does, to mount guard. Men who have not
even a thimble, give a thimblefull,—were it but of invention.
One Citoyen has wrought out the scheme of a wooden
cannon; which France shall exclusively profit by, in the first
instance. It is to be made of *staves*, by the coopers;—of
almost boundless calibre, but uncertain as to strength! Thus
they: hammering, scheming, stitching, founding, with all their
heart and with all their soul. Two bells only are to remain in
each Parish,—for tocsin and other purposes.

But mark also, precisely while the Prussian batteries were
playing their briskest at Longwi in the Northeast, and our
dastardly Lavergne saw nothing for it but surrender,—south-
westward, in remote, patriarchal La Vendée, that sour ferment
about Nonjuring Priests, after long working, is ripe, and
explodes: at the wrong moment for us! And so we have
'eight-thousand Peasants at Châtillon-sur-Sèvre' who will not

be balloted for soldiers; will not have their Curates molested.
To whom Bonchamps, Larochejaquelins, and Seigneurs
enough of a Royalist turn, will join themselves; with Stofflets
and Charettes; with Heroes and Chouan Smugglers; and the
loyal warmth of a simple people, blown into flame and fury
by theological and seignorial bellows! So that there shall be
fighting from behind ditches, death-volleys bursting out of
thickets and ravines of rivers; huts burning, feet of the pitiful
women hurrying to refuge with their children on their back;
seed-fields fallow, whitened with human bones;—'eighty-
thousand, of all ages, ranks, sexes, flying at once across the
Loire,' with wail borne far on the winds: and in brief, for
years coming, such a suite of scenes as glorious war has not
offered in these late ages, not since our Albigenses and
Crusadings were over,—save indeed some chance Palatinate,
or so, we might have to 'burn,' by way of exception. The
'eight-thousand at Châtillon' will be got dispelled for the
moment; the fire scattered, not extinguished. To the dints
and bruises of outward battle there is to be added henceforth
a deadlier internal gangrene.

This rising in La Vendée reports itself at Paris on Wednesday the 29th of August;—just as we had got our Electors
elected; and, in spite of Brunswick and Longwi, were hoping
still to have a National Convention, if it pleased Heaven.
But indeed otherwise this Wednesday is to be regarded as one
of the notablest Paris had yet seen: gloomy tidings come
successively, like Job's messengers; are met by gloomy
answers. Of Sardinia rising to invade the Southeast, and
Spain threatening the South, we do not speak. But are not
the Prussians masters of Longwi (treacherously yielded, one
would say); and preparing to besiege Verdun? Clairfait and
his Austrians are encompassing Thionville; darkening the
North. Not Metzland now, but the Clermontais is getting
harried; flying hulans and hussars have been seen on the
Châlons Road, almost as far as Sainte-Menehould. Heart,
ye Patriots; if ye lose heart, ye lose all!

It is not without a dramatic emotion that one reads in the
Parliamentary Debates of this Wednesday evening 'past seven
o'clock,' the scene with the military fugitives from Longwi.
Wayworn, dusty, disheartened, these poor men enter the
Legislative, about sunset or after; give the most pathetic
detail of the frightful pass they were in: Prussians billowing
round by the myriad, volcanically spouting fire for fifteen

hours: we, scattered sparse on the ramparts, hardly a
cannoneer to two guns; our dastard Commandant Lavergne
nowhere showing face; the priming would not catch; there
was no powder in the bombs,—what could we do? "*Mourir*
Die!" answer prompt voices; and the dusty fugitives must
shrink elsewhither for comfort.—Yes, *Mourir*, that is now the
word. Be Longwi a proverb and a hissing among French
strong-places: let it (says the Legislative) be obliterated rather
from the shamed face of the Earth;—and so there has gone
forth Decree, that Longwi shall, were the Prussians once out
of it, 'be rased,' and exist only as ploughed ground.

Nor are the Jacobins milder; as how could they, the flower
of Patriotism? Poor Dame Lavergne, wife of the poor
Commandant, took her parasol one evening, and escorted by
her Father came over to the Hall of the mighty Mother; and
'reads a memoir tending to justify the Commandant of
Longwi.' *Lafarge, Président*, makes answer; "Citoyenne, the
Nation will judge Lavergne; the Jacobins are bound to tell
him the truth. He would have ended his course there
(*terminé sa carrière*), if he had loved the honour of his
country."

CHAPTER II

DANTON

BUT better than rasing of Longwi, or rebuking poor dusty
soldiers or soldiers' wives, Danton had come over, last night,
and demanded a Decree to *search* for arms, since they were
not yielded voluntarily. Let 'Domiciliary visits,' with rigour
of authority, be made to this end. To search for arms; for
horses,—Aristocratism rolls in its carriage, while Patriotism
cannot trail its cannon. To search generally for munitions of
war, 'in the houses of persons suspect,'—and even, if it seem
proper, to seize and imprison the suspect persons themselves!
In the Prisons their plots will be harmless; in the Prisons
they will be as hostages for us, and not without use. This
Decree the energetic Minister of Justice demanded last night,
and got; and this same night it is to be executed; it is being
executed at the moment when these dusty soldiers get saluted
with *Mourir*. Two-thousand stand of arms, as they count,
are foraged in this way; and some four-hundred head of new
Prisoners; and, on the whole, such a terror and damp is
struck through the Aristocrat heart, as all but Patriotism, and

even Patriotism were it out of this agony, might pity. Yes, Messieurs! if Brunswick blast Paris to ashes, he probably will blast the Prisons of Paris too; pale Terror, if we have got it, we will also give it, and the depth of horrors that lie in it; the same leaky bottom, in these wild waters, bears us all.

One can judge what stir there was now among the 'thirty-thousand Royalists:' how the Plotters, or the accused of Plotting, shrank each closer into his lurking-place,—like Bertrand-Moleville, looking eager towards Longwi, hoping the weather would keep fair. Or how they dressed themselves in valet's clothes, like Narbonne, and 'got to England as Dr. Bollman's famulus:' how Dame de Staël bestirred herself, pleading with Manuel as a Sister in Literature, pleading even with Clerk Tallien; a prey to nameless chagrins! Royalist Peltier, the Pamphleteer, gives a touching Narrative (not deficient in height of colouring) of the terrors of that night. From five in the afternoon, a great city is struck suddenly silent; except for the beating of drums, for the tramp of marching feet; and ever and anon the dread thunder of the knocker at some door, a Tricolor Commissioner with his blue Guards (*black*-guards!) arriving. All streets are vacant, says Peltier; beset by Guards at each end: all Citizens are ordered to be within doors. On the River float sentinel barges: lest we escape by water: the Barriers hermetically closed. Frightful! The Sun shines; serenely westering, in smokeless mackerel-sky; Paris is as if sleeping, as if dead:—Paris is holding its breath, to see what stroke will fall on it. Poor Peltier! *Acts of Apostles*, and all jocundity of Leading-Articles, are gone out, and it is become bitter earnest instead; polished satire changed now into coarse pike-points (hammered out of railing); all logic reduced to this one primitive thesis, An eye for an eye, a tooth for a tooth!—Peltier, dolefully aware of it, ducks low; escapes unscathed to England; to urge there the inky war anew;—to have Trial by Jury, in due season, and deliverance by young Whig eloquence, world-celebrated for a day.

Of 'thirty-thousand,' naturally, great multitudes were left unmolested: but, as we said, some four-hundred, designated as 'persons suspect,' were seized; and an unspeakable terror fell on all. Woe to him who is guilty of Plotting, of Anti-civism, Royalism, Feuillantism; who, guilty or not guilty, has an enemy in his Section to call him guilty! Poor old M. de Cazotte is seized; his young loved Daughter with him, refusing to quit him. Why, O Cazotte, wouldst thou quit romancing and *Diable Amoureux*, for such reality as this? Poor old M. de Sombreuil, he of the *Invalides*, is seized; a man seen askance by Patriotism ever since the Bastille days; whom also a fond Daughter will not quit. With young tears hardly suppressed, and old wavering weakness rousing itself once more,—O my brothers, O my sisters!

The famed and named go; the nameless, if they have an accuser. Necklace Lamotte's Husband is in these Prisons (*she* long since squelched on the London Pavements); but gets delivered. Gross de Morande, of the *Courrier de l'Europe*, hobbles distractedly to and fro there: but they let him hobble out; on right nimble crutches;—his hour not being yet come. Advocate Maton de la Varenne, very weak in health, is snatched off from mother and kin; Tricolor Rossignol (journeyman goldsmith and scoundrel lately, a risen man now) remembers an old Pleading of Maton's! Jourgniac de Saint-Méard goes; the brisk frank soldier: he was in the Mutiny of Nancy, in that 'effervescent Régiment du Roi,'— on the wrong side. Saddest of all: Abbé Sicard goes; a Priest who could not take the Oath, but who could teach the Deaf and Dumb: in his Section one man, he says, had a grudge at him; one man, at the fit hour, launches an arrest against him; which hits. In the Arsenal quarter, there are dumb hearts making wail, with signs, with wild gestures; he their miraculous healer and speech-bringer is rapt away.

What with the arrestments on this night of the Twenty-ninth, what with those that have gone on more or less, day and night, ever since the Tenth, one may fancy what the Prisons now were. Crowding and confusion; jostle, hurry, vehemence and terror! Of the poor Queen's Friends, who had followed her to the Temple, and been committed else-whither to prison, some, as Governess de Tourzelle, are to be let go: one, the poor Princess de Lamballe, is not let go; but waits in the strong-rooms of La Force there, what will betide further.

Among so many hundreds whom the launched arrest hits, who are rolled off to Townhall or Sectionhall, to preliminary Houses of Detention, and hurled in thither as into cattle-pens, we must mention one other: Caron de Beaumarchais, Author of *Figaro*; vanquisher of Maupeou Parlements and Goezman helldogs (i. 35); once numbered among the demigods; and

now—? We left him in his culminant state; what dreadful
decline is this, when we again catch a glimpse of him! 'At
midnight' (it was but the 12th of August yet), 'the servant,
in his shirt,' with wide-staring eyes, enters your room:—
Monsieur, rise, all the people are come to seek you, they are
knocking, like to break-in the door! 'And they were in fact
knocking in a terrible manner (*d'une façon terrible*). I fling
on my coat, forgetting even the waistcoat, nothing on my feet
but slippers; and say to him'—And *he*, alas, answers mere
negatory incoherences, panic interjections. And through the
shutters and crevices, in front or rearward, the dull street-
lamps disclose only streetfuls of haggard countenances;
clamorous, bristling with pikes: and you rush distracted for
an outlet, finding none;—and have to take refuge in the
crockery-press, down stairs; and stand there, palpitating, in
that imperfect costume, lights dancing past your key-hole,
tramp of feet overhead, and the tumult of Satan, 'for four
hours and more!' And old ladies, of the quarter, started up
(as we hear next morning); rang for their *bonnes* and cordial-
drops, with shrill interjections: and old gentlemen, in their
shirts, 'leapt garden-walls;' flying while none pursued; one of
whom unfortunately broke his leg. Those sixty-thousand
stand of Dutch Arms (which never arrive), and the bold
stroke of trade, have turned out so ill!—

Beaumarchais escaped for this time; but not for the next
time, ten days after. On the evening of the Twenty-ninth he
is still in that chaos of the Prisons, in saddest wrestling condition; unable to get justice, even to get audience; 'Panis
scratching his head' when you speak to him, and making off.
Nevertheless let the lover of Figaro know that Procureur
Manuel, a Brother in Literature, found him, and delivered
him once more. But how the lean demigod, now shorn of
his splendour, had to lurk in barns, to roam over harrowed
fields, panting for life; and to wait under eaves-drops, and
sit in darkness 'on the Boulevard amid paving-stones and
boulders,' longing for one word of any Minister, or Minister's
Clerk, about those accursed Dutch muskets, and getting none,
—with heart fuming in spleen, and terror, and suppressed
canine-madness; alas, how the swift sharp hound, once fit to
be Diana's, breaks his old teeth now, gnawing mere whinstones; and must 'fly to England;' and, returning from
England, must creep into the corner, and lie quiet, toothless
(moneyless),—all this let the lover of Figaro fancy, and weep

for. We here, without weeping, not without sadness, wave the withered tough fellow-mortal our farewell. His Figaro has returned to the French stage; nay is, at this day, sometimes named the best piece there. And indeed, so long as Man's Life can ground itself only on artificiality and aridity; each new Revolt and Change of Dynasty turning up only a new stratum of *dry-rubbish*, and no *soil* yet coming to view,—may it not be good to protest against such a Life, in many ways, and even in the Figaro way?

CHAPTER III

DUMOURIEZ

SUCH are the last days of August 1792; days gloomy, disastrous and of evil omen. What will become of this poor France? Dumouriez rode from the Camp of Maulde, eastward to Sedan, on Tuesday last, the 28th of the month; reviewed that so-called Army left forlorn there by Lafayette: the forlorn soldiers gloomed on him; were heard growling on him, "This is one of them, *ce b—e là*, that made War be declared." Unpromising Army! Recruits flow in, filtering through Dépôt after Dépôt: but recruits merely: in want of all; happy if they have so much as arms. And Longwi has fallen basely; and Brunswick, and the Prussian King, with his sixty-thousand, will beleaguer Verdun: and Clairfait and Austrians press deeper in, over the Northern Marches: 'a hundred and fifty thousand' as fear counts, 'eighty-thousand' as the returns show, do hem us in; Cimmerian Europe behind them. There is Castries and Broglie chivalry; Royalist foot 'in red facing or nankeen trousers;' breathing death and the gallows.

And lo, finally! at Verdun on Sunday the 2d of September 1792, Brunswick is here. With his King and sixty-thousand, glittering over the heights, from beyond the winding Meuse River, he looks down on us, on our 'high citadel' and all our confectionary-ovens (for we are celebrated for confectionary); has sent courteous summons, in order to spare the effusion of blood!—Resist him to the death? Every day of retardation precious? How, O General Beaurepaire (asks the amazed Municipality) shall we resist him? We, the Verdun Municipals, see no resistance possible. Has he not sixty-thousand, and artillery without end? Retardation, Patriotism is good;

ut so likewise is peaceable baking of pastry, and sleeping in whole skin.—Hapless Beaurepaire stretches out his hands, and pleads passionately, in the name of country, honour, of Heaven and of Earth: to no purpose. The Municipals have, by law, the power of ordering it;—with an Army officered by Royalism or Crypto-Royalism, such a Law seemed needful: and they order it, as pacific Pastry-cooks, not as heroic Patriots would, —To surrender! Beaurepaire strides home, with long steps: his valet, entering the room, sees him 'writing eagerly,' and withdraws. His valet hears then, in few minutes, the report of a pistol: Beaurepaire is lying dead; his eager writing had been a brief suicidal farewell. In this manner died Beaurepaire, wept of France; buried in the Pantheon, with honourable Pension to his Widow, and for Epitaph these words, *He chose Death rather than yield to Despots*. The Prussians, descending from the heights, are peaceable masters of Verdun.

And so Brunswick advances, from stage to stage: who shall now stay him,—covering forty miles of country? Foragers fly far; the villages of the Northeast are harried; your Hessian forager has only 'three sous a-day:" the very Emigrants, it is said, will take silver-plate,—by way of revenge. Clermont, Sainte-Menehould, Varennes especially, ye Towns of the *Night of Spurs*, tremble ye! Procureur Sausse and the Magistracy of Varennes have fled; brave Boniface Le Blanc of the *Bras d'Or* is to the woods: Mrs. Le Blanc, a young woman fair to look upon, with her young infant, has to live in greenwood, like a beautiful Bessy Bell of Song, her bower thatched with rushes;—catching premature rheumatism. Clermont may ring the tocsin now, and illuminate itself! Clermont lies at the foot of its *Cow* (or *Vache*, so they name that Mountain), a prey to the Hessian spoiler: its fair women, fairer than most, are robbed; not of life, or what is dearer, yet of all that is cheaper and portable; for Necessity, on three half-pence a-day, has no law. At Sainte-Menehould the enemy has been expected more than once,—our Nationals all turning out in arms; but was not yet seen. Postmaster Drouet, he is not in the woods, but minding his Election; and will sit in the Convention, notable King-taker, and bold Old-Dragoon as he is.

Thus on the Northeast all roams and runs; and on a set day, the *date* of which is irrecoverable by History, Brunswick 'has engaged to dine in Paris,'—the Powers willing. And at

Paris, in the centre, it is as we saw; and in La Vendée Southwest, it is as we saw; and Sardinia is in the Southeast, and Spain is in the South, and Clairfait with Austria and sieged Thionville is in the North;—and all France leaps distracted, like the winnowed Sahara waltzing in sand-colonnades! More desperate posture no country ever stood in. A country, one would say, which the Majesty of Prussia (if it so pleased him) might partition and clip in pieces, like a Poland; flinging the remainder to poor Brother Louis,—with directions to keep it quiet, or else *we* will keep it for him!

Or perhaps the Upper Powers, minded that a new Chapter in Universal History shall begin here and not further on, may have ordered it all otherwise? In that case, Brunswick will not dine in Paris on the set day; nor, indeed, one knows not when!—Verily, amid this wreckage, where poor France seems grinding itself down to dust and bottomless ruin, who knows what miraculous salient point of Deliverance and Newlife may have already come into existence there; and be already working there, though as yet human eye discern it not! On the night of that same twenty-eighth of August, the unpromising Review-day in Sedan, Dumouriez assembles a Council of War at his lodgings there. He spreads out the map of this forlorn war-district; Prussians here, Austrians there; triumphant both, with broad highway, and little hinderance, all the way to Paris: we scattered, helpless, here and here: what to advise? The Generals, strangers to Dumouriez, look blank enough; know not well what to advise, —if it be not retreating, and retreating till our recruits accumulate; till perhaps the chapter of chances turn up some leaf for us; or Paris, at all events, be sacked at the latest day possible. The Many-counselled, who 'has not closed an eye for three nights,' listens with little speech to these long cheerless speeches; merely watching the speaker, that he may know him; then wishes them all good-night;—but beckons a certain young Thouvenot, the fire of whose looks had pleased him, to wait a moment. Thouvenot waits: *Voilà*, says Polymetis, pointing to the map! that is the Forest of Argonne, that long strip of rocky Mountain and wild Wood; forty miles long with but five, or say even three practicable Passes through it this, for they have forgotten it, might one not still seize though Clairfait sits so nigh? Once seized;—the Champagne called the Hungry (or worse, Champagne *Pouilleuse*) on their side of it; the fat Three Bishopricks, and willing France, o▶

ours; and the Equinox-rains not far;—this Argonne "might be the Thermopylæ of France!"

O brisk Dumouriez Polymetis with thy teeming head, may the gods grant it!—Polymetis, at any rate, folds his map together, and flings himself on bed; resolved to try, on the morrow morning. With astucity, with swiftness, with audacity! One had need to be a lion-fox, and have luck on one's side.

CHAPTER IV

SEPTEMBER IN PARIS

AT Paris, by lying Rumour which proved prophetic and veridical, the fall of Verdun was known some hours *before* it happened. It is Sunday the second of September; handiwork hinders not the speculations of the mind. Verdun gone (though some still deny it); the Prussians in full march, with gallows-ropes, with fire and faggot! Thirty-thousand Aristo-crats within our own walls; and but the merest quarter-tithe of them yet put in Prison! Nay there goes a word that even these will revolt. Sieur Jean Julien, wagoner of Vaugirard, being set in the Pillory last Friday, took all at once to crying, That he would be well revenged ere long; that the King's Friends in Prison would burst out, force the Temple, set the King on horseback, and, joined by the unimprisoned, ride rough-shod over us all. This unfortunate wagoner of Vaugirard did bawl, at the top of his lungs; when snatched off to the town-hall, he persisted in it, still bawling; yesternight, when they guillotined him, he died with the froth of it on his lips. For a man's mind, padlocked to the Pillory, may go mad; and all men's minds may go mad, and 'believe him,' as the frenetic will do, '*because* it is impossible.'

So that apparently the knot of the crisis and last agony of France is come? Make front to this, thou Improvised Commune, strong Danton, whatsoever man is strong! Readers can judge whether the Flag of Country in Danger flapped soothingly or distractively on the souls of men, that day.

But the Improvised Commune, but strong Danton is not wanting, each after his kind. Huge Placards are getting plastered to the walls; at two o'clock the stormbell shall be sounded, the alarm-cannon fired; all Paris shall rush to the Champ-de-Mars, and have itself enrolled. Unarmed, truly, and undrilled; but desperate, in the strength of frenzy Haste, ye men; ye very women, offer to mount guard and shoulder the brown musket: weak clucking-hens, in a state of desperation, will fly at the muzzle of the mastiff; and even conquer him,—by vehemence of character! Terror itself, when once grown transcendental, becomes a kind of courage; as frost sufficiently intense, according to Poet Milton, will *burn*.—Danton, the other night, in the Legislative Committee of General Defence, when the other Ministers and Legislators had all opined, said, It would not do to quit Paris, and fly to Saumur; that they must abide by Paris; and take such attitude as would put their enemies in fear,—*faire peur;* a word of his which has been often repeated, and reprinted —in italics.

At two of the clock, Beaurepaire, as we saw, has shot himself at Verdun; and, over Europe, mortals are going in for afternoon sermon. But at Paris, all steeples are clangouring not for sermon; the alarm-gun booming from minute to minute, Champ de-Mars and Fatherland's Altar boiling with desperate terror-courage: what a *miserere* going up to Heaven from this once Capital of the Most Christian King! The Legislative sits in alternate awe and effervescence; Vergniaud proposing that Twelve shall go and dig personally on Montmartre; which is decreed by acclaim.

But better than digging personally with acclaim, see Danton enter;—the black brows clouded, the colossus figure tramping heavy; grim energy looking from all features of the rugged man! Strong is that grim Son of France and Son of Earth; a Reality and not a Formula he too: and surely now if ever, being hurled *low* enough, it is on the Earth and on Realities that he rests. "Legislators!" so speaks the stentor-voice, as the Newspapers yet preserve it for us, "it is not the alarm-cannon that you hear: it is the *pas-de-charge* against our enemies. To conquer them, to hurl them back, what do we require? *Il nous faut de l'audace, et encore de l'audace, et toujours de l'audace,* To dare, and again to dare, and without end to dare!"—Right so, thou brawny Titan; there is nothing left for thee but that. Old men, who heard it, will still tell you how the reverberating voice made all hearts swell, in that moment; and braced them to the sticking-place; and thrilled abroad over France, like electric virtue, as a word spoken in season.

But the Commune, enrolling in the Champ-de-Mars? But the Committee of Watchfulness, become now Committee of

Public Salvation; whose conscience is Marat? The Commune enrolling enrolls many; provides Tents for them in that Mars'-Field, that they may march with dawn on the morrow: praise to this part of the Commune! To Marat and the Committee of Watchfulness not praise;—not even blame, such as could be meted out in these insufficient dialects of ours; expressive silence rather! Lone Marat, the man forbid, meditating long in his Cellars of refuge, on his Stylites Pillar, could see salvation in one thing only: in the fall of 'two-hundred and sixty thousand Aristocrat heads' (i. 245). With so many score of Naples Bravoes, each a dirk in his right-hand, a muff on his left, he would traverse France, and do it. But the world laughed, mocking the severe-benevolence of a People's-Friend; and his idea could not become an action, but only a fixed-idea. Lo, now, however, he has come down from his Stylites Pillar, to a *Tribune particulière;* here now, without the dirks, without the *muffs* at least, were it not grown possible,—now in the knot of the crisis, when salvation or destruction hangs in the hour!

The Ice-Tower of Avignon was noised of sufficiently, and lives in all memories; but the authors were not punished: nay we saw Jourdan Coupe-tête borne on men's shoulders, like a copper Portent, 'traversing the Cities of the South' (p. 56).—What Phantasms, squalid-horrid, shaking their dirk and muff, may dance through the brain of a Marat, in this dizzy pealing of tocsin-miserere and universal frenzy, seek not to guess, O Reader! Nor what the cruel Billaud 'in his short brown coat' was thinking; nor Sergent, not yet *Agate*-Sergent; nor Panis the confidant of Danton;—nor, in a word, how gloomy Orcus does breed in her gloomy womb, and fashion her monsters and prodigies of Events, which thou seest her visibly bear! Terror is on these streets of Paris; terror and rage, tears and frenzy: tocsin-miserere pealing through the air; fierce desperation rushing to battle; mothers, with streaming eyes and wild hearts, sending forth their sons to die. 'Carriage-horses are seized by the bridle,' that they may draw cannon; 'the traces cut, the carriages left standing.' In such tocsin-miserere, and murky bewilderment of Frenzy, are not Murder, Ate, and all Furies near at hand? On slight hint— who knows on how slight?—may not Murder come; and with *her* snaky-sparkling head, illuminate this murk!

How it was, and went, what part might be premeditated, what was improvised and accidental, man will never know, till the great Day of Judgment make it known. But with a Marat for keeper of the Sovereign's Conscience—and we know what the *ultima ratio* of Sovereigns, when they are driven to it, is! In this Paris there are as wicked men, say a hundred or more, as exist in all the Earth : to be hired, and set on : to set on, of their own accord, unhired.—And yet we will remark that premeditation itself is not performance, is not surety of performance ; that it is perhaps, at most, surety of *letting* whosoever wills perform. From the purpose of crime to the act of crime there is an abyss ; wonderful to think of. The finger lies on the pistol ; but the man is not yet a murderer : nay, his whole nature staggering at such consummation, is there not a confused pause rather,—one last instant of possibility for him ? Not yet a murderer ; it is at the mercy of light trifles whether the most fixed idea may not yet become unfixed. One slight twitch of a muscle, the death-flash bursts ; and he is it, and will for Eternity be it ;—and Earth has become a penal Tartarus for him ; his horizon girdled now not with golden hope, but with red flames of remorse ; voices from the depths of Nature sounding, Wo, wo on him !

Of such stuff are we all made ; on such powder-mines of bottomless guilt and criminality,—'if God restrained not,' as is well said,—does the purest of us walk. There are depths in man that go the length of lowest Hell, as there are heights that reach highest Heaven ;—for are not both Heaven and Hell made out of him, made by him, everlasting Miracle and Mystery as he is ?—But looking on this Champ-de-Mars, with its tent-buildings and frantic enrolments ; on this murky-simmering Paris, with its crammed Prisons (supposed about to burst), with its tocsin-miserere, its mothers' tears, and soldiers' farewell shoutings,—the pious soul might have prayed, that day, that God's grace would restrain, and greatly restrain ; lest on slight hest or hint, Madness, Horror and Murder rose, and this Sabbathday of September became a Day black in the Annals of men.

The tocsin is pealing its loudest, the clocks inaudibly striking *Three*, when poor Abbé Sicard, with some thirty other Nonjurant Priests, in six carriages, fare along the streets, from their preliminary House of Detention at the Townhall, westward towards the Prison of the Abbaye. Carriages enough stand deserted on the streets ; these six move on, through angry multitudes, cursing as they move. Accursed Aristocrat Tartuffes, this is the pass ye have brought us to ! And now ye will break the Prisons, and set Capet Veto on horseback to ride over us? Out upon you, Priests of Beelzebub and Moloch; of Tartuffery, Mammon and the Prussian Gallows, —which ye name Mother-Church and God!—Such reproaches have the poor Nonjurants to endure, and worse; spoken in on them by frantic Patriots, who mount even on the carriage-steps; the very guards hardly refraining. Pull up your carriage-blinds?—No! answers Patriotism, clapping its horny paw on the carriage-blind, and crushing it down again. Patience in oppression has limits: we are close on the Abbaye, it has lasted long: a poor Nonjurant, of quicker temper, smites the horny paw with his cane; nay, finding solacement in it, smites the unkempt head, sharply and again more sharply, twice over,—seen clearly of us, and of the world. It is the last that we see clearly. Alas, next moment the carriages are locked and blocked in endless raging tumults; in yells deaf to the cry for mercy, which answer the cry for mercy with sabre-thrusts through the heart. The thirty Priests are torn out, are massacred about the Prison-Gate, one after one,—only the poor Abbé Sicard, whom one Moton a watchmaker, knowing him, heroically tried to save and secrete in the Prison, escapes to tell;—and it is Night and Orcus, and Murder's snaky-sparkling head *has* risen in the murk!—

From Sunday afternoon (exclusive of intervals and pauses not final) till Thursday evening, there follow consecutively a Hundred Hours. Which hundred hours are to be reckoned with the hours of the Bartholomew Butchery, of the Armagnac Massacres, Sicilian Vespers, or whatsoever is savagest in the annals of this world. Horrible the hour when man's soul, in its paroxysm, spurns asunder the barriers and rules; and shows what dens and depths are in it! For Night and Orcus, as we say, as was long prophesied, have burst forth, here in this Paris, from their subterranean imprisonment: hideous, dim-confused; which it is painful to look on; and yet which cannot, and indeed which should not, be forgotten.

The Reader, who looks earnestly through this dim Phantas-magory of the Pit, will discern few fixed certain objects; and yet still a few. He will observe, in this Abbaye Prison, the sudden massacre of the Priests being once over, a strange Court of Justice, or call it Court of Revenge and Wild-Justice, swiftly fashion itself, and take seat round a table, with the Prison-Registers spread before it;—Stanislas Maillard, Bastille-hero, famed Leader of the Menads, presiding. O

Stanislas, one hoped to meet thee elsewhere than here; thou shifty Riding-Usher, with an inkling of Law! This work also thou hadst to do; and then—to depart forever from our eyes. At *La Force*, at the *Châtelet*, the *Conciergerie*, the like Court forms itself, with the like accompaniments: the thing that one man does, other men can do. There are some Seven Prisons in Paris, full of Aristocrats with conspiracies;—nay not even *Bicêtre* and *Salpêtrière* shall escape, with their Forgers of Assignats: and there are seventy times seven hundred Patriot hearts in a state of frenzy. Scoundrel hearts also there are; as perfect, say, as the Earth holds,—if such be needed. To whom, in this mood, law is as no-law; and killing, by what name soever called, is but work to be done.

So sit these sudden Courts of Wild-Justice, with the Prison-Registers before them; unwonted wild tumult howling all round; the Prisoners in dread expectancy within. Swift: a name is called; bolts jingle, a Prisoner is there. A few questions are put; swiftly this sudden jury decides: Royalist Plotter or not? Clearly not; in that case, Let the Prisoner be enlarged with *Vive la Nation*. Probably yea; then still, Let the Prisoner be enlarged, but without *Vive la Nation;* or else it may run, Let the Prisoner be conducted to La Force. At La Force again their Formula is, Let the Prisoner be conducted to the Abbaye.—"To La Force then!" Volunteer baliffs seize the doomed man; he is at the outer gate; 'enlarged,' or 'conducted,' not into La Force, but into a howling sea; forth under an arch of wild sabres, axes and pikes; and sinks, hewn asunder. And another sinks, and another; and there forms itself a piled heap of corpses, and the kennels begin to run red. Fancy the yells of these men, their faces of sweat and blood; the crueller shrieks of these women, for there are women too; and a fellow-mortal hurled naked into it all! Jourgniac de Saint-Méard has seen battle, has seen an effervescent Régiment du Roi in mutiny; but the bravest heart may quail at this. The Swiss Prisoners, remnants of the Tenth of August, 'clasped each other spasmodically, and hung back; gray veterans crying: "Mercy, Messieurs; ah, mercy!" But there was no mercy. Suddenly, however, one of these men steps forward. He had on a blue frock-coat; he seemed about thirty, his stature was above common, his look noble and martial. "I go first," said he, "since it must be so: adieu!" Then dashing his hat sharply behind him: "Which way?" cried he to the Brigands: "Show it me, then." They opened the folding gate : he is announced to the multitude. He stands a moment motionless ; then plunges forth among the pikes, and dies of a thousand wounds.'

Man after man is cut down ; the sabres need sharpening, the killers refresh themselves from wine-jugs. Onward and onward goes the butchery ; the loud yells wearying down into bass growls. A sombre-faced shifting multitude looks on ; in dull approval, or dull disapproval ; in dull recognition that it is Necessity. ' An *Anglais* in drab greatcoat ' was seen, or seemed to be seen, serving liquor from his own dram-bottle ;— for what purpose, 'if not set on by Pitt,' Satan and himself know best ! Witty Dr. Moore grew sick on approaching, and turned into another street.—Quick enough goes this Jury-Court ; and rigorous. The brave are not spared, nor the beautiful, nor the weak. Old M. de Montmorin, the Minister's Brother, was acquitted by the Tribunal of the Seventeenth ; and conducted back, elbowed by howling galleries ; but is not acquitted here. Princess de Lamballe has lain down on bed ; "Madame, you are to be removed to the Abbaye." "I do not wish to remove ; I am well enough here." There is a need-be for removing. She will arrange her dress a little, then ; rude voices answer, "You have not far to go." She too is led to the hell-gate ; a manifest Queen's-Friend. She shivers back, at the sight of bloody sabres ; but there is no return : Onward ! That fair hind head is cleft with the axe ; the neck is severed. That fair body is cut in fragments ; with indignities, and obscene horrors of moustachio *grands lèvres*, which human nature would fain find incredible, which shall be read in the original language only. She was beautiful, she was good, she had known no happiness. Young hearts, generation after generation, will think with themselves : O worthy of worship, thou king-descended, god-descended, and poor sister-woman ! why was I not there ; and some Sword Balmung or Thor's Hammer in my hand ? Her head is fixed on a pike ; paraded under the windows of the Temple ; that a still more hated, a Marie Antoinette, may see. One Municipal, in the Temple with the Royal Prisoners at the moment, said, "Look out." Another eagerly whispered, "Do not look." The circuit of the Temple is guarded, in these hours, by a long stretched tricolor riband : terror enters, and the clangour of infinite tumult ; hitherto not regicide, though that too may come.

But it is more edifying to note what thrillings of affec-

tion, what fragments of wild virtues turn up in this shaking
asunder of man's existence; for of these too there is a proportion. Note old Marquis Cazotte: he is doomed to die;
but his young Daughter clasps him in her arms, with an
inspiration of eloquence, with a love which is stronger than
very death: the heart of the killers themselves is touched by
it; the old man is spared. Yet he was guilty, if plotting for
his King is guilt: in ten days more, a Court of Law condemned him, and he had to die elsewhere; bequeathing his
Daughter a lock of his old gray hair. Or note old M. de
Sombreuil, who also had a Daughter:—My Father is not
an Aristocrat: O good gentlemen, I will swear it, and testify
it, and in all ways prove it; we are not; we hate Aristocrats!
"Wilt thou drink Aristocrats' blood?" The man lifts blood
(if universal Rumour can be credited): the poor maiden does
drink. "This Sombreuil is innocent then!" Yes, indeed,—
and now note, most of all, how the bloody pikes, at this news,
do rattle to the ground; and the tiger-yells become bursts
of jubilee over a brother saved; and the old man and his
daughter are clasped to bloody bosoms, with hot tears; and
borne home in triumph of *Vive la Nation*, the killers refusing
even money! Does it seem strange, this temper of theirs? It
seems very certain, well proved by Royalist testimony in other
instances; and very significant.

CHAPTER V

A TRILOGY

As all Delineation, in these ages, were it never so Epic,
'speaking itself and not singing itself,' must either found on
Belief and provable Fact, or have no foundation at all (nor,
except as floating cobweb, any existence at all),—the Reader
will perhaps prefer to take a glance with the very eyes of eye-
witnesses; and see, in that way, for himself, how it was.
Brave Jourgniac, innocent Abbé Sicard, judicious Advocate
Maton, these, greatly compressing themselves, shall speak,
each an instant. Jourgniac's *Agony of Thirty-eight hours* went
through 'above a hundred editions,' though intrinsically a
poor work. Some portion of it may here go through above
the hundred-and-first, for want of a better.

'*Towards seven o'clock*' (Sunday night at the Abbaye; for
Jourgniac goes by dates): 'We saw two men enter, their

A Trilogy

hands bloody and armed with sabres; a turnkey, with a torch,
lighted them; he pointed to the bed of the unfortunate Swiss,
Reding. Reding spoke with a dying voice. One of them
paused; but the other cried, *Allons donc;* lifted the unfortunate man; carried him out on his back to the street.
He was massacred there.

'We all looked at one another in silence, we clasped each
other's hands. Motionless, with fixed eyes, we gazed on the
pavement of our prison; on which lay the moonlight,
checkered with the triple stancheons of our windows.'

'*Three in the morning:* They were breaking-in one of the
prison-doors. We at first thought they were coming to kill us
in our room; but heard, by voices on the staircase, that it was
a room where some Prisoners had barricaded themselves.
They were all butchered there, as we shortly gathered.'

'*Ten o'clock:* The Abbé Lenfant and the Abbé de Chapt-
Rastignac appeared in the pulpit of the Chapel, which was
our prison; they had entered by a door from the stairs. They
said to us that our end was at hand; that we must compose
ourselves, and receive their last blessing. An electric movement, not to be defined, threw us all on our knees, and we
received it. These two whitehaired old men, blessing us from
their place above; death hovering over our heads, on all
hands environing us; the moment is never to be forgotten.
Half an hour after, they were both massacred, and we heard
their cries.'—Thus Jourgniac in his *Agony* in the Abbaye.

But now let the good Maton speak, what he, over in La
Force, in the same hours, is suffering and witnessing. This
Résurrection by him is greatly the best, the least theatrical of
these Pamphlets; and stands testing by documents:

'Towards seven o'clock,' on Sunday night, 'prisoners were
called frequently, and they did not reappear. Each of us
reasoned, in his own way, on this singularity: but our ideas
became calm, as we persuaded ourselves that the Memorial
I had drawn up for the National Assembly was producing
effect.'

'At one in the morning, the grate which led to our quarter
opened anew. Four men in uniform, each with a drawn sabre
and blazing torch, came up to our corridor, preceded by a
turnkey; and entered an apartment close to ours, to investigate a box there, which we heard them break up. This done,
they stept into the gallery, and questioned the man Cuissa,
to know where Lamotte' (Necklace's Widower) 'was. Lamotte,

they said, had some months ago, under pretext of a treasure he knew of, swindled a sum of three-hundred livres from one of them, inviting him to dinner for that purpose. The wretched Cuissa, now in their hands, who indeed lost his life this night, answered trembling, That he remembered the fact well, but could not tell what was become of Lamotte. Determined to find Lamotte and confront him with Cuissa, they rummaged, along with this latter, through various other apartments; but without effect, for we heard them say: "Come search among the corpses then; for, *nom de Dieu!* we must find where he is."

'At this same time, I heard Louis Bardy, the Abbé Bardy's name called: he was brought out; and directly massacred, as I learnt. He had been accused, along with his concubine, five or six years before, of having murdered and cut in pieces his own Brother, Auditor of the *Chambre des Comptes* of Montpelier; but had by his subtlety, his dexterity, nay his eloquence, outwitted the judges, and escaped.

'One may fancy what terror these words, "Come search among the corpses then," had thrown me into. I saw nothing for it now but resigning myself to die. I wrote my last-will; concluding it by a petition and adjuration, that the paper should be sent to its address. Scarcely had I quitted the pen, when there came two other men in uniform; one of them, whose arm and sleeve up to the very shoulder, as well as his sabre, were covered with blood, said, He was as weary as a hodman that had been beating plaster.'

'Baudin de la Chenaye was called; sixty years of virtues could not save him. They said, *A l'Abbaye:* he passed the fatal outer-gate; gave a cry of terror, at sight of the heaped corpses; covered his eyes with his hands, and died of innumerable wounds. At every new opening of the grate, I thought I should hear my own name called, and see Rossignol enter.'

'I flung off my night-gown and cap; I put-on a coarse unwashed shirt, a worn frock without waistcoat, an old round hat; these things I had sent for, some days ago, in the fear of what might happen.

'The rooms of this corridor had been all emptied but ours. We were four together; whom they seemed to have forgotten: we addressed our prayers in common to the Eternal to be delivered from this peril.'

'Baptiste the turnkey came up by himself, to see us. I

took him by the hands ; I conjured him to save us ; promised
him a hundred louis, if he would conduct me home. A noise
coming from the grates made him hastily withdraw.

'It was the noise of some dozen or fifteen men, armed to
the teeth ; as we, lying flat to escape being seen, could see
from our windows. "Upstairs!" said they : "Let not one
remain." I took out my penknife ; I considered where I
should strike myself,'—but reflected ' that the blade was too
short,' and also ' on religion.'

Finally, however, between seven and eight o'clock in the
morning, enter four men with bludgeons and sabres !—'To
one of whom Gérard my comrade whispered, earnestly, apart.
During their colloquy I searched everywhere for shoes, that
I might lay off the Advocate pumps (*pantoufles de Palais*) I
had on,' but could find none.—'Constant, called le Sauvage,
Gérard, and a third whose name escapes me, they let clear
off : as for me, four sabres were crossed over my breast, and
they led me down. I was brought to their bar ; to the
Personage with the scarf, who sat as judge there. He was
a lame man, of tall lank stature. He recognised me on the
streets and spoke to me, seven months after. I have been
assured that he was son of a retired attorney, and named
Chepy. Crossing the Court called *Des Nourrices*, I saw
Manuel haranguing in tricolor scarf.' The trial, as we see,
ends in acquittal and *resurrection*.

Poor Sicard, from the *violon* of the Abbaye, shall say but
a few words ; true-looking, though tremulous. Towards three
in the morning, the killers bethink them of this little *violon ;*
and knock from the court. 'I tapped gently, trembling lest
the murderers might hear, on the opposite door, where the
Section Committee was sitting : they answered gruffly, that
they had no key. There were three of us in this *violon ;* my
companions thought they perceived a kind of loft overhead.
But it was very high ; only one of us could reach it by mounting on the shoulders of both the others. One of them said
to me, that my life was usefuller than theirs : I resisted, they
insisted : no denial ! I fling myself on the neck of these two
deliverers ; never was scene more touching. I mount on the
shoulders of the first, then on those of the second, finally on
the loft ; and address to my two comrades the expression of
a soul overwhelmed with natural emotions.'

The two generous companions, we rejoice to find, did not
perish. But it is time that Jourgniac de Saint-Méard should

speak his last words, and end this singular trilogy. The night had become day; and the day has again become night. Jourgniac, worn down with uttermost agitation, was fallen asleep, and had a cheering dream: he has also contrived to make acquaintance with one of the volunteer bailiffs, and spoken in native Provençal with him. On Tuesday, about one in the morning, his *Agony* is reaching its crisis.

'By the glare of two torches, I now descried the terrible tribunal, where lay my life or my death. The President, in gray coat, with a sabre at his side, stood leaning with his hands against a table, on which were papers, an inkstand, tobacco-pipes and bottles. Some ten persons were around, seated or standing; two of whom had jackets and aprons: others were sleeping stretched on benches. Two men, in bloody shirts, guarded the door of the place; an old turnkey had his hand on the lock. In front of the President three men held a Prisoner, who might be about sixty' (or seventy: he was old Marshall Maillé, of the Tuileries and August Tenth). 'They stationed me in a corner; my guards crossed their sabres on my breast. I looked on all sides for my Provençal: two National Guards, one of them drunk, presented some appeal from the Section of Croix Rouge in favour of the Prisoner: the Man in Gray answered: "They are useless, these appeals for traitors." Then the Prisoner exclaimed: "It is frightful; your judgment is a murder." The President answered: "My hands are washed of it; take M. Maillé away." They drove him into the street; where, through the opening of the door, I saw him massacred.

'The President sat down to write; registering, I suppose, the name of this one whom they had finished; then I heard him say: "Another, *A un autre?*"

'Behold me then haled before this swift and bloody judgment-bar, where the best protection was to have no protection, and all resources of ingenuity became null if they were not founded on truth. Two of my guards held me each by a hand, the third by the collar of my coat. "Your name, your profession?" said the President. "The smallest lie ruins you," added one of the Judges.—"My name is Jourgniac Saint-Méard; I have served, as an officer, twenty years: and I appear at your tribunal with the assurance of an innocent man, who therefore will not lie."—"We shall see that," said the President: "Do you know why you are arrested?"— "Yes, Monsieur le Président; I am accused of editing the

Journal *De la Cour et de la Ville.* But I hope to prove the falsity." '—

But no; Jourgniac's proof of the falsity, and defence generally, though of excellent result as a defence, is not interesting to read. It is long-winded; there is a loose theatricality in the reporting of it, which does not amount to unveracity, yet which tends that way. We shall suppose him successful, beyond hope, in proving and disproving; and skip largely,— to the catastrophe, almost at two steps.

' "But after all," said one of the Judges, "there is no smoke without kindling; tell us why they accuse you of that."—" I was about to do so " '—Jourgniac does so; with more and more success.

' "Nay," continued I, "they accuse me even of recruiting for the Emigrants!" At these words there arose a general murmur. "O Messieurs, Messieurs," I exclaimed, raising my voice, "it is my turn to speak; I beg M. le Président to have the kindness to maintain it for me; I never needed it more." —"True enough, true enough," said almost all the Judges with a laugh : "Silence!"

'While they were examining the testimonials I had produced, a new Prisoner was brought in and placed before the President. "It was one Priest more," they said, "whom they had ferreted out of the Chapelle." After very few questions : "*A la Force!*" He flung his breviary on the table; was hurled forth, and massacred. I reappeared before the tribunal.

' "You tell us always," cried one of the Judges, with a tone of impatience, "that you are not this, that you are not that; what are you then?"—"I was an open Royalist."—There arose a general murmur; which was miraculously appeased by another of the men, who had seemed to take an interest in me : "We are not here to judge opinions," said he, "but to judge the results of them." Could Rousseau and Voltaire both in one, pleading for me, have said better?—"Yes, Messieurs," cried I, "always till the Tenth of August I was an open Royalist. Ever since the Tenth of August that cause has been finished. I am a Frenchman, true to my country. I was always a man of honour." '

' "My soldiers never distrusted me. Nay, two days before that business of Nanci, when their suspicion of their officers was at its height, they chose me for commander, to lead them to Lunéville, to get back the prisoners of the Regiment

Mestre-de-Camp, and seize General Malseigne."' Which fact there is, most luckily, an individual present who by a certain token can confirm.

'The President, this cross-questioning being over, took off his hat and said: "I see nothing to suspect in this man: I am for granting him his liberty. Is that your vote?" To which all the Judges answered: "*Oui, Oui;* it is just!"'

And there arose vivats within doors and without; 'escort of three,' amid shoutings and embracings: thus Jourgniac escaped from jury-trial and the jaws of death. Maton and Sicard did, either by trial and no bill found, lank President Chepy finding 'absolutely nothing;' or else by evasion, and new favour of Moton the brave watchmaker, likewise escape; and were embraced and wept over; weeping in return, as they well might

Thus they three, in wondrous trilogy, or triple soliloquy: uttering simultaneously, through the dread night-watches, their Night-thoughts,—grown audible to us! They Three are become audible: but the other 'Thousand and Eighty-nine, of whom Two-hundred and two were Priests,' who also had Night-thoughts, remain inaudible; choked for ever in black Death. Heard only of President Chepy and the Man in Gray!—

CHAPTER VI

THE CIRCULAR

BUT the Constituted Authorities, all this while? The Legislative Assembly; the Six Ministers; the Townhall; Santerre with the National Guard?—It is very curious to think what a City is. Theatres, to the number of some twenty-three, were open every night during these prodigies; while right-arms here grew weary with slaying, right-arms there were twiddledeeing on melodious catgut: at the very instant when Abbé Sicard was clambering up his second pair of shoulders, three-men high, five hundred thousand human individuals were lying horizontal, as if nothing were amiss.

As for the poor Legislative, the sceptre had departed from it. The Legislative did send Deputation to the Prisons, to these Street-Courts; and poor M. Dusaulx did harangue there; but produced no conviction whatsoever: nay at last, as he continued haranguing, the Street-Court interposed, not without threats; and he had to cease, and withdraw. This is the same poor worthy old M. Dusaulx who told, or indeed almost sang (though with cracked voice), the *Taking of the Bastille*, to our satisfaction, long since. He was wont to announce himself, on such and on all occasions, as *the Translator of Juvenal.* "Good Citizens, you see before you a man who loves his country, who is the Translator of Juvenal," said he once.—"Juvenal?" interrupts Sansculottism: "Who the devil is Juvenal? One of your *sacrés Aristocrates?* To the *Lanterne!*" From an orator of this kind, conviction was not to be expected. The Legislative had much ado to save one of its own Members, or Ex-Members, Deputy Jouneau, who chanced to be lying in arrest for mere Parliamentary delinquencies, in these Prisons. As for poor old Dusaulx and Company, they returned to the Salle de Manége, saying, "It was dark; and they could not see well what was going on."

Roland writes indignant messages, in the name of Order, Humanity and the Law; but there is no Force at his disposal. Santerre's National Force seems lazy to rise: though he made requisitions, he says,—which always dispersed again. Nay did not we, with Advocate Maton's eyes, see 'men in uniform' too, with their 'sleeves bloody to the shoulder?' Pétion goes in tricolor scarf; speaks 'the austere language of the law': the killers give up, while he is there; when his back is turned, recommence. Manuel too in scarf we, with Maton's eyes, transiently saw haranguing, in the Court called of Nurses, *Cour des Nourrices.* On the other hand, cruel Billaud, likewise in scarf, 'with that small puce coat and black wig we are used to on him,' audibly delivers, 'standing among corpses,' at the Abbaye, a short but ever-memorable harangue, reported in various phraseology, but always to this purpose: "Brave Citizens, you are extirpating the Enemies of Liberty; you are at your duty. A grateful Commune and Country would wish to recompense you adequately; but cannot, for you know its want of funds. Whoever shall have worked (*travaillé*) in a Prison shall receive a draft of one louis, payable by our cashier. Continue your work." The Constituted Authorities are of yesterday: all pulling different ways: there is properly no Constituted Authority, but every man is his own King; and all are kinglets, belligerent, allied, or armed-neutral, without king over them.

'O everlasting infamy,' exclaims Montgaillard, 'that Paris stood looking on in stupor for four days, and did not interfere!'

Very desirable indeed that Paris had interfered; yet not un-natural that it stood even so, looking on in stupor. Paris is in death-panic, the enemy and gibbets at its door: whoso-ever in Paris has the heart to front death, finds it more pressing to do it fighting the Prussians, than fighting the killers of Aristocrats. Indignant abhorrence, as in Roland, may be here; gloomy sanction, premeditation or not, as in Marat and Committee of Salvation, may be there; dull dis-approval, dull approval, and acquiescence in Necessity and Destiny, is the general temper. The Sons of Darkness, 'two-hundred or so,' risen from their lurking-places, have scope to do their work. Urged on by fever-frenzy of Patriotism, and the madness of Terror;—urged on by lucre, and the gold louis of wages? Nay, not lucre; for the gold watches, rings, money of the Massacred are punctually brought to the Townhall, by Killers sans-indispensables, who higgle afterwards for their twenty shillings of wages; and Sergent sticking an un-commonly fine agate on his finger (fully 'meaning to account for it') becomes *Agate*-Sergent. But the temper, as we say, is dull acquiescence. Not till the Patriotic or Frenetic part of the work is finished for want of material; and Sons of Dark-ness, bent clearly on lucre alone, begin wrenching watches and purses, brooches from ladies' necks, "to equip volunteers," in daylight, on the streets,—does the temper from dull grow vehement; does the Constable raise his truncheon, and striking heartily (like a cattle-driver in earnest) beat the 'course of things' back into its old regulated drove-roads. The *Garde-Meuble* itself was surreptitiously plundered, on the 17th of the month, to Roland's new horror; who anew bestirs himself, and is, as Sieyès says, 'the veto of scoundrels,' Roland *veto des coquins.*—

This is the September Massacre, otherwise called 'Severe Justice of the People.' These are the Septemberers (*Septem-briseurs*); a name of some note and lucency,—but lucency of the Nether-fire sort; very different from that of our Bastille Heroes, who shone, disputable by no Friend of Freedom, as in Heavenly light-radiance: to such phasis of the business have we advanced since then! The numbers massacred are, in the Historical *fantasy*, 'between two and three thousand;' or indeed they are 'upwards of six thousand,' for Peltier (in vision) saw them massacring the very patients of the Bicêtre Madhouse 'with grapeshot;' nay, finally they are 'twelve thousand' and odd hundreds,—not more than that. In

Arithmetical ciphers, and Lists drawn up by accurate Advocate Maton, the number, including two-hundred and two priests, three 'persons unknown,' and 'one thief killed at the Bernardins,' is, as above hinted, a Thousand and Eighty-nine,— not less than that.

A thousand and eighty-nine lie dead, 'two hundred and sixty heaped carcasses on the Pont au Change' itself;—among which, Robespierre pleading afterwards will 'nearly weep' to reflect that there was said to be one slain innocent. One, not two, O thou seagreen Incorruptible? If so, Themis Sansculotte must be lucky; for she was brief!—In the dim Registers of the Townhall, which are preserved to this day, men read, with a certain sickness of heart, items and entries not usual in Town Books: 'To workers employed in preserving the salubrity of the air in the Prisons, and persons who presided over these dangerous operations,'so much,—in various items, nearly seven hundred pounds sterling. To carters employed to 'the Burying-grounds of Clamart, Montrouge, and Vaugirard,' at so much a journey, per cart; this also is an entry. Then so many francs and odd sous 'for the necessary quantity of quicklime!' Carts go along the streets; full of stript human corpses, thrown pellmell; limbs sticking-up:—seest thou that cold Hand sticking-up, through the heaped embrace of brother corpses, in its yellow paleness, in its cold rigour; the palm opened towards Heaven, as if in dumb prayer, in expostulation *de profundis*, Take pity on the Sons of Men!—Mercier saw it, as he walked down 'the Rue Saint-Jacques from Montrouge, on the morrow of the Massacres:' but not a Hand; it was a Foot,—which he reckons still more significant, one understands not well why. Or was it as the foot of one *spurning* Heaven? Rushing like a wild diver, in disgust and despair, towards the depths of Annihilation? Even there shall His hand find thee, and His right hand hold thee,—surely for right not for wrong, for good not evil! 'I saw that Foot,' says Mercier; 'I shall know it again at the great Day of Judgment, when the Eternal, throned on his thunders, shall judge both Kings and Septemberers.'

That a shriek of inarticulate horror rose over this thing, not only from French Aristocrats and Moderates, but from all Europe, and has prolonged itself to the present day, was most natural and right. The thing lay done, irrevocable; a thing to be counted beside some other things, which lie very black in our Earth's Annals, yet which will not erase therefrom. For man, as was remarked, has transcendentalisms in him; standing, as he does, poor creature, every way 'in the confluence of Infinitudes;' a mystery to himself and others: in the centre of two Eternities, of three Immensities,—in the intersection of primeval Light with the everlasting Dark!—Thus have there been, especially by vehement tempers reduced to a state of desperation, very miserable things done. Sicilian Vespers, and 'eight thousand slaughtered in two hours,' are a known thing. Kings themselves, not in desperation, but only in difficulty, have sat hatching, for year and day (nay De Thou says for seven years), their Bartholomew Business; and then, at the right moment, also on an Autumn Sunday, this very Bell (they say it is the identical metal) of Saint-Germain l'Auxerrois was set a-pealing—with effect. Nay the same black boulder-stones of these Paris Prisons have seen Prison-massacres before now; men massacring countrymen, Burgundies massacring Armagnacs, whom they had suddenly imprisoned, till, as now, there were piled heaps of carcasses, and the streets ran red;—the Mayor Pétion of the time speaking the austere language of the law, and answered by the Killers, in old French (it is some four hundred years old): "*Maugré bieu, Sire*,—Sir, God's malison on your 'justice,' your 'pity,' your 'right reason.' Cursed be of God whoso shall have pity on these false traitorous Armagnacs, English; dogs they are; they have destroyed us, wasted this realm of France, and sold it to the English." And so they slay, and fling aside the slain, to the extent of 'fifteen hundred and eighteen, among whom are found four Bishops of false and damnable counsel, and two Presidents of Parlement.' For though it is not Satan's world this that we live in, Satan always has his place in it (underground properly); and from time to time bursts up. Well may mankind shriek, inarticulately anathematising as they can. There are actions of such emphasis that no shrieking can be too emphatic for them. Shriek ye; acted have they.

Shriek who might in this France, in this Paris Legislative or Paris Townhall, there are Ten Men who do not shriek. A Circular goes out from the Committee of *Salut Public*, dated 3d of September 1792; directed to all Townhalls: a State-paper too remarkable to be overlooked. 'A part of the ferocious conspirators detained in the Prisons,' it says, 'have been put to death by the People; and we cannot doubt but

he whole Nation, driven to the edge of ruin by such endless
eries of treasons, will make haste to adopt *this* means of public
alvation; and all Frenchmen will cry as the men of Paris:
Ve go to fight the enemy; but we will not leave robbers
ehind us, to butcher our wives and children.' To which are
egibly appended these signatures: Panis; Sergent; Marat,
riend of the People; with Seven others;—carried down
hereby, in a strange way, to the late remembrance of Anti-
quarians. We remark, however, that their Circular rather
ecoiled on themselves. The Townhalls made no use of it;
even the distracted Sansculottes made little; they only howled
and bellowed, but did not bite. At Rheims 'about eight
persons' were killed; and two afterwards were hanged for
doing it. At Lyons, and a few other places, some attempt
vas made; but with hardly any effect, being quickly put
down.

Less fortunate were the Prisoners of Orleans; was the good
Duke de La Rochefoucault. He journeying, by quick stages,
with his Mother and Wife, towards the Waters of Forges, or
some quieter country, was arrested at Gisors; conducted along
he streets, amid effervescing multitudes, and killed dead 'by
he stroke of a paving-stone hurled through the coach-window.'
Killed as a once Liberal, now Aristocrat; Protector of Priests,
Suspender of virtuous Pétions, and most unfortunate Hot-
grown-cold, detestable to Patriotism. He dies lamented of
Europe; his blood spattering the cheeks of his old Mother,
ninety-three years old.

As for the Orleans Prisoners, they are State Criminals:
Royalist Ministers, Delessarts, Montmorins; who have been
accumulating on the High Court of Orleans, ever since that
Tribunal was set up. Whom now it seems good that we
should get transferred to our new Paris Court of the Seventeenth; which proceeds far quicker. Accordingly hot Fournier from Martinique, Fournier *l'Américain*, is off, missioned
by Constituted Authority; with stanch National Guards,
with Lazouski the Pole; sparingly provided with road-money.
These, through bad quarters, through difficulties, perils, for
Authorities cross each other in this time,—do triumphantly
bring off the Fifty or Fifty-three Orleans Prisoners, towards
Paris; where a swifter Court of the Seventeenth will do
justice on them. But lo, at Paris, in the interim, a still
swifter and swiftest Court of the *Second*, and of *September*, has
instituted itself: enter not Paris, or that will judge you!—

What shall hot Fournier do? It was his duty, as voluntee
Constable, had he been a perfect character, to guard thos
men's lives never so Aristocratic, at the expense of his ow
valuable life never so Sansculottic, till some Constituted Cou
had disposed of them. But he was an imperfect character an
Constable; perhaps one of the more imperfect.

Hot Fournier, ordered to turn hither by one Authority
to turn thither by another Authority, is in a perplexing multi
plicity of orders; but finally he strikes off for Versailles. Hi
Prisoners fare in tumbrils, or open carts, himself and Guard
riding and marching around: and at the last village, th
worthy Mayor of Versailles comes to meet him, anxious tha
the arrival and locking up were well over. It is Sunday, th
ninth day of the month. Lo, on entering the Avenue
Versailles, what multitudes, stirring, swarming in the Septembe
sun, under the dull-green September foliage; the Four-rowe
Avenue all humming and swarming, as if the Town ha
emptied itself! Our tumbrils roll heavily through the livin
sea; the Guards and Fournier making way with ever mor
difficulty; the Mayor speaking and gesturing his persuasivest
amid the inarticulate growling hum, which growls ever th
deeper even by hearing itself growl, not without sharp yelping
here and there:—Would to God we were out of this strai
place, and wind and separation had cooled the heat, whic
seems about igniting here!

And yet if the wide Avenue is too strait, what will th
Street *de Surintendance* be, at leaving of the same? At th
corner of Surintendance Street, the compressed yelping
become a continuous yell: savage figures spring on th
tumbril-shafts; first spray of an endless coming tide! Th
Mayor pleads, pushes, half-desperate; is pushed, carried o
in men's arms: the savage tide has entrance, has master
Amid horrid noise, and tumult as of fierce wolves, th
Prisoners sink massacred,—all but some eleven, who escape
into houses, and found mercy. The Prisons, and what othe
Prisoners they held, were with difficulty saved. The strip
clothes are burnt in bonfire; the corpses lie heaped in th
ditch on the morrow morning. All France, except it be th
Ten Men of the Circular and their people, moans and rage
inarticulately shrieking; all Europe rings.

But neither did Danton shriek; though, as Minister
Justice, it was more his part to do so. Brawny Danton
in the breach, as of stormed Cities and Nations; amid th

weep of Tenth-of-August cannon, the rustle of Prussian
gallows-ropes, the smiting of September sabres; destruction
all round him, and the rushing-down of worlds: Minister of
Justice is his name; but Titan of the Forlorn Hope, and
Enfant Perdu of the Revolution is his quality,—and the man
acts according to that. "We must put our enemies in fear!"
Deep fear, is it not, as of its own accord, falling on our
enemies? The Titan of the Forlorn Hope, he is not the
man that would swiftest of all prevent its so falling. Forward,
thou lost Titan of an *Enfant Perdu;* thou must dare, and
again dare, and without end dare; there is nothing left for
thee but that! "*Que mon nom soit flétri,* Let my name be
blighted:" what am I? The Cause alone is great; and shall
live and not perish.—So, on the whole, here too is a Swallower
of Formulas; of still wider gulp than Mirabeau: this Danton,
Mirabeau of the Sansculottes. In the September days, this
Minister was not heard of as co-operating with strict Roland;
his business might lie elsewhere,—with Brunswick and the
Hôtel-de-Ville. When applied to by an official person, about
the Orleans Prisoners, and the risks they ran, he answered
gloomily, twice over, "Are not these men guilty?"—When
pressed, he 'answered in a terrible voice,' and turned his back.
A thousand slain in the Prisons; horrible if you will: but
Brunswick is within a day's journey of us; and there are Five-
and-twenty Millions yet, to slay or to save. Some men have
tasks,—frightfuller than ours! It seems strange, but is not
strange, that this Minister of Moloch-Justice, when any
suppliant for a friend's life got access to him, was found to
have human compassion; and yielded and granted 'always;'
neither did one personal enemy of Danton perish in these
days.'

To shriek, we say, when certain things are acted, is proper
and unavoidable. Nevertheless, articulate speech, not shrieking, is the faculty of man: when speech is not yet possible, let
there be, with the shortest delay, at least—silence. Silence,
accordingly, in this forty-fourth year of the business, and
eighteen hundred and thirty-sixth of an 'Era called Christian
as *lucus à non,*' is the thing we recommend and practise.
Nay, instead of shrieking more, it were perhaps edifying to
remark, on the other side, what a singular thing Customs (in
Latin, *Mores*) are; and how fitly the Virtue, *Vir-tus,* Man-hood
or Worth, that is in a man, is called his *Morality* or *Customari-*

ness. Fell Slaughter, one of the most authentic products o
the Pit you would say, once give it Customs, becomes Wai
with Laws of War; and is Customary and Moral enough
and red individuals carry the tools of it girt round thei
haunches, not without an air of pride,—which do thou nowis
blame. While, see! so long as it is but dressed in hodden o
russet; and Revolution, less frequent than War, has not ye
got its Laws of Revolution, but the hodden or russet in
dividuals are Uncustomary—O shrieking beloved brothe
blockheads of Mankind, let us close those wide mouths o
ours; let us cease shrieking, and begin considering!

CHAPTER VII

SEPTEMBER IN ARGONNE

PLAIN, at any rate, is one thing: that the *fear*, whatever c
fear those Aristocrat enemies might need, has been brough
about. The matter is getting serious then! Sansculottisr
too has become a Fact, and seems minded to assert itse
as such! This huge mooncalf of Sansculottism, staggerin
about, as young calves do, is not mockable only, and soi
like another calf; but terrible too, if you prick it; and
through its hideous nostrils, blows fire!—Aristocrats, wit
pale panic in their hearts, fly towards covert; and a light rise
to them over several things; or rather a confused transitio
towards light, whereby for the moment darkness is only darke
than ever. But what will become of this France? Her
is a question! France is dancing its desert-waltz, as Saha
does when the winds waken; in whirl-blasts twenty-five millior
in number; waltzing towards Townhalls, Aristocrat Prison
and Election Committee-rooms; towards Brunswick and th
frontiers;—towards a new Chapter of Universal History;
indeed it be not the *Finis,* and winding-up of that!

In Election Committee-rooms there is now no dubiety: bu
the work goes bravely along. The Convention is gettin
chosen,—really in a decisive spirit; in the Townhall w
already date *First year of the Republic.* Some Two hundred c
our best Legislators may be re-elected, the Mountain bodily
Robespierre, with Mayor Pétion, Buzot, Curate Grégoire
Rabaut, some three-score old Constituents; though we onc
had only 'thirty voices.' All these; and along with then

friends long known to Revolutionary fame: Camille Desmoulins, though he stutters in speech; Manuel, Tallien and
Company; Journalists Gorsas, Carra, Mercier, Louvet of
Faublas; Clootz Speaker of Mankind; Collot d'Herbois,
tearing a passion to rags; Fabre d'Eglantine, speculative
Pamphleteer; Legendre the solid butcher; nay Marat, though
rural France can hardly believe it, or even believe that there
is a Marat, except in print. Of minister Danton, who will
lay down his Ministry for a Membership, we need not speak.
Paris is fervent: nor is the Country wanting to itself. Barbaroux, Rebecqui, and fervid Patriots are coming from Marseilles. Seven-hundred and forty-five men (or indeed forty-
nine, for Avignon now sends Four) are gathering: so many
are to meet; not so many are to part!

Attorney Carrier from Aurillac, Ex-Priest Lebon from Arras,
these shall both gain a *name.* Mountainous Auvergne re-elects
her Romme; hardy tiller of the soil, once Mathematical
Professor; who, unconscious, carries in petto a remarkable
New Calendar, with Messidors, Pluvioses, and such like;—
and having given it well forth, shall depart by the death they
call Roman. Sieyès Old-Constituent comes; to make new
Constitutions as many as wanted; for the rest, peering out of
his clear cautious eyes, he will cower low in many an
emergency, and find silence safest. Young Saint-Just is
coming, deputed by Aisne in the North; more like a Student
than a Senator; not four-and-twenty yet; who has written
Books; a youth of slight stature, with mild mellow voice,
enthusiast olive-complexion and long black hair. Féraud,
from the far valley D'Aure in the folds of the Pyrenees, is
coming; an ardent Republican; doomed to fame, at least in
death.

All manner of Patriot men are coming: Teachers, Hus-
bandmen, Priests and Ex-Priests, Traders, Doctors; above all,
Talkers, or the Attorney-species. Man-midwives, as Levasseur
of the Sarthe, are not wanting. Nor Artists: gross David
with the swoln cheek, has long painted, with genius in a
state of convulsion; and will now legislate. The swoln cheek,
choking his words in the birth, totally disqualifies him as an
orator; but his pencil, his head, his gross hot heart, with
genius in a state of convulsion, will be there. A man bodily
and mentally, swoln-cheeked, disproportionate; flabby-large,
instead of great; weak withal, as in a state of a convulsion,
not strong in a state of composure: so let him play his part.

Nor are naturalised Benefactors of the Species forgotten
Priestley, elected by the Orne Department, but declining
Paine the rebellious Needleman, by the Pas-de-Calais, who
accepts.

Few Nobles come, and yet not none. Paul François
Barras 'noble as the Barrases, old as the rocks of Provence,'
he is one. The reckless, ship-wrecked man: flung ashore on
the coast of the Maldives long ago, while sailing and soldiering
as Indian Fighter: flung ashore since then, as hungry Parisian
Pleasure-hunter and Half-pay, on many a Circe Island, with
temporary enchantment, temporary conversion into beasthood
and hoghood;—the remote Var Department has now sent
him hither. A man of heat and haste; defective in utterance,
defective indeed in any thing to utter; yet not without a
certain rapidity of glance, a certain swift transient courage;
who in these times, Fortune favouring, may go far. He is
tall, handsome to the eye, 'only the complexion a little yellow;'
but 'with a robe of purple, with a scarlet cloak and plume of
tricolor, on occasions of solemnity,' the man will look well.
Lepelletier Saint-Fargeau, Old-Constituent, is a kind of noble,
and of enormous wealth; he too has come hither :—to have
the pain of Death *abolished?* Hapless Ex-Parlementeer !
Nay, among our Sixty Old-Constituents, see Philippe d'Orléans,
a Prince of the Blood ! Not now *D'Orléans :* for, Feudalism
being swept from the world, he demands of his worthy friends
the Electors of Paris, to have a new name of their choosing ;
whereupon Procureur Manuel, like an antithetic literary man,
recommends *Equality*, Égalité. A Philippe Égalité therefore
will sit ; seen of the Earth and Heaven.

Such a Convention is gathering itself together. Mere angry
poultry in moulting season ; whom Brunswick's grenadiers and
cannoneers will give short account of. Would the weather, as
Bertrand is always praying, only mend a little !

In vain, O Bertrand ! The weather will not mend a whit :
nay even if it did ? Dumouriez Polymetis, though Bertrand
knows it not, started from brief slumber at Sedan, on that
morning of the 29th of August ; with stealthiness, with
promptitude, audacity. Some three mornings after that, Brunswick, opening wide eyes, perceives the Passes of the Argonne
all seized ; blocked with felled trees, fortified with camps ;
and that it is a most shifty swift Dumouriez this, who has
outwitted him !

The manœuvre may cost Brunswick 'a loss of three weeks,' very fatal in these circumstances. A Mountain-wall of forty miles lying between him and Paris : which he should have preoccupied ;—which how now to get possession of ? Also the rain it raineth every day ; and we are in a hungry Champagne Pouilleuse, a land flowing only with ditchwater. How to cross this Mountain-wall of the Argonne ; or what in the world to do with it ?—There are marchings and wet splashings by steep paths, with *sackerments* and guttural interjections ; forcings of Argonne Passes,—which unhappily will not force. Through the woods, volleying War reverberates, like huge gong-music, or Moloch's kettledrum, borne by the echoes ; swoln torrents boil angrily round the foot of rocks, floating pale carcasses of men. In vain ! Islettes Village, with its church-steeple, rises intact in the Mountain-pass, between the embosoming heights : your forced marchings and climbings have become forced slidings and tumblings back. From the hill-tops thou seest nothing but dumb crags, and endless wet moaning woods ; the Clermont *Vache* (huge Cow that she is) disclosing herself at intervals ; flinging off her cloud-blanket, and soon taking it on again, drowned in the pouring Heaven. The Argonne Passes will not force : you must *skirt* the Argonne : go round by the end of it.

But fancy whether the Emigrant Seigneurs have not got their brilliancy dulled a little ; whether that 'Foot Regiment in red-facings with nankeen trousers' could be in field-day order ! In place of gasconading, a sort of desperation, and hydrophobia from *excess* of water, is threatening to supervene. Young Prince de Ligne, son of that brave literary De Ligne the Thundergod of Dandies, fell backwards ; shot dead in Grand-Pré, the Northmost of the Passes : Brunswick is skirting and rounding, laboriously, by the extremity of the South. Four days ; days of a rain as of Noah,—without fire, without food ! For fire you cut down green trees, and produce smoke ; for food you eat green grapes, and produce cholic, pestilential dysentery, ὀλέκοντο δὲ λαοί. And the Peasants assassinate us, they do not join us ; shrill women cry shame on us, threaten to draw their very scissors on us ! O ye hapless dulled-bright Seigneurs, and hydrophobic splashed Nankeens ; but O, ten times more, ye poor *sackerment*ing ghastly-visaged Hessians and Hulans, fallen on your backs ; who had no call to die there, except compulsion and three-halfpence a-day ! Nor has Mrs. Le Blanc of the Golden Arm a good time of it, in

her bower of dripping rushes. Assassinating Peasants are
hanged; Old-Constituent Honourable Members, though of
venerable age, ride in carts with their hands tied: these are
the woes of war.

Thus they; sprawling and wriggling, far and wide, on the
slopes and passes of the Argonne;—a loss to Brunswick of
five-and-twenty disastrous days. There is wriggling and
struggling; facing, backing and right-about facing; as the
positions shift, and the Argonne gets partly rounded, partly
forced:—but still Dumouriez, force him, round him as
you will, sticks like a rooted fixture on the ground
fixture with many *hinges;* wheeling now this way, now
that; showing always new front, in the most unexpected
manner: nowise consenting to take himself away. Recruits
stream up on him: full of heart; yet rather difficult to deal
with. Behind Grand-Pré, for example, Grand-Pré which is on
the wrong-side of the Argonne, for we are now forced and
rounded,—the full heart, in one of those wheelings and show
ings of new front, did as it were overset itself, as full hearts
are liable to do; and there arose a shriek of *sauve qui peut,*
and a death-panic which had nigh ruined all! So that the
General had to come galloping; and with thunder-words, with
gesture, stroke of drawn sword even, check and rally, and
bring back the sense of shame;—nay to seize the first
shriekers and ringleaders; 'shave their heads and eyebrows,'
and pack them forth into the world as a sign. Thus too (for
really the rations are short, and wet camping with hungry
stomach brings bad humour) there is like to be mutiny.
Whereupon again Dumouriez 'arrives at the head of their
line, with his staff, and an escort of a hundred hussars. He
had placed some squadrons behind them, the artillery in
front! he said to them: "As for you, for I will neither call
you citizens, nor soldiers, nor my men (*ni mes enfans*), you
see before you this artillery, behind you this cavalry. You
have dishonoured yourselves by crimes. If you amend, and
grow to behave like this brave Army which you have the
honour of belonging to, you will find in me a good father.
But plunderers and assassins I do not suffer here. At the
smallest mutiny I will have you shivered in pieces (*hacher en
pièces*). Seek out the Scoundrels that are among you, and
dismiss them yourselves; I hold you responsible for them."'

Patience, O Dumouriez! This uncertain heap of shriekers,
mutineers, were they once drilled and inured, will become

a phalanxed mass of Fighters; and wheel and whirl, to order, swiftly like the wind or the whirlwind: tanned mustachio-figures; often barefoot, even bare-backed; with sinews of iron; who require only bread and gunpowder: very Sons of Fire, the adroitest, hastiest, hottest ever seen perhaps since Attila's time. They may conquer and overrun amazingly, much as that same Attila did;—whose Attila's-Camp and Battlefield thou now seest, on this very ground; who, after sweeping bare the world, was, with difficulty, and days of tough fighting, checked *here* by Roman Ætius and Fortune; and his dust-cloud made to vanish in the East again!—

Strangely enough, in this shrieking Confusion of a Soldiery, which we saw long since fallen all suicidally out of square, in suicidal collision,—at Nanci, or on the streets of Metz, where brave Bouillé stood with drawn sword; and which has collided and ground itself to pieces worse and worse ever since, down now to such a state: in this shrieking Confusion, and not elsewhere, lies the first germ of returning Order for France! Round which, we say, poor France nearly all ground down suicidally likewise into rubbish and Chaos, will be glad to rally; to begin growing, and newshaping her inorganic dust; very slowly, through centuries, through Napoleons, Louis-Philippes, and other the like media and phases,—into a new, infinitely preferable France, we can hope!—

These wheelings and movements in the region of the Argonne, which are all faithfully described by Dumouriez himself, and more interesting to us than Hoyle's or Philidor's best Game of Chess, let us, nevertheless, O Reader, entirely omit;—and hasten to remark two things: the first a minute private, the second a large public thing. Our minute private thing is: the presence, in the Prussian host, in that war-game of the Argonne, of a certain Man, belonging to the sort called Immortal; who, in days since then, is becoming visible more and more in that character, as the Transitory more and more vanishes: for from of old it was remarked that when the Gods appear among men, it is seldom in recognisable shape; thus Admetus's neatherds give Apollo a draught of their goatskin whey-bottle (well if they do not give him strokes with their oxrungs), not dreaming that he is the Sungod! This man's name is *Johann Wolfgang von Goethe*. He is Herzog Weimar's Minister, come with the small contingent of Weimar; to do insignificant unmilitary duty here; very irrecognisable to nearly all! He stands at present, with drawn bridle, on the height near Sainte-Menehould, making an experiment on the 'cannon-fever;' having ridden thither against persuasion, into the dance and firing of the cannon-balls, with a scientific desire to understand what that same cannon-fever may be: 'The sound of them,' says he, 'is curious enough; as if it were compounded of the humming of tops, the gurgling of water and the whistle of birds. By degrees you get a very uncommon sensation; which can only be described by similitude. It seems as if you were in some place extremely hot, and at the same time were completely penetrated by the heat of it; so that you feel as if you and this element you are in were perfectly on a par. The eyesight loses nothing of its strength or distinctness; and yet it is as if all things had got a kind of brown-red colour, which makes the situation and the objects still more impressive on you.'

This is the cannon-fever, as a World-Poet feels it.—A man entirely irrecognisable! In whose irrecognisable head, meanwhile, there verily is the spiritual counterpart (and call it complement) of this same huge Death-Birth of the World; which now effectuates itself, outwardly, in the Argonne, in such cannon-thunder; inwardly, in the irrecognisable head, quite otherwise than by thunder! Mark that man, O Reader, as the memorablest of all the memorable in this Argonne Campaign. What we say of him is not dream, nor flourish of rhetoric, but scientific historic fact, as many men, now at this distance, see or begin to see.

But the large public thing we had to remark is this: That the Twentieth of September 1792 was a raw morning covered with mist; that from three in the morning, Sainte-Menehould and those Villages and homesteads we know of old, were stirred by the rumble of artillery-wagons, by the clatter of hoofs and many-footed tramp of men: all manner of military Patriot and Prussian, taking up positions, on the Heights of La Lune and other Heights; shifting and shoving,—seemingly in some dread chess-game; which may the Heavens turn to good! The Miller of Valmy has fled dusty under ground; his Mill, were it never so windy, will have rest to-day. At seven in the morning the mist clears off: see Kellermann, Dumouriez' second in command, with 'eighteen pieces of cannon,' and deep-serried ranks, drawn up round that same silent Windmill, on his knoll of strength; Brunswick, also with serried ranks and cannon, glooming over to him from the

Height of La Lune: only the little brook and its little dell now parting them.

So that the much-longed-for has come at last! Instead of hunger and dysentery, we shall have sharp shot; and then!—Dumouriez, with force and firm front, looks on from a neighbouring height; can help only with his wishes, in silence. Lo, the eighteen pieces do bluster and bark, responsive to the bluster of La Lune; and thunder-clouds mount into the air; and echoes roar through all dells, far into the depths of Argonne Wood (deserted now); and limbs and lives of men fly dissipated, this way and that. Can Brunswick make an impression on them? The dulled-bright Seigneurs stand biting their thumbs; these Sansculottes seem *not* to fly like poultry! Towards noontide a cannon-shot blows Kellermann's horse from under him; there bursts a powder-cart high into the air, with knell heard over all: some swagging and swaying observable;—Brunswick will try! "*Camarades*," cries Kellermann, "*Vive la Patrie! Allons vaincre pour elle*, Come let us conquer for her." "Live the Fatherland!" rings responsive to the welkin, like rolling-fire from side to side: our ranks are as firm as rocks; and Brunswick may *re*cross the dell, ineffectual; regain his old position on La Lune; not unbattered by the way. And so, for the length of a September day,—with bluster and bark; with bellow far-echoing! The cannonade lasts till sunset; and no impression made. Till an hour after sunset, the few remaining Clocks of the District striking Seven; at this late time of day Brunswick tries again. With not a whit better fortune! He is met by rock-ranks, by shout of *Vive la Patrie;* and driven back, not unbattered. Whereupon he ceases; retires 'to the Tavern of La Lune;' and sets to raising a redoute lest *he* be attacked!

Verily so, ye dulled-bright Seigneurs, make of it what ye may. Ah, and France does not rise round us in mass; and the Peasants do not join us, but assassinate us: neither hanging nor any persuasion will induce them! They have lost their old distinguishing love of King, and King's-cloak,—I fear, altogether; and will even fight to be rid of it: that seems now their humour. Nor does Austria prosper, nor the siege of Thionville. The Thionvillers, carrying their insolence to the epigrammatic pitch, have put a Wooden Horse on their walls, with a bundle of Hay hung from him, and this Inscription: "When I finish my hay, you will take Thionville." To such height has the frenzy of mankind risen.

The trenches of 'Thionville may shut; and what though those of Lille open? The Earth smiles not on us, nor the Heaven; but weeps and blears itself, in sour rain, and worse. Our very friends insult us; we are wounded in the house of our friends: 'His Majesty of Prussia had a greatcoat when the rain came; and (contrary to all known laws) he put it on, though our two French Princes, the hope of their country, had none!' To which indeed, as Goethe admits, what answer could be made?—Cold and Hunger and Affront, Colic and Dysentery and Death; and we here, cowering *redouted*, most unredoubtable, amid the 'tattered corn-shocks and deformed stubble,' on the splashy Height of La Lune, round the mean Tavern de la Lune!—

This is the Cannonade of Valmy; wherein the World-Poet experimented on the cannon-fever; wherein the French Sansculottes did not fly like poultry. Precious to France! Every soldier did his duty, and Alsatian Kellermann (how preferable to old Lückner the dismissed!) began to become greater; and *Égalité Fils*, Equality Junior, a light gallant Field-Officer, distinguished himself by intrepidity:—it is the same intrepid individual who now, as Louis Philippe, without the Equality, struggles, under sad circumstances, to be called King of the French for a season.

CHAPTER VIII

EXEUNT

But this Twentieth of September is otherwise a great day. For, observe, while Kellermann's horse was flying blown from under him at the Mill of Valmy, our new National Deputies, that shall be a NATIONAL CONVENTION, are hovering and gathering about the Hall of the Hundred Swiss: with intent to constitute themselves!

On the morrow, about noontide, Camus the Archivist is busy 'verifying their powers;' several hundreds of them already here. Whereupon the Old Legislative comes solemnly over, to merge its old ashes Phœnix-like in the body of the new;—and so forthwith, returning all solemnly back to the Salle de Manége, there sits a National Convention, Seven-hundred and Forty-nine complete. or complete enough; presided by Pétion;—which proceeds directly to do business.

Read that reported afternoon's-debate, O Reader; there are few debates like it: dull reporting *Moniteur* itself becomes more dramatic than a very Shakespeare. For epigrammatic Manuel rises, speaks strange things; how the President shall have a guard of honour, and lodge in the Tuileries:—*rejected*. And Danton rises and speaks; and Collot d'Herbois rises, and Curate Grégoire, and lame Couthon of the Mountain rises; and in rapid Meliboean stanzas, only a few lines each, they propose motions not a few: That the corner-stone of our new Constitution is, Sovereignty of the People; that our Constitution shall be accepted by the People or be null; further that the People ought to be avenged, and have right Judges; that the Imposts must continue till new order; that Landed and other Property be sacred forever; finally that 'Royalty from this day is abolished in France:'—*Decreed* all, before four o'clock strike, with acclamation of the world! The tree was all so ripe; only shake it, and there fall such yellow cart-loads.

And so over in the Valmy Region, as soon as the news come, what stir is this, audible, visible from our Muddy Heights of La Lune? Universal shouting of the French on their opposite hillside; caps raised on bayonets: and a sound as of *République: Vive la République* borne dubious on the winds!—On the morrow morning, so to speak, Brunswick slings his knapsacks before day, lights any fires he has; and marches without tap of drum. Dumouriez finds ghastly symptoms in that camp; '*latrines* full of blood!' The chivalrous King of Prussia, for he, as we saw, is here in person, may long rue the day; may look colder than ever on these dulled-bright Seigneurs, and French Princes their Country's hope;—and, on the whole, put on his greatcoat without ceremony, happy that he has one. They retire, all retire with convenient despatch, through a Champagne trodden into a quagmire, the wild weather pouring on them: Dumouriez, through his Kellermanns and Dillons, pricking them a little in the hinder parts. A little, not much; now pricking, now negotiating: for Brunswick has his eyes opened; and the Majesty of Prussia is a repentant Majesty.

Nor has Austria prospered, nor the Wooden Horse of Thionville bitten his hay; nor Lille City surrendered itself. The Lille trenches opened, on the 29th of the month; with balls and shells, and redhot balls; as if not trenches but

Vesuvius and the Pit had opened. It was frightful, say all eye-witnesses; but it is ineffectual. The Lillers have risen to such temper; especially after these news from Argonne and the East. Not a Sans-indispensables in Lille that would surrender for a King's ransom. Redhot balls rain, day and night; 'six-thousand,' or so, and bombs 'filled internally with oil of turpentine which splashes up in flame;'—mainly on the dwellings of the Sansculottes and Poor; the streets of the Rich being spared. But the Sansculottes get water-pails; form quenching-regulations: "The ball is in Peter's house!" "The ball is in John's!" They divide their lodging and substance with each other; shout *Vive la République;* and faint not in heart. A ball thunders through the main chamber of the Hôtel-de-Ville while the Commune is there assembled: "We are in permanence," says one, coldly, proceeding with his business; and the ball remains permanent too, sticking in the wall, probably to this day.

The Austrian Archduchess (Queen's Sister) will herself see red artillery fired: in their overhaste to satisfy an Archduchess, 'two mortars explode and kill thirty persons.' It is in vain; Lille, often burning, is always quenched again; Lille will not yield. The very boys deftly wrench the matches out of fallen bombs: 'a man clutches a rolling ball with his hat, which takes fire; when cool, they crown it with a *bonnet rouge.*' Memorable also be that nimble Barber, who when the bomb burst beside him, snatched up a sherd of it, introduced soap and lather into it, crying, "*Voilà mon plat à barbe,* My new shaving-dish!" and shaved 'fourteen people' on the spot. Bravo, thou nimble Shaver; worthy to shave old spectral Redcloak, and find treasures!—On the eighth day of this desperate siege, the sixth day of October, Austria finds it fruitless, draws off, with no pleasurable consciousness; rapidly, Dumouriez tending thitherward; and Lille too, black with ashes and smoulder, but jubilant sky-high, flings its gates open. The *Plat à barbe* became fashionable; 'no Patriot of an elegant turn,' says Mercier several years afterwards, 'but shaves himself out of the splinter of a Lille bomb.'

Quid multa, Why many words? The Invaders are in flight; Brunswick's Host, the third part of it gone to death, staggers disastrous along the deep highways of Champagne; spreading out also into 'the fields of a tough spongy red-coloured clay:'—'like Pharaoh through a Red Sea of mud,' says Goethe; 'for here also lay broken chariots, and riders and foot seemed sinking around.' On the eleventh morning of October, the World-Poet, struggling northwards out of Verdun, which he had entered Southwards, some five weeks ago, in quite other order, discerned the following Phenomenon and formed part of it:

'Towards three in the morning, without having had any sleep, we were about mounting our carriage drawn up at the door; when an insuperable obstacle disclosed itself: for there rolled on already, between the pavement-stones which were crushed up into a ridge on each side, an uninterrupted column of sick-wagons through the Town, and all was trodden as into a morass. While we stood waiting what could be made of it, our Landlord the Knight of Saint-Louis pressed past us, without salutation.' He had been a Calonne's Notable in 1787, an Emigrant since; had returned to his home, jubilant, with the Prussians; but must now forth again into the wide world, 'followed by a servant carrying a little bundle on his stick.'

'The activity of our alert Lisieux shone eminent, and on this occasion too brought us on: for he struck into a small gap of the wagon-row; and held the advancing team back till we, with our six and our four horses, got intercalated; after which, in my light little coachlet, I could breathe freer. We were now under way; at a funeral pace, but still under way. The day broke; we found ourselves at the outlet of the Town, in a tumult and turmoil without measure. All sorts of vehicles, few horsemen, innumerable foot-people, were crossing each other on the great esplanade before the Gate. We turned to the right, with our Column, towards Estain, on a limited highway, with ditches at each side. Self-preservation, in so monstrous a press, knew now no pity, no respect of aught. Not far before us there fell down a horse of an ammunition-wagon, they cut the traces, and let it lie. And now as the three others could not bring their load along, they cut them also loose, tumbled the heavily-packed vehicle into the ditch; and with the smallest retardation, we had to drive on right over the horse, which was just about to rise; and I saw too clearly how its legs, under the wheels, went crashing and quivering.

'Horse and foot endeavoured to escape ·from the narrow laborious highway into the meadows: but these too were rained to ruin; overflowed by full ditches, the connexion of the footpaths everywhere interrupted. Four gentlemanlike, handsome, well-dressed soldiers waded for a time beside our carriage; wonderfully clean and neat: and had such art of picking their steps, that their footgear testified no higher than the ancle to the muddy pilgrimage these good people found themselves engaged in.

'That under such circumstances one saw, in ditches, in meadows, in fields and crofts, dead horses enough, was natural to the case: by and by, however, you found them also flayed, the fleshy parts even cut away; sad token of the universal distress.

'Thus we fared on; every moment in danger, at the smallest stoppage on our own part, of being ourselves tumbled overboard; under which circumstances, truly, the careful dexterity of our Lisieux could not be sufficiently praised. The same talent showed itself at Estain; where we arrived towards noon; and descried, over the beautiful well-built little Town, through streets and on squares, around and beside us, one sense-confusing tumult: the mass rolled this way and that; and, all struggling forward, each hindered the other. Unexpectedly our carriage drew up before a stately house in the marketplace; master and mistress of the mansion saluted us in reverent distance.' Dexterous Lisieux, though we knew it not, had said we were the King of Prussia's Brother!

'But now, from the ground-floor windows, looking over the whole marketplace, we had the endless tumult lying, as it were, palpable. All sorts of walkers, soldiers in uniform, marauders, stout but sorrowing citizens and peasants, women and children, crushed and jostled each other, amid vehicles of all forms: ammunition-wagons, baggage-wagons; carriages, single, double and multiplex; such hundredfold miscellany of teams, requisitioned or lawfully owned, making way, hitting together, hindering each other, rolled here to right and to left. Horned-cattle too were struggling on; probably herds that had been put in requisition. Riders you saw few; but the elegant carriages of the Emigrants, many-coloured, lackered, gilt and silvered, evidently by the best builders, caught your eye.

'The crisis of the strait, however, arose further on a little; where the crowded marketplace had to introduce itself into a street,—straight indeed and good, but proportionably far too narrow. I have, in my life, seen nothing like it: the aspect of it might perhaps be compared to that of a swoln river which has been raging over meadows and fields, and is now again

obliged to press itself through a narrow bridge, and flow on in
its bounded channel. Down the long street, all visible from
our windows, there swelled continually the strangest tide:
a high double-seated travelling coach towered visible over the
flood of things. We thought of the fair Frenchwomen we
had seen in the morning. It was not they, however; it was
Count Haugwitz; him you could look at, with a kind of
sardonic malice, rocking onwards, step by step, there.'

In such untriumphant Procession has the Brunswick Manifesto issued! Nay in worse, 'in Negotiation with these
miscreants,'—the first news of which produced such a revulsion
in the Emigrant nature, as put our scientific World-Poet 'in
fear for the wits of several.' There is no help: they must fare
on, these poor Emigrants, angry with all persons and things,
and making all persons angry in the hapless course they struck
into. Landlord and landlady testify to you at *tables-d'hôte*,
how insupportable these Frenchmen are: how, in spite of such
humiliation, of poverty and probable beggary, there is ever
the same struggle for precedence, the same forwardness and
want of discretion. High in honour, at the head of the table,
you with your own eyes observe not a Seigneur, but the
automaton of a Seigneur fallen into dotage; still worshipped,
reverently waited on and fed. In miscellaneous seats is a
miscellany of soldiers, commissaries, adventurers; consuming
silently their barbarian victuals. 'On all brows is to be read
a hard destiny; all are silent, for each has his own sufferings
to bear, and looks forth into misery without bounds.' One
hasty wanderer, coming in, and eating without ungraciousness
what is set before him, the landlord lets off almost scot-free.
"He is," whispered the landlord to me, "the first of these
cursed people I have seen condescend to taste our German
black bread."

And Dumouriez is in Paris; lauded and feasted; paraded
in glittering saloons, floods of beautifullest blonde-dresses and
broad-cloth-coats flowing past him, endless, in admiring joy.
One night, nevertheless, in the splendour of one such scene,
he sees himself suddenly apostrophised by a squalid unjoyful
Figure, who has come in *un*invited, nay, despite of all lackeys;
an unjoyful Figure! The Figure is come "in express mission
from the Jacobins," to inquire sharply, better then than later,
touching certain things: "Shaven eyebrows of Volunteer
Patriots, for instance?" Also "your threats of shivering

in pieces?" Also, "why you have not chased Brunswick hotly enough?" Thus, with sharp croak, inquires the Figure. —"*Ah, c'est vous qu'on appelle Marat*, You are he they call Marat!" answers the General, and turns coldly on his heel,— "Marat!" The blonde-gowns quiver like aspens; the dress-coats gather round; Actor Talma (for it is his house), Actor Talma, and almost the very chandelier-lights, are blue: till this obscene Spectrum, swart unearthly Visual-Appearance, vanish, back into its native Night.

General Dumouriez, in few brief days, is gone again, towards the Netherlands; will attack the Netherlands, winter though it be. And General Montesquiou, on the Southeast, has driven in the Sardinian Majesty; nay, almost without a shot fired, has taken Savoy from him, which longs to become a piece of the Republic. And General Custine, on the Northeast, has dashed forth on Spires and its Arsenal; and then on Electoral Mentz, not uninvited, wherein are German Democrats and no shadow of an Elector now: so that in the last days of October, Frau Forster, a daughter of Heyne's, somewhat democratic, walking out of the Gate of Mentz with her Husband, finds French Soldiers playing at bowls with cannon-balls there. Forster trips cheerfully over one iron bomb, with "Live the Republic!" A black-bearded National Guard answers: "*Elle vivra bien sans vous*, It will probably live independently of you."

BOOK II

REGICIDE

CHAPTER I

THE DELIBERATIVE

FRANCE therefore has done two things very completely: she has hurled back her Cimmerian Invaders far over the marches; and likewise she has shattered her own internal Social Constitution, even to the minutest fibre of it, into wreck and dissolution. Utterly it is all altered: from King down to Parish Constable, all Authorities, Magistrates, Judges, persons that bore rule, have had, on the sudden, to alter themselves, so far as needful; or else, on the sudden, and not without violence, to be altered; a Patriot 'Executive Council of Ministers,' with a Patriot Danton in it, and then a whole Nation and National Convention, have taken care of that. Not a Parish Constable, in the farthest hamlet, who has said, *De par le Roi*, and shown loyalty, but must retire, making way for a new improved Parish Constable who can say *De par la République*.

It is a change such as History must beg her readers to imagine, *un*described. An instantaneous change of the whole body-politic, the soul-politic being all changed; such a change as few bodies, politic or other, can experience in this world. Say, perhaps, such as poor Nymph Semele's body did experience, when she would needs, with woman's humour, see her Olympian Jove as very Jove;—and so stood, poor Nymph, this moment Semele, next moment not Semele, but Flame and a Statue of red-hot Ashes! France has looked upon Democracy; seen it face to face.—The Cimmerian Invaders will rally, in humbler temper, with better or worse luck: the wreck and dissolution must *re*shape itself into a social Arrangement as it can and may. But as for this National Convention, which is to settle everything, if it do, as Deputy Paine and France generally expects, get all finished 'in a few months,' we shall call it a most deft Convention.

In truth, it is very singular to see how this mercurial French

People plunges suddenly from *Vive le Roi* to *Vive la République*; and goes simmering and dancing, shaking off daily (so to speak), and trampling into the dust, its old social garnitures, ways of thinking, rules of existing; and cheerfully dances towards the Ruleless, Unknown, with such hope in its heart, and nothing but *Freedom, Equality and Brotherhood* in its mouth. Is it two centuries, or is it only two years, since all France roared simultaneously to the welkin, bursting forth into sound and smoke at its *Feast of Pikes*, "Live the Restorer of French Liberty?" Three short years ago there was still Versailles and an Œil-de-Bœuf: now there is that watched Circuit of the Temple, girt with dragon-eyed Municipals, where, as in its final limbo, Royalty lies extinct. In the year 1789, Constituent Deputy Barrère, 'wept,' in his *Break-of-Day* Newspaper, at sight of a reconciled King Louis; and now in 1792, Convention Deputy Barrère, perfectly tearless, may be considering, whether the reconciled King Louis shall be guillotined or not!

Old garnitures and social vestures drop off (we say) so fast, being indeed quite decayed, and are trodden under the National dance. And the new vestures, where are they; the new modes and rules? Liberty, Equality, Fraternity: not vestures, but the wish for vestures! The nation is for the present, figuratively speaking, *naked;* it has no rule or vesture; but is naked,—a Sansculottic Nation.

So far, therefore, and in such manner, have our Patriot Brissots, Guadets triumphed. Vergniaud's Ezekiel-visions of the fall of thrones and crowns (p. 133), which he spake hypothetically and prophetically in the Spring of the year, have suddenly come to fulfilment in the Autumn. Our eloquent Patriots of the Legislative, like strong Conjurors, by the word of their mouth, have swept Royalism with its old modes and formulas to the winds; and shall now govern a France free of formulas. Free of formulas! And yet man lives not except with formulas; with customs, *ways* of doing and living: no text truer than this; which will hold true from the Tea-table and Tailor's shopboard up to the High Senate-houses, Solemn Temples, nay through all provinces of Mind and Imagination, onwards to the outmost confines of articulate Being,—*Ubi homines sunt modi sunt.* There are modes wherever there are men. It is the deepest law of man's nature; whereby man is a craftsman and 'tool-using animal;' not the slave of Impulse, Chance and brute Nature, but in some measure their lord. Twenty-five millions of men, suddenly stript bare of their *modi*, and dancing them down in that manner, are a terrible thing to govern!

Eloquent Patriots of the Legislative, meanwhile, have precisely this problem to solve. Under the name and nickname of 'statesmen, *hommes d'état*,' of 'moderate men, *modérantins*,' of Brissotins, Rolandins, finally of *Girondins*, they shall become world-famous in solving it. For the Twenty-five millions are Gallic effervescent too;—filled both with hope of the unutterable, of universal Fraternity and Golden Age; and with terror of the unutterable, Cimmerian Europe all rallying on us. It is a problem like few. Truly, if man, as the Philosophers brag, did to any extent look before and after, what, one may ask, in many cases would become of him? What, in this case, would become of these Seven-hundred and Forty-nine men? The Convention, seeing clearly before and after, were a paralysed Convention. Seeing clearly to the length of its own nose, it is not paralysed.

To the Convention itself neither the work nor the method of doing it is doubtful: To make the Constitution; to defend the Republic till that be made. Speedily enough, accordingly, there has been a 'Committee of the Constitution' got together. Sieyès, Old-Constituent, Constitution-builder by trade; Condorcet, fit for better things; Deputy Paine, foreign Benefactor of the Species, with that 'red carbuncled face, and the black beaming eyes;' Hérault de Séchelles, Ex-Parlementeer, one of the handsomest men in France: these, with inferior guild-brethren, are girt cheerfully to the work; will once more 'make the Constitution;' let us hope, more effectually than last time. For that the Constitution can be made, who doubts,—unless the Gospel of Jean-Jacques came into the world in vain? True, our last Constitution did tumble within the year, so lamentably. But what then; except sort the rubbish and boulders, and build them up again better? 'Widen your basis,' for one thing,—to Universal Suffrage, if need be; exclude rotten materials, Royalism and such like, for another thing. And in brief, *build*, O unspeakable Sieyès and Company, unwearied! Frequent perilous downrushing of scaffolding and rubblework, be that an irritation, no discouragement. Start ye always again, clearing aside the wreck; if with broken limbs, yet with whole hearts; and build, we say, in the name of Heaven, —till either the work do stand; or else mankind abandon it, and the Constitution-builders be paid off, with laughter and tears! One good time, in the course of Eternity, it was appointed that this of Social Contract too should try itself out. And so the Committee of Constitution shall toil: with hope and faith;—with no disturbance from any reader of these pages.

To make the Constitution, then, and return home joyfully in a few months; this is the prophecy our National Convention gives of itself; by this scientific program shall its operations and events go on. But from the best scientific program, in such a case, to the actual fulfilment, what a difference! Every reunion of men, is it not, as we often say, a reunion of incalculable Influences; every unit of it a microcosm of Influences;—of which how shall Science calculate or prophesy? Science, which cannot, with all its calculuses, differential, integral and of variations, calculate the Problem of Three gravitating Bodies, ought to hold her peace here, and say only: In this National Convention there are Seven-hundred and Forty-nine very singular Bodies, that gravitate and do much else;—who, probably in an amazing manner, will work the appointment of Heaven.

Of National Assemblages, Parliaments, Congresses, which have long sat; which are of saturnine temperament; above all, which are not 'dreadfully in earnest,' something may be computed or conjectured: yet even these are a kind of Mystery in progress,—whereby accordingly we see the Journalist Reporter find livelihood: even these jolt madly out of the ruts, frome time to time. How much more a poor National Convention, of French vehemence; urged on at such velocity; without routine, without rut, track or landmark; and dreadfully in earnest every man of them! It is a Parliament literally such as there was never elsewhere in the world. Themselves are new, unarranged; they are the Heart and presiding centre of a France fallen wholly into maddest disarrangement. From all cities, hamlets, from the utmost ends of this France with its Twenty-five million vehement souls, thick-streaming influences storm-in on that same Heart, in the Salle de Manége, and storm-out again: such fiery venous-arterial circulation is the function of that Heart. Seven-hundred and Forty-nine human individuals, we say, never sat together on our Earth under more original circumstances. Common individuals most of them, or not far from common: yet in virtue of the position they occupied, so notable. How, in this wild piping of the whirlwind of human passions, with death, victory, terror, valour, and all height and all depth pealing and piping, these men, left to their own guidance, will speak and act?

Readers know well that this French National Convention (quite contrary to its own Program) became the astonishment and horror of mankind; a kind of Apocalyptic Convention, or black *Dream become real;* concerning which History seldom speaks except in the way of interjection: how it covered France with wo, delusion and delirium; and from its bosom there went forth Death on the pale Horse. To hate this poor National Convention is easy; to praise and love it has not been found impossible. It is, as we say, a Parliament in the most original circumstances. To us, in these pages, be it as a fuliginous fiery mystery, where Upper has met Nether, and in such alternate glare and blackness of darkness poor bedazzled mortals know not which is Upper, which is Nether; but rage and plunge distractedly, as mortals in that case will do. A Convention which has to consume itself, suicidally; and become dead ashes—with its World! Behoves us, not to enter exploratively its dim embroiled deeps; yet to stand with unwavering eyes, looking how it welters; what notable phrases and occurrences it will successively throw up.

One general superficial circumstance we remark with praise: the force of Politeness. To such depth has the sense of civilisation penetrated man's life; no Drouet, no Legendre, in the maddest tug of war, can altogether shake it off. Debates of Senates dreadfully in earnest are seldom given frankly to the world; else perhaps they would surprise it. Did not the Grand Monarque himself once chase his Louvois with a pair of brandished tongs? (i. 180). But reading long volumes of these Convention Debates, all in a foam with furious earnestness, earnest many times to the extent of life and death, one is struck rather with the degree of continence they manifest in speech; and how in such wild ebullition, there is still a kind of polite rule struggling for mastery, and the forms of social life never altogether disappear. These men, though they menace with clenched right-hands, do not clutch one another by the collar; they draw no daggers, except for oratorical purposes, and this not often; profane swearing is almost unknown, though the Reports are frank enough; we find only one or two oaths, oaths by Marat, reported in all.

For the rest, that there is 'effervescence' who doubts. Effervescence enough; Decrees passed by acclamation today, repealed by vociferation tomorrow: temper fitful, most rotatory changeful, always headlong! The 'voice of the orator is covered with rumours;' a hundred 'honourable Members rush with menaces towards the Left side of the Hall;' President has 'broken three bells in succession,'—claps on his hat, as signal that the country is near ruined. A fiercely effervescent Old-Gallic Assemblage!—Ah, how the loud sick sounds of Debate, and of Life, which is a *debate*, sink silent one after another: so loud now, and in a little while so low! Brennus, and those antique Gael Captains, in their way to Rome, to Galatia and such places, whither they were in the habit of marching in the most fiery manner, had Debates as effervescent, doubt it not; though no *Moniteur* has reported them. They scolded in Celtic Welsh, those Brennuses! neither were they Sansculotte; nay rather breeches (*braccæ*, say of felt or rough leather) were the only thing they had; being, as Livy testifies, naked down *to* the haunches:—and, see, it is the same sort of work and of men still, now when they have got coats, and speak nasally a kind of broken Latin! But, on the whole, does not TIME envelope this present National Convention; as it did those Brennuses, and ancient august Senates in felt breeches?—Time surely; and also Eternity. Dim dusk of Time,—or noon which will be dusk; and then there is night, and silence; and Time with all its sick noises is swallowed in the still sea. Pity thy brother, O son of Adam! The angriest frothy jargon that he utters, is it not properly the whimpering of an infant which cannot *speak* what ails it, but is in distress clearly, in the inwards of it; and so must squall and whimper continually, till its Mother take it, and it get—to sleep!

This Convention is not four days old, and the melodious Melibœan stanzas that shook down Royalty are still fresh in our ear, when there bursts out a new diapason,—unhappily, of Discord, this time. For speech has been made of a thing difficult to speak of well: the September Massacres. How deal with these September Massacres; with the Paris Commune that presided over them? A Paris Commune hateful-terrible; before which the poor effete Legislative had to quail, and sit quiet. And now if a young omnipotent Convention will not so quail and sit, what steps shall it take? Have a Departmental Guard in its pay, answer the Girondins, and

Friends of Order! A Guard of National Volunteers, missioned from all the Eighty-three or Eighty-five Departments, for that express end; these will keep Septemberers, tumultuous Communes in a due state of submissiveness, the Convention in a due state of sovereignty. So have the Friends of Order answered, sitting in Committee, and reporting; and even a Decree has been passed of the required tenour. Nay certain Departments, as the Var or Marseilles, in mere expectation and assurance of a Decree, have their contingent of Volunteers already on march; brave Marseillese, foremost on the Tenth of August, will not be hindmost here; 'fathers gave their sons a musket and twenty-five louis,' says Barbaroux, 'and bade them march.'

Can any thing be properer? A Republic that will found itself on justice must needs investigate September Massacres; a Convention calling itself National, ought it not to be guarded by a National force?—Alas, Reader, it seems so to the eye: and yet there is much to be said and argued. Thou beholdest here the small beginning of a Controversy, which mere logic will not settle. Two small well-springs, September, Departmental Guard, or rather at bottom they are but one and the same small well-spring; which will swell and widen into waters of bitterness; all manner of subsidiary streams and brooks of bitterness flowing in, from this side and that; till it become a wide river of bitterness, of rage and separation, —which can subside only into the Catacombs. The Departmental Guard, decreed by overwhelming majorities, and then repealed for peace's sake, and not to insult Paris, is again decreed more than once; nay it is partially executed, and the very men that are to be of it are seen visibly parading the Paris streets,—shouting once, being overtaken with liquor: *A bas Marat*, Down with Marat!" Nevertheless, decreed never so often, it is repealed just as often; and continues, for some seven months, an angry noisy Hypothesis only: a fair Possibility struggling to become a Reality, but which shall never be one; which, after endless struggling, shall, in February next, sink into sad rest,—dragging much along with it. So singular are the ways of men and honourable Members.

But on this fourth day of the Convention's existence, as we said, which is the 25th of September 1792, there comes Committee Report on that Decree of the Departmental Guard, and speech of repealing it; there come denunciations of Anarchy, of a Dictatorship,—which let the incorruptible Robespierre consider: there come denunciations of a certain *Journal de la République*, once called *Ami du Peuple* ; and so thereupon there comes, visibly stepping up, visibly standing aloft on the Tribune, ready to speak,—the Bodily Spectrum of People's-Friend Marat! Shriek, ye Seven-hundred and Forty-nine ; it is verily Marat, he and not another. Marat is no phantasm of the brain, or mere lying impress of Printer's Types; but a thing material, of joint and sinew and a certain small stature ; ye behold him there, in his blackness, in his dingy squalor, a living fraction of Chaos and Old Night ; visibly incarnate, desirous to speak. "It appears," says Marat to the shrieking Assembly, "that a great many persons here are enemies of mine."—"All! All!" shriek hundreds of voices: enough to drown any People's-Friend. But Marat will not drown: he speaks and croaks explanation ; croaks with such reasonableness, air of sincerity, that repentant pity smothers anger, and the shrieks subside, or even become applauses. For this Convention is unfortunately the crankest of machines : it shall be pointing eastward with stiff violence, this moment ; and then do but touch some spring dexterously, the whole machine, clattering and jerking seven-hundred-fold, will whirl with huge crash, and, next moment, is pointing westward ! Thus Marat, absolved and applauded, victorious in this turn of fence, is, as the Debate goes on, prickt at again by some dexterous Girondin ; and then the shrieks rise anew, and Decree of Accusation is on the point of passing ; till the dingy People's-Friend bobs aloft once more ; croaks once more persuasive stillness, and the Decree of Accusation sinks. Whereupon he draws forth —a Pistol ; and setting it to his Head, the seat of such thought and prophecy, says : 'If they had passed their Accusation Decree, he, the People's-Friend, would have blown his brains out.' A People's-Friend has that faculty in him. For the rest, as to this of the two-hundred and sixty-thousand Aristocrat Heads, Marat candidly says, "*C'est là mon avis.* Such is my opinion." Also is it not indisputable : "No power on Earth can prevent me from seeing into traitors, and unmasking them,"—by my superior originality of mind? An honourable member like this Friend of the People few terrestrial Parliaments have had.

We observe, however, that this first onslaught by the Friends of Order, as sharp and prompt as it was, has failed. For neither can Robespierre, summoned out by talk of Dictatorship, and greeted with the like rumour on showing himself, be

thrown into Prison, into Accusation; not though Barbaroux
openly bear testimony against him, and sign it on paper.
With such sanctified meekness does the Incorruptible lift his
seagreen cheek to the smiter; lift his thin voice, and with
jesuitical dexterity plead, and prosper; asking at last, in a
prosperous manner: "But what witnesses has the Citoyen
Barbaroux to support his testimony?" "*Moi!*" cries hot
Rebecqui, standing up, striking his breast with both hands,
and answering "Me!" Nevertheless the Seagreen pleads
again, and makes it good: the long hurlyburly, 'personal
merely,' while so much public matter lies fallow, has ended in
the order of the day. O Friends of the Gironde, why will
you occupy our august sessions with mere paltry Personalities,
while the grand Nationality lies in such a state?—The Gironde
has touched, this day, on the foul black-spot of its fair Convention Domain; has trodden on it, and yet *not* trodden it
down. Alas, it is a *well-spring*, as we said, this black-spot;
and will not tread down!

CHAPTER II

THE EXECUTIVE

MAY we not conjecture therefore that round this grand enterprise of Making the Constitution, there will, as heretofore,
very strange embroilments gather, and question and interests
complicate themselves; so that after a few or even several
months, the Convention will not have settled everything?
Alas, a whole tide of questions comes rolling, boiling; growing ever wider, without end! Among which, apart from this
question of September and Anarchy, let us notice three,
which emerge oftener than the others, and promise to become
Leading Questions; Of the Armies; of the Subsistences;
thirdly, of the Dethroned King.

As to the Armies, Public Defence must evidently be put on
a proper footing; for Europe seems coalising itself again;
one is apprehensive even England will join it. Happily
Dumouriez prospers in the North;—nay, what if he should
prove *too* prosperous, and become *Liberticide*, Murderer of
Freedom!—Dumouriez prospers, through this winter season;
yet not without lamentable complaints. Sleek Pache, the
Swiss Schoolmaster, he that sat frugal in his Alley, the
wonder of neighbours, has got lately—whither thinks the

Reader? To be Minister of War! Madame Roland, struck with his sleek ways, recommended him to her husband as Clerk; the sleek clerk had no need of salary, being of true Patriotic temper; he would come with a bit of bread in his pocket, to save dinner and time; and munching incidentally, do three men's work in a day; punctual, silent, frugal,—the sleek Tartuffe that he was. Wherefore Roland, in the late Overturn, recommended him to be War-Minister. And now, it would seem, he is secretly undermining Roland; playing into the hands of your hotter Jacobins and September Commune; and cannot, like strict Roland, be the *Veto des Coquins!*

How the sleek Pache might mine and undermine, one knows not well; this however one does know; that his War-Office has become a den of thieves and confusion, such as all men shudder to behold. That the Citizen Hassenfratz, as Head-Clerk, sits there in *bonnet rouge*, in rapine, in violence, and some Mathematical calculation; a most insolent, red-nightcapped man. That Pache munches his pocket-loaf, amid head-clerks and sub-clerks, and has spent all the War-Estimates. That Furnishers scour in gigs, over all districts of France, and drive bargains. And lastly, that the Army gets next to no furniture: no shoes, though it is winter; no clothes; some have not even arms; 'in the Army of the South,' complains an honourable Member, 'there are thirty-thousand pairs of breeches wanting,'—a most scandalous want.

Roland's strict soul is sick to see the course things take: but what can he do? Keep his own Department strict; rebuke, and repress wheresoever possible; at lowest complain. He can complain in Letter after Letter, to a National Convention, to France, to Posterity, the Universe; grow ever more querulous-indignant;—till at last, may he not grow wearisome! For is not this continual text of his, at bottom, a rather barren one: How astonishing that in a time of Revolt and abrogation of all Law but Cannon Law, there should be such Unlawfulness? Intrepid Veto-of-Scoundrels, narrow-faithful, respectable, methodic man, work thou in that manner, since happily it is thy manner, and wear thyself away; though ineffectual, not profitless in it—then nor *now!* —The brave Dame Roland, bravest of all Frenchwomen, begins to have misgivings: the figure of Danton has too much of the 'Sardanapalus character,' at a Republican

Rolandin Dinner-table: Clootz, Speaker of Mankind, proses sad stuff about a Universal Republic, or union of all Peoples and Kindreds in one and the same Fraternal Bond; of which Bond, how it is to be *tied*, one unhappily sees not.

It is also an indisputable, unaccountable or accountable fact, that Grains are becoming scarcer and scarcer. Riots for grain, tumultuous Assemblages demanding to have the price of grain fixed, abound far and near. The Mayor of Paris and other poor Mayors are like to have their difficulties. Pétion was reelected Mayor of Paris; but has declined; being now a Convention Legislator. Wise surely to decline: for, besides this of Grains and all the rest, there is in these times an Improvised Insurrectionary Commune passing into an Elected legal one; getting their accounts settled,—not without irritancy! Pétion has declined: nevertheless many do covet and canvass. After months of scrutinising, balloting, arguing and jargoning, one Doctor Chambon gets the post of honour: who will not long keep it; but be, as we shall see, literally *crushed* out of it.

Think also if the private Sansculotte has not his difficulties, in a time of dearth! Bread, according to the People's-Friend, may be some 'six sous per pound, a day's wages some fifteen:' and grim winter here. How the Poor Man continues living, and so seldom starves; by miracle! Happily, in these days, he can enlist, and have himself shot by the Austrians, in an unusually satisfactory manner: for the Rights of Man.—But Commandant Santerre, in this so straightened condition of the flour-market, and state of Equality and Liberty, proposes, through the Newspapers, two remedies, or at least palliatives: *First*, that all classes of men should live two days of the week on potatoes: then *second*, that every man should hang his dog. Hereby, as the Commandant thinks, the saving, which indeed he computes to so many sacks, would be very considerable. Cheerfuller form of inventive-stupidity than Commandant Santerre's dwells in no human soul. Inventive-stupidity, imbedded in health, courage and good-nature: much to be commended. "My whole strength," he tells the Convention once, "is, day and night, at the service of my fellow-Citizens: if they find me worthless, they will dismiss me; I will return, and brew beer."

Or figure what correspondences a poor Roland, Minister of the Interior, must have, on this of Grains alone! Free-trade in Grain, impossibility to fix the Prices of Grain; on the other hand, clamour and necessity to fix them : Political Economy lecturing from the Home Office, with demonstration clear as Scripture ;—ineffectual for the empty National Stomach. The Mayor of Chartres, like to be eaten himself, cries to the Convention ; the Convention sends honourable Members in Deputation; who endeavour to feed the multitude by miraculous spiritual methods ; but cannot. The multitude, in spite of all Eloquence, come bellowing round ; will have the Grain-Prices fixed, and at a moderate elevation ; or else—the honourable Deputies hanged on the spot ! The honourable Deputies, reporting this business, admit that, on the edge of horrid death, they did fix, or affect to fix the Price of Grain : for which, be it also noted, the Convention, a Convention that will not be trifled with, sees good to reprimand them.

But as to the origin of these Grain-Riots, is it not most probably your secret Royalists again ? Glimpses of Priests were discernible in this of Chartres,—to the eye of Patriotism. Or indeed may not 'the root of it all lie in the Temple Prison, in the heart of a perjured King,' well as we guard him ? Unhappy perjured King !—And so there shall be Bakers' Queues, by and by, more sharp-tempered than ever : on every Baker's door-rabbet an iron ring, and coil of rope ; whereon, with firm grip, on this side and that, we form our Queue : but mischievous deceitful persons cut the rope, and our Queue becomes a ravelment ; wherefore the coil must be made of iron chain. Also there shall be Prices of Grain well fixed ; but then no grain purchasable by them : bread not to be had except by Ticket from the Mayor, few ounces per mouth daily ; after long swaying, with firm grip, on the chain of the Queue. And Hunger shall stalk direful ; and Wrath and Suspicion, whetted to the Preternatural pitch, shall stalk ; as those other preternatural 'shapes of Gods in their wrathfulness' were discerned stalking, 'in glare and gloom of that fire-ocean,' when Troy Town fell !—

CHAPTER III

DISCROWNED

But the question more pressing than all on the Legislator, as yet, is this third : What shall be done with King Louis ?

King Louis, now King and Majesty to his own family alone, in their own Prison Apartment alone, has been Louis Capet and the Traitor Veto with the rest of France. Shut in his Circuit of the Temple, he has heard and seen the loud whirl of things; yells of September Massacres, Brunswick war-thunders dying off in disaster and discomfiture; he passive, a spectator merely; waiting whither it would please to whirl with him. From the neighbouring windows, the curious, not without pity, might see him walk daily, at a certain hour, in the Temple Garden, with his Queen, Sister and two Children, all that now belongs to him in this Earth. Quietly he walks and waits; for he is not of lively feelings, and is of a devout heart. The wearied Irresolute has, at least, no need of resolving now. His daily meals, lessons to his Son, daily walk in the Garden, daily game at ombre or drafts, fill up the day: the morrow will provide for itself.

The morrow indeed; and yet How? Louis asks, How? France, with perhaps still more solicitude, asks, How? A King dethroned by insurrection is verily not easy to dispose of. Keep him prisoner, he is a secret centre for the Dis-affected, for endless plots, attempts and hopes of theirs. Banish him, he is an open centre for them; his royal war-standard, with what of divinity it has, unrolls itself, sum-moning the world. Put him to death? A cruel questionable extremity that too: and yet the likeliest in these extreme cir-cumstánces of insurrectionary men, whose own life and death lies staked: accordingly it is said, from the last step of the throne to the first of the scaffold there is short distance.

But, on the whole, we will remark here that this business of Louis looks altogether different now, as seen over Seas and at the distance of forty-four years, from what it looked then, in France, and struggling confused all round one. For indeed it is a most lying thing that same Past Tense always: so beautiful, sad, almost Elysian-sacred, 'in the moonlight of Memory,' it seems; and *seems* only. For observe, always one most important element is surreptitiously (we not noticing it) withdrawn from the Past Time: the haggard element of Fear! Not *there* does Fear dwell, nor Uncertainty, nor Anxiety; but it dwells *here*; haunting us, tracking us; running like an accursed ground-discord through all the music-tones of our Existence:—making the Tense a mere Present one! Just so is it with this of Louis. Why smite the fallen? asks Magna-nimity, out of danger now. He is fallen so low this once-high man; no criminal nor traitor, how far from it; but the un-

happiest of Human Solecisms: whom if abstract Justice had
to pronounce upon, she might well become concrete Pity,
and pronounce only sobs and dismissal!

So argues retrospective Magnanimity: but Pusillanimity,
present, prospective? Reader, thou hast never lived, for
months, under the rustle of Prussian gallows-ropes; never wert
thou portion of a National Sahara-waltz, Twenty-five millions
running distracted to fight Brunswick! Knights Errant themselves, when they conquered Giants, usually slew the Giants:
quarter was only for other Knights Errant, who knew courtesy
and the laws of battle. The French Nation, in simultaneous,
desperate dead-pull, and as if by miracle of madness, has
pulled down the most dread Goliath, huge with the growth of
ten centuries; and cannot believe, though his giant bulk,
covering acres, lies prostrate, bound with peg and packthread,
that he will not rise again, man-devouring; that the victory is
not partly a dream. Terror has its scepticism; miraculous
victory its rage of vengeance. Then as to criminality, is the
prostrated Giant, who will devour us if he rise, an innocent
Giant? Curate Grégoire, who indeed is now Constitutional
Bishop Grégoire, asserts, in the heat of eloquence, that Kingship by the very nature of it is a crime capital; that Kings'
Houses are as wild-beasts' dens. Lastly consider this: that
there is on record a Trial of Charles First! This printed
Trial of Charles First is sold and read everywhere at present:
—*Quelle spectacle!* Thus did the English People judge their
Tyrant, and become the first of Free Peoples: which feat, by
the grace of Destiny, may not France now rival? Scepticism
of terror, rage of miraculous victory, sublime spectacle to the
universe,—all things point one fatal way.

Such leading questions, and their endless incidental ones,—
of September Anarchists and Departmental Guard; of Grain-
Riots, plaintive Interior Ministers; of Armies, Hassenfratz
dilapidations; and what is to be done with Louis,—beleaguer
and embroil this Convention; which would so gladly make
the constitution rather. All which questions too, as we often
urge of such things, are in *growth;* they grow in every French
head; and can be *seen* growing also, very curiously, in this
mighty welter of Parliamentary Debate, of Public Business
which the Convention has to do. A question emerges, so small
at first; is put off, submerged; but always re-emerges bigger
than before. It is a curious, indeed an indescribable sort of
growth which such things have.

We perceive, however, both by its frequent re-emergence and by its rapid enlargement of bulk, that this Question of King Louis will take the lead of all the rest. And truly, in that case, it will take the *lead* in a much deeper sense. For as Aaron's Rod swallowed all the other serpents; so will the Foremost Question, whichever may get foremost, absorb all other questions and interests: and from it and the decision of it will they all, so to speak, be *born*, or new-born, and have shape, physiognomy and destiny corresponding. It was appointed of Fate that, in this wide-weltering, strangely growing, monstrous stupendous imbroglio of Convention Business, the grand First-Parent of all the questions, controversies, measures and enterprises which were to be evolved there to the world's astonishment, should be this question of King Louis.

CHAPTER IV

THE LOSER PAYS

THE Sixth of November 1792 was a great day for the Republic: outwardly, over the Frontiers; inwardly, in the *Salle de Manège*.

Outwardly: for Dumouriez, overrunning the Netherlands, did, on that day, come in contact with Saxe-Teschen and the Austrians; Dumouriez wide-winged, they wide-winged; at and around the village of Jemappes, near Mons. And fire-hail is whistling far and wide there, the great guns playing, and the small; so many green Heights getting fringed and maned with red Fire. And Dumouriez is swept back on this wing, and swept back on that, and is like to be swept back utterly; when he rushes up in person, the prompt Polymetis; speaks a prompt word or two; and then, with clear tenor-pipe, 'uplifts the Hymn of the Marseillese, *entonna la Marseillaise*,' ten-thousand tenor or bass pipes joining; or say, some Forty-thousand in all; for every heart leaps at the sound, and so with rhythmic march-melody, waxing ever quicker, to double and to treble quick, they rally, they advance, they rush, death-defying, man-devouring; carry batteries, redoutes, whatsoever is to be carried; and, like the fire-whirlwind, sweep all manner of Austrians from the scene of action. Thus, through the hands of Dumouriez, may Rouget de Lille, in figurative speech, be said to have gained, miraculously, like another

Orpheus, by his Marseillese fiddle-strings (*fidibus canoris*), a Victory of Jemappes; and conquered the Low Countries.

Young General Égalité, it would seem, shone brave among the bravest on this occasion. Doubtless a brave Égalité;— whom however does not Dumouriez rather talk of oftener than need were? The Mother-Society has her own thoughts. As for the Elder Égalité he flies low at this time; appears in the Convention for some half-hour daily, with rubicund, pre occupied or impassive quasi-contemptuous countenance; and then takes himself away. The Netherlands are conquered, at least overrun. Jacobin missionaries, your Prolys, Pereiras follow in the train of the Armies; also Convention Commis sioners, melting church-plate, revolutionising and remodelling —among whom Danton, in brief space, does immensities o business; not neglecting his own wages and trade-profits, i is thought. Hassenfratz dilapidates at home; Dumourie. grumbles and they dilapidate abroad: within the walls there is sinning, and without the walls there is sinning.

But in the Hall of the Convention, at the same hour with this victory of Jemappes, there went another thing forward Report, of great length, from the proper appointed Committee on the Crimes of Louis. The Galleries listen breathless; take comfort, ye Galleries: Deputy Valazé, Reporter on thi occasion, thinks Louis very criminal; and that, if convenient he should be tried;—poor Girondin Valazé, who may be trie himself, one day! Comfortable so far. Nay here come a second Committee-Reporter, Deputy Mailhe, with a Lega Argument, very prosy to read now, very refreshing to hea then, That, by the Law of the Country, Louis Capet was onl called Inviolable by a figure of rhetoric; but at bottom wa perfectly violable, triable; that he can, and even should b tried. This Question of Louis, emerging so often as an angr confused possibility, and submerging again, has emerged nov in an articulate shape.

Patriotism growls indignant joy. The so-called reign o equality is not to be a mere name, then, but a thing! Tr Louis Capet? scornfully ejaculates Patriotism: Mean crimina go to the gallows for a purse cut; and this chief crimina guilty of a France cut; of a France slashed asunder wit Clotho-scissors and Civil war; with his victims 'twelve-hundre on the Tenth of August alone' lying low in the Catacomb fattening the passes of Argonne Wood, of Valmy and fa Fields; *he*, such chief criminal, shall not even come to th

ar?—For, alas, O Patriotism! add we, it was from of old
aid, *The loser pays!* It is he who has to pay *all* scores, run
p by whomsoever; on him must all breakages and charges
all; and the twelve-hundred on the Tenth of August are not
ebel traitors, but victims and martyrs: such is the law of
quarrel.

Patriotism, nothing doubting, watches over this Question of
the trial, now happily emerged in an articulate shape; and will
see it to maturity, if the gods permit. With a keen solicitude
Patriotism watches; getting ever keener, at every new difficulty, as Girondins and false brothers interpose delays; till
t get a keenness as of fixed-idea, and will have this Trial and
no earthly thing instead of it,—if Equality be not a name.
Love of Equality; then scepticism of terror, rage of victory,
sublime spectacle to the universe: all these things are strong.

But indeed this Question of the Trial, is it not to all
persons a most grave one; filling with dubiety many a Legislative head! Regicide? asks the Gironde Respectability: To
kill a king, and become the horror of respectable nations and
persons? But then also, to save a king; to lose one's footing
with the decided Patriot; the undecided Patriot, though never
so respectable, being mere hypothetic froth and no footing?—
The dilemma presses sore; and between the horns of it you
wriggle round and round. Decision is nowhere, save in the
Mother-Society and her Sons. These have decided and go
forward: the others wriggle round uneasily within their
dilemma-horns, and make way no-whither.

CHAPTER V

STRETCHING OF FORMULAS

BUT how this Question of the Trial grew laboriously, through
the weeks of gestation, now that it has been articulated or
conceived, were superfluous to trace here. It emerged and
submerged among the infinite of questions and embroilments.
The Veto of Scoundrels writes plaintive Letters as to
Anarchy; 'concealed Royalists,' aided by Hunger, produce
Riots about Grain. Alas, it is but a week ago, these Girondins
made a new fierce onslaught on the September Massacres?

For, one day, among the last of October, Robespierre,
being summoned to the Tribune by some new hint of that
old calumny of the Dictatorship, was speaking and pleading

there, with more and more comfort to himself; till rising high in heart, he cried out valiantly: Is there any man here that dare specifically accuse me? " *Moi!* " exclaimed one. Pause of deep silence: a lean angry little Figure, with broad bald brow, strode swiftly towards the tribune, taking papers from its pocket: "I accuse thee, Robespierre,"—I, Jean Baptiste Louvet! The Seagreen became tallowgreen; shrinking to a corner of the tribune: Danton cried, "Speak, Robespierre, there are many good citizens that listen;" but the tongue refused its office. And so Louvet, with a shrill tone, read and recited crime after crime: dictatorial temper, exclusive popularity, bullying at elections, mob-retinue, September Massacres;—till all the Convention shrieked again, and had almost indicted the Incorruptible there on the spot. Never did the Incorruptible run such a risk. Louvet, to his dying day, will regret that the Gironde did not take a bolder attitude and extinguish him there and then.

Not so, however: the Incorruptible, about to be indicted in this sudden manner, could not be refused a week of delay. That week he is not idle; nor is the Mother-Society idle,— fierce-tremulous for her chosen son. He is ready at the day, with his written Speech; smooth as a Jesuit Doctor's; and convinces some. And now? Why now lazy Vergniaud does *not* rise with Demosthenic thunder; poor Louvet, unprepared, can do little or nothing: Barrère proposes that these comparatively despicable ' personalities ' be dismissed by order of the day! Order of the day it accordingly is. Barbaroux cannot even get a hearing; not though he rush down to the Bar, and demand to be heard there as a petitioner. The Convention, eager for public business (with that first articulate emergence of the Trial just coming on), dismisses these comparative *misères* and despicabilities: splenetic Louvet must digest his spleen, regretfully forever: Robespierre, dear to Patriotism, is dearer for the dangers he has run.

This is the second grand attempt by our Girondin Friends of Order, to extinguish that black-spot in their domain; and we see they have made it far blacker and wider than before. Anarchy, September Massacre: it is a thing that lies hideous in the general imagination; very detestable to the undecided Patriot, of Respectability: a thing to be harped on as often as need is. Harp on it, denounce it, trample it, ye Girondin Patriots :—and yet behold, the black-spot will not trample down ; it will only, as we say, trample blacker and wider :

Stretching of Formulas 201

fools, it is no black-spot of the surface, but a well-spring of the deep! Consider rightly, it is the Apex of the everlasting Abyss, this black-spot, looking up as water through thin ice;—say, as the region of Nether Darkness through your thin film of Gironde Regulation and Respectability: trample it *not*, lest the film break, and then——!

The truth is, if our Gironde Friends had an understanding of it, where were French Patriotism, with all its eloquence, at this moment, had *not* that same great Nether Deep, of Bedlam, Fanaticism and Popular wrath and madness, risen unfathomable on the Tenth of August? French Patriotism were an eloquent Reminiscence; swinging on Prussian gibbets. Nay, where, in few months, were it still, should the same great Nether Deep subside?—Nay, as readers of Newspapers pretend to recollect, this hatefulness of the September Massacre is itself partly an after-thought: readers of Newspapers can quote Gorsas and various Brissotins approving of the September Massacre, at the time it happened; and calling it a salutary vengeance. So that the real grief, after all, were not so much righteous horror, as grief that one's own power was departing?—Unhappy Girondins!

In the Jacobin Society, therefore, the decided Patriot complains that here are men who with their private ambitions and animosities will ruin Liberty, Equality and Brotherhood, all three: they check the spirit of Patriotism; throw stumbling-blocks in its way; and instead of pushing on, all shoulders at the wheel, will stand idle there, spitefully clamouring what foul ruts there are, what rude jolts we give! To which the Jacobin Society answers with angry roar;—with angry shriek, for there are Citoyennes too, thick crowded in the galleries here. Citoyennes who bring their seam with them, or their knitting-needles: and shriek or knit as the case needs; famed *Tricoteuses*, Patriot Knitters; *Mère Duchesse*, or the like Deborah and mother of the Faubourgs, giving the key-note. It is a changed Jacobin Society; and a still changing. Where Mother Duchess now sits, authentic Duchesses have sat. High-rouged dames went once in jewels and spangles; now, instead of jewels, you may take the knitting-needles and leave the rouge: the rouge will gradually give place to natural brown, clean washed or even unwashed: and Demoiselle Théroigne herself get scandalously fustigated. Strange enough; it is the same tribune raised in mid-air, where a high Mirabeau, a high Barnave and Aristocrat

Lameths once thundered; whom gradually your Brissots
Gaudets, Vergniauds, a hotter style of Patriots in *bonne
rouge*, did displace; red heat, as one may say, supercedin
light.   And now your Brissots in turn, and Brissotins
Rolandins, Girondins, are becoming supernumerary; mus
desert the sittings, or be expelled: the light of the Might
Mother is burning not red but blue!—Provincial Daughter
Societies loudly disapprove these things; loudly demand th
swift reinstatement of such eloquent Girondins, the swif
'erasure of Marat, *radiation de Marat*.' The Mother-Society
so far as natural reason can predict, seems ruining herself
Nevertheless she has at all crises seemed so; she has a
*preter*natural life in her, and will not ruin.

But, in a fortnight more, this great Question of the Trial
while the fit Committee is assiduously but silently working o
it, receives an unexpected stimulus. Our readers remembe
poor Louis's turn for smith-work: how, in old happier day
a certain Sieur Gamain of Versailles was wont to come ove
and instruct him in lock-making;—often scolding him, the
say, for his numbness. By whom, nevertheless, the roya
Apprentice had learned something of that craft. Haples
Apprentice: perfidious Master-Smith! For now, on this 20tl
of November 1792, dingy Smith Gamain comes over to th
Paris Municipality, over to Minister Roland, with hints tha
he, Smith Gamain, knows a thing; that, in May last, when
traitorous Correspondence was so brisk, he and the roya
Apprentice fabricated an 'Iron Press, *Armoire de Fer*,
cunningly inserting the same in a wall of the Royal chambe
in the Tuileries; invisible under the wainscot; where doubt
less it still sticks! Perfidious Gamain, attended by the prope
Authorities, finds the wainscot panel which none else car
find; wrenches it up; discloses the Iron Press,—full of Letter
and Papers! Roland clutches them out; conveys them ove
in towels to the fit assiduous Committee, which sits hard by
In towels, we say, and without notarial inventory; an oversigh
on the part of Roland.

Here, however, are Letters enough: which disclose to
a demonstration the Correspondence of a traitorous self
preserving Court; and this not with Traitors only, but ever
with Patriots, so-called! Barnave's treason, of Correspondence
with the Queen, and friendly advice to her, ever since that
Varennes Business, is hereby manifest: how happy that we
have him, this Barnave, lying safe in the Prison of Grenoble,

since September last, for he had long been suspect! Talleyrand's treason, many a man's treason, if not manifest hereby,
s next to it. Mirabeau's treason: wherefore his Bust in the
Hall of the Convention 'is veiled with gauze,' till we ascertain.
Alas, it is too ascertainable! His Bust in the Hall of the
Jacobins, denounced by Robespierre from the tribune in
mid-air, is not veiled, it is instantly broken to sherds;
a Patriot mounting swiftly with a ladder, and shivering it
down on the floor;—it and others: amid shouts. Such is
their recompense and amount of wages, at this date: on the
principle of supply and demand. Smith Gamain, inadequately
recompensed for the present, comes, some fifteen months after,
with a humble Petition; setting forth that no sooner was that
important Iron Press finished off by him, than (as he now
bethinks himself) Louis gave him a large glass of wine.
Which large glass of wine did produce in the stomach of
Sieur Gamain the terriblest effects, evidently tending towards
death, and was then brought up by an emetic; but has,
notwithstanding, entirely ruined the constitution of Sieur
Gamain; so that he cannot work for his family (as he now
bethinks himself). The recompense of *which* is 'Pension
of Twelve-hundred Francs,' and 'honourable mention.' So
different is the ratio of demand and supply at different times.

Thus, amid obstructions and stimulating furtherances, has
the question of the Trial to grow : emerging and submerging;
fostered by solicitous Patriotism. Of the Orations that were
spoken on it, of the painfully devised Forms of Process for
managing it, the Law Arguments to prove it lawful, and all
the infinite floods of Juridical and other ingenuity and oratory,
be no syllable reported in this History. Lawyer ingenuity is
good : but what can it profit here? If the truth must be
spoken, O august Senators, the only law in this case is : *Væ
victis*, The loser pays! Seldom did Robespierre say a wiser
word than the hint he gave to that effect, in his oration, That
it was needless to speak of Law ; that here, if never elsewhere,
our Right was Might. An oration admired almost to ecstasy,
by the Jacobin Patriot : who shall say that Robespierre is not
a thorough-going man ; bold in Logic at least? To the like
effect, or still more plainly, spake young Saint-Just, the black-
haired, mild-toned youth. Danton is on mission, in the
Netherlands, during this preliminary work. The rest, far as
one reads, welter amid Law of Nations, Social Contract,

Juristics, Syllogistics; to us barren as the East wind. In fact, what can be more unprofitable than the sight of Seven-hundred and Forty-nine ingenious men struggling with their whole force and industry, for a long course of weeks, to do at bottom this: To stretch out the old Formula and Law Phraseology, so that it may cover the new, contradictory, entirely *un*coverable Thing? Whereby the poor Formula does but *crack*, and one's honesty along with it! The thing that is palpably *hot*, burning, wilt thou prove it, by syllogism, to be a freezing-mixture? This of stretching out Formulas till they crack, is, especially in times of swift change, one of the sorrowfullest tasks poor Humanity has.

CHAPTER VI

AT THE BAR

MEANWHILE, in a space of some five weeks, we have got to another emerging of the Trial, and a more practical one than ever.

On Tuesday, eleventh of December, the King's Trial has *emerged*, very decidedly: into the streets of Paris; in the shape of that green Carriage, of Mayor Chambon, within which sits the King himself, with attendants, on his way to the Convention Hall! Attended, in that green carriage, by Mayors Chambon, Procureurs Chaumette; and outside of it by Commandants Santerre, with cannon, cavalry, and double row of infantry; all Sections under arms, strong Patrols scouring all streets; so fares he, slowly through the dull drizzling weather: and about two o'clock we behold him, 'in walnut-coloured greatcoat, *redingote noisette*,' descending through the Place Vendôme, towards the Salle de Manége; to be indicted, and judicially interrogated. The mysterious Temple Circuit has given up its secret; which now, in this walnut-coloured coat, men behold with eyes. The same bodily Louis who was once Louis the Desired, fares there: hapless King, he is getting now towards port; his deplorable farings and voyagings draw to a close. What duty remains to him henceforth, that of placidly enduring, he is fit to do.

The singular Procession fares on; in silence, says Prud-homme, or amid growlings of the Marseilles Hymn; in silence, ushers itself into the Hall of the Convention, Santerre holding Louis's arm with his hand. Louis looks round him, with composed air, to see what kind of Convention and

Parliament it is. Much changed indeed:—since February gone two years, when our Constituent, then busy, spread fleur-de-lys velvet for us; and we came over to say a kind word here, and they all started up swearing Fidelity; and all France started up swearing, and made it a Feast of Pikes; which has ended in this! Barrère, who once 'wept' looking up from his Editor's-Desk, looks down now from his President's-Chair, with a list of Fifty-seven Questions; and says, dry-eyed: "Louis, you may sit down." Louis sits down: it is the very seat, they say, same timber and stuffing, from which he accepted the Constitution, amid dancing and illumination, autumn gone a year. So much woodwork remains identical; so much else is not identical. Louis sits and listens, with a composed look and mind.

Of the Fifty-seven Questions we shall not give so much as one. They are questions captiously embracing all the main Documents seized on the Tenth of August, or found lately in the Iron Press; embracing all the main incidents of the Revolution History; and they ask, in substance, this: Louis, who wert King, art thou not guilty to a certain extent, by act and written document, of trying to continue King? Neither in the Answers is there much notable. Mere quiet negations, for most part; an accused man standing on the simple basis of *No:* I do not recognise that document; I did not do that act; or did it according to the law that then was. Whereupon the Fifty-seven Questions, and Documents to the number of a Hundred and Sixty-two, being exhausted in this manner, Barrère finishes, after some three hours, with his: "Louis, I invite you to withdraw."

Louis withdraws, under Municipal escort, into a neighbouring Committee-room; having first, in leaving the bar, demanded to have Legal Counsel. He declines refreshment, in this Committee-room; then, seeing Chaumette busy with a small loaf which a grenadier had divided with him, says, he will take a bit of bread. It is five o'clock; and he had breakfasted but slightly, in a morning of such drumming and alarm. Chaumette breaks his half-loaf: the King eats of the crust; mounts the green Carriage, eating; asks now, What he shall do with the crumb? Chaumette's clerk takes it from him; flings it out into the street. Louis says, It is a pity to fling out bread, in a time of dearth. "My grandmother," remarks Chaumette, "used to say to me, Little boy, never waste a crumb of bread; you cannot make one." "Monsieur Chaumette," answers Louis, "your grandmother seems to have been a sensible woman." Poor innocent mortal; so quietly he waits the drawing of the lot;—fit to do this at least well Passivity alone, without Activity, sufficing for it! He talks once of travelling over France by and by, to have a geographical and topographical view of it; being from of old fond of geography.—The Temple Circuit again receives him, closes on him; gazing Paris may retire to its hearths and coffee-houses, to its clubs and theatres: the damp Darkness has sunk, and with it the drumming and patrolling of this strange Day

Louis is now separated from his Queen and Family; given up to his simple reflections and resources. Dull lie these stone walls round him; of his loved ones none with him. 'In this state of uncertainty,' providing for the worst, he writes his Will: a Paper which can still be read; full of placidity, simplicity, pious sweetness. The Convention, after debate, has granted him Legal Counsel, of his own choosing. Advocate Target feels himself 'too old,' being turned of fifty-four; and declines. He had gained great honour once, defending Rohan the Necklace-Cardinal; but will gain none here. Advocate Tronchet, some ten years older, does not decline. Nay behold, good old Malesherbes steps forward voluntarily; to the last of his fields, the good old hero! He is gray with seventy years: he says, "I was twice called to the Council of him who was my Master, when all the world coveted that honour; and I owe him the same service now, when it has become one which many reckon dangerous." These two, with a younger Desèze, whom they will select for pleading, are busy over that Fifty-and-sevenfold Indictment, over the Hundred and Sixty-two Documents; Louis aiding them as he can.

A great Thing is now therefore in open progress; all men, in all lands, watching it. By what Forms and Methods shall the Convention acquit itself, in such manner that there rest not on it even the suspicion of blame? Difficult that will be! The Convention, really much at a loss, discusses and deliberates. All day from morning to night, day after day, the Tribune drones with oratory on this matter; one must stretch the old Formula to cover the new Thing. The Patriots of the Mountain, whetted ever keener, clamour for despatch above all; the only good Form will be a swift one. Nevertheless the Convention deliberates; the Tribune drones,—drowned indeed in tenor, and even in treble, from time to time; the whole Hall shrilling up round it into pretty frequent wrath and provocation. It has droned and shrilled wellnigh a fortnight, before we can decide, this shrillness getting ever shriller, That on Wednesday 26th of December, Louis shall appear and plead. His Advocates complain that it is fatally soon; which they well might as Advocates: but without remedy; to Patriotism it seems endlessly late.

On Wednesday therefore, at the cold dark hour of eight in the morning, all Senators are at their post. Indeed they warm the cold hour, as we find, by a violent effervescence, such as is too common now; some Louvet or Buzot attacking some Tallien, Chabot; and so the whole Mountain effervescing against the whole Gironde. Scarcely is this done, at nine, when Louis and his three Advocates, escorted by the clang of arms and Santerre's National Force, enter the Hall.

Desèze unfolds his papers; honourably fulfilling his perilous office pleads for the space of three hours. An honourable Pleading, 'composed almost overnight;' courageous yet discreet; not without ingenuity, and soft pathetic eloquence: Louis fell on his neck, when they had withdrawn, and said with tears, "*Mon pauvre Desèze !*" Louis himself, before withdrawing, had added a few words, "perhaps the last he would utter to them:" how it pained his heart, above all things, to be held guilty of that bloodshed on the Tenth of August; or of ever shedding or wishing to shed French blood. So saying, he withdrew from that Hall;—having indeed finished his work there. Many are the strange errands he has had thither; but this strange one is the last.

And now, why will the Convention loiter? Here is the Indictment and Evidence; here is the Pleading: does not the rest follow of itself? The Mountain, and Patriotism in general, clamours still louder for despatch; for Permanent-session, till the task be done. Nevertheless a doubting, apprehensive Convention decides that it will still deliberate first; that all Members, who desire it, shall have leave to speak.—To your desks, therefore, ye eloquent Members! Down with your thoughts, your echoes and hearsays of thoughts; now is the time to show oneself; France and the Universe listens! Members are not wanting: Oration, spoken Pamphlet follows spoken Pamphlet, with what eloquence it can: President's

List swells ever higher with names claiming to speak; from day to day, all days and all hours, the constant Tribune drones;—shrill Galleries supplying, very variably, the tenor and treble. It were a dull tone otherwise.

The Patriots, in Mountain and Galleries, or taking counsel nightly in Section-house, in Mother-Society, amid their shrill *Tricoteuses*, have to watch lynx-eyed! to give voice when needful; occasionally very loud. Deputy Thuriot, he who was Advocate Thuriot, who was Elector Thuriot, and from the top of the Bastille saw Saint-Antoine rising like the ocean; this Thuriot can stretch a Formula as heartily as most men. Cruel Billaud is not silent, if you incite him. Nor is cruel Jean-Bon silent; a kind of Jesuit he too;—write him not, as the Dictionaries too often do, *Jambon*, which signifies mere *Ham!*

But, on the whole, let no man conceive it possible that Louis is not guilty. The only question for a reasonable man is, or was: Can the Convention judge Louis? Or must it be the whole People; in Primary Assembly, and with delay? Always delay, ye Girondins, false *hommes d'état!* so bellows Patriotism, its patience almost failing.—But indeed, if we consider it, what shall these poor Girondins do? Speak their conviction that Louis is a Prisoner of War, and cannot be put to death without injustice, solecism, peril? Speak such conviction; and lose utterly your footing with the decided Patriot! Nay properly it is not even a conviction, but a conjecture and dim puzzle. How many poor Girondins are sure of but one thing: That a man and Girondin ought to *have* footing somewhere, and to stand firmly on it; keeping well with the respectable Classes! *This* is what conviction and assurance of faith they have. They must wriggle painfully between their dilemma-horns.

Nor is France idle, nor Europe. It is a Heart this Convention, as we said, which sends out influences, and receives them. A King's Execution, call it Martyrdom, call it Punishment, were an influence!—Two notable influences this Convention has already sent forth over all Nations; much to its own detriment. On the 19th of November, it emitted a Decree, and has since confirmed and unfolded the details of it, That any Nation which might see good to shake off the fetters of Despotism was thereby, so to speak the Sister of France, and should have help and countenance. A Decree much oised of by Diplomatists, Editors, International Lawyers; such a Decree as no living Fetter of Despotism, nor Person in Authority anywhere, can approve of! It was Deputy Chambon the Girondin who propounded this Decree;—at bottom perhaps as a flourish of rhetoric.

The second influence we speak of had a still poorer origin: in the restless loud-rattling slightly-furnished head of one Jacob Dupont from the Loire country. The Convention is speculating on a plan of National Education: Deputy Dupont in his speech says, "I am free to avow, M. le Président, that I for my part am an atheist,"—thinking the world might like to know that. The French world received it without commentary; or with no audible commentary, so *loud* was France otherwise. The Foreign world received it with confutation, with horror and astonishment; a most miserable influence this! And now if to these two were added a third influence and sent pulsing abroad over all the Earth: that of Regicide?

Foreign Courts interfere in this Trial of Louis; Spain, England: not to be listened to; though they come, as it were, at least Spain comes, with the olive-branch in one hand, and the sword without scabbard in the other. But at home too, from out of this circumambient Paris and France, what influences come thick-pulsing! Petitions flow in; pleading for equal justice, in a reign of so-called Equality. The living Patriot pleads;—O ye National Deputies, do not the dead Patriots plead? The Twelve-hundred that lie in cold obstruction, do not they plead; and petition, in Death's dumb-show, from their narrow house there, more eloquently than speech? Crippled Patriots hop on crutches round the Salle de Manége, demanding justice. The wounded of the Tenth of August, the Widows and Orphans of the Killed petition in a body; and hop and defile, eloquently mute, through the Hall: one wounded Patriot, unable to hop, is borne on his bed thither, and passes shoulder-high, in the horizontal posture. The Convention Tribune, which has paused at such sight, commences again,—droning mere Juristic Oratory. But out of doors Paris is piping ever higher. Bull-voiced St.-Huruge is heard; and the hysteric eloquence of Mother Duchess; 'Varlet, Apostle of Liberty,' with pike and red cap, flies hastily, carrying his oratorical folding-stool. Justice on the traitor! cries all the Patriot world. Consider also this other cry, heard loud on the streets: "Give us Bread, or else kill

us!" Bread and Equality; Justice on the Traitor, that w•
may have Bread!

The Limited or undecided Patriot is set against the Decided
Mayor Chambon heard of dreadful rioting at the *Théâtre de l•
Nation:* it had come to rioting, and even to fist-work, betweer
the Decided and the Undecided, touching a new Drama callec
Ami des Lois (Friend of the Laws). One of the poores
Dramas ever written; but which had didactic applications in it
wherefore powdered wigs of Friends of Order and black hair o•
Jacobin heads are flying there; and Mayor Chambon hasten
with Santerre, in hopes to quell it. Far from quelling it, ou
poor Mayor gets so 'squeezed,' says the Report, and likewis•
so blamed and bullied, say we,—that he, with regret, quits the
brief Mayoralty altogether, 'his lungs being affected.' Thi
miserable *Ami des Lois* is debated of in the Convention itself
so violent, mutually-enraged, are the Limited Patriots and the
Unlimited.

Between which two classes, are not Aristocrats enough, anc
Crypto-Aristocrats, busy? Spies running over from Londor
with important Packets; spies pretending to run! One o
these latter, Viard was the name of him, pretended to accuse
Roland, and even the Wife of Roland: to the joy of Chabo•
and the Mountain. But the Wife of Roland came, being
summoned, on the instant, to the Convention Hall; came, ir
her high clearness; and, with few clear words, dissipated thi
Viard, into despicability and air, all Friends of Order applaud
ing. So, with Theatre-riots, and 'Bread, or else kill us;
with Rage, Hunger, preternatural Suspicion, does this wild
Paris pipe. Roland grows ever more querulous, in his
Messages and Letters; rising almost to the hysterical pitch.
Marat, whom no power on earth can prevent seeing into
traitors and Rolands, takes to bed for three days; almos•
dead, the invaluable People's-Friend, with heart-break, with
fever and headache: '*O Peuple babillard, si tu savais agir,
People of Babblers, if thou couldst but *act!*'

To crown all, victorious Dumouriez, in these New-year's
days, is arrived in Paris;—one fears for no good. He pretends
to be complaining of Minister Pache, and Hassenfratz dilapidations; to be concerting measures for the spring Campaign
one finds him much in the company of the Girondins.
Plotting with them against Jacobinism, against Equality, and
the Punishment of Louis? We have Letters of his to the

Convention itself. Will he act the old Lafayette part, this new victorious General? Let him withdraw again; not undenounced!

And still, in the Convention tribune, it drones continually, mere Juristic Eloquence, and Hypothesis without Action; and there are still fifties on the President's List. Nay these Gironde Presidents give their own party preference: we suspect they play foul with the List; men of the Mountain cannot be heard. And still it drones, all through December into January and a New year; and there is no end! Paris pipes round it; multitudinous; ever higher, to the note of the whirlwind. Paris will 'bring cannon from Saint-Denis;' there is talk of 'shutting the Barriers,'—to Roland's horror.

Whereupon, behold, the convention Tribune suddenly ceases droning: we cut short, be on the List who likes; and make end. On Tuesday next, the Fifteenth of January 1793, it shall go to the Vote, name by name; and one way or other, this great game play itself out!

CHAPTER VII

THE THREE VOTINGS

Is Louis Capet guilty of conspiring against Liberty? Shall our Sentence be itself final, or need ratifying by Appeal to the People? If guilty, what Punishment? This is the form agreed to, after uproar and 'several hours of tumultuous indecision:' these are the Three successive Questions, whereon the Convention shall now pronounce. Paris floods round their Hall; multitudinous, many-sounding. Europe and all nations listen for their answer. Deputy after Deputy shall answer to his name: Guilty or Not guilty?

As to the Guilt, there is, as above hinted, no doubt in the mind of Patriot men. Overwhelming majority pronounces Guilt; the unanimous Convention votes for Guilt, only some feeble twenty-eight voting not Innocence, but refusing to vote at all. Neither does the Second Question prove doubtful, whatever the Girondins might calculate. Would not Appeal to the People be another name for civil war? Majority of two to one answers that there shall be no Appeal: this also is settled. Loud Patriotism, now at ten o'clock, may hush itself for the night; and retire to its bed not without hope. Tuesday has gone well. On the morrow comes, What Punishment? On the morrow is the tug of war.

Consider therefore if, on this Wednesday morning, there is an affluence of Patriotism; if Paris stands a-tiptoe, and all Deputies are at their post! Seven-hundred and Forty-nine honourable Deputies; only some twenty absent on mission, Duchâtel and some seven others absent by sickness. Meanwhile expectant Patriotism and Paris standing a-tiptoe, have need of patience. For this Wednesday again passes in debate and effervescence; Girondins proposing that a 'majority of three-fourths' shall be required; Patriots fiercely resisting them. Danton, who has just got back from mission in the Netherlands, does obtain 'order of the day' on this Girondin proposal; nay he obtains further that we decide *sans désemparer*, in Permanent-session, till we have done.

And so, finally, at eight in the evening this Third stupendous Voting, by roll-call or *appel-nominal*, does begin. What Punishment? Girondins undecided, Patriots decided, men afraid of Royalty, men afraid of Anarchy, must answer here and now. Infinite Patriotism, dusky in the lamp-light, floods all corridors, crowds all galleries; sternly waiting to hear. Shrill-sounding Ushers summon you by Name and Department; you may rise to the Tribune, and say.

Eye-witnesses have represented this scene of the Third Voting, and of the votings that grew out of it; a scene protracted, like to be endless, lasting, with few brief intervals, from Wednesday till Sunday morning,—as one of the strangest seen in the Revolution. Long night wears itself into day, morning's paleness is spread over all faces; and again the wintry shadows sink, and the dim lamps are lit: but through day and night and the vicissitudes of hours, Member after Member is mounting continually those Tribune-steps; pausing aloft there, in the clearer upper light, to speak his Fate-word; then diving down into the dusk and throng again. Like Phantoms in the hour of midnight; most spectral, pandemonial! Never did President Vergniaud, or any terrestrial President, superintend the like. A King's Life, and so much else that depends thereon, hangs trembling in the balance. Man after man mounts; the buzz hushes itself till he have spoken: Death; Banishment; Imprisonment till the Peace. Many say, Death; with what cautious well-studied phrases and paragraphs they could devise, of explanation, of enforcement, of faint recommendation to mercy. Many too say, Banishment; something short of Death. The balance trembles, none can yet guess whitherward. Whereat anxious Patriotism bellows; irrepressible by Ushers.

The poor Girondins, many of them, under such fierce bellowing of Patriotism, say Death; justifying, *motivant*, that most miserable word of theirs by some brief casuistry and jesuitry. Vergniaud himself says, Death; justifying by jesuitry. Rich Lepelletier Saint-Fargeau had been of the Noblesse, and then of the Patriot Left Side, in the Constituent; and had argued and reported, there and elsewhere, not a little, *against* Capital Punishment: nevertheless he now says, Death; a word which may cost him dear. Manuel did surely rank with the Decided in August last; but he has been sinking and backsliding ever since September and the scenes of September. In this Convention, above all, no word he could speak would find favour; he says now, Banishment; and in mute wrath quits the place forever,—much hustled in the corridors. Philippe Égalité votes, in his soul and conscience, Death: at the sound of which and of whom, even Patriotism shakes its head; and there runs a groan and shudder through this Hall of Doom. Robespierre's vote cannot be doubtful; his speech is long. Men see the figure of shrill Sieyès ascend; hardly pausing, passing merely, this figure says, "*La Mort sans phrase*, Death without phrases;" and fares onward and downward. Most spectral, pandemonial!

And yet if the Reader fancy it of a funereal, sorrowful or even grave character, he is far mistaken: 'the Ushers in the Mountain quarter,' says Mercier, 'had become as Box-keepers at the Opera;' opening and shutting of Galleries for privileged persons, for 'D'Orléans Égalité's mistresses,' or other high-dizened women of condition, rustling with laces and tricolor. Gallant Deputies pass and repass thitherward, treating them with ices, refreshments and small-talk; the high-dizened heads beck responsive; some have their card and pin, pricking down the Ayes and Noes, as at a game of *Rouge-et-Noir*. Further aloft reigns Mère Duchesse with her unrouged Amazons; she cannot be prevented making long *Hahas*, when the vote is not *La Mort*. In these Galleries there is refection, drinking of wine and brandy 'as in open tavern, *en pleine tabagie*.' Betting goes on in all coffeehouses of the neighbourhood. But within doors, fatigue, impatience, uttermost weariness sits now on all visages; lighted up only from time to time by turns of the game. Members have fallen asleep; Ushers come and awaken them to vote; other Members calculate whether they shall not have time to run and dine. Figures rise, like phantoms, pale in the dusky lamp-light; utter from this Tribune, only one word: Death. '*Tout est optique*,' says Mercier, 'The world is all an optical shadow.' Deep in the Thursday night, when the Voting is done, and Secretaries are summing it up, sick Duchâtel, more spectral than another, comes borne on a chair, wrapt in blankets, in 'nightgown and nightcap,' to vote for Mercy: one vote it is thought may turn the scale.

Ah no! In profoundest silence, President Vergniaud, with a voice full of sorrow, has to say: "I declare, in the name of the Convention, that the punishment it pronounces on Louis Capet is that of Death." Death by a small majority of Fifty-three. Nay, if we deduct from the one side, and add to the other, a certain Twenty-six, who said Death but coupled some faintest ineffectual surmise of mercy with it, the majority will be but *One*.

Death is the sentence: but its execution? It is not executed yet! Scarcely is the vote declared when Louis's Three Advocates enter; with Protest in his name, with demand for Delay, for Appeal to the People. For this do Desèze and Tronchet plead, with brief eloquence: brave old Malesherbes pleads for it with eloquent want of eloquence, in broken sentences, in embarrassment and sobs; that brave time-honoured face, with its gray strength, its broad sagacity and honesty, is mastered with emotion, melts into dumb tears.— They reject the Appeal to the People; that having been already settled. But as to the delay, what they call *Sursis*, it *shall* be considered: shall be voted for tomorrow: at present we adjourn. Whereupon Patriotism 'hisses' from the Mountain: but a 'tyrannical majority' has so decided, and adjourns.

There is still this *fourth* Vote then, growls indignant Patriotism:—this vote, and who knows what other votes, and adjournments of voting; and the whole matter still hovering hypothetical! And at every new vote those Jesuit Girondins, even they who voted for Death, would so fain find a loophole! Patriotism must watch and rage. Tyrannical adjournments there have been; one, and now another at midnight on plea of fatigue,—all Friday wasted in hesitation and higgling; in *re*counting of the votes, which are found correct as they stood ! Patriotism bays fiercer than ever; Patriotism, by long watching, has become red-eyed, almost rabid.

"Delay: yes or no ?" men do vote it finally, all Saturday, all day and night. Men's nerves are worn out, men's hearts are desperate; now it shall end. Vergniaud, spite of the baying, ventures to say Yes, Delay; though he had voted Death. Philippe Égalité says, in his soul and conscience, No. The next Member mounting: "Since Philippe says No, I for my part say Yes, *moi je dis Oui*." The balance still trembles. Till finally, at three o'clock on Sunday morning, we have : *No delay*, by a majority of Seventy; *Death within four-and-twenty hours !*

Garat, Minister of Justice, has to go to the Temple with this stern message: he ejaculates repeatedly, "*Quelle commission affreuse*, What a frightful function !" Louis begs for a Confessor: for yet three days of life, to prepare himself to die. The Confessor is granted; the three days and all respite are refused.

There is no deliverance, then ? Thick stone walls answer, None. Has King Louis no friends ? Men of action, of courage grown desperate, in this his extreme need ? King Louis's friends are feeble and far. Not even a voice in the coffeehouses rises for him. At Méot the Restaurateur's no Captain Dampmartin now dines; or sees death-doing whiskerandoes on furlough exhibit daggers of improved structure. Méot's gallant Royalists on furlough are far across the marches; they are wandering distracted over the world : or their bones lie whitening Argonne Wood. Only some weak Priests 'leave Pamphlets on all the bourne-stones,' this night, calling for a rescue : calling for the pious women to rise ; or are taken distributing Pamphlets, and sent to prison.

Nay there is one death-doer, of the ancient Méot sort, who, with effort, has done even less and worse : slain a Deputy, and set all the Patriotism of Paris on edge ! It was five on Saturday evening when Lepelletier St. Fargeau, having given his vote, *No Delay*, ran over to Février's in the Palais-Royal to snatch a morsel of dinner. He had dined, and was paying. A thickset man 'with black hair and blue beard,' in a loose kind of frock, stept up to him; it was, as Février and the bystanders bethought them, one Pâris of the old King's-Guard. "Are you Lepelletier?" asks he.—"Yes."—"You

voted in the King's Business——?"—"I voted Death."—
"*Scélérat*, take that!" cries Pâris, flashing out a sabre from
under his frock, and plunging it deep in Lepelletier's side.
Février clutches him: but he breaks off; is gone.

The voter Lepelletier lies dead; he has expired in great
pain, at one in the morning;—two hours before that Vote of
No Delay was fully summed up. Guardsman Pâris is flying
over France; cannot be taken; will be found some months
after, self-shot in a remote inn.—Robespierre sees reason to
think that Prince d'Artois himself is privately in Town; that
the Convention will be butchered in the lump. Patriotism
sounds mere wail and vengeance: Santerre doubles and
trebles all his patrols. Pity is lost in rage and fear; the Convention has refused the three days of life and all respite.

CHAPTER VIII

PLACE DE LA RÉVOLUTION

To this conclusion, then, hast thou come, O hapless Louis!
The Son of Sixty Kings is to die on the Scaffold by form of
Law. Under Sixty Kings this same form of Law, form of
Society, has been fashioning itself together, these thousand
years; and has become, one way and other, a most strange
Machine. Surely, if needful, it is also frightful, this Machine;
dead, blind; not what it should be; which, with swift stroke,
or by cold slow torture, has wasted the lives and souls of innumerable men. And behold now a King himself, or say
rather Kinghood in his person, is to expire here in cruel tor-
tures;—like a Phalaris shut in the belly of his own red-heated
Brazen Bull! It is ever so; and thou shouldst know it, O
haughty tyrannous man: injustice breeds injustice; curses and
falsehoods do verily return 'always *home*,' wide as they may
wander. Innocent Louis bears the sins of many generations:
he too experiences that man's tribunal is not in this Earth;
that if he had no Higher one, it were not well with him.

A King dying by such violence appeals impressively to the
imagination; as the like must do, and ought to do. And yet
at bottom it is not the King dying, but the man! Kingship
is a coat: the grand loss is of the skin. The man from whom
you take his Life, to him can the whole combined world do
more? Lally went on his hurdle; his mouth filled with a gag
(i. 70). Miserablest mortals, doomed for pi king pockets, have

a whole five-act Tragedy in them, in that dumb pain, as they go to the gallows, unregarded ; they consume the cup of trembling down to the lees. For Kings and for Beggars, for the justly doomed and the unjustly, it is a hard thing to die. Pity them all : thy utmost pity, with all aids and appliances and throne-and-scaffold contrasts, how far short is it of the thing pitied !

A Confessor has come; Abbé Edgeworth, of Irish extraction, whom the King knew by good report, has come promptly on this solemn mission. Leave the Earth alone, then, thou hapless King ; it with its malice will go its way, thou also canst go thine. A hard scene yet remains : the parting with our loved ones. Kind hearts, environed in the same grim peril with us ; to be left *here !* Let the Reader look with the eyes of Valet Cléry, through these glass-doors, where also the Municipality watches ; and see the cruellest of scenes:

'At half-past eight, the door of the ante-room opened : the Queen appeared first, leading her Son by the hand ; then Madame Royale and Madame Elizabeth : they all flung themselves into the arms of the King. Silence reigned for some minutes ; interrupted only by sobs. The Queen made a movement to lead his Majesty towards the inner room, where M. Edgeworth was waiting unknown to them : "No," said the King, "let us go into the dining-room, it is there only that I can see you." They entered there ; I shut the door of it, which was of glass. The King sat down, the Queen on his left hand, Madame Elizabeth on his right, Madame Royale almost in front ; the young Prince remained standing between his Father's legs. They all leaned towards him, and often held him embraced. This scene of wo, lasted an hour and three quarters ; during which we could hear nothing ; we could see only that always when the King spoke, the sobbings of the Princesses redoubled, continued for some minutes ; and that then the King began again to speak.' And so our meetings and our partings do now end ! The sorrows we gave each other ; the poor joys we faithfully shared, and all our lovings and our sufferings, and confused toilings under the earthly Sun, are over. Thou good soul, I shall never, never through all ages of Time, see thee any more !—NEVER ! O Reader, knowest thou that hard word ?

For nearly two hours this agony lasts ; then they tear themselves asunder. "Promise that you will see us on the morrow."

He promises :—Ah yes, yes ; yet once ; and go now, ye loved ones ; cry to God for yourselves and me !—It was a hard scene, but it is over. He will not see them on the morrow. The Queen, in passing through the ante-room, glanced at the Cerberus Municipals ; and, with woman's vehemence, said through her tears, " *Vous êtes tous des scélérats.*"

King Louis slept sound, till five in the morning, when Cléry, as he had been ordered, awoke him. Cléry dressed his hair : while this went forward, Louis took a ring from his watch, and kept trying it on his finger ; it was his wedding-ring, which he is now to return to the Queen as a mute farewell. At half-past six, he took the Sacrament ; and continued in devotion, and conference with Abbé Edgeworth. He will not see his Family : it were too hard to bear.

At eight, the Municipals enter : the King gives them his Will, and messages and effects ; which they, at first, brutally refuse to take charge of : he gives them a roll of gold pieces, a hundred and twenty-five louis ; these are to be returned to Malesherbes, who had lent them. At nine, Santerre says the hour is come. The King begs yet to retire for three minutes. At the end of three minutes, Santerre again says the hour is come. ' Stamping on the ground with his right-foot, Louis answers : "*Partons*, Let us go."'—How the rolling of those drums comes in, through the Temple bastions and bulwarks, on the heart of a queenly wife ; soon to be a widow ! He is gone, then, and has not seen us ? A Queen weeps bitterly ; a King's Sister and Children. Over all these Four does Death also hover : all shall perish miserably save one ; she, as Duchesse d'Angoulême, will live,—not happily.

At the Temple Gate were some faint cries, perhaps from voices of pitiful women : " *Grace ! Grace !*" Through the rest of the streets there is silence as of the grave. No man not armed is allowed to be there : the armed, did any even pity, dare not express it, each man overawed by all his neighbours. All windows are down, none seen looking through them. All shops are shut. No wheel-carriage rolls, this morning, in these streets but one only. Eighty-thousand armed men stand ranked, like armed statues of men ; cannons bristle, cannoneers with match burning, but no word or movement : it is as a city enchanted into silence and stone : one carriage with its escort, slowly rumbling, is the only sound. Louis reads, in his Book of Devotion, the Prayers of the Dying : clatter of this death-march falls sharp on the ear, in

the great silence ; but the thought would fain struggle heavenward, and forget the Earth.

As the clocks strike ten, behold the Place de la Révolution,
once Place de Louis Quinze : the Guillotine, mounted near
the old Pedestal where once stood the Statue of that Louis !
Far round, all bristles with cannons and armed men : spectators crowding in the rear ; d'Orléans Égalité there in cabriolet. Swift messengers, *boquetons*, speed to the townhall, every
three minutes : near by is the Convention sitting,—vengeful
for Lepelletier. Heedless of all, Louis reads his Prayers of
the Dying ; not till five minutes yet has he finished ; then the
Carriage opens. What temper he is in ? Ten different witnesses will give ten different accounts of it. He is in the
collision of all tempers ; arrived now at the black Mahlstrom
and descent of Death : in sorrow, in indignation, in resignation struggling to be resigned. "Take care of M. Edgeworth,"
he straitly charges the Lieutenant who is sitting with them :
then they two descend.

The drums are beating : " *Taisez-vous*, Silence ! " he cries
' in a terrible voice, *d'une voix terrible.*' He mounts the
scaffold, not without delay ; he is in puce coat, breeches of
gray, white stockings. He strips off the coat ; stands disclosed in a sleeve-waistcoat of white flannel. The Executioners approach to bind him : he spurns, resists ; Abbé Edgeworth has to remind him how the Saviour, in whom men trust,
submitted to be bound. His hands are tied, his head bare ;
the fatal moment is come. He advances to the edge of the
Scaffold, ' his face very red,' and says : " Frenchmen, I die
innocent : it is from the Scaffold and near appearing before
God that I tell you so. I pardon my enemies ; I desire that
France——" A General on horseback, Santerre or another,
prances out, with uplifted hand : " *Tambours !* " The drums
drown the voice. "Executioners, do your duty ! " The Executioners, desperate lest themselves be murdered (for Santerre
and his Armed Ranks will strike, if they do not), seize the
hapless Louis : six of them desperate, him singly desperate,
struggling there ; and bind him to their plank. Abbé Edgeworth, stooping, bespeaks him : " Son of Saint Louis, ascend
to Heaven." The Axe clanks down ; a King's Life is shorn
away. It is Monday the 21st of January 1793. He was aged
Thirty-eight years four months and twenty-eight days.

Executioner Samson shows the Head : fierce shout of *Vive
la République* rises, and swells ; caps raised on bayonets, hats

waving: students of the College of Four Nations take it up, on the far Quais; fling it over Paris. D'Orléans drives off in his cabriolet: the Townhall Councillors rub their hands, saying, "It is done, It is done." There is dipping of handkerchiefs, of pike-points in the blood. Headsman Samson, though he afterwards denied it, sells locks of the hair: fractions of the puce coat are long after worn in rings.—And so, in some half-hour it is done; and the multitude has all departed. Pastrycooks, coffee-sellers, milkmen sing out their trivial quotidian cries: the world wags on, as if this were a common day. In the coffee-houses that evening, says Prudhomme, Patriot shook hands with Patriot in a more cordial manner than usual. Not till some days after, according to Mercier, did public men see what a grave thing it was.

A grave thing it indisputably is; and will have consequences. On the morrow morning, Roland, so long steeped to the lips in disgust and chagrin, sends in his demission. His accounts lie all ready, correct in black-on-white to the uttermost farthing: these he wants but to have audited, that he might retire to remote obscurity, to the country and his books. They will never be audited, those accounts; he will never get retired thither.

It was on Tuesday that Roland demitted. On Thursday comes Lepelletier St. Fargeau's Funeral, and passage to the Pantheon of Great Men. Notable as the wild pageant of a winter day. The Body is borne aloft, half-bare; the winding-sheet disclosing the death-wound; sabre and bloody clothes parade themselves; a 'lugubrious music' wailing harsh *næniæ*. Oak-crowns shower down from windows; President Vergniaud walks there, with Convention, with Jacobin Society, and all Patriots of every colour, all mourning brotherlike.

Notable also for another thing, this Burial of Lepelletier: it was the last act these men ever did with concert! All Parties and figures of Opinion, that agitate this distracted France and its Convention, now stand, as it were, face to face, and dagger to dagger; the King's Life, round which they all struck and battled, being hurled down. Dumouriez, conquering Holland, growls ominous discontent, at the head of Armies. Men say Dumouriez will have a King; that young D'Orléans Égalité shall be his King. Deputy Fauchet, in the *Journal des Amis*, curses his day, more bitterly than Job did; invokes the poniards of Regicides, of 'Arras Vipers' or Robespierres, of Pluto Dantons, of horrid Butchers Legendre and Simulacra d'Herbois, to send him swiftly to another world than *theirs*. This is *Te-Deum* Fauchet, of the Bastille Victory, of the *Cercle Social*. Sharp was the death-hail rattling round one's Flag-of-truce, on that Bastille day: but it was soft to such wreckage of high Hope as this; one's New Golden Era going down in leaden dross, and sulphurous black of the Everlasting Darkness!

At home this Killing of a King has divided all friends; and abroad it has united all enemies. Fraternity of Peoples, Revolutionary Propagandism; Atheism, Regicide; total destruction of social order in this world! All Kings, and lovers of Kings, and haters of Anarchy, rank in coalition; as in a war for life. England signifies to Citizen Chauvelin, the Ambassador or rather Ambassador's-Cloak, that he must quit the country in eight days. Ambassador's-Cloak and Ambassador, Chauvelin and Talleyrand, depart accordingly. Talleyrand, implicated in that Iron Press of the Tuileries, thinks it safest to make for America.

England has cast out the Embassy: England declares war, —being shocked principally, it would seem, at the condition of the River Scheldt. Spain declares war; being shocked principally at some other thing; which doubtless the Manifesto indicates. Nay we find it was not England that declared war first, or Spain first; but that France herself declared war first on both of them;—a point of immense Parliamentary and Journalistic interest in those days, but which has become of no interest whatever in these. They all declare war. The sword is drawn, the scabbard thrown away. It is even as Danton said, in one of his all-too gigantic figures: "The coalised Kings threaten us; we hurl at their feet, as gage of battle, the Head of a King."

BOOK III

THE GIRONDINS

CHAPTER I

CAUSE AND EFFECT

THIS huge Insurrectionary Movement, which we liken to a breaking out of Tophet and the Abyss, has swept away Royalty, Aristocracy, and a King's life. The question is, What will it next do; how will it henceforth shape itself? Settle down into a reign of Law and Liberty; according as the habits, persuasions and endeavours of the educated, monied, respectable class prescribe? That is to say: the volcanic lava-flood, bursting up in the manner described, will explode and flow according to Girondin Formula and pre-established rule of Philosophy? If so, for our Girondin friends it will be well.

Meanwhile were not the prophecy rather, that as no external force, Royal or other, now remains which could control this Movement, the Movement will follow a course of its own; probably a very original one? Further, that whatsoever man or men can best interpret the inward tendencies it has, and give them voice and activity, will obtain the lead of it? For the rest, that as a thing *without* order, a thing proceeding from beyond and beneath the region of order, it must work and welter, not as a Regularity but as a Chaos; destructive and self-destructive; always till something that *has* order arise, strong enough to bind it into subjection again? Which something, we may further conjecture, will not be a Formula, with philosophical propositions and forensic eloquence; but a Reality, probably with a sword in its hand!

As for the Girondin Formula, of a respectable Republic for the Middle Classes, all manner of Aristocracies being now sufficiently demolished, there seems little reason to expect that the business will stop there. *Liberty, Equality, Fraternity*, these are the words; enunciative and prophetic. Republic for the respectable washed Middle Classes, how can that be the fulfilment thereof? Hunger and nakedness, and nightmare oppression lying heavy on Twenty-five million hearts;

222

this, not the wounded vanities or contradicted philosophies of philosophical Advocates, rich Shopkeepers, rural Noblesse, was the prime mover in the French Revolution; as the like will be in all such Revolutions, in all countries. Feudal Fleur-de-lys had become an insupportably bad marching-banner, and needed to be torn and trampled: but Moneybag of Mammon (for that, in these times, is what the respectable Republic for the Middle Classes will signify) is a still worse, while it lasts. Properly, indeed, it is the worst and basest of all banners, and symbols of dominion among men; and indeed is possible only in a time of general Atheism, and Unbelief in anything save in brute Force and Sensualism; pride of birth, pride of office, any known kind of pride being a degree better than purse-pride. Freedom, Equality, Brotherhood: not in the Money-bag, but far elsewhere, will Sansculottism seek these things.

We say therefore that an insurrectionary France, loose of control from without, destitute of supreme order from within, will form one of the most tumultuous Activities ever seen on this Earth; such as no Girondin Formula can regulate. An immeasurable force, made up of forces manifold, heterogeneous, compatible and incompatible. In plainer words, this France must needs split into Parties; each of which seeking to make itself good, contradiction, exasperation will arise; and Parties on Parties find that they cannot work together, cannot exist together.

As for the number of Parties, there will, strictly counting, be as many Parties as there are opinions. According to which rule, in this National Convention itself, to say nothing of France generally, the number of Parties ought to be Seven-hundred and Forty-nine; for every unit entertains his opinion. But now, as every unit has at once an individual nature or necessity to follow his own road, and a gregarious nature or necessity to see himself travelling by the side of others,—what can there be but dissolutions, precipitations, endless turbulence of attracting and repelling; till once the master-element get evolved, and this wild alchemy arrange itself again?

To the length of Seven-hundred and Forty-nine Parties, however, no Nation was ever yet seen to go. Nor indeed much beyond the length of Two Parties; two at a time;—so invincible is man's tendency to unite, with all the invincible divisiveness he has! Two Parties, we say, are the usual number at one time: let these two fight it out, all minor

shades of party rallying under the shade likest them; when
the one has fought down the other, then it, in its turn, may
divide, self-destructive; and so the process continue, as far as
needful. This is the way of Revolutions, which spring up as
the French one has done; when the so-called Bonds of Society
snap asunder; and all Laws that are not Laws of Nature become naught and Formulas merely.

But, quitting these somewhat abstract considerations, let
History note this concrete reality which the streets of Paris
exhibit, on Monday the 25th of February 1793. Long before
daylight that morning, these streets are noisy and angry.
Petitioning enough there has been; a Convention often
solicited. It was but yesterday there came a Deputation of
Washerwomen with Petition; complaining that not so much
as soap could be had; to say nothing of bread, and condi-
ments of bread. The cry of women, round the Salle de
Manège, was heard plaintive: "*Du pain et du savon*, Bread
and soap."

And now from six o'clock, this Monday morning, one perceives the Baker's Queues unusually expanded, angrily agitating themselves. Not the Baker alone, but two Section
Commissioners to help him, manage with difficulty the daily
distribution of loaves. Soft-spoken assiduous, in the early
candle-light, are Baker and Commissioners: and yet the pale
chill February sunrise discloses an unpromising scene. Indignant Female Patriots, partly supplied with bread, rush now
to the shops, declaring that they will have groceries. Groceries
enough: sugar-barrels rolled forth into the street, Patriot
Citoyennes weighing it out at a just rate of elevenpence a
pound; likewise coffee-chests, soap-chests, nay cinnamon and
cloves-chests, with *aquavitæ* and other forms of alcohol,—at a
just rate, which some do not pay; the pale-faced Grocer silently
wringing his hands! What help? The distributive Citoyennes
are of violent speech and gesture, their long Eumenides-hair
hanging out of curl; nay in their girdles pistols are seen sticking: some, it is even said, have *beards*,—male Patriots in
petticoats and mob-cap. Thus, in the street of Lombards, in
the street of Five-Diamonds, street of Pulleys, in most streets
of Paris does it effervesce, the livelong day; no Municipality,
no Mayor Pache, though he was War-Minister lately, sends
military against it, or aught against it but persuasive-eloquence,
till seven at night, or later.

On Monday gone five weeks, which was the twenty-first of January, we saw Paris, beheading its King, stand silent, like a petrified City of Enchantment: and now on this Monday it is so noisy, selling sugar! Cities, especially Cities in Revolution, are subject to these alternations; the secret courses of civic business and existence effervescing and efflorescing, in this manner, as a concrete Phenomenon to the eye. Of which Phenomenon, when secret existence becoming public effloresces on the street, the philosophical cause and effect is not so easy to find. What, for example, may be the accurate philosophical meaning, and meanings, of this sale of sugar? These things that have become visible in the street of Pulleys and over Paris, whence are they, we say; and whither?—

That Pitt has a hand in it, the gold of Pitt: so much, to all reasonable Patriot men, may seem clear. But then, through what agents of Pitt? Varlet, Apostle of Liberty, was discerned again of late, with his pike and red nightcap. Deputy Marat published in his Journal, this very day, complaining of the bitter scarcity, and sufferings of the people, till he seemed to get wroth; 'If your Rights of Man were anything but a piece of written paper, the plunder of a few shops, and a forestaller or two hung up at the door-lintels, would put an end to such things.' Are not these, say the Girondins, pregnant indications? Pitt has bribed the Anarchists; Marat is the agent of Pitt: hence this sale of sugar. To the Mother-Society, again, it is clear that the scarcity is factitious; is the work of Girondins, and such like; a set of men sold partly to Pitt; sold wholly to their own ambitions, and hard-hearted pedantries; who will not fix the grain-prices, but prate pedantically of free-trade; wishing to starve Paris into violence, and embroil it with the Departments: *hence* this sale of sugar.

And, alas, if to these two notabilities, of a Phenomenon and such Theories of a Phenomenon, we add this third notability, That the French Nation has believed, for several years now, in the possibility, nay certainty and near advent, of a universal Millennium, or reign of Freedom, Equality, Fraternity, wherein man should be the brother of man, and sorrow and sin flee away? Not bread to eat, nor soap to wash with; and the reign of Perfect Felicity ready to arrive, due always since the Bastille fell! How did our hearts burn within us, at that Feast of Pikes, when brother flung himself on brother's bosom; and in sunny jubilee, Twenty-five millions burst forth into sound and cannon-smoke! Bright was our Hope then, as sunlight; red-angry is our Hope grown now, as consuming fire. But, O Heavens, what enchantment is it, or devilish legerdemain, of such effect, that Perfect Felicity, always within arm's length, could never be laid hold of, but only in her stead Controversy and Scarcity? This set of traitors after that set! Tremble, ye traitors; dread a People which calls itself patient, long-suffering; but which cannot always submit to have its pockets picked, in this way,—of a Millennium!

Yes, Reader, here is a miracle. Out of that putrescent rubbish of Scepticism, Sensualism, Sentimentalism, hollow Machiavelism, such a Faith has verily risen; flaming in the heart of a People. A whole People, awakening as it were to consciousness in deep misery, believes that it is within reach of a Fraternal Heaven-on-Earth. With longing arms, it struggles to embrace the Unspeakable; cannot embrace it, owing to certain causes.—Seldom do we find that a whole People can be said to have any Faith at all; except in things which it can eat and handle. Whensoever it gets any Faith, its history becomes spirit-stirring, noteworthy. But since the time when steel Europe shook itself simultaneously at the word of Hermit Peter, and rushed towards the Sepulchre where God had lain, there was no universal impulse of Faith that one could note. Since Protestantism went silent, no Luther's voice, no Zisca's drum any longer proclaiming that God's Truth was *not* the Devil's Lie; and the Last of the Cameronians (Renwick was the name of him; honour to the name of the brave!) sank, shot, on the Castle-hill of Edinburgh, there was no partial impulse of Faith among Nations. Till now, behold, once more, this French Nation believes! Herein, we say, in that astonishing Faith of theirs, lies the miracle. It is a Faith undoubtedly of the more prodigious sort, even among Faiths; and will embody itself in prodigies. It is the soul of that world-prodigy named French Revolution; whereat the world still gazes and shudders.

But, for the rest, let no man ask History to explain by cause and effect how the business proceeded henceforth. This battle of Mountain and Gironde, and what follows, is the battle of Fanaticisms and Miracles; unsuitable for cause and effect. The sound of it, to the mind, is as a hubbub of voices in distraction; little of articulate is to be gathered by long listening and studying; only battle-tumult, shouts of triumph, shrieks of despair. The Mountain has left no

Memoirs; the Girondins have left Memoirs, which are too often little other than long-drawn Interjections, of *Woe is me*, and *Cursed be ye*. So soon as History can philosophically delineate the conflagration of a kindled Fireship, she may try this other task. Here lay the bitumen-stratum, there the brimstone one; so ran the vein of gunpowder, of nitre, tere-binth and foul grease: this, were she inquisitive enough, History might partly know. But how they acted and reacted below decks, one fire-stratum playing into the other, by its nature and the art of man, now when all hands ran raging, and the flames lashed high over shrouds and topmast: this let not History attempt.

The Fireship is old France, the old French Form of Life; her crew a Generation of men. Wild are their cries and their ragings there, like spirits tormented in that flame. But, on the whole, are they not *gone*, O Reader? Their Fireship and they, frightening the world, have sailed away; its flames and its thunders quite away, into the Deep of Time. One thing therefore History will do: pity them all; for it went hard with them all. Not even the seagreen Incorruptible but shall have some pity, some human love, though it takes an effort. And now, so much once thoroughly attained, the rest will become easier. To the eye of equal brotherly pity, innumerable per-versions dissipate themselves; exaggerations and execrations fall off, of their own accord. Standing wistfully on the safe shore, we will look, and see, what is of interest to us, what is adapted to us.

CHAPTER II

CULOTTIC AND SANSCULOTTIC

GIRONDE and Mountain are now in full quarrel; their mutual rage, says Toulongeon, is growing a 'pale' rage. Curious, lamentable: all these men have the word Republic on their lips; in the heart of every one of them is a passionate wish for something which he calls Republic: yet see their death-quarrel! So, however, are men made. Creatures who live in confusion; who, once thrown together, can readily fall into that confusion of confusions which quarrel is, simply because their confusions differ from one another; still more because they seem to differ! Men's words are a poor exponent of their thought; nay their thought itself is a poor exponent of the inward unnamed Mystery, wherefrom both thought and

action have their birth. No man can explain himself, can get
himself explained; men see not one another, but distorted
phantasms which they call one another; which they hate and
go to battle with: for all battle is well said to be *misunder
standing*.

But indeed that similitude of the Fireship; of our poor
French brethren, so fiery themselves, working also in an
element of fire, was not insignificant. Consider it well, there
is a shade of the truth in it. For a man, once committed
headlong to republican or any other Transcendentalism, and
fighting and fanaticising amid a Nation of his like, becomes
as it were enveloped in an ambient atmosphere of Transcen
dentalism and Delirium: his individual self is lost in some
thing that is not himself, but foreign though inseparable from
him. Strange to think of, the man's cloak still seems to hold
the same man: and yet the man is not there, his volition is
not there; nor the source of what he will do and devise;
instead of the man and his volition there is a piece of
Fanaticism and Fatalism incarnated in the shape of him.
He, the hapless incarnated Fanaticism, goes his road; no
man can help him, he himself least of all. It is a wonderful,
tragical predicament;—such as human language, unused to
deal with these things, being contrived for the uses of common
life, struggles to shadow out in figures. The ambient element
of material fire is not wilder than this of Fanaticism; nor,
though visible to the eye, is it more real. Volition bursts
forth involuntary-voluntary; rapt along; the movement of free
human minds becomes a raging tornado of fatalism, blind as
the winds; and Mountain and Gironde, when they recover
themselves, are alike astounded to see *where* it has flung and
dropt them. To such height of miracle can men work on
men; the Conscious and the Unconscious blended inscrutably
in this our inscrutable Life; endless Necessity environing
Freewill!

The weapons of the Girondins are Political Philosophy,
Respectability and Eloquence. Eloquence, or call it rhetoric
really of a superior order; Vergniaud, for instance, turns a
period as sweetly as any man of that generation. The
weapons of the Mountain are those of mere Nature; Audacity
and Impetuosity which may become Ferocity, as of men
complete in their determination, in their conviction; nay of
men, in some cases, who as Septemberers must either prevail

or perish. The ground to be fought for is Popularity: further you may either seek Popularity with the friends of Freedom and Order, or with the friends of Freedom Simple; to seek it with both has unhappily become impossible. With the former sort, and generally with the Authorities of the Departments, and such as read Parliamentary Debates, and are of Respectability, and of a peace-loving monied nature, the Girondins carry it. With the extreme Patriot again, with the indigent Millions, especially with the Population of Paris who do not read so much as hear and see, the Girondins altogether lose it, and the Mountain carries it.

Egoism, nor meanness of mind, is not wanting on either side. Surely not on the Girondin side; where in fact the instinct of self-preservation, too prominently unfolded by circumstances, cuts almost a sorry figure; where also a certain finesse, to the length even of shuffling and shamming, now and then shows itself. They are men skilful in Advocate-fence. They have been called the Jesuits of the Revolution; but that is too hard a name. It must be owned likewise that this rude blustering Mountain has a sense in it of what the Revolution means; which these eloquent Girondins are totally void of. Was the Revolution made, and fought for, against the world, these four weary years, that a Formula might be substantiated; that Society might become *methodic*, demonstrable by logic; and the old Noblesse with their pretensions vanish? Or ought it not withal to bring some glimmering of light and alleviation to the Twenty-five Millions, who sat in darkness, heavy-leaden, till they rose with pikes in their hands? At least and lowest, one would think, it should bring them a proportion of bread to live on? There is in the Mountain here and there; in Marat People's-friend; in the incorruptible Seagreen himself, though otherwise so lean and formulary, a heartfelt knowledge of this latter fact;—without which knowledge all other knowledge here is naught, and the choicest forensic eloquence is as sounding brass and a tinkling cymbal. Most cold, on the other hand, most patronising, unsubstantial is the tone of the Girondins towards ' our poorer brethren;'—those brethren whom one often hears of under the collective name of 'the masses,' as if they were not persons at all, but mounds of combustible explosive material, for blowing down Bastilles with! In very truth, a Revolutionist of this kind, is he not a Solecism? Disowned by Nature and Art; deserving only to be erased, and disappear!

Surely, to our poorer brethren of Paris, all this Girondin patronage sounds deadening and killing: if fine-spoken and incontrovertible in logic, then all the falser, all the hatefuller in fact.

Nay doubtless, pleading for Popularity, here among our poorer brethren of Paris, the Girondin has a hard game to play. If he gain the ear of the Respectable at a distance, it is by insisting on September and such like; it is at the expense of this Paris where he dwells and perorates. Hard to perorate in such an auditory! Wherefore the question arises: Could we not get ourselves out of this Paris? Twice or oftener such an attempt is made. If not we ourselves, thinks Guadet, then at least our *Suppléans* might do it. For every Deputy has his *Suppléant*, or Substitute, who will take his place if need be: might not these assemble, say at Bourges, which is a quiet episcopal Town, in quiet Berri, forty good leagues off? In that case, what profit were it for the Paris Sansculottery to insult us; our *Suppléans* sitting quiet at Bourges, to whom we could run? Nay, even the Primary electoral Assemblies, thinks Guadet, might be reconvoked, and a New Convention got, with new orders from the Sovereign People; and right glad were Lyons, were Bourdeaux, Rouen, Marseilles, as yet Provincial Towns, to welcome us in their turn, and become a sort of Capital Towns; and teach these Parisians reason.

Fond schemes; which all misgo! If decreed, in heat of eloquent logic, to-day, they are repealed, by clamour and passionate wider considerations, on the morrow. Will you, O Girondins, parcel us into separate Republics, then; like the Swiss, like your Americans; so that there be no Metropolis or indivisible French Nation any more? Your Departmental Guard seemed to point that way! Federal Republic? Federalist? Men and Knitting-women repeat *Fédéraliste*, with or without much Dictionary-meaning; but go on repeating it, as is usual in such cases, till the meaning of it becomes almost magical, fit to designate all mystery of Iniquity; and *Fédéraliste* has grown a word of Exorcism and *Apage-Satanas*. But furthermore, consider what 'poisoning of public opinion' in the Departments, by these Brissot, Gorsas, Caritat-Condorcet Newspapers! And then also what counter-poisoning, still feller in quality, by a *Père Duchesne* of Hébert, brutallest Newspaper yet published on Earth; by a *Rougiff* of Guffroy; by the 'incendiary leaves of Marat!' More than once, on

complaint given and effervescence rising, it is decreed that a
man cannot both be Legislator and Editor; that he shall
choose between the one function and the other. But this too,
which indeed could help little, is revoked or eluded; remains
a pious wish mainly.

Meanwhile, as the sad fruit of such strife, behold, O ye
National Representatives, how between the friends of Law
and the friends of Freedom everywhere, mere heats and
jealousies have arisen; fevering the whole Republic! Department, Provincial Town is set against Metropolis, Rich against
Poor, Culottic against Sansculottic, man against man. From
the Southern Cities come Addresses of an almost inculpatory
character; for Paris has long suffered Newspaper calumny.
Bourdeaux demands a reign of Law and Respectability,
meaning Girondism, with emphasis. With emphasis Marseilles demands the like. Nay, from Marseilles there come
two Addresses: one Girondin; one Jacobin Sansculottic.
Hot Rebecqui, sick of this Convention-work, has given place
to his Substitute, and gone home; where also, with such
jarrings, there is work to be sick of.

Lyons, a place of Capitalists and Aristocrats, is in still
worse state; almost in revolt. Chalier the Jacobin Town-
Councillor has got, too literally, to daggers-drawn with Nièvre-
Chol the *Modérantin* Mayor; one of your Moderate, perhaps
Aristocrat, Royalist or Federalist Mayors! Chalier, who
pilgrimed to Paris 'to behold Marat and the Mountain,' has
verily kindled himself at their sacred urn: for on the 6th of
February last, History or Rumour has seen him haranguing
his Lyons Jacobins in a quite transcendental manner, with
a drawn dagger in his hand; recommending (they say) sheer
September-methods, patience being worn out; and that the
Jacobin Brethren should, impromptu, work the Guillotine
themselves! One sees him still, in Engravings: mounted on
a table; foot advanced, body contorted; a bald, rude, slope-
browed, infuriated visage of the canine species, the eyes
starting from their sockets; in his puissant right-hand the
brandished dagger, or horse-pistol, as some give it; other
dog-visages kindling under him:—a man not likely to end
well! However, the Guillotine was *not* got together impromptu, that day, 'on the Pont Saint-Clair,' or elsewhere;
but indeed continued lying rusty in its loft: Nièvre-Chol with
military went about, rumbling cannon, in the most confused

manner; and the 'nine hundred prisoners' received no hurt.
So distracted is Lyons grown, with its cannons rumbling.
Convention Commissioners must be sent thither forthwith:
if even they can appease it, and keep the Guillotine in its
loft?

Consider finally if, on all these mad jarrings of the
Southern Cities, and of France generally, a traitorous Crypto-
Royalist class is not looking and watching; ready to strike
in, at the right season! Neither is there bread; neither is
there soap: see the Patriot women selling out sugar, at a just
rate of twenty-two sous per pound! Citizen Representatives,
it were verily well that your quarrels finished, and the reign
of Perfect Felicity began.

CHAPTER III

GROWING SHRILL

ON the whole, one cannot say that the Girondins are wanting
to themselves, so far as goodwill might go. They prick
assiduously into the sore-places of the Mountain; from
principle, and also from Jesuitism.

Besides September, of which there is now little to be made
except effervescence, we discern two sore-places where the
Mountain often suffers: Marat and Orléans Égalité. Squalid
Marat for his own sake and for the Mountain's, is assaulted
ever and anon; held up to France, as a squalid bloodthirsty
Portent, inciting to the pillage of shops; of whom let the
Mountain have the credit! The Mountain murmurs, ill at
ease: this 'Maximum of Patriotism,' how shall they either own
him or disown him? As for Marat personally, he, with his
fixed-idea, remains invulnerable to such things; nay the
People's-friend is very evidently rising in importance, as his
befriended People rises. No shrieks now, when he goes to
speak; occasional applauses rather, furtherance which breeds
confidence. The day when the Girondins proposed to 'decree
him accused' (décréter d'accusation, as they phrase it) for that
February Paragraph, of 'hanging up a Forestaller or two at
the door-lintels,' Marat proposes to have *them* 'decreed
insane;' and, descending the Tribune-steps, is heard to
articulate these most unsenatorial ejaculations: "*Les cochons,
les imbéciles*, Pigs, idiots!" Oftentimes he croaks harsh sarcasm, having really a rough rasping tongue, and a very deep fund

of contempt for fine outsides; and once or twice, he even laughs,
nay 'explodes into laughter, *rit aux éclats*,' at the gentilities
and superfine airs of these Girondin "men of statesmanship,"
with their pedantries, plausibilities, pusillanimities : "these
two years," says he, "you have been whining about attacks,
and plots, and danger from Paris; and you have not a scratch
to show for yourselves."—Danton gruffly rebukes him, from
time to time: a Maximum of Patriotism, whom one can
neither own nor disown !

But the second sore-place of the Mountain is this anomalous
Monseigneur Equality Prince d'Orléans. Behold these men,
says the Gironde ; with a whilom Bourbon Prince among
them : they are creatures of the d'Orléans Faction ; they will
have Philippe made King ; one King no sooner guillotined
than another made in his stead ! Girondins have moved,
Buzot moved long ago, from principle and also from jesuitism,
that the whole race of Bourbons should be marched forth from
the soil of France; this Prince Égalité to bring up the rear.
Motions which might produce some effect on the public ;
—which the Mountain, ill at ease, knows not what to do with.

And poor Orléans Égalité himself, for one begins to pity
even him, what does he do with them ? The disowned of all
parties, the rejected and foolishly bedrifted hither and thither,
to what corner of Nature can he now drift with advantage ?
Feasible hope remains not for him : unfeasible hope, in pallid
doubtful glimmers, there may still come, bewildering, not
cheering or illuminating,—from the Dumouriez quarter ; and
how, if not the timewasted Orléans Égalité, then perhaps the
young unworn Chartres Égalité might rise to be a kind of
King ? Sheltered, if sheltered it be, in the clefts of the
Mountain, poor Égalité will wait : one refuge in Jacobinism,
one in Dumouriez and Counter-Revolution, are there not two
chances ? However, the look of him, Dame Genlis says, is
grown gloomy ; sad to see. Sillery also, the Genlis's Husband,
who hovers about the Mountain, not on it, is in a bad way.
Dame Genlis has come to Raincy, out of England and Bury
St. Edmunds, in these days ; being summoned by Égalité,
with her young charge, Mademoiselle Égalité, — that so
Mademoiselle might not be counted among Emigrants and
hardly dealt with. But it proves a ravelled business : Genlis
and charge find that they must retire to the Netherlands ;
must wait on the Frontiers, for a week or two ; till Monseigneur, by Jacobin help, get it wound up. 'Next morning,'

says Dame Genlis, 'Monseigneur, gloomier than ever, gave me his arm, to lead me to the carriage. I was greatly troubled; Mademoiselle burst into tears; her Father was pale and trembling. After I had got seated, he stood immovable at the carriage-door, with his eyes fixed on me; his mournful and painful look seemed to implore pity;—"*Adieu, Madame!*" said he. The altered sound of his voice completely overcame me; unable to utter a word, I held out my hand; he grasped it close; then turning, and advancing sharply towards the postilions, he gave them a sign, and we rolled away.'

Nor are Peace-makers wanting; of whom likewise we mention two; one fast on the crown of the Mountain, the other not yet alighted anywhere : Danton and Barrère. Ingenious Barrère, Old-Constituent and Editor, from the slopes of the Pyrenees, is one of the usefullest men of this Convention, in his way. Truth may lie on both sides, on either side, or on neither side; my friends, ye must give and take : for the rest, success to the winning side! This is the motto of Barrère. Ingenious, almost genial; quick-sighted, supple, graceful; a man that will prosper. Scarcely Belial in the assembled Pandemonium was plausibler to ear and eye. An indispensable man : in the great *Art of Varnish* he may be said to seek his fellow. Has there an explosion arisen, as many do arise, a confusion, unsightliness, which no tongue can speak of, nor eye look on; give it to Barrère; Barrère shall be Committee-Reporter of it; you shall see it transmute itself into a regularity, into the very beauty and improvement that was needed. Without one such man, we say, how were this Convention bested? Call him not, as exaggerative Mercier does, 'the greatest liar in France:' nay it may be argued there is not truth enough in him to make a real lie of. Call him, with Burke, Anacreon of the Guillotine, and a man serviceable to this Convention.

The other Peace-maker whom we name is Danton. Peace, O peace with one another! cries Danton often enough : Are we not alone against the world; a little band of brothers? Broad Danton is loved by all the Mountain; but they think him too easy-tempered, deficient in suspicion : he has stood between Dumouriez and much censure, anxious not to exasperate our only General : in the shrill tumult Danton's strong voice reverberates, for union and pacification. Meetings there are; dinings with the Girondins : it is so pressingly essential that there be union. But the Girondins are haughty and respectable: this Titan Danton is not a man of Formulas, and there rests on him a shadow of September. "Your Girondins have no confidence in me:" this is the answer a conciliatory Meillan gets from him; to all the argument and pleadings this conciliatory Meillan can bring, the repeated answer is, "*Ils n'ont point de confiance.*"—The tumult will get ever shriller; rage is growing pale.

In fact, what a pang is it to the heart of a Girondin, this first withering probability that the despicable unphilosophic anarchic Mountain, after all, may triumph! Real Septemberers, a fifth-floor Tallien, 'a Robespierre without an idea in his head,' as Condorcet says, 'or a feeling in his heart:' and yet we, the flower of France, cannot stand against them; behold the sceptre departs from us; from us and goes to them! Eloquence, Philosophism, Respectability avail not: 'against Stupidity the very gods fight to no purpose,'

'*Mit der Dummheit kämpfen Götter selbst vergebens!*'

Shrill are the plaints of Louvet; his thin existence all acidified into rage, and preternatural insight of suspicion. Wroth is young Barbaroux; wroth and scornful. Silent, like a Queen with the aspic on her bosom, sits the wife of Roland; Roland's Accounts never yet got audited, his name become a byword. Such is the fortune of war, especially of revolution. The great gulf of Tophet, and Tenth of August, opened itself at the magic of your eloquent voice; and lo now, it will not close at your voice! It is a dangerous thing such magic. The Magician's Famulus got hold of the forbidden Book, and summoned a goblin: *Plait-il*, What is your will? said the goblin. The Famulus, somewhat struck, bade him fetch water: the swift goblin fetched it, pail in each hand; but lo, would not cease fetching it! Desperate, the Famulus shrieks at him, smites at him, cuts him in two; lo, *two* goblin watercarriers ply; and the house will be swum away in Deucalion Deluges.

CHAPTER IV
FATHERLAND IN DANGER

OR rather we will say, this Senatorial war might have lasted long; and Party tugging and throttling with Party might have suppressed and smothered one another, in the ordinary bloodless Parliamentary way; on one condition: that France had been at least able to exist, all the while. But this Sovereign People has a digestive faculty, and cannot do without bread Also we are at war, and must have victory; at war with Europe, with Fate and Famine: and behold, in the spring of the year, all victory deserts us.

Dumouriez had his outposts stretched as far as Aix-la-Chapelle, and the beautifullest plan for pouncing on Holland, by stratagem, flat-bottomed boats and rapid intrepidity; wherein too he had prospered so far; but unhappily could prosper no further. Aix-la-Chapelle is lost; Maestricht will not surrender to mere smoke and noise: the flat-bottomed boats must launch themselves again, and return the way they came. Steady now, ye rapidly intrepid men; retreat with firmness, Parthian-like! Alas, were it General Miranda's fault; were it the War-minister's fault; or were it Dumouriez's own fault and that of Fortune: enough, there is nothing for it but retreat,—well if it be not even flight; for already terror-stricken cohorts and stragglers pour off, not waiting for order; flow disastrous, as many as ten thousand of them, without halt till they see France again. Nay, worse: Dumouriez himself is perhaps secretly turning traitor? Very sharp is the tone in which he writes to our Committees. Commissioners and Jacobin Pillagers have done such incalculable mischief; Hassenfratz sends neither cartridges nor clothing; shoes we have, deceptively 'soled with wood and paste-board.' Nothing in short is right. Danton and Lacroix, when it was they that were Commissioners, would needs join Belgium to France;—of which Dumouriez might have made the prettiest little Duchy for his own secret behoof! With all these things the General is wroth; and writes to us in a sharp tone. Who knows what this hot little General is meditating? Dumouriez Duke of Belgium or Brabant; and say, Égalité the Younger King of France: there were an end for our Revolution!—Committee of Defence gazes, and shakes its head: who except Danton, defective in suspicion, could still struggle to be of hope?

And General Custine is rolling back from the Rhine Country; conquered Mentz will be reconquered, the Prussians gathering round to bombard it with shot and shell. Mentz may resist, Commissioner Merlin, the Thionviller, 'making sallies, at the head of the besieged;'—resist to the death; but not longer than that. How sad a reverse for Mentz!

Brave Forster, brave Lux planted Liberty-trees, amid *ça-ira*-ing music, in the snow-slush of last winter, there; and made Jacobin Societies; and got the Territory incorporated with France; they came hither to Paris, as Deputies or Delegates, and have their eighteen francs a-day: but see, before once the Liberty-tree is got rightly in leaf, Mentz is changing into an explosive crater; vomiting fire, bevomited with fire!

Neither of these men shall again see Mentz; they have come hither only to die. Forster has been round the Globe; he saw Cook perish under Owyhee clubs; but like this Paris he has yet seen or suffered nothing. Poverty escorts him: from home there can nothing come, except Job's-news; the eighteen daily francs, which we here as Deputy or Delegate with difficulty 'touch,' are in paper *assignats*, and sink fast in value. Poverty, disappointment, inaction, obloquy; the brave heart slowly breaking! Such is Forster's lot. For the rest, Demoiselle Théroigne smiles on you in the Soirées; 'a beautiful brownlocked face,' of an exalted temper; and contrives to keep her carriage. Prussian Trenck, the poor subterranean Baron, jargons and jangles in an unmelodious manner. Thomas Paine's face is red-pustuled, 'but the eyes uncommonly bright.' Convention Deputies ask you to dinner: very courteous; and 'we all play at *plumpsack*.' 'It is the Explosion and New-creation of a World,' says Forster; 'and the actors in it, such small mean objects, buzzing round one like a handful of flies.'—

Likewise there is war with Spain. Spain will advance through the gorges of the Pyrenees; rustling with Bourbon banners, jingling with artillery and menace. And England has donned the red coat; and marches, with Royal Highness of York,—whom some once spake of inviting to be our King. Changed that humour now: and ever more changing; till no hatefuller thing walk this Earth than a denizen of that tyrannous Island; and Pitt be declared and decreed, with effervescence, '*L'ennemi du genre humain,* The enemy of mankind;' and, very singular to say, you make order that no Soldier of Liberty give quarter to an Englishman. Which order, however, the Soldier of Liberty does but partially obey. We will take no Prisoners then, say the Soldiers of Liberty; they shall all be 'Deserters' that we take. It is a frantic order; and attended with inconvenience. For surely, if you give no quarter, the plain issue is that you will get none; and so the business become as broad as it was long.—Our

'recruitment of Three-hundred Thousand men,' which was the
decreed force for this year, is like to have work enough laid to
its hand.

So many enemies come wending on; penetrating through
throats of mountains, steering over the salt sea; towards al
points of our territory; rattling chains at us. Nay, worst o
all: there is an enemy within our own territory itself. In
the early days of March, the Nantes Postbags do not arrive
there arrive only instead of them Conjecture, Apprehension
bodeful wind of Rumour. The bodefullest proves true
Those fanatic Peoples of La Vendée will no longer keep
under: their fire of insurrection, heretofore dissipated with
difficulty, blazes out anew, after the King's Death, as a wide
conflagration; not riot, but civil war. Your Cathelineaus
your Stofflets, Charettes, are other men than was thought
behold how their Peasants, in mere russet and hodden, with
their rude arms, rude array, with their fanatic Gaelic frenzy
and wild-yelling battle-cry of *God and the King*, dash at us like
a dark whirlwind; and blow the best-disciplined Nationals we
can get into panic and *sauve-qui-peut!* Field after field is
theirs; one sees not where it will end. Commandant Santerre
may be sent there; but with non-effect; he might as well have
returned and brewed beer.

It has become peremptorily necessary that a National Con
vention cease arguing, and begin acting. Yield one party o
you to the other, and do it swiftly. No theoretic outlook is
here, but the close certainty of ruin; the very day that is
passing over us must be provided for.

It was Friday the Eighth of March when this Job's-post
from Dumouriez, thickly preceded and escorted by so many
other Job's-posts, reached the National Convention. Blank
enough are most faces. Little will it avail whether our Sep
temberers be punished or go unpunished; if Pitt and Cobourg
are coming in, with one punishment for us all; nothing now
between Paris itself and the Tyrants but a doubtful Dumouriez,
and hosts in loose-flowing loud retreat!—Danton the Titan
rises in this hour, as always in the hour of need. Great is his
voice, reverberating from the domes:—Citizen-Representatives,
shall we not, in such crisis of Fate, lay aside discords? Re
putation: O what is the reputation of this man or of that?
"*Que mon nom soit flétri; que la France soit libre:* Let my
name be blighted; let France be free!" It is necessary now

again that France rise, in swift vengeance, with her million
right-hands, with her heart as of one man. Instantaneous
recruitment in Paris; let every Section of Paris furnish its
thousands; every Section of France! Ninety-six Commissioners of us, two for each Section of the Forty-eight, they
must go forthwith, and tell Paris what the Country needs of
her. Let Eighty more of us be sent, post haste, over France;
to spread the fire-cross, to call forth the might of men. Let
the Eighty also be on the road, before this sitting rise. Let
them go, and think what their errand is. Speedy Camp of
Fifty-thousand between Paris and the North Frontier; for
Paris will pour forth her volunteers! Shoulder to shoulder;
one strong universal death-defiant rising and rushing; we shall
hurl back these Sons of Night yet again; and France, in spite
of the world, be free!—So sounds the Titan's voice: into all
Section-houses; into all French hearts. Sections sit in Permanence, for recruitment, enrolment, that very night. Convention Commissioners, on swift wheels, are carrying the fire-
cross from Town to Town, till all France blaze.

And so there is Flag of *Fatherland in Danger* waving from
the Townhall, Black Flag from the top of Notre-Dame Cathedral; there is Proclamation, hot eloquence; Paris rushing out
once again to strike its enemies down. That, in such circumstances, Paris was in no mild humour can be conjectured.
Agitated streets; still more agitated round the Salle de
Manége! Feuillans-Terrace crowds itself with angry Citizens,
angrier Citizenesses; Varlet perambulates with portable chair:
ejaculations of no measured kind, as to perfidious fine-spoken
Hommes d'état, friends of Dumouriez, secret-friends of Pitt
and Cobourg, burst from the hearts and lips of men. To
fight the enemy? Yes, and even to 'freeze him with terror,
glacer d'effroi:' but first to have domestic Traitors punished!
Who are they that, carping and quarrelling, in their jesuitic
most *moderate* way, seek to shackle the Patriotic movement?
That divide France against Paris, and poison public opinion
in the Departments? That when we ask for bread, and a
Maximum fixed-price, treat us with lectures on Free-trade in
grains? Can the human stomach satisfy itself with lectures
on Free-Trade; and are we to fight the Austrians in a moderate
manner, or in an immoderate? This Convention must be
purged.

"Set up a swift Tribunal for Traitors, a Maximum for
Grains:" thus speak with energy the Patriot Volunteers, as

they defile through the Convention Hall, just on the wing
to the Frontiers ;—perorating in that heroical Cambyses' vein
of theirs : beshouted by the Galleries and Mountain ; be
murmured by the Right-side and Plain. Nor are prodigies
wanting : lo, while a Captain of the Section Poissonnière
perorates with vehemence about Dumouriez, Maximum and
Crypto-Royalist Traitors, and his troop beat chorus with him
waving their Banner overhead, the eye of a Deputy discerns
in this same Banner, that the *cravates* or streamers of it have
Royal fleurs-de-lys ! The Section-Captain shrieks ; his troop
shriek, horrorstruck, and 'trample the Banner under foot :
seemingly the work of some Crypto-Royalist Plotter? Most
probable :—or perhaps at bottom, only the *old* Banner of the
Section, manufactured prior to the Tenth of August, when
such streamers were according to rule !

History, looking over the Girondin Memoirs, anxious to
disentangle the truth of them from the hysterics, finds these
days of March, especially this Sunday the Tenth of March,
play a great part. Plots, plots ; a plot for murdering the
Girondin Deputies ; Anarchists and Secret-Royalists plotting
in hellish concert, for that end ! The far greater part of which
is hysterics. What we do find indisputable is, that Louvet
and certain Girondins were apprehensive they might be
murdered on Saturday, and did not go to the evening sitting,
but held council with one another, each inciting his fellow to
do something resolute, and end these Anarchists : to which,
however, Pétion, opening the window, and finding the night
very wet, answered only, "*Ils ne feront rien,*" and 'composedly
resumed his violin,' says Louvet ; thereby, with soft Lydian
tweedledeeing, to wrap himself against eating cares. Also
that Louvet felt especially liable to being killed ; that several
Girondins went abroad to seek beds : liable to being killed ;
but were not. Further that, in very truth, Journalist Deputy
Gorsas, poisoner of the Departments, he and his Printer had
their houses broken into (by a tumult of Patriots, among
whom redcapped Varlet, American Fournier loom forth, in the
darkness of the rain and riot) ; had their wives put in fear ;
their presses, types and circumjacent equipments beaten to
ruin ; no Mayor interfering in time ; Gorsas himself escaping,
pistol in hand, 'along the coping of the back wall.' Further
that Sunday, the morrow, was not a work-day ; and the streets
were more agitated than ever : Is it a new September, then,

that these Anarchists intend? Finally, that no September came;—and also that hysterics, not unnaturally, had reached almost their acme.

Vergniaud denounces and deplores; in sweetly turned periods. Section Bonconseil, *Good-counsel* so-named, not Mauconseil or *Ill-counsel* as it once was,—does a far notabler thing; demands that Vergniaud, Brissot, Guadet, and other denunciatory fine-spoken Girondins, to the number of Twenty-two, be put under arrest! Section Good-counsel, so named ever since the Tenth of August, is sharply rebuked, like a section of Ill-Counsel: but its word is spoken, and will not fall to the ground.

In fact, one thing strikes us in these poor Girondins; their fatal shortness of vision; nay fatal poorness of character, for that is the root of it. They are as strangers to the People they would govern; to the thing they have come to work in. Formulas, Philosophies, Respectabilities, what has been written in Books, and admitted by the Cultivated Classes: *this* inadequate *Scheme* of Nature's working is all that Nature, let her work as she will, can reveal to these men. So they perorate and speculate; and call on the Friends of Law, when the question is not Law or No-Law, but Life or No-Life. Pedants of the Revolution, if not Jesuits of it! Their Formalism is great; great also is their Egoism. France rising to fight Austria has been raised only by plot of the Tenth of March, to kill Twenty-two of *them!* This Revolution Prodigy, unfolding itself into terrific stature and articulation, by its own laws and Nature's, not by the laws of Formula, has become unintelligible, incredible as an impossibility, 'the waste chaos of a Dream.' A Republic founded on what they call the Virtues; on what we call the Decencies and Respectabilities; this they will have, and nothing but this. Whatsoever other Republic Nature and Reality send, shall be considered as not sent; as a kind of Nightmare Vision, and thing non-extant; disowned by the Laws of Nature, and of Formula. Alas! dim for the best eyes is this Reality; and as for these men, they will not look at it with eyes at all, but only through 'facetted spectacles' of Pedantry, wounded Vanity; which yield the most portentous fallacious spectrum. Carping and complaining forever of Plots and Anarchy, they will do one thing; prove, to demonstration, that the Reality will not translate into their Formula; that they and their Formula are incompatible with the Reality: and, in its dark wrath the

Reality will extinguish it and them! What a man *kens* he *cans.* But the beginning of a man's doom is, that vision be withdrawn from him; that he sees not the reality, but a false spectrum of the reality; and following that, step darkly, with more or less velocity, downwards to the utter Dark; to Ruin, which is the great Sea of Darkness, whither all falsehoods, winding or direct, continually flow!

This Tenth of March we may mark as an epoch in the Girondin destinies the rage so exasperated itself, the misconception so darkened itself. Many desert the sittings; many come to them armed. An honourable Deputy, setting out after breakfast, must now, besides taking his Notes, see whether his Priming is in order.

Meanwhile with Dumouriez in Belgium it fares ever worse. Were it again General Miranda's fault, or some other's fault, there is no doubt whatever but the 'Battle of Nerwinden,' on the 18th of March, is lost; and our rapid retreat has become a far too rapid one. Victorious Cobourg, with his Austrian prickers, hangs like a dark cloud on the rear of us: Dumouriez never off horseback night or day; engagement every three hours; our whole discomfited Host rolling rapidly inwards, full of rage, suspicion and *sauve-qui-peut!* And then Dumouriez himself, what his intents may be? Wicked seemingly and not charitable! His despatches to Committee openly denounce a factious Convention, for the woes it has brought on France and him. And his speeches—for the General has no reticence! The execution of the Tyrant this Dumouriez calls the Murder of the King. Danton and Lacroix, flying thither as Commissioners once more, return very doubtful; even Danton now doubts.

Three Jacobin Missionaries, Proly, Dubuisson, Pereyra, have flown forth; sped by a wakeful Mother Society: they are struck dumb to hear the General speak. The Convention, according to this General, consists of three-hundred scoundrels and four-hundred imbeciles: France cannot do without a King. "But we have executed our King." "And what is it to me," hastily cries Dumouriez, a General of no reticence, "whether the King's name be *Ludovicus* or *Jacobus?*" "Or *Philippus!*" rejoins Proly;—and hastens to report progress. Over the Frontiers such hope is there.

CHAPTER V

SANSCULOTTISM ACCOUTRED

LET us look, however, at the grand international Sansculottism and Revolution Prodigy, whether it stirs and waxes: there and not elsewhere may hope still be for France. The Revolution Prodigy, as Decree after Decree issues from the Mountain, like creative *fiats*, accordant with the nature of the Thing,—is shaping itself rapidly, in these days, into terrific stature and articulation, limb after limb. Last March, 1792, we saw all France flowing in blind terror; shutting town-barriers, boiling pitch for Brigands: happier, this March, that it is a seeing terror; that a creative Mountain exists, which can say *fiat*! Recruitment proceeds with fierce celerity: nevertheless our Volunteers hesitate to set out, till Treason be punished at home; they do not fly to the frontiers; but only fly hither and thither, demanding and denouncing. The Mountain must speak new *fiat*, and new *fiats*.

And does it not speak such? Take, as first example, those *Comités Révolutionnaires* for the arrestment of Persons Suspect. Revolutionary Committee, of Twelve chosen Patriots, sits in every Township of France; examining the Suspect, seeking arms, making domiciliary visits and arrestments;—caring, generally, that the Republic suffer no detriment. Chosen by universal suffrage, each in its Section, they are a kind of elixir of Jacobinism; some Forty-four Thousand of them awake and alive over France! In Paris and all Towns, every house-door must have the names of the inmates legibly printed on it, 'at a height not exceeding five feet from the ground;' every Citizen must produce his certificatory *Carte de Civisme*, signed by Section-President; every man be ready to give account of the faith that is in him. Persons Suspect had as well depart this soil of Liberty! And yet departure too is bad: all Emigrants are declared Traitors, their property become National; they are 'dead in Law,'—save indeed that for *our* behoof they shall 'live yet fifty years in Law,' and what heritages may fall to them in that time become National too! A mad vitality of Jacobinism, with Forty-four Thousand centres of activity, circulates through all fibres of France.

Very notable also is the *Tribunal Extraordinaire :* decreed by the Mountain; some Girondins dissenting, for surely such a Court contradicts every formula;—other Girondins assent-

ing, nay co-operating, for do not we all hate Traitors, O ye
people of Paris?—Tribunal of the Seventeenth, in Autumn
last, was swift (pp. 127, 136); but this shall be swifter.   Five
Judges; a standing Jury, which is named from Paris and the
Neighbourhood, that there be not delay in naming it: they
are subject to no Appeal; to hardly any Law-forms, but must
'get themselves convinced' in all readiest ways; and for
security are bound 'to vote audibly;' audibly, in the hearing
of a Paris Public.   This is the *Tribunal Extraordinaire;*
which, in few months, getting into most lively action, shall
be entitled *Tribunal Révolutionnaire;* as indeed it from the
very first has entitled itself: with a Herman or a Dumas for
Judge President, with a Fouquier-Tinville for Attorney-
General, and a Jury of such as Citizen Leroi, who has sur-
named himself *Dix-Août,* 'Leroi *August-Tenth,*' it will become
the wonder of the world.   Herein has Sansculottism fashioned
for itself a Sword of Sharpness: a weapon magical; tempered
in the Stygian hell-waters; to the edge of it all armour, and
defence of strength or of cunning shall be soft; it shall mow
down Lives and Brazen-gates; and the waving of it shed terror
through the souls of men.

But speaking of an amorphous Sansculottism taking form,
ought we not, above all things, to specify how the Amorphous
gets itself a Head?   Without metaphor, this Revolution
Government continues hitherto in a very anarchic state.
Executive Council of Ministers, Six in number, there is: but
they, especially since Roland's retreat, have hardly known
whether they were Ministers or not.   Convention Committees
sit supreme over them; but then each Committee as supreme
as the others: Committee of Twenty-one, of Defence, of
General Surety; simultaneous or successive, for specific purposes.   The Convention alone is all-powerful,—especially if
the Commune go with it; but is too numerous for an adminis-
trative body.   Wherefore, in this perilous quick-whirling condition of the Republic, before the end of March we obtain
our small *Comité de Salut Public;* as it were, for miscellaneous
accidental purposes requiring despatch;—as it proves, for a
sort of universal supervision, and universal subjection.   They
are to report weekly, these new Committee-men; but to deliberate in secret.   Their number is Nine, firm Patriots all,
Danton one of them; renewable every month;—yet why not
re-elect them if they turn out well?   The flower of the matter
is, that they are but nine; that they sit in secret.   An insig-

nificant-looking thing at first, this Committee; but with a principle of growth in it! Forwarded by fortune, by internal Jacobin energy, it will reduce all Committees and the Convention itself to mute obedience, the Six Ministers to Six assiduous Clerks; and work its will on the Earth and under Heaven, for a season. A 'Committee of Public Salvation,' whereat the world still shrieks and shudders.

If we call that Revolutionary Tribunal a Sword, which Sansculottism has provided for itself, then let us call the 'Law of the Maximum,' a Provender-scrip, or Haversack, wherein, better or worse, some ration of bread may be found. It is true, Political Economy, Girondin free-trade, and all law of supply and demand, are hereby hurled topsyturvy: but what help? Patriotism must live; the 'cupidity of farmers' seems to have no bowels. Wherefore this Law of the Maximum, fixing the highest price of grains, is, with infinite effort, got passed; and shall gradually extend itself into a Maximum for all manner of *comestibles* and commodities: with such scrambling and topsyturvying as may be fancied! For now, if, for example, the farmer will not sell? The farmer shall be forced to sell. An accurate Account of what grain he has shall be delivered in to the Constituted Authorities: let him see that he say not too much; for in that case, his rents, taxes and contributions will rise proportionally: let him see that he say not too little; for, on or before a set day, we shall suppose in April, *less* than one-third of this declared quantity must remain in his barns, more than two-thirds of it must have been thrashed and sold. One can denounce him, and raise penalties.

By such inextricable overturning of all Commercial relations will Sansculottism keep life in; since not otherwise. On the whole, as Camille Desmoulins says once, "while the Sansculottes fight, the Monsieurs must pay." So there come *Impôts Progressifs*, Ascending taxes; which consume, with fast-increasing voracity, the 'superfluous-revenue' of men: beyond fifty-pounds a-year, you are not exempt; rising into the hundreds, you bleed freely; into the thousands and tens of thousands, you bleed gushing. Also there come Requisitions; there comes 'Forced Loan of a Milliard,' some Fifty-Millions Sterling; which of course they that *have* must lend. Unexampled enough; it has grown to be no country for the Rich, this; but a country for the Poor? And then if one fly, what steads it? Dead in Law; nay kept alive fifty years yet, for *their* accursed behoof! In this manner therefore it goes; topsyturvying, *ça-ira*-ing;—and withal there is endless sale of Emigrant National-Property, there is Cambon with endless cornucopia of Assignats. The Trade and Finance of Sansculottism; and how, with Maximum and Bakers'-queues, with Cupidity, Hunger, Denunciation and Paper-money, it led its galvanic-life, and began and ended,— remains the most interesting of all Chapters in Political Economy: still to be written.

All which things, are they not clean against Formula? O Girondin Friends, it is not a Republic of the virtues we are getting; but only a Republic of the Strengths, virtuous and other!

CHAPTER VI

THE TRAITOR

BUT Dumouriez, with his fugitive Host, with his King *Ludovicus* or King *Philippus?* There lies the crisis; there hangs the question: Revolution Prodigy, or Counter-Revolution?—One wide shriek covers that North-east region. Soldiers, full of rage, suspicion and terror, flock hither and thither; Dumouriez, the many counselled, never off horseback, knows now no counsel that were not worse than none: the counsel, namely of joining himself with Cobourg; marching to Paris, extinguishing Jacobinism, and, with some new King Ludovicus or King Philippus, restoring the Constitution of 1791!

Is Wisdom quitting Dumouriez; the herald of Fortune quitting him? Principle, faith, political or other, beyond a certain faith of mess-rooms, and honour of an officer, had him not to quit. At any rate his quarters in the Burgh of Saint-Amand; his head-quarters in the Village of Saint-Amand des Boues, a short way off,—have become a Bedlam. National Representatives, Jacobin Missionaries are riding and running; of the 'three Towns,' Lille, Valenciennes or even Condé, which Dumouriez wanted to snatch for himself, not one can be snatched; your Captain is admitted, but the Town-gate is closed on him, and then alas the Prison-gate, and 'his men wander about the ramparts.' Couriers gallop breathless; men wait, or seem waiting, to assassinate, to be assassinated; Battalions nigh frantic with such suspicion and uncertainty, with *Vive-la-République* and *Sauve-qui-peut*, rush this way and that;—Ruin and Desperation in the shape of Cobourg lying entrenched close by.

Dame Genlis and her fair Princess d'Orléans find this Burgh of Saint-Amand no fit place for them; Dumouriez's protection is grown worse than none. Tough Genlis, one of the toughest women; a woman, as it were, with nine lives in her; whom nothing will beat: she packs her bandboxes; clear for flight in a private manner. Her beloved Princess she will—leave here, with the Prince Chartres Égalité her Brother. In the cold gray of the April morning, we find her accordingly established in her hired vehicle, on the street of Saint-Amand; postilions just cracking their whips to go,—when behold the young Princely Brother, struggling hitherward, hastily calling; bearing the Princess in his arms! Hastily he has clutched the poor young lady up, in her very night-gown, nothing saved of her goods except the watch from the pillow: with brotherly despair he flings her in, among the bandboxes, into Genlis's chaise, into Genlis's arms: Leave her not, in the name of Mercy and Heaven! A shrill scene, but a brief one:—the postilions crack and go. Ah, whither? Through by-roads and broken hill-passes; seeking their way with lanterns after nightfall; through perils, and Cobourg Austrians, and suspicious French Nationals: finally, into Switzerland; safe though nigh moneyless. The brave young Égalité has a most wild Morrow to look for; but now only himself to carry through it.

For indeed over at that Village named *of the Mudbaths*, Saint-Amand des Boues, matters are still worse. About four o'clock on Tuesday afternoon, the 2d of April 1793, two Couriers come galloping as if for life; *Mon Général!* Four National Representatives, War-Minister at their head, are posting hitherward from Valenciennes; are close at hand,— with what intents one may guess! While the Couriers are yet speaking, War-Minster and National Representatives, old Camus the Archivist for chief speaker of them, arrive. Hardly has *Mon Général* had time to order out the Hussar Regiment de Berchigny; that it take rank and wait near by, in case of accident. And so, enter War-Minister Beurnonville, with an embrace of friendship, for he is an old friend; enter Archivist Camus and the other three following him.

They produce Papers, invite the General to the bar of the Convention: merely to give an explanation or two. The

General finds it unsuitable, not to say impossible, and that
" the service will suffer." Then comes reasoning; the voice
of the old Archivist getting loud. Vain to reason loud with
this Dumouriez; he answers mere angry irreverences. And
so, amid plumed staff-officers, very gloomy-looking; in jeopardy
and uncertainty, these poor National messengers debate and
consult, retire and re-enter, for the space of some two hours:
without effect. Whereupon Archivist Camus, getting quite
loud, proclaims, in the name of the National Convention, for
he has the power to do it, That General Dumouriez is
arrested: "Will you obey the National mandate, General!"—
"*Pas dans ce moment-ci,* Not at this particular moment,"
answers the General also aloud; then glancing the other way,
utters certain unknown vocables, in a mandatory manner;
seemingly a German word-of-command. Hussars clutch the
Four National Representatives, and Beurnonville the War-
Minister! pack them out of the apartment; out of the
Village, over the lines to Cobourg, in two chaises that very
night,—as hostages, prisoners; to lie long in Maestricht and
Austrian strongholds! *Jacta est alea.*

This night Dumouriez prints his 'Proclamation;' this night
and the morrow the Dumouriez Army, in such darkness
visible, and rage of semi-desperation as there is, shall meditate
what the General is doing, what they themselves will do in it.
Judge whether this Wednesday was of halcyon nature, for any
one! But on the Thursday morning, we discern Dumouriez
with small escort, with Chartres Egalité and a few staff-
officers, ambling along the Condé Highway: perhaps they are
for Condé, and trying to persuade the Garrison there; at all
events, they are for an interview with Cobourg, who waits in
the woods by appointment, in that quarter. Nigh the Village
of Doumet, three National Battalions, a set of men always
full of Jacobinism, sweep past us; marching rather swiftly,—
seemingly in mistake, by a way we had not ordered. The
General dismounts, steps into a cottage, a little from the wayside; will give them right order in writing. Hark! what
strange growling is heard; what barkings are heard, loud yells
of "*Traitors,*" of "*Arrest:*" the National Battalions have
wheeled round, are emitting shot! Mount, Dumouriez, and
spring for life! Dumouriez and Staff strike the spurs in,
deep; vault over ditches, into the fields, which prove to
be morasses; sprawl and plunge for life; bewhistled with
curses and lead. Sunk to the middle, with or without horses,

several servants killed, they escape out of shot-range, to General Mack the Austrian's quarters. Nay they return on the morrow, to Saint-Amand and faithful foreign Berchigny; but what boots it? The Artillery has all revolted, is jingling off to Valenciennes; all have revolted, are revolting; except only foreign Berchigny, to the extent of some poor fifteen hundred, none will follow Dumouriez against France and Indivisible Republic: Dumouriez's occupation's gone.

Such an instinct of Frenchhood and Sansculottism dwells in these men: they will follow no Dumouriez nor Lafayette, nor any mortal on such errand. Shriek may be of *Sauve-qui-peut*, but will also be of *Vive-la-République*. New National Representatives arrive; new General Dampierre, soon killed in battle; new General Custine: the agitated Hosts draw back to some Camp of Famars; make head against Cobourg as they can.

And so Dumouriez is in the Austrian quarters; his drama ended, in this rather sorry manner. A most shifty, wiry man; one of Heaven's Swiss; that wanted only work. Fifty years of unnoticed toil and valour; one year of toil and valour, not unnoticed, but seen of all countries and centuries; then thirty other years again unnoticed, of Memoir-writing, English Pension, scheming and projecting to no purpose: Adieu thou Swiss of Heaven, worthy to have been something else!

His Staff go different ways. Brave young Égalité reaches Switzerland and the Genlis Cottage; with a strong crabstick in his hand, a strong heart in his body: his Princedom is now reduced to that. Égalité the Father sat playing whist, in his Palais Égalité, at Paris, on the 6th day of this same month of April, when a catchpole entered: Citoyen Égalité is wanted at the Convention Committee! Examination, requiring Arrestment; finally requiring Imprisonment, transference to Marseilles and the Castle of If! Orleansdom has sunk in the black waters; Palais Égalité, which was Palais Royal, is like to become Palais National.

CHAPTER VII

IN FIGHT

OUR Republic, by paper Decree, may be 'One and Indivisible;' but what profits it while these things are? Federalists in the Senate, renegadoes in the Army, traitors everywhere! France, all in desperate recruitment since the Tenth of March, does not fly to the frontier, but only flies hither and thither. This defection of contemptuous diplomatic Dumouriez falls heavy on the fine-spoken high-sniffing *Hommes d'état* whom he consorted with; forms a second epoch in their destinies.

Or perhaps more strictly we might say, the second Girondin epoch, though little noticed then, began on the day when, in reference to this defection, the Girondins broke with Danton. It was the first day of April; Dumouriez had not yet plunged across the morasses to Cobourg, but was evidently meaning to do it, and our Commissioners were off to arrest him; when what does the Girondin Lasource see good to do, but rise, and jesuitically question and insinuate at great length, whether a main accomplice of Dumouriez had not probably been— Danton! Gironde grins sardonic assent; Mountain holds its breath. The figure of Danton, Levasseur says, while this speech went on, was noteworthy. He sat erect with a kind of internal convulsion struggling to keep itself motionless; his eye from time to time flashing wilder, his lip curling in Titanic scorn. Lasource, in a fine-spoken attorney-manner, proceeds: there is this probability to his mind, and there is that; probabilities which press painfully on him, which cast the Patriotism of Danton under a painful shade;—which painful shade, he, Lasource, will hope that Danton may find it not impossible to dispel.

"*Les Scélérats!*" cries Danton, starting up, with clenched right hand, Lasource having done; and descends from the Mountain, like a lava-flood: his answer not unready. Lasource's probabilities fly like idle dust, but leave a result behind them. "Ye were right, friends of the Mountain," begins Danton, "and I was wrong: there is no peace possible with these men. Let it be war then! They will not save the Republic with us: it shall be saved without them; saved in spite of them." Really a burst of rude Parliamentary eloquence this; which is still worth reading, in the old *Moniteur*. With fire-words the exasperated rude Titan rives and smites these Girondins; at every hit the glad Mountain utters chorus! Marat, like a musical *bis*, repeating the last phrase. Lasource's probabilities are gone; but Danton's pledge of battle remains lying.

A third epoch, or scene in the Girondin Drama, or rather it

is but the completion of this second epoch, we reckon from the day when the patience of virtuous Pétion finally boiled over; and the Girondins, so to speak, took up this battle pledge of Danton's, and decreed Marat accused. It was the eleventh of the same month of April, on some effervescence rising, such as often rose; and President had covered himself, mere Bedlam now ruling; and Mountain and Gironde were rushing on one another with clenched right-hands, and even with pistols in them; when, behold, the Girondin Duperret drew a sword! Shriek of horror rose, instantly quenching all other effervescence, at sight of the clear murderous steel; whereupon Duperret returned it to the leather again;—confessing that he did indeed draw it, being instigated by a kind of sacred madness, "*sainte fureur*," and pistols held at him; but that if he parricidally had chanced to scratch the outmost skin of National Representation with it, he too carried pistols, and would have blown his brains out on the spot.

But now in such posture of affairs, virtuous Pétion rose, next morning, to lament these effervescences, this endless Anarchy invading the Legislative Sanctuary itself; and here, being growled at and howled at by the Mountain, his patience, long tried, did as we say, boil over; and he spake vehemently, in high key, with foam on his lips; "whence," says Marat, "I concluded he had got *la rage*," the rabidity, or dog-madness. Rabidity smites others rabid: so there rises new foam-lipped demand to have Anarchists extinguished; and specially to have Marat put under Accusation. Send a representative to the Revolutionary Tribunal? Violate the inviolability of a Representative? Have a care, O Friends! This poor Marat has faults enough; but against Liberty or Equality, what Fault? That he has loved and fought for it, not wisely but too well. In dungeons and cellars, in pinching poverty, under anathema of men; even so, in such fight, has he grown so dingy, bleared; even so has his head become a Stylites one! Him you will fling to your Sword of Sharpness; while Cobourg and Pitt advance on us, fire-spitting?

The Mountain is loud, the Gironde is loud and deaf; all lips are foamy. With 'Permanent-Session of twenty-four hours,' with vote by rollcall, and a deadlift effort, the Gironde carries it: Marat is ordered to the Revolutionary Tribunal, to answer for that February Paragraph of Forestallers at the door-lintel (p. 225), with other offences; and, after a little hesitation, he obeys.

Thus is Danton's battle-pledge taken up; there is, as he said there would be, 'war without truce or treaty, *ni trève ni composition.*' Wherefore, close now with one another, Formula and Reality, in death-grips, and wrestle it out; both of you cannot live, but only one!

CHAPTER VIII

IN DEATH-GRIPS

IT proves what strength, were it only of inertia, there is in established Formulas, what weakness in nascent Realities, and illustrates several things, that this death-wrestle should still have lasted some six weeks or more. National business, discussion of the Constitutional Act, for our Constitution should decidedly be got ready, proceeds along with it. We even change our Locality; we shift, on the Tenth of May, from the old Salle de Manége into our new Hall, in the Palace, once a King's but now the Republic's, of the Tuileries. Hope and ruth, flickering against despair and rage, still struggle in the minds of men.

It is a most dark confused death-wrestle, this of the six weeks. Formalist frenzy against Realist frenzy; Patriotism, Egoism, Pride, Anger, Vanity, Hope and Despair, all raised to the frenetic pitch: Frenzy meets Frenzy, like dark clashing whirlwinds; neither understands the other; the weaker, one day, will understand that *it* is verily swept down! Girondism is strong as established Formula and Respectability: do not as many as Seventy-two of the Departments, or say respectable Heads of Departments, declare for us? Calvados, which loves its Buzot, will even rise in revolt, so hint the Addresses; Marseilles, cradle of Patriotism, will rise; Bordeaux will rise, and the Gironde Department, as one man; in a word, who will *not* rise, were our *Représentation Nationale* to be insulted, or one hair of a Deputy's head harmed! The Mountain, again, is strong as Reality and Audacity. To the Reality of the Mountain are not all furthersome things possible? A new Tenth of August, if needful; nay a new Second of September!—

But, on Wednesday afternoon, Twenty-fourth day of April, year 1793, what tumult as of fierce jubilee is this? It is Marat returning from the Revolutionary Tribunal! A week

or more of death-peril: and now there is triumphant acquittal;
Revolutionary Tribunal can find no accusation against this
man. And so the eye of History beholds Patriotism, which
had gloomed unutterable things all week, break into loud
jubilee, embrace its Marat; lift him into a chair of triumph,
bear him shoulder-high through the streets. Shoulder-high is
the injured People's-friend, crowned with an oak-garland;
amid the wavy sea of red nightcaps, carmagnole jackets,
grenadier bonnets and female mobcaps; far sounding like a
sea! The injured People's-friend has here reached his
culminating point; he too strikes the stars with his sublime
head.

But the Reader can judge with what face President Lasource, he of the 'painful probabilities,' who presides in this
Convention Hall, might welcome such jubilee-tide, when it got
thither, and the Decreed of Accusation floating on the top of
it! A National Sapper, spokesman on the occasion, says, the
People know their Friend, and love his life as their own;
"whosoever wants Marat's head must get the Sapper's first."
Lasource answered with some vague painful mumblement,—
which, says Levasseur, one could not help tittering at. Patriot
Sections, Volunteers not yet gone to the Frontiers, come
demanding the "purgation of traitors from your own bosom;"
the expulsion, or even the trial and sentence, of a factious
Twenty-two.

Nevertheless the Gironde has got its Commission of
Twelve; a Commission specially appointed for investigating
these troubles of the Legislative Sanctuary: let Sansculottism
say what it will, Law shall triumph. Old-Constituent Rabaut
Saint-Étienne presides over this Commission: "it is the last
plank whereon a wrecked Republic may perhaps still save
herself." Rabaut and they therefore sit, intent; examining
witnesses; launching arrestments; looking out into a waste
dim sea of troubles,—the womb of *Formula*, or perhaps her
grave! Enter not that sea, O Reader! There are dim
desolation and confusion; raging women and raging men.
Sections come demanding Twenty-two; for the *number* first
given by Section Bonconseil still holds, though the names
should even vary. Other Sections, of the wealthier kind,
come denouncing such demand; nay the same Section will
demand today, and denounce the demand tomorrow, according as the wealthier sit, or the poorer. Wherefore, indeed,
the Girondins decree that all Sections shall close 'at ten in

the evening;' before the working people come : which Decree remains without effect. And nightly the Mother of Patriotism wails doleful; doleful, but her eye kindling! And Fournier l'Américain is busy, and the two banker Freys, and Varlet Apostle of Liberty; the bull-voice of Marquis St.-Huruge is heard. And shrill women vociferate from all Galleries, the Convention ones and downwards. Nay a 'Central Committee' of all the Forty-eight Sections looms forth huge and dubious; sitting dim in the *Archevêché*, sending Resolutions, receiving them : a Centre of the Sections; in dread deliberation as to a New Tenth of August!

One thing we will specify, to throw light on many : the aspect under which, seen through the eyes of these Girondin Twelve, or even seen through one's own eyes, the Patriotism of the softer sex presents itself. There are Female Patriots, whom the Girondins call Megæras, and count to the extent of eight thousand; with serpent-hair, all out of curl; who have changed the distaff for the dagger. They are of 'the Society called Brotherly, *Fraternelle*, say *Sisterly*, which meets under the roof of the Jacobins. 'Two thousand daggers,' or *so*, have been ordered,—doubtless for them. They rush to Versailles, to raise more women; but the Versailles women will not rise.

Nay behold, in National Garden of Tuileries,—Demoiselle Théroigne herself is become as a brownlocked Diana (were that possible) attacked by her own dogs, or she-dogs! The Demoiselle, keeping her carriage, is for Liberty indeed, as she has full well shown; but then for Liberty with Respectability : whereupon these serpent-haired Extreme She-Patriots do now fasten on her, tatter her, shamefully fustigate her, in their shameful way; almost fling her into the Garden-ponds, had not help intervened. Help, alas, to small purpose. The poor Demoiselle's head and nervous-system, none of the soundest, is so tattered and fluttered that it will never recover; but flutter worse and worse, till it crack; and within year and day we hear of her in madhouse and straitwaistcoat, which proves permanent!—Such brownlocked Figure did flutter, and inarticulately jabber and gesticulate, little able to *speak* the obscure meaning it had, through some segment of the Eighteenth Century of Time. She disappears here from the Revolution and Public History forevermore.

Another thing we will not again specify, yet again beseech the Reader to imagine : the reign of Fraternity and Perfection.

Imagine, we say, O Reader, that the Millennium were struggling on the threshold, and yet not so much as groceries
could be had,—owing to traitors. With what impetus would
a man strike traitors, in that case! Ah, thou canst not
imagine it; thou hast thy groceries safe in the shops, and little
or no hope of a Millennium ever coming!—But indeed, as to
the temper there was in men and women, does not this one
fact say enough: the height SUSPICION had risen to? Preternatural we often called it; seemingly in the language of
exaggeration: but listen to the cold deposition of witnesses.
Not a musical Patriot can blow himself a snatch of melody
from the French Horn, sitting mildly pensive on the housetop,
but Mercier will recognise it to be a signal which one Plotting
Committee is making to another. Distraction has possessed
Harmony herself; lurks in the sound of *Marseillaise* and
Ça-ira. Louvet, who can see as deep into a millstone as the
most, discerns that we shall be invited back to our old Hall of
the Manége, by a Deputation; and then the Anarchists will
massacre Twenty-two of us, as we walk over. It is Pitt and
Cobourg; the gold of Pitt.—Poor Pitt! They little know
what work he has with his own Friends of the People; getting
them bespied, beheaded, their habeas-corpuses suspended,
and his own Social Order and strong-boxes kept tight,—to
fancy him raising mobs among his neighbours!

But the strangest fact connected with French or indeed with
human Suspicion, is perhaps this of Camille Desmoulins.
Camille's head, one of the clearest in France, has got itself so
saturated through every fibre with Preternaturalism of Suspicion, that looking back on that Twelfth of July 1789, when
the thousands rose round him, yelling responsive at his word
in the Palais-Royal Garden, and took cockades, he finds it
explicable only on this hypothesis, That they were all hired
to do it, and set on by the Foreign and other Plotters. "It
was not for nothing," says Camille with insight, "that this
multitude burst up round me when I spoke!" No, not for
nothing. Behind, around before, it is one huge Preternatural
Puppet-play of Plots; Pitt pulling the wires. Almost I conjecture that I, Camille myself, am a Plot, and wooden with
wires.—The force of insight could no furthur go.

Be this as it will, History remarks that the Commission of
Twelve, now clear enough as to the Plots; and luckily having
'got the threads of them all by the end,' as they say,—are

launching Mandates of Arrest rapidly in these May days; and carrying matters with a high hand; resolute that the sea of troubles shall be restrained. What chief Patriot, Section-President even, is safe? They can arrest him; tear him from his warm bed, because he has made irregular Section Arrestments! They arrest Varlet Apostle of Liberty. They arrest Procureur-Substitute Hébert, *Père Duchesne;* a Magistrate of the People, sitting in Townhall; who, with high solemnity of martyrdom, takes leave of his colleagues; prompt he, to obey the Law; and solemnly acquiescent, disappears into prison.

The swifter fly the Sections, energetically demanding him back; demanding not arrestment of Popular Magistrates, but of a traitorous Twenty-two. Section comes flying after Section;—defiling energetic, with their Cambyses-vein of oratory: nay the Commune itself comes, with Mayor Pache at its head; and with question not of Hébert and the Twenty-two alone, but with this ominous old question made new, "Can you save the Republic, or must we do it?" To whom President Max Isnard makes fiery answer: If by fatal chance, in any of those tumults which since the Tenth of March are ever returning, Paris were to lift a sacrilegious finger against the National Representation, France would rise as one man, in never-imagined vengeance, and shortly 'the traveller would ask, on which side of the Seine Paris had stood!' Whereat the Mountain bellows only louder, and every Gallery; Patriot Paris boiling round.

And Girondin Valazé has nightly conclaves at his house; sends billets, 'Come punctually, and well armed, for there is to be business.' And Megæra women perambulate the streets, with flags, with lamentable *alleleu*. And the Convention-doors are obstructed by roaring multitudes: fine-spoken *Hommes d'état* are hustled, maltreated, as they pass; Marat will apostrophise you, in such death-peril, and say, Thou too art of them. If Roland ask leave to quit Paris, there is order of the day. What help? Substitute Hébert, Apostle Varlet, must be given back; to be crowned with oak-garlands. The Commission of Twelve, in a Convention overwhelmed with roaring Sections, is broken; then on the morrow, in a Convention of rallied Girondins, is reinstated. Dim Chaos, or the sea of troubles, is struggling through all its elements; writhing and chafing towards some Creation.

CHAPTER IX

EXTINCT

Accordingly, on Friday, the Thirty-first of May 1793, there comes forth into the summer sunlight one of the strangest scenes. Mayor Pache with Municipality arrives at the Tuileries Hall of Convention; sent for, Paris being in visible ferment; and gives the strangest news.

How, in the gray of this morning, while we sat Permanent in Townhall, watchful for the commonweal, there entered, precisely as on a Tenth of August, some Ninety-six extraneous persons; who declared themselves to be in a state of Insurrection; to be plenipotentiary Commissioners from the Forty-eight Sections, sections or members of the Sovereign People, all in a state of Insurrection; and further that we, in the name of said Sovereign in Insurrection, were dismissed from office. How we thereupon laid off our sashes, and withdrew into the adjacent Saloon of Liberty. How, in a moment or two, we were called back; and reinstated; the Sovereign pleasing to think us still worthy of confidence. Whereby, having taken new oath of office, we on a sudden find ourselves Insurrectionary Magistrates, with extraneous Committee of Ninety-six sitting by us; and a Citoyen Henriot, one whom some accuse of Septemberism, is made Generalissimo of the National Guard; and, since six o'clock, the tocsins ring, and the drums beat:—Under which peculiar circumstances, what would an august National Convention please to direct us to do?

Yes, there is the question! "Break the Insurrectionary Authorities," answer some with vehemence. Vergniaud at least will have "the National Representatives all die at their post;" this is sworn to, with ready loud acclaim. But as to breaking the Insurrectionary Authorities,—alas, while we yet debate, what sound is that? Sound of the Alarm-Cannon on the Pont Neuf; which it is death by the Law to fire without order from us!

It does boom off there, nevertheless; sending a stound through all hearts. And the tocsins discourse stern music; and Henriot with his Armed Force has enveloped us! And Section succeeds Section, the livelong day; demanding with Cambyses-oratory, with the rattle of muskets, That traitors, Twenty-two or more, be punished; that the Commission of Twelve be irrecoverably broken. The heart of the Gironde dies within it; distant are the Seventy-two respectable Departments, this fiery Municipality is near! Barrère is for a middle course; granting something. The Commission of Twelve declares that, not waiting to be broken, it hereby breaks itself, and is no more. Fain would Reporter Rabaut speak his and its last-words; but he is bellowed off. Too happy that the Twenty-two are still left unviolated!—Vergniaud, carrying the laws of refinement to a great length, moves, to the amazement of some, that 'the Sections of Paris have deserved well of their country.' Whereupon, at a late hour of the evening, the deserving Sections retire to their respective places of abode. Barrère shall report on it. With busy quill and brain he sits, secluded; for him no sleep tonight. Friday the last of May has ended in this manner.

The Sections have deserved well: but ought they not to deserve better? Faction and Girondism is struck down for the moment, and consents to be a nullity; but will it not, at another favourabler moment rise, still feller; and the Republic have to be saved in spite of it? So reasons Patriotism, still Permanent; so reasons the Figure of Marat, visible in the dim Section-world, on the morrow. To the conviction of men!—And so at eventide of Saturday, when Barrère had just got the thing all varnished by the labour of a night and day, and his report was setting off in the evening mail-bags, tocsin peals out *again*. *Générale* is beating; armed men taking station in the Place Vendôme and elsewhere, for the night; supplied with provisions and liquor. There, under the summer stars, will they wait, this night, what is to be seen and to be done, Henriot and Townhall giving due signal.

The Convention, at sound of *générale*, hastens back to its Hall; but to the number only of a Hundred; and does little business, puts off business till the morrow. The Girondins do not stir out thither, the Girondins are abroad seeking beds.—Poor Rabaut, on the morrow morning, returning to his post, with Louvet and some others, through streets all in ferment, wrings his hands, ejaculating, "*Illa suprema dies !*" It has become Sunday, the second day of June, year 1793, by the old style; by the new style, year One of Liberty, Equality, Fraternity. We have got to the last scene of all, that ends this history of the Girondin Senatorship.

It seems doubtful whether any terrestrial Convention had ever met in such circumstances as this National one now does.

Tocsin is pealing; Barriers shut; all Paris is on the gaze, or under arms. As many as a Hundred Thousand under arms they count: National Force; and the Armed Volunteers, who should have flown to the Frontiers and La Vendée; but would not, treason being unpunished; and only flew hither and thither! So many, steady under arms, environ the National Tuileries and Garden. There are horse, foot, artillery, sappers with beards: the artillery one can see with their camp-furnaces in this National Garden, heating bullets red, and their match is lighted. Henriot in plumes rides, amid a plumed Staff: all posts and issues are safe; reserves lie out, as far as the Wood of Boulogne; the choicest Patriots nearest the scene. One other circumstance we will note: that a careful Municipality, liberal of camp-furnaces, has not forgotten provision-carts. No member of the Sovereign need now go home to dinner; but can keep rank,—plentiful victual circulating unsought. Does not this People understand Insurrection? Ye, *not* un-inventive, *Gualches!*—

Therefore let a National Representation, 'mandatories of the Sovereign,' take thought of it. Expulsion of your Twenty-two, and your Commission of Twelve: we stand here till it be done! Deputation after Deputation, in ever stronger language, comes with that message. Barrère proposes a middle course: —Will not perhaps the inculpated Deputies consent to with-draw voluntarily; to make a generous demission, and self-sacrifice for the sake of one's country? Isnard, repentant of that search on which river-bank Paris stood, declares himself ready to demit. Ready also is *Te-Deum* Fauchet; old Dusaulx of the Bastille, '*vieux radoteur*, old dotard,' as Marat calls him, is still readier. On the contrary, Lanjuinais the Breton declares that there is one man who never will demit volun-tarily; but will protest to the uttermost, while a voice is left him. And he accordingly goes on protesting; amid rage and clangour; Legendre crying at last: "Lanjuinais, come down from the Tribune, or I will fling thee down, *ou je te jette en bas!*" For matters are come to extremity. Nay they do clutch hold of Lanjuinais, certain zealous Mountainmen; but cannot fling him down, for he 'cramps himself on the railing;' and 'his clothes get torn.' Brave Senator, worthy of pity! Neither will Barbaroux demit; he "has sworn to die at his post, and will keep that oath." Whereupon the Galleries all rise with explosion; brandishing weapons, some of them; and rush out, saying: "*Allons*, then; we must save our

country!" Such a Session is this of Sunday the second o
June.

Churches fill, over Christian Europe, and then empty them
selves; but this Convention empties not, the while: a day o
shrieking contention, of agony, humiliation and tearing o
coat-skirts; *illa suprema dies !* Round stand Henriot and his
Hundred Thousand, copiously refreshed from tray and basket;
nay he is 'distributing five francs a-piece,' we Girondins saw it
with our eyes; five francs to keep them in heart! And distraction of armed riot encumbers our borders, jangles at our
Bar; we are prisoners in our own Hall: Bishop Grégoire
could not get out for a *besoin actuel* without four gendarmes to
wait on him! What is the character of a National Representative become? And now the sunlight falls yellower on western
windows, and the chimney-tops are flinging longer shadows;
the refreshed Hundred Thousand, nor their shadows stir not!
What to resolve on? Motion rises, superfluous one would
think, That the Convention go forth in a body; ascertain with
its own eyes whether it is free or not. Lo, therefore, from the
Eastern Gate of the Tuileries, a distressed Convention issuing;
handsome Hérault Sechelles at their head; he with hat on, in
sign of public calamity, the rest bareheaded,—towards the
Gate of the Carrousel; wondrous to see: towards Henriot
and his plumed staff. "In the name of the National Convention, make way!" Not an inch of way does Henriot make:
"I receive no orders, till the Sovereign, yours and mine, have
been obeyed." The Convention presses on; Henriot prances
back, with his staff, some fifteen paces, "To arms! Cannoneers,
to your guns!"—flashes out his puissant sword, as the Staff all
do, and the Hussars all do. Cannoneers brandish the lit
match; Infantry present arms,—alas, in the level way, as if
for firing! Hatted Hérault leads his distressed flock, through
their pinfold of a Tuileries again; across the Garden, to the
Gate on the opposite side. Here is Feuillans-Terrace, alas,
there is our old Salle de Manége; but neither at this Gate of
the Pont Tournant is there egress. Try the other; and the
other; no egress! We wander disconsolate through armed
ranks; who indeed salute with *Live the Republic*, but also
with *Die the Gironde*. Other such sight, in the year One of
Liberty, the westering sun never saw.

And now behold Marat meets us; for he lagged in this
Suppliant Procession of ours: he has got some hundred elect
Patriots at his heels; he orders us, in the Sovereign's name, to

return to our place, and do as we are bidden and bound. The Convention returns. "Does not the Convention," says Couthon with a singular power of face, "see that it is free," —none but friends round it? The Convention, overflowing with friends and armed Sectioners, proceeds to vote as bidden. Many will not vote, but remain silent; some one or two protest, in words; the Mountain has a clear unanimity. Commission of Twelve, and the denounced Twenty-two, to whom we add Ex-Ministers Clavière and Lebrun: these, with some slight extempore alterations (this or that orator proposing, but Marat disposing), are voted to be under 'Arrestment in their own houses.' Brissot, Buzot, Vergniaud, Guadet, Louvet, Gensonné, Barbaroux, Lasource, Lanjuinais, Rabaut,—Thirty-two, by the tale; all that we have known as Girondins, and more than we have known. They, 'under the safeguard of the French People;' by and by, under the safeguard of two Gendarmes each, shall dwell peaceably in their own houses; as Non-Senators; till further order. Herewith ends *Séance* of Sunday the second of June 1793.

At ten o'clock, under mild stars, the Hundred Thousand, their work well finished, turn homewards. Already yesterday, Central Insurrection Committee had arrested Madame Roland; imprisoned her in the Abbaye. Roland has fled, no man knows whither.

Thus fell the Girondins, by Insurrection; and became extinct as a Party: not without a sigh from most Historians. The men were men of parts, of Philosophic culture, decent behaviour; not condemnable in that they were but Pedants, and had not better parts; not condemnable, but most unfortunate. They wanted a Republic of the Virtues, wherein themselves should be head; and they could only get a Republic of the Strengths, wherein others than they were head.

For the rest, Barrère shall make Report of it. The night concludes with a 'civic promenade by torchlight:' surely the true reign of Fraternity is now not far?

BOOK IV

TERROR

CHAPTER I

CHARLOTTE CORDAY

IN the leafy months of June and July, several French Depart
ments germinate a set of rebellious *paper*-leaves, named
Proclamations, Resolutions, Journals, or Diurnals, 'of the
Union for Resistance to Oppression.' In particular, the
Town of Caen, in Calvados, sees its paper-leaf of *Bulletin de
Caen* suddenly bud, suddenly establish itself as Newspaper
there; under the Editorship of Girondin National Repre-
sentatives!

For among the proscribed Girondins are certain of a more
desperate humour. Some, as Vergniaud, Valazé, Gensonné,
'arrested in their own houses,' will await with stoical resignation what the issue may be. Some, as Brissot, Rabaut, will
take to flight, to concealment; which, as the Paris Barriers are
opened again in a day or two, is not yet difficult. But others
there are who will rush, with Buzot, to Calvados; or far over
France, to Lyons, Toulon, Nantes and elsewhither, and then
rendezvous at Caen: to awaken as with war-trumpet the
respectable Departments; and strike down an anarchic Mountain Faction; at least not yield without a stroke at it. Of
this latter temper we count some score or more, of the
Arrested, and of the Not-yet-arrested: a Buzot, a Barbaroux,
Louvet, Guadet, Pétion, who have escaped from Arrestment
in their own homes; a Salles, a Pythagorean Valady, a
Duchâtel, the Duchâtel that came in blanket and nightcap to
vote for the life of Louis, who have escaped from danger and
likelihood of Arrestment. These, to the number at one time
of Twenty-seven, do accordingly lodge here at the '*Intendance*,
or Departmental Mansion,' of the town of Caen in Calvados;
welcomed by Persons in Authority; welcomed and defrayed,
having no money of their own. And the *Bulletin de Caen*
comes forth, with the most animating paragraphs: How the
Bourdeaux Department, the Lyons Department, this Depart-

ment after the other is declaring itself; sixty, or say sixty-nine,
or seventy-two respectable Departments either declaring, or
ready to declare. Nay Marseilles, it seems, will march on
Paris by itself, if need be. So has Marseilles Town said,
That she will march. But on the other hand, that Montélimart
Town has said, No thoroughfare; and means even to 'bury
herself' under her own stone and mortar first,—of this be no
mention in *Bulletin de Caen*.

Such animating paragraphs we read in this new Newspaper;
and fervours and eloquent sarcasm: tirades against the Mountain, from the pen of Deputy Salles; which resemble, say
friends, Pascal's *Provincials*. What is more to the purpose,
these Girondins have got a General in chief, one Wimpfen,
formerly under Dumouriez; also a secondary questionable
General Puisaye, and others; and are doing their best to raise
a force for war. National Volunteers, whosoever is of right
heart: gather in, ye national Volunteers, friends of Liberty;
from our Calvados Townships, from the Eure, from Brittany,
from far and near: forward to Paris, and extinguish Anarchy!
Thus at Caen, in the early July days, there is a drumming and
parading, a perorating and consulting: Staff and Army;
Council; Club of *Carabots*, Antijacobin friends of Freedom,
to denounce atrocious Marat. With all which, and the editing
of *Bulletins*, a National Representative has his hands full.

At Caen it is most animated; and, as one hopes, more or
less animated in the 'Seventy-two Departments that adhere to
us.' And in a France begirt with Cimmerian invading Coalitions, and torn with an internal La Vendée, *this* is the conclusion we have arrived at: To put down Anarchy by Civil
War! *Durum et durum*, the Proverb says, *non faciunt murum*.
La Vendée burns: Santerre can do nothing there; he may
return home and brew beer. Cimmerian bombshells fly all
along the North. That Siege of Mentz is become famed;—
lovers of the Picturesque (as Goethe will testify), washed
country-people of both sexes, stroll thither on Sundays, to see
the artillery work and counterwork; 'you only duck a little
while the shot whizzes past.' Condé is capitulating to the
Austrians; Royal Highness of York, these several weeks,
fiercely batters Valenciennes. For, alas, our fortified Camp of
Famers was stormed; General Dampierre was killed; General
Custine was blamed,—and indeed is now come to Paris to
give 'explanations.'

Against all which the Mountain and atrocious Marat must

even make head as they can. They, anarchic Convention as they are, publish Decrees, expostulatory, explanatory, yet not without severity; they ray forth Commissioners, singly or in pairs, the olive-branch in one hand, yet the sword in the other. Commissioners come even to Caen; but without effect. Mathematical Romme, and Prieur named of the Côte d'Or, venturing thither, with their olive and sword, are packed into prison: there may Romme lie, under lock and key, 'for fifty days;' and meditate his New Calendar, if he please. Cimmeria, La Vendée, and Civil War! Never was Republic One and Indivisible at a lower ebb.—

Amid which dim ferment of Caen and the World, History specially notices one thing: in the lobby of the Mansion *de l'Intendance*, where busy Deputies are coming and going, a young Lady with an aged valet, taking grave graceful leave of Deputy Barbaroux. She is of stately Norman figure; in her twenty-fifth year; of beautiful still countenance: her name is Charlotte Corday, heretofore styled D'Armans, while Nobility still was. Barbaroux has given her a Note to Deputy Duperret,—him who once drew his sword in the effervescence (p. 251). Apparently she will to Paris on some errand? 'She was a Republican before the Revolution, and never wanted energy.' A completeness, a decision is in this fair female Figure: 'by energy she means the spirit that will prompt one to sacrifice himself for his country.' What if she, this fair young Charlotte, had emerged from her secluded stillness, suddenly like a Star; cruel-lovely, with half-angelic, half-dæmonic splendour; to gleam for a moment, and in a moment be extinguished: to be held in memory, so bright complete was she, through long centuries!—Quitting Cimmerian Coalitions without, and the dim-simmering Twenty-five millions within, History will look fixedly at this one fair Apparition of a Charlotte Corday; will note whither Charlotte moves, how the little Life burns forth so radiant, then vanishes swallowed of the Night.

With Barbaroux's Note of Introduction, and slight stock of luggage, we see Charlotte on Tuesday the ninth of July seated in the Caen Diligence, with a place for Paris. None takes farewell of her, wishes her Good-journey: her Father will find a line left, signifying that she is gone to England, that he must pardon her, and forget her. The drowsy Diligence lumbers along; amid drowsy talk of Politics, and raise of the Mountain; in which she mingles not: all night, all day, and again all night. On Thursday, not long before noon, we are at the bridge of Neuilly; here is Paris with her thousand black domes, the goal and purpose of thy journey! Arrived at the Inn de la Providence in the Rue des Vieux Augustins, Charlotte demands a room; hastens to bed; sleeps all afternoon and night, till the morrow morning.

On the morrow morning, she delivers her Note to Duperret. It relates to certain Family Papers which are in the Minister of the Interior's hand; which a Nun at Caen, an old Convent-friend of Charlotte's, has need of; which Duperret shall assist her in getting: this then was Charlotte's errand to Paris? She has finished this, in the course of Friday; yet says nothing of returning. She has seen and silently investigated several things. The Convention, in bodily reality, she has seen; what the Mountain is like. The living physiognomy of Marat she could not see; he is sick at present, and confined to home.

About eight on the Saturday morning, she purchases a large sheath-knife in the Palais Royal; then straightway, in the Place des Victoires, takes a hackney-coach: "To the Rue de l'École de Médecine, No. 44." It is the residence of the Citoyen Marat! —The Citoyen Marat is ill, and cannot be seen; which seems to disappoint her much. Her business is with Marat, then? Hapless beautiful Charlotte; hapless squalid Marat! From Caen in the utmost West, from Neuchâtel in the utmost East, they two are drawing nigh each other; they two have, very strangely, business together.—Charlotte, returning to her Inn, despatches a short Note to Marat; signifying that she is from Caen, the seat of rebellion; that she desires earnestly to see him, and 'will put it in his power to do France a great service.' No answer. Charlotte writes another Note, still more pressing; sets out with it by coach, about seven in the evening, herself. Tired day-labourers have again finished their Week; huge Paris is circling and simmering, manifold, according to its vague wont: this one fair Figure has decision in it; drives straight,—towards a purpose.

It is yellow July evening, we say, the thirteenth of the month; eve of the Bastille day,—when 'M. Marat,' four years ago, in the crowd of the Pont Neuf, shrewdly required of that Besenval Hussar-party, which had such friendly dispositions, "to dismount, and give up their arms, then;" and became notable among Patriot men (i. 156). Four years: what a road he has travelled;—and sits now about half-past seven of the clock, stewing in slipper-bath; sore afflicted; ill of Revolution Fever,—of what other malady this History had rather not name. Excessively sick and worn, poor man: with precisely eleven-pence-halfpenny of ready-money in paper; with slipper-bath; strong three-footed stool for writing on, the while; and a squalid—Washerwoman, one may call her: that is his civic establishment in Medical-School Street; thither and not else-whither has his road led him. Not to the reign of Brother-hood and Perfect Felicity; yet surely on the way towards that? —Hark, a rap again! A musical woman's voice, refusing to be rejected: it is the Citoyenne who would do France a ser-vice. Marat, recognising from within, cries, Admit her. Charlotte Corday is admitted.

Citoyen Marat, I am from Caen the seat of rebellion, and wished to speak with you.—Be seated, *mon enfant.* Now what are the Traitors doing at Caen? What Deputies are at Caen? —Charlotte names some Deputies. "Their heads shall fall within a fortnight," croaks the eager People's-friend, clutching his tablets to write: *Barbaroux, Pétion,* writes he with bare shrunk arm, turning aside in the bath: *Pétion,* and *Louvet,* and—Charlotte has drawn her knife from the sheath; plunges it, with one sure stroke, into the writer's heart. " *À moi, chère amie,* Help, dear!" no more could the Death-choked say or shriek. The helpful Washerwoman running in, there is no Friend of the People, or Friend of the Washerwoman left; but his life with a groan gushes out, indignant, to the shades below.

And so Marat People's-friend is ended; the lone Stylites has got hurled down suddenly from his Pillar—*whitherward* He that made him knows. Patriot Paris may sound triple and tenfold, in dole and wail; re-echoed by Patriot France; and the Convention, 'Chabot pale with terror, declaring that they are to be all assassinated,' may decree him Pantheon Honours, Public Funeral, Mirabeau's dust making way for him; and Jacobin Societies, in lamentable oratory, summing up his character, parallel him to One, whom they think it honour to call 'the good Sansculotte,'—whom we name not here; also a Chapel may be made, for the urn that holds his Heart, in the Place du Carrousel; and new-born children be named Marat; and Lago-di-Como Hawkers bake mountains of stucco into unbeautiful Busts; and David paint his Picture, or Death-Scene; and such other Apotheosis take place as the

human genius, in these circumstances, can devise: but Marat
returns no more to the light of this Sun. One sole circumstance we have read with clear sympathy, in the old *Moniteur*
Newspaper: how Marat's Brother comes from Neuchâtel to
ask of the Convention, 'that the deceased Jean-Paul Marat's
musket be given him.' For Marat too had a brother, and
natural affections; and was wrapt once in swaddling clothes,
and slept safe in a cradle like the rest of us. Ye children of
men!—A sister of his, they say, lives still to this day in Paris.

As for Charlotte Corday, her work is accomplished; the
recompense of it is near and sure. The *chère amie*, and
neighbours of the house, flying at her, she 'overturns some
movables,' entrenches herself till the gendarmes arrive; then
quietly surrenders; goes quietly to the Abbaye Prison: she
alone quiet, all Paris sounding, in wonder, in rage or admiration, round her. Duperret is put in arrest, on account of
her; his Papers sealed,—which may lead to consequences.
Fauchet, in like manner; though Fauchet had not so much as
heard of her. Charlotte, confronted with these two Deputies,
praises the grave firmness of Duperret, censures the dejection
of Fauchet.

On Wednesday morning, the thronged Palais de Justice
and Revolutionary Tribunal can see her face; beautiful and
calm: she dates it 'fourth day of the Preparation of Peace.'
A strange murmur ran through the Hall, at sight of her; you
could not say of what character. Tinville has his indictments
and tape-papers: the cutler of the Palais Royal will testify
that he sold her the sheath-knife; "All these details are needless," interrupted Charlotte; "it is I that killed Marat." By
whose instigation?—"By no one's." What tempted you,
then? His crimes. "I killed one man," added she, raising
her voice extremely (*extrêmement*), as they went on with their
questions, "I killed one man to save a hundred thousand; a
villain to save innocents; a savage wild beast to give repose
to my country. I was a Republican before the Revolution; I
never wanted energy." There is therefore nothing to be said.
The public gazes astonished: the hasty limners sketch her
features, Charlotte not disapproving: the men of law proceed
with their formalities. The doom is Death as a murderess.
To her Advocate she gives thanks; in gentle phrase, in highflown classical spirit. To the priest they send her she gives
thanks; but needs not any shriving, any ghostly or other aid
from him.

On this same evening therefore, about half-past seven o'clock, from the gate of the Conciergerie, to a City all on tiptoe, the fatal Cart issues; seated on it a fair young creature, sheeted in red smock of murderess; so beautiful, serene, so full of life; journeying towards death,—alone amid the World. Many take off their hats, saluting reverently; for what heart but must be touched? Others growl and howl. Adam Lux, of Mentz, declares that she is greater than Brutus; that it were beautiful to die with her: the head of this young man seems turned. At the Place de la Révolution, the countenance of Charlotte wears the same still smile. The executioners proceed to bind her feet; she resists, thinking it meant as an insult; on a word of explanation, she submits with cheerful apology. As the last act, all being now ready, they take the neckerchief from her neck; a blush of maidenly shame overspreads that fair face and neck; the cheeks were still tinged with it when the executioner lifted the severed head, to show it to the people. 'It is most true,' says Forster, 'that he struck the cheek insultingly; for I saw it with my eyes: the Police imprisoned him for it.'

In this manner have the Beautifullest and the Squalidest come in collision, and extinguished one another. Jean-Paul Marat and Marie-Anne Charlotte Corday both, suddenly, are no more. 'Day of the Preparation of Peace?' Alas, how were peace possible or preparable, while, for example, the heart of lovely Maidens, in their convent-stillness, are dreaming not of Love-paradises, and the light of Life; but of Codrus'-sacrifices, and Death well-earned? That Twenty-five million hearts have got to such temper, this *is* the Anarchy; the soul of it lies in this: whereof not peace can be the embodiment! The death of Marat, whetting old animosities tenfold, will be worse than any life. O ye hapless Two, mutually extinctive, the Beautiful and the Squalid, sleep ye well,—in the Mother's bosom that bore you both!

This is the history of Charlotte Corday; most definite, most complete; angelic-dæmonic: like a Star! Adam Lux goes home, half-delirious; to pour forth his Apotheosis of her, in paper and print; to propose that she have a statue with this inscription, *Greater than Brutus.* Friends represent his danger; Lux is reckless; thinks it were beautiful to die with her.

CHAPTER II

IN CIVIL WAR

But during these same hours, another guillotine is at work. on another : Charlotte, for the Girondins, dies at Paris to-day ; Chalier, by the Girondins, dies at Lyons to-morrow.

From rumbling of cannon along the streets of that City, it has come to firing of them, to rabid fighting : Nièvre Chol and the Girondins triumph ;—behind whom there is, as everywhere, a Royalist Faction waiting to strike in. Trouble enough at Lyons, and the dominant party carrying it with a high hand ! For, indeed, the whole South is astir ; incarcerating Jacobins ; arming for Girondins : wherefore we have got a 'Congress of Lyons ;' also a 'Revolutionary Tribunal of Lyons,' and Anarchists shall tremble. So Chalier was soon found guilty, of Jacobinism, of murderous Plot, 'address with drawn dagger on the sixth of February last' (p. 231) ; and, on the morrow, he also travels his final road, along the streets of Lyons, 'by the side of an ecclesiastic, with whom he seems to speak earnestly,'—the axe now glittering nigh. He could weep, in old years, this man, and 'fall on his knees on the pavement,' blessing Heaven at sight of Federation Programs or the like ; then he pilgrimed to Paris, to worship Marat and the Mountain : now Marat and he are both gone ;—we said he could not end well. Jacobinism groans inwardly, at Lyons ; but dare not outwardly. Chalier, when the Tribunal sentenced him, made answer : " My death will cost this City dear."

Montélimart Town is not buried under its ruins ; yet Marseilles is actually marching, under order of a 'Lyons Congress ;' is incarcerating Patriots ; the very Royalists now showing face. Against which a General Cartaux fights, though in small force ; and with him an Artillery Major, of the name of—Napoleon Buonaparte. This Napoleon, to prove that the Marseillese have no chance ultimately, not only fights, but writes ; publishes his *Supper of Beaucaire*, a Dialogue which has become curious. Unfortunate Cities, with their actions and their reactions ! Violence to be paid with violence in geometrical ratio ; Royalism and Anarchism both striking in ;—the final net-amount of which geometrical series, what man shall sum ?

The Bar of Iron has never yet floated in Marseilles Harbour ; but the Body of Rebecqui was found floating, self-drowned there. Hot Rebecqui, seeing how confusion deepened, and Respectability grew poisoned with Royalism, felt that there was no refuge for a Republican but death. Rebecqui disappeared: no one knew whither; till, one morning, they found the empty case or body of him risen to the top, tumbling on the salt waves; and perceived that Rebecqui had withdrawn forever.—Toulon likewise is incarcerating Patriots; sending delegates to Congress; intriguing, in case of necessity, with the Royalists and English. Montpellier, Bourdeaux, Nantes: all France, that is not under the swoop of Austria and Cimmeria, seems rushing into madness, and suicidal ruin. The Mountain labours; like a volcano in a burning volcanic Land. Convention Committees, of Surety, of Salvation, are busy night and day: Convention Commissioners whirl on all high-ways; bearing olive-branch and sword, or now perhaps sword only. Chaumette and Municipals come daily to the Tuileries demanding a Constitution: it is some weeks now since he resolved, in Townhall, that a Deputation 'should go every day,' and demand a Constitution, till one were got; whereby suicidal France might rally and pacify itself; a thing inexpressibly desirable.

This then is the fruit your Anti-anarchic Girondins have got from that Levying of War in Calvados? This fruit, we may say; and no other whatsoever. For indeed, before either Charlotte's or Chalier's head had fallen, the Calvados War itself had, as it were, vanished, dreamlike, in a shriek! With 'seventy-two Departments' on our side, one might have hoped better things. But it turns out that Respectabilities, though they will vote, will not fight. Possession always is nine points in Law; but in Lawsuits of *this* kind, one may say, it is ninety-and-nine points. Men do what they were wont to do; and have immense irresolution and inertia: they obey him who has the symbols that claim obedience. Consider what, in modern society, this one fact means: the Metropolis is with our enemies! Metropolis, *Mother-city*; rightly so named: all the rest are but as her children, her nurslings. Why, there is not a leathern Diligence, with its post-bags and luggage-boots, that lumbers out from her, but is as a huge life-pulse; she is the heart of all. Cut short that one leathern Diligence, how much is cut short!—General Wimpfen, looking practically into the matter, can see nothing for it but that one should fall back on Royalism; get into communication with Pitt! Dark innuendos he flings out, to that effect: whereat we

Girondins start, horror-struck. He produces as his Second in command a certain 'Ci-devant,' one Comte Puisaye; entirely unknown to Louvet; greatly suspected by him.

Few wars, accordingly, were ever levied of a more insufficient character than this of Calvados. He that is curious in such things may read the details of it in the Memoirs of that same Ci-devant Puisaye, the much-enduring man and Royalist: How our Girondin National forces, marching off with plenty of wind-music, were drawn out about the old Château of Brécourt, in the wood country near Vernon, to meet the Mountain National forces advancing from Paris. How on the fifteenth afternoon of July, they did meet;—and, as it were, shrieked mutually, and took mutually to flight, without loss. How Puisaye thereafter,—for the Mountain Nationals fled first, and we thought ourselves the victors,—was roused from his warm bed in the Castle of Brécourt, and had to gallop without boots; our Nationals, in the night-watches, having fallen unexpectedly into *sauve-qui-peut:*—and in brief the Calvados War had burnt priming; and the only question now was, Whitherward to vanish, in what hole to hide oneself!

The National Volunteers rush homewards, faster than they came. The Seventy-two Respectable Departments, says Meillan, 'all turned round and forsook us, in the space of four-and-twenty hours.' Unhappy those who, as at Lyons for instance, have gone too far for turning! 'One morning,' we find placarded on our Intendance Mansion, the Decree of Convention which casts us *Hors la loi*, into Outlawry; placarded by our Caen Magistrates;—clear hint that we also are to vanish. Vanish indeed: but whitherward? Gorsas has friends in Rennes; he will hide there,—unhappily will not lie hid. Guadet, Lanjuinais are on cross roads; making for Bourdeaux. To Bourdeaux! cries the general voice, of Valour alike and of Despair. Some flag of Respectability still floats there, or is thought to float.

Thitherward therefore; each as he can! Eleven of these ill-fated Deputies, among whom we may count as twelfth, Friend Riouffe the Man of Letters, do an original thing: Take the uniform of National Volunteers, and retreat southward with the Breton Battalion, as private soldiers of that corps. These brave Bretons had stood truer by us than any other. Nevertheless, at the end of a day or two, they also do now get dubious, self-divided; we must part from them; and, with some half-dozen as convoy or guide, retreat by ourselves, —a solitary marching detachment, through waste regions of the West.

CHAPTER III

RETREAT OF THE ELEVEN

It is one of the notablest Retreats, this of the Eleven, that History presents : The handful of forlorn Legislators retreating there, continually, with shouldered firelock and well-filled cartridge-box, in the yellow autumn ; long hundreds of miles between them and Bourdeaux ; the country all getting hostile, suspicious of the truth ; simmering and buzzing on all sides, more and more. Louvet has preserved the Itinerary of it ; a piece worth all the rest he ever wrote.

O virtuous Pétion, with thy early-white head, O brave young Barbaroux, has it come to this ? Weary ways, worn shoes, light purse ;—encompassed with perils as with a sea ! Revolutionary Committees are in every Township ; of Jacobin temper ; our friends all cowed, our cause the losing one. In the Borough of Moncontour, by ill chance, it is market-day : to the gaping public such transit of a solitary Marching Detachment is suspicious ; we have need of energy, of promptitude and luck, to be allowed to march through. Hasten, ye weary pilgrims ! The country is getting up ; noise of you is bruited day after day, a solitary Twelve retreating in this mysterious manner : with every new day, a wider wave of inquisitive pursuing tumult is stirred up, till the whole west will be in motion. 'Cussy is tormented with gout, Buzot is too fat for marching.' Riouffe, blistered, bleeding, marches only on tiptoe ; Barbaroux limps with sprained ancle, yet ever cheery, full of hope and valour. Light Louvet glances hare-eyed, not hare-hearted : only virtuous Pétion's serenity 'was but once seen ruffled.' They lie in straw-lofts, in woody brakes ; rudest paillasse on the floor of a secret friend is luxury. They are seized in the dead of night by Jacobin mayors and tap of drum ; get off by firm countenance, rattle of muskets, and ready wit.

Of Bourdeaux, through fiery La Vendée and the long geographical spaces that remain, it were madness to think : well, if you can get to Quimper on the sea-coast, and take shipping there. Faster, ever faster ! Before the end of the march, so hot has the country grown, it is found advisable to march all night. They do it ; under the still night-canopy they plod along ;—and yet behold, Rumour has outplodded them. In the paltry Village of Carhaix (be its thatched huts and bottomless peat-bogs long notable to the Traveller), one is astonished to find light still glimmering : citizens are awake, with rushlights burning, in that nook of the terrestrial Planet ; as we traverse swiftly the one poor street, a voice is heard saying, "There they are, *Les voilà qui passent !*" Swifter, ye doomed lame Twelve : speed ere they can arm ; gain the Woods of Quimper before day, and lie squatted there !

The doomed Twelve do it ; though with difficulty, with loss of road, with peril and the mistakes of a night. In Quimper are Girondin friends, who perhaps will harbour the homeless, till a Bourdeaux ship weigh. Wayworn, heartworn, in agony of suspense, till Quimper friendship get warning, they lie there, squatted under the thick wet boscage ; suspicious of the face of man. Some pity to the brave ; to the unhappy ! Unhappiest of all Legislators, O when ye packed your luggage, some score or two-score months ago, and mounted this or the other leathern vehicle, to be Conscript Fathers of a regenerated France, and reap deathless laurels,—did ye think your journey was to lead *hither ?* The Quimper Samaritans find them squatted ; lift them up to help and comfort ; will hide them in sure places. Thence let them dissipate gradually ; or there they can lie quiet, and write *Memoirs*, till a Bourdeaux ship sail.

And thus, in Calvados all is dissipated ; Romme is out of prison, meditating his Calendar ; ringleaders are locked in his room. At Caen the Corday family mourns in silence : Buzot's House is a heap of dust and demolition ; and amid the rubbish sticks a Gallows ; with this inscription, *Here dwelt the Traitor Buzot who conspired against the Republic.* Buzot and the other vanished Deputies are *hors la loi,* as we saw ; their lives free to take where they can be found. The worse fares it with the poor Arrested visible Deputies at Paris. 'Arrestment at home' threatens to become 'Confinement in the Luxembourg ;' to end : *where ?* For example, what pale-visaged thin man is this, journeying towards Switzerland as a Merchant of Neuchâtel, whom they arrest in the town of Moulins ? To Revolutionary Committee he is suspect. To Revolutionary Committee, on probing the matter, he is evidently : Deputy Brissot ! Back to thy Arrestment, poor Brissot ; or indeed to strait confinement,—whither others are fated to follow. Rabaut has built himself a false-partition, in a friend's house; lives in invisible darkness, between two walls. It will end, this same Arrestment business, in Prison, and the Revolutionary Tribunal.

Nor must we forget Duperret, and the seal put on his papers by reason of Charlotte. One Paper is there, fit to breed woe enough: A secret solemn Protest against that *suprema dies* of the Second of June! This Secret Protest our poor Duperret had drawn up, the same week, in all plainness of speech; waiting the time for publishing it: to which Secret Protest his signature, and that of other honourable Deputies not a few, stands legibly appended. And now, if the seals were once broken, the Mountain still victorious? Such Protesters, your Merciers, Bailleuls, Seventy-three by the tale, what yet remains of Respectable Girondism in the Convention, may tremble to think!—These are the fruits of levying civil war.

Also we find, that in these last days of July, the famed Siege of Mentz is *finished*: the Garrison to march out with honours of war; not to serve against the Coalition for a year. Lovers of the Picturesque, and Goethe standing on the Chaussée of Mentz, saw, with due interest, the Procession issuing forth, in all solemnity:

'Escorted by Prussian horse came first the French Garrison. Nothing could look stranger than this latter; a column of Marseillese, slight, swarthy parti-coloured, in patched clothes, came tripping on;—as if King Edwin had opened the Dwarf Hill, and sent out his nimble Host of Dwarfs. Next followed regular troops; serious, sullen; not as if downcast or ashamed. But the remarkablest appearance, which struck every one, was that of the Chasers (*Chasseurs*) coming out mounted: they had advanced quite silent to where we stood, when their Band struck up the *Marseillaise*. This revolutionary *Te-Deum* has in itself something mournful and bodeful, however briskly played; but at present they gave it in altogether slow time, proportionate to the creeping step they rode at. It was piercing and fearful, and a most serious-looking thing, as these cavaliers, long, lean men, of a certain age, with mien suitable to the music, came pacing on: singly you might have likened them to Don Quixote; in mass, they were highly dignified.

'But now a single troop became notable: that of the Commissioners or *Représentans*. Merlin of Thionville, in hussar uniform, distinguishing himself by wild beard and look, had another person in similar costume on his left; the crowd shouted out, with rage, at sight of this latter, the name of a

Jacobin Townsman and Clubbist; and shook itself to seize him Merlin drew bridle; referred to his dignity as French Representative, to the vengeance that should follow any injury done; he would advise every one to compose himself, for this was not the *last time* they would see him here.' Thus rode Merlin; threatening in defeat. But what now shall stem that tide of Prussians setting-in through the open Northeast? Lucky if fortified Lines of Weissembourg, and impassabilities of Vosges Mountains confine it to French Alsace, keep it from submerging the very heart of the country!

Furthermore, precisely in the same days, Valenciennes Siege is finished, in the Northwest:—fallen, under the red hail of York! Condé fell some fortnight since. Cimmerian Coalition presses on. What seems very notable too, on all these captured French Towns there flies not the Royalist fleur-de-lys, in the name of a new Louis the Pretender; but the Austrian flag flies; as if Austria meant to keep them for herself! Perhaps General Custine, still in Paris, can give some explanation of the fall of these strong-places? Mother-Society, from tribune and gallery, growls loud that he ought to do it;—remarks, however, in a splenetic manner that 'the *Monsieurs* of the Palais Royal' are calling Long-life to this General.

The Mother-Society, purged now, by successive 'scrutinies or *épurations*,' from all taint of Girondism, has become a great Authority: what we can call shield-bearer, or bottle-holder, nay call it fugleman, to the purged National Convention itself. The Jacobins Debates are reported in the *Moniteur*, like Parliamentary ones.

CHAPTER IV

O NATURE

But looking more specially into Paris City, what is this that History, on the 10th of August, Year One of Liberty, 'by old style, year 1793,' discerns there? Praised be the Heavens, a new Feast of Pikes!

For Chaumette's 'Deputation every day' has worked out its result: a Constitution. It was one of the rapidest Constitutions ever put together; made, some say in eight days, by Hérault Séchelles and others; probably a workmanlike, road-worthy Constitution enough;—on which point, however, we are for some reasons, little called to form a judgment. Work-manlike or not, the Forty-four Thousand Communes of

France, by overwhelming majorities, did hasten to accept it; glad of any Constitution whatsoever. Nay Departmental Deputies have come, the venerablest Republicans of each Department, with solemn message of Acceptance; and now what remains but that our new Final Constitution be proclaimed, and sworn to, in Feast of Pikes? The Departmental Deputies, we say, are come some time ago; Chaumette very anxious about them, lest Girondin *Monsieurs*, Agio-jobbers, or were it even *Filles de joie* of a Girondin temper, corrupt their morals. Tenth of August, immortal Anniversary, greater almost than Bastille July, is the Day.

Painter David has not been idle. Thanks to David and the French genius, there steps forth into the sunlight, this day, a Scenic Phantasmagory unexampled :—whereof History, so occupied with Real Phantasmagories, will say but little.

For one thing, History can notice with satisfaction, on the ruins of the Bastille, a *Statue of Nature*; gigantic, spouting water from her two *mammelles*. Not a Dream this; but a fact, palpable visible. There she spouts, great Nature; dim, before daybreak. But as the coming Sun ruddies the East, come countless Multitudes, regulated and unregulated; come Departmental Deputies, come Mother-Society and Daughters; comes National Convention, led on by handsome Hérault; soft wind-music breathing note of expectation. Lo, as great Sol scatters his first fire-handful, tipping the hills and chimney-heads with gold, Hérault is at great Nature's feet (she is Plaster of Paris merely); Hérault lifts, in an iron saucer, water spouted from the sacred breasts; drinks of it, with an eloquent Pagan Prayer, beginning, "O Nature!" and all the Departmental Deputies drink, each with what best suitable ejaculation or prophetic-utterance is in him;—amid breathings, which become blasts, of wind-music; and the roar of artillery and human throats: finishing well the first act of this solemnity.

Next are processionings along the Boulevards: Deputies or Officials bound together by long indivisible tricolor riband; general 'members of the Sovereign' walking pell-mell, with hammers, with the tools and emblems of their crafts; among which we notice a Plough, and ancient Baucis and Philemon seated on it, drawn by their children. Many-voiced harmony and dissonance filling the air. Through Triumphal Arches enough : at the basis of the first of which, we descry—whom thinkest thou?—the Heroines of the Insurrection of Women.

Strong Dames of the Market, they sit there (Théroigne too ill to attend, one fears), with oak-branches, tricolor bedizenment; firm seated on their Cannons. To whom handsome Hérault, making pause of admiration, addresses soothing eloquence; whereupon they rise and fall into the march.

And now mark, in the Place de la Révolution, what other august Statue may this be; veiled in canvass,—which swiftly we shear off by pulley and cord? The *Statue of Liberty!* She too is of Plaster, hoping to become of metal; stands where a Tyrant Louis Quinze once stood. 'Three thousand birds' are let loose, into the whole world, with labels round their neck, *We are free; imitate us.* Holocaust of Royalist and *ci-devant* trumpery, such as one could still gather, is burnt; pontifical eloquence must be uttered, by handsome Hérault, and Pagan orisons offered up.

And then forward across the River; where is new enormous Statuary; enormous plaster Mountain; Hercules-*Peuple*, with uplifted all-conquering club; 'many-headed Dragon of Girondin Federalism rising from fetid marsh:'—needing new eloquence from Hérault. To say nothing of Champ-de-Mars, and Fatherland's Altar there; with urn of slain Defenders, Carpenter's-level of the Law; and such exploding, gesticulating and perorating, that Hérault's lips must be growing white, and his tongue cleaving to the roof of his mouth.

Towards six o'clock let the wearied President, let Paris Patriotism generally sit down to what repast, and social repasts, can be had; and with flowing tankard or light-mantling glass, usher in this New and Newest Era. In fact, is not Romme's New Calendar getting ready? On all housetops flicker little tricolor Flags, their flagstaff a Pike and Liberty-Cap. On all house-walls, for no Patriot, not suspect, will be behind another, there stand printed these words: *Republic one and indivisible, Liberty, Equality, Fraternity, or Death.*

As to the New Calendar, we may say here rather than elsewhere that speculative men have long been struck with the inequalities and incongruities of the Old Calendar; that a New one has long been as good as determined on. Maréchal the Atheist, almost ten years ago, proposed a New Calendar, free at least from superstition: this the Paris Municipality would now adopt, in defect of a better; at all events, let us have either this of Maréchal's or a better,—the New Era being come. Petitions, more than once, have been sent to that effect; and indeed, for a year past, all Public Bodies, Journalists, and Patriots in general, have dated *First Year of the Republic*. It is a subject not without difficulties. But the Convention has taken it up; and Romme, as we say, has been meditating it; not Maréchal's New Calendar, but a better New one of Romme's and our own. Romme, aided by a Monge, a Lagrange and others, furnishes mathematics; Fabre d'Églantine furnishes poetic nomenclature: and so, on the 5th of October 1793, after trouble enough, they bring forth this New Republican Calendar of theirs, in a complete state; and by Law, get it put in action.

Four equal Seasons, Twelve equal Months of Thirty days each; this makes three hundred and sixty days; and five odd days remain to be disposed of. The five odd days we will make Festivals, and name the five *Sansculottides*, or Days without Breeches. Festival of Genius; Festival of Labour; of Actions; of Rewards; of Opinion: these are the five Sansculottides. Whereby the great Circle, or Year, is made complete: solely every fourth year, whilom called Leap-year, we introduce a sixth Sansculottide: and name it Festival of the Revolution. Now as to the day of commencement, which offers difficulties, is it not one of the luckiest coincidences that the Republic herself commenced on the 21st of September; close on the Vernal Equinox? Vernal Equinox, at midnight for the meridian of Paris, in the year whilom Christian 1792, from that moment shall the New Era reckon itself to begin. *Vendémiaire, Brumaire, Frimaire;* or as one might say, in mixed English, *Vintagearious, Fogarious, Frostarious:* these are our three Autumn months. *Nivose, Pluviose, Ventose,* or say, *Snowous, Rainous, Windous,* make our Winter season. *Germinal, Floréal, Prairial,* or *Buddal, Floweral, Meadowal,* are our Spring season. *Messidor, Thermidor, Fructidor,* that is to say (*dor* being Greek for *gift*) *Reapidor, Heatidor, Fruitidor,* are Republican Summer. These Twelve, in a singular manner, divide the Republican Year. Then as to minuter subdivisions, let us venture at once on a bold stroke: adopt your decimal subdivision; and instead of the world-old Week, or *Se'ennight*, make it a *Tennight*, or *Décade;*—not without Results. There are three Decades, then, in each of the months; which is very regular; and the *Décadi*, or Tenth-day, shall always be the 'Day of Rest.' And the Christian Sabbath, in that case? Shall shift for itself!

This, in brief, is the New Calendar of Romme and the Convention; calculated for the meridian of Paris, and Gospel of Jean-Jacques: not one of the least afflicting occurrences for the actual British reader of French History;—confusing the soul with *Messidors, Meadowals;* till at last, in self-defence, one is forced to construct some ground-scheme, or rule of Commutation from New-style to Old-style, and have it lying by him. Such ground-scheme, almost worn out in our service, but still legible and printable, we shall now, in a Note,[1] present to the reader. For the Romme Calendar, in so many Newspapers, Memoirs, Public Acts, has stamped itself deep into that section of Time: a New Era that lasts some Twelve years and odd is not to be despised. Let the Reader, therefore, with such ground-scheme, help himself where needful, out of New-style into Old-style, called also 'slave-style, *stile-esclave;*' —whereof we, in these pages, shall as much as possible use the latter only.

Thus with new Feast of Pikes, and New Era or New Calendar, did France accept her New Constitution: the most Democratic Constitution ever committed to paper. How it will work in practice? Patriot Deputations, from time to time, solicit fruition of it, that it be set a-going. Always, however, this seems questionable; for the moment, unsuitable. Till, in some weeks, *Salut Public,* through the organ of Saint-Just, makes report, that, in the present alarming circumstances, the state of France is Revolutionary; that her 'Government must be Revolutionary till the Peace!' Solely as Paper, then, and as a Hope, must this poor new Constitution exist;—in which shape we may conceive it lying, even now, with an infinity of other things, in that Limbo near the Moon. Further than paper it never got, nor ever will get.

CHAPTER V

SWORD OF SHARPNESS

IN fact it is something quite other than paper theorems, it is iron and audacity that France now needs.

Is not La Vendée still blazing;—alas too literally; rogue Rossignol burning the very cornmills? General Santerre could do nothing there; General Rossignol, in blind fury, often in liquor, can do less than nothing. Rebellion spreads, grows ever madder. Happily those lean Quixote-figures, whom we

[1] *See page x.*

saw retreating out of Mentz, 'bound not to serve against the Coalition for a year,' have got to Paris. National Convention packs them into post-vehicles and conveyances; sends them swiftly, by post, into La Vendée. There valiantly struggling, in obscure battle and skirmish, under rogue Rossignol, let them, unlaureled, save the Republic, and 'be cut down gradually to the last man.'

Does not the Coalition, like a fire-tide, pour in; Prussia through the opened Northeast; Austria, England through the Northwest? General Houchard prospers no better there than General Custine did: let him look to it! Through the Eastern and the Western Pyrenees Spain has deployed itself; spreads, rustling with Bourbon banners, over the face of the South. Ashes and embers of confused Girondin civil war covered that region already. Marseilles is damped down, not quenched; to be quenched in blood. Toulon, terrorstruck, too far gone for turning, has flung itself, ye righteous Powers, —into the hands of the English! On Toulon Arsenal there flies a flag,—nay not even the Fleur-de-lys of a Louis Pretender, there flies that accursed St. George's Cross of the English and Admiral Hood! What remnant of sea-craft, arsenals, roperies, war-navy France had, has given itself to these enemies of human nature, 'ennemis du genre humain.' Beleaguer it, bombard it, ye Commissioners Barras, Fréron, Robespierre Junior; thou General Cartaux, General Dugommier: above all, thou remarkable Artillery-Major, Napoleon Buonaparte! Hood is fortifying himself, victualling himself; means, apparently, to make a new Gibraltar of it.

But lo, in the Autumn night, late night, among the last of August, what sudden red sunblaze is this that has risen over Lyons City; with a noise to deafen the world? It is the Powder-tower of Lyons, nay the Arsenal with four Powder-towers, which has caught fire in the Bombardment; and sprung into the air, carrying 'a hundred and seventeen houses' after it. With a light, one fancies, as of the noon sun; with a roar second only to the Last Trumpet! All living sleepers far and wide it has awakened. What a sight was that, which the eye of History saw, in the sudden nocturnal sunblaze! The roofs of hapless Lyons, and all its domes and steeples made momentarily clear; Rhone and Soane streams flashing suddenly visible; and height and hollow, hamlet and smooth stubblefield, and all the region round;—heights, alas, all

scarped and counterscarped, into trenches, curtains, redoubts;
blue Artillery-men, little Powder-devilkins, plying their hell-
trade there, through the *not* ambrosial night! Let the darkness cover it again; for it pains the eye. Of a truth, Chalier's
death is costing the City dear. Convention Commissioners,
Lyons Congresses have come and gone; and action there was
and reaction; bad ever growing worse; till it has come to
this; Commissioner Dubois-Crancé, 'with seventy thousand
men, and all the Artillery of several Provinces,' bombarding
Lyons day and night.

Worse things still are in store. Famine is in Lyons, and
ruin and fire. Desperate are the sallies of the besieged;
brave Précy, their National Colonel and Commandant, doing
what is in man: desperate but ineffectual. Provisions cut
off; nothing entering our city but shot and shells! The
Arsenal has roared aloft; the very Hospital will be battered
down, and the sick buried alive. A black Flag hung on this
latter noble Edifice, appealing to the pity of the besiegers, for
though maddened, were they not still our brethren? In their
blind wrath, they took it for a flag of defiance, and aimed
thitherward the more. Bad is growing ever worse here: and
how will the worse stop, till it have grown worst of all?
Commissioner Dubois will listen to no pleading, to no speech,
save this only, We surrender at discretion. Lyons contains in
it subdued Jacobins; dominant Girondins; secret Royalists.
And now, mere deaf madness and cannon-shot enveloping
them, will not the desperate Municipality fly, at last, into the
arms of Royalism itself? Majesty of Sardinia was to bring
help, but it failed. Emigrant d'Autichamp, in name of the
Two Pretender Royal Highnesses, is coming through Switzerland with help; coming, not yet come: Précy hoists the
Fleur-de-lys!

At sight of which, all true Girondins sorrowfully fling down
their arms:—Let our Tricolor brethren storm us, then, and
slay us in their wrath; with *you* we conquer not. The famishing women and children are sent forth: deaf Dubois sends
them back;—rains in mere fire and madness. Our 'redoubts
of cotton-bags' are taken, retaken; Précy under his Fleur-
de-lys is valiant as Despair. What will become of Lyons?
It is a siege of seventy days.

Or see, in these same weeks, far in the Western waters:
breasting through the Bay of Biscay, a greasy dingy little

Merchant-ship, with Scotch skipper; under hatches whereof sit, disconsolate,—the last forlorn nucleus of Girondism, the Deputies from Quimper! Several have dissipated themselves, whithersoever they could. Poor Riouffe fell into the talons of Revolutionary Committee and Paris Prison. The rest sit here under hatches; reverend Pétion with his gray hair, angry Buzot, suspicious Louvet, brave young Barbaroux, and others. They have escaped from Quimper, in this sad craft; are now tacking and struggling; in danger from the waves, in danger from the English, in still worse danger from the French;— banished by Heaven and Earth to the greasy belly of this Scotch skipper's Merchant-vessel, unfruitful Atlantic raving round. They are for Bourdeaux, if peradventure hope yet linger there. Enter not Bourdeaux, O Friends! Bloody Convention Representatives, Tallien and such like, with their Edicts, with their Guillotine, have arrived there; Respectability is driven under ground; Jacobinism lords it on high. From that Réole landing-place, or *Beak of Ambès*, as it were, pale Death, waving his Revolutionary Sword of Sharpness, waves you elsewhither!

On one side or the other of that Bec d'Ambès, the Scotch Skipper with difficulty moors, a dexterous greasy man; with difficulty lands his Girondins;—who, after reconnoitring, must rapidly burrow in the Earth; and so, in subterranean ways, in friends' back-closets, in cellars, barn-lofts, in caves of Saint-Emilion and Libourne, stave off cruel Death. Unhappiest of all Senators!

CHAPTER VI

RISEN AGAINST TYRANTS

AGAINST all which incalculable impediments, horrors and disasters, what can a Jacobin Convention oppose? The uncalculating Spirit of Jacobinism, and Sansculottic sans-formulistic Frenzy! Our Enemies press-in on us, says Danton, but they shall not conquer us, "we will burn France to ashes rather, *nous brûlerons la France.*"

Committees, of *Sûreté*, of *Salut*, have raised themselves, '*à la hauteur*, to the height of circumstances.' Let all mortals raise themselves *à la hauteur*. Let the Forty-four thousand Sections and their Revolutionary Committees stir every fibre of the Republic; and every Frenchman feel that he is to do or die. They are the life-circulation of Jacobinism, these Sections and Committees: Danton, through the organ of Barrère and *Salut Public*, gets decreed. That there be in Paris, by law, two meetings of Section weekly; also, that the Poorer Citizen be *paid* for attending, and have his day's-wages of Forty Sous. This is the celebrated .'Law of the Forty Sous;' fiercely stimulant to Sansculottism, to the life-circulation of Jacobinism.

On the twenty-third of August, Committee of Public Salvation, as usual through Barrère, had promulgated, in words not unworthy of remembering, their Report, which is soon made into a Law, of *Levy in Mass.* 'All France, and whatsoever it contains of men or resources, is put under requisition,' says Barrère; really in Tyrtæan words, the best we know of his. 'The Republic is one vast besieged city.' Two-hundred and fifty Forges shall, in these days, be set up in the Luxembourg Garden, and round the outer wall of the Tuileries; to make gun-barrels; in sight of Earth and Heaven! From all hamlets, towards their Departmental Town; from all Departmental Towns, towards the appointed Camp and seat of war, the Sons of Freedom shall march; their banner is to bear: '*Le Peuple Français debout contre les Tyrans*, The French People risen against Tyrants. The young men shall go to the battle; it is their task to conquer: the married men shall forge arms, transport baggage and artillery; provide subsistence: the women shall work at soldiers' clothes, make tents; serve in the hospitals: the children shall scrape old-linen into surgeon's-lint: the aged men shall have themselves carried into public places; and there, by their words, excite the courage of the young; preach hatred to Kings and unity to the Republic.' Tyrtæan words; which tingle through all French hearts.

In this humour, then, since no other serves, will France rush against its enemies. Headlong, reckoning no cost or consequence, heeding no law or rule but that supreme law, Salvation of the People! The weapons are, all the iron that is in France; the strength is, that of all the men, women, and children that are in France. There, in their two-hundred and fifty shed-smithies, in Garden of Luxembourg or Tuileries, let them forge gun-barrels, in sight of Heaven and Earth.

Nor with heroic daring against the Foreign foe, can black vengeance against the Domestic be wanting. Life-circulation of the Revolutionary Committees being quickened by that *Law of the Forty Sous*, Deputy Merlin, not the Thionviller, whom we saw ride out of Mentz, but Merlin of Douai, named subsequently Merlin *Suspect*,—comes, about a week after, with his world-famous *Law of the Suspect:* ordering all Sections, by their Committees, instantly to arrest all Persons Suspect ; and explaining withal who the Arrestable and Suspect specially are. 'Are suspect,' says he, 'all who by their actions, by their connexions, speakings, writings have'—in short become Suspect. Nay Chaumette, illuminating the matter still further, in his Municipal Placards and Proclama tions, will bring it about that you may almost recognise a Suspect on the streets, and clutch him there,—off to Committee, and Prison. Watch well your words, watch well your looks: if Suspect of nothing else, you may grow, as came to be a saying, 'Suspect of being Suspect!' For are we not in a State of Revolution?

No frightfuller Law ever ruled in a Nation of men. All Prisons and Houses of Arrest in French land are getting crowded to the ridge-tile: Forty-four thousand Committees, like as many companies of reapers or gleaners, gleaning France, are gathering their harvest, and storing it in these Houses. Harvest of Aristocrat tares ! Nay lest the Forty-four thousand, each on its own harvest-field, prove insufficient, we are to have an ambulant 'Revolutionary Army:' six-thousand strong, under right captains, this shall perambulate the country at large, and strike in wherever it finds such harvest-work slack. So have Municipality and Mother-Society petitioned; so has Convention decreed. Let Aristocrats, Federalists, Monsieurs vanish, and all men tremble: 'the Soil of Liberty shall be purged,'—with a vengeance !

Neither hitherto has the Revolutionary Tribunal been keeping holyday. Blanchelande, for losing Saint-Domingo ; 'Conspirators of Orleans,' for 'assassinating,' for assaulting the sacred Deputy Léonard-Bourdon : these with many Nameless, to whom life was sweet, have died. Daily the great Guillotine has its due. Like a black Spectre, daily at eventide, glides the Death-tumbril through the variegated throng of things. The variegated street shudders at it, for the moment; next moment forgets it: The Aristocrats ! They were guilty against the Republic; their death, were it only that their goods are confiscated, will be useful to the Republic; *Vive la République !*

In the last days of August fell a notabler head: General Custine's. Custine was accused of harshness, of unskilfulness, perfidiousness; accused of many things: found guilty, we may say, of one thing, unsuccessfulness. Hearing his unexpected Sentence, 'Custine fell down before the Crucifix,' silent for the space of two hours: he fared, with moist eyes and a look of prayer, towards the Place de la Révolution; glanced upwards at the clear suspended axe; then mounted swiftly aloft, swiftly was struck away from the lists of the Living. He had fought in America; he was a proud, brave man; and his fortune led him *hither*.

On the 2d of this same month, at three in the morning, a vehicle rolled off, with closed blinds, from the Temple to the Conciergerie. Within it were two Municipals; and Marie-Antoinette, once Queen of France! There in that Conciergerie, in ignominious dreary cell, she, secluded from children, kindred, friend and hope, sits long weeks; expecting when the end will be.

The Guillotine, we find, gets always a quicker motion, as other things are quickening. The Guillotine, by its speed of going, will give index of the general velocity of the Republic. The clanking of its huge axe, rising and falling there, in horrid systole-diastole, is portion of the whole enormous Life-movement and pulsation of the Sansculottic System!—'Orleans Conspirators' and Assaulters had to die, in spite of much weeping and entreating; so sacred is the person of a Deputy. Yet the sacred can become desecrated: your very Deputy is not greater than the Guillotine. Poor Deputy Journalist Gorsas: we saw him hide at Rennes, when the Calvados War burnt priming. He stole, afterwards, in August, to Paris; lurked several weeks about the Palais *ci-devant* Royal; was seen there, one day; was clutched, identified, and without ceremony, being already 'out of the Law,' was sent to the Place de la Révolution. He died, recommending his wife and children to the pity of the Republic. It is the ninth day of October 1793. Gorsas is the first Deputy that dies on the scaffold; he will not be the last.

Ex-Mayor Bailly is in Prison; Ex-Procureur Manuel. Brissot and our poor Arrested Girondins have become Incarcerated Indicted Girondins; universal Jacobinism clamouring for their punishment. Duperret's Seals are *broken* (p. 274)! Those Seventy-three Secret Protesters, suddenly one day, are reported upon, are decreed accused; the Convention-doors being 'previously shut,' that none implicated might escape. They were marched, in a very rough manner, to Prison that evening. Happy those of them who chanced to be absent! Condorcet has vanished into darkness ; perhaps, like Rabaut, sits between two walls, in the house of a friend.

CHAPTER VII

MARIE-ANTOINETTE

On Monday the Fourteenth of October 1793, a Cause is pending in the Palais de Justice, in the new Revolutionary Court, such as these old stone-walls never witnessed : the Trial of Marie-Antoinette. The once brightest of Queens, now tarnished, defaced, forsaken, stands here at Fouquier-Tinville's Judgment bar ; answering for her life. The Indictment was delivered her last night. To such changes of human fortune what words are adequate ? Silence alone is adequate.

There are few Printed things one meets with, of such tragic, almost ghastly, significance as those bald Pages of the *Bulletin du Tribunal Révolutionnaire*, which bear Title, *Trial of the Widow Capet*. Dim, dim, as if in disastrous eclipse ; like the pale kingdoms of Dis ! Plutonic Judges, Plutonic Tinville ; encircled, nine times, with Styx and Lethe, with Fire-Phlegethon and Cocytus named of Lamentation ! The very witnesses summoned are like Ghosts : exculpatory, inculpatory, they themselves are all hovering over death and doom ; they are known, in our imagination, as the prey of the Guillotine. Tall *ci-devant* Count d'Estaing, anxious to show himself Patriot, cannot escape ; nor Bailly, who, when asked If he knows the Accused, answers with a reverent inclination towards her, " Ah, yes, I know Madame." Ex-Patriots are here, sharply dealt with, as Procureur Manuel ; Ex-Ministers, shorn of their splendour. We have cold Aristocratic impassivity, faithful to itself even in Tartarus ; rabid stupidity, of Patriot Corporals, Patriot Washerwomen, who have much to say of Plots, Treasons, August Tenth, old Insurrection of Women. For all now has become a crime, in her who has *lost*.

Marie-Antoinette, in this her utter abandonment, and hour of extreme need, is not wanting to herself, the imperial woman. Her look, they say, as that hideous Indictment was reading, continued calm ; ' she was sometimes observed moving her fingers, as when one plays on the Piano.' You discern, not without interest, across that dim Revolutionary Bulletin itself, how she bears herself queenlike. Her answers are prompt, clear, often of Laconic brevity ; resolution, which has grown contemptuous without ceasing to be dignified, veils itself in calm words. "You persist then in denial?"—"My plan is not denial: it is the truth I have said, and I persist in that." Scandalous Hébert has borne his testimony as to many things: as to one thing, concerning Marie-Antoinette and her little Son,—wherewith Human Speech had better not further be soiled. She has answered Hébert; a Juryman begs to observe that she has not answered as to *this*. "I have not answered," she exclaims with noble emotion, "because Nature refuses to answer such a charge brought against a Mother. I appeal to all the Mothers that are here." Robespierre, when he heard of it, broke out into something almost like swearing at the brutish blockheadism of this Hébert; on whose foul head his foul lie has recoiled. At four o'clock on Wednesday morning, after two days and two nights of interrogating, jury-charging, and other darkening of counsel, the result comes out: sentence of Death. "Have you anything to say?" The Accused shook her head, without speech. Night's candles are burning out; and with her too Time is finishing, and it will be Eternity and Day. This Hall of Tinville's is dark, ill-lighted except where she stands. Silently she withdraws from it, to die.

Two Processions, or Royal Progresses, three-and-twenty years apart, have often struck us with a strange feeling of contrast. The first is of a beautiful Archduchess and Dauphiness, quitting her Mother's City, at the age of Fifteen; towards hopes such as no other Daughter of Eve then had: 'On the morrow,' says Weber an eye-witness, 'the Dauphiness left Vienna. The whole city crowded out; at first with a sorrow which was silent. She appeared: you saw her sunk back into her carriage; her face bathed in tears; hiding her eyes now with her handkerchief, now with her hands; several times putting out her head to see yet again this Palace of her Fathers, whither she was to return no more. She motioned her regret, her gratitude to the good Nation, which was crowding here to bid her farewell. Then arose not only tears; but piercing cries, on all sides. Men and women alike abandoned themselves to such expression of their sorrow. It was an audible sound of wail, in the streets and avenues of Vienna. The last Courier that followed her disappeared, and the crowd melted away.

The young imperial Maiden of Fifteen has now become a worn discrowned Widow of Thirty-eight; gray before her time: This is the last Procession: 'Few minutes after the Trial ended, the drums were beating to arms in all Sections; at sunrise the armed force was on foot, cannons getting placed at the extremities of the Bridges, in the Squares, Crossways, all along from the Palais de Justice to the Place de la Révolution. By ten o'clock, numerous patrols were circulating in the Streets; thirty thousand foot and horse drawn up under arms. At eleven Marie-Antoinette was brought out. She had on an undress of *piqué blanc*: she was led to the place of execution, in the same manner as an ordinary criminal; bound, on a Cart; accompanied by a Constitutional Priest in Lay dress; escorted by numerous detachments of infantry and cavalry. These, and the double row of troops all along her road, she appeared to regard with indifference. On her countenance there was visible neither abashment nor pride. To the cries of *Vive la République* and *Down with Tyranny*, which attended her all the way, she seemed to pay no heed. She spoke little to her Confessor. The tricolor Streamers on the housetops occupied her attention, in the Streets du Roule and Saint-Honoré; she also noticed the Inscriptions on the house-fronts. On reaching the Place de la Révolution, her looks turned towards the *Jardin National,* whilom Tuileries; her face at that moment gave signs of lively emotion. She mounted the Scaffold with courage enough; at a quarter past Twelve, her head fell; the Executioner showed it to the people, amid universal long-continued cries of *Vive la République.*'

CHAPTER VIII

THE TWENTY-TWO

WHOM next, O Tinville! The next are of a different colour: our poor Arrested Girondin Deputies. What of them could still be laid hold of; our Vergniaud, Brissot, Fauchet, Valazé, Gensonné; the once flower of French Patriotism, Twenty-two by the tale: *hither*, at Tinville's Bar, onward from 'safeguard of the French People,' from confinement in the Luxembourg, imprisonment in the Conciergerie, have they now, by the course of things, arrived. Fouquier-Tinville must give what account of them he can.

Undoubtedly this Trial of the Girondins is the greatest that Fouquier has yet had to do. Twenty-two, all chief Republicans, ranged in a line there; the most eloquent in France; Lawyers too; not without friends in the auditory. How will Tinville prove these men guilty of Royalism, Federalism, Conspiracy against the Republic? Vergniaud's eloquence awakes once more; 'draws tears,' they say. And Journalists report, and the Trial lengthens itself out day-after day; 'threatens to become eternal,' murmur many. Jacobinism and Municipality rise to the aid of Fouquier. On the 28th of the month, Hébert and others come in deputation to inform a Patriot Convention that the Revolutionary Tribunal is quite 'shackled by Forms of Law;' that a Patriot Jury ought to have 'the power of cutting short, of *terminer les débats*, when they feel themselves convinced.' Which pregnant suggestion, of cutting short, passes itself, with all despatch, into a Decree.

Accordingly, at ten o'clock on the night of the 30th of October, the Twenty-two, summoned back once more, receive this information, That the Jury feeling themselves convinced have cut short, have brought in their verdict; that the Accused are found guilty, and the Sentence on one and all of them is, Death with confiscation of goods.

Loud natural clamour rises among the poor Girondins; tumult; which can only be repressed by the gendarmes. Valazé stabs himself; falls down dead on the spot. The rest, amid loud clamour and confusion, are driven back to their Conciergerie; Lasource exclaiming, "I die on the day when the People have lost their reason; ye will die when they recover it." No help! Yielding to violence, the Doomed uplift the Hymn of the Marseillese; return singing to their dungeon.

Riouffe, who was their Prison-mate in these last days, has lovingly recorded what death they made. To our notions, it is not an edifying death. Gay satirical *Pot-pourri* by Ducos; rhymed Scenes of Tragedy, wherein Barrère and Robespierre discourse with Satan; death's eve spent in 'singing' and 'sallies of gaiety,' with 'discourses on the happiness of peoples;' these things, and the like of these, we have to accept for what they are worth. It is the manner in which the Girondins make *their* Last Supper. Valazé with bloody breast, sleeps cold in death; hears not the singing. Vergniaud has his dose of poison; but it is not enough for his friends, it is enough only for himself; wherefore he flings it from him; presides at this Last Supper of the Girondins, with wild coruscations of eloquence, with song and mirth. Poor human Will struggles to assert itself; if not in this way, then in that.

But on the morrow morning all Paris is out; such a crowd

as no man had seen. The Death-carts, Valazé's cold corpse stretched among the yet living Twenty-one, roll along. Bareheaded, hands bound; in their shirt-sleeves, coat flung loosely round the neck: so fare the eloquent of France; bemurmured, beshouted. To the shouts of *Vive la République*, some of them keep answering with counter-shouts of *Vive la République*. Others, as Brissot, sit sunk in silence. At the foot of the scaffold they again strike up, with appropriate variations, the Hymn of the Marseillese. Such an act of music; conceive it well! The yet Living chant there; the chorus so rapidly wearing weak! Samson's axe is rapid; one head per minute, or little less. The chorus is wearing weak! the chorus is worn *out*;—farewell forevermore, ye Girondins. Te-Deum Fauchet has become silent; Valazé's dead head is lopped: the sickle of the Guillotine has reaped the Girondins all away. 'The eloquent, the young, the beautiful and brave!' exclaims Riouffe. O Death, what feast is toward in thy ghastly Halls?

Nor, alas, in the far Bourdeaux region will Girondism fare better. In caves of Saint-Emilion, in loft and cellar, the weariest months roll on; apparel worn, purse empty; wintry November come; under Tallien and his Guillotine, all hope now gone. Danger drawing ever nigher, difficulty pressing ever straiter, they determine to separate. Not unpathetic the farewell; tall Barbaroux, cheeriest of brave men, stoops to clasp his Louvet: "In what place soever thou findest my Mother," cries he, "try to be instead of a son to her: no resource of mine but I will share with thy Wife, should chance ever lead me where she is."

Louvet went with Guadet, with Salles and Valadi; Barbaroux with Buzot and Pétion. Valadi soon went southward, on a way of his own. The two friends and Louvet had a miserable day and night; the 14th of the November month, 1793. Sunk in wet, weariness and hunger, they knock, on the morrow, for help, at a friend's country-house; the fainthearted friend refuses to admit them. They stood therefore under trees, in the pouring rain. Flying desperate, Louvet thereupon will to Paris. He sets forth, there and then, splashing the mud on each side of him, with a fresh strength gathered from fury or frenzy. He passes villages, finding 'the sentry asleep in his box in the thick rain;' he is gone, before the man can call after him. He bilks Revolutionary Committe es; rides in carriers' carts, covered carts and

open; lies hidden in one, under knapsacks and cloaks of
soldiers' wives on the Street of Orleans, while men search for
him; has hairbreadth escapes that would fill three romances:
finally he gets to Paris to his fair Helpmate; gets to Switzerland, and waits better days.

Poor Guadet and Salles were both taken, ere long; they
died by the Guillotine in Bourdeaux; drums beating to drown
their voice. Valadi also is caught, and guillotined. Barbaroux and his two comrades weathered it longer, into the
summer of 1794; but not long enough. One July morning,
changing their hiding-place, as they have often to do, 'about
a league from Saint-Emilion, they observe a great crowd of
country-people:' doubtless Jacobins come to take them?
Barbaroux draws a pistol, shoots himself dead. Alas, and it
was not Jacobins; it was harmless villagers going to a village
wake. Two days afterwards, Buzot and Pétion were found in
a Corn-field, their bodies half-eaten by dogs.

Such was the end of Girondism. They arose to regenerate
France, these men; and have accomplished *this*. Alas, whatever quarrel we had with them, has not their cruel fate
abolished it? Pity only survives. So many excellent souls of
heroes sent down to Hades; they themselves given as a prey
of dogs and all manner of birds! But, here too, the will of
the Supreme Power was accomplished. As Vergniaud said:
'the Revolution, like Saturn, is devouring its own children.'

BOOK V

TERROR THE ORDER OF THE DAY

CHAPTER I

RUSHING DOWN

WE are now, therefore, got to that black precipitous Abyss; whither all things have long been tending; where, having now arrived on the giddy verge, they hurl down, in confused ruin; headlong, pellmell, down, down;—till Sansculottism have consummated itself; and in this wondrous French Revolution, as in a Doomsday, a World have been rapidly, if not born again, yet destroyed and engulfed. Terror has long been terrible: but to the actors themselves it has now become manifest that their appointed course is one of Terror; and they say, Be it so. "*Que la Terreur soit à l'ordre du jour.*"

So many centuries, say only from Hugh Capet downwards, had been adding together, century transmitting it with increase to century, the sum of Wickedness, of Falsehood, Oppression of man by man. Kings were sinners, and Priests were, and People. Open Scoundrels rode triumphant, bediademed, becoronetted, bemitred; or the still fataller species of Secret-Scoundrels, in their fair-sounding formulas, speciosities, respectabilities, hollow within: the race of Quacks was grown many as the sands of the sea. Till at length such a sum of Quackery had accumulated itself as, in brief, the Earth and the Heavens were weary of. Slow seemed the Day of Settlement; coming on, all imperceptible, across the bluster and fanfaronade of Courtierisms, Conquering-Heroisms, Most Christian *Grand Monarque*-isms, Well-beloved Pompadourisms: yet behold it was always coming; behold it has come, suddenly, unlooked for by any man! The harvest of long centuries was ripening and whitening so rapidly of late; and now it is grown *white*, and is reaped rapidly, as it were, in one day. Reaped, in this Reign of Terror; and carried home, to Hades and the Pit!—Unhappy Sons of Adam: it is ever so; and never do they know it, nor will they know it. With cheerfully smoothed countenances, day after day, and generation after generation, they, calling cheerfully to one another, Well-speed-ye, are at work, *sowing the wind*. And yet, as God lives, they *shall reap the whirlwind:* no other thing, we say, is possible,—since God is a Truth and His World is a Truth.

History, however, in dealing with this Reign of Terror, has had her own difficulties. While the Phenomenon continued in its primary state, as mere 'Horrors of the French Revolution,' there was abundance to be said and shrieked. With and also without profit. Heaven knows, there were terrors and horrors enough: yet that was not all the Phenomenon; nay, more properly, that was not the Phenomenon at all, but rather was the *shadow* of it, the negative part of it. And now, in a new stage of the business, when History, ceasing to shriek, would try rather to include under her old Forms of speech or speculation this new amazing Thing; that so some accredited scientific Law of Nature might suffice for the unexpected Product of Nature, and History might get to speak of it articulately, and draw inferences and profit from it; in this new stage, History, we may say, babbles and flounders perhaps in a still painfuller manner. Take, for example, the latest Form of speech we have seen propounded on the subject as adequate to it, almost in these months, by our worthy M. Roux, in his *Histoire Parlementaire*. The latest and the strangest: that the French Revolution was a deadlift effort, after eighteen hundred years of preparation, to realise —the Christian Religion! *Unity, Indivisibility, Brotherhood or Death*, did indeed stand printed on all Houses of the Living; also, on Cemeteries, or Houses of the Dead, stood printed, by order of Procureur Chaumette, *Here is Eternal Sleep:* but a Christian Religion realised by the Guillotine and Death-Eternal 'is suspect to me,' as Robespierre was wont to say, '*m'est suspecte*.'

Alas, no, M. Roux! A Gospel of Brotherhood, not according to any of the Four old Evangelists, and calling on men to repent, and amend *each his own* wicked existence, that they might be saved; but a Gospel rather, as we often hint, according to a new Fifth Evangelist Jean-Jacques, calling on men to amend *each the whole world's* wicked existence, and be saved by making the Constitution. A thing different and distant *toto cælo*, as they say: the whole breadth of the sky, and further if possible! It is thus, however, that History, and indeed all human Speech and Reason does yet, what Father Adam began life by doing : strive to *name* the new Things it sees of Nature's producing,—often helplessly enough.

But what if History were to admit, for once, that all the Names and Theorems yet known to her fall short ? That this grand Product of Nature was even grand, and new, in that it came not to range itself under old recorded Laws of Nature at all, but to disclose new ones ? In that case, History renouncing the pretension to *name* it at present, will *look* honestly at it, and name what she can of it ! Any approximation to the right Name has value : were the right Name itself once here, the Thing is known henceforth ; the Thing is then ours, and can be dealt with.

Now surely not realisation, of Christianity, or of aught earthly, do we discern in this Reign of Terror, in this French Revolution of which it is the consummating. Destruction rather we discern,—of all that was destructible. It is as if Twenty-five millions, risen at length into the Pythian mood, had stood up simultaneously to say, with a sound which goes through far lands and times, that this Untruth of an Existence had become insupportable. O ye Hypocrisies and Speciosities, Royal mantles, Cardinal plush-cloaks, ye Credos, Formulas, Respectabilities, fair-painted Sepulchres full of dead men's bones,—behold, ye appear to us to be altogether a Lie. Yet our Life is not a Lie ; yet our Hunger and Misery is not a Lie ! Behold we lift up, one and all, our Twenty-five million right-hands ; and take the Heavens, and the Earth and also the Pit of Tophet to witness, that either ye shall be abolished, or else we shall be abolished !

No inconsiderable Oath, truly ; forming, as has been often said, the most remarkable transaction in these last thousand years. Wherefrom likewise there follow, and will follow, results. The fulfilment of this Oath ; that is to say, the black desperate battle of Men against their whole Condition and Environment,—a battle, alas, withal, against the Sin and Darkness that was in themselves as in others : this is the Reign of Terror. Transcendental despair was the purport of it, though not consciously so. False hopes, of Fraternity, Political Millennium, and what not, we have always seen : but the unseen heart of the whole, the transcendental despair, was not false ; neither has it been of no effect. Despair, pushed far enough, completes the circle, so to speak ; and becomes a kind of genuine productive hope again.

Doctrine of Fraternity, out of old Catholicism, does, it is true, very strangely in the vehicle of a Jean-Jacques Evangel, suddenly plump down out of its cloud-firmament; and from a theorem determine to make itself a practice. But just so do all creeds, intentions, customs, knowledges, thoughts and things, which the French have, suddenly plump down; Catholicism, Classicism, Sentimentalism, Cannibalism: all *isms* that make up Man in France, are rushing and roaring in that gulf; and the theorem has become a practice, and whatsoever cannot swim sinks. Not Evangelist Jean-Jacques alone; there is not a Village Schoolmaster but has contributed his quota: do we not *thou* one another, according to the Free Peoples of Antiquity? The French Patriot, in red Phrygian night-cap of Liberty, christens his poor little red infant Cato, —Censor, or else of Utica. Gracchus has become Babœuf, and edits Newspapers; Mutius Scævola, Cordwainer of that ilk, presides in the Section Mutius-Scævola: and in brief, there is a world wholly jumbling itself, to try what will swim.

Wherefore we will, at all events, call this Reign of Terror a very strange one. Dominant Sansculottism makes, as it were, free arena; one of the strangest temporary states Humanity was ever seen in. A nation of men, full of wants and void of habits! The old habits are gone to wreck because they were old: men, driven forward by Necessity and fierce Pythian Madness, have, on the spur of the instant, to devise for the want the *way* of satisfying it. The Wonted tumbles down: by imitation, by invention, the Unwonted hastily builds itself up. What the French National head has in it comes out: if not a great result, surely one of the strangest.

Neither shall the Reader fancy that it was all black, this Reign of Terror: far from it. How many hammermen and squaremen, bakers and brewers, washers and wringers, over this France, must ply their old daily work, let the Government be one of Terror or one of Joy! In this Paris there are Twenty-three Theatres nightly; some count as many as Sixty places of Dancing. The Playwright manufactures,—pieces of a strictly Republican character. Ever fresh Novel-garbage, as of old, fodders the Circulating Libraries. The 'Cesspool of *Agio*,' now in a time of Paper Money, works with a vivacity unexampled, unimagined; exhales from itself 'sudden fortunes,' like Aladdin-Palaces: really a kind of miraculous Fata-Morganas, since you *can* live in them, for a time. Terror is as a sable ground, on which the most variegated of scenes paints itself. In startling transitions, in colours all intensated, the sublime, the ludicrous, the horrible succeed one another; or rather, in crowding tumult, accompany one another.

Here, accordingly, if anywhere, the 'hundred tongues,' which the old Poets often clamour for, were of supreme service! In defect of any such organ on our part, let the Reader stir up his own imaginative organ: let us snatch for him this or the other significant glimpse of things, in the fittest sequence we can.

CHAPTER II

DEATH

IN the early days of November, there is one transient glimpse of things that is to be noted: the last transit to his long home of Philippe d'Orléans Égalité. Philippe was 'decreed accused,' along with the Girondins, much to his and their surprise; but not tried along with them. They are doomed and dead, some three days, when Philippe, after his long half-year of durance at Marseilles, arrives in Paris. It is, as we calculate, the third of November 1793.

On which same day, two notable Female Prisoners are also put in ward there: Dame Dubarry, and Josephine Beauharnais. Dame whilom Countess Dubarry, Unfortunate-female, had returned from London; they snatched her, not only as Ex-harlot of a whilom Majesty, and therefore suspect; but as having 'furnished the Emigrants with money.' Contemporaneously with whom there comes the wife Beauharnais, soon to be the widow: she that is Josephine Tascher Beauharnais; that shall be Josephine Empress Buonaparte,—for a black Divineress of the Tropics prophesied long since that she should be a Queen and more. Likewise, in the same hours, poor Adam Lux, nigh turned in the head, who, according to Forster, 'has taken no food these three weeks,' marches to the Guillotine for his Pamphlet on Charlotte Corday: he 'sprang to the scaffold;' said 'he died for her with great joy.' Amid such fellow-travellers does Philippe arrive. For, be the month named Brumaire year 2 of Liberty, or November year 1793 of Slavery, the Guillotine goes always, *Guillotine va toujours*.

Enough, Philippe's indictment is soon drawn, his jury soon convinced. He finds himself made guilty of Royalism, Conpiracy and much else; nay, it is a guilt in him that he voted Louis's Death, though he answers, "I voted in my soul and conscience." The doom he finds is death forthwith; this present sixth dim day of November is the last day that Philippe is to see. Philippe, says Montgaillard, thereupon called for breakfast: sufficiency of 'oysters, two cutlets, best part of an excellent bottle of claret;' and consumed the same with apparent relish. A Revolutionary Judge or some official Convention Emissary, then arrived, to signify that he might still do the State some service by revealing the truth about a plot or two. Philippe answered that, on him, in the pass things had come to, the State had, he thought, small claim; that nevertheless, in the interest of Liberty he, having still some leisure on his hands, was willing, were a reasonable question asked him, to give a reasonable answer. And so, says Montgaillard, he leant his elbow on the mantel-piece, and conversed in an undertone, with great seeming composure; till the leisure was done, or the Emissary went his ways.

At the door of the Conciergerie, Philippe's attitude was erect and easy, almost commanding. It is five years, all but a few days, since Philippe, within these same stone walls, stood up with an air of graciosity, and asked King Louis, "Whether it was a Royal Session, then, or a Bed of Justice?" (i. 75.) O Heaven!—Three poor blackguards were to ride and die with him: some say, they objected to such company and had to be flung in, neck and heels; but it seems not true. Objecting or not objecting, the gallows-vehicle gets under way. Philippe's dress is remarked for its elegance; green frock, waistcoat of white *piqué*, yellow buckskins, boots clear as Warren: his air, as before, entirely composed, impassive, not to say easy and Brummellean-polite. Through street after street; slowly, amid execrations;—past the Palais Égalité, whilom Palais Royal! The cruel Populace stopped him there, some minutes: Dame de Buffon, it is said, looked out on him, in Jezebel head-tire; along the ashlar Wall there ran these words in huge tricolor print, REPUBLIC ONE AND INDIVISIBLE; LIBERTY, EQUALITY, FRATERNITY, OR DEATH: *National Property*. Philippe's eyes flashed hell-fire one instant; but the next instant it was gone, and he sat impassive, Brummellean-polite. On the scaffold, Samson was for drawing off his boots: "Tush," said Philippe, "they will come better off *after*; let us have done, *dépêchons-nous!*"

So Philippe was not without virtue, then? God forbid that

there should be any living man without it! He had the virtue
to keep living for five-and-forty years;—other virtues perhaps
more than we know of. But probably no mortal ever had such
things recorded of him: such facts, and also such lies. For
he was a *Jacobin Prince of the Blood*; consider what a combination! Also, unlike any Nero, any Borgia, he lived in the
Age of Pamphlets. Enough for us: Chaos *has* reabsorbed
him; may it late or never bear his like again!—Brave young
Orleans Égalité, deprived of all, only not deprived of himself, is gone to Coire in the Grisons, under the name of Corby,
to teach Mathematics. The Égalité Family is at the darkest
depths of the Nadir.

A far nobler victim follows; one who will claim remembrance for several centuries: Jeanne-Marie Phlipon, the Wife
of Roland. Queenly, sublime in her uncomplaining sorrow,
seemed she to Riouffe in her Prison. 'Something more
than is usually found in the looks of women painted itself,'
says Riouffe, 'in those large black eyes of hers, full of
expression and sweetness. She spoke to me often, at the
Grate: we were all attentive round her, in a sort of admiration and astonishment; she expressed herself with a purity,
with a harmony and prosody that made her language like
music, of which the ear could never have enough. Her con-
versation was serious, not cold; coming from the mouth of a
beautiful woman, it was frank and courageous as that of a great
man.' 'And yet her maid said: "Before you, she collects her
strength; but in her own room, she will sit three hours
sometimes leaning on the window, and weeping."' She has
been in Prison, liberated once, but recaptured the same hour
ever since the first of June: in agitation and uncertainty
which has gradually settled down into the last stern certainty,
that of death. In the Abbaye Prison, she occupied Charlotte
Corday's apartment. Here in the Conciergerie, she speaks with
Riouffe, with Ex-Minister Clavière; calls the beheaded
Twenty-two "*Nos amis*, our Friends,"—whom we are soon
to follow. During these five months, those *Memoirs* of hers
were written, which all the world still reads.

But now, on the 8th of November, 'clad in white,' says
Riouffe, 'with her long black hair hanging down to her
girdle,' she is gone to the Judgment-bar. She returned with a
quick step; lifted her finger, to signify to us that she was
doomed: her eyes seemed to have been wet. Fouquier-
Tinville's questions had been 'brutal;' offended female

onour flung them back on him, with scorn, not without
ars. And now, short preparation soon done, she too shall
o her last road. There went with her a certain Lamarche,
Director of Assignat-printing;' whose dejection she en-
eavoured to cheer. Arrived at the foot of the scaffold, she
sked for pen and paper, "to write the strange thoughts that
ere rising in her:" a remarkable request; which was refused.
ooking at the Statue of Liberty which stands there, she says
itterly: "O Liberty, what things are done in thy name!"
or Lamarche's sake, she will die first; show him how easy it
s to die: "Contrary to the order," said Samson.—"Pshaw,
ou cannot refuse the last request of a Lady;" and Samson
ielded.

Noble white Vision, with its high queenly face, its soft
roud eyes, long black hair flowing down to the girdle; and
s brave a heart as ever beat in woman's bosom! Like a white
Grecian Statue, serenely complete, she shines in that black
rreck of things;—long memorable. Honour to great Nature
ho, in Paris City, in the Era of Noble-Sentiment and Pompa-
ourism, can make a Jeanne Phlipon and nourish her to clear
erennial Womanhood, though but on Logics, *Encyclopédies*,
nd the Gospel according to Jean-Jacques! Biography will
ong remember that trait of asking for a pen "to write the
trange thoughts that were rising in her." It is as a little light-
eam, shedding softness, and a kind of sacredness, over all
hat preceded: so in her too there was an Unnameable; she
oo was a Daughter of the Infinite; there were mysteries
hich Philosophism had not dreamt of!—She left long written
ounsels to her little Girl; she said her Husband would not
urvive her.

Still crueller was the fate of poor Bailly, First National
resident, First Mayor of Paris: doomed now for Royalism,
ayettism; for that Red-Flag Business of the Champ-de-
Mars;—one may say in general, for leaving his Astronomy to
neddle with Revolution. It is the 10th of November 1793,
cold bitter drizzling rain, as poor Bailly is led through the
treets; howling Populace covering him with curses, with
nud; waving over his face a burning or smoking mockery of
Red Flag. Silent, unpitied, sits the innocent old man.
low faring through the sleety drizzle, they have got to the
Champ-de-Mars: Not there! vociferates the cursing Populace;
uch Blood ought not to stain an Altar of the Fatherland: not
here; but on that dung-heap by the River-side! So vocifer-

ates the cursing Populace; Officiality gives ear to them. Th
Guillotine is taken down, though with hands numbed by th
sleety drizzle; is carried to the River-side; is there set up
again, with slow numbness; pulse after pulse still counting
itself out in the old man's weary heart. For hours long; amid
curses and bitter frost-rain! "Bailly, thou tremblest," said
one. "*Mon ami*, it is for cold," said Bailly, "*c'est de froid.*"
Crueller end had no mortal.

Some days afterwards, Roland, hearing the news of what
happened on the 8th, embraces his kind Friends at Rouen
leaves their kind house which had given him refuge; goes
forth, with farewell too sad for tears. On the morrow morning
16th of the month, 'some four leagues from Rouen, Paris
ward, near Bourg-Baudoin, in M. Normand's Avenue,' there
is seen sitting leant against a tree the figure of a rigorous
wrinkled man; stiff now in the rigour of death; a cane-sword
run through his heart; and at his feet this writing: 'Whoever
thou art that findest me lying, respect my remains: they are
those of a man who consecrated all his life to being useful
and who has died as he lived, virtuous and honest.' 'Not
fear, but indignation, made me quit my retreat, on learning
that my Wife had been murdered. I wished not to remain
longer on an Earth polluted with crimes.'

Barnave's appearance at the Revolutionary Tribunal was o
the bravest; but it could not stead him. They have sent for
him from Grenoble; to pay the common smart. Vain is eloquence, forensic or other, against the dumb Clotho-shears o
Tinville. He is still but two-and-thirty, this Barnave, and has
known such changes. Short while ago, we saw him at the top
of Fortune's wheel, his word a law to all Patriots: and now
surely he is at the *bottom* of the wheel: in stormful altercation
with a Tinville Tribunal, which is dooming him to die! And
Pétion, once also of the Extreme Left, and named *Pétion
Virtue*, where is he? Civilly dead; in the Caves of Saint-
Emilion; to be devoured of dogs. And Robespierre, who
rode along with him on the shoulders of the people, is in
Committee of *Salut*; civilly alive: not to live always. So
giddy-swift whirls and spins this immeasurable *tormentum* of
a Revolution; wild-booming; not to be followed by the eye.
Barnave, on the Scaffold, stamped with his foot; and looking
upwards was heard to ejaculate, "This then is my reward?"

Deputy Ex-Procureur Manuel is already gone; and Deputy
Osselin, famed also in August and September, is about to go;

and Rabaut, discovered treacherously between his two walls, and the Brother of Rabaut. National Deputies not a few! And Generals: the memory of General Custine cannot be defended by his Son; his Son is already guillotined. Custine the Ex-noble was replaced by Houchard the Plebeian: he too could not prosper in the North; for him too there was no mercy; he has perished in the Place de la Révolution, after attempting suicide in Prison. And Generals Biron, Beauharnais, Brunet, whatsoever General prospers not; tough old Lückner, with his eyes grown rheumy; Alsatian Westermann, valiant and diligent in La Vendée: *none of them can*, as the Psalmist sings, *his soul from death deliver*.

How busy are the Revolutionary Committees; Sections with their Forty Halfpence a-day! Arrestment on arrestment falls quick, continual; followed by death. Ex-Minister Clavière has killed himself in Prison. Ex-Minister Lebrun, seized in a hayloft, under the disguise of a working-man, is instantly conducted to death. Nay, withal, is it not what Barrère calls ' coining money on the Place de la Révolution?' For always the 'property of the guilty, if property he have,' is confiscated. To avoid accidents, we even make a Law that suicide shall not defraud us; that a criminal who kills himself does not the less incur forfeiture of goods. Let the guilty tremble, therefore, and the suspect, and the rich. and in a word all manner of Culottic men! Luxembourg Palace, once Monsieur's, has become a huge loathsome Prison; Chantilly Palace too, once Condé's:—And their Landlords are at Blankenberg, on the wrong side of the Rhine. In Paris are now some Twelve Prisons; in France some Forty-four Thousand: thitherward, thick as brown leaves in Autumn, rustle and travel the suspect; shaken down by Revolutionary Committees, they are swept thitherward, as into their storehouse,—to be consumed by Samson and Tinville. 'The Guillotine goes not ill, *La Guillotine ne va pas mal*.'

CHAPTER III

DESTRUCTION

The suspect may well tremble; but how much more the open rebels;—the Girondin Cities of the South! Revolutionary Army is gone forth, under Ronsin the Playwright; six thousand strong; 'in red nightcap, in tricolor waistcoat, in black shag trousers, black-shag-spencer, with enormous moustachioes enormous sabre,—in *carmagnole complète;* and has portabl guillotines. Representative Carrier has got to Nantes, by th edge of blazing La Vendée, which Rossignol has literally se on fire: Carrier will try what captives you make; what accom plices they have, Royalist or Girondin: his guillotine goe always, *va toujours;* and his wool-capped 'Company o Marat.' Little children are guillotined, and aged men. Swif as the machine is, it will not serve; the Headsman and al his valets sink, worn down with work; declare that the human muscles can no more. Whereupon you must try fusillading to which perhaps still frightfuller methods may succeed.

In Brest, to like purpose, rules Jean-Bon Saint-André; with an Army of Red Nightcaps. In Bourdeaux rules Tallien, with his Isabeau and henchmen; Guadets, Cussys, Salleses, many fall; the bloody Pike and Nightcap bearing supreme sway; the Guillotine coining money. Bristly fox-haired Tallien, once Able Editor, still young in years, is now become most gloomy, potent; a Pluto on Earth, and has the keys of Tartarus. One remarks, however, that a certain Senhorina Cabarus, or call her rather *Senhora* and wedded not yet widowed, *Dame de Fontenai*, brown beautiful woman, daughter of Cabarus the Spanish Merchant,—has softened the red bristly countenance; pleading for herself and friends; and prevailing. The keys of Tartarus, or any kind of power, are something to a woman; gloomy Pluto himself is not insensible to love. Like a new Proserpine, she, by this red gloomy Dis, is gathered; and, they say, softens his stone heart a little.

Maignet, at Orange in the South; Lebon, at Arras in the North, become world's wonders. Jacobin Popular Tribunal, with its National Representative, perhaps where Girondin Popular Tribunal had lately been, rises here and rises there; wheresoever needed. Fouchés, Maignets, Barrases, Frèrons scour the Southern Departments; like reapers, with their guillotine-sickle. Many are the labourers, great is the harvest. By the hundred and the thousand, men's lives are cropt; cast like brands into the burning.

Marseilles is taken, and put under martial law: lo, at Marseilles, what one besmutted red-bearded corn-ear is this which they cut;—one gross Man, we mean, with copper-studded face; plenteous beard, or beard-stubble, of a tile-

:olour? By Nemesis and the Fatal Sisters, it is Jourdan Coupe-tête! Him they have clutched, in these martial-law districts; him too, with their 'national razor,' their *rasoir national*, they sternly shave away. Low now is Jourdan the Headsman's own head;—low as Deshuttes's and Varigny's, which he sent on pikes, in the Insurrection of Women! No more shall he, as a copper Portent, be seen gyrating through the Cities of the South; no more sit judging, with pipes and brandy, in the Ice-tower of Avignon. The all-hiding Earth has received him, the bloated Tilebeard: may we never look upon his like again!—Jourdan one names; the other Hundreds are not named. Alas, they, like confused faggots, lie massed together for us; counted by the cart-load: and yet not an individual faggot-twig of them but had a Life and History; and was cut, not without pangs as when a Kaiser dies!

Least of all cities can Lyons escape. Lyons, which we saw in dread sunblaze, that Autumn night when the Powder-tower sprang aloft (p. 280), was clearly verging towards a sad end. Inevitable: what could desperate valour and Précy do; Dubois-Crancé, deaf as Destiny, stern as Doom, capturing their 'redoubts of cotton-bags;' hemming them in, ever closer, with his Artillery-lava? Never would that *ci-devant* D'Autichamp arrive; never any help from Blankenberg. The Lyons Jacobins were hidden in cellars; the Girondin Municipality waxed pale, in famine, treason and red fire. Précy drew his sword, and some Fifteen Hundred with him; sprang to saddle, to cut their way to Switzerland. They cut fiercely; and were fiercely cut, and cut down; not hundreds, hardly units of them ever saw Switzerland. Lyons, on the 9th of October, surrenders at discretion; it is become a devoted Town. Abbé Lamourette, now Bishop Lamourette, whilom Legislator, he of the old *Baiser-l'Amourette* or Delilah-Kiss, is seized here; is sent to Paris to be guillotined: 'he made the sign of the cross,' they say, when Tinville intimated his death-sentence to him; and died as an eloquent Constitutional Bishop. But wo now to all Bishops, Priests, Aristocrats and Federalists that are in Lyons! The *manes* of Chalier are to be appeased; the Republic, maddened to the Sibylline pitch, has bared her right arm. Behold! Representative Fouché, it is Fouché of Nantes, a name to become well known; he with a Patriot company goes duly, in wondrous

Procession, to raise the corpse of Chalier. An Ass housed in Priest's cloak, with a mitre on his head, and trailing the Mass-Books, some say the very Bible, at its tail, paces through Lyons streets: escorted by multitudinous Patriotism, by clangour as of the Pit; towards the grave of Martyr Chalier. The body is dug up, and burnt: the ashes are collected in an Urn; to be worshipped of Paris Patriotism. The Holy Books were part of the funeral pile; their ashes are scattered to the wind. Amid cries of "Vengeance! Vengeance!"—which, writes Fouché, shall be satisfied.

Lyons in fact is a Town to be abolished; not Lyons henceforth, but 'Commune Affranchie, Township Freed:' the very name of it shall perish. It is to be razed, this once great City, if Jacobinism prophesy right; and a Pillar to be erected on the ruins, with this Inscription, Lyons rebelled against the Republic; Lyons is no more. Fouché, Couthon, Collot, Convention Representatives succeed one another: there is work for the hangman; work for the hammerman, not in building. The very Houses of Aristocrats, we say, are doomed. Paralytic Couthon, borne in a chair, taps on the wall, with emblematic mallet, saying, "La Loi te frappe, The Law strikes thee;" masons, with wedge and crowbar, begin demolition. Crash of downfal, dim ruin and dust-clouds fly in the winter wind. Had Lyons been of soft stuff, it had all vanished in those weeks, and the Jacobin prophecy had been fulfilled. But Towns are not built of soap-froth; Lyons Town is built of stone. Lyons, though it rebelled against the Republic, is to this day.

Neither have the Lyons Girondins all one neck, that you could despatch it at one swoop. Revolutionary Tribunal here, and Military Commission, guillotining, fusillading, do what they can: the kennels of the Place des Terreaux run red; mangled corpses roll down the Rhone. Collot d'Herbois, they say, was once hissed on the Lyons stage: but with what sibilation, of world-catcall or hoarse Tartarean Trumpet, will ye hiss him now, in this his new character of Convention Representative,—not to be repeated! Two-hundred and nine men are marched forth over the River, to be shot in mass, by musket and cannon, in the Promenade of the Brotteaux. It is the second of such scenes; the first was of some Seventy. The corpses of the first were flung into the Rhone, but the Rhone stranded some; so these now, of the second lot, are to be buried on land. Their one long grave is dug; they stand ranked, by the loose mould-ridge; the younger of them singing the Marseillese. Jacobin National Guards give fire; but have again to give fire, and again; and to take the bayonet and the spade, for though the doomed all fall, they do not all die;—and it becomes a butchery too horrible for speech. So that the very Nationals, as they fire, turn away their faces. Collot, snatching the musket from one such National, and levelling it with unmoved courtenance, says, "It is thus a Republican ought to fire."

This is the second Fusillade, and happily the last: it is found too hideous; even inconvenient. There were Two-hundred and nine marched out; one escaped at the end of the Bridge: yet behold, when you count the corpses, they are Two-hundred and *ten*. Rede us this riddle, O Collot? After long guessing, it is called to mind that two individuals, here in the Brotteaux ground, did attempt to leave the rank, pro-testing with agony that they were not condemned men, that they were Police Commissaries: which two we repulsed, and disbelieved, and shot with the rest! Such is the vengeance of an enraged Republic. Surely this, according to Barrère's phrase, is Justice "under rough forms, *sous des formes acerbes.*" But the Republic, as Fouché says, must "march to Liberty over corpses." Or again, as Barrère has it: "None but the dead do not come back, *Il n'y a que les morts qui ne reviennent pas.*" Terror hovers far and wide: 'the Guillotine goes not ill.'

But before quitting those Southern regions, over which His-tory can cast only glances from aloft, she will alight for a moment, and look fixedly at one point: the Siege of Toulon. Much battering and bombarding, heating of balls in furnaces or farmhouses, serving of artillery well and ill, attacking of Ollioules Passes, Forts Malbosquet, there has been: as yet to small purpose. We have had General Cartaux here, a whilom Painter elevated in the troubles of Marseilles; General Doppet, a whilom Medical man elevated in the troubles of Piémont, who, under Crancé, took Lyons, but cannot take Toulon. Finally we have General Dugommier, a pupil of Washington. Convention *Représentans* also we have had; Barrases, Salicettis, Robespierres the Younger:—also an Artillery *Chef de brigade*, of extreme diligence, who often takes his nap of sleep among the guns; a short, taciturn, olive-complexioned young man, not unknown to us, by name Buonaparte; one of the best Artillery-officers yet met with. And still Toulon is not taken. It is the fourth month now; December, in slave-style; *Fros-*

tarious or *Frimaire*, in new-style: and still their cursed Red-Blue Flag flies there. They are provisioned from the Sea; they have seized all heights, felling wood, and fortifying themselves; like the coney, they have built their nest in the rocks.

Meanwhile, *Frostarious* is not yet become *Snowous* or *Nivose*, when a Council of War is called; Instructions have just arrived from Government and *Salut Public*. Carnot, in *Salut Public*, has sent us a plan of siege: on which plan General Dugommier has this criticism to make, Commissioner Salicetti has that; and criticisms and plans are very various; when that young Artillery-Officer ventures to speak; the same whom we saw snatching sleep among the guns, who has emerged several times in this History,—the name of him Napoleon Buonaparte. It is his humble opinion, for he has been gliding about with spy-glasses, with thoughts, That a certain Fort l'Eguillette can be clutched, as with lion-spring, on the sudden; wherefrom, were it once ours, the very heart of Toulon might be battered; the English Lines were, so to speak, turned inside out, and Hood and our Natural Enemies must next day either put to sea, or be burnt to ashes. Commissioners arch their eye-brows, with negatory sniff: who is this young gentleman with more wit than we all? Brave veteran Dugommier, however, thinks the idea worth a word; questions the young gentleman; becomes convinced; and there is for issue, Try it.

On the taciturn bronze-countenance therefore, things being now all ready, there sits a grimmer gravity than ever, compressing a hotter central-fire than ever. Yonder, thou seest is Fort l'Eguillette; a desperate lion-spring, yet a possible one; this day to be tried!—Tried it is; and found *good*. By stratagem and valour stealing through ravines, plunging fiery through the fire-tempest Fort l'Eguillette is clutched at, is carried; the smoke having cleared, we see the Tricolor fly on it: the bronze-complexioned young man was right. Next morning, Hood, finding the interior of his lines exposed, his defences turned inside out, makes for his shipping. Taking such Royalists as wished it on board with him he weighs anchor; on this 19th of December 1793, Toulon is once more the Republic's!

Cannonading has ceased at Toulon; and now the guillotining and fusillading may begin. Civil horrors, truly; but at least that infamy of an English domination is purged away. Let there be Civic Feast universally over France: so reports Barrère, or Painter David; and the Convention assist in a body. Nay, it is said, these infamous English (with an attention rather to their own interests than to ours) set fire to our store-houses, arsenals, war-ships in Toulon Harbour, before weighing; some score of brave war-ships, the only ones we now had! However, it did not prosper, though the flame spread far and high; some two ships were burned, not more; the very galley-slaves ran with buckets to quench. These same proud Ships, Ship *l'Orient* and the rest, have to carry this same young Man to Egypt first: not yet can they be changed to ashes, or to Sea-Nymphs; not yet to sky-rockets, O ship *l'Orient*; nor become the prey of England,—before their time!

And so, over France universally, there is Civic Feast and high-tide: and Toulon sees fusillading, grapeshotting in mass, as Lyons saw; and death 'is poured out in great floods, *vomie à grands flots;*' and Twelve-thousand Masons are requisitioned from the neighbouring country, to raze Toulon from the face of the Earth. For it is to be razed, so reports Barrère; all but the National Shipping Establishments; and to be called henceforth not Toulon, but *Port of the Mountain.* There in black death-cloud we must leave it;—hoping only that Toulon too is built of stone; that perhaps even Twelve-thousand Masons cannot pull it down, till the fit pass.

One begins to be sick of 'death vomited in great floods.' Nevertheless, hearest thou not, O Reader (for the sound reaches through centuries), in the dead December and January nights, over Nantes Town,—confused noises, as of musketry and tumult, as of rage and lamentation; mingling with the everlasting moan of the Loire waters there? Nantes Town is sunk in sleep; but *Représentant* Carrier is not sleeping, the wool-capped Company of Marat is not sleeping. Why unmoors that flatbottomed craft, that *gabarre;* about eleven at night; with Ninety Priests under hatches? They are going to Belle Isle? In the middle of the Loire stream, on signal given, the gabarre is scuttled; she sinks with all her cargo. 'Sentence of Deportation,' writes Carrier, 'was executed *vertically.*' The Ninety Priests, with their gabarre-coffin lie deep! It is the first of the *Noyades*, what we may call *Drownages*, of Carrier; which have become famous forever.

Guillotining there was at Nantes, till the Headsman sank worn out: then fusillading 'in the Plain of Saint-Mauve;' little children fusilladed, and women with children at the breast; children and women, by the hundred and twenty;

and by the five hundred, so hot is La Vendée: till the very
Jacobins grew sick, and all but the Company of Marat cried,
Hold! Wherefore now we have got Noyading; and on the
24th night of *Frostarious* year 2, which is 14th of December
1793, we have a second Noyade; consisting of 'a Hundred
and Thirty-eight persons.'

Or why waste a gabarre, sinking it with them? Fling them
out; fling them out, with their hands tied: pour a continual
hail of lead over all the space, till the last struggler of them be
sunk! Unsound sleepers of Nantes, and the Sea-Villages
thereabouts, hear the musketry amid the night-winds; wonder
what the meaning of it is. And women were in that gabarre;
whom the Red Nightcaps were stripping naked; who begged,
in their agony, that their smocks might not be stript from
them. And young children were thrown in, their mothers
vainly pleading: "Wolflings," answered the Company of Marat,
"who would grow to be wolves."

By degrees, daylight itself witnesses Noyades: women and
men are tied together, feet and feet, hands and hands; and
flung in: this they call *Mariage Républicain*, Republican
Marriage. Cruel is the panther of the woods, the she-bear
bereaved of her whelps: but there is in man a hatred crueller
than that. Dumb, out of suffering now, as pale swoln corpses,
the victims tumble confusedly seaward along the Loire stream;
the tide rolling them back: clouds of ravens darken the
River; wolves prowl on the shoal-places: Carrier writes,
'*Quel torrent révolutionnaire*, What a torrent of Revolution!'
For the man is rabid; and the Time is rabid. These are the
Noyades of Carrier; twenty-five by the tale, for what is done
in darkness comes to be investigated in sunlight: not to be
forgotten for centuries.—We will turn to another aspect of
the Consummation of Sansculottism; leaving this as the
blackest.

But indeed men are all rabid; as the Time is. Representative Lebon, at Arras, dashes his sword into the blood
flowing from the Guillotine; exclaims, "How I like it!"
Mothers, they say, by his order, have to stand by while the
Guillotine devours their children: a band of music is stationed
near; and, at the fall of every head, strikes up its *Ça ira*. In
the Burgh of Bedouin, in the Orange region, the Liberty-tree
has been cut down overnight. Representative Maignet, at
Orange, hears of it; burns Bedouin Burgh to the last doghutch; guillotines the inhabitants, or drives them into the

caves and hills. Republic One and Indivisible! She is the newest Birth of Nature's waste inorganic Deep, which men name Orcus, Chaos, primeval Night; and knows one law, that of self-preservation. *Tigresse Nationale;* meddle not with a whisker of her! Swift-rending is her stroke; look what a paw she spreads;—pity has not entered into her heart.

Prudhomme, the dull-blustering Printer and Able Editor, as yet a Jacobin Editor, will become a renegade one, and publish large volumes, on these matters, *Crimes of the Revolution;* adding innumerable lies withal, as if the truth were not sufficient. We, for our part, find it more edifying to know, one good time, that this Republic and National Tigress *is* a New-Birth; a Fact of Nature among Formulas, in an Age of Formulas; and to look, oftenest in silence, how the so genuine Nature-Fact will demean itself among these. For the Formulas are partly genuine, partly delusive, supposititious: we call them, in the language of metaphor, regulated modelled *shapes;* some of which have bodies and life still in them; most of which, according to a German Writer, have only emptiness, 'glass-eyes glaring on you with a ghastly affectation of life, and in their interior unclean accumulation of beetles and spiders!' But the Fact, let all men observe, is a genuine and sincere one; the sincerest of Facts; terrible in its sincerity, as very Death. Whatsoever is equally sincere may front it, and beard it; but whatsoever is *not?*—

CHAPTER IV

CARMAGNOLE COMPLETE

SIMULTANEOUSLY with this Tophet-black aspect, there unfolds another aspect, which one may call a Tophet-red aspect, the Destruction of the Catholic Religion; and indeed, for the time being, of Religion itself. We saw Romme's New Calendar establish its *Tenth* Day of Rest; and asked, what would become of the Christian Sabbath? The Calendar is hardly a month old, till all this is set at rest. Very singular, as Mercier observes: last *Corpus-Christi* Day 1792, the whole world, and Sovereign Authority itself, walked in religious gala, with a quite devout air;—Butcher Legendre, supposed to be irreverent, was like to be massacred in his Gig, as the thing went by. A Gallican Hierarchy, and Church, and Church Formulas seemed to flourish, a little brown-leaved or so, but not browner than of late years or decades; to flourish far and wide, in the sympathies of an unsophisticated People; defying Philosophism, Legislature and the Encyclopédie. Far and wide, alas, like a brown-leaved Vallombrosa: which waits but one whirl-blast of the November wind, and in an hour stands bare! Since that *Corpus-Christi* Day, Brunswick has come, and the Emigrants, and La Vendée, and eighteen months of Time: to all flourishing, especially to brown-leaved flourishing, there comes, were it never so slowly, an end.

On the 7th of November, a certain Citoyen Parens, Curate of Boissise-le-Bertrand, writes to the Convention that he has all his life been preaching a lie, and is grown weary of doing it; wherefore he will now lay down his Curacy and stipend, and begs that an august Convention would give him something else to live upon. '*Mention honorable,*' shall we give him? Or 'reference to Committee of Finances?' Hardly is this got decided, when goose Gobel, Constitutional Bishop of Paris, with his Chapter, with Municipal and Departmental escort in red nightcaps, makes his appearance, to do as Parens had done. Goose Gobel will now acknowledge 'no Religion but Liberty;' therefore he doffs his Priest-gear, and receives the Fraternal embrace. To the joy of Departmental Momoro, of Municipal Chaumettes and Héberts, of Vincent and the Revolutionary army! Chaumette asks, Ought there not, in these circumstances, to be among our intercalary Days Sans-breeches, a Feast of Reason? Proper surely! Let Atheist Maréchal Lalande, and little Atheist Naigeon rejoice; let Clootz, Speaker of Mankind, present to the Convention his *Evidences of the Mahometan Religion,* 'a work evincing the nullity of all Religions,'—with thanks. There shall be Universal Republic now, thinks Clootz; and 'one God only, *Le Peuple.*'

The French Nation is of gregarious imitative nature; it needed but a fugle-motion in this matter; and goose Gobel, driven by Municipality and force of circumstances, has given one. What Curé will be behind him of Boissise; what Bishop behind him of Paris? Bishop Grégoire, indeed, courageously declines; to the sound of "We force no one; let Grégoire consult his conscience;" but Protestant and Romish by the hundred volunteer and assent. From far and near, all through November into December, till the work is accomplished, come Letters of renegation, come Curates who 'are learning to be Carpenters,' Curates with their new-wedded

Nuns: has not the day of Reason dawned, very swiftly, and become noon? From sequestered Townships come Addresses, stating plainly, though in Patois dialect, That 'they will have no more to do with the black animal called Curay, *animal noir appelé Curay.*'

Above all things, there come Patriotic Gifts, of Church-furniture. The remnant of bells, except for tocsin, descend from their belfries, into the National meltingpot to make cannon. Censers and all sacred vessels are beaten broad; of silver, they are fit for the poverty-stricken Mint; of pewter, let them become bullets, to shoot the 'enemies *du genre humain.*' Dalmatics of plush make breeches for him who had none; linen stoles will clip into shirts for the Defenders of the Country: old-clothesmen, Jew or Heathen, drive the briskest trade. Chalier's Ass-Procession, at Lyons (p. 304), was but a type of what went on, in those same days, in all Towns. In all Towns and Townships as quick as the guillotine may go, so quick goes the axe and the wrench: sacristies, lutrins, altar-rails are pulled down; the Mass-Books torn into cartridge-papers: men dance the Carmagnole all night about the bonfire. All highways jingle with metallic Priest-tackle, beaten broad; sent to the Convention, to the poverty-stricken Mint. Good Sainte Geneviève *Chasse* is let down: alas, to be burst open, this time, and burnt on the Place de Grève. Saint Louis's Shirt is burnt;—might not a Defender of the Country have had it? At Saint-Denis Town, no longer Saint-Denis but *Franciade*, Patriotism has been down among the Tombs, rummaging; the Revolutionary Army has taken spoil. This, accordingly, is what the streets of Paris saw:

'Most of these persons were still drunk, with the brandy they had swallowed out of chalices;—eating mackerel on the patenas! Mounted on Asses, which were housed with Priests' cloaks, they reined them with Priests' stoles; they held clutched with the same hand communion-cup and sacred wafer. They stopped at the doors of Dramshops; held out ciboriums; and the landlord, stoop in hand, had to fill them thrice. Next came Mules highladen with crosses, chandeliers, censers, holy-water vessels, hyssops;—recalling to mind the Priests of Cybele, whose panniers, filled with the instruments of their worship, served at once as storehouse, sacristy and temple. In such equipage did these profaners advance towards the Convention. They enter there, in an immense train, ranged in two rows; all masked like mummers in fantastic sacerdotal vestments; bearing on hand-barrows their heaped plunder,—ciboriums, suns, candelabras, plates of gold and silver.'

The Address we do not give; for indeed it was in strophes, sung *vivâ voce*, with all the parts;—Danton glooming considerably, in his place; and demanding that there be prose and decency in future. Nevertheless the captors of such *spolia opima* crave, not untouched with liquor, permission to dance the Carmagnole also on the spot: whereto an exhilarated Convention cannot but accede. Nay 'several Members,' continues the exaggerative Mercier, who was not there to witness, being in Limbo now, as one of Duperret's *Seventy-three*, 'several Members, quitting their curule chairs, took the hand of girls flaunting in Priests' vestures, and danced the Carmagnole along with them.' Such Old-Hallowtide have they, in this year, once named of Grace 1793.

Out of which strange fall of Formulas, tumbling there in confused welter, betrampled by the Patriotic dance, is it not passing strange to see a *new* Formula arise? For the human tongue is not adequate to speak what 'triviality run distracted' there is in human nature. Black Mumbo-Jumbo of the woods, and most Indian Wau-waus, one can understand: but this of Procureur *Anaxagoras*, whilom John-Peter, Chaumette? We will say only: Man is a born idol-worshipper, *sight*-worshipper, so sensuous-imaginative is he; and also partakes much of the nature of an ape.

For the same day, while this brave Carmagnole-dance has hardly jigged itself out, there arrive Procureur Chaumette and Municipals and Departmentals, and with them the strangest freightage: a New Religion! Demoiselle Candeille, of the Opera; a woman fair to look upon, when well rouged; she, borne on palanquin shoulder high; with red woollen nightcap; in azure mantle; garlanded with oak; holding in her hand the Pike of the Jupiter-*Peuple*, sails in: heralded by white young women girt in tricolor. Let the world consider it. This, O National Convention wonder of the universe, is our New Divinity; *Goddess of Reason*, worthy, and alone worthy of revering. Her henceforth we adore. Nay, were it too much to ask of an august National Representation that it also went with us to the *ci-devant* Cathedral called of Notre-Dame, and executed a few strophes in worship of her?

President and Secretaries give Goddess Candeille, borne at

due height round their platform, successively the Fraternal kiss; whereupon she, by decree, sails to the right-hand of the President and there alights. And now, after due pause and flourishes of oratory, the Convention, gathering its limbs, does get under way in the required procession towards Notre-Dame;—Reason, again in her litter, sitting in the van of them, borne, as one judges, by men in the Roman costume; escorted by wind-music, red nightcaps, and the madness of the world. And so, straightway, Reason taking seat on the high-altar of Notre-Dame, the requisite worship or quasi-worship is, say the Newspapers, *executed;* National Convention chanting 'the *Hymn to Liberty,* words by Chénier, music by Gossec.' It is the first of the *Feasts of Reason;* first communion-service of the New Religion of Chaumette.

'The corresponding Festival in the Church of Saint-Eustache,' says Mercier, 'offered the spectacle of a great tavern. The interior of the choir represented a landscape decorated with cottages and boskets of trees. Round the choir stood tables overloaded with bottles, with sausages, pork-puddings, pastries and other meats. The guests flowed in and out through all doors: whosoever presented himself took part of the good things: children of eight, girls as well as boys, put hand to plate, in sign of Liberty; they drank also of the bottles, and their prompt intoxication created laughter. Reason sat in azure mantle aloft, in a serene manner; Cannoneers, pipe in mouth, serving her as acolytes. And out of doors,' continues the exaggerative man, 'were mad multitudes dancing round the bonfire of Chapel-balustrades, of Priests' and Canons' stalls; and the dancers,—I exaggerate nothing,—the dancers nigh bare of breeches, neck and breast naked, stockings down, went whirling and spinning, like those Dustvortexes, forerunners of Tempest and Destruction.' At Saint-Gervais Church, again, there was a terrible 'smell of herrings;' Section or Municipality having provided no food, no condiment, but left it to chance. Other mysteries, seemingly of a Cabiric or even Paphian character, we leave under the Veil, which appropriately stretches itself 'along the pillars of the aisles,'—not to be lifted aside by the hand of History.

But there is one thing we should like almost better to understand than any other: what Reason herself thought of it, all the while. What articulate words poor Mrs. Momoro, for example, uttered; when she had become ungoddessed again, and the Bibliopolist and she sat quiet at home, at supper? For he was an earnest man, Bookseller Momoro; and had notions of Agrarian Law. Mrs. Momoro, it is admitted, made one of the best Goddesses of Reason; though her teeth were a little defective.—And now if the Reader will represent to himself that such visible Adoration of Reason went on 'all over the Republic,' through these November and December weeks, till the Church woodwork was burnt out, and the business otherwise completed, he will perhaps feel sufficiently what an adoring Republic it was, and without reluctance quit this part of the subject.

Such gifts of Church-spoil are chiefly the work of the *Armée Révolutionnaire;* raised, as we said, some time ago (p. 284). It is an army with portable guillotine: commanded by Playwright Ronsin in terrible moustachioes; and even by some uncertain shadow of Usher Maillard, the old Bastille Hero, Leader of the Menads, September Man in Gray! Clerk Vincent of the War-Office, one of Pache's old Clerks, 'with a head heated by the ancient orators,' had a main hand in the appointments, at least in the staff-appointments.

But of the marchings and retreatings of these Six-thousand no Xenophon exists. Nothing, but an inarticulate hum, of cursing, and sooty frenzy, surviving dubious in the memory of ages! They scour the country round Paris; seeking Prisoners; raising Requisitions; seeing that Edicts are executed, that the Farmers have thrashed sufficiently; lowering Church-bells or metallic Virgins. Detachments shoot forth dim, towards remote parts of France; nay new Provincial Revolutionary Armies rise dim, here and there, as Carrier's Company of Marat, as Tallien's Bourdeaux Troop; like sympathetic clouds in an atmosphere all electric. Ronsin, they say, admitted, in candid moments, that his troops were the elixir of the Rascality of the Earth. One sees them drawn up in market-places; travel-splashed, rough-bearded, in *carmagnole complète:* the first exploit is to prostrate what Royal or Ecclesiastical monument, crucifix or the like, there may be: to plant a cannon at the steeple; fetch down the bell without climbing for it, bell and belfry together. This, however, it is said, depends somewhat on the size of the town: if the town contains much population, and these perhaps of a dubious choleric aspect, the Revolutionary Army will do its work gently, by ladder and wrench; nay perhaps will take its billet without work at all; and, refreshing itself with a little liquor and sleep, pass on to the next stage. Pipe in cheek, sabre on thigh; in Carmagnole complete!

Such things have been; and may again be. Charles Second sent out his Highland Host over the Western Scotch Whigs; Jamaica Planters got Dogs from the Spanish Main to hunt their Maroons with: France too is bescoured with a Devil's Pack, the baying of which, at this distance of half a century, still sounds in the mind's ear.

CHAPTER V

LIKE A THUNDER-CLOUD

But the grand, and indeed substantially primary and generic aspect of the Consummation of Terror remains still to be looked at; nay blinkard History has for most part all but *over*looked this aspect, the soul of the whole; that which makes it terrible to the Enemies of France. Let Despotism and Cimmerian Coalitions consider. All French men and French things are in a State of Requisition; Fourteen Armies are got on foot; Patriotism, with all that it has of faculty in heart or in head, in soul or body or breeches-pocket, is rushing to the Frontiers, to prevail or die! Busy sits Carnot, in *Salut Public*; busy, for his share, in 'organising victory.' Not swifter pulses that Guillotine, in dread systole-diastole in the Place de la Révolution, than smites the Sword of Patriotism, smiting Cimmeria back to its own borders, from the sacred soil.

In fact, the Government is what we can call Revolutionary; and some men are 'à la hauteur,' on a level with circumstances; and others are not à la hauteur,—so much the worse for them. But the Anarchy, we may say, has *organised* itself: Society is literally overset; its old forces working with mad activity, but in the inverse order; destructive and self-destructive.

Curious to see how all still refers itself to some head and fountain; not even an Anarchy but must have a centre to revolve round. It is now some six months since the Committee of *Salut Public* came into existence; some three months since Danton proposed that all power should be given it, and 'a sum of fifty millions,' and the 'Government be declared Revolutionary.' He himself, since that day, would take no hand in it, though again and again solicited; but sits private in his place on the Mountain. Since that day, the Nine, or if they should even rise to Twelve, have become permanent, always re-elected when their term runs out; *Salut Public*, *Sûreté Générale* have assumed their ulterior form and mode of operating.

Committee of Public Salvation, as supreme; of General surety, as subaltern: these, like a Lesser and Greater Council, most harmonious hitherto, have become the centre of all things. They ride this Whirlwind; they, raised by force of circumstances, insensibly, very strangely, thither to that dread height;—and guide it, and seem to guide it. Stranger set of Cloud-Compellers the Earth never saw. A Robespierre, a Billaud, a Collot, Couthon, Saint-Just; not to mention still meaner Amars, Vadiers, in *Sûreté Générale:* these are your Cloud-Compellers. Small intellectual talent is necessary: indeed where among them, except in the head of Carnot, busied organising victory, would you find any? The talent is one of instinct rather. It is that of divining aright what this great dumb Whirlwind wishes and wills; that of willing, with more frenzy than any one, what all the world wills. To stand at no obstacles; to heed no considerations, human or divine, to know well that, of divine or human, there is one thing needful, Triumph of the Republic, Destruction of the enemies of the Republic! With this one spiritual endowment, and so few others, it is strange to see how a dumb inarticulately storming Whirlwind of things puts, as it were, its reins into your hand, and invites and compels you to be leader of it.

Hard by, sits a Municipality of Paris; all in red nightcaps since the fourth of November last: a set of men fully 'on a level with circumstances,' or even beyond it. Sleek Mayor Pache, studious to be safe in the middle; Chaumettes, Héberts, Varlets, and Henriot their great Commandant; not to speak of Vincent the War-clerk, of Momoros, Dobsents and such like: all intent to have Churches plundered, to have Reason adored, Suspects cut down, and the Revolution triumph. Perhaps carrying the matter *too* far? Danton was heard to grumble at the civic strophes; and to recommend prose and decency. Robespierre also grumbles that, in overturning Superstition, we did not mean to make a religion of Atheism. In fact, your Chaumette and Company constitute a kind of Hyper-Jacobinism, or rabid 'Faction *des Enragés;*' which has given orthodox Patriotism some umbrage, of late months. To 'know a Suspect on the streets;' what is this but bringing the *Law of the Suspect* itself into ill odour? Men half-frantic, men zealous overmuch,—they toil there, in their red night-caps, restlessly, rapidly, accomplishing what of Life is allotted them.

And the Forty-four Thousand other Townships, each with Revolutionary Committee, based on Jacobin Daughter-Society; enlightened by the spirit of Jacobinism; quickened by the Forty Sous a-day!—The French Constitution spurned always at anything like Two Chambers; and yet behold, has it not verily got Two Chambers? National Convention, elected, for one; Mother of Patriotism, self-elected, for another! Mother of Patriotism has her Debates reported in the *Moniteur*, as important state-procedures; which indisputably they are. A Second Chamber of Legislature we call this Mother-Society; —if perhaps it were not rather comparable to that old Scotch Body named *Lords of the Articles*, without whose origination, and signal given, the so-called Parliament could introduce no bill, could do no work? Robespierre himself, whose words are a law, opens his incorruptible lips copiously in the Jacobins Hall. Smaller Council of *Salut Public*, Greater Council of *Sûreté Générale*, all active Parties, come here to plead; to shape beforehand what decision they must arrive at, what destiny they have to expect. Now if a question arose, Which of those Two Chambers, Convention, or Lords of the Articles, was the *stronger?* Happily they as yet go hand in hand.

As for the National Convention, truly it has become a most composed Body. Quenched now the old effervescence; the Seventy-three locked in ward; once noisy Friends of the Girondins sunk all into silent men of the Plain, called even 'Frogs of the Marsh,' *Crapauds du Marais!* Addresses come, Revolutionary Church-plunder comes; Deputations, with prose or strophes: these the Convention receives. But beyond this, the Convention has one thing mainly to do: to listen what *Salut Public* proposes, and say, Yea.

Bazire followed by Chabot, with some impetuosity, declared, one morning, that this was not the way of a Free Assembly. "There ought to be an Opposition side, a *Côté Droit*," cried Chabot: "if none else will form it, I will. People say to me, You will all get guillotined in your turn, first you and Bazire, then Danton, then Robespierre himself." So spake the Dis-frocked, with a loud voice: next week, Bazire and he lie in the Abbaye; wending, one may fear, towards Tinville and the

Axe; and 'people say to me'—what seems to be proving true! Bazire's blood was all inflamed with Revolution Fever; with coffee and spasmodic dreams. Chabot, again, how happy with his rich Jew-Austrian wife, late Fräulein Frey! But he lies in Prison; and his two Jew-Austrian Brothers-in-Law, the Bankers Frey, lie with him; waiting the urn of doom. Let a National Convention, therefore, take warning, and know its function. Let the Convention, all as one man, set its shoulder to the work; not with bursts of Parliamentary eloquence, but in quite other and serviceabler ways!

Convention Commissioners, what we ought to call Representatives, '*Représentans* on mission,' fly, like the Herald Mercury, to all points of the Territory; carrying your behests far and wide. In their 'round hat, plumed with tricolor feathers, girt with flowing tricolor taffeta; in close frock, tricolor sash, sword and jack-boots,' these men are powerfuller than King or Kaiser. They say to whomso they meet, Do; and he must do it: all men's goods are at their disposal; for France is as one huge City in Siege. They smite with Requisitions, and Forced-loan; they have the power of life and death. Saint-Just and Lebas order the rich classes of Strasburg to 'strip off their shoes,' and send them to the Armies, where as many as 'ten-thousand pairs' are needed. Also, that within four-and-twenty hours, 'a thousand beds' be got ready; wrapt in matting, and sent under way. For the time presses!— Like swift bolts, issuing from the fuliginous Olympus of *Salut Public*, rush these men, oftenest in pairs; scatter your thunder-orders over France; make France one enormous Revolutionary thunder-cloud.

CHAPTER VI

DO THY DUTY

Accordingly, alongside of these bonfires of Church-balustrades, and sounds of fusillading and noyading, there rise quite another sort of fires and sounds: Smithy-fires and Proof-volleys for the manufacture of arms.

Cut off from Sweden and the world, the Republic must learn to make steel for itself; and, by aid of Chemists, she has learnt it. Towns that knew only iron, now know steel: from their new dungeons at Chantilly, Aristocrats may hear the rustle of our new steel furnace there. Do not bells transmute themselves into cannon; iron stancheons into the white-weapon (*arme blanche*), by sword-cutlery? The wheels of Langres scream, amid their spluttering fire-halo; grinding mere swords. The stithies of Charleville ring with gun-making. What say we, Charleville? Two hundred and fifty-eight Forges stand in the open spaces of Paris itself; a hundred and forty of them in the Esplanade of the Invalides, fifty-four in the Luxembourg Garden: so many Forges stand; grim Smiths beating and forging at lock and barrel there. The Clockmakers have come, requisitioned, to do the touch-holes, the hard-solder and file-work. Five great Barges swing at anchor on the Seine Stream, loud with boring; the great press-drills grating harsh thunder to the general ear and heart. And deft Stock-makers do gouge and rasp; and all men bestir themselves, according to their cunning:—in the language of hope, it is reckoned that 'a thousand finished muskets can be delivered daily.' Chemists of the Republic have taught us miracles of swift tanning: the cordwainer bores and stitches; —*not* of 'wood and pasteboard,' or he shall answer it to Tinville! The women sew tents and coats, the children scrape surgeons'-lint, the old men sit in the market-places; able men are on march; all men in requisition: from Town to Town flutters, on the Heaven's winds, this Banner, THE FRENCH PEOPLE RISEN AGAINST TYRANTS.

All which is well. But now arises the question: What is to be done for saltpetre? Interrupted Commerce and the English Navy shut us out from saltpetre; and without salt-petre there is no gunpowder. Republican Science again sits meditative; discovers that saltpetre exists here and there, though in attenuated quantity; that old plaster of walls holds a sprinkling of it;—that the earth of the Paris Cellars holds a sprinkling of it, diffused through the common rubbish; that were these dug up and washed, saltpetre might be had. Whereupon, swiftly, see! the Citoyens, with up-shoved *bonnet rouge*, or with doffed bonnet, and hair toil-wetted; digging fiercely, each in his own cellar, for saltpetre. The Earth-heap rises at every door; the Citoyennes with hod and bucket carrying it up; the Citoyens, pith in every muscle, shovelling and digging: for life and saltpetre. Dig, my *braves;* and right well speed ye! What of saltpetre is essential the Republic shall not want.

Consummation of Sansculottism has many aspects and tints: but the brightest tint, really of a solar or stellar bright-ness, is this which the Armies give it. That same fervour of

Jacobinism, which internally fills France with hatreds, suspicions, scaffolds and Reason-worship, does, on the Frontiers, show itself as a glorious *Pro patria mori*. Ever since Dumouriez's defection, three Convention Representatives attend every General. Committee of *Salut* has sent them; often with this Laconic order only: "Do thy duty, *Fais ton devoir*." It is strange, under what impediments the fire of Jacobinism, like other such fires, will burn. These soldiers have shoes of wood and pasteboard, or go booted in hay-ropes, in dead of winter; they skewer a bast mat round their shoulders, and are destitute of most things. What then? It is for Rights of Frenchhood, of Manhood, that they fight: the unquenchable spirit, here as elsewhere, works miracles. "With steel and bread," says the Convention Representative, "one may get to China." The Generals go fast to the guillotine; justly and unjustly. From which what inference? This, among others: That ill-success is death; that in victory alone is life! To conquer or die is no theatrical palabra, in these circumstances, but a practical truth and necessity. All Girondism, Halfness, Compromise is swept away. Forward, ye Soldiers of the Republic, captain and man! Dash, with your Gaelic impetuosity, on Austria, England, Prussia, Spain, Sardinia, Pitt, Cobourg, York, and the Devil and the World! Behind us is but the Guillotine; before us is Victory, Apotheosis and Millennium without end!

See, accordingly, on all Frontiers, how the Sons of Night, astonished after short triumph, do recoil;—the Sons of the Republic flying at them, with wild *Ça-ira* or Marseillese *Aux armes*, with the temper of cat-o'-mountain, or demon incarnate; which no Son of Night can stand! Spain, which came bursting through the Pyrenees, rustling with Bourbon banners, and went conquering here and there for a season, falters at such cat-o'-mountain welcome; draws itself in again; too happy now were the Pyrenees impassable. Not only does Dugommier, conqueror of Toulon, drive Spain back; he invades Spain. General Dugommier invades it by the Eastern Pyrenees; General Müller shall invade it by the Western. *Shall,* that is the word: Committee of *Salut Public* has said it; Representative Cavaignac, on mission there, must see it done. Impossible! cries Müller.—Infallible! answers Cavaignac. Difficulty, impossibility, is to no purpose. "The Committee is deaf on that side of its head," answers Cavaignac, "*n'entend pas de cette oreille là.* How many wantest thou, of men, of horses, cannons? Thou shalt have them. Conquerors, conquered or hanged, forward we must." Which things also, even as the Representatives spake them, were *done*. The Spring of the new Year sees Spain invaded: and redoubts are carried, and Passes and Heights of the most scarped description; Spanish Field-officerism struck mute at such cat-o'-mountain spirit, the cannon forgetting to fire. Swept are the Pyrenees; Town after Town flies open, burst by terror or the petard. In the course of another year, Spain will crave Peace; acknowledge its sins and the Republic; nay, in Madrid, there will be joy as for a victory, that even Peace is got.

Few things, we repeat, can be notabler than these Convention Representatives, with their power more than kingly. Nay at bottom are they not Kings, *Able-men*, of a sort; chosen from the Seven-hundred and Forty-nine French Kings; with this order, Do thy duty? Representative Levasseur, of small stature, by trade a mere pacific Surgeon-Accoucheur, has mutinies to quell; mad hosts (mad at the Doom of Custine) bellowing far and wide; he alone amid them, the one small Representative,—small, but as hard as flint, which also carries *fire* in it! So too, at Hondschooten, far in the afternoon, he declares that the Battle is not lost; that it must be gained; and fights, himself, with his own obstetric hand;—horse shot under him, or say on foot, 'up to the haunches in tide-water;' cutting stoccado and passado there, in defiance of Water, Earth, Air and Fire, the choleric little Representative that he was! Whereby, as natural, Royal Highness of York had to withdraw,—occasionally at full gallop; like to be swallowed by the tide: and his Siege of Dunkirk became a dream, realising only much loss of beautiful siege-artillery and of brave lives.

General Houchard, it would appear, stood behind a hedge on this Hondschooten occasion; wherefore they have since guillotined him. A new General Jourdan, late Sergeant Jourdan, commands in his stead: he, in long-winded Battles of Watigny, 'murderous artillery-fire mingling itself with sound of Revolutionary battle-hymns,' forces Austria behind the Sambre again; has hopes of purging the soil of Liberty. With hard wrestling, with artillerying and *ça-ira*-ing, it shall be done. In the course of a new Summer, Valenciennes will see itself beleaguered; Condé beleaguered; whatsoever is yet in the hands of Austria beleaguered and bombarded: nay, by Convention Decree, we even summon them *all* 'either to surrender in twenty-four hours, or else be put to the sword;'—

a high saying, which, though it remains unfulfilled, may show what spirit one is of.

Representative Drouet, as an Old-dragoon, could fight by a kind of second nature : but he was unlucky. Him, in a night-foray at Maubeuge, the Austrians took alive, in October last. They stript him almost naked, he says; making a show of him, as King-taker of Varennes. They flung him into carts; sent him far into the interior of Cimmeria, to 'a Fortress called Spitzberg' on the Danube River; and left him there, at an elevation of perhaps a hundred and fifty feet, to his own bitter reflections. Reflections; and also devices! For the indomitable Old-dragoon constructs wing-machinery, of Paperkite; saws window-bars; determines to fly down. He will seize a boat, will follow the River's course; land somewhere in Crim Tartary, in the Black-Sea or Constantinople region : *à la* Sindbad ! Authentic History, accordingly, looking far into Cimmeria, discerns dimly a phenomenon. In the dead night-watches, the Spitzberg sentry is near fainting with terror :—Is it a huge vague Portent descending through the night-air ? It is a huge National Representative Old-dragoon, descending by Paperkite; too rapidly, alas ! For Drouet had taken with him 'a small provision-store, twenty pounds weight or thereby;' which proved accelerative : so he fell, fracturing his leg; and lay there, moaning, till day dawned, till you could discern clearly that he was not a Portent but a Representative.

Or see Saint-Just, in the Lines of Weissembourg, though physically of a timid apprehensive nature, how he charges with his 'Alsatian Peasants armed hastily' for the nonce; the solemn face of him blazing into flame; his black hair and tri-color hat-taffeta flowing in the breeze ! These our Lines of Weissembourg were indeed forced, and Prussia and the Emigrants rolled through : but we *re*-force the Lines of Weissembourg; and Prussia and the Emigrants roll back again still faster,—hurled with bayonet-charges and fiery *ça-ira*-ing.

Ci-devant Sergeant Pichegru, *ci-devant* Sergeant Hoche, risen now to be Generals, have done wonders here. Tall Pichegru was meant for the Church ; was Teacher of Mathematics once, in Brienne School,—his remarkablest Pupil there was the Boy Napoleon Buonaparte. He then, not in the sweetest humour, enlisted, exchanging ferula for musket, and had got the length of the halberd, beyond which nothing could be hoped; when the Bastille barrier falling made passage for him, and he is here. Hoche bore a hand at the literal overturn of the Bastille; he was, as we saw, a Sergeant of the *Gardes Françaises*, spending his pay in rushlights and cheap editions of books. How the Mountains are burst, and many an Enceladus is disemprisoned; and Captains founding on Four parchments of Nobility are blown with their parchments across the Rhine, into Lunar Limbo!

What high feats of arms, therefore, were done in these Fourteen Armies; and how, for love of Liberty and hope of Promotion, lowborn valour cut its desperate way to Generalship; and, from the central Carnot in *Salut Public* to the outmost drummer on the Frontiers, men strove for their Republic, let Readers fancy. The snows of Winter, the flowers of Summer continue to be stained with warlike blood. Gaelic impetuosity mounts ever higher with victory; spirit of Jacobinism weds itself to national vanity: the Soldiers of the Republic are becoming, as we prophesied, very Sons of Fire. Barefooted, barebacked: but with bread and iron you can get to China! It is one Nation against the whole world; but the Nation has that within her which the whole world will not conquer. Cimmeria, astonished, recoils faster or slower; all round the Republic there rises fiery, as it were, a magic ring of musket-volleying and *ça-ira*-ing. Majesty of Prussia, as Majesty of Spain, will by and by acknowledge his sins and the Republic; and make a Peace of Bâle.

Foreign Commerce, Colonies, Factories in the East and in the West, are fallen or falling into the hands of sea-ruling Pitt, enemy of human nature. Nevertheless what sound is this that we hear, on the first of June 1794; sound as of war-thunder borne from the Ocean too, of tone most piercing? War-thunders from off the Brest waters: Villaret-Joyeuse and English Howe, after long manœuvring, have ranked themselves there; and are belching fire. The enemies of human nature are on their own element; cannot be conquered; cannot be kept from conquering. Twelve hours of raging cannonade; sun now sinking westward through the battle-smoke: six French Ships taken, the Battle lost; what Ship soever can still sail, making off! But how is it, then, with that *Vengeur* Ship, she neither strikes nor makes off? She is lamed, she cannot make off; strike she will not. Fire rakes her fore and aft from victorious enemies; the *Vengeur* is sinking. Strong are ye, Tyrants of the sea; yet we also, are we weak? Lo!

all flags, streamers, jacks, every rag of tricolor that will yet run on rope, fly rustling aloft: the whole crew crowds to the upper deck; and with universal soul-maddening yell, shouts *Vive la République*,—sinking, sinking. She staggers, she lurches, her last drunk whirl; Ocean yawns abysmal; down rushes the *Vengeur*, carrying *Vive la République* along with her, unconquerable, into Eternity. Let foreign Despots think of that. There is an Unconquerable in man, when he stands on his Rights of Man: let Despots and Slaves and all people know this, and only them that stand on the Wrongs of Man tremble to know it.—So has History written, nothing doubting, of the sunk *Vengeur*.

—— Reader! Mendez Pinto, Münchäusen, Cagliostro, Psalmanazar have been great; but they are not the greatest. O Barrère, Barrère, Anacreon of the Guillotine! must inquisitive pictorial History, in a new edition, ask again, 'How *is* it with the *Vengeur*,' in this its glorious suicidal sinking; and, with resentful brush, dash a bend-sinister of contumelious lampblack through thee and it? Alas, alas! The *Vengeur*, after fighting bravely, did sink altogether as other ships do, her captain and above two-hundred of her crew escaping gladly in British boats; and this same enormous inspiring Feat, and rumour 'of sound most piercing,' turns out to be an enormous inspiring Non-entity, extant nowhere save, as falsehood, in the brain of Barrère! Actually so. Founded, like the World itself, on *Nothing;* proved by Convention Report, by solemn Convention Decree and Decrees, and wooden ' *Model of the Vengeur;*' believed, bewept, besung by the whole French People to this hour, it may be regarded as Barrère's masterpiece; the largest, most inspiring piece of *blague* manufactured, for some centuries, by any man or nation. As such, and not otherwise, be it henceforth memorable.

CHAPTER VII

FLAME-PICTURE

IN this manner, mad-blazing with flame of all imaginable tints, from the red of Tophet to the stellar-bright, blazes off this Consummation of Sansculottism.

But the hundredth part of the things that were done, and the thousandth part of the things that were projected and decreed to be done, would tire the tongue of History. Statue of the *Peuple Souverain*, high as Strasburg Steeple; which shall fling its shadow from the Pont Neuf over Jardin National and Convention Hall;—enormous, in Painter David's Head! With other the like enormous Statues not a few: realised in paper Decree. For, indeed, the Statue of Liberty herself is still but Plaster, in the Place de la Révolution. Then Equalisation of Weights and Measures, with decimal division; Institutions, of Music and of much else; Institute in general; School of Arts, School of Mars, *Élèves de la Patrie*, Normal Schools: amid such Gun-boring, Altar-burning, Saltpetre-digging, and miraculous improvements in Tannery!

What, for example, is this that Engineer Chappe is doing, in the Park of Vincennes? In the Park of Vincennes; and onwards, they say, in the Park of Lepelletier Saint-Fargeau the assassinated Deputy; and still onwards to the Heights of Écouen and further, he has scaffolding set up, has posts driven in; wooden arms with elbow-joints are jerking and fugling in the air, in the most rapid mysterious manner! Citoyens ran up, suspicious. Yes, O Citoyens, we are signalling: it is a device this, worthy of the Republic; a thing for what we will call *Far-writing* without the aid of postbags; in Greek it shall be named Telegraph.—*Télégraphe sacré!* answers Citoyenism: For writing to Traitors, to Austria?—and tears it down. Chappe had to escape, and get a new Legislative Decree. Nevertheless he has accomplished it, the indefatigable Chappe: this his *Far-writer*, with its wooden arms and elbow-joints, can intelligibly signal; and lines of them are set up, to the North Frontiers and elsewhither. On an Autumn evening of the Year Two, Far-writer having just written that Condé Town has surrendered to us, we send from the Tuileries Convention-Hall this response in the shape of Decree: 'The name of Condé is changed to *Nord-Libre*, North-Free. The Army of the North ceases not to merit well of the country.'—To the admiration of men! For lo, in some half hour, while the Convention yet debates, there arrives this new answer: 'I inform thee, *je t'annonce*, Citizen President, that the Decree of Convention, ordering change of the name Condé into *North-Free;* and the other, declaring that the Army of the North ceases not to merit well of the country; are transmitted and acknowledged by Telegraph. I have instructed my Officer at Lille to forward them to North-Free by express. *Signed*, CHAPPE.'

Or see, over Fleurus in the Netherlands, where General
Jourdan, having now swept the soil of Liberty, and advanced
thus far, is just about to fight, and sweep or be swept, hangs
there not in the Heaven's Vault, some Prodigy, seen by
Austrian eyes and spy-glasses: in the similitude of an enormous Windbag, with netting and enormous Saucer depending
from it? A Jove's Balance, O ye Austrian spy-glasses? One
saucer-scale of a Jove's Balance; *your* poor Austrian scale
having kicked itself quite aloft, out of sight? By Heaven,
answer the spy-glasses, it is a Montgolfier, a Balloon, and they
are making signals! Austrian cannon battery barks at this
Montgolfier; harmless as dog at the Moon: the Montgolfier
makes its signals; detects what Austrian ambuscade there
may be, and descends at its ease.—What will not these devils
incarnate contrive?

On the whole, is it not, O Reader, one of the strangest
Flame-Pictures that ever painted itself; flaming off there, on
its ground of Guillotine-black? And the nightly Theatres
are Twenty-three; and the *Salons de danse* are Sixty; full of
mere *Égalité*, *Fraternité* and *Carmagnole*. And Section
Committee-rooms are Forty-eight, redolent of tobacco and
brandy: vigorous with twenty-pence a-day, coercing the Suspect. And the Houses of Arrest are Twelve, for Paris alone;
crowded and even crammed. And at all turns, you need your
'Certificate of Civism;' be it for going out, or for coming in;
nay without it you cannot, for money, get your daily ounces
of bread. Dusky red-capped Bakers'-queues; wagging themselves; not in silence! For we still live by Maximum, in all
things; waited on by these two, Scarcity and Confusion.
The faces of men are darkened with suspicion; with suspect-
ing, or being suspect. The streets lie unswept; the ways
unmended. Law has shut her Books; speaks little, save
impromptu, through the throat of Tinville. Crimes go unpunished; not crimes against the Revolution. 'The number
of foundling children,' as some compute, 'is doubled.'

How silent now sits Royalism; sits all Aristocratism;
Respectability that kept its Gig! The honour now, and the
safety, is to Poverty, not to Wealth. Your Citizen, who would
be fashionable, walks abroad, with his Wife on his arm, in red
wool nightcap, black-shag spencer, and carmagnole complete.
Aristocratism crouches low, in what shelter is still left;
submitting to all requisitions, vexations; too happy to escape
with life. Ghastly châteaus stare on you by the wayside;

disroofed, diswindowed; which the National Housebroker is peeling for the lead and ashlar. The old tenants hover disconsolate, over the Rhine with Condé; a spectacle to men. *Ci-devant* Seigneur, exquisite in palate, will become an exquisite Restaurateur Cook in Hamburg; *Ci-devant* Madame, exquisite in dress, a successful *Marchande des Modes* in London. In Newgate-Street, you meet M. le Marquis, with a rough deal on his shoulder, adze and jack-plane under arm; he has taken to the joiner trade; it being necessary to live (*faut vivre*).—Higher than all Frenchmen the domestic Stock-jobber flourishes,—in a day of Paper-money. The Farmer also flourishes: 'Farmers' houses,' says Mercier, 'have become like Pawnbrokers' shops;' all manner of furniture, apparel, vessels of gold and silver accumulate themselves there: bread is precious. The Farmer's rent is Paper-money, and he alone of men has bread: Farmer is better than Landlord, and will himself become Landlord.

And daily, we say, like a black Spectre, silently through that Life-tumult, passes the Revolution Cart; writing on the walls its MENE, MENE, *Thou art weighed, and found wanting!* A Spectre with which one has grown familiar. Men have adjusted themselves: complaint issues not from that Death-tumbril. Weak women and *ci-devants*, their plumage and finery all tarnished, sit there; with a silent gaze, as if looking into the Infinite Black. The once light lip wears a curl of irony, uttering no word; and the Tumbril fares along. They may be guilty before Heaven, or not; they are guilty, we suppose, before the Revolution. Then, does not the Republic 'coin money' of them, with its great axe? Red nightcaps howl dire approval: the rest of Paris looks on; if with a sigh, that is much: Fellow-creatures whom sighing cannot help; whom black Necessity and Tinville have clutched.

One other thing, or rather two other things, we will still mention; and no more: The Blond Perukes; the Tannery at Meudon. Great talk is of these *Perruques blondes:* O Reader, they are made from the Heads of Guillotined women! The locks of a Duchess, in this way, may come to cover the scalp of a Cordwainer; her blonde German Frankism his black Gaelic poll, if it be bald. Or they may be worn affectionately, as relics; rendering one Suspect? Citizens use them, not without mockery; of a rather cannibal sort.

Still deeper into one's heart goes that Tannery at Meudon; not mentioned among the other miracles of tanning! 'At

Meudon,' says Montgaillard with considerable calmness, 'ther
was a Tannery of Human Skins; such of the Guillotined a
seemed worth flaying : of which perfectly good wash-leathe
was made ; ' for breeches, and other uses. The skin of th
men, he remarks, was superior in toughness (*consistance*) an
quality to shamoy; that of the women was good for almos
nothing, being so soft in texture !—History looking back ove
Cannibalism, through *Purchas's Pilgrims* and all early and lat
Records, will perhaps find no terrestrial Cannibalism of a sort
on the whole, so detestable. It is a manufactured, soft-feeling
quietly elegant sort; a sort *perfide !* Alas then, is man
civilisation only a wrappage, through which the savage natur
of him can still burst, infernal as ever ? Nature still make
him ; and has an Infernal in her as well as a Celestial.

BOOK VI
THERMIDOR

CHAPTER I
THE GODS ARE ATHIRST

WHAT then is this Thing, called *La Révolution*, which, like an Angel of Death, hangs over France, noyading, fusillading, fighting, gun-boring, tanning human skins? *La Révolution* is but so many Alphabetic Letters; a thing nowhere to be laid hands on, to be clapt under lock and key: where is it? what is it? It is the Madness that dwells in the hearts of men. In this man it is, and in that man; as a rage or as a terror, it is in all men. Invisible, impalpable; and yet no black Azrael, with wings spread over half a continent, with sword sweeping from sea to sea, could be a truer Reality.

To explain, what is called explaining, the march of this Revolutionary Government, be no task of ours. Man cannot explain it. A paralytic Couthon, asking in the Jacobins, 'What hast thou done to be hanged if Counter-Revolution should arrive?' a sombre Saint-Just, not yet six-and-twenty, declaring that 'for Revolutionists there is no rest but in the tomb;' a seagreen Robespierre converted into vinegar and gall; much more an Amar and Vadier, a Collot and Billaud: to inquire what thoughts, predetermination or prevision, might be in the head of these men! Record of their thought remains not; Death and Darkness have swept it out utterly. Nay, if we even had their thought, all that they could have articulately spoken to us, how insignificant a fraction were that of the Thing which realised itself, which decreed itself, on signal given by them! As has been said more than once, this Revolutionary Government is not a self-conscious but a blind fatal one. Each man, enveloped in his ambient-atmosphere of revolutionary fanatic Madness, rushes on, impelled and impelling; and has become a blind brute Force; no rest for him but in the grave! Darkness and the mystery of horrid cruelty cover it for us, in History; as they did in Nature. The chaotic Thunder-cloud, with its pitchy black, and its tumult of dazzling jagged fire, in a world all electric : thou wi' not undertake to show how that comported itself,—what th secrets of its dark womb were ; from what sources, with wha specialties, the lightning it held did, in confused brightnes of terror, strike forth, destructive and self-destructive, till i ended? Like a blackness naturally of Erebus, which by wi' of Providence had for once mounted itself into dominion an the Azure : is not this properly the nature of Sansculottisr consummating itself? Of which Erebus Blackness be i enough to discern that this and the other dazzling fire-bol dazzling fire-torrent, does by small Volition and great Necessity verily issue,—in such and such succession ; destructive so an so, self-destructive so and so : till it end.

Royalism is extinct, 'sunk,' as they say, 'in the mud of th Loire ;' Republicanism dominates without and within : what therefore, on the 15th day of March, 1794, is this? Arrest ment, sudden really as a bolt out of the Blue, has hit strang victims : Hébert *Père Duchesne*, Bibliopolist Momoro, Cler Vincent, General Ronsin ; high Cordelier Patriots, redcappe Magistrates of Paris, Worshippers of Reason, Commanders o Revolutionary Army ! Eight short days ago, their Cordelie Club was loud, and louder than ever, with Patriot denuncia tions. Hébert *Père Duchesne* had " held his tongue and hi heart these two months, at sight of Moderates, Crypto-Aristo crats, Camilles, *Scélérats* in the Convention itself : but coul not do it any longer : would, if other remedy were not, invok the sacred right of Insurrection." So spake Hébert in Cor delier Session ; with vivats, till the roofs rang again. Eigh short days ago ; and now already ! They rub their eyes : it i no dream : they find themselves in the Luxembourg. Goos Gobel too ; and they that burnt Churches ! Chaumette him self, potent Procureur, *Agent National* as they now call it, wh could 'recognise the Suspect by the very face of them,' h lingers but three days ; on the third day he too is hurled in Most chopfallen, blue, enters the National Agent this Limb whither he has sent so many. Prisoners crowd round, jibin and jeering ; " Sublime National Agent," says one, " in virtu of thy immortal Proclamation, lo there ! I am suspect, thou art suspect, he is suspect, we are suspect, ye are suspect, the are suspect !"

The meaning of these things? Meaning ! It is a Plot Plot of the most extensive ramifications ; which, however

Barrère holds the threads of. Such Church-burning and scandalous masquerades of Atheism, fit to make the Revolution odious: where indeed could they originate but in the gold of Pitt? Pitt indubitably, as Preternatural Insight will teach one, did hire this Faction of *Enragés*, to play their fantastic tricks; to roar in their Cordeliers Club about Moderatism; to print their *Père Duchesne;* worship skyblue Reason in red nightcap; rob all Altars,—and bring the spoil to *us!*

Still more indubitable, visible to the mere bodily sight, is this: that the Cordeliers Club sits pale, with anger and terror; and has 'veiled the Rights of Man,'—without effect. Likewise that the Jacobins are in considerable confusion: busy 'purging themselves, *s'épurant,*' as in times of Plot and public Calamity they have repeatedly had to do. Not even Camille Desmoulins but has given offence: nay there have risen murmurs against Danton himself; though he bellowed them down, and Robespierre finished the matter by 'embracing him in the Tribune.'

Whom shall the Republic and a jealous Mother-Society trust? In these times of temptation, of Preternatural Insight! For there are, Factions of the Stranger, '*de l'étranger,*' Factions of Moderates, of Enraged; all manner of Factions: we walk in a world of Plots; strings universally spread, of deadly gins and falltraps, baited by the gold of Pitt! Cloots, Speaker of Mankind so-called, with his *Evidences of Mahometan Religion,* and babble of Universal Republic, him an incorruptible Robespierre has purged away. Baron Clootz, and Paine rebellious Needleman lie, these two months, in the Luxembourg; limbs of the Faction *de l'étranger.* Representative Phélippeaux is purged out: he came back from La Vendée with an ill report in his mouth against rogue Rossignol, and our method of warfare there. Recant it, O Phélippeaux, we entreat thee! Phélippeaux will not recant; and is purged out. Representative Fabre d'Églantine, famed Nomenclator of Romme's Calendar, is purged out; nay, is cast into the Luxembourg: accused of Legislative Swindling 'in regard to moneys of the India Company.' There with his Chabots, Bazires, guilty of the like, let Fabre wait his destiny. And Westermann, friend of Danton, he who led the Marseillese on the Tenth of August, and fought well in La Vendée, but spoke not well of rogue Rossignol, is purged out. Lucky, if he too go not to the Luxembourg. And your Prolys, Guzmans, of the Faction of the Stranger, they have gone; Pereyra, though he fled, is gone, 'taken in the disguise of a Tavern Cook.' I am suspect, thou art suspect, he is suspect!—

The great heart of Danton is weary of it. Danton is gone to native Arcis, for a little breathing-time of peace : Away, black Arachne-webs, thou world of Fury, Terror and Suspicion : welcome, thou everlasting Mother, with thy spring greenness, thy kind household loves and memories ; true art thou, were all else untrue ! The great Titan walks silent, by the banks of the murmuring Aube, in young native haunts that knew him when a boy ; wonders what the end of these things may be.

But strangest of all, Camille Desmoulins is purged out. Couthon gave as a test in regard to Jacobin purgation the question, 'What hast thou done to be hanged if Counter-Revolution should arrive?' Yet Camille, who could so well answer this question, is purged out ! The truth is, Camille, early in December last, began publishing a new Journal, or Series of Pamphlets, entitled the *Vieux Cordelier*, Old Cordelier. Camille, not afraid at one time to 'embrace Liberty on a heap of dead bodies,' begins to ask now, Whether among so many arresting and punishing Committees, there ought not to be a 'Committee of Mercy?' Saint-Just, he observes, is an extremely solemn young Republican, who 'carries his head as if it were a *Saint-Sacrement*,' adorable Hostie, or divine Real-Presence ! Sharply enough, this *old* Cordelier,—Danton and he were of the earliest primary Cordeliers,—shoots his glittering war-shafts into your *new* Cordeliers, your Héberts, Momoros, with their brawling brutalities and despicabilities ; say, as the Sun god (for poor Camille is a Poet) shot into that Python Serpent, sprung of mud.

Whereat, as was natural, the Hébertist Python did hiss and writhe amazingly ; and threaten 'sacred right of Insurrection;' —and, as we saw, get cast into Prison. Nay, with all the old wit, dexterity and light graceful poignancy, Camille, translating 'out of *Tacitus*, from the Reign of Tiberius,' pricks into the *Law of the Suspect* itself ; making it odious ! Twice, in the Decade, his wild Leaves issue ; full of wit, nay of humour, of harmonious ingenuity and insight,—one of the strangest phenomena of that dark time ; and smite, in their wild-sparkling way, at various monstrosities, Saint-Sacrement heads, and Juggernaut idols, in a rather reckless manner. To the great joy of Josephine Beauharnais, and the other Five-thousand and odd Suspect, who fill the Twelve Houses of Arrest ; on whom a ray of hope dawns ! Robespierre, at first

pprobatory, knew not at last what to think; then thought,
with his Jacobins, that Camille must be expelled. A man
of true Revolutionary spirit, this Camille; but with the un-
wisest sallies; whom Aristocrats and Moderates have the art
to corrupt; Jacobinism is in uttermost crisis and struggle;
enmeshed wholly in plots, corruptibilities, neck-gins and baited
falltraps of Pitt *Ennemi du Genre Humain.* Camille's First
Number begins with '*O Pitt!*'—his last is dated 15 Pluviose
Year 2, 3d February 1794, and ends with these words of
Montezuma's, '*Les dieux ont soif,* The gods are athirst.'

Be this as it may, the Hébertists lie in Prison only some
nine days. On the 24th of March, therefore, the Revolution
Tumbrils carry through that Life-tumult a new cargo: Hébert,
Vincent, Momoro, Ronsin, Nineteen of them in all; with
whom, curious enough, sits Clootz Speaker of Mankind. They
have been massed swiftly into a lump, this miscellany of
Nondescripts; and travel now their last road. No help. They
too must 'look through the little window;' they too must
sneeze into the sack,' *éternuer dans le sac;* as they have done
to others, so is it done to them. *Sainte-Guillotine,* meseems,
is worse than the old Saints of Superstition, a man-devouring
Saint? Clootz, still with an air of polished sarcasm, endeavours to jest, to offer cheering 'arguments of Materialism;'
he requested to be executed last, 'in order to establish certain
principles,'—which hitherto, I think, Philosophy has got no
good of. General Ronsin too, he still looks forth with some
air of defiance, eye of command: the rest are sunk in a stony
paleness of despair. Momoro, poor Bibliopolist, no Agrarian
Law yet realised,—they might as well have hanged thee at
Evreux, twenty months ago, when Girondin Buzot hindered
them. Hébert *Père Duchesne* shall never in this world rise in
sacred right of insurrection; he sits there low enough, head
sunk on breast; Red Nightcaps shouting round him, in frightful
parody of his Newspaper Articles, "Grand choler of the Père
Duchesne!" Thus perish they; the sack receives all their
heads. Through some section of History, Nineteen spectre-
chimeras shall flit, squeaking and gibbering; till Oblivion
swallow them.

In the course of a week, the Revolutionary Army itself
is disbanded; the General having become spectral. This
Faction of Rabids, therefore, is also purged from the Republican soil; here also the baited falltraps of that Pitt have

been wrenched up harmless; and anew there is joy over a Plo
Discovered. The Revolution then is verily devouring its own
children? All Anarchy, by the nature of it, is not only destruc
tive but *self*-destructive.

CHAPTER II

DANTON, NO WEAKNESS

DANTON, meanwhile, has been pressingly sent for from Arcis
he must return instantly, cried Camille, cried Phélippeaux and
Friends, who scented danger in the wind. Danger enough
A Danton, a Robespierre, chief-products of a victorious Revo
lution, are now arrived in immediate front of one another
must ascertain how they will live together, rule together. One
conceives easily the deep mutual incompatibility that divided
these two: with what terror of feminine hatred the poor sea
green Formula looked at the monstrous colossal Reality, and
grew greener to behold him;—the Reality, again, struggling to
think no ill of a chief-product of the Revolution; yet feeling
at bottom that such chief-product was little other than a chie
windbag, blown large by Popular air; not a man, with the
heart of a man, but a poor spasmodic incorruptible pedant,
with a logic-formula instead of heart; of Jesuit or Methodist
Parson nature; full of sincere-cant, incorruptibility, of viru
lence, poltroonery; barren as the eastwind! Two such
chief-products are too much for one Revolution.

Friends, trembling at the results of a quarrel on their part,
brought them to meet. "It is right," said Danton, swallowing much indignation, "to repress the Royalists: but we
should not strike except where it is useful to the Republic; we
should not confound the innocent and the guilty."—"And
who told you," replied Robespierre with a poisonous look,
"that one innocent person had perished?"—"*Quoi*," said
Danton, turning round to Friend Pâris self-named Fabricius,
Juryman in the Revolutionary Tribunal: "*Quoi*, not one
innocent? What sayest thou of it, Fabricius?"—Friends.
Westermann, this Pâris and others urged him to show himself,
to ascend the Tribune and act. The man Danton was not
prone to show himself; to act, or uproar for his own safety.
A man of careless, large, hoping nature; a large nature that
could rest: he would sit whole hours, they say, hearing
Camille talk, and liked nothing so well. Friends urged him

to fly; his Wife urged him: "Whither fly?" answered he:
"If freed France cast me out, there are only dungeons for me
elsewhere. One carries not his country with him at the sole of
his shoe!" The man Danton sat still. Not even the arrestment of Friend Hérault, a member of *Salut*, yet arrested by
Salut, can rouse Danton.—On the night of the 30th of March
Juryman Pâris came rushing in; haste looking through his
eyes: A clerk of the *Salut* Committee had told him Danton's
warrant was made out, he is to be arrested this very night!
Entreaties there are and trepidation, of poor Wife, of Pâris
and Friends: Danton sat silent for a while; then answered,
"*Ils n'oseraient*, They dare not;" and would take no measures.
Murmuring "They dare not," he goes to sleep as usual.

And yet, on the morrow morning, strange rumour spreads
over Paris City:- Danton, Camille, Phélippeaux, Lacroix have
been arrested overnight! It is verily so: the corridors of the
Luxembourg were all crowded, Prisoners crowding forth to see
this giant of the Revolution enter among them. "Messieurs,"
said Danton politely, "I hoped soon to have got you all out
of this: but here I am myself; and one sees not where it will
end."—Rumour may spread over Paris: the Convention clusters
itself into groups, wide-eyed, whispering, "Danton arrested!"
Who then is safe? Legendre, mounting the Tribune, utters,
at his own peril, a feeble word for him; moving that he be
heard at that Bar before indictment; but Robespierre frowns
him down: "Did you hear Chabot, or Bazire? Would you
have two weights and measures?" Legendre cowers low:
Danton, like the others, must take his doom.

Danton's Prison-thoughts were curious to have, but are not
given in any quantity: indeed few such remarkable men have
been left so obscure to us as this Titan of the Revolution. He
was heard to ejaculate: "This time twelvemonth, I was moving
the creation of that same Revolutionary Tribunal. I crave
pardon for it of God and man. They are all Brothers Cain;
Brissot would have had me guillotined as Robespierre now
will. I leave the whole business in a frightful welter (*gâchis
épouvantable*): not one of them understands anything of government. Robespierre will follow me; I drag down Robespierre.
O, it were better to be a poor fisherman than to meddle with
governing of men."—Camille's young beautiful Wife, who had
made him rich not in money alone, hovers round the Luxembourg, like a disembodied spirit, day and night. Camille's
stolen letters to her still exist; stained with the mark of his

tears. "I carry my head like a Saint-Sacrament?" so Saint-Just was heard to mutter: "perhaps he will carry his like a Saint-Dennis."

Unhappy Danton, thou still unhappier light Camille, once light *Procureur de la Lanterne*, ye also have arrived, then, at the Bourne of Creation, where, like Ulysses Polytlas at the limit and utmost Gades of his voyage, gazing into that dim Waste beyond Creation, a man does see *the Shade of his Mother*, pale, ineffectual;—and days when his Mother nursed and wrapped him are all-too sternly contrasted with this day! Danton, Camille, Hérault, Westermann, and the others, very strangely massed up with Bazires, Swindler Chabots, Fabre d'Églantines, Banker Freys, a most motley Batch, '*Fournée*' as such things will be called, stand ranked at the Bar of Tinville. It is the 2d of April 1794. Danton has had but three days to lie in Prison; for the time presses.

What is your name? place of abode? and the like, Fouquier asks; according to formality. "My name is Danton," answers he; "a name tolerably known in the Revolution: my abode will soon be Annihilation (*dans le Néant*); but I shall live in the Pantheon of History." A man will endeavour to say something forcible, be it by nature or not! Hérault mentions epigrammatically that he "sat in this Hall, and was detested of Parlementeers." Camille makes answer, "My age is that of the *bon Sansculotte Jésus*; an age fatal to Revolutionists." O Camille, Camille! And yet in that Divine Transaction, let us say, there did lie, among other things, the fatallest Reproof ever uttered here below to Worldly Right-honourableness; 'the highest fact,' so devout Novalis calls it, 'in the Rights of Man.' Camille's real age, it would seem, is thirty-four. Danton is one year older.

Some five months ago, the Trial of the Twenty-two Girondins was the greatest that Fouquier had then done. But here is a still greater to do; a thing which tasks the whole faculty of Fouquier; which makes the very heart of him waver. For it is the voice of Danton that reverberates now from these domes; in passionate words, piercing with their wild sincerity, winged with wrath. Your best Witnesses he shivers into ruin at one stroke. He demands that the Committee-men themselves come as Witnesses, as Accusers; he "will cover them with ignominy." He raises his huge stature, he shakes his huge black head, fire flashes from the eyes of him,—piercing to all Republican hearts: so that the very Galleries, though we filled them by ticket, murmur sympathy; and are like to burst down, and raise the People, and deliver him! He complains loudly that he is classed with Chabots, with swindling Stock-jobbers; that his Indictment is a list of platitudes and horrors. "Danton hidden on the 10th of August?" reverberates he, with the roar of a lion in the toils: "where are the men that had to press Danton to show himself, that day? Where are these high-gifted souls of whom he borrowed energy? Let them appear, these Accusers of mine: I have all the clearness of my self-possession when I demand them. I will unmask the three shallow scoundrels," *les trois plats coquins,* Saint-Just, Couthon, Lebas, "who fawn on Robespierre, and lead him towards his destruction. Let them produce themselves here; I will plunge them into Nothingness, out of which they ought never to have risen." The agitated President agitates his bell; enjoins calmness, in a vehement manner: "What is it to thee how I defend myself?" cries the other: "the right of *dooming* me is thine always. The voice of a man speaking for his honour and his life may well drown the jingling of thy bell!" Thus Danton, higher and higher; till the lion-voice of him 'dies away in his throat:' speech will not utter what is in that man. The Galleries murmur ominously; the first day's Session is over.

O Tinville, President Herman, what will ye do? They have two days more of it, by strictest Revolutionary Law. The Galleries already murmur. If this Danton were to burst your meshwork!—Very curious indeed to consider. It turns on a hair: and what a Hoitytoity were *there,* Justice and Culprit changing places; and the whole History of France running changed! For in France there is this Danton only that could still try to govern France. He only, the wild amorphous Titan;—and perhaps that other olive-complexioned individual, the Artillery-Officer at Toulon, whom we left pushing his fortune in the South?

On the evening of the second day, matters looking not better but worse and worse, Fouquier and Herman, distraction in their aspect, rush over to *Salut Public.* What is to be done? *Salut Public* rapidly concocts a new Decree; whereby if men 'insult Justice,' they may be 'thrown out of the Debates.' For indeed, withal, is there not 'a Plot in the Luxembourg Prison?' *Ci-devant* General Dillon, and others of the Suspect, plotting with Camille's Wife to distribute *assignats;* to force the Prisons, overset the Republic? Citizen Laflotte, himself Suspect but desiring enfranchisement, has reported said Plot for us:—a report that may bear fruit! Enough, on the morrow morning, an obedient Convention passes this Decree. *Salut* rushes off with it to the aid of Tinville, reduced now almost to extremities. And so, *Hors de Débats*, Out of the Debates, ye insolents! Policemen do your duty! In such manner, with a dead-lift effort, *Salut*, Tinville, Herman, Leroi *Dix-Août*, and all stanch jurymen setting heart and shoulder to it, the Jury becomes 'sufficiently instructed;' Sentence is passed, is sent by an Official, and torn and trampled on: *Death this day.* It is the 5th of April 1794. Camille's poor Wife may cease hovering about this Prison. Nay, let her kiss her poor children; and prepare to enter it, and to follow!—

Danton carried a high look in the Death-cart. Not so Camille; it is but one week, and all is so topsyturvied; angel Wife left weeping; love, riches, Revolutionary fame, left all at the Prison-gate; carnivorous Rabble now howling round. Palpable, and yet incredible; like a madman's dream! Camille struggles and writhes; his shoulders shuffle the loose coat off them, which hangs knotted, the hands tied: "Calm, my friend," said Danton; "heed not that vile canaille (*laissez là cette vile canaille*)." At the foot of the Scaffold, Danton was heard to ejaculate: "O my Wife, my well-beloved, I shall never see thee more then!"—but, interrupting himself: "Danton, no weakness!" He said to Hérault-Séchelles stepping forward to embrace him: "Our heads will meet *there*," in the Headsman's sack. His last words were to Samson the Headsman himself: "Thou wilt show my head to the people; it is worth showing."

So passes, like a gigantic mass, of valour, ostentation, fury, affection and wild revolutionary force and manhood, this Danton, to his unknown home. He was of Arcis-sur-Aube; born of 'good farmer-people' there. He had many sins; but one worst sin he had not, that of Cant. No hollow Formalist, deceptive and self-deceptive, *ghastly* to the natural sense, was this; but a very Man: with all his dross he was a Man; fiery-real, from the great fire-bosom of Nature herself. He saved France from Brunswick; he walked straight his own wild road, whither it led him. He may live for some generations in the memory of men.

CHAPTER III

THE TUMBRILS

NEXT week, it is still but the 10th of April, there comes a new Nineteen; Chaumette, Gobel, Hébert's Widow, the Widow of Camille: these also roll their fated journey; black death devours them. Mean Hébert's Widow was weeping, Camille's Widow tried to speak comfort to her. O ye kind Heavens, azure, beautiful, eternal behind your tempests and Time-clouds, is there not pity in store for all! Gobel, it seems, was repentant; he begged absolution of a Priest; died as a Gobel best could. For Anaxagoras Chaumette, the sleek head now stript of its *bonnet rouge*, what hope is there? Unless death *were* 'an eternal sleep?' Wretched Anaxagoras, God shall judge thee, not I.

Hébert, therefore, is gone, and the Hébertists; they that robbed Churches, and adored blue Reason in red nightcap. Great Danton, and the Dantonists; they also are gone. Down to the catacombs; they are become silent men! Let no Paris Municipality, no Sect or Party of this hue or that, resist the will of Robespierre and *Salut*. Mayor Pache, not prompt enough in denouncing these Pitt Plots, may congratulate about them now. Never so heartily; it skills not! His course likewise is to the Luxembourg. We appoint one Fleuriot-Lescot Interim-Mayor in his stead: an 'architect from Belgium,' they say, this Fleuriot; he is a man one can depend on. Our new Agent-National is Payan, lately Jury-man; whose cynosure also is Robespierre.

Thus then, we perceive, this confusedly electric Erebus-cloud of Revolutionary Government has altered its shape somewhat. Two masses, or wings, belonging to it; an over-electric mass of Cordelier Rabids, and an under-electric of Dantonist Moderates and Clemency-men,—these two masses, shooting bolts at one another, so to speak, have annihilated one another. For the Erebus-cloud, as we often remark, is of suicidal nature; and, in jagged irregularity, darts its lightning withal into itself. But now these two discrepant masses being mutually annihilated, it is as if the Erebus-cloud had got to internal composure; and did only pour its hell-fire lightning on the World that lay under it. In plain words, Terror of the Guillotine was never terrible till now. Systole, diastole, swift and ever swifter goes the Axe of Samson. Indictments cease by degrees to have so much as plausibility : Fouquier chooses from the Twelve Houses of Arrest what he calls Batches, 'Fournées,' a score or more at a time ; his Jurymen are charged to make *feu de file*, file-firing till the ground be *clear*. Citizen Laflotte's report of Plot in the Luxembourg is verily bearing fruit ! If no speakable charge exist against a man, or Batch of men, Fouquier has always this : a Plot in the Prison. Swift and ever swifter goes Samson ; up, finally, to three score and more at a Batch. It is the highday of Death : none but the Dead return not.

O dusky D'Espréménil, what a day is this, the 22d of April, thy last day ! The Palais Hall here is the same stone Hall, where thou, five years ago, stoodest perorating, amid endless pathos of rebellious Parlement, in the gray of the morning ; bound to march with D'Agoust to the Isles of Hières (i. 83). The stones are the same stones : but the rest, Men, Rebellion, Pathos, Peroration, see ! it has all fled, like a gibbering troop of ghosts, like the phantasms of a dying brain. With D'Espréménil, in the same line of Tumbrils, goes the mournfullest medley. Chapelier goes, *ci-devant* popular President of the Constituent ; whom the Menads and Maillard met in his carriage, on the Versailles Road (i. 206). Thouret likewise, *ci-devant* President, father of Constitutional Law-acts ; he whom we heard saying, long since, with a loud voice, "The Constituent Assembly has fulfilled its mission !" (ii. 42.) And the noble old Malesherbes, who defended Louis and could not speak, like a gray old rock dissolving into sudden water : he journeys here now, with his kindred, daughters, sons and grandsons, his Lamoignons, Châteaubriands ; silent, towards Death.—One young Châteaubriand alone is wandering amid the Natchez, by the roar of Niagara Falls, the moan of endless forests : Welcome thou great Nature, savage, but not false, not unkind, unmotherly ; no Formula thou, or rabid jangle of Hypothesis, Parliamentary Eloquence, Constitution-building and the Guillotine ; speak thou to me, O Mother, and sing my sick heart thy mystic everlasting lullaby-song, and let all the rest be far !—

Another row of Tumbrils we must notice : that which holds Elizabeth, the Sister of Louis. Her Trial was like the rest ; for Plots, for Plots. She was among the kindliest, most innocent of women. There sat with her, amid four-and-twenty others, a once timorous Marchioness de Crussol ; courageous now ; expressing towards her the liveliest loyalty. At the foot of the Scaffold, Elizabeth with tears in her eyes thanked this Marchioness; said she was grieved she could not reward her. "Ah, Madame, would your Royal Highness deign to embrace me, my wishes were complete!"—"Right willingly, Marquise de Crussol, and with my whole heart." Thus they: at the foot of the Scaffold. The Royal Family is now reduced to two: a girl and a little boy. The boy, once named Dauphin, was taken from his mother while she yet lived; and given to one Simon, by trade a Cordwainer, on service then about the Temple-Prison, to bring him up in principles of Sansculottism. Simon taught him to drink, to swear, to sing the *carmagnole*. Simon is now gone to the Municipality: and the poor boy, hidden in a tower of the Temple, from which in his fright and bewilderment and early decrepitude he wishes not to stir out, lies perishing, 'his shirt not changed for six months;' amid squalor and darkness, lamentably,—so as none but poor Factory Children and the like are wont to perish, and *not* be lamented!

The Spring sends its green leaves and bright weather, bright May, brighter than ever: Death pauses not. Lavoisier, famed Chemist, shall die and not live: Chemist Lavoisier was Farmer-General Lavoisier too, and now 'all the Farmers-General are arrested;' all, and shall give an account of their moneys and incomings; and die for 'putting water in the tobacco' they sold. Lavoisier begged a fortnight more of life, to finish some experiments: but "the Republic does not need such;" the axe must do its work. Cynic Chamfort, reading these inscriptions of *Brotherhood or Death*, says "it is a Brotherhood of Cain:" arrested, then liberated; then about to be arrested again, this Chamfort cuts and slashes himself with frantic uncertain hand; gains, not without difficulty, the refuge of death. Condorcet has lurked deep, these many months; Argus-eyes watching and searching for him. His concealment is become dangerous to others and himself; he has to fly again, to skulk, round Paris, in thickets and stone-quarries. And so at the Village of Clamars, one bleared May morning, there enters a Figure, ragged, rough-bearded, hunger-stricken; asks breakfast in the tavern there. Suspect, by the look of him! "Servant out of place, sayest thou?" Committee-President of Forty-Sous finds a Latin Horace on him: "Art thou not one of those *Ci-devants* that were wont to keep servants? *Suspect!*" He is haled forthwith, breakfast unfinished, towards Bourg-la-Reine, on foot: he faints with exhaustion; is set on a peasant's horse; is flung into his damp prison-cell: on the

morrow, recollecting him, you enter; Condorcet lies dead on
the floor. They die fast, and disappear: the Notabilities of
France disappear, one after one, like lights in a Theatre, which
you are snuffing out.

Under which circumstances, is it not singular, and almost
touching, to see Paris City drawn out, in the meek May nights,
in civic ceremony, which they call '*Souper Fraternel*,' Brotherly
Supper? Spontaneous, or partially spontaneous, in the twelfth,
thirteenth, fourteenth nights of this May month, it is seen.
Along the Rue Saint-Honoré, and main Streets and Spaces,
each Citoyen brings forth what of supper the stingy *Maximum*
has yielded him, to the open air; joins it to his neighbour's
supper; and with common table, cheerful light burning
frequent, and what due modicum of cut-glass and other
garnish and relish is convenient, they eat frugally together,
under the kind stars. See it, O Night! With cheerfully
pledged wine-cup, hobnobbing to the Reign of Liberty,
Equality, Brotherhood, with their wives in best ribands, with
their little ones romping round, the Citoyens, in frugal Love-
feast, sit there. Night in her wide empire sees nothing
similar. O my brothers, why is the reign of Brotherhood *not*
come! It is come, it shall have come, say the Citoyens
frugally hobnobbing.—Ah me! these everlasting stars, do they
not look down 'like glistening eyes, bright with immortal pity,
over the lot of man!'—

One lamentable thing, however, is, that individuals will
attempt assassination—of Representatives of the People.
Representative Collot, Member even of *Salut*, returning home,
'about one in the morning,' probably touched with liquor, as
he is apt to be, meets on the stairs the cry "*Scélérat!*" and
also the snap of a pistol: which latter flashes in the pan; disclosing to him, momentarily, a pair of truculent saucer-eyes,
swart grim-clenched countenance; recognisable as that of our
little fellow-lodger, Citoyen Amiral, formerly 'a clerk in the
Lotteries!' Collot shouts *Murder*, with lungs fit to awaken
all the *Rue Favart*; Amiral snaps a second time; a second
time flashes in the pan; then darts up into his apartment; and,
after there firing, still with inadequate effect, one musket at
himself and another at his captor, is clutched and locked in
Prison. An indignant little man this Amiral, of Southern
temper and complexion, of 'considerable muscular force.' He
denies not that he meant to "purge France of a tyrant;" nay

avows that he had an eye to the Incorruptible himself, but took Collot as more convenient!

Rumour enough hereupon; heaven-high congratulation of Collot, fraternal embracing, at the Jacobins and elsewhere. And yet, it would seem, the assassin mood proves catching. Two days more, it is still but the 23rd of May, and towards nine in the evening, Cécile Rénault, Paper-dealer's daughter, a young woman of soft blooming look, presents herself at the Cabinet-maker's in the Rue Saint-Honoré; desires to see Robespierre. Robespierre cannot be seen; she grumbles irreverently. They lay hold of her. She has left a basket in a shop hard by: in the basket are female change of raiment and two knives! Poor Cécile, examined by Committee, declares she "wanted to see what a tyrant was like:" the change of raiment was "for my own use in the place I am surely going to."—"What place?"—"Prison: and then the Guillotine," answered she.—Such things come of Charlotte Corday; in a people prone to imitation, and monomania! Swart choleric men try Charlotte's feat, and their pistols miss fire; soft blooming young women try it, and, only half-resolute, leave their knives in a shop.

O Pitt, and ye Faction of the Stranger, shall the Republic never have rest; but be torn continually by baited springes, by wires of explosive spring-guns? Swart Amiral, fair young Cécile, and all that knew them, and many that did not know them, lie locked, waiting the scrutiny of Tinville.

CHAPTER IV

MUMBO-JUMBO

BUT on the day they call *Décadi*, New-Sabbath, 20 *Prairial*, 8th June by old style, what thing is this going forward in the Jardin National, whilom Tuileries Garden?

All the world is there, in holyday clothes: foul linen went out with the Hébertists; nay Robespierre, for one, would never once countenance that; but went always elegant and frizzled, not without vanity even,—and had his room hung round with seagreen Portraits and Busts. In holyday clothes, we say, are the innumerable Citoyens and Citoyennes: the weather is of the brightest; cheerful expectation lights all countenances. Juryman Vilate gives breakfast to many a Deputy, in his official Apartment, in the Pavillon *ci-devant* of

Flora; rejoices in the bright-looking multitudes, in the bright-
ness of leafy June, in the auspicious *Décadi*, or New-Sabbath.
This day, if it please Heaven, we are to have, on improved
Anti-Chaumette principles : a New Religion.

Catholicism being burned out, and Reason-worship guillotined, was there not need of one? Incorruptible Robespierre,
not unlike the Ancients, as Legislator of a free people, will
now also be Priest and Prophet. He has donned his sky-blue
coat, made for the occasion; white silk waistcoat broidered
with silver, black silk breeches, white stockings, shoe-buckles
of gold. He is President of the Convention; he has made
the Convention *decree*, so they name it, *décréter*, the ' Existence
of the Supreme Being,' and likewise ' *ce principe consolateur* of
the Immortality of the Soul.' These consolatory principles,
the basis of rational Republican Religion, are getting decreed;
and here, on this blessed *Décadi*, by help of Heaven and Painter
David, is to be our first act of worship.

See, accordingly, how after Decree passed, and what has
been called ' the scraggiest Prophetic Discourse ever uttered
by man,'—Mahomet Robespierre, in sky-blue coat and black
breeches, frizzled and powdered to perfection, bearing in his
hand a bouquet of flowers and wheat-ears, issues proudly from
the Convention Hall; Convention following him, yet, as is
remarked, with an interval. Amphitheatre has been raised,
or at least *Monticule* or Elevation, hideous Statues of Atheism,
Anarchy and such like, thanks to Heaven and Painter David,
strike abhorrence into the heart. Unluckily, however, our
Monticule is too small. On the top of it not half of us can
stand; wherefore there arises indecent shoving, nay treasonous
irreverent growling. Peace, thou Bourdon de l'Oise : peace,
or it may be worse for thee !

The seagreen Pontiff takes a torch, Painter David handing
it; mouths some other froth-rant of vocables, which happily
one cannot hear; strides resolutely forward, in sight of expectant France; sets his torch to Atheism and Company,
which are but made of pasteboard steeped in turpentine.
They burn up rapidly; and, from within, there rises ' by
machinery,' an incombustible Statue of Wisdom, which,
by ill hap, gets besmoked a little; but does stand there visible
in as serene attitude as it can.

And then? Why, then, there is other Processioning, scraggy
Discoursing, and—this *is* our Feast of the *Être Suprême*; our

new Religion, better or worse, is come!—Look at it one moment, O Reader, not two. The shabbiest page of Human Annals: or is there, that thou wottest of, one shabbier? Mumbo-Jumbo of the African woods to me seems venerable beside this new Deity of Robespierre; for this is a *conscious* Mumbo-Jumbo, and *knows* that he is machinery. O seagreen Prophet, unhappiest of windbags blown nigh to bursting, what distracted Chimera among realities art thou growing to! This then, this common pitch-link for artificial fireworks of turpentine and pasteboard; *this* is the miraculous Aaron's Rod thou wilt stretch over a hag-ridden hell-ridden France, and bid her plagues cease? Vanish, thou and it!—"*Avec ton Être Suprême*," said Billaud, "*tu commences m'embêter:* With thy Être Suprême thou beginnest to be a bore to me."

Catherine Théot, on the other hand, 'an ancient serving-maid seventy-nine years of age,' inured to Prophecy and the Bastille from of old, sits in an upper room in the Rue de Contrescarpe, poring over the Book of Revelations, with an eye to Robespierre; finds that this astonishing thrice-potent Maximilien really is the Man spoken of by Prophets, who is to make the Earth young again. With her sit devout old Marchionesses, *ci-devant* honourable women; among whom Old-Constituent Dom Gerle, with his addle head, cannot be wanting. They sit there, in the Rue de Contrescarpe; in mysterious adoration: Mumbo is Mumbo, and Robespierre is his Prophet. A conspicuous man this Robespierre. He has his volunteer Bodyguard of *Tappe-durs*, let us say *Strike-sharps*, fierce Patriots with feruled sticks; and Jacobins kissing the hem of his garment. He enjoys the admiration of many, the worship of some; and is well worth the wonder of one and all.

The grand question and hope, however, is: Will not this Feast of the Tuileries Mumbo Jumbo be a sign perhaps that the Guillotine is to abate? Far enough from that! Precisely on the second day after it, Couthon, one of the 'three shallow scoundrels,' gets himself lifted into the Tribune; produces a bundle of papers. Couthon proposes that, as Plots still abound, the *Law of the Suspect* shall have extension, and Arrestment new vigour and facility. Further that, as in such case business is like to be heavy, our Revolutionary Tribunal too shall have extension; be divided, say, into Four Tribunals, each with its President, each with its Fouquier or Substitute of Fouquier, all labouring at once, and any remnant of shackle or dilatory formality be struck off: in this way it may perhaps still overtake the work. Such is Couthon's *Decree of the Twenty-second Prairial*, famed in those times. At hearing of which Decree, the very Mountain gasped, awestruck; and one Ruamps ventured to say that if it passed without adjournment and discussion, he, as one Representative, "would blow his brains out." Vain saying! The Incorruptible knit his brows; spoke a prophetic fateful word or two: the *Law of Prairial* is Law; Ruamps glad to leave his rash brains where they are. Death then, and always Death! Even so. Fouquier is enlarging his borders; making room for Batches of a Hundred and fifty at once;—getting a Guillotine set up of improved velocity, and to work under cover, in the apartment close by. So that *Salut* itself has to intervene, and forbid him: "Wilt thou *demoralise* the Guillotine," asks Collot, reproachfully, "*démoraliser le supplice!*"

There is indeed danger of that; were not the Republican faith great, it were already done. See, for example, on the 17th of June, what a *Batch*, Fifty-four at once! Swart Amiral is here, he of the pistol that missed fire; young Cécile Rénault, with her father, family, entire kith and kin; the Widow of D'Espréménil; old M. de Sombreuil of the Invalides, with his Son,—poor old Sombreuil, seventy-three years old, his Daughter saved him in September, and it was but for *this*. Faction of the Stranger, fifty-four of them! In red shirts and smocks, as Assassins and Faction of the Stranger, they flit along there; red baleful Phantasmagory, towards the land of Phantoms.

Meanwhile will not the People of the Place de la Révolution, the inhabitants along the Rue Saint-Honoré, as these continual Tumbrils pass, begin to look gloomy? Republicans too have bowels. The Guillotine is shifted, then again shifted; finally set up at the remote extremity of the Southeast: Suburbs Saint-Antoine and Saint-Marceau, it is to be hoped, if they have bowels, have very tough ones.

CHAPTER V

THE PRISONS

It is time now, however, to cast a glance into the Prisons. When Desmoulins moved for his Committee of Mercy, these Twelve Houses of Arrest held five-thousand persons. Continually arriving since then, there have now accumulated twelve-thousand. They are Ci-devants, Royalists; in far greater part, they are Republicans, of various Girondin, Fayettish, Un-Jacobin colour. Perhaps no human Habitation or Prison ever equalled in squalor, in noisome horror, these Twelve Houses of Arrest. There exist records of personal experience in them, *Mémoires sur les Prisons;* one of the strangest Chapters in the Biography of Man.

Very singular to look into it: how a kind of order rises up in all conditions of human existence; and wherever two or three are gathered together, there are formed modes of existing together, habitudes, observances, nay gracefulnesses, joys! Citoyen Coittant will explain fully how our lean dinner, of herbs and carrion, was consumed not without politeness and *place-aux-dames:* how Seigneur and Shoeblack, Duchess and Doll-Tearsheet, flung pellmell into a heap, ranked themselves according to method: at what hour 'the Citoyennes took to their needlework;' and we, yielding the chairs to them, endeavoured to talk gallantly in a standing posture, or even to sing and harp more or less. Jealousies, enmities, are not wanting; nor flirtations, of an effective character.

Alas, by degrees, even needlework must cease: Plot in the Prison rises, by Citoyen Laflotte and Preternatural Suspicion. Suspicious Municipality snatches from us all implements; all money and possession, of means or metal, is ruthlessly searched for, in pocket, in pillow and paillasse, and snatched away: red-capped Commissaries entering every cell. Indignation, temporary desperation, at robbery of its very thimble, fills the gentle heart. Old Nuns shriek shrill discord; demand to be killed forthwith. No help from shrieking! Better was that of the two shifty male Citizens, who, eager to preserve an implement or two, were it but a pipe-picker, or needle to darn hose with, determined to defend themselves: by tobacco. Swift then, as your fell Red Caps are heard in the Corridor rummaging and slamming, the two Citoyens light their pipes, and begin smoking. Thick darkness envelops them. The Red Nightcaps, opening the cell, breathe but one mouthful; burst forth into chorus of barking and coughing. "*Quoi, Messieurs,*" cry the two Citoyens, "you don't smoke? Is the pipe disagreeable? *Est-ce que vous ne fumez pas?*" But the Red Nightcaps have fled, with slight search. "*Vous n'aimez pas la pipe?*" cry the Citoyens, as their door slams-to again. My poor brother Citoyens, O surely, in a reign of Brotherhood, you are not the two I would guillotine!

Rigour grows, stiffens into horrid tyranny; Plot in the Prison getting ever rifer. This Plot in the Prison, as we said, is now the stereotype formula of Tinville: against whomsoever he knows no crime, this is a ready-made crime. His Judgment-bar has become unspeakable; a recognised mockery; known only as the wicket one passes through, towards Death. His Indictments are drawn out in blank; you insert the Names after. He has his *moutons*, detestable traitor jackals, who report and bear witness; that they themselves may be allowed to live,—for a time. His *Fournées*, says the reproachful Collot, 'shall in no case exceed three-score;' that is his *maximum*. Nightly come his Tumbrils to the Luxembourg, with the fatal Roll-call; list of the *Fournée* of tomorrow. Men rush towards the Grate: listen, if their name be in it? One deep-drawn breath, when the name is not in; we live still one day! And yet some score or scores of names were in. Quick these, they clasp their loved ones to their heart, one last time; with brief adieu, wet-eyed or dry-eyed, they mount, and are away. This night to the Conciergerie; through the Palais misnamed *of Justice*, to the Guillotine, tomorrow.

Recklessness, defiant levity, the Stoicism if not of strength yet of weakness, has possessed all hearts. Weak women and *Ci-devants*, their locks not yet made into blond perukes, their skins not yet tanned into breeches, are accustomed to 'act the Guillotine' by way of pastime. In fantastic mummery, with towel-turbans, blanket-ermine, a mock Sanhedrim of Judges sits, a mock Tinville pleads; a culprit is doomed, is guillotined by the oversetting of two chairs. Sometimes we carry it further: Tinville himself, in his turn, is doomed, and not to the Guillotine alone. With blackened face, hirsute, horned, a shaggy Satan snatches him not unshrieking; shows him, with outstretched arm and voice, the fire that is not quenched, the worm that dies not; the monotony of Hell-pain, and the *What hour?* answered by, *It is Eternity*.

And still the Prisons fill fuller, and still the Guillotine goes faster. On the high roads march flights of Prisoners, wending towards Paris. Not *Ci-devants* now; they, the noisy of them, are mown down; it is Republicans now. Chained two and two they march; in exasperated moments singing their *Marseillaise*. A hundred and thirty-two men of Nantes, for instance, march towards Paris, in these same days: Republicans, or say even Jacobins to the marrow of the bone; but Jacobins who had not approved Noyading. *Vive la République* rises from them in all streets of towns: they rest by night in unutterable noisome dens, crowded to choking; one or two dead on the morrow. They are wayworn, weary of heart; can only shout: *Live the Republic;* we, as under horrid enchantment, dying in this way for it!

Some Four-hundred Priests, of whom also there is record, ride at anchor, 'in the roads of the Isle of Aix,' long months; looking out on misery, vacuity, waste Sands of Oleron and the ever-moaning brine. Ragged, sordid, hungry; wasted to shadows: eating their unclean ration on deck, circularly, in parties of a dozen, with finger and thumb; beating their scandalous clothes between two stones; choked in horrible miasmata, closed under hatches, seventy of them in a berth, through night; so that the 'aged Priest is found lying dead in the morning, in the attitude of prayer!'—How long, O Lord!

Not forever; no. All Anarchy, all Evil, Injustice, is, by the nature of it, *dragon's-teeth;* suicidal, and cannot endure.

CHAPTER VI

TO FINISH THE TERROR

IT is very remarkable, indeed, that since the *Être-Suprême* Feast, and the sublime continued harangues on it, which Billaud feared would become a bore to him, Robespierre has gone little to Committee: but held himself apart, as if in a kind of pet. Nay they have made a Report on that old Catherine Théot, and her Regenerative Man spoken of by the Prophets; not in the best spirit. This Théot mystery they affect to regard as a Plot; but have evidently introduced a vein of satire, of irreverent banter, not against the Spinster alone, but obliquely against her Regenerative Man! Barrère's light pen was perhaps at the bottom of it; read through the solemn snuffling organs of old Vadier of the *Sûreté Générale*, the Théot Report had its effect; wrinkling the general Republican visage into an iron grin. Ought these things to be?

We note further, that among the Prisoners in the Twelve Houses of Arrest, there is one whom we have seen before— Senhora Fontenai, *born* Cabarus, the fair Proserpine whom

Representative Tallien Pluto-like did gather at Bourdeaux, not without effect on himself! (p. 302.) Tallien is home, by recall, long since, from Bourdeaux; and in the most alarming position. Vain that he sounded, louder even than ever, the note of Jacobinism, to hide past shortcomings: the Jacobins purged him out; two times has Robespierre growled at him words of omen from the Convention Tribune. And now his fair Cabarus, hit by denunciation, lies Arrested, Suspect, in spite of all he could do!—Shut in horrid pinfold of death, the Senhora smuggles out to her red-gloomy Tallien the most pressing entreaties and conjurings: Save me; save thyself. Seest thou not that thy own head is doomed; thou with a too fiery audacity; a Dantonist withal; against whom lie grudges? Are ye not all doomed, as in the Polyphemus Cavern: the fawningest slave of you will be but eaten last!—Tallien feels with a shudder that it is true. Tallien has had words of omen, Bourdon has had words, Fréron is hated and Barras: each man 'feels his head if it yet stick on his shoulders.'

Meanwhile Robespierre, we still observe, goes little to Convention, not at all to Committee; speaks nothing except to his Jacobin House of Lords, amid his body-guard of *Tappedurs*. These 'forty-days,' for we are now far in July, he has not showed face in Committee; could only work there by his three shallow scoundrels, and the terror there was of him. The Incorruptible himself sits apart; or is seen stalking in solitary places in the fields, with an intensely meditative air; some say, 'with eyes red-spotted,' fruit of extreme bile: the lamentablest seagreen Chimera that walks the Earth that July! O hapless Chimera; for thou too hadst a life, and heart of flesh,—what is this that the stern gods, seeming to smile all the way, have led and let thee to! Art not thou he, who, few years ago, was a young Advocate of promise, and gave up the Arras Judgeship rather than sentence one man to die?—

What his thoughts might be? His plans for finishing the Terror? One knows not. Dim vestiges there flit of Agrarian Law; a victorious Sansculottism become Landed Proprietor; old Soldiers sitting in National Mansions, in Hospital Palaces of Chambord and Chantilly; peace bought by victory; breaches healed by Feast of *Être Suprême*;—and so, through seas of blood, to Equality, Frugality, worksome Blessedness, Fraternity, and Republic of the virtues. Blessed shore, of such a sea of Aristocrat blood: but how to land on it?

Through one last wave: blood of corrupt Sansculottists; traitorous or semi-traitorous Conventionals, rebellious Talliens, Billauds, to whom with my *Être Suprême* I have become a bore; with my Apocalyptic Old Woman a laughing-stock!— So stalks he, this poor Robespierre, like a seagreen ghost, through the blooming July. Vestiges of schemes flit dim. But *what* his schemes or his thoughts were will never be known to man.

New Catacombs, some say, are digging for a huge simultaneous butchery. Convention to be butchered, down to the right pitch, by General Henriot and Company: Jacobin House of Lords made dominant; and Robespierre Dictator. There is actually, or else there is not actually, a List made out; which the Hairdresser has got eye on, as he frizzled the Incorruptible locks. Each man asks himself, Is it I?

Nay, as Tradition and rumour of Anecdote still convey it, there was a remarkable bachelor's dinner, one hot day, at Barrère's. For doubt not, O Reader, this Barrère and others of them gave dinners; had 'country-house at Clichy,' with elegant enough sumptuosities, and pleasures high-rouged. But at this dinner we speak of, the day being so hot, it is said, the guests all stript their coats, and left them in the drawing-room: whereupon Carnot glided out; groped in Robespierre's pocket; found a list of Forty, his own name among them; and tarried not at the wine-cup that day!—Ye must bestir yourselves, O Friends; ye dull Frogs of the Marsh, mute ever since Girondism sank under, even you now must croak or die! Councils are held, with word and beck; nocturnal, mysterious as death. Does not a feline Maximilien stalk there; voiceless as yet; his green eyes red-spotted; back bent, and hair up? Rash Tallien, with his rash temper and audacity of tongue; he shall *bell the cat*. Fix a day; and be it soon, lest never!

Lo, before the fixed day, on the day which they call Eighth of Thermidor, 26th July 1794, Robespierre himself reappears in Convention; mounts to the Tribune! The biliary face seems clouded with new gloom: judge whether your Talliens, Bourdons, listened with interest. It is a voice bodeful of death or of life. Long-winded unmelodious as the screech-owl's, sounds that prophetic voice: Degenerate condition of Republican spirit; corrupt Moderatism; *Sûreté, Salut* Committees themselves infected; backsliding on this hand and on that; I, Maximilien, alone left incorruptible, ready to die at a moment's warning. For all which what remedy is there? The

Guillotine; new vigour to the all-healing Guillotine; death to
traitors of every hue! So sings the prophetic voice; into its
Convention sounding-board. The old song this: but today,
O Heavens! has the sounding-board ceased to act? There is
not resonance in this Convention; there is, so to speak, a gasp
of silence; nay a certain grating of one knows not what?—
Lecointre, our old Draper of Versailles, in these questionable
circumstances, sees nothing he can do so safe as rise, 'insidiously' or not insidiously, and move, according to established
wont, that the Robespierre Speech be 'printed and sent to the
Departments.' Hark: gratings, even of dissonance! Honourable Members hint dissonance; Committee-Members, inculpated in the Speech, utter dissonance, demand 'delay in
printing.' Ever higher rises the note of dissonance; inquiry
is even made by Editor Fréron: "What has become of the
Liberty of Opinions in this Convention?" The Order to
print and transmit, which had got passed, is rescinded.
Robespierre, greener than ever before, has to retire, foiled;
discerning that it is mutiny, that evil is nigh!

Mutiny is a thing of the fatallest nature in all enterprises
whatsoever; a thing so incalcuable, swift-frightful: not to be
dealt with in *fright*. But mutiny in a Robespierre Convention, above all,—it is like fire seen sputtering in the ship's
powder-room! One death-defiant plunge at it, this moment,
and you may still tread it out: hesitate till next moment,—
ship and ship's captain, crew and cargo are shivered far; the
ship's voyage has suddenly ended between sea and sky. If
Robespierre can, tonight, produce his Henriot and Company,
and get his work done by them, he and Sansculottism may
still subsist some time; if not, probably not. Oliver Cromwell, when that Agitator Sergeant stept forth from the ranks,
with plea of grievances, and began gesticulating and demonstrating, as the mouthpiece of Thousands expectant there,—
discerned, with those truculent eyes of his, how the matter
lay; plucked a pistol from his holsters; blew Agitator and
Agitation instantly out. Noll was a man fit for such things.
Robespierre, for his part, glides over at evening to his
Jacobin House of Lords; unfolds there, instead of some
adequate resolution, his woes, his uncommon virtues, in-
corruptibilities; then, secondly, his rejected screech-owl
Oration;—reads this latter over again; and declares that he
is ready to die at a moment's warning. Thou shalt not die!

shouts Jacobinism from its thousand throats. "Robespierre, I will drink the hemlock with thee," cries Painter David, "*Je boirai la cigue avec toi;*"—a thing not essential to *do*, but which, in the fire of the moment, can be said.

Our Jacobin sounding-board, therefore, does act! Applauses heaven-high cover the rejected Oration; fire-eyed fury lights all Jacobin features: Insurrection a sacred duty; the Convention to be purged; Sovereign People under Henriot and Municipality; we will make a new June-Second of it: To your tents, O Israel! In this key pipes Jacobinism; in sheer tumult of revolt. Let Tallien and all Opposition men make off. Collot d'Herbois, though of the supreme *Salut*, and so lately near shot, is elbowed, bullied; is glad to escape alive. Entering Committee-room of *Salut*, all dishevelled, he finds sleek sombre Saint-Just there, among the rest; who in his sleek way asks, "What is passing at the Jacobins?"— "What is passing?" repeats Collot, in the unhistrionic Cambyses' vein: "What is passing? Nothing but revolt and horrors are passing. Ye want our lives; ye shall not have them." Saint-Just stutters at such Cambyses-oratory; takes his hat to withdraw. That *Report* he had been speaking of, Report on Republican Things in General we may say, which is to be read in Convention on the morrow, he cannot show it them, at this moment: a friend has it; he, Saint-Just, will get it, and send it, were he once home. Once home, he sends not it, but an answer that he will not send it; that they will hear it from the Tribune tomorrow.

Let every man, therefore, according to a well-known good-advice, 'pray to Heaven, and keep his powder dry!' Paris, on the morrow, will see a thing. Swift scouts fly dim or invisible, all night, from *Sûreté* and *Salut;* from conclave to conclave; from Mother-Society to Townhall. Sleep, can it fall on the eyes of Talliens, Frérons, Collots? Puissant Henriot, Mayor Fleuriot, Judge Coffinhal, Procureur Payan, Robespierre and all the Jacobins are getting ready.

CHAPTER VII

GO DOWN TO

TALLIEN'S eyes beamed bright, on the morrow, Ninth of Thermidor 'about nine o'clock,' to see that the Convention had actually met. Paris is in rumour: but at least we are met, in Legal Convention here; we have not been snatched seriatim; treated with a *Pride's Purge* at the door. "*Allons*, brave men of the Plain," late Frogs of the Marsh! cried Tallien with a squeeze of the hand, as he passed in; Saint-Just's sonorous voice being now audible from the Tribune, and the game of games begun.

Saint-Just is verily reading that Report of his; green Vengeance, in the shape of Robespierre, watching nigh; Behold, however, Saint-Just has read but few sentences, when interruption rises, rapid *crescendo*; when Tallien starts to his feet, and Billaud, and this man starts and that,—and Tallien, a second time, with his: "Citoyens, at the Jacobins last night, I trembled for the Republic. I said to myself, if the Convention dare not strike the Tyrant, then I myself dare; and with this I will do it, if need be," said he, whisking out a clear-gleaming Dagger, and brandishing it there; the Steel of Brutus, as we call it. Whereat we all bellow, and brandish, impetuous acclaim. "Tyranny! Dictatorship! Triumvirate!" And the *Salut* Committee-men accuse, and all men accuse, and uproar, and impetuously acclaim. And Saint-Just is standing motionless, pale of face; Couthon ejaculating, "Triumvir?" with a look at his paralytic legs. And Robespierre is struggling to speak, but President Thuriot is jingling the bell against him, but the Hall is sounding against him like an Æolus-Hall: and Robespierre is mounting the Tribune-steps and descending again; going and coming, like to choke with rage, terror, desperation:—and mutiny is the order of the day!

O President Thuriot, thou that wert Elector Thuriot, and from the Bastille battlements sawest Saint-Antoine rising like the Ocean-tide, and hast seen much since, sawest thou ever the like of this? Jingle of bell, which thou jinglest against Robespierre, is hardly audible amid the Bedlam-storm; and men rage for life. "President of Assassins," shrieks Robespierre, "I demand speech of thee for the last time!" It cannot be had. "To you, O virtuous men of the Plain," cries he, finding audience one moment, "I appeal to you!" The virtuous men of the Plain sit silent as stones. And Thuriot's bell jingles, and the Hall sounds like Æolus's Hall. Robespierre's frothing lips are grown 'blue;' his tongue dry, cleaving to the roof of his mouth. "The blood of Danton chokes him," cry they. "Accusation! Decree of Accusation!" Thuriot swiftly puts that question. Accusation passes; the incorruptible Maximilien is decreed Accused.

"I demand to share my Brother's fate, as I have striven to share his virtues," cries Augustin, the Younger Robespierre: Augustin also is decreed. And Couthon, and Saint-Just, and Lebas, they are all decreed; and packed forth,—not without difficulty, the Ushers almost trembling to obey. Triumvirate and Company are packed forth, into *Salut* Committee-room; their tongue cleaving to the roof of their mouth. You have but to summon the Municipality; to cashier Commandant Henriot, and launch Arrest at him; to regulate formalities; hand Tinville his victims. It is noon: the Æolus-Hall has delivered itself; blows now victorious, harmonious, as one irresistible wind.

And so the work is finished? One thinks so: and yet it is not so. Alas, there is yet but the first-act finished; three or four other acts still to come; and an uncertain catastrophe! A huge City holds in it so many confusions: seven hundred thousand human heads; not one of which knows what its neighbour is doing, nay not what itself is doing.—See, accordingly, about three in the afternoon, Commandant Henriot, how instead of sitting cashiered, arrested, he gallops along the Quais, followed by Municipal Gendarmes, 'trampling down several persons!' For the Townhall sits deliberating, openly insurgent: Barriers to be shut; no Gaoler to admit any Prisoner this day;—and Henriot is galloping towards the Tuileries, to deliver Robespierre. On the Quai de la Ferraillerie, a young Citoyen, walking with his wife, says aloud: "Gendarmes, that man is not your Commandant; he is under arrest." The Gendarmes strike down the young Citoyen with the flat of their swords.

Representatives themselves (as Merlin the Thionviller), who accost him, this puissant Henriot flings into guardhouses. He bursts towards the Tuileries Committee-room, "to speak with Robespierre:" with difficulty, the Ushers and Tuileries Gendarmes, earnestly pleading and drawing sabre, seize this Henriot; get the Henriot Gendarmes persuaded not to fight;

get Robespierre and Company packed into hackney-coaches, sent off under escort, to the Luxembourg and other Prisons. This then *is* the end? May not an exhausted Convention adjourn now, for a little repose and sustenance, 'at five o'clock?'

An exhausted Convention did it; and repented it. The end was not come; only the end of the *second-act*. Hark, while exhausted Representatives sit at victuals,—tocsin bursting from all steeples, drums rolling, in the summer evening: Judge Coffinhal is galloping with new Gendarmes, to deliver Henriot from Tuileries Committee-room; and does deliver him! Puissant Henriot vaults on horseback; sets to haranguing the Tuileries Gendarmes; corrupts the Tuileries Gendarmes too; trots off with them to Townhall. Alas, and Robespierre is not in Prison: the Gaoler showed his Municipal order, durst not, on pain of his life, admit any Prisoner; the Robespierre Hackney-coaches, in this confused jangle and whirl of uncertain Gendarmes, have floated safe—into the Townhall! There sit Robespierre and Company, embraced by Municipals and Jacobins, in sacred right of Insurrection; redacting Proclamations; sounding tocsins; corresponding with Sections and Mother-Society. Is not here a pretty enough third-act of a *natural* Greek Drama; catastrophe more uncertain than ever?

The hasty Convention rushes together again, in the ominous nightfall: President Collot, for the chair is his, enters with long strides, paleness on his face; claps-on his hat; says with solemn tone: "Citoyens, armed Villains have beset the Committee-rooms, and got possession of them. The hour is come, to die at our post!" "*Oui*," answer one and all: "We swear it!" It is no rhodomontade, this time, but a sad fact and necessity; unless we *do* at our posts, we must verily die. Swift therefore, Robespierre, Henriot, the Municipality, are declared Rebels; put *Hors la Loi*, Out of Law. Better still, we appoint Barras Commandant of what Armed-force is to be had; send Missionary Representatives to all Sections and quarters, to preach, and raise force; will die at least with harness on our back.

What a distracted City; men riding and running, reporting and hearsaying; the Hour clearly in travail,—child not to be *named* till born! The poor Prisoners in the Luxembourg hear the rumour; tremble for a new September. They see men making signals to them, on skylights and roofs, apparently signals of hope; cannot in the least make out what it is. We observe, however, in the eventide, as usual, the Death-tumbrils faring Southeastward, through Saint-Antoine, towards their Barrier du Trône. Saint-Antoine's tough bowels melt; Saint-Antoine surrounds the Tumbrils; says, It shall not be. O Heavens, why should it! Henriot and Gendarmes, scouring the streets that way, bellow, with waved sabres, that it must. Quit hope, ye poor Doomed! The Tumbrils move on.

But in this set of Tumbrils there are two other things notable: one notable person; and one want of a notable person. The notable person is Lieutenant-General Loiserolles, a nobleman by birth and by nature; laying down his life here for his son. In the Prison of Saint-Lazare, the night before last, hurrying to the Grate to hear the Death-list read, he caught the name of his son. The son was asleep at the moment. "I am Loiserolles," cried the old man: at Tinville's bar, an error in the Christian name is little; small objection was made.—The want of the notable person, again, is that of Deputy Paine! Paine has sat in the Luxembourg since January, and seemed forgotten; but Fouquier had pricked him at last. The Turnkey, List in hand, is marking with chalk the outer doors of to-morrow's *Fournée*. Paine's outer door happened to be open, turned back on the wall; the Turnkey marked it on the side next him, and hurried on: another Turnkey came, and shut it; no chalk-mark now visible, the *Fournée* went without Paine. Paine's life lay not there.—

Our fifth-act, of this natural Greek Drama, with its natural unities, can only be painted in gross; somewhat as that antique Painter, driven desperate, did the *foam*. For through this blessed July night, there is clangour, confusion very great, of marching troops; of Sections going this way, Sections going that; of Missionary Representatives reading Proclamations by torchlight; Missionary Legendre, who has raised force somewhere, emptying out the Jacobins, and flinging their key on the Convention table: " I have locked their door; it shall be Virtue that reopens it." Paris, we say, is set against itself, rushing confused, as Ocean-currents do; a huge Mahl-strom, sounding there, under cloud of night. Convention sits permanent on this hand; Municipality most permanent on that. The poor prisoners hear tocsin and rumour; strive to bethink them of the signals apparently of hope. Meek continual Twilight streaming up, which will be Dawn and a Tomorrow, silvers the Northern hem of Night; it wends and wends there, that meek brightness, like a silent prophecy, along the great ring-dial of the Heaven. So still, eternal! and on Earth all is confused shadow and conflict; dissidence, tumultuous gloom and glare; and 'Destiny as yet sits wavering, and shakes her doubtful urn.'

About three in the morning, the dissident Armed Forces have *met*. Henriot's Armed Force stood ranked in the Place de Grève; and now Barras's, which he has recruited, arrives there; and they front each other, cannon bristling against cannon. Citoyens! cries the voice of Discretion loudly enough, Before coming to bloodshed, to endless civil-war, hear the Convention Decree read: 'Robespierre and all rebels Out of Law!'—Out of Law? There is terror in the sound. Unarmed Citoyens disperse rapidly home. Municipal Cannoneers, in sudden whirl, anxiously unanimous, range themselves on the Convention side, with shouting. At which shout, Henriot descends from his upper room, far gone in drink as some say; finds his Place de Grève empty; the cannons' mouth turned *towards* him; and on the whole,—that it is now the catastrophe!

Stumbling in again, the wretched drunk-sobered Henriot announces: "All is lost!" "*Misérable*, it is thou that hast lost it!" cry they; and fling him, or else he flings himself, out of window: far enough down; into masonwork and horror of cesspool; not into death but worse. Augustin Robespierre follows him; with the like fate. Saint-Just, they say, called on Lebas to kill him; who would not. Couthon crept under a table; attempting to kill himself; not doing it.—On entering that Sanhedrim of Insurrection, we find all as good as extinct; undone, ready for seizure. Robespierre was sitting on a chair, with pistol-shot blown through not his head but his under-jaw; the suicidal hand had failed. With prompt zeal, not without trouble, we gather these wrecked Conspirators; fish up even Henriot and Augustin, bleeding and foul; pack them all, rudely enough, into carts; and shall, before sunrise, have them safe under lock and key. Amid shoutings and embracings.

Robespierre lay in an anteroom of the Convention Hall, while his Prison-escort was getting ready; the mangled jaw bound up rudely with bloody linen: a spectacle to men. He lies stretched on a table, a deal-box his pillow; the sheath of the pistol is still clenched convulsively in his hand. Men bully him, insult him: his eyes still indicate intelligence; he speaks no word. 'He had on the sky-blue coat he had got made for the Feast of the *Être Suprême*'—O Reader, can thy hard heart hold out against that? His trousers were nankeen; the stockings had fallen down over the ankles. He spake no word more in this world.

And so, at six in the morning, a victorious Convention adjourns. Report flies over Paris as on golden wings; penetrates the Prisons; irradiates the faces of those that were ready to perish: turnkeys and *moutons*, fallen from their high estate, look mute and blue. It is the 28th day of July, called 10th of Thermidor, year 1794.

Fouquier had but to identify; his Prisoners being already Out of Law. At four in the afternoon, never before were the streets of Paris seen so crowded. From the Palais de Justice to the Place de la Révolution, for *thither* again go the Tumbrils this time, it is one dense stirring mass; all windows crammed; the very roofs and ridge-tiles budding forth human Curiosity, in strange gladness. The Death-tumbrils, with their motley Batch of Outlaws, some Twenty-three or so, from Maximilien to Mayor Fleuriot and Simon the Cordwainer, roll on. All eyes are on Robespierre's Tumbril, where he, his jaw bound in dirty linen, with his half-dead Brother, and half-dead Henriot, lie shattered; their 'seventeen hours' of agony about to end. The Gendarmes point their swords at him, to show the people which is he. A woman springs on the Tumbril; clutching the side of it with one hand; waving the other Sibyl-like; and exclaims: "The death of thee gladdens my very heart, *m'enivre de joie;*" Robespierre opened his eyes; "*Scélérat*, go down to Hell, with the curses of all wives and mothers!"—At the foot of the scaffold, they stretched him on the ground till his turn came. Lifted aloft, his eyes again opened; caught the bloody axe. Samson wrenched the coat off him; wrenched the dirty linen from his jaw: the jaw fell powerless, there burst from him a cry; hideous to hear and see. Samson, thou canst not be too quick.

Samson's work done, there bursts forth shout on shout of applause. Shout, which prolongs itself not only over Paris, but over France, but over Europe, and down to this generation. Deservedly, and also undeservedly. O unhappiest Advocate of Arras, wert thou worse than other Advocates? Stricter man, according to his Formula, to his Credo and his Cant, of probities, benevolences, pleasures-of-virtue, and such like, lived not in that age. A man fitted, in some luckier settled age, to have become one of those incorruptible barren Pattern-Figures, and have had marble-tablets and funeral-sermons. His poor landlord, the Cabinet-maker in the Rue Saint-Honoré, loved him; his Brother died for him. May God be merciful to him, and to us!

This is the end of the Reign of Terror; new glorious *Revolution* named *of Thermidor*; of Thermidor 9th, year **2**; which being interpreted into old slave-style means 27th of July 1794. Terror is ended; and death in the Place de la Révolution, were the '*Tail* of Robespierre' once executed; which service Fouquier in large Batches is swiftly managing.

BOOK VII

VENDÉMIAIRE

CHAPTER I

DECADENT

How little did any one suppose that here was the end not of Robespierre only, but of the Revolution System itself! Least of all did the mutinying Committee-men suppose it; who had mutinied with no view whatever except to continue the National Regeneration with their own heads on their shoulders. And yet so it verily was. The insignificant stone they had struck out, so insignificant anywhere else, proved to be the Keystone; the whole arch-work and edifice of Sansculottism began to loosen, to crack, to yawn; and tumbled piecemeal, with considerable rapidity, plunge after plunge; till the Abyss had swallowed it all, and in this upper world Sansculottism was no more.

For despicable as Robespierre himself might be, the death of Robespierre was a signal at which great multitudes of men, struck dumb with terror heretofore, rose out of their hiding-places; and, as it were, saw one another, how multitudinous they were; and began speaking and complaining. They are countable by the thousand and the million; who have suffered cruel wrong. Ever louder rises the plaint of such a multitude; into a universal sound, into a universal continuous peal, of what they call Public Opinion. Camille had demanded a 'Committee of Mercy,' and could not get it; but now the whole Nation resolves itself into a Committee of Mercy: the Nation has tried Sansculottism, and is weary of it. Force of Public Opinion! What King or Convention can withstand it? You in vain struggle: the thing that is rejected as 'calumnious' today must pass as veracious with triumph another day: gods and men have declared that Sansculottism cannot be. Sansculottism, on the Ninth night of Thermidor suicidally 'fractured its under-jaw;' and lies writhing, never to rise more.

Through the next fifteen months, it is what we may call the

death-agony of Sansculottism. Sansculottism, Anarchy of the Jean-Jacques Evangel, having now got deep enough, is to perish in a new singular system of Culottism and Arrangement. For Arrangement is indispensable to man; Arrangement, were it grounded only on that old primary Evangel of Force, with Sceptre in the shape of Hammer! Be there method, be there order, cry all men; were it that of the Drill-sergeant! More tolerable is the drilled Bayonet-rank, than that undrilled Guillotine, incalculable as the wind.—How Sansculottism, writhing in death-throes, strove some twice, or even three times, to get on its feet again; but fell always, and was flung resupine, the next instant; and finally breathed out the life of it, and stirred no more: this we are now, from a due distance, with due brevity, to glance at; and then—O Reader! —Courage, I see land!

Two of the first acts of the Convention, very natural for it after this Thermidor, are to be specified here: the first is, renewal of the Governing Committees. Both *Sûreté Générale* and *Salut Public*, thinned by the Guillotine, need filling up: we naturally fill them up with Talliens, Fréons, victorious Thermidorian men. Still more to the purpose, we appoint that they shall, as Law directs, not in name only but in deed, be renewed and changed from period to period; a fourth part of them going out monthly. The Convention will no more lie under bondage of Committees, under terror of death; but be a free Convention; free to follow its own judgment, and the Force of Public Opinion. Not less natural is it to enact that Prisoners and Persons under Accusation shall have right to demand some 'Writ of Accusation,' and see clearly what they are accused of. Very natural acts: the harbingers of hundreds not less so.

For now Fouquier's trade, shackled by Writ of Accusation, and legal proof, is as good as gone; effectual only against Robespierre's Tail. The Prisons give up their Suspect; emit them faster and faster. The Committees see themselves besieged with Prisoners' friends; complain that they are hindered in their work: it is as with men rushing out of a crowded place; and obstructing one another. Turned are the tables: Prisoners pouring out in floods; Jailors, *Moutons* and the Tail of Robespierre going now whither they were wont to send!—The Hundred and thirty-two Nantese Republicans, whom we saw marching in irons, have arrived; shrunk to

Ninety-four, the fifth man of them choked by the road. They arrive: and suddenly find themselves not pleaders for life, but denouncers to death. Their Trial is for acquittal, and more. As the voice of a trumpet, their testimony sounds far and wide, mere atrocities of a Reign of Terror. For a space of nineteen days; with all solemnity and publicity. Representative Carrier, Company of Marat; Noyadings, Loire Marriages, things done in darkness, come forth into light: clear is the voice of these poor resuscitated Nantese; and Journals, and Speech, and universal Committee of Mercy reverberate it loud enough, into all ears and hearts. Deputation arrives from Arras; denouncing the atrocities of Representative Lebon. A tamed Convention loves its own life: yet what help? Representative Lebon, Representative Carrier must wend towards the Revolutionary Tribunal; struggle and delay as we will, the cry of a Nation pursues them louder and louder. Them also Tinville must abolish;—if indeed Tinville himself be not abolished.

We must note moreover the decrepit condition into which a once omnipotent Mother-Society has fallen. Legendre flung her keys on the Convention table, that Thermidor night; her President was guillotined with Robespierre. The once mighty Mother came, some time after, with a subdued countenance, begging back her keys: the keys were restored her; but the strength could not be restored her; the strength had departed forever. Alas, one's day is done. Vain that the Tribune in mid-air sounds as of old: to the general ear it has become a horror, and even a weariness. By and by, Affiliation is prohibited: the mighty Mother sees herself suddenly childless; mourns as so hoarse a Rachel may.

The Revolutionary Committees, without Suspects to prey upon, perish fast; as it were, of famine. In Paris the old Forty-eight of them are reduced to Twelve; their *Forty sous* are abolished: yet a little while, and Revolutionary Committees are no more. *Maximum* will be abolished; let Sansculottism find food where it can. Neither is there now any Municipality; any centre at the Townhall. Mayor Fleuriot and Company perished; whom we shall not be in haste to replace. The Townhall remains in a broken submissive state; knows not well what it is growing to; knows only that it is grown weak, and must obey. What if we should split Paris into, say, a Dozen separate Municipalities; incapable of concert! The Sections were thus rendered safe to act with :—or indeed might not the Sections themselves be abolished? You had then merely your Twelve manageable pacific Townships, without centre or subdivision; and sacred right of Insurrection fell into abeyance!

So much is getting abolished; fleeting swiftly into the Inane. For the Press speaks, and the human tongue; Journals, heavy and light, in Philippic and Burlesque: a renegade Fréron, a renegade Prudhomme, loud they as ever, only the contrary way. And *Ci-devants* show themselves, almost parade themselves; resuscitated as from death-sleep; publish what death-pains they have had. The very Frogs of the Marsh croak with emphasis. Your protesting Seventy-three shall, with a struggle, be emitted out of Prison, back to their seats; your Louvets, Isnards, Lanjuinais, and wrecks of Girondism, recalled from their haylofts, and caves in Switzerland, will resume their place in the Convention: natural foes of Terror!

Thermidorian Talliens, and mere foes of Terror, rule in this Convention, and out of it. The compressed Mountain shrinks silent more and more. Moderatism rises louder and louder: not as a tempest, with threatenings; say rather, as the rushing of a mighty organ-blast, and melodious deafening Force of Public Opinion, from the Twenty-five million windpipes of a Nation all in Committee of Mercy: which how shall any detached body of individuals withstand?

CHAPTER II

LA CABARUS

How, above all, shall a poor National Convention withstand it? In this poor National Convention, broken, bewildered by long terror, perturbations and guillotinement, there is no Pilot, there is not now even a Danton, who could undertake to steer you anywhither, in such press of weather. The utmost a bewildered Convention can do, is to veer, and trim, and try to keep itself steady; and rush, undrowned, before the wind. Needless to struggle; to fling helm a-lee, and make '*bout ship*! A bewildered Convention sails not in the teeth of the wind; but is rapidly blown round again. So strong is the wind, we say; and so changed; blowing fresher and fresher, as from the sweet Southwest; your devastating Northeasters, and wild Tornado-gusts of Terror, blown utterly out! All Sansculottic things are passing away; all things are becoming Culottic.

Do but look at the cut of clothes; that light visible Result, significant of a thousand things which are not so visible. In winter 1793, men went in red nightcap; Municipals themselves in *sabots;* the very Citoyennes had to petition against such headgear. But now in this winter 1794, where is the red nightcap? With the things beyond the Flood. Your moneyed Citoyen ponders in what elegantest style he shall dress himself; whether he shall not even dress himself as the Free Peoples of Antiquity. The more adventurous Citoyenne has already done it. Behold her, that beautiful adventurous Citoyenne: in costume of the Ancient Greeks, such Greek as Painter David could teach; her sweeping tresses snooded by glittering antique fillet; bright-dyed tunic of the Greek women; her little feet naked, as in Antique Statues, with mere sandals, and winding-strings of riband,—defying the frost!

There is such an effervescence of Luxury. For your Emigrant *Ci-devants* carried not their mansions and furnitures out of the country with them; but left them standing here: and in the swift changes of property, what with money coined on the Place de la Révolution, what with Army-furnishings, sales of Emigrant Domains and Church Lands and King's Lands, and then with the Aladdin's-lamp of Agio in the time of Paper-money, such mansions have found new occupants. Old wine, drawn from *Ci-devant* bottles, descends new throats. Paris has swept herself, relighted herself; Salons, Soupers not Fraternal, beam once more with suitable effulgence, very singular in colour. The fair Cabarus is come out of Prison; wedded to her red-gloomy Dis, whom they say she treats too loftily: fair Cabarus gives the most brilliant soirées. Round her is gathered a new Republican Army, of Citoyennes in sandals; *Ci-devants* or other: what remnants soever of the old grace survive are rallied there. At her right-hand, in this cause, labours fair Josephine the Widow Beauharnais, though in straitened circumstances: intent, both of them, to blandish down the grimness of Republican austerity, and recivilise mankind.

Recivilise, even as of old they were civilised: by witchery of the Orphic fiddle-bow, and Euterpean rhythm; by the Graces, by the Smiles! Thermidorian Deputies are there in those soirées: Editor Fréron, *Orateur du Peuple;* Barras, who has known other dances than the Carmagnole. Grim

Generals of the Republic are there; in enormous horse-collar neckcloth, good against sabre-cuts; the hair gathered all into one knot, 'flowing down behind, fixed with a comb.' Among which latter do we not recognise, once more, that little bronze-complexioned Artillery-Officer of Toulon, home from the Italian Wars! Grim enough; of lean, almost cruel aspect: for he has been in trouble, in ill health; also in ill favour, as a man promoted, deservingly or not, by the Terrorists and Robespierre Junior. But does not Barras know him? Will not Barras speak a word for him? Yes,—if at any time it will serve Barras so to do. Somewhat forlorn of fortune, for the present, stands that Artillery-Officer; looks, with those deep earnest eyes of his, into a future as waste as the most. Taciturn; yet with the strangest utterances in him, if you awaken him, which smite home, like light or lightning;—on the whole, rather dangerous? A 'dissocial' man? Dissocial enough; a natural terror and horror to all Phantasms, being himself of the genus Reality! He stands here, without work or out-look, in this forsaken manner;—glances nevertheless, it would seem, at the kind glance of Josephine Beauharnais; and, for the rest, with severe countenance, with open eyes, and closed lips, waits what will betide.

That the Balls, therefore, have a new figure this winter, we can see. Not Carmagnoles, rude 'whirlblasts of rags,' as Mercier called them, 'precursors of storm and destruction:' no, soft Ionic motions; fit for the light sandal, and antique Grecian tunic! Efflorescence of Luxury has come out: for men have wealth; nay new-got wealth; and under the Terror you durst not dance, except in rags. Among the innumerable kinds of Balls, let the hasty reader mark only this single one: the kind they call Victim Balls, *Bals à Victime*. The dancers, in choice costume, have all crape round the left arm: to be admitted, it needs that you be a *Victime;* that you have lost a relative under the Terror. Peace to the Dead; let us *dance* to their memory! For in all ways one must dance.

It is very remarkable, according to Mercier, under what varieties of figure this great business of dancing goes on. 'The women,' says he, 'are Nymphs, Sultanas; sometimes Minervas, Junos, even Dianas. In lightly-unerring gyrations they swim there; with such earnestness of purpose; with perfect silence, so absorbed are they. What is singular,' continues he, 'the on-lookers are as it were mingled with the dancers; form, as it were, a circumambient element round the different contredances, yet without deranging them. It is rare, in fact, that a Sultana in such circumstances experiences the smallest collision. Her pretty foot darts down, an inch from mine; she is off again; she is as a flash of light: but soon the measure recalls her to the point she set out from. Like a glittering comet she travels her ellipse; revolving on herself, as by a double effect of gravitation and attraction.' Looking forward a little way, into Time, the same Mercier discerns *Merveilleuses* in 'flesh-coloured drawers' with gold circlets; mere dancing Houris of an artificial Mahomet's-Paradise: much too Mahometan. Montgaillard, with his splenetic eye, notes a no less strange thing; that every fashionable Citoyenne you meet is in an interesting situation. Good Heavens, *every !* Mere pillows and stuffing! adds the acrid man;—such in a time of depopulation by war and guillotine, being the fashion. No further seek its merits to disclose.

Behold also, instead of the old grim *Tappe-durs* of Robespierre, what new street-groups are these? Young men habited not in black-shag Carmagnole spencer, but in superfine *habit carré*, or spencer with rectangular tail appended to it; 'square-tailed coat,' with elegant anti-guillotinish specialty of collar; 'the hair plaited at the temples,' and knotted back, long-flowing, in military wise: young men of what they call the *Muscadin* or Dandy species! Fréron, in his fondness, names them *Jeunesse Dorée*, Golden or Gilt Youth. They have come out, these Gilt Youths, in a kind of resuscitated state; they wear crape round the left arm, such of them as were *Victims.* More, they carry clubs loaded with lead; in an angry manner: any *Tappe-dur*, or remnant of Jacobinism they may fall in with, shall fare the worse. They have suffered much: their friends guillotined; their pleasures, frolics, superfine collars ruthlessly repressed: 'ware now the base Red Nightcaps who did it! Fair Cabarus and the Army of Greek sandals smile approval. In the Théâtre Feydeau, young Valour in square-tailed coat eyes Beauty in Greek sandals, and kindles by her glances: Down with Jacobinism! No Jacobin hymn or demonstration, only Thermidorian ones, shall be permitted here: we beat down Jacobinism with clubs loaded with lead.

But let any one who has examined the Dandy nature, how petulant it is, especially in the gregarious state, think what an element, in sacred right of insurrection, this Gilt Youth was!

Broils and battery; war without truce or measure! Hateful is Sanculottism, as Death and Night. For indeed is not the Dandy *culottic*, habilatory, by law of existence; 'a cloth-animal; one that lives, moves, and has his being in cloth?'

So goes it, waltzing, bickering; fair Cabarus, by Orphic witchery, struggling to recivilise mankind. Not unsuccessfully, we hear. What utmost Republican grimness can resist Greek sandals, in Ionic motion, the very toes covered with gold rings? By degrees the indisputablest new-politeness rises; grows, with vigour. And yet, whether, even to this day, that inexpressible tone of society known under the old Kings, when Sin had 'lost all his deformity' (with or without advantage to us), and airy Nothing had obtained such a local habitation and establishment as she never had,—be recovered? Or even, whether it be not lost beyond recovery?—Either way, the world must contrive to struggle on.

CHAPTER III

QUIBERON

BUT indeed do not these long-flowing hair-queues of a *Jeunesse Dorée* in semi-military costume betoken, unconsciously, another still more important tendency? The Republic, abhorrent of her Guillotine, loves her Army.

And with cause. For, surely, if good fighting be a kind of honour, as it is in its season; and be with the vulgar of men, even the chief kind of honour; then here is good fighting, in good season, if there ever was. These Sons of the Republic, they rose, in mad wrath, to deliver her from Slavery and Cimmeria. And have they not done it? Through Maritime Alps, through gorges of Pyrenees, through Low Countries, Northward along the Rhine-valley, far is Cimmeria hurled back from the Sacred Motherland. Fierce as fire, they have carried her Tricolor over the faces of all her enemies;—over scarped heights, over cannon-batteries, it has flown victorious, winged with rage. She has 'Eleven hundred thousand fighters on foot,' this Republic: 'at one particular moment she had,' or supposed she had, 'Seventeen-hundred thousand.' Like a ring of lightning, they, volleying and *ça-ira*-ing, begirdle her from shore to shore. Cimmerian Coalition of Despots recoils, smitten with astonishment and strange pangs.

Such a fire is in these Gaelic Republican men; high-blazing; which no Coalition can withstand! Not scutcheons, with four degrees of nobility; but *ci-devant* Sergeants, who have had to clutch Generalship out of the cannon's throat, a Pichegru, a Jourdan, a Hoche lead them on. They have bread, they have iron; 'with bread and iron you can get to China.'—See Pichegru's soldiers, this hard winter, in their looped and windowed destitution, in their 'straw-rope shoes and cloaks of bastmat,' how they overrun Holland, like a demon-host, the ice having bridged all waters; and rush shouting from victory to victory! Ships in the Texel are taken by hussars on horseback: fled is York; fled is the Stadtholder, glad to escape to England, and leave Holland to fraternise. Such a Gaelic fire, we say, blazes in this People, like the conflagration of grass and dry-jungle; which no mortal can withstand—for the moment.

And even so it will blaze and run, scorching all things; and, from Cadiz to Archangel, mad Sansculottism, drilled now into Soldiership, led on by some 'armed Soldier of Democracy' (say, that monosyllabic Artillery-Officer), will set its foot cruelly on the necks of its enemies; and its shouting and their shrieking shall fill the world!—Rash Coalised Kings, such a fire have ye kindled; yourselves fireless, *your* fighters animated only by drill-sergeants, mess-room moralities, and the drummer's cat! However, it is begun, and will not end: not for a matter of twenty years. So long, this Gaelic fire, through its successive changes of colour and character, will blaze over the face of Europe, and afflict and scorch all men: —till it provoke all men; till it kindle another kind of fire, the Teutonic kind, namely; and be swallowed up, so to speak, in a day! For there is a fire comparable to the burning of dry-jungle and grass; most sudden, high-blazing: and another fire which we liken to the burning of coal, or even of anthracite coal; difficult to kindle, but then which no known thing will put out. The ready Gaelic fire, we can remark further,—and remark not in Pichegrus only, but in innumerable Voltaires, Racines, Laplaces, no less; for a man, whether he fight, or sing, or think, will remain the same unity of a man,—is admirable for roasting eggs, in every conceivable sense. The Teutonic anthracite again, as we see in Luthers, Leibnitzes, Shakespeares, is preferable for smelting metals. How happy is our Europe that has both kinds!—

But be this as it may, the Republic is clearly triumphing.

In the spring of the year, Mentz Town again sees itself besieged; will again change master: did not Merlin the Thionviller, 'with wild beard and look,' say it was not for the last time they saw him there? The Elector of Mentz circulates among his brother Potentates this pertinent query, Were it not advisable to treat of Peace? Yes! answers many an Elector from the bottom of his heart. But, on the other hand, Austria hesitates; finally refuses, being subsidied by Pitt. As to Pitt, whoever hesitate, he, suspending his Habeas-corpus, suspending his Cash-payments, stands inflexible,—spite of foreign reverses; spite of domestic obstacles, of Scotch National Conventions and English Friends of the People, whom he is obliged to arraign, to hang, or even to see acquitted with jubilee: a lean inflexible man. The Majesty of Spain, as we predicted, makes Peace; also the Majesty of Prussia: and there is a Treaty of Bâle. Treaty with black Anarchists and Regicides! Alas, what help? You cannot hang this Anarchy; it is like to hang you: you must needs treat with it.

Likewise, General Hoche has even succeeded in pacificating La Vendée. Rogue Rossignol and his 'Infernal Columns' have vanished: by firmness and justice, by sagacity and industry, General Hoche has done it. Taking 'Movable Columns,' not infernal; girdling-in the Country; pardoning the submissive, cutting down the resistive, limb after limb of the Revolt is brought under. La Rochejacquelin, last of our Nobles, fell in battle; Stofflet himself makes terms; Georges-Cadoudal is back to Brittany, among his Chouans: the frightful gangrene of La Vendée seems veritably extirpated. It has cost, as they reckon in round numbers, the lives of a Hundred-thousand fellow-mortals; with noyadings, conflagratings by infernal column, which defy arithmetic. This is the La Vendée War.

Nay in few months, it does burst up once more, but once only;—blown upon by Pitt, by our Ci-devant Puisaye of Calvados, and others. In the month of July 1795, English ships will ride in Quiberon Roads. There will be debarkation of chivalrous Ci-devants, of volunteer Prisoners-of-war—eager to desert; of fire-arms, Proclamations, clothes-chests, Royalists and specie. Whereupon also, on the Republican side, there will be rapid stand-to-arms; with ambuscade marchings by Quiberon beach, at midnight; storming of Fort Penthièvre; war-thunder mingling with the roar of the nightly main; and such a morning light as has seldom dawned: debarkation hurled back into its boats, or into the devouring billows, with wreck and wail ;—in one word, a Ci-devant Puisaye as totally ineffectual here as he was in Calvados, when he rode from Vernon Castle without boots.

Again, therefore, it has cost the lives of many a brave man. Among whom the whole world laments the brave Son of Sombreuil. Ill-fated family! The father and younger son went to the guillotine ; the heroic daughter languishes, reduced to want, hides her woes from History : the elder son perishes here ; shot by military tribunal as an Emigrant ; Hoche himself cannot save him. If all wars, civil and other, are misunderstandings, what a thing must right-understanding be!

CHAPTER IV

LION NOT DEAD

The Convention, borne on the tide of Fortune towards foreign Victory, and driven by the strong wind of Public Opinion towards Clemency and Luxury, is rushing fast ; all skill of pilotage is needed, and more than all, in such a velocity.

Curious to see, how we veer and whirl, yet must ever whirl round again, and scud before the wind. If, on the one hand, we re-admit the Protesting Seventy-three, we, on the other hand, agree to consummate the Apotheosis of Marat ; lift his body from the Cordeliers Church, and transport it to the Pantheon of Great Men,—flinging out Mirabeau to make room for him. To no purpose : so strong blows Public Opinion! A Gilt Youthhood, in plaited hair-tresses, tears down his Busts from the Théâtre Feydeau ; tramples them under foot ; scatters them, with vociferation, into the Cesspool of Montmartre. Swept is his Chapel from the Place du Carrousel ; the Cesspool of Montmartre will receive his very dust. Shorter godhood had no divine man. Some four months in this Pantheon, Temple of All the Immortals ; then to the Cesspool, grand *Cloaca* of Paris and the World! 'His Busts at one time amounted to four thousand.' Between Temple of All the Immortals and Cloaca of the World, how are poor human creatures whirled!

Furthermore the question arises, When will the Constitution of *Ninety-three*, of 1793, come into action? Considerate heads surmise, in all privacy, that the Constitution of Ninety-three will never come into action. Let them busy themselves to get ready a better.

Or, again, where now are the Jacobins? Childless, most decrepit, as we saw, sat the mighty Mother; gnashing not teeth, but empty gums, against a traitorous Thermidorian Convention and the current of things. Twice were Billaud, Collot and Company accused in Convention, by a Lecointre, by a Legendre; and the second time, it was not voted calumnious. Billaud from the Jacobin tribune says, "The lion is not dead, he is only sleeping." They ask him in Convention, What he means by the awakening of the lion? And bickerings, of an extensive sort, arose in the Palais-Égalité between *Tappe-durs* and the Gilt Youthhood; cries of "Down with the Jacobins, the *Jacoquins*," *coquin* meaning scoundrel! The Tribune in mid-air gave battle-sound; answered only by silence and uncertain gasps. Talk was, in Government Committees, of 'suspending' the Jacobin Sessions. Hark, there!—it is in Allhallow-time, or on the Hallow-eve itself, month *ci-devant* November, year once named of Grace 1794, sad eve for Jacobinism,—volley of stones dashing through our windows, with jingle and execration! The female Jacobins, famed *Tricoteuses* with knitting-needles, take flight; are met at the doors by a Gilt Youthhood and 'mob of four thousand persons;' are hooted, flouted, hustled; fustigated, in a scandalous manner, *cotillons retroussés;*—and vanish in mere hysterics. Sally out, ye male Jacobins! The male Jacobins sally out; but only to battle, disaster and confusion. So that armed Authority has to intervene: and again on the morrow to intervene; and suspend the Jacobin Sessions forever and a day.—Gone are the Jacobins; into invisibility; in a storm of laughter and howls. Their Place is made a Normal School, the first of the kind seen; it then vanishes into a 'Market of Thermidor Ninth;' into a Market of Saint-Honoré, where is now peaceable chaffering for poultry and greens. The solemn temples, the great globe itself; the baseless fabric! Are not we such stuff, we and this world of ours, as Dreams are made of?

Maximum being abrogated, Trade was to take its own free course. Alas, Trade, shackled, topsyturvied in the way we saw, and now suddenly let-go again, can for the present take no course at all; but only reel and stagger. There is, so to speak, no Trade whatever for the time being. Assignats, long sinking, emitted in such quantities, sink now with an

alacrity beyond parallel. " *Combien ?* " said one, to a
Hackney-coachman, "What fare ? " " Six thousand livres,"
answered he : some three hundred pounds sterling, in Paper-
money. Pressure of Maximum withdrawn, the things it compressed likewise withdraw. 'Two ounces of bread per day'
is the modicum allotted : wide-waving, doleful are the Bakers'
Queues ; Farmers' houses are become pawnbrokers' shops.

One can imagine, in these circumstances, with what humour
Sansculottism growled in its throat, " *La Cabarus ;* " beheld
Ci-devants return dancing, the Thermidor effulgence of re-
civilisation, and Balls in flesh-coloured drawers. Greek tunics
and sandals ; hosts of *Muscadins* parading, with their clubs
loaded with lead ;—and we here, cast out, abhorred, 'picking
offals from the street ;' agitating in Baker's Queue for our two
ounces of bread ! Will the Jacobin lion, which they say is
meeting secretly 'at the Archevêché, in *bonnet rouge* with
loaded pistols,' not awaken ? Seemingly, not. Our Collot,
our Billaud, Barrère, Vadier, in these last days of March 1795,
are found worthy of *Déportation*, of Banishment beyond seas ;
and shall, for the present, be trundled off to the Castle of
Ham. The lion is dead ;—or writhing in death-throes !

Behold, accordingly, on the day they call Twelfth of
Germinal (which is also called First of April, not a lucky
day), how lively are these streets of Paris once more ! Floods
of hungry women, of squalid hungry men ; ejaculating :
" Bread, bread, and the Constitution of Ninety-three ! "
Paris has risen, once again, like the Ocean-tide ; is flowing
towards the Tuileries, for Bread and a Constitution. Tuileries
Sentries do their best ; but it serves not : the Ocean-tide
sweeps them away ; inundates the Convention Hall itself ;
howling, " Bread and the Constitution ! "

Unhappy Senators, unhappy People, there is yet, after all
toils and broils, no Bread, no Constitution. " *Du pain, pas
tant de longs discours*, Bread, not bursts of Parliamentary
eloquence ! " so wailed the Menads of Maillard, five years ago
and more ; so wail ye to this hour. The Convention, with
unalterable countenance, with what thought one knows not,
keeps its seat in this waste howling chaos ; rings its storm-bell
from the Pavilion of Unity. Section Lepelletier, old *Filles
Saint-Thomas*, who are of the money-changing species ; these
and Gilt Youthhood fly to the rescue : sweep chaos forth
again, with levelled bayonets. Paris is declared ' in a state

of siege.' Pichegru, Conqueror of Holland, who happens to be here, is named Commandant, till the disturbance end. He, in one day so to speak, ends it. He accomplishes the transfer of Billaud, Collot and Company; dissipating all opposition 'by two cannon-shots,' blank cannon-shots, and the terror of his name; and thereupon, announcing, with a Laconicism which should be imitated, "Representatives, your decrees are executed," lays down his Commandantship.

This Revolt of Germinal, therefore, has passed, like a vain cry. The Prisoners rest safe in Ham, waiting for ships; some nine-hundred 'chief Terrorists of Paris' are disarmed. Sansculottism, swept forth with bayonets, has vanished, with its misery, to the bottom of Saint-Antoine and Saint-Marceau. —Time was when Usher Maillard with Menads could alter the course of Legislation; but that time is not. Legislation seems to have got bayonets, Section Lepelletier takes its firelock, not for us! We retire to our dark dens; our cry of hunger is called a Plot of Pitt; the Saloons glitter, the flesh-coloured Drawers gyrate as before. It was for " *The Cabarus* " then, and her *Muscadins* and Money-changers that we fought? It was for Balls in flesh-coloured' drawers that we took Feudalism by the beard, and did, and dared, shedding our blood like water? Expressive Silence, muse thou their praise!—

CHAPTER V

LION SPRAWLING ITS LAST

Representative Carrier went to the Guillotine, in December last; protesting that he acted by orders. The Revolutionary Tribunal, after all it has devoured, has now only, as Anarchic things do, to devour itself. In the early days of May, men see a remarkable thing: Fouquier-Tinville pleading at the Bar once his own. He and his chief Jurymen, Leroi *August-Tenth*, Juryman Vilate, a Batch of Sixteen; pleading hard, protesting that they acted by orders: but pleading in vain. Thus men break the axe with which they have done hateful things; the axe itself having grown hateful. For the rest Fouquier died hard enough: "Where are thy Batches?" howled the people.—"Hungry *canaille*," asked Fouquier, " is thy Bread cheaper, wanting them?"

Remarkable Fouquier; once but as other Attorneys and

Law-beagles, which hunt ravenous on this Earth, a well-known phasis of human nature; and now thou art and remainest the most remarkable Attorney that ever lived and hunted in the Upper Air! For, in this terrestrial Course of Time, there was to be an *Avatar* of Attorneyism; the Heavens had said, Let there be an Incarnation, not divine, of the venatory Attorney-spirit which keeps its eye on the bond only;—and lo, this was it; and they have attorneyed it in its turn. Vanish, then, thou rat-eyed Incarnation of Attorneyism; who at bottom wert but as other Attorneys, and too hungry sons of Adam! Juryman Vilate had striven hard for life, and published, from his Prison, an ingenious Book, not unknown to us; but it would not stead: he also had to vanish; and this his Book of the *Secret Causes of Thermidor*, full of lies, with particles of truth in it undiscoverable otherwise, is all that remains of him.

Revolutionary Tribunal has done; but vengeance has not done. Representative Lebon, after long struggling, is handed over to the ordinary Law Courts, and by them guillotined. Nay at Lyons and elsewhere, resuscitated Moderatism, in its vengeance, will not wait the slow process of Law; but bursts into the Prisons, sets fire to the Prisons; burns some three-score imprisoned Jacobins to dire death, or chokes them 'with the smoke of straw.' There go vengeful truculent 'Companies of Jesus,' 'Companies of the Sun;' slaying Jacobinism wherever they meet with it; flinging it into the Rhone-stream; which once more bears seaward a horrid cargo. Whereupon, at Toulon, Jacobinism rises in revolt; and is like to hang the National Representatives.—With such action and reaction, is not a poor National Convention hard bested? It is like the settlement of winds and waters, of seas long tornado-beaten; and goes on with jumble and with jangle. Now flung aloft, now sunk in trough of the sea, your Vessel of the Republic has need of all pilotage and more.

What Parliament that ever sat under the Moon had such a series of destinies as this National Convention of France? It came together to make the Constitution; and instead of that, it has had to make nothing but destruction and confusion: to burn up Catholicisms, Aristocratisms; to worship Reason and dig Saltpetre; to fight Titanically with itself and with the whole world. A Convention decimated by the Guillotine; above the tenth man has bowed his neck to the axe. Which has seen Carmagnoles danced before it, and patriotic strophes sung amid Church-spoils; the wounded of the Tenth of August defile in handbarrows; and, in the Pandemonial Midnight, Égalité's dames in tricolor drink lemonade, and spectrum of Sieyès mount, saying, *Death sans phrase.* A Convention which has effervesced, and which has congealed; which has been red with rage, and also pale with rage; sitting with pistols in its pocket, drawing sword (in a moment of effervescence): now storming to the four winds, through a Danton-voice, Awake, O France, and smite the tyrants; now frozen mute under its Robespierre, and answering his dirge-voice by a dubious gasp. Assassinated, decimated; stabbed at, shot at, in baths, on streets and staircases; which has been the nucleus of Chaos. Has it not heard the chimes at midnight? It has deliberated, beset by a Hundred-thousand armed men with artillery-furnaces and provision-carts. It has been betocsined, bestormed; over-flooded by black deluges of Sansculottism; and has heard the shrill cry, *Bread and Soap.* For, as we say, it was the nucleus of Chaos: it sat as the centre of Sansculottism; and had spread its pavilion on the waste Deep, where is neither path nor landmark, neither bottom nor shore. In intrinsic valour, ingenuity, fidelity, and general force and manhood, it has perhaps not far surpassed the average of Parliaments; but in frankness of purpose, in singularity of position, it seeks its fellow. One other Sansculottic submersion, or at most two, and this wearied vessel of a Convention reaches land.

Revolt of Germinal Twelfth ended as a vain cry; moribund Sansculottism was swept back into invisibility. There it has lain moaning, these six weeks: moaning, and also scheming. Jacobins disarmed, flung forth from their Tribune in mid-air, must needs try to help themselves, in secret conclave under ground. Lo therefore, on the First day of the Month *Prairial*, 20th of May 1795, sound of the *générale* once more; beating sharp, ran-tan, To arms, To arms!

Sansculottism has risen, yet again, from its death-lair; waste, wild-flowing, as the unfruitful Sea. Saint-Antoine is afoot: "Bread and the Constitution of Ninety-three," so sounds it; so stands it written with chalk on the hats of men. They have their pikes, their firelocks; Paper of Grievances; standards; printed Proclamation, drawn up in quite official manner, —considering this, and also considering that, they, a much-enduring Sovereign People, are in Insurrection; will have Bread and the Constitution of Ninety-three. And so the Barriers are seized, and the *générale* beats, and tocsins discourse discord. Black deluges overflow the Tuileries; spite of sentries, the Sanctuary itself is invaded: enter, to our Order of the Day, a torrent of dishevelled women, wailing, "Bread! Bread!" President may well cover himself; and have his own tocsin rung in 'the Pavilion of Unity;' the ship of the State again labours and leaks; overwashed, near to swamping, with unfruitful brine.

What a day, once more! Women are driven out: men storm irresistibly in; choke all corridors, thunder at all gates. Deputies, putting forth head, obtest, conjure; Saint-Antoine rages, "Bread and Constitution." Report has risen that the 'Convention is assassinating the women:' crushing and rushing, clangor and furor! The oak doors have become as oak tambourines, sounding under the axe of Saint-Antoine; plasterwork crackles, woodwork booms and jingles; door starts up; —bursts-in Saint-Antoine with frenzy and vociferation, with Rag-standards, printed Proclamation, drum-music: astonishment to eye and ear. Gendarmes, loyal Sectioners charge through the other door; they are recharged; musketry exploding: Saint-Antoine cannot be expelled. Obtesting Deputies obtest vainly: Respect the President; approach not the President! Deputy Féraud, stretching out his hands, baring his bosom scarred in the Spanish wars, obtests vainly; threatens and resists vainly. Rebellious Deputy of the Sovereign, if thou have fought, have not we too? We have no Bread, no Constitution! They wrench poor Féraud; they tumble him, trample him, wrath waxing to see itself work: they drag him into the corridor, dead or near it; sever his head, and fix it on a pike. Ah, did an unexampled Convention want this variety of destiny, too, then? Féraud's bloody head goes on a pike. Such a game has begun; Paris and the Earth may wait how it will end.

And so it billows free through all Corridors; within and without, far as the eye reaches, nothing but Bedlam, and the great Deep broken loose! President Boissy d'Anglas sits like a rock: the rest of the Convention is floated 'to the upper benches;' Sectioners and Gendarmes still ranking there to form a kind of wall for them. And Insurrection rages; rolls its drums; will read its Paper of Grievances, will have this decreed, will have that. Covered sits President Boissy; unyielding; like a rock in the beating of seas. They menace him, level muskets at him, he yields not; they hold up Féraud's bloody head to him, with grave stern air he bows to it, and yields not.

And the Paper of Grievances cannot get itself read for uproar: and the drums roll, and the throats bawl; and Insurrection, like sphere-music, is inaudible for very noise: Decree us this, Decree us that. One man we discern bawling 'for the space of an hour at all intervals,' "*Je demande l'arrestation des coquins et des lâches*." Really one of the most comprehensive Petitions ever put up; which indeed, to this hour, includes all that you can reasonably ask Constitution of the Year One, Rotten-Borough, Ballot-Box, or other miraculous Political Ark of the Covenant to do for you to the end of the world! I also *demand arrestment of the Knaves and Dastards*, and nothing more whatever.—National Representation, deluged with black Sansculottism, glides out; for help elsewhere, for safety elsewhere; here is no help.

About four in the afternoon, there remain hardly more than some Sixty Members: mere friends, or even secret-leaders; a remnant of the Mountain-crest, held in silence by Thermidorian thraldom. Now is the time for them; now or never let them descend, and speak! They descend, these Sixty, invited by Sansculottism: Romme of the New Calendar, Ruhl of the Sacred Phial, Goujon, Duquesnoy, Soubrany, and the rest. Glad Sansculottism forms a ring for them; Romme takes the President's chair; they begin resolving and decreeing. Fast enough now comes Decree after Decree, in alternate brief strains, or strophe and antistrophe,—what will cheapen bread, what will awaken the dormant lion. And at every new decree, Sansculottism shouts "Decreed, decreed!" and rolls its drums.

Fast enough; the work of months in hours,—when see, a Figure enters, whom in the lamp-light we recognise to be Legendre; and utters words: fit to be hissed out! And then see, Section Lepelletier or other Muscadin Section enters, and Gilt Youth, with levelled bayonets, countenances screwed to the sticking-place! Tramp, tramp, with bayonets gleaming in the lamp-light: what can one do, worn down with long riot, grown heartless, dark, hungry, but roll back, but rush back, and escape who can? The very windows need to be thrown up, that Sansculottism may escape fast enough. Money-changer Sections and Gilt Youth sweep them forth, with steel besom, far into the depths of Saint-Antoine. Triumph once more! The Decrees of that Sixty are not so much as rescinded; they are declared null and non-extant. Romme,

Ruhl, Goujon and the ringleaders, some thirteen in all, are decreed Accused. Permanent-session ends at three in the morning. Sansculottism, once more flung resupine, lies sprawling; sprawling its *last*.

Such was the first of Prairial, 20th of May, 1795. Second and Third of Prairial, during which Sansculottism still sprawled, and unexpectedly rang its tocsin, and assembled in arms, availed Sansculottism nothing. What though with our Rommes and Ruhls, accused but not yet arrested, we make a new 'True National Convention' of our own, over in the East; and put the others Out of Law? What though we rank in arms and march? Armed Force and Muscadin Sections, some thirty-thousand men, environ that old False Convention: we can but bully one another; bandying nicknames, "*Muscadins*," against "Blood-drinkers, *Buveurs de Sang*." Féraud's Assassin, taken with the red hand, and sentenced, and now near to Guillotine, and Place de Grève, is retaken; is carried back into Saint-Antoine:—to no purpose. Convention Sectionaries and Gilt Youth come, according to Decree, to seek him; nay to disarm Saint-Antoine! And they do disarm it: by rolling of cannon, by springing upon enemy's cannon; by military audacity, and terror of the Law. Saint-Antoine surrenders its arms; Santerre even advising it, anxious for life and brewhouse. Féraud's Assassin flings himself from a high roof: and all is lost.

Discerning which things, old Ruhl shot a pistol through his old white head; dashed his life in pieces, as he had done the Sacred Phial of Rheims (p. 48). Romme, Goujon and the others stand ranked before a swiftly-appointed, swift Military Tribunal. Hearing the sentence, Goujon drew a knife, struck it into his breast, passed it to his neighbour Romme; and fell dead. Romme did the like; and another all-but did it; Roman-death rushing on there, as in electric-chain, before your Bailiffs could intervene! The Guillotine had the rest.

They were the *Ultimi Romanorum*. Billaud, Collot and Company are now ordered to be tried for life; but are found to be already off, shipped for Sinamarri, and the hot mud of Surinam. There let Billaud surround himself with flocks of tame parrots; Collot take the yellow fever, and drinking a whole bottle of brandy, burn up his entrails. Sansculottism sprawls no more. The dormant lion has become a dead one; and now, as we see, any hoof may smite him.

CHAPTER VI

GRILLED HERRINGS

So dies Sansculottism, the *body* of Sansculottism; or is changed. Its ragged Pythian Carmagnole-dance has transformed itself into a Pyrrhic, into a dance of Cabarus Balls. Sansculottism is dead; extinguished by new *isms* of that kind, which were its own natural progeny: and is buried, we may say, with such deafening jubilation and disharmony of funeral knell on their part, that only after some half-century or so does one begin to learn clearly why it ever was alive.

And yet a meaning lay in it: Sansculottism verily was alive, a New-Birth of TIME; nay it still lives, and is not dead but changed. The *soul* of it still lives; still works far and wide, through one bodily shape into another less amorphous, as is the way of cunning Time with his New-Births:—till, in some perfected shape, it embrace the whole circuit of the world! For the wise man may now everywhere discern that he must found on his manhood, not on the garnitures of his manhood. He who, in these Epochs of our Europe, founds on garnitures, formulas, culottisms of what sort soever, is founding on old cloth and sheepskin, and cannot endure. But as for the body of Sansculottism, that is dead and buried,—and, one hopes, need not reappear, in primary amorphous shape, for another thousand years.

It was the frightfullest thing ever born of Time? One of the frightfullest. This Convention, now grown Antijacobin, did, with an eye to justify and fortify itself, publish Lists of what the Reign of Terror had perpetrated: Lists of Persons Guillotined. The Lists, cries splenetic Abbé Montgaillard, were not complete. They contain the names of, How many persons thinks the Reader?—Two-thousand all but a few. There were above Four-thousand, cries Montgaillard: so many were guillotined, fusilladed, noyaded, done to dire death; of whom Nine-Hundred were women. It is a horrible sum of human lives, M. l'Abbé:—some ten times as many shot rightly on a field of battle, and one might have had his Glorious-Victory with *Te-Deum*. It is not far from the two-hundredth part of what perished in the entire Seven-Years War. By which Seven-Years War, did not the great Fritz wrench Silesia from the great Theresa; and a Pompadour, stung by epigrams, satisfy herself that she could not be an Agnes Sorel? The head of man is a strange vacant sounding-shell, M. l'Abbé; and studies Cocker to small purpose.

But what if History somewhere on this Planet were to hear of a Nation, the third soul of whom had not, for thirty weeks each year, as many third-rate potatoes as would sustain him? History, in that case, feels bound to consider that starvation is starvation; that starvation from age to age presupposes much; History ventures to assert that the French Sansculotte of Ninety-three, who, roused from long death-sleep, could rush at once to the frontiers, and die fighting for an immortal Hope and Faith of Deliverance for him and his, was but the *second*-miserablest of men! The Irish Sans-potato, had he not senses then, nay a soul! In his frozen darkness, it was bitter for him to die famishing; bitter to see his children famish. It was bitter for him to be a beggar, a liar and a knave. Nay, if that dreary Greenland-wind of benighted Want, perennial from sire to son, had frozen him into a kind of torpor and numb callosity, so that he saw not, felt not,—was this, for a creature with a soul in it, some assuagement; or the cruellest wretchedness of all?

Such things were; such things are; and they go on in silence peaceably:—and Sansculottisms follow them. History, looking back over this France through long times, back to Turgot's time for instance, when dumb Drudgery staggered up to its King's Palace, and in wide expanse of sallow faces, squalor and winged raggedness, presented hieroglyphically its Petition of Grievances; and for answer got hanged on a 'new gallows forty feet high,'—confesses mournfully that there is no period to be met with, in which the general Twenty-five Millions of France suffered *less* than in this period which they name Reign of Terror! But it was not the Dumb Millions that suffered here; it was the Speaking Thousands, and Hundreds and Units; who shrieked and published, and made the world ring with their wail, as they could and should: that is the grand peculiarity. The frightfullest Births of Time are never the loud-speaking ones, for these soon die; they are the silent ones, which can live from century to century! Anarchy, hateful as Death, is abhorrent to the whole nature of man; and so must itself soon die.

Wherefore let all men know what of depth and of height is still revealed in man; and, with fear and wonder, with just sympathy and just antipathy, with clear eye and open heart, contemplate it and appropriate it; and draw innumerable inferences from it. This inference, for example, among the first : That 'if the gods of this lower world will sit on their glittering thrones, indolent as Epicurus' gods, with the living Chaos of Ignorance and Hunger weltering uncared-for at their feet, and smooth Parasites preaching, Peace, peace, when there is no peace,' then the dark Chaos, it would seem, will rise ;—has risen, and O Heavens ! has it not tanned their skins into breeches for itself? That there be no second Sansculottism in our Earth for a thousand years, let us understand well what the first was ; and let Rich and Poor of us go and do *otherwise*.—But to our tale.

The Muscadin Sections greatly rejoice ; Cabarus Balls gyrate : the well-nigh insoluble problem, *Republic without Anarchy*, have we not solved it ?—Law of Fraternity or Death is gone : chimerical *Obtain-who-need* has become practical *Hold-who-have*. To anarchic Republic of the Poverties there has succeeded orderly Republic of the Luxuries ; which will continue as long as it can.

On the Pont au Change, on the Place de Grève, in long sheds, Mercier, in these summer evenings, saw working men at their repast. One's allotment of daily bread has sunk to an ounce and a half. 'Plates containing each three grilled herrings, sprinkled with shorn onions, wetted with a little vinegar ; to this add some morsel of boiled prunes, and lentils swimming in a clear sauce : at these frugal tables, the cook's gridiron hissing near by, and the pot simmering on a fire between two stones, I have seen them ranged by the hundred ; consuming, without bread, their scant messes, far too moderate for the keenness of their appetite, and the extent of their stomach.' Seine water, rushing plenteous by, will supply the deficiency.

O Man of Toil, thy struggling and thy daring, these six long years of insurrection and tribulation, thou hast profited nothing by it, then? Thou consumest thy herring and water, in the blessed gold-red of evening. O why was the Earth so beautiful, be-crimsoned with dawn and twilight, if man's dealings with man were to make it a vale of scarcity, of tears, not even soft tears ? Destroying of Bastilles, discomfiting of Brunswicks, fronting of Principalities and Powers, of Earth and Tophet, all that thou hast dared and endured,—it was for a Republic of the Cabarus Saloons? Patience ; thou must have patience ; the end is not yet.

CHAPTER VII

THE WHIFF OF GRAPESHOT

In fact, what can be more natural, one may say inevitable, as a Post-Sansculottic transitionary state, than even this? Confused wreck of a Republic of the Poverties, which ended in Reign of Terror, is arranging itself into such composure as it can. Evangel of Jean-Jacques, and most other Evangels, becoming incredible, what is there for it but return to the old Evangel of Mammon? *Contrat-Social* is true or untrue, Brotherhood is Brotherhood or Death; but money always will buy money's worth: in the wreck of human dubitations, this remains indubitable, that Pleasure is pleasant. Aristocracy of Feudal Parchment has passed away with a mighty rushing; and now, by a natural course we arrive at Aristocracy of the Moneybag. It is the course through which all European Societies are, at this hour, travelling. Apparently a still baser sort of Aristocracy? An infinitely baser; the basest yet known.

In which, however, there is this advantage, that, like Anarchy itself, it cannot continue. Hast thou considered how Thought is stronger than Artillery-parks, and (were it fifty years after death and martyrdom, or were it two thousand years) writes and unwrites Acts of Parliament, removes mountains; models the World like soft clay? Also how the beginning of all Thought, worth the name, is Love; and the wise head never yet was, without first the generous heart. The Heavens cease not their bounty; they send us generous hearts into every generation. And now what generous heart can pretend to itself, or be hoodwinked into believing, that Loyalty to the Moneybag is a noble Loyalty? Mammon, cries the generous heart out of all ages and countries, is the basest of known Gods, even of known Devils. In him what glory is there, that ye should worship him? No glory discernible; not even terror: at best, detestability, ill-matched with despicability!—Generous hearts, discerning, on this hand, widespread Wretchedness, dark without and within, moistening its ounce-and-half of bread with tears; and, on that hand, mere Balls in flesh-coloured drawers, and inane or foul glitter of such sort,—cannot but ejaculate, cannot but announce: Too much, O divine Mammon; somewhat too much!—The voice of these, once announcing itself, carries *fiat* and *pereat* in it, for all things here below.

Meanwhile we will hate Anarchy as Death, which it is; and the things worse than Anarchy shall be hated *more*. Surely Peace alone is fruitful. Anarchy is destruction; a burning up, say, of Shams and Insupportabilities; but which leaves Vacancy behind. Know this also, that out of a world of Unwise nothing but an Unwisdom can be made. Arrange it, constitution-build it, sift it through ballot-boxes as thou wilt, it is and remains an Unwisdom,—the new prey of new quacks and unclean things, the latter end of it slightly better than the beginning. Who can bring a wise thing out of men unwise? Not one. And so Vacancy and general Abolition having come for this France, what can Anarchy do more? Let there be Order, were it under the Soldier's Sword: let there be Peace, that the bounty of the Heavens be not split; that what of Wisdom they do send us bring fruit in its season!—It remains to be seen how the quellers of Sansculottism were themselves quelled, and sacred right of Insurrection was blown away by gunpowder; wherewith this singular eventful History called *French Revolution* ends.

The Convention, driven such a course by wild wind, wild tide and steerage and non-steerage, these three years, has become weary of its own existence, sees all men weary of it; and wishes heartily to finish. To the last, it has to strive with contradictions: it is now getting fast ready with a Constitution, yet knows no peace. Sieyès, we say, is making the Constitution once more; has as good as made it. Warned by experience, the great Architect alters much, admits much. Distinction of Active and Passive Citizen, that is, Money-qualification for Electors: nay Two Chambers, 'Council of Ancients,' as well as 'Council of Five-hundred;' to that conclusion have we come! In a like spirit, eschewing that fatal self-denying ordinance of your Old Constituents, we enact not only that actual Convention Members are re-eligible, but that Two-thirds of them must be re-elected. The Active Citizen Electors shall for this time have free choice of only One-third of their National Assembly. Such enactment, of Two-thirds to be re-elected, we append to our Constitution; we submit our Constitution to the Townships of France, and say, Accept *both*, or reject both. Unsavoury as this appendix may be, the Townships, by the overwhelming majority, accept and ratify.

With Directory of Five: with Two good Chambers, double-majority of them nominated by ourselves, one hopes this Constitution may prove final. *March* it will; for the legs of it, the re-elected Two-thirds, are already here, able to march. Sieyès looks at his paper-fabric with just pride.

But now see how the contumacious Sections, Lepelletier foremost, kick against the pricks! Is it not manifest infraction of one's Elective Franchise, Rights of Man, and Sovereignty of the People, this appendix of re-electing *your* Two-thirds? Greedy tyrants who would perpetuate yourselves!—For the truth is, victory over Saint-Antoine, and long right of Insurrection, has spoiled these men. Nay spoiled all men. Consider too how each man was free to hope what he liked; and now there is to be no hope, there is to be fruition, fruition of *this*.

In men spoiled by long right of Insurrection, what confused ferments will rise, tongues once begun wagging! Journalists declaim, your Lacretelles, Laharpes; Orators spout. There is Royalism traceable in it, and Jacobinism. On the West Frontier, in deep secrecy, Pichegru, durst he trust his Army, is treating with Condé: in these Sections, there spout wolves in sheep's clothing, masked Emigrants and Royalists. All men, as we say, had hoped, each that the Election would do something for his own side: and now there is no Election, or only the third of one. Black is united with white against this clause of the Two-thirds; all the Unruly of France, who see their trade thereby near ending.

Section Lepelletier, after Addresses enough, finds that such clause is a manifest infraction; that it, Lepelletier, for one, will simply not conform thereto; and invites all other free Sections to join it, 'in central Committee,' in resistance to oppression. The Sections join it, nearly all; strong with their Forty-thousand fighting men. The Convention therefore may look to itself! Lepelletier, on this 12th day of Vendémiaire, 4th of October, 1795, is sitting in open contravention, in its Convent of Filles Saint-Thomas, Rue Vivienne, with guns primed. The Convention has some Five-thousand regular troops at hand; Generals in abundance; and a Fifteen-hundred of miscellaneous persecuted Ultra-Jacobins, whom in this crisis it has hastily got together and armed, under the title *Patroits of Eighty-nine*. Strong in Law, it sends its General Menou to disarm Lepelletier.

General Menou marches accordingly, with due summons and demonstration; with no result. General Menou, about eight in the evening, finds that he is standing ranked in the Rue Vivienne, emitting vain summonses; with primed guns pointed out of every window at him; and that he cannot disarm Lepelletier. He has to return, with whole skin, but without success; and be thrown into arrest, as 'a traitor.' Whereupon the whole Forty-thousand join this Lepelletier which cannot be vanquished: to what hand shall a quaking Convention now turn? Our poor Convention, after such voyaging, just entering harbour, so to speak, has *struck on the bar ;*—and labours there frightfully, with breakers roaring round it, Forty-thousand of them, like to wash it, and its Sieyès Cargo and the whole future of France, into the deep! Yet one last time, it struggles, ready to perish.

Some call for Barras to be made Commandant; he conquered in Thermidor. Some, what is more to the purpose, bethink them of the Citizen Buonaparte, unemployed Artillery-Officer, who took Toulon. A man of head, a man of action: Barras is named Commandment's-Cloak; this young Artillery-Officer is named Commandant. He was in the Gallery at the moment, and heard it; he withdrew, some half-hour, to consider with himself: after a half-hour of grim compressed considering, to be or not to be, he answers *Yea.*

And now, a man of head being at the centre of it, the whole matter gets vital. Swift, to Camp of Sablons; to secure the Artillery, there are not twenty men guarding it! A swift Adjutant, Murat is the name of him, gallops; gets thither some minutes within time, for Lepelletier was also on march that way: the Cannon are ours. And now beset this post, and beset that; rapid and firm: at Wicket of the Louvre, in Cul-de-sac Dauphin, in Rue Saint-Honoré, from Pont-Neuf all along the north Quays, southward to Pont *ci-devant* Royal,—rank round the Sanctuary of the Tuileries, a ring of steel discipline; let every gunner have his match burning, and all men stand to their arms!

Thus there is Permanent-session through the night; and thus at sunrise of the morrow, there is seen sacred Insurrection once again: vessel of State labouring on the bar; and tumultuous sea all round her, beating *générale*, arming and sounding, —not ringing tocsin, for we have left no tocsin but our own in the Pavilion of Unity. It is an imminence of shipwreck, for the whole world to gaze at. Frightfully she labours, that poor ship, within cable-length of port; huge peril for her. However, she has a man at the helm. Insurgent messages, received and not received; messenger admitted blindfolded; counsel and counter-counsel: the poor ship labours!—Vendémiaire 13th, year 4: curious enough, of all days, it is the Fifth day of October, anniversary of that Menad-march, six years ago; by sacred right of Insurrection we are got thus far.

Lepelletier has seized the Church of Saint-Roch; has seized the Pont-Neuf, our piquet there retreating without fire. Stray shots fall from Lepelletier; rattle down on the very Tuileries Staircase. On the other hand, women advance dishevelled, shrieking, Peace; Lepelletier behind them waving its hat in sign that we shall fraternise. Steady! The Artillery-Officer is steady as bronze; can, if need were, be quick as lightning. He sends eight-hundred muskets with ball-cartridges to the Convention itself; honourable Members shall act with these in case of extremity: whereat they look grave enough. Four of the afternoon is struck. Lepelletier, making nothing by messengers, by fraternity or hat-waving, bursts out, along the Southern Quai Voltaire, along streets and passages, treble-quick, in huge veritable onslaught! Whereupon, thou bronze Artillery-Officer—? "Fire!" say the bronze lips. And roar and thunder, roar and again roar, continual, volcano-like, goes his great gun, in the Cul-de-sac Dauphin against the Church of Saint-Roch; go his great guns on the Pont-Royal; go all his great guns;—blow to air some two-hundred men, mainly about the Church of Saint-Roch! Lepelletier cannot stand such horse-play; no Sectioner can stand it: the Forty-thousand yield on all sides, scour towards covert. 'Some hundred or so of them gathered about the Théâtre de la République; but,' says he, 'a few shells dislodged them. It was all finished at six.'

The Ship is *over* the bar, then; free she bounds shoreward, —amid shouting and vivats! Citoyen Buonaparte is 'named General of the Interior, by acclamation;' quelled Sections have to disarm in such humour as they may; sacred right of Insurrection is gone forever! The Sieyès Constitution can disembark itself, and begin marching. The miraculous Convention Ship has got to land;—and is there, shall we figuratively say, changed, as Epic Ships are wont, into a kind of *Sea Nymph*, never to sail more; to roam the waste Azure, a Miracle in History!

'It is false,' says Napoleon, 'that we fired first with blank charge; it had been a waste of life to do that.' Most false: the firing was with sharp and sharpest shot: to all men it was plain that here was no sport; the rabbets and plinths of Saint-Roch Church show splintered by it to this hour.—Singular: in old Broglie's time, six years ago, this Whiff of Grapeshot was promised; but it could not be given then; could not have profited then. Now, however, the time is come for it, and the man; and behold, you have it; and the thing we specifically call *French Revolution* is blown into space by it, and become a thing that was!—

CHAPTER VIII

FINIS

HOMER'S Epos, it is remarked, is like a Bas-Relief sculpture: it does not conclude, but merely ceases. Such, indeed, is the Epos of Universal History itself. Directorates, Consulates, Emperorships, Restorations, Citizen-Kingships succeeded this Business in due series, in due genesis one out of the other. Nevertheless the First-parent of all these may be said to have gone to air in the way we see. A Babœuf Insurrection, next year, will die in the birth; stifled by the Soldiery. A Senate, if tinged with Royalism, can be purged by the Soldiery; and an Eighteenth of Fructidor transacted by the mere show of bayonets. Nay Soldiers' bayonets can be used *à posteriori* on a Senate, and make it leap out of window,—still bloodless; and produce an Eighteenth of Brumaire. Such changes must happen: but they are managed by intriguings, caballings, and then by orderly word of command; almost like mere changes of Ministry. Not in general by sacred right of Insurrection, but by milder methods growing ever milder, shall the events of French History be henceforth brought to pass.

It is admitted that this Directorate, which owned, at its starting, these three things, an 'old table, a sheet of paper, and an ink-bottle,' and no visible money or arrangement whatever, did wonders: that France, since the Reign of Terror hushed itself, has been a new France awakened like a giant out of torpor: and has gone on in the Internal Life of it, with continual progress. As for the External form and forms of Life, what can we say, except that out of the Eater there comes Strength; out of the Unwise there comes *not* Wisdom!— Shams are burnt up; nay, what as yet is the peculiarity of France, the very Cant of them is burnt up. The new Realities are not yet come: ah no, only Phantasms, Paper models, tentative Prefigurements of such! In France there are now Four Million Landed Properties; that black portent of an Agrarian Law is, as it were, *realised*. What is still stranger, we understand all Frenchmen have 'the right of duel;' the Hackney-coachman with the Peer, if insult be given: such is the law of Public Opinion. Equality at least in death! The Form of Government is by Citizen-King, frequently shot at, not yet shot.

On the whole, therefore, has it not been fulfilled what was prophesied, *ex-post facto* indeed, by the Arch-quack Cagliostro, or another? He, as he looked in rapt vision and amazement into these things thus spake: 'Ha! What is *this?* Angels, Uriel, Anachiel, and ye other Five; Pentagon of Rejuvenescence; Power that destroyedst Original Sin; Earth, Heaven, and thou Outer Limbo, which men name Hell! Does the EMPIRE OF IMPOSTURE waver? Burst there, in starry sheen updarting, Light-rays from out of *its* dark foundations; as it rocks and heaves, not in travail-throes but in death-throes? Yea, Light-rays, piercing, clear, that salute the Heavens,—lo, they *kindle* it; their starry clearness becomes as red Hell-fire!

'IMPOSTURE is in flames, Imposture is burnt up: one red sea of Fire, wild-bellowing, enwraps the World: with its fire-tongue licks at the very Stars. Thrones are hurled into it and Dubois Mitres, and Prebendal Stalls that drop fatness, and—ha! what see I?—all the *Gigs* of Creation: all, all! Wo is me! Never since Pharaoh's Chariots, in the Red Sea of water, was there wreck of Wheel-vehicles like this in the Sea of Fire. Desolate, as ashes, as gases, shall they wander in the wind.

'Higher, higher, yet flames the Fire-Sea; crackling with new dislocated timber; hissing with leather and prunella. The metal Images are molten; the marble Images become mortar-lime; the stone Mountains sulkily explode. RESPECTABILITY, with her collected Gigs inflamed for funeral pyre, wailing, leaves the Earth: not to return save under new Avatar. Imposture how it burns, through generations: how it is burnt up; for a time. The World is black ashes;— which, ah, when will they grow green? The Images all run into amorphous Corinthian brass; all Dwellings of men destroyed; the very mountains peeled and riven, the valleys black and dead: it is an empty World! Wo to them that shall be born then!——A King, a Queen (ah me!) were hurled in; did rustle once; flew aloft, crackling, like paper-scroll. Iscariot Égalité was hurled in ; thou grim de Launay, with thy grim Bastille; whole kindreds and peoples : five millions of mutually destroying Men. For it is the End of the dominion of IMPOSTURE (which is Darkness and opaque Firedamp); and the burning up, with unquenchable fire, of all the Gigs that are in the Earth.' This Prophecy, we say, has it not been fulfilled, is it not fulfilling?

And so here, O Reader, has the time come for us two to part. Toilsome was our journeying together; not without offence; but it is done. To me thou wert as a beloved shade, the disembodied or not yet embodied spirit of a Brother. To thee I was but as a Voice. Yet was our relation a kind of sacred one; doubt not that! For whatsoever once sacred things become hollow jargons, yet while the Voice of Man speaks with Man, hast thou not there the living fountain out of which all sacrednesses sprang, and will yet spring? Man, by the nature of him, is definable as 'an incarnated Word.' Ill stands it with me if I have spoken falsely: thine also it was to hear truly. Farewell.

GENERAL INDEX

ABBAYE, massacres at, ii. 151.

Acceptation, grande, by Louis XVI., ii. 38–44

Aiguillon, Duke d', account of, i. 2

Altar, of Fatherland, in Champ-de-ars, i. 276

America : see United States

Angoulême, Duchesse d', ii. 218

Antoinette, Marie, splendour of, i. 26; compromised by Diamond Necklace, 46; unpopular, 180; courage of, 221; Fifth October, at Versailles; 224; shows herself to mob, 227; and Louis at Tuileries, 236; and Mirabeau, 331, 343; flight from Tuileries, ii. 10; captured, 26; during twentieth June, 92; during tenth August, 118, 120; behaviour as captive, 127; and Princess de Lamballe, 153; in Temple Prison, 195; parting scene with King, 218; to the Conciergerie, 285; trial of, 286; guillotined, 288

Aristocrats, officers in French army, i 291; seized, ii. 141; condition in 1794, 326

Arms, smiths making, i. 145, 147; search for, 145

Army, French, after Bastille, i. 290; officered by aristocrats, 291; to be disbanded, 295; demands arrears, 295–8; general mutiny of, 296; bad state of, ii. 70, 85, 144; in want, 192; Revolutionary, 237, 283, 284, 301; fourteen armies on foot, 322, 369

Arsenal, attempt to burn, i. 152

Artois, M. d', i. 26, 71, 163

Assemblies, French, Primary and Secondary, i. 98

Assembly, National, Third Estate becomes, i. 129 (see Estate, Third); ratified by King, 135; cannon pointed at, 136; after Bastille, 161

Assembly, Constituent, National, becomes, i. 172; what it can do, 173; Left and Right Side, 177; raises money, 193; on the Veto, 193; Fifth October, women, 209; on deficit, assignats, 239; on clergy, 239; and Riot, 246; prepares for Louis's visit, 260; on Federation, 273; on Emigrants, 337; on death of Mirabeau, 347; on escape of King, ii. 14; completes Constitution, 38; dissolves itself, 42; what it has done, 43

Assembly, Legislative, First French Parliament, doings of, ii. 45–51; decrees vetoed, 73; scenes in, 74; reprimands, King's ministers, 75; declares war, 83, 88; 20th June, 92; declares France in danger, 100, 103; King and Swiss, August Tenth, 119–125; becoming

defunct, 128, 132; September massacres, 160; dissolved, 176. See Convention, National

Assignats, origin of, i. 239; forgers of, ii. 152

Atheism and Dupont, ii. 209

August Tenth (1792), ii. 112–127

Austria, its quarrel with France, ii. 66. See Brunswick, Duke

Austrian Committee, at Tuileries, ii. 64

Austrian Army, invades France, ii. 139; unsuccessful there, 178; defeated at Jemappes, 198; Dumouriez escapes to, 248; repulsed, Watigny, 321

Avignon, Union of, ii. 41; state of, 52; occupied by Jourdan, 54; massacre at, 55

BAILLY, astronomer, i. 116; President of National Assembly, 129; Mayor of Paris, 162; receives Louis in Paris, 164; and Paris Parlement, guillotined, ii. 77; in prison, 285; at Queen's trial, 286; guillotined cruelly, 299

Balloons invented, i. 41; used as spies, ii. 326

Barbaroux, and Marat, i. 245; and the Rolands, ii. 57; Marseilles, 89; in National Convention, 169; against Robespierre, 191; the Girondins declining, 235; arrested, 261; and Charlotte Corday, 264; retreats to Bordeaux, 272; 262; farewell of, 290; shoots himself, 291

Barentin, Keeper of Seals, i. 128

Barnave, at Grenoble, i. 85; duel with Cazalès, 325; escorts the King from Varennes, ii. 31; treason, in prison, 202; guillotined, 300

Barras, Paul-François, in National Convention, ii. 170; commands in Thermidor, 356; appoints Napoleon, in Vendémiairie 386

Bastille, Linguet's Book on, i. 45; meaning of, 105; besieged, 153; capitulates, 158; demolished, Key sent to Washington, 169; dance on ruins of, 286

Battles, nature of, i. 202. See Valmy, Jemappes, Neerwinden, Hondschooten, Watigny, Howe

Béarn, riot at, i. 85

Beauharnais, i. 218; ii. 296, 365

Bed of Justice, i. 67

Belief, French, i. 120

Bentham, Jeremy, naturalised, ii. 134

Berline (see Fersen), towards Varennes, ii. 16–20

Berthier, Commandant, at Versailles, i. 334

Besenval, Baron, Commandant of Paris,

on French Finance, i. 52; decamps, 161; and Louis XVI., 180

Béthune, riot at, i. 138

Bill-stickers, Paris, i. 254, 318

Billaud-Varennes, Jacobin, ii. 76; accuses Robespierre, 354; accused, 372; banished, 374

Birmingham riot, ii. 65

Blanc, Le, landlord at Varennes, ii. 26

Blood, baths of, i. 11

Bouillé, at Metz, i. 288; his troops mutinous, 295; would liberate king, ii. 29; emigrates, 30

Brest, sailors revolt, i. 313; state of, in 1791, ii. 60

Breton Club, germ of Jacobins, i. 85

Brézé, Marquis de, i. 106; and National Assembly, 129, 133

Brienne, Loménie, anti-protestant, i. 30; Controller of Finance, 62; incapacity of, 63; failure of, 67; arrests Paris Parlement, 69; secret scheme, 80; scheme discovered, 80; arrests two Parlementeers, 83; desperate shifts by, 87, 88

Brigands, the, origin of, i. 101; in Paris, 102; ii. 72

Brissac, Duke de, commands Constitutional Guard, ii. 38

Brissot, edits Moniteur, i. 109; friend of Blacks, 241; in First Parliament, ii. 47; pelted in Assembly, 103; arrested, ii. 261, 273; trial of, 288; guillotined, 290

Brittany, commotions in, i. 11, 85, 99, 100

Broglie, Marshal, i. 86, 126, 137, 141, 163

Brunout, M., among Menads, i. 214

Brunswick, Duke, marches on France, ii. 85; (ii. 137). Proclamation, 105; retreats, 177

Buonaparte: see Napoleon

Burke on French Revolution, ii. 64

Buttafuoco, Napoleon's letter to, i. 294

ÇA-IRA, origin of, i. 260

Calendar, Romme's new, ii. 277-9

Calonne, M. de financier, character of, i. 54; his difficulties, 57, 58; dismissed, 61

Cambon, notice of, ii. 48

Candeille, Mlle., Goddess of Reason, ii. 312

Cannon, Siamese, i. 145; wooden, ii. 138; fever, Goethe on, 174

Cant defined, i. 44

Carmagnole, ii. 302, 312

Carnot, Hippolyte, ii. 47, 306, 315

Carra, on plots for King's flight, i. 333

Castries, Duke de, duel with Lameth, i. 326

Cazalès, Royalist, i. 114, 177, 236, 325; ii. 15, 66

Cercle Social, of Fauchet, i. 321

Cerutti, his funeral oration on Mirabeau, i. 348

Cevennes, revolt of, i. 348

Chabray, Louison, at Versailles, October Fifth, i. 213, 218

Chambon, Dr., Mayor of Paris, ii. 193; retires, 210

Champ-de-Mars, Federation, i. 271; preparations for, 272; anecdotes of, 279; Federation-scene at, 281-7; riot, Patriot petition, 1791, ii. 36; new Federation (1792), 103; enlisting in, 147

Champs Elysées, i. 205, 286

Chantilly Palace, a prison, ii. 301

Charenton, Marseillese at, ii. 108

Charles I., Trial of, sold in Paris, ii. 196

Chartres, Duke de. (See Orleans)

Chartres, grain-riot at, ii. 104

Châteaubriands, in French Revolution, ii. 340

Châtelet, Achille de, ii. 15

Châtillon-sur-Sèvre, insurrection at, ii. 138

Chemists, French, inventions of, ii. 319

Chesterfield, Lord, predicts French Revolution, i. 12

Choiseul, Duke, i. 12

Choiseul, Colonel Duke, ii. 9, 17, 25, 28

Choisi, General, at Avignon, ii. 55

Christianity. (See Religion, Christian)

Church, spiritual guidance, i. 7; of Rome, decay of, 9; of Rome, dead in France, ii. 2, 7

Citizens, French, active and passive, i. 253

Clergy, French, in States-General, i. 118; joins Third Estate, 124-8; lands, national? 239, 243; power of, constitution for, 240

Clermont, ii. 23, 145

Cléry, valet, on Louis's last scene, ii. 217

Clootz, Anacharsis, Baron de, account of, 250; collects human species, 273; in National Convention, ii. 169; universal republic of, 193; on nullity of religion, 310; purged from the Jacobins, 331; guillotined, 333

Clovis, in Champ-de-Mars, i. 8

Club, Electoral, at Paris, i. 140, 159, 144, 151

Club: see Breton, Jacobin, Enraged, Cordeliers,

Clubs in Paris, 1788, i. 94, 124; in 1790, 256

Clugny, M., as Finance Minister, i. 37

Coblentz, Royalist Emigrants at, ii. 58, 62, 67-9

Cobourg and Dumouriez, ii. 246, 248

Cockades, i. 141, 145, 196, 199

Coigny, Duke de, i. 53

Collot d'Herbois, 353

Commerce, new Noblesse of, i. 11

Commissioners, Convention, like Kings, ii. 318, 321

Committee, Electoral: see Club, Electoral, Austrian

Committee of Defence, ii. 106; Central, 110, 115; of Watchfulness, of Public Salvation, 134, 143; Circular of, 164; of the Constitution, 185; Revolutionary, 243; of Sections, 254; Revolutionary, busy, 301

Committees, Forty-four Thousand, ii. 284

Commune, Council General of the, ii. 128, 133, 148

Communes, of France, ii. 275

Condé, Prince de, i. 14, 163
Condé, Town, surrendered, ii. 257
Condorcet, Marquis, i. 109; ii. 47, 76, 235, , 342
Conscience, leaders of, i. 9
Constituent Assembly: see Assembly
Constitution, French, ii. 38–44, 51, 60, 64, 125, 276, 279. See Committee
Constitution, new, of, 1793, ii. 275, 279. See Sieyès
Constitutions, how built, i. 175
Contrat Social: see Rousseau
Convention, National, determined on, ii. 127; constituted, 176; work to be done, 185; on September Massacres, 188; try the King, 206; invite to revolt, 208; condemn Louis, 211–16; power of, 245 (see Mountain, Girondins); removes to Tuileries, 252; besieged, 2 June, 1793, extinction of Girondins, 259, 261; Carmagnole, Goddess of Reason, 312; awed to silence, 317; at Feast of Être Suprême, 344; to be butchered?, 350; end of Robespierre, 352, 354, 356; retrospect of, 274, 376
Corday, Charlotte, account of, ii. 264; in Paris, 265; stabs Marat, 266; examined, 267; executed, 268
Cordeliers, Club, i. 258 (see Danton)
Council of Ancients, of Five Hundred, ii. 384
Court, French Plenary, i. 80, 85
Covenant, Scotch, ii. 266, 271; French, 266, 271
Crime, purpose and act of, ii. 150
Crussol, Marquise de, ii. 340
Cuissa, massacred at La Force, ii. 156
Curates abolished, ii. 310
Customs and morals, ii. 168

Damas, Colonel Comte de, at Clermont, ii. 23; at Varennes, 28
Dampierre, General, killed, ii. 263
Dampmartin, Captain, i. 104, 293, 319; ii. 55
Dandoins, Captain, Flight to Varennes, ii. 19–23
Danton, notice of, i. 110; President of Cordeliers, 191; and Marat, 247, 252; in Cordeliers Club, 258; elected Councillor, 341; Mirabeau of Sansculottes, ii. 46; in Jacobins, 79; for Deposition, 99; of Committee, August Tenth, 106, 111; Minister of Justice, 127, 136; after September Massacre, 166; after Jemappes, 198; and Robespierre, 200; in Netherlands, 203; at King's Trial, 212; on war, 231; rebukes Marat, 233; peacemaker, 234; and Dumouriez, 242; in Salut Committee. 244; breaks with Girondins, 250; and Revolutionary Government, 315; and Paris Municipality, 316; suspect, 331; retires to Arcis, 332; and Robespierre, 334; arrested, 335; trial of, 336–8; guillotined, 338
David, Painter, ii. 169, 276, 325, 344, 353
Death, kingly idea of, i. 15

Deficit, Mirabeau on, i. 193
Democracy, on Bunker Hill, i. 6; spread of, in France, 36, 37, 95
Departments, France divided into, i. 239
Desmoulins, Camille, notice of, i. 110; in arms at Café de Foy, 141; Insurrection of women, 203; in National Convention, ii. 169; on Sansculottism, 245; on plots, 255; suspect, 332; for a committee of mercy, 332; ridicules law of the suspect, 332; his Journal, 333; his wife, 335; guillotined. 338
Diderot, prisoner in Vincennes, ii. 335
Directorate, feats of, ii. 388
Discipline, Army, nature of, ii. 290–1
Douai: see Parlement
Drouet, Jean B., ii. 20, 25, 28, 42
Dubarry, Dame, and Louis XV., i. 2; flight of. 18; imprisoned, ii. 296
Dubois-Crancé, bombards Lyons, ii. 281; takes Lyons, 303
Duelling, in French Revolution, i. 325
Dumouriez, notice by, i. 2; account of him, 248; in La Vendée, ii. 58; sent for to Paris, 70; Foreign Minister, 80; dismissed, to Army, 87; disobeys Lückner, 99; Commander-in-Chief, 129; his army, 144; Council of War, 146; seizes Argonne Forest, 146, 170; Grand-Pré, 172; and mutineers, 172; and Marat in Paris, 181; to Netherlands, 182; at Jemappes, 197; in Paris, 210; discontented, 220; retreats, 236; traitor? 242; will join the enemy, 246; arrests his arresters, 248; escapes to Austrians, 249
Duperret, Girondin draws sword in Convention, ii. 251; papers sealed, Charlotte Corday, 274
Dupont, Deputy, Atheist, ii. 209
Duport, Adrien, i. 66, 178, 237

Edgeworth, Abbé, ii. 217, 219
Editors, in 1789, i. 189
Égalité: see Orléans, Duke, d'
Election for States-General, i. 97
Emigrants, law against, i. 337; ii. 67, 171, 180
Emigration, first French, i. 163, 186; second, 229, 317; ii. 34
England declares war on France, ii. 221, 257; gains Toulon, 280
Enraged Club, the, i. 94
Equality, reign of, ii. 137
Esprémenil, Duval d', notice of, i. 66; patriot, speaker in Paris Parlement. 68, 70; discovers Brienne's plot, 80; arrest and speech of, 80–3; turncoat, 117; beaten by populace, guillotined, ii. 340
Estaing, Count d', i. 196, 210, 213; ii. 286
Estate, Third, i. 95, 96, 116, 123, 129
Estate, Fourth, of Editors, &c., i. 189
Etiquette, acme of: see Brézé
Étoile, beginning of Federation at, i. 267
Evil, nature of, i. 29

FALSEHOOD, doom of, i. 172

Famine in France, i. 28, 44, 87, 128, 136, 181, 216, 323; ii. 193. 245

Fanaticism and Formula, i. 171

Fatherland : *see* Altar

Fauchet, Abbé, at Siege of Bastille, i. 155; famous for Te-Deums, 187; his Cercle Social, 321; in First Parliament, ii. 47; King's death, lamentation, 221; will demit, 259; trial of, 288

Feast, of Reason, ii. 311–14; of Etre Suprême, 344

Federation, i. 268, 272. 280; ii. 97, 102

Féraud, in National Convention, ii. 169; massacred there, 377

Fersen, Count, ii. 9

Feudalism, death of, in France, i. 108

Finances, bad state of, i. 37, 52, 72, 88; how to be improved, 80, 239

Flanders, how Louis XV. conquers, i. 5

Flandre, régiment de, at Versailles, i. 196, 197, 212

Fleury, Joly de, Controller of Finance, i. 52

Formula, i. 171, 181; ii. 184

Fouché, at Lyons, ii. 304

Foulon, i. 54, 73, 90, 163, 166

France, abject, under Louis XV., i. 4, 10–12; on accession of Louis XVI., 24; famine in, 1775, 27, 43; state of, prior Revolution, 29; aids America, 35; in 1788, 86; inflammable, July 1789, 140; how to be regenerated, 245; Mirabeau and, 343; after King's flight, ii. 15; Europe leagues against, 66; decree of War, 83; country in danger, 99, 103; Marat's Circular, September, 164; Sans-culottic, 184: declaration of war, 221; Mountain and Girondins divide, 231; communes of, 275; coalition against, 280; levy in mass, 283; one large 'Committee of Mercy,' in 1795, 364; state of, since the Revolution, 388

Franklin, Ambassador to France, i. 35

Fraternity, doctrine of, ii. 292

Freedom, meaning of, i. 148

French, Anglomania, i. 39

Fréron, i. 254, 364, 367

Freys, the Jew brokers, imprisoned, ii. 248

GALLOIS, to La Vendée, ii. 58

Gamain, Sieur, locksmith, informer, ii. 202

Game, i. 186

Garat, Minister of Justice, ii. 215

Gazette, origin of the term, i. 256

German, meaning of term, i. 320

Germinal Twelfth, First of April 1795, ii. 373

Gibraltar besieged, i. 37

Gifts, patriotic, ii. 138

Girondins, origin of term, ii. 47; in National Convention, 188; against Robespierre, 190; King's trial, 199, 211–14; and Jacobins, 199–202; formula of, 213; favourers of, 228; schemes of, 230–40; to be seized? 240; break with Danton, 250; armed against Mountain, 251;

accuse Marat, 251; departments, 252; commission of twelve, 257; war by, 269; retreat of eleven, 272; trial of, 288; last supper of, 289; guillotined, 290

Gobel, Archbishop to be, i. 237, 347; renounces religion, ii. 310; arrested, 330; guillotined, 339

Goethe, ii. 173, 179–81, 274

Gouvion, Major-General, i. 203; ii. 8, 9, 14, 85

Government, Maurepas's, i. 32; bad state of French, 95; real, 174; French revolutionary, ii. 315, 329; Danton on, 335

Grenoble, riot at, i. 85

Grievances, writ of, i. 97

Guards, Swiss, and French, i. 104; French won't fire, 134, 138; fire on Royal-Allemand, 143; to Bastille, 147, 156, 158; name changed, 160; Body at Versailles, October Fifth, 214; fight there, 223; fly in Château, 224; National, at Nanci, 303; French, last appearance of, ii. 39; Constitutional, dismissed, 74; routed, 110; Swiss at Tuileries, 114, 121; fire, 122; ordered to cease, destroyed, 123; Departmental, for National Convention, 189

Guillaume, Clerk, pursues King, ii. 22. *See* Drouet.

Guillotin, Doctor, i. 101, 115, 211, 217, 260

Guillotine invented, i. 115; described, ii. 136; in action, 285, 296, 301; to be improved, 346; number of sufferers by, 380

HÉBERT, Editor of *Père Duchesne*, i. 318; signs petition, ii. 36; arrested, 256; at Queen's trial, 287; quickens Revolutionary Tribunal, 289; arrested, 330; guillotined, 333

Hénault, President, on Surnames, i. 1

Héritier, Jerôme l', i. 223

Hoche, Sergeant Lazare, i. 138; ii. 323, 370

Holland invaded by Prussia, 1787, i. 72

Hondschooten, Battle of, ii. 321

Hope and Man, i. 32

Hôtel des Invalides, i. 158

Hôtel de Ville, i. 158, 162, 204, 232

Houchard, General, ii. 279, 301

Howe, Lord, beats French navy, ii. 323

Huguenin, Patriot, ii. 75, 91

Hulin, half-pay, at siege of Bastille, i. 158

Huns, Attila's, long arms of, ii. 131

IDEALS, realised, i. 6

Inisdal's, Count d', plot, i. 330

Insurrection, most sacred of duties, i. 201; of Women, 192–232; of August Tenth, ii. 100–6; of Paris, against Girondins, 1793, ii. 257–61; sacred right of, 330; last Sansculottic, 376. *See* Riot

Irish Sans-Potato, ii. 381

Isnard, Max, i. 268 ; ii. 46, 76, 256, 259, 364

Jacob, Jean Claude, i. 275
Jacobins, Society, germ of, i. 85 ; Hall, described, and members, 257 ; at Nanci, suppressed, 312 ; and Mirabeau, 323, 342 ; extinguishes Feuillans, ii. 78 ; and Marseillese, 109 ; missionaries in Army, 198 ; on accusation of Robespierre, 200 ; against Girondins, 200, 253 ; National Convention and, 275, 317 ; Popular Tribunals of, 302 ; Couthon's Question in, 329 ; purges members, 330 ; to become dominant, 350 ; locked out by Legendre, 357 ; begs back its keys, 364 ; decline of, 372 ; hunted down, 374
Jacobinism, spirit of, ii. 320
Jalès, Camp of, i. 241 ; ii. 71
Jaucourt, Chevalier, ii. 47
Jemappes, battle of, ii. 198
Jesuitism and Dame Dubarry, i. 12
Jokéi, French, described, i. 39
Jones, Paul, i. 36, 249, 273 ; ii. 103
Jourdan, General, repels Austria, ii. 321
Jourdan, Coupe-tête, i. 212 ; ii. 52, 54-6, 56, 303
Journals (see Paris), ii. 253, 318
Julien, Sieur Jean, ii. 147
June Twentieth, 1792, ii. 93
Justice, bed of, i. 67

Kaunitz, Prince, ii. 78
Kings, primitive, i. 7
King : see Louis
Kingship, decline of, in France, i. 9 : see Royalty
Klopstock, naturalized, ii. 134
Knox, John, and the Virgin, i. 312
Korff, Baroness de, ii. 9, 12

Lafarge, President of Jacobins, Madame Lavergne and, ii. 140
Lafayette, against Calonne, i. 59 ; demands by, in Notables, 64 ; Bastille time, Vice-President of National Assembly, 149, 161 ; General of National Guard, 162 ; resigns and reaccepts, 168 ; French Guards and, 206 ; to Versailles, 207 ; at Versailles, Fifth October, 220 ; swears the Guards, 228 ; Feuillant, 259 ; on abolition of Titles, 274 ; at Champ-de-Mars Federation, 283 ; at De Castries' Riot, 327 ; in Day of Poniards, 338 ; difficult position of, 339 ; at King's going to St. Cloud, ii. 3 ; at flight from Tuileries, 10 ; on Petition for Deposition moves for amnesty, 41 ; resigns, 44 ; decline of, 77 ; fruitless journey to Paris, 95 ; flies to Holland, 129
Laflotte, prison-plot, informer, ii. 340, 347
La Force : see Prison
Lamarche, guillotined, ii. 299
Lamarck's, Mirabeau sick at, i. 345
Lamballe, Princess de, ii. 17, 64, 81, 142, 153

Lambesc, Prince, i. 142
Lameth, in Constituent Assembly, one of a trio, i. 178 ; brothers, 237, 257. 326 ; ii. 33, 47
Lamoignon, Keeper of Seals, i. 60, 74, 79, 90, 91
Lamotte, Countess de, i. 46, 56, 76 ; ii. 74, 142, 155
Lanterne, death by the, i. 167
Lasource, ii. 250
Launay, Marquis de, Governor of Bastille, i. 150, 152, 153, 156
Lavergne, surrenders Longwi, ii. 138
Lavoisier, Chemist, ii. 341
Law, Martial, in Paris, i. 246 ; Book of the, ii. 37, 49
Lawyers, their influence on the Revolution, i. 11 ; number of, in Tiers Etat, 119 ; in Parliament First, ii. 46
Lazare, Maison de St., i. 146
Lebrun, forger of Assignats, ii. 68
Lechapelier, Deputy, and Insurrection of Women, i. 206
Lecointre, National Major, i. 197, 213, 199, 216 ; ii. 48
Legendre, Butcher, ii. 87, 169, 259, 335, 357, 372
Legislation : see Assembly
Lepelletier, ii. 373, 378
Lettres-de-Cachet, and Parlement of Paris, i. 75
Liancourt, Duke de, Liberal, i. 117 ; not a revolt, but a revolution, 161 ; Royalist, in Normandy, ii. 97
Liberty, on, i. 253 ; tree of, 285 ; ii. 89, 102 ; and Equality 82 ; Statue of, 277
Lies, Philosophism on, i. 12 ; to be extinguished, how, 31 ; cant, a double power of, 44 ; their doom, 184
Ligne, Prince de, death of, ii. 171
Lille, Colonel Rouget de, Marseillese Hymn, ii. 101
Lille city besieged, ii. 177
Literature, its influence on the Revolution, i. 11 ; in France in 1781-7, 45, 48, 77
Loan, Successive, scheme of, i. 73
Longwi, surrendered, ii. 138 ; fugitives at Paris, 139
Lords of the Articles, Jacobins as, ii. 317
Lorraine Fédérés and the Queen, i. 280 ; state of, in 1790, 295
Louis XIV., l'état c'est moi, i. 8 ; booted in Parlement, 73 ; pursues Louvois with tongs, ii. 187
Louis XV., origin of his surname, i. 1 ; last illness of, 20 ; dismisses Dame Dubarry, 18 ; his mode of conquest, 5 ; impoverishes France, 11 ; his daughters, 13 ; on death, 15 ; on ministerial capacity. 17 ; death of, 20 ; burial of, 20
Louis XVI., at his accession, i. 20 ; difficulties of, 33, 77 ; holds Royal Session, 73-5 ; receives States-General Deputies, 106 ; speech to States-General, 120 ; National Assembly, 135 ; dismisses Necker, 141 ; apprised of the Revolution, 161 ; visits Assembly,

162; visits Paris, 164; deserted, will fly, 180, 197; deposition of, proposed, 207; grants the acceptance, 218; Paris propositions to, 220; in the Chateau tumult (Oct. 6), 225; will go to Paris, 228; procession to Paris, 230–6; review of his position, 233; lodged at Tuileries, 234; Restorer of French Liberty, 235; visits Assembly, 260; will fly, 329; Mirabeau, 341; indecision of, ii. 1; prepares for St. Cloud, 3; hindered by populace, 4; flies, 9; letter to Assembly, 14; manner of flight, 16; detected by Drouet, 21; captured at Varennes. 26; return to Paris, 30; reception there, 31; to be deposed? 33–5; reinstated, 38; reception of Legislative, 50; position of, 61; proposes war, 83; vetoes, dissolves Roland Ministry, 87; in riot of Twentieth June, 92; declared forfeited, 111, 127; last levee of, 111; Tenth August, 117, 120; quits Tuileries for Assembly, 121; in Assembly, 126; sent to Temple prison, 128; in Temple, ii. 195; to be tried, 197–204; at the bar, 204; his will, 206; condemned, 211–216; parting scene, 217; execution of, 218–19

Louis-Philippe, King of the French, i. 258; ii. 176, 198, 246, 247, 297

Louvet, i. 48, 254; ii. 29, 169, 200, 235, 272, 282, 290

Lückner, Supreme General, i. 289; ii. 86; and Dumouriez, 99; guillotined, 301

Lunéville, Inspector Malseigne at, i. 304

Lux, Adam, on death of Charlotte Corday, ii. 268; guillotined, 296

Luxembourg, forges at, ii. 283; Palace, a prison, 301

Lyons, Federation at, i. 268; disorders in, ii. 231; Chalier, Jacobin, executed at, 269; bombarded, powder-tower of, 280; captured, 303; massacres at, 304

MAILLARD, Usher, i. 156, 158, 204, 211; ii. 36, 151

Malesherbes, M. de, i. 71, 76; ii. 206, 214, 218, 340

Malseigne, Army Inspector, i. 302–5, 308

Man, rights and mights of, i. 176, 183; ii. 65

Mandat, Commander of Guards, ii. 113; 116

Manège, Salle de, Constituent Assembly occupies, i. 236

Marat, Jean Paul, horseleech to D'Artois, i. 40; notice of, 110; against violence, 140; at siege of Bastille, 156; summoned by Constituent, 189; how to regenerate France, 244, 319; on abolition of titles, 274; would gibbet Mirabeau, 319; concealed in cellars, ii. 107; pulls tocsin rope, 114; in seat of honour, 135; signs circular, 165; elected to Convention, 169; oaths by, in Convention, 187; against Roland, 210; on sufferings of People, 225; and Girondins, 232; arrested, 251; returns in triumph,

252; fall of Girondins, 261; sick, his residence, 265; and Charlotte Corday, 266; honours to, 266. 371

Marat, Company of, ii. 302

Maréchal, Atheist, Calendar by, ii. 277

Maréchale, the Lady, on nobility, i. 10

Marie Antoinette : see Antoinette

Marseilles, Brigands at, i. 137; on Déchéance, the bar of iron, ii. 34; for Girondism, 252, 263, 269; guillotine at, 302

Marseillese, March and Hymn of, ii. 100, 109, 111, 116, 121–4

Massacre, Avignon, ii. 54; September, 151–163; compared to Bartholomew, 164; Convention on, 188

Maton, Advocate, ii. 155

Mauconseil, section, on forfeiture of King, ii. 111; on Girondins, 241

Maurepas, Prime Minister, i. 25, 32, 51

Maury, Abbé, 118, 177, 230, 236, 244, 324; ii. 43

Menads, the, i. 201–4, 231

Mentz, occupied by French, ii. 182; siege of, 263, 370; surrender of, Goethe describes, 274

Mercier, i. 137, 190; ii. 163, 214

Merlin of Douai, Law of Suspect, ii. 283

Mesmer, Dr., glance at, i. 42

Métra the Newsman, ii. 255

Metropolis, importance of a, ii. 270

Metz, Bouillé at, i. 288; troops mutinous at, 296

Millennium, French idea of, ii. 225

Mirabeau, Marquis, i. 28, 45, 150

Mirabeau, Count, his pamphlets, i. 58–9; expelled by the Provence Noblesse, 101; is Deputy for Aix, 101; king of Frenchmen, 111; his future course, 113; groaned at, in Assembly, 124; his newspaper suppressed, 126; silences Usher de Brézé, 133; at Bastille ruins, 169; on Robespierre, 178; on French deficit, 193; Mounier, October Fifth, 206; insight of, defends veto, 237; and Danton, on Constitution, 247; at Jacobins, 257; Marat would gibbet, 319; his power in France, 323; on duelling, 325; interview with Queen, 331; speech on emigrants, 337; in Council, 341–2; probable career of, 343; sickens, yet works, 345; last sayings of, 346; death of, 347; public funeral of, 348; character of, 349; last of Mirabeaus, 351; bust in Jacobins, ii. 78; bust demolished, 203; his remains turned out of the Pantheon, 371

Mirabeau the younger, i. 117, 135, 177

Miranda, General, attempts Holland, ii. 236

Mobs on, i. 201

Moleville, Bertrand de, Historian, i. 85; ii. 60–2. 76, 111, 137

Monge, Mathematician, ii. 127, 278

Monsabert, G. de, President of Paris Parlement, i. 80, 83

Montélimart, covenant sworn at, i. 267

Montesquiou, General, ii. 182

Moudon, Abbé confessor to Louis XV., i. 13, 18

Mounier, i. 85, 131, 206, 211, 218, 229

Mountain, members of the, ii. 48; re-elected in National Convention, ii. 168; Gironde and, 227–30; favourers of the, 229; vulnerable points of, 232; prevails, 235; after Gironde dispersed, 261; in labour, 270

Municipality of Paris, to be abolished, ii. 363

Murat, in Vendémiaire, revolt, ii. 386

Mutiny, military, nature of, i. 290

NANCI, i. 288–313

Nantes, ii. 15, 302; noyades, 307

Napoleon Buonaparte, studying mathematics, i. 87; pamphlet by, 294; democratic, in Corsica, 329; August Tenth, ii. 123; under General Cartaux, 269; at Toulon, 280, 306–7; was pupil of Pichegru, 322; Josephine and, at La Cabarus's, 366; Vendémiaire, 386, 387

Nature, statue of, ii. 276

Navy, Louis XV. on French, i. 36; French, rots, ii, 61

Necker, and finance, account of, i. 37; dismissed, 38; refuses Brienne, 88; recalled, 90; difficulty as to States-General, 96; reconvokes Notables, 96; opinion of himself, 109; popular, 134; dismissed, 141; recalled, 163; returns in in glory, 186; his plans, 193; getting unpopular, 241; departs, with difficulty, 311

Necklace, Diamond, i. 43, 56

Neerwinden, battle of, ii. 242

Netherlands, occupied by French, ii. 197

Nobles, state of the, under Louis XV., i. 10; new, 11; join Third Estate, 135; Emigrant, errors of, ii. 68

Notables, Calonne's convocation of, i. 56; assembled, 22 Feb., 1787, 57; organed out, 64; effects of dismissal of, 64; reconvoked, 64; and dismissed again, 96, 97

OATH, of the Tennis-Court, i. 131; National, 261

October Fifth, 1789, i. 201–4

Orléans, Philippe (Egalité), Duc d', i. 58; wealth, debauchery, Palais-Royal buildings, 46; in Notables, 58; looks of, Bed-of-Justice, 1787, 74–5; liberated, 77; in States-General Procession, 117; joins Third Estate, 155; his party, in Constituent Assembly, 178; Fifth October and, 230; accused by Royalists, 340; in National Convention, ii. 170; decline of, in Convention, 198, 233; vote on King's trial, 213, 215, 217; at King's execution, 219; arrested, imprisoned, 249; condemned, 296; execution, 297

PAINE, 'Common Sense,' i. 249; ii. 15, 134, 170, 357

Pantheon, first occupant of, i. 348

Paper, Age of, uses of, i. 23

Paris, origin of city. i. 6; police in 1750, 11; ship Ville-de- Paris, 36; riot at Palais-de-Justice, 70; election, 1789, 98; troops called to, 126; military preparations in, 136; July Fourteenth, cry for arms, 143, 151; Bailly, mayor of, 162; Lafayette patrols, 195; October Fifth, propositions to Louis, 220; Louis in, 232; foreigners flock to, 248; Journals, 253–6; bill-stickers, 254, 318; on Nanci affair, 310; on death of Mirabeau, 347; on Flight to Varennes, ii. 13–15; on King's return, 32; on forfeiture of King, 111; Sections, rising of, 112; August Tenth, prepares for insurrection, 112–18; statues torn down, King and Queen to prison, 128; September 1792, 161; names printed on house-door, 243; in insurrection, Girondins, May 1793, 257; like a Mahlstrom, Thermidor, 357; Sections to be abolished, 364; brightened up, 1795, 365–7; Gilt youth, 368

Parlement of Paris, re-established, i. 24; patriotic, 50, 67; arrested, 70; Royal Session in, 73–4; how to be tamed, 79; oath and declaration of, 81; scene in, and dismissal of, 83–4; reinstated, 90; unpopular, 93; summons Dr. Guillotin, 101; abolished, 240

Parlements, Provincial, i. adhere to Paris, 68, 76; rebellious, 78, 82; exiled, 86; grand deputations of, 90; abolished, 240

Past, the, and Fear, ii. 195

Pétion, account of, i. 114; to be mayor, 341; Varennes, see King, ii. 31; Mayor of Paris, 76; in Twentieth June, 92; August Tenth, in Tuileries, 114; in National Convention, 168

Pétion-National-Pique, christening of, ii. 85

Petition, of famishing French, i. 28; at Fatherland's altar, ii. 36; of the Eight Thousand, 86; of washerwomen, 224

Petitions, on capture of King, ii. 35; for deposition, &c., 111

Philosophes, French, i. 24, 251

Philosophism, influence of, on Revolution, i. 11; what it has done with Church, 30; with Religion, 47; disappointment on succeeding, 251

Pikes, fabricated; see Arms; Feast of, i. 286; in 1793, 275–7

Pitt, against France, ii. 66; and Girondins, 225; inflexible, 370

Plots, of King's flight, i. 196, 328–5; ii. 9–12; various, of Aristocrats, October Fifth, i. 201–8; Royalist, of Favras, and others, 243; cartels, Twelve bullies from Switzerland, 325; D'Inisdal, willo'-wisp, 330; Mirabeau and Queen, 331; poniards, 335; against Girondins, ii. 240; Desmoulins on, 255; prison, 340, 345–7

Poniards, Royalist, i. 330; Day of, 335

Prisons, Paris, in Bastille time, i 146 number of, 301; state of, in Terror 346–9; after Terror, 363

Procession, of States-General Deputies, i. 108; of Louis to Paris, 230-2; of Black Breeches, ii. 90-3; of Louis to trial, 204; at Constitution of 1793, 276

Reason, Goddess of, ii. 312-15
Rebecqui, of Marseilles, ii. 57, 169, 191, 269
Religion, Christian, and French Revolution, ii. 293; abolished, 309-12; a new, 312-43
Republic, French, ii. 16, 168, 177, 183, 193, 241, 249, 277, 368-71
Revolt, Paris in, i. 145; becomes Revolution, 161
Revolution, French, causes of the, i. 10, 29, 47, 78; not a Revolt, 161; general commencement of, 183; progress of, 315; Republic decided on, ii. 15; cardinal movements in, 131; Danton and the, 166; changes produced by the, 183; effect of King's death on, 222-4; Terror and, 292; and Christian religion, 203; Robespierre essential to, 361; end of, 388
Riot, Paris, in May 1750, i. 11; at Palais de Justice, 70; of Rue St. Antoine, 104; of July Fourteenth (1789), and Bastille, 142-61; Paris, on the veto, 193; Versailles Château, October Fifth (1789), 202-7; at Vincennes, 336; on King's proposed journey to St. Cloud, ii. 3; in Champ-de-Mars, with sharp shot, 36; Paris, Twentieth June, 1792, 92; August Tenth, 1792, 113-28; Grain, 193; of Thermidor, 1794, 354-60; of Germinal, 1795, 373; of Prairial, 376; final, of Vendémiaire, 385-9
Robespierre, Maximilien, account of, i. 114; Jacobin, 257, 323; chief priest of Jacobins, ii. 79; on September Massacre, 163; accused by Girondins, 190; accused by Louvet, 200; Condorcet on, 235; and Paris Municipality, 316; Desmoulins and, 332; and Danton, 334; Danton on, at trial, 337; supreme, 339; to be assassinated, 343; at Feast of Etre Suprême, 344-5; reserved, 350; fails in Convention, 351; accused, 354; rescued, 356; at Townhall, declared out of Law, 356; half-killed, 358; guillotined, 359; essential to Revolution, 361
Rochefoucault, Duke de la, i. 117; ii. 97, 165
Rohan, Cardinal, Diamond Necklace and, i. 46
Roland, Madame, at, i. 269; ii. 16, 57, 81, 192, 210, 261, 298-9
Roland, M., i. 269; ii. 57, 80, 87, 192, 220, 300
Romœuf, pursues the King, ii. 16; at Varennes, 29
Rosière, Thuriot de la, i. 152; ii. 48, 208, 354
Rousseau, Jean-Jacques, Contrat Social of, i. 43; Gospel according to, 262; ii. 42

Royalty, signs of demolished, ii. 15, 127; abolished in France, 177

St. Just, ii. 169 322, 329; in Committee-room, Thermidor, 353; his report, 353; arrested, 354
Salm, regiment, at Nanci, i. 296
Salut Public: see Committee
Sansculottism, apparition of, i. 171; effects of, 186; origin of term, 331; and Royalty, ii. 91; French Nation and, 184; how it lives, 245; consummated, 308, 319; fall of, 361; last rising of, 376-9
Santerre, Brewer, i. 156; ii. 118, 193, 378
Savoy, occupied by French, ii. 182
Séchelles, Hérault, de, ii. 185, 260, 335, 338
Sieyès, Abbé, i. 116, 173; ii. 169, 213, 384
Spain, against France, ii. 66; invaded by France, 221, 320
Spurs, night of, ii. 214
Staël, Mme. de, i. 109; ii. 63, 137, 141
States-General, first mooted, i. 64, 67, 73; how constituted, 93; representatives to, 97; Parlements against, 101; number of Deputies, 106; place of assembling, 106; procession of, 108-18; union of orders, 124-7
Suspect, Law, of the, ii. 284, 330
Suspicion, in France, 1788, i. 102; in Revolution, ii. 255
Swiss Guards, ii. 83, 152

Talleyrand-Périgord, Bishop, i. 118; ii. 6, 43; in London, 221
Tallien accuses Robespierre, ii. 354
Tax, Ascending, ii. 245
Telegraph invented, ii. 325
Terror, consummation of, ii. 292; reign of, designated, 294; number guillotined in, 380
Tinville, Fouquier, Attorney-General in Tribunal Révolutionnaire, ii. 244; at trial of Danton, 336; his prison-plots, 348; accused, guillotined, 374
Tithes, titles, &c., abolished, i. 177, 274
Toulon, Girondin, ii. 270; occupied by English, 280; besieged, 305; surrenders, 307
Tribunal, Extraordinaire, ii. 243; Révolutionnaire, doings of, 284; extended, 345
Tuileries, i. 234, 236; ii. 91, 107, 109, 112, 121, 123, 252
Tyrants, French People risen against, ii. 283, 319

United States, i. 6, 35, 36, 179

Varennes, ii. 25-8, 145
Vendée, La, Commissioners to, i. 58; state of, in 1792, 71; insurrection in, 138; war, after King's death, 233; on fire, 302; pacificated, 370
Vendémiaire, Thirteenth, Oct. 4, 1795, ii. 385-8

Vengeur, sinking of the, ii. 323

Verbs, Irregular, National Assembly at, i. 173

Verdun, to be besieged, ii. 139, 144; surrendered, 145

Vergennes, M. de, Prime Minister, i. 51; death of, 60

Vergniaud, notice of, ii. 46; too languid, 76; during June Twentieth, 92; orations of, 133; President at King's condemnation, 212; in fall of Girondins, 257; trial of, 288; at last supper of Girondins, 289

Versailles, death of Louis XV. at, i. 2, 20; in Bastille time, National Assembly at, 149, 161; march of women on, 204; insurrection scene at, 210; Orléans prisoners massacred at, 165

Veto, question of the, i. 193; ii. 73, 89, 92; eluded, 97

Voltaire, i. 34; ii. 348

WAR, civil, manual and lingual, i. 244; French, becomes general, 310

Washington, key of Bastille sent to, i. 169; formula for Lafayette, 117; ii. 129

Women, patriotic gifts by, i. 193; revolutionary speeches by, 200; Insurrection of, 201; at Hôtel-de-Ville, 202; march to Versailles, 204; deputation of, to Assembly, 211; to King, 211; corrupt the Guards, 212; would hang their deputy, 213; in fight at Versailles, 223; selling sugar, cry of soap, ii. 224; 'Megæras,' 254; Hérault and Heroines, 276

YOUNG, ARTHUR, at French Revolution, i. 181-6

Youth, Gilt, ii. 367, 378

EVERYMAN'S LIBRARY AND EVERYMAN PAPERBACKS: A Selection

indicates the volumes also in paperback: for their series numbers in Everyman Paperbacks add 1000 to the EML numbers given.

EUL stands for Everyman's University Library.

For copyright reasons some of the following titles are not available in the U.S.A.

BIOGRAPHY

*Brontë, Charlotte. *Life* by Mrs Gaskell   318
Byron, Lord. *Letters*   931
*Johnson, Dr Samuel. *Life of Dr Johnson* by James Boswell   1, 2
*Keats, John. *Life and Letters* by Lord Houghton   801
*Lives of the English Poets. (A selection) by Dr Samuel Johnson   770
Pepys, Samuel. *Diary*   53–5

ESSAYS AND CRITICISM

*Bacon, Frances. *Essays* (EUL)   10
Coleridge, Samuel Taylor. *Shakespearean Criticism*   162, 183
Hazlitt, William. *Lectures on the English Comic Writers*   411
*Lawrence, D. H. *Stories, Essays and Poems*   958
*Milton, John. *Prose Writings*   795
*Paine, Thomas. *The Rights of Man*   718
*Writing of the 'Nineties. From Wilde to Beerbohm   773

FICTION

Austen, Jane. The principal novels including:
    Emma   24
    Pride and Prejudice   22
    Sense and Sensibility   21
Balzac, Honoré de
    Eugénie Grandet   169
    Old Goriot   170
Bennett, Arnold. *The Old Wives' Tale*   919
*Boccaccio, Giovanni. *Decameron*   845–6
Brontë, Charlotte
    Jane Eyre   287
    The Professor and *Emma* (a fragment)   417
    Shirley   288
    Villette   351

*Brontë, Emily. *Wuthering Heights* and *Poems*

*Bunyan, John. *Pilgrim's Progress*. Parts I and II

Cervantes, Miguel de. *Don Quixote de la Mancha*   3

*Conrad, Joseph. *Lord Jim*

Dickens, Charles. The principal novels including:
    David Copperfield
    Great Expectations
    Hard Times
    Nicholas Nickleby
    Oliver Twist
    The Pickwick Papers

Dostoyevsky, Fyodor. The principal novels including:
    Crime and Punishment
    The Idiot

Dumas, Alexandre. The principal novels including:
    The Black Tulip
    The Count of Monte Cristo   3
    The Three Musketeers

Eliot, George. The principal novels including:
    Adam Bede
    Felix Holt
    Middlemarch   85
    The Mill on the Floss
    Silas Marner

Fielding, Henry
    Amelia
    Joseph Andrews and *Shamela* (EUL)
    Journey from this World to the Next
    Tom Jones   35

Flaubert, Gustave
    Salammbô
    Sentimental Education

Forster, E. M. *A Passage to India*

Gaskell, Mrs Elizabeth. The principal novels including:
    Cranford
    Mary Barton
    North and South

*Gissing. *The Nether World*

*Hardy, Thomas. *Stories and Poems*

*Jerome, Jerome K. *Three Men in a Boat*

*Kipling, Rudyard. *Stories and Poems*

*Maupassant, Guy de. *Short Stories*

*Pushkin, Alexander. *The Captain's Daughter* and *Other
    Stories*   8

Rabelais, François. *The Heroic Deeds of Gargantua and
    Pantagruel*   826

Stevenson, R. L.
  *Dr Jekyll and Mr Hyde; The Merry Men; Will
    o 'the Mill; Markheim; Thrawn Janet; Olalla;
    The Treasure of Franchard   767
  *Treasure Island and New Arabian Nights   763
Strindberg, Johann August. The Red Room   348
Thackeray, W. M.
  *Henry Esmond   73
  *Vanity Fair   298
Tolstoy, Count Leo
  Anne Karenina   612–13
  War and Peace   525–7
Trollope, Anthony. The Barsetshire novels including:
  *Barchester Towers   30
  *Framley Parsonage   181
  *The Warden   182
*Voltaire. Candide, and Other Tales   936
*Woolf, Virginia. To the Lighthouse   949

HISTORY

*Anglo-Saxon Chronicle (EUL)   624
Gibbon, Edward. The Decline and Fall of the Roman
  Empire   434–6, 474–6
*Prescott, W. H. History of the Conquest of Mexico   397–8

LEGENDS AND SAGAS

*Chrétien de Troyes. Arthurian Romances   698
*The Mabinogion   97
*The Story of Burnt Njal   558

POETRY AND DRAMA

Anglo-Saxon Poetry   794
*Browning, Robert. Men and Women and Other Poems (EUL)   427
Chaucer, Geoffrey
  *Canterbury Tales (EUL)   307
  *Troilus and Criseyde (EUL)   992
Ibsen, Henrik
  *A Doll's House; The Wild Duck; The Lady from the
    Sea   494
  *Ghosts; The Warriors at Helgeland; An Enemy of the
    People   552
  Peer Gynt   747
*Keats, John. Poems   101

Marlowe, Christopher. *Plays and Poems* (EUL)
*Milton, John. *Poems*
*Restoration Plays
Shakespeare, William. *Plays*   1
*Tchekhov, Anton. *Plays and Stories*
*Thomas, Dylan. *Collected Poems: 1934–1952*
   (Aldine Paperback 87)
*Wilde, Oscar. *Plays, Prose Writings and Poems*
*Wordsworth, William. *Selected Poems* (EUL)

RELIGION AND PHILOSOPHY

*Aristotle. *Metaphysics*
*Augustine, Saint. *Confessions*
*Browne, Sir Thomas. *Religio Medici, and Other Writings*
*The Koran
*Law, William. *A Serious Call to a Devout and Holy Life*
*Locke, John. *An Essay Concerning Human Understanding*   332,
Marcus Aurelius Antoninus. *The Meditations of Marcus
    Aurelius*
Plato
   The Republic
   The Trial and Death of Socrates

SCIENCES: POLITICAL AND GENERAL

*Aristotle. *Ethics*
*Darwin, Charles. *The Origin of Species* (EUL)
*Locke, John. *Two Treatises of Government*
*Marx, Karl. *Capital. Volume 1*
Owen, Robert. *A New View of Society* and *Other Writings*
*Rousseau, J-J. *Émile*
Smith, Adam. *The Wealth of Nations*   412–

TRAVEL AND TOPOGRAPHY

Boswell, James. *Journal of a Tour to the Hebrides with
    Samuel Johnson*   3
Calderón de la Barca, Frances. *Life in Mexico*   6
Cobbett, William. *Rural Rides*   6
*Darwin, Charles. *The Voyage of the 'Beagle'*   1
Defoe, Daniel. *A Tour Through the Whole Island of
    Great Britain* (EUL)   8
*Polo, Marco. *Travels*   3
Stevenson, R. L. *An Inland Voyage*; *Travels with a Donkey*;
    The Silverado Squatters   7
*White, Gilbert. *A Natural History of Selborne*